D1200489

VIOLENCE
IN AMERICA

An Encyclopedia

Editorial Board

EDITOR IN CHIEF

RONALD GOTTESMAN, Department of English, University of Southern California

CONSULTING EDITOR

RICHARD MAXWELL BROWN, Department of History, University of Oregon

THE ADVISORY BOARD

LAURA A. BAKER, Department of Psychology, University of Southern California

HOWARD BECKER, Department of Sociology, University of California, Santa Barbara

ERIC FONER, Department of History, Columbia University

JAMES GILLIGAN, Cambridge Hospital, Cambridge, Massachusetts

SANDER L. GILMAN, Departments of Germanic Studies and Psychiatry, University of Chicago

JAMES A. INCIARDI, Center for Drug and Alcohol Studies, University of Delaware

W. J. T. MITCHELL, Departments of English and Art History, University of Chicago

ALEX PIQUERO, Department of Criminal Justice, Temple University

VIOLENCE
IN AMERICA
An Encyclopedia

RONALD GOTTESMAN

Editor in Chief

RICHARD MAXWELL BROWN

Consulting Editor

VOLUME 1

Charles Scribner's Sons

An Imprint of The Gale Group
New York

Cover illustration credits

Front
Center: Corbis. Clockwise from lower left: UPI/Corbis-Bettmann; Reuters/Corbis-Bettmann; Corbis-Bettmann; Corbis-Bettmann.

Back
Clockwise from top right: Reuters/Corbis-Bettmann; Corbis-Bettmann; Reuters/Rob Taggart/Archive Photos; The Granger Collection; Corbis-Bettmann; UPI/Corbis-Bettmann.

Copyright © 1999 by Charles Scribner's Sons

Charles Scribner's Sons
An Imprint of The Gale Group
1633 Broadway
New York, New York 10019

All rights reserved. No part of this book may be reprinted or reproduced or utilized in any form or by any electronic, mechanical, or other means, now known or hereafter invented, including photocopying and recording, or in any information storage or retrieval system, without permission in writing from Charles Scribner's Sons.

3   5   7   9   11   13   15   17   19   20   18   16   14   12   10   8   6   4

PRINTED IN THE UNITED STATES OF AMERICA

Library of Congress Cataloging-in-Publication Data

Violence in America : an encyclopedia / Ronald Gottesman, editor ; Richard Maxwell Brown, Consulting editor . . . [et al.].
      p.   cm.
   Includes bibliographical references and index.
      ISBN 0-684-80487-5 (set : alk. paper) — ISBN 0-684-80488-3 (vol. I : alk. paper)
         1. Violence — United States — Encyclopedias. 2. Violent crimes — United States — Encyclopedias. 3. Violence in popular culture — United States — Encyclopedias. I. Gottesman, Ronald.

   HN90.V5 V5474   1999
   303.6'0973'03 — dc21   99-052027

ISBN 0-684-80489-1 (vol. 2)   ISBN 0-684-80490-5 (vol. 3)

The paper used in this publication meets the requirements of ANSI/NISO Z39.48-1992 (Permanence of Paper).

Editorial Staff

Project Editor
Jeffrey H. Chen

Associate Project Editors
Laura Kathleen Smid   Deborah A. Gershenowitz

Editorial Assistants
Rabindar N. Kapoor   Gina J. Magadia-McGandy
Vaidwattie M. Seewah   Adrianne Wadewitz

Copy Editors
Melissa A. Dobson   Jessica Hornik Evans   Gretchen Gordon
Louise B. Ketz   Evangeline Legones   Ingrid Sterner
Jeffrey L. Beneke   Hannah Borgeson   Susanna Daniel
Sarah Hannah Goldstein   William Kaufman   Andrew Libby   Toni Mortimer

Fact-Checkers
Barbara Julie   Doreen Kallfisch   Sabine Louissaint
Nicholas Okrent   Sudhindra R. Swamy   Elizabeth Yuen

Proofreaders
Dorothy Bauhoff   Gretchen Gordon   Catherine Langevin-Falcon
Vida Petronis   Helen W. Wallace

Picture Editor
Carmel Gabbay

Index
M. L. Coughlin Editorial Services

Manufacturing
Rose Capozzelli, Production Manager
Robert Freese, Interior Design
Irina Lubenskya, Cover Design

Senior Editor
John Fitzpatrick

Executive Editor
Sylvia K. Miller

Publisher
Karen Day

Contents

CONTENTS

Preface

Violence in America: An Encyclopedia takes as its point of departure the German polymath Alexander von Humboldt's observation that "in order to explore any one thing, one needs to approach it from all sides." This encyclopedia has thus attempted to surround American violence, not to oblige it to yield an essence but rather to expose the multifaceted nature of the subject of our explorations. For purposes of this encyclopedia, violence is broadly construed to include injury, or threat of injury, inflicted by one or more people on human beings, other species, the natural environment, or property. The injury may be physical, emotional, or psychological; direct or implied; legally authorized or criminal; and intentional or not. If murder is unarguably violence because it destroys the potential for further ontological development, so too, for many people, are various kinds of experimentation on animals, dumping toxic wastes without regard for environmental consequences, and illegally burning down buildings. Hate speech inflicts psychological damage and may also instigate physical violence—gay bashing, for example. Violence need not be overtly enacted; it may, as in certain forms of sexual harassment, be implicit and still cause injury. Human beings, after all, are mental, emotional, imaginative, and spiritual beings as well as physical ones, and harm to one strand of being vibrates across all others.

Violence in America concerns itself, too, with the wide range of legally authorized violence, war and capital punishment being only two obvious instances. By way of example, the carelessness or negligence of health professionals may cause harm or even death; even though the health practitioner did not set out deliberately to injure a patient, violence has been done. Many other examples of violence could be provided, but perhaps these few will be sufficiently suggestive of the range of actions we have considered. Violence, in sum, may occur even if cause and effect are separated in time, even if deliberate intent to injure is not present, even if psychological or emotional rather than physical damage has been done.

The editors are aware that this broad construction of violence will not satisfy everyone, but we have deliberately chosen to err in the direction of inclusiveness, since to do so is consistent with our desire to call attention to the way violence of many kinds and degrees permeates—and always has permeated—American life. In any event, we trust that this unprecedented inventory of what scholarship and research now know about violence in America will make a contribution to the public good. This encyclopedia also addresses the remarkably wide range of ways violence in American society has been represented in American culture. Our dance, music, painting, sculpture, and literature as well as our comics, print and broadcast media, movies, television programming, folklore, sports, and even

our everyday language all bear witness to American practices of violence. Images of violence in our high as well as popular culture have always testified to one of our central national preoccupations. Indeed much creative energy and ingenuity of technique have been invested in encountering and bringing to consciousness the violence we repeatedly experience but just as repeatedly suppress, forget, or deny. And as W. T. J. Mitchell reminds us in his penetrating contribution, "Representation of Violence," representation has political as well as aesthetic meanings.

One way to appreciate the scope of *Violence in America,* in fact, is to acknowledge the ubiquity, continuity, and variousness of violence in America. From the first encounters between indigenous peoples and Europeans in the late fifteenth century to the present day, violence has been one of the defining facts of life in what we now call the United States. (Indeed, among American Indians violence was a commonplace from before the earliest encounters.) Outlaws, vigilantes, mobs, feuds, riots, protests, rebellions, land wars, assassinations, slavery, gangsters, military interventions, and violent crime have been central features of the territory for five hundred years. In fact, some American historians have identified conquests large and small as the basic reality of American life on and off the frontier.

Users of this encyclopedia should not conclude, however, that because it concentrates on the darker aspects of life in the United States, the editors are, to paraphrase the poet John Keats, half in love with murder and mayhem. In the final years of the twentieth century agencies such as the Centers for Disease Control and Prevention and the American Medical Association recognized that the psychiatrist James Gilligan was not being merely metaphorical or engaging in hyperbole when he titled his important study *Violence: An American Epidemic and What We Can Do About It* (1996). Indeed, legal, medical, and other professionals who study violence have increasingly suggested that before the "web of violence" can be treated as a national health problem, its biological, sociological, psychological, historical, and cultural components must be clearly identified. The editors would argue that one central purpose of this project is precisely to make the darkness of American violence highly visible. It might be helpful to know, for example, that tangible economic losses from crime victimization are estimated at $105 billion a year. Perhaps even more striking is the estimate that on average each of the more than fifty thousand nonfatal gunshot wounds seen annually in emergency rooms costs $375,000 to treat. Only when we can see and understand the multidetermined nature of violence in America will we be in a position to make policy and other kinds of interventions in what is a spiritual as well as a public health problem. At the same time, *Violence in America* also gives some attention to alternatives to violence. Peace studies, conscientious objection, negotiated settlements of interpersonal and international conflicts, disarmament, and pacifism are all addressed here to some degree. Nevertheless, it was apparent to us from the outset that these and related topics deserve a separate reference work.

Although the present work is arranged alphabetically, it may also be thought of as a set of nesting boxes. The outermost box—the thirty or so major essays of 5,000 to 12,000 words—is distinguished by its attempt to provide overviews of often vast domains of research and scholarship. Richard Maxwell Brown's magisterial introductory "Overview of Violence in the United States," for example, offers an integrated conspectus of the "varieties," the "values and images," and the "processes" of American violence. It locates the topic in its social, intellectual, legal, political, and cultural contexts and is thus a useful point of entry for anyone who wishes to understand what is distinctive about the nature and history of violence in America as it has unfolded over the past five centuries. This essay should be required reading for legislators, administrators, students, and their par-

ents. Similarly, Lawrence M. Friedman's entry, "Crime and Punishment in American History," condenses a lifetime of scholarship devoted to the legal and judicial history of the ongoing tension between those who commit crimes and the ideas and institutions that have evolved to deal with them. Many other exemplary integrative entries might be cited: Joseph A. Vorrasi and James Garbarino on poverty, Don Scheese on the environment, and Mary P. Koss and Carolyn House-Higgins on women come to mind. Every reader will find many vistas opened by these overview essays. All of these articles interpret as well as summarize research on the most basic questions faced by biologists, social scientists, medical and legal scholars and practitioners, and cultural critics who study violence in all of its multifariousness. These interpretive essays offer contexts—social, historical, and cultural—for understanding current developments in violence research in such varied fields as history, criminology, sociology, psychiatry, penology, psychobiology, folklore, popular culture, art history, gender studies, social work, law enforcement, public policy, media studies, and many others.

While some consultation was required to decide on these major topics, in most cases simply to name the topic was to understand that its scope required extended treatment. It should be possible to provide a meaningful 2,500-word entry on the Ku Klux Klan (which we have done), but it would be hard to imagine an essay of less than 5,000 words that would even begin to address the tangled and deadly yoking of race and violence in the United States over the past five centuries. Indeed, as the cross-references and index reveal, race and violence, like other major strands of violence in the United States, receive substantial historical and interpretive treatment under several rubrics, including slavery, riots, abolition, lynching, and slave rebellions as well as in entries on immigration, class, and particular ethnic and racial groups. Inevitably some overlap and repetition will also be apparent, but reinforcement of core facts of American history requires no apology. Can we be told too often, for instance, that "a twenty-five-year-old black man is nine times more likely to be stabbed or shot than his white counterpart" (see Schriger, "Emergency Medicine")? Or that more than a third of "all violent crimes are committed by offenders under the influence of alcohol at the time of the incident" (see Slutske, "Alcohol and Alcoholism")?

Violence in America has been conceived also as a tool for understanding conceptually the ubiquity and complexity of American violence. It is with this objective in mind that we have invited leading thinkers to address theories of the origins and social functions of violence, especially as these have been developed in the United States. Our notions of where human violence comes from have changed over time, and taken together, these reflections on the several—and often competing—accounts of the origins and nature of violence should at least help readers to understand the terminological and methodological differences that have made the serious study of violence so complicated. At the very least, for instance, demonstrating just how anthropologists, behavioral scientists, historians, philosophers, theologians and depth psychologists, have differently theorized violence should prove instructive to those who seek single and simple solutions to complex problems.

Every contributor is expert in the subject he or she covers, and no attempt has been made to impose any ideology or single point of view on our colleagues, though we did offer suggestions about the scope of each essay. Doubtless this procedure will, as noted above, result in some overlap (since violence is both legion and indivisible), and at times even contradictions may appear. This plurality of views seems to us to be a virtue rather than a flaw. We should also like to observe that different levels of discourse will be apparent from entry to entry. These differences were inevitable given the variety of writing tasks we assigned.

Theoretical articles require one level of argument and vocabulary, while those devoted, for instance, to medical and biological subjects demand other modes of treatment. We have attempted, nonetheless, to assure clarity in all cases. At the same time we entertain no illusions of having resolved all conflicts, removed all ambiguities, stabilized all interpretations, settled all meanings.

The thirty major essays—historical, interpretive, and theoretical—offer overviews of subjects that seemed to us to demand extended analysis. A reader should expect to come away from Allen D. Grimshaw's remarkable essay on riots, for example, with an understanding of how and why riots have been, and still are, a continuous and periodically highly visible feature in American history. To cite another example, Jomills Henry Braddock, Robin F. Bachin, and Jan Sokol-Katz's fine essay on sports and violence should be instructive on violence among and between participants and spectators, on the ways in which gender and class inflect violence in sport, and on the ways, often subtle, that the media erase or heighten violence associated with sports and their representation.

The encyclopedia's second set of nested boxes provides close examinations of some two hundred more circumscribed topics in treatments of 1,000–5,000 words apiece. Sometimes these finer-grained essays appear as parts of a composite article, sometimes as separate entries with appropriate cross-references. Violence represented in animated or documentary films makes sense as a subdivision within a composite article on violence and film, whereas violence and photography or dance seemed to call for separate treatment. And even though Charles Wolfe's overview of film violence or James Goodwin's on photography are relatively short, both of these entries manage remarkably to provide greatly enlarged understanding of these topics. In any case, anyone who reads the longer and shorter essays on violence and the fine and popular arts and consults the cross-references and the index may be surprised by the pervasiveness of violence as a subject and by the way forms themselves may participate in violence. Art, after all, is one of the best ways human beings have devised for bringing to consciousness, interrogating, and clarifying the uses of coercive force that so mark our species and perhaps especially our species as it has operated on this continent in modern times.

If enriched understanding of violence as a continuous and widespread feature of American life is the object of the longer overview essays as well as the shorter but substantial articles, information is the objective of the third "box," the 366 shorter entries of 500–1,000 words apiece. Even here, though, we have tried to avoid offering mere undigested information by being selective rather than comprehensive in our choice of items. Incidents, individuals, and titles have been chosen with the large sweep of American history in mind. In the case of incidents we asked this question: Has this incident become so much a part of common cultural currency that most educated Americans would at least recognize the event by name even if they could not offer much factual information about it? My Lai and Wounded Knee, we decided, were such events, but many other battles and massacres we concluded were not, although they may well be mentioned in the text of longer entries. Of individuals as potential entries we asked: Has the person entered the public imagination, usually as the result of becoming the subject of fiction, film, or television? Our answer in the case of Al Capone, John Brown, and Lizzie Borden, for instance, was yes. On the other hand, very few of the hundreds of serial murderers, including most of those who murdered dozens or even scores of people, appear as separate entries, although many can be found in the index because they too are mentioned in other contexts. The same is true for most mobsters, regardless of how much power they wielded or how ruthless they were in exercising it. If they have not achieved something like legendary status, their place in history will have to be sought in the vast secondary literature and in the many reference works devoted to such aspects of American life.

The reader should also understand that many of these shorter entries are essentially factual and provide basic information about a person, event, or work. Anyone who wants to find out about the Earp family can do so by consulting the entry in its alphabetical order. Any reader, however, who seeks to understand this family in the context of the frontier and in reference to gunslingers should read the latter entries as well.

Composite entries gather together related articles. For example, readers will find under "Drugs" four subentries: Drugs and Violence, Drugs and Crime, Drug Prevention and Violence, and Drug Trade. Virtually all types of writings are discussed in the literature composite.

Another way to clarify the informing conceptual organization of *Violence in America* is to observe that it is designed generally to address four broad and interrelated questions. First, what explanations for violence have been offered over the years? This question is addressed especially in the entries on theories of violence as well as the entries on biological and psychological topics. Second, how has violence manifested itself in the continental nation-state we now call the United States? Here, of course, the answer is to be found in the explicitly historical pieces. Third, how and with what consequences has violence been represented in the fine and popular arts produced in the United States? These questions are engaged in the many individual entries as well as the composite ones on film, literature, and the other arts. Finally, what have been the official (and unofficial) political and judicial responses to violence? The many articles on the criminal justice system—from government acts and prisons to laws and methods of execution—speak to this question. We are aware that violence was not invented in North America and that all of the arts and sciences have their roots and branches in other parts of the globe. This awareness is reflected in the attempt to contextualize historically and cross-culturally all but the very shortest entries.

The editors, finally, are also aware that virtually every assertion about violence is hotly contested. We have therefore tried to be evenhanded in the coverage of controversial subjects and issues. We asked contributors to try to clarify and summarize rather than to attempt to settle scholarly debates. Opinion and speculation should be easily identified by any attentive reader, and the bibliographies at the end of entries refer the reader to various sources that will further explore contested issues.

Many of the 595 entries by 444 contributors are supplemented by sidebars that highlight a subtopic (a person, an incident, a court case, a statistical matrix) in order to illuminate the main topics. The approximately 460 photographs, charts, graphs, and other illustrative materials are included to extend and enrich the verbal information. Both verbal and visual information are made more readily accessible by a full analytical index that includes categories (e.g., criminal justice, weapons, biographies) and concepts (e.g., censorship, methodologies) as well as names, titles, and places (e.g., Lee Harvey Oswald, *Obedience to Authority*, Waco). Together with blind entries (the blind entry for "Joseph, Chief," for example, tells the reader to look under "Chief Joseph") and extensive cross-references, all these features should enhance the usefulness of the volumes and underscore the interconnectedness of many kinds of violence in America.

The frontmatter in volume 1 contains a chronology of selected significant violent events in American history: wars, riots, assassinations, murders, executions, trials, terrorist attacks, and government violence. The appendix in volume 3 lists organizations and publications that in one capacity or another are concerned with violence prevention and reduction. The alphabetical lists are followed by a short subject index that helps readers locate a particular group or publication. Although not exhaustive, the lists will lead readers to many pertinent sources of information. Contact information, including Web site if available, is provided for each organization.

Ronald Gottesman
November 1999

Acknowledgments

My debt to students, scholars, researchers, clinical experts, friends, and family for assistance of every sort is commensurate with the magnitude of this project. These positive acts of patience, help, and support, in fact, have made several years of immersion in the destructive element not only bearable but the source of new knowledge and new and renewed friendships.

Violence in America: An Encyclopedia had its immediate origins in an experimental graduate seminar at the University of Southern California titled "American Media and Discourses of Violence," which I organized in 1994. Three seminarians in particular helped me to comprehend the implications and complications of the seminar topic: Barbara Williams Lewis, Diane McDaniel, and Nikki Senecal. They have led me to believe that even professors are educable. To those colleagues from a dozen disciplines who made presentations to the seminar, I once again express my gratitude.

Other current or recent USC graduate students, either by giving me what Walt Whitman called "good heart" or by contributing entries, have eased my editorial task. These students include Arnab Chakladar, Andrew Durkin, Dean Franco, Naomi Guttman, Paul Hansom, Desmond Harding, Valerie Karno, Barbara Williams Lewis, Chris Lippard, Kathleen Lonsdale, Ketura Persellin, Giovanna Pompele, David Ramsey, Michael Reynolds, Nancy Sanders, and Nikki Senecal.

One of the first and best things I did to initiate this project was to consult with my friend and USC colleague Steve Ross; his recommendations and advice were invaluable. Early on, Bruce Jackson and Mauricio Mazón contributed greatly to conceptualizing the project and to identifying potential topics and contributors. I am grateful to them for their friendship as well as for their willingness to share their extraordinary learning and extensive professional networks.

Sylvia K. Miller welcomed my initial inquiry regarding a reference work on violence in America soon after she assumed her position as Executive Editor of Charles Scribner's Sons. Since then she has helped me to clarify my intentions and at every step along the way has offered good advice, concrete suggestions, and editorial support. Without her this encyclopedia could not have been begun, nor could it have been concluded. I appreciate as well the enthusiastic engagement of Publisher Karen Day. Senior Editor John Fitzpatrick and Associate Project Editor Laura Kathleen Smid were instrumental in helping to bring the project to completion.

Many of my colleagues at USC (and elsewhere) were convinced that to undertake an interdisciplinary project of this magnitude was madness. Several of them not only refrained from saying so but even encouraged me to take it on in spite of what others said. For their belief in me I wish to thank my English Department colleagues Paul Alkon, Leo Braudy, Tim Gustafson, and Jim Kincaid, all of whom have practiced interdisciplinary scholarship of the most liberating kind. I am even more beholden to my USC faculty colleagues who contributed entries. They are identified in the List of Contributors.

I welcome the opportunity to thank dear friends Elaine Attias, Warren Bennis, Clayton Eshleman, Alan Jay Friedman, Grace Gabe, Lil Hara, Roger Jackson, Marsha Kinder, Edward Lehrner, Hal Lieberman, Jay Martin, Hank Plone, Alan Shucard, Al Silver, Anna Silver, Myron Simon, Bob Snyder, and June Wayne, all of whom encouraged me and believed in the value of the project.

My greatest debt is to Jeff Chen, Project Editor at Scribners. Jeff computerized the infinitely detailed information required to make an encyclopedia of this kind, handled most of the correspondence, exercised his daunting diplomatic and editorial skills day in and year out by e-mail, snail mail, phone, and fax, and did so with equanimity and good humor. He has been both the collaborator and guardian angel every editor dreams of yet seldom finds. It is a pleasure to salute him in this public way.

Many other colleagues—too numerous to name—recommended experts or otherwise assisted in the completion of this encyclopedia; I wish especially to acknowledge members of USC's Violence Study Group, now numbering nearly one hundred researchers and clinicians across the disciplines of a large university devoted to connecting theoretical and critical studies with professional practitioners of nearly every sort. I am happy, too, to acknowledge a grant from the College of Letters, Arts and Sciences at USC. Dean of Faculty Joseph Aoun and Dean of the College Morton O. Schapiro have been encouraging from start to finish and I am pleased to express my appreciation to them.

I am particularly pleased to give credit to Consulting Editor Richard Maxwell Brown, our leading historian of American violence. We consulted him with shameless frequency and he never failed us. Professor Brown is a scholar, a gentleman, and a fine judge of academic horseflesh. The remarkable group of scholars who served as an Editorial Board engaged in everything from recruiting contributors to reading and commenting on essays with a fine critical eye. Indeed, their constructive critiques were invaluable in the long (and sometimes painful) editorial process we have now happily completed.

Allison McCabe was my first invaluable research assistant, word-processor, files organizer, and Net navigator. Allison's work was continued with equal skill by Caline Evans. My children, Lann and Grant, have kept faith with me as always.

Finally, Beth Shube was my partner in this enterprise as she has been in so many others over the past two decades. It would be hard to exaggerate her sound judgment, her skill, her equanimity, and her loving patience.

Ronald Gottesman
November 1999

Chronology

The chronology below is highly selective and is intended only to suggest the pervasiveness and the seemingly endless variety of individual and collective violence in American history from the first encounters between Native Americans and Europeans. Many events in the chronology are titled entries in the encyclopedia; others can be found in the index at the end of volume 3.

1622	Powhatan uprising against Jamestown.
1675–1676	King Philip's War.
1676	Bacon's Rebellion in Virginia.
1680	Only successful Native American insurrection (against the Spanish) in North America, led by a Tewa holy man, Pope.
1692	Salem witch trials.
1754–1763	French and Indian War.
1770	Boston Massacre.
1773	Boston Tea Party.
1775	Start of American Revolution.
1782	Shawnees and Delawares, and their allies, inflict bloody defeat on Americans at the Battle of Blue Licks in Kentucky.
1783	End of American Revolution.
1786–1787	Shays's Rebellion in Massachusetts.
1791	Slave rebellion in Haiti.
1793	First Fugitive Slave Act.
1794	Whiskey Rebellion.
1798	Alien and Sedition Acts.

1804	Alexander Hamilton killed by Vice President Aaron Burr in a pistol duel.
1812	War of 1812.
1823	Monroe Doctrine.
1823–1841	James Fenimore Cooper's Leatherstocking novels published.
1830	Indian Removal Act.
1830–1859	Trail of Tears.
1831	Slave revolt led by Nat Turner in Southampton, Virginia.
1836	Battle of the Alamo.
	Revolver by Samuel Colt patented in the United States.
1839	*Amistad* mutiny.
1840s–1854	Anti-immigration and nativist Know-Nothing movement.
1844	Mormon leader Joseph Smith killed by mob.
1846–1848	Mexican War.
1847	Remington pistol marketed by Eliphalet Remington.
1849	Riots outside New York City's Astor Place Opera House,

resulting in between twenty-two and thirty deaths

1850   Second Fugitive Slave Act.

1851   Filibustering expedition to Cuba led by Narciso López.

John A. Quitman resigns as governor of Mississippi when he is indicted by the federal government for aiding Narciso López's filibustering expedition to Cuba.

c. 1852   Short-barreled, large-bore percussion pocket pistol invented by Henry Deringer.

1855   William Walker and band capture Nicaragua on filibustering expedition.

1855–1858   Violence between proslavery and abolitionist groups in Kansas earns the state the title Bleeding Kansas.

1857   Dred Scott case decided in the Supreme Court.

1859   John Brown's raid on Harpers Ferry in Virginia.

1860   Henry repeating rifle produced by Oliver Fisher Winchester.

1861   Start of Civil War.

1862   Rapid-fire gun patented by Richard Jordan Gatling.

1863   Emancipation Proclamation.

Battle of Gettysburg.

Draft riots in New York City produce a thousand casualties, the worst civil disorder in U.S. history.

Quantrill's Raid.

1863–1865   More than twelve thousand Union soldiers die in Andersonville Prison in Georgia during the Civil War.

1864   Long Walk of the Navajo.

General William Tecumseh Sherman's "march to the sea."

Sand Creek massacre, in which at least 150 Cheyenne Indians are killed by a Colorado militia.

1865   End of Civil War.

President Abraham Lincoln assassinated.

1865–1867   Black Codes passed by former Confederate states.

1866   Incorporation of the American Society for the Prevention of Cruelty to Animals.

Race riot in New Orleans, in which at least thirty-four blacks are killed and more than one hundred injured.

Ku Klux Klan formed in Tennessee.

1870   Suffrage granted to black men by Fifteenth Amendment.

First Enforcement Act, in conformity with the Fourteenth and Fifteenth Amendments.

1871   Incorporation of the National Rifle Association.

Second and third Enforcement Acts signed, giving the federal government further authority to enforce civil rights in the Reconstruction era.

1876   Battle of Little Bighorn, in which Crazy Horse, with the help of Sitting Bull, leads Sioux to defeat General George Custer and his troops.

1877   Nez Percé War.

Anti-Chinese riots in San Francisco.

1880   Conflict in Mussel Slough, California, between the Southern Pacific Railroad and the farmers of the Lower Kings River.

1880–1930   More than three thousand blacks lynched in the South.

1881   O. K. Corral gunfight.

President James Garfield shot, dies two months later.

1882 Chinese Exclusion Act banning Chinese immigration for ten years.

Jesse James killed by fellow gang member.

1886 Haymarket Square riot in Chicago.

1889 Last bare-knuckle championship boxing fight.

1890 Massacre of two hundred Indians at Wounded Knee, South Dakota.

First execution by electric chair, at Auburn Prison in New York State.

1892 Lizzie Borden accused of killing her father and stepmother; found innocent in 1893.

In New Orleans, first boxing match under the Marquess of Queensbury rules.

Homestead strike.

1894 Pullman strike.

1896 Herman Mudgett (also known as Dr. H. H. Holmes), considered America's first serial killer, hanged after confessing to twenty-seven murders.

Plessy v. Ferguson, upholding social segregation of the races.

1898 Spanish-American War.

Attack at San Juan Hill in Cuba by Theodore Roosevelt and Rough Riders.

Treaty of Paris ends Spanish-American War and transfers Philippines to United States; Filipino resistance leads to guerrilla warfare.

1901 President William McKinley assassinated.

1902 Owen Wister's *The Virginian,* the novel that set the conventions for the Western, published.

1903 Release of Edwin S. Porter's film *The Great Train Robbery.*

1905 Industrial Workers of the World cofounded by Eugene V. Debs.

1910 Bombing of *Los Angeles Times* Building kills twenty people.

1911 Unsafe working conditions at New York City's Triangle Shirtwaist Company contribute to the death of 146 workers during a fire.

1913 Leo Frank, a northern Jew, accused of murdering a fourteen-year-old girl in Atlanta; although his death sentence is commuted to life imprisonment, twenty-five armed men take him from jail and hang him in 1915.

1915 Sinking of the *Lusitania,* in which 128 U.S. citizens die, helping to precipitate U.S. involvement in World War I.

Release of D. W. Griffith's film *The Birth of a Nation.*

1917 Espionage Act.

U.S. entry into World War I.

Race riots in East Saint Louis, in which approximately thirty-nine blacks and nine whites are killed.

1918 End of World War I.

1919 Prohibition established by Eighteenth Amendment.

Race riot in Chicago leaves thirty-eight dead.

1919–1920 The first Red Scare.

1920 Nationwide suffrage granted to women by Nineteenth Amendment.

Bombing of Wall Street (most likely by the anarchist Mario Buda) leaves thirty-three dead and more than two hundred injured.

1921 Sacco and Vanzetti arrested.

1924 Fourteen-year-old Bobby Franks kidnapped and murdered in Chicago by Richard Loeb and Nathan Leopold, who are sentenced to life imprisonment.

1927   Sacco and Vanzetti executed.

1929   St. Valentine's Day Massacre.

1930   Carl Panzram executed after killing at least twenty-one people and committing more than one thousand acts of sodomy.

Motion Picture Producers and Distributors of America, under the leadership of William H. Hays, announces Motion Picture Production Code.

1931   Gambling legalized in Nevada.

Scottsboro Case.

1932   Charles Lindbergh's baby son kidnapped and murdered.

Release of Howard Hawks's film *Scarface*.

1932–1972   Government-endorsed Tuskegee study to examine the effects of untreated syphilis on some four hundred impoverished black men.

1933   Attempted assassination of President-elect Franklin D. Roosevelt.

Union Station Massacre in Kansas City.

Prohibition repealed by Twenty-first Amendment.

1934   Clyde Barrow and Bonnie Parker killed in a shoot-out in Gibsland, Louisiana, after killing at least twelve people, including law-enforcement officers, and injuring at least three.

John Dillinger, dubbed public enemy number one by the FBI, killed by FBI agents.

1935   U.S. Senator Huey Long assassinated.

1938   Creation of the House Committee on Un-American Activities.

The radio program *The War of the Worlds* airs on Columbia Broadcasting System, causing nationwide panic.

1941   Attack at Pearl Harbor by Japanese; U.S. entry into World War II.

1942–1946   Internment of Japanese Americans in relocation centers.

1943   Zoot-Suit Riot in Los Angeles.

1944   Normandy campaign of World War II initiated on 6 June, D-Day.

1945   Landing of U.S. Marines on Iwo Jima.

Invasion of Okinawa by U.S. forces.

Atomic bombs dropped on Hiroshima and Nagasaki.

End of World War II.

1947   Creation of the Central Intelligence Agency, the National Security Council, and the Department of Defense; legal status given to the Joint Chiefs of Staff.

House Committee on Un-American Activities hearings on communists in the film industry.

Elizabeth Short, known as Black Dahlia, found murdered and cut in half in a vacant lot near Hollywood, California.

1949   Thirteen people killed in Camden, New Jersey, by Howard Unruh.

1950   Beginning of the Korean War.

Senate Special Committee to Investigate Organized Crime, headed by Estes Kefauver, formed; report issued in 1951.

1952   First hydrogen bomb exploded by United States.

1953   Julius and Ethel Rosenberg executed for treason.

End of Korean War.

1954   Kefauver Commission, established to determine causes of juvenile delinquency, examines possible effects of popular culture.

1955 — Fourteen-year-old Emmett Till lynched in Money, Mississippi, for allegedly approaching a white woman.

1955–1956 — Bus boycott in Montgomery, Alabama.

1957 — Ed Gein arrested for the murder and dismemberment of two women.

1959 — Charles Starkweather electrocuted for killing eleven people in 1957–1958; his accomplice, Caril Ann Fugate, imprisoned until 1976.

1960 — Sit-in at a lunch counter in Greensboro, North Carolina, by four black college students.

Release of Alfred Hitchcock's film *Psycho*.

1961 — Bay of Pigs Invasion.

Arrival of U.S. troops in South Vietnam.

1962 — Cuban Missile Crisis.

Students for a Democratic Society founded; holds antiwar protests throughout the decade.

1963 — Four black girls killed in bombing of Sixteenth Street Baptist Church in Birmingham, Alabama.

March on Washington and speech by Martin Luther King, Jr.

President John F. Kennedy assassinated.

1964 — Kitty Genovese murdered in Queens, New York City, while thirty-eight people stand by and do nothing.

1965 — Malcolm X assassinated.

Watts riots in Los Angeles, leaving thirty-four people dead.

March from Selma, Alabama, to Montgomery, led by Martin Luther King, Jr.

First government warnings that smoking may be hazardous to health appear on cigarette packages.

Eight nurses murdered in a Chicago suburb by Richard Speck.

1966 — Sixteen people killed by sniper Charles Whitman shooting from a tower at the University of Texas; ninety-six minutes later Whitman is killed by police.

Truman Capote's *In Cold Blood* published.

1967 — 150 U.S. cities erupt in racial violence during the "long hot summer."

National Advisory Commission on Civil Disorders (the Kerner Commission) established.

Release of Arthur Penn's film *Bonnie and Clyde*.

1968 — Tet offensive in South Vietnam.

Martin Luther King, Jr., assassinated.

Six days of violence, looting, and burning in Washington, D.C., following the assassination of Martin Luther King, Jr.; similar outbreaks in many other cities.

Robert F. Kennedy assassinated.

Violent clashes between police and demonstrators at the National Democratic Convention in Chicago.

Founding of the American Indian Movement.

The Motion Picture Association of America introduces a new classification system based on letter ratings.

National Commission on the Causes and Prevention of Violence (the Violence Commission) established.

My Lai Massacre in South Vietnam (exposed 1969).

1969   Aerial bombing campaign over Cambodia begun by United States.

Charles Manson and his followers arrested and eventually charged with killing nine people, including Sharon Tate, wife of director Roman Polanski.

Release of Sam Peckinpah's film *The Wild Bunch.*

Weatherman created out of remains of Students for a Democratic Society.

1970   Four people killed by Ohio National Guard during anti–Vietnam War protests at Kent State University.

Two black students shot by city and state police at antiwar and antiracism demonstrations at Jackson State College in Mississippi.

Chicano Moratorium, a massive anti–Vietnam War protest, takes place in Los Angeles.

1971   Riots at Attica prison in New York State.

Juan Corona arrested after killing twenty-five migrant workers and drifters in Yuba City, California.

Cigarette advertisements on radio and television banned by Congress.

Release of Stanley Kubrick's film *A Clockwork Orange.*

1972   *Furman v. Georgia,* decided by the U.S. Supreme Court, effectively invalidating current capital punishment statutes.

Bombing of North Vietnam halted by United States.

Release of Francis Ford Coppola's film *The Godfather.*

1973   *Roe v. Wade* removes most government restrictions on abortion.

Bombing of Cambodia halted by United States.

1974   Patty Hearst kidnapped by Symbionese Liberation Army.

Stanley Milgram's *Obedience to Authority* published.

1975   Disappearance and presumed murder of labor leader Jimmy Hoffa.

Two attempted assassinations of President Gerald Ford.

Oglala firefight at Pine Ridge Reservation.

1976   *Gregg v. Georgia* enables some states to resume capital punishment.

Release of Martin Scorsese's film *Taxi Driver.*

1977   David "Son of Sam" Berkowitz arrested after yearlong killing spree in New York City.

Gary Gilmore, executed by firing squad in Utah, becomes the first person executed in the United States in ten years.

Lethal injection first used to execute a prisoner.

1978   Mass suicide-murder of the Reverend Jim Jones and 912 followers in Jonestown, Guyana.

John Wayne Gacy arrested in Chicago after having killed more than thirty young males.

San Francisco mayor George Moscone and city supervisor Harvey Milk assassinated.

1979   Accident at Three Mile Island nuclear power plant.

1979–1981   Iran hostage crisis.

1980   John Lennon murdered.

1980s   Iran-Contra affair.

1981   Attempted assassination of President Ronald Reagan.

1983   Strategic Defense Initiative announced by President Reagan.

Landing of U.S. troops in Grenada.

Arrested for gun possession, Henry Lee Lucas admits to having killed more than 350 people; he probably killed at least 200, some of them with his accomplice, Ottis Toole.

1984   Four black youths shot by Bernhard Goetz on a New York City subway.

1985   Police bomb MOVE headquarters in Philadelphia.

1986   Howard Beach incident in New York City.

U.S. bombing raid on Tripoli and Benghazi after two U.S. servicemen are killed in the bombing (thought to have been sponsored by Libya) of a West Berlin nightclub.

1988   Terrorist bombing of Pan Am flight 103 over Lockerbie, Scotland.

1989   Murder of parents by Erik and Lyle Menendez in Beverly Hills, California; they are eventually convicted and sentenced to life imprisonment.

Ted Bundy electrocuted after killing at least twenty-eight young women from 1974 to 1978.

U.S. troops invade Panama City, leading to surrender of Manuel Noriega in 1990.

The *Exxon Valdez* leaks more than ten million gallons of oil into the waters of Prince William Sound in Alaska, causing massive environmental damage.

1991   Aileen Wuornos, considered America's first female serial killer, arrested after killing seven men in Florida.

Persian Gulf War.

Riot in the Crown Heights section of Brooklyn in New York City.

1992   Riots in Los Angeles after police are found not guilty in the beating of motorist Rodney King.

Federal siege at Ruby Ridge, Idaho.

Wisconsin police discover Jeffrey Dahmer's crimes, killing and dismembering seventeen African American and Asian American boys.

1993   Bombing of World Trade Center, New York City.

FBI siege of Branch Davidian complex in Waco, Texas, leaving seventy-four people dead.

The television series *NYPD Blue* premieres.

1994   Release of Oliver Stone's film *Natural Born Killers* and Quentin Tarrantino's film *Pulp Fiction*.

1995   O. J. Simpson tried for 1994 murders of Nicole Brown Simpson and Ronald Goldman.

Bombing of Alfred P. Murrah Federal Building in Oklahoma City, which left 168 dead.

Susan Smith sentenced to life imprisonment for killing her two young sons.

1996   Bombing of Atlanta Centennial Olympic Park kills one and injures more than one hundred.

Theodore Kaczynski (the so-called Unabomber) arrested after a series of bombings that killed three people and injured twenty-three.

Telecommunications law mandating v-chip in all newly manufactured television sets.

1997   Mass suicide of thirty-nine members of the Heaven's Gate cult in California.

Suicide of Andrew Cunanan after his killing of clothing designer Gianni Versace and four others.

1998 Bombing of New Woman All Women Health Care Center in Birmingham, Alabama, killing one man and seriously injuring a woman.

Explosion of bombs at U.S. embassies in Nairobi, Kenya, and Dar es Salaam, Tanzania.

Abner Louima severely beaten by police in a Brooklyn, New York, precinct house.

Barnett Slepian, an abortion provider, shot to death at his home in Amherst, New York.

Suicide of Thomas Youk, with the assistance of Jack Kevorkian, airs on *60 Minutes*.

1999 Twelve students and one teacher killed by two fellow students at Columbine High School in Colorado.

Assisted-suicide advocate Jack Kevorkian convicted of second-degree murder.

VIOLENCE
IN AMERICA

An Encyclopedia

Overview of Violence in the United States

In 1837 Abraham Lincoln declared that the mortal threat to American democracy was not foreign military power but an internal flaw: violence. Lincoln spoke a home truth, but it was a lonely viewpoint. Despite a mountain of evidence to the contrary, Americans as late as the 1940s still refused to think of themselves as essentially violent. Centuries of white-Indian warfare, race riots, agrarian uprisings, frontier vigilantism, and industrial conflict were all complacently excused as exceptions to the self-perception of the overwhelmingly peaceable and law-abiding character of American citizens. Then came the 1950s, one of the calmest decades in U.S. history, and Americans' conception of themselves as a basically nonviolent people seemed to be confirmed; the major causes of violence in the United States had apparently withered away. The era of white-Indian warfare was long gone as was frontier vigilantism, and there had not been a major agrarian uprising since the 1930s. The excruciatingly violent industrial conflict of six decades tailed off after 1940. Even the enduring nemesis of combative white-black race relations faded in the 1950s as the lynching of African Americans all but disappeared, and the last big race riot had occurred in 1943. With the Supreme Court outlawing southern school segregation in 1954, the most intractable of all American social pathologies seemed to be in the sunset stage. Meanwhile, crime dropped off, and the homicide rate reached a twenty-year low in the 1950s.

The 1950s were, however, only the calm before the storm of the 1960s—one of the most violent decades in U.S. history, replete with massive urban riots, outbursts of racial antagonism, a presidential assassination and other notable assassinations, campus violence, antiwar disorder, and a spectacular increase in crime and homicide rates. At last Americans acknowledged themselves as a violent nation. For a century historians had written much about violence but not as something central to the American experience. Instead, violence was viewed as merely an unfortunate by-product of racial, religious, ethnic, frontier, agrarian, and industrial conflict that did not really diminish the national achievements of freedom and democracy. In the crisis mood of the 1960s, immediate enlightenment was needed, and a series of presidential commissions were appointed to make sense of the raging violence and disorder. The most ambitious effort was the National Commission on the Causes and Prevention of Violence (1968–1969), headed by Milton Eisenhower, a university president and the brother of President Dwight Eisenhower. With twelve scholarly teams at work on virtually all aspects of historical and contemporary American violence, the Eisenhower Commission issued sixteen learned volumes written by historians, humanists, and social and behavioral scientists. A public eager

1

for knowledge purchased more than three hundred thousand copies of the original edition and three reprints of the commission's cornerstone publication, *Violence in America: Historical and Contemporary Perspectives* (1969). The field of American-violence studies emerged in the 1970s and 1980s as an interdisciplinary effort of scholarship to describe, analyze, and explain America's irrepressibly violent heritage and behavior. Since 1969, the result was the publication of thousands of books and articles in which violence was treated as central to the American story. The present encyclopedia, also entitled *Violence in America,* is a culmination of three decades of American-violence studies.

Scholars have concluded that during the nineteenth and twentieth centuries the United States was by far the most violent of its peer group of nations—the economically advanced democracies of the world. This is not because Americans are an innately violent people, but because a combination of factors from the colonial period on have created the juggernaut of American violence. Other comparable nations had many of the major causes of modern violence, but only in America had all been present and on a large scale: racial, ethnic, religious, agrarian, and industrial conflict; crime, vigilantism, revolution, civil war, terrorism, and assassination; urban riots and rural feuds; youth violence and violence against women; and a heavily armed, violence-prone civilian population. These factors reinforced each other to produce a deeply rooted tradition in which through the last decades of the twentieth century it was natural for Americans to react to stress or provocation with violence.

Attitudes excusing and justifying violence coexisted with and often overwhelmed what the Swedish social scientist Gunnar Myrdal characterized as the "American creed" of freedom, equality, and democracy. In a nation born in the violence of the American Revolution and preserved in the Civil War, Americans absorbed and acted upon the lessons of the Revolution and the Civil War that violence in what is seen as an urgently good cause is, although regrettable, praiseworthy. In our past the patriot, the frontier settler, the farmer, the worker, the industrialist, the capitalist, the solid member of the middle class, the rebel, and the aggrieved of various types all undertook violence imbued with the notion that it was an entirely proper last resort to satisfy a legitimate grievance or rectify a glaring injustice.

VARIETIES OF AMERICAN VIOLENCE

White-Indian Warfare

The oldest mode of American violence was warfare between white intruders and Indian defenders. These conflicts afflicted all regions and almost every state. As far back as the sixteenth century, Indians fought the first Spanish colonists in the Southwest and Florida. In the same century, North Carolina Indians wiped out the English colony on Roanoke Island, and the early-seventeenth-century Opechancanough uprising almost destroyed the Virginia colony. In the seventeenth century, the mass outbreak of Indians behind Metacom in the so-called King Philip's War was a near disaster for the colonies of Massachusetts and Rhode Island. In the Southeast in the eighteenth and nineteenth centuries, great wars were waged by the Yamassee, Seminoles, Cherokees, and Creeks. In the Midwest the Shawnees fought to the bitter end, which finally came in the 1810s, while the Great Sioux Wars were fought in the 1860s and 1870s from Minnesota to Montana and Wyoming. The Great Plains from Texas to the Dakotas were heavily conflicted, thanks to uprisings and wars that went back to the time of the conquistador Francisco Vásquez de Coronado and featured, among others, the Comanche, Kiowa, Cheyenne, and Arikara Indians. The Southwest was noted for the wars of the Apaches, but they were preceded by the bitter campaigns of the Pueblos and the Navajos. In the Rocky Mountain region, the Blackfoot Indians were relentless in their opposition to American intruders, while the Utes and the Shoshone resisted white inroads. The Pacific Northwest had its own Thirty Years' War of whites versus Indians from the 1840s to the 1870s. All of California was a huge battleground, with repeated Indian uprisings against the Spanish and Mexican colonists in southern and central California. In northern California white American violence against the natives became genocidal—one tribe was hunted down and exterminated to the last man, Ishi, who in the early twentieth century was found nearly starved on the outskirts of a sizable Sierra Nevada town.

The white-Indian wars produced notable Indian leaders who were feared in their time but became for whites icons of bravery: Pontiac, Tecumseh, Sitting Bull, Chief Joseph, and Geronimo are among the best known. Yet white-Indian warfare entered the American language with tropes of extermination like "nits make lice," a phrase meaning that

The Ottawa chief Pontiac. HULTON GETTY/LIAISON AGENCY

often began uprisings against white intrusion or dominance with massacres—for example, the Pueblo uprising of 1680 in New Mexico and the Great Sioux War in Minnesota, which began in 1862 with a massacre of settlers. Loss of white life was heavy in such outbursts, but it pales before the casualties of Indian men, women, and children who were on the receiving end of such massacres as the following:

1860: Humboldt Bay, California—nearly 200 Wyots killed

1864: Sand Creek, Colorado—some 200 Cheyennes killed

1868: Washita River, Oklahoma—103 Cheyennes killed

1870: Marias River, Montana—173 Blackfoot killed

1890: Wounded Knee, South Dakota—at least 300 Lakotas killed

In the late twentieth century scholarship focused more and more on what some call the American Indian Holocaust, in which Indians massively succumbed not only to warfare and outright genocide but also to white diseases against which they had no immunity. These maladies were often insidious killers that infected Indian nations long before whites actually appeared on the scene. The settlers who thronged into the Willamette Valley of Oregon, for example, found the rich, riverine land virtually deserted of its native inhabitants, who had fallen victim to prepioneer epidemics. According to a conservative conjecture, a population loss of "between three and four million people occurred" in what is now the United States and Canada—just part of the 90 percent of Indian population decline that, as a result of "disease diffusion," occurred during the four post-Columbian centuries in North and South America. Meanwhile, white-Indian warfare in the United States too often consisted of the "ethnic cleansing" of Indians by whites long before the Yugoslavian civil war in the 1990s gave rise to that term.

White-Black Violence

White-Indian warfare and violence largely ended with the Wounded Knee massacre of 1890, but the violence of whites versus African Americans that started later lasted into the late twentieth century. The first slave revolt occurred in Rappahannock County, Virginia, in 1691, but the first major slave uprising was an urban one in New York City in 1712. Not until 1739 in South Carolina

the only assurance of extermination was to kill babies and not just men and women. The nadir of white-Indian warfare was the massacre, a technique of violence that was present at the beginning of the long-term conflict. English colonists brought with them the European massacre tradition, which was, however, bound by some restraints. As the colonists fought Indians, they quickly gave way to the unrestrained Mystic, Connecticut, massacre of 1637, in which only a few Pequots escaped from their fortified village that was burned to the ground. Of some four hundred or more Pequots who met fiery deaths at Mystic, most were old men, women, and children. All too often the merciless assault, like that at Mystic, was the norm for future massacres of Indians. Indians themselves

along the Stono River did the first major rebellion of southern plantation slaves erupt. Periodically thereafter, slave uprisings or conspiracies to revolt occurred in the southern colonies and states. Among the biggest were the Gabriel Prosser conspiracy in Richmond, Virginia, in 1800; Louisiana uprisings in two rural parishes in 1811; the Denmark Vesey conspiracy in Charleston, South Carolina, in 1822; and the Nat Turner rebellion in Southampton County, Virginia, in 1831, in which some sixty to eighty slaves killed some sixty-five whites. The outcome of the Nat Turner rebellion was typical: the uprising was suppressed in forty-eight hours and a huge vigilante roundup of slave and free blacks produced at least sixty African American fatalities and perhaps hundreds more. Some twenty-one of the known rebels were tried, convicted, and executed, of which the last was Turner himself, who died on 11 November 1831.

Meanwhile, a steady stream of runaway southern slaves known as maroons escaped to lives of freedom, which they defended with violence. In the North, free blacks were increasingly subjected to pogrom-style white riots against them from the 1830s to the 1850s. Most of these occurred in big cities like New York, Philadelphia, and Cincinnati, but one of the worst cases was two-and-a-half months of rioting in 1834 against the African Americans who composed one-quarter of the two thousand residents of Columbia, Pennsylvania.

The nineteenth-century wave of northern antiblack riots climaxed in one of the greatest urban uprisings in American history: the July 1863 rioting in New York City. This outbreak was a protest of lower- and working-class whites against a military draft to raise troops for the Union Army, but the city's African Americans were the scapegoats and by far the greatest victims of roving mobs that took some 110 lives.

During Reconstruction, as southern whites sought to subdue the former slaves, pogrom-style riots of whites against blacks took place with such major outbreaks as those in 1866 in New Orleans, Louisiana, and Memphis, Tennessee (34 and 36 killed, respectively), and in 1873 in Colfax, Louisiana (103 killed). Pogrom-style riots also took place later in Wilmington, North Carolina, in 1898 (30 dead) and Atlanta in 1906 (25 dead). It was outside the big cities like New Orleans, Memphis, and Atlanta, however, that the worst carnage occurred as a lynch-law frenzy against mainly rural and small-town southern blacks produced 2,460 African American fatalities in the South from 1889 to 1918. In the 1890s, when a total of 1,111 blacks were lynched in the United States, almost all of them were in the South. Beginning with the lynching of over four hundred African Americans by the Ku Klux Klan between 1868 and 1871, the application of lynch law to southern blacks was so incessant that by the 1890s it was institutionalized in

A scene from the draft riots in New York City in 1863. In the background, an orphan asylum for black children burns. Engraving from the illustrated *London News.* CORBIS/BETTMANN

a horrid ritual that was repeated again and again —one typically witnessed by a mass of white men, women, and children who festively gathered to cheer on the prolonged torture of an accused African American whose life was finally ended by burning at the stake. It is often said that people commit the most hideous violence against others only when they first dehumanize their victims. Such atrocities have often occurred in American history, but the worst example was the ritualistic lynching of southern blacks in the late nineteenth and early twentieth centuries.

Pogrom-style riots in which whites freely assaulted African Americans occurred at least seven times, North and South, from 1908 to 1951, but during World War I a new type of riot emerged: the "communal," or contested-area, riot in which whites, although still generally dominant, were opposed by relatively equal bands of blacks, with the mobs of each race attacking the other's neighborhoods. The greatest such riots took place in 1919 in Chicago and Washington, D.C., and in 1943 in Detroit. The growing combative spirit of blacks and their ability to fight back escalated to the huge wave of black-ghetto uprisings in the 1960s in which African Americans were the aggressors. Sometimes termed "commodity riots" because blacks mainly destroyed and looted white-owned ghetto property rather than taking lives, the prototype of a series of huge riots was the 11–18 August 1965 riot in the Watts section of South Central Los Angeles, in which thirty-four people were killed. Those killed in the Watts uprising and other such large-scale riots as Newark and Detroit in 1967 were mainly African American rioters who died from the efforts of police and military forces to contain the disorder. From 1963 to 1970 there were well over five hundred riots of the commodity type, with thousands of urban African Americans destroying property worth up to $200 million or more, yet most of the 263 persons killed were black rioters. Relative deprivation in a time of national prosperity and long-simmering civil rights grievances were the root causes of these riots, but with one huge exception they were triggered by specific local events. The exception was the assassination of Martin Luther King, Jr., on 4 April 1968, which incited a massive wave of 125 riots (headed by those in Washington, D.C., Baltimore, Chicago, and Kansas City, Missouri), resulting in forty-six deaths and leaving block after block of ghetto property in fire-blackened shambles.

The greatest urban rioting of the twentieth century occurred in Los Angeles in 1992, following the not-guilty verdict given by an all-white suburban

Police use tear gas against rioting whites in a Detroit race riot on 21 June 1943. CORBIS/
BETTMANN

5

jury to white policemen accused of brutally attacking an African American motorist, Rodney King. This verdict inspired a giant, spontaneous black protest in South Central Los Angeles. The riot rapidly spread to other Los Angeles ethnic groups—Hispanics, Asians, and whites—and ramified throughout the city as its identity rapidly changed from a black protest action to the sort of mob nihilism envisioned by the writer Nathanael West in his 1939 novel, *The Day of the Locust*, with its apocalyptic vision of the burning of Los Angeles.

Agrarian Violence

Agrarian violence surfaced in colonial Virginia with Bacon's Rebellion in 1676 and thereafter endured as a sustained tradition of forceful protest for more than two and a half centuries. Many rural rebels had much to protest, especially an economic and landholding system that seemed to be—and often was—rigged against them. Living close to the soil and the hunt, American frontier farmers and planters were well armed and ready and willing to defend themselves or attack those whom they viewed as their oppressors. This they did in one uprising after another, including the eighteenth-century New Jersey land rioters, the upstate New York antirent movement of the nineteenth century, the antimonopolistic tobacco-farming Kentucky Night Riders of the early twentieth century, the poverty-stricken Green Corn rebels of Oklahoma in 1917, and the midwestern Farmers' Holiday Association movement of the 1930s aroused by Depression-era low farm prices.

There were, however, peak periods of agrarian violence: the first was a wave of backcountry rebellions in the colonies and states along the Atlantic Coast from 1740 to 1799 and later; the second was a similar wave of insurgency in the far-flung American West of the 1870s–1890s. Both peaks were brought on by a crisis of land, population, and wealth. In the first instance, the root cause stemmed mainly from a combination of the fastest growing population in the Western world with a limited, nonexpanding land base restricted to the narrow belt of colonies-states along the East Coast. The result was ten backcountry rebel movements spread out among New Jersey, New York, Pennsylvania, Vermont, Massachusetts, Maine, and the Carolinas. Although grievances varied, many members of these movements suffered from onerous taxation and debt. Others lived in fear of Indians or were afflicted by outlaws. In almost every case they thought—often with good reason—that

the governors and legislatures located in such long-settled coastal capitals as Boston, New York City, Philadelphia, and Charleston were indifferent or hostile to their grievances. By this time these backcountry residents had formulated a "homestead ethic" that included three key beliefs:

- the right to have and to hold a family-size farm
- the right to enjoy such a "homestead" free of ruinous economic burden
- the right of peaceful occupancy without fear of violence to person or property

The early American yeomanry was ready to fight any violation of the homestead ethic, and to these farmers it was being roundly contradicted: the shortage of good land made possession of a farm increasingly difficult and problematical; harsh taxation and debt fell as a ruinous burden on the farmer; and, as the case might be, Indians and outlaws posed grave threats to life and property. These violent East Coast protest movements were largely successful until, finally, the crisis of land, population, and wealth faded away as backcountry people poured westward across the Appalachian Mountains after 1800.

The homestead ethic was often invoked in the "garden of the world" between the Appalachian and Rocky Mountains, where once again a new crisis of land, population, and wealth occurred, this time in the Far West. It had been assumed that there was plenty of land available for homesteaders in the vast region from the Missouri River to the Pacific Ocean, but in the 1870s and 1880s, the California economist and reformer Henry George pointed out that in the Golden State and elsewhere in the West, huge blocks of land were increasingly monopolized by greedy railroads favored with vast federal land grants and by wealthy landholders and ranchers. Once again the homestead ethic was being massively violated, and the small farmers and ranchers of the West were fighting mad.

Along with the perceived violation of the homestead ethic in California and the West, aggrieved farmers found themselves fighting for their economic and social lives in the Western Civil War of Incorporation (discussed below). Of many sensational episodes of agrarian violence, a prototypical example was the Mussel Slough conflict in California on 11 May 1880, in which small farmers and the monopolistic Southern Pacific Railroad fell into violent conflict over a lush belt of irrigated land to which each side had laid claim. The Mussel Slough farmers embodied what the historian Catherine McNicol Stock called "rural producer radicalism." When the conflict turned violent, even Karl Marx in faraway London took notice and later in 1880 wrote to Freidrich Sorge, an American correspondent, that California "is very important for me because nowhere else" in the world "has the upheaval most shamelessly caused" by capitalist oppression "taken place with such speed" (Marx and Engels 1953, p. 126). Violent resistance failed and most of the Mussel Slough settlers lost their land, but in California at large the economic boom of the 1880s banked the fires of rebellious fervor that had aroused Marx's hopes. The Mussel Slough dissidents lost their bout, but the moral edge was all theirs in the fictionalized version of the conflict that appeared in a classic of literary naturalism, Frank Norris's powerful antirailroad novel, *The Octopus: A Story of California* (1901).

The agrarian-protest movement of the late nineteenth and early twentieth centuries had its peaceful political wing in the Farmers Alliance, Populist Party, Nonpartisan League, and Farmer-Labor Party. In uneasy and troubled juxtaposition was the movement's violent wing of Mussel Slough settlers, Kentucky Night Riders, and violence-prone small farmers and ranchers of the West. Both wings of the agrarian-reform movement were largely failures. The agricultural policy of President Franklin D. Roosevelt's New Deal in the 1930s finally ended some 250 years of agrarian discontent and violence. Yet memories were short, and it was the descendants of the agrarian rebels (along with their blue-collar allies in the labor-union movement) who were often stonily unsympathetic to and least able to understand the grievances of the black-ghetto rebels and youthful dissidents of the 1960s.

Vigilante Violence

Although there were precedents for vigilantism in European and British history, they were isolated and generated no vigilante tradition. Thus, vigilantism was an original American contribution to the worldwide repertoire of violence. (Not until the 1960s did vigilante movements spring up outside the United States.) The first American vigilantes, who called themselves Regulators, operated in the South Carolina backcountry from 1767 to 1769. Not until the second half of the nineteenth century did the generic "vigilante" and "vigilance committee" begin to supersede their term. From 1767

to 1904, there were more than three hundred vigilante movements. About one-third were in the eastern half of the United States, while the remainder were in the western half. A large majority of the western movements were founded after 1850.

The objective of the preponderance of the vigilante movements was to reconstruct in new frontier areas the old-settled societies from which the vigilantes came—to establish the values of life and property against the misdeeds and threats of thugs, thieves, murderers, and outlaws. Extensive outlaw bands circulated at will east of the Mississippi until the vigilantes broke them up with strong doses of South Carolina–style "regulation." From the Great Plains to the Pacific, the lawless organized themselves in gangs of horse and cattle thieves or plagued the new towns and cities of the region with crime and mayhem. Whether east or west of the Mississippi, vigilante bands were a coalition of the frontier upper class and middle class; the former provided the leadership and the latter formed the rank and file. Vigilante groups could have fewer than one hundred members, but the largest numbered in the thousands, and even more had members in the hundreds. The "instant cities"—San Francisco and Denver—spawned vigilante organizations, and the largest in American history was the San Francisco movement of 1856, with its six thousand to eight thousand members. All western states had vigilante movements, but the three most significant vigilante states were California, whose gold rush–era vigilantes became a prized part of the state's pioneer heritage; Texas, with more vigilante movements than any other state; and Montana, in which the pervasive vigilante mystique was memorialized in statuary at both the front and rear entrances to the state capitol in Helena.

Since leading men of property founded vigilante movements in order to uphold law and order, they organized carefully, elected officers, adopted constitutions, and held trials for their victims before expelling or whipping them or, as became more and more common, hanging them. (A total of at least 729 lives, overwhelmingly white, were snuffed out by vigilante executions from 1767 to 1904.) Rather rapidly an ideology of vigilantism began to emerge and garner widespread support from the orderly minded. Well aware that vigilantism was breaking the law even though its aim was to establish and support lawfulness, the vigilantes justified themselves with a threefold philosophy frequently expressed in their constitutions and declarations: (1) self-preservation is the first law of nature, (2) the right of revolution justifies a temporary usurpation of legal authority in the interest of punishing the criminal and establishing order, and (3) popular sovereignty in a time of social crisis legitimizes the action of the people as being above the law in temporarily reclaiming from government the power to punish the lawless. There was also an economic rationale for vigilantism: it was much cheaper than the regular functioning of the law with its cumbersome, costly, and often frustrating legal due process for the accused. *No EXPENSE TO THE COUNTY* was the slogan on one vigilante banner in Indiana, while a leading Denver pioneer and city builder reminisced approvingly that in the days of the vigilantes "there were no appeals" and "no writs of errors; no attorney's fees; no pardon in six months. Punishment was swift, sure and certain!"

The pillars of frontier society often joined or supported vigilante movements. At one time in the late nineteenth century, five former vigilantes served in the U.S. Senate. These senators never repudiated their vigilantism and were proud of it. Eight territorial or state governors had been vigilantes, as had two founding first presidents of state bar associations. One prominent attorney was so proud of having been a late-nineteenth-century urban vigilante that he put it in his entry in *Who's Who in America*. In presidential correspondence, Andrew Jackson once approved a band of Iowa settlers' use of vigilantism to deal with crime and disorder.

As a young rancher in North Dakota, the aristocratic Harvard graduate Theodore Roosevelt tried with all his might to join a Montana vigilante movement that turned out to be the most lethal in American history. The vigilante chieftains slyly rebuffed the loquacious twenty-five-year-old Roosevelt, because they feared he would talk too much about vigilante operations. Until the end of his life, Roosevelt regretted that he had never been a frontier vigilante. As a former president who had headed a strongly imperialist administration, Roosevelt in a private letter enthusiastically and favorably compared vigilantism to imperialism. Leading members of the late-nineteenth- and early-twentieth-century American illuminati of judges, lawyers, and legal experts praised frontier vigilantism and went so far as to advocate (unsuccessfully) procedural revisions in the law that would have moved the legal system much closer to the swiftness, sureness, and certainty of vigilan-

tism. By the early twentieth century, vigilantism (with prior precedents) evolved from the frontier variety into neovigilantism. Largely a response to modern America, neovigilantism was much more urban than rural. In the early and middle twentieth century, it found its victims chiefly among racial, ethnic, and religious minorities; laboring men and labor leaders; political radicals; and proponents of civil liberties.

As neovigilantism thrived, respectable leaders of American public opinion shifted from approval to strong condemnation of vigilantism. The evolution in attitudes is exemplified by the contrasting response to two popular and significant novels: Owen Wister's *The Virginian* (1902) and Walter Van Tilburg Clark's *The Ox-Bow Incident* (1940). Wister was, like his good friend Theodore Roosevelt (to whom he dedicated the novel), an eastern aristocrat and Harvard graduate with strong ties to the West. Later filmed three times, *The Virginian* was a widely read and influential American novel. It tells the tale of a heroic young Wyoming cowboy in the age of frontier ranching and outlaw villainies. One of the climaxes of the strongly provigilante novel finds the cowboy-hero heading a lynching party in the implacable execution of a cattle rustler who was no less than the hero's friend gone bad. Quite different is Clark's powerful classic published some forty years later and made into an equally unforgettable 1943 film of the same title. *The Ox-Bow Incident*, set in the Nevada of 1885, focuses on the tragic lynching of three men by vigilantes who stubbornly insist on hanging them despite their pleas of innocence, later proved correct. *The Ox-Bow Incident* leaves the reader in no doubt that its author wholeheartedly opposed vigilantism. It was a mark of changing times that in the 1930s and 1940s an increasingly due process–minded American public was ready to embrace a forceful antivigilante novel and film. Yet notions of vigilantism were still so deeply incised in American consciousness that in the high-crime decades of the 1970s and 1980s, graphic fantasies of updated vigilantism found an audience in Hollywood films and television productions, as was the case with the popular, chilling 1974 movie *Death Wish* (and its four sequels), starring Charles Bronson as a vengeful vigilante at war with crime in New York City.

Urban Riots and Industrial Violence

The colonial- and Revolutionary-era tradition of anti-British urban rioting in the leading Atlantic Coast cities fell dormant in the late eighteenth and early nineteenth centuries, but in the relatively calm decades from 1800 to 1830, growing ethnic and religious diversity, increasing immigration, a widening gap between rich and poor, and a democratic egalitarianism among the city masses sowed the seeds of a remarkable burst of urban rioting from the 1830s to the 1850s. The prototypical American slum, Lower Manhattan's Five Points, emerged as a festering district of poverty, crime, and discontent. Similar ghettos of the poor rose in other big cities, and the antiquated colonial watch-and-ward system of preserving order was outstripped by growing turbulence that flamed into the first great riot decade of the nineteenth century, the 1830s. On through the 1850s, the variety of riot types was notable: anti–African American, anti-immigrant, anti-Catholic, and antiabolitionist as well as election and labor riots all became common in New York City, Philadelphia, Boston, Baltimore, and Cincinnati; altogether they were shaken by thirty-nine major riots from 1830 to 1859. Extending the period to 1865, U.S. cities of twenty thousand or more suffered eighty major riots. In response, the modern American institution of city police arose in emulation of the London police force created by Robert Peel in 1829.

Following the Civil War the American industrial system began its climb to twentieth-century status as the greatest in the world. After 1865, the profusion of urban group conflict narrowed mainly to two immensely important types: race riots (see above) and industrial disputes. With a prelude in the Molly Maguire Pennsylvania labor troubles of the 1860s and 1870s, the Sixty Years' War of industrial conflict opened with the great transcontinental railroad strike that made 1877 "the year of violence." Incited by wage cuts in a time of severe economic depression, unorganized railroad workers in Baltimore and Pittsburgh spontaneously launched what one scholar called "the most spectacular and widespread" strike in American history—one that produced violence and disorder all the way to San Francisco. In Pittsburgh radical agitators called for war between capital and labor. Before federal troops could arrive to restore order in that city, a militant strike turned into a revolutionary insurrection that left a railroad roundhouse, shops, 104 locomotives, and thousands of freight and passenger cars in a flaming shambles. The Pennsylvania Railroad sustained $5 million worth of damage, and at least twenty-four people lost their lives. Stunned observers were reminded of the proletarian uprising that established the revolutionary Paris Commune in 1871.

A battle-scarred city during these six decades, Chicago was the locale of the next great explosion of violence: the Haymarket Square riot of 1886. The violence-prone anarchist movement in Chicago joined a citywide campaign for the eight-hour working day. As an orderly prolabor meeting broke up, a bomb was suddenly hurled into the midst of a contingent of policemen. Frightened and enraged, the police fired on the crowd, and the riot was on. Although estimates vary, approximately eight policemen and eight rioters died, and for years a huge controversy about the violence raged. Labor relations in Chicago were still embittered when another episode of industrial violence rocked the city with a weekend of rioting and protest on behalf of the 1894 national strike of the American Railway Union (ARU) against the many railroads that hauled sleeping cars manufactured by the antilabor Pullman Company in a Chicago suburb. Twelve were killed in the Chicago outburst, and a wave of riots in support of the striking railroad rolled west to San Francisco. As in 1877, the intervention of federal troops broke the Pullman strike. Reared in the heartland of Indiana to believe in a classless America, a disillusioned Eugene V. Debs, the ARU leader, became a socialist and soon moved into the realm of political protest as a perennial Socialist candidate for president.

Defeats by organized labor in its campaign to obtain the right to organize and bargain collectively piled up in a succession of agonizing industrial disputes. Two years before the Pullman strike, Andrew Carnegie and Henry Clay Frick used a lockout that turned violent to destroy a long-established union of their steelworkers. Ten lost their lives at Homestead, Pennsylvania, in what was a demoralizing setback for labor at the hands of one of the nation's greatest industrialists, Carnegie. By the turn of the century, the mounting impact of industrial violence created an unsettling specter of class conflict in America. Jack London's monitory novel *The Iron Heel* (1907) caught the foreboding of the nation on the verge of civil war between the upper and lower classes. Some felt that the murderous dynamiting of the *Los Angeles Times* in Los Angeles in 1910 by labor-union zealots angered by the newspaper's reactionary publisher, Harrison Gray Otis, was a portent of the revolution to come.

Things got worse. To many, London's nightmarish vision of the oppressive "iron heel" of capitalism become a reality in 1913–1914 when America's prototypical robber baron, John D. Rockefeller, Sr., won a smashing victory in the "Great Coalfield War" of southern Colorado. With John D., Jr., in charge of details, the senior Rockefeller staunchly approved an unyielding policy in the face of a strike by the United Mine Workers (UMW) against the Rockefeller-controlled Colorado Fuel and Iron (CFI) and smaller companies. With the indispensable support of the state militia and local officials, CFI and its corporate allies fought off the UMW effort by withstanding thirty-eight skirmishes (with eighteen deaths) during the first five weeks of the strike. But the miners refused to give up, and at Ludlow, Colorado, union families, having been expelled from the Rockefeller company town, settled down in a tent city on the outskirts of CFI property during the winter of 1913–1914. They were still there on Easter Sunday 1914. The next day, Monday, 20 April, brought a tragedy that greatly pained John D. Rockefeller, Jr. The event went down in history as the infamous "Black Hole of Ludlow." On the morning of the twentieth, a gun battle erupted between the miners and the militia who were on duty to guard CFI property and keep the tent city under surveillance. The militia gradually gained control and began setting fire to the tents. Having foreseen just such a tactic, many union families had pits below their tents in which to take refuge. Beneath one tent, two mothers led their eleven young children down into what they thought was the safety of a pit, while flames crackled above them. Instead of surviving, all thirteen women and children suffocated. Their bodies were found the next morning, 21 April, when George S. McGovern, the historian of the episode, wrote, "the sun shone on what might well be considered the most pathetic scene" in the history of American industrial warfare. Following this tragedy, maddened miners struck back in a ten-day onslaught of violence over a 250-square-mile area of southern Colorado before the neutral intervention of federal soldiers restored peace. Yet, the UMW lost the strike, and cosmetic reforms by the Rockefellers did not alleviate the basic grievance: continued control of the lives of the miners and their families by the company.

More violence and more defeats for strikers and their unions came in the remainder of the 1910s and on into the 1920s. Baleful premonitions of all-out class conflict revived in 1932, the last year of President Herbert Hoover's administration, when many sober citizens feared that the "crisis of the old order" in the deepest depths of the worst depression in American history had the nation poised on the abyss of social revolution. It may have been a near miss, but instead of social revolution came Franklin D. Roosevelt's New Deal for labor, which was nevertheless accompanied by the last great spasm of U.S. industrial conflict.

Encouraged by the federal government's new prolabor policy, numerous job actions in the major mass-production industries won victories for a revitalized and expanded labor-union movement in the turbulent 1930s. The worst episode of violence was in connection with a steelworkers' strike, when in the tragic Memorial Day massacre in Chicago in 1937, police shot down fleeing picketers, killing ten. Labor's overall triumph in the 1930s would never have occurred but for a Depression-born national consensus in favor of Roosevelt's reform of labor relations that resulted in what workers had fruitlessly fought for in the previous five decades: union recognition and collective bargaining.

United Mine Workers involved in the coal strike war of the Ludlow mines, 1914, shown here at their military headquarters in Trinidad, Colorado. CORBIS/BETTMANN

Paradoxically, however, the profusion of riots and violent strikes and lockouts in the classic age of urban industrialism, 1870s–1930s, was counterpointed by a very different trend at the level of the individual. This was a trend in which Americans were, as a result of the constraints of industrial society, becoming more orderly in their personal behavior—a trend that was cognate with the "incorporation of America" that accompanied industrialization. (See the following sections "Incorporation and American Violence" and on the transition from the industrial to the information society.)

Women and Violence

During the 1980s and 1990s, scholars began to give more attention to women, the most neglected topic in the history of American violence. It is a subject that is often inseparable from marital and family violence. In 1987 Elizabeth Pleck published a landmark study entitled *Domestic Tyranny: The Making of Social Policy Against Family Violence from Colonial Times to the Present*—a treatment that showed the ebb and flow over the centuries of public concern with family violence, culminating in the late-twentieth-century era of heightened consciousness that began in the 1960s after seventy years of neglect. The linkage of violence against wives with the broader subject of family violence was continued in 1988 with another pioneering book, Linda Gordon's *Heroes of Their Own Lives: The Politics and History of Family Violence, Boston, 1880–1960*. Geographically balancing this East Coast study is a monograph on the West Coast, *What Trouble I Have Seen: A History of Violence Against Wives* (1996), by David Peterson del Mar, that focused on Oregon in the nineteenth and twentieth centuries and disclosed a broad historical pattern in the propensity of husbands to beat their wives: In the early and middle nineteenth century, a traditional patriarchal society produced a relatively high incidence of violence against wives. But with the decline of patriarchy in the late nineteenth century, a period that was both more industrialized and more orderly in personal relations, male self-restraint toward women increased, and the prevalence of violence against wives went down. From the 1920s on, however, violence against wives rose in accord with a burgeoning American mood of "expressive individualism" that gradually reduced the prior male generations' self-imposed barriers to wife abuse. After 1945 the situation grew even worse: in a society that increasingly emphasized personal gratification, self-indulgent violence by husbands against wives significantly escalated the beating of wives to the high levels of the late twentieth century.

The other side of the coin is, of course, that in the late twentieth century women had become more violent, although the level of their violence was still far below that of men. Going back to the colonial period, there have always been notable women murderers, although the most famous accused female murderer, Lizzie Borden, was never convicted. At the end of the twentieth century, scholars attempted to go beyond famous but oversensationalized women outlaws and murderers to understand more generally criminal women. Such women were fruitfully studied through research on female prison inmates of the nineteenth and early twentieth centuries, the majority of whom never achieved great notoriety. A provocative study of women in western penitentiaries from 1865 to 1915 by Anne M. Butler punctured stereotypes of criminal women and women prisoners to depict a system of "gendered justice" that was more accurately one of gendered injustice to women. These women were discriminated against by the legal culture that sent them to prison and by the predominantly male culture that presided over them in prison.

VALUES AND IMAGES OF AMERICAN VIOLENCE

Values—Mentally Armed for Violence: Male Honor and No-Duty-to-Retreat

While the intergroup violence discussed in the sections "White-Indian Warfare" through "Urban Riots and Industrial Violence" was usually on behalf of ardently held causes, it was a general phenomenon of male honor that often led American men to fight each other in the nineteenth century—personal combat that led to many a tragic death and a high homicide rate. In the antebellum South, the "code duello" punctiliously governed the etiquette of the duel in which gentlemen fought to avenge perceived insults to their honor. In the postbellum American West, the gentlemanly combat of Dixie was democratized and broadened, resulting in the "code of the West." The code defined rules of man-to-man gunfights epitomized by the "walkdown" along the dusty street of a frontier town in which armed rivals confronted one another, drew, fired, and killed. Not all approved; one jaundiced observer, Joseph H. Beale, Jr., of the Harvard Law School, denounced such combat as a barbaric survival mired in a morally deficient notion of "hip-pocket ethics." The phrase was in reference to where a western man often carried his pistol. To Beale's extreme distaste, questions of cowardice and honor supplanted the more truly honorable concept of reverence for life. Gerald F. Linderman's study of courage in the Civil War showed that it was individual allegiance to personal honor that kept soldiers fighting in the front lines even though they were slaughtered by the thousands in such appalling bloodbaths as Shiloh, Antietam, Fredericksburg, Gettysburg, and many others. Elliot J. Gorn's book on the cult of bare-knuckle prizefighting revealed how boxing focused the meaning of honor for members of the urban and industrial working class of the North and East.

The historian Roger Lane succinctly defined honor "as a matter of reputation as judged by the community"—a small, local community or group in which an individual's peers take the measure of his honor. Closely related to the codes of combat-oriented male honor in the nineteenth century was the concept of "no duty to retreat." The doctrine of no-duty-to-retreat emerged in the nineteenth century when the nation largely turned away from the English common law of homicide and self-defense in which retreat was legally required in potentially lethal confrontations of combative individuals. From medieval times to Sir William Blackstone in the eighteenth century, English common-law doctrine had a bias against killing in self-defense out of its concern that the right to defend might be mistaken for the right to kill. Crucial to the English common law was the notion of escape: in a personal dispute that threatened to become violent, one must flee from the scene. Should it be impossible to get away, however, the common law required that one must retreat as far as possible—"to the wall" was the legal phrase—before one could use violence or kill in an act of lawful self-defense.

Following the westward movement of settlers beyond the Appalachians, a succession of state supreme courts—eventually upheld by the U.S. Supreme Court—repudiated the English duty to retreat in favor of no-duty-to-retreat: the American right to stand one's ground and kill in self-defense. The Ohio Supreme Court held in 1876 that a "true man" was not obligated to flee from an assailant, while the supreme court in neighboring Indiana announced in the following year that "the tendency of the American mind seems to be very strongly against the enforcement of any rule which requires a person to flee when assailed." In effect, the Indiana court held that the English duty to retreat was a legal rationale for cowardice and was, therefore, simply un-American.

The American doctrine of no-duty-to-retreat was strictly speaking a self-defense concept, but it was highly compatible with the spirit of aggressive violence linked to such formulations of personal honor as the code duello and the code of the West. Nor were such notions of male honor restricted to white men or the nineteenth century. Edward L. Ayers and Fox Butterfield found that post–Civil War southern blacks had similar values of honor that made them likewise prone to violence. As Butterfield, Elijah Anderson, and Lane indicated, these notions of honor persisted into late-twentieth-century urban life as embodied in the African American "code of the streets," with its violence-prone insistence on "respect" by one's peers among the gang-ridden streets of black ghettos. Meanwhile, after twenty-five years of clinical work with violent men, the psychiatrist James Gilligan concluded in 1996 that a twisted notion of male honor, rooted in the persistent institution of patriarchy, was the ultimate cause of their violence. The late-twentieth-century status of no-duty-to-retreat was that while some judges and legal scholars were embarrassed by what they saw as the atavistic concept of no-duty-to-retreat, others were not. In 1999, for example, the Florida Supreme Court held that it was allowable for married women to use deadly force on husbands if wives were in mortal danger, even if such wives did not attempt to leave the house first; this repealed a former court order saying that abused wives could not use deadly force unless they attempted first to flee. In the much broader realm of foreign affairs and war, America was always a no-duty-to-retreat nation.

Images: Crime, Social Bandits, and Conservative Heroes

Often ambivalent in their attitudes, Americans were of two minds about crime and criminals. Murderers, rapists, thugs, and brutal robbers were viewed with fear and loathing, but a host of nineteenth- and twentieth-century outlaws and gangsters were among the most romanticized social types in American history. The likes of Billy the Kid and Jesse James were immortalized in the

American heritage as what scholars call "social bandits." Conceptualized by the British historian Eric J. Hobsbawm, "social bandits" worldwide became heroes because their crimes appealed to the social discontents and grievances of ordinary people who would never commit such crimes on their own. In Hobsbawm's formulation, the model social bandit was the medieval English outlaw Robin Hood, who, according to legend, took from the rich to give to the poor.

There were many American social bandits. Leading the list, Jesse and Frank James were widely admired for their robberies of banks and trains by law-abiding farmers and townspeople of the Midwest who suffered the oppression of railroads' excessive freight rates and high-handed conduct and of banks' onerous lending policies. Billy the Kid, the prototypical bandit of the Southwest, was idolized by Anglo and Hispanic small ranchers and farmers for his gunslinging skill against the economic tyranny of a mercantile clique in the bloody Lincoln County War of New Mexico. A never-ending succession of dime novels and romantic films thereafter forged the mighty myth of Billy the Kid. The celluloid saga of the Kid includes incarnations in the *Young Guns* movies of 1988 and 1990, and the James brothers were depicted in the classic films *Jesse James* (1939) and *The Long Riders* (1980). In short, American social bandits were outlaw heroes whose actions spoke to the hopes and dreams of the downtrodden—as did, among many examples, Joaquín Murieta, the California brigand out of Mexico, who appealed to the native "Californios" disinherited from land and status by the American takeover in the Gold Rush era. Of similar attraction was the South Texas *bandido* Gregorio Cortez, whose violent deeds "with his pistol in his hand" made him a folk hero to the poor villagers under the sway of Anglo hegemony and lawless actions by the Texas Rangers.

The daring 1930s midwestern bank robberies of the "public enemy" John Dillinger struck a chord with middle Americans, many of whom had lost their lifetime savings in the numerous bank failures early in the decade. Another Depression-era desperado, "Pretty Boy" Floyd, had a Robin Hood image among the hard-pressed rural Oklahoma stock from which he sprang. Two good-natured turn-of-the-twentieth-century outlaws, Butch Cassidy and Harry Longabaugh, alias the "Sundance Kid," had their contemporary sympathizers, but it was a 1969 film—*Butch Cassidy and the Sundance Kid*—that elevated these two almost-forgotten

western outlaws into instant social-bandit status among 1960s Americans captivated by the anti-establishment movie mystique of Butch and Sundance. Likewise, the kill-crazy robbery team of Clyde Barrow and Bonnie Parker had a following among alienated hardscrabble Texans in the "dirty thirties," but it was the unique combination of crime and tragedy in the hit film *Bonnie and Clyde* (1967) that captured for them a bright spot in the pantheon of American social bandits.

Bonnie and Clyde and *Butch Cassidy and the Sundance Kid* graphically illustrate the point that western outlaws have been a highly profitable genre for the Hollywood film industry since its earliest days. Long chronicled in popular novels and romanticized biographies as well as in movies, there is, in contrast to the social bandit, the socially conservative hero, represented, for example, by the western lawmen "Wild Bill" Hickok and Wyatt Earp. The Hollywood director Cecil B. DeMille glorified Hickok in a wildly inaccurate but ingeniously entertaining box-office success, *The Plainsman* (1936), while Earp was featured in or portrayed in about thirty-six films, including the classic *My Darling Clementine* (1946) as well as *Gunfight at the O. K. Corral* (1957) and an appealing, although gory, update, *Tombstone* (1993). The aspect of the American

Paul Newman as Butch Cassidy, in the 1969 film *Butch Cassidy and the Sundance Kid.* CORBIS/BETTMANN

psychology that values order and security responds to the reassuring movie myth of the socially conservative hero who always defeats evil. The social-bandit hero evokes, conversely, the instinctive American distrust of established power and fondness for dissent. These two competing versions of popular-media mythology expressed in images of violence endure because they represent a deep ambivalence—a cognitive split—in American attitudes to established power and dissident protest. One outstanding movie deftly combined both: *High Noon* featured a heroic local marshal in a winning walkdown with an evil pistoleer who held a town hostage to its fear of him. The film appearing in 1952 at the height of McCarthyism, *High Noon's* heroic marshal also stood for dissent and protest in that he was the only man in town strong and responsible enough to stand up to the McCarthy-like threats and bullying of the murderous gunfighter.

PROCESSES OF AMERICAN VIOLENCE

Incorporation and American Violence

The period after the Civil War was, according to the scholar Alan Trachtenberg, an age of incorporation. By this he meant that potent industrial elements were not merely organizing themselves in legal institutions known as "corporations." Rather, in the most sweeping "general process of change," such corporations with their commercial and financial allies were taking the lead in "the expansion of an industrial capitalist system across the continent" highlighted by "the spread of a market economy into all regions." The result was "the emergence of a changed, more tightly structured society with new hierarchies of control" in business, finance, and industry (Trachtenberg 1982, pp. 3–4). Aside from core factors of economic and class interest, there were strong racial and ethnic overtones to the frequently violent and unremitting trend of incorporation. America had been a nation of immigrants since the colonial period of the English along the Atlantic Coast and the Spanish and Mexicans in the Southwest. Yet the pace and variety of immigration to the United States dramatically altered after the Civil War. The predominant "old immigration" of the prewar era was from northern and western Europe, but after the war, Ellis Island became the principal gateway for a booming "new immigration" from southern

and eastern Europe, especially Poles, Russians, Jews, Hungarians, Slavs, Greeks, and Italians. Anglo prejudice was heavy against these new immigrants and was even more hostile to the Chinese immigrants who flowed into the American West. Similarly discriminated against, especially in California and Texas, was the Hispanic population that went back to colonial times but was heavily augmented by later immigrants from Mexico. (Hispanics were, however, too numerous in New Mexico to be as victimized as their *compadres* in California and Texas.)

Yet incorporation was not simply an alignment of Anglos against non-Anglos; Anglos nationwide were split by the process of incorporation. Among those who most spiritedly resisted the trend everywhere were Americans of Anglo and old immigrant stock. The incorporating movement was highly politicized. Its cutting edge in politics and the judiciary were incorporation-minded Republicans and conservative Democrats who were opposed by liberal Democrats, third-party movements like the Populists, and a dwindling band of reform-minded Republicans. In the South white dirt farmers and sharecroppers, to say nothing of former slaves, most acutely felt the pressure of incorporation. A radical Populist Party faction led by Tom Watson of Georgia, an Anglo, attempted to form an anti-incorporation coalition of white and black farmers, but a vindictive bloc of moneyed whites used corruption at the polls to crush this reform movement.

Behind much of the industrial violence in the East and Midwest and the agrarian violence in the Midwest was the bête noire of incorporation. It was in the West, however, that polarization over the trend of incorporation was especially widespread and violent. Indeed, a veritable "Western Civil War of Incorporation" raged from Missouri to the West Coast from the 1850s to 1920. In this far-flung regional civil war, much of the violence usually and rightly understood under the headings of Indian dispossession, vigilantism, outlaw exploits, gunfights and shootouts, Hispanic dissidence, boomtown turmoil, land and range wars, and agrarian and industrial conflict is more broadly and collectively subsumed under the trend of incorporation. Opposing the incorporating aggression in more than forty episodes was an anti-incorporating element of small ranchers, homesteading farmers, and small-town folk as well as, here and there, workers, miners, and mill hands. There was also an extensive and unintimidated element of rustlers and outlaws whose robbery victims were often banks, railroads, and big ranches. The law-abiding rural anti-incorporators tolerated the outlaw opponents of incorporation, because the latter usually behaved with courtesy and respect to them. Lawfully or lawlessly, the anti-incorporating people fought to preserve traditional ways of life at the grass roots; in their worldview, the bonds of kin and locality were precious, and they disdained the impersonal market forces that often ruined them. Anti-incorporating men and women in the West were, on the other hand, regarded by the incorporating element as socially retrograde, as barriers to commercial and civic progress spearheaded by the modern trend of incorporation.

Although strongly opposed by both peaceful and violent means, the western incorporators sought with great success to sew up willing legislatures, acquiescent governors, and sympathetic judges. Sensational episodes of late-nineteenth- and early-twentieth-century violence in the Western Civil War of Incorporation included the Lincoln County War in New Mexico; the conflict in Tombstone and Cochise County, Arizona; the Mus-

sel Slough uprising in California; Colorado's Thirty Years' War of industrial strife (1884–1914); the Johnson County War in Wyoming; and the ill-fated 1917 Green Corn Rebellion in Oklahoma. A final, desperate campaign against incorporation in the West was mounted by the Industrial Workers of the World from 1916 to 1919, but the "Wobblies," as its members were called, were crushed by violence and intimidation in notable outbreaks in Everett and Centralia, Washington; Butte, Montana; and Bisbee, Arizona.

Disincorporation and Deauthoritization in the 1960s

Despite the New Deal reforms of Franklin D. Roosevelt, a solidly incorporated America survived through the 1930s, 1940s, and 1950s. Curbed in significant ways by the New Deal, America's leading industrial and financial institutions yet retained great wealth and standing during the Depression of the 1930s and even more so during the prosperity of World War II and the postwar period. By the 1950s and 1960s, the leaders of incorporated America were referred to as "the establishment."

A group of men stand guard outside the Industrial Workers of the World headquarters in Seattle, Washington, on 18 July 1913, after U.S. Navy sailors rioted and burned the hall the night before. Corbis/PEMCO — Webster and Stevens Collection; Museum of History and Industry, Seattle

It swiftly came apart in the 1960s. California's example is a microcosm of America's experience with incorporation and violence. During the 1920s–1950s, California was a strongly incorporated society dominated by the great private and public economic, political, educational, and media organizations and institutions of the time—among them the ultraconservative *Los Angeles Times* and the equally conservative press lord William Randolph Hearst; the Associated Farmers of California in the forefront of aggressive agribusiness; the Bank of America; powerful electric utilities and oil interests; the great Hollywood film companies; the University of California, resolutely led by Robert Gordon Sproull from 1930 to 1958; governmental bodies like the Los Angeles Department of Water and Light; and the giant aerospace companies of the 1940s and 1950s. There were some ugly episodes of violence in California in the 1920–1959 period, but with the lid of incorporation tightly on there was not much compared to what came in the 1960s.

A key factor in the large-scale 1960s renewal of violence in California and the nation as a whole was the sudden onset of widespread disincorporation. The sociologist Lewis Feuer described the process of "deauthoritization" by which in America during the 1960s a wide panoply of society's citadels of power—among them, the presidency, the Pentagon, and the State Department—lost credibility and authority by their actions in regard to the Vietnam War. In California the powerful organs of "the establishment" were by 1970 greatly weakened, altered, or under sustained attack. Standing out in the almost incessant events of shocking violence that plagued California after 1960 were political assassinations, race riots, homicidal and suicidal cults, mass killings and serial murder, lethal youth gangs, sickening sex crimes, and sensational show trials of accused killers. In the nation at large, not only the presidency and the Pentagon suffered from deauthoritization but so did great corporations like General Motors. Just as great violence attended the long-term trend of incorporation, great violence accompanied the rapid disincorporation of the 1960s.

Crime and Homicide in the Transition from the Industrial to the Information Society, 1960s–1990s

The disincorporation of the 1960s and after converged with the transition from the industrial society to the information society. This transitional era is often spoken of as the postindustrial period. It was marked by the loss of structure governing the full-fledged industrial society that came to an end in the 1960s. Reinforced by the conjoined trend of incorporation, the emergence of an urbanized, industrial society in the last three decades of the nineteenth century produced a structured order in which crime and homicide fell significantly, remained relatively low during the first half of the twentieth century, and bottomed out in 1955, with the lowest murder rate of all. With the onset of the postindustrial era, the murder rate began a steep climb in the 1960s and 1970s and reached a four-decades peak in 1974.

The industrial revolution in America as elsewhere produced the dominance of mass-produced manufactured products. Not only the labor system but all of society and the economy were organized around industrialization and the closely related factor of urbanization. The successful functioning of the industrial system was based on a highly disciplined people performing their daily work in thousands of factories, mills, mines, offices, and shops. In such a society there was little tolerance of the drunken, the idle, the disorderly, and the criminal. Closely knit families, effective police, demanding schools, and a pervasive middle-class ethos of work and decorum produced the most orderly society in the realm of personal behavior experienced by America in the long period from the 1830s to the 1990s. In the highly structured industrial era, wrote Roger Lane, the "moral lessons of self-control and the private and governmental institutions of social control reinforced each other" (Lane 1997, p. 299). With the waning of industrial society in the 1960s and the rise of an "aggressive hedonism," declared Ted Robert Gurr, "a sense of resentment against large, impersonal or indeed any external source of authority" broke through nearly a century of staunch restraints on antisocial behavior, unleashing the high crime and homicide rates of the 1960s–1980s (Graham and Gurr, eds. 1979, p. 370). Thus, the U.S. murder rate more than doubled in only twenty years, from a low of 4.5 homicides per 100,000 population in 1955 to 10.2 in 1974. Through the 1970s, the homicide rate remained high, varying from 8.5 to over 10.0. It fell off during the middle and late 1980s and then rose to 9.0 at the end of the decade before soaring to 10.2 for the 1991–1992 biennium.

It should be noted, however, that although a number of nations in South America and Africa have had double or triple the U.S. homicide rates, the latter, when compared with those of other economically advanced democracies of the world, are spectacularly high: during the late twentieth century, Japan's homicide rate averaged well under 1.0; Germany, France, and England averaged around 1.0; Canada occasionally went over 2.0; and Italy exceeded 2.5; but, said Lane, no developed nation averaged anything as high as American homicide rates during the 1970s and 1980s. Lane cogently argued that the three main causes of America's very high homicide rate in the late twentieth century were historical: the "decay" of urban industrial society; the American gun culture "in part born of, and long nurtured by, the nearly two centuries of racial warfare that followed European invasion of long-established native peoples"; and, "above all," the heritage of "slavery and the resulting racial hostilities" as well as "habits, values, attitudes, and even institutions that have made Americans historically more likely than other developed peoples to tolerate and even admire the kind of belligerence that leads to violence" (Lane 1997, pp. 313, 353).

Yet, one scholar's 1990 prediction of significantly reduced crime and homicide in the 1990s was correct. The Federal Bureau of Investigation reported that for six years in a row, from 1992 to 1997, serious crime in America steadily declined. Most striking of all was that the homicide rate fell 28 percent, to a low level not seen since the late 1960s. Americans in the late 1990s were, however, still mostly uneasy about crime, for the reduced rates of crime and homicide were still unacceptably high. Moreover, Lane noted that "even as homicides by ordinary adults" were falling, "the most troubling kinds" were rising, "from ideological bombings and serial killings to the more common murders by strangers, criminals, and deeply alienated teenagers" (Lane 1997, p. 353).

CONCLUSION: A BAD DAY AT COLUMBINE HIGH

Among other ideological bombings, Lane was referring to the 1995 destruction of the Alfred P. Murrah Federal Building in Oklahoma City (which killed 168), but his reference to "deeply alienated teenagers" was written well before the vengeful 20 April 1999 attack on Columbine High School in Littleton, Colorado, by two heavily armed students, eighteen-year-old Eric Harris and seventeen-year-old Dylan Klebold, who took delight in the mass murder of twelve of their peers and one teacher before killing themselves. This tragedy was preceded by a series of similar but much less deadly school shootings:

1997: Pearl, Mississippi (sixteen-year-old killed three); and Paducah, Kentucky (fourteen-year-old killed three)

1998: Jonesboro, Arkansas (eleven-year-old and thirteen-year-old killed five); Edinboro, Pennsylvania (fourteen-year-old killed one); Fayetteville, Tennessee (eighteen-year-old killed one); and Springfield, Oregon (fifteen-year-old killed two)

In these six 1997–1998 shootings, forty-six people were wounded. The 1999 Littleton shooting equaled that figure in a single day. The Columbine massacre, with its body count of thirteen killed and forty-six wounded, shocked America as had no other outburst of violence since the Oklahoma City catastrophe four years before.

By 1999 the information society was an accomplished fact. On the eve of the second millennium, Europeans feared the end of the world, but in 1999, as the third millennium approached, Americans feared "Y2K"—that is, a potentially massive breakdown of society and the economy due to the "crashing" of preprogrammed computers unable to adapt to the numerals of the year 2000. Contrary to manifest events of violence, latent trends in the middle and late 1990s revealed impersonal statistics giving hope to some that the information

Eric Harris and Dylan Klebold, in yearbook photos from Columbine High School in Littleton, Colorado.
CORBIS/AFP

society was beginning to achieve a modicum of order and stability: examples were the significant decline of crime and homicide noted above; a drop in teenage pregnancy; and a six-year increase in the test scores of high school seniors. Even the Littleton massacre was counterbalanced by the declining national rate of violence in the schools and a drop in teenage crime.

There is evidence that the cornerstone of the information society, the computer, revitalized student interest in learning during the teen and pre-teen years. The remarkable 1990s megaexpansion of the computerized Internet truly created an information society, realizing, at last, an electronically connected national, if not worldwide "village." The communication of both practical and scholarly information over the Internet had an incalculably positive effect on knowledge and learning in America. (To be noted, too, is that the use of the computer and the Internet made law enforcement more adept, versatile, and quick to react to crime.) Yet, there was a negative impact. The suicidal Littleton mass murderers, Harris and Klebold, were fully fledged children of the information society. For a classroom assignment they used their skill as moviemakers to film in advance a simulation of their murderous fantasy of massacring fellow students. Harris, the leader, operated his own Internet home page and used it to vent his nihilistic, avowedly Hitlerian, hatred and desire to "KILL 'EM AAAAALLLL!!!!" The Internet was used by scholars to exchange the latest information on all manner of research, but it was also used by the likes of Harris and Klebold to receive and purvey know-how for bomb making. Examples of the way in which the Internet was a significant enabler of the dysfunctional and the antisocial, not to say the violence-prone, could be multiplied. Homicidal individuals aside, computers exist in a proximate world of electronic violence in which computer "viruses" thrive.

In the last years of the twentieth century, Americans haltingly confronted the destructive effects of the Internet and an entertainment industry of music, film, and television increasingly obsessed with violence. At the same time, Americans grappled with the much more tangible problem of gun regulation in a massively armed and historically violence-prone civilian society. With well over two hundred million guns in circulation among the civilian population, and with half of the households in the United States possessing firearms, the abun-

The Gun in America. CORBIS/HANNAH GAL

dant holding of guns is an almost incredibly important explanation of American violence. Shaken by such events as the Littleton massacre and the frequency of mass murders, Americans in the 1990s were ever more in favor of increased gun regulation. It was not, however, just the National Rifle Association, but also significant representatives of the poor and of minority groups that prized the notion of the constitutionally protected right to bear arms.

As this overview, other thematic overviews (see, for example, "American Violence in Comparative Perspective" "Crime and Punishment in American History," "Immigration," "Race and Ethnicity," and "Representation of Violence"), and many, many specific entries in this encyclopedia underscore, America has a tenacious tradition and pattern of violence. What history has taken so long to create will not be easily or quickly reversed. This must be done, but how long will it take? Only time and history will tell.

BIBLIOGRAPHY

The general works below often contain important specialized material on violence. By the same token, the works listed under specialized headings also have broad implications for understanding American violence.

GENERAL WORKS

Brown, Richard Maxwell. *No Duty to Retreat: Violence and Values in American History and Society.* New York: Oxford University Press, 1991.

———. *Strain of Violence: Historical Studies of American Violence and Vigilantism.* New York: Oxford University Press, 1986.

Clarke, James W. *American Assassins: The Darker Side of American Politics.* Princeton, N.J.: Princeton University Press, 1982.

Gilje, Paul A. *Rioting in America.* Bloomington: Indiana University Press, 1996.

Gilligan, James. *Violence: Our Deadly Epidemic and Its Causes.* New York: Putnam, 1996.

Graham, Hugh Davis, and Ted Robert Gurr, eds. *Violence in America: Historical and Contemporary Perspectives.* 2 vols. Washington, D.C.: U.S. Government Printing Office, 1969. Reprint, New York: Bantam, 1969. Reprint, New York: New American Library, 1969. Reprint with revised title, *The History of Violence in America,* New York, Praeger, 1969.

———. *Violence in America: Historical and Comparative Perspectives.* 2d ed., revised. Beverly Hills, Calif.: Sage, 1979.

Gurr, Ted Robert, ed. *Violence in America.* Vol. 1, *The History of Crime.* Vol. 2, *Protest, Rebellion, Reform.* Newbury Park, Calif.: Sage, 1989.

Hofstadter, Richard, and Michael Wallace, eds. *American Violence: A Documentary History.* New York: Knopf, 1970.

Lane, Roger. *Murder in America: A History.* Columbus: Ohio State University Press, 1997.

Lane, Roger, and John J. Turner, eds. *Riot, Rout, and Tumult: Readings in American Social and Political Violence.* Westport, Conn.: Greenwood, 1978.

Limerick, Patricia N. *The Legacy of Conquest: The Unbroken Past of the American West.* New York: Norton, 1987.

Slotkin, Richard. *Fatal Environment: The Myth of the Frontier in the Age of Industrialization, 1800–1890.* New York: Atheneum, 1985.

———. *Gunfighter Nation: The Myth of the Frontier in Twentieth-Century America.* New York: Atheneum, 1992.

———. *Regeneration Through Violence: The Mythology of the American Frontier, 1600–1860.* Middletown, Conn.: Wesleyan University Press, 1973.

WHITE–INDIAN WARFARE

Carranco, Lynwood, and Estle Beard. *Genocide and Vendetta: The Round Valley Wars of Northern California.* Norman: University of Oklahoma Press, 1981.

Drinnon, Richard. *Facing West: The Metaphysics of Indian Hating and Empire Building.* Minneapolis: University of Minnesota Press, 1980.

Edmunds, R. David. *Tecumseh and the Quest for Indian Leadership.* Boston: Little, Brown, 1984.

Karr, Ronald Dale. "'Why Should You Be So Furious?': The Violence of the Pequot War." *Journal of American History* 85 (December 1998).

Stanard, David E. *American Holocaust: Columbus and the Conquest of the New World.* New York: Oxford University Press, 1992.

Utley, Robert M. *The Indian Frontier of the American West, 1846–1890.* Albuquerque: University of New Mexico Press, 1984.

WHITE–BLACK VIOLENCE

Bernstein, Iver. *The New York City Draft Riots: Their Significance for American Society and Politics in the Age of the Civil War.* New York: Oxford University Press, 1990.

Brundage, W. Fitzhugh, ed. *Under Sentence of Death: Lynching in the South.* Chapel Hill: University of North Carolina Press, 1997.

Clarke, James W. *The Lineaments of Wrath: Race, Violent Crime, and American Culture.* New Brunswick, N.J.: Transaction, 1998.

Foner, Eric. *Reconstruction: America's Unfinished Revolution, 1863–1877.* New York: Harper and Row, 1988.

Genovese, Eugene D. *From Rebellion to Revolution: Afro-American Slave Revolts in the Modern World.* Baton Rouge: Louisiana State University Press, 1979.

Trelease, Allen W. *White Terror: The Ku Klux Klan Conspiracy and Southern Reconstruction.* New York: Harper and Row, 1971.

AGRARIAN VIOLENCE

Brown, Richard Maxwell. "Back Country Rebellions and the Homestead Ethic in America, 1740–1799." In *Tradition, Conflict, and Modernization: Perspectives on the American Revolution,* edited by Richard Maxwell Brown and Don E. Fehrenbacher. New York: Academic, 1977.

Marx, Karl, and Frederick Engels. *Letters to Americans, 1848–1895: A Selection,* edited by Alexander Trachtenberg. New York: International, 1953.

Slaughter, Thomas P. *The Whiskey Rebellion: Frontier Epilogue to the American Revolution.* New York: Oxford University Press, 1986.

Stock, Catherine McNicol. *Rural Radicals: Righteous Rage in the American Grain.* Ithaca, N.Y.: Cornell University Press, 1996.

Taylor, Alan. *Liberty Men and Great Proprietors: The Revolutionary Settlement on the Maine Frontier, 1760–1820.* Chapel Hill: University of North Carolina Press, 1990.

Waldrep, Christopher. *Night Riders: Defending Community in the Black Patch, 1890–1915.* Durham, N.C.: Duke University Press, 1993.

VIGILANTE VIOLENCE

Caughey, John W., ed. *Their Majesties the Mob.* Chicago: University of Chicago Press, 1960.

Ingalls, Robert P. *Urban Vigilantes in the New South: Tampa, 1882–1936.* Knoxville: University of Tennessee Press, 1988.

Rosenbaum, H. Jon, and Peter C. Sederberg, eds. *Vigilante Politics.* Philadelphia: University of Pennsylvania Press, 1976.

Senkewicz, Robert M. *Vigilantes in Gold Rush San Francisco.* Stanford, Calif.: Stanford University Press, 1985.

URBAN RIOTS AND INDUSTRIAL VIOLENCE

Avrich, Paul. *The Haymarket Tragedy.* Princeton, N.J.: Princeton University Press, 1984.

Bruce, Robert V. *1877: The Year of Violence*. Indianapolis: Bobbs-Merrill, 1959.

Kenny, Kevin. *Making Sense of the Molly Maguires*. New York: Oxford University Press, 1998.

Krause, Paul. *The Battle for Homestead, 1880–1892: Politics, Culture, and Steel*. Pittsburgh: University of Pittsburgh Press, 1992.

McGovern, George S. "The Colorado Coal Strike, 1913–1914." Ph.D. diss., Northwestern University, 1953.

McGovern, George S., and Leonard F. Guttridge. *The Great Coalfield War*. Boston: Houghton Mifflin, 1972.

WOMEN AND VIOLENCE

Butler, Anne M. *Gendered Justice in the American West: Women Prisoners in Men's Penitentiaries*. Urbana: University of Illinois Press, 1997.

Gordon, Linda. *Heroes of Their Own Lives: The Politics and History of Family Violence, Boston, 1880–1960*. New York: Viking, 1988.

Peterson del Mar, David. *What Trouble I Have Seen: A History of Violence Against Wives*. Cambridge, Mass.: Harvard University Press, 1996.

Pleck, Elizabeth. *Domestic Tyranny: The Making of Social Policy Against Family Violence from Colonial Times to the Present*. New York: Oxford University Press, 1987.

MALE HONOR

Anderson, Elijah. "The Code of the Streets." *Atlantic Monthly* 273 (May 1994).

Ayers, Edward L. *Vengeance and Justice: Crime and Punishment in the Nineteenth-Century South*. New York: Oxford University Press, 1984.

Butterfield, Fox. *All God's Children: The Bosket Family and the American Tradition of Violence*. New York: Knopf, 1995.

Gorn, Elliott J. *The Manly Art: Bareknuckle Prize Fighting in America*. Ithaca, N.Y.: Cornell University Press, 1986.

Linderman, Gerald F. *Embattled Courage: The Experience of Combat in the American Civil War*. New York: Free Press, 1987.

Wyatt-Brown, Bertram. *Southern Honor: Ethics and Behavior in the Old South*. New York: Oxford University Press, 1982.

SOCIAL BANDITS AND CONSERVATIVE HEROES

Hobsbawm, Eric J. *Bandits*. New York: Penguin, 1985.

Hutton, Paul Andrew. "Showdown at the Hollywood Corral." *Montana: The Magazine of Western History* 45 (summer 1995).

Patterson, Richard. *Butch Cassidy: A Biography*. Lincoln: University of Nebraska Press, 1998.

Phillips, John Neal. *Running with Bonnie and Clyde: The Ten Fast Years of Ralph Fults*. Norman: University of Oklahoma Press, 1996.

Rosa, Joseph G. *Wild Bill Hickok: The Man and His Myth*. Lawrence: University Press of Kansas, 1996.

Tatum, Stephen. *Inventing Billy the Kid: Visions of the Outlaw in America, 1881–1981*. Albuquerque: University of New Mexico Press, 1982.

White, Richard. "Outlaw Gangs of the Middle Border: American Social Bandits." *Western Historical Quarterly* 12 (October 1981).

INCORPORATION AND DISINCORPORATION

Brown, Richard Maxwell. "Law and Order on the American Frontier: The Western Civil War of Incorporation." In *Law for the Elephant, Law for the Beaver: Essays in the Legal History of the North American West*, edited by John McLaren et al. Pasadena, Calif.: Ninth Judicial Circuit Historical Society, 1992.

Dubofsky, Melvin. *We Shall Be All: A History of the Industrial Workers of the World*. Urbana: University of Illinois Press, 1988.

Feuer, Lewis. *The Conflict of Generations: The Character and Significance of Student Movements*. New York: Basic, 1969.

Saxton, Alexander. *The Indispensable Enemy: Labor and the Anti-Chinese Movement in California*. Berkeley: University of California Press, 1971.

Thelen, David. *Paths of Resistance: Tradition and Dignity in Industrializing Missouri*. New York: Oxford University Press, 1986.

Trachtenberg, Alan. *The Incorporation of America: Culture and Society in the Gilded Age*. New York: Hill and Wang, 1982.

FROM THE INDUSTRIAL TO THE INFORMATION SOCIETY

Brown, Richard Maxwell. "Crime, Law, and Society: From the Industrial to the Information Society." In *Violence in America*. Vol. 1, *The History of Crime*, edited by Ted Robert Gurr. Newbury Park, Calif.: Sage, 1989.

Gurr, Ted Robert. "On the History of Crime in Europe and America." In *Violence in America: Historical and Contemporary Perspectives*, edited by Hugh Davis Graham and Ted Robert Gurr. 2d ed., revised. Beverly Hills, Calif.: Sage, 1979.

Lane, Roger. "On the Social Meaning of Homicide Trends in America." In *Violence in America*. Vol. 1, *The History of Crime*, edited by Ted Robert Gurr. Newbury Park, Calif.: Sage, 1989.

THE LITTLETON MASSACRE

Bai, Matt, et al. "Death at Columbine High." *Newsweek*, 3 May 1999.

Dizard, Jan, et al., eds. *Guns in America: A Reader*. New York: New York University Press, 1999.

Gegax, T. Trent, and Matt Bai. "The Colorado Tragedy." *Newsweek*, 10 May 1999.

Kantrowitz, Barbara, et al. "Beyond Littleton." *Newsweek*, 10 May 1999.

Malcolm, Joyce Lee. *To Keep and Bear Arms: The Origins of an Anglo-American Right*. Cambridge, Mass.: Harvard University Press, 1994.

RICHARD MAXWELL BROWN

ABOLITION

No political issue or institution in the history of the United States has matched slavery in its power to provoke violent responses. During the antebellum period slavery dominated the nation's economy and, increasingly, its politics, leading to the Civil War. Because of its signal importance, the institution of slavery engendered passionate, defensive, and often violent responses from both its supporters and detractors. As a result, the movement to abolish slavery in the United States was permeated by violence.

Violence inflicted on slaves prompted thousands of free blacks and whites to join the movement for immediate emancipation. Slaves, too, used violence and even murder to protest a system that kept them in bondage. Countless mobs—in the North as well as the South—subjected abolitionists themselves to violence. And some radical abolitionists launched their own violent crusade against slavery's defenders.

Antislavery feelings were strong during the American Revolution and in the Upper South in the 1820s, but abolitionists did not coalesce into a militant movement until the 1830s. By that time the rise of commercial agriculture and manufacturing in much of the North had led to profound economic and social transformations including powerful religious movements aimed at ending sinful practices and "perfecting" human society. In what became known as the Second Great Awakening, preachers like Lyman Beecher and Charles Gran-

dison Finney stressed each individual's responsibility for upholding God's will. Many of Beecher's and Finney's northern followers launched a variety of reforming crusades against such perceived evils as the abuse of alcohol, war, and the subjugation of women. But it was the movement against slavery that emerged as the most significant reform movement of the nineteenth century.

In 1831 William Lloyd Garrison published the first issue of *The Liberator,* setting abolitionism on a radical new course. Before Garrison's publication, most white opponents of slavery had advocated gradual emancipation by individual slave owners. Garrison, already a veteran of several reform movements, called for the immediate emancipation of the nation's slaves. "I am in earnest," he declared in the paper's first editorial. "I will not equivocate—I will not excuse—I will not retreat a single inch—AND I WILL BE HEARD." Although radical, the movement championed by Garrison was mostly nonviolent. The Garrisonian abolitionists' preferred tactic was "moral suasion"; they hoped to persuade slaveholders to recognize their sin and emancipate their property voluntarily.

Yet even these pacifist abolitionists employed violence, at least rhetorically, to make their case against slavery. In the mid-1830s abolitionists flooded the U.S. postal system with more than one million pieces of antislavery literature, much of it chronicling the vicious whippings, sexual assaults on slave women, and the destruction of slave families common on southern plantations. Despised by slaveholders as "inflammatory," publications like *American Slavery as It Is* by the Reverend Theodore Dwight Weld (1839) described in graphic and repetitive detail every conceivable form of slave abuse.

A minority of abolitionists believed that only slave rebellion, not moral suasion, would bring an end to the institution of slavery. David Walker, a free African American living in Boston, openly advocated rebellion in his famous *Appeal*, published in 1829. The Reverend Henry Highland Garnet of New York called for similar action in a speech in 1843. But it was the enslaved blacks of Southampton County in Virginia's Tidewater region who launched the most violent slave revolt in American history (although there had been numerous earlier plots and rebellions). In August 1831 about sixty Southampton slaves shot and hacked to death fifty-five white men, women, and children. Their leader was Nat Turner, a Baptist lay preacher who saw himself as an instrument of God's wrath. Turner had experienced religious visions since childhood, and after a particularly vivid dream around 1830 (where he saw white and black spirits engaged in battle), Turner began to recruit other slaves for his methodical and murderous revolt. White forces caught up with Turner's band the next day and executed more than fifty blacks, including Turner, whose revolt convinced every southern slaveholder of the potential for extreme violence among even the most trusted slaves.

Disagreement over tactics—including whether or not violence was acceptable—split the abolitionist movement in the late 1830s. Those who continued to favor moral suasion stuck with Garrison; others more interested in political action followed leaders like Lewis Tappan and James G. Birney into the new Liberty Party. Others, like the escaped slave and African American abolitionist Frederick Douglass, were concerned about white domination of the movement. Douglass eventually split with Garrison and endorsed political action and even, as a last resort, slave rebellion.

It was the abolitionists' foes, however, that were far more likely to resort to violence to express their fear and racial hatred. Anti-abolitionist mob violence was common in the 1830s, especially in northern cities, where abolitionists there were showered with stones, burned out of their businesses and homes, dragged through the streets, and even murdered by mobs led or encouraged by leading citizens. Weld was famous as the "most mobbed man in the United States," and Douglass and Garrison were very nearly the victims of murderous plots. In 1837 Elijah Lovejoy, an abolitionist editor in Alton, Illinois, became a martyr to the cause when a proslavery mob killed him and threw his printing press into the Mississippi River.

It was exactly this type of anti-abolitionist activity that spurred radicals like John Brown to action. Brown was an abolitionist and upstate New York tanner who became increasingly radical in his attacks on slavery. When the federal government opened Kansas Territory for settlement in the 1850s, Brown and several of his sons moved there in an attempt to claim the territory as free soil. Proslavery settlers also headed to Kansas, and by 1856 the two factions were at each other's throats. When a proslavery mob sacked the free-state town of Lawrence and smashed the presses of its antislavery newspaper, Brown vowed revenge. Claiming, like Nat Turner, to be acting out the will of God, in 1856 Brown and his sons rode to a proslavery settlement near Pottawatomie Creek, dragged five men out of their cabins, and split open their heads with broadswords. The same week, the antislavery senator Charles Sumner was nearly beaten to death in the Senate chamber with a cane wielded by a South Carolina congressman. The caning, the massacre at Pottawatomie, and the sack of Lawrence set off a small-scale civil war, dubbed "Bleeding Kansas" by historians, a title that made it abundantly clear that abolition would never be accomplished without violence. In the end, it took the deaths of more than six hundred thousand Confederate and Union troops (including thousands of black soldiers) to end slavery in North America.

BIBLIOGRAPHY

Quarles, Benjamin. *The Black Abolitionists*. New York: Oxford University Press, 1970.

Richard, Leonard L. *"Gentlemen of Property and Standing": Anti-Abolitionist Mobs in Jacksonian America*. New York: Oxford University Press, 1970.

Stewart, James Brewer. *Holy Warriors: The Abolitionists and American Slavery*. New York: Hill and Wang, 1986.

JONATHAN H. EARLE

See also **Brown, John; Civil War; Slave Rebellions; Slavery.**

ABORTION

Prior to the twentieth century, abortion in the United States was defined as occurring only after, roughly, the end of the second trimester. Catholic and legal thought had held since the early church fathers that "ensoulment" (the point at which the soul was implanted in the fetus by the Divine) did not occur until there was fetal movement, or quickening. Prior to that moment, a woman did not know whether she was pregnant or some other internal or reproductive "problem" was causing the end of her menses and the attendant symptoms. Thus, into the second decade of the twentieth century, popular over-the-counter drugs included a large number of patent medicine potions (some of which occasionally worked) designed to "restore regularity," which was not a reference to one's bowels but to the menses.

In 1821 Connecticut became the first state to outlaw abortion. However, abortion did not figure as a social or legal problem until the 1860s and 1870s. The first effort to restrict abortion arose with the formation of the American Medical Association (AMA) in 1847. At that time abortions were frequently performed by midwives. Seeking to establish the status of physicians as professionals with the right to control the practice of medicine, the AMA began to lobby in the states for laws prohibiting abortions by anyone other than physicians. The AMA effort was fueled by several sensational newspaper articles about women dying while undergoing abortion procedures. One of the AMA arguments against abortion even as performed by physicians was the high rate of complications and death associated with the procedure; medical practitioners as yet had no comprehension of sepsis, the spread of harmful bacteria from the site of an infection.

The AMA was joined in its efforts by nativists of the period. The last half of the nineteenth century saw a high rate of immigration from eastern European countries of non-Protestants, Jews, Catholics, and non-English speakers, all with a high birthrate. At the same time, urbanization and a developing middle class led to a declining birthrate among urban Protestants. Fearing the loss of their hegemony, nativists supported legal restrictions on abortion so as to force middle-class Protestant women to increase their birthrate.

By 1880 virtually every state had laws prohibiting abortion, frequently even outlawing abortions that might be necessary in order to save the mother's life. However, patent medicines to "restore regularity" remained available until the early twentieth century, when the federal government enacted pure food and drug laws.

Twentieth-Century Medical Developments

In the twentieth century scientists learned the details of conception and fetal development. This knowledge made it clear that the "quickening" distinction was false, that fetal development was a continuous process. The Catholic Church thus declared that ensoulment occurs with conception.

A second development of major significance was the introduction of effective birth-control devices—first, condoms and later, diaphragms, spermicides, and oral contraceptives. The Catholic Church responded by equating birth control with abortion under the Thomistic theology of natural law. The doctrine of natural law, propounded by Thomas Aquinas, holds that some moral proscriptions can be derived by human reason's examination of nature, that some eternal truths do not require biblical revelation. In this view, animals have sexual intercourse solely in order to procreate, and any interference with conception is "unnatural" and therefore prohibited. (The anthropological argument, by contrast, holds that anything humans do, for good or ill, is "natural" because such actions grow out of human nature and inherent human capabilities. Thus, contraceptives are viewed as "natural" because they are a product of the human mind.) In some states, primarily those with a Catholic majority, birth-control devices were legally equated with abortion and hence outlawed.

A third important advance was the development, by midcentury, of extremely effective antibiotics, especially the sulfa- and penicillin-based drugs, which practically eliminated the problem of sepsis in surgeries and other invasive practices. These new drugs, combined with improved surgical techniques based on clearer understandings of anatomy, led to the near-absolute safety of abortion as performed by physicians—the procedure being safer, in fact, than carrying a fetus to term.

By 1960 a number of physicians, having observed in emergency rooms the severe effects, including deaths, of illegal, nonmedical abortions not performed in hospitals or under antiseptic conditions, were performing illegal abortions themselves. Many states permitted abortions when the woman's health was endangered; some physicians interpreted that stipulation to include her mental health, giving them broad license to abort. However, those states allowing abortion for the sake of the woman's health generally required approval by a panel of physicians, usually including a psychiatrist, before an abortion could be performed.

All legal (and a number of illegal) abortions were still performed in hospitals, which meant that the cost of an abortion was often prohibitively expensive (an abortion in a hospital costs roughly ten times one in a clinic setting) when the procedure was available at all. But the number of abortions actually available to women at any cost was also severely limited, since most hospitals did not want to come under state investigation or to be known as an easy source of abortion.

Legalization

Into the 1960s abortion remained basically a medical decision circumscribed by legal limitations. But a dramatic shift in public attitudes toward abortion was in progress. Several events and circumstances propelled this shift.

First, a small but increasing number of physicians were offering, in effect, abortions on demand. A few openly offered abortions, even advertising the service, courting arrest and the chance to contest state restrictions.

Second, with the initiative of Lawrence Lader and others, the National Abortion Rights Action League (NARAL) was organized and began lobbying for liberalized state laws. NARAL's efforts served to put abortion into public discussion and debate and to begin mobilization of public opinion for liberalization.

Third, the American Law Institute (ALI), an independent organization of attorneys that suggests changes in state laws to make them more rational and compatible with one another, had recommended to the states in 1959 a model law regulating abortion. Much more open than the laws of a number of states, the model law would allow for abortion in cases of rape, incest, and severe fetal deformity, and to benefit the woman's health, including her psychological health. Although abortion would thus become somewhat more available, the law would not have a dramatic effect on access, for the procedure would remain a restricted medical decision.

Fourth, in 1962 a resident of Arizona, Sherri Finkbine, who had been taking the drug thalidomide, discovered she was pregnant. Thalidomide was not approved for use in the United States; its use in Europe had resulted in a relatively large number of severe fetal abnormalities. (Finkbine's husband, a military serviceman, had brought the drug back from Europe.) An Arizona hospital had approved an abortion for Finkbine, but two days before she was scheduled to terminate the preg-

nancy news of her pending abortion hit the media: the hospital withdrew its approval under the glare of publicity that was exacerbated by the fact that Finkbine was a television personality who hosted the children's program *Romper Room*. Finkbine ultimately went to Sweden for an abortion. The case stirred a strong public reaction in favor of legal reforms and stimulated the efforts of those seeking to have them implemented.

Finally, in 1964 an epidemic of German measles (rubella) swept the country, resulting in a large number of fetal abnormalities and making abortion access a much more pressing public concern. Accordingly, between 1967 and 1970 regulation of abortion was liberalized in twelve states, usually using some or all of the ALI guidelines; abortion regulation was abolished altogether in New York, while in Hawaii, Alaska, and Washington abortion was deregulated except for the fact that women seeking the procedure had to prove that they were legal residents of the state.

As the effort to liberalize access was primarily an issue focused at the state level, organized opposition was also emerging at the state level. In most states the opposition was limited to relatively small groups. Massive mobilization was apparently deemed unnecessary, under the assumption that no enlightened person could support abortion, especially not abortion on demand. However, with several state legislatures voting overwhelmingly for liberalization, it soon became clear that this was a mistaken assumption, and more organized opposition developed. The early opponents willing to organize were primarily professionals, physicians, nurses, and social workers. Once liberalized access became a reality, the opposition quickly developed into a more working-class movement (Luker 1984). Of the early state-based, antiabortion organizations, the most effective were Right to Life committees, led and funded by Catholic churches under the urging and financial support of the Catholic Bishops' Conference.

On 22 January 1973 the nation, including abortion supporters, was shocked at the Supreme Court decisions in *Roe v. Wade* and *Doe v. Bolton*. Those decisions effectively threw out all state laws regulating abortion, even the liberal laws following the ALI model and laws that merely consisted of a residency requirement. The short-term effect of these decisions was a deflation of the abortion rights movement, since its supporters felt they had "won." On the other hand, the antiabortion countermovement was rapidly mobilized by the decisions and began developing national organizations.

The Antiabortion Movement

The first major antiabortion organization was the National Right to Life Committee (NRLC), which remains today the largest organization opposing abortion (reportedly having more than eleven million members). An outgrowth of Catholic organizations within the states and still primarily Catholic today, the NRLC uses social-movement methods traditionally associated with the middle class, such as lobbying in national and state legislatures and promoting the election of compatible candidates for public office. Early efforts sought to overturn *Roe* and *Doe* with the passage of a "pro-life" amendment to the U.S. Constitution. Despite the support of some politically influential legislators, every one of these efforts failed. In the late 1990s legislators proposed and passed a law banning the so-called partial-birth abortion; however, they were unable to muster support sufficient to override the subsequent presidential veto.

Other early antiabortion efforts included the picketing of abortion clinics, a tactic with labor union associations and working-class appeal. Clinics quickly arose following *Roe* and *Doe*, replacing hospitals and private physicians in general practice as the primary delivery system for abortion and other reproductive services, which reduced the costs of such services dramatically. But the clinics also served to isolate abortion services, making them far easier targets for picketing and violence.

Joseph Scheidler of the Pro-Life Action League (PLAL), headquartered in Chicago, escalated the tactics of opposition, encouraging direct action in the form of clinic sit-ins. Scheidler, a former Benedictine monk who had worked previously for two Chicago-area antiabortion organizations, was fired by one and left the other just before being discharged, in both cases for acting in more direct and aggressive ways than those organizations approved. Scheidler penned the major early tactical manual of the movement, *Closed: Ninety-nine Ways to Stop Abortion*, published in 1985. (The original title, *Ninety-nine Ways to Close an Abortion Clinic*, was changed, probably for reasons of legal liability.) In the book Scheidler outlines in broad strokes a number of ways to harass clinic personnel and their clients. Although he is careful to state that he does not recommend illegal behavior, for those so motivated he reviews illegal methods.

The Rising Tide of Violence

It is difficult to exaggerate the importance of Scheidler to the subsequent developments in movement tactics, especially those that became

Roe v. Wade

Keith Cassidy

In *Roe v. Wade*, announced on 22 January 1973, the Supreme Court found that a right to privacy was implicit in the Fourteenth Amendment to the Constitution and that this right extended to a woman's right to abortion. "Jane Roe" was the pseudonym of Norma McCovey, a Texas woman who was prevented from terminating her pregnancy by a state statute prohibiting abortion. The Court's seven-to-two decision, taken in conjunction with that in the companion case of *Doe v. Bolton,* not only struck down the Texas law but invalidated virtually all state regulations. The Court said the prohibition of abortion in the last three months of pregnancy remained a possibility, if there was no threat to the life or health of the mother, but the very broad definition of "health" given in the *Doe* decision in practice precluded this option. Subsequent Supreme Court decisions, especially *Planned Parenthood of Southeastern Pennsylvania v. Casey* (1992), decisively reaffirmed the *Roe* decision but permitted some limited state restrictions.

Abortion rights referendums had been defeated in North Dakota and Michigan just a few months before *Roe*, and while a majority of Americans supported some access to abortion, only a minority favored a framework as sweeping as that created by the Court. Because there was no public consensus on the issue, *Roe* seemed to some to short-circuit the democratic process. As a result, many saw *Roe* as illegitimate—"an exercise in raw judicial power," as one of the dissenting justices put it—and compared it to the proslavery *Dred Scott* decision of 1857. Those favoring abortion and those opposed to it both saw the issue as one of absolute rights—a woman's liberty on one side and an unborn child's right to life on the other—with little room for compromise. These factors produced a polarization in the American abortion debate that was unique in the Western world.

Police officers stand guard between the two sides of the abortion debate outside a clinic in Little Rock, Arkansas, in July 1994. REUTERS/JEFF MITCHELL/ARCHIVE PHOTOS

violent. The vast majority of activist organizations can in fact be traced back to Scheidler's activities and organization. Scheidler undertakes to visit all those imprisoned for violent acts against abortion clinics and their personnel, to attend their trials, and to hold national meetings and celebrations at which law violators receive a Defender of Life award upon their release from prison. As of 1999 more than thirty antiabortion activists had been sentenced to state and federal prisons for violent acts against abortion clinics and their personnel, including bombings, arsons, and murders. PLAL meetings and ceremonies gave rise to activist networks across the nation.

A number of radical activists came out of PLAL. Randall Terry was serving on Scheidler's board of directors when he initiated Operation Rescue. John Brockhoeft, who bombed several Cincinnati-area clinics between 1986 and 1988, drove a bomb to Pensacola, Florida, to hit a clinic, the Ladies Center, having been shown its location by John Burt at a Scheidler event in Chicago. Scheidler "soldiers" stole a large number of aborted fetuses from a Chicago-area site and mailed them all over the na-

tion for a variety of symbolic uses, including an attempt to hand one to Bill Clinton during the 1992 Democratic Convention.

The National Abortion Federation (NAF) is an association of clinic owners and physicians across the nation to which about a third of abortion providers belong. (Planned Parenthood Federation of America has the largest "chain" of clinics, some of which do not provide abortions, but all of which offer other reproductive health services. The National Coalition of Abortion Providers is not a chain but is composed of individual clinics.) The NAF has kept statistics on clinic incidents, based on the Federal Bureau of Investigation and clinic self-reports, since 1977. Analysis of those data reveals an interesting pattern of the rise and fall of a variety of violent tactics against abortion providers. Periodically, new tactics and methods are introduced, while the old ones continue but less frequently. Overall, however, the new tactics introduced indicate a gradual escalation in the degree of violence.

With the failure of picketing, clearly a legal and nonviolent form of protest, and political efforts, both of which were prevalent in the 1970s, some activists turned to illegal tactics: death threats; anonymous phone calls, letters, and postcards; vandalism of property; bomb threats; stink bombs released inside clinics; and other forms of harassment of providers, clinic personnel, and patients.

These methods, too, failed to reduce access to abortion, and 1982 saw the beginning of an increase in bombings and arson, both attempted and achieved. These methods reached a peak in 1984–1985, with thirty arsons or bombings in 1984 and twenty-two the following year. Many of these did not end in convictions because of the statute of limitations. In 1985–1986 approximately thirty bombers and arsonists were tried, convicted, and given lengthy prison sentences. These arrests and convictions appear to have dampened the enthusiasm for such tactics.

On Thanksgiving weekend in 1986, Randall Terry announced to a gathering of antiabortion leaders the formation of Operation Rescue (OR). In 1987 he held his first invasion and blockade of a clinic at Cherry Hill, New Jersey. OR quickly picked up momentum and began staging blockades and invasions weekly and in multiple locations. Special concentrations of efforts were begun in the summer in several cities at the same time. The height of OR's efforts came at the Democratic convention of 1988 in Atlanta. Waves of OR protesters were arrested, the OR attempting purposely to overload the Atlanta jails. Police used rough tactics to move limp protesters into school buses, which deposited them at football stadiums. Certain (perhaps naive) OR followers were shocked at the unsympathetic handling by the police and the failure of OR representatives to bail them out of jail as promised.

The year 1992 marked the beginning of a new rise in bombings and arsons, an increase that continued into 1994. Meanwhile, in 1993 a new and even more violent tactic was introduced: the assassination of physicians and clinic personnel. In March 1993 Dr. David Gunn was murdered with a shot in the back by Michael Griffin in Pensacola, Florida. In August of the same year Rachelle Shannon superficially wounded Dr. George Tiller of Wichita, Kansas. In 1994 in Pensacola, the Reverend Paul Hill used a shotgun to murder Dr. John Britton and his escort, James Barrett. John Salvi walked into two clinics in Brookline, Massachusetts, firing wildly from a rifle and killing two clinic receptionists, while wounding several oth-

ers. Griffin and Salvi (who later committed suicide in prison) received life prison sentences, and Hill was sentenced to death.

By the late 1990s antiabortion violence had taken yet another form, in which snipers with high-powered rifles attempted to assassinate physicians in their homes. Targets included Canadian abortion providers in Vancouver, British Columbia, and Hamilton, Ontario. In October 1998 Barnett Slepian was murdered by a bullet fired through his kitchen window in Amherst, New York, near Buffalo, where he worked as an abortion provider. Although Slepian was the first abortion provider to be fatally wounded by an antiabortion sniper, he was not the first victim of sniper violence; before Slepian's murder, five other providers in Canada and the United States were wounded by antiabortion sniper assaults, two of them so seriously they could not continue their practice. Whereas in the early to mid-1990s antiabortion murderers had made weak, if any, attempts to avoid capture and trial, the snipers attacking physicians in their homes managed to avoid apprehension. James Kopp, a frequent protester in the United States and Canada, is wanted by the FBI for the Slepian murder.

Likewise, a manhunt ensued after an off-duty policeman (working as a security guard) was killed by a bomb at a Birmingham, Alabama, clinic in January 1998. The suspect in the bombing, Eric Rudolph, was also charged with having set off a fatal bomb in Atlanta, Georgia's Centennial Olympic Park during the 1996 Olympic Games and with bombings at another family planning clinic and at a lesbian bar, also in Atlanta, both in 1997, that left several people injured. Months after the charges were filed, Rudolph remained on the FBI's "Ten Most Wanted Fugitives" list, his whereabouts unknown.

Assuming Rudolph is guilty, he is representative of a major development in abortion-clinic violence: an increasing association with the antiestablishment militias. As early as the 1980s, some antiabortion organizations had demonstrated an affinity for the tenets of militias that may be described as racist or that expressed a deep hostility to the federal government—for example, Human Life International's anti-Semitism. There are indications that militia groups trained some antiabortion radicals in the use of explosives and heavy weapons in the 1980s. After the Gunn assassination in 1993, a distinction arose in the antiabortion movement between those persons and organizations supporting the murder of abortion services providers and those who condemned such "tactics." A new organization, the American Coalition of Life Activists, was composed primarily of homicide justifiers.

The increasing violence by some antiabortion activists led to a dramatic decrease in the numbers of those willing to be identified with the movement, even through simple clinic picketing. Operation Rescue, in particular, underwent a significant decline in support. The Gunn murder hastened the passage of the Freedom of Access to Clinic Entrances Act (FACE) of 1994, making many of OR's tactics now a violation of federal law, carrying much stiffer sentences than the state and local laws that had previously been in force. Although OR sought to develop new attention-getting tactics such as picketing, with large posters depicting fetuses, outside high schools across the country, such actions were counterproductive, angering parents, students, and the public.

Few individuals and organizations were prosecuted under FACE, to the chagrin and condemnation of clinics and pro-choice organizations. But because FACE allows for civil, as well as criminal, penalties, several civil and criminal suits filed under FACE did result in multimillion-dollar judgments against antiabortion groups and individuals. However, during the OR blockades and invasions, most antiabortionists had made themselves judgment-proof by divesting themselves of assets. Furthermore, organizations similar to OR soon became skilled at money "laundering" to prevent seizure of their assets.

Who Commits the Violence?

By 1999 more than forty thousand persons had been arrested for commission of clinic "incidents." The majority of perpetrators of any form of violence in the United States are male, under thirty-five years of age, and working class; perpetrators of antiabortion violence fit this "normal" violence profile, but in addition, they have a larger agenda, one that extends even beyond abortion.

The more violent the individual or group, the more likely they are to adhere to the views of Christian reconstructionism, a doctrine originating from the Reformed tradition of John Calvin. This radical expression of fundamentalism seeks to establish an American theocracy in which only reconstructionists would hold office, males would

occupy positions of authority, Old Testament biblical law would be the public law, crime and sin would be the same thing, and most crimes, including adultery, abortion, homosexuality, pornography, and juvenile delinquency, would result in death. The government would be reduced to courts, police, and an army. There would be no welfare or public education or any other public program. Control of the media, so as to prevent any public expression outside reconstructionism, is a primary goal.

Those antiabortion activists who commit violence also tend to be encapsulated, that is, their meaningful relationships are limited to those who agree with them and share their worldview. Although participants in the broad antiabortion movement are diverse in their motivations, belief systems, religious orientations, age, and choice of tactics, those espousing and using violence have a singular profile, operating out of a similar motivational and belief system, and have gained particular prominence because of the dangers they pose.

BIBLIOGRAPHY

Blanchard, Dallas A. *The Anti-Abortion Movement: References and Resources.* New York: Hall, 1996.

———. *The Anti-Abortion Movement and the Rise of the Religious Right: From Polite to Fiery Protest.* New York: Twayne, 1994.

Blanchard, Dallas A., and Terry J. Prewitt. *Religious Violence and Abortion: The Gideon Project.* Gainesville: University Press of Florida, 1993.

Bray, Michael. *A Time to Kill.* Gaithersburg, Md.: Reformation Press, 1995.

Clarkson, Frederick. *Eternal Hostility: The Struggle Between Theocracy and Democracy.* Monroe, Maine: Common Courage Press, 1997.

Conway, Flo, and Jim Siegelman. *Holy Terror: The Fundamentalist War on America's Freedoms in Religion, Politics, and Our Private Lives.* New York: Delta, 1982.

Crutcher, Mark. *Firestorm: A Guerrilla Strategy for a Pro-Life America.* Lewisville, Tex.: Life Dynamics, 1992.

Diamond, Sara. *Spiritual Warfare: The Politics of the Christian Right.* Boston: South End Press, 1989.

Ginsberg, Faye. *Contested Lives: The Abortion Debate in an American Community.* Berkeley: University of California Press, 1990.

Hunter, James Davison. *Culture Wars: The Struggle to Define America.* New York: Basic Books, 1991.

Joffe, Carol. *Doctors of Conscience: The Struggle to Provide Abortion Before and After Roe v. Wade.* Boston: Beacon, 1995.

Lader, Lawrence. *Abortion.* New York: Bobbs-Merrill, 1966.

Lawrence, Bruce B. *Defenders of God: The Fundamentalist Revolt Against the Modern Age.* New York: Harper and Row, 1989.

Life Advocate (magazine). Portland, Ore.: Advocates for Life Ministries.

Luker, Kristin. *Abortion and the Politics of Motherhood.* Berkeley: University of California Press, 1984.

Mohr, James C. *Abortion in America: The Origins and Evolution of National Policy.* New York: Oxford University Press, 1978.

Neitz, Mary Jo. "Family, State, and God: Ideologies of the Right-to-Life Movement." *Sociological Analysis* 42 (spring 1981).

Petchetsky, Rosalind P. *Abortion and Woman's Choice: The State, Sexuality, and Reproductive Freedom.* New York: Longman, 1984.

Russo, Nancy Felipe, and Jean E. Denious. "Why Is Abortion Such a Controversial Issue in the United States?" In *The New Civil War: The Psychology, Culture, and Politics of Abortion,* edited by Linda J. Beckman and S. Marie Harvey. Washington, D.C.: American Psychological Association, 1998.

Scheidler, Joseph M. *Closed: Ninety-nine Ways to Stop Abortion.* Westchester, Ill.: Crossway, 1985.

Terry, Randall. *Operation Rescue.* Springdale, Penn.: Whitaker House, 1988.

DALLAS A. BLANCHARD

See also **Civil Liberties; Religion; Women.**

ADDICTION. *See* Alcohol and Alcoholism; Drugs.

ADVERTISING

Historically, the creators, users, and defenders of American advertising have portrayed commercial publicity as a pacific institution. Advertising, they have reasoned, is persuasion, and persuasion is the opposite of coercion. Advertising, therefore, is antithetical to the physical force and violence that are elements of coercive power. More broadly, as an institution of the market, advertising has been depicted as part of a system that prizes voluntary choice above command, freedom rather than compulsion. As the financial support of a free press, advertising has contributed to informed dialogue and peaceful means of dispute resolution. There are certainly elements of truth in these assertions. Yet the relationship between advertising and violence historically and at present has been both closer and more complex than this contrast would have it.

Historical Perspectives

Advertising in the United States underwent a series of fundamental transformations in the decades around the turn of the twentieth century. Advertising in the post–Civil War era was only a faint harbinger of promotion today. With few exceptions, advertisements were announcements of goods for sale, sometimes sprinkled with perfunctory superlatives, rarely designed to attract attention or persuade potential buyers effectively. Patent medicines, usually of dubious merit, dominated the advertising columns. Yet American advertising took on a recognizably modern form by about 1920. Advertising agencies, their corporate clients, and the media formed a contentious triad not dissimilar to that in the 1990s: the major trade organizations had taken shape and the advertising industry contended with issues of government control and self-regulation; a vigorous, if severely limited, reform movement had rallied advertising men to march in parades and sing hymns to "truth in advertising"; and the concepts of advertising as an element of marketing and particular advertisements as part of a strategic campaign were well-established.

The emerging advertising of the early twentieth century in general manifested few violent themes. Examination of a randomly chosen issue from each decade of the *Saturday Evening Post*, the most popular mass-circulation magazine of the era, reveals only a handful of display advertisements with any intimations of physical force or harm, and none of interpersonal acts of violence. Ads for firearms, for example, refer to hunting and target shooting. An ad in the 17 May 1930 issue for the Hartford Fire Insurance Company personifies fire as a devilish figure lurking around a building and asking, "You're not afraid of me, are you? You have fire insurance to replace the value of your property. . . ." Another advertisement in the same issue, published by a plumbing supplies manufacturer, praised plumbers for standing "on guard" against the "foemen" of civilization. In the illustration a sturdy, shirtless man stands over a city, shaking his fists at fire, drought, cold, and dirt, all of which are depicted as threatening gods descending on horseback from the sky.

It is not surprising that the advertisements of this era aimed at a broad middle-class readership were so free of violence. Mainstream advertising, for the most part, was product-centered. Indeed, as historian Roland Marchand noted in his magisterial study, *Advertising the American Dream,*

A 1909 advertisement for the Daisy air rifle. CORBIS/BETTMANN

advertisers often depicted their products as objects of reverence. Beams of light illuminated automobiles. Refrigerators emanated halo-like glows. Friends and neighbors convened around vacuum cleaners in worshipful attention. These advertisements were not about to admit unsettling elements like violence into the tableaux they displayed. Their objective was to soothe, not perturb, Americans' transition to a commercially dominated modern era.

Wartime Advertising and Collective Violence

To a certain degree, wartime conditions altered this pattern. When the United States entered World War I in April 1917, advertising practitioners wanted to demonstrate the value of their persuasive skills for the war effort. Even here they warned against implausible linkages between advertised products and the military struggle: "Dragging a patriotic note as a selling point into advertising copy is neither good taste nor sound

business," warned one trade periodical (*Printers' Ink,* 26 April 1917, p. 118). But martial appeals tempted many advertisers, and logic often gave way to flag-draped proclamations. Fould's Spaghetti, for instance, posed a riddle: Why was their product like the American flag? "Because there are so many ways to serve it," was the reply (cited in *Printers' Ink,* 10 January 1918, pp. 124–125). Advertisements in mass-circulation magazines in the first years of World War I rarely offered visual portrayals of combat or bloodshed, but the themes and language of wartime publicity were colored by the international conflict and frequently assumed a martial tone.

Ironically, the advertising industry, which had prided itself on its pacific methods, began in the era of World War I to emphasize its ability to force responses. Professionally applied, persuasion itself would become compulsion: "In those dim and distant days before the war, reformers were wont to say, 'Oh, if the people would only do so and so!'

An American World War I recruiting poster, 1917.
THE GRANGER COLLECTION

Under the rigorous prod of Mars, they have learned to say, 'The people *must* do this and that —go out and advertise and make them come through'" (*Printers' Ink,* 13 December 1917, p. 148). This formulation did not equate advertising with violence, nor did it suggest the use of violent imagery in advertisements, but it suggested that practitioners could use advertising for much the same purpose. War—large-scale collective violence—had altered the discourse of persuasion.

World War II again indicated the complex relationship between institutional violence and American advertising. This time, advertising agencies seemed less hesitant to show the violent face of warfare. As historian Frank W. Fox pointed out, it was easy to find ads featuring pilots boasting of their latest skirmishes or bombing runs. It was also common to find frightening reminders of war's violence—"pictures of slain soldiers, face down

in the mud ... the National War Fund's heart-rending photograph of a woman lying dead amid her torn shopping bags ... a small boy on the beach quizzically picking a ragged sailor hat from the water." Another motif was the threat to Americans if the enemy were not stopped. Leering Nazis, for example, examined attractive young women, selecting them for an ominous "High Honor" (Fox 1975, p. 35).

As it had a generation earlier, warfare affected advertising indirectly as well. The industry used the war to call for a halt to the attacks on business and advertising that had hounded it during the Depression era. It maintained that the global struggle required advertising skills. "Not to understand the place advertising plays in a total war is the equivalent of a military error," proclaimed Chester La Roche, chairman of the industry's War Advertising Council (Fox 1975, p. 50). Fox also noted a reciprocal influence of advertising on warfare and violence. Wartime advertising in the United States, he contends, often depicted warfare as a test of character, almost an inevitable and necessary rite of masculine passage. Second, advertising linked World War II with earlier American traditions, incorporating the violent myths of westward expansion into modern warfare. In both ways, advertising themes may have inured audiences to the destructiveness and pain of contemporary collective violence.

Another exception to the rule that advertising's presence was largely nonviolent can be seen in commercial media portrayals of people of color and "exotic" foreigners. Depictions of African Americans in which advertisers used violent imagery in racial stereotyping were all too common and pernicious. Blacks were portrayed as quick to fight, usually with straight-edge razors as weapons. Rotund "mammy" figures disciplined irresponsible males with blows to the head from frying pans. Adults and children suffered accidents by their ignorance and carelessness. A racist culture intended these representations to be "humorous" depictions of African American inferiority and, by contrast, white supremacy. If they bore any relation to the product promoted, the link was almost always tenuous. It should be noted that these portrayals permeated aspects of consumer culture in the late nineteenth and much of the twentieth century. They are to be found not only in advertisements but also in vaudeville and minstrelsy, movies, sheet music, comic strips, and cartoons. (The 1986 documentary video *Ethnic Notions,* produced and directed by Marlon Riggs, is an exceptionally powerful presentation and analysis of this racial stereotyping in popular culture.)

The Era of Market Segmentation

The advent of commercial television caused massive changes in advertising and in the relationship between advertising and violence. By the 1960s television was omnipresent in U.S. households and the prevalent family leisure-time activity. Moving images supplanted static pictures and words, giving television commercials new kinds of persuasive methods. But as powerful as television advertising was in its early years, commercials generally remained focused on the product and promoted its desirable features. The dominance of the major networks limited programming choice and tended to reduce advertising strategies to rather bland "lowest common denominator" styles. Violence that could upset or offend some viewers would be a dangerous tactic for an advertiser in this environment.

By the 1960s, however, several developments coalesced to give violent themes and images more prominence in television advertising. In the first place, advertising, like virtually all cultural institutions, responded to a decade marked by social conflict and collective violence. Advertisements often absorbed the visual and verbal rhetoric of rebelliousness, distrust of authority, and social tension. Changes in the advertising industry brought about a so-called creative revolution; copywriters and art directors used fantasy, irony, and self-mockery to counteract consumer cynicism and tedium. The new advertising could evoke unsettling associations. The flamboyant art director and agency head George Lois, debating a colleague who maintained that advertising provided information to consumers, replied, "You and I are in different businesses. I spray poison gas" (Price 1978, p. 80).

The rise of market segmentation, another fundamental change in advertising since the 1950s, also has raised concern about violence in advertising. More and more advertising has been tailored for particular audiences in media designed to reach those groups. If, indeed, males in the eighteen-to-thirty-four age bracket like to watch action-adventure shows and contact sports, programmers and advertisers will respond to this demand. Commercials on these shows are likely to share some of the violent characteristics of the entertainment. It should be noted, however, that American viewer demand is not the sole force driving violent programming. Television program producers seldom make a profit on their initial domestic broadcasts. They aim for foreign sales to put their accounts in the black. Language barriers put a premium on action-adventure shows, where visual images and noise, unlike dialogue, need no translation.

Finally, the number of commercials has grown while their average length has shrunk. Advertising specialists worry about "clutter" and seek new ways to make their messages stand out from the constant flow of persuasion. Remote controls with mute buttons and videocassette recorders give viewers new ways to tune out advertisements. For these reasons, too, the advertisement as announcement of product benefits has tended to give way to the commercial as spectacle. This environment tempts advertisers to employ violence to grab a share of viewers' limited supply of attention.

Media Violence as a Social Problem

Both as an intellectual challenge and as a problem for social policy, the issue of media representations' impact on behavior has concerned scholars as well as citizens. Television has been the focus of concern for nearly half a century. In its bluntest form, the concern is whether or not violence in the media causes viewers to perform violent acts. From the reporting of terrorism to the images in children's cartoons, media depictions of violence have shouldered the blame for inciting acts of violence among members of their audiences. In a 1992 report, *Big World, Small Screen: The Role of Television in American Society*, a task force of the American Psychological Association offered a clear-cut verdict: "The accumulated research clearly demonstrates a correlation between viewing violence and aggressive behavior" (Huston et al. 1992, p. 54). Studies with a wide range of methodologies and definitions generally reinforce this conclusion.

Some researchers nonetheless consider the APA claim of a correlation between watching violence and acting violently to be a misleading answer to a question posed too narrowly. For George Gerbner, a renowned researcher on violence and the media, "The question is not what 'causes' violence and crime. . . . the question is what contributions do media policies and frequent exposure to media scenarios of violence and terror make to people's conceptions of reality, to some behavioural patterns, and to the pursuit of institutional interests" (Gerbner 1988, p. 21). Gerbner and his associates maintain that media portrayals of violence cause people to exaggerate the actual danger of violence, legitimate the violence of those who hold power, and help produce a "mean world" syndrome. People construe the world as hostile and conflict-ridden. These responses, they contend, are the main effects of media violence.

In Gerbner's framework, it would be hard to separate advertising from other media messages and images in accounting for the cultural patterns that Gerbner links to media violence. But this is not to say that violence and advertising are unrelated. Even the question of how much violence appears in television commercials is not simple to answer. There are few quantitative studies, and indeed most treatments of television violence pay scant attention to commercials. However, one 1994 study of food advertisements on children's programs found violent themes in 62 percent of commercials examined, both live and cartoon format (Rajecki et al. 1994, pp. 1685–1700). One might expect that concern about violence in children's television would reduce the incidence of violent themes; one might also think that food products do not especially lend themselves to violent promotion. Yet the study's results suggest that the extent of advertising violence may be broader than commonly believed.

In the case of television commercials, we can ask if decontextualized violence poses special problems. Does a shooting, for example, shown in a thirty-second spot for a movie differ in its effects from the same scene in a two-hour movie that reveals the causes and consequences of the action? One major study, the University of California at Los Angeles–sponsored *Television Violence Monitoring Project* (1999), notes that the problem seems especially acute in promotional messages for networks' forthcoming shows: "Many television writers and producers complain that they carefully craft their shows to deal with violence responsibly and then are dismayed to see a promotion eliminate all of the context and only feature the violence." As an example, the report points to a promo for *Walker: Texas Ranger,* consisting of a series of karate kicks and the voice-over proclaiming, "It's a butt-kicking season finale."

A related concern about violence in short commercial messages on television is that they may reach inappropriate and vulnerable audiences. In a 1997 article noting the frequency of violent imagery, a family physician in Minnesota recounts the experience of watching the 1996 baseball playoffs with his children. He videotaped 1,528 commercials and found that 104 (6.8 percent) contained violent interactions, defined as threats, acts, and consequences of violence. Significantly, over two-thirds of these advertisements were promotions for other television programs. Including promotions for cable-television events and motion pictures, 97 of 104 could be considered entertainment promotions. The author points out that parents cannot reasonably predict if or when violent commercials will appear in family-oriented programming. Thus, children almost unavoidably see these advertisements (Anderson 1997).

Commercials aired during the National Football League's annual Super Bowl, the most expensive spots on television, have come under intensive scrutiny since the 1980s. The bellicose nature of professional football has been a backdrop to objections to violent advertisements. Claims that reports of domestic violence cases against women peak around the time of the Super Bowl have also increased scrutiny of the ads. Two cases in 1999 suggest both the variety of violent messages and the sensitivity of audiences to these issues. One commercial drawing fire was a spot for the World Wrestling Federation jokingly purporting to show a typical day at the organization's headquarters. A wrestler announced that the WWF offered a "nonviolent form of entertainment" but then hit a passerby with a folding chair. Other images included officials fighting in the lobby and bodies shattering glass office partitions.

Significantly, however, complaints from conservative media criticism groups focused on sexual imagery in the ad. The American Family Association notified the Federal Communications Commission that it considered the ad a violation of the agency's standards of decency and unsuitable for broadcast in an early evening time slot on a show children were likely to be watching. These critics apparently found the violent scenarios unobjectionable, but the commercial indicates that sex and violence are often hard to separate in advertising themes. Violence in professional wrestling itself, however parodic, is often coupled with exaggerated sexual intimations. The ad also reinforces the point that advertising often transmits images of a product that is in itself violent. Critics often take aim at the advertisement when the underlying product or service is considered objectionable. Since television targets segmented audiences, the problem becomes most noticeable when the advertising message reaches a group other than the intended viewers of the program.

The other controversial 1999 Super Bowl commercial was an advertisement for a shoe-store chain showing a barefoot Kenyan runner hunted like an animal. Captured, he is drugged into unconsciousness by his trackers, who then put running shoes on his feet. Following complaints that the commercial was insulting and racist, the firm withdrew it from the air and apologized (*Washington Post*, 8 February 1999, p. C7). Here, the racial connotations of the spot heightened sensitivity to the hunters' attack on the runner.

Unlike the World Wrestling Federation's ad, the running shoe spot adopted a violent scenario to promote a nonviolent product. This is a relatively new development in television advertising. Advertisements in which a narrator describes and demonstrates the product's advantages or where typical product users are depicted in everyday situations dominated television in its earlier decades. These advertisements rarely had occasion to show scenes of violence. Now, however, television advertising's ability to escape the confines of realism and the pressure to create eye-catching commercials mean that ads can and will often portray fantasies, dreams, and even nightmares. Advertising is no longer confined to presenting conventional product benefits but often promises escape, wish-fulfillment, or the violation of social taboos. A 1999 advertisement for the ESPN network's telecasts of the National Hockey League features an elderly man sitting on a park bench. Annoyed by a skater crossing in front of him with a loud boom box, he reaches out with his cane and trips the young man; the ad then cuts to flashes of violence on the hockey rink. The verbal message explicitly links viewing violence to wish-fulfillment. Tripping someone is not permissible in daily life, but viewers can enjoy it in televised hockey.

That same year a cable network was forced to withdraw a promotional message for its Super Bowl Sunday "counter-programming" for women. The Court TV network, planning a five-hour block of programs about domestic violence by women against men, advertised it with a commercial showing a woman picking up a large knife when her football-watching husband complains that he is hungry. "Don't get angry, ladies, get even," was the voice-over message ("Court TV Changes Promo," *New York Newsday*, 30 January 1999, p. A47). Although the promotional announcement was clearly not meant as a prescription for spousal stabbing, even its mock advocacy of a violent cure for marital conflict raised angry protests. Although

it seems unlikely that a barbed but humorous allusion to gender conflict over the nation's annual football spectacle would serve as a direct incitement to viewer violence, the ad's highlighting of domestic violence clearly unsettled audiences and critics.

Advertising as Solution

Yet if advertising is part of the problem of media violence, it may also prove to be part of the solution. This, at least, is the hope of those who feel that the techniques that sell running shoes and breakfast cereals can also promote prosocial behavior. In the 1990s, television networks and the Advertising Council, the ad industry's voluntary association that produces and distributes public-service announcements (PSAs), turned their attention to antiviolence messages. Celebrities and others warn of the destructive consequences of violence and urge nonviolent methods of conflict resolution. Difficult as it is to judge the effectiveness of a conventional commercial campaign, it is still harder to measure the impact of these PSAs. The *National Television Violence Study* was not encouraging, concluding in 1997 that "no evidence was found that either the anti-violence programs or PSAs significantly altered . . . adolescents' attitudes toward the appropriateness of using violence to resolve conflicts" (vol. 1, p. 415). The sheer volume of violent media images and messages may simply drown out the limited efforts to deglamorize violence that media and the advertising industry have undertaken.

Advertising may be able to contribute to alleviating the problems of media violence in a less direct way. In television's earlier days, sponsoring advertisers often directly controlled program content. Today the power of spot advertisers to affect the shows where they place their commercials is more limited. Still, advertising is the financial base of commercial television, and the withdrawal of advertiser support hardly augurs well for a show's survival. Pressure groups that use letter-writing campaigns and boycotts to stop advertisers' support of programs the groups deem objectionable have hoped to influence content in this way. However, sexuality and related cultural issues, not violence, have been the main focus of pressures on television advertisers. Most notably, the religious right objected to the ABC network's comedy series *Ellen* when the lead character (as well as the actress portraying her, Ellen DeGeneres) came out as a lesbian in a 1997 episode. Their campaign proved unsuccessful, as just one advertiser, Chrysler, pulled out of the show, only to return by the next episode. This points to a limitation on advertiser boycotts in a segmented marketplace. Those who find a program objectionable are unlikely to be the show's target audience, and hence will lack leverage to pressure the kinds of advertisers who want to reach those viewers.

Still, other things being equal, it may not pay for advertisers to air their spots on violent programs. A 1998 study found that viewers remembered advertised brands and their commercial messages better when they appeared on nonviolent programs than on violent ones. The experiments indicated that violent programming raised the audience's level of anger, and that anger interfered with memory (Bushman 1998). A 1993 survey of public opinion found that about three out of five viewers were personally disturbed by televised violence in entertainment programming. Four out of five considered entertainment violence harmful to society. Even local station managers considered the level of television violence to be excessive. That these sentiments will translate into change, however, is doubtful. The economic and political forces (advertising among them) perpetuating media violence are formidable. It appears likely that advertising will continue both to reflect and to reinforce media violence unless there are fundamental changes in the media and American culture.

BIBLIOGRAPHY

Anderson, Charles. "Violence in Television Commercials During Nonviolent Programming: The 1996 Major League Baseball Playoffs." *Journal of the American Medical Association* 278, no. 13 (1 October 1997).

Bok, Sissela. *Mayhem: Violence as Public Entertainment.* Reading, Mass.: Addison-Wesley, 1998.

Bushman, Brad J. "Effects of Television Violence on Memory for Commercial Messages." *Journal of Experimental Psychology: Applied* 4, no. 4 (December 1998).

Fox, Frank W. *Madison Avenue Goes to War: The Strange Military Career of American Advertising, 1941–45.* Provo, Utah: Brigham Young University Press, 1975.

Gerbner, George. *Violence and Terror in the Mass Media.* UNESCO Reports and Papers on Mass Communication No. 102. Paris: United Nations Educational, Scientific, and Cultural Organization, 1988.

Hamilton, James T. *Channeling Violence: The Economic Market for Violent Television Programming.* Princeton, N.J.: Princeton University Press, 1998.

Huston, Aletha C., et al. *Big World, Small Screen: The Role of Television in American Society.* Lincoln: University of Nebraska Press, 1992.

Lears, Jackson. *Fables of Abundance: A Cultural History of Advertising in America.* New York: Basic, 1994.

Marchand, Roland. *Advertising the American Dream.* Berkeley: University of California Press, 1985.

National Television Violence Study. Vol. 1. Thousand Oaks, Calif.: Sage, 1997.

Price, Jonathan. *The Best Thing on TV, Commercials.* New York: Viking, 1978.

Rajecki, D. W., et al. "Violence, Conflict, Trickery, and Other Story Themes in TV Ads for Food for Children." *Journal of Applied Social Psychology* 24, no. 19 (October 1994).

Schudson, Michael. *Advertising, the Uneasy Persuasion: Its Dubious Impact on American Society.* New York: Basic, 1984.

UCLA Center for Communication Policy. *Television Violence Monitoring Project 1997.* University of California at Los Angeles. 17 February 1999. URL: *ccp.ucla.edu/network .htm#Promos.*

DANIEL POPE

See also **Television.**

AFRICAN AMERICANS

From the forced migration of Africans to the Americas to the police beating of Rodney King captured on videotape for the world to see, blacks have been the object of violence both physically and psychologically. Through branding, whipping, maiming, raping, bulldozing, lynching, rioting, stereotyping, and impoverishment, violence has been a means to maintain white dominance and black subordination in the United States. The rise of chattel slavery in the late seventeenth century brought with it a justification among Europeans for dehumanizing black people. Proponents of slavery defended the inhumane system on the ground that black people were inferior; black bodies could therefore be violated with impunity. Even after emancipation, the black body was devalued through minstrelsy and caricatures of African Americans in popular culture. Violence, both overt and subtle, has been used as a means of social control to support white supremacy and to keep African Americans "in their place." African Americans have employed violence as a form of resistance, whether via arson, poisoning, rioting, and looting. Because violence permeates American society, intraracial violence has also affected black family and community life.

The Trade in African Captives

Between twelve and fifteen million Africans were transported across the Atlantic Ocean during the four-hundred-year period of the Atlantic slave

A daguerreotype depicting the bark *Wildfire* carrying five hundred African slaves to Key West, Florida, in April 1860. LIBRARY OF CONGRESS

tives. The loss of their freedom and separation from family and friends took its toll psychologically. Unlike servitude in Africa, where captives retained rights as persons and were absorbed into society, the Africans captured for export faced a decidedly harsh fate.

The typical voyage across the Atlantic took six to eight weeks. The mortality rate aboard ship was as high as 24 percent during the seventeenth century but declined to about 15 percent during the eighteenth and nineteenth centuries due to better ships, shorter passage time, and more attention to the health of the captives. The captives typically had to lie belowdecks on their backs or sides and could not sit or stand, because the average ship packed in about four hundred Africans. Men were generally in chains; women and children generally were not. Ventilation was poor, and captives often wallowed in human waste. Under these conditions, disease could spread rapidly. To preserve the health of their most valuable human cargo, black males, ship captains during good weather forced the captives, who were chained together, on deck to exercise by way of dancing. On these occasions the compartments below decks were cleaned, and African women were particularly vulnerable to sexual predation on the part of the ship's crew.

Many Africans rebelled during the so-called middle passage by committing suicide or by throwing themselves overboard and trying to swim back home, while others attacked their captors and even attempted to gain control of the ships. There was at least one slave ship uprising a year during the period from 1699 to 1845; the historian Jay Coughtry has estimated that there was about one rebellion for every fifty-five voyages of Rhode Island vessels. Captured Africans stood greater chance of escape while vessels were anchored near the African coast. In 1730 during the sixth day at sea, ninety-six Africans aboard the ship *Little George* broke their chains, seized the ship, and steered it back to Africa.

The two most noted slave mutinies took place off the coast of the United States, on the *Amistad* and the *Creole*. Both of these rebellions occurred after 1808, when Congress outlawed American participation in the Atlantic slave trade. The *Amistad* sailed from Havana to the Cuban port of Guanaja on 27 June 1839 with fifty-three captives; under the leadership of one of the captives, Joseph Cinqué, the Africans seized control of the ship and ordered the sailors to sail to Africa. For seven weeks the crew steered the ship eastward by day

trade, which reached a peak between the years 1650 and 1850. Approximately half a million Africans were sold in North America, where the black population increased primarily through reproduction, rather than replacement as was the case in the Caribbean. The process of capture in Africa and transport across the ocean was especially brutal. Because Africans controlled the interior of the western coast, slave traders had to purchase human cargo from African rulers rather than capturing them directly. Those captives were generally marched in shackles from the interior to the coast, where they were held in dungeons, stockades, or barracoons until sold to ship captains. There has been very little calculation of the number of Africans who died during the process of capture in the interior, march to the coast, and confinement until sale. The estimate of upwards of twelve million Africans who were shipped to the Americas is based primarily on maritime records.

The dungeons were often damp and the stockades and barracoons were generally crowded, with unsanitary conditions. The rainy season, from June to August, was especially harsh on the cap-

but northwestward by night; the ship was then seized in United States' waters and the captives imprisoned. In a case that reached the Supreme Court in 1841, the justices ruled that the Africans aboard the *Amistad* had the right to rebel for their freedom because they had been taken to Cuba illegally and had never been slaves in the eyes of the law. The *Amistad* captives returned to Africa.

The *Creole* in 1841 sailed from Hampton Roads, Virginia, to New Orleans with a cargo of 135 slaves. Under the direction of a slave named Madison Washington, the captives gained control of the ship and forced the crew to sail to Nassau, where the British, who had outlawed the slave trade in 1807, refused to return them to the United States, ruling that slaves became free persons once they set foot on British soil.

Enslavement

The captives who were forcefully brought to North America from Africa or the Caribbean underwent a process of seasoning that involved the captive's acquiring some familiarity with the language, responding to a name given to him or her by the slaveholder, learning the labor routine, and acquiescing to the authority of the slaveholder and indeed of all whites. Slaveholders sought to instill in African captives a sense of inferiority, powerlessness, and dependence on their will.

The institution of slavery evolved slowly in North America. Africans experienced an uncertain condition prior to the 1660s. Some of them even became free men and women after a term of service similar to that required of white indentured servants. By the 1660s, however, the British colonies of North America had passed laws that distinguished Africans and that confined them to perpetual bondage. They declared that baptism did not free slaves; that slave masters, or those appointed by them to punish their slaves, could not be prosecuted for a crime if slaves died in the process of being disciplined; that neither blacks nor slaves could carry weapons or travel without permission, subject to twenty lashes; that any black person who lifted a hand against a white person should receive thirty lashes; and that any fugitive slave who resisted capture could be killed.

The lash was the major means of coercion in forcing slaves to work. Although Robert W. Fogel and Stanley L. Engerman hypothesize that plantation slavery was a profitable economic system in which slaves were hardworking and efficient laborers who internalized the Protestant work ethic, Herbert G. Gutman demonstrated that slaveholders employed physical coercion more than incentives and rewards to maximize slave productivity. Drawing on evidence from the plantation records of Bennet H. Barrow, a Louisiana planter, Gutman concludes that on average male slaves were whipped once a week and females once every other week. Slaveholders or their surrogates usually whipped recalcitrant slaves in front of all their slaves as a form of warning and a means of social control. Slaves received fifteen to twenty lashes for moderate infractions such as clumsiness, and thirty-nine or more lashes for serious offenses such as any form of insubordination. Sometimes slaveholders poured salt into the lash wounds as further punishment. During the eighteenth and even the nineteenth century, slaves might be branded, mutilated, castrated, or placed in stocks.

Living conditions for slaves were especially harsh. They were housed in small, generally windowless cabins that were inadequately ventilated and poorly maintained. Slaves received minimal clothing and food. The average adult ration was a peck (eight quarts) of cornmeal and three to four pounds of salt pork or bacon a week. Some slaveholders allowed slaves to tend vegetable gardens to supplement their diets. As a form of punishment, slaveholders often withheld meat rations. Given the poor living conditions and diet, slaves suffered from disease and malnutrition. When American participation in the slave trade was outlawed in 1808, slaveholders began to pay greater attention to the health of their enslaved property.

Although the Revolutionary War had led to the abolition of slavery in the North, the new nation protected the institution of slavery through Article IV of the U.S. Constitution, which provided that no person held to labor or service in one state could be discharged from that obligation by escaping to another state. Moreover, for purposes of states' representation in Congress, Article I of the Constitution referred to slaves as three-fifths of a person. The three-fifths clause perpetuated the idea of African Americans as less than human and therefore not entitled to the same rights and privileges of citizens of the United States. Even those African Americans who were not enslaved experienced restrictions, since they could not become naturalized citizens of the United States. If there was any ambiguity about the status of African Americans, Chief Justice Roger B. Taney in the 1857 Dred Scott decision declared that blacks had been considered inferior beings for more than a century and therefore had no rights that white men were bound to respect.

Given that the Europeans who migrated to what became the United States came as settlers rather than sojourners, the institution of slavery in North America differed from that in the Caribbean. Many of the planters in the Caribbean were absentee owners or sojourners who sought to make a quick profit. Day-to-day conditions of enslavement were therefore more harsh, as slaveholders often worked their slaves to death and replaced their labor force every seven to eight years. The ratio of male to female slaves was very high and did not lend itself to the development of black families. In contrast, slave labor in the United States was organized primarily by family unit. To increase their property value, slaveholders encouraged slaves to reproduce. However, although enslaved African Americans were able to form families, they were at the mercy of the slaveholder. Slave families were often broken apart due to slaveholders' financial circumstances or as a form of punishment.

Slave Resistance and Rebellions

The demographics of slavery in the United States encouraged the reproduction and expansion of the slave population; slavery was thus self-perpetuating, a factor that inhibited slave rebellion. Nevertheless, slaves resisted brutalization and dehumanization in numerous covert and overt ways. Covertly, they slowed their pace of work, abused farm animals, feigned illness, broke tools, and stole crops. Overtly, they poisoned slaveholders, burned storehouses, escaped, and staged violent revolts. In the nineteenth century, up until the time of emancipation in 1863, about fifty thousand slaves a year ran away for varying lengths of time. Some established organized groups of fugitive slaves who periodically raided plantations for food and supplies. The largest and most successful maroon (fugitive slave community) settlement was in Florida, where fugitive slaves settled among the Seminole Indians and were instrumental in fighting the Seminole Wars of 1817–1818 and 1835–1842. Many of the African Americans in Florida were slaves purchased by the Seminoles but allowed to live like tenant farmers.

The Seminole Negroes, as both the slaves and maroons were called, lived in their own villages, cultivated crops, and tended cattle. During the War of 1812, about a thousand black people sought refuge in Florida and built a settlement called Negro Fort along the Apalachicola River. American forces destroyed Negro Fort in 1816. Those who escaped were later pursued by General Andrew Jackson during the First Seminole War. The status of the maroons was an important part of the conflict between the Americans and the Seminoles. A major point of contention in Seminole refusal to resettle in Oklahoma was the absence of a guarantee that the maroons would be permitted to leave with the tribe without being reenslaved. The Second Seminole War was as much a slave-catching expedition as a battle against the Indians. After three years of fierce fighting, with the maroons in the forefront, American forces agreed that they would not be reenslaved and could accompany the Indians to Oklahoma.

The Seminole Wars were perhaps the most successful armed rebellion among the slaves. Armed struggle was more difficult in the United States than in the Caribbean or South America because whites outnumbered blacks, the terrain was not as mountainous, and there were more acculturated slaves who were less likely to rebel than African-born slaves. Although the circumstances were not favorable for uprisings, there were at least forty-three important slave revolts or conspiracies in North America from the seventeenth century to the Civil War. One of the earliest revolts took place in New York City in 1712 when about two dozen slaves set fire to a building and ambushed whites who came to put it out, killing nine and wounding seven others. In retaliation, twenty slaves were hanged, three were burned at the stake, one broken on the wheel, and one starved to death. Six slaves committed suicide before being taken into custody.

In September 1739 about twenty-one slaves along the Stono River in South Carolina under the leadership of a slave named Jemmy rose up, raided a store for arms and ammunition, and marched toward Florida, killing more than twenty whites and burning their homes. A military force under Lieutenant Governor William Bull of South Carolina routed the slaves, killed about fourteen of them, cut off their heads, and placed them on mile posts. About twenty-five whites and fifty Africans were killed in the uprising. One of the largest slave rebellions in the United States took place in Louisiana in January 1811. Some four to five hundred slaves under the leadership of a free mulatto from Haiti, Charles Deslondes, invaded a plantation about thirty-five miles north of New Orleans and marched with guns, drums, and flags from plantation to plantation. The governor led a military force that stopped the revolt and killed sixty-six of the slaves immediately. Sixteen slaves were tried and convicted in New Orleans, beheaded, and their heads placed on poles along the Mississippi River from the city to the location of the uprising as a warning to other slaves.

The slave insurrection in Haiti in 1791 under the direction of Toussaint Louverture inspired American slaves to rebel, especially Gabriel Prosser, an enslaved black man in Virginia. Together with his wife and his brothers Solomon and Martin, Prosser planned to attack Richmond, the state's capital, on 30 August 1800, seize the armory, capture the governor, James Monroe, and negotiate for the slaves' freedom. As many as two thousand slaves were probably recruited to participate in the revolt, which was brought to the attention of authorities by slave informers. More than two dozen slaves, including Prosser, were executed for participating in the conspiracy. Twenty-two years later Denmark Vesey, a free black carpenter in Charleston, South Carolina, sought assistance from Haiti in staging a revolt against slavery. His conspiracy involved thousands of slaves and free blacks and like Prosser's was revealed to white authorities by slave informants. As a result of the conspiracy, thirty-seven African Americans were executed and forty-three were deported from the state.

The last major slave uprising prior to John Brown's raid on Harpers Ferry, Virginia, on 16 October 1859, took place in Southampton County, Virginia, on 21 August 1831. A slave named Nat Turner believed that it was God's will for him to rise up and end slavery. Together with five other slaves, Turner killed the members of his slaveholder's household and then marched from farm to farm, slaughtering the owners, gathering recruits, and heading for Jerusalem, the county seat. Over a span of about twenty miles and forty hours, Turner's band of some seventy slaves killed at least fifty-seven whites. Initially, Turner's rebels repulsed the militia that pursued them, but the militia surprised the insurgents when they stopped to rest about three miles from Jerusalem. Turner escaped capture but nearly a hundred slaves were killed, and similar to other uprisings, the heads of more than two dozen were severed and placed atop poles as a warning to other slaves. Turner was captured about two months later and executed on 11 November 1831.

In the aftermath of Vesey's conspiracy and Turner's rebellion, in particular, the slave states strengthened their slave codes. The Negro Seamen Act (1822) required that black sailors be held in jail while their ships were in port, although federal courts ruled the law unconstitutional a year later. It was against the law for slaves and even free blacks in many states to learn how to read and write. Manumission became more difficult, and the growth of the free black population slowed. Not more than five African Americans, slave or free, could meet together even for prayer services without a white person being present. Slaves could not leave plantations without passes and could not blow horns or beat drums. Unless proven otherwise, every black person was assumed to be a slave and was subject to the authority of slave patrols, or "paderollers," as the slaves called them, who could chastise them with impunity. The South was an armed camp where practically every white person, adult or child, was committed to upholding the institution of slavery and to keeping African Americans in their place. Violence was prevalent throughout the region, where dueling and fighting were a part of life. The subordination of African Americans through violence affected other areas of southern life in relations between husbands and wives, parents and children, and rich and poor.

Slavery took both a physical and psychological toll on African Americans. Child abuse, sexual molestation, rape, and beatings, according to Nell Irvin Painter, resulted in "soul murder," which produced self-doubt and self-hatred among the slaves, robbed them of their vitality and creativity, and crushed their self-esteem. John W. Blassingame has suggested that there were three stereotypes of the slave personality—Sambo, Jack, and Nat. Sambo was the loyal, faithful, docile, and dependent slave; Jack was hardworking but manipulative, doing just what was needed to get by; and Nat was the rebel, the incorrigible runaway who took vengeance on slaveholders, their property, and families. These stereotypes tell us as much about slaveholders as they do about slaves. They express slaveholders' fears and anxieties about keeping a people in bondage and treating them as chattel. Despite the grim realities of enslavement, African Americans maintained their integrity as a people through a culture that emphasized families, folklore, religion, and spirituals.

Antebellum Race Riots

After the American Revolution, each northern state by 1804 had taken steps to abolish slavery, although it continued to exist in the North well into the 1830s, given the general provisions for gradual emancipation. As the free black population grew in the North, African Americans began to live in small black neighborhoods in urban areas. Faced with competition from blacks for jobs and housing and out of fear of social equality, especially intermarriage and miscegenation, white northerners often attacked black communities. These attacks on vastly outnumbered African Americans often took the form of pogroms.

One of the worst riots took place in Cincinnati, Ohio, in late August 1829, when several hundred whites invaded the black community. By the 1820s most African Americans in Cincinnati lived in a small neighborhood known as Bucktown, or Little Africa. Ohio's Black Laws required that African Americans provide written proof of freedom to settle in the state and that they post bond of five hundred dollars to guarantee good behavior. The laws were loosely enforced and the black population in Cincinnati grew to almost 10 percent by 1829, when white men who feared that the black population was growing too fast insisted on enforcement of the laws. For three days, whites attacked and killed African Americans, forcing more than a thousand to flee their homes for Canada, where they established the settlement of Wilberforce.

In May 1838 Philadelphia whites destroyed black churches, meeting halls, homes, and a shelter for black orphans. It seems ironic that northern whites were particularly hostile to examples of black self-improvement such as churches, schools, businesses, and benevolent organizations. Although the North generally opposed the institution of slavery, it did not welcome African Americans. Between 1824 and 1849 there were at least thirty-nine riots against African Americans in the North. The bloodiest race riot took place in New York City during the Civil War. The so-called draft riots took place in July 1863, instigated by poor white men who were angered that they were subject to the draft, while the well-to-do could pay three hundred dollars for a substitute to take their place in the war. Working-class and poor whites went on a rampage for five days, destroying property and taking out their rage on African Americans, hanging, burning, shooting, and beating to death hundreds of black people. They even attacked the Colored Orphan Asylum, which they burned to the ground, and looted the Colored Seamen's Home. Almost half the city's black population fled their homes for refuge elsewhere.

This pattern of violence spread to the South immediately after the Civil War, when two riots took place in Memphis, Tennessee, and New Orleans, Louisiana, in 1866. During the war, the Union Army had set up a camp for newly freed slaves near Memphis. Many African Americans remained at this camp after the war. Tension arose between African American and Irish residents of the same neighborhoods. The Irish settlers, who were struggling economically, took out their frustration on the freedmen and freedwomen in a riot in which they killed forty-six African Americans, raped five women, and destroyed ninety-one black homes, four churches, and all twelve black schools. In July 1866 African Americans in New Orleans sought to attend the Radical Republican Convention, which was meeting to change the state constitution to allow black men the right to vote. A white protester fired at a group of African Americans, who shot back. The city police then attacked the African Americans and antiblack violence spread throughout the city. Thirty-four African Americans were killed and 119 were wounded.

Bulldozing

Violence was so widespread against the former slaves in the South that Congress began an eleven-month investigation in March 1871. Between 1865 and 1877 an estimated forty thousand African Americans were murdered by white vigilante groups such as the Ku Klux Klan, Red Shirts, and Rifle Clubs. General Oliver Otis Howard, head of the Freedmen's Bureau, testified before Congress that the white population of the South seemed determined to exterminate the black population.

Through vagrancy laws, apprenticeship regulations, the convict-lease system, and peonage, the white South tried to return African Americans to a slavelike status. Any black persons who could not prove that they were gainfully employed could be arrested and hired out to employers who paid their fines. These blacks usually worked without compensation until the employers determined that they had satisfied their debts. Apprenticeship laws placed black children, whom the courts decided could not be supported by their parents, in the custody of guardians who could work them and punish them at will. The convict-lease system saw black men entrapped for and then convicted of petty crimes, then leased out to work on plantations, railroad construction, lumber mills, and in mines. The lessees agreed to feed, clothe, house, and provide security for the prisoners. The system was worse than slavery because lessees had no investment in the convicts, as slaveholders had in slaves. Peonage bound black families to the soil as sharecroppers and tenant farmers cultivating cotton, which they associated with their lives in slavery. In fact, the system of debt peonage replaced slavery. African Americans could not leave the land until they had paid for the credit extended to them until the harvest. Their crops never seemed to exceed the credit as determined by planters and store owners.

The Ku Klux Klan, organized in Pulaski, Tennessee, in 1866, espoused the superiority of whites over blacks and targeted black politicians, prosperous farmers, and any African American who appeared to defy this social order for beatings, torture, and murder. Bulldozing was a strategy of violence to keep African Americans subordinate after emancipation. The term *bulldoze*, or *bulldose*, originated after the Civil War and referred to the severe flogging of an African American—literally, the infliction of a "doze" or a "dose" sufficient to subdue a bull. Bulldozing was primarily a rural phenomenon, used to prevent African Americans from voting, holding office, and even owning land.

To escape the terror that gripped the South during Reconstruction, many African Americans sought to emigrate to Africa or to safe territory within the United States. Blacks organized the National Colored Colonization Society during the 1870s and in 1877 inscribed a list of ninety-eight thousand African Americans from Arkansas, Louisiana, Mississippi, and Texas who were prepared to leave the South. Many of them were among the twenty-five thousand African Americans who migrated to Kansas in 1879 in search of a better life. Others moved to Oklahoma, where African Americans created some thirty-two black towns during the 1890s.

Lynching

Riots and pogroms against African Americans became less frequent between 1880 and 1900 as lynching became the major form of violence. Lynching, or summary and illegal mob execution usually by burning, hanging, or both, was a form of violence that unified the white population in the maintenance of white supremacy and that terrorized African Americans into observing the etiquette of race relations in the South. Preserving the chastity of white womanhood was the pretext for most lynchings. In fact, Ida B. Wells, a fearless black newspaper owner, discovered in her investigations, most of which took place between 1892 and 1902, that even the charge of rape was present

in only about 20 percent of the cases. During the 1890s there was an average of 188 lynchings per year, a number that exceeded legal executions by two to one. The number of African Americans—men, women, and children—lynched in the former slave states from 1889 to 1918 was 2,460.

After the Civil War bulldozing had been a means to curb the freedom of the recently emancipated slaves. Through a series of Supreme Court decisions, African Americans in the South lost the few rights that they gained during the Reconstruction era. But during the 1890s, a new generation of whites and blacks who had not experienced the institution of slavery and its control of black life came of age. Lynching became the preferred means of social control, to keep African Americans in their place, and to serve as a lesson especially to young black men about what awaited African Americans who showed less than total deference to all white people. According to Leon Litwack (1998), this new generation of free blacks was "more questioning of their 'place' and less inclined to render absolute deference to whites"; they therefore "encountered (and in a certain sense helped to provoke) the most violent and repressive period in the history of race relations in the United States" (p. xiv).

During the late nineteenth and early twentieth century, lynchings were public spectacles or rituals advertised in advance. They attracted mobs of thousands; people often came by special trains scheduled for the occasion. All strata of white society, not just uneducated males, took part in lynchings. Families brought their young children to witness the rituals and to be indoctrinated into the culture of white supremacy. The subjects of lynchings were generally black males accused of rape, but the "crime" for which victims stood accused could as well be disputing a white person or making boastful comments. The lynchers often cut off parts of the victim's body—fingers, toes, genitals, eyeballs, ears—that members of the mob took home for souvenirs. The tortured body might be dragged through town for spectators to kick and stone before being hung from a pole and burned. The corpse was usually left dangling for a few days as a warning, reminder, and lesson to onlookers, both black and white.

Twentieth-Century Race Riots

Lynchings declined in the second decade of the twentieth century as many African Americans moved to urban areas in both the South and the North. Once there, however, and competing with whites for jobs and housing, they faced race riots similar to the pogroms of the antebellum era. One of the most brutal race riots ever recorded took place in East Saint Louis, Illinois, on 2 July 1917. The riots were set off when some blacks opened fire on a police car, believing it was the return of previous marauders to the neighborhood, and a white police officer was killed. A mob of whites, already angry about the hiring of African Americans for government-contract factory work, invaded black neighborhoods, beating and killing black people and destroying their homes. Thousands of African Americans fled the city for safety in nearby towns. At least thirty-nine African Americans and nine whites were killed in the riot.

There were twenty-five major race riots across the country during the summer of 1919. So much black blood flowed in the streets of America that writers referred to it as the Red Summer of 1919. With the end of World War I, many soldiers returned home to find that their former jobs were now held by African Americans hired during the wartime labor shortage. Tensions in the cities ran high. The worst riot of the summer took place in Chicago, Illinois, where violence broke out after whites drowned a black youth who, while swimming in Lake Michigan, unwittingly crossed an in-visible boundary between the black and white sections of the beach. Whites attacked African Americans on their way to work and on the fringes of black neighborhoods. Unlike the earlier pogroms, the riots of 1919 became interracial wars in which African Americans fought back in pitched battles. Twenty-three blacks and fifteen whites were killed, more than five hundred were injured, and thousands were left homeless during almost two weeks of violence in Chicago.

Two years later, white mobs destroyed the black neighborhood of Greenwood in Tulsa, Oklahoma, leaving eleven thousand African Americans homeless. A white elevator operator reported that Dick Rowland, a black man who allegedly jostled her in the elevator, had tried to rape her. The black man was arrested, and the next day the *Tulsa Tribune* revealed that he was to be lynched that night. Seventy-five armed black men offered to help the police protect the defendant, but the police rejected their offer and tried to disarm them. An argument took place and shots were fired, with the black men, who were outnumbered by a white mob, retreating to Greenwood. Whites invaded the neighborhood and blacks exchanged gunfire with them. African Americans were burned out of their homes and shot as they tried to escape. There were even reports of two airplanes dropping bombs on the neighborhood, which was completely destroyed.

A May 1944 parade in Detroit demonstrating against "Jim Crow" segregation laws. LIBRARY OF CONGRESS

The death toll was at least twenty-six African Americans and ten whites, with some estimates much higher. African Americans rebuilt Greenwood, a prosperous and self-sufficient black community. The small black town of Rosewood in western Florida, with one hundred and fifty inhabitants, suffered a similar fate in 1923; it was wiped off the map. Unlike in the Greenwood case, the state of Florida later paid survivors of Rosewood reparations for the destruction of their town.

Interracial violence continued during the Great Depression, with the New York City Riot of 1935, and during World War II, with riots in Detroit, Harlem, Los Angeles, and Beaumont, Texas. After the war, pitched battles continued to characterize race riots in the North until the 1960s, while in the South lynching and pogroms continued to be the most common forms of violence against blacks. The campaign by southern whites of "massive resistance" to *Brown v. Board of Education of Topeka, Kansas*, the 1954 Supreme Court decision that overturned the doctrine of "separate but equal," led to the murder of civil rights activists, especially black leaders, and to the bombing of black homes and churches. The Southern Poverty Law Center's Civil Rights Memorial (designed in the late 1980s by Maya Lin, who created the Vietnam Veterans Memorial in Washington, D.C.) in Montgomery, Alabama, includes the names of forty men, women, and children, including six whites, who were killed between 1955 and 1968 in the cause of civil rights.

Urban Rebellions

Racial violence took on new dimensions after 1963, when there were over five hundred uprisings in America, which left at least 263 dead and $160 billion worth of property damage. These disturbances were more assaults on property than on persons, and were less incidents of interracial strife than of racial unrest. The National Advisory Commission on Civil Disorders (the Kerner Commission) reported in 1968 that police practices were the major grievance among African Americans in communities that had experienced urban rebellions between 1963 and 1967. Concerns about police brutality surpassed those for other issues such as unemployment, substandard housing, and inadequate education.

Among inner-city African Americans, the police were perceived as an army of occupation similar to the "paderollers" during slavery and "bulldozers" during Reconstruction. They were symbols of oppression and emblematic of the political repression and impoverishment that African Americans suffered. They represented psychological as well as physical violence. The Black Panther Party, organized in Oakland, California, in 1966, developed a ten-point platform and program; point seven stated: "We want an immediate end to Police Brutality and Murder of Black people." The Black Panthers advocated arming African Americans for self-defense and began a practice of following the police, observing them in questioning suspects, reading suspects their rights, following them to the police station if arrested, and posting bail. They engaged in several violent confrontations with the police and soon became the object of nationwide police repression. J. Edgar Hoover, director of the Federal Bureau of Investigation, considered the Black Panthers the greatest threat to internal security in the United States and sought to destroy them through COINTELPRO, a counterintelligence program. In just two years, 1968 and 1969, the police killed at least twenty-eight members of the Black Panther Party, most notably Fred Hampton and Mark Clark, Illinois Panther leaders, murdered in their sleep by officers from the state attorney's office in Cook County, Illinois. By 1969 most of the Black Panther leadership had been killed, jailed, or exiled.

Many law-enforcement officials assumed that the urban rebellions were part of an organized conspiracy, but the Kerner Commission concluded that they stemmed from African Americans being left behind in the tide of economic progress sweeping across the nation. In an oft-quoted statement, the Kerner Commission reported that America was becoming two nations, black and white, separate and unequal. The urban rebellions were a form of political insurgency, of collective violence, releasing pent-up resentment over economic exploitation, racial discrimination, and police brutality. Although in the late twentieth century much progress was made in the United States in reducing the level of black poverty, which once stood at one-third of the black population, and black unemployment, which in 1999 remained twice as high as white unemployment but had dropped to the single digits for the first time, the issues of police brutality and inequitable law enforcement continued to be major concerns for African Americans.

Actions by some white police officers, in particular, led to the widely held perception among blacks and whites that white police have little regard for African Americans as fellow citizens

Members of the Black Panther Party march in New York City, preceded by mounted police officers, circa 1970. CORBIS/BETTMANN

whom they are dutybound to serve and to protect. The legacy of slavery, bulldozing, and lynching seemed to some to have left white society with little regard for the black body, which was assaulted in the past with impunity. The police beating of Rodney King in Los Angeles, captured on videotape in 1992, outraged African Americans, who assumed that the police would be held responsible. When an all-white jury in Simi Valley (to which the proceedings had been moved because of pretrial publicity) acquitted the police of excessive force, assault with a deadly weapon, and filing of false reports, African Americans in Los Angeles went on a rampage. (Fresh in their minds was the recent killing of a fifteen-year-old black girl, Latasha Harlins, by Soon Ja Du, a Korean store owner, for allegedly trying to steal a bottle of orange juice, a killing that was also captured on videotape. For the latter crime, Du received only five years probation and community service as punishment.) In lives lost, about fifty-eight, and property damage, almost $1 billion, the Los Angeles riot was the worst uprising ever.

In the late 1990s, police brutality continued in the beating and sodomizing of Abner Louima in New York, the killing of Tyisha Miller, shot fourteen times in her car in Riverside, California, and the death of Amadou Diallo, who was shot at forty-one times while standing unarmed at the entrance to his apartment in New York.

African Americans have also suffered from the inequitable administration of justice in the United States. In 1999 one in three young black men was under the supervision of the criminal justice system. Black males are ten times more likely than whites to be imprisoned. Although African Americans account for 15 percent of the nation's drug users, they make up one-third of those arrested for drug use and 57 percent of those convicted on drug charges. African Americans are targeted as potential criminals through racial profiling, arrested more frequently, generally have less than adequate legal representation, are convicted at higher rates, and receive longer sentences for the same crimes committed by whites. Almost half the nation's prison population is black, as are 40 percent of those on death row. These high rates of incarceration deprive black communities of husbands and fathers and contribute to family instability and neighborhood deterioration.

Intraracial Violence

Black-on-black violence became more prevalent during the twentieth century as African Americans became more concentrated in urban areas of the country. In the 1990s young black males were four times more likely than white males to be the victims of homicide. Although only 1.3 percent of the population, they committed 17.2 percent of the homicides in 1992. Black children were disproportionately victims of child abuse and neglect, and spousal abuse was more frequent among African Americans.

Some social scientists suggested that a subculture of violence emerged among African Americans during the twentieth century. They argued that violence begets violence and that racial subjugation and violent oppression shaped a violent climate in which honor and respect come from physical intimidation and domination of others. The socialization process and what some scholars have called "forceful parenting" in the disciplining of children were suggested as factors contributing to violent behavior. As James W. Clarke concluded in his 1998 book *The Lineaments of Wrath*, "It would be a mistake to assume that the behavior of black children today, who have no personal memory and probably little knowledge of the experiences of their forebears, is unaffected by the history of victimization" (p. 287).

The existence of a violent subculture among blacks is a controversial and much contested finding. Research suggests that physical abuse takes place more frequently in black families that are poor with single-parent mothers and stepfathers (consensual or legal), on welfare, have more family members, and with little formal education. High-risk environments, stress, poverty, unemployment, substandard housing, and unstable kinship networks are argued to be more predictive of criminal and family violence than is race.

Conclusion

Both physical and psychological violence have been used against black people in the United States to enslave them, to segregate and disfranchise them, to "keep them in their place" as separate and distinct from the rest of society, and to make them "a part of" but "apart from" the dominant society.

Given emancipation, Reconstruction, and civil rights, violence against African Americans at the close of the twentieth century, except with respect to police brutality, was more subtle than overt. The problem was less interracial than intraracial physical violence in the African American community. Psychological violence continued to take its toll in the high rates of black poverty, unemployment, family instability, inequitable education, crime, and underserved inner-city neighborhoods. But given the assault on the black body and soul over almost four hundred years, the resilience of the African American community and spirit is nothing less than remarkable.

BIBLIOGRAPHY

Berlin, Ira. *Many Thousands Gone: The First Two Centuries of Slavery in North America.* Cambridge, Mass.: Harvard University Press, 1998.

Blassingame, John W. *The Slave Community: Plantation Life in the Antebellum South.* Rev. and enl. ed. New York: Oxford University Press, 1979.

Brown, Richard Maxwell. *Strain of Violence: Historical Studies of American Violence and Vigilantism.* New York: Oxford University Press, 1975.

Clarke, James W. *The Lineaments of Wrath: Race, Violent Crime, and American Culture.* New Brunswick, N.J.: Transaction, 1998.

Coughtry, Jay. *The Notorious Triangle: Rhode Island and the African Slave Trade, 1700–1807.* Philadelphia: Temple University Press, 1981.

Fogel, Robert W., and Stanley L. Engerman. *Time on the Cross: The Economics of American Negro Slavery.* Boston: Little, Brown, 1974.

Goode, Stephen. *Violence in America.* New York: Messner, 1984.

Gutman, Herbert G. "Time on the Cross: The Economics of American Negro Slavery: The World Two Cliometricians Made." *Journal of Negro History* 60, no. 1 (January 1975).

Hampton, Robert L., ed. *Violence in the Black Family: Correlates and Consequences.* Lexington, Mass.: Lexington Books, 1987.

Kolchin, Peter. *American Slavery, 1619–1877.* New York: Hill and Wang, 1993.

Litwack, Leon F. *Trouble in Mind: Black Southerners in the Age of Jim Crow.* New York: Knopf, 1998.

McMurry, Linda O. *To Keep the Waters Troubled: The Life of Ida B. Wells.* New York: Oxford University Press, 1998.

Painter, Nell Irvin. "Soul Murder and Slavery: Toward a Fully Loaded Cost Accounting." In *U.S. History as Women's History: Knowledge, Power, and State Formation,* edited by Linda K. Kerber et al. Chapel Hill: University of North Carolina Press, 1995.

Pearson, Hugh. *The Shadow of the Panther: Huey Newton and the Price of Black Power in America.* Reading, Mass.: Addison-Wesley, 1994.

Pinkney, Alphonso. *The American Way of Violence*. New York: Random House, 1972.

Rawley, James A. *The Transatlantic Slave Trade: A History*. New York: Norton, 1981.

Shapiro, Herbert. *White Violence and Black Response: From Reconstruction to Montgomery*. Amherst: University of Massachusetts Press, 1988.

Wade, Wyn Craig. *The Fiery Cross: The Ku Klux Klan in America*. New York: Simon and Schuster, 1987.

ROBERT L. HARRIS, JR.

See also **Amistad Case; Black Codes; Black Panthers; Civil Rights Movements; Draft Riots; Dred Scott Decision; Fugitive Slave Acts; King, Martin Luther, Jr.; Los Angeles Riots of 1992; Lynching; Malcolm X; Police: Police Brutality; Race and Ethnicity; Reconstruction; Riots; Slave Rebellions; Slavery; Structural Violence; Urban Violence; Watts Riot.**

AGE AND THE LIFE CYCLE

As far back as 1831 Adolphe Quetelet, in his *Research on the Propensity for Crime at Different Ages*, concluded that the variable most correlated with criminal offending is age: "*Age* is without contradiction the cause which acts with the most energy to develop or moderate the propensity for crime" (p. 64). Across cities, countries, and time periods, criminal behavior generally rises in early adolescence, peaks in late adolescence, and declines during early adulthood. For the most part, the relationship between age and crime is the same with respect to both violent and nonviolent offenses, with violent offenses exhibiting a somewhat later (in age of perpetrator) increase and peak. Studies examining the relationship between age and crime at the individual level reveal a substantively similar conclusion.

The study of the relationship between age and crime has brought evidence to bear on the characteristics of victims and perpetrators. For example, late-twentieth-century studies indicated that the incidence of violent behavior is increasing more rapidly for juveniles than for any other subgroup. According to the Uniform Crime Reports compiled by the Federal Bureau of Investigation, between 1985 and 1994 the number of persons arrested for murder and nonnegligent manslaughter increased by 150 percent for persons under eighteen, whereas an increase of a little over 11 percent was evidenced for persons over eighteen. Data from the 1992 National Crime Victimization Survey, administered by the U.S. Department of

Justice, reveals a similar story. For whites, the rate of violent victimization was highest in the twelve-to-fifteen age group (75 per 1,000), while for blacks, it peaked in the sixteen-to-nineteen age group (125 per 1,000). Moreover, teenagers were most at risk for fatal victimizations.

These findings may give the false impression that aggressive impulses first surface in adolescence. Research has shown, however, that aggressive tendencies can be identified as early as infancy (i.e., three to six months) and that aggression is manifested in different forms throughout development, for instance as biting and pushing in infancy, bullying in childhood, assault in adolescence, and domestic battery in adulthood. Lee Robins (1978) qualifies this view, suggesting that although "adult antisocial behavior virtually *requires* childhood antisocial behavior," most juvenile delinquents do not go on to become serious adult offenders (p. 611, emphasis in original).

While the nature of the relationship between age and crime is in little dispute, the reason for the covariation has been the subject of intense debate. For example, is the peak in criminal behavior observed in late adolescence a function of the increasing number of adolescent offenders engaging in criminal acts (prevalence), or is it a function of a relatively small number of offenders engaging in a large amount of criminal acts (incidence)? Why does criminal behavior decrease in early adulthood? Is the decrease due to maturation, a change in social bonds, or simply a process of self-selection whereby individuals choose to cease their criminal involvement? Are the reasons for the cessation the same for both violent and nonviolent offenders? Clearly, the study of age and crime has far-reaching implications on both theoretical and policy grounds. Answers to questions like the ones posed above would be able to both test the leading theories of crime and inform policy decisions made by the juvenile and criminal justice systems.

This essay explores three central components of the study of age and crime, with a particular emphasis on the relationship between age and violent crime: (1) statistical and data analysis; (2) manifestations of violence over the life cycle; and (3) theoretical explanations. The essay closes with a discussion of future research directions in the study of age and violence over the life course.

Statistical and Data Analysis

This section presents what is known about the relationship between age and crime in general, and age and violence in particular, from the three major sources of information on criminal behavior: official data, victimization surveys, and self-report surveys. All three forms of data collection have comparable advantages and disadvantages; their collective use may provide the most complete picture of the relationship between age and violence.

Official Data. One of the most widely accepted facts in criminology is that crime varies substantially with age. It is well known that age and crime are negatively correlated. Property crime rates peak between the ages of thirteen and sixteen, drop in half by age twenty, then continue a steady decline throughout adulthood. In the age–violent crime relationship, a negative correlation is still observed, yet the peak age for violent offenses rises to about age eighteen, then follows a gradual but steady decline throughout adulthood. Figure 1 presents the cross-sectional relationship between age and criminal arrests (for both property and violent crime) for 1995, while figure 2 presents violent-crime arrest rates per 100,000 for juveniles (under age fourteen and ages fifteen to seventeen) and adults (ages eighteen to twenty, twenty-one to twenty-four, and twenty-five and older) for the period 1970–1996. It should be noted that since both of these figures involve arrest rates, they focus on the frequency (incidence), as opposed to the prevalence, of offending, which may obscure the presence of repeat offenders. In practice, however, the relationships between age and incidence and prev-

alence generally point to similar substantive conclusions. Importantly, both figures suggest that a preponderance of crimes are committed by youths between the ages of thirteen and eighteen.

Between 1970 and 1995 the rate of adolescents arrested for homicide more than doubled, while homicide arrest rates for adults actually declined. The "youngness" of the crime problem is not necessarily attributable to adolescent offenders. In fact, offenders under age fifteen represent the leading edge of the juvenile crime problem, such that between 1980 and 1995 violent-crime arrests grew 94 percent for this group, while for older youths the increase was only 47 percent. In 1995 juveniles aged twelve or younger accounted for 8 percent of arrests for violent-crime index offenses (i.e., murder and nonnegligent manslaughter, forcible rape, robbery, and aggravated assault) and 13 percent of property-crime index offenses (i.e., burglary, larceny-theft, motor vehicle theft, and arson). Youths aged thirteen and fourteen accounted for 23 percent and 28 percent of such arrests, respectively, and juveniles aged fifteen or older accounted for 70 percent and 58 percent, respectively.

A comparison of the percentage change in the number of arrests for juveniles aged twelve and younger, juveniles aged thirteen and fourteen, and juveniles aged fifteen or older between 1980 and 1995 reveals some interesting trends. For violent-crime index offenses, there were increases of 102 percent, 92 percent, and 47 percent across the three

FIGURE 1. **Arrests by Offense Charged and Age, 1995**

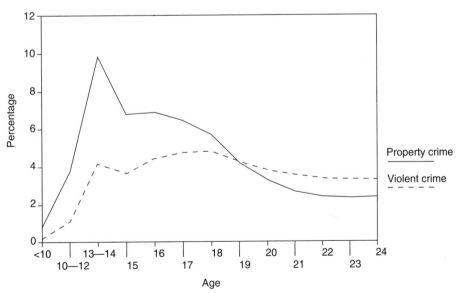

SOURCE: Uniform Crime Reports 1995

FIGURE 2.   Violent-Crime Arrest Rates per 100,000, 1970–1996

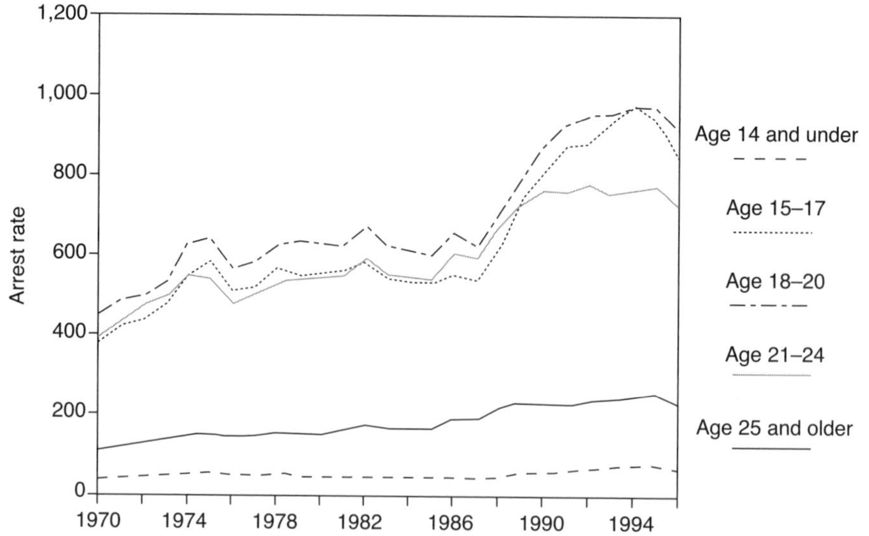

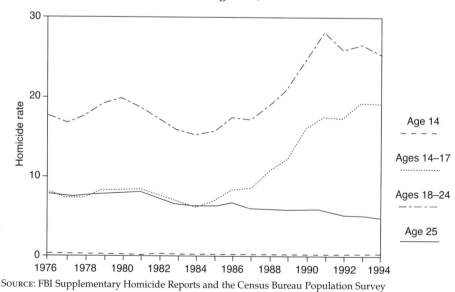

SOURCE: Uniform Crime Reports 1997

age groups, while for property crimes the percentage change figures were −1 percent, 16 percent, and −9 percent for these groups. Still, between 1992 and 1995 violent-crime index arrests for murder, forcible rape, and aggravated assault decreased.

James Alan Fox (1996) reported that from 1985 to 1994 the rate of murder committed by juveniles aged fourteen to seventeen increased 172 percent, with the highest rate increase evidenced for both black and white male teenagers. To examine the trend in homicide offending rates (per 100,000 population) by age, figure 3 presents a time plot

for the years 1976 through 1994 based on the FBI Supplementary Homicide Reports and the Census Bureau Current Population Report. As can be seen, there were fairly substantial increases in the homicide offending rate around 1987–1988 for those individuals in the fourteen-to-seventeen and eighteen-to-twenty-four age groups, while decreases were found for the twenty-five-and-over age group. Interestingly, the eighteen-to-twenty-four age group had the largest rate (28.2 percent) per 100,000, peaking in 1991. Moreover, according to the Supplementary Homicide Reports, the increases observed around 1987–1988 were consis-

FIGURE 3.   Trends in Homicide Offending Rates, 1976–1994

SOURCE: FBI Supplementary Homicide Reports and the Census Bureau Population Survey

tent with a substantial increase in handgun usage in juvenile homicides. Although not shown here, across the entire time span, males and blacks had higher homicide offending rates than females and whites.

Much has been made of the apparent decrease in crime that began in the mid-1990s. While this trend has been observed across the United States, researchers tend to disagree about its causes. Does it indicate a change in the age demographics of the criminal population? Is it due to a change in other societal factors such as community policing and a strong economy? Is it a function of both demographic and societal changes? Whatever the decrease is attributed to, it must be kept in mind that as the age demographics change in the early years of the twenty-first century, there will be a significantly higher number of youngsters within the crime-prone ages. Is a crime boom on the horizon? Will this boom impact both property and violent crimes?

Victimization Data. Vulnerability to crime victimization varies across the age spectrum. Similar to offending and arrest rates, victimization rates increase through adolescence, peak in the late teens and early twenties (depending on the type of offense), and steadily decrease throughout adulthood. With some minor exceptions, this pattern is invariant across race, sex, and ethnicity.

To provide some sense of the victimization rates for violent crimes (i.e., homicide, rape, robbery, and both simple and aggravated assault), figure 4 portrays the victimization rate per 1,000 persons,

by age category, from 1973 through 1994. As can be seen, younger individuals, especially those in the twelve-to-fifteen and sixteen-to-nineteen age categories, are substantially more likely to be victims of violent crimes than are individuals in older age categories. Persons between the ages of twelve and twenty-four, less than a quarter of the U.S. population age twelve or older, represent half of all serious victimizations, while persons age forty or older, comprising almost half of the population age twelve or older, represent less than a fifth of the serious violent victimizations.

Turning our attention to homicide victimization rates per 100,000, data presented in figure 5 from the FBI Supplementary Homicide Reports and Census Bureau Current Population Report show that the highest rates are found in the age categories of eighteen to twenty-four and twenty-five to thirty-four. Throughout the 1980s and 1990s increases in homicide victimization were most pronounced for individuals in the former category. Across all years, the homicide victimization rates were higher for males than females, and for blacks relative to whites.

Self-Report Data. In the United States, there are three major longitudinal self-report studies (i.e., studies that interview subjects over a period of at least a couple of years) that contain information on violent offending. In comparing official and self-report data on serious violent offenders, Delbert Elliott (1994) has used the National Youth Survey to argue that the two methods differ in several respects. Elliott observes that, with self-report

FIGURE 4. **Victimization Rates per 1,000 Persons, 1973–1994**

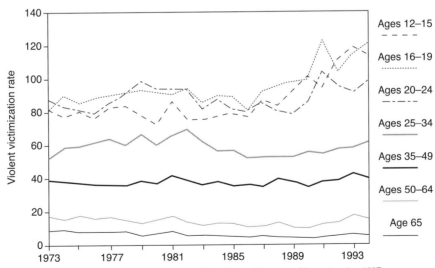

SOURCE: National Crime Victimization Survey and the Federal Bureau of Investigation 1997

FIGURE 5. Homicide Victimization Rates per 100,000, 1976–1996

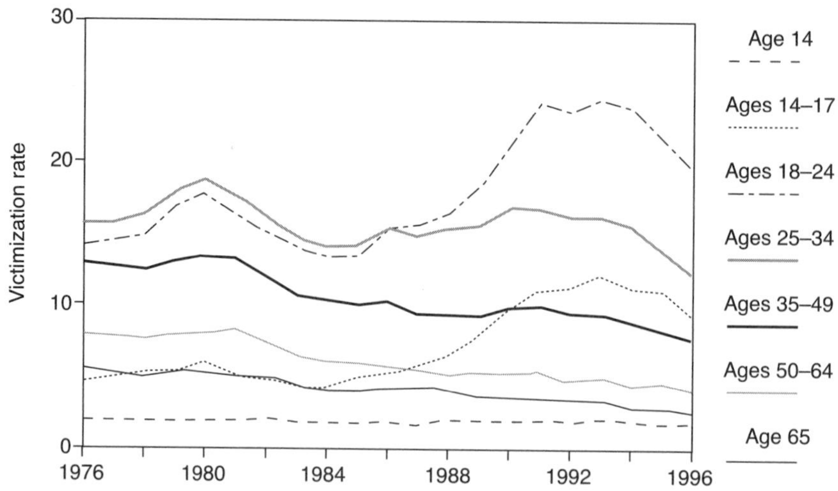

SOURCE: FBI Supplementary Homicide Reports and the Census Bureau Population Report

surveys, "the prevalence of serious violent offenders is substantially higher, onset occurs much earlier, the demographic correlates are substantially weaker, evidence for escalation in frequency, seriousness, and variety of offenses over the career is much stronger, evidence for the sequencing of serious forms of violent behavior is stronger, and the continuity of serious violent offending from the juvenile into the adult years is similar for males and females" (p. 18). Importantly, Elliott found that serious-violent-offender prevalence increases after age twenty-five for black males, while it continues to decline or remains stable for white males and for females of both racial groups.

Since 1978 the Monitoring the Future study, conducted by the Institute for Social Research of the University of Michigan at Ann Arbor, has engaged in a national self-report study of twenty-five hundred high school seniors to provide information on self-reported delinquent activity during a twelve-month period. According to the 1995 study, about 30 percent of high school seniors reported having engaged in theft, 20 percent had been involved in a gang fight, and more than 10 percent had injured someone so badly that the victim had to seek medical attention.

The Causes and Correlates of Crime Study, a large-scale research project funded by the Office of Juvenile Justice and Delinquency Prevention since 1986, is a three-site project designed to examine the factors responsible for criminal behavior. In Denver, Rochester, and Pittsburgh, a team of researchers has been following a number of individuals from late childhood/early adolescence through early adulthood in an effort to gauge their self-reported involvement in serious delinquency and drug use over time. The study sites were selected to capture inner-city youth considered at high risk for involvement in delinquency and substance abuse.

Information on self-reported involvement in serious violence has been gathered that includes questions on aggravated assault, robbery, rape, and gang fights. In Denver, the prevalence of males involved in serious violence shows a gradual increase from age ten (about 2 percent) to age nineteen (a little over 20 percent). The prevalence of females involved in serious violence, however, peaks around the ages of fourteen and fifteen (between 6 and 7 percent) and declines thereafter. The findings in Rochester do not reveal the same gradual trends found in Denver. The first wave of data collection in Rochester, for twelve-year-olds, showed that males (about 20 percent) and females (about 15 percent) began with relatively high prevalence rates of serious violence. While the trend begins to decline for females after age fourteen, the male prevalence rate increases to age fourteen, decreases between fifteen and eighteen, and then increases again to about 20 percent by age eighteen. In Pittsburgh, information was collected only for males. The prevalence rates of serious violence at age ten were around 7 percent, with increases to about 16 percent around ages thirteen and fourteen, decreases at ages fifteen and sixteen, and another increase at age seventeen to 16 percent.

In general, three interesting findings have emerged from the Causes and Correlates study. First, across all three sites, the cumulative prevalence of serious violence by age sixteen is rather high: 39 percent for Denver males, 41 percent for Pittsburgh males, 40 percent for Rochester males, 16 percent for Denver females, and 32 percent for Rochester females. Second, involvement in serious violent behavior seems to begin at a very young age for some of the children in the three sites (before age eleven). Third, through age eighteen, boys in the three study sites have failed to exhibit decreased prevalence of serious violence during their late teenage years. As these studies continue into the future, more information will be known about violent behavior over the life course.

Manifestations of Violence over the Life Cycle

Research on aggression, defined as a category of behavior that causes or threatens physical harm to others, indicates that there is continuity between childhood aggression and adult violence, suggesting the persistence of an underlying construct. Yet as was stated previously, aggression is manifested differently throughout the life course, taking different forms in infancy, childhood, adolescence, and adulthood.

Some scholars trace aggression back as far as the perinatal period, suggesting that complications arising from pregnancy and birth are related to aggression and criminal behavior throughout the life course. Beginning in infancy, many if not most infants show signs of frustration and rage, and research indicates that infants' reactions to frustration are stable over time. Moreover, aggression in infancy has been found to be related to boys' externalizing problems (i.e., hyperactivity, aggression) at age three, and studies report that boys with high levels of aggression in laboratory observations at two years of age have high rates of aggression when observed in similar situations three years later.

During the second and third years of life (i.e., toddlerhood), temper tantrums and aggression toward adults and peers can be observed, and individual differences in anger expression emerge. R. B. Cairns (1979) has pointed out that, in terms of frequency of aggressive acts, humans are at their most aggressive during the toddler years, and there is a decrease in frequency of aggression with advancing age.

Aggression during adolescence and early adulthood has received a great deal of research attention, and two important findings have emerged. First, aggressive acts increase in their harmfulness (infliction of injury) during this stage of development, due in part to the increasing physical

strength of the offenders and their increasing access to weapons. Second, communal delinquency becomes common during this time period. Adolescence is a time when same-sex peer groups prey on other same-sex peer groups, and aggressive juveniles tend to associate with other aggressive juveniles. Most organized gangs emerge in early adolescence. Research has shown that (1) the presence of gangs in schools is associated with a doubling of reports of weapons in schools; (2) youths who join a gang are more heavily involved in violent crime than those who do not; and (3) delinquent behavior increases upon entering a gang and decreases upon exiting a gang.

As late adolescence and adulthood approach, the manifestations of aggression alter due to changes in normative situations (e.g., situational contexts such as school, employment, dating) as well as general age-graded changes (e.g. puberty, entry into or exit from high school). With further increase in physical size and ability (as well as even greater access to weapons), older juveniles tend to engage in a host of property and violent offenses. Some scholars suggest that increased criminal behavior is a function of teenagers' reach for adult status.

These findings lead to an important question: are the acts observed in infancy, childhood, adolescence, and adulthood reflective of an underlying aggressive propensity? In other words, is "criminal" behavior manifested differently at varying stages of the life course?

A fair amount of research has focused on the connection between childhood misbehavior and adult criminal behavior. Avshalom Caspi and Daryl Bem (1990) have devised the term *heterotypic continuity* to explain the existence of a latent attribute (e.g., aggression) that is presumed to underlie diverse but related phenomena. The key point is that while a specific form of antisocial activity in childhood (i.e., kicking or biting) may not appear in adulthood, other actions may be conceptually consistent with that earlier behavior. This argument is consistent with one advanced by Travis Hirschi and Michael Gottfredson (1990, 1994), who hypothesized that adult criminal behavior results from a common underlying factor—low self-control. As Robert Sampson and John Laub (1993) suggested, the important point behind heterotypic continuity "is that individual characteristics in childhood (for example, ill-tempered behavior) will not only appear across time but will be manifested in a number of diverse situations" (p. 124).

Evidence for heterotypic continuity is found by a number of researchers. L. Rowell Huesmann and colleagues (1984) reported that childhood aggression was related not only to adult criminal activity but to commonly unprosecuted adult behaviors such as spousal abuse, child abuse, and drunk driving. Lee Robins also found that childhood antisocial behavior detrimentally affected adult occupational status, job stability, income, and residential mobility.

Theoretical Explanations

One of the most innovative and provocative interdisciplinary models (taking into account biological, psychological, and sociological factors) explaining the relationship between age and crime is Terrie Moffitt's (1993, 1994) dual taxonomy of antisocial behavior. Moffitt hypothesized that there are two types of criminal offenders. The first type, the life-course-persistent offenders, begin engaging in antisocial and criminal behavior early in life, demonstrate a high incidence of criminal activity throughout the life cycle, and face numerous obstacles with respect to cessation of criminal and antisocial activity. Comprising about 5 to 8 percent of all offenders, the proposed cause of antisocial activity for these individuals is the interaction between neuropsychological deficits, including biological and psychological deficiencies, and deficient home environments (e.g., poor socioeconomic status or weak familial structure). Opportunities for desistance for this group are few because of the cumulative effects that they are subject to over the life course.

The second type of offender in Moffitt's model, the adolescence-limited offenders, engage in antisocial behavior and criminal activity only in the teenage years. According to Moffitt (1997), the cause of such behavior in this group is "the emerging appreciation of desirable adult privileges met with the awareness that those privileges are yet forbidden" (p. 43). Adolescence-limited offenders tend to mimic their antisocial peers' solution to this problem—antisocial and criminal behavior—until late adolescence/early adulthood, when they develop prosocial skills.

Moffitt (1993, 1994) makes explicit predictions about the types of offenses these two groups will become involved in. The adolescence-limited offenders will engage in crimes that symbolize adult privilege or that demonstrate personal autonomy and freedom from parental control. Examples of these kinds of acts include vandalism, substance abuse, and "status" crimes such as running away and theft. Life-course-persistent offenders will engage in a wider variety of crimes including victim-oriented violent offenses.

A second interdisciplinary theory is Adrian Raine and colleagues' (1997) biosocial model of violence, which focuses on the interaction between genetics and the environment. In this theory, "environmental factors can give rise to the expression of a latent genetic trait (e.g., poor environment magnifying genetically predisposed low IQ), while genetic factors can alter the environment (e.g., a low IQ individual drifts into more criminogenic environments)" (p. 14). Genetic factors may also give rise to biological risk factors and environmental risk factors may give rise to social risk factors. As well, environmental factors may give rise to biological risks (e.g., an accident may cause brain damage) and genetic factors may give rise to social risks (e.g., child abuse potential).

The model then hypothesizes reciprocal relationships between biological and social risk factors. For example, the biological risk factor of low arousal may push a stimulus-seeking child into the social risk factor of a delinquent gang. Similarly, a social risk factor such as weak parental control may give rise to a child suffering a serious head trauma after a fall from a bicycle while left unattended. Importantly, the biological and social risk factors do not have to interact to create violence; their influence can be additive as well as interactive.

Next, the model incorporates the role of protective factors. In other words, biological (e.g., increased health care) and social (e.g., protective familial environments) factors may act to prevent the occurrence of violence by reducing the negative impact of biological or social risk factors or both. In this sense, the model is not deterministic but rather probabilistic. Finally, the model allows for violence to affect risk and protection status. For example, involvement in violence could lead to a jail term, which could then create a new risk factor (e.g., unemployment), which could increase the risk for later violence.

The biosocial model proposed by Raine and colleagues poses a number of interesting questions that have specific bearing on the age-violence relationship. One of the most interesting questions concerns whether different biosocial models are needed for different developmental stages. For example, the Raine et al. model was originally designed to explain general adult violence. However, given what is known about heterotypic continuity, it may be appropriate to develop models that take into account varying manifestations of violence at different stages of the life course. For example, since infants do not engage in "adult-like" violence, examination of aggressive temperament may be more appropriate for this developmental stage. When early childhood violence or aggression becomes the focus, a particular set of aggression-type outcomes may be of interest (for example, bullying on the playground, etc.). Another interesting examination would be a longitudinal investigation of the Raine et al. model, following individuals from birth through adulthood. For example, one could specify the risk and protective risk factors, and identify outcomes with respect to the particular life-course stage under investigation.

Conclusion

A number of potential research directions could bring further evidence to light on the age-violence relationship. One avenue for future research would be to further examine the relationship between age and victimization. This area of research is underdeveloped; however, the incorporation of the routine-activities perspective (a theory that incorporates the meeting in time and space of offenders, victims, and targets) could help provide information on the characteristics of individuals who are violently victimized, as well as the factors associated with their victimization.

A second potential research direction is the study of desistance from violent crime, or an offender's cessation of criminal activity. Researchers disagree about the developmental course of desistance, and the rate of desistance of aggression with age has been insufficiently studied. The little research that has accumulated shows that a proportion of juveniles desist in aggressive and criminal behavior over time, with a substantial concentration of desistance occurring during the transition from preschool to elementary school and during late adolescence. As such, a number of unanswered questions remain: Are the causes of desistance the same for both violent and nonviolent offending? For different types of violent offending? For females and males? For those who exhibit a late onset of criminal behavior and those who incur an early onset? The problem with studying desistance, of course, is that a one- or five-year crime-free period is no guarantee that offending has terminated. Typically, there are stops and starts throughout a criminal career. Such bouts of "intermittency" are in need of explanation, especially as they relate to the association between age and violence.

A third avenue of future research may concentrate on how individual offending frequency (1) changes over time within offenders, (2) changes with increasing age, and (3) varies by type of crime. Alfred Blumstein and colleagues (1986) found a general absence of offending frequencies (i.e., a lack of criminal acts) with age for specific types of crimes among juveniles and youths, especially for violent index offenses. However, a self-report study of California prison inmates shows that while the number of active crime types declines with age, crime-specific frequencies (reflected by an intensity-scale score) are stable over age. That study also found that total frequencies, reflecting the combination of all offense types combined, varied more with age, increasing during the juvenile years and decreasing during the adult years.

Given the increasing emphasis at the federal level on understanding the causes of violence, and the National Science Foundation's creation of the National Consortium on Violence Research to aid in this task, the study of age and violence is likely to gain in research attention in the years to come as theoretical models are designed and redesigned to account for violence. It is likely that this line of research will emphasize changes in the patterns of crime and aggression within individuals over the developmental years and will attempt to establish common patterns of development so that those most at risk for violent activity can be identified and treated.

BIBLIOGRAPHY

Blumstein, Alfred, Jacqueline Cohen, Jeffrey A. Roth, and Christy A. Visher, eds. *Criminal Careers and Career Criminals.* Vol. 1. Washington, D.C.: National Academy Press, 1986.

Cairns, R. B. *Social Development: The Origins and Plasticity of Interactions.* San Francisco, Calif.: Freeman, 1979.

Caspi, Avshalom, and Daryl J. Bem. "Personality Continuity and Change Across the Life Course." In *Handbook of Personality: Theory and Research,* edited by L. A. Pervin. New York: Guilford, 1990.

Elliott, Delbert S. "1993 Presidential Address: Serious Violent Offenders: Onset, Developmental Course, and Termination." *Criminology* 32 (February 1994): 1–21.

Farrington, David P. "Age and Crime." In *Crime and Justice: An Annual Review of Research,* edited by Michael Tonry and Norval Morris. Chicago: University of Chicago Press, 1986.

Fox, James Alan. *Trends in Juvenile Violence: A Report to the United States Attorney General on Current and Future Rates of Juvenile Offending.* Washington, D.C.: U.S. Department of Justice, Bureau of Justice Statistics, 1996.

Gottfredson, Michael, and Travis Hirschi. *A General Theory of Crime.* Stanford, Calif.: Stanford University Press, 1990.

Hirschi, Travis, and Michael Gottfredson. *The Generality of Deviance.* New Brunswick, N.J.: Transaction, 1994.

Huesmann, L. Rowell, Leonard D. Eron, Monroe M. Leftkowitz, and Leopold O. Walder. "Stability of Aggression over Time and Generations." *Developmental Psychology* 20 (1984): 1120–1134.

Loeber, Rolf, and Dale Hay. "Key Issues in the Development of Aggression and Violence from Childhood to Early Adulthood." *Annual Review of Psychology* 48 (1997): 371–410.

Moffitt, Terrie E. "Adolescence-Limited and Life-Course-Persistent Offending: A Complementary Pair of Developmental Theories." In *Advances in Criminological Theory.* Vol. 7, *Developmental Theories of Crime and Delinquency,* edited by Terrence Thornberry. New Brunswick, N.J.: Transaction, 1997.

———. "Life-Course Persistent and 'Adolescence-Limited' Antisocial Behavior: A Developmental Taxonomy." *Psychological Review* 100 (1993): 674–701.

———. "Natural Histories of Delinquency." In *Cross-National Longitudinal Research on Human Development and Criminal Behavior,* edited by H. J. Kerner and E. Weitekamp. Dordrecht, Holland: Kluwer Academic Press, 1994.

Olweus, D. "Stability of Aggressive Reaction Patterns in Males: A Review." *Psychological Bulletin* 86 (1979): 852–857.

Raine, Adrian, Patricia Brennan, and David P. Farrington. "Biosocial Bases of Violence: Conceptual and Theoretical Issues." In *Biosocial Bases of Violence,* edited by Adrian Raine et al. New York: Plenum, 1997.

Reiss, Albert, and Jeffrey A. Roth, eds. *Understanding and Preventing Violence.* Washington, D.C.: National Academy Press, 1993.

Robins, Lee. *Deviant Children Grown Up: A Sociological and Psychiatric Study of Sociopathic Personality.* Baltimore, Md.: Williams and Wilkins, 1966.

———. "Sturdy Childhood Predictors of Adult Antisocial Behavior." *Psychological Medicine* 8 (1978): 611–622.

Sampson, Robert, and John Laub. *Crime in the Making.* Cambridge, Mass.: Harvard University Press, 1993.

West, Donald J., and David P. Farrington. *The Delinquent Way of Life.* London: Heinemann, 1977.

ALEX PIQUERO

See also **Birth Order and Birth Spacing; Child Abuse; Children; Developmental Factors; Domestic Violence; Elder Abuse; Teenagers.**

AGGRESSION

The terms *aggression* and *violence* are used with enormous flexibility sometimes even interchange-ably, but they have distinct meanings that must be understood in order to elucidate their relationships to biological, psychological, and other factors.

Defining Aggression

Definitions of aggression have varied historically as well as with respect to different organisms. Early studies of animal aggression emphasized innate drives (e.g., fear and anger) that triggered individual responses designed to maximize gain and avoid pain. Animal aggression may largely reflect evolved, adaptive responses that enhance the survival of the individual. Animal researchers often distinguish between two types of aggression: "predatory attack," which is often quiet, planned, and instrumental, versus "affective defense," which is often based on reactions to fear and anger and is often explosive. In the latter part of the twentieth century, ethologists started to recognize the importance of the behavior of nearby others in eliciting aggressive behavior. In defining aggression, it is therefore important to understand the context in which aggressive behavior occurs as well as the properties (e.g., motivations) of the individual perpetrator of aggressive acts.

In contrast, the distinction between attack and defense behaviors is not as clearly made in defining and measuring human aggression. In fact, the definition and use of the word *aggression* in humans varies widely among researchers. One distinction in human-aggression studies, however, that is similar to the attack-defense one in animal studies, is that made between "proactive" and "reactive" aggression. (The former type of aggression is sometimes referred to as "appetitive" aggression, since the goal is often territory- or feeding-related.) Although not completely parallel as theoretical constructs, the animal and human typologies share many features, including the notion that defensive (reactive) versus predatory (proactive) forms of aggression may have distinct biological pathways and may be elicited through different mechanisms.

An important alternative distinction in humans is often made between "adaptive" versus "maladaptive" aggression, although much of (researched) human violence and aggression often falls somewhere between these two extremes. Aggression may be adaptive to the extent that it enhances survival and reproduction. For example, aggressive individuals may be more likely to acquire and maintain resources (e.g., food, shelter) and may have increased chances for desirable mates. Aggression might be a particularly important asset to individuals with limited cognitive abilities. However, to the extent that aggression limits access to resources and mates (e.g., if the aggressor becomes injured, incarcerated, or ostracized), aggressive behavior would be considered maladaptive. In nonhuman animals, there are often clear benefits that result from aggression (e.g., killing prey, dominant males having greater sexual access). Whether violent offending in humans should be generally considered as instrumental and adaptive is open to question.

Several important features of human aggression are apparent across various definitions. First, there is general agreement that aggressive actions must have the potential for harm, damage, or discomfort. This could be broadly defined, however, to include physical, emotional, or reproductive harm, for example. However, because some defensive actions may also cause harm to oneself, the potential for harm and damage is not a sufficient condition for classifying actions as aggressive.

Intent to cause harm or damage is another important aspect of aggressive acts. It is difficult, however, to establish the intentions of others. This results in problems for individuals attempting to judge the degree of threat being made by another individual as well as difficulties in measuring aggression in scientific investigations.

Many researchers consider physiological arousal to be another important component of aggression. That is, aggression may involve alterations in autonomic responses, including heart rate, respiration, and the distribution of blood in the tissues. There is considerable research in support of the relationship of autonomic arousal and aggression in humans, but the degree of the relationship may depend on the type of aggression being studied. For example, affective (defensive or reactive) forms of aggression produce a greater autonomic reaction, perhaps as a "hot-blooded" response to fear or anger, while instrumental (predatory or proactive) aggression may produce little or no autonomic reaction but may instead be highly organized, planned, and "cold-blooded."

Some researchers also set as a condition for aggression that the victim evaluate the action as being aversive (something to be avoided). Evaluating the perceptions of the victim, like the judgment of intentions, results in problems in clearly defining and measuring aggression.

Many forms of human aggression have these characteristics. David Buss (1971) attempted to classify aggressive behavior on three dimensions: physical versus verbal, active versus passive, and direct versus indirect. Other categorizations have also been suggested, such as proactive versus reactive aggression. In the 1990s, the concept of "relational" aggression gained attention from psychologists (Crick and Grotpeter 1995) as a distinct form of aggression that concerns the social manipulation of peers through gossip and exclusion, for example. One unanswered question, however, is how these various types of aggressive behavior may relate to one another. Do individuals demonstrating strong relational aggression also display high frequencies of physical aggression? How correlated are reactive and proactive forms of aggression within individuals? Some studies suggest they are not completely independent of one another, but that they may be at least moderately correlated within individuals. Still, these correlations are far from perfect, and there is support for different etiologies of varying forms of aggression. For example, Emil Coccaro and colleagues (1993) reported that genetic variations and serotonin deficiencies are greatest for a subcategory of irritable impulsiveness.

Measurement of Aggression

The measurement of aggression in animals involves simple, highly reliable, and almost stereotypic motor behaviors. Predatory behaviors include the sequence of stalking of prey followed by biting the back of the victim's neck, while affective defense behaviors involve noticeable signs—such as piloerection, retraction of the ears, arching of the back, marked pupillary dilation, vocalization, unsheathing of claws—that are usually explosive in nature.

In humans, measurement of aggression is much less precise and is often confusing and controversial. In research, aggression may be measured by eliciting opinions of peers, teachers, parents, or other relatives or, most commonly, by questioning an individual about his or her own aggressive behavior. Both interview and self-report questionnaires have been developed for use with subjects of varying ages, although questionnaires are by far the most popular means of measuring human aggression. Observation of social interactions in natural or laboratory settings is an alternative but less often used measuring scheme. The method of measuring and defining human aggression is especially important to consider, since it affects the results. For example, genetic influences come across more strongly in questionnaire surveys than in studies using observational methods (see Plomin, Nitz and Rowe 1990).

Distinction Between Violence and Aggression

How does aggression relate to violence? One view is that violent behavior is simply an extreme manifestation of normal-varying aggression. Violence may also represent aggressive actions that attract greater than normal social disapproval. Given the broadly varying definitions of aggression described here, however, not all forms of aggression, even in extreme forms, may be considered as violence.

One of the more useful definitions of violence comes from the Panel on Understanding and Control of Violent Behavior. It specifies that violent behaviors "intentionally threaten, attempt, or inflict physical harm on others" (Reiss and Roth 1993–1994, p. 2). Thus, though the term *aggression* may include nonphysical forms of bringing pain or discomfort to others (e.g., relational, indirect, or verbal aggression), *violence* is generally more narrowly defined as behaviors that involve overt, physical acts. Several distinctions may still be made, similar to those in the more general concept of aggression, such as between proactive (unprovoked) and reactive (provoked) violent behaviors. In general, specific clarification of the various forms of aggression and violence needs to be made in evaluating individual studies in this area.

BIBLIOGRAPHY

Brain, Paul F. "Hormonal Aspects of Aggression and Violence." In *Understanding and Preventing Violence.* Vol. 2, *Biobehavioral Influences,* edited by Albert J. Reiss, Jr., Klaus A. Miczek, and Jeffrey A. Roth. Washington, D.C.: National Academy Press, 1994.

Buss, David. "Aggression Pays." In *The Control of Aggression and Violence: Cognitive and Physiological Factors,* edited by Jerome L. Singer. New York: Academic Press, 1971.

Carey, Gregory, and David Goldman. "The Genetics of Antisocial Behavior." In *Handbook of Antisocial Behavior,* edited by David M. Stoff, James Breiling, and Jack Maser. New York: Wiley, 1996.

Coccaro, Emil, Cindy S. Bergeman, and Gerald E. McClearn. "Heritability of Irritable Impulsiveness: A Study of Twins Reared Together and Apart." *Psychiatry Research* 48, no. 3 (1993): 229–242.

Crick, Nicky R., and Jennifer K. Grotpeter. "Relational Aggression, Gender, and Social-Psychological Adjustment." *Child Development* 66, no. 3 (1995): 710–722.

Dodge, Kenneth. "The Structure and Function of Reactive and Proactive Aggression." In *The Development and Treatment of Childhood Aggression,* edited by Debra J. Pepler and Kenneth H. Rubin. Hillsdale, N.J.: L. Erlbaum Associates, 1991.

Niehoff, Debra. *The Biology of Violence: How Understanding the Brain, Behavior, and Environment Can Break the Vicious Circle of Aggression.* New York: Free Press, 1998.

Plomin, Robert, Katherine Nitz, and David C. Rowe. "Behavioral Genetics and Aggressive Behavior in Childhood." In *Handbook of Developmental Psychology,* edited by Michael Lewis and Suzanne M. Miller. New York: Plenum, 1990.

Reiss, Albert J., and Jeffrey A. Roth. *Understanding and Preventing Violence.* Washington, D.C.: National Academy, 1993–1994.

LAURA A. BAKER

See also **Animal Studies of Aggression and Violence; Fight-or-Flight Syndrome; Psychophysiology: Autonomic Activity; Temperament; Theories of Violence.**

AGRARIAN VIOLENCE

Since the seventeenth century American farmers have taken up arms to protest perceived injustices in society. In some cases they rose up to put right an aspect of the "moral economy" that disadvantaged them. Even more often, however, they retaliated against political inequities. Usually the groups established by farmers to foment violence were short-lived, single-issue oriented, and homogenous in their racial and ethnic composition. Moreover, the majority of those who acted out violent impulses on behalf of agrarian ideals were men. However, women also played critical roles in the leadership structures and support networks of these organizations.

Between 1650 and 1750 colonists in British North America—and particularly those on the frontier—rose up in violence more than forty times. Generally they protested local land laws and targeted local landlords, but they also rose up against unresponsive governments in faraway coastal capitals. So frequent and serious were these violent incidences that, at the time of the Revolutionary War, American urban leaders were not sure they could count on their country cousins to form a union with them.

A booming population trying to settle a relatively small strip of land between the east coast and the Appalachians would have spelled trouble even if all that land had actually been available for purchase. The fact that Native Americans held by treaty the fertile lands west of Jamestown led to the first major incidence of agrarian violence in the colonies, Bacon's Rebellion of 1676. Nathaniel

Bacon led freed indentured servants on a series of raids, killing members of the local tribes whom, whether peaceful or not, Bacon considered "all Enemies." When Virginia's governor Sir William Berkeley refused to reinstate Bacon on the local council and refused to violate land treaties, Bacon and his men marched on Jamestown and burned it to the ground. The rebellion ended on 26 October 1676 when Bacon died of dysentery.

In colonial New York, New Jersey, Maryland, and the Carolinas, hungry settlers discovered that lands were held on a proprietary model; that is, several wealthy families owned enormous tracts of land that they had been granted by the British crown and that were only available for lease. In each of these colonies, squatters organized mobs, burned landlords' manors, and tried to establish separate governments. In Vermont they succeeded when in 1770 Ethan Allen organized the Green Mountain Boys to protest the granting of lands to wealthy New York proprietors. After shutting down local courts and lashing local officials, Allen and others established the independent Republic of New Connecticut, which joined the Union in 1791.

In the immediate post-Revolutionary era, farmers continued to worry about "who would rule at home" (Becker 1909). These concerns were expressed first throughout the Connecticut River Valley and particularly in western Massachusetts by the nearly eight thousand fighting farmers of Shays's Rebellion of 1786–1787. Due to the post-Revolutionary monetary crisis, many frontier farmers were deeply in debt, and thousands were forced into debtors' prison until they could pay their loans. All this, they claimed, was made possible by a state constitution that allowed only property holders to vote or hold office. Still wearing their Patriot uniforms, Shays's men marched on the Springfield armory, where they were soundly defeated by troops under the command of General William Shepard. However short-lived their "little rebellion," Shays and his men convinced many leaders that the new American constitution should provide for a closer regulation of the economy—as well as for a standing army to cope with future domestic uprisings.

This army would stay busy throughout the late eighteenth and early nineteenth centuries, as access to land and political power were contested in Maine, Ohio, Kentucky, Tennessee, and Maryland. The Whiskey Rebellion of 1793–1794, for example, pitted angry western Pennsylvanians protesting the new tax on whiskey (imposed by Alexander Hamilton) against the Washington administration's "Watermelon Army" of poor boys from the New Jersey shore. Before their defeat, the whiskey rebels had kidnapped, beaten, and tortured several tax collectors and marched on Pittsburgh and burned it to the ground.

Universal white male suffrage and access to land in the Homestead Act of 1862 kept organized agrarian violence to a minimum in the nineteenth century. Not until the economic downturn at the end of the century did farmers feel again that the promise of American life had unfairly eluded them. They organized the Populist Party in the South, Midwest, and Rocky Mountain region. Usually nonviolent, Populists in Kansas took up arms to protect their supporters and candidates in the 1890s.

The vicissitudes of the Great Depression provided the twentieth century's first example of sustained agrarian violence. Beginning with the Cow War in Iowa in 1930, and continuing with the farm strikes of the Farmers' Holiday Association (FHA) and its women's auxiliaries, farmers banded together to protest low crop prices and government interference with their businesses and to protect property from foreclosure. The FHA supporter "Wild Bill" Langer, governor of North Dakota, was rumored to have said, "Treat the banker like a chicken thief. Shoot him on sight." No bankers were shot, but in Le Mars, Iowa, a local judge was kidnapped, tied, and beaten for refusing to sign a pledge to stop farm foreclosures. Likewise, farmers who did not cooperate in farm strikes and tried to sell their products were threatened and attacked. One was shot to death in Racine, Wisconsin.

During the farm crisis of the 1980s, bankers and government officials were again targets of rural violence. These incidents, however, were not organized mob actions, as in previous generations, but more often individual random acts, like the murder in 1982 of Rudy Blythe, a local banker in Ruthton, Minnesota, who had foreclosed on a farmer's property. Nevertheless, dispirited farmers became fresh recruits for other violent organizations of the late twentieth century that did not have strictly agrarian aims but which promoted Identity Christianity (a right-wing extremist belief system that claims that Jews, African Americans, and members of other ethnic minorities are "diluting" racial purity in the United States) and antigovernment violence. These included the Covenant, the Sword, and the Arm of the Lord; the Aryan Nation; the Posse Comitatus; and a variety of small militia groups.

BIBLIOGRAPHY

Becker, Carl. *The History of Political Parties in the Province of New York, 1760–1776*. Madison: University of Wisconsin Press, 1909.

Brown, Richard Maxwell. "Back Country Rebellions and the Homestead Ethic in America, 1740–1799." In *Tradition, Conflict, and Modernization: Perspectives on the American Revolution*, edited by Richard Maxwell Brown and Don E. Fehrenbacher. New York: Academic Press, 1977.

Coates, James. *Armed and Dangerous: The Rise of the Survivalist Right*. New York: Hill and Wang, 1987.

Davidson, Osha Gray. *Broken Heartland: The Rise of America's Rural Ghetto*. New York: Free Press, 1990.

Saloutos, Theodore, and John D. Hicks. *Agricultural Discontent in the Middle West, 1900–1939*. Madison: University of Wisconsin Press, 1951.

CATHERINE McNICOL STOCK

See also **Civil Disorder; Militias, Unauthorized; Riots; Rural Violence.**

AIR FORCE. *See* Military.

ALAMO

Located in San Antonio, Texas, the Alamo was originally the fortified Spanish mission San Antonio de Valero. During the Texas Revolution (1835–1836) it became the site of the bloodiest battle in Texas history.

When Texas colonists revolted against Mexico in 1835, Mexican troops were forced to withdraw from the Alamo, and Ben Milam, a leader of the colonists, took command of the fort. On 23 February 1836, a force of 145 Texans, under the joint command of Colonels William B. Travis and James Bowie, prepared to defend the fort against a siege by Mexican troops who had crossed the Rio Grande under the command of Mexico's dictator, General Antonio López de Santa Anna, who was determined to recapture the fortification. After Santa Anna's demand for surrender, to which Travis replied with a cannon shot, a thirteen-day siege began. A courier was dispatched to Sam Houston, commander in chief of all Texas forces, with a plea from Travis for reinforcements: "I have sustained a continual bombardment and a cannon-

A late-nineteenth-century wood engraving depicting the siege of the Alamo, 23 February–6 March 1836. THE GRANGER COLLECTION

ade for 24 hours and have not lost a man. . . . I shall never surrender or retreat. . . . Victory or death." No reinforcements were forthcoming, but on 2 March thirty-two men made it through Mexican lines into the fort, joining the Texas troops, the frontiersman Davy Crockett, and twelve Tennessee volunteers.

The Americans held off the Mexicans, primarily with cannon fire, without the loss of a single man (only Bowie was down, because of a fall), killing approximately fifteen hundred Mexican troops. Before dawn on 6 March, with the Americans' ammunition running low, the Mexicans launched assaults on all sides. On the third assault, they stormed the walls. Hand-to-hand combat ensued, with the exhausted Americans drawing knives and using their rifles as clubs. Santa Anna had ordered that no prisoners be taken, and almost all of the defenders were killed within the compound. Those who surrendered were ordered executed by Santa

Anna, although about thirty noncombatants were spared.

The massacre at the Alamo inspired Texans, who were rallied by the cry "Remember the Alamo" when they defeated the Mexicans and captured Santa Anna at the Battle of San Jacinto in April, driving the Mexicans from their borders and thereby gaining independence for Texas.

Jim Bowie was one of the thousands of non-Mexican Texas colonists. His heroism during several battles for Texas independence became legendary through songs and ballads, as did his (or his brother's) invention of the Bowie knife. Davy Crockett was already a heroic figure by the time of the Alamo, owing to his exaggerated exploits as a backwoodsman and his anecdotal storytelling style while serving in the House of Representatives. (He joined the Texas independence forces following his defeat for reelection in 1835.) His purported death at the Alamo led to even greater renown for Crockett as a folk hero. The diary of José Enrique de la Peña, a Mexican officer who fought at the Alamo, states that Crockett did not die in the Alamo but was among the captured who were later tortured to death.

BIBLIOGRAPHY

Davis, William C. *Three Roads to the Alamo: The Lives and Fortunes of David Crockett, James Bowie, and William Barret Travis.* New York: HarperCollins, 1998.

Hatch, Thom. *Encyclopedia of the Alamo and the Texas Revolution.* Jefferson, N.C.: McFarland, 1999.

Hoyt, Edwin P. *The Alamo: An Illustrated History.* Dallas: Taylor, 1999.

Long, Jeff. *Duel of Eagles: The Mexican and U.S. Fight for the Alamo.* Vol. 1. New York: Morrow, 1991.

Peña, José Enrique de la. *With Santa Anna in Texas: A Personal Narrative of the Revolution.* Translated and edited by Carmen Perry. College Station: Texas A&M University Press, 1975.

Tinkle, Lon. *Thirteen Days to Glory: The Siege of the Alamo.* College Station: Texas A&M University Press, 1958.

LOUISE B. KETZ

See also **Bowie, James; Frontier.**

ALCOHOL AND ALCOHOLISM

Alcohol is second only to caffeine as the drug of choice of Americans. At least 80–95 percent of Americans have consumed alcohol at some point in their lives, and about two-thirds use alcohol in any given year. Even if alcohol plays only a minor role in violent crime, its impact could potentially be quite substantial given how ubiquitous its use is in U.S. society. Evidence concerning the role of alcohol in violent crime comes from (1) records of alcohol involvement in actual criminal events, (2) "natural experiments" in which the effect of changes in the availability of alcohol on crime rates is observed, (3) experimental studies of aggression in which alcohol use is directly manipulated among research participants, and (4) surveys of individuals who report about their history of alcohol use and involvement in criminal activities. Although the combined evidence suggests that alcohol may play an important role in violent crime, it is clear that alcohol use is not always associated with violent behavior. In fact, it is only in some situations and among a minority of people that alcohol use is associated with aggressive, violent behavior.

Alcohol Use and Alcoholism in the United States

Despite the pervasiveness of alcohol use in American society, certain segments of society are much more likely to drink alcohol more frequently and in greater quantities than others. Men drink more than women, younger adults drink more than older adults, and Caucasian individuals tend to drink more than African Americans, Hispanic Americans, and Asian Americans. For many other demographic factors, the association with alcohol use is more complex. For example, individuals from lower income groups are less likely to drink alcohol at all, but on average those who do drink are more likely to drink heavily and more frequently.

The most widely accepted definition of alcoholism in the United States is that outlined in the American Psychiatric Association's *Diagnostic and Statistical Manual of Mental Disorders* (*DSM*). Individuals receive a diagnosis of "alcohol dependence" when they evidence multiple problems attributable to alcohol such as: (1) problems at home, school, or work, or with their physical health; (2) loss of control over drinking; and (3) physical dependence. A nationally representative survey conducted in the early 1990s in the United States found that 20 percent of men and 8 percent of women reported a history of problems with alcohol consistent with a diagnosis of alcohol dependence, and that an additional 13 percent of men and 6 percent of women had a history of harmful consequences of their alcohol use ("alcohol abuse"). Perhaps more striking is the fact that 14 percent of men and 5 percent of women reported that they had experienced problems with alcohol *in the past year*. These data suggest that overall, nearly 10 percent of the general population experience some degree of problems with alcohol in a given year—meaning that a significant fraction of individuals who drink alcohol have problems associated with using alcohol. Because men, younger individuals, Caucasian individuals, and those from lower income groups who are drinkers drink alcohol more frequently and in greater quantities, they are also more likely to develop problems such as alcoholism.

Unlike many other psychotropic drugs—drugs that target specific parts of the brain—alcohol appears to affect nearly all parts of the brain. Thus the effects of alcohol on feelings and behavior are complex and varying because alcohol can mimic the effects of stimulants, anxiolytics (anxiety-relieving drugs), sedatives, and analgesics. Some of the various effects of alcohol on behavior are more common at lower versus higher doses of alcohol or when the level of alcohol in the bloodstream is increasing (soon after drinking is initiated) versus decreasing (about an hour after drinking has ceased). When the level of alcohol in the bloodstream is increasing, alcohol has a stimulant effect, causing feelings of euphoria and gregariousness. In contrast, when the level of alcohol in the bloodstream is decreasing, alcohol has a sedating effect, causing feelings of dysphoria and anxiety. In addition, ingestion of alcohol can lead to impaired thinking and judgment.

Studying the Association Between Alcohol Use and Violence

In order to better understand the association between alcohol use and violence, it would be ideal to take a representative group of men and women from the general population, give half of them a standard dose of alcohol, and observe whether the ones who have been administered alcohol are more likely than the ones who were not given alcohol to become violent. The main obstacle to this approach is that, in contrast to alcohol use and alcoholism, violence, at least at the level of the individual, is quite rare. In other words, the vast majority of people do not commit violent acts, and the vast majority of people drink alcohol without committing violent acts. So one would need to study many individuals to observe an association

between alcohol use and violent behavior. The other problem with this approach, of course, is that it would not be ethical to elicit and observe interpersonal violence in a research setting. One solution to this dilemma is to identify naturally occurring violent acts and then attempt to determine whether alcohol was involved.

There are several sources of information on the association of alcohol use and violence. First, the Department of Justice conducts a yearly National Crime Victimization Survey that questions a nationally representative sample of individuals about their experiences as victims of crime. When instances of crime are reported, victims are asked to judge whether the offender was under the influence of alcohol or drugs. Second, the Federal Bureau of Investigation maintains a database of crimes. Included in this database is the investigating officer's perception of whether alcohol was a contributing factor in the incident. Third, the Bureau of Justice Statistics conducts national surveys of individuals on probation or in state or federal prisons. Offenders are asked to report their use of alcohol at the time of their offense.

The available data on the association between alcohol use and violence are imperfect. For example, the role of alcohol in the violent act is not measured objectively (by conducting, for example, a breathalyzer test), but instead is based on the victim's, the officer's, or the offender's report. Perhaps more problematic is the lack of a control or comparison group essential for drawing conclusions about an association between alcohol use and violence. For example, it might seem impressive to learn that 40 percent of violent offenders were under the influence of alcohol at the time of their offense. But this would not be nearly as impressive if we were to learn that 40 percent of similar individuals in similar circumstances (including those who *do not* commit violent offenses) were also under the influence of alcohol. Indeed, victims of violence are nearly as likely to be under the influence of alcohol as offenders.

Alcohol-Related Violence: Where, When, and Who

The U.S. Bureau of Justice Statistics reported in 1998 that about 37 percent of violent crimes, according to both victim's and offender's reports, were committed by offenders who were under the influence of alcohol at the time of the incident (other studies report rates of alcohol use among violent offenders ranging from as low as 6 percent to as high as 87 percent). The similarity of the rates of alcohol-related violent crimes using victim's versus offender's reports is reassuring because it suggests that reports of alcohol use by victims and offenders may not be especially biased compared with an objective index of alcohol use. It also suggests that relying on reports of crimes that have come to the attention of the police (reports of convicted offenders) may not be especially biased compared with relying on incidents of both reported and unreported crimes (reports from a victimization survey). Clearly victim's reports do not include the most serious of violent offenses—homicide. It has been estimated that nearly three million crimes per year in the United States are committed by offenders who are under the influence of alcohol at the time of the incident. Alcohol use is associated with the entire spectrum of violence, from simple assault to aggravated assault, robbery, rape, and homicide. In 1997 alone, more than seven thousand people in the United States were killed by offenders under the influence of alcohol—that is about twenty homicides per day that were alcohol-related.

If one considers all alcohol-related violent incidents reported by victims, the majority (about 70 percent) occur in a residence, whereas a minority (about 10 percent) occur in a bar or restaurant. The reason why most alcohol-related violent incidents occur in a residence is because most violent incidents (alcohol-related and non-alcohol-related combined) occur in residences. If one considers all violent incidents that occur at home, a minority are alcohol-related (about 15 percent). Similarly, if one considers all violent incidents that occur at a bar or tavern, a majority (about 80 percent) are alcohol-related. Most alcohol-related violent incidents occur at home, but the probability of a violent incident being alcohol-related is much higher at a drinking establishment than anywhere else. Neighborhoods with a higher density of liquor stores tend to have higher violent-crime rates, and liquor store employees are at a relatively high risk compared to other types of service workers of being a victim of violence. Not surprisingly, alcohol-related violence also tends to occur most commonly at times of the day when people are most likely to have been drinking heavily, that is, between 11 P.M. and midnight and on the weekends. Alcohol-related violence is at its lowest point around 9:00 in the morning.

Men are more likely to commit violent crimes and are also more likely to commit alcohol-related violent crimes. If one considers all violent crimes committed by men and women, it appears that alcohol use is more likely to have preceded the violent behavior of the men than the women. Nearly two-thirds of convicted violent offenders report a prior history of alcohol problems severe enough to require some kind of intervention (usually participation in a detoxification program), and they report consuming very large amounts of alcohol on average (equivalent to nine to eighteen beers) prior to the violent incident for which they were arrested. Clearly the large majority of individuals who commit alcohol-related violent crimes are alcohol dependent. The victims of alcohol-related violent crimes are usually intimate partners (e.g., spouses, boyfriends, girlfriends), former partners, or acquaintances of the offender.

Does Alcohol Use Cause Violence?

Teetotalers rarely commit violent acts, but this does not necessarily mean that if everyone stopped drinking alcohol the rate of violence would decrease. Determining whether the association between alcohol use and violence is (at least partially) explained by a *causal* influence of alcohol use on violence is important because it tells us whether reducing alcohol use is likely to reduce the frequency of violent acts. Studying naturally occurring violent acts in the community is important for characterizing the scope and nature of the association between alcohol use and violence, but it cannot answer the important question of whether alcohol use *causes* violence. Although this interpretation would be consistent with a link found between alcohol use and violent crime, there are other possible explanations. The ideal study, described above, in which violent behaviors are observed among a representative group of men and women who are randomly assigned either to drink alcohol or not to drink alcohol, would bring us closer to establishing whether there is a causal relationship between alcohol use and violence. Random assignment of subjects to experimental groups allows one to rule out a host of extraneous variables. For example, it is possible that the type of person who drinks alcohol frequently is also the type of person who engages in violent or aggressive behaviors, and as a consequence of this link, more violent acts will be committed by individuals who have been drinking. By randomly assigning people to groups, we could break any potential naturally occurring links between alcohol use and violent behavior.

Even random assignment of people to experimental groups would not ensure that we would be able to establish whether there is a causal link between alcohol use and violence. In the ideal study described above, we would also need to be certain that it is the alcohol itself that is the "active ingredient" in causing increased rates of violence. For example, it may be that whether one drinks alcohol is not the active ingredient, but rather *thinking* that one is drinking alcohol. Participants in the experiment who are given alcohol to drink may expect to become more violent based on their preconceived notions about how alcohol affects behavior. To control for such expectations or preconceptions in drug-administration studies, a placebo condition is often used. Thus, both the alcohol and no-alcohol groups might both believe that they are drinking alcohol because the no-alcohol group is given a placebo. Only when all possible extraneous variables are ruled out is a causal link between alcohol use and violence established.

Occasionally, "natural experiments" occur. Due to a change in public policy (such as an increased tax on alcohol or a change in the legal drinking age) or a change or disruption in the production of alcohol (such as a strike at a state-run distillery in Scandinavian countries like Sweden, Finland, and Norway), the availability of alcohol may be temporarily or permanently altered. For example, the period of Prohibition in the United States (1919–1933) could be considered a natural experiment, because it marked a period in American history when the availability of alcohol was drastically reduced. A reduced rate of violent crime during Prohibition compared to the preceding and succeeding years would suggest a causal link between alcohol and violence. Unfortunately, the Prohibition period is not very informative about the role of alcohol in violence—the rate of violence in America during Prohibition may have actually increased because of the illegal means that people went to in order to obtain alcohol. However, more recently occurring and less drastic changes in alcohol availability have been linked to changes in the rates of violent crime and therefore suggest that changing the availability of alcohol at the community level would be likely to have an effect on the rate of violent crime. Natural experiments can be extremely informative but do not rule out extraneous factors as well as do true experiments. For example, in the case of the period of Prohibition, one could incorrectly infer that a reduction in

An alcoholic sleeps on a Chicago street, circa 1950. CORBIS/HULTON-DEUTSCH COLLECTION

alcohol use actually increases the frequency of violent behavior. In addition, a true experiment, unlike a natural experiment, can sometimes shed light on *how* and *why* alcohol use causes violence.

From 1972 to 1995 over fifty experimental studies were conducted to determine whether alcohol use causes violence or, rather, whether alcohol use causes *interpersonal aggression* (as mentioned above, there are limits to what can be ethically studied in the laboratory). In the typical experimental study a participant is brought into the lab; given either a standard dose of alcohol, a placebo, or no alcohol; and told that the purpose of the experiment is to study the effects of alcohol on reaction time. Participants are led to believe that they will be competing with an unseen opponent in responding to a cue by releasing a button on a control panel in front of them more quickly than their opponent. After each trial, the loser of the trial receives a shock of an intensity previously determined before the trial by the opponent. In fact, there really is no opponent and the occurrence of and the level of the shock administered to the participant is preprogrammed by the experimenter. The variable of interest in the study is the average intensity of shock that the participant has chosen to administer to the sham opponent. The average intensity of shock selected for the opponent is used as an indicator of the level of interpersonal aggression.

The results of experimental studies of the relation between alcohol use and interpersonal aggression have been quite variable. Some studies find that participants who receive alcohol choose higher levels of shock for their sham opponent (on average) than participants who do not receive alcohol, whereas other studies find that prior ingestion of alcohol has no effect on the level of shock chosen by participants in the experiment. Several researchers have used a statistical technique called meta-analysis in an attempt to combine objectively the results of the various experimental studies in a way that a more definitive conclusion about the effect of alcohol use on aggression can be reached. The results suggest that, on average, participants who receive alcohol choose higher levels of shock than participants who receive a placebo or no alcohol, but that the strength of the association between alcohol use and aggression is not particularly large. Most of the studies summarized included only men as participants; a minority of studies (about six) examined the effect of alcohol on interpersonal aggression among women. Over-

all, the results of these few studies do not provide strong evidence for a similar effect of alcohol on aggression among women.

How Alcohol Use Causes Violence

In the experiment on alcohol and interpersonal aggression, comparisons of participants who receive a placebo (who believe that they are drinking alcohol but actually are not drinking alcohol) with those who receive no alcohol (who believe that they are not drinking alcohol and are really not drinking alcohol) can test whether *expectancies* about the effects of alcohol (preconceived notions about how alcohol affects behavior) explain the effect of alcohol on interpersonal aggression. Meta-analyses of studies that have made this comparison suggest that expectancies cannot explain much of the effect of alcohol on interpersonal aggression. Further support for this conclusion comes from the studies of other species, such as mice, rats, and monkeys, in which alcohol has also been associated with increased aggression; expectancies clearly cannot explain the association between alcohol use and aggression in these other species.

Comparisons of participants who receive alcohol (who believe that they are drinking alcohol and actually are drinking alcohol) with those who receive a placebo can test whether there are effects of alcohol on aggression over and above those that can be explained by expectancies. Meta-analyses of studies that have made this comparison suggest that alcohol does have an effect on aggression that cannot be explained by expectancies. These effects of alcohol may be due to the direct or indirect *pharmacological* properties of alcohol (i.e., that it can act as a stimulant or sedative and can impair thinking and judgment).

There is no definitive answer yet concerning exactly how alcohol increases aggression. Any theory advanced to explain this association must account for the fact that alcohol does not *always* increase aggression, and so there must be certain circumstances in which aggression is more or less likely to follow the consumption of alcohol. Most theories implicate alcohol's effects on attention, thinking, and judgment as playing an important role in leading to aggressive behavior. Individuals under the influence of alcohol may not process information accurately. In complex interpersonal situations (where interpersonal aggression takes place), individuals under the influence of alcohol may only see part of the picture (the part that might trigger an aggressive response) but may not attend to other parts of the picture (the part that would inhibit the aggressive response). In essence, an individual under the influence of alcohol is like a car with faulty brakes.

Extraneous Factors Revisited

Above, the possibility was raised that alcohol use may be associated with violence because of extraneous factors. For example, a devoutly religious person may avoid drinking alcohol and also avoid engaging in violent behaviors. In this case, it is not the abstention from alcohol that causes this person to be nonviolent, but rather his or her strong religious proscriptions against certain behaviors, including violence. Conversely, individuals who engage in heavy alcohol use are more likely to engage in many other forms of problem behaviors, including getting involved in physical fights and committing crimes.

Studies of violent criminals are hampered by two limitations: the low prevalence of violent criminals in the general population (less than 1 percent of individuals in the general population have been convicted of a violent crime), and the possible biases introduced when focusing only on those individuals who have been identified by law-enforcement agencies. In the American Psychiatric Association's *DSM* there is a syndrome called "antisocial personality disorder." Individuals with antisocial personality disorder have a long-standing pattern of disregarding and violating the rights of others. Although not all individuals with antisocial personality disorder are violent, as a group they are much more likely to act aggressively than individuals without the disorder. In fact, one of the indicators leading to a diagnosis of antisocial personality disorder is a history of repeated physical fights or assaults. Although antisocial personality disorder is not synonymous with being a violent offender, studies of individuals with antisocial personality disorder may shed some light on the roots of violent behavior.

Individuals who are most likely to be diagnosed with antisocial personality disorder are similar to individuals who are most likely to be heavy drinkers and to be diagnosed with alcohol dependence, that is, they are younger men from lower income groups. There is a great degree of overlap between having a history of antisocial personality disorder and alcohol dependence. In fact, 63 percent of individuals with antisocial personality disorder have a history of alcohol dependence, and an additional 14 percent have a history of alcohol abuse.

Alcohol-related problems are extremely common in individuals with a history of criminal offending and with a history of antisocial personality disorder. Conversely, individuals with a history of alcohol dependence or abuse are also more likely to have a history of antisocial personality disorder. Seventeen percent of men and 8 percent of women with a lifetime history of alcohol dependence would also meet the criteria for a diagnosis of antisocial personality disorder, compared to rates of antisocial personality disorder in the general population of 6 percent among men and 1 percent among women.

It is unlikely that the association between antisocial personality disorder and alcohol dependence can be completely or even predominantly explained by the causal role of alcohol on interpersonal aggression. Symptoms of antisocial personality disorder typically emerge before the age of ten, most often before the onset of alcohol use. In addition, the effect of alcohol on interpersonal aggression is not nearly strong enough or consistent enough to account for the degree of overlap between antisocial personality disorder and alcohol dependence. At best, the causal effect of alcohol use on aggression can account for only a small part of the association between antisocial personality disorder and alcohol dependence.

Another possibility is that the association between antisocial personality disorder and alcohol dependence is due to the causal effect of aggression on alcohol use. One hypothesis is that individuals who intend to commit a violent act can muster up the courage to do so through the use of "liquid courage," that is, alcohol. This hypothesis, however, cannot explain the vast majority of violent acts that are not premeditated but that are carried out in the heat of the moment.

The strongest evidence that supports the possibility that aggressive behavior causes alcohol use is mostly based on temporal information—children who are aggressive are more likely to drink alcohol at an earlier age, to become heavy drinkers, and to eventually develop alcohol dependence than other children. In fact, one of the strongest childhood predictors of the development of alcohol dependence as an adult is a history of aggressive and disinhibited behavior. Establishing that aggression causes alcohol use is not nearly as easy as establishing that alcohol use causes aggression, because *aggression* is not nearly as easy to manipulate experimentally as is *alcohol use*. In other words, in order to firmly establish that aggression causes alcohol use, one would need to conduct a study in which aggression could somehow be directly manipulated in people randomly assigned to "aggression" and "no aggression" groups. Therefore, it is unclear how much of the association between antisocial personality disorder and alcohol dependence can be explained by the causal influence of aggression on alcohol use.

It is quite likely that antisocial personality disorder and alcohol dependence co-occur so frequently in part because of extraneous factors that cause both disorders. There is a growing body of evidence that suggests that some of the precursors of antisocial personality disorder are the same as those of alcohol dependence. Individuals at risk for either antisocial personality disorder or alcohol dependence are more likely than other individuals: (1) to come from families in which there has been divorce and marital conflict; (2) to have received harsh parental discipline or to have been poorly supervised as children; (3) to have been impulsive, restless, and distractible as children; (4) to have had problems in school as children; and (5) to have associated with delinquent, alcohol-using peers as children. The personality precursors of antisocial personality disorder and alcohol dependence are also quite similar. Individuals at risk for either antisocial personality disorder or alcohol dependence are on average more impulsive, risk-taking, aggressive, and rebellious, and less trusting of others than individuals who do not develop these disorders as adults.

Both antisocial personality disorder and alcohol dependence run in families. Individuals with a parent who has a history of antisocial personality disorder or alcohol dependence are at a greater risk for developing the same disorder as their parent. In addition, it appears that antisocial personality disorder and alcohol dependence tend to run in the *same* families. Having a parent with a history of antisocial personality disorder puts one at risk for alcohol dependence as well as antisocial personality disorder, and having a parent with a history of alcohol dependence puts one at risk for antisocial personality disorder as well as alcohol dependence. This suggests that the common causes of both antisocial personality disorder and alcohol dependence must be something that also runs in families, that is, either shared life experiences or shared genes.

There is no definitive answer yet concerning which specific life experiences or genes jointly increase the risk for both antisocial personality dis-

order and alcohol dependence. Some of the risk factors described above are likely to be important, but the mechanisms that lead to the final outcome of interest are still unknown. There are many important discoveries yet to be made in identifying how and why some people develop problems with antisocial behavior and alcohol while others do not. Understanding the causes of both antisocial personality disorder and alcohol dependence, and their common causes, should lead to a greater understanding of alcohol-related violence, because these are the individuals who account for the majority of these offenses.

Conclusion

Between 1993 and 1997, at least four complete scientific monographs were devoted to the issue of the association between alcohol, alcoholism, and violence, including contributions from economists, criminologists, sociologists, epidemiologists, psychologists, and psychiatrists—all surveying the problem from their special perspective. The National Institute on Alcohol Abuse and Alcoholism, an agency of the federal government that makes decisions about where research dollars should be spent, has identified alcohol-related violence as a priority for future research. There are many more unanswered questions than there are answers concerning this thorny problem. This entry attempted to highlight the things that we do understand about alcohol, alcoholism, and violence, and some of the reasons why this is such a difficult question to study. Given the increasing level of research activity focused on alcohol-related violence, it is likely that there will be many more important insights still to come in the years ahead.

BIBLIOGRAPHY

Alcohol Health and Research World 17, no. 2 (1993). "Special Focus: Alcohol, Aggression, and Injury."

Braun, Stephen. *Buzz: The Science and Lore of Alcohol and Caffeine.* New York: Oxford University Press, 1996.

Bushman, Brad J., and Harris M. Cooper. "Effects of Alcohol on Human Aggression: An Integrative Research Review." *Psychological Bulletin* 107, no. 3 (1990): 341–354.

Galanter, Marc, ed. *Recent Developments in Alcoholism.* Vol. 13, *Alcohol and Violence.* New York: Plenum, 1997.

Greenfield, Lawrence A. *Alcohol and Crime: An Analysis of National Data on the Prevalence of Alcohol Involvement in Crime.* Washington, D.C.: U.S. Department of Justice, Bureau of Justice Statistics, 1998.

Ito, Tiffany A., Norman Miller, and Vicki E. Pollock. "Alcohol and Aggression: A Meta-Analysis on the Effects of

Inhibitory Cues, Triggering Events, and Self-Focused Attention." *Psychological Bulletin* 120, no. 1 (1996): 60–82.

Kessler, Ronald C., et al. "Lifetime and Twelve-Month Prevalence of DSM-III-R Psychiatric Disorders in the United States: Results from the National Comorbidity Survey." *Archives of General Psychiatry* 51 (1994): 8–19.

Martin, Susan E., ed. *Alcohol and Interpersonal Violence: Fostering Multidisciplinary Perspectives.* National Institute on Alcohol Abuse and Alcoholism Research monograph 24. Rockville, Md.: U.S. Department of Health and Human Services, 1993.

Pohorecky, Larissa A., John Brick, and Gail Gleason Milgram, eds. *Journal of Studies on Alcohol,* supplement 11, *Alcohol and Aggression* (1993).

WENDY S. SLUTSKE

See also **Developmental Factors: Prenatal; Drugs; Drunk Driving; Prohibition and Temperance; Self-Destructiveness.**

ALIEN AND SEDITION ACTS

The Alien and Sedition Acts were passed by a Federalist Party congressional majority under the John Adams administration in the wake of the 1797–1798 XYZ affair. One of the new republic's first international scandals, the XYZ affair erupted into widespread anti-French public opinion when it was disclosed in the American press that agents of the French government (dubbed X, Y, and Z) had attempted to extort money from U.S. ambassadors, rather than openly negotiating a treaty with them. The acts were initially proposed as a series of crisis measures because the United States seemed on the verge of war with France. Ultimately, though, they were used on a partisan basis to suppress numerous immigrant populations who evinced Jeffersonian Republican (anti-Federalist) leanings and to intimidate native-born Republicans who expressed opinions the Federalists found just as suspiciously "un-American" as those of alien immigrants.

The legislation had four key components: the Naturalization Act, the Alien Act, the Alien Enemies Act, and the Sedition Act (all passed in 1798). The first three of these, as their names suggest, were targeted at immigrant populations and created self-constituting standards for Americanness that, on the one hand, dictated new procedures for how American citizenship status was to be achieved and, on the other, created a category of outsiders, or aliens, against which to define authentic Americans and Americanness. These acts were passed in a decade during which the boundaries of the new nation were still being settled, both literally and figuratively.

The Naturalization Act made it harder to become a naturalized American citizen, by raising the residency requirement from five to fourteen years and by requiring would-be Americans to declare their intent to naturalize five years in advance. The Alien Enemies Act, essentially a war measure that was never implemented, gave the president broad powers to seek out and expel any persons who had come from nations that the United States might oppose in war. The Alien Act extended the president's prerogative to deport *any* nonnative person whom the president deemed a threat to the safety and security of the United States, regardless of his or her country of origin.

The final of these four laws, the Sedition Act, became the most infamous and ultimately cemented the popular sense that these acts (and Adams's administration) were devoted to curtailing freedom of speech and freedom of the press. The Sedition Act extended the question of what constituted Americanness beyond one's country of origin to include one's ideological position. The act targeted allegedly seditious or unpatriotic speech, seeking to regulate "any person [who] shall write, print, utter, or publish, or shall cause or procure to be written, printed, uttered or published . . . any false, scandalous and malicious writing or writings against" the government of the United States, the Congress, or the president. Thus the four acts taken together gave the president broad powers to seek out and suppress anyone, American or not, who expressed views critical of his administration's party and its policies.

Regardless of the strong line they seemed to draw between insider and outsider, American and non- or un-American, the acts were unevenly enforced, even under Adams. For instance, while the "alien" provisions of the acts did create some anxiety among immigrant populations, and even caused some political refugees from France, Ireland, and Britain to go into hiding, none of these provisions was ever officially enforced during Adams's administration. There was in fact a generalized sense of the unconstitutionality and hence unenforceability of the Alien Acts. The Sedition Act, on the other hand, was broadly enforced, though on a partisan basis. Between 1798 and 1800, approximately twenty-five defendants were charged with seditious offenses and ten were convicted—including, most famously, Thomas

Cooper, a British émigré and newspaper editor with radical Republican political ideals; James Thomson Callender, an émigré Scotsman and pamphleteer who routinely criticized Adams personally and publicly; and Matthew Lyon, a congressman from Vermont who had openly criticized the Adams administration's policies toward his constituents. In addition to the official enforcement of the Sedition Act, an unofficial system of harassment and violence emerged, particularly in the streets of major cities, where mobs of young Federalists dressed in black cockades roamed the streets harassing and in some cases beating radical editors and other perceived enemies of the state.

Remembered today as artifacts from the fierce partisan politics of the 1790s between Anglophile Federalist Party affiliates and Francophile Jeffersonian Republicans, the acts languished after the so-called Revolution of 1800, when Adams lost the presidency to Thomas Jefferson. While he did not outright repeal them, Jefferson did not use the acts to suppress alien populations, immigration, or speech, and he pardoned all defendants who had been previously convicted under them. Indeed, Jefferson's inauguration speech marked an attempt to end the practice of rampant partisanship that had marked Federalist hegemony—particularly the practice of creating insiders and outsiders—by sympathetically proclaiming "we are all federalists; we are all republicans." While the Sedition Act expired, never to be reinstated, in March 1801, the Alien Acts were intermittently revived in later wartime situations.

BIBLIOGRAPHY

Elkins, Stanley, and Eric McKitrick. *The Age of Federalism.* New York: Oxford University Press, 1993.
Miller, John C. *Crisis in Freedom: The Alien and Sedition Acts.* Boston: Little, Brown, 1951.
Smith, James Morton. *Freedom's Fetters: The Alien and Sedition Laws and American Civil Liberties.* Ithaca, N.Y.: Cornell University Press, 1956.

TRISH LOUGHRAN

See also **Foreign Intervention, Fear of; Government Commissions; Immigration; Nativism.**

AMERICAN INDIAN MOVEMENT

The American Indian Movement (AIM) was founded in July 1968 by a group of urbanized Chippewas that included Dennis Banks, George Mitchell, and Pat Ballanger. Modeling itself after the Black Panther Party, the organization initially focused on forming street patrols to quell the violence routinely visited by Minneapolis police upon the local Indian community. A number of service programs similar to that of the Panthers followed over the next two years. These ranged from alternative schools to low-cost housing initiatives, several of which were ongoing three decades later.

By 1971 AIM had reoriented itself to Indian land and treaty issues, shifting its emphasis from the urban to reservation context. This change of focus lent the group further credibility and precipitated dramatic increases in both the size and diversity of its membership. Chapters sprouted from Oklahoma to South Dakota, Iowa to California and Washington State. According to Geroge Mitchell there were sixty-seven active chapters with about 4,500 members by the end of 1972 (Rolland Dewing, *Wounded Knee II*, 1995, p. 36). Growth also brought in some of AIM's most capable leaders, including Russell Means (Oglala Lakota), John Trudell (Santee Dakota), and Carter Camp (Ponca).

For a time, AIM pursued a strategy of forcing highly visible confrontations with federal, state, and local authorities. The most spectacular of these clashes was undoubtedly the weeklong occupation, called the Trail of Broken Treaties, of the Bureau of Indian Affairs headquarters in Washington, D.C., on the eve of the 1972 presidential election—although grassroots Indians were likely more impressed with the militancy of AIM's responses to the murders of Raymond Yellow Thunder and Wesley Bad Heart Bull near the Pine Ridge Reservation in South Dakota.

A climax of sorts was reached in early 1973 when traditional Oglala leaders on Pine Ridge requested AIM's help in opposing a federally installed and viciously corrupt tribal government headed by Richard Wilson. Among other things, Wilson maintained a GOON squad—an acronym for Guardians of the Oglala Nation—to physically intimidate his opponents, leading Justice Department civil rights investigators to conclude later that he had imposed a "reign of terror" on reservation residents and that federal authorities had funded him to do so.

AIM's intervention led to a seventy-one-day armed standoff at the reservation hamlet of Wounded Knee, during which the Wilsonites together with several hundred federal marshals, Federal Bureau of Investigation agents, and military advisers besieged the dissidents and poured more than five hundred thousand shots into their flimsy defenses. Although two Indians were killed and another dozen badly wounded during the fighting, it ended only when federal officials finally agreed to discuss violations of U.S. treaty obligations with the Oglala chiefs.

International attention was captured by the events at Wounded Knee, and AIM was widely admired as "the shock troops of Indian sovereignty" (from the pro-AIM tribal council member Birgil Kills Straight, photocopied and distributed on Pine Ridge during March 1973). Embarrassed by bad press at home and abroad yet unable to finesse the movement's demands—to comply in any real sense with the terms of its Indian treaties would, as one senior official admitted at the time, "require dismantling the United States"—the government quietly targeted AIM for what counterintelligence operatives refer to as "neutralization" (unnamed source, as quoted in Jimmie Durham, *A Certain Lack of Coherence*, 1993, p. 174).

In part, this stategy was accomplished by the time-honored expedient of using the judicial system for extralegal purposes. In the aftermath of Wounded Knee, 562 federal felony charges were lodged against AIM members. While a paltry fifteen of these resulted in convictions, the expense of continuously posting bail and paying attorneys literally bankrupted the movement while diverting its members' attention from their work for years on end. The diminishing of AIM's grassroots efforts, rather than dispensing justice, was clearly the government's motive. Federal authorities would eventually "win" such a contest, the army adviser Colonel Volney Warner said in 1974, "even if no one goes to prison."

Other counterintelligence techniques heavily employed against AIM included a comprehensive campaign to plant false and derogatory stories in the media and infiltration by agents provocateurs to spread rumors, instigate disputes, and otherwise disrupt the movement's internal workings. The FBI also adapted the tactics of counterinsurgency warfare. As the GOON leader Duane Brewer subsequently confirmed, agents converted Wilson's thugs into outright death squads, providing them with weapons, explosives, communications gear, field intelligence, and immunity from prosecution (Churchill 1996, pp. 231–270). The results were predictably horrific.

From March 1973 to March 1976, at least sixty-nine AIM members and supporters died violently on Pine Ridge, while some 340 others suffered serious physical assaults. "Using only documented political deaths, the yearly murder rate on the Pine Ridge Reservation between March 1, 1973 and March 1, 1976 was 170 per 100,000. By comparison, Detroit, the reputed 'murder capital of the United States,' had a rate of 20.2 per 100,000" (Johansen and Maestas 1978, p. 83). In twenty-one of the AIM homicides, eyewitnesses identified the killers as known GOON squad members. Although the FBI exercises primary jurisdiction on Indian reservations, not one of these crimes was ever brought to trial as the result of a federal investigation.

By early summer 1975, the situation on Pine Ridge was so grim that many activists had disengaged. Those who did not were compelled to rely on armed self-defense for their very survival. The upshot was the so-called Oglala Firefight of 26 June, in which two FBI agents and the AIM member Joe Killsright died. The event was then used as a pretext to send a force of 250 militarily equipped agents onto the reservation to finish the job that steady attrition had failed to accomplish. By fall, their work was mostly complete.

A year later Bob Robideau and Darrelle "Dino" Butler, members of an AIM security team, were tried in Cedar Rapids, Iowa, for killing the agents. They were acquitted on the basis of self-defense after an all-white jury concluded that the nature of the FBI's operations on Pine Ridge would have led any reasonable person to do as they had done. Nonetheless, a third member of the group, Leonard Peltier, was tried in 1977. He was convicted and sentenced to a double-life term after prosecutors introduced much tainted evidence and the judge ruled that he could not present a case for self-defense.

Peltier remained in prison in 1999 despite the prosecutor Lynn Crooks's acknowledgment during a 1987 appeal hearing that Crooks "really has no idea who shot those agents." The Eighth Circuit Court has also ruled that the case presented against him was invalid. It has thus been argued that Peltier serves his time not for any crime he has committed but as a symbol of the arbitrary ability of the federal government to repress the legitimate aspirations to liberation of native people within its borders.

As for AIM, the relentless and often lethal repression of the mid-1970s left it decimated, wracked by internal dissension, and therefore unable to regain its former momentum. Since then, it has displayed only occasional flashes of its original promise, as with its 1978 "Longest Walk" from

San Francisco to Washington, D.C., undertaken to draw attention to Indian issues; the Yellow Thunder Camp occupation near Rapid City, South Dakota, during the early 1980s, which was a successful challenge to the Forest Service's consistent denial of use permits to Indians in the Black Hills; and Colorado AIM's anti-Columbus demonstrations in the early 1990s.

BIBLIOGRAPHY

Churchill, Ward. *From a Native Son: Selected Essays in Indigenism, 1985–1995.* Cambridge, Mass.: South End Press, 1996.

Churchill, Ward, and Jim Vander Wall. *Agents of Repression: The FBI's Secret Wars Against the Black Panther Party and the American Indian Movement.* Cambridge, Mass.: South End Press, 1988.

Deloria, Vine, Jr. *Behind the Trail of Broken Treaties: An Indian Declaration of Independence.* 2d ed. Austin: University of Texas Press, 1984.

Johansen, Bruce, and Roberto Maestas. *Wasi'chu: The Continuing Indian Wars.* New York: Monthly Review, 1978.

Matthiessen, Peter. *In the Spirit of Crazy Horse: The Story of Leonard Peltier.* 2d ed. New York: Viking, 1991.

Smith, Paul Chaat, and Robert Allen Warrior. *Like a Hurricane: The American Indian Movement from Alcatraz to Wounded Knee.* New York: New Press, 1996.

Weyler, Rex. *Blood of the Land: The U.S. Government and Corporate War Against the American Indian Movement.* 2d ed. Philadelphia: New Society, 1992.

WARD CHURCHILL

See also **American Indians; Wounded Knee, 1973.**

AMERICAN INDIANS

Following the **Overview***, there are two subentries:* **American Indian Holocaust** *and* **American Indian Wars.**

OVERVIEW

In the fifteenth and sixteenth centuries, Europe learned about American Indians by indirect means. The few Indians captured and carried across the Atlantic came as slaves or as exhibits in shows. The image of Indians for Europeans came almost entirely from the various accounts of Spanish conquerors, various colonizers, and travelers, whose purposes and visions diverged widely.

Believing the American natives to be a subhuman people who deserved conquest, the Spanish concluded it was their duty as righteous men to persuade these heathens to submit to a Christian monarch and to convert them to the true religion. Thus Christopher Columbus, in his reports to the Spanish crown, justified his seizure and enslavement of thousands of peaceful, conspicuously nonviolent Taino natives of Hispaniola. Lurking in the background, however, were other Indians of a very different kind, the warlike Caribs whose name became corrupted to "cannibals." A good Christian could not deny the duty of suppressing these natives who ate human flesh.

From the days of earliest contact, attributed cannibalism became a major feature of the image of Indians that took shape in Europe. It loomed as strong justification for Hernando Cortés's 1519 conquest in Mexico, when there might otherwise have been some difficulty in proclaiming a "just war" simply for plunder. Cortés's Aztec opponents were not easily categorized as wild men; they were civilized builders of great cities, but they were also pagans who practiced human sacrifice in their high temples. After paying tribute to their gods with human hearts ripped out of living bodies, they kicked the rest of the sacrificial victims down the pyramids' stairs to be taken home for dinner by the rituals' sponsors.

The great Aztec emperor (*tlatoani*) Moctezuma II (Montezuma II, 1466–1520) regularly received for his own repast one of the more "delectable" thighs from each tribute. Cortés remonstrated with Moctezuma, who promised to change his ways—or so we are told in surviving accounts. The tales become more sensational when the Aztecs rise against Cortés and capture some of his men to be sacrificed in full view on top of a pyramid.

These accounts of the Aztecs diverted attention from the slaughters and cruelties of the conquistadores and stimulated an appetite in Europe for titillation.

Savage Imagery: Cannibalism and Scalping

In 1590 the first picture books about Spanish conquests appeared, beginning with volume I of Theodor de Bry's *Collected Travels in the East Indies and West Indies.* De Bry, an engraver and printer at Frankfurt am Main (in present-day Germany), was a Protestant with no love for Spanish Catholics. His large-format, multilingual books show conscientious reportage of conquerors' journals, with much attention to the Spaniards' cruelties and atrocities. These books caught the public's attention and sold briskly, but, as it seems, not profitably enough to satisfy de Bry's sons. After de Bry died in 1598, they took over the enterprise and subtly reoriented its pictures for greater sensationalism. Successive editions increasingly show full frontal nudity of Indians and stress their cannibal-

The Black Legend

The Black Legend of Spanish atrocities in America began to form when the Spanish missionary and historian Friar Bartolomé de Las Casas voiced his protests to the crown in his book *The Tears of the Indians* (1552). Hoping to get royal intervention on behalf of the Indians, Las Casas and his followers told how conquistadores treated horses and dogs better than their Indian captives. One horrid example related how a Spaniard wagered that he could sever the head of an Indian standing nearby with one slash of his sword—and then proceeded to do so. Hostile Englishmen, trying to persuade Irishmen that Spanish conquest would be worse than English rule, propagated such gory details.

Worse even than direct brutality was the heavy workload and deprivation of food that the Indians endured. In their weakened state the Indians succumbed to epidemic diseases, such as smallpox, that were imported with the Europeans. The ensuing undeniable decline in Indian numbers came to be accepted as evidence of truth in the Black Legend of cruelty. In 1498 one and a half million tribute-paying Indians were counted on the island of Santo Domingo by its founder, Bartolomé Columbus. And there were many more hidden in the hills. Yet, within decades there were none on the island; genocide was complete.

ism. The later pictures show family parties happily eating dismembered arms and legs in the midst of scattered body parts. These pictures sold books.

New editions continued to appear until 1634. Based on reports of cannibalism among Brazilian natives, these editions gave an impression that the practice prevailed everywhere in America. It should be stressed that these were the very first visual images of American Indians to shape European minds, and they surely did not contribute to a conception of "noble savages." Even today, scholars make faulty inferences when they consult only one edition of the sequence.

Human sacrifice and cannibalism by natives were suppressed by the conquistadores, whose own sadistic practices became known as the Black Legend. For the French and English the distinguishing characteristic of the natives was their wildness; they were therefore described as *savage*

(*sauvage*, in French). At first this term was ambiguous. The French writer Marc Lescarbot protested against an "abusive and unmerited" interpretation of *sauvage.* The Englishman George Johnson, at Jamestown in 1609, called the Indians "wild and savage" but "loving and gentle" like "herds of deer in a forest."

This ambiguity turned ugly in the reporting of Captain John Smith. In 1616 Smith called the Indians "poore innocent souls," but after the Powhatan uprising in 1622, he made them "cruel beasts" with "a more unnatural brutishness than beasts." Thus he established an image of Indian violence in English literature that became irrationally animal-like. The historian Francis Parkman, famed as America's finest nineteenth-century chronicler, conceived Indians "as a troublesome and dangerous species of wild beast." He called the Indian allies of Canada's Count Frontenac, "this heterogeneous multitude . . . like a vast managerie [*sic*] of wild animals; and the lynx bristled at the wolf, and the panther grinned fury at the bear." In combat with scalp bounty hunters from Massachusetts, "the Indians howled like wolves, yelled like enraged cougars"; and the bounty hunters "were much like hunters of wolves, catamounts, or other dangerous beasts, except that the chase of this fierce and wily game demanded far more hardihood and skill." In the three hundred years from John Smith to Francis Parkman, Indians were persistently portrayed as beasts of predation—violent, brutal, and bloodthirsty.

The horror of cannibalism, varying somewhat from Aztec conduct, emerged again among some of the northern tribes. Instead of being a climax to regular rituals of human sacrifice, cannibalism occurred erratically among some tribes when victors in battle ritually devoured their most admired fallen enemies in the belief that some of the victim's "power" would be absorbed with his flesh. Jesuit missionaries reported on such occurrences and used them as compelling reasons for righteous persons to support the missions that contended against such practices. Such souls surely needed to be saved.

In light of all the sensational reporting, it often seemed that all Indians practiced cannibalism, but this was far from true. Indians of the Algonquian family group living near the Atlantic coast were contemptuous of interior Iroquoians, whom they identified to the Dutch and English as Minquas, Mengwe, and Maqua, names that meant "man-eaters." *Maquas* evolved gradually to *Mohawks*, but the Iroquoians called themselves *Kaniengahaga*. At the multitribal siege of Detroit in 1763, the ritual cannibalism of the Ottawas was denounced by a Chippewa chief and an Erie chief who spoke also for the Delawares. This sort of information, however, did not reach Europe, where the fiendishness of cannibalism cast Indians in monstrous shapes and where Parkman's view was given much prominence.

Stories of scalping aroused much horror among colonials and Europeans who read about it. Histories that tell of strings of scalps hanging at the entrances of great warriors' homes still provoke strong reactions. In the twentieth century, Indians who regarded the practice as shameful even denied it was originally an Indian cultural trait and asserted it had been taught to them by Europeans. True enough, east coast Narragansetts are recorded in King Philip's War (1675–1676) as bringing severed heads, rather than scalps, as a peace offering to the feared English, but this proves only that they were doing what New England's colonials wanted them to do at the time. (In later years these colonials offered bounties for scalps.) At most, one may infer some difference between those Narragansetts and other tribes whose custom of scalping has been demonstrated in a study by James Axtell and William C. Sturtevant.

This practice has obsessed some writers. It has been reported that no Indian male could attain the status of manhood until he had taken a scalp. Simple calculation shows that if that were true, no Indians would have survived until Europeans arrived.

Torture

Indians have suffered from often inaccurate accounts of scalping and torture. In the 1956 film *Around the World in Eighty Days*, for example, the servant Passepartout is shown tied to a stake with faggots beginning to take flame, before he is rescued by a charge of the U.S. Calvary—an especially ironic portrayal of Indians, given that this peculiar form of execution had indeed been learned from Europeans. Nathaniel Knowles, in a careful, systematic examination of sources for the southeast-coast region of North America, found that "there are no expressions by the early explorers and colonizers indicating any fear of such treatment [though] the Europeans were only too willing in most cases to call attention to the barbarity of the Indians and thus justify their need for either salvation or extermination." Knowles published this in the *Proceedings of the American Philosophical Society* in 1940. To this day it has not been contradicted.

As for the Northeast, New France's Marc Lescarbot in 1618 wrote positively that "our sea-coast Indians" did not practice torture, and he was confirmed in the twentieth century by the historian and translator W. L. Grant in one of the conscientiously edited *Publications of the Champlain Society.*

The earliest references to torturing and burning at the stake point to Indians of the interior, especially those who used the Iroquoian family of languages, and there are vague hints that the practice had diffused with them from the Southwest. The practice spread among Canadian Indians as testified by horrific reports in the *Jesuit Relations.* An interesting incident occurred in 1719 in Pennsylvania. A report came to Philadelphia that an Indian raiding party had tortured a captive to death in one of the villages along the Susquehanna River. Colonel John French was sent to command the sachems (chiefs) of all the Indian towns that "no person whatever offer after this time to put any man to Death by Torture here, for whoever does it must answer to the Governour and Government at their peril." He seems to have been obeyed. The accounts of such brutality so common to New England, New York, Canada, and Virginia simply do not exist in Pennsylvania's annals; one must ask to what extent torture continued because of approbation by those governments, which sometimes instigated the torture as a form of management by realpolitik.

Torture was nothing new to Europeans. One may visit museums and other places, like Madame Tussaud's waxworks in London, to see exhibits of devices once used to inflict excruciating pain. Generally, European torture was conducted out of sight in specially equipped dungeons. By contrast, Indians made it a spectacle for public participation, as did American lynching mobs in pursuit of black victims and as did European executioners on edifying special occasions, as well as medieval and early modern Inquisitors, who "saved souls" by burning people, such as Joan of Arc, at the stake. In the twentieth century Amnesty International has documented torture practices all over the world.

The differences between Indian and European torture originated in their different kinds of laws. Torture in Europe was inflicted by specialists under orders from established authority; and crowds, when invited to observe, were cordoned off from the "performance." Among Indian communities punishment of a crime was the responsibility of families, and the torture of a captive regarded as a criminal was democratic. Participation was open to everyone. Even old women often joined in wholeheartedly in the horrid acts: thrusting fire-brands at the victim's genitals or chewing off the joints of his fingers after promising to "caress" him. Such behavior was reported to Europe by horrified missionary observers.

Captives were not always tortured, because of two considerations. First, colonial captives (unlike Indian captives) might be held for ransom if they survived the grueling march back to their captors' villages. Retreat was always hasty, and those too infirm to keep up the pace were hatcheted to death because their captors, in fear of revenge, did not want to leave them behind to guide pursuers. Second, of the survivors, those not ransomed might be taken permanently as adoptees into their captors' families and tribe.

Those marked for possible adoption were forced to run the gauntlet between two lines of persons beating at them with sticks or weapons. The runner who got through to the end without collapsing became a member of the captors' tribe. Particularly desirable captives received very light strokes along the gauntlet; those who succumbed to blows might be taken to the stake afterward.

Treatment of adoptees, however, was kind. They ceased to be regarded as captives and instead took the place of lost family members. Captured and adopted Indians took on their new identities to the extent that they regarded themselves as dead in their former tribes. Many colonial adoptees became so fond of their new families that they refused to return to their natal relatives. For colonials generally this was incomprehensibly scandalous conduct, even though widely practiced.

Torture was practiced by colonials as well as by their sponsoring empires, and colonial experts in Indian affairs (with the exception of Quakers) not only accepted the idea of torture by their Indian allies but sometimes selectively instigated it for political purposes. To precipitate a desired war between two tribes, it was enough to persuade one's ally to torture conspicuously a warrior from the other tribe, thereby ensuring that the tribes would not come to terms with each other at one's own expense.

French officials excelled in this sort of management. Englishmen were less skillful, but they played the same game when the opportunity offered itself. The government of New France had a superb intelligence network of traders scattered and intermarried in Indian villages, and some of these agents actually led tribal raids to punish Indians showing too much independence from French policies.

A portrayal of the 1778 Massacre of Wyoming Valley, Pennsylvania, taken from the original painting by Alonzo Chappel. LIBRARY OF CONGRESS

Collaboration and Conflict

In 1752 the Indian agent Charles Langlade, who was of mixed ancestry, led a large party of Ottawas and Chippewas and some Potawatomis in an attack on the Miami town Pickawillany (in present-day western Ohio). Langlade's purpose was to prevent the Miamis from leaving the French alliance to join the British, and he succeeded. The raiders killed Chief Memeskia and feasted ritually on his corpse to gain his "power." Governor General Duquesne soon after recommended Langlade for an annual pension from the French crown. In such situations Indian cannibalism aroused thrills of horror among Europeans; the official nature of the maneuver escaped attention.

Earlier, French policy had turned violently against the Outagami, or Fox, Nation, and in 1712 an official at Detroit had recruited Ottawas and Potawatomis to massacre Foxes trying to escape. The reason was commercial. The French would not tolerate the Foxes as an obstacle to trade with western tribes, and the Foxes rejected orders from Montreal. The massacre was reported as done by Indians to other Indians; the French organizer was portrayed merely as an adviser.

Englishmen also were not above such behavior. After Charlestown, South Carolina, was founded in 1670, Spanish troops from Florida raided it and were rebuffed. Annoyed Carolinians retaliated by striking at the Spanish Catholic missions in Florida. A handful of Carolinians from Goose Creek organized and bribed traditionalist Creek Indians to raid the missions, and by 1708 as many as ten to twelve thousand Catholic converts had been seized and sold into West Indian slavery to the great profit of Goose Creek and somewhat less of the Creek Indians. The violence was Indian; the direction of it was English colonial.

In the turbulent era of invasion and colonialism, such occasions for violence took various forms but shared the common substance of teamwork between Indians and the agents of the empire. Parkman wrote a sensational account of the destruction of the Huron confederacy by its rivals, the Iroquois Five Nations, from 1649 to 1655. He made much of the ferocity of the Iroquoians that forced the Hurons to flee from their homeland. The fighting was fierce and ugly, but it did not arise from mere bloodthirstiness; it followed a rational strategy. Motivation was provided by Huron domination of a great circuit of trade with other Indians for final exchange with the French; the Iroquoians aimed at breaking up these arrangements and picking up the pieces for themselves.

The Iroquoians were able to triumph because they had firearms, which the Hurons lacked; the Iroquoians had those firearms because their Dutch trading partners, who shared the Iroquois objective, provided them. Combat was as furious as in Europe's Thirty Years' War (1618–1648), but the Indians were more specific in their aims, as is shown by Seneca victors who "adopted" the entire Tahontaenrat band of defeated Hurons and assigned them to their own village of Gandougarae. There they were permitted to take in other refugees and maintain their own customs, and they gradually assimilated with their hosts. Thus, as an incidental by-product of a literal trade war, the Senecas became the largest tribe of the Iroquois Five Nations, and they acted with great independence within the Iroquois league.

Powhatan Uprising of 1622. Independent race wars of Indians against Europeans were few. Probably the most notorious was the Powhatan uprising of 1622 against Jamestown. English war propaganda made a furious response to these "perfidious and inhumane people" (as Captain John Smith described them). Stories were told of Indians being accepted in Englishmen's homes, only to treacherously tomahawk their host's entire family. So far as they went, these stories were probably true. Statistics, however, suggest a qualified interpretation. When casualties were finally counted, 347 colonials died under the hatchet, and it seems relevant to state that at least 4,500 transported colonials had been allowed to die of neglect and indifference by the founding Virginia company. Starving colonists had fled to the Indians for succor "but were taken again, and hung, shot, or broken upon the wheel: one man for stealing meal had a bodkin thrust through his tongue, and was chained to a tree until he starved." This other side to the war propaganda is found in the official records of the Virginia Company, but it made no waves elsewhere in recorded histories.

The Pequots. In early-seventeenth-century New England the Pequots tried to negotiate "civilized" rules of combat before launching their raids against the Connecticut Colony. In a colloquy shouted to the commander of Fort Saybrook on the Connecticut River, "They asked if we did use to kill women and children." They were answered, "They should see that hereafter." Accepting that as a statement of total war, the Pequots then an-

73

nounced their determination to spare no noncombatants. In Boston's subsequent mobilization of its Narragansett allies, those Indians requested Roger Williams, the Puritan clergyman and founder of Rhode Island, to notify Boston "that it would be pleasing to all natives, that women and children be spared."

Such efforts were in vain. When Connecticut's Captain John Mason campaigned against the Pequots in 1637, he chose to attack the "Mystic" fort that contained only women, children, and old men who had been sent there while the warriors waited for battle five miles away. Mason and his colleague Captain John Underhill surrounded the Mystic stockade. Relegating Narragansett allies to an outer ring, they charged at daybreak. Swinging swords against fleeing Indians, the attackers tired themselves. Mason declared, "we should never kill them after that manner . . . WE MUST BURN THEM," and he set the wigwams on fire. (The quotation is from Mason's manuscript.)

Fleeing victims tried to break through the surrounding ring of soldiers to refuge among the Narragansetts, "but not above five of them escaped out of *our* hands," according to Captain Underhill. He also noted that the Narragansetts protested, "It is too furious, and slays too many men."

Miantonomo. The Pequot and Narragansett tribes became embroiled in war against each other in the context of rivalry between the two colonies of Connecticut and Massachusetts Bay. Another tribe, the Mohegans, took on the role of clients to Connecticut and helped that colony, as Narragansetts helped Massachusetts, to war against the Pequots. After defeat and suppression of the Pequots, Mohegans challenged Narragansetts for the spoils, and in combat they captured the Narragansett chief Miantonomo in 1643. He offered ransom to be delivered to his Massachusetts allies, a transaction done in accordance with Indian customary law.

The colonists, however, regarded Miantonomo as too strong and independent. Boston's governor John Winthrop thought "it would not be safe to set him at liberty, neither had we sufficient ground for us to put him to death." He and his colleagues solved their problem by ordering the Mohegan leader Uncas to kill him "according to justice and prudence"; and to make sure that Uncas would not succumb to the justice of Indian custom about ransom, they ordered some Englishmen to accompany the Indians to prudently oversee the "execution."

It had to be done with finesse: Uncas was not to kill until he had departed from the jurisdiction of the English and had arrived in his own territory, and Winthrop's judges decreed that "the English meddle not with the head or body at all." Thus, New England's most eminent men absolved themselves of guilt for judicial murder, and Uncas was charged with responsibility for murderous violation of Miantonomo's ransom, which had been fully paid.

King Philip's War. In 1675 New England's greatest Indian war broke out when desperate "King Philip"—the Wampanoag chief Metacom—rose against the colonists who were in the process of seizing the last of his tribe's territory. Narragansetts hoped to avoid conflict with the English, so their chief, Pessicus, assailed the Wampanoags to demonstrate more than neutrality. Pessicus delivered to an English agent on Narragansett Bay the severed heads of seven of Metacom's warriors. In addition, he brought in alive the Wampanoag "squaw sachem" Weetamoo and a hundred of her band. Although these prisoners had not joined Metacom's fighting men, it was enough for the New Englanders that they belonged to the same tribe. They were summarily sold off to slavery in the West Indies—all of them, that is, except Weetamoo, whose head was kept to decorate a stake.

The unfortunate Narragansetts, who had tried so hard to isolate the uprising exclusively among the Wampanoags, soon discovered the futility of their strategy. They occupied choice real estate for which both Massachusetts and Connecticut hoped to acquire "rights of conquest." Boston hired a company of buccaneers under Captain John Moseley to do the colony's fighting. Moseley's men paid no heed to niceties of distinction between tribe and tribe. On the principle that all Indians were eligible to be plundered, they killed and captured sixty Narragansetts who had deluded themselves into thinking the war was not theirs. After that, however, some Narragansetts forgot their differences with Wampanoags and joined Metacom's warriors against what had become their joint enemy.

Boston sent the Reverend William Hubbard to England to denounce Indian savages and the terrible menace they had presented to pious New England. Roger Williams's earlier unpublicized protest to the Massachusetts General Court went without response:

> Hath not the God of peace and Father of mercies made these natives more friendly in this, than our native

countrymen in our own land to us? Have they not entered leagues of love, and to this day [1654] continued peaceable commerce with us? Are not our families grown up in peace amongst them? Upon which I humbly ask, how it can suit with Christian ingenuity to take hold of some seeming occasions for their destructions.

Even after the raid of Captain Moseley and his buccaneers, responsible Narragansett leaders hoped to hide away and wait out the war. They made a fort in what seemed like an impenetrable swamp, but the implacable New Englanders learned from a turncoat the intricate path to the fort, and there they once again massacred without mercy. Warriors who escaped became the colonists' most bitter enemies.

With such unintended assistance from the colonists, Metacom attracted supporters from many tribes, most remarkably from Massachusetts's mission Indians. In the winter of 1675, Metacom regrouped his forces in the upper Hudson Valley to prepare for an immense, organized campaign, but

An 1883 print in the *Harper's* magazine depicting the death of the Wampanoag chief Metacom, also called King Philip, in 1676 in Massachusetts. HULTON GETTY/ LIAISON AGENCY

this was a fatal error. His presence attracted attention from New York's governor, Edmund Andros, who greatly feared the possibility of widespread uprising against all English colonies. Andros rushed upriver to engage the Mohawks against Metacom, and they dealt a devastating blow that effectively ended Metacom's ability to fight.

New Englanders wrote the histories, and the histories show Indians with bloody, uplifted hatchets, which was true enough in the heat of combat and horrible enough for farmers within reach. Victims of Indian raids were not likely to take an indifferent view of what motivated the warriors to torture and burn their families. For historians, however, it is patent that such parital truth is not only tendentious but in fact a lie. In seventeenth-century New England, Indian violence was retaliation for casualties many times greater that the colonists had inflicted on the Indians.

French and Indian War. Alliances between Europeans and Indians came to a climax in the eighteenth century's Seven Years' War (1754–1763), usually referred to in textbooks as the French and Indian War. The Governor of New France understood very well that English colonials outnumbered his Frenchmen twenty to one. He therefore recruited Indians to create havoc among backwoods settlers. Frenchmen prided themselves on being the most civilized people in Europe, and they held Indian-style war in contempt. "The cruelties and the insolence of these barbarians is horrible," wrote the Comte de Bougainville. "Their souls are as black as pitch. It is an abominable way to make war." But he grew accustomed to it. A year later he wrote, "What a scourge! Humanity shudders at being obliged to make use of such monsters. But without them the war would be too much against us."

Stories about the Indians' raids in the Seven Years' War are rife with atrocities, but they did not occur at random. Targets were chosen by French generals, and each band of raiders was accompanied and supervised by a French officer (in disguise) who urged the raiders on and promised rewards for satisfactory results. When the gallant Marquis de Montcalm attacked the British forts Oswego and William Henry, he preceded the campaigns by negotiating arrangements with Indian chiefs to permit seizure and scalping of prisoners, and he thus recruited necessary warrior allies. Massacres occurred, and Montcalm stayed out of sight long enough to fulfill his agreement. Then he made a great show of saving the surviving English for ransom.

At both Fort Oswego and Fort William Henry, the unleashed Indians rushed first to the hospitals and took scalps as tokens of bravery from helpless patients. At Fort William Henry they even dug up some recently buried casualties to gain more scalps, but retribution came soon for such counterfeit bravery. Smallpox had claimed victims in that hospital, and it claimed victims again when the warriors returned home.

The Uses of Propaganda

The goals of Europeans and their descendants in North America led to the need to portray Indians as enemies when the Indians were only defending their territories from conquest. The violence of the armed resistance by Indians allowed misrepresentations of the cause of that violence to be used by Europeans as war propaganda. The images of brutality lasted as long as there were Indians defending their tribal territories.

Some examples show with special clarity why and how the images were primarily propaganda. For instance, whether the Shawnee chief Tecumseh (1768–1813) is venerated as a hero or reviled as a savage, he appears in histories as a warrior in arms and the organizer of a multitribal war (1811–1813) against the United States. This warrior image has spread to all Shawnees, and it hides awareness of the policies of the legitimate head of the Shawnee, Black Hoof. This thoughtful man had become convinced that the Shawnees must accommodate the Americans instead of fighting them in vain. In 1807 he renounced armed resistance, accepted assistance from a Quaker missionary, and followed a plan to become "civilized." Black Hoof's five hundred followers cleared 430 acres of land in Indiana, planted orchards, acquired breeding stock of swine and cattle, hired a blacksmith, and built mills—all in one year. Black Hoof's neighbors petitioned Washington, D.C., on his behalf, but Washington's officials saw Black Hoof and his followers as a threat. If his program succeeded, his Shawnees would be able to keep their land. It was against national policy to let Indians settle on their own land, so Washington ordered the missionary away, and the yet untutored Shawnee project fell into ruin.

Our American past is filled with images of the Overland Trail, showing covered wagons on their way to Oregon and California, and the images often involve circled wagons being attacked by mounted, howling warriors. This persevering image is largely false. John D. Unruh, in his great study *The Plains Across* (1979), examined contemporary newspapers of the period and discovered that in many cases multiple accounts of the same conflicts were written to arouse public anger. In fact, from 1840 to 1844 throughout the territories, not a single emigrant was killed by Indians, though two Indians were killed by emigrants. Total deaths from 1840 to 1860 were 363 emigrants and 426 Indians.

There was conflict, of course. Under the circumstances, how could there not be? But reporting was entirely one-sided, as in the case of nine thousand emigrants who signed a paper stating "that they have been most kindly treated by the [Shoshoni] Indians"; their story was not reported.

Indians are now getting fairer treatment, and since tribes no longer rise in arms—all tribal territory has been lost except for the "reservations" allotted by the conqueror—reasons for war propaganda are past. Yet little children still play "cowboys and Indians," and generations will pass before accurate histories—those called mainstream simply repeat old slurs—catch up to new opinion.

BIBLIOGRAPHY

Axtell, James. *The European and the Indian*. New York: Oxford University Press, 1981.

Jennings, Francis. *Empire of Fortune*. New York: Norton, 1988.

———. *The Invasion of America*. New York: Norton, 1975.

Knowles, Nathaniel. "The Torture of Captives by the Indians of Eastern North America." *Proceedings of the American Philosophical Society* 82 (1940): 151–225.

Trigger, Bruce G. *The Children of Aataentsic*. Montreal: McGill-Queen's University Press, 1976. Indispensable for studies of seventeenth-century northern Indians.

FRANCIS JENNINGS

See also **American Indian Holocaust; American Indian Wars; Custer, George Armstrong; Sand Creek Massacre; Scalping; Trail of Tears.**

AMERICAN INDIAN HOLOCAUST

Much remains controversial about the Euramerican destruction of the indigenous peoples of the Americas, including the magnitude of the holocaust, its causes, and whether or not *genocide* is an accurate term to use in characterizing it. There is no longer any question, however, that the near annihilation of the Western Hemisphere's native peoples during the four centuries following Christopher Columbus's voyages to the Caribbean constitutes the most massive human eradication in the history of the world.

Magnitude and Causes of the Holocaust

Determining the size of the population crash that followed in the wake of the European invasion of the Americas is an ongoing and difficult task. One of the more prominent, if conservative, estimates puts the proportional population decline throughout North and South America at roughly 90 percent, or close to 50 million people and perhaps as many as 60 million, between 1492 and the end of the nineteenth century. According to this conjecture, a decline of between three and four million people occurred in what is today the United States and Canada (Denevan 1992).

What makes this estimate far too low is that, like virtually all general assessments, it derives from a review of numerous regional calculations that are themselves based almost entirely on projected mortality rates from epidemic-disease outbreaks and, even more limiting, on only those epidemic-disease outbreaks that are known to have occurred *after* extensive face-to-face contact between Europeans and natives.

Two crucial matters are ignored in these appraisals. The first is a growing body of archaeological evidence showing that the introduced European diseases that so devastated entire regions of the Americas commonly raced on well ahead of the European explorers, with the consequence that—time and time again—when Europeans arrived in a given area, disease had long since preceded them in exterminating vast numbers of physically uncontacted indigenous inhabitants. For example, the various Caddoan peoples of what is now the southeastern United States endured a population collapse estimated at more than 95 percent from introduced diseases *before* they encountered the Europeans who had released those diseases into neighboring areas (Perttula 1991). This phenomenon of disease diffusion, now known to have occurred in numerous other locales (see, for example, Dobyns 1983; Ramenofsky 1987; Borah 1992), is entirely overlooked by those relying solely on the written record for their population and depopulation estimates.

The second essential element absent from conventional estimates of post-Columbian New World depopulation magnitudes is any serious consideration of the great variety of other factors that contributed to population decline—factors of enormous importance ranging from outright mass murder, enslavement, and starvation to psychological trauma and infertility as a consequence of both disease and gross mistreatment (Stannard 1991, 1992). An indication of how crucial just one of these additional phenomena can be is provided by the case of the Hawaiians, an isolated indigenous people who suffered a massive post-contact population free fall even during periods when violence and epidemics were absent; this collapse was brought on largely by introduced endemic (as opposed to epidemic) disease and consequent devastation of the birthrate due to pathologically induced infertility and subfecundity (Stannard 1990).

Moreover, the impact of these various population-decline causes cannot be measured simply by piling one newly recognized contributing factor on top of the others, because they invariably operate interactively, multiplying rather than merely adding to the devastation. Thus a pattern is becoming evident that occurred literally thousands of times over four centuries of conquest: epidemic diseases were introduced to populations that had no previous exposure, and thus no immunity, to them; consequent population crashes and general debilitation made the affected indigenous communities easy prey to enslavement, forced labor, violent dispersal, or outright genocide; these actions, in turn, wiped out food supplies and undermined traditional public-health practices, caused death by overwork and exposure, destroyed tribal or national leadership, and obliterated cultural support systems; and all of this, in its turn, caused psychological despair and increased epidemiological vulnerability, thereby making people even less resistant to the next round of inevitable disease and violent assault. This deadly cycle continued, chopping entire complex societies down to, at most, small and imperiled remnants of what they once were.

Projections made by several scholars suggest that the pre-Columbian hemispheric population totals were in the neighborhood of 100 million, with 15 to 18 million indigenous people residing in the present-day United States and Canada (e.g., Borah 1962; Dobyns 1966, 1983; Ramenofsky 1987). As numbers in this range become more widely accepted, and as researchers calculating the causes of depopulation continue to take into account factors in addition to epidemic disease, the conclusion that will inevitably be reached is that between 95 and 98 percent of North and South America's 1492 population was wiped out by the post-Columbian holocaust.

Was It Genocide?

With one extreme exception (Kroeber 1939), the lowest scholarly estimates made in the past of

This nineteenth-century wood engraving portrays the massacre of American Indians by the backwoodsmen of the upper Ohio River Valley. LIBRARY OF CONGRESS

indigenous-population decline in the Americas—estimates that are only one-third to one-quarter of today's conservative conventional wisdom—produce a hemispheric population collapse of approximately 65 percent. That is identical to the proportion of European Jews who perished in the Holocaust: for every three who were alive before the killing began, one was left standing when it stopped. Using today's conventional estimates, the figures for the Americas are far worse: for every ten who were alive on the eve of the American holocaust, one was left standing when the killing was over. And this is a conservative estimate; more likely, the extermination ratio endured by the native peoples of the Americas was twice this number. Thus in terms of both total numbers killed and proportion of population destroyed, there is no comparison: no event of mass killing in human history—the Crusades, the Black Death, the African slave trade, the Irish famine, the Holocaust, the genocides in Cambodia or Rwanda—came close to destroying human life on a scale such as this.

Of course, there are important differences among these events—differences ranging from the speed and means of the killing to the perceived intent, if any, of the killers. But all comparisons of this sort mean nothing to the dead, and far too often such exercises are transparently intended to do little more than minimize and demean the historical suffering of some groups while perversely exalting the victimization of others (for more ex-

tensive discussion of this, see Vidal-Naquet 1992 and Stannard 1996). Moreover, even within the borders of specific killing zones universally acknowledged to be genocidal, the causes of death invariably differ, while hard data to prove perpetrator intent are not always easy to come by, even when genocide is circumstantially evident.

During the Holocaust, for example, more than eight hundred thousand Jews living outside the concentration and extermination camps died prematurely from what the Holocaust historian Raul Hilberg calls "ghettoization and general privation," while even more Jews (and others) died within the camps from overwork, starvation, and disease. At one point in 1942, the SS became so alarmed at the death rate from disease that it ordered better treatment of camp inmates in order to "lower mortality figures" (Hilberg 1985; Hackett 1995). Neither of these facts, however, minimizes the reality that the Holocaust was a heinous, purposeful, and massive extermination campaign and that those who died from starvation or disease or forced labor were as much victims of genocide as were those who died from shooting, gassing, or phenol injection. A similar recognition is due the victims of other genocides, including those that swept across the Americas for four centuries and more.

From one continent to the other, from one century to the next, the repeated cruelties of the killers—as recorded in their own words—defy explanation in terms other than those of psychopathology. Such common sixteenth-century Spanish military practices as testing the sharpness of blades on the bodies of infants, slicing off ears, noses, hands, and women's breasts, and slaughtering the inhabitants of entire villages for no apparent purpose other than pure sadism were matched repeatedly by British and American settlers and troops one, two, and three centuries later. One such venue was Sand Creek in Colorado—where, in 1864, U.S. soldiers, with no provocation and to no military purpose, massacred hundreds of Indian women and children and then mutilated their bodies: hacking off women's breasts and cutting out their genitals, then decorating their own hats and saddlebows with the excised flesh; scalping and gutting small children and gratuitously crushing their skulls. (President Theodore Roosevelt later said that the Sand Creek massacre was "as righteous and beneficial a deed as ever took place on the frontier.")

In the mid-sixteenth century devastating diseases swept through the coastal regions of Brazil, killing the majority of native people, and in the wake of the epidemics the Portuguese enslaved the survivors by the hundreds of thousands and worked them to death. Similarly, in New England a century later, following in the wake of debilitating smallpox epidemics that wiped out vast numbers of Indians while leaving the European colonists largely unaffected, the settlers waged all-out war against the Pequots, the Narraganset, the Wampanoag, and other native peoples—again slaughtering women and children and selling the few survivors into slavery in the Caribbean.

For every form of outrage perpetrated by the Spanish and the Portuguese in Mesoamerica and Central and South America, its equivalent—although the numbers were smaller—was carried out by the British and the Americans in North America. The exception was mass enslavement. Whereas the conquistadores to the south captured vast armies of native people and subjected them to forced labor (and imminent death) in gold and silver mines and on subtropical plantations, by the time labor was needed in North America in large supply—two centuries after Columbus landed on Hispaniola—Africa was providing all the slaves that were required. Indians, then, were merely an impediment to Euramerican land seizure and settlement. And that is why President Thomas Jefferson (like George Washington before him) repeatedly warned Indian tribes either to remove themselves "beyond the Mississippi" or "beyond our reach" or else to suffer "the hatchet" and military pursuit destined to end in "extermination."

The common practice of killing Indian women, and especially children, was therefore intentional and was justified in terms that were openly genocidal. An everyday saying on the frontier was that Indians were no better than vermin—lice, specifically—and thus they deserved to be exterminated. Since "nits make lice," it was essential to kill the nits—the children—if true eradication was to be effected. No less a light than President Andrew Jackson—who had a private collection of Indian scalps and who as a general during the Creek War of 1814 personally supervised the postmortem mutilation of hundreds of Creek Indians killed by his troops—urged the systematic mass murder of Indian women and children, comparing them to "wolves" and "whelps" in an 1837 letter to the Secretary of War, Joel Roberts Poinsett.

Not surprisingly, the governors of colonies, territories, and states also issued edicts of extermination. In the seventeenth century the governor of Virginia, Sir William Berkeley, called for the elimination of all the Indians within his reach—killing the men and selling the surviving women and children into distant slavery, thereby having the genocide pay for itself. By the end of the seventeenth century, 95 percent of the original indigenous population of Virginia had been wiped out. Two centuries later successive governors of California, Peter Burnett and John McDougal, officially urged settler "wars of extermination" against the new state's native people and received federal appropriations to carry out the task. Within just eight years of the first of these proclamations, the Indian population of California had plunged by 60 percent. By the end of the nineteenth century, at least 95 percent of the original indigenous population of California had been eliminated.

The Killing Continues

For every incident noted here—from fifteenth- and sixteenth-century Mexico and Brazil to seventeenth-, eighteenth-, and nineteenth-century Virginia, Massachusetts, and California—there were thousands of others of equal ferocity that occurred in virtually every corner of the sixteen million square miles of land that make up North and South America. Outside of oral histories of survivor descendants or buried bones and razed habitation sites awaiting archaeological discovery, the killing is largely undocumented. The magnitude of the slaughter is incomprehensible.

And the killing continues today. In Central and South America—from Chiapas to Guatemala to the Amazon—the techniques are the same as before: disease, exposure, starvation, raw violence. On the reservations and in the Indian ghettos to the north, the assault is more refined, more constrained by the rule of law: impoverishment, malnutrition, unemployment, and despair leading directly to staggering rates of alcoholism, suicide, and other causes of premature death. What Alexis de Tocqueville once said of the United States regarding its treating native people "with the most chaste affection for legal formalities" remains true today: "It is impossible to destroy men with more respect to the laws of humanity."

BIBLIOGRAPHY

Borah, Woodrow. "America as Model: The Demographic Impact of European Expansion upon the Non-Western World." In *Actas y Memorias del XXXV Congreso Internacional de Americanistas*. Vol. 3. Mexico City, 1964.
———. Introduction to *"Secret Judgments of God": Old World Disease in Colonial Spanish America*, edited by Noble David Cook and W. George Lovell. Norman: University of Oklahoma Press, 1992.
Denevan, William M., ed. *The Native Population of the Americas in 1492*. 2d ed. Madison: University of Wisconsin Press, 1992.
Dobyns, Henry F. "Estimating Aboriginal American Population: An Appraisal of Techniques with a New Hemispheric Estimate." *Current Anthropology* 7 (1966).
———. *Their Number Become Thinned: Native American Population Dynamics in Eastern North America*. Knoxville: University of Tennessee Press, 1983.
Hackett, David A., ed. *The Buchenwald Report*. Boulder, Colo.: Westview, 1995.
Hilberg, Raul. *The Destruction of the European Jews*. Vol. 3. Rev. ed. New York: Holmes and Meier, 1985.
Kroeber, Alfred L. *Cultural and Natural Areas of Native North America*. Berkeley: University of California Press, 1939.
Perttula, Timothy K. "European Contact and Its Effects on Aboriginal Caddoan Populations Between A.D. 1520 and A.D. 1680." In *Columbian Consequences*. Vol. 3, *The Spanish Borderlands in Pan-American Perspective*, edited by David Hurst Thomas. Washington, D.C.: Smithsonian Institution Press, 1991.
Ramenofsky, Ann F. *Vectors of Death: The Archaeology of European Contact*. Albuquerque: University of New Mexico Press, 1987.
Stannard, David E. *American Holocaust: Columbus and the Conquest of the New World*. New York: Oxford University Press, 1992.
———. "The Consequences of Contact: Toward an Interdisciplinary Theory of Native Responses to Biological and Cultural Invasion." In *Columbian Consequences*. Vol. 3,
The Spanish Borderlands in Pan-American Perspective, edited by David Hurst Thomas. Washington, D.C.: Smithsonian Institution Press, 1991.
———. "Disease and Infertility: A New Look at the Demographic Collapse of Native Populations in the Wake of Western Contact." *Journal of American Studies* 24 (1990).
———. "Uniqueness as Denial: The Politics of Genocide Scholarship." In *Is the Holocaust Unique? Perspectives on Comparative Genocide*, edited by Alan S. Rosenbaum. Boulder, Colo.: Westview, 1996.
Vidal-Naquet, Pierre. *Assassins of Memory: Essays on the Denial of the Holocaust*. New York: Columbia University Press, 1992.

DAVID E. STANNARD

See also **American Indian Wars; American Indians; Long Walk of the Navajo; Trail of Tears.**

AMERICAN INDIAN WARS

When European peoples invaded what is now the United States early in the seventeenth century, Native Americans responded with both interest and resistance. During the next three centuries, Indians and European Americans met, mingled, and fought a series of bloody conflicts. The Indian wars revealed much about the broader forces undermining Native American independence. Although defeated militarily, Indian peoples emerged with their cultures intact. Survivors of the wars and their descendants today play vital roles in American life.

Early Colonial Wars

The earliest English contact along the Atlantic coast followed a pattern that would become familiar over the next generations. After a period of generally friendly relations came a time of rising tension, then open conflict. Native peoples around the first permanent English settlement at Jamestown, Virginia, were united under a confederation led by Powhatan. This Pamunkey leader first aided the struggling settlers probably to keep open the flow of trade, but within a few years English demands and occasional raids soured relations and led to a period of mutual assaults. The marriage of a prominent Virginian, John Rolfe, to Powhatan's daughter, Pocahontas, cemented a peace that lasted until 1622. On Good Friday of that year Opechancanough, Powhatan's brother-in-law and successor, led a withering surprise assault on the outlying Virginia settlements. Out of 1,200 colonists, 347—more than a quarter—died before a retaliatory campaign forced an uneasy truce. The next twenty years saw intermittent hostilities as the English population grew prodigiously, encouraged by a dramatic rise in tobacco production. In 1644 Opechancanough launched a second, even bloodier war. This one ended in his coalition's defeat. By 1669 the Indian population in the Chesapeake Bay region had shrunk from about thirty thousand to two thousand.

A similar story unfolded in the first New England colonies. Puritan separatists in Plymouth (the Pilgrims of 1620) and the far larger emigrant population around Massachusetts Bay after 1629 at first were aided by local Narragansett and Wampanoag peoples. Some Indians soon felt pressure from the several thousand new arrivals, however. Puritan farmers were especially interested in the fertile Connecticut River watershed. Soon they were at odds with the Pequots over use of the land, and with the Narragansetts as allies the English virtually annihilated the Pequots at their main settlement on the Mystic River in 1637. Nearly forty years after the Pequot War the Narragansetts, Wampanoags, and Nipmucks battled with Puritan forces in perhaps the most vicious conflict of the colonial period. The Wampanoag leader Metacom, "King Philip" to the English, after several years of growing hostility led an attack on the Puritans, and an English counterassault brought the Narragansetts into King Philip's War. An Indian campaign had the English reeling until the Great Swamp Fight, a winter offensive against the main Narragansett settlement, turned the tide. In the end Metacom was killed, and his head was displayed on a pike in Plymouth for twenty-five years. The cost of the fourteen-month war was enormous. Twelve of ninety Puritan towns were destroyed, and hundreds of people were killed on both sides.

Behind these recurring conflicts were a few causes. With little resistance to the contact diseases brought by Europeans, Indian populations were devastated. The number of natives in New England shrank from about seventy thousand in 1600 to about nine thousand in 1675. The natives who survived were deeply resentful and suspicious when settlers, especially the Puritans, pressed them to adopt the English religion and way of life and to bend to English laws. Cultural friction and resentment from Indian political and spiritual leaders often led to open violence. The rapidly growing English population generated tremendous environmental pressures. Tobacco cultivation expanded voraciously into the interior; Puritan farmers disrupted hunting habitats as their herds of cattle and swine invaded Indian fields.

Friendlier exchanges also led to some difficulties. Religious conversions and cultural adaptations to English ways fractured Indian societies. King Philip's War was triggered when Wampanoags killed a Harvard-educated tribal member who was thought to have betrayed tribal interests. Powerful spiritual leaders, who felt threatened by missionary activities, were especially resentful. Indians bartered valuable furs for pots, blankets, awls, knives, seines, firearms, and other manufactures, but the same vigorous trade that drew the two cultures together, in time, set them at cross-purposes. English expansion, environmental changes, and the Indians' own overhunting depleted the animals they needed for exchange and left natives deeply in debt and increasingly reliant on trade, which in turn made them terribly vulnerable. The Yamassees of South Carolina owed English merchants more than a hundred thousand deerskins by 1715. The traders' escalating demands and abuses sparked a war in that year that devastated the Yamassees and opened the colony's backcountry to full occupation by white farmers.

European colonizers spawned other wars in what became the United States. Spanish rule in New Mexico, especially the rigorous efforts of Franciscan priests to convert the native populations, produced a simmering anger among the several Pueblo villages of the upper Rio Grande valley. In 1680 a Tewa holy man, Pope, organized the only successful Native American insurrection in North America. The united Pueblos killed twenty-one priests and more than four hundred settlers and soldiers and drove the remaining Spaniards southward to El Paso del Norte. Churches and other vestiges of the Spanish presence were destroyed in a determined effort at cultural regeneration. After divisions among the Pueblos reappeared, Spanish forces reconquered the area in 1692. The French generally cultivated friendly relations to facilitate their lucrative fur trade, but their presence too provoked wars among Indians who resisted. A growing French presence, disputes over trade goods, and mistreatment of Indian women brought a stiffening opposition among the Natchez, one of the most powerful peoples of the lower Mississippi Valley. In a coordinated attack in November 1729, the Natchez killed more than three hundred French and captured at least as many. A determined counteroffensive the next year smashed the elaborate Natchez villages, sites of impressive ceremonial mounds, and killed or dispersed most of the warriors. Nearly four hundred persons, including the leader who was considered to be a descendant of the sun, were sold into slavery in the West Indies. The Natchez War was one of the few instances of a purposeful annihilation of an entire tribe.

Wars of Indian and Colonial Independence

European colonizers eventually fought among themselves for control of the continent. Indian peoples took part in these wars not so much as allies but as independent peoples pursuing their own interests. In the four colonial wars between France and England in eastern North America (1689–1763), most tribes fought with the French, reasoning that the English colonies, with their far larger populations and expansive agrarian economies, posed a much greater threat. There were exceptions. The powerful Iroquois confederacy of western New York aligned with the English, as did some of the most populous group of the Southeast, the Cherokees. In these colonial wars some of the most vicious fighting took place along the outermost edge of English settlement, especially in New England, where various Algonquian tribes lashed out against encroaching frontier settlement.

The defeat of France therefore was a devastating blow to Indian interests. With England in control of Canada and of all country east of the Mississippi River, the tribes of the Ohio Valley and Great Lakes region were suddenly more vulnerable than ever to the pressures of white expansion. Native Americans responded with the most widespread resistance of the colonial era. This war usually has been called Pontiac's Rebellion, named for the Ottawa chief closely involved with its beginnings. One historian has called it the War of Indian Independence, emphasizing the effort by many tribes to find some autonomy in the face of the English threat—dramatically illustrated by the hostile and offensive policies of the administrator Jeffrey Amherst.

The war began when Pontiac led an unsuccessful attack on Fort Detroit in May 1763. The assault and the following five-month siege of the post inspired Potawatomis, Ojibwas, Hurons, Miamis, Shawnees, Delawares, and other tribes to strike at British positions throughout the region. Except for Fort Pitt, which was also besieged, every major post in the West fell to the Indians. Badly stung, the English launched retaliatory expeditions and worked to unsettle the native coalition. By the end of 1763 most of the posts were recaptured, the sieges of Detroit and Pitt broken, and Pontiac had

withdrawn to the Illinois country. To a degree, however, this war was an Indian victory. The British, worried by their own vulnerability and by the costs of the war, turned to policies much more in line with tribal interests, including an order (largely ignored) that lands beyond the Appalachians be closed indefinitely to white settlement.

Consequently, as divisions deepened between England and the American colonies, Indians leaned toward the British and away from the Americans, whose hungry interest in western lands now posed the greater threat. At the outbreak of the Revolutionary War in April 1775, English agents nonetheless urged tribal leaders to refrain from fighting. Except on the southern frontier, where Cherokees were repulsed and badly mauled in attacks against Tennessee settlements, Indians stayed mostly on the sidelines until England saw it could not force a quick victory. In 1777 Shawnees, Delawares, and other Ohio Valley tribes launched ferocious assaults on Boonesboro and other Kentucky towns. Mohawks and other Iroquois nations, led by the brilliant native commander Joseph Brant, killed or captured several hundred settlers in blistering campaigns against western New York and northwestern Pennsylvania. George Washington responded by sending General John Sullivan on a scorched-earth assault into the Mohawk homeland. By war's end Iroquois power was broken.

The surprise campaign by George Rogers Clark into the Illinois country diverted Indian pressure against Kentucky, but by 1782, as fighting wound down in the east, the Shawnees, Delawares, and allies were again slashing into the settlements. At the Battle of Blue Licks they ambushed a large force of Kentuckians and inflicted the worst defeat of the war. By then mutual hostility had reached an unprecedented pitch. After a fruitless pursuit into Ohio, Pennsylvanians turned on a village of Delaware Christian converts at Gnadenhutten and slaughtered ninety-six men, women, and children. A subsequent campaign into Ohio country turned into a rout when Indians divided the invading force, inflicted heavy casualties, and captured many more. The war ended in 1783 with no clear victors in the crucial Ohio Valley region. If anything, Native American forces were on the ascendant.

The next twelve years were some of the bloodiest in the history of Indian wars. The new government's bumbling efforts at finding an effective policy; its ill-conceived treaties with the Iroquois,

Shawnees, and other tribes north of the Ohio; and the mounting pressure of white settlers to move into that region led to misunderstandings and mutual anger. British traders meantime continued their lucrative business in the Great Lakes region, and although England had ceded that country to the new nation, its troops remained in its military posts there, and its agents strongly encouraged tribes to form a confederation and a Native American buffer state to resist American expansion. Under the new Constitution after 1789, President George Washington tried but failed to keep his constituents from invading the Ohio country to farm its fertile lands.

In 1790 President Washington ordered General Josiah Harmar into Ohio against Indians united under the Miami chief Little Turtle. When confederation warriors badly mauled this column, the president quickly sent a larger force under Arthur St. Clair. In western Ohio, on 7 November 1791, Little Turtle's men routed these poorly disciplined recruits. Nearly 650 whites died, more than in any battle during the Indian wars. By some measures it was the worst defeat in American military history. After fruitless negotiations for a new compromise with Native American leaders, Washington ordered a third expedition, this one under General Anthony Wayne, a skilled veteran of the Revolutionary War. Wayne raised and trained troops in Kentucky and marched them methodically into Ohio, building forts to hold his positions. Near the western end of Lake Erie in August 1794, Wayne's troops engaged the confederated warriors at the Battle of Fallen Timbers, so called because of trees scattered by a recent tornado. The sharp fighting ended when the Indians fled the field and retreated to the nearby British Fort Miami, whose commander refused to give them refuge. Demoralized, their confederation splintering, Little Turtle and other chiefs surrendered much of Ohio at the Treaty of Greenville a year later. In 1796 British troops finally abandoned their posts.

Tecumseh and the War of 1812

As a flood of white settlers began to wash down the Ohio Valley, tribes surrendered millions of acres in a patchwork of treaties between 1796 and 1809. The forces at work since the earliest colonial days—the aggressive push on the agrarian frontier, environmental transformation, decimation of animal populations, cultural tensions, and the dynamic of trade that left Indians increasingly vulnerable—undercut the Native American posi-

The Shawnee chief Tecumseh is slain at the Battle of the Thames in October 1813. A lithograph by Nathaniel Currier after J. McGee. HULTON GETTY/LIAISON AGENCY

tion. Out of this precarious situation arose a remarkable attempt to unify Indian peoples of eastern America to save what remained of their lands.

Its leaders were Tecumseh, a charismatic Shawnee warrior and orator, and his brother, Tenskwatawa, a spiritual leader and holy man also called the Prophet. After fighting for the Native American confederation at Fallen Timbers, Tecumseh became increasingly angry at the steady loss of Indian territory. After 1809 he traveled extensively among the tribes from the Gulf Coast to the Great Lakes to promote a unified Indian resistance to further cessions of lands. Tenskwatawa expressed his assurance of divine support for this pan-Indian movement. Thousands of supporters flocked to Prophetstown, a village the brothers founded on Tippecanoe Creek in central Indiana, making it by some estimates the largest town in the territory by 1811. Whites naturally feared a full-scale assault; meanwhile, Tecumseh, realizing the poor odds of military victory, was planning on a solid but peaceful tribal opposition against further white

Conquest and Cultural Exchange

The extraordinary diplomatic and religious crusade by Tecumseh and Tenskwatawa highlights another revealing aspect of the Indian wars. The Shawnee brothers were two of many Native American leaders who had come to understand the dangers inherent in the economic and cultural exchanges between Indians and whites. Native peoples were increasingly reliant on trade goods they could not produce for themselves, and the decline of animal populations persistently undermined their bargaining position. Cultural contact compromised the tribes' identities and fractured their unity. Within a generation or two after the first settlements, some Indian leaders were calling for a disengagement with Europeans and a revitalization of their own religions and traditional way of life. These movements of cultural renaissance often were closely linked to military confrontations, as in the Pueblo rebellion against the Spanish led by Popé. Although historians often have stressed the importance of the leadership of warriors, spiritual figures seem to have played at least as significant a role as inspirations of resistance. The great war associated with Pontiac was kindled by Neolin, a Delaware prophet, who urged Indians to unite in rejecting European culture.

Ironically, these new religions of cultural defiance often drew heavily on Christianity. Native "messiahs" found especially appealing the Christian concepts of resurrection and a violent "end time" when the righteous would triumph and the sinful would be banished. Holy men like Neolin, usually telling of visions and describing his communion with a divine power, assured followers that faith, rejection of white culture, and the practice of inspired ceremonies would bring otherworldly intervention, destruction of European-Americans, and the return of departed kinsmen and vanished game. These holy men often promised, as well, protection from the enemies' weapons. The language and rites reflected religious influences at their core from the very culture that Native American holy men so bitterly condemned. Tenskwatawa taught a ritual closely resembling prayer with a rosary, and his name, translated as "the Open Door," seems to have been taken from Christian scripture. These revivalist movements reveal the cultural give-and-take of the era as well as the tensions behind the Indian wars and the natives' powerful sense of inspiration for armed resistance.

expansion. This plan was undone in November 1811, however, when Tenskwatawa launched an attack on a militia force headed to Prophetstown led by the future U.S. president William Henry Harrison while Tecumseh was on a diplomatic mission to the south. The militia routed the Indians, who were demoralized when the holy man's prayers did not protect them as promised, and burned Prophetstown.

With the fighting begun prematurely and Tenskwatawa in disgrace, Tecumseh chose to ally his followers with English forces who went to war against the United States the following year. During the War of 1812, Indians aided the British in several victories in the Great Lakes region, including the American surrender of Detroit. To the south, Tecumseh's most enthusiastic supporters, the Red Sticks faction of the Creeks, overran Fort Mims in northern Alabama and killed between 250 and 350 settlers who had taken refuge there. The war's latter stage, however, was disastrous for Native Americans. Tecumseh was killed in October 1813 at the Battle of the Thames while protecting British troops withdrawing into Canada, and on 27 March 1814 Andrew Jackson's combined force of white, Cherokee, and Chickasaw troops cornered Red Stick warriors in their village of Tohopeka on the Horseshoe Bend of the Tallapoosa River. Nearly eight hundred persons died. This campaign broke the power of the Creeks, the most formidable Indian force of the Southeast. In treaties after the war more than forty million acres of Indian land were surrendered.

Last Stand in the East

Native American military power nonetheless was crippled during the War of 1812, and later conflicts did not seriously challenge white control east of the Mississippi. As demands to open Indian lands to white settlement increased, federal and state governments insisted that most tribes emigrate west of the Mississippi. About seventy thousand members of more than a score of tribes were removed with great suffering but generally without resistance along several routes known collectively as the Trail of Tears. The so-called Creek Rebellion of 1836 was used as a pretext for troops to seize those refusing to emigrate. In 1838, following a nonviolent legal campaign by Cherokee leaders, troops began the roundup, confinement, and forced march of sixteen thousand Cherokees—the most infamous episode of the Trail of Tears.

The great exception to this pattern, one of the continent's longest Indian wars, occurred close to one of the earliest points of European contact. The Seminoles, close relatives of the Creeks, had retreated from northern Florida down the peninsula after a punitive expedition by Andrew Jackson in 1818. As pressure grew to open Florida to cotton planters, some Seminoles agreed in 1835 to remove themselves and settle in Indian Territory, but a large faction led by Osceola refused. Their decimation of an army column in 1835 began a lengthy conflict in which Indians raided and harassed military posts and settlements while frustrated troops chased elusive warriors through swamps and woodlands, ideal terrain for guerrilla warfare. Osceola, captured under a flag of truce, died in prison, but the Seminoles continued to fight under Bowlegs and Wildcat until 1842, when the federal government allowed a remnant of the tribe to remain in the Everglades of southern Florida. It was one of the costliest wars in American history. Three thousand Seminoles were forced from their homes at the cost of between $40 million and $60 million, and one soldier was lost for every two Seminoles removed.

Tribes of the Ohio Valley and Great Lakes meanwhile were also being moved across the Mississippi, often by treaty and sometimes by force, and here, too, the pressure at times flashed into violence. In 1831 the Sac and Fox of western Illinois

were forced by federal troops to migrate into Iowa. The following spring a leader of one of their bands, Black Hawk, led his people back to their Illinois villages, probably to plant corn. White farmers in Illinois and others who had been drawn to the newly dug lead mines there feared an attack. Black Hawk's War began with several inconclusive skirmishes between Indians and militia. Then regular army units arrived and Black Hawk's band fled into Wisconsin, where soldiers caught up with them along the Bad Axe River. In the battle that followed more than three hundred hungry and exhausted Sac and Fox were killed, and Black Hawk was captured. Thirty years later an even bloodier war erupted when the eastern Sioux, or Dakotas, increasingly desperate because of inadequate government support and encroachments on their reservation, lashed out against settlers around New Ulm, Minnesota. Warriors led by Little Crow killed between four hundred and eight hundred men, women, and children before a counterassault by troops reversed the tide, killing several hundred Dakotas. Little Crow was shot to death by a farm boy. Thirty-eight Dakota leaders were hanged the day after Christmas in 1862, many more were imprisoned, and most eastern Sioux were removed to Iowa and South Dakota. In this, the last episode of Indian removal from east of the Mississippi, some eastern Sioux joined their far western relatives, the Lakotas, living on the Great Plains. As the last fighting flickered out east of the river, these exiled warriors would join the resistance that had already begun to the west.

Civil War and the Northern Plains

Some Native Americans participated directly in the Civil War. The so-called civilized tribes recently removed from the Southeast, especially the Cherokees and Creeks, fought generally with the Confederacy, although a minority sent soldiers to fight with the Union. Indians played important roles in some battles west of the Mississippi, notably Pea Ridge in northern Arkansas, and some resisted the victors until the end. Stand Watie, a Creek, was the last Confederate general to surrender. Elsewhere the Civil War unsettled relations even more than usual and helped set in motion the final stage of Indian wars between 1860 and 1890.

The most famous Indian wars, those on the Great Plains, arose from causes familiar from almost three centuries of conflict to the east. An expanding white population, now hundreds of times that of Native Americans, pressed in on Indian lands, consumed irreplaceable resources, and undermined the tribes' cultural integrity. More sedentary peoples, such as the Pawnees and others in the Missouri River drainage, offered little military resistance. Much stiffer opposition came from the western Sioux (Lakotas), Cheyennes, Arapahoes, Kiowas, Comanches, and other groups. Superb horsemen who commanded large herds, these peoples used their considerable military skills to defend a nomadic and pastoral way of life that was under siege by the middle of the nineteenth century.

Tensions were greatest where Indians and whites came in closest contact—on the overland trails along the Platte and Arkansas Rivers. The valleys were essential to the survival of Indians and their horses. The quarter million white emigrants who took these routes to the Pacific coast between 1840 and 1865 wore away steadily at these vital habitats. The first serious clash occurred in 1854 when a few hundred Sioux killed Lieutenant John Grattan and twenty-nine soldiers who rashly attacked their camp. The next year General William Harney's punitive assault on another village killed eighty-five Sioux. The Indians' anxiety deepened when the discovery of gold in Colorado triggered a rush of more than a hundred thousand persons across the plains on the eve of the Civil War. Soon Denver and other towns sprang up along the base of the Rocky Mountains in some of the prime territory of the nomads, while merchants, ranchers, and farmers began to settle the plains along the trails.

With the Indians' situation deteriorating and Colorado's white population suspecting Confederate plotting among the tribes, relations grew increasingly hostile, erupting into mutual raiding in the summer of 1864. An uneasy peace in autumn was shattered when militia from Denver led by Colonel John Chivington attacked a peaceful Cheyenne village on Sand Creek in southeast Colorado. About 180 Indians, mostly women and children, died in a butchery later condemned by both Congress and the army. In the months after the Sand Creek massacre Cheyennes, Arapahoes, and Sioux struck furiously at outposts along the Platte, but these assaults could not stop the tide of settlement in Colorado and western Kansas. Intermittent fighting between troops and the more militant bands of Indians continued for another four years, punctuated by an attack by the Seventh U.S. Cavalry under the leadership of George Custer on an-

other peaceful Cheyenne village on the Washita River in western Indian Territory. At the Battle of Summit Springs in July 1869, the most formidable band of warriors, the Cheyenne Dog Soldiers, were crushed by a column led by Major Eugene Carr. With that, fighting on the central plains was over.

On the rich grasslands north of the Platte, however, the Sioux and Cheyennes lived unchallenged until new gold strikes in Montana in 1863 prompted white gold seekers to blaze the Bozeman Trail through some of the best of their territory. Led by Red Cloud, the brilliant Sioux strategist, war parties harassed travelers, and when troops were stationed along the trail, a force of Sioux, Cheyennes, and Arapahoes annihilated eighty cavalrymen when their young commander, Captain William Fetterman, was lured into an ambush near the newly constructed Fort Phil Kearney. More forts were built and skirmishes fought, but once alternative routes were found to the gold fields, the army withdrew, and in 1868 the Bozeman Trail was abandoned. Like the Pueblo revolt of 1680, Red Cloud's War was the only one Indians could call a victory.

This success was short-lived. In 1872, when eastern chemists learned to process bison hide into leather for industrial uses, hundreds of white hide hunters began slaughtering millions of the animals that plains nomads required for both subsistence and trade. Bison populations, in steep decline for thirty years before this great hunting orgy, plummeted. By 1874 the huge herd on the central plains was gone, and commercial hunters turned north and south in search of more. Then gold was found in South Dakota's Black Hills in 1875. This country, granted to the Sioux and Northern Cheyennes by treaty in 1868, was sacred ground to both tribes; but now the government was unable to stem the flood of prospectors chasing dreams of instant wealth. As the predictable incidents accumulated, the military in November 1875 ordered all Indians in the region onto reservations by the end of January. Few answered the call, and the stage was set for the Great Sioux War, the culminating confrontation of the northern plains, and the most famous battle of the western Indian wars.

In the late spring of 1876 Sioux and Northern Cheyennes came together on the Montana plains in probably the largest concentration of that era. Three large commands of white troops converged on this area in June, hoping to trap the nomads and force them onto reservations. General George Crook held back his column after a sharp fight

The Battle of the Rosebud, 25 June 1876. Sioux warriors, led by Crazy Horse, charge General George Crook's troops on the Rosebud River in Montana. HULTON GETTY/ LIAISON AGENCY

with warriors led by Crazy Horse along the Rosebud River. A second command approaching from the east sent George Custer and twelve companies to locate the Indians. On 25 June they found a village on the Little Big Horn River, and although Custer's Crow scouts warned him it was far too large to challenge, Custer divided his forces and ordered an attack on a camp with at least two thousand Sioux and Cheyenne warriors. Three companies attempting a frontal assault were repulsed with heavy casualties. Custer, with five companies, had planned a coordinated attack on the opposite end of the village, but he was driven back, his troops were divided, and all were killed—more than two hundred soldiers. Indian losses were low, perhaps as few as twenty-five.

The defeat and death of the famous and flamboyant George Custer made him a national martyr—and his legend overshadowed the successful army campaign that followed. The great concentration of Sioux and Cheyennes had dispersed; over the winter and into the spring the army harassed the nomadic bands until some, led by Sitting Bull, fled into Canada and others, including Crazy Horse, surrendered and were put onto reservations. By the summer of 1877 resistance on the northern plains had ceased and the

largest Native American military force on the plains had been contained or exiled.

The Southern Plains and Southwest

Meanwhile a similar story had unfolded on the southern plains. The Comanches, the most populous tribe and most formidable Native American force, were superb mounted warriors. With their Kiowa allies they had preyed for generations on the Pueblo Indians and Hispanic settlements in the Southwest and more recently on the ranches and farms of the Texas frontier. By the 1850s, however, they were feeling the same effects of westward expansion that were driving other plains tribes to the edge of disaster. The herds of bison were shrinking and pioneer emigrants were occupying more and more of the pasturage and winter shelters essential for the nomads and their horses. Their unease turned to rage when white buffalo hunters shifted their operations onto the south plains below the Arkansas and Canadian Rivers in 1874. In June of that year, inspired by the mixed-blood leader Quanah Parker and Isa-tai (Wolf Dung), a holy man promising protection from enemy bullets, warriors fell on the hunting outpost of Adobe Walls in the Texas panhandle. The failed attack precipitated the Red River, or Buffalo, War.

The Piegan Massacre

One of the least known incidents in the Indian wars—but one of the most appalling and costly in human life—occurred in far northern Montana in 1870. Some among the Piegan branch of the Blackfeet had been raiding white settlers who were pressing into the region around the Marias River. Pressured to bring the raids to a halt, Lieutenant General Phil Sheridan ordered a winter assault to chastise the hostile Piegans. When Major Eugene M. Baker located a large band camped in the brutal cold along the Marias River, he ordered an immediate attack. At the first shots the camp's chief, Heavy Runner, ran from his lodge waving a document from the Indian Bureau testifying to his band's friendship, but he was shot down. The camp was first raked by vicious rifle fire, then overrun with a direct assault. By official count 173 persons were left dead, 53 of them women and children. Only one of Baker's soldiers was killed. Baker soon discovered, as the bureau document attested, that Heavy Runner's band had taken no part in the raiding. Ten miles upstream was the Piegan camp Baker had been seeking, with the warriors who had attacked white settlements. By the time Baker realized his error and sent his men on a second attack, that band had escaped across the nearby border into Canada.

Army strategists took an approach that they soon would try again on the northern plains against the Sioux. They first declared that all Indians not reporting to reservations in Indian Territory were assumed to be hostile; then six columns were sent on converging routes into the heartland of resistance, the Texas panhandle. By keeping the nomads on the move and denying them the chance to hunt, the army eventually would force recalcitrant bands to terms. Indians in camps ran the risk of full attack. In late September 1874 Colonel Ranald Mackenzie found a large encampment on the floor of Palo Duro Canyon, a traditional refuge. After the cavalry's charge and a spirited fight, the Comanches and Kiowas were forced to abandon their village and, more important, most of their horses. Mackenzie's men burned the lodges and shot more than a thousand of the Indians' mounts, leaving the fleeing warriors without the means either to fight or hunt. Pursuit and harassment continued through the winter and spring until the last holdouts under Quanah Parker surrendered. With many Comanche and Kiowa leaders imprisoned in Florida, resistance on the southern plains was at an end.

Conflict persisted later in the southwestern deserts than anywhere else in the far West, largely because terrain and isolation worked to the advantage of mobile and well-adapted warriors. The causes of conflict, however, were basically the same as those elsewhere. The same geography that gave them sanctuary required that native peoples either move and hunt freely and widely or occupy sites that could support some irrigated agriculture, or both. Ranching on the frontier and the discovery of gold and silver at Prescott, Tombstone, and other spots disrupted the movement of the natives and reduced the land available to them for farming. This environmental and economic stress, added to the existing friction between the two cultures, once more led to mutual antagonism—and eventually to war.

The Southwest had long been one of the most conflicted parts of the continent. Long before the Spanish arrival, Navajos and Utes had preyed on village peoples, and the Apaches, driven from the plains by the Comanches, had more recently come to raid settlements in New Mexico and Arizona and far into Mexico. Shortly after taking the region from Mexico in 1846, the United States ruthlessly suppressed an uprising of Pueblo Indians in Taos. Thereafter the sedentary peoples remained mostly at peace, but the army spent nearly forty years trying to control the region's horseborne tribes. Whereas in other regions warfare consisted only of large campaigns and pitched battles, here forays against small bands of these elusive nomadic warriors were more successful.

More than ten campaigns between 1846 and 1861 failed to diminish significantly the power of the raiding native peoples. As on the plains and in Minnesota, however, expanded military power during the Civil War was used to break or curtail Native American strength. One of the most formidable Apache groups, the Mescaleros, were forced onto a reservation. In northern Arizona during 1863–1864, a more ambitious campaign, led by the famous mountain man and scout Christopher "Kit" Carson, sought out the scattered Navajo bands, destroyed their supplies and seized their sheep, and kept them on the run. This effort culminated when Carson's command fell on the Navajo stronghold at Canyon de Chelly, taking its stores of corn and burning its peach orchards. Hungry and hounded, most Navajos finally surrendered. On the infamous Long March, a southwestern version of the Trail of Tears, about eight thousand Indians walked more than four hundred miles to a desolate internment at Bosque Redondo in eastern New Mexico.

Apaches, moving easily back and forth across the Mexican border and finding refuge in rugged desert mountains, proved a more difficult quarry. Cochise, a Chiricahua Apache who had been friendly to the United States until he was mistreated in 1861, led raids throughout southern Arizona for the next decade. After fruitless attempts to stop him, the government offered peace in 1872 in exchange for a large reservation close to the border, which the government took back in 1876 following Cochise's death. The most persistent opposition for the next generation came from another Chiricahua leader, Goyakla (translated as He Who Yawns), better known to whites as Geronimo. He had struck viciously at ranches and settlements in Mexico ever since soldiers there killed his family

in 1858, and in the United States he alternated between periods of uneasy accord and ferocious hit-and-run campaigns in which he inflicted heavy losses in life and property in the face of extraordinary efforts to capture him. In 1877 he was confined to the San Carlos reservation, but he broke out after four years and again raided on both sides of the border. He returned to the reservation in 1884 and the next year left for another year of raiding before surrendering for good to General Nelson Miles in 1886. After five years of imprisonment in Florida, he was sent to Fort Sill in Oklahoma.

Final Confrontations

During this long-running Apache resistance other western tribes engaged government troops in briefer, but dramatic conflicts. A small faction of Modocs refused to return to an Oregon reservation in 1872 and retired to the rough terrain of northern California lava beds after they killed several soldiers who were trying to force them. After evading troops for months, their leader, Kintpuash, also known as Captain Jack, pressed by militant

---

Conflicts in the Pacific Northwest

The well-known wars with the Modocs in 1872 and with the Nez Percé five years later were the culmination of many conflicts that plagued the Pacific Northwest in the mid-nineteenth century. In 1847 Cayuse Indians killed the Presbyterian missionaries Marcus and Narcissa Whitman and eleven others after half their number died from measles carried in by white emigrants passing through their Oregon mission. In the two-year conflict that followed, the Cayuses were hounded nearly to starvation. Invasion of Indian lands by gold seekers and farmers led to rising tension and finally warfare in 1856 with the Yakimas and bands in the Rogue River region of southern Oregon. Two years later fighting broke out again between the army and a coalition of several tribes of the Columbia River basin. After an initial stunning victory by the Indians in this so-called Yakima War, a large and well-armed force of army regulars made a systematic and destructive march through the country, hanging native leaders, killing hundreds of horses, and dispersing all opposition.

One of the region's most tragic moments came from a continuing source of strife—travel on the overland trails. Shoshonis of southern Idaho chafed at the tens of thousands of emigrants and their teams who crossed their lands, overgrazing the grassbeds and cutting the timber. Overlanders sometimes shot at Indians, who sometimes attacked wagons and often stole stock. In January 1863 a command of California volunteers under Colonel Patrick Conner, who was ordered to subdue the Shoshonis, attacked a camp on the Bear River. In one of the bloodiest episodes of the western Indian wars, between two and four hundred Indians were killed, many of them women and children. Only twenty-three soldiers died.

Modocs, murdered General Edward Canby during truce negotiations. A predictably furious response drove the Modocs from their sanctuary, and the militants surrendered finally and turned Captain Jack over to the authorities, who hanged him. A similar scenario unfolded in the fall of 1879 in western Colorado. Ute warriors killed their reservation agent, Nathan Meeker, who had insisted they abandon their hunting way of life. They then held off an army column for a week before retreating. The next year they were removed to Utah.

The same years witnessed one of the most dramatic episodes of the Indian wars. Its origin once again was the government's insistence that native peoples, in this case the Nez Percé of northeast Oregon, surrender their hunting lands and their homelands in exchange for a reservation in May 1877. Troops were sent in when some angry young men killed a few settlers. After warriors badly mauled the army column, killing more than thirty, the Nez Percé embarked on a remarkably audacious attempt to escape to the same part of southern Canada to which the Lakota Sitting Bull had recently fled. They almost made it. During the summer they crossed the Rocky Mountains and followed a circuitous route of more than a thousand miles, including a dash through the newly created park at Yellowstone. With a large military force in pursuit, the Nez Percé fought several skirmishes and two battles, the fiercest in the Big Hole valley of Montana on 9 and 10 August. The extraordinary running fight ended on 5 October at the Bear Paw Mountains, just below the Canadian border, where the exhausted survivors, led by Chief Joseph, surrendered. This "peace chief" had overseen defense of the camps but had taken no part in the fighting; he became something of a folk hero among white people, a symbol of the Native Americans' final capitulation.

Although these campaigns and the Apache raids were the last significant military resistance, a final tragic event is usually regarded as the last episode of the Indian wars. A messianic religious movement arose in the Great Basin in 1889. Its prophet, Wovoka, was a Paiute who told of a divine message: If native peoples would love one another and keep their traditions while following new rituals, including a Ghost Dance, the dead would return, whites would disappear, and a golden age would begin. Wovoka's message spread rapidly to many tribes, among them the Sioux, who shifted from a pacifist stance to a more aggressive one. White authorities, worried about

an uprising, were especially nervous because Sitting Bull had returned from Canada in 1881. Sitting Bull was killed during a clash between his followers and Indian police sent to arrest him. Several bands fled the reservation in fear of retaliation. When soldiers caught a band of Miniconjou Sioux along Wounded Knee Creek, firing began during the disarming—there has been argument ever since as to who fired first—and about 150 Sioux died. Twenty-five troopers were killed, most of them apparently by crossfire from their fellow soldiers. The Wounded Knee massacre, as so often during the previous three centuries the result of misunderstanding and Native Americans' striving for cultural independence, was the last violent engagement of the century.

Casualties in the Indian wars, although difficult to calculate, were quite low compared with those in other conflicts. One historian has estimated that about seven thousand whites and four thousand Indians were killed between 1789 and 1898. Between 1866 and 1891 the army recorded an almost equal number of fights and deaths—932 soldiers killed in 930 clashes with Indians. In shaping the nation and the relations of its peoples, however, the impact of the Indian wars was incalculable.

BIBLIOGRAPHY

Andrist, Ralph K. *The Long Death: The Last Days of the Plains Indians*. New York: Macmillan, 1964.

Debo, Angie. *Geronimo: The Man, His Time, His Place*. Norman: University of Oklahoma Press, 1976.

Dowd, Gregory Evans. *A Spirited Resistance: The North American Indian Struggle for Unity, 1745–1815*. Baltimore: Johns Hopkins University Press, 1992.

Edmunds, R. David. *The Shawnee Prophet*. Lincoln: University of Nebraska Press, 1983.

———. *Tecumseh and the Quest for Indian Leadership*. Boston: Little, Brown, 1984.

Ehle, John. *Trail of Tears: The Rise and Fall of the Cherokee Nation*. New York: Anchor, 1988.

Hampton, Bruce. *Children of Grace: The Nez Percé War of 1877*. New York: Henry Holt, 1994.

Jennings, Francis. *Empire of Fortune: Crowns, Colonies, and Tribes in the Seven Years War in America*. New York: Norton, 1988.

———. *The Invasion of America: Indians, Colonialism, and the Cant of Conquest*. Chapel Hill: University of North Carolina Press, 1975.

Josephy, Alvin. *The Indian Heritage of America*. New York: Knopf, 1968.

———. *The Nez Percé Indians and the Opening of the Northwest*. New Haven, Conn.: Yale University Press, 1965.

———. *The Patriot Chiefs: A Chronicle of American Indian Leadership*. New York: Viking, 1961.

Leach, Douglas. *Flintlock and Tomahawk: New England in King Philip's War.* New York: Macmillan, 1958.

Lepore, Jill. *The Name of the War: King Philip's War and the Origins of American Identity.* New York: Knopf, 1998.

Prucha, Francis Paul. *The Great Father: The United States Government and the American Indians.* Lincoln: University of Nebraska Press, 1984.

Steele, Ian. *Warpaths: Invasions of North America.* New York: Oxford University Press, 1994.

Stewart, Edgar Irving. *Custer's Luck.* Norman: University of Oklahoma Press, 1955.

Sugden, John. *Tecumseh.* New York: Henry Holt, 1997.

Thornton, Russell. *American Indian Holocaust and Survival: Population History Since 1492.* Norman: University of Oklahoma Press, 1987.

Utley, Robert M. *The Indian Frontier of the American West, 1846–1890.* Albuquerque: University of New Mexico Press, 1984.

———. *The Lance and the Shield: The Life and Times of Sitting Bull.* New York: Henry Holt, 1993.

———. *The Last Days of the Sioux Nation.* New Haven, Conn.: Yale University Press, 1963.

Vaughan, Alden T. *The New England Frontier: Puritans and Indians, 1620–1675.* Boston: Little, Brown, 1965.

White, Richard. *The Middle Ground: Indians, Empires, and Republics in the Great Lakes Region, 1650–1815.* New York: Cambridge University Press, 1991.

ELLIOTT WEST

See also **American Indian Holocaust; American Indian Movement; American Indians; Custer, George Armstrong; Sitting Bull; Trail of Tears; Wovoka; Wounded Knee, 1890.**

AMERICAN REVOLUTION

A subentry on **Military Campaigns** *follows the Overview.*

OVERVIEW

By comparison with its French counterpart, the American Revolution might seem an unviolent affair. No castles were stormed, no guillotines were set up, no mass executions took place. Yet among major American military conflicts, the War of Independence (1775–1783) stands second only to the Civil War in its ratio of casualties to population. The whole period of revolution is usually taken to stretch from 1763, the year of the first inklings of trouble between Great Britain and the thirteen colonies, to ratification of the Constitution in 1788. That quarter century saw outbreak after outbreak of both organized and unorganized violence.

White colonials entered the crisis with a deeply rooted tradition of legitimate popular uprisings. In part, these actions expressed the lower-class, economic self-defense that E. P. Thompson calls "the moral economy" of the eighteenth-century English crowd. As Thompson describes it, people faced with shortage might distribute what they needed from a "hoarder's" stores, paying what they regarded as a fair price. The European tradition of *charivari*, which the English called "rough music" or "riding skimmington," was closely related, but it tended to focus on violators of community norms rather than challenges to material welfare. Charivari normally aimed at shaming the offender. A cuckold or a wife beater or an adulterous couple might find a crowd in disguise serenading them with pots and pans for accompaniment. Such characteristically American forms as tarring and feathering (whose first known revolutionary instance happened in Salem, Massachusetts, on 7 September 1768) and riding the rail stem directly from the version practiced in Europe.

Pauline Maier has demonstrated that American uprisings also drew upon the undeveloped American political condition, in which crowd action received offical sanction, provided that a fire chief, sheriff, or militia officer led it. (A volunteer fire company, posse, or militia unit amounted to a crowd with official leadership and legal authority.) Popular celebrations contributed as well, particularly Pope's Day (5 November). That day's anti-Catholic street parades and impromptu brawls amounted to a Protestant-inflected carnival that kept alive popular memories of seventeenth-century English upheavals and that temporarily inverted social relations.

All these fused in the crucible of the northern American port cities between the Stamp Act Crisis (1765–1766) and the Boston Tea Party (1773). The initial event, Boston's uprising of 14 August 1765, drew directly both on the Pope's Day pageantry of effigies and parades and on the generalized understanding that (in the words of Massachusetts Lieutenant Governor Thomas Hutchinson) "mobs, a sort of them at least, are constitutional." But it also introduced a new element: politically conscious leadership from the Sons of Liberty, who sought to nullify Britain's attempt to tax the colonies rather than merely protest against it. The day of 14 August saw a controlled but powerful assault on the property of Massachusetts' stamp distributor: he got the message and resigned. All of the other stamp distributors save Georgia's did as well, rendering the act unenforceable.

Twelve days later, another crowd sacked the elegant Boston home of Lieutenant Governor

In New York City, Americans tear down a statue of King George III during the War of Independence. An 1857 painting by William Walcutt. CORBIS/BETTMANN

Hutchinson, who privately opposed the act. One explanation for this attack is class resentment against Hutchinson's ostentatious display of wealth in a town suffering economic depression. Another is that the leaders simply lost control. That tension among imperial political issues, together with domestic economic and cultural conflicts, continued through the decade of protest and upheaval that followed. In some events, such as New Yorkers' destruction of a theater on 5 May 1766, the domestic issues of consumption and poverty were at the fore. In others, such as the Boston Tea Party, the prime issue was imperial relations. But all urban violence of the revolutionary era drew upon this mix.

In the countryside the fundamental issue was land. Unlike modern America, the boundaries that defined real estate and established its ownership were unclear in the late eighteenth century. Where settler-owned land ended and Native American land began, the lines between one settler's political unit and another's, and the limits of a great landlord's holdings were all sources of conflict and open to negotiation. The terms of Indian-white conflict were laid out starkly by the Cherokee Old Tassel, who told Carolinians in 1776 that it was "our land we are talking about," and by the South Carolina leader William Henry Drayton, who in the same year rallied backcountry patriots with the

promise that they would enslave defeated Cherokees and seize their tribal lands. The struggle over land neither began nor ended during the Revolution, but in the southern backcountry and in the Great Lakes region whites and Indians battled ferociously. In the long run, the dispossesion of Indians east of the Mississippi River may have been the Revolution's most fundamental social change. It took place under conditions of great violence, including both guerrilla conflict between settlers and Indians and carefully planned campaigns. In 1779 the New York State legislature decreed the "sovereignty" of New Yorkers "in respect of all property"—including the property of Indians—within the state's boundaries. That same year Congress and New York State's government jointly sponsored a major armed invasion of Iroquois Confederacy country. White troops destroyed towns, fields, and crops in huge quantities. At the end of the Revolutionary War the Iroquois had the choice of either accepting submission and dispossession or going into exile, as the rich land that had been theirs was transformed into the Empire State. What happened in New York prefigured the conflicts that would follow elsewhere, as "Indian Country" became the "West."

Among whites, ill-drawn political boundaries and unclear land titles led both landlords and would-be freeholders to claim the same land, each side convinced that right and law were with them. As with the Indian-white conflict, the issue both preceded the revolutionary era and extended beyond it. Mid-eighteenth-century land rioting in New Jersey and the Hudson Valley, the 1770s North Carolina Regulator movement, much wartime rural loyalism, and continuing postwar conflicts in eastern New York State and in Maine all sprang from the question of who rightfully held the land and on what terms. Land rioters dispossessed tenants, destroyed landlords' property, frustrated surveying parties, disrupted court sessions, opened courts of their own, and rescued condemned prisoners. New Jersey insurgents built a "gaol back in the woods" as early as 1749. In 1761 rioters in the mountain country along the Massachusetts–New York line captured the sheriff of Albany when he was sent to arrest them and carted him off to jail in Springfield. The Green Mountain Boys whipped a New York justice of the peace fiercely when he defied their orders and tried to open his court in 1774.

Landords and political authorities took these matters most seriously, calling on militiamen, on British redcoats, and, later, on state and federal troops to put down the insurrections. Observing New York leaders responding to the Hudson Valley tenant rising of 1766, one British officer quipped that they were of the opinion that nobody was entitled to riot except themselves. The same province's "Bloody Act" of 1774 condemned the leaders of the Green Mountain movement by name, allowing anybody to kill them on sight, and imposed the death penalty for actions committed in the region that were considered minor elsewhere. Almost always, the authorities, not the rioters, won the struggle. The Green Mountain Boys were alone among backcountry rioters in getting what they wanted, breaking free of New York in 1777 and maintaining their independence in a two-sided struggle against both New York and the British. Their state of Vermont did not win recognition and admission to the Union until 1791.

In town and in country alike, there were people who chose the British side. Prior to the independence crisis of 1774–1776, such people might be socially ostracized, tarred and feathered, or have their property damaged, but outright violence against them was sporadic and unorganized. The war changed matters by turning political opposition into armed enmity. Overall, committed loyalists comprised about one-fifth of the white population. In a few places, such as New York's Long Island, a loyalist majority actively resisted the revolutionary movement. In most places they bided their time until the course of the war brought British armed forces near. Loyalists fought when they could, particularly in western New York and, after the British adopted a southern strategy in 1779, in the Georgia and Carolina backcountry. Native Americans calculating their own best interests and slaves seeking freedom joined in on both sides. Wherever the conflict pitted Americans of any sort against other Americans, it was fierce, with no quarter likely to be given.

The greatest violence in early America was the institution of slavery, which rested entirely upon the willingness of enslavers to maim or kill the people they enslaved. The British writer Samuel Johnson caught the irony perfectly in 1776: "How is it that we hear the loudest *yelps* for liberty among the drivers of Negroes?" The previous year Virginia's last royal governor, Lord Dunmore, had addressed the issue with the promise of action, offering freedom to slaves belonging to "rebels" who rallied to the British cause. By 1775, however, popular upheaval had driven Dunmore from his governor's palace in Williamsburg to the security of a British warship in Chesapeake Bay. Slaves pressed Dunmore to make good on the offer, but given the circumstances, few could get to his ship. Approximately eight hundred did so, and the soldiers of Dunmore's "Ethiopian Regiment" bore the slogan "Liberty to Slaves" upon their breastplates. Through such episodes did the Revolution produce the partial destruction of slavery—not just by the action of the British but also because some white Americans did find themselves conscience-ridden and some slaves found a moment in which they could shake if not destroy their enslavement. The frightened response of such Virginia leaders as Patrick Henry and Dunmore's offer to the slaves, calling for redoubled patrols for the sake of the "public safety," illustrate both the seriousness and the complexities of the issue. Many white revolutionaries came to comprehend the contradiction and freed their slaves. Others agonized while actually doing little or nothing. But the war's end saw the spectacle of victorious Americans boarding British ships in order to forcibly prevent the departure of slaves who had found their own freedom among the Revolution's enemies.

The war's aftermath also saw significant violence against former loyalists, especially in New York, whose southern district had been under British occupation since 1776. One New York law

A nineteenth-century line engraving of the Shays's Rebellion, 1786. THE GRANGER COLLECTION

declared supporters of the British to be outside "the protection of the laws of this state," which seemed to lay them open to whatever the revolutionary side wanted to do. Loyalists suffered exile, confiscation of their property, and mob action, but these incidents rapidly dwindled, perhaps because of the unquestionable quality of the Revolution's triumph and perhaps because some sixty thousand chose exile rather than submission. More important from the point of view of the Revolution's outcome is its final instance of the social-political violence with which it had begun—Shays's Rebellion, which ripped across the western counties of Massachusetts late in 1786.

The rebellion's initial course virtually repeated the collapse of royal government in the same province a dozen years earlier. The fundamental issue was the state government's policy of hard money, insistent tax collections, and firm enforcement of contractual obligations, whoever the parties might be, including Britons and former loyalists. Local grievances, which centered on a fear that farmers would lose their land, led to popular committees assembling and then to verbal protest. These actions combined with a generalized sense that the Revolution's gains were being squandered. Under the leadership of county conventions and town meetings, an impromptu militia gathered under former Continental Captain Daniel Shays, to close the courts and prevent further legal action. A better-trained and better-equipped army led by former General Benjamin Lincoln outmarched and outmaneuvered the rebels and put down the insurgency. Shays himself went into permanent exile. Other leaders were tried for treason, condemned to death, and given melodramatic last-minute reprieves. Most of the rebels turned from armed violence to electoral politics to find solutions for their problems.

The U.S. Constitution's explicitly stated goal of securing "domestic tranquillity" to "ourselves and our posterity" rested on its framers' understanding that continuing popular unrest of the sort the revolutionary era had known was incompatible with a stable social order. In principle the government that the framers created would seek to establish the "monopoly of violence" that Max Weber characterized as one of the prime hallmarks of a modern state. In terms of economic relations, that goal was largely achieved. In terms of "race," however, the Revolution's legacy of small, supposedly beleaguered, white communities using any means at their disposal to protect their own interests continued, almost without challenge. Sad though it is to say, lynch mobs and the Ku Klux Klan stand among the heirs of what the Revolution's patriotic violence bequeathed.

BIBLIOGRAPHY

Bailyn, Bernard. *The Ordeal of Thomas Hutchinson.* Cambridge, Mass.: Harvard University Press, 1975.

Bellesiles, Michael. *Revolutionary Outlaws: Ethan Allen and the Struggle for Independence on the Early American Frontier.* Charlottesville: University Press of Virginia, 1993.

Countryman, Edward. *The American Revolution.* New York: Hill and Wang, 1985.

Gross, Robert A., ed. *In Debt to Shays: The Bicentennial of an Agrarian Rebellion.* Charlottesville: University Press of Virginia, 1993.

Hoffman, Ronald. "The 'Disaffected' in the Revolutionary South." In *The American Revolution: Explorations in the History of American Radicalism,* edited by Alfred F. Young. De Kalb: Northern Illinois University Press, 1976.

Maier, Pauline. *From Resistance to Revolution: Colonial Radicals and the Development of American Opposition to Britain, 1765–1776.* New York: Knopf, 1972.

Nash, Gary B. *The Urban Crucible: Social Change, Political Consciousness, and the Origins of the American Revolution.* Cambridge, Mass.: Harvard University Press, 1979.

Smith, Barbara Clark. "Food Rioters and the American Revolution." *William and Mary Quarterly* 3d ser., 51 (1994).

Thompson, E. P. "The Moral Economy of the English Crowd in the Eighteenth Century." In *Customs in Common.* London: Merlin Press, 1991.

Young, Alfred F. "English Plebeian Culture and Eighteenth-Century American Radicalism." In *The Origins of Anglo-American Radicalism,* edited by Margaret Jacob and James Jacob. London: Allen and Unwin, 1983.

EDWARD COUNTRYMAN

See also **Boston Massacre; Civil Disorder; Militias; Slavery; War.**

MILITARY CAMPAIGNS

Between 1775 and 1781, British and German (Hessian) regulars, American loyalist militias, and British-allied Indians fought a bloody war against the Continental army, patriot militias, and—beginning in 1778—French regulars. Yet the war's outcome depended less on campaigns than on the uncommitted portion of the colonial population, who may have numbered as many as 40 percent of all colonists in 1775. Violence, more than any other factor, determined whether the patriots or the British crown would win the hearts and minds of these neutrals.

Prior to the war New England was the region most fervent in its resistance to Britain, but in April 1775 the British high command believed that only mobs, not an outraged population in arms, needed to be controlled. The Continental Congress, meeting at Philadelphia, understood the potential for unbridled violence, and after the Battles of Lexington and Concord (19 April) and Bunker Hill (17 June) adopted the New England troops as the nucleus of the Continental army, which would be under congressional authority and the command of George Washington. Their goal was to restrain a rapidly-developing guerrilla conflict, and instead to fight a controllable war.

British commanders first assumed that their regular troops—of whom 7,000 were present at Boston, and who in three years' time would number 40,000 in America as a whole—would disperse the untrained Americans. But during the Battle of Bunker Hill redcoat frontal assaults on rebel entrenchments resulted in a 45 percent casualty rate for the British and forced their generals to rethink the war as a confrontation between armies. The British commander, General William Howe, believed that a few battlefield defeats would force Congress to negotiate; indeed, his principal goal was to bring about a negotiated peace. Thus he shifted the British base of operations from Boston to New York, a strategically superior location, and without much difficulty dislodged the rebels from defensive positions on Long Island and Manhattan

in the late summer and fall of 1776. Washington, having lost more than eleven hundred men as casualties and four thousand as prisoners, retreated across New Jersey with a disintegrating army. He crossed the Delaware River on 7 December with perhaps five thousand troops fit for duty.

But Howe's successes were working against him. British and Hessian regulars regarded all civilians who did not appear in arms to support the crown as enemies, and frequently subjected them to theft, rape, and summary execution. Howe's loyalist auxiliary troops used the occupation of New Jersey to settle scores with members of patriot groups who had until recently controlled Tory opposition by means of ostracism, physical coercion, and imprisonment. When Howe sent his men into winter quarters across central New Jersey in December, therefore, he was not garrisoning a defeated province so much as dispersing his troops across a countryside filled with angry colonists. Thus, Washington's successful attacks on two vulnerable enemy posts (Trenton on 26 December and Princeton on 3 January 1777) not only restored Continental morale but encouraged guerrilla attacks that soon made New Jersey untenable for the British. Even so, Howe expected to renew his pursuit of Washington's main force in 1777, while General John Burgoyne would invade New York from Canada. Both commanders expected loyalist support to emerge wherever the redcoats appeared. Both were mistaken.

Burgoyne reached the upper Hudson Valley in New York in July 1777, but his use of Hessians and Indians, whom the colonists regarded as equally barbaric in their readiness to plunder, maltreat, and kill civilians, had turned most New Yorkers against him. The supplies and loyalist supporters he expected never materialized, and Continentals and militiamen overwhelmed his expeditionary force at the Battles of Saratoga (19 September and 7 October). Howe failed to destroy Washington's army in Pennsylvania, but he seized Philadelphia in September—only to find that, as Franklin quipped, "Philadelphia ha[d] captured Howe." His conventional-war strategy failed because redcoat, loyalist, and Hessian abuses of civilians drove neutrals into alliance with the patriots. Thus Howe, whose 17,000 men at Philadelphia outnumbered Washington's Continentals at nearby Valley Forge by nearly two to one, was able to venture into the countryside only with large, heavily-armed foraging parties—groups whose aggressive behavior toward civilians only reinforced popular revulsion at redcoat tactics. By contrast, Washington dealt cautiously with civilians, refusing to confiscate food and clothing even when his ragged Continentals were starving. Patriot authorities tolerated the indifference of neutrals as no more than evidence of America's general tendency to distrust all power not rooted in local structures of authority. They therefore required only minimal support: anyone who paid his taxes, kept his mouth shut, and performed militia duty would be left alone. This policy helped win the neutrals' acquiescence, as did the selective application of force in making examples of notorious Tories by imprisonment, exile, the confiscation of property, and on rare occasions even execution.

Burgoyne's surrender at Saratoga on 17 October convinced the French to enter into an open alliance with the United States and transformed the war into a transatlantic struggle that required Britain to defend its homeland against invasion and to protect its West Indian sugar islands from attack. Thus, the new British commander, General Henry Clinton, who replaced Howe in May 1778, was short on men and supplies and was no longer able to count on naval superiority in American waters. He decided on a new strategy. Knowing that rice planters in the Carolina-Georgia low country feared slave rebellions and that long-standing animosities divided this lowland aristocracy from the poorer, more numerous backcountry farmers, Clinton decided to move the war to that vulnerable region. Once the regulars cleared out rebel opposition, he believed, loyalist militia would pacify the countryside by moving into conquered regions and establishing martial law. When they had succeeded in creating physical security for loyalist lives and property, civil government and courts could be reinstituted at colony and local levels.

The southern campaign was successful for the British and resulted in several reversals for the Continental army. Pacification worked so well in Georgia following the invasion of November 1778 that civil government could be established in 1779 under a royal governor and an elected assembly; yet it failed in South Carolina, where a civil war erupted in 1780. Bands of patriot partisans could no more be rooted out of the swamps and mountains than the loyalists could be restrained from settling old scores. Both sides employed terror freely. In two of the best-known atrocities of a savage guerrilla war, patriot militiamen massacred loyalist prisoners after the Battle of King's Mountain (7 October 1780) in retaliation for an earlier massacre of patriots at the Battle of Waxhaws (29 May). While loyalist attacks swelled patriot ranks with former neutrals throughout the backcountry during the summer and fall of 1780, Clinton's policy of accepting slaves as refugees brought tens of thousands of runaways to British camps and effectually alienated the low country elite. By year's end, pacification was doomed. Unable to control the situation, the local British commander, General Charles Cornwallis, concentrated on trying to destroy General Nathanael Greene's small force of Continentals when the latter invaded South Carolina in December.

Cornwallis pursued Greene from December 1780 through the spring of 1781, wearing down his own men in indecisive battles and grueling marches but never destroying his enemy. In May, Cornwallis relocated his forces to Virginia, to attack the French troops under the Marquis de Lafayette. Cornwallis assumed that Greene would move north, but Greene remained in South Carolina, attacking the scattered British garrisons, forcing British troops to withdraw to coastal enclaves, and restoring patriot control of the countryside. Meanwhile, Cornwallis, failing to trap Lafayette in Virginia, unleashed his loyalist irregulars against the estates of patriots. These raids built civilian support for Lafayette, who shadowed Cornwallis as he moved to establish a base with access to the sea at Yorktown.

The Battle of Yorktown ended British hopes in America. Cut off from resupply by the French fleet, which blockaded Chesapeake Bay, and confronted by thousands of Continentals and French soldiers that Washington had quickly marched down from New York to join Lafayette, Cornwallis surrendered on 20 October 1781. Pressed by demands in other theaters, the British government suspended military operations in North America and replaced Clinton with Sir Guy Carleton. He reached New York in May 1782 and observed a truce with Washington until peace negotiations in Europe officially ended the war in 1783.

BIBLIOGRAPHY

Boatner, Mark Mayo, III. *Encyclopedia of the American Revolution.* Rev. ed. New York: D. McKay, 1974.
Ferling, John C., ed. *The World Turned Upside Down: The American Victory in the War of Independence.* New York: Greenwood, 1988.
Fray, Sylvia. *Water from the Rock: Black Resistance in a Revolutionary Age.* Princeton, N.J.: Princeton University Press, 1991.

Higginbotham, Don. *The War of American Independence: Military Attitudes, Policies, and Practices, 1763–1789*. New York: Macmillan, 1971.

Higginbotham, Don, ed., *War and Society in Revolutionary America*. Columbia: University of South Carolina Press, 1988.

Hoffman, Ronald, and Peter J. Albert, eds. *Arms and Independence: The Military Character of the American Revolution*. Charlottesville: University of Virginia Press, 1984.

Hoffman, Ronald, Thad W. Tate, and Peter J. Albert, eds. *An Uncivil War: The Southern Backcountry During the American Revolution*. Charlottesville: University of Virginia Press, 1985.

Kwasny, Mark. *Washington's Partisan War, 1775–1783*. Kent, Ohio: Kent State University Press, 1996.

Martin, James Kirby, and Mark E. Lender. *A Respectable Army: The Military Origins of the Republic, 1763–1789*. Arlington Heights, Ill.: H. Davidson, 1982.

Middlekauff, Robert. *The Glorious Cause: The American Revolution, 1763–1789*. New York: Oxford University Press, 1982.

Royster, Charles. *A Revolutionary People at War: The Continental Army and American Character*. Chapel Hill: University of North Carolina Press, 1979.

Shy, John W., ed. *A People Numerous and Armed: Reflections on the Military Struggle for American Independence*. New York: Oxford University Press, 1976.

Ward, Christopher. *The War of the Revolution*, edited by John Richard Alden. New York: Macmillan, 1952.

FRED ANDERSON

See also **Militias, Authorized; War.**

AMERICAN VIOLENCE IN COMPARATIVE PERSPECTIVE

Like that of other countries, violence in the United States follows the rhythm of national politics and economic development. Changes induced by colonial revolution, civil war, and two world wars as well as industrialization and urbanization threatened established groups while newly emerging groups sought to consolidate their hold. On occasion both established and challenging groups turned to violence. Rather than attempting to set the United States in a true world perspective—an unrealistic goal within the scope of this article—this essay examines the role of state structures in violence through a paired comparison of case studies.

Comparative analysis reveals that political decentralization has exerted important and enduring influence on the character of U.S. violence. Violent colonial protest borrowed from contemporary London radicals, but, confronting new social and economic circumstances, Americans developed their own distinctive methods of violence. International comparison suggests that the most distinctive contemporary characteristic of U.S. violence—its high rate of homicides—is historically rooted in tolerance in the United States for widespread gun ownership, a decentralized law-enforcement system, and enduring racial hostilities.

State Structure and Violence

In his classic study of comparative violence, *Histoire de la violence en Occident* (1981), Jean-Claude Chesnais writes that "in regard to violence, no two countries are less similar than France and the United States," owing to France's powerful centralized state, cultural unity, and strict gun control. To reveal the strengths and weaknesses of his analysis, we might briefly compare two violent regions—one in France and one in the United States—over two centuries: in the United States, the southern Illinois region, roughly the bottom quarter of the state, south from East Saint Louis; and in France, the area known as the Stéphanois, around Saint-Étienne in southeastern France. Although industrialization in the Stéphanois was much greater and widespread, both areas were poorly endowed agricultural areas that became major coal-mining centers.

In 1800 southern Illinois already had a violent reputation. Cave-in-Rock near the Ohio River was a haunt of the Harpe brothers, Micajah and Wiley, river pirates and ruthless murderers. Defending their land, Indians killed adult males in isolated settlements and kidnapped their families; in retaliation, southern Illinois furnished recruits to every Indian war.

During the same period, the urbanized Stéphanois region of France was far bloodier and more riotous than the American frontier. In 1789, ten days after the fall of the Bastille, local artisans rioted against state engineers who had sought to impose a new industrial discipline in its arms manufactories; by December, the engineers were in full flight. In 1793–1794, Claude Javogues, representing the revolutionary government, set up a guillotine in the Stéphanois and executed several hundred for the area's halfhearted support of the counterrevolutionary uprising in Lyons.

Meanwhile southern Illinois felt the tremors of civil war and its aftermath. In the prewar years, fleeing slaves attracted slave catchers, and one vigilante campaign was undertaken against these bounty hunters who often consorted with local criminals and kidnapped or attacked freed African Americans. In 1837 in Alton, a proslavery mob killed the abolitionist editor Elijah Lovejoy while trying to burn his press. Southern Illinois was mainly settled from the south and, although majority opinion finally swung behind the Union, was a center of antiwar sentiment. Stemming from such war-bred tension, the "Bloody Vendetta" of 1868–1876 paralyzed law enforcement; the state's attorney of Williamson County had ties to one faction, the sheriff to the other.

In the Stéphanois the 1840s and 1850s witnessed new forms of violence as the region industrialized and responded to Parisian revolutions. In 1846, near Saint-Étienne, soldiers called to repress a miners' strike fired into a crowd and killed six. In 1848, unruly local crowds greeted the news of revolution in Paris: miners seized mines to institute a "republican regime" below ground, while ribbon weavers sacked a convent workshop where young women were trained in ribbon weaving and worked below the established scale. In 1851 hundreds of armed volunteers marched toward Lyons to resist Louis-Napoléon's coup, turning back only when they learned the town had been secured by imperial forces. In 1869 soldiers again intervened against strikers and shot fourteen dead at La Ricamarie. In 1871, in solidarity with Paris, workers in Saint-Étienne briefly took over the town and proclaimed their own commune and, in the confusion, the department's chief official, the prefect, was killed.

After 1890, as coal mining expanded rapidly and East Saint Louis urbanized, southern Illinois oscillated wildly between intense class struggles and murderous ethnic and racial conflicts. Urbanization contributed African American migrants, and coal mining brought foreign Catholics, mainly Italians and Slavs, to an overwhelmingly fundamentalist Protestant, white region. Although murderous conflicts occurred in Carterville in 1899 and Zeigler in 1905, the best-known incident of class struggle was the massacre that took place near Herrin in 1922.

The Herrin massacre happened in the context of coal overproduction encouraged by wartime demand and local support for a national miners' strike. While the strike was still under way, an outside coal operator attempted to mine coal, an act of folly in an area where 60 percent of the male population were members of the union and the rest, including the mercantile classes, were dependent upon them. Soon crowds raided local hardware stores for guns, and the union-busting mine superintendent was besieged by hundreds of well-armed miners. His frantic phone calls went unreturned by the local sheriff, then running for county treasurer. In despair, the superintendent surrendered and was one of twenty nonunion men killed by an exultant crowd. The local chapter of the United Mine Workers of America (UMWA) provided electric fans for the jailed defendants and, in two successive trials, local juries found every defendant innocent on every count.

Bracketing the Herrin massacre were incidents of racial and ethnic violence in 1917 and in the years from 1923 to 1924. In 1917 East Saint Louis was a center of stockyards and packing plants supplemented by metal manufacturing and pro-

Left: **A lynch mob attacks the warehouse of the abolitionists Godfrey Gilman and Elijah Lovejoy in Alton, Illinois, on 7 November 1837.** CORBIS *Right:* **French troops storm the Bastille during the French Revolution, 14 July 1789.** HULTON GETTY/LIAISON AGENCY

cessing. Rapid wartime growth attracted African American migrants. Local Democrats demagogically accused Republicans of colonizing the city with Republican voters. To dampen the demands of white trade unionists, a local company hired African Americans and broke a subsequent strike. Increasingly, white mobs attacked African Americans. On 2 July 1917 the murder of two policemen, mistaken for men who had fired on blacks' homes, led to attacks of white mobs in the downtown area; at a minimum, thirty-nine blacks and nine whites were killed. The mayor's efforts to get military reinforcements encountered obstacles from state and local politicians.

In 1923–1924 in the southeast coal-mining region around West Frankfort and Herrin, Ku Klux Klan activity focused on native gangsters as well as local Italian communities that made wine for personal consumption and sometimes supplied bootleggers. In a prolonged period of harassment targeting Catholic migrants, hundreds of Italian families were roused out of their beds by white-robed Klansmen searching for evidence of wine-making. In the summer of 1924, Klan action practically supplanted local law enforcement, but the campaign of intimidation was eventually curtailed by violent shoot-outs that left dead both leading Klansmen and principal supporters of the bootleggers. As the Klan declined, gang war broke out among bootleg gangs, only ending with the capital conviction and execution of the most notorious gang leader in April 1927. Between 1926 and 1932, the UMWA was split by violent conflicts between left-wing dissidents and the brutal and undemocratic leadership of John L. Lewis. Major organizing attempts of the leftist National Miners Union and the Progressive Miners Union were crushed by UMWA thugs acting under Lewis's instructions and supported by local authorities.

While southern Illinois authorities allowed right-wing authorities to attack leftists, Stéphanois authorities engaged directly in repression. In the 1940s, in the wake of French military defeat, still greater violence swept the Stéphanois as a divided labor movement and politically polarized communities provided supporters for the Vichy regime as well as supporters for the resistance violently opposing Vichy, and later German, rule. Arresting local citizens, mainly Jews, leftists, and members of the resistance, sending them to concentration camps and to work in Germany, and executing them as hostages, Vichy authorities captured and killed resisters and were, in turn, assassinated by

their resistance comrades. On 26 May 1944, American planes bombed Saint-Étienne's arms works and working class neighborhoods indiscriminately, killing 957. Reliable estimates for the communist dead in the resistance are hard to obtain, but during the last years of the war, 125 members of the noncommunist resistance were killed. When the resistance finally captured Saint-Étienne in August 1944, 61 collaborators were summarily executed; later, 108 were tried and condemned to death, but only 17 were actually executed.

In the post–World War II years, violence declined sharply in both the Stéphanois and in southern Illinois as deindustrialization and out-migration diminished the capacity for collective action.

This quick survey suggests that Jean-Claude Chesnais's generalization about the dissimilarity of violence in the United States and France is not so much wrong as one-sided. French centralization led to different enduring patterns of violence from those of American decentralization. French centralization made agents of the national state both highly visible and very important actors on the local scene. With the aid of well-informed spies and a developed administrative apparatus, it protected the interests of groups that were influential at the national level, and it did so forcefully; the state was the perpetrator of all mass killings in the Stéphanois region. In turn, the periodic collapse of this overreaching state opened up opportunities for those who had formerly been the targets of state repression. In France, whether violently or peacefully, protestors generally confronted directly the omnipresent national government.

In contrast, local governments were largely responsible for law enforcement in the United States, and a local government was liable to become paralyzed when a region was deeply divided or when local feeling conflicted with national laws. Local governments buffered populations from national political events, and violent responses to national events were often deferred until these found local supporters willing to inflict violence. Only then did local divisions over national issues become deadly, but with the intimate hatred possible only among neighbors. In southern Illinois, nativist mobs, mine police, and unionists were the major agents of mass killing.

Comparative Violent Repertoires

Colonial Americans, predominantly from Great Britain and Ireland, brought with them the British legal and policing systems as well as repertoires of protest for contesting these systems. Colonists adapted old-country repertoires to their own purposes. The colonies witnessed food riots but more important were crowd actions against infringements on colonial autonomy such as impressment, the British navy's commandeering of pine trees for masts, and customs regulations. As important, Boston, New York, and Philadelphia were in close contact with London, at that time a center of innovative collective action. Emulating London, colonial radicals created formal organizations such as Boston's Sons of Liberty as well as adopting Wilkite political symbols, such as a boot held on a pole, a symbol of the Earl of Bute, a hated enemy of both John Wilkes and the colonists. From the great American port cities, the latest London tools for fighting for popular rights spread through the agrarian hinterlands.

Many migrant groups brought their own protest repertoires to the United States, but successful repertoires were based on shared understandings between both protestors and government. For this reason, methods of protest developed in the peasant societies of Europe seldom succeeded in the context of the industrializing and democratic societies of America. Between 1862 and 1874 in the Pennsylvania anthracite areas, some Gaelic-speaking Donegal miners turned the methods of Irish agrarian secret societies to industrial purposes, but "Molly Maguireism" proved ultimately disastrous. Secret societies could never withstand sustained scrutiny by the authorities; as in the case of the Molly Maguires, informers or provocateurs inevitably emerged. Southern Italians introduced the Mafia; but whereas in Italy mafiosi were violent mediators between Italian republican laws and the hierarchical southern agrarian order, in the United States, they harnessed ethnic solidarity and a code of secrecy for personal crime. Germans and Eastern European Jews were more influential in introducing their own traditions of labor organization and socialism, but even though their models were derived from relatively industrial societies, they were unable to fundamentally alter the character of U.S. protest.

American born and bred, the practice of lynching was the most infamous U.S. contribution to the repertoire of violence. Its persistence into the twentieth century reflected its growing association with the continuing high level of racial violence required to enforce white supremacy. Increasingly, as the nineteenth century wore on, the summary punishment of alleged lawbreakers by popular violence (or the threat thereof) increasingly concentrated in the South, where the term *lynching* had originated during the Revolutionary War to describe informal punishment visited on Loyalists; in the post–Civil War period it centered on the murder of blacks accused of crimes by white mobs. The rhetoric of lynching portrayed it as a form of popular justice, but in practice, successful lynching depended on some level of tacit cooperation with local authorities and on the toleration of local elites.

The United States also developed its own characteristic forms of strike action. A Franco-American comparison allows us to observe the origins of a protest repertoire that involved violence. Between 1870 and 1914 in France, elites were hopelessly split on the desirability of a parliamentary republic based on universal manhood suffrage. To maintain their rule, middle-class republicans found it necessary to make tacit alliances with a labor movement that, while committed to radical doctrines, was also loyal to the republic. When confronted with massive strikes, republican French governments often intervened to promote compromises and prevent republican-oriented trade unions from being destroyed by capitalist monarchists. In France large-scale strikes more often than small-scale strikes ended in success or compromise, and national governments that had formerly shot workers began to protect them. In time massive solidarity strikes and brief national work stoppages were recognized as a method for exerting pressure for government attention.

The trend in the United States was the opposite. Having triumphed nationally with the Civil War, U.S. elites had no reason to conciliate labor. American political decentralization might allow trade unions to occupy powerful positions within a region, but national rulers were hostile to the labor movement and lacked the administrative apparatus to intervene in local labor negotiations had they so willed. Strikes large enough to attract the attention of the federal government were violently repressed, while local strikes were more likely to end in success or in compromise; strikes tended to avoid appeals to politicians and ended up as slugouts between labor and capital.

The strike repertoires formed in France and the United States between 1870 and 1914 still powerfully shape strike activity in these countries because they have been embodied in the tactics of trade unions and institutionalized in labor laws.

Distinctive Features of U.S. Violence

Perhaps the most distinctive feature of American violence is its high homicide rate. At or near its historic high in the 1980s, the homicide rate was approximately fifteen times that of such industrial nations as France, Germany, Japan, and the United Kingdom. Half of U.S. homicides were committed with handguns, over five hundred times the rate of the United Kingdom, where handguns are strictly regulated. While remaining many times higher than that of other industrial nations, the U.S. homicide rate declined by a quarter in the 1980s and 1990s. Explanations for this decline differ, although increased incarceration rates, a decline in the size of violence-prone younger demographic cohorts, and economic prosperity all contributed.

Increased incarceration rates, the size of demographic cohorts, and economic prosperity, however, are not sufficient to explain American violence because to some degree Europe followed the same evolution and remained less prone to violence. Analysis locates several distinctive features of violence in the United States that account for its continuing high homicide levels—all of them rooted in the past. One of the important reasons why widespread unrest led to revolution in the American colonies and failed in contemporary Ireland, Scotland, and England is that Americans possessed their own long-standing, experienced militias drawn from a general male population who, initially at least, had been motivated by fear of Amerindian attacks. American militias were popular institutions made up of rural recruits who possessed firearms and were accustomed to their use; before the Napoleonic era militias in the British Isles were unable to recruit successfully from the ranks of merchants and artisans, for these groups lacked familiarity with weapons and a compelling reason for participation. When more broad-based militias were formed, as in Ireland in the late 1770s, they quickly raised demands and were disbanded. The American Revolution made many patriots fearful of a standing army and, while the Constitution provided for such an army, the Second Amendment also guaranteed the rights of militia conceived as a military group of the armed citizenry. The guarantee that citizens could carry guns was intended to differentiate America from degraded continental nations like France, where armsbearing was an aristocratic prerogative.

A second distinctive feature is the decentralized character of U.S. law enforcement, a characteristic feature of the entire U.S. political system. National police forces have consolidated repressive power in all the world's industrial nations save the United States. The Federal Bureau of Investigation's jurisdiction is a pale shadow of that of the French Sûreté Nationale and even of the more weakly centralized British police. Elected law-enforcement officials are far more susceptible to local pressure and more likely to condone violence against minorities. Local law enforcement is generally more poorly trained than national law enforcement and inherently less efficient.

Finally, racial violence has always been more significant in the United States than in other industrial nations, with race riots, lynchings, and ghetto rebellions playing a large role. In part, this tradition of violence was developed by southerners to maintain slavery and, later, white domination, but it was quickly adapted by white urban northerners. Extremely high levels of violence were used to enforce informal discrimination in the face of laws granting equality.

BIBLIOGRAPHY

Angle, Paul M. *Bloody Williamson: A Chapter in American Lawlessness.* 1952. Reprint, Urbana: University of Illinois Press, 1992.

Bernstein, Iver. *The New York City Draft Riots: Their Significance for American Society and Politics in the Age of the Civil War.* New York: Oxford University Press, 1990.

Brown, Richard Maxwell. *Strain of Violence: Historical Studies of American Violence and Vigilantism.* New York: Oxford University Press, 1975.

Brundage, W. Fitzhugh, ed. *Under Sentence of Death: Lynching in the South.* Chapel Hill: University of North Carolina Press.

Chesnais, Jean-Claude. *Histoire de la violence en Occident de 1800 à nos jours.* Paris: Robert Laffont, 1981.

Friedman, Gerald. "The State and the Making of the Working Class: France and the United States, 1880–1914." *Theory and Society* 17, no. 3 (1988).

Kenny, Kevin. *Making Sense of the Molly Maguires.* New York: Oxford University Press, 1998.

McAdam, Doug. *Political Process and the Development of Black Insurgency, 1930–1970.* Chicago: University of Chicago Press, 1982.

Rule, James B. *Theories of Civil Violence.* Berkeley: University of California Press, 1988.

Tilly, Charles. "Collective Action in England and America, 1765–1775." In *Tradition, Conflict, and Modernization: Perspectives on the American Revolution*, edited by Richard Maxwell Brown and Don E. Fehrenbacher. New York: Academic Press, 1977.

Tilly, Charles, Louise Tilly, and Richard Tilly. *The Rebellious Century, 1830–1930.* Cambridge, Mass.: Harvard University Press, 1975.

MICHAEL P. HANAGAN

See also **Overview of Violence in the United States (vol. 1); Gun Control; Ku Klux Klan; Labor and Unions; Lynching; Molly Maguires.**

AMISTAD CASE

In the waters off northern Cuba during the stormy early morning of 2 July 1839, Joseph Cinqué, a-Mende, led fifty-three West Africans in a revolt on the Spanish slaver *Amistad*, killing the captain and the cook and sparing only the two Spanish slave owners to navigate the vessel to Africa. Two sailors disappeared; they probably jumped overboard and drowned in an attempt to reach shore twenty-one miles away. The two Spaniards, however, sailed the ship in a zigzag course, hoping for rescue by a passing vessel. Instead, the *Amistad* headed northward and arrived off the coast of Long Island, New York, with only forty-three of the blacks still alive. While Cinqué and others foraged ashore for provisions, Lieutenant Thomas Gedney of the U.S.S. *Washington* spotted their activity and, after a brief skirmish, seized the blacks, the ship, and its cargo as salvage and took the entire cache to an admiralty court in New London, Connecticut. Had Gedney taken the ship to a New York court, the blacks would not have been subject to assessment as property since the state had abolished slavery. Connecticut, however, did not officially end slavery until 1848.

The *Amistad* story might have ended here had it not been for the abolitionists. Believing slavery to be a sin, they advocated immediate emancipation of all slaves without compensation to owners. The abolitionists solicited the assistance of New York businessman Lewis Tappan, who underwrote the Amistad Committee and hired attorney Roger S. Baldwin of Connecticut to defend the blacks as "kidnapped Africans" who had the inherent right of self-defense in seeking their freedom.

At this point the case became thoroughly entangled. The two Spaniards filed a suit for their slave property, legally purchased in Cuba, and the government of Madrid invoked Pinckney's Treaty of 1795 and the Adams-Onís Treaty of 1819 in demanding the return of the blacks both as Spanish property and as assassins. The abolitionists warned of a "judicial massacre" and insisted that the blacks' birthplace was not Cuba: the captives spoke no Spanish and had phony names assigned to conceal their African origin. Cinqué's real name, for example, was Sengbe Pieh. President Martin Van Buren, however, headed a Democratic party made up of northerners and southerners and could not win reelection in 1840 if a public confrontation developed over slavery. He opted to comply with Spain's demand.

The defense fought this outcome. In the circuit court in Connecticut, Baldwin sought a writ of habeas corpus, aimed at forcing the Spaniards to charge the blacks with murder and thereby admit to their status as human beings. The abolitionists could meanwhile sear the national conscience by exposing the horrors of the African slave trade and perhaps slavery itself. A great chasm existed between morality and the law—between the natural rights doctrine underpinning the Declaration of Independence and the protection of slavery afforded by the due process guarantees in the Constitution. But even though the presiding justice, Smith Thompson of the U.S. Supreme Court, found slavery morally repugnant, he realized that American law protected a slave owner in his property and denied the writ.

The case went before the district court in Connecticut, where Judge Andrew Judson presided and where the prognosis for the abolitionists was not good. Judson was a white supremacist and a political opportunist. So sure was President Van Buren of a favorable decision that he stationed a ship nearby, ready to whisk the blacks to Cuba without allowing them their constitutional right of

An engraving from John W. Barber's *A History of the Amistad Captives* (1840), depicting the 1839 revolt.
LIBRARY OF CONGRESS

appeal. But Judson's position was complicated by some of his contemporaries who sympathized with the captives. Baldwin had located a Mende by the name of James Covey, who translated Cinqué's testimony. In the most dramatic moment of the trial, Cinqué lay on the floor of the courtroom as if in chains to demonstrate the brutal treatment he and his fellow captives received, both on the Portuguese slaver *Tecora* during the Middle Passage and on the *Amistad* before the revolt.

Judson delivered a political verdict. He stunned everyone by agreeing that the blacks were kidnapped Africans and therefore entitled to freedom; but he twisted the Congressional Law of 1819 in authorizing government transportation back to Africa by asserting that they were slaves brought illegally into the United States. Although the law empowered the president to send illegally imported slaves back to Africa, the *Amistad* blacks had entered the United States while in control of the ship and were not slaves. Judson hoped to satisfy his peers by releasing the blacks while placating the White House by ushering them out of the country.

Judson's decision settled nothing. The president appealed to the Supreme Court, where the chief justice was Roger Taney, who would later hand down the Dred Scott decision, which denied any rights to blacks. Further, five of the nine justices owned or had owned slaves.

Now needing a lawyer of national prominence, the abolitionists persuaded John Quincy Adams, former U.S. president and now congressman from Massachusetts, to lead the defense. Seventy-three years old and nearly deaf, Adams acceded, regarding this confrontation as an opportunity to win the blacks their freedom as well as to expose executive interference. Moreover, he intended to appeal to the Declaration of Independence in registering a call for human rights.

Adams delivered an impassioned eight-and-a-half-hour argument over the course of two days that in March 1841 resulted in freedom for the Africans. Justice Joseph Story wrote the decision, referring to "the eternal principles of justice" in affirming the inherent right of all human beings to escape unlawful captivity. The ownership papers were fraudulent. The Court reversed Judson's use of the Congressional Act of 1819 in providing the blacks with a way home. They had entered the United States as free people, not slaves.

Story's decision is notable for several reasons. He did not respond to Adams's charges of executive interference. Indeed, he wrote his wife that Adams had presented an "extraordinary argument . . . extraordinary . . . for its power, for its bitter sarcasm, and its dealing with topics far beyond the record and points of discussion." Story did not base his decision on slavery. Although he considered the institution immoral, he recognized its legality. In essence the blacks were freed on a technicality, and yet Story surely must have realized that the abolitionists would broadly interpret "eternal principles of justice" to mean an assault on slavery.

The *Amistad* decision marked the first civil rights case in America's history. Blacks had testified in antebellum American courts and were set free. The abolitionists had exposed the brutalities of the African slave trade while suggesting the horrors of slavery itself. The death of slavery could come only after a lengthy series of sustained blows. Blacks had worked together with whites within the American legal system in winning the freedom of Africans, shattering one of the central myths of the period—that blacks passively accepted captivity.

The *Amistad* decision had a mixed impact. The freed blacks had no means of getting home and found refuge in Farmington, Connecticut, where black and white church groups worked together in building a place to live for Cinqué and his companions and in helping them raise money for passage home. Eight months after the trial, and almost three years after their departure from West Africa, the thirty-five survivors sailed home on the barque *Gentleman*—making this the only time in history that blacks captured in Africa and brought to the New World made their way back home. Accompanied by James Covey and five missionaries, two of them black, they established a Christian mission at Kaw-Mende in Sierra Leone, which became the basis in 1846 for the American Missionary Association, the first of its kind in Africa. Cinqué never found his wife and three children, perhaps themselves victims of the slave trade. No evidence substantiates the charge that Cinqué engaged in the trade; in fact, for over three decades there is no record of his activities. It appears that he returned to the mission in the late 1870s and died there in 1879.

BIBLIOGRAPHY

Cable, Mary. *Black Odyssey: The Case of the Slave Ship Amistad.* New York: Viking, 1971.

Hoyt, Edwin P. *The "Amistad" Affair.* New York: Abelard-Schuman, 1970.

Jones, Howard. "All We Want Is Make Us Free!" *American History* (February 1998).

———. *Mutiny on the Amistad: The Saga of a Slave Revolt and Its Impact on American Abolition, Law, and Diplomacy.* Rev. ed. New York: Oxford University Press, 1997.

HOWARD JONES

See also **Slave Rebellions; Slavery.**

AMNESTY INTERNATIONAL

Amnesty International, the world's largest human rights organization, was founded in 1961 when a British barrister, Peter Benenson, learned of the imprisonment of two students in Portugal (then under the rule of the dictator Antonio Salazar) for the crime of raising their beers in a toast to freedom. In an editorial in a London newspaper, Benenson urged his fellow British to write Salazar's government demanding the students' release. Hundreds responded, and the world's first grassroots international human rights organization was born. In 1977 Amnesty International was awarded the Nobel Peace Prize.

As of 1999 Amnesty had more than a million members in more than 150 countries and territories. There are formal national sections of the organization in 55 countries, including the United States. The international headquarters is in London.

The mandate of the organization is precise: to free all prisoners of conscience (POCs; a term introduced by Amnesty to refer to people detained because of their ethnic origin, gender, sexual orientation, color, language, national or social origin, or economic status who have not used or advocated violence); to ensure prompt and fair trials for political prisoners; to end torture and other cruel, inhuman, or degrading treatment of prisoners; to abolish the death penalty; and to end extrajudicial executions and "disappearances." Amnesty also promotes through education the Universal Declaration of Human Rights. It maintains strict impartiality, opposing human rights violations committed both by governments and by opposition groups, and takes no position on the political or economic system of a country.

The information upon which Amnesty acts is obtained through research conducted by experts based in London and elsewhere and through more than a hundred missions a year to countries in which human rights violations take place. This in-

formation (on approximately 150 countries) is forwarded to members around the world who then petition the governments or opposition groups involved to respect human rights. Members may also conduct demonstrations, mount educational campaigns, pressure businesses to support human rights, pressure their home governments to intervene, and so on.

The United States section of Amnesty was founded in 1966. In the late 1980s it experienced a major growth in membership as a result of a series of concerts by such musicians as Bruce Springsteen and Sting given to publicize human rights violations and urge support for Amnesty. Today about three hundred thousand people belong to Amnesty International USA (AIUSA). The organization maintains a presence as well on approximately eighteen hundred high school and college campuses. Its administrative headquarters are in New York City, a legislative office is maintained in Washington, D.C., and six regional offices can be found in major cities around the country.

Among the domestic issues addressed by AIUSA are excessive use of force by police (frequently against people of color); ill treatment of prisoners, including abuse of women prisoners; and the treatment of immigrants and refugees, particularly political-asylum seekers. Although there were no POCs in the United States at the end of the twentieth century, in 1999 Amnesty called for the release of Leonard Peltier, a member of the American Indian Movement serving two life sentences for murder, who may have been denied a fair trial on political grounds. It also raised similar concerns about Geronimo Pratt, the former Black Panther Party leader convicted of murder in 1972; his conviction was overturned in 1998.

Amnesty is opposed to the death penalty in all circumstances as a violation of international human rights standards; the organization has therefore been particularly active in efforts to stem the ever-increasing tide of executions in this country. More than five hundred people have been executed since the death penalty was reintroduced in 1978. Amnesty believes that the death penalty risks the execution of innocent people, is applied in a racially discriminatory fashion, has never been proved to be a deterrent to violent crime, and, paradoxically, contributes to violence in society by institutionalizing its use by the state.

In Washington, Amnesty focuses on U.S. foreign policy as it affects international human rights. The organization has taken a leadership role in opposing U.S. military and security assistance to countries where there is "a consistent pattern of gross violations of internationally recognized human rights," assistance that is outlawed by Section 502B of the Foreign Assistance Act. It has called for the cutoff of military equipment to Colombia and Turkey because it believes those countries are using U.S.-supplied equipment to commit human rights violations.

AIUSA has also been in the forefront of efforts to expose violations committed by U.S. intelligence agencies, particularly in Latin America; to bring alleged war criminals to justice in Bosnia and Rwanda; to support the establishment of a permanent International Criminal Court (ICC); and to ratify the Convention on the Elimination of Discrimination Against Women (CEDAW). Though Amnesty does not take a position on economic sanctions nor advocate boycotts of companies, it believes that corporations have a major role to play both in respecting human rights themselves and influencing governments in which their operations are located. Amnesty participates in a dialogue with the U.S. government and corporations about the relationship between trade and human rights, maintaining that respect for human rights is not antithetical to U.S. economic interests but congruent with them.

Amnesty takes no position on the production of military arms per se or the use of military force—it is not a pacifist organization—but contends that such arms and force must be utilized within a framework of respect for human rights standards and covenants. The organization, particularly in the United States, has been outspoken in its criticism of companies that produce electroshock weapons and that may export such weapons to countries that have records of using them for torture.

Amnesty has been criticized for not ranking countries that are the worst offenders and for not addressing social and economic rights. Until 1991 Amnesty limited its criticism to violations committed by governments, but in that year it took up abuses by nonstate actors, including armed opposition groups. In 1998–1999 Amnesty for the first time focused one of its comprehensive international campaigns on human rights violations in the United States.

BIBLIGRAPHY

Forrest, Duncan, ed. *A Glimpse of Hell: Reports on Torture Worldwide.* New York: New York University Press, 1996.

Power, Jonathan. *Amnesty International: The Human Story.* New York: Pergamon, 1981.

Staunton, Marie, et al. *The Amnesty International Handbook.* Claremont, Calif.: Hunter House, 1991.

Winner, David. *Peter Benenson: Taking a Stand Against Injustice—Amnesty International.* Milwaukee, Wis.: Gareth Stevens, 1991.

WILLIAM F. SCHULZ

See also **Capital Punishment; Human Rights; Nonviolence; Torture.**

ANARCHISM

Stereotypes of bearded bomb throwers clutching infernal machines beneath their shabby coats still shape most peoples' image of anarchists, those individuals who reject the authority of the centralized state. (Many anarchists also repudiate capitalism for fostering inequalities of wealth and power.) Yet most anarchists were not terrorists, and many were explicitly nonviolent because violence seemed to them an illegitimate form of coercion. When desperate men—and virtually all violent activists were male—did resort to violence, it was usually to respond to the vastly greater force of the authorities. Nevertheless, it is true that in the heyday of the anarchist movement, from 1880 to 1920, terrorism appealed to anarchists as a means of redressing social injustice. Anarchists were more prone to individual acts of violence than were their socialist brethren on the left, both because anarchists explicitly repudiated the political process and because they emphasized individual will more than collective action. Since the effect of the violent deed depended on its dissemination through the popular press, terrorists were also publicists, a fact recognized by the contemporary term *propaganda by the deed*.

About 1880 two major changes occurred. Anarchism shifted from individualist to communist, advocating the revolutionary seizure of private property; and its adherents shifted from native-born to mostly immigrants from central, eastern, and southern Europe—initially Germans and Czechs, many of whom settled in Chicago in the 1880s, and later, from 1890 to 1920, mainly Italians and Jews. Johann Most arrived in 1882, a refugee from Bismarck's repression of the German left and the original apostle of violence. In 1885 Most published the notorious *Science of Revolutionary Warfare: A Manual in the Use and Preparation of Nitroglycerin, Dynamite, Gun-Cotton, Fulminating*

Mercury, Bombs, Poisons, etc., etc. So strong was the association between aliens and anarchists that, when President William McKinley was assassinated by Leon Czolgosz in 1901, Congress responded by passing a law banning all individuals who "disbelieve in or are opposed to all organized governments" from entering the United States—this despite the fact that Czolgosz was native-born.

The anarchist apogee from the 1880s to the 1920s began and ended with causes célèbres. On 3 May 1886 the Chicago police broke up a mass meeting of striking workers outside the McCormick Reaper Works and killed at least two workers. Five thousand copies of a revenge circular were printed in English and German, and the next day August Spies, the editor of a German-language anarchist paper, addressed the crowd outside the factory. As the police moved in, a bomb was thrown and seven policemen were killed; sixteen workers were shot that night, of whom four died. Eight prominent anarchists were tried, including Spies and Albert Parsons, editor of *Alarm.* Parsons had written the previous year: "Dynamite! Of all the good stuff, that is the stuff! Stuff several pounds of this sublime stuff into an inch pipe . . . place this in the immediate vicinity of a lot of rich loafers who live by the sweat of other people's brows, and light the fuse. A most cheerful and gratifying result will follow." Parsons and three others were hanged for inciting a riot in which several people were killed. Their execution caused worldwide condemnation, and their memorial in Waldheim Cemetery in Chicago became a radical pilgrimage site. In 1905 Albert Parsons's widow, Lucy Parsons, led a delegation there, after which Lucy Parsons and Big Bill Haywood founded an anarcho-syndicalist union, the Industrial Workers of the World, which favored direct action and the general strike.

The Homestead Strike of 1892 pitted the steelworkers of Pittsburgh against the giant Carnegie Steel Corporation. Carnegie's manager, Henry Clay Frick, locked out the workers and surrounded the plant with a fifteen-foot-high fence. On 6 July three hundred Pinkerton guards sailed on barges up the Monongahela River to the Homestead Plant; a pitched battle ensued, with the expulsion that night of all remaining Pinkertons. Later that month, a young Russian-Jewish immigrant named Alexander Berkman, the lover of Emma Goldman, traveled to Pittsburgh, entered the Homestead offices and shot Frick several times at close range. Frick managed to survive; Berkman

---

Emma Goldman

For a quarter of a century, from 1894 to 1919, Emma Goldman personified anarchism in America. As well as contributing articles to *Mother Earth,* she made numerous lecture tours, speaking in favor of birth control and, during World War I, against the draft; she was imprisoned for speaking on both of these causes. Goldman was also a strong proponent of women's social and sexual emancipation, although, as an anarchist, she did not campaign for women's suffrage. Throughout her life she never renounced violence as a means of achieving social revolution.

---

spent the next fourteen years in prison, emerging to rejoin Goldman as an editor of *Mother Earth* in 1906. The two were eventually deported to Russia, along with 246 other radicals, during the Red Scare of 1919. As he was awaiting deportation, Berkman heard of Frick's death. "Deported by God," he commented laconically.

The Russian Revolution and the Bolsheviks' peace treaty with the Germans, concluded in March 1918, greatly increased hostility to socialists and anarchists in the wartime United States. In October 1918 Congress passed a law barring all anarchists from entering the United States; any resident alien who harbored such beliefs might be deported. Government repression combined with labor unrest in 1919 led to an upsurge in left-wing violence. A general strike was called in Seattle in February 1919, and although the workers remained peaceful, the mayor, Ole Hanson, capitalized on fears of revolution by calling out the police and the army. Two months later, a package bomb was sent to his office, and in the following days thirty-five similar packages were discovered, addressed to prominent government officials and timed to reach their targets on May Day. In June a bomb exploded on the steps of Attorney General A. Mitchell Palmer's home in Washington, D.C., killing the would-be terrorist, an Italian immigrant from Philadelphia whose exact identity was never established. Leaflets signed by the Anarchist Fighters were found nearby. In September 1920 a horse-drawn carriage exploded in the heart of New York's financial district, killing thirty-three and wounding two hundred more. No Wall Street tycoons were hurt, but J. P. Morgan's offices were badly damaged. The police failed to identify the perpetrator (widely suspected to be an anarchist), and the lack of a trial diminished the fame of the deed. Greater attention was paid to the robbery and murder at a shoe factory in South Braintree, Massachusetts, for which two Italian immigrants, Nicola Sacco and Bartolomeo Vanzetti, were arrested and, in July 1921, sentenced to death. It was widely believed Sacco and Vanzetti were convicted for being alien anarchists. When they were finally executed in 1927, protesting their innocence but reaffirming their anarchist convictions, American embassies were attacked in many countries. If ineffective revolutionaries, anarchists made great martyrs.

Leftist violence exploded again in the New Left of the late 1960s, although the student radicals rarely identified themselves overtly as anarchists. The level of violence was significant, and the targets—draft centers, corporate and university bureaucracies, and war-research facilities—fit perfectly with an anarchist critique of a militarized society. The Bureau of Alcohol, Tobacco, and Firearms estimated that between January 1969 and April 1970, 4,330 bombings were actually carried out and forty-three persons killed. Reminiscent of the work of Johann Most, William Powell's *The Anarchist Cookbook* (1971) included chapters on recreational drugs as well as advice on bombs and firearms.

More explicitly anarchistic and violence-prone, the radical ecological group Earth First! followed in the Thoreauvian tradition of favoring wilderness over civilization. They were inspired by Edward Abbey's 1975 novel *The Monkey Wrench Gang*, which advocates sabotage to protect the natural environment. Where mainstream environmental organizations lobbied Congress, the radical ecologists resorted to direct action, spiking trees to prevent logging and pouring sand into the gas tanks of bulldozers. The radical movements of the 1960s to 1990s suggest that anarchist violence may not be confined to the distant past, to grievances involving labor, or to immigrants with alien traditions.

BIBLIOGRAPHY

Adamic, Louis. *Dynamite: The Story of Class Violence in America*. Gloucester, Mass.: P. Smith, 1934.

Avrich, Paul. *The Haymarket Tragedy*. Princeton, N.J.: Princeton University Press, 1984.

Falk, Candace. *Love, Anarchy, and Emma Goldman*. New York: Holt, Rinehart, and Winston, 1984.

Murray, Robert. *Red Scare: A Study in National Hysteria, 1919–1920*. Minneapolis: University of Minnesota Press, 1955.

Nelson, Bruce. *Beyond the Martyrs: A Social History of Chicago's Anarchists*. New Brunswick, N.J.: Rutgers University Press, 1988.

Runkle, Gerald. *Anarchism: Old and New*. New York: Delacorte, 1972.

RICHARD D. SONN

See also **Civil Disorder; Haymarket Square Riot; Industrial Workers of the World; Red Scare; Sacco-Vanzetti Case.**

ANIMALS, VIOLENCE AGAINST

An enormous amount of violence is directed toward nonhuman animals. Although some animals certainly act in violent ways toward each other, it is the use and treatment of animals by humans that is responsible for the overwhelming amount of violence toward animals. Humans use animals for food and clothing, in experiments and product testing, and for sport and entertainment. In the United States alone, these uses involve billions of animals annually and result in an enormous amount of animal pain and suffering.

Our moral thinking about violence toward animals is marked by a fundamental contradiction. On the one hand, we claim to take animal interests seriously and to regard animals as having some moral significance, which would suggest that there are meaningful limits on our use and treatment of animals. On the other hand, we tend to ignore animal interests whenever it benefits us to do so, and there appear to be no consistently observed limits on our use and treatment of animals.

Animals as Things

Until the nineteenth century, Western culture explicitly regarded animals as things that had no morally significant interests and to which humans had no direct moral or legal obligations. That is, animals were viewed as not having any preferences, wants, or desires, and as indistinguishable from inanimate objects. The view that animals were merely things was expressed in two categories of thinking.

Into one category fall claims that animals were literally like stones because they were not the sorts of beings that could have any interests. For example, René Descartes (1596–1650), considered to be one of the founders of modern philosophy,

107

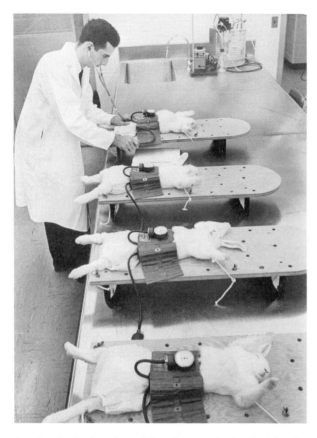

A scientist in Cranbury, New Jersey, checks the blood pressure of four New Zealand white rabbits during a test of hypertension medicine in October 1961. CORBIS/BETTMANN

maintained that animals were not conscious—they had no mind whatsoever—because they did not have souls, which God had invested only in human beings. As support for the idea that animals were not conscious, Descartes argued that animals did not use verbal or sign language.

Descartes maintained that because animals were not conscious, they were not sentient, that is, they could not experience pain, pleasure, or anything else. Descartes and his colleagues conducted experiments in which animals were nailed by their paws onto boards and were cut, burned, scalded, and mutilated in every conceivable manner. When the animals reacted as though they were suffering, Descartes dismissed their reactions as no different from the sound of a machine that was functioning improperly and that needed to be oiled. Animals were nothing more than "automatons" or moving machines. Under Descartes's view, it was as senseless to talk about our moral obligations to animals, machines created by God, as it was to talk about

our moral obligations to clocks, machines created by humans.

Into the second category falls the view that although animals were sentient and had interests in avoiding pain and suffering, sentience was not sufficient for moral significance and people might treat animals as if they were Cartesian automatons. For example, the German philosopher Immanuel Kant (1724–1804) recognized that animals could suffer, but he maintained that because animals supposedly lacked rationality and self-consciousness, humans could treat animals exclusively as means to their ends and that people had no moral obligations that they owed directly to animals.

The Humane-Treatment Principle and Animal Welfare Laws

Since the late nineteenth century, Anglo-American culture has very explicitly rejected the view that animals are merely things that lack moral value or have no morally significant interests. Although we continue to use animals for human purposes, most of us accept as a completely uncontroversial matter that our use and treatment of animals are guided by the humane-treatment principle, or that because animals, like humans, can suffer, humans have a moral obligation that they owe directly to animals to treat them with compassion and sympathy, and not to impose unnecessary suffering on them.

The humane-treatment principle finds its origins in the theories of the English lawyer and philosopher Jeremy Bentham (1748–1832). Bentham argued that although there were differences between humans and animals, there was an important similarity: both humans and animals can suffer and the ability to suffer—and not the ability to talk or to reason or any other capacity—is all that is required for animal interests to be morally significant.

Not all animals may be sentient, and it may be difficult to draw the line separating those that are capable of having conscious experiences of pain and suffering from those that are not, but there is no doubt that most of the animals that humans exploit are sentient. That is, although we may not know whether insects are capable of having conscious experiences of pain, we know that primates, cows, pigs, chickens, and rodents are sentient and capable of subjective mental experiences. Indeed, it is now becoming widely accepted by scientists that fish are sentient. Further, although we may not know whether a dog or cow feels pain or suffers

"Pets" and Other Animals

It is clear that at least some Americans already attribute moral status and rights to some animals. Over 50 percent of Americans live with cats or dogs. Ninety percent of those people regard their companion animals as members of their families and claim that they would risk injury or death to save the life of their animal. Americans spend approximately $7 billion annually on veterinary care for their companion animals, and over $20 billion on food and accessories.

There is, however, no difference between a companion animal (a dog or cat) and a cow or pig or many of the other animals that we eat. All of these animals are sentient and intelligent creatures that possess interests and personalities. It is a curious feature of our culture that we regard some animals as members of our families and that we stick dinner forks into other animals.

in exactly the same way that humans do, we do not know whether all humans experience pain or suffering in exactly the same way. We have no access to the minds of other humans that would permit us to prove that our experiences of pain and suffering are identical or even similar. What matters morally is that to be a sentient being—human or nonhuman—is to be the sort of being who has subjective experiences of pain and suffering and who has an interest in not having such experiences. In this sense, all sentient beings are, despite any differences, similar to each other and dissimilar from everything else in the world that is not sentient.

The humane-treatment principle is so entrenched in our moral culture that the state and federal laws of the United States, and the laws of other nations, purport to establish the principle as a legal standard in animal welfare laws. There are two kinds of such laws. General animal welfare laws, such as anticruelty laws, supposedly prohibit cruelty or the infliction of unnecessary pain, suffering, or death on animals without distinguishing between various uses of animals. For example, the state of New York prohibits the "torture" of or "cruelty" toward animals, and these terms are defined to include every act or omission "whereby unjustifiable physical pain, suffering or death is caused or permitted." Specific animal welfare laws

purport to apply the humane-treatment principle to a particular animal use. For example, the American Animal Welfare Act, enacted in 1966, and the British Cruelty to Animals Act, enacted in 1876, concern the treatment of animals used in experiments. The American Humane Slaughter Act, enacted in 1958, regulates methods for the killing of animals used for food purposes.

The humane-treatment principle and the animal welfare laws that reflect it require that humans balance the interests of animals in avoiding pain and suffering against their interests in using animals for a particular purpose. To balance interests means to assess the relative strengths of conflicting interests. If our interests in inflicting suffering outweigh the animal interests, then our interests prevail and the animal suffering is regarded as necessary. If no justifiable human interests are at stake, then the imposition of suffering on animals in that situation must be regarded as unnecessary. In other words, we may use animals but only when it is necessary to do so, and we should impose only the minimum amount of pain and suffering that is required for the purpose.

Although we may disagree about whether animal use or suffering is necessary in any particular context, it is clear that if a prohibition against unnecessary suffering means anything, it means that we cannot rely on our amusement, pleasure, or convenience to justify our exploitation of animals.

Human Uses of Animals

Our actual use and treatment of animals differ greatly from the moral and legal norms represented by the humane-treatment principle. Some uses of animals, such as for fur, are unquestionably gratuitous. The same observation, however, may be made about the overwhelming portion of our animal use, which cannot be described as necessary but merely furthers the satisfaction of human amusement, pleasure, or convenience.

Animal Agriculture. Animal agriculture comprises the major use of animals by humans. According to statistics from the U.S. Department of Agriculture, the United States slaughters approximately eight billion animals annually for food. Animal agriculture results in considerable suffering on the part of animals, many of which are castrated, branded, dehorned, debeaked, and ultimately slaughtered under conditions the best of which are quite brutal.

Most animals used for food are bred, raised, and killed on enormous mechanized farms that

Avoiding Violence at Your Local Supermarket

Two remarks commonly made by those who eat meat are: "If I had to kill the animal myself, I would probably be a vegetarian," and "Don't tell me how they raise animals for food—you'll put me off my dinner." Such remarks are indicative of the fact that many Americans are uncomfortable with violence toward animals used for food and prefer to avoid the issue altogether. Most Americans do not hunt and more than half oppose sport hunting; most Americans have never been in a slaughterhouse and have little if any knowledge about the way that animals are raised for food.

Meat products are sold at the local supermarket, neatly packaged in cellophane containers often under cartoon displays that show smiling pigs or cows promoting these products. Hamburgers and fried chicken are sold by friendly and familiar faces, such as Ronald McDonald or Colonel Sanders, at restaurants that often have special promotions aimed at children and that are generally considered as wholesome places for the family. Indeed, much of the marketing surrounding the sale of meat can be construed as attempting to sanitize animal agriculture and absolve the consumer of any guilt in connection with the support of the meat industry.

specialize in one species and house hundreds of thousands of animals at a time. This practice is known as factory farming. Factory farms are usually owned by large corporations and are operated on economies of scale; they are highly automated, and the concepts of profit and efficiency that drive factory farms require that animals be viewed as nothing more than economic commodities. The animals are raised in a manner that requires the least possible manual handling by humans. They are crammed in small spaces in the cheapest possible facilities and are fed the least expensive food. For example, most beef cows are squeezed shoulder to shoulder in large dirt corrals called feedlots. Broiler chickens are crammed into buildings holding thousands of birds, while chickens used in egg production are confined four to a wire cage that measures 144 square inches, often with cages stacked three to five layers high. These animals

have no place to nest or to exercise for their entire lives, and they often injure their feet and break their bones by catching their necks, wings, and toes on the cramped wire cages. Female pigs used for breeding are kept in metal farrowing stalls that are two feet wide.

No one maintains that it is necessary to eat meat or other animal products. Indeed, voices as mainstream as the U.S. Department of Agriculture and the American Dietetic Association have now recognized that a completely plant-based diet, supplemented by vitamin B_{12}, can provide the human body with sufficient protein, vitamins, minerals, and other nutrients to maintain excellent health. Animal foods have been coming under greater suspicion within the mainstream scientific community. Even the most traditional health-care professionals are urging a reduction in our consumption of meat and other animal products; others are calling for the elimination of such products from our diet. It is an uncontested fact that vegetarians have lower rates of many forms of cancer, heart disease, diabetes, hypertension, gallstones, kidney stones, and other diseases.

Moreover, animal agriculture has serious environmental consequences. Animals consume more protein than they produce. According to David Pimental (1997), for every kilogram (2.2 pounds) of animal protein produced, animals consume almost 6 kilograms, or over 13 pounds, of plant protein from grains and forage. More than 50 percent of U.S. grain and 40 percent of world grain is fed to animals to produce meat, rather than consumed directly by people. Because we need so many crops to feed the billions of animals we consume, we use an enormous amount of land to grow those crops. Although estimates vary, a conservative assessment is that approximately a third of the land area in the United States is devoted to the production of livestock. Our unlimited need for land to produce crops for animals has resulted in devastation of topsoil. Approximately 90 percent of cropland in the United States is losing topsoil at a rate thirteen times above the sustainable rate. Erosion may exceed a hundred times the sustainable rate on severely overgrazed pastures, and approximately 54 percent of American pasture land is overgrazed. Moreover, the need for land to produce grain and forage for animals has resulted in forest destruction throughout the world; as older pastures are destroyed through overgrazing, new land is cleared to replace them. It takes only one-sixth of an acre to supply a vegetarian with food for one year; it takes three and one-quarter acres to supply a meat eater with food for a year. That means an acre of land can feed twenty times more vegetarians than meat eaters.

Animal agriculture also consumes enormous amounts of other resources, such as water and energy. It takes up to one hundred times more water to produce one kilogram of animal protein than is required for one kilogram of plant protein. For example, it takes more than 25,000 gallons of water to produce one kilogram of beef, and approximately 240 gallons of water to produce one kilogram of wheat. On rangeland, it takes more than 50,000 gallons of water to produce one kilogram of beef flesh. It takes approximately 925 gallons of water to produce one kilogram of chicken flesh, and 130 gallons of water to produce one kilogram of potatoes. The average amount of fossil energy used for animal-protein production is more than eight times the average for grain-protein production.

In addition to the consumption of huge amounts of water and energy, animal agriculture results in serious water pollution because animals produce about 1.4 billion tons of waste per year—130 times more than the human population—and much of this waste is not and cannot be recycled and is instead dumped into our waters, with the result that the nitrogen in the wastes reduces the amount of dissolved oxygen in the water and causes levels of ammonia, nitrates, phosphates, and bacteria to increase. Animal agriculture also contributes significantly to global warming because cattle, sheep, and goats, in their flatulence and waste, emit seventy to eighty million tons of methane—one of the greenhouse gases—every year, accounting for as much as 30 percent of the methane released into the atmosphere.

In sum, animal agriculture cannot be described as necessary in any sense; our best justification for the violence that we inflict on farm animals is that we enjoy eating their flesh.

Hunting. The second largest source of institutionalized animal exploitation and slaughter in the United States is sport hunting. Conservative estimates are that approximately two hundred million animals, including doves, squirrels, rabbits, quail, pheasants, ducks, deer, elk, and bears, are killed annually by American hunters. These numbers do not include animals killed on commercial game ranches or those killed or wounded by hunters without being retrieved. It is estimated that bow-

hunters do not retrieve 50 percent of the animals hit with their arrows, and this underreporting increases the true death toll of hunting by at least tens of millions of animals. Many animals have been hunted to the point of extinction or near extinction.

Although hunters claim that their activity is necessary to reduce the overpopulation of animals, the overwhelming number of animals pursued by hunters are purposely nourished, sheltered, and restocked to ensure that their populations remain high enough to meet hunter demand. Because hunters spend large amounts of money every year buying licenses, permits, and equipment and because the U.S. government dispenses funds to state and wildlife agencies based on the number of licenses that they sell, these agencies view so-called game animals as economic resources to be maintained for "maximum harvest."

Federal and state wildlife agencies manipulate populations and ecosystems through a variety of techniques: clearcutting and burning of wooded areas to provide grazing ground for deer and other game animals, destroying predator populations, digging and diverting waterways and damming streams and rivers to provide lakes and marshes for ducks, planting berry bushes and fruit trees to attract deer and bear, winter feeding, providing roost structures and nesting grounds to attract popular species, restocking areas when populations get low, fencing in tracts of land to increase population density, and limiting hunting to the killing of bucks to ensure that there will be more does to increase population size.

Again, use of animals for sport hunting is not necessary in any sense; the best justification for the considerable violence that hunters impose on animals is that they derive pleasure from such activity.

Animals for Entertainment. Millions of animals are used for the sole purpose of providing entertainment. Animal "actors" are used in film and television. There are thousands of zoos, circuses, carnivals, horse and dog racetracks, marine mammal shows, rodeos, and live-bird shoots. Animals used in entertainment are often forced to endure lifelong incarceration and confinement, poor living conditions, extreme physical danger and hardship, and brutal treatment. Most animals used for entertainment purposes are killed when no longer useful. If a prohibition against unnecessary suffering is in any way meaningful, the use of animals for human entertainment must be considered as wholly unnecessary.

Although zoos are often justified on the grounds of education and protection and reintroduction of endangered species, studies show that the average zoo visitor spends little time in reading any information that may accompany an animal display. Endangered species often do not fare well in captivity, and zoo programs to reintroduce endangered species in the wild have been largely unsuccessful.

Animals in Biomedical Research. The most ostensibly compelling use of animals in terms of necessity is the use of animals in biomedical research. The exact numbers of animals used for this purpose in the United States is not known because the government does not require reporting of numbers of commonly used species, such as rats and mice, but government reports cite estimates that range from ten million to one hundred million animals annually. Experimenters use animals to measure the effects of toxins, diseases, drugs, radiation, bullets, and all forms of physical and psychological deprivations. Animals are burned, poisoned, irradiated, blinded, starved, given electric shocks and diseases (such as cancer) and infections (such as pneumonia), deprived of sleep, kept in solitary

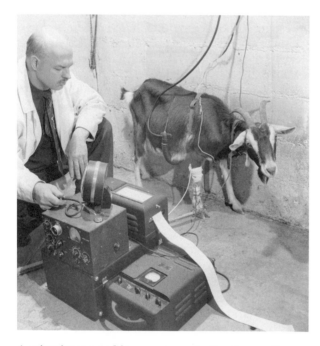

A scientist researching neuroses studies the reactions of a goat to a series of electric shocks, around 1950. CORBIS/HULTON-DEUTSCH COLLECTION

confinement, subjected to the removal of limbs and eyes, addicted to drugs, forced to withdraw from drug addiction, and caged for the duration of their lives. The animals that do not die during experimental procedures are almost always killed immediately afterward or are recycled for other experiments or tests until they are finally killed.

Even in this context, however, the necessity of animal use is questionable for at least four reasons. First, animals are routinely used to develop medical procedures or therapies; therefore, it is difficult to make any accurate factual representation about the actual causal role that animal use has played in any particular medical discovery. Since animals are always used as models of disease or to test procedures or drugs, it is difficult to know whether the procedures or discoveries that are attributed to animal use would not have occurred in its absence.

Second, to say that animal use is necessary is to say that there is no way to solve human health problems in the absence of animal use. But even if animal experiments produce some information that is beneficial to human health, it does not follow that animal experiments are the only way, or the most efficient way, to solve human health problems. For example, there is considerable controversy about whether the dollars expended on AIDS research involving animals would have been more effectively used on safe-sex education programs and needle exchanges. There are limited financial resources available to address any particular human problem, and the choice to spend these resources on animal experiments rather than other possible solutions often represents a political judgment as much as a scientific one.

Third, a growing number of scientists and health-care professionals are challenging the notion that animal experiments are necessary for human health purposes, and are maintaining that in many instances animal use has actually been useless and even counterproductive. For example, by 1963, various studies had demonstrated a strong correlation between cigarette smoking and lung cancer, but virtually all attempts to create an animal model of lung cancer through smoking had failed. As a result, leading cancer researchers proclaimed that the failure to induce experimental cancers in animals indicated doubt that smoking caused lung cancer. Because the animal experiments did not agree with the human data, the cigarette industry was able to delay health warnings about cigarettes for years, and many humans died as a result. Similarly, it was clear by the early 1940s that asbestos caused cancer in humans, but, once again, since animal experiments did not confirm the dangers of asbestos, this substance went unregulated in the United States for decades.

Certain medical discoveries attributed to animal use often were made despite animal use and not because of it. For example, polio experiments involving monkeys falsely indicated that the virus infected only the nervous system, and this mistake—directly related to reliance on animal models—delayed the discovery of the polio vaccine. Indeed, it was research with human cell cultures that led researchers to understand that the polio virus infected nonneural tissue and that the virus could be cultivated on nonneural tissue. Similarly, the use of a human's own veins to replace clogged arteries was delayed because animal experiments with dogs indicated that veins could not be used.

Fourth, even those who defend the use of animals in experiments intended to find cures for diseases agree that many animal experiments do not fall into this category. For example, some scientists criticize the use of animals in aggression studies, addiction studies, other psychological research, and for military research. Moreover, many animals are used in testing for the purpose of producing more consumer goods, which are arguably unnecessary except to increase corporate profits.

Animals as Property

The disparity between what we say about animals—that they possess morally significant interests and are not merely things—and our treatment of animals as nothing more than things is attributable to the status of animals as human property. In virtually all modern political and economic systems, animals are regarded as economic commodities that have no value apart from that which is accorded to them by their owners, whether individuals, corporations, or governments. The status of animals as property has been with humans for thousands of years. Indeed, there is historical evidence that the domestication and ownership of animals are closely related to the development of the very ideas of property and money. For example, the word *cattle* comes from the same etymological root as *capital*.

The law regards animals as objects that are assigned to human owners. The owner is entitled to exclusive physical possession of the animal. The owner may use the animal for economic or other gain and has the right to manage the animal by making contracts with respect to the animal or to use the animal as collateral for a loan. Animal owners have a duty to ensure that their property does not harm others, but as property, the animal can be sold, bequeathed, given away, or taken away as part of the execution of a legal judgment against the owner. The owner can also kill the animal for no reason whatsoever. Wild animals are generally regarded as owned by the state and held in trust for the benefit of the people; they may be reduced to private property through hunting or confining and taming them.

The legal status of animals as property means that animals can be treated as if they were things with no protectable interests, even though we claim to accord moral significance to at least some animal interests. The humane-treatment principle's balance of human and animal interests becomes, in effect, a balance of the interest of the property owner against the interest of the property. Such a balance cannot be achieved; as a general matter, the property has no interests that the property owner does not choose to recognize. The animal loses the balance even when the human interests at stake are clearly trivial (as in the case of animals used for entertainment purposes or for fur) and the animal interests are considerable.

For the most part, we allow animal interests to be ignored whenever it is economically beneficial for animal owners to do so, and we allow the owners of animals to determine how to value their animal property. For example, farmers in the United States are allowed to castrate, dehorn, and brand cattle—all very painful procedures—without providing any pain relief. Castrating cattle makes them more docile and easy to handle, dehorning permits more animals to be confined together without causing injury to one another or to human cattle handlers, and branding allows for the identification of animal property. Cattle ranchers have decided that these procedures do not decrease the value of the animals, and that the use of pain relief or alternative methods of raising cattle will only increase the costs of meat production without any corresponding economic benefit for producers or consumers.

Many state anticruelty laws specifically exempt major uses of animals, such as for food or hunting. Federal statutes that regulate animal experiments or slaughter impose few actual restrictions on the use of animals. As a general matter, the only time that animal abuse or mistreatment is restricted or

A hog being slaughtered in Chimayo, New Mexico. Corbis/Craig Aurness

prohibited is when humans inflict pain and suffering on animals that is not part of an accepted institutionalized use of animals. For example, when teenagers set fire to a dog, they may be prosecuted for violating an anticruelty law. The same conduct, however, by researchers engaged in burn experiments would be protected under the law.

In the 1990s many states made the violation of anticruelty laws punishable as felonies rather than as misdemeanors, and this means that the criminal penalties for violating these laws has been increased. Nevertheless, there is no indication that these laws are being enforced more vigorously or that they are being interpreted to apply to a broader range of conduct than in the past.

Speciesism

Humans treat animals in ways in which they do not treat their own kind. We do not regard it as morally or legally acceptable to use humans in experiments in which they do not give informed consent, and we limit the circumstances under which we permit humans to give such consent. We do not eat humans, hunt them, force them to perform in circuses and rodeos, or exhibit them in zoos. We no longer regard it as acceptable for some humans to be the property of others; the U.S. Constitution explicitly prohibits slavery.

How can we justify this differential treatment?

The usual response is to claim that some factual difference between humans and animals justifies our treating animals as resources. For example, we maintain that animals cannot think rationally or abstractly, or that animals are not self-conscious, and it is therefore acceptable for us to treat them as commodities. Reliance on such factual differences is problematic for two reasons. First, cognitive ethologists—people who study the thought processes and consciousness of animals—continually find more and more evidence that animals possess considerable intelligence and are able to think in sophisticated and complex ways. Second, many humans, such as young children, the severely retarded, or the senile, cannot think rationally or in abstract terms, and we would never think of using such humans as subjects in painful biomedical experiments, as forced organ donors, or as sources of food or clothing.

There is no characteristic that serves to distinguish humans from all other animals. Whatever attribute we may think makes humans special or distinctive and thereby different from other animals is shared by some group of nonhumans. Whatever defect we may think makes animals inferior to us is shared by some group of humans. In short, the only characteristic that we can point to that distinguishes humans from nonhumans is species. And species is in itself no more relevant than race, sex, or sexual orientation as a criterion for membership in the moral community. To exclude sentient nonhumans from the moral community simply on the basis of species is *speciesism*, just as to exclude humans from the moral community and treat them as things on the basis of race is racism.

There are some who argue that speciesism is justified on religious grounds, such as the notion that God created animals for human use. Apart from other difficulties involved in resting moral arguments on religious doctrines, such doctrines have also been used historically to justify discrimination against groups of humans.

Modern Animal Ethics

Most modern theories of animal ethics reject speciesism and recognize that we cannot morally justify treating animals solely as economic commodities. Theories of animal ethics can be grouped by the position they take on how to address the moral shortcomings of speciesism.

The animal rights position maintains that we ought to abolish the institution of animal property and recognize that animals have at least one right—the right not to be treated exclusively as the resources of humans. Our recognition of this one basic right would mean that we could no longer justify our use of animals for food, experiments, product testing, clothing, or entertainment.

The utilitarian position maintains that we may still treat animals as property but that we should not treat animals merely as economic commodities and allow humans to impose suffering on animals whenever it produces a property-related benefit. For example, in *Animal Liberation* (1975, 1990), Peter Singer does not challenge the status of animals as property per se, and he rejects the concept of animal rights. Rather, Singer argues that we may use animals as long as we attach greater weight to animal interests in not suffering. Yet Singer does not explain how we can respect animal interests if animals remain property. Similarly, feminist writers known as ecofeminists argue that we can retain animals as property as long as we apply an "ethic of care" in our treatment of animals. Again, these writers do not explain how we can accord moral significance to animal interests at the same time that we continue to treat them as property. A similar problem faced those who sought to regulate rather than abolish human slavery. Although there were reformist laws that sought to attach greater weight to slave interests and thereby modify the status of slaves as property, those laws were largely ineffective precisely because slaves remained property and the law was unwilling to interfere to any significant degree with the valuation of slaves by their owners.

There is a great diversity of views within the environmental movement, but virtually no environmental theory advocates the abolition of animal exploitation reflected in the animal rights position. The environmental position has its roots in conservationism, or the notion that we should preserve biodiversity for our own purposes. For example, the environmentalist concern for endangered species seeks to ensure that species are preserved for purposes of ecological balance and so that future generations of humans will be able to use members of the species as a resource. As soon as a species' population stabilizes, individual members of the species may be "harvested" or killed to the extent that the species itself is not threatened.

The debate about violence toward animals is not new. There was controversy about the issue among the ancient Greeks and the matter has been part of moral discourse in virtually every age and in every society. Given technological changes, such as factory farming and cloning, and human population increases, we are exploiting more animals than ever before in human history. It is unlikely that the treatment of animals is likely to change significantly as long as we continue to accept that violence toward other humans is either inevitable or morally acceptable, and our record in this regard does not bode well for animals.

BIBLIOGRAPHY

Bekoff, Marc, with Carron A. Meaney, eds. *Encyclopedia of Animal Rights and Animal Welfare*. Westport, Conn.: Greenwood, 1998.

Bencke, Adrian. *The Bowhunting Alternative*. San Antonio, Tex.: B. Todd, 1989.

Benton, Ted. *Natural Relations: Ecology, Animal Rights, and Social Justice*. London: Verso, 1993.

Carruthers, Peter. *The Animals Issue: Moral Theory in Practice*. Cambridge, U.K.: Cambridge University Press, 1992.

Clark, Stephen R. L. *The Moral Status of Animals*. Oxford, U.K.: Clarendon, 1977.

Clarke, Paul A. B., and Andrew Linzey, eds. *Political Theory and Animal Rights*. London: Pluto, 1990.

DeGrazia, David. *Taking Animals Seriously: Mental Life and Moral Status*. Cambridge, U.K.: Cambridge University Press, 1996.

Fox, Michael Allen. *Deep Vegetarianism*. Philadelphia: Temple University Press, 1999.

Francione, Gary L. *Animals, Property, and the Law*. Philadelphia: Temple University Press, 1995.

———. "Ecofeminism and Animal Rights." *Women's Rights Law Reporter* 18 (1996): 95–106.

———. *Introduction to Animal Rights: Your Child or the Dog?* Philadelphia: Temple University Press, 1999.

———. *Rain Without Thunder: The Ideology of the Animal Rights Movement*. Philadelphia: Temple University Press, 1996.

Francione, Gary L., and Anna E. Charlton. *Vivisection and Dissection in the Classroom: A Guide to Conscientious Objection.* Jenkintown, Pa.: AAVS, 1992.

Frey, R. G. *Interests and Rights: The Case Against Animals.* Oxford, U.K.: Clarendon, 1980.

Linzey, Andrew. *Christianity and the Rights of Animals.* London: S.P.C.K., 1987.

Midgely, Mary. *Animals and Why They Matter.* Athens: University of Georgia Press, 1984.

Masson, Jeffrey Moussaieff, with Susan McCarthy. *When Elephants Weep: The Emotional Lives of Animals.* New York: Delacorte, 1995.

Noske, Barbara. *Beyond Boundaries: Humans and Animals.* Montreal: Black Rose, 1997.

Pimental, David. "Livestock Production: Energy Inputs and the Environment." In *Proceedings of the Canadian Society of Animal Science: 47th Annual Meeting,* edited by Shannon L. Scott and Xin Zhao. Montreal: Canadian Society of Animal Science, 1997.

Pluhar, Evelyn. *Beyond Prejudice: The Moral Significance of Human and Nonhuman Animals.* Durham, N.C.: Duke University Press, 1995.

Rachels, James. *Created from Animals: The Moral Implications of Darwinism.* New York: Oxford University Press, 1990.

Regan, Tom. *The Case for Animal Rights.* Berkeley: University of California Press, 1983.

Rollin, Bernard E. *Animal Rights and Human Morality.* Rev. ed. Buffalo, N.Y.: Prometheus, 1992.

Sapontzis, S. F. *Morals, Reason, and Animals.* Philadelphia: Temple University Press, 1987.

Singer, Peter. *Animal Liberation.* 2d. ed. New York: New York Review of Books, 1990.

Sorabji, Richard. *Animal Minds and Human Morals.* Ithaca, N.Y.: Cornell University Press, 1993.

Swan, James A. *In Defense of Hunting.* New York: HarperCollins, 1995.

GARY L. FRANCIONE

See also **Environment, Violence Against; Fashion.**

ANIMAL STUDIES OF AGGRESSION AND VIOLENCE

The scientific study of aggression and violence in animals begins with the writings of Charles Darwin. Since then, the findings on aggression and violence in animals have been related to aspects of these behaviors in humans. Here, the article discusses four relevant topics: (1) Are humans more aggressive or violent than animals? (2) Are male animals usually more aggressive or violent than females? (3) Are aggression and violence in animals typically adaptive or pathological? and (4) Do genes as well as environment affect variation and development of aggression and violence in animals? These topics are preceded by a discussion of the types of aggression and violence in animals and followed by a discussion about animal models for human aggression and violence.

Types of Aggression and Violence

Since the early 1970s, it was recognized that there is more than one type of aggression in animals. Widely used classification schemes have been proposed by K. E. Moyer (1976) and by Paul F. Brain (1979). Moyer lists seven kinds of aggression: predatory, intermale, fear-induced, maternal, irritable, sex-related, and instrumental. Distinctions are made on the basis of type of response, eliciting stimuli, reinforcing properties, and physiological mechanisms. Brain lists five types of aggression: self-defensive, maternal, predatory, reproductive termination, and social. Self-defensive includes escape-directed, pain-induced, and proximity-related forms of aggression; and social includes rank-related, territorial, and mate-selection forms of aggression. Distinctions are based primarily on behavioral function and emotional tone. John Archer (1988) has proposed a system for resolving conflicts between the two classification systems. Also, if the aggressive behavior inflicts serious injury or death, any of these types of aggression may be a type of violence. The answers to the questions raised above and their relevance to human behavior may not be the same for each type of aggression or violence in animals.

Humans Compared with Animals

Aggressive behavior is widespread throughout the animal kingdom. Fighting among adults occurs in all multicellular animal phyla and vertebrate classes. However, it was long thought that, in contrast to humans, such fighting in animals rarely led to injury or death. Thus, humans but not animals were seen by Konrad Lorenz as violent, and animals but not humans appeared to inhabit a nonviolent world. However, by the 1980s, it was recognized that animals live in a world of violence. Across the animal phyla, there are accounts that attacks of one adult species member on another inflict serious injury and death. Lethal attacks on adult members of the same species have been reported for ants, bees, gulls and other birds, lions, cougars, wolves, hyenas, black bears, grizzly bears, macaque monkeys, langur monkeys, and chimpanzees. For many phyla, there are also reports of adults killing infants of the same species. These include insects, crustaceans, fish, amphibians, birds, rodents, carnivores, and primates.

Two grizzly bears fight over fishing territory while a third watches at Brooks Falls, Katmai National Park, Alaska, July 1992. CORBIS/PAUL A. SOUDERS

Males Versus Females

Many believe that across species, males are more aggressive and violent than females. (See, for example, Barash and Lipton 1997). This alleged sex difference in animals has been viewed as consistent with, as well as providing, a phylogenetic explantion for an alleged sex difference in human aggression and violence. However, such sex differences in animals depend on the type of aggression and on the species. There may be, for example, no sex differences in frequency or intensity of any type of aggression or violence in mice. However, there are differences in the circumstances and situations in which males and females attack. On the one hand, adult males primarily attack adult males, whereas adult females attack both adult males and females. On the other hand, both male and female mice attack and kill infants of either sex. In contrast, there are sex differences in aggression and violence in hyenas. Female hyenas are more aggressive toward adults than are males, and females are more likely than males to kill female siblings. However, female lions are more likely than males to kill same-sex intruders, whereas males are more likely than females to kill infants. These species and behavior differences provide a new context for suggestions that male and female humans may be equally aggressive, violent, and warlike, or that sex differences in humans may depend on the type of aggression or violence.

Adaptive or Pathological?

There was a tendency before the 1970s to see animal violence as pathological, and there still was a tendency in the 1990s to view human violence as pathological. Violence in animals was first reported in captive or crowded populations, and it was inferred that this violence was an abnormal response to the stress of these situations. However, by the 1980s, it was recognized that animal aggression and violence are usually adaptive.

Aggression among adults of the same species may be "defensive" or "offensive." Defensive aggression serves to protect the individual or his or her progeny from attacks by others. Offensive aggression enables an individual to obtain and retain resources, such as space, food, and mates. Thus, aggressive behavior has an obvious survival value. It might be expected that it would be most adaptive for an individual to be highly aggressive and violent. Yet across most, if not all, species, many disputes among adult animals are resolved with little or no overt fighting or injury or death. However, some disputes do escalate to overt attacks with injury or death of an opponent. Game theory has been used to develop ecological and evolutionary explanations for these findings. Game theory shows that for social behaviors, such as aggression, what is optimal for one individual to do depends on what the other is likely to do. For example, if two individuals are likely to engage in fighting with the potential for injury or death, it

---

Intraspecies Killings

The incidence of killing another member of the same species may be as high or higher in some animals as it is in humans, even if our episodic wars are included. The incidence of homicides in Western cultures is about 1 per 10,000, whereas in lions the incident of one adult lion killing another is 20 to 2,000 times as high as that for homicides. Similar findings have been reported for mountain gorillas. Thus, it may be that no unique explanations for human violence are needed; rather, they may be needed to account for the relative nonviolence or peacefulness of humans in comparison to other animals.

---

may be advantageous to settle a dispute before its escalation. The decision of whether to settle or escalate a dispute depends on mutual assessment of fighting ability (resource-holding power, or RHP), which is an indicator of who is likely to win an escalated fight. Game theory has predicted and observations have confirmed that when RHP is equal, fights often escalate from display to attacks; when RHP is unequal, the dispute may be resolved without escalation to attack. The early models assumed that information of RHP was acquired at the start of a dispute. Other models propose that an object of the gradual escalation is to obtain accurate information at the lowest cost about the RHP of the opponent. The decision of whether to settle or escalate a dispute also depends on assessment by each individual of the value of a resource. Again, game theory has predicted and observation has confirmed that disputes often escalate to potentially injurious or lethal fights when the value of the resource is high for both combatants. It has been argued that game theory models for escalation of disputes also apply to humans.

Infanticide is another type of aggression and violence in animals and humans. Several adaptive functions have been proposed for infanticide. These include sexual selection (e.g., killing of infants by male lions when they take over a pride of female lions); exploitation (e.g., killing infants for food by female land crabs); competition (e.g., killing wild dog infants of subordinate female by dominate female to remove food competition for her pups); and parental manipulation (the killing of offspring if conditions for their survival are

poor). Similarly, it has been suggested that some infanticide by humans may be understood in the context of the theory of evolved adaptations.

Genes or Environment?

Genes are known to influence variation in aggression in some species of fish, birds, and mammals, and it is very likely that they do so in all multicellular animals. Since the genetics of mice is well characterized, most research on the genetics of aggression and violence in mammals has been done with mice. Inbred strains, selected strains, and crosses of these strains have been used to show that individual differences for offense and other types of aggression in males or females are in part due to genetic variation. Also, some of the individual chromosomes and genes causing this variation have been identified. There are genes with effects on offense on the male-specific part of the Y chromosome and of chromosome 17; these genes have not been identified. The individual and identified genes (sixteen of them by 1998) include those with effects on hormone receptors, neurotransmitters, enzymes, or development. A gene for a hormone receptor affects not only the male but also the female offense. Its null mutant (no functional protein) decreases offense in males but increases it in females. In contrast, the null mutant for the serotonin receptor gene increases aggression in male and female mice. It has been reported that male mice with the null mutant of the gene for nitric oxide synthase not only attack but also kill other adult males.

However, it should not be thought that since genes affect aggression in mice, there is no influence of the environment on aggression in mice. In 1942, it was shown that the experience of winning or losing a fight can change aggressive behavior. Highly aggressive mice become pacific after a series of defeats, and highly pacific mice become very aggressive after a series of wins. In the 1990s, it was shown that extreme stress enhances aggression of mice. Also, after extreme stress, some mice attack and also kill other mice. In fact, every aspect of the environment and life history of a mouse can and does influence its aggressive behavior.

It is clear that both genes and environment play a role in individual differences and development of offense and other types of aggression in mice. This was not an issue in the 1990s. Rather, the issues were what the genes and environments alone and in interaction do to affect aggression and violence. It is reasonable to assume that both play a role in the aggressive behaviors of other species, including those of humans. However, much remains to be done to show that in humans, a type of aggression or violence is heritable and to identify genes with effects on these behaviors. Research with mice may assist in finding genes with effects on aggression in other species, since most genes in mice are homologous with genes in other mammalian species. By the late 1990s, it was possible to determine whether the homologue of a gene with an effect on a type of aggression or violence in mice affects a type of aggression or violence in other mammalian species, including humans.

Animal Models

There are two main types of animal models for human aggression and violence. These are behavioral and biological models, which are the basis for developing and testing exact hypotheses about the behavior and its biology in humans.

For behavioral models, it should be recognized that any animal behavior will always be, at best, both similar and different in comparison to that of humans. For this reason, Paul Scott has recommended that no animal species can serve as an exact model for human aggression and violence, but, rather, that some aspects of animal behavior in a species will appear relevant to human aggression. Consequently, he proposed that information should be accumulated on the various kinds of aggression in a wide range of species. Scott has carried out part of this program by considering the advantages and disadvantages of dogs and mice as potential models for some aspects of human aggression and violence. D. Caroline Blanchard and Robert J. Blanchard (1984) have taken a similar approach in their research program on animal models of human aggression and violence. In their two-part strategy, they first describe, examine, and analyze aggressive behaviors in the context of a species' ecology and evolution. The second part is a systematic comparison of the behaviors in humans and the animal model in order to determine the extent of point-by-point correspondence. They have done this for offense and defense aggression in rats and humans, as well as to some degree in several mammalian species. Stephen C. Maxson's 1998 study discusses the advantages and limitations of behavioral models for human aggression and violence in the context of mouse models for impulsive aggression in humans.

Biological models are used to develop hypotheses about the role of anatomical, physiological, or neurochemical systems in human aggression and violence. For example, effects of testosterone or serotonin on offense in animals are studied, and hypotheses are generated about their possible effects on similar behaviors in humans. For these, the methods of endocrinology and pharmacology are widely used in developing the respective animal models. Single-gene mutants in mice may have value as biological models for human aggression and violence.

Genic models are a special case of biological models. These are based on effects of homologous genes on a behavior in animals and humans. An example of this type of model is the effect of mutants for the monoamine oxidase A gene on aggression in mice and humans. Monoamine oxidase A is an enzyme that degrades such neurotransmitters as serotonin. If other genes with effects on a type of aggression or violence in mice have an effect on a type of aggression or violence in humans, these may also become genic models.

Research on aggression and violence in animals has relevance to the understanding of these behaviors in humans. The animal research provides a cross-species context for thinking about aggression and violence in humans. Also, it suggests that both genes and environment are causes of variation in these behaviors, that sex differences in these behaviors depend on the type of aggression and environmental circumstances, and that these behaviors may be adaptive as well as pathological. Animal research can also provide hypotheses about the genetic, endocrine, and neural mechanisms involved in these behaviors. These in turn can be related to the powerful effects of the environment on the development and occurrence of aggression and violence in animals and humans.

BIBLIOGRAPHY

Archer, John. *The Behavioral Biology of Aggression.* Cambridge: Cambridge University Press, 1988.

Archer, John, and Felicity Huntingford. "Game Theory Models and Escalation of Animal Fights." In *The Dynamics of Aggression,* edited by Michael Potegal and John F. Knutson. Hillsdale, N.J.: Lawrence Erlbaum, 1994.

Albert, D. J., M. L. Walsh, and R. H. Jonik. "Aggression in Humans: What Is Its Biological Foundation?" *Neuroscience and Biobehavioral Reviews* 17 (1993).

Barash, David P., and Judith Eve Lipton. *Making Sense of Sex: How Genes and Gender Influence Our Relationships.* Washington, D.C.: Island Press, 1997.

Berkowitz, Leonard. *Aggression: Its Causes, Consequences, and Control.* Philadelphia: Temple University Press, 1993.

Bjorkqvist, Kaj, and Pirkko Niemela. *Of Mice and Women: Aspects of Female Aggression.* San Diego, Calif.: Academic, 1992.

Blanchard, D. Caroline, and Robert J. Blanchard. "Affect and Aggression: An Animal Model Applied to Human Behavior." In *Advances in the Study of Aggression.* Vol. 1, edited by Robert J. Blanchard and D. Caroline Blanchard. New York: Academic, 1984.

Brain, Paul F. *Hormones and Aggression.* Vol. 2. St. Albans, U.K.: Eden Press, 1979.

Brunner, Han G. "MAOA Deficiency and Abnormal Behavior: Perspectives on Aggression." In *Genetics of Criminal and Antisocial Behaviour,* edited by Gregory R. Bock and Jamie A. Goode. New York: Wiley, 1996.

Cook, Philip W. *Abused Men: The Hidden Side of Domestic Violence.* Westport, Conn.: Praeger, 1997.

Daly, Martin, and Margo Wilson. *Homicide.* New York: Aldine de Gruyter, 1988.

Frank, Laurence G., Stephen E. Glickman, and Paul Light. "Fatal Sibling Aggression, Precocial Development, and Androgens in Neonatal Spotted Hyenas." *Science* 252 (1991).

Hrdy, Sarah Blaffer. *The Woman Who Never Evolved.* Cambridge, Mass.: Harvard University Press, 1981.

Huntingford, Felicity, and Angela Turner. *Animal Conflict.* New York: Chapman and Hall, 1987.

Jones, David E. *Women Warriors: A History.* Washington, D.C.: Brassesy's, 1997.

Lorenz, Konrad. *On Aggression.* New York: Harcourt, Brace, and World, 1963.

Maxson, Stephen C. "The Genetics of Aggression in Vertebrates." In *The Biology of Aggression,* edited by Paul F. Brain and David Benton. Rockville, Md.: Skjthoff and Noordhoff, 1981.

———. "Homologous Genes, Aggression, and Animal Models." *Developmental Neuropsychology* 14, no. 1 (1998).

———. "Methodological Issues in Genetic Analyses of an Agonistic Behavior (Offense) in Male Mice." In *Techniques for the Genetic Analysis of Brain and Behavior: Focus on the Mouse,* edited by David Goldowitz, Richard E. Wimer, and Douglas Wahlsten. New York: Elsevier, 1992.

———. "Potential Genetic Models of Aggression and Violence in Males." In *Genetically Defined Animal Models of Neurobehavioral Dysfunctions,* edited by Peter Driscoll. Boston: Birkhauser, 1992.

Moyer, K. E. *The Psychobiology of Aggression.* New York: Harper and Row, 1976.

Pearson, Patricia. *When She Was Bad: Violent Women and the Myth of Innocence.* New York: Viking, 1997.

Rensberger, Boyce. *The Cult of the Wild.* New York: Doubleday, 1977.

Scott, Paul. "Agonistic Behavior of Mice and Rats: A Review." *American Zoologist* 6 (1966).

———. "The Dog as a Model for Human Aggression." In *Biological Perspectives on Aggression,* edited by Kevin J. Flannelly, Robert J. Blanchard, and D. Caroline Blanchard. New York: Alan R. Liss, 1984.

Southwick, Charles H. "Conflict and Violence in Animal Societies." In *Animal Aggression: Selected Readings,* edited by Charles H. Southwick. New York: Van Nostrand Reinhold, 1969.

Wrangham, Richard, and Dale Peterson. *Demonic Males: Apes and the Origin of Human Violence.* Boston: Houghton Mifflin, 1996.

STEPHEN C. MAXSON

See also **Aggression; Endocrinology; Genetics; Methodologies of Violence Research; Theories of Violence.**

ANOREXIA AND BULIMIA

The current Western ideal of feminine beauty requires that women be unrealistically thin, even gaunt. Such a standard has been linked to pervasive struggles with weight and body image among women in the United States. This "normative discontent" characterizes one end of a continuum of eating and weight concerns, with actual eating disorders (EDs) at the opposite end of the spectrum.

EDs affect approximately 2 percent of the population, of which 95 percent are women; onset occurs mostly in adolescence or early adulthood. EDs are multidetermined phenomena influenced by social and cultural pressures, life events, family environment, personality, and genetic predisposition. The American Psychiatric Association lists among the EDs anorexia nervosa (AN), bulimia nervosa (BN), and eating disorders not otherwise specified (NOS), a group that includes binge eating disorder (BED). AN involves weight loss and maintenance of body weight below 85 percent of that expected for one's age and height and is subtyped into *restricting* (A-R) and *bingeing-purging* (A-BP) groups. BN refers to a chaotic pattern of eating involving repeat episodes of bingeing followed by some form of compensatory behavior (that is, vomiting, exercising excessively, and abusing laxatives, diet pills, or diuretics). BED entails repeat bingeing without compensatory behavior. Prevalence rates for AN and BN are, respectively, .5 percent to 1 percent and 1 percent to 3 percent among adolescent and young adult women, and for BED roughly 2 percent among the general population. Were these rates to include subclinical eating patterns (that is, those meeting less than full diagnostic criteria), the numbers would more than double.

Women with eating disorders are, in general, not regarded as overtly violent toward others. Their aggression is typically turned inward in the form of self-destructive action and a passive-aggressive interpersonal style. Because of the potential harm to the body, self-destructiveness is embedded in the definition of EDs. These women commonly suffer digestive problems, muscle atrophy, dental problems, and tissue damage to the throat, esophagus, and stomach. More severe self-harm can include heart problems, electrolyte imbalance, diabetes, and even death. The long-term mortality rate from BN and BED is unknown, but it is over 10 percent from AN.

For a number of individuals with EDs the embattled relationship with their bodies extends beyond the manipulation of food and weight to involve other self-destructive acts, including self-cutting, substance abuse, involvement in physically and verbally abusive relationships, and suicide. In 1997 Angela Favaro and Paolo Santonastaso found that of 495 patients with EDs, 29 percent reported current suicidal ideation and 26 percent reported multiple attempts. This evidently more disturbed subgroup displayed pathology that, although shaped by cultural ideals, was likely compounded by more psychologically debilitating life experiences.

Self-destructive behavior has been generally associated with trauma, namely sexual and physical abuse, findings that have influenced ED research. Studies report sexual abuse, including rape, in about 30 percent of outpatient ED samples. Estimates of physical battery in women with BN range from 23 percent to 40 percent. Maria Root (1991) notes that symptoms associated with EDs—namely major depression, anxiety, dissociation, powerlessness, lack of control, cognitive distortions, low self-esteem, and interpersonal difficulties—overlap with those of post-traumatic stress disorder (PTSD). She argues that EDs constitute a gender-specific post-traumatic stress response to physical victimization and that their symptoms serve important coping functions.

Methodological limitations and similarly high base rates of abuse in other clinical and nonclinical samples of women caution against assuming any causal connection. Yet the co-morbidity of abuse and EDs is compelling and continues to foster research. Research in the 1990s began to explore the relation between victimization and EDs by focusing on possible mediating variables. Attention has been drawn to the impact of abuse frequency, duration, and severity; verbal and emotional abuse; features of family environment in which abuse occurs; response of significant others; and the role of post-traumatic stress. Another emerging focus was type of ED symptom involved. Reports show the prevalence of sexual abuse, aggravated assault, and PTSD to be significantly higher in women with

BN than in other ED subgroups. Similarly, compared with other subgroups, prevalence of suicide attempts is reportedly higher in A-BP and BN. These results suggest that, of the ED symptoms, compensatory behavior in particular may be most strongly linked to victimization. Clearly more research is needed to understand the complex ways in which EDs and victimization are related.

ED symptoms have multiple functions. Typically individuals with EDs have great difficulty identifying, expressing, and regulating internal states. Without the words to speak their inner life, communication is rendered through symptomatic behaviors, or enactments, that simultaneously limit self-awareness. Bingeing, for example, may at once express and "cover over" intolerable rage; purging may act to punish perceived wrongdoing; and restricting may be an anorexic's only way of fending off feelings of intrusion by means of overcontrol. Strikingly bereft of nonfood-related methods of coping, many women with EDs use eating as a way to self-soothe or regulate tension. ED symptoms are, in essence, what Freud termed "compromise formations" (1923), at once expressing inner strife through action, while keeping it from consciousness.

The goal of psychotherapy is to increase a person's capacity for self-awareness and self-expression through the use of language, thereby decreasing reliance on symptomatic enactments. Such behaviors only perpetuate a way of life whose misguided end has been to restore control and power through the pursuit of thinness. Outpatient psychotherapy, including individual and group modalities, is commonly used to treat EDs. Group work is often psychoeducational and may provide a less threatening entrée into the pychotherapeutic process. Individuals severely at risk of self-injury require hospitalization. In cases where there is a history of abuse, working through the trauma, attendant shame, and self-blame is essential to intercept the cycle of victimization rendered by others and by the individual. The long-term, self-destructive nature of these disorders is a challenge to psychotherapists. Because successful treatment hinges on a strong alliance, health practitioners must, in order to remain empathic, stay cognizant of the terrors both expressed and defended against by these symptoms.

BIBLIOGRAPHY

American Psychiatric Association. *Diagnostic and Statistical Manual of Mental Disorders.* 4th ed. Washington, D.C.: American Psychiatric Association, 1994.

Bulik, Cynthia M., Patrick F. Sullivan, and Marcia Rorty. "Childhood Sexual Abuse in Women with Bulimia." *Journal of Clinical Psychiatry* 50 (1987): 460–464.

Cross, Lisa. "Body and Self in Feminine Development: Implications for Eating Disorders and Delicate Self-Mutilation." *Bulletin of the Menninger Clinic* 57 (1983): 41–68.

Dansky, Bonnie S., et al. "The National Women's Study: Relationship of Victimization and Posttraumatic Stress Disorder to Bulimia Nervosa." *International Journal of Eating Disorders* 21 (1997): 213–228.

Favaro, Angela, and Paolo Santonastaso. "Suicidality in Eating Disorders: Clinical and Psychological Correlates." *Acta Psychiatrica Scandinavia* 85 (1997): 508–514.

Freud, Sigmund. Two Encyclopedia Articles. *Standard Edition of the Complete Psychological Works of Sigmund Freud.* Vol. 18. 1923, p. 242.

Garfinkel, Paul E., et al. "Should Amenorrhoea Be Necessary for the Diagnosis of Anorexia Nervosa?" *British Journal of Psychiatry* 168 (1996): 500–506.

Garner, David M., and Lionel W. Rosen. "Eating Disorders." In *Handbook of Aggressive and Destructive Behavior in Psychiatric Patients*, edited by M. Hersen, R. T. Ammerman, and L. A. Sisson. New York: Plenum, 1994.

Hastings, Theresa, and Jeffrey M. Kern. "Relationships Between Bulimia, Childhood Sexual Abuse, and Family Environment." *International Journal of Eating Disorders* 15, no. 2 (1994): 103–111.

Kaner, Angelica, Cunthia M. Bulik, and Patrick F. Sullivan. "Abuse in Adult Relationships of Bulimic Women." *Journal of Interpersonal Violence* 8, no. 1 (1993): 52–63.

Kearney-Cooke, Anne, and Ruth H. Striegel-Moore. "Treatment of Child Sexual Abuse in Anorexia Nervosa and Bulimia Nervosa: A Feminist Psychodynamic Approach." *International Journal of Eating Disorders* 15, no. 4 (1994): 305–319.

Lacey, J. Hubert. "Self-Damaging and Addictive Behaviour in Bulimia Nervosa." *British Journal of Psychiatry* 163 (1993): 190–194.

Rodin, Judith, Lisa Silberstein, and Ruth H. Striegel-Moore. "Women and Weight: A Normative Discontent." *Psychology and Gender. Nebraska Symposium on Motivation* 32 (1985): 267–307.

Root, Maria P. P. "Persistent, Disordered Eating as a Gender-Specific, Post-Traumatic Stress Response to Sexual Assault." *Psychotherapy* 28 (1991): 96–101.

Root, Maria P. P., and Patricia Fallon. "The Incidence of Victimization Experiences in a Bulimic Sample." *Journal of Interpersonal Violence* 3, no. 2 (1988): 161–173.

Spitzer, Robert L., et al. "Binge Eating Disorder: A Multisite Field Trial of the Diagnostic Criteria." *International Journal of Eating Disorders* 11 (1991): 191–203.

Weiner, Kristi E., and J. Kevin Thompson. "Overt and Covert Sexual Abuse: Relationship to Body Image and Eating Disturbance." *International Journal of Eating Disorders* 22 (1997): 273–284.

ANGELICA KANER

See also **Health and Medical Factors: Diet and Nutrition; Self-Destructiveness; Suicide.**

ANTI-SEMITISM. *See* Holocaust; Jews; Race and Ethnicity; Religion.

ANTIWAR PROTESTS

A survey of antiwar dissent from the American Revolution to the Vietnam War permits one to make several observations. First, government authorities—and not protesters—have tended to be the perpetrators of violence. In World War I federal agencies and vigilantes suppressed antiwar dissent. Fifty years later, however, thousands of antiwar activists embraced violent protest. Significantly, on the one occasion in the nineteenth century when antiwar partisans initiated violence (New York City, 1863), the demonstrators were not affiliated with any peace group. Second, when it was expedient, some peace activists have adopted a pro-war stance. This was true in the 1860s and the 1930s. Third, antiwar demonstrators often hailed from the upper middle class and had little connection with working-class citizens—the very people most likely to be drafted. Finally, peace organizations usually experienced their greatest period of growth *after* a war broke out. In the history of the United States, however, dissenters, for the most part, have had little effect on the conduct of foreign policy during wartime. The exception is the Vietnam War. Although the 1960s antiwar movement caused enough domestic disruption to make the wider escalation of the conflict untenable, the violent behavior of many peace partisans limited their appeal.

At any given moment in American history there never existed an ideologically monolithic peace movement. Some protesters might vigorously oppose a particular war but just as enthusiastically support another armed conflict if they believed the cause was just. Such people are better described as antiwar protesters and not necessarily as peace activists. Antiwar protesters sometimes include among their ranks individuals who do not wish to be drafted as well as those who would advocate America's military defeat at the hands of its foes. Pacifist peace advocates, on the other hand, oppose war under all circumstances and are prepared to be jailed for their opposition to America's military involvement overseas. Radical pacifists would proceed one step further, opting to engage in forms of civil disobedience that might include the destruction of property and the inadvertent injury of those who stand in their way. When engaged in provocative acts, antiwar protesters and radical pacifists often provoke a violent response from local and federal government officials. Although pacifist peace activists try to avoid confrontational tactics, they, nonetheless, sometimes also find themselves being violently repressed.

The American Revolution to the Civil War

In 1776 Anthony Benezet, a Pennsylvania Quaker and pacifist, published an appeal to the Continental Congress calling for an end to the Revolutionary War. Although revolutionaries ignored Benezet's "Thoughts on the Nature of War," they gave pacifists a respectful hearing. Four states—Delaware, New Hampshire, New York, and Pennsylvania—would not coerce conscientious objectors into bearing arms. Indeed, General George Washington insisted that pacifists be left alone. Any violence directed against antiwar dissenters was sporadic and not sanctioned by state representatives.

Angered by the outbreak of a second war between Great Britain and the United States (1812–1815), David Low Dodge, a wealthy New Yorker, established the New York Peace Society. In 1815 Dodge also wrote a critique of American foreign policy entitled *War Inconsistent with the Religion of Jesus Christ*. Meanwhile in New England, twenty-two clergymen, college presidents, and essayists founded the Massachusetts Peace Society. Thirteen years later, in 1828, the peace societies of New York, Massachusetts, Maine, New Hampshire, and Pennsylvania merged to form the American Peace Society (APS). Led by William Ladd, a Harvard graduate, the APS had three hundred partisans, including the writer Ralph Waldo Emerson. Although primarily concerned with foreign policy, these peace activists embraced other causes of moral reform in the antebellum period—notably, temperance, restriction of Irish Catholic immigration, and the abolition of slavery.

The APS experienced its first ideological schism in 1838 when William Lloyd Garrison, an antislavery publisher and radical pacifist, issued his "Declaration of Sentiments of the New England Non-Resistant Society." Garrison urged citizens to engage in massive acts of civil disobedience in the event America once again went to war. Unlike the members of the APS, Garrison denied that there could ever be a "just war" that would permit citizens to take up arms with a clean conscience. Garrison's ideas influenced elite college leaders, Protestant clergy, and writers in New England and the Western Reserve of Ohio. His greatest convert was the essayist Henry David Thoreau. In 1848 Thoreau wrote "Civil Disobedience." Charging that Southerners had conspired to spread slavery into the western territories won by the United States in the Mexican War (1846–1848), Thoreau exhorted people not to pay their taxes and to engage in other forms of nonviolent protest.

Both Thoreau and Garrison ultimately abandoned their nonviolent principles. The efforts of Democratic Party leaders to permit slavery to enter the Kansas-Nebraska territories (1854), as well as the U.S. Supreme Court's ruling in *Dred Scott* (1857) that northern states could not prohibit slavery, turned peace partisans into war-minded militants. Indeed, Thoreau cheered in 1859 when the abolitionist John Brown seized a federal arsenal at Harpers Ferry, Virginia, with the intent of arming slaves for revolution. When eleven southern states left the Union between 1860 and 1861, APS leaders like Senator Charles Sumner of Massachusetts and nonviolent pacifists like Garrison urged President Abraham Lincoln to put down the rebellion and abolish slavery. Peace activists rationalized their support for war by arguing that the antislavery cause superseded all other reforms. Moreover, they contended, since Americans were only killing other Americans, the rebellion was not like a real war in which foreigners were slain.

Many northern Democrats opposed going to war with the South. Overall public support for the war rose or fell depending upon the Union's military fortunes. Most "Peace Democrats" hailed from sections of the North that had cultural ties to Dixie. Lancaster, Ohio, for instance, the home of the Union general William Tecumseh Sherman, sent Edson Olds, an antiwar Democrat, to the state legislature in 1863. Southern Ohio in general, having been settled by Virginians, opposed any military action that might end slavery and promote racial equality. In eastern cities like New York, Irish Catholics resented the nativist sentiment of the abolitionists and the Republican Party. Hundreds of New York City's Irish rioted against the draft in July 1863. Rioters, who complained that poor working-class Catholics bore the brunt of the draft because middle-class Protestants could afford to pay someone to take their place, lynched several blacks and attacked federal draft boards. Union troops fresh from the Gettysburg battlefield fired cannon into the mob. Ultimately 105 people died, making the New York City antidraft riots the bloodiest urban uprising ever in American history.

The World War I Era

By the end of the nineteenth century America was becoming a global military and economic power. In 1898 the United States fought a hundred-day war against Spain, winning Puerto Rico and the Philippines in the process. A subsequent guerrilla insurgency that lasted until 1902 resulted in the deaths of 250,000 Filipinos and 7,000 Americans. The novelist Mark Twain denounced both the Spanish-American War and the Filipino conflict, while thirty thousand citizens established the Anti-Imperialist League. Some antiwar activists feared that America was becoming an imperialist power like Great Britain; others did not want "black" Puerto Ricans and Filipinos potentially acquiring American citizenship. In 1900 former Nebraska congressman William Jennings Bryan ran as a presidential peace candidate on the Democratic ticket. He lost. Fifteen years later, as the U.S. secretary of state, Bryan resigned in protest because he thought President Woodrow Wilson was leading America into war with Germany. Americans who traveled into European combat zones, Bryan argued, did not merit the protection of the United States.

In 1910 the industrialist Andrew Carnegie established the Carnegie Endowment for International Peace. A year after the outbreak of World War I in Europe (1914–1918), Jane Addams, a prominent Chicago social worker, founded the Women's Peace Party. (By 1919 the organization changed its name to the Women's International League for Peace and Freedom.) In 1915 peace activists who embraced the pacifism and economic reform agenda of the Protestant Social Gospel organized the Fellowship of Reconciliation (FOR). Antiwar activists between 1914 and 1917 typically included social workers, Protestant clergy, journalists, and teachers. William Lloyd Garrison's daughter, Fanny Garrison Villard, was one such pacifist. Roger Baldwin, a peace partisan who went on to found the American Civil Liberties Union after World War I, created the People's Council of America for Peace and Democracy in 1917.

Once Wilson declared war on Germany in April 1917, federal, state, and local patriotic groups hounded peace activists. Since fifty-six congressmen (out of 511) had voted against going to war, the highest number ever recorded, and millions of Americans of Irish and German descent were of an anti-British and isolationist bent, government officials felt it necessary to suppress dissent. In 1917 Congress instituted a draft and passed the Espio-

nage Act. A year later Congress enacted the Sedition Act. Taken together, these legislative initiatives criminalized all criticism of the war and American foreign policy. Roger Baldwin, who advocated total noncooperation with the war effort, went to prison in 1918. Reverend A. J. Muste, the chair of FOR, was also incarcerated.

Eugene Debs, the leader of the American Socialist Party—the only branch of the socialist international that took a stance against the war—was convicted in 1918 for giving a speech at Canton, Ohio, in which he criticized Wilson for imprisoning peace advocates. The armed forces drafted religious pacifists like the Mennonites, Quakers, and Seventh Day Adventists. When 450 drafted conscientious objectors refused to fight, they were court-martialed. Some received death sentences that were later commuted. Others were tortured in prison by overzealous guards. In all, four thousand conscientious objectors ran afoul of the federal government.

Jane Addams

Born in 1860, Jane Addams was a social activist whose career spanned six decades. In 1889 Addams helped establish Hull House in Chicago. Along with other middle-class social workers, Addams hoped to bring moral uplift and education to the masses of immigrants who flocked to America's urban centers in the late nineteenth century. Addams was a tireless advocate of local and federal legislation that would create workers' compensation and prohibit child labor. Her devoted followers included Frances Perkins, who, as President Franklin D. Roosevelt's labor secretary (1933–1945), championed labor unions and old-age pensions. Addams also embraced the causes of peace, voting rights for women, and racial equality. This latter interest led to her helping to found the National Association for the Advancement of Colored People in 1910. When America entered World War I in 1917, the U.S. Justice Department placed Addams and pacifists like her under surveillance. In 1931 Addams received the Nobel Peace Prize for her leading role in founding the Women's International League for Peace and Freedom (established in 1915). Addams died in 1935.

On the local level, vigilantes, frequently in the service of the American Legion, anti-union corporations, and police departments, assaulted German and Irish Americans and, in Arizona, rounded up at gunpoint twelve hundred copper miners who belonged to the radical, antiwar Industrial Workers of the World (IWW). They were "deported" to New Mexico. The IWW and the Socialist Party both had their offices raided by federal and state authorities and their membership lists seized. They never fully recovered. Patriotic hysteria rose to such a fever pitch that prohibitionist-minded supporters of the war persuaded millions of voters that ethnic German brewers were "un-American." The Volestead Act of 1919, which outlawed the manufacturing of alcohol, could not have become law without the wartime demonization of German-Americans.

The World War II Era

Disillusionment with America's European allies, on top of a backlash against wartime hysteria, deepened isolationist sentiment in the United States. New pacifist and social reform organizations appeared, notably the War Resisters League (1924) and the Catholic Worker Movement. Chaired by Evan Thomas—brother of the socialist activist Norman Thomas—the War Resisters League had a membership of nine hundred by 1939. The Catholic Worker Movement, established by the journalist Dorothy Day, split over the issue of military intervention in World War II. Of the 11,887 World War II conscientious objectors, just 135 were Catholic. (Conscientious objectors in World War II received better treatment than had been the case twenty years before. Many performed alternative community service and thereby avoided prison. Even those who were jailed for their unwillingness to cooperate in any way with the war effort were not beaten or tortured.)

As the prospect of a second world war loomed larger, two profoundly different peace groups emerged. In 1935 communists, socialists, and pacifists created the American Student Union (ASU). At its peak in 1937, the ASU had twenty thousand members. (Overall, one million Americans joined the Communist Party and its "front" organizations in the 1930s.) The ASU advocated military intervention to destroy Nazi Germany. When Joseph Stalin and Adolf Hitler became allied in 1939, the ASU changed course, urging Americans to eschew war. The thousands of Jews who had viewed the ASU and the Communist Party as bulwarks against anti-Semitism fled both organizations. Two years later, once Germany invaded the Soviet Union, the Communist Party again shifted gears, becoming a bulwark against fascism.

Anticommunist isolationists embraced Charles Lindbergh's America First Committee (established in 1940). America First opposed any initiatives by President Franklin Roosevelt to provide military assistance to Great Britain. Although some America First members were sympathetic to fascism, others simply did not want a repeat of the 1917–1918 experience. In 1935 Congress had enacted neutrality legislation to prohibit military aid to combatants. The 1935 Neutrality Act also informed Americans that they traveled into war zones at their own risk. As late as 1941, after the Nazi conquest of France and the invasion of the Soviet Union, a Gallup public opinion poll revealed that 80 percent of Americans did not want to get involved in another world war. Only the Japanese attack on Pearl Harbor undercut isolationist sentiment.

The Vietnam War Era

Prior to the military escalation of the Vietnam War (1965–1973), peace activists protested the arms race with the Soviet Union. In 1957 the Committee for a Sane Nuclear Policy (SANE), under the leadership of the editor Norman Cousins, championed a comprehensive atomic weapons test ban treaty. That same year the Committee for Non-Violent Action (CNVA), which followed the pacifist principles of A. J. Muste, began picketing Polaris submarine facilities. SANE grew to twenty-five thousand members by the beginning of the 1960s and helped persuade President John Kennedy to agree to an atmospheric test ban of atomic weapons. Radical pacifists like Dave Dellinger, a World War II conscientious objector and the editor of *Liberation* magazine, exhorted social activists to fill the prisons. In the aftermath of the 1968 National Democratic Convention, at which thousands of Chicago police and antiwar demonstrators clashed, Dellinger stood trial for conspiracy to riot. Although he was found guilty, a higher court overturned Dellinger's conviction, citing irregularities in the original trial proceedings.

In 1961 former members of the ASU and the Women's International League for Peace and Freedom formed Women Strike for Peace (WSP). Dagmar Wilson, a Georgetown (Washington, D.C.) artist, headed the group. Like SANE and the CNVA, the WSP claimed an upper-middle-class membership. In the 1960s the several hundred members of

Vietnam War protesters in a violent confrontation with military police at a 1968 antiwar rally. HULTON GETTY/LIAISON AGENCY

the WSP marched on Washington to support a nuclear weapons test ban treaty, and its leaders went to Hanoi to express solidarity with the Vietnamese Marxists.

The Catholic Worker Movement recruited a new generation of members, including Thomas Cornell, who founded the Catholic Peace Fellowship in 1964. Following the lead of the Fellowship of Reconciliation and Clergy and Laity Concerned About Vietnam (established in 1965), young Catholic peace activists marched against the war. Other Catholics, chiefly Fathers Daniel and Philip Berrigan, began raiding draft boards in 1967 with the intent of destroying Selective Service records. By the early 1970s the two hundred core members of the "Catholic New Left" had seized or destroyed thousands of Selective Service files.

In 1962 the Students for a Democratic Society (SDS) held its founding convention in Port Huron, Michigan. SDS denounced America's anticommunist foreign policy. By 1968 SDS had a hundred thousand members and figured prominently in many campus protests against university military research, the draft, and the Vietnam War. A year later, as SDS founder Tom Hayden prepared to join Dave Dellinger on the docket as one of the "Chicago Seven" conspiracy defendants, the organiza-

tion split. One faction, called the Revolutionary Youth Movement (or Weatherman) launched a terrorist war against "pig AmeriKKKa."

From 1969 to 1970 there were 174 actual or attempted campus bombings. Shortly after President Richard Nixon ordered the invasion of Cambodia, the governor of Ohio called up the National Guard to occupy Kent State University following the torching of its campus Reserve Officers' Training Corps building. On 4 May 1970, the Guard fired into a crowd of antiwar protesters, killing four and wounding nine. Four million college students at 1,350 campuses went on strike to protest the Kent State slayings.

Over the course of the 1960s, 26,358 students were arrested for protesting against the Vietnam War. Each successive wave of confrontations with university and local law enforcement agencies became bloodier. By 1968 the public had turned against both the war and the peace movement. Few voters made distinctions between pacifists and the less decorous members of SDS. Recognizing the need to restore domestic tranquillity, Nixon had little choice but to negotiate a peace settlement. After Vietnam, America's political and military leaders became more cautious about deploying U.S. forces overseas.

BIBLIOGRAPHY

Chatfield, Charles. *The American Peace Movement: Ideals and Activism.* New York: Twayne, 1992.

DeBenedetti, Charles, with Charles Chatfield. *An American Ordeal: The Antiwar Movement of the Vietnam Era.* Syracuse, N.Y.: Syracuse University Press, 1990.

Heineman, Kenneth J. *Campus Wars: The Peace Movement at American State Universities in the Vietnam Era.* New York: New York University Press, 1993.

Kohn, Stephen M. *Jailed for Peace: The History of American Draft Law Violators, 1658–1985.* Westport, Conn.: Greenwood, 1986.

Lewy, Guenter. *The Cause That Failed: Communism in American Political Life.* New York: Oxford University Press, 1990.

Swerdlow, Amy. *Women Strike for Peace: Traditional Motherhood and Radical Politics in the 1960s.* Chicago: University of Chicago Press, 1993.

Tyler, Alice Felt. *Freedom's Ferment: Phases of American Social History from the Colonial Period to the Outbreak of the Civil War.* New York: Harper and Row, 1962.

Zaroulis, Nancy, and Gerald Sullivan. *Who Spoke Up? American Protest Against the War in Vietnam, 1963–1975.* Garden City, N.Y.: Doubleday, 1984.

Ziegler, Valerie H. *The Advocates of Peace in Antebellum America.* Bloomington: Indiana University Press, 1992.

KEN HEINEMAN

See also **Civil Disobedience; Jackson State; Kent State; New Left; Nonviolence; Weatherman and Weather Underground.**

ARMED FORCES. *See* Military.

ARMS RACE. *See* Disarmament and Arms Control.

ARMY. *See* Military.

ARSON AND FIRE

Arson—the intentional burning of property—has been used as a weapon of violence since before recorded history. Many historians are quick to point out that the United States was born in violence and that organizations such as the Sons of Liberty (formed in 1765 to oppose the Stamp Act) used fire to suppress opposition. During the American Revolution, both the Loyalists and the Patriots used fire to terrorize and destroy their enemies. On the frontier, the Indians, encouraged by the English, conducted raids against isolated farms,

---

Molotov Cocktail

Why is fire such a choice weapon of violence? Part of the reason is the availability of supplies and the ease of use. A conventional bomb, a pipe bomb, or a stick of dynamite requires some degree of skill or knowledge and can be dangerous if not properly handled. A gasoline bomb, or Molotov cocktail, is easier to use, with materials readily available—a bottle, some gasoline mixed with some fuel oil, and a piece of cloth as a wick.

The use of a Molotov cocktail has been copied by many street-gang members. The wholesale destruction of the Bronx in New York City during the 1960s and early 1970s, followed by similar damage in many other inner cities during the 1970s and 1980s, is a good example of the destructive power of this weapon.

---

barns, and fields and even attacked and burned villages. This method of warfare continued on the frontier for the next hundred years and was practiced by both Indians and whites.

During the Civil War, fire was once again used as a weapon by both sides. In an infamous terrorist attack, Confederate forces operating out of Canada were barely prevented from burning a small Vermont village to the ground. The ever present threat of other Southern raiders, such as Nathan Bedford Forrest, Earl Van Dorn, and John Hunt Morgan, attacking Union supply lines, farms, and villages forced the Union to keep a large number of troops posted to guard against these attacks.

The worst such attack was made by a Confederate raider, William Clarke Quantrill, on 21 August 1863. With a large force of mounted men, Quantrill entered the town of Lawrence, Kansas, and set the town on fire to force the civilians to come into the open, where he conducted a systematic massacre. He left the town a charred mass of rubble.

General William Tecumseh Sherman's "march to the sea" with his Union forces left Atlanta in flames in 1864. He continued using fire as a weapon and left a trail of destruction fifty miles wide to Charleston, South Carolina. Southern morale was effectively broken by this Northern army crossing their territory and leaving a wide path of

TABLE 1.   Major U.S. Fires in the Twentieth Century

Year	Site	City	Deaths (approx.)	Cause
1903	Iroquois Theater	Chicago, Ill.	603	Carelessness
1904	*General Slocum* (ship)	New York City	1,021	Carelessness
1908	Lakeview School	Collingwood, Ohio	174	Carelessness
1911	Triangle Shirtwaist Co.	New York City	147	Unknown
1930	Ohio Penitentiary	Columbus, Ohio	320	Carelessness
1937	Texas School	New London, Tex.	297	Carelessness
1940	Rhythm Dance Club	Natchez, Miss.	207	Carelessness
1942	Cocoanut Grove (nightclub)	Boston, Mass.	492	Carelessness
1944	Ringling Brothers Circus	Hartford, Conn.	163	Arson
1946	Wincoff Hotel	Atlanta, Ga.	119	Carelessness
1947	SS *Grandcomp*	Texas City, Tex.	468	Carelessness
1949	St. Anthony's Hospital	Effinghom, Ill.	74	Carelessness
1958	Our Lady of Angels School	Chicago, Ill.	93	Carelessness
1963	Katie Jane's Nursing Home	Warrington, Mo.	72	Carelessness
1963	Home (nursing home)	Fitchville, Ohio	63	Carelessness
1977	Beverly Hills Supper Club	Southgate, Ky.	165	Carelessness
1980	MGM Grand Hotel	Las Vegas, Nev.	85	Carelessness
1986	Dupont Plaza Hotel	San Juan, P.R.	96	Arson
1990	Happy Land Social Club	New York City	87	Arson

destruction, with no Southern forces available to stop the advance. Sherman's march may have been more effective in breaking the Southern will to continue the war than the Union siege of Richmond, Virginia.

During World War I, German agents were active in the United States, both before and after the American entry into the war. Munitions plants around the United States were targeted and many were destroyed by fire. In the battlefields of Europe, destruction by fire was the norm whenever an army retreated. Cities, villages, farms, and factories were destroyed by fire and were left unproductive for years after the war ended.

In World War II, once again, cities of both the Allied and Axis nations were attacked from the air by bomb and fire, leaving behind death and destruction. Both the Russian and German armies practiced the "scorched earth" policy—that is, they burned all useful property before abandoning a site. This policy left much of eastern Europe a charred ruin at the close of the war.

Fire in the Late Twentieth Century

After years of study, the U.S. government finally stepped in and published its famous report, *America Burning*, in 1973. According to the report, issued by the National Commission on Fire Prevention

and Control, the United States had not only one of the highest per capita fire rates in the world but also the highest rate of arson. The report attributed these rates to three factors: the large transient population in the larger cities of the United States, the availability of fire insurance, and the easy settlement of claims. The United States saw the rate of arson quadruple during the 1970s, with an accompanying increase in monetary losses due to fire, although the number of actual fires increased only slightly. The direct losses due to fire—accidental or willful—exceeded $3 billion per year; coupled with the loss of business and the added living expenses, the total losses were estimated at $11 billion annually. In the 1980s and 1990s there was a slight downturn, but the losses were still staggering. Although it is difficult to estimate, approximately ten percent of all fires nationwide are deliberately set.

The human toll is even more devastating. In the 1990s, fire killed an average of 6,200 persons annually in the United States, a decrease from a high of 6,700 the 1980s. In addition, 300,000 persons a year were injured and permanently scarred by fire. Of these, 50,000 required extended specialized hospitalization. In addition to the physical trauma, a burn patient undergoes a lifetime of mental anguish dealing with permanent deformities.

Arson and the Law

Criminal burning has always been treated as a serious offense. The old Roman law of "incendium," though broader in scope than the common law, included willful burning that endangered another's property. A person convicted of incendium was burned alive. Common law defined arson as the willful burning of a dwelling of another, making it a crime against habitation. The crime contained four elements: (1) The property had to be a dwelling; (2) the dwelling had to be occupied by another person; (3) burning had to have occurred; and (4) the burning had to be intentional. In the 1950s the National Fire Protection Association proposed the Model Arson Law, and most states adopted it or passed statutes closely related to it. The law brought a measure of uniformity, recognized degrees of arson, and covered attempts and burnings to defraud.

BIBLIOGRAPHY

Cote, Arthur E., ed. *Fire Protection Handbook.* 17th ed. Quincy, Mass.: National Fire Protection Association, 1991.

Robertson, James C. *Introduction to Fire Prevention.* 4th ed. Englewood Cliffs, N.J.: Prentice-Hall, 1995.

Van Every, Dale. *A Company of Heroes: The American Frontier, 1775–1783.* New York: Morrow, 1962.

FREDERICK MERCILLIOTT

See also **Bombings and Bomb Scares; Church Bombings; Crime, Legal Definitions of; Quantrill's Raid; Vandalism and Violence Against Property.**

ARTISTIC REPRESENTATION. *See* Representation of Violence.

ASIANS

Violence against Asian immigrant groups seems to be endemic in the modern world. Asian immigrants, chiefly Asian Indians and Chinese, have suffered violence directed against them because of their race or ethnicity on every inhabited continent from at least the eighteenth century. Although this entry concentrates on the United States, more Asians have been killed in violent encounters in Mexico than in the United States, more in Cuba than in the United States and Mexico combined, and more in Peru than in all the rest of the New World. Not surprisingly, there has been even more violence in Asia itself.

In terms of national groups, Chinese, because of their much more diverse and long-standing migration, have been the most common targets for nativists. In Indonesia, for example, resident Chinese have been massacred from the eighteenth century all the way to July 1998. The Chinese there have long lived with the sporadic sacking of their businesses and churches. Indonesian jealousy of Chinese economic dominance is a factor, as is religion. In Japan it has been Koreans who have borne the brunt of intra-Asian violence, most spectacularly in the aftermath of the great Konto earthquake of 1923, in which Tokyo mobs somehow blamed Koreans for the destruction and assaulted and murdered many of them; the violence against Korean "comfort women" during World War II by the Japanese military is notorious, as is Japan's refusal to atone for its wartime crimes.

In Africa both workers imported from India and middle-class Indians suffered brutal mistreatment throughout the twentieth century. In South Africa until the end of apartheid the violence was inflicted by the white government, and afterward by black citizens. In Britain there were anti-Chinese riots in the early twentieth century and violence against Asian Indians and Pakistanis in more recent decades. In Germany most Vietnamese (who had been welcomed as workers by the former German Democratic Republic) can no longer work legally, and Vietnam has strict limits on the number of its emigrants who may return in any one year. The result is that many Vietnamese in Germany have become part of a criminal subculture and suffer violence from both the police and criminals of various ethnicities. In Australia, Chinese and later Japanese were brutally treated in the nineteenth century and excluded for more than half of the twentieth. Lethal attacks on Chinese miners similar to those that occurred in California and elsewhere in the American West began as early as 1857. During World War II, Australian troops massacred Japanese prisoners of war.

Anti-Asian Violence in the United States

In the United States, Chinese became targets of racist violence almost as soon as they arrived in the late 1840s. In the West, endemic mob violence both preceded and followed the Chinese Exclusion

Act of 1882, while in the East, Chinese suffered from sporadic urban violence, most notably during the New York City "draft riots" of 1863. More than a hundred Chinese were killed by mobs in nineteenth-century America, and enforcement of the exclusion acts led the government to resort to violence on more than one occasion.

The Japanese who began to come to the United States in considerable numbers in the 1890s suffered fewer fatalities than did Chinese. They were victims of mob violence from southern California to Vancouver in the late nineteenth and early twentieth centuries. In 1924 they also experienced legislative exclusion, and, in World War II, mass incarceration during which state-sponsored homicide killed several inmates in three different War Relocation Authority concentration camps and one Immigration and Naturalization Service internment camp. Asian Indians—mostly Sikhs—and Filipinos also suffered from mob violence in the West before World War II.

In post–World War II America, despite a much more numerous and diverse Asian American population—nearly seven million in the 1990 census, which has been followed by continued rapid growth—there has been no mob violence against Asians; but there have been many instances of anti-Asian violence directed against persons of almost every Asian American group. The most celebrated and symbolic such attack was the 1982 murder of Vincent Chin, a second-generation Chinese American killed as the result of a barroom encounter in Detroit with two white unemployed autoworkers who mistook him for Japanese and thus somehow responsible for their unemployment. Asian Indians have been assaulted systematically with at least one fatality, and refugees from Southeast Asia have been attacked, sometimes fatally, in every section of the United States. There has been considerable destruction of Asian property, most notably vandalism and arson against non-Christian religious sites.

To be sure, in modern America most violence against Asians has been committed by other Asians, often by youth gangs that prey largely on older and less acculturated immigrants. But this merely follows the standard American pattern: most violence is intraracial, intraethnic, and within families. The basic cause of most of the anti-Asian violence in the United States can be laid to racism and vicious ethnocentrism, although economic, social, and political stresses are often triggering factors.

BIBLIOGRAPHY

Daniels, Roger. *Asian America: Chinese and Japanese in the United States Since 1850.* Seattle: University of Washington Press, 1988.

———, ed. *Anti-Chinese Violence in North America.* New York: Arno, 1978.

McClain, Charles J., Jr. *In Search of Equality: The Chinese Struggle Against Discrimination in Nineteenth-Century America.* Berkeley: University of California Press, 1994.

Tinker, Hugh. *A New System of Slavery: The Export of Indian Labour Overseas, 1830–1920.* London: Oxford University Press, 1974.

U.S. Commission on Civil Rights. *Civil Rights Issues Facing Asian Americans in the 1990s.* Washington, D.C.: Government Printing Office, 1992.

ROGER DANIELS

See also **Chinese Americans; Chinese Exclusion Act; Hate Crimes; Immigration; Japanese Americans; Korean Americans; Race and Ethnicity; Vietnamese Americans.**

ASSASSINATIONS

The premeditated murder of a politician or politically influential figure for reasons associated with the victim's prominence or views or some combination of both is known as assassination. There have been eighteen such attacks on nationally prominent political figures in the United States, involving seventeen assassins and would-be assassins.

American assassinations can be divided into two eras. The first begins in 1789, when George Washington became the nation's first president, and extends through 1962. During that time eight attacks occurred, resulting in the deaths of Presidents Abraham Lincoln in 1865, James Garfield in 1881, and William McKinley in 1901. Presidents Andrew Jackson and Harry Truman survived unsuccessful attacks in 1835 and 1950 respectively, as did presidential candidate Theodore Roosevelt in 1912 and his distant cousin President-elect Franklin Roosevelt in 1933.

The filmed and televised coverage of President John F. Kennedy's assassination in 1963 marks the beginning of the modern period, establishing the precedent—and promise—of enormous notoriety that assassins have since been assured. Although Kennedy was the only president assassinated during this period the eight other attempts on the lives of nationally prominent political figures equaled the number of presidential elections from 1964 to 1992 and surpassed, in just three decades, the total

The assassination of President Abraham Lincoln at Ford's Theatre in Washington, D.C., 14 April 1865. A drawing by Currier and Ives. LIBRARY OF CONGRESS

number of such attacks recorded in the first 173 years of the nation's presidential history. Following President Kennedy's assassination, civil rights leader Martin Luther King, Jr., and the late president's brother, Senator Robert F. Kennedy, were both assassinated in 1968. Five others narrowly escaped death in the years that followed. In 1972 presidential candidate George Wallace was crippled by an assassin's bullet while campaigning. Two years later, President Richard Nixon's life was spared when his would-be assassin's attempt to crash-dive a commercial jetliner into the White House failed. Two unsuccessful attempts on the life of President Gerald Ford were made in 1975. In 1981 President Ronald Reagan suffered near-fatal wounds, and three others were wounded, in a determined effort to end his life. In 1994 a man armed with an assault rifle fired twenty-nine rounds toward the White House at a person he mistakenly believed was President Bill Clinton.

Since all but one of the assassination attempts in U.S. history involved individuals acting alone (two men were involved in the attempt on President Truman's life), attention necessarily centers on the motives and mental states of the assailants. The psychological profile of American assassins and would-be assassins extends across a continuum, ranging from rational political extremists, through those with various types of emotional disturbances, to those with severe mental disorders.

Those considered political extremists are John Wilkes Booth (Lincoln), Leon Czolgosz (McKinley), Oscar Collazo and Griselio Torresola (Truman), and Sirhan Sirhan (R. Kennedy). The emotionally troubled subjects (that is, those motivated by depression and anger following failed relationships or careers) include Giuseppe Zangara (F. Roosevelt), Lee Harvey Oswald (J. Kennedy), Arthur Bremer (Wallace), Samuel Byck (Nixon), Lynette Fromme (Ford), Sara Moore (Ford), John Hinckley, Jr. (Reagan), and Francisco Duran (Clinton). Just three subjects—Richard Lawrence (Jackson), Charles Guiteau (Garfield), and John Schrank (T. Roosevelt)—exhibited symptoms of severe mental disorder. The only two exceptions to this classification are Carl Weiss, who killed Senator Huey Long in 1935, probably for reasons of family honor, and James Earl Ray, the contract killer of Martin Luther King. Although conspiracy theories abound, to date convincing supporting evidence of conspiracies can be found only in the Lincoln and King assassinations.

BIBLIOGRAPHY

Clarke, James W. *American Assassins: The Darker Side of Politics.* Princeton, N.J.: Princeton University Press, 1990.

———. *On Being Mad or Merely Angry: John W. Hinckley, Jr., and Other Dangerous People.* Princeton, N.J.: Princeton University Press, 1990.

JAMES W. CLARKE

ASSAULT

Although there are several definitions of what constitutes assault, the event typically involves physical contact between individuals. Charges of assault can be brought without one individual's actually striking another; any deliberate, unwanted physical contact or touching between people is considered assault. In some jurisdictions, simply poking someone can bring charges. Additionally, an individual can be charged with verbal assault for threatening to harm another person.

Early English common law classified assault and battery separately. Assault was viewed as an attempted battery, that is, an attempt by an individual to do harm to another. Battery was simply a completion of this attempt. Although touching was not specifically required, simple verbal threats were not treated as assaults. Common law made no distinction between degrees of assault and battery. However, the courts were typically more punitive with cases involving severe injury. The U.S. legal definition of assault was built upon common law. Colonial law defined four categories of offenses against the person: assaultive crimes, homicidal crimes, sexual offenses, and offenses against movement, such as false imprisonment and kidnapping. As the conditions and culture of the United States changed, assault laws also evolved.

Assault is considered an offense in all jurisdictions, with most referring to battery as a crime as well. Often the phrase "assault and battery" is used to refer to one offense. Minor assaults are generally charged as misdemeanors, whereas more serious incidents are regarded as felonies. Each legal jurisdiction defines assault in subtly different ways. For example, according to California's penal code, assault is "an unlawful attempt, coupled with a present ability, to commit a violent injury on the person of another." The California statute proscribes harsher penalties for assaults committed against a person performing the duties of a nurse, police officer, paramedic, or firefighter. Assault with a deadly weapon is, as in most states, charged as a felony. Battery, under the California penal code, is defined as "any willful and unlawful use of force or violence upon the person of another." As with the crime of assault, the penal code holds for increased punishment for offenses committed against certain types of officers (e.g., police, firefighters, or paramedics).

According to the Federal Bureau of Investigation, assault is "an unlawful physical attack on a person." It is then categorized by level of severity as either simple or aggravated assault. Simple assault is an attack without a weapon involving little or minor injury. A verbal attack or attempt without a weapon is also a simple assault. An aggravated assault is an attack or attempted attack with a weapon resulting in serious injury. Serious injury can include broken bones, loss of teeth, internal injuries, and loss of consciousness.

Although categorized separately, sexual assaults form another variant of physical harm between individuals. Sexual assault encompasses a wide variety of victimizations but does not include rape or attempted rape. These victimizations may entail attacks or attempted attacks involving unwanted sexual contact between the victim and the offender. Sexual assaults may or may not involve force and include such actions as grabbing or fondling. A verbal threat can also be considered a sexual assault.

Another form of interpersonal violence is that of mayhem. Mayhem is a less commonly seen offense in today's courts and differs from assault in that it is defined as a willful attempt to injure another so as to render the individual less able to fight or defend himself. A notorious example of mayhem is Lorena Bobbitt's cutting off of her husband's penis in 1993. Most jurisdictions will charge such violent offenders with aggravated battery or attempted murder or both.

Over the history of the United States, violence has typically followed a wavelike pattern. In the nineteenth century incidents of violence generally declined, despite temporary increases during the 1860s and 1870s. Trends in the twentieth century showed a similar ebb and flow. For example, there was a steady increase between 1973 and 1991, followed by a period of decline thereafter.

The trends of aggravated assault have been different from those of violent crimes in general. In the mid-1970s rates of aggravated assault began to decline with minimal interruption until the mid-1980s. After remaining fairly constant for a number of years, rates increased from 1990 to 1993. Because of a sharp decrease during 1995, aggravated assault reached its lowest rate in a twenty-three-year period. Rates for simple assault also increased between 1974 and 1977, remaining stable until 1979. After declining until 1989, rates rose again until 1991, returning to their peak levels of the late 1970s. A decrease in 1995 was the first significant change since 1991.

Certain patterns emerge for the period from 1992 onward according to the Uniform Crime Reports. Typically most assaults occur during the summer. Over 40 percent of all aggravated assaults occur in the southern states, followed by the West (25 percent), the Midwest (19 percent), and the Northeast (16 percent). Metropolitan areas typically report higher rates than rural areas.

Domestic Assault and Child Abuse

One of the most disturbing aspects of assault is the role it plays in the American home. Children are often the victims of familial violence. It is now estimated that three million incidents of reported child abuse and neglect occur each year. These numbers are frightening enough, yet they may represent only a portion of actual occurrences as child abuse tends to remain hidden within the family unit.

What constitutes child abuse has long been debated among scholars and the public. Puritan law decreed that children could be put to death for transgressions as simple as disobeying a parental figure. Historically, punishments for unruly children have often involved some sort of physical contact between parent and child. Yet physical punishment is not in itself child abuse; where children are concerned, it becomes difficult to find a useful and widely accepted definition of assault. Are spankings and beatings the same thing? Only when children are tortured and killed is there any degree of consensus. Researchers who study child abuse define it as an act of aggravated assault in which the child is a victim. However, this definition does not cover types of abuse where there is no overt physical act—namely, neglect. More children suffer from malnourishment, poor living conditions, and lack of supervision than from direct physical abuse.

Assault of women is typically seen in two forms: spousal or domestic abuse, and sexual assault or rape. Although men have been victims of spousal abuse and rape, these occurrences are very limited. Cultural values regarding the abuse of women in domestic relationships have been slowly changing. In some parts of the modern world, it is permissible for men to beat their wives for relatively minor acts such as public drinking and tardiness in serving meals. The phrase "rule of thumb," relatively innocuous today, stood for the rule that a man was allowed to beat his wife with a switch no wider than his thumb.

During the Middle Ages, although a wife was thought of as an object to be cherished, she was often punished severely for even minor transgressions. Wife beating was so accepted by the community that men were often punished themselves if they failed to discipline their wives. It was not until the late nineteenth century that laws were passed outlawing the physical abuse of women. However, the cultural values that dictate male dominance have let the abuse continue.

As a result of changes in women's roles in society over the course of the twentieth century, women in the 1960s and 1970s moved closer to equality with men than ever before. This shift in cultural values regarding women brought greater public attention to the issue of domestic violence. Yet, although society is increasingly aware of spousal assault, this problem, like child abuse, remains partially hidden behind the veil of family privacy.

Some analyses (e.g., the National Crime Victimization Survey) estimate that incidents of spousal assault occur a half million times each year; yet we are no closer to realizing the true extent of domestic violence. Attitudes measured in a 1993 poll by the Family Violence Prevention Fund found that 44 percent of Americans believe that a man would severely beat his wife during a fight. In another sample of six thousand households, it was reported that one out of six couples experienced assault during the year the study was completed. Another survey by James Makepeace found that more than 20 percent of college females had experienced violence in their relationships.

Although rape is classified outside of assault, wives are often victims of this act in the abusive relationship. In the United States laws forbidding forcible intercourse within marriage did not appear until the late 1970s. Until then, men were allowed by law to have sex with their wives whenever they wished, effectively barring them from ever being prosecuted for rape.

As with child abuse, it is difficult to gauge the true number of spousal assaults. These crimes often go unreported because victims believe that police intervention would not help and might actually make things worse. To ease the burden on the victim, a number of states have adopted legislation making it easier to prosecute offenders and grant protection orders for victims. Also, it is common for courts to hold the police civilly liable if they fail to protect the victims of spousal assault.

Although homicide tends to dominate reporting and representation of crime in the media and popular culture, assault is much more pervasive. Our inability to deal with the great number of these incidents stems from the hidden nature of many assaults. Every day children and women are subjected to abuse at the hands of their parents and spouses, and much remains to be done in the realms of social policy, law enforcement, and legal action to remedy this overwhelming problem.

BIBLIOGRAPHY

Glick, Leonard. *Criminology*. Boston: Allyn and Bacon, 1995.

Harries, Keith D. *Serious Violence: Patterns of Homicide and Assault in America*. Springfield, Ill.: Charles C. Thomas, 1990.

Livingston, Jay. *Crime and Criminology*. 2d ed. Upper Saddle River, N.J.: Prentice Hall, 1996.

Maguire, Kathleen, and Ann L. Pastore, eds. *Sourcebook of Criminal Justice Statistics, 1996*. U.S. Department of Justice, Bureau of Justice Statistics. Washington, D.C.: U.S. Government Printing Office, 1997.

Makepeace, James. "Social-Factor and Victim-Offender Differences in Courtship Violence." *Family Relations* 33 (1987).

Rand, Michael R., et al. *Criminal Victimization, 1973–95*. Bureau of Justice Statistics, National Criminal Victimization Survey. Washington, D.C.: U.S. Department of Justice, Office of Justice Programs, 1997.

Scheb, John M., and John M. Scheb II. *Criminal Law and Procedure*. St. Paul, Minn.: West, 1989.

Siegel, Larry J. *Criminology: Theories, Patterns, and Typologies*. St. Paul, Minn.: West, 1992.

LARRY SIEGEL
ERIK DIETZ

See also **Child Abuse; Crime, Legal Definitions of; Domestic Violence; Rape; Spousal and Partner Abuse.**

ASSISTED SUICIDE AND EUTHANASIA

The word *euthanasia* was coined from the Greek (*eu* for good or noble and *thanatos* for death) in the seventeenth century by the English philosopher of science Francis Bacon to refer to an easy, painless, happy death. In modern times it has come to mean the active causation of a patient's death by a physician usually through the injection of a lethal dose of medication. In physician-assisted suicide the patient self-administers the lethal dose, which has been prescribed by a physician who knows the patient intends to use it to end his or her life.

Historical Background

Throughout Western history individual philosophers from Plato and Seneca to Michel Montaigne and David Hume justified self-induced death for those who were severely sick and suffering. The idea that physicians should assist in the suicide, however, was not seriously proposed until the discovery in the nineteenth century of analgesics and anesthetics that could relieve suffering in dying patients as well as easily and painlessly end life.

Interest in medical euthanasia also coincided with the birth at the end of the nineteenth century of the modern hospital as an institution that could provide curative medical and surgical treatment. As medicine enabled doctors to control acute infectious disease, and as life expectancy began its gradual increase from a norm of forty in 1850 to almost double that figure at the end of the twentieth century, degenerative and late-onset diseases, of which cancer was the epitome, made the discussion of end-of-life care more urgent and the role of the physician more important. By the beginning of the twentieth century the principle of the double effect was introduced into medicine; that is, in the interests of relieving suffering, it was appropriate to give treatments that risked death. The first articles advocating euthanasia in modern medicine appeared in the United States and England in the 1870s. The first proposal to legalize euthanasia was made and defeated in Ohio in 1905. Following a similar defeat in Iowa no further proposals were made in the United States for three decades.

Interest in euthanasia revived in the United States and was even stronger in England in the 1930s. Euthanasia societies were formed in both countries, while accounts of suffering patients who desired euthanasia as well as of physicians who had performed it surreptitiously began to appear. In 1936 the British House of Lords rejected by a vote of thirty-five to fourteen a bill to legalize euthanasia. In 1937 the Nebraska legislature also defeated such a proposal.

The post–World War II revulsion to news that German doctors had used euthanasia to end the lives of mentally ill people considered incurable and of Jews, gypsies, and others designated inimical to the racial and genetic potential of the German people discredited the movement. In the

1970s and 1980s, modern medical technology that makes it possible to maintain a pointless semblance of life and creates fear of painful and undignified deaths revived interest in euthanasia, which centered on compassion for suffering patients. The Netherlands was the first country to give legal sanction to physician-assisted suicide and euthanasia. In 1994 Oregon became the only state to pass a law permitting physician-assisted suicide. Legal challenges prevented the law from going into effect until its reaffirmation in November 1997 by Oregon voters.

The Modern Argument

Compassion. Contemporary advocacy for euthanasia centers on compassion for patients whose suffering is considered incapable of relief in any other way or who wish to avoid what they fear will be an undignified death. Opponents point out that the overwhelming number of patients who request euthanasia change their minds when their suffering is addressed by a knowledgeable and caring physician; in exceptional cases sedation can be used to relieve suffering. They see death as undignified only when patients are not valued or treated with respect. Proponents counter that even if it is theoretically possible to provide a painless or dignified death to suffering patients, the trained personnel and the social and medical systems that

The physician Jack Kevorkian, a vocal advocate of physician-assisted suicide, in a Michigan courtroom in December 1998. Kevorkian pleaded not guilty to charges of first-degree murder, assisted suicide, and delivering a controlled substance. Photo by Jeff Kowalsky. (For a sidebar on Kevorkian, see the entry "Euthanasia.") CORBIS/AFP

would enable this are lacking. In the meantime, they contend, patients are suffering and should be afforded relief.

Autonomy and Social Policy. Many believe that personal autonomy includes the right to die at a time and place of one's choosing, seeing assisted suicide and euthanasia as no different from withdrawing patients from unwanted treatment. Opponents point out that a patient's right to withdraw from treatment is based on the principle of informed consent that underlies the practice of medicine; that is, every patient, whether terminally ill or not, has the right to withdraw from treatment, which has nothing to do per se with hastening death. Addressing the right-to-die issue, Leon Kass (1989) maintains that "physicians serve the needs of patients not because patients exercise self-determination but because patients are sick. A patient may not insist, for example, on a treatment the physician feels is not consistent with sound medical practice."

Euthanasia advocates believe that respect for the integrity of individuals' lives and for the issues they deem important, including how they wish to die, requires that their requests for euthanasia be granted. Opponents respond that some individuals react to various life crises with depression, panic, and the desire to die, and we do not assist them in suicide. Does the fact, they ask, that a crisis is a serious or terminal illness demand that we should heed their request to die? What about those for whom the panic that accompanies serious or terminal illness is not in keeping with their character? Opponents of euthanasia point out that when the panic is addressed it usually subsides and the request for death disappears, and that if the panic is not addressed, the request for death is often mistakenly perceived as the expression of an autonomous desire.

Since euthanasia and assisted suicide entail the participation of another person, many opponents regard them as not private acts but forms of communal action, arguing that the United States does not allow killing as a form of contractual relationship between two consenting adults, just as it no longer permits people to sell themselves into slavery. The killing of another is legally sanctioned in the United States only in cases of self-defense, capital punishment, and war. A strong public interest is required to justify taking a life, which has been considered too great a power to be given to individuals to serve private ends, even good ends like compassion and the relief of suffering. Finally, opponents argue, even if a case can be made that an individual's right of self-determination extends to death, it does not follow that the right can be transformed into the right of someone else to kill that person. Proponents maintain that relieving the suffering of the terminally ill is a strong public interest. Society can also change its views of when it will sanction killing, as happened in the U.S. with capital punishment.

For U.S. society to modify its attitude toward euthanasia and assisted suicide, it would have to perceive the problem of the suffering of the terminally ill as overwhelming and treatable in no other way. The euthanasia debate is in part over whether the need to reduce suffering in those who are terminally ill requires legalizing euthanasia.

Abuse and Regulation. There is concern among opponents of legalizing euthanasia that patients would be psychologically and economically pressured to agree to it and that it would lead to physicians' ending patients' lives without their consent. Since a small but significant number of doctors in the United States admit to secretly practicing assisted suicide and euthanasia and to ending patients' lives without being requested to do so, proponents see legalization as a way to supervise and control the practice. However, opponents fear that doctors who violate laws prohibiting such practices, despite the possibility of severe penalty, are not likely to follow guidelines if euthanasia is sanctioned.

The Nature of Medicine. Proponents maintain that advances in medical technology that make it possible to prolong the dying process necessitate legalizing euthanasia. In reaction to this argument, D. J. Bakker (1992) has pointed out that "euthanasia is then chosen as the wrong solution for a wrong development in medicine. A medical science that is in need of euthanasia has to be changed as soon as possible to a medicine that cares beyond cure."

Some physicians have vigorously argued that the moral structure of the practice of medicine requires that doctors must not kill, noting that for centuries physicians have not participated in capital punishment because to do so would compromise their role as healers. Advocates of euthanasia do not see it as intrinsically opposed to healing. They insist that it can be considered proper medical care, justified when it prevents pain, incompetence, or undignified dying, because the prevention of suffering is part of a doctor's activities. Els Borst-Eilers (1992), for instance, has stated: "There are situations when the best way to heal the patient is to help him die peacefully. The doctor who, in such a situation, grants the patient's request acts as the healer par excellence." Yet opponents argue that justifying euthanasia by reference to healing and helping opens the door to ending the lives of people who have not expressed the wish to die but who appear to be suffering a great deal. Pain and suffering become all-important criteria, but since there is no objective way of determining what is unbearable pain and suffering, the decision depends on physicians' subjective assessments; such assessments have been shown to be often at variance with patients' perceptions and wishes.

The Dutch Experience

In a series of cases going back to 1973, Dutch courts have legally sanctioned assisted suicide and euthanasia provided they are practiced within certain guidelines: a voluntary, well-considered, persistent request; intolerable suffering that cannot be relieved; formal consultation with a colleague; and reporting of cases. At first sanctioned only for those who were terminally ill, it was extended to the chronically ill, who had longer to suffer; initially permitted for only suffering that was physical in origin, it was extended to suffering that was mental on the grounds that not to do so was discriminatory. Although ending the lives of patients who have not requested it was not legally sanctioned, there were widespread reports of involuntary euthanasia, sometimes justified on the grounds that it was necessary to relieve suffering in cases where patients were not capable of making decisions for themselves (Richard Fenigsen, "A Case Against Dutch Euthanasia," *Hastings Center Report, Special Supplement* 19, no. 1 [1989]: 22–30).

Charges of abuse led the Dutch government to sanction studies of assisted suicide and euthanasia. These studies revealed that virtually all of the guidelines were being violated. Fifty-nine percent of cases were not reported to the authorities, which by itself makes regulation impossible. In only 11 percent of the unreported cases was there consultation with another physician. Twenty percent of the physicians' most recent unreported cases involved ending of a life without the patient's consent: several thousand lives a year were ended in this manner. Twenty-five percent of Dutch physicians admit to having done so. Although physicians used patients' incompetence to justify such actions, in at least 20 percent of cases, the patients were competent.

Perhaps the strongest criticism to come from Dutch and foreign observers has been that legal sanction for assisted suicide and euthanasia, which were intended for exceptional cases, have become routine ways of dealing with terminal illness. Palliative care and hospice care were said to lag behind that of other countries. In testimony before the British House of Lords, Zbigniew Zylicz, one of the few palliative care experts in the Netherlands, emphasized Dutch deficiencies in palliative care, attributing them to the easier alternative of euthanasia. He saw the lack of hospice care in the Netherlands and the fact that there are only seventy palliative care beds in the country as a reflection of this option. The U.S. Supreme Court cited this specific deficiency and the Dutch experience in general as demonstrative of the dangers of giving legal sanction to euthanasia.

The U.S. Supreme Court

Advocates in the United States tried to establish a constitutional right to assisted suicide, invoking the equal protection and due process clauses of the Fourteenth Amendment. Cases challenging the New York and Washington State laws prohibiting the practice eventually reached the U.S. Supreme Court, which in a decision released on 26 June 1997 unanimously upheld the prohibitions on assisting suicide.

In the New York case the proponents argued that patients denied euthanasia were not being given the same right to hasten death as were patients who could withdraw from life support. The Supreme Court rejected their contention that the right to refuse life-sustaining medical treatment "is nothing more or less than assisted suicide."

The Court based its analysis on causation and intent, two legal principles used to distinguish acts that may have the same result. Under a causation analysis, the court reasoned that a patient refusing life-sustaining medical treatment dies from an underlying disease, while a patient ingesting lethal medication is killed by the medication. The physician's intent is different in the two situations: a doctor withdrawing or not administering treatment is only complying with a patient's wishes; a doctor assisting in a suicide, however, intends that the patient be dead. Moreover, a patient who commits suicide with the help of a doctor has the specific intention of ending his or her life, while a patient who refuses or discontinues treatment might

not have such an intention. Since the refusal of life-sustaining treatment is not identical with assisted suicide and *everyone,* regardless of physical condition, is entitled to refuse life-sustaining medical treatment while *no one* is allowed to assist a suicide, the court concluded that laws apply even-handedly to all and protect all equally. If the patient is not competent to make a decision about ending life-sustaining treatment, the decision is made by the patient's family, except in New York and Missouri, where the family can only decide to end life-sustaining treatment if they can demonstrate that they are following the patient's wishes. Finally, the Court found that New York had valid and important public interests for its law, including "maintaining physicians' role as their patients' healers" and "protecting vulnerable people from indifference, prejudice, and psychological and financial pressure to end their lives."

In upholding Washington's law against causing or aiding suicide, the Court rejected the contention that it violated a liberty protected by the due process clause of the Fourteenth Amendment. The Court pointed out that the clause protects fundamental rights and liberties rooted in U.S. history. It then traced a history of prohibition against assisted suicide in the country, noting that such prohibitions had been reexamined and reaffirmed in many states. The Court also rejected the notion that the fundamental liberty involved was the right to die. The Court felt the more precise issue was whether the due process clause included the right to commit suicide, which itself would include a right to assistance in doing so. Here the Court refused to reverse "centuries of legal doctrine and practice" to overrule the policy choices of almost every state.

The majority of the justices were more concerned with a patient's right not to suffer than with creating a right to assisted suicide. That patients involved in the two cases could obtain the relief they needed in their states was a factor in the Court's decision. The justices in essence challenged the states to provide this relief, making clear their willingness to revisit the issue if such relief was not provided.

The Future

Although the Supreme Court decision did not preclude states from accepting assisted suicide in their effort to care for terminally ill patients, and Oregon has done so, as of 1999 most states seemed unlikely to implement this practice. The legal and medical reasons the Court gave for ruling in favor of the New York and Washington prohibitions against assisted suicide seemed likely to influence other states' consideration of the practice.

All states, however, will need to address the Court's challenge that they provide relief to suffering patients. They will have to improve the education of physicians in palliative care, remove regulations that restrict the ways physicians can treat pain, widen the availability of hospice care, foster proper reimbursement for end-of-life care, and pass better-crafted surrogacy laws that, while protecting incompetent patients, permit proxies to see to it that inappropriate treatments are withdrawn. If states are successful in providing adequate palliative care to terminally ill patients, assisted suicide and euthanasia may not seem necessary, and the issue of legalization may become less relevant.

BIBLIOGRAPHY

Bakker, D. J. "Active Euthanasia: Is Mercy Killing the Killing of Mercy?" In *Euthanasia: The Good of the Patient, the Good of Society,* edited by Robert I. Misbin. Frederick, Md.: University Publishing Group, 1992.

Borst-Eilers, Els. "Euthanasia in the Netherlands: Brief Historical Review and Present Situation." In *Euthanasia: The Good of the Patient, the Good of Society,* edited by Robert I. Misbin. Frederick, Md.: University Publishing Group, 1992.

Callahan, Daniel. "Can We Return Death to Disease?" *Hastings Center Report, Special Supplement* 19, no. 1 (1989): 4–6.

Capron, Alexander. "Euthanasia in the Netherlands: American Observations." *Hastings Center Report* 22, no. 2 (1990): 30–33.

Dworkin, Ronald. *Life's Dominion: An Argument About Abortion, Euthanasia, and Individual Freedom.* New York: Vintage, 1994.

Hendin, Herbert. *Seduced by Death: Doctors, Patients, and the Dutch Cure.* New York: Norton, 1996.

Kass, Leon. "Neither for Love nor Money: Why Doctors Must Not Kill." *Public Interest* 94 (winter 1989): 25–46.

Lifton, Robert J. *The Nazi Doctors: Medical Killing and the Psychology of Genocide.* New York: Basic, 1986.

Pellegrino, Edmund. "Doctors Must Not Kill." In *Euthanasia: The Good of the Patient, the Good of Society,* edited by Robert I. Misbin. Frederick, Md.: University Publishing Group, 1992.

van der Maas, P. J., G. van der Wal, I. Haverkate, et al. "Euthanasia, Physician-Assisted Suicide, and Other Medical Practices Involving the End of Life in the Netherlands, 1990–1995." *New England Journal of Medicine* 335 (1996): 1699–1705.

van der Maas, P. J., J. J. M. van Delden, and L. Pijnenborg. *Euthanasia and Other Medical Decisions Concerning the End of Life.* New York: Elsevier Sciences, 1992.

HERBERT HENDIN

See also **Eugenics; Euthanasia; Suicide.**

ATLANTA

Violence in Atlanta, Georgia, follows patterns similar to those of many American cities that came of age in the industrial era, but it has also reflected the city's racial diversity and southern culture. Atlanta's rapid economic expansion, combined with the racial mores of the South, gave rise to tensions that often manifested themselves in violence. In the nineteenth century Atlanta's geographic location made it an important transportation center, and in the twentieth century it became a major southern manufacturing and service city. Throughout its history, racial terrorism, crowd violence, and vigilante activity have been the most common modes of violence. White racist organizations, acting alone or in conjunction with crowds, have perpetrated the majority of Atlanta's violence.

Atlanta's earliest experiences with violence were those of warfare. During the American Civil War, Atlanta was a major supplier of materials for the Confederate Army; it was also the Confederacy's transportation hub. In 1864 Union forces under the command of William Tecumseh Sherman inaugurated a strategy of total war, bringing military might against the civilian population of Atlanta. Sherman's troops earned infamy when they laid siege to Atlanta, bombarded residential areas with artillery fire, and then destroyed, via arson, much of what remained of the city.

During the Jim Crow era, racism fueled several of Atlanta's major episodes of violence. Despite the relative absence of violence during Reconstruction, crowd and racist violence marked Atlanta in the early twentieth century. A citywide race riot in 1906 garnered nationwide and global attention. Following a series of rumors that several white women had been assaulted by black men and a heated gubernatorial race in which the main issue was how to best eradicate African American political rights, white crowds attacked African Americans in residential and commercial neighborhoods. Martial law was imposed and order finally restored to the city on 26 September, four days after the riot began. The official tally of deaths is disputed, but at least ten African Americans and two whites were killed, and dozens more were injured. The 1906 riot began a series of segregationist activities and policies in the 1910s and 1920s that separated black residential and commercial space from white Atlanta. African American students from the city's black colleges who strayed too far from campus were sometimes assaulted by white thugs, and numerous Atlanta blacks were subjected to both verbal and physical abuse on the city's public transportation system well into the 1950s.

Atlanta also holds the dubious distinction of being the birthplace of the modern Ku Klux Klan. Modeled on the Reconstruction-era terrorist organization that repressed black political participation, over thirty Atlanta residents formed a new Ku Klux Klan in 1915. Atlanta served as the national headquarters of the Klan in the 1920s, and fifteen thousand Atlanta residents were members. When Atlanta's restrictive covenants and discriminatory real estate practices of the 1920s failed to restrict black expansion into white neighborhoods, the Ku Klux Klan burned and bombed African American homes, strafed black neighborhoods with gunfire, and threatened blacks with lynching.

The Klan also engaged in vigilante violence in Atlanta. Several white men who had earned reputations for drunkenness or spousal abuse were beaten by the Klan in the 1920s, and at least one union organizer was harassed and assaulted in 1938. The Klan's popularity began to decline in the 1930s, but it was not until 1940 that the city's media and political elite strongly denounced the Klan's violence.

Anti-Semitism was another source of violence in Atlanta's history. At the turn of the twentieth century, Jewish immigrants from eastern Europe arrived at the same time that Atlanta's manufacturing base dramatically expanded. Some white southerners were suspicious of both the new Jewish immigrants and factory labor, and they were particularly concerned with the employment of single white women in Jewish-owned factories. In 1913 Leo Frank, a Jewish supervisor at the National Pencil Company, was charged with the murder of Mary Phagan, a thirteen-year-old employee. Frank's arrest and trial unleashed virulent anti-Semitism in Atlanta's press and working-class neighborhoods, as well as the city's adjacent rural communities. Frank was convicted and sentenced to death, but national Jewish organizations succeeded in having his sentence reduced to life in prison. In the summer of 1915 a mob removed Frank from jail and lynched him. The Frank case marginalized Atlanta's Jewish community, leaving Jews on the outside of city politics until the 1960s.

In the early twentieth century, Atlanta's dramatic economic growth created conditions that led to violence between capital and labor. Atlanta's textile workers organized two unsuccessful and relatively peaceful strikes in 1913 and 1934. A 1916 streetcar workers' strike became more violent. Both the workers and management equipped

Leo Frank, lynched in Marietta, Georgia, in August 1915. CORBIS/UNDERWOOD & UNDERWOOD

themselves with dynamite and threatened to destroy one another. One nonstriking worker later recalled that the company had planted the dynamite on union property. On one occasion during the strike, gunfire broke out near a school, but there were no injuries. Although the 1916 streetcar strike was not a success, by 1919 the workers had won union recognition and a contract.

Racial and ethnic violence flared again in Atlanta during the civil rights struggles of the 1950s and 1960s. In comparison with other southern cities in the 1950s, such as Birmingham, Alabama, and Little Rock, Arkansas, Atlanta avoided much of the violence that erupted during the numerous campaigns to end Jim Crow segregation in the South. Atlanta's mayor William Hartsfield moved much quicker than other southern mayors to implement the desegregation of public schools. The nonviolent tactics of Atlanta resident Martin Luther King, Jr., and the Student Non-Violent Coordinating Committee successfully challenged the downtown business district's segregated facilities. However, Atlanta did not entirely escape the era's violence. Ku Klux Klan activists reappeared in public, and in 1960 an African American elementary school was bombed. Atlanta's Jewish community became more active in the local civil rights movement after anti-Semitic bigots bombed Atlanta's reform Jewish Temple in October of 1958. The temple's rabbi, Jacob Rothschild, remained a staunch critic of Jim Crow racism. Finally, riots flared in Atlanta's poorest African American neighborhoods in the summer of 1966, causing property damage and injuries, but no deaths.

Since the 1970s, Atlanta's economy has shifted to media services and tourism, and its population has become more ethnically diverse. Crowd and terrorist violence perpetrated against African Americans and Jews has declined, but in their place, Atlanta has experienced serial murders, antiabortion violence, and terrorism, such as the bombing at Atlanta Centennial Olympic Park during the 1996 Olympics.

BIBLIOGRAPHY

Greene, Melissa Fay. *The Temple Bombing*. New York: Addison-Wesley, 1996.

Kuhn, Clifford M., Harlon E. Joye, and E. Bernard West. *Living Atlanta: An Oral History of the City, 1914–1948*. Atlanta and Athens, Ga.: Atlanta Historical Society Press and the University of Georgia Press, 1990.

Roth, Darlene E., and Andy Ambrose. *Metropolitan Frontiers: A Short History of Atlanta*. Atlanta: Longstreet, 1996.

Russell, James Michael. *Atlanta, 1847–1890: City Building in the Old South and the New*. Baton Rouge: Louisiana State University, 1988.

MICHAEL JONATHAN PEBWORTH

See also **Civil War; Frank, Leo; Ku Klux Klan; Reconstruction; South; Urban Violence.**

ATLANTA CENTENNIAL OLYMPIC PARK, BOMBING OF

At about 1:20 A.M. on the morning of 27 July 1996, the first Saturday of the twenty-sixth Summer Olympic Games, a forty-pound pipe bomb exploded in downtown Atlanta's Centennial Olympic Park. The bomb sprayed shrapnel as far as one hundred yards, killed a woman, and injured 111 other people, some very seriously. It was the first terrorist attack at the Olympics since the 1972 Summer Games in Munich, Germany.

About twenty minutes before the bomb detonated, someone in a telephone bank a few blocks from the park had called 911 warning of the attack. "There is a bomb in Centennial Park," the mysterious male caller with no discernible accent told the operator at 1:06 A.M. "You have thirty minutes." A few minutes before the call, a security guard at a rock concert had observed a green knapsack lying near a light-and-sound tower across from the stage. The guard alerted a police officer,

who examined the parcel and called in a bomb-diagnosis team.

The diagnostic team, a Federal Bureau of Investigation agent and a Bureau of Alcohol, Tobacco, and Firearms (BATF) agent who were in the park, observed pipes and wires within the knapsack. With the help of state troopers they had begun at approximately 1:15 A.M. to clear people from the area when the bomb detonated. For his role in the evacuation the guard, a man named Richard Jewell, was at first hailed as a hero, but he later became a suspect and the focus of intense media and law-enforcement scrutiny because he fit the FBI's profile of a typical bomber. Almost four months passed before the U.S. Attorney's office cleared Jewell as a suspect. The Senate eventually held a hearing on the FBI's initial handling of the case and how Jewell's name got out, leading to two internal FBI probes. The head of the FBI Atlanta office was disciplined for improperly questioning Jewell; the other agent lost pay.

At the end of 1996, the FBI requested public help in solving the bombing—this time offering a $500,000 reward for information leading to the arrest and conviction of those responsible. The FBI released the audiotape recording of the telephoned bomb warning and revealed a replica of the green, military-style knapsack, commonly known as an "Alice pack," that had contained the bomb.

In 1997, bombings at an abortion clinic and a gay nightclub terrorized the Atlanta area. A letter-writer invoking the "Army of God" claimed credit, lambasting "sodomites" and "abortionists." Investigators noticed that there were similarities between the two bombings; both contained Westclox timers and both incidents involved a second bomb timed to explode and spray nails after police and rescue workers arrived. A year later a bomb at a women's clinic in Birmingham, Alabama, killed a police officer and seriously wounded a nurse. Lab reports found significant similarities in design and key components of the clinic and nightclub bombs, and a gray Nissan pickup truck registered to Eric Robert Rudolph was seen leaving the scene of the nightclub bombing, leading the FBI to suspect that Rudolph might be responsible for these bombings. Furthermore, the shrapnel from these bombings came from the same foundry that produced the shrapnel used in the Centennial Park bombing. A special FBI-BATF task force code-named "Sandbom" was formed to hunt for Rudolph. The FBI placed him on its most-wanted list and increased the reward to $1 million for his arrest and conviction. In May 1999 searchers were still hunting for Rudolph in western North Carolina, and the Centennial Park bombing remained unsolved.

BIBLIOGRAPHY

"Law Enforcement and the Media: Information Leaks and the Atlanta Olympic Bombing Investigation: Hearing Before the Subcommittee on Terrorism, Technology, and Government Information, Committee on the Judiciary, United States Senate." Washington, D.C.: United States Government Printing Office, 1997.

HARVEY W. KUSHNER

See also **Bombings and Bomb Scares; Terrorism.**

ATLANTA CHILD MURDERS

From July 1979 to June 1981 twenty-nine young African American men, boys, and girls were murdered in Atlanta, Georgia. Labeled collectively as the "Atlanta Child Murders," these killings provoked a great deal of fear and anger within Atlanta's African American community and raised disturbing questions about local law enforcement's reluctance to respond to crimes committed against impoverished racial minorities.

The perpetrator of some of these killings (those in which the victim was asphyxiated) was almost certainly Wayne Bertram Williams, sentenced to life in prison after his 1982 conviction for the murders of Jimmy Payne (age twenty-one) and Nathaniel Cater (age twenty-eight), the last two "child" victims. Williams, a self-employed twenty-three-year-old African American music executive and talent scout, was apprehended after police surveillance observed him allegedly dumping Cater's body in the Chattahoochee River. A search of Williams's home produced hair and fiber evidence linking him to twelve of the other murders.

The wide range in the victims' ages (from eight to twenty-eight) and the varied modes of their deaths (strangulation and asphyxiation, but also stabbing, shooting, and undetermined causes) raise considerable doubt that the same person committed the murders. In particular, two female victims, Angel Lenair (age twelve) and Latonya Wilson (age eight), are generally agreed to be victims of other killers. Nevertheless, they were included with twenty-seven other victims in the infamous and statistically impossible "list," which was published in the *Atlanta Journal-Constitution* on 28 June 1981. Publication of the list guaranteed that all unsolved murders of young African American males during these two years would be attributed to Williams. No other person was convicted of the murders.

The controversy surrounding the murders and the arrest and conviction of Wayne Williams must be understood in the context of the city of Atlanta at the time. Atlanta, "the city too busy to hate," was a prominent southern city that prided itself on its cosmopolitan attitude. Yet Atlanta also had a large, ghettoized African American and nonwhite population that was beginning to make significant progress breaking into city politics. The national media attention garnered by the Atlanta Child Murders spotlighted the racial issues that still existed within law enforcement. Camille Bell, the mother of a nine-year-old victim, Yusef Bell, formed an activist group with other parents, was a vocal advocate for police involvement and media scrutiny, and became an active fund-raiser to help the city defray the costs of such an expensive and exhaustive investigation.

After the broadcast of a fictionalized television movie, *The Atlanta Child Murders*, in 1985, the famed attorneys William Kunstler and Alan Dershowitz joined Williams's defense lawyers to seek a new trial based on evidence they claimed had been withheld during the 1981 trial. The new evidence—supposedly a confession by a Ku Klux Klan member to the murder of Lubie Geter (age fourteen)—could not be verified, and the petition was denied. However, Williams's conviction continues to provoke critiques of racism in serial-murder investigations. The most famous of these critiques is *Evidence of Things Not Seen* (1985) by the author James Baldwin, who argues that the focus on this particular serial killer elides the more pressing issues of racial ghettoization, poverty, and systemic malaise in large American cities.

BIBLIOGRAPHY

Baldwin, James. *Evidence of Things Not Seen*. New York: Holt, 1985.
Fisher, Joseph C. *Killer Among Us: Public Reactions to Serial Murder*. Westport, Conn.: Praeger, 1997.
Headley, Bernard D. *The Atlanta Youth Murders and the Politics of Race*. Carbondale: Southern Illinois University Press, 1998.

KATHLEEN LONSDALE

B

BACON'S REBELLION. *See* Agrarian Violence; Rebellions.

BARKER, MA "ARIZONA KATE"
(1872–1935)

Born near Springfield, Missouri, in 1872, Arizona Donnie Clark, who as a child acquired the nickname "Kate," is remembered as Ma Barker, the matriarch of a notorious gang of outlaw brothers who terrorized the Midwest during the 1920s and 1930s. Her four sons—known as the Bloody Barkers—were infamous for robbery, kidnapping, and murder.

As a young woman, Clark entertained romantic ideas about Jesse James and other outlaws of the day. At twenty she married George Barker and set out to cultivate her admiration of the outlaw in their four sons. (Some historians have argued that mental illness plagued the lineage for several generations and note that Ma was often described as "touched" by family friends.) George, a passive father, claimed that she would not let him straighten the boys out. She taught them that laws were made to be broken. The Barker boys came to view criminal life as encompassing glamour and adventure, and as teenagers they sported guns and committed small-time robberies. The Barker household in Tulsa, Oklahoma, ultimately harbored some of the most egregious and notorious outlaws in the Midwest. Each of Ma's sons was arrested numerous times, as their lives and their crimes ranged from

Minneapolis to Tulsa to Chicago. While Ma would often seek their early release, even those who served jail sentences would inevitably return to the life of robbery, kidnapping, and murder.

Ma Barker was alleged by the Federal Bureau of Investigation and its director, J. Edgar Hoover, to have been the brains behind the gang and also to have played a major role in planning the kidnappings of millionaire brewer William A. Hamm, Jr., in 1933 and millionaire banker Edward George Bremer in 1934. Others allege she also arranged for the murder of her boyfriend—Arthur V. Dunlop—in 1932. This was a crime very likely carried out by her son Freddie and his cohort Alvin Karpis. All of the Barkers, including Ma—although she was never charged with any crime—were on J. Edgar Hoover's "public enemy" list in the 1930s. Freddie was regarded as a homicidal maniac among the independent gangsters of the 1930s and had what people referred to as a pathological devotion to his mother.

Karpis and others who had close ties to the Barkers argued that Ma Barker really had little to do with the actual running of the gang and the planning of its escapades. Instead, they claimed, she used her knowledge of human nature—the dramatic impact of a woman's pleading, tantrums, tears, and promises on male authorities—to continually get her sons out of trouble with the law. Ma was infamous for flooding prison wardens with letters, appealing to them to release her sons, thus freeing the Bloody Barkers to engage in more of their infamy.

Ma Barker with her friend Arthur V. Dunlop. Barker is alleged to have ordered Dunlop's murder in 1932. CORBIS/BETTMANN

Perhaps fittingly, Ma Barker and each of her four boys came to a violent end. Freddie and Ma died in a shoot-out with officers from the FBI in Florida in 1935. Doc (Arthur) was killed in 1939 trying to escape from Alcatraz. Herman shot himself to death in 1927 after seriously wounding a police officer following a robbery. Lloyd, who served a long sentence at Leavenworth Penitentiary, was killed by his wife in 1949, two years after his release.

BIBLIOGRAPHY

Karpis, Alvin, with Bill Trent. *The Alvin Karpis Story.* New York: Coward, McCann, 1971.

JARRETT PASCHEL

See also **Women: Outlaws.**

BARROW, CLYDE, AND BONNIE PARKER. *See* Bonnie and Clyde.

BEHAVIOR GENETICS. *See* Genetics.

BERKOWITZ, DAVID "SON OF SAM"
(1953–)

Seven months before his first killing, David Berkowitz performed a homicidal experiment. On Christmas Eve in 1975, he attacked two young women with a knife. The experience was almost as traumatic for Berkowitz as it was for his two victims. The women's screaming rattled him and made him panic, prompting him to run off before finishing the job. As he explained after his arrest nearly two years later, "I didn't want to hurt them. I only wanted to kill them."

Following this botched murder attempt, Berkowitz, later to be known as the "Son of Sam," would unleash his rage against young women without any threat of unnerving personal contact. Instead, the pudgy, polite postal worker would maintain a safe distance, concealed by darkness, gun in hand, sneaking up on his victims with the cool precision of an assassin.

As one would expect of someone distressed by his victims' screams, Berkowitz, who was born in the Bronx, New York, in 1953, did not compile a record of violence while growing up—at least not personal violence. He did, however, commit arson, perhaps as many as three hundred times. His impulse to destroy overcame him once he discovered the method of murder that suited him. Primarily he targeted couples out "parking" in secluded spots, but he would also diverge from this pattern. In one instance, he shot two women sitting on a stoop. On another occasion, he murdered a woman walking home from school at night. In all, he would kill six and wound seven in the Bronx, Queens, and Brooklyn over a thirteen-month period. The news media latched onto every detail and development in his case as Berkowitz's crimes plunged the city into panic. Nightclub business dwindled; hundreds of police officers were assigned to the case. Enraged citizens, in one instance, attempted to lynch a man they considered to be a likely suspect. Berkowitz's crimes placed a chill over New York City.

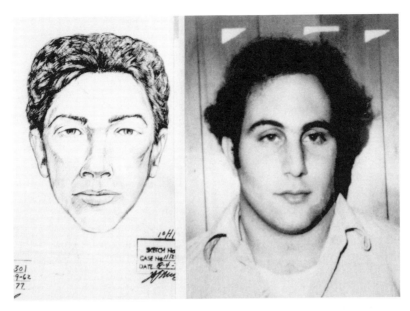

Composite police sketch and mug shot of David Berkowitz, in 1977.
CORBIS/BETTMANN

Berkowitz's cryptic moniker became known when he left a note at the scene of one of his shootings. In addition to warning that he would strike again, the note announced, "I am the 'Son of Sam.' I am a little 'Brat.'" The meaning of the nickname became clear only after his arrest in August 1977.

The police caught up with Berkowitz after the killer received a parking ticket in the vicinity of his final murder. Following up on this lead, the police located Berkowitz's home in Yonkers, and a search of his car and apartment revealed that he was about to escalate his mysterious terrorist campaign: he planned to commit mass murder with a semiautomatic rifle at a chic disco in the Hamptons on Long Island. The case took on a new, even more bizarre dimension when Berkowitz provided the reasons for his murder spree.

The "Son of Sam" moniker referred to the killer's neighbor, Sam Carr, who, Berkowitz claimed, owned a demonically possessed dog. It was the dog, Berkowitz said, that had given him the orders to kill. According to an early court-ordered evaluation, Berkowitz was afflicted with schizophrenia and was haunted by an overpowering sense of "emptiness" and a feeling of "deadness." The psychiatrist David Abrahamsen, also appointed by the court to examine the killer, did not agree. Despite the evidence of derangement that the demonic-dog story implied, he testified that Berkowitz was, in fact, too cunning to be con-

sidered legally insane. The judge in the case went along with this interpretation when he sentenced Berkowitz to life in prison.

At a press conference he held at Attica Prison in 1979, Berkowitz seemed to confirm Abrahamsen's opinion as to his sanity, and also that of the Federal Bureau of Investigation veteran Robert Ressler, who interviewed the killer three times that year: the Son of Sam now claimed that the demonic-dog story had been a fabrication. Perhaps this story had been one way for Berkowitz to avoid taking responsibility for his crimes in his own mind. Others will believe that he wanted to be thought insane to avoid a heavy sentence.

BIBLIOGRAPHY

Abrahamsen, David. *Confessions of Son of Sam.* New York: Columbia University Press, 1985.

Klausner, Lawrence D. *Son of Sam: Based on the Authorized Transcription of the Tapes, Official Documents, and Diaries of David Berkowitz.* New York: McGraw-Hill, 1981.

Newton, Michael. *Hunting Humans: An Encyclopedia of Modern Serial Killers.* Port Townsend, Wash.: Loompanics, 1990.

DAVID EVERITT

See also **Serial Killers.**

BERSERKING. *See* Wilding and Berserking.

BILLY THE KID
(1859–1881)

Few figures in the legend of the American West loom as large as the diminutive Henry F. McCarty, alias William H. Bonney, alias William Antrim, alias "Billy the Kid." His was an unlikely story from start to finish. Born in New York City in 1859 to Irish parents, he spent his childhood in Indiana and Kansas before moving to New Mexico, where his mother married a man named William Antrim. She died in 1874, and the next year McCarty got in trouble with the law over a prank involving two Chinese residents of Silver City and fled to Arizona. Near Camp Grant, where he was known as Kid Antrim, he killed the local blacksmith, Frank P. Cahill, a bully who had insulted the Kid, and returned to Mesilla, in Lincoln County of New Mexico, with yet another alias, William H. Bonney.

After working briefly for Lawrence G. Murphy, a government beef contractor in New Mexico, he

Billy the Kid. HULTON GETTY/LIAISON AGENCY

took a job on the ranch of John Tunstall, who was already involved in the escalating quarrel between John Chisum and Murphy over government beef contracts in New Mexico. When Tunstall was murdered in February 1878, Billy became a partisan against the "house of Murphy." He joined a group known as the Regulators, backers of Tunstall and his partner, Alexander McSween. Richard Brewer, the leader of the Regulators, was a duly appointed constable, which gave the group the color of legality, but when they murdered two of Tunstall's killers, they found themselves condemned as outlaws.

By then the Lincoln County War was in full swing. Billy was among the men who ambushed the county sheriff, William Brady, and his deputy, George Hindman. He was also in the engagement at Blazer's Mill, where A. L. "Buckshot" Roberts, a Murphy partisan, killed Brewer before dying of wounds himself. After Brewer's death, Billy assumed a larger role in the McSween faction. In July 1878 McSween was killed in the "five day battle" at Lincoln. After McSween's death, his followers continued the fight without a real leader.

Eventually a new governor, Lew Wallace, issued a general pardon for the participants in the Lincoln County War, but because of his role in the death of Sheriff Brady, it did not apply to Bonney. Still, the fighting stopped until Murphy's men killed a local lawyer. Governor Wallace promised Billy a full pardon in exchange for his testimony in the killing of the lawyer. Billy agreed, surrendered to officers, and remained in nominal custody for several months, but in the spring of 1879, with no sign of the promised pardon, he simply rode away.

Billy then tried to collect wages from John Chisum, who had been loosely aligned with Tunstall and McSween, and when Chisum refused, he took his wages from Chisum's herds, entering into a new phase of his career, as a cattle thief. In January 1880 he killed a Texas bully named Joe Grant and was almost captured during a gunfight at White Oaks when Jim Carlyle, a popular blacksmith, was killed. These events confirmed Billy's status as an outlaw, and the new sheriff of Lincoln County, Pat Garrett, determined to end his career.

Garrett captured Billy the Kid after a fight at Stinking Springs, twenty-five miles from Fort Sumner, in which two of Billy's friends were killed. He was charged in the deaths of Buckshot Roberts and Sheriff Brady. The Roberts charge was thrown out of court, but he was convicted in Brady's murder. Before he could be executed, the Kid made a daring escape in which he killed two deputies. On the night of 14 July 1881 Garrett caught up with him at the ranch of Pete Maxwell. Billy the Kid walked into Maxwell's darkened bedroom, unaware that Garrett was there, and Garrett shot him dead.

Three weeks later the first "biography" of Billy the Kid appeared. Later Ash Upson ghosted Pat Garrett's *The Authentic Life of Billy the Kid* (1882), a decidedly unauthentic account, and the legend of Billy the Kid as a killer was born. In 1925 Walter Noble Burns published *The Saga of Billy the Kid*, which portrayed Billy as an American Robin Hood. In both the popular literature of the Old West and the popular culture of movies and television, the legend of Billy the Kid continues to have more power than the less compelling figure of history.

BIBLIOGRAPHY

Jacobsen, Joel. *Such Men as Billy the Kid: The Lincoln County War Reconsidered*. Lincoln: University of Nebraska Press, 1994.

Nolan, Frederick. *The Lincoln County War: A Documentary History*. Norman: University of Oklahoma Press, 1992.

Tatum, Stephen. *Inventing Billy the Kid: Visions of the Outlaw in America, 1881–1981*. Albuquerque: University of New Mexico Press, 1982.

Tuska, John. *Billy the Kid: A Handbook*. Westport, Conn.: Greenwood, 1986.

Utley, Robert M. *Billy the Kid: A Short and Violent Life*. Lincoln: University of Nebraska Press, 1989.

GARY L. ROBERTS

See also **Garrett, Pat; Gunfighters and Outlaws, Western.**

BIRTH ORDER AND BIRTH SPACING

Family structure affects interaction among family members as well as their personalities. Children born into a family enter a network of relationships that were established to perform such basic family functions as provision of intimacy, socialization of young, and creation and distribution of material necessities. Newborns first engage this network as consumers who hold only the promise of future contribution. As they develop, their interests are shaped by the resources and expectations of the family. Children's access to resources, especially parental attention, and the expectations put upon

them are influenced by their age relationship to their siblings. The age difference between a child and his or her closest sibling and that child's age position (e.g., oldest, middle, youngest) both affect how a child assumes a role within the family network and what types of behaviors the child will engage in.

A small age difference between siblings means that a sibling pair will always be at proximate developmental stages and thus share many interests. They will compete with one another when resources are limited, developing strategies to appropriate these resources. Typically, these strategies include coercion and violence. Murray Straus and Richard J. Gelles in their 1976 study of American families found that 82 percent of youths who lived in a household with siblings committed an act of sibling violence—any incident of hitting, kicking, punching, or using a weapon by one sibling against another—within the past year. In most cases the violence occurred frequently, and in many cases it included severe acts.

Sibling violence is far less common between siblings spaced in wide intervals. When siblings are spaced wider than five years apart, their interactions are based less on competing interests than on complementary interests. Moreover, when conflict does arise, significantly older siblings normally can use their vast developmental advantage to resolve problems without resorting to physical violence.

It is less clear whether birth intervals influence the siblings' propensity for violence outside the sibling dyad. The interactionist school of personality development argues that personalities form as infants—who have genetically determined temperamental characteristics—and interact with their social environment. A stable personality structure crystallizes after a number of years of social interactions. Recurring and routine interactions, which involve stable relationships, are the most meaningful. Immediate family members who are in regular contact with the youth therefore have substantial influence over how the personality will develop. When young children learn that they can successfully assert themselves using violence against their siblings, they are more likely to incorporate character traits that promote violent acts later in life.

Frank J. Sulloway (1996) advanced this argument to suggest that firstborn children, especially ones with closely spaced siblings, become more "tough-minded" rather than "tender-hearted."

Firstborns aggressively assert themselves in competition with later-born children, resulting in personalities that are conservative, authoritarian, and domineering. Sulloway attributes both violent and despotic moments in history to firstborn leaders' expressing the character traits that they developed within their sibling interactions. However, empirical evidence related to the frequency of violence (such as criminal assault) has not been studied with respect to differences in birth spacing or in birth order.

BIBLIOGRAPHY

Straus, Murray, and Richard J. Gelles. *Physical Violence in American Families.* Ann Arbor, Mich.: Inter-univeristy Consortium for Political and Social Research, 1976.

Straus, Murray, Richard J. Gelles, and Suzanne K. Steinmetz. *Behind Closed Doors: Violence in the American Family.* Garden City, N.Y.: Anchor, 1980.

Sulloway, Frank J. *Born to Rebel: Birth Order, Family Dynamics, and Creative Lives.* New York: Pantheon, 1996.

Teti, Douglas M. "Sibling Interaction." In *Handbook of Social Development: A Lifespan Perspective,* edited by Vincent B. Van Hasselt and Michel Hersen. New York: Plenum, 1992.

EMORY MORRISON

See also **Age and the Life Cycle; Domestic Violence; Sibling Abuse.**

BLACKBEARD
(c. 1680–1718)

The pirate known as Blackbeard terrorized the Atlantic coastal shipping lanes from 1717 to 1718. By creating a fearsome appearance for himself, he often frightened seamen into a quick surrender.

Born Edward Teach in Bristol, England, he served as a privateer in the Royal Navy during Queen Anne's War (1702–1713). Stranded in the West Indies after the war, he chose piracy as a career around 1716. In Nassau, the Bahamas, a haven for pirates, Teach met Benjamin Hornigold, another privateer turned pirate. The two became partners, and in 1717, off St. Vincent, they attacked the French merchantman *Concorde,* which was loaded with gold dust. Teach killed half the crew, and the other half surrendered. Thus began Teach's policy of sparing crews that surrendered without a fight. Teach renamed the *Concorde* the *Queen Anne's Revenge* and began besting warships of the Royal Navy.

About this time he intentionally developed a demonic persona. He grew a coarse black beard, which he often braided with ribbons, and took the name Blackbeard. During battles, he would put long, slow-burning matches in his beard, which made for a frightening appearance. He also dressed in black and wore a bandolier with at least three pistols primed and ready to fire. Superstitious seamen usually surrendered immediately to the ship led by the devil personified. Blackbeard was an excellent navigator and a shrewd leader; he once shot a crewman in the knee, explaining that if he did not shoot one of the crew now and then, they would forget who he was.

Early in 1718 he sailed for North Carolina's Pamlico Sound. Protected by the Outer Banks, the sound provided a number of hiding places. His favorite refuge was Ocracoke Island. Blackbeard began to collect tolls forcibly from shipping in Pamlico Sound and made a prize-sharing agreement with the royal governor, Charles Eden. Blackbeard then briefly pursued an honest life: he grounded his ship, abandoned most of his crew, and gained a pardon offered to pirates by King George I. The lure of piracy was overwhelming, however, and in May 1718 he blockaded Charleston harbor, South Carolina. His first major capture was the *Crowley,* with several wealthy South Carolina citizens aboard. Blackbeard sent some of his men ashore with a ransom demand for three hundred pounds of medicine in return for the hostages. Four days passed, during which Blackbeard threatened to send in the heads of the hostages, before his men returned with the medicine and the hostages were released.

Blackbeard next headed for Bermuda and encountered two French merchantmen—one empty and one loaded with sugar. Blackbeard seized the sugar ship, which he set on fire back in Pamlico Bay, claiming the ship was empty when he found it. Governor Alexander Spotswood of Virginia knew of the sugar ship, however, and the ship's capture erased Blackbeard's pardon. Blackbeard anchored at Ocracoke Inlet, and Spotswood sent two sloops with fifty-eight men under Lieutenant Robert Maynard to capture him. At dawn on 22 November, Blackbeard, with only eighteen men aboard the *Adventure,* fired on Maynard's ship. The battle that followed after Blackbeard and his men boarded the *Ranger* is considered the bloodiest ever on the deck of a ship.

Blackbeard suffered five musket shots and twenty cutlass wounds before he fell dead. May-

Blackbeard liked to keep two slow-burning matches in his beard. HULTON GETTY/LIAISON AGENCY

nard hung Blackbeard's head on his bowsprit, and during his return to Virginia, he stopped at Bath, North Carolina, where he discovered some of Blackbeard's booty in the barn of Governor Eden's secretary. Blackbeard's skull was hung from a pole in Virginia at what is still known as Blackbeard's Point.

The dark fascination with Blackbeard, the most infamous of pirates, a demon who lacked any human kindness, has continued into the twentieth century. The myth that his decapitated body swam around Maynard's ship several times before sinking has endured. The search goes on for Blackbeard's skull (believed to have been turned into a silver-plated drinking vessel) and his legendary buried treasure. In November 1996 a private research company discovered a ship in twenty feet of water off Beaufort Inlet, North Carolina, and it is presumed to be the *Queen Anne's Revenge*.

BIBLIOGRAPHY

Hoffman, Margaret. *Blackbeard: A Tale of Villainy and Murder in Colonial America*. Columbia, S.C.: Summerhouse, 1998.

Lee, Robert Earl. *Blackbeard the Pirate: A Reappraisal of His Life and Times*. Winston-Salem, N.C.: John F. Blair, 1974. Reprint, 1984.

Pendered, Norman C. *Blackbeard: The Fiercest Pirate of All.* Manteo, N.C.: Times Printing, 1975.

Roberts, Nancy. *Blackbeard and Other Pirates of the Atlantic Coast*. Winston-Salem, N.C.: John F. Blair, 1993.

Yetter, George Humphrey. "When Blackbeard Scourged the Seas." *Colonial Williamsburg Journal* 15, no. 1 (fall 1992).

LOUISE B. KETZ

See also **Piracy; Privateers.**

BLACK CODES

In the wake of the Civil War and emancipation, southern legislatures enacted a series of repressive statutes collectively known as the Black Codes. Intended to define the meaning of freedom for African Americans on southern whites' terms, these state laws severely restricted blacks' freedom while at the same time reinforcing white control in the South. Although varied from state to state, the Black Codes generally regulated African Americans' ability to move, work, control their families, own property, make contracts, sue and be sued, and testify in court.

While southern whites initially resorted to such nonlegal means as violence to limit African Americans' recently won freedom, by the fall of 1865 they also turned to state legislatures to reassert white legal control over blacks. Educated during slavery, most whites believed that blacks were inherently inferior to whites and that unless they were subject to strict social controls they would resort to idleness and crime, refuse to labor, and thus threaten order and stability. Heightening the anxieties of white southerners in 1865 were continued fears of insurrection and blacks' seeming unwillingness to enter labor contracts for 1866. With the demise of slavery, white southerners called for the creation of a rigid system of racial control that would replace the power of the master with that of the state. Mississippi and South Carolina were the first to respond, enacting the most severe Black Codes in late 1865; Alabama, Louisiana, Florida, Virginia, Georgia, North Carolina, Texas, and Tennessee acted in 1866; and Arkansas followed in 1867. With their roots in the Slave Codes of the antebellum South, these complex laws touched every aspect of southern blacks' lives and denied them their most basic economic, legal, political, and social rights.

The object of the Black Codes was to reinforce white power by keeping African Americans in the fields as property-less agricultural laborers. Perhaps the most fundamental of the Black Codes' provisions were those regulating vagrancy and labor. African Americans throughout the South encountered harsh vagrancy laws designed to keep them working. Vagrants—in practice, former slaves who refused to enter labor contracts—were subject to stiff fines, imprisonment, and, in some states, corporal punishment. If blacks were unable to pay their fines themselves, local officials hired out vagrants to labor (without compensation) for any person who paid the fine. The codes also governed how and where African Americans labored. They punished blacks who failed to enter contracts, established criminal penalties for breach of contract, and penalized those who enticed away workers. Mississippi, for instance, each January required blacks to have written proof of employment for the year, and prohibited blacks from renting or leasing land. South Carolina barred blacks from entering occupations other than farming or service by imposing an annual licensing fee on those engaged in "any other trade, employment or business . . . besides that of husbandry, or that of a servant under a contract for service or labor." Florida made disobedience, impudence, and disrespect to the employer a crime punishable by a fine not to exceed $500, imprisonment, or forced labor for as long as one year. And Louisiana stipulated that all disputes between employers and employees "shall be settled . . . by the former." In short, vagrancy laws provided the compulsion for reluctant blacks to work on terms acceptable to whites and the means to ensure labor discipline.

Additional provisions of the Black Codes did more to perpetuate white control. African Americans were barred from entering some states and required to carry passes from their employers in others, limiting their freedom of movement. Intermarriage between races was prohibited. Many states forbade blacks to own firearms, leaving them vulnerable to white violence. Moreover, the codes made black families susceptible to white interference. Although states now legally recognized African American families, apprenticeship laws enabled state officials—at their discretion—to "bind out" black orphans and children whose parents were unable to support them. Southern officials took great advantage of these measures, removing tens of thousands of children from their families and binding them to labor-starved planters under the pretense of teaching them agricultural and domestic trades. The Black Codes also impaired African Americans' access to justice: Blacks were allowed to testify only in cases involving black parties and could not serve on juries. Penal codes provided judges and juries with the discretion to impose harsher punishments on black criminals—ensuring they would be subjected to execution, corporal punishment, forced labor, lengthy imprisonment, and heavy fines more often than whites convicted of similar crimes.

Reaction to the Black Codes was swift and profound. Northern newspapers chastised them as an effort to restore slavery in all but name, running such headlines as that of the *New York Tribune* on 14 November 1865: "South Carolina Re-establishing Slavery." To northerners, the South appeared unrepentant and unwilling to change—despite military loss. The Freedmen's Bureau prevented enforcement of the Black Codes' most flagrant laws and Congress overrode many of their provisions by passing the Civil Rights Act of 1866. African Americans resisted the codes, making them difficult to enforce and sometimes sparking increased white violence.

Northern reaction to the first Black Codes led other southern legislatures to enact statutes that were, on their face, nondiscriminatory and, theoretically, applied to blacks and whites alike. By expanding the discretionary power of judges and juries, however, southern legislatures ensured that local officials would have the authority to maintain white control. Thus, by the end of 1866 southern blacks encountered discrimination not necessarily in the law but in the way states enforced the law. Understanding this and bolstered by northern outcry over the Black Codes, Republicans in Congress reacted with more radical Reconstruction plans that ultimately included passage of the Reconstruction Act and adoption of the Fourteenth and Fifteenth Amendments. With the rights these laws granted—most notably citizenship, equality before the law, and voting—in the late 1860s southern blacks worked with and as lawmakers to dislodge all remnants of the Black Codes. Nevertheless, the spirit of racism embodied in the Black Codes would reemerge in the disenfranchisement and segregation laws adopted across the South in the decades following Reconstruction and would not be dismantled until the Civil Rights movement in the 1950s and 1960s.

BIBLIOGRAPHY

Foner, Eric. *Reconstruction: America's Unfinished Revolution, 1863–1877.* New York: Harper and Row, 1988.

Nieman, Donald G. *To Set the Law in Motion: The Freedmen's Bureau and the Legal Rights of Blacks, 1865–1868.* Millwood, N.Y.: KTO Press, 1979.

Wilson, Theodore. *The Black Codes of the South.* Tuscaloosa: University of Alabama Press, 1965.

MARY J. FARMER

See also **African Americans; Slave Rebellions; Slavery; South.**

BLACK DAHLIA CASE

On the morning of 15 January 1947 a Los Angeles housewife made the grisly discovery of a young woman's body, neatly cut in half and dumped in a vacant lot. The body was almost ceremonially arranged, with the torso completely separated from the legs, which were spread wide. Police department investigators on the scene found that her wrists had been bound, her face and breasts mutilated, and her body completely washed. Amazingly, there was no trace of blood or fluids on the ground, and the corpse bore no signs of serration marks around the separation point. The discovery set off a manhunt, which, though the largest of its day, would find no motive, no suspects, and only a few sketchy details about an itinerant inhabitant of southern California's seedier world.

Within hours of the body's discovery, the Federal Bureau of Investigation turned up a fingerprint match that identified the victim as Elizabeth Short, twenty-two years old, originally from Medford, Massachusetts, the third of five daughters of Phoebe and Cleo Short. Her record and police profile showed she was a drifter, a participant in the transient lifestyle of the Hollywood scene, and possibly a prostitute. Los Angeles police were familiar with the Hollywood scene, which included a fairly regular circle of hostesses and prostitutes. However, given the constant stream of young hopefuls who did not find the stardom they were seeking, it was often difficult for police to track a single individual. Her wardrobe of sleek black clothing had led acquaintances to nickname her "Black Dahlia." An image began to emerge of Short as an enigmatic loner, frequenting clubs and cafés, clad in tight dresses—an elusive and mysterious woman. Most of Short's acquaintances shared rooms, cosmetics, and gossip about male friends with her, but they were never close to her. Worldly wise and innocent at the same time, Short was often surprised when girls exchanged sexual

Elizabeth Short, also known as the Black Dahlia.
CORBIS/BETTMANN

favors for gifts and money, although she would become no stranger to this practice.

The gruesome case immediately fired public imagination, and the investigation was continuously hampered by the added pressure of intense scrutiny of police procedure. From the beginning the detectives essentially lost control of the case; they failed to secure key evidence at the scene, take photographs, or make imprint casts. The investigation was also hindered by the local Hearst newspapers, the *LA Examiner* and *Herald-Express*, which seized on the murder as a chance to boost sales. Not only did the reporters try to scoop the police on possible clues and suspects, but they attempted to solve the crime before the police did by offering a $10,000 reward, posing as detectives, and starting wild rumors.

At the time of the investigation, the Los Angeles Police Department was fraught with internal rivalries and ego clashes, and a high incidence of corruption resulted in low morale. Also, the increasing

Los Angeles murder rate and declining arrest records made for a gloomy and embattled mentality. Under increasing internal frustration and stung by public outrage generated by the sensational newspaper coverage, the police felt compelled to find a suspect at any cost, which resulted in several grievous procedural errors. Detectives managed to locate two of Short's last acquaintances, Leslie Dillon and Robert Manley, and tried to force confessions from them. Each man, however, passed a polygraph test, had a strong alibi, and was clearly innocent. Public disgust with the police department merely increased.

As police and reporters tried to reconstruct Black Dahlia's final days, it became clear there was a gap in her activities, a period known as the "missing week." Between 9 and 15 January, Short had simply disappeared, and none of the leads or witnesses could offer any possible solutions as to her whereabouts. Deepening the mystery, nine days after the discovery of her body the apparent killer mailed an envelope to the *Examiner* containing Short's Social Security card, birth certificate, snapshots, and an address book with pages ripped out. All of the items had been washed in gasoline to remove fingerprints. Yet despite the possible leads, the names from the address book only led the police deeper into confusion and confirmed the case was unsolvable.

While Short's killer was never found, her brutal mutilation and flighty life became an unspoken morality tale of the dangers surrounding Hollywood glitz and glamour. The sultriness, mystery, and utter ambiguity surrounding Black Dahlia was woven into the mesh of Los Angeles myth, becoming alternatively a symbol of innocence corrupted, a confirmation of the existence of predatory maniacs, and proof of police ineffectiveness.

BIBLIOGRAPHY

Gilmore, John. *Severed: The True Story of the Black Dahlia Murder.* Los Angeles: Zanja, 1994.

Harnish, Larry. "A Slaying Cloaked in Mystery and Myths." *Los Angeles Times,* 6 January 1997.

Rice, Craig, ed. *Los Angeles Murders.* New York: Duell, Sloan, and Pearce, 1947.

Webb, Jack. *The Badge.* Englewood Cliffs, N.J.: Prentice Hall, 1958.

PAUL HANSOM

See also **Homicide; Los Angeles.**

BLACK HAND

The term *Black Hand* has been employed erroneously to describe a national criminal syndicate. Black Hand gangs, operating by 1903, were not forms of syndicates; rather, they were organized gangs that engaged in extortion. Unlike syndicates, they did not provide illicit goods and services and they did not have police protection. Black Hand gangs were composed exclusively of Italian and especially Sicilian immigrants, typically originating from specific provinces in Italy; their major enterprise involved extorting money from their fellow countrymen who had settled in the United States.

The American Mafia (1971) cites data obtained from interviews with informants, victims, and close associates of gang members in the Pittsburgh area. Findings were consistent with those contained in a 1908 report of the White Hand Society, a group of Italians who studied and sought the demise of these gangs. Although the size of gangs varied according to the number of members needed in each enterprise, a gang typically consisted of six to ten members under one leader. The major feature of these gangs was their method of extorting money by sending letters that threatened victims with death or injury if they did not comply, a method commonly practiced by bandits in Sicily. Also like these bandits, Black Hand members would sometimes kidnap a person, usually a child, and hold him or her for ransom.

The modus operandi of the Black Hand gangs consisted of first gaining information about any Italians who had recently come into a fortune through an inheritance, a sale of property in Italy, or even a large monetary wedding gift. This information was obtained by members who served as spies and frequented taverns, barbershops, and other places where Italians congregated.

The letter sent to the intended victim was unique in that crude drawings of such things as daggers, skulls, coffins, and black hands were added to the margins. These drawings were meant to further intimidate the victim. The letter stated the amount of money demanded and provided directions as to where and when it was to be delivered; specific tombstones in cemeteries often were the place of choice. If the victims refused payment, they and members of their family might be killed. The killer was selected by drawing lots. Bombings of houses and businesses were also frequent methods of killing or intimidating victims. Usually ordinary citizens were selected as victims, but sometimes celebrities, such as the opera tenors Enrico Caruso and Tito Schipa, became targets.

Although they employed stealth, gang members were often known by the public, and in some cases potential victims, who were themselves skilled in the use of violence, successfully threatened the Black Hand members with retaliation, thus causing them to terminate their threats. The gangs disappeared; some killed each other off in gang wars, but most turned to the more lucrative enterprise of selling illicit alcohol during Prohibition. By 1933 Black Hand gangs had simply become another part of Italian-American history.

BIBLIOGRAPHY

Albini, Joseph L. *The American Mafia: Genesis of a Legend.* New York: Appleton-Century-Crofts, 1971.

The Italian "White Hand" Society in Chicago, Illinois: Studies, Actions, and Results. Chicago, 1908.

Pitkin, Thomas Monroe, and Francesco Cordasco. *The Black Hand: A Chapter in Ethnic Crime.* Totowa, N.J.: Littlefield, Adams, 1977.

JOSEPH L. ALBINI

See also **Mafia; Organized Crime.**

BLACK PANTHERS

On the night of 17 February 1968, more than five thousand Black Panther Party (BPP) supporters crowded into the Oakland Auditorium for a rally calling for Huey P. Newton's release from the Oakland County, California, jail. Newton was awaiting trial for the killing of an Oakland police officer. It was Newton's birthday, and a large wicker chair had been left empty in the center of the stage; Newton, who had insisted (falsely) on his innocence had become a symbol of the ills of police brutality. The party, which had been founded by Newton and Bobby Seale in October 1966 when they were students at Merritt College in Oakland, was hardly a year and a half old and already it had achieved widespread popularity, primarily among urban blacks and the radical white left.

After the large crowd settled in, Stokely Carmichael, Eldridge Cleaver, and Rap Brown spoke on Newton's behalf. Bobby Seale rose to address the audience as smoke from his cigarette curled up past his black beret. Slowly, deliberately, he re-

viewed the party's political platform, known as the Ten Point Program.

1. *We want the power to determine the destiny of our black community.* From America's founding fathers the BPP inherited the belief that a nation oppressed by a tyrannous regime had the right to liberate itself by force, and from Fidel Castro and Che Guevara it adopted the idea that a poor disfranchised people could rise up against and overthrow a wealthier elite class.

2. *We want full employment for our people.* While most of the nation experienced a prolonged postwar economic expansion, the inner cities grew poorer. Middle-class blacks and whites with money fled the cities, leaving pockets of poverty behind.

3. *We want an end to the robbery by the capitalists of our black community.* The Black Panthers saw themselves as racial proletariats, hard-working laborers who were exploited by white America and kept down by discrimination and racism.

4. *We want decent housing fit for shelter of human beings.* Among the party's initiatives was the organization of tenants to lobby for their rights against abusive slumlords.

5. *We want education for our people.* The Panthers were outraged that the public school system was failing to educate inner-city black Americans. Newton himself was illiterate even after he graduated from high school. He taught himself to read and eventually earned a Ph.D. at the University of California, Santa Cruz.

6. *We want all black men to be exempt from military service.* The Panthers did not want to support what they considered a racist government as it waged war against the Vietnamese, whom the Panthers considered people of color like themselves.

7. *We want an immediate end to police brutality and murder of black people.* The formation of the Black Panther Party for Self Defense was primarily a reaction against police brutality, a reaction in kind against the police's willingness to apply deadly force. The Panthers viewed American inner cities as "occupied territories," portions of America subdued and occupied by foreign troops. They saw black America as a nation

Black Panthers march to a news conference in New York in July 1968 to protest the trial of one of the group's founders, Huey P. Newton. HULTON GETTY/LIAISON AGENCY

intimidated and dehumanized by a brutal police force that was enforcing the will of a racist government. They saw violence as the primary means by which they could reclaim their self-respect and their humanity.

The Panthers had first gained notoriety for what they called "police patrols." Panther members intercepted police communications using a shortwave radio, rushed to the scene of the crime, and approached the arresting officers as they were apprehending individuals. The Panthers informed the arrested individuals of their constitutional rights, and they attempted to intimidate the officers. Their uniforms of black leather jackets, black berets, and shotguns became emblematic of their paramilitary disposition, and they certainly cultivated a militarist image. Confrontations between the Panthers and the police led to arrests of party members and to shoot-outs between Panthers and police.

8. *We want freedom for all black men held in federal, state, county, and city prisons and jails.* If the impoverished, decaying inner cities were occupied territories, then incarcerated blacks were prisoners of war.

9. *We want all black people when brought to trial to be tried by a jury of their peer group, by people from the black communities.* The Panthers insisted that the trial and imprisonment of millions of black Americans was unjust because they were not tried before a jury of black peers.

10. *We want land, bread, housing, education, clothing, justice, and peace.* There was more to the Black Panthers than a call to violent revolution. In the mid-1970s, with their popularity on the wane among black American leaders, the Panthers undertook several community service programs in order to improve their own prestige and the lives of inner-city black Americans. One of the most helpful programs was a free breakfast program for schoolchildren. The Black Panthers founded health clinics to provide free medical care to poor blacks, a busing program to help the friends and relatives of prisoners visit their loved ones on visiting days, and a transportation program for elderly black residents of housing projects. Other programs provided shoes and clothing to needy black Americans.

Police officers were not the only targets of the Black Panther Party. Party members also engaged in a pattern of intimidation and extortion in order to get local business owners to contribute money, goods, and services to the party's coffers. For example, in 1969 a convenience-store owner on San Pablo Avenue in North Oakland thought that the Panthers "request" for six dozen eggs for a breakfast program was unreasonable. The owner donated only one dozen eggs, and on 10 May 1969, two Panthers, Reginald Forte and John Sloan, firebombed his store. By the late 1960s the party had become a small-scale racketeering operation, demanding money from drug dealers and pimps in Oakland in exchange for keeping the police from interrupting their operations. Party members beat up or murdered those who they believed were not cooperating with their revolutionary agenda, and they often resorted to beatings or political assassinations of current members or former members of the party. In one such incident, former Panther Renee Rice was beaten when she appeared at the national office. After a friend of hers named Ron Black confronted the party leadership about the beating, he was murdered on 5 April 1969. Newton's own savagery escalated after he became a cocaine addict upon his release from prison in 1970. Among Newton's more brutal acts of violence was the sodomizing of Bobby Seale in 1973.

From its inception the BPP had been under attack by the Federal Bureau of Investigation, and it became public enemy number one after the formation of the FBI's counterintelligence program, or COINTELPRO, in the late 1960s. The FBI led frequent raids to round up and jail Black Panther members. One of the most sensational was the rounding up of the "Panther 21" in New York City in 1969. Charged with over one hundred counts of conspiracy, the twenty-one defendants were acquitted on all charges in 1971. Throughout the 1970s the FBI successfully fostered dissent within the party, and the Panthers effectively disbanded in 1982.

The concrete political gains of the Black Panthers were limited. In the early 1970s they helped elect only a handful of officials to posts in the Bay Area, and their official membership never exceeded five thousand. However, their symbolic impact on the United States during the late 1960s and early 1970s was tremendous. They served as an emblem of black power and black pride at a time when many blacks felt intimidated and dehumanized by a brutal police force.

While their ideological rhetoric may have been commendable, the tactics of the Black Panther Party members were no less ignominious than the police whom they criticized. Under the banner of black nationalism and revolutionary intercommunalism, the party leadership eventually devolved into a group of gangsters and thugs. The party's corruption and reliance on guerrilla tactics ultimately undermined any claims it might have had to widespread political legitimacy among African Americans.

BIBLIOGRAPHY

Anthony, Earl. *Picking Up the Gun: A Report on the Black Panthers.* New York: Dial, 1970.

Kempton, Murray. *The Briar Patch: The Trial of the Panther 21.* New York: Da Capo, 1997. Originally published in 1973.

Newton, Huey. *The War Against the Panthers: A Study of Repression in America.* New York and London: Harlem River Press, 1996.

Pearson, Hugh. *The Shadow of the Panther: Huey Newton and the Price of Black Power in America.* Reading, Pa.: Addison-Wesley, 1994.

Seale, Bobby. *Seize the Times: The Story of the Black Panther Party and Huey P. Newton.* Baltimore: Black Classic Press, 1970. Reprint, 1997.

Van Deburg, William L., ed. *Modern Nationalism: From Marcus Garvey to Louis Farrakhan.* New York: New York University Press, 1997.

ADAM MAX COHEN

See also **Cleaver, Eldridge; Newton, Huey.**

BOMBINGS AND BOMB SCARES

Each year in the United States there are thousands of bombings (some 2,217 in 1997) and bomb scares. Many innocent people are killed, and many more are injured because of improvised explosive devices, that is, bombs. Property damage and related medical expenses are reported to be in the millions. Bomb scares in the form of hoax bombs—bombs made to look like the real thing—are particularly troublesome. Because these devices must be addressed in an extremely cautious manner until they can be deemed harmless, they often disrupt operations longer than an anonymous threat does. Still, bomb scares in the form of anonymous threats also take a great toll. Repeated bomb scares at schools place stress on young children, and evacuating an industrial plant because of a bomb threat is expensive. Moreover, the cost of implementing security procedures to deal with bomb scares, as well as bombings themselves, is significant.

Types of Bombers and Bombs

The motives behind bombings and bomb scares may be ideological, revenge-oriented, or profit-driven. Ideological bombings have been carried out on behalf of political or social beliefs, ranging from those associated with radical animal rights groups to bombs planted by right-wing zealots who believe abortion is the work of the devil. Ideological bombers are frequently skilled bomb makers and bombers motivated by extremist beliefs. Their bombings are often symbolic and meant to strike fear in the general public. With revenge bombings, in contrast, the bomber is motivated by some personal dispute. Revenge bombers usually suffer from some form of mental illness. Profit bombings have no ideological or psychopathic motivation; they are solely for direct or indirect monetary gain. Frequently profit bombings are carried out by organized-crime operatives trying to extort money through intimidation or during a power struggle between various crime factions. Some profit bombings are used as arson to cover up theft.

Hoax bombs and anonymous bomb threats are often the work of copycat criminals who are lured by the sheer thrill of making headlines. They may see the United States in an uproar over a particularly noteworthy crime, such as a bombing, and regard threatening a similar event as a way to achieve importance. In such cases the bomb threat becomes a power trip, particularly for those who feel that they have nothing to lose.

Bombers' targets are airports and aircraft, mailboxes, vehicles, utility companies, state and local governments, the federal government, banks, and medical facilities, to name a few. Among the most popular places to plant devices for bombings are inside and immediately outside buildings, in trash cans, in parking lots, and under vehicles. Some of the most efficient types of containers used to deliver bombs include metal pipes, bottles, cans, dynamite sticks, metal and cardboard boxes, pressurized cartridges, and grenade hulls. A variety of fillers have been used to make these improvised devices, such as black powder, flammable liquid, smokeless powder, photoflash and fireworks powders, match heads, and blasting agents. Bottles filled with flammable liquids are the weapon of choice, followed in popularity by pipe bombs— metal pipes filled with black powder.

Bombing tactics vary according to the individuals or groups involved in planning the explosion. Some individuals and groups forewarn of an impending explosion. Some bombers set two explosions, with the second timed to detonate when law-enforcement and emergency personnel are at the scene, thus making the first-line responders the real target. Individual bombers generally follow certain patterns when crafting their deadly devices. Experts say that every bomb maker develops a distinguishing signature, whether it be the way in which certain wires are cut and looped, the angle of the switches of the bomb, the material used to create the bombs, or a defining identification mark inscribed on the metal parts that survive the blast.

Bomb Materials and Know-how

Stolen explosives from manufacturers, dealers, permittees, and other legitimate users as well as military bases contribute to the number of bombings in the United States each year. Some of the more favorite targets for thefts include dynamite, TNT, black powder, and smokeless powder. Law-enforcement agencies like the Bureau of Alcohol, Tobacco, and Firearms measure the yearly theft totals in tons. A substantial portion of this stolen material is never recovered and is thus assumed available for improper use. More significant, however, is the fact that most of the ingredients needed to build deadly bombs are available through normal channels, and the law does not restrict the purchase of most of these items. Many individuals— by dint of their occupation and interests—have most of the essentials for bomb assembly. In addition, the shelves of hardware stores, garden-supply centers, and chemical suppliers are full of the essential ingredients for some of the most commonly used explosive devices. The bombs that shattered the World Trade Center in New York City in 1993 and the Alfred P. Murrah Federal Building in Oklahoma City in 1995 consisted of such readily accessible ingredients.

Instructional Guides. Also contributing to the large number of bombings and bomb scares is the easy access to bomb-making information. A number of publishers, such as Paladin Press, specialize in books containing easy-to-follow bomb-making recipes, and bookstores make these books readily available to the general public. Several companies specializing in survivalist gear list in their catalogs such classic manuals on do-it-yourself mayhem as

William Powell's *The Anarchist Cookbook* (1971) and Kurt Saxon's *The Poor Man's James Bond* (1991) as well as books and videos about manufacturing explosives. A catalog popular with the survivalist crowd tempts customers with the following sales pitch for the video *Deadly Explosives: How and Why They Work*: "Imagine spending an hour with a top explosives expert while he teaches you everything you ever wanted to know. . . . Not only is it a blast to watch, you'll come away with more practical knowledge than most licensed explosives experts"(Vol. 36B; El Dorado, Arizona: Delta Press, 1996).

The Internet. More than any other source, the Internet brings bomb-making skills to the general public. A number of booksellers on the Internet have hundreds of manuals available for sale online twenty-four hours a day. Entering the key words *pipe bomb* in search engines brings up thousands of hits linking the user to a variety of Web sites offering related information, including assembly instructions as well as more links to sites on to how to construct such deadly devices as works bombs, dry-ice bombs, and Molotov cocktails, to name a few.

There are also many Internet chat rooms where participants can share their bomb-making skills on-line. These real-time conversations with other Internet users allow anonymity and the development of deadly knowledge concerning bombs, bombings, and bomb scares.

In addition to being used for sharing bomb formulas and conducting other conversations related to explosives, e-mail communications are fast replacing the telephone as the preferred method of making anonymous bomb threats. Even school-age children have employed the technology to involve themselves in bombings and bomb scares. For example, in the weeks following the 1999 Columbine High School killings in Littleton, Colorado, many teenagers across the country sent e-mail messages to schools threatening similar bomb incidents. One Web site popular with youths features *The School Stopper's Textbook*, written by unknown members of the 1960s Youth International Party (the Yippies), which advocates bomb scares to "break up the boredom especially during exams or on beautiful days."

Some Significant Bombings

Haymarket Square Bombing. On 3 May 1886 violence erupted at the McCormick Reaper Works in

Police robot picks up a suspicious briefcase found in a New York City restaurant, 20 April 1983. UPI/CORBIS-BETTMANN

Chicago during an assembly of strikers. That evening a small group of anarchists—including August Spies, whose colleague Johann Most wrote *Military Science for Revolutionaries* (1885)—met to plan a rally to protest the violence. Alarmed by the plans, the mayor of Chicago, Carter Harrison, assembled approximately two hundred policemen to keep order. During the rally at Haymarket Square, anarchist leaders called for a violent uprising. As the police advanced to disperse the vocal gathering, a dynamite bomb was thrown into their ranks and rioting ensued. The Chicago police officer Mathias J. Degan was killed instantaneously, six more policemen were mortally wounded, and sixty-eight others suffered lesser wounds.

Public indignation over the bombing rose rapidly, and punishment was demanded. All well-known anarchists and radicals were rounded up and arrested. Of the thirty-one named in the criminal indictment, eight were held for trial. Although the bomber was never identified, the eight indicted men were convicted. Judge Joseph E. Gary imposed the death sentence on seven of them, and

TABLE 1. Bombing Incidents: 1992–1996

Type of Incident	1992	1993	1994	1995	1996	Total
Nonincendiary Bombings	1,911	1,880	1,916	1,562	1,457	8,726
Attempted Nonincendiary Bombings	384	375	522	417	504	2,202
Incendiary Bombings	582	538	545	406	427	2,498
Attempted Incendiary Bombings	112	187	180	192	185	856
Total Bombings	2,989	2,980	3,163	2,577	2,573	14,282
Reported Killed	26	49	31	193	23	322
Reported Injured	349	1,323	308	744	336	3,060
Reported Property Damage*	$12.5	$518.2	$7.3	$105.0	$5.1	$648.1

*Property damage estimates in millions.

SOURCE: Bureau of Alcohol, Tobacco, and Firearms Arson and Explosion Division, *1996 Arson and Explosives Incidents Report.*

TABLE 2. Juvenile Bombing Incidents: 1992–1996

Type of Incident	1992	1993	1994	1995	1996	Total
Nonincendiary Bombings	659	803	888	698	618	3,666
Attempted Nonincendiary Bombings	61	87	151	110	129	538
Incendiary Bombings	44	72	55	77	46	294
Attempted Incendiary Bombings	10	20	32	46	25	133
Total Bombings	774	982	1,126	931	818	4,631
Reported Killed	3	4	6	2	3	18
Reported Injured	81	83	103	99	80	446
Reported Property Damage	$163,364	$1,249,328	$287,270	$418,745	$223,041	$2,341,748

SOURCE: Bureau of Alcohol, Tobacco, and Firearms Arson and Explosion Division, *1996 Arson and Explosives Incidents Report.*

the other was given fifteen years in prison. Four were hanged, including Spies; one committed suicide; and the sentences of the other two were commuted from death to life imprisonment. The three men remaining in prison were pardoned in 1893.

Ku Klux Klan Bombings. The Ku Klux Klan (KKK), a secret organization advocating white supremacy, also used bombing as a weapon of violence and destruction. The use of dynamite bombs by Klansmen began in January 1956, when the Montgomery, Alabama, home of the civil rights leader Martin Luther King, Jr., was blasted. The Klan is believed responsible for more than 150 bombings, in which dozens of innocent people were killed and untold others were injured, between the time of the King incident and 1 June 1963.

One bombing stands out in the history of the KKK and its fanatical fight against integration in the South during the 1960s. On 15 September 1963

a dynamite bomb ripped apart the Sixteenth Street Baptist Church in Birmingham, Alabama, killing four young black schoolgirls: Addie Mae Collins, Denise McNair, Carole Robertson, and Cynthia Wesley. In 1977 Robert "Dynamite Bob" Chambliss, a KKK member, was convicted in McNair's death.

All told, the Klan's campaign of violence against the Civil Rights movement resulted in hundreds of bombings throughout the South and other parts of the United States. Although southern officials made some attempts to arrest and prosecute the bombers, and southern juries sometimes convicted the defendants, the Klan thrived until federal authorities started to pursue the matter in the early 1960s.

Leftist Bombings. In the late 1960s, the more militant members of the leftist protest group Students for a Democratic Society (SDS) gave birth to the Weather Underground (WU). The latter was re-

TABLE 3. Stolen Explosives: 1992–1996

Number of Thefts*	1992	1993	1994	1995	1996	Total
Dynamite	7,983	4,409	5,320	3,234	2,620	23,566
TNT, C-4	2	74	22	16	0	114
Primers	89	25	0	78	5	197
Boosters	531	127	2,593	76	358	3,685
Black Powder	0	303	100	25	252	680
Smokeless Powder	20	24	0	0	200	244
Blasting Agents	1,063	4,022	6,905	5,300	5,703	22,993
Total	9,688	8,984	14,940	8,729	9,138	51,479
Detonator Cord/ Ignitor Cord/ Safety Fuse†	29,640	28,534	83,771	19,267	30,637	191,849
Detonators‡	11,067	7,075	5,226	7,818	5,428	36,614
Grenades‡	0	224	69	58	0	351

* in pounds
† in feet
‡ by quantity

SOURCE: Bureau of Alcohol, Tobacco, and Firearms Arson and Explosion Division, *1996 Arson and Explosives Incidents Reports.*

sponsible for numerous bombings on college campuses throughout the United States. In 1970 the group bombed the headquarters of the New York City Police Department. Soon after this incident, three members of the WU were killed in a brownstone in New York when a bomb they were making unexpectedly detonated.

In 1971 the WU bombed the U.S. Capitol in Washington, D.C. During the next five years the WU claimed responsibility for at least nineteen bombings, including the 29 January 1975 bombing of the U.S. State Department Building to protest U.S. aid to South Vietnam. For logistic purposes, the organization kept its bombing campaign mainly on the East and West Coasts.

In 1974 group leaders explained the rationale behind their bombings in *Prairie Fire: The Politics of Revolutionary Anti-Imperialism.* In addition to a list of bombings committed by the WU, *Prairie Fire* also acknowledged the group's support for any group fighting U.S. imperialism, especially members of Puerto Rican independence groups. The publication's honesty about the bombings backfired when it caused the ire of many citizens and caught the attention of different law-enforcement agencies, forcing the group's leaders to go into hiding.

In the mid-1970s former SDS and WU members formed the United Freedom Front (UFF), a Marxist-Leninist organization bent on overthrowing the government of the United States. Although it never had more than eight members, it embarked upon an almost decade-long campaign of bombings. From the spring of 1976, with the UFF's bombing of the Suffolk County Courthouse in Boston, until the group's last bombing, in September 1984, of the Union Carbide Corporation in Tarrytown, New York, the UFF is known to have committed at least nineteen bombings and is suspected of many others. By using mail drops and public telephones to communicate with one another, and by maintaining an extensive network of safe houses where group members led fairly normal lives, UFF members successfully hid from the authorities. After surveying potential targets, UFF group members selected their victims at meetings where they undertook detailed analyses, kept copious notes, and used aliases to refer to one another. The UFF was the most successful leftist terrorist organization of the 1970s and 1980s.

Abortion Clinic Bombings. Between the late 1970s and the late 1990s, antiabortion extremists were responsible for some two hundred bombings and hundreds of bomb threats. In the early 1980s the name Army of God (AOG) began surfacing as abortion clinics were bombed; it came up again when letters claiming credit for the deadly 29 January 1998 bombing of an abortion clinic in Birmingham, Alabama, were signed "Army of

God." Similar letters lambasting "sodomites" and "abortionists" and threatening to strike also had taken credit for 1997 Atlanta-area bombings of an abortion clinic and a gay nightclub.

Who—or what—the AOG is has plagued authorities for years. In 1999 they did not know whether AOG was a concrete underground terrorist group. Aside from a letter claiming victory for a bombing, the primary AOG document to reach the public was the so-called Army of God manual on destroying abortion clinics, which offers detailed instructions on how to build ammonium-nitrate bombs and homemade C-4s (a plastic explosive).

Eric Robert Rudolph was charged with the 1998 Birmingham clinic bombing, which killed an off-duty police officer working as a security guard and critically injured the clinic's head nurse. Investigators also uncovered evidence that seemed to link the Birmingham bombing with the fatal 27 July 1996 Atlanta Centennial Olympic Park bombing, which killed one and wounded more than one hundred others; and the 16 January 1997 Atlanta-area abortion clinic bombing, which injured six people. Flooring nails found near Murphy, North Carolina, in a storage shed rented by Rudolph, a part-time carpenter, matched the nails in the pipe bombs used in both the Atlanta nightclub and the Birmingham clinic bombings. Forensic evidence also revealed that both bombs contained steel plates designed to direct shrapnel and that the plates had been cut from steel found at a metal-working plant in North Carolina. The plant was an hour from Rudolph's home and employed one of his friends.

Rudolph disappeared after the Birmingham bombing, and in 1999 federal agents were still searching for him in the backwoods of western North Carolina. The Federal Bureau of Investigation offered a $1 million reward for his arrest and conviction.

Terrorist Bombings. On 26 February 1993, a bomb detonated inside a yellow rental van parked in the garage beneath the World Trade Center complex in New York City. The blast was so powerful that it left a crater two hundred by one hundred feet wide and five stories deep. The approximately twelve hundred pounds of explosives killed six people and injured more than one thousand others while causing $500 million in damage. Had the mastermind of the bombing, Ramzi Ahmed Yousef, accomplished what he intended, one of the 110-story towers would have toppled into the

other and killed many of the approximately fifty thousand people inside the complex. Had the sodium cyanide in the bomb burned instead of vaporizing, cyanide gas would have been sucked into the north tower and killed thousands. Not since the Civil War had the United States seen such a casualty-producing event. The bombing was also the worst act of international terrorism committed on U.S. soil.

In May 1994 Mohammed A. Salameh, Nidal A. Ayyad, Mahmoud Abouhalima, and Ahmad M. Ajaj were convicted for the bombing; each was sentenced to 240 years in prison and fined $250,000. Two remaining defendants, Yousef and Abdul Rahman Yasin, were indicted in absentia. In October 1995 Omar Abdel Rahman, the spiritual advisor to the men convicted of the bombing, and nine other defendants were found guilty in federal court for seditious conspiracy in plotting to bomb the World Trade Center and other landmarks to undermine U.S. support for Egypt and Israel.

Yousef was later apprehended by Pakistani and U.S. agents and released into U.S. custody in early February 1995, after federal authorities working together from the State Department, the Justice Department, the FBI, and the Central Intelligence Agency revealed his presence in Islamabad, Pakistan. He was then returned to the United States. Yousef and his accomplice, Eyad Ismoil, the driver of the bomb-laden van, were found guilty of a plot to bomb the World Trade Center. In 1999, Abdul Yasin remained the only conspirator in the bombing still at large.

On 19 April 1995, just over two years after the World Trade Center bombing, a yellow rental van with a two-ton ammonium-nitrate and fuel-oil bomb exploded in front of the Alfred P. Murrah Federal Building in Oklahoma City. The force of the explosion nearly leveled the building and ten other buildings within a three-block radius. Cars were overturned and ignited as their gas tanks exploded. Over three hundred buildings were damaged as the blast rocked the ground up to forty miles away. Property damage was assessed in the hundreds of millions of dollars. In the end, 168 people lost their lives, and about 850 others were injured. It was the single worst case of terrorism in U.S. history.

At first blush, it appeared to many that the crumbled facade of the Murrah Building was the work of international terrorists, particularly those of Middle Eastern extraction. But the world would soon learn that the perpetrator was not a foreign-born terrorist, but one of the homegrown variety.

Seventy-five minutes after the bombing Timothy James McVeigh was pulled over on the interstate by an Oklahoma highway patrol officer for driving without a car tag. When the officer noticed a pistol in a shoulder holster beneath McVeigh's jacket, he arrested him. Just before McVeigh was released from police custody on 21 April, he was recognized as a bombing suspect and turned over to the federal authorities. His army buddy Terry Lynn Nichols was held as material witness, and on 10 August McVeigh and Nichols were indicted in the bombing. The judge ordered separate trials for the two defendants.

On 2 June 1997 a Denver jury convicted McVeigh on eleven counts, and two months later Judge Richard Matsch sentenced him to death. On 23 December 1997, Nichols was convicted of conspiracy and involuntary manslaughter, but not murder, for his role in the bombing.

Serial Bombers. Starting in 1978, a series of package and mail bombs targeted university departments of technology and computer science, and airline executives. As evidence mounted in the 1980s that the bombs had clearly been produced by one man—serial bombers are predominantly males—the FBI formed a task force named UNABOM, after the targets (university and airline personnel) preferred by the bomber. The anonymous serial bomber was then dubbed the Unabomber.

Five months after the last bombing occurred in April 1995, the Unabomber sent a long letter to the *New York Times* in which he threatened that the terrorist group FC (for Freedom Club, a group he claimed to belong to) would increase its activity and the destructive power of its bombs unless a book-length political statement was published by certain newspapers. The Unabomber agreed to "permanently desist from terrorist activities" except for "sabotage" if the treatise were published. In September 1995 the *New York Times* and the *Washington Post* ran the 35,000-word manifesto criticizing technology and its effects on modern society, which have, he wrote, "made life unfulfilling, have subjected human beings to indignities, have led to widespread psychological suffering . . . and have inflicted damage on the natural world."

FBI experts identified the Unabomber as Theodore John Kaczynski by comparing the turgid rhetoric of the published manifesto with that contained in letters provided by Kaczynski's brother, David. The FBI set up a two-month stakeout of a ten-by-twelve-foot cabin located in Florence Gulch, Montana, where Kaczynski had been living like a hermit for the past twenty-five years, and in April 1996 he was apprehended by federal agents. Searches of the cabin revealed a homestyle bomb lab.

Theodore Kaczynski entered into a plea bargain with federal prosecutors in January 1998 to avoid the public investigation into his mental health that a trial would bring. The bargain also protected him from the prospect of a death sentence. Kaczynski was given a life sentence without the possibility of appeal or release and ordered to pay more than $15 million to his victims, of whom three were killed and twenty-three wounded and maimed.

BIBLIOGRAPHY

Avrich, Paul. *The Haymarket Tragedy*. Princeton, N.J.: Princeton University Press, 1984.

Brodie, Thomas G. *Bombs and Bombings: A Handbook to Detection, Disposal, and Investigation for Police and Fire Departments*. 2d ed. Springfield, Ill.: Charles C. Thomas, 1996.

Graysmith, Robert. *Unabomber: A Desire to Kill*. Washington, D.C.: Regnery, 1997.

Greene, Melissa Fay. *The Temple Bombing*. Reading, Mass.: Addison Wesley, 1996.

Harber, David. *The Anarchist Arsenal: Improvised Incendiary and Explosives Techniques*. Boulder, Colo.: Paladin, 1990.

———. *Guerrilla's Arsenal: Advanced Techniques for Making Explosives and Time-Delay Bombs*. Boulder, Colo.: Paladin, 1994.

Jenkins, Ray. *Blind Vengeance: The Roy Moody Mail Bomb Murders*. Athens: University of Georgia Press, 1997.

Mello, Michael. *The United States of America Versus Theodore John Kaczynski: Ethics, Power, and the Invention of the Unabomber*. New York: Context, 1999.

Powell, William. *The Anarchist Cookbook*. 1971. New York: Barricade, 1989.

Saxon, Kurt. *Poor Man's James Bond*. Rev. ed. Vol. 1. El Dorado, Ariz.: Desert, 1991.

Scott, Lee. *Pipe and Fire Bomb Designs: A Guide for Police Bomb Technicians*. Boulder, Colo.: Paladin, 1994.

HARVEY W. KUSHNER

See also **Abortion; Arson and Fire; Church Bombings; Hofmann, Mark; Internet; Ku Klux Klan; Letter Bombs; Oklahoma City Bombing; Strikes; Terrorism; Unabomber; Wall Street, Bombing of; Weatherman and Weather Underground; World Trade Center Bombing.**

BONNEY, WILLIAM. *See* Billy the Kid.

BONNIE AND CLYDE
Bonnie Parker (1910–1934); Clyde Barrow (1909–1934)

Products of Depression-era Texas, Bonnie Parker and Clyde Barrow embarked on a two-year crime spree between 1932 and 1934. Their names joined the ranks of 1930s public enemies that included such criminal luminaries as John Dillinger, "Machine Gun" Kelly, and "Pretty Boy" Floyd. What set Bonnie and Clyde apart from their contemporaries was not just their association as a killer couple but their toll of victims that climbed to at least one dozen, including seven peace officers and one prison guard. In spite of these killings, Bonnie and Clyde have been imbued with certain features of the social bandit tradition that persisted in rural America into the twentieth century.

The second of three children in a family with middle-class pretensions, Bonnie Parker was born in Rowena, Texas, on 1 October 1910. Less than five feet tall and barely one hundred pounds, the diminutive Parker was from all accounts a good student with an artistic bent. But when she married a school friend, Roy Thornton, at age sixteen, her life began a downward spiral that would end on a country road in Louisiana eight years later. Her marriage to Thornton was short-lived, and they soon drifted apart.

Clyde Chestnut Barrow was born on 24 March 1909. He was the sixth of eight children in a family of poor tenant farmers in rural Ellis County, Texas. At five feet seven inches and 125 pounds, Barrow reportedly possessed a volatile temper and was, according to family members, obsessed with guns from an early age.

Barrow met Parker through a mutual friend in January 1930. Their initial flirtation was soon interrupted when Barrow was sentenced to fourteen years for burglary. At the Eastham Prison Farm, near Huntsville, Barrow, with the assistance of a fellow convict, whacked off two toes with an ax in order to avoid prison labor. Much to his chagrin, he was paroled a short time later and left Huntsville aided by crutches.

Reunited with Parker in early 1932, Barrow quickly assembled a small outlaw gang and by March had returned to robbery and burglary. Despite Parker and Barrow's reputation as bank robbers during their 1932–1934 crime spree, their targets were more often small-town grocery stores, filling stations, and dry cleaners.

As their own best press agents, Parker and Barrow presaged the celebrity-driven media of the late twentieth century; they were willful partners in the creation of their own legend. While Parker assaulted Dallas newspaper editors with bits of maudlin verse and news detailing the perambulations of the notorious Barrow gang, Barrow wrote the inventor Henry Ford to endorse the Ford V-8 automobile as the only kind he would steal. Although Barrow claimed he stole them because of their speed and low maintenance, police discovered the plausible reason for Barrow's predilection when they captured one of his cars and noted signs of deflected bullets on the armorlike chassis.

Parker and Barrow survived a number of shootouts with peace officers and were wounded on several occasions. While most accounts of the criminal couple portray them as wanton killers, the work of E. R. Milner and others suggests that they only killed in the heat of battle or in one-on-one confrontations.

Bonnie Parker and Clyde Barrow. Corbis-Bettmann

The legend of Bonnie and Clyde was given another boost when police developed several rolls of film left behind following a deadly shoot-out in Joplin, Missouri. The photographs helped identify various gang members and left for posterity the indelible image of Parker brandishing weapons while firmly clenching a cigar between her teeth. Although intended as a joke, this memorable portrait contributed to the depiction of Parker as a remorseless killer.

Ending their crime spree was given more urgency following their January 1934 killing of a guard while freeing a former gang member from prison. On 23 May 1934 six men led by the retired Texas Ranger Frank Hamer waited beside Highway 154, a few miles south of Gibsland, Louisiana. Concealed behind a large mound of dirt near the roadway were members of various law-enforcement agencies that the general manager of the Texas Prison System hired to track down the Barrow gang after they had killed the prison guard. As the criminals' car approached, the six lawmen unleashed a fusillade that finally ended the lives of Parker and Barrow.

The successful release of Arthur Penn's film *Bonnie and Clyde* in 1967 reintroduced the Depression-era duo to a nation clamoring for antiestablishment heroes. The sexually provocative couple seemed just right for audiences in the 1960s, and the film was nominated for nine Academy Awards while elevating the killer couple to hero status.

Separately, Parker's and Barrow's short banal lives were bleak and uninteresting. Together, their intertwined lives contained all the ingredients of a Shakespearean drama. While on one level it is easy to fathom how their story captures the public's fascination decades after their demise, on a more visceral level it is hard to reconcile their horrific crime spree with notions of romance and derring-do.

BIBLIOGRAPHY

DeFord, Miriam Allen. *The Real Bonnie and Clyde.* New York: Ace, 1968.
Fortune, Jan I., ed. *Fugitives: The Story of Clyde Barrow and Bonnie Parker, as Told by Bonnie's Mother (Mrs. Emma Parker) and Clyde's Sister (Nell Barrow Cowan).* Dallas: Ranger, 1934.
Hinton, Ted. *Ambush: The Real Story of Bonnie and Clyde.* Austin, Tex.: Shoal Creek, 1979.
Milner, E. R. *The Lives and Times of Bonnie and Clyde.* Carbondale: Southern Illinois University Press, 1996.
Roth, Mitchel. "Bonnie and Clyde in Texas: The End of the Texas Outlaw Tradition." *East Texas Historical Journal* 35, no. 2 (1997).
Treherne, John. *The Strange History of Bonnie and Clyde.* London: Cape, 1984.

MITCHEL ROTH

See also **Film.**

BOOTH, JOHN WILKES
(1838–1865)

Even before he assassinated President Abraham Lincoln, John Wilkes Booth was famous. One of the most popular actors of his day, Booth sacrificed phenomenal critical and financial success, and ultimately his own life, to kill a man he considered an American tyrant.

John Wilkes Booth was the son of the brilliant but eccentric tragedian, Junius Brutus Booth, the nation's preeminent Shakespearean actor. His older brothers, Junius Brutus, Jr., and Edwin, also became stars, although Edwin was by far the more famous. After a childhood of horseback riding, shooting, and reciting Shakespeare to the rented slaves on the family property outside of Bel Air, Maryland, John Wilkes Booth got his first chance at professional acting in 1855, in the part of Richmond in Shakespeare's *Richard III*. The violent play remained one of Booth's most popular productions throughout his career.

In 1857 Booth joined a stock theater company in Philadelphia. In 1858 and 1859 he worked in a stock company in Richmond, Virginia, where he first began to identify with the southern cause. In December 1859 he joined a militia company called the Richmond Grays, in which he served briefly and was a guard during the execution of abolitionist John Brown. Booth toured the South in 1860, becoming a star in his own right. In that year, he also wrote his first political manifesto, an unfinished and never-delivered speech in which he blamed abolitionists for tearing the nation apart and advocated their suppression, by violence if necessary.

He spent most of the Civil War, from 1861 through the summer of 1864, on tour. During at least part of that period he worked as a southern agent, using his large income and unrestricted passage across battle lines to smuggle quinine and information into the Confederacy. In the summer of 1864 he stopped touring to devote himself to espionage full time. He began shuttling between Franklin, Pennsylvania, where he had oil well investments, and Montreal, Quebec, where he seems

John Wilkes Booth. LIBRARY OF CONGRESS

to have met with various Confederate secret agents. He conspired to kidnap Lincoln in March 1865, but the plan failed due to a last-minute change in the president's itinerary.

On 14 April 1865 Booth and several of his co-conspirators in the plan to kidnap Lincoln arranged to assassinate the president, vice president, and secretary of state. Booth would shoot Lincoln while the president attended a light comedy, *Our American Cousin,* at Ford's Theatre; David Herold would make sure Booth had a horse waiting outside. Simultaneously, Lewis Powell was supposed to assassinate Secretary of State William Seward, while George Atzerodt was assigned to kill Vice President Andrew Johnson. Atzerodt never carried out his assignment, and Powell's stabbing attack failed to kill Seward, but Booth was spectacularly successful. The assassination was deliberately dramatic. After entering the presidential box and

shooting Lincoln in the head, Booth leaped onto the stage and shouted, "Sic semper tyrannis!" ("Thus always to tyrants!") The Latin phrase was the state motto of Virginia. Before the audience or the players could react, Booth fled. When federal troops caught up with him at a Virginia farm on 26 April, one of the soldiers shot him against orders. He died a few hours later.

David Herold, Lewis Powell, George Atzerodt, and Mary Surratt (owner of the boarding house where the conspirators met) were hanged on 7 July 1865. Dr. Samuel Mudd, who treated Booth's broken leg during the assassin's flight from Washington, was sentenced to prison, along with three members of the conspiracy to kidnap Lincoln who had apparently played no role in the assassination: Samuel Arnold, Edman Spangler, and Michael O'Laughlen.

Although later accounts questioned Booth's sanity and suggested that he had lost the ability to distinguish between real life and such dramatic roles as Brutus and Richmond, his writings show that he acted with rational deliberation for a cause in which he believed.

BIBLIOGRAPHY

Booth, John Wilkes. *"Right or Wrong, God Judge Me": The Writings of John Wilkes Booth,* edited by John Rhodehamel and Louise Taper. Chicago: University of Illinois Press, 1997.

Samples, Gordon. *Lust for Fame: The Stage Career of John Wilkes Booth.* Jefferson, N.C.: McFarland, 1982.

Smith, Gene. *American Gothic: The Story of America's Legendary Theatrical Family—Junius, Edwin, and John Wilkes Booth.* New York: Simon and Schuster, 1992.

Tidwell, William A., with James O. Hall and David Winfred Gaddy. *Come Retribution: The Confederate Secret Service and the Assassination of Lincoln.* Jackson: University Press of Mississippi, 1988.

R. RUDY HIGGENS-EVENSON

See also **Assassinations; Brown, John; Lincoln, Abraham.**

BORDEN, LIZZIE
(1860–1927)

More than a century after the famous trial in Fall River, Massachusetts, the name Lizzie Borden continues to haunt the American psyche. A man and his second wife had been violently murdered. Lizzie, the man's own daughter, stood accused of the crime, rendering it not only a murder but—even more abhorrent—a parricide. Although she was acquitted, no one else was ever accused of the crime.

The Borden family were prominent citizens of some wealth who had lived in Fall River for at least eight generations. Yet, despite these facts, Andrew Borden was a notorious miser. He and his second wife, Abbey, and his two daughters, Emma and Lizzie, lived in a modest house in an unfashionable part of town. There has been much speculation that although Lizzie participated in society, she was frustrated by not being allowed to entertain as she felt a woman of her prominence should. Although Lizzie was fairly young when Andrew Borden remarried, the relationship between stepmother and stepdaughters was never very good. By 1892 the two grown daughters had begun to refer to their stepmother as "Mrs. Borden." Such stories fanned the public interest in Lizzie once her trial got under way.

Witnesses to the crime scene described a gruesome spectacle. Abbey Borden, in an upstairs bedroom, was slumped forward on her knees, her head nearly torn off her shoulders. Andrew Borden's face, hacked by what was later determined to be eleven blows, was nearly unrecognizable. One eye had been sliced in half. Blood still seeped from his wounds, an indication that death was recent. Despite the violence, the scene was surprisingly orderly. There were no signs of a struggle and relatively little blood was splattered on the walls; what blood was spilled lay within close proximity of the bodies. This fact lent an even more eerie atmosphere to the setting.

Theories about the murders were as conjectural as the violence was self-evident. The few undisputed facts included the following: On the morning of 4 August 1892, Abbey Borden was struck in the head from behind with some blunt instrument as she cleaned the guest room. While she lay dead or dying, the murderer continued to strike her at least eighteen times. Andrew Borden returned from his business rounds about 10:45. By 11:15 a handyman of one of the Borden's neighbors had notified the police of a murder; Seabury W. Bowen, the Borden's family physician and neighbor, arrived at 11:30; and by 11:45 the medical examiner and other investigators were at the house.

The events in the interval between 10:40 and 11:15 are those that remain a mystery. The Bordens' maid, Bridget Sullivan, testified that at 10:55 she went up to her room to lie down while Mr. Borden

Lizzie Borden. CORBIS-BETTMANN

settled down on the couch in the living room. Lizzie testified that, at this time, she went out to the barn to search for some lead to use as a fishing sinker. She further claimed that she did not return until 11:10, whereupon she found her father's body.

The Fall River police followed up dozens of leads. Ultimately, however, their most prominent and controversial suspect was Lizzie. Yet despite their narrowed focus, the police could do little more than construct a case based largely on circumstantial evidence. No eyewitnesses were ever produced. A murder weapon was never found. The prosecution suspected that the weapon was an ax, but they were able neither to find it nor definitively to prove that the blows that killed the Bordens were caused by an ax. Moreover, use of such a weapon would have been likely to produce an awful mess around the bodies, which clearly was not the case. Further, if Bridget was to be believed, only about twenty minutes had elapsed between the time she went upstairs and the time the bodies were found. The twenty-minute interval would hardly have been enough time for Lizzie to kill her father and mother, clean off the blood, and still hide the murder weapon. The fact that several people testified to Lizzie's spotless appearance immediately following the murders clearly undermined the prosecution's case.

The size of the house also played an important role in the muddle of theories surrounding the crime. According to Lizzie and Bridget, they were both in or around the relatively small house the entire morning. Yet neither admitted to having heard any of the blows, which were delivered forcefully enough to crush the victims' skulls. Even if this were possible, was it also possible that they did not hear the thud of a two-hundred-pound woman falling onto the floor? Nonetheless, when the two women were first questioned about Mrs. Borden's whereabouts, both claimed not to have known whether she was even in the house. It seemed incredible that two people could spend nearly three hours together in a small house without hearing any unusually loud sounds or someone climbing the front stairs or seeing an ax-wielding murderess or murderer. Do these details point to Bridget's involvement? If so, authorities have never been able to attribute a motive to her.

No single theory seemed to provide a full explanation. Whether one assumed Lizzie's innocence or guilt, more questions than answers were suggested. After about an hour of deliberation, a jury exonerated Lizzie on 19 June 1893. Members of the jury, and of Victorian society, found themselves faced with the image of an unmarried woman, whom the defense counsel referred to as a "little girl" (even though she was thirty-three at the time), as a heinous and vicious murderer. The jury was composed entirely of older men who were more inclined to think of women as delicate. One can safely say the jury was predisposed to a judgment of innocence. In other words, even if they believed Lizzie to be guilty, they were hard-pressed to convict her.

Both society and history convicted Lizzie Borden in a different way. Following her acquittal, she was ostracized from Fall River society, indicating a belief that Lizzie, even if she was not the murderer, was somehow involved. Eventually, she became estranged even from her sister, Emma.

Lizzie Borden fascinates us, as she did her contemporaries, as an indeterminate image of the innocent and the monster. The most obvious motive for the murders was the wealth she stood to inherit from her father's death. Speculators reasoned that Abbey's death was also necessary for Lizzie and Emma to inherit. (While Emma fell under suspi-

cion as well, her alibi cleared her.) Some pointed out that the strained family relations were enough motivation to kill. As plausible as these theories may seem, at the time it was difficult for many people to believe that a Victorian maiden could commit parricide for any reason. Lizzie is allowed to make the ultimate getaway—in fact, she must, in order to maintain and conform to the social requirements of feminine behavior. Yet it is also imperative that she be punished, lest she fully undermine the validity of the very structures that freed her. With no way to determine if justice was served, the case and the figure of Lizzie Borden remain intriguing and frightening.

The legend of Lizzie Borden has given birth to numerous books (with as many theories), a ballet, a made-for-television movie, and, finally, an opera. Even the house where the murders were committed has since been converted into a bed-and-breakfast. Lizzie has been portrayed as a fiend, a feminist, a victim, and a cold-blooded murderer. Somewhere amid the speculation, depictions, and stories is the Lizzie Borden who is more than our invention and the truth behind what happened that summer day in 1892.

BIBLIOGRAPHY

Adler, Gabriela S. "But She Doesn't Look Like a Fiend." www.cinema.ucla.edu/women/adler.

Beem, Edgar A. "Did Lizzie Borden Really Take an Ax and Give Her Mother Forty Whacks?" *Yankee* 56, no. 8 (August 1992).

"Butchered in Their Homes: Mr. Borden and His Wife Killed in Broad Daylight." *New York Times*, 5 August 1892.

Carlisle, Marcie R. "What Made Lizzie Borden Kill?" *American Heritage* 43, no. 4 (July 1992).

Kent, David. *Forty Whacks: New Evidence in the Life and Legend of Lizzie Borden*. Emmaus, Pa.: Yankee Books, 1992.

MacDonald, Lewis. "One Hundred Years of Lizzie Borden." *Contemporary Review* 261, no. 1523 (December 1992).

Sams, Ed. *Lizzie Borden Unlocked*. Ben Lomond, Calif.: Yellow Tulip Press, 1997.

Schofield, Ann. "Lizzie Borden Took an Axe: History, Feminism, and American Culture." *American Studies* 34, no. 1 (spring 1993).

Weafer, Don. "The Long Silence of Lizzie Borden." *Yankee* 60, no. 6 (June 1996).

BINH H. POK

See also **Parricide; Women: Women Who Kill.**

BOSKET FAMILY

In 1978 New York's governor, Hugh Carey, signed the Juvenile Offender Act, otherwise known as the

Willie Bosket Law. The act grew out of public outrage over the New York State Division for Youth's lenient handling of Willie Bosket, an angel-faced African American boy—and hardened criminal—from Harlem. In an ironic inversion of the American Dream, Bosket had followed in the footsteps of his father, grandfather, and great-grandfather, extending the family legacy of violent robberies and murders.

Originally from rural Edgefield, South Carolina, home to many esteemed though notoriously violent whites, the Bosket family exhibited brutal behavior through four generations in various locales: South Carolina; Augusta, Georgia; and the "Promised Land" of Harlem, New York. In the beginning Clifton "Pud" Bosket, son of an Edgefield deacon and sharecropper, refused to submit to the whip of his landowner and, blacklisted from farm work, turned to robbery and bootlegging. His son James grew up in Augusta, Georgia, absorbing "Pud" stories and trickster tales; emulating his now-deceased father's reputation as a "bad black man," James committed a series of small-time robberies along the East Coast.

James's son, Butch Bosket, abandoned by both parents and brutally beaten by his grandmother, hustled on the streets of Augusta, committing petty thefts and running errands for pimps, and skipped school. To evade the Georgia work farms, Butch moved to Harlem, where, after he was thrown out by his mother, a prostitute, he began careening in and out of prisons and mental hospitals. While on parole following a robbery conviction, he was responsible for a series of bank robberies, sex crimes, and murders—including the high-profile slayings of a Milwaukee pawnshop owner and a shop customer. In 1980, however, while at Leavenworth Federal Penitentiary, Butch received a B.A. degree from the University of Kansas and was elected to Phi Beta Kappa.

Although Butch's son Willie never met his father, who was imprisoned before his birth, he followed a remarkably similar path, committing violent robberies, murders, and repeated assaults on his way to some of the same mental hospitals and juvenile-detention centers that had treated Butch. When the sixteen-year-old Willie received the maximum five-year sentence for the 1978 murder of two men on the New York subway, the ensuing public outcry made Willie Bosket a symbol of a city's increasing fear and intolerance of youthful offenders. Prison life only incited him to further violent behavior: he attacked other inmates and corrections officers—stabbing one in the lung with a homemade pick—and he frequently lit his cell on fire, destroying its contents.

A leading interpretation of the Bosket family saga is the book *All God's Children: The Bosket Family and the American Tradition of Violence* by the journalist Fox Butterfield, who argues that the violence of the Bosket men resulted not from the causes suggested by conventional wisdom—urban or

A handcuffed Willie Bosket acts as his own attorney in his 1989 trial for stabbing a prison guard. *DAILY FREEMAN*, KINGSTON, NEW YORK

rural impoverishment, lack of education and opportunity, racism, genetic defect, neglectful or abusive parents—but from their paternal heritage in antebellum Edgefield. Butterfield argues that the culture of honor of the planter class thrives today in the inner city, that the planter reliance on family name, code duello, vigilante justice, and a biased, impotent legal system took hold in the former slaves of these planters. Butterfield thus proposes that, by assuming an adherence to this culture of honor, the family was emulating southern whites.

Other analysts, however, dispute Butterfield's interpretation. Orville Vernon Burton, the author of *In My Father's House Are Many Mansions: Family and Community in Edgefield, South Carolina* (a book that Butterfield relied on heavily for his history of the Bosket's southern episodes), suggests that it was not culture in the rural South but racism in both northern and southern urban areas that set the stage for crime by excluding African American men from jobs. Many freed slaves rejected the violence that slavery wrought upon them and their families. The rural South's African American culture remains even today strongly influenced by black churches and a moral value system much different from the one portrayed by Butterfield. The Edgefield ancestral home of the Boskets is also home to the mentor of the Rev. Martin Luther King, Jr., the African American apostle of peace Dr. Benjamin E. Mays.

Butterfield goes on to argue that the Bosket men sought status through their criminal behavior. In contrast to wealthy whites, who owned nearly everything, the freed persons and their descendant sharecroppers owned almost nothing; yet they treasured honor within their own communities. As Pud Bosket claimed, "Don't step on my reputation. My name is all I got, so I got to keep it. I'm a man of respect" (Butterfield 1995, p. 63). To that end, Pud used violence to achieve and maintain reputation, respect, and deference from his peers. Similarly, Willie used violent crime to attain celebrity status, a position he relished and maintained in jail, where mere parity in violence was unthinkable for Willie: he had to be the most violent, most erratic, and most feared man in the prison. Although countless whites and blacks abhorred him, Willie symbolized to his peers in crime the continued enslavement of blacks by the white legal system. He mocked and attacked the economic, social, and legal systems that had long excluded blacks, and for many in Harlem, Willie did merit respect. As Willie

Bosket proclaimed to one of the many juries and judges who have decided his fate, "I am only a monster created by the system" (Butterfield 1995, p. xiii). According to Butterfield, then, Willie Bosket and his family history symbolize a system of honor and reputation that has made monsters of the Bosket men for generations.

BIBLIOGRAPHY

Brown, Richard Maxwell. *Strain of Violence: Historical Studies of American Violence and Vigilantism.* New York: Oxford University Press, 1977.

Burton, Orville Vernon. *In My Father's House Are Many Mansions: Family and Community in Edgefield, South Carolina.* Chapel Hill: University of North Carolina Press, 1985.

Butterfield, Fox. *All God's Children: The Bosket Family and the American Tradition of Violence.* New York: Knopf, 1995.

ORVILLE VERNON BURTON

See also **Honor; Intergenerational Transmission of Violence.**

BOSTON

Boston, Massachusetts, shares with any major city a long history of violence. It is the city's history of collective political violence, however, that sets it apart from other American cities. From the angry mobs of the Revolutionary era to the struggle over school busing in the 1970s, Boston has repeatedly been the site of violent mass demonstrations.

The Revolution

In the years before the American Revolution, Boston became a flash point for protest against the British. Even as early as 1688, mobs of Bostonians menaced the unpopular governor Edmund Andros outside his home. As tensions between the colonies and the home country increased, Boston led the charge with often violent anti-British protests. Though much of the mob protest of the era was more pageantry than actual destruction, the threat of real violence was always just below the ritual.

In 1765 the Stamp Act levied a tax on all paper, including court papers and newspapers. Colonists saw it as both a restriction of their free press and an attempt by Parliament to expand its authority unfairly. As the wave of protest over the Stamp Act swept the colonies, Andrew Oliver, the crown's appointee to enforce the act, watched in horror as a large mob looted and burned his office and men-

A mob gathers on Scollay Square in Boston during the great Police Strike of September 1919. Corbis/Bettmann

aced his home until he pledged to resign his new post on 14 August 1765. On 26 August the mob turned their sights on the governor, Thomas Hutchinson, burning him in effigy, then burning his home to the ground. To combat "mob rule" in Boston, the British substantially increased the military presence in the city. A tense standoff between residents and the British Regulars continued until 5 March 1770, when the British opened fire on a group protesting the Townshend Acts of 1767, taxes imposed by Parliament on the most common colonial imports such as glass, paper, and tea. British troops killed five of the protesters. Though the actual skirmish ended quickly, its significance lived on as Paul Revere's famous etching and Samuel Adams's letters publicized the "Boston Massacre" throughout the colonies to illustrate the cruelty and excess of the crown. The Boston populace again rose up in December 1773, this time to hold the Boston Tea Party, dumping twenty thousand pounds of tea into Boston Harbor in protest of the Tea Act. Bostonians also played a role in

the Revolution itself. In 1775 the famed Battle of Bunker Hill took place just outside the city. Though the colonists lost, the tenacious Boston militia proved that victory would not come easily for the British.

Political Violence

Violence—or the threat of it—remained an important political tool in Boston throughout the city's history, and the Revolution did not mark the end of politically inspired mob violence. The outspoken *Liberator* editor William Lloyd Garrison discovered this when an antiabolitionist crowd pulled him from his office and dragged him through the city by a rope in 1835. Sadly, Garrison's treatment was far from the last time ethnic or racial tensions in Boston exploded into violence. With the huge influx of immigrants to Boston beginning in the 1840s, riots between Irish newcomers and native Bostonians raged in changing neighborhoods like South Boston and Dorchester. As new groups arrived, including southern and eastern Europeans, the participants changed, but the frequent flare-ups of gang activity and ethnic turf battles did not.

Even Boston's electoral politics have often been a rough-and-tumble affair. As the Boston Irish came to control the Democratic Party in the city between the 1860s and 1880s, many who had been gang members in the ethnic battles of the previous generation became political leaders. Before the advent of secret balloting, rival ward organizations would hire young toughs and even professional prizefighters to serve as menacing "poll sitters" who would "encourage" the electorate to see the choices their way. The great champion of the bare-knuckle era, John L. Sullivan, frequently hired himself out to candidates in his hometown. The link between boxers and politicians was strong enough that for a time around the turn of the twentieth century, a boxing career was almost a prerequisite to hold elected office.

Though Boston residents had long been used to the often violent realities of urban life, nothing prepared them for the anarchy that accompanied the early hours of the great Police Strike of 1919. After the city refused to recognize an American Federation of Labor–affiliated police union, the Boston Police Department walked off the job, leaving the city with almost no police protection on a blisteringly hot 9 September. Riots broke out throughout the city, the worst occurring in South Boston and around Scollay Square. Adolescent street gangs, like South Boston's Gustins, ruled the day. Businesses were looted, women were raped in the streets, and the few police who remained on duty found themselves barricaded in their station houses as mobs pelted the buildings with refuse and sought to break in. By the end of the first night, Boston's elite sought to restore order. Reserve Officers' Training Corps students and football players from Harvard University formed a makeshift security force, and several gentlemen's social clubs followed the students' lead. Finally Governor Calvin Coolidge called in the state militia, restored order, and prepared to deal harshly with the striking officers. The rioting quickly dissipated, and the budding link between American police departments and organized unions was torn apart. Also torn apart was the city itself; the area around Scollay Square remained gutted and pockmarked, wearing the scars of the strike for more than a generation.

The Boston Strangler

Like any major city, Boston has also seen its share of individual violence committed by notable criminals. Of these, Albert DeSalvo (1931–1973) remains the most notorious. Between 1962 and 1964 the Boston Strangler, as the press dubbed him, terrified the city with thirteen fatal attacks on women ranging in age from teens to septuagenarians. DeSalvo was convicted in 1967 and sentenced to life in prison, where he died in 1973. (See entry on DeSalvo.)

Busing

Racial and ethnic violence in Boston has continued well into the twentieth century. With the exception of the old West End, a slum neighborhood razed in a 1950s urban renewal project, Boston has long been a city divided into coherent and homogeneous ethnic enclaves. A 1974 federal district court ruling ordering Boston's schools to desegregate through an aggressive busing program unleashed a storm of protest and sporadic rioting and bias attacks, particularly in white working-class enclaves like Charleston and South Boston. Even into the 1990s scuffles between students at South Boston High School and others continued.

BIBLIOGRAPHY

Levesque, George A. *Black Boston: African-American Life and Culture in Urban America, 1750–1866.* New York: Garland, 1994.

Lukas, Anthony J. *Common Ground: A Turbulent Decade in the Lives of Three American Families.* New York: Knopf, 1985.

Mayer, Henry. *All on Fire: William Lloyd Garrison and the Abolition of Slavery.* New York: St. Martin's, 1998.

Russell, Francis. *A City in Terror: 1919, the Boston Police Strike.* New York: Viking, 1975.

Thomas, Peter David Garner. *Tea Party to Independence.* New York: Oxford University Press, 1991.

MATTHEW TAYLOR RAFFETY

See also **DeSalvo, Albert; Urban Violence.**

BOSTON MASSACRE

On 5 March 1770, British soldiers of the Twenty-ninth Regiment of Foot opened fire on a crowd in

King Street (now State Street) in Boston. Five colonials died. The event received enormous publicity and its anniversary was commemorated with a public oration until 4 July emerged as the American holiday of nationhood. Although actual war was still five years in the future, the massacre marked the point when the conflict between Great Britain and the colonies turned lethal.

The popular image of this "Boston Massacre" was shaped almost immediately by the *Short Narrative of the Horrid Massacre* that the town commissioned from James Bowdoin, Joseph Warren, and Samuel Pemberton, and by the engraving that Paul Revere produced for mass circulation. Revere shows the soldiers drawn up in a disciplined line as Captain Thomas Preston raises his sword and gives the order to fire; a sniper fires from a nearby building as well. The unarmed and innocent Bostonians fall back in horror. As propaganda, the engraving was superb. As history, it neither portrays the shooting nor explains it.

The soldiers were guarding the Customs House (now the Old State House Museum), where the British-appointed American Board of Customs Commissioners had maintained its headquarters since 1767. One historian has described the com-

missioners' activities as "racketeering," because of the way they and their employees used legal technicalities to prey upon colonial commerce. On 26 February customs man Ebenezer Richardson had fired into a hostile street crowd, killing eleven-year-old Christopher Snider (or Seider), whose funeral became a political event. The Customs House guard was no mere ornamentation.

Like the customs service, the British army had made itself deeply unpopular. Until 1768 no troops had been stationed in Boston. The several regiments that arrived that year to protect British officials behaved like an army of occupation, although martial law was not in effect. A significant Boston grievance was the competition that off-duty soldiers offered for scarce jobs. Only three days prior to the shooting, rope workers, including one victim-to-be, had brawled with soldiers from the Twenty-ninth who were seeking employment at John Gray's rope walk. Boston workingmen had a history of clashing with Britain's other armed service, the Royal Navy, especially regarding forced impressment from merchant vessels into naval service. All of these issues meshed with general colonial hostility to Britain's continuing attempts to increase its control over colonial

Paul Revere's well-circulated but inaccurate engraving of the Boston Massacre. LIBRARY OF CONGRESS

economic and political life, with the determination of colonial popular leaders to resist those attempts with force, and with the eighteenth-century notion that popular uprisings were not necessarily illegitimate.

The Bostonians angrily confronted the soldiers on 5 March. Although they had no firearms, they pelted the guard with hard snowballs scraped off the street. The panic-stricken soldiers responded with a ragged volley after they thought they had received an order, rather than with the discipline Revere attributed to them. Together with Captain Preston, the soldiers were tried for murder in a civilian court. They were acquitted, Preston because he had not given the order and the soldiers because they thought he had.

BIBLIOGRAPHY

Bowdoin, James, Joseph Warren, and Samuel Pemberton. *A Short Narrative of the Horrid Massacre in Boston.* 1770. Reprint, Williamstown, Mass.: Corner House, 1973.

Lemisch, Jesse. "Radical Plot in Boston (1770): A Study in the Use of Evidence." *Harvard Law Review* 84 (1970–1971).

Zobel, Hiller B. *The Boston Massacre.* New York: Norton, 1970.

EDWARD COUNTRYMAN

See also **American Revolution; Civil Disorder.**

BOSTON STRANGLER. *See* DeSalvo, Albert.

BOUNTY HUNTERS

In history and folklore, the term *bounty hunter* conjures up images of gunfighters in the American West riding from one dusty town to the next carrying in their saddlebags posters that read WANTED DEAD OR ALIVE. Anyone could be a bounty hunter by strapping on a Colt .45 and lying in wait for the outlaw with a "price on his head." Although this Hollywood image of the bounty hunter has some basis in fact, contemporary bounty hunters, now referred to as bail-enforcement agents, "skip tracers," or fugitive-recovery agents, are linked to the U.S. system of bail.

The Bail Process

The purpose of bail is to ensure that a defendant in a criminal proceeding will be present in court at all times as required. In return for being released from jail, the accused guarantees his or her future appearance by posting funds or some other form of security with the court. When the defendant appears in court, the security is returned; if he or she fails to appear, the security is forfeited.

The modern U.S. bail system has its roots deep in English history, well before the Norman conquest in 1066. It emerged at a time when there were few prisons, and the only places secure enough to detain an accused awaiting trial were the dungeons and strong rooms in the many castles around the countryside. Magistrates often called upon respected local noblemen to serve as jailers, trusting them to produce the accused on the day of trial. As the land became more populated and the castles fewer in number, magistrates were no longer able to locate jailers known to them. Volunteers were sought, but to ensure that they would be proper custodians, they were required to sign a bond. Known as private sureties, these jailers would forfeit to the king a specified sum of money or property if they failed to live up to their obligations of keeping defendants secure and producing them in court on the day required. As the system was transferred to the New World, it shifted from a procedure of confinement to one of freedom under financial control. In current practice it is the accused that posts the bond or has some third party—a surety—post it on his or her behalf.

The Bail Bond Business

Keeping in mind that the purpose of bail is to ensure that the accused appears in court for trial, the magistrate is required to fix bail at a level calculated to guarantee the defendant's presence at future court hearings. Once bail has been set there are three ways it may be exercised. The first is for the accused to post the full amount of the bond in cash with the court. Under a second method that is allowed in many jurisdictions, a defendant (or family and friends) may put up property as collateral and, thus, post a property bond. In either case the money or property is returned when all court appearances are satisfied, or it is forfeited if the defendant fails to appear.

Neither cash bail nor property bonds are commonly used, however. Most defendants do not have the necessary cash funds to meet the full bond, and the majority of courts require that the equity in the property held as collateral be at least double the amount of bond, putting that method out of reach for many defendants as well. Thus the most common method—the third alternative—is to use the services of a bail bonds-agent.

Clustered around urban courthouses across the nation are the storefront offices of the bail bonds-agents. Often aglow with bright neon lights, their signs boldly proclaim: BAIL BONDS — 24-HOUR SERVICE. Or sometimes, during the late-night hours on local television, the viewer is confronted with commercials for twenty-four hour bail-bond services. In either case, the message is quite clear: freedom is available—for a price.

Commercial bonds-agents are essentially small-business entrepreneurs who serve as liaisons with the courts. For a nonrefundable fee of 10 percent of the bail that has been set, the bonds-agent posts a surety bond with the court. If the defendant "jumps bail" by failing to appear at trial, the bonds-agent (or an insurance company) is responsible for the full amount of the bond, and the offender forfeits the amount he or she put up as collateral for the 90 percent of the bail posted by the bonds-agent. This is where the bail-enforcement agent or "skip tracer" comes into play. If the skip tracer brings in the offender, the bonds-agent keeps what the offender put up, less the skip tracer's fee.

Bail-Enforcement Agents

Bail bonds-agents have extraordinary legal powers over bailed defendants who "jump bond" and flee. When a bond is issued, the client is required to sign a contract waiving the right to extradition and allowing the bonds-agent—or the bonds-agent's agent or deputy—to retrieve the defendant from wherever he or she has fled. This results in law-enforcement powers that exceed those of police officers. Bonds-agents need no warrants, nor are they prevented from taking bond jumpers across state lines. Moreover, since most bonds-agents are ill-equipped to seek out bond jumpers personally, they use professional skip tracers who are essentially armed bounty hunters.

Nationally there are several thousand men and women who work as professional fugitive-recovery agents. Typically they receive 10 percent of the bond for the services rendered. Most of the fees they receive range from a few hundred to a few thousand dollars, but on occasion there are some considerably larger ones.

Television and film tend to emphasize the force and violence that is associated with apprehending "skips," as the fugitives are called. However, it is estimated that less than 3 percent of all apprehensions require force, and only a small proportion of those result in uncontrolled violence. Few modern-day bounty hunters kick down doors or become involved in car chases and gunfights. Most flush out their "skips" with tactics similar to those used by Sherlock Holmes. Such general detective work includes surveillance, checking phone bills and use of credit cards, and contacting relatives.

BIBLIOGRAPHY

Abramsky, Sasha. "Citizen's Arrest." *New York Magazine,* 5 January 1998, pp. 32–39.
Drimmer, Jonathan. "When Man Hunts Man: The Rights and Duties of Bounty Hunters in the American Criminal Justice System." *Houston Law Review* 33 (fall 1996): 731–793.
Goldkamp, John S. *Two Classes of Accused: A Study of Bail and Detention in American Justice.* Cambridge, Mass.: Ballinger, 1979.

JAMES A. INCIARDI

BOWIE, JAMES
(1796–1836)

James Bowie was a defender of the Alamo during the thirteen-day siege by Mexicans in which all members of the Texas revolutionary forces were killed on or before 6 March 1836. Bowie, an American adventurer, was a slave trader and land speculator prior to assuming command of the Alamo volunteers (Colonel William Travis commanded the regular army).

Bowie arrived in San Antonio (then a part of Mexico) in 1828 from Bayou Boeuf, Rapides Parish, Louisiana. (Sources vary as to whether he was born in Tennessee, Kentucky, or Georgia.) A flamboyant, wealthy, handsome, and eligible young bachelor, he married Ursula Veramendi, daughter of Juan Martin de Veramendi, vice governor of San Antonio, on 23 April 1831. Bowie became a Mexican citizen and a Catholic. While Bowie was away on a business trip in September 1833, his wife and children died in a cholera epidemic.

Bowie was said to have been absolutely fearless. Much of this reputation stemmed from a fight near Natchez, Mississippi, on 19 September 1827. Using what was to become the "Bowie knife," Bowie eviscerated Major Norris Wright of Alexandria, Louisiana, transforming himself and the knife into legendary figures. The Bowie knife, designed for

James Bowie. <small>LIBRARY OF CONGRESS</small>

hunting but often used in fights, had a blade fifteen inches long. It was said that it had to be as sharp as a razor, broad as a paddle, and heavy as a hatchet. Perhaps the most interesting thing about the Bowie knife is that it was not invented by James Bowie. Rather, according to a document signed in the presence of a notary public in Marksville, Louisiana, on 10 April 1827, the design was actually created by Jim's brother, Rezin P. Bowie.

Legend claims that Bowie was the last to die at the Alamo, and nothing to the contrary has ever been proved. The most credible story is that sometime around 21 February 1836 Bowie fell from a scaffold as he attempted to help build a lookout post. He broke either his hip or his leg and was confined to his cot for the siege. He took to his bed prior to the fighting, so it is highly unlikely that he participated in actual combat. By some accounts, Davy Crockett stole into Bowie's room and gave him two pistols for his defense on the thirteenth day, 6 March. Other stories claim that Crockett killed Bowie as a show of mercy. Most accounts agree that Bowie was found dead in his cot, but

there is a report that while the Mexicans heaped the dead Texans onto a burning pyre, some soldiers carried Bowie and tossed him, still alive, onto the pile with the rest.

BIBLIOGRAPHY

Davis, William C. *Three Roads to the Alamo: The Lives and Fortunes of David Crockett, James Bowie, and William Barret Travis.* New York: HarperCollins, 1998.
Hopewell, Clifford. *James Bowie: Texas Fighting Man.* Austin, Tex.: Eakin Press, 1994.
Thorp, Raymond W. *Bowie Knife.* Albuquerque: University of New Mexico Press, 1948.

BARBARA WILLIAMS LEWIS

See also **Alamo.**

BOXING

In the late 1980s, after listening to an essay on boxing read at the New York Public Library, a young boxer complained of writers' preoccupation with the sport's violence. Boxing, he insisted, is more about controlling than unleashing brute force, and he called attention to aspects of the sport that he thought were central: stylistic grace, mental alertness, and discipline under pressure. Although these qualities do distinguish the trained boxer, as most trainers, promoters, and fighters concede, they exist in boxing only in the context of physical assault. Unlike most other dangerous sports and entertainments, boxing is explicit in its violence, a fact that has always made it ethically marginal and intertwined its history with periods of abolition or self-imposed and governmental regulations. It is an appropriate irony that Jack Broughton's Rules of 1743, the earliest of their kind, were named for a champion whose challenger George Stevenson died two years earlier in the first fatality of the modern ring.

From Bare-Knuckle to Queensberry

Although there is scattered evidence of pugilism in seventeenth-century England, modern boxing dates from its revival in 1719 by the English cudgeler and fencer James Figg. It first appeared in the United States in the late eighteenth century as staged bouts between Virginia slaves; soon after, there were the well-publicized bouts of Bill Richmond and Tom Molineaux in England. Richmond, a son of slaves, had emigrated from America to England as the valet of a British general after the outbreak of the Revolutionary War; Molineaux, a Virginia slave, won his freedom after defeating a boxer owned by a rival master. Both fought successfully, but both were defeated by the English heavyweight champion Tom Cribb; Molineaux was defeated twice (in 1810 and 1811) in exhausting contests illustrated by artists such as Théodore Géricault and George Cruikshank.

Boxing as a relatively formalized sport took shape in the United States in 1816, continuing intermittently for the first half of the century. Under Broughton's Rules—designed to regulate crowd behavior and gambling as much as to ensure the boxers' safety—blows to a fallen fighter and seizing below the waist were outlawed, but wide latitude for mayhem remained. The London Prize Ring Rules of 1838 and 1853 more closely restricted fouls such as butting, gouging, biting, kicking, and deliberately falling knee first on a dropped opponent. But rounds ended only when a man was thrown or punched off his feet, and the fight ended only when he was too battered to return to combat within thirty-eight seconds. Despite rudimentary lightweight and middleweight divisions, little accommodation was made for size until the second half of the nineteenth century. As late as 1860, an international championship bout featured the six-foot-two American John Heenan at 195 pounds outweighing the five-foot-eight British champion Tom Sayers, who was 152 pounds.

Lighterweight divisions gradually evolved, and by the end of the century the welterweight Kid McCoy, the lightweight Joe Gans, and the featherweights George Dixon and "Terrible" Terry McGovern emerged as American stars, as did the heavyweight John Morrissey (who went on to two terms in the U.S. Congress). The greatest figure of this era was John L. Sullivan, the heavyweight champion from 1882 to 1892 and one of the first national sports celebrities. By the end of his reign, boxing had entered a new, gloved era. Padded "mufflers" had been introduced long before by Broughton to protect his aristocratic students, and professionals occasionally fought with skintight gloves. The Marquess of Queensberry Rules, named for their sponsor but compiled, and then published in 1867, by John Graham Chambers of England's Amateur Athletic Club, gave boxing its modern shape by mandating padded gloves, abolishing wrestling, and specifying three-minute rounds and ten-second knockouts. These rules applied primarily to amateurs, but after the seventy-five round, two-hour-and-sixteen-minute bout between Sullivan and Jake Kilrain in 1889, the London Prize Ring Rules were abandoned for Queensberry's. With Sullivan's defeat three years later by "Gentleman" Jim Corbett, the era of bareknuckle boxing ended.

Twentieth-Century Boxing

The Queensberry Rules established the basic structure of boxing, and with its legal status uncontested by 1920, the scope of professional boxing progressively widened through shrewd promotion, cultural trends (including the so-called Golden Age of Sport), and mass media. Immigration patterns highlighted Irish, Jewish, and Italian boxers at various weights—Mickey Walker, Benny Leonard, and Tony Canzoneri, among others—whose impressive skills provoked deep ethnic loyalties and rivalries. But it was among the heavyweights that broad and sometimes violent identifications, especially racial conflicts, became most visible.

Boxing already had had black champions with Dixon and Gans, but when Jack Johnson became the first African American to capture the heavyweight prize in 1908, he exposed wounds beyond the ring. Black fighters had been, and continued to be, denied championship opportunities. Johnson broke the color barrier with a vengeance: a superb tactician, he mocked and tormented white opponents, while his personal flamboyance and relations with white women struck the racial nerve. When the retired champion Jim Jeffries returned to the ring as a white hope, the promoter Tex Rickard exploited the racial angle so effectively that Johnson's protracted and humiliating beating of Jeffries on 4 July 1910 caused race riots across the nation. Films of the bout were banned in several states and in England and South Africa; a more general ban of fight films followed, and no black fighter would get a heavyweight shot until Joe Louis, almost three decades later.

The first million-dollar gates were engineered in the 1920s by Rickard, whose main attraction, Jack Dempsey, broke that mark five times, despite his never meeting his leading contender, the black fighter Harry Wills. Small for a heavyweight but agile and powerful, Dempsey waged some of the most sensational bouts ever. At the New York Polo Grounds in 1923, Dempsey, weighing in at 192.5 pounds, was punched through the ropes and out of the ring by Luis Firpo, at 216.5 pounds, in the first round (a moment immortalized in a 1924 painting by George Bellows, *Demsey and Firpo*), but

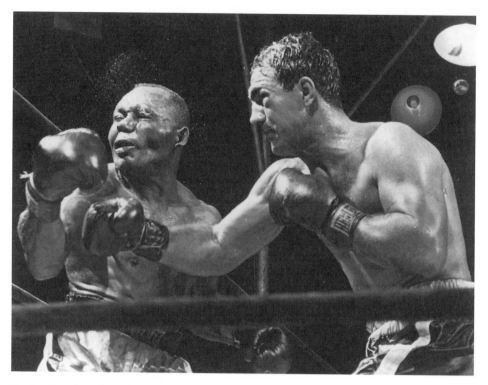

Rocky Marciano knocks out Jersey Joe Walcott on 23 September 1952 in the world heavyweight championship bout. LIBRARY OF CONGRESS

Demsey in turn hammered his foe to the canvas nine times in two rounds to win by a knockout. Fighters had scored exciting wins before, but Dempsey, sometimes credited with coining the phrase "killer instinct," helped transform the boxer's stance from a relatively static, wide-legged posture to one of propulsive assault.

Skill always evolves to counter or redefine aggression, however, and Gene Tunney, who twice defeated an aging but still dangerous Dempsey, was one of the first fighters to be dubbed the "father of scientific boxing." Some fighters are known as pure punchers or pure stylists, and puncher-stylist matchups (Joe Frazier–Muhammad Ali, Sandy Saddler–Willie Pep) are as legendary as head-to-head brawls (Tony Zale–Rocky Graziano, Carmen Basilio–Tony DeMarco). But most great boxers are both. Joe Louis was more controlled than Dempsey, fighting patiently behind a jab and taking careful measure before releasing precise and devastating combinations.

Louis's victories assumed national, even international, importance. The first black heavyweight champion since Johnson, he projected an image of quiet, personal modesty that was scrupulously crafted to avoid controversy, while his prodigious skills and championship longevity—his uninterrupted reign lasted from 1937 to 1948, with a record twenty-five successful defenses—cast him, along with the smaller but comparably talented Henry Armstrong, as a black hero. Louis emerged as an international symbol with the stunning one-round knockout in 1938 of his previous conqueror, the German boxer Max Schmeling, a victory projected by many into a morality play refuting Nazi master-race ideology.

During Louis's reign boxing's popularity and revenues were enhanced by radio coverage, a development that later extended to network, closed-circuit, and cable television, though at the cost of choking off the small clubs where young fighters traditionally learned their trade. Media coverage also increased pressure for abolition of the sport; a national outcry followed the deaths of Benny Paret in 1962 and Deuk-Koo Kim in 1982 after televised bouts. Yet outstanding fighters repeatedly revived interest; the era of Rocky Marciano, Sugar Ray Robinson, and Archie Moore was succeeded by that of Roberto Duran and crossover attractions such as Sugar Ray Leonard and Oscar De La Hoya. But only Muhammad Ali reached beyond the ring to Louis's national and international status.

By the 1960s and 1970s Ali's unorthodox boxing performances, by turns frivolous, courageous, and cruel, were admired and attacked as embodiments of his defiance outside the ring. His early improvisational style and prefight boasting (borrowed from professional wrestling) seemed to represent the youthful insolence of the 1960s in the face of faded Eisenhower-era decorum. His embracing of Black Muslims and refusal of the military draft turned his bouts into more threatening enactments of America's racial and political conflicts, as witnessed by the brutal beating Ali gave Ernie Terrell for calling him by his "slave name" (Cassius Clay). The later stages of Ali's career—forced exile, triumphant comeback bouts (against Joe Frazier and George Foreman), and physical deterioration—allowed writers to blur the boundaries between sports reporting and political, aesthetic, and ethical commentary.

By the end of the century, the once-promising Mike Tyson—a tangle of frustrated rage and compulsive self-destructiveness packaged for a curious public by entertainment juggernauts—offered yet another reflection of national culture and its values. "Boxing has become America's tragic theater," Joyce Carol Oates wrote in 1987, a "magical space" within which "moral and political complexities" are momentarily suspended to focus on "man . . . *in extremis*." But like tragedy itself, boxing also reflected those complexities, as major fights continued to be read—sometimes absurdly, yet irresistibly—as cultural allegories.

Amateur boxing also flourished in the twentieth century. Established in the United States in the late nineteenth century and admitted to the Olympic Games in 1904, it expanded through the Golden Gloves tournaments under the newspaper sponsorship of the *Chicago Tribune* and the *New York Daily News* in 1926 and 1927, respectively. At the end of the century amateur boxing was conducted on local, national, and international levels, with the most prestigious tournament held every four years at the Olympics. Followers of and participants in amateur boxing often insist on its difference from professional boxing. Shorter distances (three-minute rounds or four or five two-minute rounds) encourage a faster pace; the emphasis on scoring points—clean contact counts as much as a knockdown—promotes skill over punishment; and safety measures such as head guards, gloves that absorb shock, and stricter enforcement of regulations foster greater safety. The referee Mills Lane has claimed that amateurs preserve boxing

---

The Marquess of Queensberry Rules (1867)

Rule 1. To be a fair stand-up boxing match in a twenty-four-foot ring, or as near that size as practicable.

Rule 2. No wrestling or hugging allowed.

Rule 3. The rounds to be of three minutes' duration, and one minute's time between rounds.

Rule 4. If either man fall through weakness or otherwise, he must get up unassisted, ten seconds to be allowed him to do so, the other man meanwhile to return to his corner, and when the fallen man is on his legs the round is to be resumed and continued until three minutes have expired. If one man fails to come to the scratch in the ten seconds allowed, it shall be in the power of the referee to give his award in favor of the other man.

Rule 5. A man hanging on the ropes in a helpless state, with his toes off the ground, shall be considered down.

Rule 6. No seconds or any other person to be allowed in the ring during the rounds.

Rule 7. Should the contest be stopped by any unavoidable interference, the referee to name the time and place as soon as possible for finishing the contest; so that the match must be won and lost, unless the backers of both men agree to draw the stakes.

Rule 8. The gloves to be fair-sized boxing gloves of the best quality and new.

Rule 9. Should a glove burst, or come off, it must be replaced to the referee's satisfaction.

Rule 10. A man on one knee is considered down, and if struck is entitled to the stakes.

Rule 11. No shoes or boots with springs allowed.

Rule 12. The contest in all other respects to be governed by revised rules of the London Prize Ring.

---

as a sport, while professionals are part of the entertainment business. (For a useful tabulation of these and other differences, see Cantu 1995.) Differences are, however, sometimes a matter more of emphasis than of sharp demarcation. A scoring

Professional Weight Classes and World Championships

Weight divisions evolved in the second half of the nineteenth century into six classes. With the Walker Law of 1920, which returned legalized boxing to New York, a system of eight classes was agreed on by U.S. and British authorities. These eight traditional classes are identified by an asterisk (*) below. Intermediary, or junior, divisions between welterweight and lightweight also appeared in the 1920s but faded by the mid-1930s. They revived in the 1940s and faded once more before they revived again in 1959, and soon they were joined by others, expanding the traditional eight to seventeen. In addition, the number of "world" sanctioning bodies has increased and as of 1999 stood at ten—three major (World Boxing Council, World Boxing Association, and International Boxing Federation), one moderately influential (World Boxing Organization), and six minor (World Boxing Union, International Boxing Union, World Boxing Federation, International Boxing Council, International Boxing Organization, and International Boxing Association), called collectively the "alphabet-soup organizations" by critics because they are usually referred to by their initials. Each has its own set of rankings, general regulations, and world champions, increasing the number of potential world title-holders from 8 to at least 170.

Weight Class	Limit (pounds)
Heavyweight*	Unlimited
Cruiser Weight	190
Light Heavyweight*	175
Super Middleweight	168
Middleweight*	160
Junior Middleweight (or Super Welterweight)	154
Welterweight*	147
Junior Welterweight (or Super Lightweight)	140
Lightweight*	135
Junior Lightweight (or Super Featherweight)	130
Featherweight*	126
Junior Featherweight (or Super Bantamweight)	122
Bantamweight*	118
Junior Bantamweight (or Super Flyweight)	115
Flyweight*	112
Junior Flyweight (or Light Flyweight)	108
Strawweight (or Minimum Weight)	105

Source: Web sites for World Boxing Council (www.wbcboxing.com), World Boxing Association (www.wbaonline.com), and International Boxing Federation (www.ibf-usba-boxing.com).

blow, defined as a punch delivered with the knuckle part of the glove, "with the weight of the body or shoulder" behind it, leaves room for risk and knockouts: witness the crushing victories of the Cuban heavyweight Teofilo Stevenson in 1972, 1976, and 1980 and David Reid's dramatic one-punch victory in the 1998 Olympics. Medical observers argue that head guards offer better protection against external lacerations than against internal injury. Furthermore, the sporting nature of amateurism is sometimes compromised by external pressures, most observable in politically biased decisions rendered during Olympic competitions and in the premature recruitment of prospects by professional managers and promoters.

Modern Controversy

Throughout the history of boxing, ambivalence has characterized public perception of the sport. Boxing continues to be the only major sport in the United States whose abolition is an essential part of conversation about it. A criminal element was suspected in its operation as early as Jack Slack's championship reign (1750–1760), and fixed fights, bizarre decisions, rigged ratings (usually determining which fighters get lucrative championship opportunities), and the financial exploitation of fighters have raised eyebrows and protests ever since. Organized crime became associated with boxing in the late 1940s and the 1950s with the near monopoly enjoyed by the International Boxing Club (IBC, a.k.a. the Octopus), the chief promotional player in the booming television market. The IBC's ties to underworld figures such as Frankie Carbo and "Blinky" Palermo had a coercive effect on fighters, managers, and matchmakers, with details made public by the Kefauver Senate hearings in 1950. At the end of the century contemporary boxing was still plagued by manipulation and exploitation, although the centralized Octopus had been replaced by a patchwork of large and small promoters. Their bitter rivalries and temporary alliances were fueled by lucrative cable contracts and sometimes involved questionable favoritism bestowed by ratings and sanctioning organizations. Talented and savvy boxers could earn spectacular sums, but they were a small minority, and even top performers could find themselves trapped in adverse, long-term contracts. Campaigns for stricter regulation were mounted periodically, for example, in 1998 in the so-called Muhammad Ali Boxing Reform Act sponsored by Senator John McCain of Arizona.

Amateur Weight Classes and Regulations

Amateur boxing is regulated in the United States by United States Amateur Boxing, Inc., and internationally by the Amateur International Boxing Association. Twelve weight divisions for competition in the United States are defined by pounds and kilograms.

Weight Class	Limit (pounds / kilograms)
Super Heavyweight	Unlimited
Heavyweight	201 / 91
Light Heavyweight	178 / 81
Middleweight	165 / 75
Light Middleweight	156 / 75
Welterweight	147 / 67
Light Welterweight	139 / 63.5
Lightweight	132 / 60
Featherweight	125 / 57
Bantamweight	119 / 54
Flyweight	112 / 51
Light Flyweight	106 / 48

Source: United States Amateur Boxing, Inc.

One constant concern is for the grave medical consequences of boxing. As the promoter Mike Jacobs once remarked, fans "come to see a man hurt." Modern protections—mouthpiece, foul cup, fight stoppages called by referees, additional ring ropes, fewer rounds (maximums dropping from twenty to fifteen to twelve), an automatic count to eight after a knockdown, a limit of three knockdowns in a single round—have not silenced debate. Even gloves provoke controversy. They protect the hands, critics note, but they also allow the fragile human fist to strike more powerful blows to the head. Statistics on deaths and injuries in the media are inconsistent or selective, in part because statistics are often deployed as rhetorical ammunition by apologists or abolitionists, with both sides drawing comparisons to football, rugby, automobile racing, and so on. *The Ring Record Book and Boxing Encyclopedia,* which used to keep records on all aspects of boxing, lists the highest number of fatalities as occurring from the mid-1940s to the mid-1960s (the worst, twenty-two deaths in 1953), followed by a general tapering off. Yet it records the rate from 1970 to 1978 (and after) as about six per year, while a news-service article in 1980, claiming boxing to be the deadliest contact sport, put the average for the same period at twenty-one per year. A thorough 1987 study of medical consequences reported a much lower rate, below that of several other sports, at four per year from 1979 to 1985. Rapid medical response has helped reduce fatalities, but still high is the rate of injury for boxers with long, punishing careers, including injuries to eyes, ears, and teeth and assorted fractures and lacerations. Most serious is the cumulative brain damage caused by repeated concussive and subconcussive blows, *dementia pugilistica,* or punch-drunk syndrome, that may become apparent only after retirement. (For fuller information, and for medical, ethical, and social arguments on both sides of the controversy, see Cantu 1995.)

The mingled exhilaration and dismay that boxing inspires have long attracted writers, artists, and filmmakers. William Hazlitt, Ernest Hemingway, A. J. Liebling, Norman Mailer, and Oates are some of the prominent writers who have explored it in fiction and essays. Powerful films such as *Body and Soul* (1947), *The Set-Up* (1949), *Champion* (1949), *The Harder They Fall* (1956), *Requiem for a Heavyweight* (1962), *The Great White Hope* (1970), *Fat City* (1972), the documentary *When We Were Kings* (1996) and the sometimes ludicrous Rocky series (1976–1990) testify to its exceptional drama, even when treatments are scathing. Film biographies reveal the fascination with fighters themselves; some are sanitized to varying degrees—*Gentleman Jim* (1942), *The Great John L.* (1945), *The Greatest* (1977) —but others are unflinching, such as *Raging Bull* (1980), Martin Scorsese's grim portrait of the middleweight champion Jake La Motta. In 1999 two films concerning the menacing and enigmatic heavyweight champion Sonny Liston were in production.

The strange appeal continues. Muhammad Ali's affliction with Parkinson's disease, the progression of which was likely accelerated by injury to his brain sustained over many years of boxing, spurred the House of Delegates for the American Medical Association in 1984 to call for an end to the sport. Yet Ali also enjoyed extraordinary adulation as an international celebrity and goodwill ambassador. In 1998 he received the Messenger of Peace award from Kofi Annan, the secretary-general of the United Nations, who confessed to admiring him throughout his career. Ali presented Annan, in return, with a pair of boxing gloves.

BIBLIOGRAPHY

Berger, Phil. *Blood Season: Tyson and the World of Boxing.* New York: Morrow, 1989.

Cantu, Robert C., ed. *Boxing and Medicine.* Champaign, Ill.: Human Kinetics, 1995.

Fleischer, Nat. *Black Dynamite: The Story of the Negro in the Prize Ring from 1782 to 1938.* 5 vols. New York: C. J. O'Brien, 1938–1947.

Fleischer, Nat, and Sam Andre. *A Pictorial History of Boxing.* 2d rev. ed. 1959. Secaucus, N.J.: Citadel, 1987.

Fleischer, Nat, et al., eds. *The Ring Record Book and Boxing Encyclopedia.* New York: Ring Book Shop/Ring, 1941–1987.

Hauser, Thomas. *Muhammad Ali: His Life and Times.* New York: Simon and Schuster, 1991.

Heinz, W. C., ed. *The Fireside Book of Boxing.* New York: Simon and Schuster, 1961. Contains selections from Homer, Virgil, Lord Byron, William Hazlitt, George Bernard Shaw, Ernest Hemingway, Ring Lardner, Damon Runyon, Clifford Odets, and others.

Liebling, A. J. *The Sweet Science.* New York: Viking, 1956.

Nagler, Barney. *James Norris and the Decline of Boxing.* Indianapolis: Bobbs-Merrill, 1964.

Oates, Joyce Carol. *On Boxing.* Garden City, N.Y.: Doubleday, 1987.

Oates, Joyce Carol, and Daniel Halperin, eds. *Reading the Fights.* New York: Henry Holt, 1988. Contains selections from A. J. Liebling, Norman Mailer, Hugh McIlvanney, Leonard Gardner, Pete Hamill, Joyce Carol Oates, and others.

Remnick, David. *The King of the World: The Rise of Muhammad Ali.* New York: Random House, 1998.

Sammons, Jeffrey T. *Beyond the Ring: The Role of Boxing in American Society.* Urbana and Chicago: University of Illinois Press, 1988.

RONALD LEVAO

See also **Spectacle, Violence as; Sports; Ultimate Fighting; Wrestling, Professional.**

BRADY BILL. *See* Gun Control.

BRIDGER, JIM
(1804–1881)

Jim Bridger was one of the most famous guides, trappers, and Indian fighters in the American West. Born in Richmond, Virginia, he was orphaned at fourteen near Saint Louis, Missouri. In 1822 he accompanied William H. Ashley on his first expedition into the Rocky Mountains. Though illiterate, Bridger became a shrewd frontiersman who cheated death several times. He did not, however, escape a life of violence, which was so much a part of the American frontier.

Bridger was a man capable of cruelty on many levels. In 1823, while accompanying Major Andrew Henry's expedition up the Missouri River, he was assigned to care for Hugh Glass, a trapper who had been seriously mauled by a grizzly bear. Bridger and a companion, John Fitzgerald, however, decided to abandon Glass's mutilated body. As they believed he would not live, they even took away his gun. Glass, however, survived and swore vengeance against both men.

Bridger was familiar with Indian ways and successively married the daughter of a Flathead chief, Cora, who bore him three children; a Ute woman, who died after giving birth to a daughter; and a Shoshone, Mary, who bore him two more children. Nevertheless, Indians were a constant danger. In what later became Washington state, one of Bridger's daughters was taken captive and killed. In 1824 Bridger followed the Bear River to its outlet into the Great Salt Lake. He thought he had reached the Pacific Ocean. Four years later, he was again trapping in the area near Bear Lake. On that occasion four of his men were killed and several others wounded by the Blackfeet tribe. Bridger's party brought this violence upon itself after one member shot a local chieftain and fled with the chief's robe.

On 18 July 1832, Bridger took part in a skirmish known as the Battle of Pierre's Hole against the Blackfeet. In 1833 a band of Indians crept into his camp on snowshoes and stole eighteen horses, including his favorite mount, Grohean. Although Bridger doubled his guard after this incident, in 1833 a Blackfoot shot him in the back with an iron arrowhead, which was removed two years later by the medical missionary Dr. Marcus Whitman. The frontiersman Kit Carson was also wounded in the skirmish.

Further encounters with danger on America's western frontier were inevitable for Jim Bridger. In 1853 a group of Mormons accused Bridger of inciting Indian attacks against their remote settlements. He had failed to comply with Brigham Young's order that no trade be conducted with local natives during Walker's War, the conflict between the Ute tribe and the Mormons. The Mormons had their revenge in August 1853 when an armed Mormon posse descended upon Fort Bridger (an outpost founded by Bridger in 1843) to arrest the frontiersman. Bridger, who was fore-

Jim Bridger. Line cut from *Outing* magazine, May 1884, from an original by Frederic Remington. LIBRARY OF CONGRESS

warned, escaped to Fort Leavenworth, a federal installation. Next, Brigham Young's armed Danites chased him out of the Green River region, a rich beaver-trapping area.

Bridger then joined the 1857 government expedition of Colonel Albert Sidney Johnston as a guide. Johnston led twenty-five hundred troops into what would later become Utah in order to enforce U.S. sovereignty. As tensions had arisen between the Mormons and all "Gentiles," Bridger's relations with "Mormonia" continued to be strained. In fact, Mormons continued to accuse Bridger of selling guns and ammunition to Indians. On one occasion, he was indicted by a Salt Lake City court for selling stolen horses. As late as 1868, Bridger continued to guide government expeditions through Mormon and Indian areas. On one such foray he boasted that his party had killed thirty Indians and dozens of buffalo.

Bridger spent his last days peacefully on a farm near Santa Fe, Missouri. He died an honored hero of America's frontier West, the very symbol of the mountain man: shrewd, rough—a man shaped by the dangers he faced.

BIBLIOGRAPHY

Alter, J. Cecil. *James Bridger: Trapper, Frontiersman, Scout, and Guide.* Norman: University of Oklahoma Press, 1962.

Gowans, Fred. *Fort Bridger: Island in the Wilderness.* Provo, Utah: Frontier, 1975.

Ismert, Cornelius. "James Bridger." In *Mountain Men . . . ,* edited by LeRoy R. Hafen. Vol. 6. Glendale, Calif.: Clark, 1968.

Vestal, Stanley. *Jim Bridger: Mountain Man.* New York: Morrow, 1946.

ANDREW ROLLE

See also **Frontier; Mormons.**

BROWN, JOHN
(1800–1859)

One of the most controversial personalities in nineteenth-century America, John Brown has been dismissed as a lunatic, reviled as a terrorist, and glorified as a martyr for his leadership of a guerrilla band in the Kansas civil war of 1856 and for his spectacular failure to ignite a slave revolt at Harpers Ferry, Virginia, in 1859.

Brown was a puritanical Congregationalist who believed that God had appointed him for a special purpose. After an eye problem in his youth kept him from pursuing a career in the ministry, he became a moderately successful tanner. Despite repeated financial disasters between 1835 and 1855, Brown helped escaped slaves flee northward on the Underground Railroad and gained the confidence of well-connected abolitionists such as the newspaper editor Frederick Douglass and the millionaire Gerrit Smith. Brown believed that slavery was a war in which even the most heinous brutalities against slave owners could be vindicated as self-defense on behalf of the slaves.

In 1855 Brown followed five of his sons to Kansas to help defend antislavery, or "free soil," settlers against the proslavery territorial government fraudulently established by Missouri "border ruffians." On the night of 23 May 1856 he and seven men, including four of his sons, headed up Pottawatomie Creek, intent on executing the area's leading proslavery settlers. Brown ordered his band to drag five proslavery men from their beds and hack them to death with broadswords. After the killings were done, he led his group back into the Kansas wilderness for several months of raiding in the intermittent guerrilla warfare that became known as Bleeding Kansas. Brown's exploits included his victory over a Missouri militia company com-manded by Henry Clay Pate at Black Jack on 2 June and his defeat on 30 August at Osawatomie.

Notorious now, with a $250 federal bounty on his head and a Broadway play, *Osawatomie Brown,* popularizing his victories and blaming his enemies for the Pottawatomie massacre, Brown schemed with six wealthy abolitionists (Gerrit Smith, Reverend Theodore Parker, Frank B. Sanborn, Dr. Samuel G. Howe, George Luther Stearns, and Reverend Thomas Wentworth Higginson) to provoke a massive slave uprising in the South itself, beginning with a takeover of the federal arsenal in Harpers Ferry, Virginia. On the night of 16 October 1859 Brown led a force of eighteen men into Harpers Ferry and captured the armory and a rifle factory. But contrary to his predictions, no hordes of freed slaves flocked to his side. Instead, Brown was captured after two days of fighting. Seventeen men, including ten of his recruits, were killed.

In his trial Brown rejected his lawyers' suggestion that he plead insanity, despite the fact that sev-

John Brown. LIBRARY OF CONGRESS

eral of his relatives signed affidavits testifying that there was insanity in his family. Brown's many interviews and letters from prison, however, show that he was thinking clearly in the last month of his life.

John Brown was convicted on 31 October and hanged on 2 December 1859. For abolitionists he was a martyr in the cause. For slave owners he became a terrorist and a madman. For both sides his life symbolized the irreconcilable passions that divided Americans on the eve of the Civil War.

BIBLIOGRAPHY

Boyer, Richard O. *The Legend of John Brown.* New York: Knopf, 1972.

Finkelman, Paul, ed. *His Soul Goes Marching On: Responses to John Brown and the Harpers Ferry Raid.* Charlottesville: University Press of Virginia, 1995.

Oates, Stephen B. *To Purge This Land with Blood.* New York: Harper and Row, 1970.

Renehan, Edward J., Jr. *The Secret Six: The True Tale of the Men Who Conspired with John Brown.* New York: Random House, 1995.

R. RUDY HIGGENS-EVENSON

See also **Harpers Ferry, Raid on; Slavery.**

BUCHALTER, LOUIS "LEPKE." *See* Lepke, Louis.

BUFFALO BILL. *See* Cody, William "Buffalo Bill."

BULIMIA. *See* Anorexia and Bulimia.

BUNDY, TED
(1946–1989)

Serial killers are commonly characterized as the mythic monsters of our era. In countless novels and films, they come across as the modern-day equivalent of the Victorian-age boogeyman, always ready to pounce on unsuspecting victims who are foolhardy enough to let down their guard, no matter how brief the mental lapse may be. This contemporary demon, though, does not have to be a snaggle-toothed grotesque. Ted Bundy, more than any other serial killer, taught us that.

Bundy was an attractive man with a disarming manner. In the early 1970s, while enrolled as a psy-chology major at the University of Washington, he created the impression of a studious and civic-minded young man. He once ran down a purse snatcher and turned him over to the police. Another time he pulled a drowning child out of a lake. Even a closer inspection of his life would not have revealed any indication of the savage crimes to come. It would, however, have uncovered certain traits that did not jibe with his clean-cut persona.

As a child, he was a habitual liar and petty thief. More important, though, were the sexual obsessions that had already begun to take hold by the time Bundy had reached college. When not attending classes or campaigning for local Republican candidates, he was a Peeping Tom. This unsavory, alternate personality he would later call "the hunchback," his distorted, grotesque mirror image.

Bundy's brutality gradually emerged from his sexual fantasies. No longer content to peer at young women through windows, he began to make tentative, clumsy attempts at abduction and assault. In 1974 his fantasies about violence against women exploded into reality.

Over a seven-month period, Bundy murdered at least eight young women in the Seattle area. At first he would sneak into his victims' bedrooms. Later he would meet women in public places and convince them to get into his car. His victims' bodies were all found raped and battered. He then moved on to Salt Lake City, where he enrolled as a law student at the University of Utah. There the police began to find the mutilated corpses of young women, as would the police in Colorado when Bundy moved there in 1975. One night, Bundy, who had returned to Utah, was picked up by the police for prowling in a Salt Lake City neighborhood. This incident led to his being identified by one of his victims, a young woman who had escaped his seduction attempt. Bundy's affable appearance had in the past deflected suspicion. After receiving a conviction for kidnapping in Utah, however, evidence against him began to mount, and Bundy was extradited to Colorado to face murder charges.

Even in prison Bundy relied on his personable manner and his gift for lying to win people's trust. Vigilance slackened enough to allow him to escape from the Aspen courthouse; during a recess in his trial, Bundy was allowed to visit the courthouse library and he escaped through a library window. He was soon recaptured, but within six months he

Ted Bundy, in 1986. CORBIS/BETTMANN

escaped again—this time through a hole he had sawed through the ceiling of his prison cell—and succeeded in crossing the country to Florida. His murder rampage there, brutal even by his standards, would be his last. The teeth marks that he left in the flesh of one of his victims were matched to an impression of his teeth, thus providing the damning physical evidence that would lead to his death sentence in 1979. He had murdered at least twenty-eight women.

Acting as his own attorney, the ever-conniving Bundy managed to put off his execution for ten years. In that time, the media seized upon the case, feeding the public's fascination with the handsome college boy capable of such ugly, unspeakable crimes. Several books about the case were published, one of which, *Bundy: The Deliberate Stranger*, became the basis for a television miniseries in 1986. Bundy himself, exploiting his rather dubious star status, tried to use the media for his own deceitful ends. Hours before his execution, he arranged an interview with James Dobson, a psychiatrist and radio personality on the religious right. Bundy ex-

plained that his exposure to pornography as a child had warped his mind and had led to his murderous career, as if in his last moments he felt he could lay the responsibility for his crimes outside himself. Dobson and other activists targeting sex and violence in the media were a credulous audience for this argument. Others were not interested in self-serving explanations; they wanted revenge. Bundy died in the electric chair on 24 January 1989. Outside the prison, a crowd of three hundred people cheered when they heard the news.

At the time of Bundy's execution, one of the prosecutors remarked that he could not grasp what had driven Bundy to commit such horrible crimes. Since then, some writers have revealed aspects of the killer's childhood that might have disordered his mind, but nothing seems commensurate with the savage nature of his crimes. Bundy was an illegitimate child who never enjoyed a close relationship with his mother. During his earliest years, while living with his mother and her parents, he was exposed to domestic violence when he witnessed his grandfather beating his grandmother. As damaging as these experiences may have been to a young boy, they do not compare to the childhood brutality experienced by the likes of Henry Lee Lucas, Albert DeSalvo, or Charles Manson. In the end the explanation for Ted Bundy's violent criminal behavior remains a mystery.

BIBLIOGRAPHY

Larsen, Richard W. *Bundy: The Deliberate Stranger*. Englewood Cliffs, N.J.: Prentice-Hall, 1980.
Michaud, Stephen G., and Hugh Aynesworth. *The Only Living Witness*. New York: Simon and Schuster, 1983.
Rule, Ann. *The Stranger Beside Me*. New York: Norton, 1980.

DAVID EVERITT

See also **DeSalvo, Albert; Lucas, Henry Lee; Manson, Charles; Psychopathy, Biology of; Serial Killers.**

BUREAU OF ALCOHOL, TOBACCO, AND FIREARMS

Since its earliest days, the United States has required some federal entity to enforce federal excise taxation in the face of organized resistance—some of it violent. To quell armed resistance to the first federal excise tax on liquor, passed in 1791 to raise much-needed revenue, George Washington dispatched militiamen to put down the Whiskey Rebellion, thus enforcing the right of the federal government to levy such taxes. Excise taxes on alcoholic beverages then came and went with the needs of the Treasury until the Civil War. In 1862 financial exigency prompted Congress to create the Office of Internal Revenue (which in 1953 became the Internal Revenue Service) and the following year to authorize the hiring of three agents to hunt down tax evaders. The pattern for enforcing excise taxes was essentially set.

In the 1920s, during Prohibition, Internal Revenue's Prohibition Unit, created by the Volstead Prohibition Enforcement Act, was transformed into the Bureau of Prohibition, with responsibility for bringing to justice the violent bootlegging gangs of the era. Among the bureau's special squads of enforcement agents was that led by Eliot Ness and his "untouchables" in Chicago, whom current agents of the Bureau of Alcohol, Tobacco, and Firearms (BATF) consider their professional forebears. With the repeal of Prohibition, the Bureau of Prohibition, which had been under the supervision of the Justice Department since 1919, effectively became the Alcohol Tax Unit (ATU) in the Bureau of Internal Revenue. In 1940 the ATU was combined with the Federal Alcohol Administration, the Treasury Department's alcohol regulatory arm, to fuse regulatory and enforcement functions into a single agency.

In 1942 the ATU, which by then had considerable experience in enforcing liquor laws and in regulating the liquor industry, was chosen to enforce the first national gun control laws: the ATF/2 National Firearms Act (passed in 1934), directed at "gangster type" weapons (e.g., sawed-off shotguns and machine guns); and the 1938 Federal Firearms Act, which made some inroads into regulation of the firearms industry and banned the use of interstate commerce to supply arms to fugitives and felons. In 1951 enforcement of tobacco taxes was added to the ATU's responsibilities for alcohol and firearms laws, and the ATU became the Alcohol and Tobacco Tax Division (ATTD) of the Internal Revenue Service (IRS).

With crime increasing in the 1960s and in the wake of the shocking assassinations of that decade, ATTD was given further enforcement powers under the Omnibus Crime Control and Safe Streets Act and the Gun Control Act (both 1968). Now bombs and other weapons of terror were added to ATTD's list of weapons to be suppressed, and it was charged with enforcing tighter regulation of the firearms industry and sanctions against additional illegal uses of guns. In recognition of its additional responsibilities, the agency's name was changed to the Alcohol, Tobacco, and Firearms Division (ATFD) of the IRS.

ATFD became the Bureau of Alcohol, Tobacco, and Firearms in the Treasury Department in 1972. It was assigned the enforcement of the federal law against bombing and arson (under the 1970 Explosives Control Act) and cigarette smuggling (under the 1978 Contraband Cigarettes Act); provisions of the Anti-Arson Act of 1982 involving incendiary fires; further federal limitations on criminal use of firearms (including the Brady Bill of 1993); the 1996 Antiterrorism and Effective Death Penalty Act; and the 1996 Church Arson Prevention Act (resulting from a rash of church bombings, many of them racially motivated).

BATF's involvement in the Ruby Ridge incident in 1992 and the deadly destruction of the Branch Davidian compound at Waco, Texas, in 1993 aroused the ire of the gun lobby and militantly antigovernment "militia" groups. These controversies notwithstanding, BATF has remained active and effective in countering threats of international and domestic terrorism and in investigating the illegal firearms trade, arson, and crimes in which explosives were used.

BIBLIOGRAPHY

Kurian, George T., ed. *A Historical Guide to the U.S. Government.* New York and London: Oxford University Press, 1998.

Moore, Jim. *Very Special Agents: The Inside Story of America's Most Controversial Law Enforcement Agency—the Bureau of Alcohol, Tobacco, and Firearms.* New York: Pocket Books, 1997.

A Report on the Bureau of Alcohol, Tobacco, and Firearms: Its History, Progress, and Programs. Washington, D.C.: U.S. Government Printing Office, 1995.

ALAN SHUCARD

See also **Government Violence Against Citizens; Ruby Ridge; Waco.**

BYSTANDERS

Bystanders—individuals, groups, or nations—are witnesses to events to which they are in a position to respond. When they remain passive in the face of harmdoing, aggression, or violence against individuals or groups, this passivity encourages the perpetrators. Bystanders have great potential to halt and prevent violence. They can play important roles in the face of various situations: violence committed against groups of people, such as genocide, mass killing, and ethnic violence; sexual and physical abuse of children; the unnecessary use of violence by police against civilians; and emergency situations in public settings. Passive bystanding in these and other situations means that witnesses or people (individuals or groups) that have access to information take no action and even go on with business as usual, as if nothing were happening. They may even actively avoid using or even accessing relevant information. Active bystanding means responding in ways that might reduce or stop harmdoing or violence or help people who are victimized, suffer, or need help for other reasons.

Violence by Groups Against Other Groups

Usually, extreme collective violence like genocide or mass killing evolves step by step. Smaller acts of discrimination and violence against a victim group gradually change perpetrators and the group or society they are part of. The norms of acceptable conduct change. Institutions change, or new ones are established that serve violence. The victims are increasingly devalued. It is often the case that perpetrators develop an intense commitment to an ideology that guides them to the destruction of the ideological "enemy." In some cases mutual violence between two groups leads to the dominance of one, and this group or the previously dominant group turns to genocide.

Unfortunately, both internal bystanders—members of the population who are not themselves perpetrators—and external bystanders—outsiders—tend to remain passive rather than making an effort to stop this evolution. At times, guided by their view of national interests or historical ties, nations even support the perpetrators. In the 1930s, during the increasing persecution of Jews in Nazi Germany, the German people obediently boycotted Jewish stores, ended relationships with Jewish friends and lovers, and took over Jewish jobs and businesses. Like the Germans, many Turks became "semiactive participants" in the genocide against the Armenians in 1915 and 1916 carried out by the Young Turk government of the Ottoman Empire. U.S. corporations were busy in the 1930s developing business in Germany, and in 1936 the whole world went to Berlin to participate in the Olympics. The United States, to-

gether with many other countries, supported Iraq before its invasion of Kuwait, with military weapons and economic credit, in its war against Iran. This was the case even though Iraq started the war, and the support continued even though the Iraqi government used chemical weapons against its Kurdish citizens. Perpetrators more often than not go unpunished by the passive community of nations.

The U.S. role in El Salvador during that country's civil war affords a notable instance of bystander behavior. According to Amnesty International, about forty thousand people were killed there between 1979 and 1983, a large percentage of them in extrajudicial executions by government security forces. Yet in 1984 the United States, which backed the government's efforts to put down the rebel guerrillas, increased its military aid to El Salvador for that year to nearly $197 million. The U.S. actions in both El Salvador and Iraq may be seen as going beyond passive bystanding, as complicity with governments that engage in mass killing. A few years later, however, after Salvadoran government forces killed groups of nuns and Jesuit priests, intense international pressure, including pressure from the United States, was brought to bear on the Salvadoran regime to end the civil war. Seemingly the combination of this pressure—a form of active bystandership—and a successful offensive by the guerrillas compelled the government to engage in serious negotiations. With effective UN participation, the long civil war was brought to resolution.

A shocking example of passivity by the international community was in response to the 1994 genocide in Rwanda. Human Rights Watch and other organizations reported the danger of intense violence. The head of the UN peacekeeping force received information about impending plans of genocide by the ruling circle of Hutus against the Tutsi minority, but his superiors at the UN ordered him to take no action. In the years preceding the genocide, the French supported the Hutu government militarily in a civil war against Tutsi-led rebels without reacting to occasional massacres of Tutsi peasants. After the genocide began in April 1994, most of the UN peacekeepers were withdrawn. The international community, with U.S. participation and to some extent leadership, refused to use the term "genocide," apparently to avoid the pressure for action that the acknowledgment of a genocide in progress would have created. When sending back UN peacekeepers was contemplated, action was slowed by negotiation of how much the United States was going to charge the UN for equipment it was going to lease to UN peacekeepers.

Why are bystanders passive in the face of group violence? Internal bystanders fear retribution. They are usually also part of a society that has long devalued the group that has come to be victimized. This, together with other aspects of the culture, reduces the motivation to act. When responsibility is diffused among many bystanders, individuals feel absolved of action. Nations often follow a tradition of regarding what happens in another country as that country's internal affair. Historically, nations have not seen themselves as moral agents who have obligations for the lives and welfare of people beyond their borders. They pursue national self-interest, usually defined as wealth, power, and influence.

Inaction changes bystanders. Over time, passive bystanders tend psychologically to distance themselves from victims. This diminishes their guilt and whatever empathy they might once have felt, together with their distress or empathic suffering. Like perpetrators, they blame and increasingly devalue victims. In the end they exclude victims from the human and moral universe. The bystanders' passivity also affects the victims who, abandoned, feel helpless to act in their own behalf. Action, helpful responding, also changes. During the Holocaust, there were people who endangered their lives to save Jews. Such rescuers, once they began to act, tended to become increasingly committed to helping.

The passivity of bystanders encourages and even confirms perpetrators' belief in the rightness of their cause. By contrast, when bystanders act, they can make a difference. A person can greatly influence the behavior of others by remaining passive or taking action. What one person says can lead others either to help or not to help someone in distress.

At the Huguenot village La Chambon in France, the heroic actions of the villagers during World War II in saving Jewish refugees affected some of the perpetrators, who in turn helped the villagers. Although examples are rare, the great potential power of nations and the international community was seen in South Africa, which experienced sanctions and boycotts imposed by several nations against the apartheid system, and in Bosnia, where after much hesitation U.S. initiatives led to limited military action by the North Atlantic Treaty Or-

ganization against Serbian aggressors, followed by diplomatic efforts. In such situations, concentrated follow-up is required to prevent renewed violence. Having made a commitment in Bosnia, and perhaps also motivated by its failure to respond in Rwanda, the international community, represented by NATO and led by the United States, responded in another part of the former Yugoslavia, Kosovo. That a response took place was extremely important. But lack of understanding of the roots of genocide and lack of experience in how to respond in such situations led to a mode of response, extended bombing, that was probably less than optimal in minimizing human suffering. A flexible response that combined bombing with acknowledgment of past Serb suffering and actions that affirmed Serb identity would have been more effective.

The international climate must undergo a change so that bystander nations will be expected to act. Standards for action must be developed that specify who is to act and the timing and method of action. Actions can include offers of help with mediation and conflict resolution and high-level diplomacy; withholding aid; condemnation, sanctions, and boycotts; and, if unavoidable, a military response. Early reactions increase the potential of halting violence without the use of violence in kind. Bystanders at the international level can also work to prevent violence by helping historically antagonistic groups to reconcile; nations can help previously victimized groups to heal, lessening the likelihood that they will become perpetrators themselves.

Violence By and Against Individuals

Child Abuse. Although both boys and girls are sexually abused, more is known about the sexual abuse of girls. Father-daughter incest is the consequence in part of perpetrator characteristics, in part of the characteristics of the particular family system. In a family type with a needy, dependent father and a wife-mother who already in childhood was overburdened by caring for others, she may withdraw, leaving a daughter to become the caretaker. In another system, the father treats his family like chattel, thus feeling justified in doing whatever he wishes to people he sees as his property.

The extent to which mothers or other relatives know about sexual abuse by fathers (or other family members) is often difficult to determine. Some wives and other relatives are probably motivated not to know. When daughters tell their mothers of

187

abuse, some refuse to believe it or blame their daughters and do nothing. The passivity of bystanders, and even more their refusal to help or their harmdoing as they blame victims, increases the traumatic impact of abuse. It is likely that both sexual and physical abuse of children are encouraged by the passivity or complicity of bystanders—in most instances within the family itself.

Police Violence. The passivity of fellow officers and superiors, together with insufficient community response, increases the likelihood that police will use unnecessary force against citizens. In New York City in 1997, Abner Louima, a Haitian immigrant, was handcuffed and savagely abused by an officer in a station-house restroom while his fellow officers did nothing to intervene. Frequently, police officers engage in such violence with impunity. Without punishment, admonishment, or even disapproval from superiors and fellow officers, the standards of a police unit will shift. Violence against citizens becomes acceptable, especially against devalued minorities.

Training police officers to be active bystanders is one way to reduce police violence. Officers need to believe that diffusing the tension of a heated interaction between a fellow officer and a civilian, or stopping violence as it begins, is effective teamwork. It may not only help a citizen but also protect a fellow officer from potential punishment. But given the strong inclination of police officers to protect each other, such active bystandership can be achieved only with support by superiors.

Public Emergencies. When someone has a minor accident or a sudden attack of illness or some other sudden need, witnesses often remain passive. When a number of witnesses are present, each becomes less likely to act, due to diffusion of responsibility or to feeling inhibited in public. In the well-known instance of bystander passivity that has become a sad American legend, the murder of Kitty Genovese, thirty-eight witnesses heard her screams in the adjoining apartment houses in the middle of the night in Queens, New York, as a man attacked her, left, returned again, left again, and returned to finally finish the murder. In a public emergency involving violence against individuals, the victims' need for help can be even greater than that of accident victims or persons taken ill. The potential cost of helping the victims of violence is also greater.

By what he or she says, a bystander can define a situation for others as one that requires action. A bystander can recruit others as allies, thereby achieving safety in numbers and increasing the likelihood that these allies will take action. Even without physical interference, bystanders can influence perpetrators. Simply screaming at, say, an adolescent who is holding and hitting another, telling him or her to stop, can immediately defuse a scene of violence. A more difficult, and all too common, situation is one in which a bystander witnesses a parent verbally or physically abusing his or her child in public. The rights of parents to mistreat their children have come under increasing scrutiny, making it more appropriate for bystanders to respond. They can do this in nonconfrontational ways, such as by offering to help an impatient parent at a supermarket by keeping watch over the child, by complimenting the parent on the child's appearance, or by simply making their presence known by engaging the parent (or any other adult mistreating a child) in some way.

How can bystander behavior in general be changed? The public must be made aware of strategies for action and must learn about conditions that lead to passivity, such as diffusion of responsibility or people looking unconcerned in public, leading others to believe that there is no need for action. Heightened sensitivity to cues of distress can increase bystander response. All would benefit from a climate in which individuals and nations are expected to act. If people are to become active bystanders, it is necessary that children be raised in ways that lead them to care about the welfare of all people and be instilled with the moral courage to act on their caring in the midst of the uncertainty that surrounds many situations of need or in opposition to forces that encourage violence.

BIBLIOGRAPHY

Latane, Bibb, and John Darley. *The Unresponsive Bystander: Why Doesn't He Help?* New York: Appleton-Crofts, 1970.

Staub, Ervin. "Preventing Genocide: Activating Bystanders, Helping Victims, and the Creation of Caring." *Peace and Conflict: Journal of Peace Psychology* 2, no. 2 (1996):189–201.

———. *The Roots of Evil: The Origins of Genocide and Other Group Violence.* New York: Cambridge University Press, 1989.

Wyman, David S. *The Abandonment of Jews: America and the Holocaust, 1941–1945.* New York: Pantheon, 1984.

ERVIN STAUB

See also **Genovese, Kitty, Murder of; Mass Muder: Collective Murder.**

C

CALAMITY JANE
(1852–1903)

Although her origins are obscure, historians generally agree that Martha Jane Cannary, the woman destined to become a legend in the West as Calamity Jane, was born on 1 May 1852 in Princeton, Missouri. Around 1865 she went with her family to Virginia City, Montana, where she worked as a bull-whacker, cracking a whip over teams of oxen. She was also at times a horse tender, laundress, cook, and prostitute. In early adolescence she was already frequenting frontier army posts and hells-on-wheels, the raucous towns at the ends of the tracks during the transcontinental railroad construction. Big-boned and possessing masculine features, she often dressed in male attire and passed herself off as a man to gain employment. She obviously enjoyed the company of rough men and in later years became notorious as a two-fisted drinker able to hold her own with the most hardened habitués of frontier saloons. Her claims of having served as a scout with noted military leaders in various Indian campaigns are unsubstantiated.

She apparently acquired her memorable nickname sometime in the early 1870s because of her propensity for bringing misfortune to those around her. It caught on with fabricators of sensational dime novels, who began churning out tales of the frontier heroine Calamity Jane by 1877. A more respectable novel, *Calamity Jane: A Story of the Black Hills*, by Mrs. William Loring Spencer, appeared in 1887. These publications had little fac-

tual basis, but contributed greatly to the legend of Calamity Jane. Although she was present in some of the wildest towns of the West during their most violent periods, including, most notably, Deadwood, Dakota Territory, in 1876, historians have uncovered no authenticated instances of Calamity Jane's involvement in the gunplay that made these rough camps infamous. Her claim to a close association with Wild Bill Hickok, including a reported marriage, was greatly exaggerated. She evidently arrived in Deadwood with Hickok's party in June 1876 and "followed him around like a dog," according to one source, until he was murdered less than six weeks later. The story she told of chasing Hickok's assassin down and capturing him with a meat cleaver was an invention. Historians have dismissed assertions she made that Hickok fathered her daughter after a secret marriage.

In later years Jane lived with a series of men, with and without benefit of marriage. A man named Clinton Burke reportedly married her in El Paso in the 1880s and she used the surname Burke (or Burk) the rest of her life. She is said to have given birth to a son around 1882 and a daughter in 1887, but researchers have never confirmed these reports. She took increasingly to the bottle until her death on 1 August 1903 in Terry, Dakota, near Deadwood. Her last request was to be buried beside Wild Bill at Mount Moriah Cemetery in Deadwood. The wish was granted, and today the two frontier legends lie together.

The Calamity Jane myth, with special focus on her purported relationship with Hickok, was further enhanced in the twentieth century by several

Calamity Jane in 1895. LIBRARY OF CONGRESS

motion pictures in which beautiful women, Ethel Grey Terry (*Wild Bill Hickok*, 1923), Jean Arthur (*The Plainsman*, 1936), Jane Russell (*The Paleface*, 1948), Doris Day (*Calamity Jane*, 1953), and Yvonne DeCarlo (*Calamity Jane and Sam Bass*, 1959), portrayed the rough-hewn frontier female. A novel of the period by Ethel Hueston, *Calamity Jane of Deadwood Gulch* (1937), retold the fable. Pete Dexter's *Deadwood* (1986) and Larry McMurtry's *Buffalo Girls: A Novel* (1990) were debunking attempts, but deeply embedded in the American mythology, the Calamity Jane legend lives on.

BIBLIOGRAPHY

Burk, Martha. *Life and Adventures of Calamity Jane by Herself.* N.p., 1896.
Clairmonte, Glenn. *Calamity Was the Name for Jane.* Denver: Sage, 1959.
Sollid, Roberta Beed. *Calamity Jane: A Study in Historical Criticism.* Helena, Mont.: Montana Historical Society Press, 1995.

ROBERT K. DEARMENT

See also **Gunfighters and Outlaws, Western; Hickok, James Butler "Wild Bill".**

CAMPUS VIOLENCE

College campuses in the United States have a long history of violence. The peak of violent activity in the campus setting was the 1960s, when political protests against the Vietnam War and in support of the Civil Rights movement, involving clashes with law enforcement, resulted in death and injuries. Other notable campus incidents that have entailed violence, both nonlethal and lethal, include rape and sexual assault, nonsexual physical assault, hazing, and bias-related crime. Yet crime statistics indicate that violent crime on campus is a relatively rare event compared both to national and statewide violent-crime figures and to campus property-crime figures.

In European history, campus violence dates back to medieval conflicts between state and church. Some of the bloodiest battles were between townspeople and students, referred to as "town and gown" conflicts and arising out of competing interests, namely, who possessed economic power. In an effort to moderate the violence, England, for example, granted universities their legal independence, allowing university tribunals to hear cases against students.

Political Activism

In the United States in the early 1800s, campuses turned violent with protests against such things as "bad butter in the commons" and bans on student drinking, resulting in destruction of university property, injury, and the death of one university professor (at the University of Virginia in Charlottesville). Student antiwar activism continued through the early 1900s, but most of the protests during this time were peaceful. It was not until the 1960s, at the height of the Civil Rights movement and during the Vietnam War, that campus protests regularly resulted in extreme violence; at the same time, such violence was more widely publicized than ever before, with reports broadcast on television to a nationwide audience. Campus disorder, including bombings and attempted bombings; arson and suspected arson; general destruction of furniture and windows; marches, rallies, teach-ins, and pickets; occupation of buildings, streets, and offices; class boycotts and disruption of extracurricular activities; and the taking of hostages, characterized the unrest that reached its height in the late 1960s. The Berkeley Free Speech Movement, the Kent State antiwar demonstrations, and the Jackson State College civil rights demonstrations led to violent confrontations between students and law enforcement. At Kent State University, four antiwar demonstrators were killed after the National Guard was called in by Ohio governor James Rhodes to stop the student protests. At Jackson State College in Mississippi, two people died in the shooting as police overreacted to civil rights demonstrations. The late 1960s and early 1970s marked an ideological shift in how colleges and universities related to students. A more participatory governance was emerging. Faculty, students, and staff shared in decision making, and there was a concerted effort to bring due process to campuses, which resulted in fewer violent protests. In the 1980s renewed awareness of social concerns among college students resulted in a resurgence of student activism, with protests centering on racial tensions, presidential campaigns, abortion rights, civil liberties, and affirmative action—but the activism was never again on the level of the late 1960s. The policy of apartheid in South Africa was especially a focal point of student activism. Students demonstrated for college administrators to withdraw their school's financial investments from South African business enterprises. Protests included building replica shanties on campus, circulating petitions, and staging sitins, sleep-ins, and marches. Although nonviolent in conception, these forms of protest did at times result in violence when students and administration disagreed on their appropriateness. The level

of violence, however, never matched or exceeded that of Kent State or Jackson State. By the end of the twentieth century, protests, especially those resulting in violence, were quite rare. Some universities and colleges experienced students protesting political and environmental issues, but there was no mass activism on the scale of the protests of the 1960s.

Campus Violent Crime

Violent crime on campus became a national concern with the 1986 murder of Jeanne Ann Clery, a freshman at Lehigh University, a small liberal arts college in Easton, Pennsylvania. Clery was raped, sodomized, and murdered in her dormitory by an assailant who gained entrance through an exterior residence-hall door that was carelessly left propped open. Clery's parents sought redress against the college, alleging that the campus security force was unprofessional and that the college failed to offer clear and easily obtainable literature about campus safety policies and procedures and also failed to reveal crime-rate statistics to prospective students. The Clerys demanded that not only Lehigh but all college campuses across the United States make crime statistics available to all potential students, faculty, and staff; on 26 May 1988 Pennsylvania enacted legislation requiring all public and private colleges and universities to do just that.

National Guard troops enter the University of Maryland campus to quell an antiwar demonstration. CORBIS/BETTMANN

The essence of such legislation is that college administrators have a moral and ethical obligation to preserve personal safety and that the public has the right to know how safe each campus is. Similar legislation was adopted in other states, but problems arose when uniformity in reporting was not achieved. Different reporting criteria and requirements led to the introduction of a bill at the national level requiring all colleges and universities to participate in the Federal Bureau of Investigation's Uniform Crime Reports (UCR) program. This bill, in modified form, was signed into law by President George Bush in November 1990 and became known as the Student Right-to-Know and Campus Security Act. It mandates that anyone desiring to know the level of campus violence at any university or college has the right to that information. Ongoing research indicates a general level of compliance with the spirit of the law; but some researchers question the accuracy of campus statistics, suggesting that there may be more violence than is being revealed.

Hazing

Since 1973 more than sixty-eight deaths on campuses occurred as a result of hazing, that is, rites of initiation into organizations such as campus fraternities. Hazing most often involves the humiliation of "pledges"—aspiring members of a fraternity—who are commanded by fraternity "brothers" to engage in physically demanding, disgusting, or otherwise disagreeable actions. Some sororities also use hazing, but less commonly. Although the tradition of hazing has existed on college campuses since at least the late nineteenth century, it is only since the 1970s that hazing has seemed to become more severe, with often tragic results.

Hazing can produce injuries that are physical, psychological, or both (Richmond 1990). Videotapes released to CNN and NBC capture the hazing behavior of U.S. Marine graduates from a paratrooper school in North Carolina. The tapes show Marine pledges screaming in pain as fellow Marines pound metal insignia into their chests. In Athens, Georgia, three members of a fraternity were suspended after they paddled a fraternity pledge more than fifty times in an initiation rite held off campus. Other students have endured kidney slaps or back punches resulting in internal bleeding; fallen from balconies, down steps, and off roofs; lapsed into comas after drinking excessive amounts of alcohol, or even died of alcohol

poisoning; suffered concussions, bruises, and broken bones; and tolerated electrical shocks and subsequent burns as part of hazing practices. In response, thirty-eight states have enacted antihazing measures, and the National Interfraternity Council has sponsored workshops and undertaken awareness programs to promote a change in fraternity rituals, calling for less hazing and partying and more civic-minded activities.

Sexual Violence

Many studies indicate that a significant number of college students experience some form of violence in their dating relationships. In a 1981 study of physical aggression in dating situations among college students, 21 percent of those surveyed reported either experiencing or initiating at least one of these violent acts: threats, pushing, slapping, punching, assault with a weapon, and striking with an object (Makepeace 1981). In a 1987 study, the rate of violence increased to 73 percent for females and 79 percent for males (Marshall and Rose 1987). Some researchers attribute the varying levels of violence across studies to measurement and sampling differences. On the average, studies suggest that more than one-third of males and females surveyed report expressing violence toward a dating partner.

Factors involving sexuality and gender roles are among the explanations most commonly put forth to account for dating violence. Sexuality and violence are often portrayed in American culture as legitimately connected. Television shows, movies, and novels often blur the line between rape and consensual sexual activity, but rape is an act of power; it is not an aspect of sexuality but a violent act. The notion that women want to be "taken" by force and that violence is natural to men and thus an acceptable part of the male domain, has often skewed the debate about violence and sexuality—including, and perhaps especially, debates about sex and violence in the campus setting.

Researchers once thought that there were few differences between male- and female-inflicted dating violence; however, it appears that risk factors for dating violence by females may be quite different from those for dating violence by males. One predictor of dating violence in general is attitudes toward violence: those who have experienced dating violence have a less negative attitude toward it. Male perpetrators of dating violence exhibit greater acceptance of violence than do female perpetrators. This relationship is not found when examining males and females who have not experienced dating violence.

Sex-role attitudes also play an important part in understanding dating violence. Males who have traditional sex-role expectations are more likely to inflict violence in dating situations. Generally, research has found that males support traditional sex roles more than do females. Romantic jealousy is a widely cited source of dating violence. Individuals with a history of combativeness (men report more violence in nondating contexts than do women) are more likely to engage in dating violence. A tendency to engage in both verbal aggression and physical violence is a predictor of dating violence.

Reasons for Campus Crime

Much of the research on campus crime and its causes focuses on nonviolent property crime (including such acts as motor-vehicle theft and theft from automobiles). Some researchers cite the adjacent city's crime rates, reasoning that campus crime is a result of city residents crossing over to the campus to commit crimes there. Others argue that city crime rates do not explain campus crime rates, thereby shifting the focus from external campus variables to internal campus variables, namely characteristics of the campus and the student body.

Explanations for violent campus crime include precipitating factors involving sexuality and gender roles, discussed above (in relation to dating violence), as well as a number of other precipitating factors. Of these, the most campus-specific is the age of the typical university population. Crime statistics indicate that young people (ages seventeen to twenty-four) are more likely to be both victims and perpetrators of violent crime. This age vulnerability is key on college campuses, where most college students are young, have little experience living away from home without parental supervision, and may tend to be naive and subject to the influence of peer pressure. For many, the challenges of college life, that is, being fully responsible for oneself, create a higher level of vulnerability to victimization.

At the same time, societal tolerance of violence likely contributes to an escalating cycle of violence. The degree to which society legitimizes violence is reflected in portrayals of violent activities and events in the movies, on television, and in print media. The abundance of violent images may have a desensitizing effect on the viewer or reader; this may be particularly true of young people.

Other significant factors associated with campus violence, as with violence generally, include (1) alcohol abuse—excessive drinking has been associated with a great deal of violent behavior on campus; (2) denial—both offender and victim may try to hide or discount the severity of violent acts; and (3) inequality and prejudice—racial hatred or unequal status among individuals sometimes results in hate-crime violence.

Despite certain periods of increased and highly visible campus violence in U.S. history, and the real issues related to the safety of campuses in the United States, campus crime remains a relatively rare event. Victimization surveys indicate that students are more likely to become a victim of a property crime than a violent crime. At the turn of the twenty-first century, campus activism was a peaceful endeavor, and publicity and discussion of issues surrounding dating violence and other forms of aggression led to greater awareness at campuses across the country.

BIBLIOGRAPHY

Bookwala, Jamila, et al. "Predictors of Dating Violence: A Multivariate Analysis." *Violence and Victims* 7, no. 4 (1992).

Brownmiller, Susan. *Against Our Will: Men, Women, and Rape.* New York: Simon and Schuster, 1975.

Gibbs, Annette, and James J. Szablewicz. "The Judicial View of Apartheid Protests on Campus." *NASPA Journal* 26, no. 2 (1989).

McLaughlin, Colleen. "Normalization, Expectation, and Glamorization: The Media's Role in Perpetuating the Cycle of Violence." Paper presented at the American Society of Criminology annual meeting, Washington, D.C., November 1998.

Makepeace, James M. "Courtship Violence Among College Students." *Family Relations* 30 (1981).

Marshall, Linda L., and Patricia Rose. "Gender, Stress, and Violence in Adult Relationships of a Sample of College Students." *Journal of Social and Personal Relationships* 4, no. 3 (1987).

Moriarty, Laura J., and William V. Pelfrey. "Exploring Explanations for Campus Crime: Examining Internal and External Factors." *Journal of Contemporary Criminal Justice* 12, no. 1 (February 1996).

Patterson, Brent G. "Freedom of Expression and Campus Dissent." *NASPA Journal* 31, no. 3 (spring 1994).

Richmond, Douglas. "Crime on Campus: When Is a University Liable?" *NASPA Journal* 27, no. 4 (summer 1990).

Roark, Mary L. "Conceptualizing Campus Violence: Definitions, Underlying Factors, and Effects." *Journal of College Student Psychotherapy* 8, no. 12 (1993).

Smith, Michael Clay. *Coping with Crime on Campus.* New York: Macmillan, 1988.

Sugarman, David B., and Gerald T. Hotaling. "Dating Violence: Prevalence, Context, and Risk Markers." In *Violence in Dating Relationships: Emerging Social Issues,* edited by Maureen A. Pirog-Good and Jan E. Stets. New York: Praeger, 1989.

LAURA J. MORIARTY

See also **Antiwar Protests; Jackson State; Kent State; Rape; Schools; Teenagers.**

CANNARY, MARTHA JANE. *See* Calamity Jane.

CANNIBALISM

Eating people is wrong—or so runs the title of one satire of academia. Obediently, Americans have not eaten one another very often, though they have talked about it a great deal.

Cannibalism is usually classified according to the circumstances that gave rise to it: cultural, psychopathological, or survivalist. Cultural cannibalism takes place in societies that approve of eating flesh—as a form of mourning, a battlefield privilege, or a source of protein. Ever since Europeans discovered America, writers such as Montaigne depicted the New World as the home of this sort of people-eater. But in 1979 the anthropologist W. R. Arens attacked this centuries-old notion as a myth of European superiority. Arens could find no verified eyewitness reports of cannibalism and no conclusive physical evidence. However, Arens himself has been impressed by the work of archaeologist Christy Turner II. In a 1998 book Turner showed that the Chaco Anasazi, ancestors to the modern Hopi, cannibalized systematically in the region that is now the southwestern United States, perhaps using the terror that cannibalism inspired as a form of social control.

Psychotic individuals, usually serial killers such as Jeffrey Dahmer, compose the second class of cannibals. These criminals are prosecuted for murder rather than for cannibalism per se, which is against the law in only one state, Idaho.

Dahmer and his ilk capture the popular imagination, but of greater interest to legal scholars are cases of the third sort, survival cannibalism. Cannibalism in the face of imminent starvation is one of the few situations in which a necessity defense might clear a charge of premeditated murder. As A. W. Brian Simpson has written, "maritime survival cannibalism, preceded by the drawing of lots and killing, was a socially accepted practice among seamen until the end of the days of sail"—that is, well into the nineteenth century (p. 145). Cannibalism at this time was understood to be a hazard of the nautical profession and was well documented in newspaper accounts, sailors' ballads, and literary tales such as Edgar Allan Poe's *The Narrative of Arthur Gordon Pym* (1838). However, the case that set the common-law precedent on the issue, *Regina v. Dudley and Stephens* (1884), was decided against this prevailing social norm—that is, against the cannibals.

Cannibalism was also a hazard of the American frontier. In the winter of 1846–1847 a group of westward-bound families known as the Donner Party became, in the words of historian C. F. McGlashan, "pioneer martyrs of California" when they resorted to cannibalism while snowbound in the Sierra Nevada. In 1874 a guide named Alferd G. Packer led five prospectors into the San Juan mountains; two months later, only Packer emerged, looking a little too well nourished. Convicted but never hanged, Packer became a tourist attraction as the Colorado Man-Eater.

Cannibalism today is rare, although it figures rhetorically in debates over fetal tissue transplants, false memory syndrome (as an example of the patently unreal horrors that people can be tricked into "remembering"), human organ sales, and homosexual marriage (as an extreme example of what cultural relativism will lead to). The literature of cannibalism is rich. American writers such as Herman Melville, Charles Warren Stoddard, and Tobias Schneebaum have written travelogues of their visits to cannibals in South America and the Pacific, which literary critics such as David Bergman and Geoffrey Sanborn have examined for the indirect light they shed on sexuality, cultural difference, and imperialism. Popular culture is, of course, also rife with cannibalism (e.g., the fictional Hannibal Lecter of the 1991 film *The Silence of the Lambs*).

BIBLIOGRAPHY

Arens, W. R. *The Man-Eating Myth: Anthropology and Anthropophagy.* New York: Oxford University Press, 1979.

Bergman, David. *Gaiety Transfigured.* Madison: University of Wisconsin Press, 1991.

McGlashan, C. F. *History of the Donner Party: A Tragedy of the Sierra.* Rev. ed. Edited by George Henry Hinkle and Bliss

McGlashan Hinkle. Stanford, Calif.: Stanford University Press, 1947.

Sanborn, Geoffrey. *Sign of the Cannibal*. Durham, N.C.: Duke University Press, 1998.

Simpson, A. W. Brian. *Cannibalism and the Common Law*. Chicago: University of Chicago Press, 1984.

Turner II, Christy, and Jacqueline Turner. *Man Corn: Cannibalism and Violence in the Prehistoric American Southwest*. Salt Lake City: University of Utah Press, 1998.

CALEB CRAIN

See also **Dahmer, Jeffrey.**

CANTON, FRANK
(1849–1927)

Frank M. Canton was born Josiah W. Horner in Virginia in 1849. His father was a wanderer, and the family had lived in Iowa, Indiana, Missouri, Kansas, and Arkansas before the outbreak of the Civil War in 1861. At war's end Joe Horner struck out on his own as a government teamster. Within a short time, he killed a man and was tried and acquitted of murder. He joined his brother in Texas and began a brief life as a cowboy and Indian fighter. By 1874 he was part of the horse-stealing operations that helped to bring on the Red River War with the southern Plains tribes.

Operating out of Jacksboro, Texas, Joe Horner killed a black soldier in 1875 and was believed to be the head of a gang of cutthroats in the area. Arrested, he quickly escaped. In January 1876 he and his confederates robbed a bank in Comanche, Texas. He was arrested, convicted, and sentenced to ten years in jail, but he escaped again. He then robbed a stage, was captured, and tried again to escape. This time he was incarcerated at the Huntsville State Penitentiary, but on 4 August 1879 he escaped from a prison work detail.

Horner assumed the name of Frank M. Canton and settled in Wyoming. He was still a hard man with violent proclivities, but this time he fell in with powerful men. In 1881 he became an inspector for the Wyoming Stock Growers Association (WSGA) and a deputy sheriff for Johnson County. The following year, he was elected sheriff. He served two terms as sheriff and then took a job as chief of the detective bureau of the WSGA. By then he had become a controversial figure. In 1891, a time of building tension between big cattlemen and small ranchers, Canton was accused of murdering John A. Tisdale, a Texas homesteader who openly defied the WSGA. While he was still embroiled in the legal fight over that case, Canton took a leading role in the WSGA's invasion of Johnson County, which was organized in order to kill a large number of alleged rustlers. He was later among those charged with the murders of Nate Champion and Nick Ray, two of the men on the death list. In the charged environment of Johnson County, the case was dismissed.

In 1894 Canton left Wyoming for Oklahoma, where he served as both deputy sheriff and deputy U.S. marshal. That same year he sought and received a pardon for his crimes in Texas. Canton was dismissed as deputy U.S. marshal in 1897 because of alleged fraud, but he managed to secure an appointment as a federal deputy marshal in Alaska. He lost that job two years later because the Oklahoma charges had come to light. Returning to Oklahoma, he worked as a bounty hunter. When Oklahoma became a state in 1907 he was appointed the state's first adjutant general, a post he held until 1916. He later worked for the Texas Cattle Raisers' Association.

Although he left the criminal life in Texas as he left his true name, Frank Canton always inspired fear as well as admiration. Across the years he consistently hid or lied about the unpleasant parts of his life. He even wrote an autobiography in which he whitewashed his criminal past. Published after his death under the title *Frontier Trails* (1930), the book became a classic although it did not tell the truth about Canton's life.

BIBLIOGRAPHY

DeArment, Robert K. *Alias Frank Canton*. Norman: University of Oklahoma Press, 1996.

GARY L. ROBERTS

See also **Gunfighters and Outlaws, Western.**

CAPITALISM

Capitalism refers to a system of social organization for the production and distribution of goods and services. Its distinctive features are "free market pricing, production for profit, competition between independent producers, a free labor market, and private ownership of the means of production" (Wrong 1992, p. 153). The capitalist system can be contrasted with other economic systems, such as socialism, feudalism, tribal communism, state communism, slave systems of production, and monopolistic production; each of these systems contains a dominant logic, suggesting a structure of social relationships that shape actors' interests, strategies available to pursue them, and the probability that one set of actors will prevail over others in advancing those interests. Capitalism orders social relationships according to a dichotomous class structure—workers who sell their labor for a wage and capitalists who own the resources necessary for production.

Members of these two classes behave toward others in their own class as a function of pressures that emanate from the logic of the system—that is, the orientation toward exchange for the pursuit of profit and material gain. This behavior, along with the way members of one class interact with those in the other, shapes the relationship between capitalism and violence. The behavior of the two classes can best be studied at three distinct "moments" in the operation of capitalism: its development, its performance, and its diffusion. Although violence plays a part at each of these moments, in the end it is difficult to assess whether the logic of capitalism promotes violent activity relative to the logic of any other economic system.

Capitalism developed at a historically unique time and place. Karl Marx, Max Weber, and Fernand Braudel suggest that capitalism emerged slowly out of feudal Western Europe with its roots in the fifteenth or sixteenth century. The capitalist spirit arose in the towns of Europe among the artisans—especially those, as Weber emphasizes, of reformist religious movements. These burghers rationalized their productive activity by keeping careful accounts of their transactions in monetary terms, attending to such issues as profit margins. During this early period, however, labor was rarely commodified; burghers did not yet purchase the labor of workers for a price fixed by labor market forces. Instead, within the towns most work remained organized around traditional guild relationships; in Europe in general, a vast majority of the work occurred in rural areas governed by traditional feudal norms.

The wide-scale free-labor market first emerged in the late eighteenth century in England. State interventions into the life of the English rural poor were the necessary conditions both to effect this transformation and to sustain the new order. Such interventions included violence and other forms of coercion. In England the mass of people who were willing to sell their labor for a wage appeared only after the landed aristocracy, with state support, forcibly displaced peasants from traditional common land. When the aristocracy created enclo-

sures, instituting large-scale ranching and renting of lands, peasants lost their means to provide for their own material subsistence. Peasants resisted this appropriation of the common land, but the English state used military force to quell incidents of popular insurgence. In order to survive, peasants relocated to urban centers and traded their labor for wages, becoming the original proletariat. According to the theorist Anthony Giddens, this creation of a pool of "free" labor, along with the political institutions to promote this new organization of work, marks the advent of capitalist society. These institutions include a judicial system that adjudicates disputes over contracts and labor market arrangements. They also include domestic police forces. Both are established to protect individual property rights.

The historian E. P. Thompson documents how the English masses resisted the new institutions of capitalist society and their transformation to the role of wage laborer. For example, Thompson details peasant uprisings against the market-pricing mechanism, in which food prices rose as a function of supply and demand. During times of inflation, the new working class rioted, seized goods, and then distributed these goods at traditional prices. Again the English state responded with repressive tactics, mobilizing coercive forces to protect the new institutions of capitalism. However, the most contested arena in the new social order was the workplace, where members of the proletariat reluctantly submitted to what they viewed as exploitation in order to gain a subsistence wage. The social order, though despised by many workers, was maintained through state institutions of control: "the [English] commercial expansion, the enclosure movement, the early years of the Industrial Revolution—all took place within the shadows of the gallows" (Thompson 1963, p. 61). Other states followed different pathways to capitalism, but common to all were the displacement of large numbers of rural poor and the advent of new state institutions for social control.

Some have speculated that, once the new institutions of capitalism are fixed, the normal performance of capitalism promotes violence. Two theoretical perspectives, in different ways, argue that it does. Strain theory attempts to explain violent behavior common to the urban poor in some capitalist countries. The sociologist Robert Merton, an early developer of this school, suggests that societies define for their members life-orienting goals and legitimate strategies for working toward those goals. Capitalist societies instill the value of material gain and consumption. However, not everybody will be able to achieve these goals through legitimate behavior. Instead, some will be frustrated and turn to antisocial forms of behavior. Later strain theorists, like Albert Cohen, have used this theory to account for violence within urban youth gangs.

The second theoretical orientation, Marxist conflict theory, suggests a different way in which capitalism may promote violence. In this perspective, capitalism provides an incentive structure that encourages actors to pursue individual material gain at the expense of other members of society. Conflict theory draws attention to the consequences of this incentive system for the behavior of those who have wealth and power—notably, corruption on the part of the wealthy to obtain unfair market advantages and their use of political influence to monopolize sectors and undermine market pricing mechanisms through the control of information. The most important difference between the two views is that, whereas strain theory focuses on violence committed by the poor, conflict theory focuses on the activity of the agents of the capitalist system. Thus, conflict theorists examine how state agencies like the police, the courts, and the schools act in order to control populations that present problems to the capitalist social order. A system of private property depends on these agencies and the threat of violence that they pose.

Although one might infer from strain and conflict theory that capitalist societies experience heightened rates of violence relative to societies based on other modes of economic organization, such a conclusion is not supported by empirical evidence. First, though it is true that some capitalist nations like the United States do have high rates of violence, others such as Switzerland and Singapore have relatively low rates of violence. Second, quantitative, cross-cultural analyses of violence are difficult to conduct, as many measures of violence are not reliable, especially in noncapitalist societies. However, qualitative data from anthropological and historical sources indicate that, in traditional societies as compared to modern states, "daily life was very often a much more tenuous, and potentially violent, affair. . . . [T]he level of casual violence in day-to-day life seems to have been high" (Giddens 1985, p. 60).

The third moment in which the relationship between capitalism and violence may be assessed is in its diffusion across the globe. War plays an integral role in the history of the expansion of capitalism. The cause of World War I, for example, in which some ten million combatants died and total casualties among combatants numbered more than thirty million, may be seen as conflict among national interests to control colonial resources so as to fuel their internal capitalist economies. The Cold War also can be interpreted as the outcome of capitalist expansion. Although the two main players, the Soviet Union and the United States, never battled each other directly in the forty-year détente that followed World War II, each attempted to further its own interests through involvement in a number of civil wars, as in Korea and Vietnam, that emerged around the globe. Modernization and the organization of political and economic institutional structures, it can be argued, were central issues in these wars.

Although much of the warfare during the twentieth century may be interpreted as a function of capitalist expansion, other interpretations are as tenable. For example, the organization of economies may have had less to do with the fighting of wars than did the impetus toward expansion of state interests. This interpretation is sufficient to account for the warfare in World War I and for superpower involvement during the Cold War. Moreover, this mode of thinking helps explain why warfare is a more common element in traditional states than in modern ones. That warfare is more common in traditional states than in modern ones is an empirical fact that can be verified in the historical record. For example, a look at feudal Europe shows states constantly at war in order to expand state interests, thus demonstrating that this is not a function of capitalist organization but rather of state leaders who have something to gain by conquering neighbors. On the other hand, the destructive force of twentieth-century warfare is historically unprecedented, and that magnitude of violence is undeniably a function of capitalist society. As the capitalist system has improved the efficiency of production in almost all spheres, it has improved the efficiency of war making.

Capitalist social organization certainly has an effect on the amount of violent activity that a society experiences. The size and direction of that effect, however, are much easier to theorize about than to demonstrate empirically. Capitalism is too highly correlated with other features of societies, such as a democratic form of government, industrial modes of production, Western culture (e.g., Christianity, Roman law, rock music), urbanization, modernization, and so on, to isolate an independent effect of the logic of capitalism on the behavior of individuals. Moreover, capitalism itself is too complex to conclude that outcomes (such as levels of violent activity) derive from the realization of any one of its dimensions.

BIBLIOGRAPHY

Braudel, Fernand. *Civilization and Capitalism, Fifteenth–Eighteenth Century.* Vol. 2, *The Wheels of Commerce.* London: Collins, 1982.

Foucault, Michel. *Discipline and Punish: The Birth of the Prison.* London: Allan Lane, 1977.

Giddens, Anthony. *The Nation State and Violence.* Berkeley: University of California Press, 1985.

Marx, Karl. *Capital.* London: Dent, 1957.

Merton, Robert. *Social Theory and Social Structure.* Glencoe, Ill.: Free Press, 1957.

Thompson, E. P. *The Making of the English Working Class.* London: V. Gollancz, 1963.

Wallerstein, Immanuel. *The Modern World System.* New York: Academic Press, 1974.

Weber, Max. *The Protestant Ethic and the Spirit of Capitalism.* London: Allen and Unwin, 1976.

Wrong, Dennis. "Disaggregating the Idea of Capitalism." In *Cultural Theory and Cultural Change,* edited by Mike Featherstone. Newbury Park, Calif.: Sage, 1992.

EMORY MORRISON

See also **Corporations; Costs of Violent Crime; Depressions, Economic; Poverty; Structural Violence.**

CAPITAL PUNISHMENT

The history of capital punishment in America records over several centuries the social fears and concerns of lawmakers, voters, judges, jurors, and politically active Americans. It is a tangled story, with conflicting views of the seriousness of various crimes and of the value of human life, views often differing on the basis of race, age, sex, and condition. As the ultimate exercise of civil authority, the death penalty entails emotional concerns, legal complexities, and moral challenges.

English Law and Practices

Under the English common law inherited by the first American colonists, all felonies were subject to the death penalty. In the thirteenth century, the king of England was the first ruler in the western world to establish a judicial monopoly over felonious crime, a key step in the development of the nation-state. The list of offenses thought deserving of punishment by death is essentially the same as those the Federal Bureau of Investigation now defines as "major crimes": homicide, robbery, burglary, larceny, arson, and rape. By the fourteenth century a variety of local methods, from burying the felon alive to pushing him off a cliff, had been generally replaced by hanging. Treason, a big criminal category that included counterfeiting, required a special humiliation—dragging a convict behind a cart to the gallows. So did petit treason, the killing of one's lord, master, or husband; convicted wives were, uniquely, condemned to death by fire.

In the abstract no basis for dissent to the death penalty existed. Catholic theologians cited the Book of Genesis on retribution: "Whoso sheddeth man's blood, by man shall his blood be shed." To have ordinary felonies decided by the royal courts was some insurance against the earlier alternative, a continual round of local feuds. Owing to the belief in deterrence, an execution was a highly public event conducted at a prominent site, usually within hours or even minutes of a sentence, with the body sometimes gibbeted, that is, left to rot for months as a warning to anyone tempted to defy the laws of God and man. The judicial system was also driven by simple greed: the goods of all convicts reverted to the king.

Legal rules did allow some felons to escape the fate of hanging. Common law followed church doctrine in calling for pardon, after conviction, of those incapable of "felonious intent" either because of insanity or being under twelve years of age, the recognized "age of reason." The king himself often pardoned sturdy felons who agreed to serve in his army. In a compromise with the church dating from the twelfth century, not only priests but also wandering friars, university students, and a host of others who had taken minor orders might plead "benefit of clergy," proving their clerical status simply by demonstrating their ability to read. The church called on the state to burn those convicted, in its own courts, of the crime of heresy; reciprocally, convicted clerics were remanded by the state to the church, which imposed not death but penance.

Medieval men had no theoretical objections to capital punishment, but they clearly found it distasteful in practice. The hangman was generally shunned. Thus, the ordinary free men who made up trial juries provided the more significant escapes from hanging. And while the law recognized no distinctions among either victims or perpetrators of felony, just as the church ranked all souls as equal, jurors were moved by their own morality, prejudices, and fears. If "not guilty" was the only way to save a prisoner from hanging, "not guilty" it was, even in cases where the evidence was powerful. This form of "pious perjury" in practice freed the great majority of those in the dock.

The more immediate sixteenth- and early-seventeenth-century background of English settlement in America was the turbulent Tudor period and Protestant Reformation. One result of King Henry VIII's break with Rome in 1534 (he reigned from 1509 to 1547) was a fear for the monarch's legitimacy, in an age in which religious difference was close to treason. Henry feared Catholic claimants to his throne, spies, and invasions from the continent; conversely, his Catholic daughter, Queen Mary (r. 1553–1558), feared Protestant and domestic rebellion, and during the 1550s the nation for the first time witnessed mass burnings of heretics. Monarchical paranoia then and later led to reliance on secret "Star Chamber" courts, held without juries, in which suspected traitors were tried and condemned to grisly new penalties: their genitals would be cut off and their bowels burned before their eyes, after which their bodies were quartered and spiked in public places. At the same time, as a reflection of the contemporary witchcraft scare, beginning in 1542 ordinary villagers often turned on odd or unpopular neighbors, many of them lone women.

In this era fewer felonies and certainly fewer routine acts of violence were committed than in the Middle Ages; yet public and official fears are evidenced by the facts that a higher proportion of those tried were convicted and that in some years more witches were hanged than ordinary criminals. The "benefit of clergy" plea was allowed even after the Reformation, as the social standing of literates gave them, in effect, one free ticket to commit a serious crime with no greater penalty than branding. But some crimes were ruled not "clergyable": murder with "malice aforethought" was made one of them, distinguished now from simple manslaughter, and so of course were heresy and treason. It is estimated that as many as seventy-five thousand people—routine criminals, heretics, and traitors—were executed in England from 1530 to 1630.

In the Colonies

It was this gory legacy, then, that the first British Americans brought with them in the early seventeenth century. Naturally concerned with the need for social order, especially in the first decades of settlement, the colonial elite took felony seriously. And whether using their memories of common law or, in Massachusetts, the Mosaic Code, they convicted the great majority of prisoners, hanging masters as well as servants and abandoned girls accused of infanticide. Capital cases everywhere were tried in the highest courts, in some places before the colonial assembly or governor's council. The Massachusetts authorities, more fearful of internal demons than of external threats, were distinguished for imposing the death sentence on a pair of adulterers, on a farmboy accused of buggery with a cow, on four Quakers who persistently refused to leave the colony, and, most famously, in 1692, on twenty Salem witches.

In dealing with their white fellows, the colonial authorities in fact moved increasingly away from the death penalty. During the eighteenth century, just as the English Parliament was multiplying the number of capital crimes out of concern for property, the several colonies seized on alternatives. Death for sexual offenses and for witchcraft virtually disappeared. Plagued by a chronic shortage of labor, in strong contrast to the mother country, county magistrates imposed new or additional terms of indentured servitude rather than hanging. And despite their horror of "popery," or in New England even Anglicanism, they not only kept the right to "benefit of clergy" but also extended it to women and even slaves who could memorize and recite a single verse; in effect, any sane adult not convicted of murder or treason was simply branded on thumb or forehead. Official pardons, too, were common, granted to about half of all condemned Pennsylvanians in the eighteenth century.

At the same time the colonists customarily abandoned the more barbarous official methods of killing. Jacob Leisler, convicted in 1690 of leading a major rebellion against the new English rulers in New York, was read the full Tudor sentence for treason but then simply hanged. Salem's Giles Corey, convicted in 1692 of witchcraft, elected—under a medieval provision that would save his goods from confiscation—to be pressed to death, but his is the only such death known on this side of the water. One white woman, in 1731, is known to have been burned for petit treason; in the early days a few Indians were beheaded. Elsewhere hanging was used exclusively. The usual crimes varied somewhat by colony: homicide everywhere, piracy in seafaring New England, persistent robbery in the Middle Colonies. But nowhere was execution of white colonials common. In Pennsylvania, which probably led the rest of the colonies in capital offenses, the average was fewer than one hanging a year; a little over half of those hangings were for property crime.

Much of the fear and violence in colonial society was in effect directed downward. While it was potential treason and assaults on property that inspired official fears in England, in America the fear was over race and slavery. Blacks were thus subjected to unique Black and Slave Codes. During the eighteenth century, not counting known pardons, an estimated 555 slaves were hanged in Virginia alone, a total that dwarfs all others anywhere. The crimes spanned the spectrum, but while killing whites was rare, paranoia was not. Above all, the colonials' fear was of mass conspiracy or rebellion. In 1712, of nineteen blacks convicted in New York City of setting fire to a building and shooting at whites, thirteen were hanged, one was left in chains to die of thirst, four were burned to death, and one was broken on a wheel.

After the Revolution

The American Revolution and the early Republic brought much change. Proud of their new nation and born in a more humanitarian age, Americans eliminated "cruel and unusual punishments" when the Bill of Rights was added to the U.S. Constitution in 1791, in effect making hanging the only legal form of execution. Following the thinking of Cesare Beccaria and other figures of the European Enlightenment, a few revolutionaries, such as Benjamin Rush, opposed capital punishment altogether. This remained minority sentiment, yet nevertheless capital offenses, in sharp contrast to the law in England, were in general reduced to four: murder, treason, arson, and rape, the last rarely charged against whites. The number of executions plummeted from a peak of perhaps thirty-five per one hundred thousand of the colonial population annually to about three or four. Blacks were still victimized disproportionately, but even slaves were not often hanged, given such alternatives as transportation farther south. The northern states, too, eliminated such irrationalities as "benefit of clergy," and by the 1820s were build-

ing reformatory penitentiaries as alternatives. Low, nonthreatening homicide rates among whites helped fuel this new movement. By the 1830s and 1840s, in a new era of Romantic reform, the voices first raised against capital punishment in the Revolutionary era had become a chorus.

Appeal to the Bible, as the dominant Calvinism gave way to less literal versions of Protestantism, was no longer enough; the Book of Leviticus, it was noted, provided death for a whole range of offenses, from adultery through gathering sticks on the Sabbath, which were no longer thought worthy of capital punishment. Reformers appealed not only to humane sentiment but to a new weapon, social statistics, to show that capital punishment had no real deterrent effect. And all could see that the ongoing revolt against official authority that marked much of American history had long undermined the moral effect of the ancient hanging rituals: last meal, followed by last words and clerical benediction or sermon. Where once contrition had been the invariant rule, now fierce denial was often heard; by the time of the early Republic, the printed pamphlets that accompanied every major execution were not reaffirming but challenging the whole procedure, suggesting the innocence of the accused, while clerics on the gallows often commanded more derision than respect. Furthermore, a competent hanging required calculating the drop needed (based on body weight) to break a convict's neck, causing instant death, but few hangmen outside of slave country had much experience; a few convicts were decapitated by a long drop, whereas a short drop, more commonly, left men to strangle violently for several minutes, their breeches soaking, while the crowd hooted.

All agreed that public hanging was a brutalizing spectacle, and reformers considered it an affront to human dignity. Pennsylvania in 1834 led the way in conducting executions behind prison walls, a move that quickly spread north, east, and west. Several southern states began a movement to make death a discretionary judgment by the jury, which would use its own criteria, even in first-degree murder cases. Virtually all states required a waiting period, after a signed warrant from the governor. In 1846 Michigan, followed shortly by Wisconsin and Rhode Island, eliminated capital punishment altogether. This was the peak of the nineteenth-century opposition movement.

Renewed Popular Support

Beginning in the 1830s and 1840s, mass Irish immigration, mob violence, Colt revolvers, and the heightened racial tension preceding the Civil War all contributed to rising homicide rates and mounting middle class fears. Penny papers and the *National Police Gazette* fed an increasingly literate public on crime news. Even in peaceful New Hampshire, in 1844, a unique referendum proposing the elimination of the death penalty was voted down two to one. For the rest of the century, with poorly run penitentiaries having long lost their luster and fears of labor violence scaring northerners just as the need to suppress freed blacks obsessed southerners, the abolition movement sputtered. And although the number of legal hangings, from which the public was barred, continued slowly to decline, especially in the industrial North, sensational newspapers fed readers' appetites for the ancient ritual. The only real innovation was the advent of the electric chair, billed as a humane alternative to the gallows, a proposition hard to sell to those reporters and officials who on 6 August 1890 watched William Kemmler die amid sparks, smoke, and the odor of burning flesh at New York's Auburn prison.

The technological efficiency of the electric chair nonetheless appealed to the Progressive movement, and early in the twentieth century the chair rapidly replaced the noose across most states. At the same time the prestige of social science, which generated new statistics about the death penalty's lack of deterrence, and the fundamental humanitarianism of the movement, prompted nine new states to end capital punishment altogether and several more to make it discretionary rather than mandatory. But although this second wave of abolition lasted longer than the first, it died, together with the Progressive movement itself, during World War I and its aftermath, as violent emotions led not only to race riots and the Red Scare of 1919 but to reinstitution of the death penalty in four western states that had just abolished it. In some states new capital offenses, such as assault by a life prisoner, were in fact added to old ones, almost never invoked, such as arson, burglary, train wrecking, and in some southern states obsessed with black-white sexual relations, "carnal knowledge." There was no real decline in the proportionate number of executions, which continued to hover round two per one hundred thousand annually, as it had since the late nineteenth century.

Not only the usual sex-and-violence killers but also bootleggers and then bank robbers generated more crime news than ever in the 1920s and 1930s.

Two cases in particular focused on the death penalty. In a Chicago courtroom in the summer of 1924, Clarence Darrow built his entire defense of the brilliant but "morally insane" teenage "fun killers" Nathan Leopold and Richard Loeb around a multi-pronged attack on capital punishment. Whereas the judge's decision to spare Leopold and Loeb on account of their youth was highly unpopular, the 1927 execution of Nicola Sacco and Bartolomeo Vanzetti (two anarchists convicted of a 1920 robbery and murder in Massachusetts) was widely approved, despite huge demonstrations in protest. A few states followed Nevada, beginning in 1921, in moving to lethal gas chambers; but whatever the method, support was strong. The kidnap-murder of twenty-month-old Charles A. Lindbergh, Jr., in 1932 led the majority of states to add kidnapping to the list of their capital offenses, and several convicted kidnappers were put to death.

The nation emerged from World War II with less racial and economic turmoil than had followed World War I. As the result of the Cold War, the most publicized executions of the period involved not killers but spies—Ethel and Julius Rosenberg, convicted of passing atomic-weapons secrets to the Soviet Union and electrocuted in 1953. But at home during the later 1940s and 1950s, a long period of full industrial employment helped to drive the annual murder rate to all-time lows—well below five per one hundred thousand. Homicides were not only rare but in effect "domesticated"—that is, compared to earlier eras, proportionately more of them involved fights with family, friends, and acquaintances, rather than strangers or robbers. In this nonthreatening atmosphere the last holdouts among the states moved to make capital punishment discretionary, and with the number of annual executions dropping to double digits by 1950 and a mere trickle in the early 1960s, public opinion polls showing rising opposition to the death penalty approached a majority. For the first time in decades, five states joined the abolition ranks, in 1965, making a total of eleven.

Law and Order

These moves occurred just as the nation entered the turmoil of the 1960s. During the war in Vietnam, urban riots and the assassinations of the Kennedy brothers and Martin Luther King, Jr., were accompanied by such repellent killers as the Boston Strangler, Richard Speck, and the Manson "family." With the loss of industrial jobs, too, the

A hanging in the early twentieth century. LIBRARY OF CONGRESS

ordinary homicide rate went up. Nineteen sixty-eight, the year in which the "law and order" issue helped Richard Nixon win the presidency, "was the first that no American officially suffered the death penalty; ironically it was also the last in which a majority of polled citizens opposed it" (Bowers 1984).

The effective suspension of executions was the work not of legislatures but of courts, which were impressed by new sets of arguments. For decades after *Powell v. Alabama* in 1932 eased the right of federal appeal in ordinary criminal cases, the U. S. Supreme Court had been sympathetic to the rights of defendants. During the 1960s lawyers for the National Association for the Advancement of Colored People presented overwhelming evidence that blacks suffered disproportionately from the death penalty. In 1968 *Witherspoon v. Illinois* held it unconstitutional to bar prospective jurors simply on the ground that they opposed capital punishment, a practice so routine that no state dared execute convicts until the rules were clarified. Finally,

in *Furman v. Georgia* in 1972, a bare majority of five justices ruled in effect against all existing state death penalty laws, partly on the grounds that execution had become so rare as to be "unusual" (and so barred under the Eighth Amendment prohibition against cruel and unusual punishments), and partly on the grounds that it had become a kind of lottery, in which juries might condemn one convict, often black, while freeing others guilty of nearly identical crimes.

With law and order now a winning political issue, the states scrambled to tighten their legislation, and in *Gregg v. Georgia* in 1976, the court upheld a law that spelled out carefully, in advance, special "aggravating circumstances"—such as murder for hire, or as part of robbery or rape—that would distinguish a capital case. Under intense media scrutiny, on 17 January 1977 the nine-year moratorium on execution was ended when the unrepentant robber-killer Gary Gilmore faced a firing squad in Utah, where the law had long called literally for blood atonement.

Later that year *Coker v. Georgia* ruled that death was a "disproportionate" penalty for rape, and one used almost exclusively against blacks in the South. Since then, first-degree murder under aggravating circumstances has been effectively the only capital offense in the United States. Whatever its actual applications, the death penalty has remained invulnerable to legislative attack because of the popular appeal of the crime issue. Although the homicide rate has rarely risen over its 1974 peak of 10.3 per 100,000, and began a marked decline in the middle of the 1990s, voters have been sensitive to increases in the kinds of killings that have historically scared or repelled them—serial murders, gang murders, mass murders, and, perhaps above all, ideologically driven murders such as the 1995 bombing of the Alfred P. Murrah Federal Building in Oklahoma City, which took 168 lives. Each election year since the mid-1980s the Congress has passed a crime bill that, among other things, has often made certain types of homicide, such as gangland hits or assassination of a federal officer, capital federal offenses. The most notable case was that of Timothy McVeigh, convicted in 1997 of the Oklahoma City bombing; he would in any case have been subject to death under state law.

The 1990s saw little serious argument about method, with lethal injection gaining on both the gas chamber and the electric chair. And with opponents of the death penalty largely reduced to battling for individual lives through postconviction legal pleas, supporters have decried the delay between sentence and execution, which by 1996 averaged fully eight years. The 1996 federal crime bill sought to meet this complaint by setting deadlines and limiting the number of federal appeals.

The rationale for capital punishment has shifted dramatically since the Middle Ages, but in practice some elements have remained relatively constant. Arguments against it have not changed greatly since the opposition was first heard over two centuries ago. The effectiveness of its use as a deterrent to further crime is still debated, indeed with increasing sophistication, opponents for the most part having more proof on their side. Simple revenge is now rarely cited in public or philosophical debate, nor is the Book of Genesis, although the demand for retribution is still a powerful force in practice. The Roman Catholic hierarchy is now the most visible organization that condemns capital punishment, as part of its insistence on life's sanctity; some governors and prosecutors have attempted to follow its teachings. In the late twentieth century, in fact, with the death penalty for practical purposes restricted to killers, both sides now emphasize the value of life—one arguing that killing by the state devalues life, the other that some kinds of murder require the most severe penalties. In the contemporary world this last position is expressed less in terms of atonement than of popular psychology: the need for "closure," public and private, as provided by the long-familiar final rituals, still carefully chronicled by the media. Jurors, too, of all faiths and none, despite the narrowed discretion allowed under *Gregg,* have continued to decide on death according to their own fears, values, and prejudices, many of which, except for the characteristically American emphasis on race, resemble those of the thirteenth century. Federal laws and many state laws now require a separate penalty trial after a murder conviction; such a trial provides legal sanction for jurors to do what they have always done, that is, to decide on emotional grounds, based on evidence about the lives and character of victims as well as of alleged killers, that in effect some lives are more valuable than others.

While blacks and women tend to be more opposed to the death penalty than whites and men, the capital punishment issue cuts across all the lines of race, religion, class, and gender. Under *Gregg* the actual number of annual executions should remain well under those of the 1930s and early 1940s, and, as always, should not match the number of crimes deemed capital offenses. In the late 1990s, in fact, several convicts on death row were conclusively proven innocent and freed through the highly publicized activities of law professors or journalists. Nevertheless, the curve has been rising raggedly since the 1970s. In a troubled nation, with a heavy majority of polled voters in its favor, capital punishment in the millennial era is very much alive and well.

BIBLIOGRAPHY

Bedau, Hugo Adam, ed. *The Death Penalty in America: Current Controversies.* New York: Oxford University Press, 1997.

Bowers, William J. *Legal Homicide: Death as Punishment in America, 1864–1982.* Boston: Northeastern University Press, 1984.

Lane, Roger. *Murder in America: A History.* Columbus: Ohio State University Press, 1997.

Gatrell, V. A. C. *The Hanging Tree: Execution and the English People, 1770–1868.* New York: Oxford University Press, 1994.

Teeters, Negley K. *Hang by the Neck: The Legal Use of Scaffold and Noose, Gibbet, Stake, and Firing Squad from Colonial Times to the Present.* Springfield, Ill: Charles C. Thomas, 1967.

ROGER LANE

See also **Crime and Punishment in American History; Cruel and Unusual Punishment; Death Row; Execution, Methods of; Gilmore, Gary; Nonviolence; Sacco-Vanzetti Case.**

CAPONE, AL
(1899–1947)

Al Capone is probably the most widely recognized name in organized crime. Born Alphonse Capone into modest circumstances in Brooklyn, New York, he was the fourth of nine children of Italian immigrant parents. Capone ended his formal education at age fourteen in the sixth grade when he assaulted his teacher, leaving school behind to further his education in the streets. He began his life of crime as a minor hoodlum. By his mid-twenties, he was able to boast that he "owned" Chicago. His organization, later known as the Outfit, at its peak had over one thousand members and numerous associates. His span of control, moreover, went far beyond the mob. Law-enforcement officials, politicians, agency heads at state and local levels, and even governors and congressmen made deals with Capone. His operation typified organized crime's potential for widespread corruption.

Capone had absolute control of criminal activities in an empire that included Chicago and most of its suburbs, most notably Cicero, Illinois. Capone was ever ready to meet competitors in warlike fashion. He designed and built a house in one suburb, Michigan City, Indiana, that operated in design and function as a safe house during wars with rival gangs. The house reflected Capone's

---

"Outfit" and Other Monikers of Organized Crime

The term *Outfit* is used exclusively to describe the Italian criminal organization based in Chicago. The "family" is most often used to describe the Patriarca mob that operates on the East Coast north of New York City. New York City's crime families are referred to by their respective leaders' names. Few mafiosi would refer to their group as the Mafia. The mob, the Mafia, and La Cosa Nostra are terms used most often by the popular press.

---

lifestyle: ostentatious (it had a hand-cut marble waterfall in the pool), pragmatic (the basement kitchen had gun-ports for windows), and "old-school" (there were six bocci courts in the backyard). Next door, the house of one of his lieutenants included a forty-car garage, concealed in the basement. The entire neighborhood, effectively a fortified compound, was designed and paid for by Capone.

His initiation into crime and violence began when, as a teenager, Capone was hired as a bouncer in a brothel owned by Johnny Torrio, a well-known Brooklyn mobster. In this capacity Capone received the knife wound from which came his nickname, Scarface. When Torrio relocated to Chicago, he took young Al along. Under the mobster's tutelage, Capone's rise to power seemed preordained. In the mid-1920s Jim Colosimo, the boss of the Outfit at the time, controlled the prostitution trade. Content with the income from vice, Colosimo was reluctant to traffic in prohibited liquor. Torrio and Capone disagreed, so they hired Frankie Yale to murder Colosimo. Later, when his mentor, Torrio, was badly wounded in a war with the O'Bannion gang, the twenty-six-year-old Capone inherited the criminal organization that would supply America with bootleg whiskey during Prohibition.

Although Capone's income was largely derived from the distribution of illegal alcohol, he controlled the entire vice sector in Chicago and environs. Once he became the boss, Capone realized that the successful management of the Outfit would require administrative skills and savvy. His impact has forever altered our perceptions of organized crime.

Capone operated on two major premises: give the people what they want—liquor, gambling, and prostitution—and make deals with whoever can further the ends of the Outfit; when that fails, eliminate the opposition forcibly. By 1929 the only surviving leader of the North Side mob of any notoriety was George "Bugs" Moran. To get rid of Moran, Capone concocted a scheme by which a mobster from Detroit contacted Moran about a load of illegal whiskey. Delivery was scheduled for a garage at 2122 North Clark Street on 14 February 1929. Posing as police officers, five of Capone's henchmen entered the garage and, using tommy-guns, shot seven of the North Side gang to death. Moran escaped, but the St. Valentine's Day Massacre effectively made Al Capone the crime czar of Chicago.

Al Capone, left, in Chicago being greeted by Chief of Detectives John Stege in March 1930. LIBRARY OF CONGRESS

Capone achieved an almost heroic status, probably because, in defiance of the authorities, he supplied alcohol during Prohibition. He has left us with the popular conception of a crime family as a hierarchical structure ruled by a powerful boss who possesses far-reaching criminal networks and the ability to violently eliminate all who oppose him. One characteristic of organized crime is its ability to endure even after its main income source and its leaders have disappeared; the organization put together by Al Capone still flourishes, a testament to his entrepreneurial as well as his organizational skill, however violent his methods may have been.

In the end Capone fell victim to federal law enforcement and a social disease. Although he could not be convicted for the St. Valentine's Day murders, the killings aroused intense pressure from federal law-enforcement agencies. In 1931 Capone was convicted for income tax evasion and sentenced to eleven years in prison. He began serving his time in Atlanta, and in 1934 he was transferred to Alcatraz in San Francisco Bay. By the time of his release in 1939, Capone's health had deteriorated greatly from a syphilitic condition contracted during his early years in Brooklyn. He retired to Miami Beach, where he died 25 January 1947.

BIBLIOGRAPHY

Abadinsky, Howard. *Organized Crime.* 5th ed. Chicago: Nelson Hall, 1997.
Ryan, Patrick J. *Organized Crime: A Reference Handbook.* Santa Barbara, Calif.: ABC-CLIO, 1995.
Sifakis, Carl. *The Encyclopedia of Crime.* New York: Smithmark, 1982.

PATRICK J. RYAN

See also **Chicago; Ness, Eliot; Organized Crime; St. Valentine's Day Massacre.**

CARJACKING

Since the first automobiles took to the roadways in the early twentieth century, auto theft has been a concern, notwithstanding the fact that early auto theft was hindered by the time-consuming auto-cranking needed to start the car. With few vehicles on the road in the early days, detection of stolen vehicles was not difficult. As mass production of vehicles increased, so did auto theft. According to Federal Bureau of Investigation statistics, 1.4 million vehicles were reported stolen in 1996. Because of nonuniform reporting by various police agencies throughout the country, the statistics do not reveal how many of these thefts were carjackings. An agency might classify a carjacking as a "joy ride," as "auto theft," or simply as "unauthorized use." It is also possible that one agency might classify an armed carjacking as "armed robbery," while another agency would identify the same type of crime as "auto theft." The classification might also depend on political funding.

While the term *carjacking* was coined during the 1990s, the somewhat similar crime of hijacking has been noted since the Prohibition era, when trucks transporting illegal alcohol were often hijacked. However, this form of hijacking diminished in 1933 with the repeal of the Eighteenth Amendment. Armored cars that transported large sums of money or other valuables have also been targets of hijackings, but bulletproof exteriors and armed drivers have helped to make such crimes rare. Before the automobile era, horses were the targets of theft instead of cars; in the 1990s carjackings became (often armed) confrontations to obtain a vehicle.

Purpose of Carjacking

Unlike ordinary car thieves, who break into unoccupied cars and steal the vehicle or parts without confrontation, armed carjackers prey upon their victims using whatever force is necessary to obtain the vehicle. The majority of carjacked vehicles are used for "joyriding" or to commit other crimes, including other robberies and drug transactions. (According to the 1993 *FBI Law Enforcement Bulletin* it has been estimated that 90 percent of the vehicles carjacked are eventually recovered.) Like most conventional auto thieves, some carjackers use "chop shops" to extract and sell stolen auto parts. Some carjackers strip the vehicles themselves for such unmarked parts as tires, wheels, stereos, batteries, air bags, and car phones—all of which can be sold on the street for easy profit. A few carjackers work for professional criminals who ship luxury cars out of the country. Some criminals may order luxury vehicles through intermediaries who purchase the stolen car directly from the carjacker.

In the 1990s, it was not uncommon for carjackers to demand such personal valuables as wallets, jewelry, and pocketbooks during the violent encounter. In 1996, for instance, in the Lake Tahoe region on the California-Nevada border, two carjackers blocked the roadway to force their victim to stop his vehicle. As one man remained in the roadway to prevent the vehicle from moving, the other thief produced a handgun and pulled the victim from his vehicle. The victim reported his wallet and two gold rings stolen, as well as his station wagon.

Carjacker Strategies

In the popular carjacking method known as "bump and rob," the thief stages a minor car accident with the victim. When the victim stops to investigate the damage, the carjacking takes place. Carjackers also fake personal injury or pretend to be stranded motorists in order to lure the victims into stopping their vehicle. Some carjackers stalk victims by waiting for them to return to their vehicle. This is often the method used by professional carjackers who have an "order" to steal a particular car.

Carjacking Statistics

By examining the characteristics of both victims and carjackers, we may be better able to make predictions and suggest precautions concerning carjackings. According to the U.S. Department of Justice National Crime Victimization Survey (1987–1992), which is based only on self-reported data, of the 35,000 annual carjackings (or attempted carjackings), the thief succeeded in stealing the vehicle 52 percent of the time. The 1994 National Crime Victimization Survey on Carjacking reported that each year, two in ten thousand people aged twelve and older were victims of an attempted or completed carjacking. Ninety percent of the completed and 60 percent of the attempted carjackings were reported to the police. Victims of carjackings were predominantly males under thirty-five.

In 77 percent of all attempted and completed carjackings, the offender(s) used a weapon. The most common weapon used was the handgun, which accounted for 59 percent of completed carjackings and 17 percent of those attempted. Victims were injured in 24 percent of the completed carjackings and in 18 percent of the attempted carjackings. Only 4 percent of all victims of attempted or completed carjackings suffered serious injury—gunshot or knife wounds, broken bones, loss of teeth, internal injuries, loss of consciousness, or undetermined injuries requiring two or more days of hospitalization.

The majority of carjackings took place on the street or in a garage area during evening hours. Approximately two-thirds of all carjackings occurred at night.

Eighty-seven percent of all carjackings were committed by men and 6 percent by men and women together; only 1 percent of all carjackings are committed by women alone. About 50 percent of the carjackers were between the ages of twenty-one and twenty-nine. More than half of all carjackings (54 percent) were committed by groups of two or more offenders. Accomplices often provided transportation to the scene or assisted in the robbery. People residing in urban areas were more likely to be victims of carjacking than those living in suburban or rural areas. Rural areas have the fewest attempted carjackings.

Method of Operation

Armed carjackers approach their victims using a variety of methods. Many armed confrontations have occurred while victims were at red lights,

Comparative Statistics

Statistics indicate that a person's lifetime chances of being carjacked (2 per 10,000) are minimal compared with other life-threatening events. For instance, the chances of being a victim of an assault (31 per 1,000 adults), being injured in a motor vehicle accident (25 per 1,000), being robbed (8 per 1,000), or dying of heart disease (5 per 1,000) all outweigh the possibility of becoming a carjacking victim. (U.S. Department of Justice, National Crime Victimization Survey, 1987–1992)

stop signs, fast food drive-through lines, automated teller machines (ATMs), self-service gas stations, convenience stores, parking lots, garages, shopping centers, pay telephones, private driveways, and self-service car washes. Some carjackers commit "home robberies" (combination burglary and robbery) where victims are confronted in their home and forced to turn over their valuables, including their car keys.

The following cases illustrate the diverse methods used by carjackers:

- On Tuesday, 8 September 1992, carjacking received national attention when Pamela Basu, a thirty-four-year-old woman, and her twenty-two-month-old infant daughter were carjacked near their suburban Maryland home. The carjackers forcibly removed Ms. Basu from her BMW while she was at a stop sign. While attempting to free her child, who was strapped into a baby seat, Ms. Basu's left arm became entangled in the vehicle's safety belt and she was dragged for approximately two miles. The carjackers stopped long enough to toss the baby, who was still strapped into the car seat, into the roadway. Ms. Basu was killed, but her daughter survived the tragedy.

- A twenty-year-old man was confronted on the steps of his Washington, D.C., home by robbers brandishing a handgun and demanding his car keys, wallet, and money. The carjackers fled in his 1986 Chrysler LeBaron.

- A Raleigh, North Carolina, man was abducted, beaten, and shot at by carjackers when he was approached in a parking lot while getting into his vehicle. The victim stopped when he heard one of the suspects yell, "Yo, man, don't I know you?" At that point, two accomplices held the victim at gunpoint and forced him into his car. They drove him to a dirt road, ordered him out of the vehicle, and pistol-whipped him. The carjackers fired six shots near the victim and then fled in his 1989 Subaru.

Motives

The motives for carjacking are debatable. One popular hypothesis concerns advances in vehicle manufacturer alarm and locking devices (known as the "anti-theft device" hypothesis). Many car thieves believe that the most effective way to obtain possession of a vehicle is to wait until the alarm system is deactivated by the driver. Since the 1980s and 1990s critics have proposed that crime prevention tactics are necessary and that car manufacturers and police agencies should continue their efforts to discourage auto theft through improved devices, such as Lojack and TeleTrac, which aid law enforcement in tracking and recovering stolen vehicles.

- The "desperation theory" proposes that carjackers act because vehicles represent instant cash and have immediate functional value. The vehicle or parts can be converted into cash for drug purchases or the vehicle can be used in other crimes.
- The "availability theory" assumes that carjacking is a crime of opportunity. Unlike conventional auto theft, carjacking requires little skill. Vehicles and their drivers are easy prey compared with other targets (especially since the proliferation of surveillance cameras).
- The "brazen theory" is based upon the arrogant self-confidence of carjackers, who often believe that they are invincible and that the police are not intelligent enough to apprehend them. Even FBI agents have been victims of carjackings, which have continued even after the carjackers recognized their victims' status.
- The "sociological theory" argues that the availability of guns in the United States affords greater opportunity to commit carjackings. Additionally, carjacking has become a status crime among thieves. Armed carjacking serves as a form of "one-upmanship"

Recommendations

The following carjacking-awareness techniques are recommended by most police agencies throughout the nation:

If loiterers are present in a parking lot or garage, do not approach your vehicle until they have left the area. If necessary, contact the police.

Check inside and under the vehicle before entering. Approach with keys in hand. (Keep house keys and car keys separate.)

Once inside the vehicle, lock all doors and secure all windows.

It is advisable to have a cellular phone (or CB radio) in your vehicle, but do not keep the registration card in the vehicle.

Be alert to your surroundings and be particularly suspicious of people who may approach your vehicle asking directions or soliciting money.

Always maintain sufficient distance between your vehicle and other vehicles at stoplights and stop signs to allow yourself free movement in case you are confronted.

Do not leave keys in the vehicle while stopped at a convenience store or gas station (13 percent of all stolen vehicles have the keys in the car).

Drive in the center lane. Rarely will a carjacker parade through lanes of traffic to steal a car.

Stay out of high-crime areas whenever possible. Take freeways whenever available.

If you believe that you may be a victim of a "bump and rob" scam, do not get out of your vehicle. Write down the license plate number and drive to the nearest police station. Communicate with the driver of the other vehicle via hand signals or by a note in the window.

Do not stop at isolated phones or ATMs.

Vary your routine. Some carjackers will look for a pattern in your behavior.

If an armed confrontation occurs, cooperate with the robber. Do not resist.

over the conventional car thief, providing achievement, danger, and challenge.

• The "depersonalization theory" proposes that some carjackers possess a total disregard for human life. It is a matter of the ends justifying the means.

The motives and theories presented are not exhaustive, nor are they mutually exclusive. Preventive measures may influence motives of carjackers. For instance, the Anti-Car Theft Act of 1992 made armed carjacking a federal offense. The act imposes severe penalties for convicted carjackers, including sentences up to life imprisonment if an armed carjacking results in death. Aside from legislation, it is imperative that citizens incorporate the necessary prevention measures to minimize the dangers of carjackings.

BIBLIOGRAPHY

Beekman, Mary Ellen. "Auto Theft: Countering Violent Trends." *FBI Law Enforcement Bulletin* 62 (October 1993).

Burke, Tod W., and Charles E. O'Rear. "Armed Carjacking: The Latest Nightmare." *Law and Order* (October 1992).

———. "Armed Carjacking: A Violent Problem in Need of a Solution." *Police Chief* (January 1993).

Donahue, Michael E., C. Vance McLaughlin, and Loretta V. Damm. "Accounting for Carjackings: An Analysis of Police Records in a Southeastern City." *American Journal of Police* 13, no. 4 (1994).

Rand, Michael R. "National Crime Victimization Survey: Carjacking." *U.S. Department of Justice, Office of Justice Programs, Bureau of Justice Statistics*, NCJ-147002 (March 1994).

"Two Teens Charged in Carjacking." *Washington Post*, 1 October 1997.

Tod W. Burke

See also **Road Rage.**

CARTOONS. *See* Comics; Film: Animation; Television: Children's Television.

CASSIDY, BUTCH, AND THE SUNDANCE KID
Cassidy (1866–c. 1909); Sundance Kid (1870–c. 1909)

Butch Cassidy was born Robert LeRoy Parker on 13 April 1866. Living with his nine brothers and sisters on a small farm in Utah, he was raised in the Mormon faith by his caring parents. To the disappointment of his family, Cassidy began his career as a cattle rustler during his friendship with neighbor Mike Cassidy, from whom Butch would later take the name Cassidy. After he met well-known robbers Matt Warner and Tom and Bill McCarty in Robber's Roost, Utah, he graduated to train and bank robberies. A remarkably skilled gunman, Butch Cassidy was reluctant to use his gun. He had an easygoing, calm, and friendly nature. Even in his years as an outlaw, he was known as an honest man with a good sense of humor.

Harry Longabaugh, the Sundance Kid, who was known to have a similar personality, had served time in the Sundance, Wyoming, jail, from which he received his nickname. Longabaugh, along with his two sisters and brother, had been raised in Pennsylvania by his parents. It is possible that he and Cassidy worked together as early as 1889, in the robbery of the bank in Telluride, Colorado. The two men met many of their future accomplices at the Hole-in-the-Wall, a common Wyoming hideout for western outlaws of the time. Together, the group became known as the Wild Bunch and became famous for their daring robberies. Cassidy was the leader at first, but the group was so loosely organized that it was not unusual for members to split off into smaller groups or to go out on their own for various jobs. The group included William Carver, Harvey Logan (better known as Kid Curry), O. C. Hanks, Ben Kilpatrick, Elzy Lay, and many more well-known criminals. Kid Curry was

known for being trigger-happy, and Cassidy was rumored to have intervened frequently to save the lives of innocent victims. In a train robbery in Wilcox, Wyoming, the Wild Bunch used dynamite to blast a train car and empty the safe. The train car was completely demolished.

In 1900 five of the members sat for a group photo. It was a virtual gift to lawmen, into whose hands it quickly fell. The photo helped in the quick capture of many of the men pictured. In an attempt to give up their life of crime and evade the law, Butch Cassidy and the Sundance Kid moved to South America with Sundance's girlfriend, Etta Place, who had assisted the men in their robberies. They returned to bank robbing in South America, and in 1909 they made their final stand near San Vicente, Bolivia. Trapped in a cabin by lawmen, the two men were presumed to have been shot and killed after a long shoot-out. Many claim that Cassidy escaped and lived for another twenty-eight years. Others contend that the men killed were not Cassidy and Sundance and that the two retired,

A portrait of the Wild Bunch, around 1900. Seated left to right: the Sundance Kid, Ben Kilpatrick, Butch Cassidy. Standing from left: William Carver, Kid Curry. CORBIS/ JONATHAN BLAIR

having evaded the law forever. In any case, Butch Cassidy and the Sundance Kid quickly became legendary outlaws, later immortalized in films such as *Butch Cassidy and the Sundance Kid* (1969), which portrayed Cassidy and Sundance as a comedic and charismatic pair. Viewed as Robin Hoods of the Old West, they appealed to the growing sixties culture of nonviolence and defiance of authority.

BIBLIOGRAPHY

Meadows, Anne. *Digging Up Butch and Sundance.* New York: St. Martin's, 1994.

O'Neill, Eamonn. *Outlaws: A Quest for Butch and Sundance.* Edinburgh, U.K.: Mainstream, 1997.

Patterson, Richard M. *Butch Cassidy: A Biography.* Lincoln: University of Nebraska Press, 1998.

TRACY W. PETERS

See also **Frontier; Gunfighters and Outlaws, Western.**

CATHOLICS

Fear and hatred of Catholics was for centuries a staple of American life. In the colonial era this was especially the case in New England, whose Puritan settlers had left Europe to distance themselves from the Catholic trappings of the Church of England. That the colonists' principal enemies—the French and the Spanish—were also Catholics further contributed to colonial anti-Catholic sentiment and convinced English settlers that English North America was threatened by their enemies' desire to spread Catholicism there.

Although overt American anti-Catholicism waned during and after the American Revolution, it revived and became violent in the 1830s owing to a number of factors. The Catholic presence in the United States began to grow as immigration from predominantly Catholic Ireland increased. The spread of the Second Great Awakening (a resurgence of Protestant religious enthusiasm) during the 1830s was also important, because the movement's leading ministers cited Catholicism as an evil whose persistence would impede the coming of the millennium. One of the staples of this anti-Catholicism was the belief that the cloistered secrecy of Catholic convents made them "hotbeds of lust and debauchery" where priests could exercise the most "shocking licentiousness and most unmitigated despotism over the hearts, minds, and persons of the nuns" (according to anti-

Catholic publications of the 1850s). Thus, the first large-scale anti-Catholic violence in the United States was aimed at a convent. In August 1834 a mob in Charlestown, Massachusetts (just across the Charles River from Boston), burned the Ursuline convent there after a rumor spread that priests were confining a nun against her will.

Educational Disputes

As the Catholic population of the United States continued to increase, animosity against Catholics spread to the political realm. Much of nineteenth-century anti-Catholicism stemmed from Catholic dissatisfaction with American public schools. In most schools Protestant hymns and prayers were recited, the Protestant King James Bible was read in the classroom, and textbooks were tinged with anti-Catholic biases. Some Catholics asked that the Bible no longer be read in the schools and that the hymns and prayers be eliminated. Others instead asked that the state finance Catholic parochial schools. Much of the anti-Catholic violence of the antebellum years resulted from these educational disputes. In 1842, the year these issues were first addressed by New York lawmakers, riots broke out between Protestants and Catholics during an April election in New York City. The rioters attacked both Catholic voters and the home of John Hughes (a Catholic bishop whose outspoken stand on educational issues had infuriated many Protestants), damaging windows, furniture, and blinds before police drove them off in what one observer called "a grand no-popery riot."

Inspired by Hughes's efforts in New York, the Philadelphia bishop Francis Kenrick pressed school officials to allow Catholic students to use the Catholic Douay Bible during school Bible reading. The school board voted down Kenrick's request, but the school director in the predominantly Irish-Catholic suburb of Kensington defied the board and ordered Bible reading stopped anyway. When Protestants tried to organize an avowedly anti-Catholic political party in Kensington to ensure that Bible reading remained part of the curriculum, these efforts were violently rebuffed by the suburb's Irish-Catholic inhabitants; skirmishes between the two groups in May 1844 escalated into a bloody three-day riot, in which Protestants burned and destroyed two Catholic churches. In July, after Protestants found guns stored in a Catholic church in the Southwark neighborhood, another riot erupted in which thirteen were killed and more than fifty were seriously injured.

The potato blight in Ireland, which first appeared in 1845, led to widespread starvation and dramatically increased the number of Irish Catholics immigrating to the United States. By the early 1850s record numbers of Germans (a majority of whom were Catholics) immigrated to the United States as well. Consequently, the educational controversies revived, again with violent consequences. In mid-1854 a Catholic priest in Ellsworth, Maine, who had incurred the wrath of Protestants by telling Catholic children not to participate in school Bible readings, was tarred and feathered and carried out of town on a rail.

Political Problems

Protestant Americans increasingly believed that Catholics posed a political as well as an educational threat. Catholics would soon make up the majority of citizens in large immigrant cities such as New York, and Protestants believed that the tendency of Catholics to follow the dictates of their priests and the pope did not give them the independence of thought necessary for the ideal citizen in a republic. Consequently, when the papal nuncio Gaetano Bedini visited the United States in the winter of 1853–1854, the possibility that he might forge diplomatic relations between the United States and the papal states led riotous mobs to assail him in Wheeling (Virginia, now a part of West Virginia), Pittsburgh, Baltimore, and Cincinnati. Many (and in some cases most) of those who demonstrated against Bedini's visit were themselves immigrants, sometimes Protestants but often lapsed Catholics whose devotion to the church had ended when the pope acted to prevent the formation of republics in Italy, Hungary, and the German states.

The best-known manifestation of anti-Catholicism in the 1850s, the Know-Nothing Party, was not an overtly violent organization. One of its founders' most consistent criticisms of Irish-Catholic immigrants was that they had made violence an endemic part of American elections, a charge that had some foundation in truth. In some places, however, Know-Nothings and Catholics engaged in ugly election-day clashes for control of the polling places. In the autumn and winter of 1854–1855, bloody riots took place in cities such as Brooklyn, New Orleans, and St. Louis. In some others, such as Lawrence, Massachusetts, and Baltimore, Know-Nothings seemed to bear most of the blame, while in Louisville and Cincinnati, Catholics seem to have been the instigators of the violence.

The climax of Catholic-Protestant violence in the United States came in New York in 1870 and 1871. When members of Protestant-Irish "Orange" lodges paraded on 12 July 1870 to celebrate the anniversary of the victory of the Protestant prince William of Orange (thus the lodge names) over the Catholic king James II at the Battle of the Boyne in 1690, Irish Catholics objected to this celebration of Protestant ascendancy in Ireland. The ensuing melee between the two groups left six dead. A year later, New York's mayor tried to ban the scheduled Orange march, only to be overruled by the governor. When Catholics attacked the marchers, troops fired at the predominantly Catholic crowds that lined the path of the march, and in the fighting that followed sixty were killed.

The Orange riots marked the end of large-scale violence against Catholics inspired specifically by their religion. Catholics were still subject to attacks in the late nineteenth and early twentieth centuries, but attackers tended to choose victims because they were Italian or Filipino rather than because they were Catholic (in fact, in some cases the attackers themselves were Catholics of Irish ancestry). The revived Ku Klux Klan of the 1920s also targeted Catholics, but not with the same violence they aimed at African Americans. Although specifically anti-Catholic violence has faded from the collective memory of most Americans, it was once an important facet of U.S. history.

BIBLIOGRAPHY

Billington, Ray A. *The Protestant Crusade, 1800–1860: A Study of the Origins of American Nativism.* Chicago: Quadrangle, 1938.

Feldberg, Michael. *The Philadelphia Riots of 1844: A Study in Ethnic Conflict.* Westport, Conn.: Greenwood, 1975.

Gordon, Michael A. *The Orange Riots: Irish Political Violence in New York City, 1870 and 1871.* Ithaca, N.Y.: Cornell University Press, 1993.

TYLER ANBINDER

See also **Irish Americans; Religion.**

CENTRAL INTELLIGENCE AGENCY

On 7 December 1941 Japanese warplanes struck Pearl Harbor in a surprise attack. Five U.S. battleships and two destroyers sank at their piers; two hundred aircraft were damaged; more than two thousand soldiers, sailors, and civilians died. Stunned by this sudden use of violence by the

Japanese military against the U.S. fleet, the government of the United States vowed to improve its intelligence capabilities as soon as possible. Investigations into the disaster at Pearl Harbor indicated that intelligence about a possible Japanese strike lay buried in the bowels of the U.S. bureaucracy but had never been consolidated and provided to the White House or even key naval officers. Clearly America required a more extensive intelligence apparatus, with less institutional fragmentation and greater coordination.

The exigencies of World War II delayed major intelligence reform, but after the war the Truman administration proposed the creation of an agency that could provide the president with more sophisticated and better coordinated intelligence. The National Security Act of 1947 established the Central Intelligence Agency, to be led by a director of central intelligence. For the first time in American history, the nation had a well-funded strategic intelligence agency with the ear of the president, an agency conceived in the crucible of violence at Pearl Harbor and soon to have a violent agenda of its own.

The CIA's statutory mandate was to gather, evaluate, and disseminate intelligence within the federal government, reporting to the president through the newly created National Security Council (NSC). An ambiguous catchall phrase included in its founding law allowed the president and the NSC to use the CIA for the performance of "other functions and duties" beyond those related to its core mission of intelligence collection and interpretation ("analysis" in spy argot). Within months the Truman administration relied on this wording to turn the CIA in quite a different direction. In addition to its collection and analysis duties, the new agency was charged with a leading role in the incipient war against global communism.

The Truman Doctrine of 1947 vowed that the United States would "help free peoples to maintain their free institutions and their national integrity against aggressive movements seeking to impose on them totalitarian regimes." A cold war had begun against America's erstwhile ally, the Soviet Union. The United States aimed to contain the spread of communism through a variety of overt means: political, economic, propaganda, and, if necessary, military (as with the Berlin airlift); the CIA became the spearhead for many similar activities conducted in a secret fashion known by intelligence officers as "covert action."

This new mission for the CIA, never explicitly stated in the National Security Act, soon took on a life of its own. An extensive covert-action bureaucracy grew inside the agency and in its embassy-based "stations" in almost every country. As the Cold War intensified, funding priorities shifted from collection and analysis to covert action as the CIA engaged (at the president's behest) in a broad range of secret political, economic, propaganda, and paramilitary activities designed to thwart the spread of communism. The agency was charged with accomplishing its goals by any means necessary.

From the relatively benign task of spying overseas, the CIA had become an aggressive warrior in the Cold War against the Soviets that transfixed U.S. national security officials. As a now-declassified, top-secret study from the Hoover Commission stated in 1954:

> It is now clear that we are facing an implacable enemy whose avowed objective is world domination by whatever means and at whatever cost. There are no rules in such a game. Hitherto acceptable norms of human conduct do not apply. If the U.S. is to survive, long-standing American concepts of "fair play" must be reconsidered. We must develop effective espionage and counterespionage services. We must learn to subvert, sabotage and destroy our enemies by more clear, more sophisticated and more effective methods than those used against us. It may become necessary that the American people will be made acquainted with, understand and support this fundamentally repugnant philosophy.

If the Soviet secret services, the KGB and the GRU (military intelligence), would play tough, so would the CIA.

The most critical duel was over hearts and minds: the use of propaganda to sway the world toward Western, democratic doctrines and against the beguiling slogans of Marxism. A second category, political covert action, involved helping pro-U.S. factions win democratic elections around the world or promoting pro-Western dictators when necessary—sometimes by organizing rallies that turned violent. Economic covert action, in its extreme forms, included the mining of enemy harbors to disrupt commerce (Vietnam), inciting labor strikes (Chile), and dynamiting electrical power lines and storage tanks (Nicaragua). On occasion, the results of the CIA's interventions were less sanguine than expected; the Iranian Shah proved an unpopular leader, and governments in Vietnam, Guatemala, Chile, and Nicaragua (among other locations) remained dictatorial and often unresponsive to the agency's wishes.

Ratcheting up the violence further, the CIA employed paramilitary activities as well—nothing less than full-scale secret wars against indigenous Communists in places like Iran (1953), Guatemala (1954), Cuba (1960–1962), Laos (1963–1973), Nicaragua (1983–1987), Afghanistan (1980–1988), and Iraq (1994–1999). In Afghanistan the CIA introduced advanced shoulder-held Stinger missiles capable of bringing down Soviet aircraft (several of the missiles have never been recovered by the agency). During the Vietnam War the CIA conducted the Phoenix Program, a counterintelligence plan to subdue Communists in the South Vietnamese countryside. Many Communists died as a result of this program, although these casualties were considered part of the open warfare in which the United States pitted itself against the North Vietnamese government and its surrogates in South Vietnam.

The CIA also attempted a series of assassination plots against pro-Moscow leaders in the developing world, including Fidel Castro of Cuba (1961–1962) and Patrice Lumumba of the Congo (1961). Castro eluded his assassins, and Lumumba was killed by a rival African faction apart from the CIA's plotting. By executive order in 1976, President Gerald R. Ford prohibited assassination plots.

The CIA has suffered sharp criticism for its activities, especially for the excesses of its domestic spying in the 1960s and its involvement in the Iran-Contra affair in the 1980s. For the most part, however, the agency has proven to be a valuable tool for presidents in the war against foreign enemies, from KGB agents during the Cold War to modern-day terrorists. Although not particularly large (its budget is about $3 billion, or around 10 percent of the total U.S. funding for intelligence), the CIA is the president's preeminent secret instrument in the defense against hostile threats to the United States.

BIBLIOGRAPHY

Johnson, Loch K. *America's Secret Agencies: U.S. Intelligence in a Hostile World.* New Haven, Conn.: Yale University Press, 1986.

Snepp, Frank. *Decent Interval.* New York: Random House, 1979.

Stockwell, John. *In Search of Enemies: A CIA Story.* New York: Norton, 1978.

Treverton, Gregory F. *Covert Action: The Limits of Intervention in the Postwar World.* New York: Basic, 1987.

Turner, Stansfield. *Secrecy and Democracy: The CIA in Transition.* Boston: Houghton Mifflin, 1985.

LOCH K. JOHNSON

See also **Cold War; Contras; Federal Bureau of Investigation; Military Interventions: Overview.**

CHICAGO

From its founding in the 1830s as a western outpost of the young American republic, Chicago has been the location of considerable violence. As the city grew from a small boomtown to the great metropolis of the Midwest, its growing pains often took a violent form. Labor upheavals, organized crime, racial strife, and political violence have all made their mark on Chicago.

Labor Struggles

Perhaps the most persistent form of violence in Chicago's history resulted from the changing relationship between workers and bosses as the nation industrialized over the nineteenth century. Chicago's tremendous growth and rapid industrialization made it the stage upon which the nation's struggles between labor and management played out.

During the summer of 1877, a national rail strike that had started in the East shut Chicago down as workers from numerous industries walked off the job in solidarity with the railroaders. Over the course of weeklong actions and skirmishes, Chicago police killed nearly thirty strikers and sympathizers before the strike finally failed. Nine years later, a strike at the McCormick Reaper Works again brought Chicago's workers to national attention. Violence erupted between police and strikers in the morning hours of 3 May 1886 after the strikers tried to block the path of strikebreakers. Numerous injuries to strikers outraged Chicago's radicals. A small group of anarchists planned reprisals. The following night, as police sought to clear Chicago's Haymarket Square at the end of an evening rally for strikers, a bomb was thrown amid the officers and exploded. In the ensuing confusion, one officer was killed (six more died later from injuries suffered in the melee) and sixty others were injured, many as a result of guns fired by panicked officers.

The attack proved disastrous for the labor movement and for radicals throughout the United States. The strike collapsed, and revolutionaries

What was meant to be a peaceful antiwar protest in Chicago during the 1968 Democratic National Convention turned violent when demonstrators clashed with police. LIBRARY OF CONGRESS

and radicals throughout the nation faced increased persecution. In Chicago, although the bomb throwers were never apprehended, thirty-one indictments were handed down in connection with the bombing. Of the eight men—identified as anarchist labor leaders—tried, all were convicted. Four were hanged, and one committed suicide when an appeal postponed execution. Although in 1893 the governor of Massachusetts pardoned the three anarchists who had been sentenced to life in prison for the Haymarket riot, the legacy of the event silenced would-be activists and critics nationwide. Many saw the Haymarket disaster as a loss of innocence for America; no longer was the nation immune to the kinds of rancorous and violent class conflicts that had been associated with Europe.

Chicago was the site of another major labor action in 1894. A strike at the railcar factory in the company town of Pullman began 11 May and garnered support from workers around the nation. Strikers held out for months during an armed and often tense standoff with police and factory security forces. Finally, federal troops were called out by President Grover Cleveland, who applied the Sherman Anti-Trust Act to labor for the first time. Federal involvement outraged strikers and sparked citywide looting and violence until the

leaders were arrested, and the strike ended in failure on 2 August.

Al Capone and Organized Crime

In the 1920s, after passage of the Volstead Act in 1919 led to the enforcement of Prohibition, Chicago developed a reputation as a gangland. A young New York mobster, Al "Scarface" Capone, saw an opportunity in the then underdeveloped rackets of the city. Aided by a pliable City Hall, bootleggers and racketeers came to rule Chicago through violence and intimidation. During the 1920s, more than five hundred mobsters were shot in Chicago. On 14 February 1929 Capone lieutenants posing as police officers machine-gunned several members of the rival bootlegger George "Bugs" Moran's gang in a city garage. Dubbed by the press the "St. Valentine's Day Massacre," the attack brought Chicago's organized crime—and Capone himself—to the eyes of the nation. Capone reveled in his new fame, hired journalist Damon Runyon as his publicist, and proceeded to lead a very swank and public life. Despite the best efforts of Capone's nemesis, Treasury agent Eliot Ness and his team of "Untouchables," Capone's criminal career ended in 1931 with a conviction for the decidedly unglamorous and nonviolent crime of tax fraud.

Race Riots and Ethnic Violence

Racially and ethnically motivated violence also scars Chicago's history. The Lager Beer Riots of 1855 began as a protest by German saloonkeepers angered over the enforcement of Sunday closing laws. The foreign-born barmen felt that Mayor Levi Boone, a supporter of the anti-immigrant Know-Nothing Party, had singled them out for persecution. When hundreds of saloonkeepers were arrested, German Chicagoans flocked in protest to the courthouse, where they had a violent altercation with police that left at least one officer and one professor dead and scores wounded.

Although tensions among white ethnic groups remained a strong force in Chicago, it was racial difference that sparked the most violent outbursts. A long series of race riots began in the summer of 1919, after Eugene Williams, a young black man who was swimming in Lake Michigan, drowned from exhaustion after white children on the shore pelted him with rocks. When the story spread through town, the response was five days of rioting that left 291 people injured and 38 dead.

The 1960s saw a resurgence of racial violence both in Chicago and in cities around the nation. Both Puerto Rican and black Chicagoans rioted and found themselves targets of riots throughout the 1960s. The largest riot came following the assassination of Martin Luther King, Jr., in April 1968. Nine people were killed.

Political Violence

Chicago has also seen its share of politically motivated violence. A statue memorializing the police killed in the Haymarket Square riot has been the target of numerous symbolic attacks, with paint, bombs, and, in 1927, even a streetcar. The controversial statue was removed to Chicago police headquarters in 1972 to protect it from further attack.

Two Chicago mayors have fallen victim to assassins' bullets. Carter Harrison, Sr., was gunned down by a disgruntled office-seeker in October 1893. Forty years later, in 1933, a bullet meant for President Franklin D. Roosevelt felled Mayor Anton Cermak, who was riding beside the president in a Miami, Florida, motorcade.

Chicago's most famous moment of political violence, however, came in 1968. The demonstrations at the Democratic National Convention became one of the most contested and controversial protests of the 1960s. Led by antiwar "yippies" including Jerry Rubin and Abbie Hoffman, protesters sought to disrupt the convention and turn it into political protest theater. Mayor Richard Daley responded by deploying Chicago police to disperse the protesters. The nation watched as the demonstrations turned violent, with both police and protesters losing control in the melee. Described by one observer as "a police riot," the American public initially backed law-enforcement officers, seeing the yippies as an example of the decadence and selfishness of American youth. The violence surrounding the protests, and the ensuing trial of the instigators, dubbed by the press the "Chicago Seven," changed the tenor of both protest and political life in the nation. In a year of violence and confusion nationwide, the fiasco at

Whites pursue a black man during race riots in Chicago in 1919. Photographed by Jun Fujita. COURTESY OF CHICAGO HISTORICAL SOCIETY

the Chicago convention became a symbol of the increasingly confusing and rancorous public life of the nation.

BIBLIOGRAPHY

Avrich, Paul. *The Haymarket Tragedy*. Princeton, N.J.: Princeton University Press, 1984.

Bergreen, Laurence. *Capone*. New York: Simon and Schuster, 1996.

Cohen, Lizabeth. *Making a New Deal: Industrial Workers in Chicago, 1919–1939*. New York: Cambridge University Press, 1990.

Cronon, William. *Nature's Metropolis*. New York: Norton, 1991.

Farber, David. *Chicago '68*. Chicago: University of Chicago Press, 1988.

Miller, Donald L. *City of the Century*. New York: Simon and Schuster, 1996.

Painter, Nell Irvin. *Standing at Armageddon: The United States, 1877–1919*. New York: Norton, 1987.

Schoenburg, Robert J. *Mr. Capone*. New York: William Morrow, 1993.

MATTHEW TAYLOR RAFFETY

See also **Capone, Al; Giancana, Sam; Haymarket Square Riot; Organized Crime; Politics: Government; Riots; St. Valentine's Day Massacre; Urban Violence.**

CHICANO MORATORIUM

The Chicano Moratorium was primarily a protest movement against Chicano participation in the Vietnam War. Statistics demonstrated that a disproportionate number of young Chicano males were casualties of the war when compared with the percentage of resident Chicanos, particularly in Texas, California, and other states in the American southwest. Several draftees, among the first of whom (in 1963) were Rosalio Muñoz, Ernesto Vigil, and Sal Baldenegro, refused to be drafted into the Vietnam War. Community activists and organizations responded with preparations for protest. The Brown Berets (a group that utilized a militant image to promote community development and self-sufficiency for Latinos), with the support of the Chicano Youth Liberation Committee and Movimiento Estudiantil Chicano de Aztlán, formed the National Chicano Moratorium Committee in 1969. Immediately after the formation of this committee, several local moratorium marches took place in such areas as McAllen, Texas, and San Bernardino and East Los Angeles, California. In March 1970 at the second annual Chicano Youth Conference, the National Chicano Moratorium was planned for 29 August 1970 in East Los Angeles.

The national moratorium began as a two-and-a-half-mile march to the rallying ground at Laguna Park in East Los Angeles, where such prominent Chicano activists as César Chavez and Corky Gonzáles were scheduled to speak. Approximately twenty to thirty thousand people were in attendance. The event, which began peacefully, ended violently when police officers attempted to apprehend teenagers accused of shoplifting in nearby stores. The perpetrators escaped into the crowd at Laguna Park, and officers who had previously been standing outside the park entered the rally. In the ensuing confusion, protesters threw rocks and bottles at the officers while the police fired tear gas into the crowd and used clubs on individuals. The subsequent melee produced many injuries and three fatalities (Ángel Díaz, Lynn Ward, and Rubén Salazar). More than 250 rally participants were arrested. A subsequent riot in the surrounding area resulted in over $1 million in property damage.

The most notorious fatality was that of Rubén Salazar, a popular reporter for the *Los Angeles Times* and the news director of KMEX, a Spanish-language television station in Los Angeles. Salazar was with friends at the Silver Dollar Cafe on Whittier Boulevard when police officers, allegedly searching for a gunman, surrounded the building. There are varying reports on whether police ordered those within the bar to evacuate; in any event, it is known that people were still in the bar when two tear-gas projectiles were fired into the establishment. One of them, a ten-inch Flite Rite projectile, struck Salazar in the head and killed him instantly. Some believe that Salazar was intentionally killed in response to the increasingly activist stance he took in his articles. An inquest began on 10 September 1970; however, no criminal charges were filed against the officer who shot the projectile that killed Salazar. Because of inconsistencies in the police reports, many questioned the fairness of the inquest.

After the events of 29 August 1970, several demonstrations took place in other areas of Los Angeles, but these actions often turned into rioting and other violent activities and incurred the disapproval of the media. Later demonstrations were also unsuccessful in that they tended to turn popular support away from the demonstrators. Police harassment and media criticism were common, and the assemblies often ended violently and without resolving any problems. Nevertheless, the demonstrations did promote an awareness of difficulties within and surrounding the Mexican community. The National Chicano Moratorium Committee broadened the agenda of these protests to include issues of police harassment and brutality, low educational standards, and governmental harassment of Chicano immigrants. This organization remains dedicated to the uplifting of Mexican Americans.

BIBLIOGRAPHY

Acuna, Rodolfo. *Occupied America: A History of Chicanos*. 2d ed. New York: Harper and Row, 1981.

Borjon, Patricia, et al., eds. *La Raza* 1, nos. 1–3 (1970).

Castro, Tony. *Chicano Power: The Emergence of Mexican America*. New York: Saturday Review Press, 1974.

Griswold del Castillo, Richard, and Arnoldo De León. *North to Aztlán: A History of Mexican-Americans in the United States*. New York: Twayne, 1996.

Machado, Manuel A., Jr. *Listen Chicano! An Informal History of the Mexican-American*. Chicago: Nelson Hall, 1978.

ROSIE BANKS

See also **Antiwar Protests; Mexican Americans.**

CHIEF JOSEPH
(c. 1840–1904)

One of the most famous Indians in American history, Chief Joseph was born probably in 1840 near the Grande Ronde River in present-day northeast Oregon. Son of Old Chief Joseph (Tuekakas), a Cayuse-Umatilla, and Khapkhaponimi, a Nez Percé woman, Young Joseph was named Hinmahtooyahlatkekht (Thunder Rising over Loftier Mountain Heights). His parents had been married in 1839 by a Presbyterian missionary, Henry H. Spalding, who established a mission at Lapwai in 1836 near present-day Lewiston, Idaho. At the behest of his father, who had converted to Christianity, Young Joseph was baptized with the biblical name Ephraim. During his youth, the Wallowa band of Nez Percé in northeast Oregon numbered around three hundred people and spent their days in relative peace, breeding and herding horses, fishing for salmon, hunting, and gathering *camas* and other foods native to the plateau.

That peace was interrupted in 1847 when the missionary Marcus Whitman, his wife, Narcissa, and twelve other whites were killed by the Cayuse near present-day Walla Walla, Washington, following a severe outbreak of measles which killed many Indians and for which the missionaries were blamed. The Nez Percé remained neutral in the conflict, subsequently harboring several white survivors and conducting them to safety. In 1855, Governor Isaac I. Stevens gathered the region's chiefs together at Walla Walla for a treaty council. Old Joseph is reported to have carried a Bible at the convention and he, along with all other Nez Percé leaders present, agreed to cede land in exchange for a large reservation and the right to live, hunt, and fish on their former territory.

What began as a potentially workable solution to white demands for fertile farmlands and Native need to preserve sacred sites and resource habitats soon turned violent. The Yakima and other Columbia River tribes rose in revolt, feeling betrayed by Stevens, whose treaty had not been ratified by the U.S. Senate, but who had already opened up Indian lands for white settlement. The Nez Percé remained noncombatants in the Yakima War, which lasted from September 1855 to November 1856 and resulted in several dozen deaths on both sides. Soon thereafter, the Nez Percé experienced

Chief Joseph. HULTON GETTY/LIAISON AGENCY

trespass on their own reserved territory when in 1860 gold was discovered on their land. Hundreds of miners invaded the Nez Percé Reservation and a supply point was illegally established at Lewiston in 1861. By 1862, over eighteen thousand whites had settled on Nez Percé land. Fearing violence, federal Indian commissioners arrived in 1863, determined to reduce the size of the original 1855 Nez Percé Reservation. Old Joseph and two-thirds of the Nez Percé band chiefs refused to sign this second "steal (or thief) treaty" of 1863. However, cooperative headmen were designated as signatories for the entire tribe, and the reserve was reduced by seven million acres, leaving the Nez Percé approximately one-fourth of the lands originally negotiated in 1855.

Old Joseph died in 1871, having renounced Christianity and all treaties, at which time his people remained in the Wallowa Valley on their ancestral lands, but outside the official boundaries of the 1863 reservation. Hinmahtooyahlatkekht succeeded his father as chief of the Wallowa Band and was known thereafter as Chief Joseph by non-Indians. An 1873 executive order gave the title to the Wallowa Lake region to Joseph's descendants, but white homesteaders demanded that these fertile lands be renegotiated. In 1875, the Wallowa country was reopened to non-Indian settlement. A commission met with Nez Percé leaders in 1876 and recommended to the Indian Bureau that all nontreaty bands be persuaded to move into the formal 1863 reservation boundaries, and that they be forced to do so after 1 April 1877. General Oliver O. Howard was placed in charge of relocation.

A striking, broad-shouldered man possessing unusual oratorical skills, Joseph held his own against Howard, but he eventually acquiesced, arguing that it was "better to live at peace than to begin a war and lie dead." The die was cast before Joseph and his brother Ollokot, a warrior and leader of buffalo hunters, could move the entire band to Idaho. After leaving Oregon by crossing the swollen Snake River, where many horses and cattle were lost, the band rested at Tolo Lake, only a two-day ride from the Indian agency at Lapwai and not far from locations where whites had committed depredations and homicides against Nez Percé without subsequent prosecution. On 12 June 1877, several young Nez Percé killed the murderer of one of their relatives as well as three other whites in the Salmon River area. Joseph and Ollokot were absent from the camp. When they re-

turned, fourteen additional whites had been slain to avenge the deaths of at least forty Nez Percé in recent months at the hands of white ranchers and miners from settlements along the Snake and Salmon Rivers. The Nez Percé War had begun.

Fearing retribution, the Nez Percé sought refuge in White Bird Canyon, but were attacked by civilians and soldiers on 17 June. At the end of the day, thirty-four soldiers were dead, but only two Nez Percé were wounded and none were killed. Skirmishes and a battle within the new reservation boundaries on the Clearwater River in July convinced Nez Percé leaders that they would have no peace in Idaho. Joseph opposed continued violence and further flight and hoped to negotiate with Howard, but the war council, led by Looking Glass, overruled him. By now, the Nez Percé patriots consisted of 200 hundred men and approximately 550 women and children. They rounded up, packed two thousand horses, and fled toward the buffalo country in Montana, intent upon reaching friends among the Crow.

During the next four months, they trekked through Montana and Wyoming's Yellowstone country, pursued by O. O. Howard and Nelson Miles. A surprise attack against the Nez Percé encampment at the Big Hole River on 9 August left eighty-nine Nez Percé dead, mostly women and children. Sixty Nez Percé sharpshooters held off a superior force of the U.S. Seventh Infantry under Colonel John Gibbon, while Joseph led survivors out of immediate harm's way. By the end of the battle, thirty-three Nez Percé warriors had died killing thirty-one soldiers and wounding thirty-eight. Of the seventeen officers with Gibbon, fourteen were killed or wounded. Although Looking Glass survived this battle, faith in his leadership had been shaken. From this point on, the people placed more authority and responsibility in the hands of Chief Hototo (Lean Elk) and Joseph. By late September, a weary group of survivors struggled to reach the Canadian border, only forty miles away. They hoped to find refuge there with Sitting Bull's exiles, who had been given temporary sanctuary by the Royal Canadian Mounted Police after the Battle of Little Bighorn. A final battle in the Bear's Paw Mountains held off U.S. troops long enough for some Nez Percé to escape to Canada; 60 women, 8 children, and 103 men under the charge of Chief White Bird eluded detection and slipped across the border. On 5 October, with Ollokot and Looking Glass dead, Joseph was left with complete authority. Chief Joseph surrendered himself, 86 other men, 184 women, and 147 children, with a pledge from U.S. officials that his people could spend the winter on Tongue River and return to Idaho in the spring to live on their reservation in peace.

That promise was broken. For the next eight years, Joseph and most of his people remained prisoners of war in Indian territory, where many died of disease and despondency. In 1885, non-Christian Nez Percé were allowed to return to the Northwest, but not to the Wallowa Valley or to Lapwai. Joseph and 150 of his band were sent to the Colville Reservation in eastern central Washington, where the chief lived out the rest of his life and died—of a broken heart, it was reported—on 21 September 1904. By then, Joseph had raised an extended family and had made many friends in Washington and among Indian reform groups.

Ironically, among white Americans and Europeans, he was regarded as a celebrated war chief and was called the Red Napoleon. Today, Chief Joseph, America's favorite patriot chief of the late-nineteenth-century Indian wars, is remembered as a statesman and diplomat, an advocate of peace and justice who resorted to violence only to protect the women, children, and elderly in his care throughout the fifteen-hundred-mile ordeal of the Nez Percé in 1877.

BIBLIOGRAPHY

Gidley, Mick. *Kopet: A Documentary Narrative of Chief Joseph's Last Years*. Seattle: University of Washington Press, 1981.

Gulick, Bill. *Chief Joseph: Land of the Nez Percé*. Caldwell, Idaho: Caxton Printers, 1985.

Hinmahtooyahlatkekht (Chief Joseph). "Chief Joseph's Own Story." *North American Review* 128 (April 1879): 412–433.

Howard, Oliver O. *Famous Indian Chiefs I Have Known*. New York: Century Company, 1907.

Josephy, Alvin M., Jr. *The Nez Percé Indians and the Opening of the Pacific Northwest*. New Haven, Conn.: Yale University Press, 1965.

McWhorter, Lucullus V. *Hear Me My Chiefs! Nez Percé History and Legend*. Caldwell, Idaho: Caxton, 1952.

Slickpoo, Allen P., Sr., with Deward E. Walker, Jr. *Noon Nee-Me-Poo (We, the Nez Percés): Culture and History of the Nez Percés*. Lapwai, Idaho: Nez Percé Tribe of Idaho, 1973.

Trafzer, Clifford E. *The Nez Percé*. New York: Chelsea House, 1992.

WILLIAM R. SWAGERTY

See also **American Indian Wars.**

CHILD ABUSE

*This entry is dividied into three parts: **Physical, Ritual, and Sexual.***

PHYSICAL

Examples of extreme physical child maltreatment can be found throughout history, but the 1874 case of Mary Ellen, a ten-year-old girl who was severely beaten and neglected by her parents, was one of the first to receive widespread newspaper coverage. The case prompted the development of the Society for the Prevention of Cruelty to Children in 1874. Formal efforts to describe and combat the physical abuse of children, however, were not evident until the 1970s, as a consequence of the work of the pediatrician C. Henry Kempe and his colleagues. They described a pattern of nonaccidental physical injuries, termed the battered child syndrome, that they had observed in an increasing number of children presented at pediatric clinics. By 1970 mandatory reporting laws were adopted in the United States that require professionals (such as doctors or teachers) to report any suspected child abuse to the authorities. State-run agencies such as the Department of Social Services have been developed to investigate and handle such reports.

Definition and Description

The physical abuse of children is defined as any avoidable and nonaccidental act that causes physical injury to a child and is inflicted by someone who is responsible for that child's welfare. This may include acts such as scalding, beating with an object, slapping, punching, and kicking. Injuries may be minor (small cuts, welts, or bruises) or major (bone fractures or internal injuries). According to the 1994 U.S. Bureau of the Census, approximately 25 percent of all substantiated cases of child maltreatment involve physical abuse. This represents about 250,000 children for whom an abusive incident is reported, investigated, and confirmed each year. It is difficult to estimate the total number of children experiencing physical abuse, because of those cases that have not been reported to authorities, but studies using self-report measures (surveys, as opposed to counts of cases that are officially reported) have estimated victimization rates ranging from 300,000 to 1,500,000 in the United States each year (Finkelhor and Dziuba-Leatherman 1994).

Factors Contributing to Abuse

The psychological, biological, social, and environmental characteristics of both the abusive guardian and the child contribute to physical child abuse. These characteristics often work in combination to increase the risk of child abuse.

Characteristics of the Abusive Caregiver. Being abused as a child increases the chances of being an abusive parent or guardian. The parent who is abusive may have learned to behave aggressively, developed a hostile attitude toward others, or adopted a harsh philosophy of parenting in response to his or her own childhood experiences. There is also a greater incidence of abuse in families where the caregiver experiences a psychiatric or emotional disturbance, such as depression, anxiety, marital distress, or substance abuse. Such disturbances may diminish the caregiver's ability to cope with stress, which in turn may impair judgment and decrease impulse control, leading to parenting practices that are inadequate or hostile. Some abusive parents may have unrealistic expectations of their child's abilities. For example, a caregiver may overestimate a child's ability to control his or her emotions. When the child does not meet such expectations, an abusive caregiver may become frustrated or angry and any attempts at discipline may quickly escalate to abuse.

Some abusive parents may have a genetic predisposition to negative emotionality, psychiatric disturbance, or aggressive behavior, which may contribute to their ineffective parenting. Some experimental research has shown that physically abusive parents have a stronger physiological reaction to the sounds of children crying than do parents who are not abusive. These parents report feeling more irritated, more annoyed, and less sympathetic toward the child's crying. These studies suggest that abusive parents may be especially prone to react negatively in response to signals of a child in distress. It is unclear what causes this type of reaction to distress, but it could arise from a parent's own abuse in childhood, which in turn leads to oversensitivity to aversive signals and threatening stimuli, or the abusive parent may have a genetic predisposition for negative reactions and hostility.

Psychological and biological risk factors in caregivers need to be viewed within the social or environmental context in which the abusive relationship takes place. Social factors that increase the stress placed upon the family and decrease the family's ability to cope with such stress are associated with the physical abuse of children. Higher rates of abuse occur in families experiencing stress factors such as poverty, disorganization or chaos, crowding, frequent changes in residence, social isolation, and lack of social support networks. Young, single parents, while encountering the stresses of single-parenting, financial hardship, and social isolation, are especially vulnerable because they may have little knowledge of behavior appropriate to their child's age or of proper parenting skills. These factors may be compounded by a physiological inclination to react negatively to distress or by the presence of psychological difficulties such as emotional disturbances or the inability to avoid repetition of abusive behavior learned from childhood.

Characteristics of the Child. Characteristics of the child that increase his or her risk of being abused have also been delineated. These characteristics are intended to clarify possible parent-child interactions that could lead to abuse, rather than to place responsibility upon the child for the abuse. They are viewed as variables that make some children more challenging to raise than other children, and that therefore might increase negative behavior associated with parental frustration and stress in caregivers.

Psychological factors that place a child at risk include behavior problems such as a tendency to be distracted, hyperactive, impulsive, noncompliant, or aggressive. The direction of causality, however, is unclear. Some studies indicate that aversive child behavior can provoke coercive hostile parenting, while other studies find an increase in a child's behavior problems only after abuse has occurred. Regardless of timing, a child's behavior problems and negative parental responses are both heightened in abusive families and may have the effect of maintaining one another.

Biological risk factors for the child include age, physical health, and temperament. Very young children, from infancy to age four, are at greater risk of physical abuse than other age groups. Some possible explanations for the increased risk at these ages are the child's increased dependency on others for care, an increased vulnerability to physical injury, and a decreased capacity to regulate his or her emotions. All these factors serve to increase demands placed upon the caregiver, which can lead to increasing frustration and reactivity on the part of the caregiver. Physical health problems have been studied primarily in terms of premature birth and sleep difficulties in infancy. The high-pitched cries and irregular sleep patterns of these infants are thought to be potential elicitors of abuse in some caregivers, but results of the research are inconclusive. Finally, temperamental qualities of the child may be risk factors. For example, infants who are consistently irritable, difficult to soothe or to calm, and irregular in terms of sleeping, eating, and elimination may increase the chances of evoking hostile behavior from their caregivers.

Social factors regarding the child involve general societal and cultural attitudes toward violence and children. It has been suggested that the United States has a more tolerant attitude toward violence and physical punishment than other countries where child physical abuse is less common. Historically, physical punishment has been viewed as a disciplinary strategy that was necessary for the proper upbringing of children, and children were viewed as the property of their parents. Thus, parents were seen as having the right, even the duty, to treat their child severely, without intervention from others. Although these attitudes are changing, one may still hear today "spare the rod, spoil the child" or "what goes on in their family is none of my business." These general attitudes impact children by creating an atmosphere where acts of abuse can be tolerated or ignored.

Consequences of Abuse on Children

The physical abuse of children leads to both current difficulties as well as long-standing problems into adulthood for many children.

Biological and Psychological Consequences. Biological consequences of physical abuse that are experienced by children include medical problems, neurological or neuropsychological impairments, and unusual hormonal changes. Medical problems range from minor sprains and bruises to serious internal bleeding, broken bones, or even death. Concussions or blows to the head in these children can lead to neurological insult and neuropsychological problems that subtly impair academic capabilities, cognitive functioning, ability to plan ahead, impulse control, emotional regulation, and other self-regulating functions. Hormonal changes involve the stress-hormone cortisol, which is the primary hormone produced as part of the hypothalamic-pituitary-adrenal (HPA) axis controlled by the central nervous system. The few studies that

have examined cortisol in maltreated children included primarily both physically abused children and neglected children, as well as some sexually abused children. Results from these studies have indicated that the HPA system does not function normally in maltreated children, which may impair their ability to handle mildly stressful situations.

Psychological consequences of physical child abuse include an increased likelihood of experiencing depression, anxiety, and disruptive behavior disorders. It is estimated that 18 to 22 percent of physically abused children will meet criteria for a diagnosis of depression. Physically abused children are also more likely to experience low self-esteem, feelings of hopelessness, and suicidal or self-destructive behavior compared with non-abused children. Prolonged exposure to abuse, especially if coupled with sexual abuse, may lead to anxiety symptoms related to post-traumatic stress disorder. Some studies also have found higher rates of physical abuse in samples of children diagnosed with disruptive behavior problems, such as attention deficit hyperactivity disorder, oppositional defiant disorder (a pattern of negativity, hostile, and defiant behavior), and conduct disorder (a pattern of antisocial behavior). Physical abuse in childhood is also related to heightened rates of delinquency in adolescents.

Disruptive behavior problems can also be understood within the context of social difficulties experienced by physically abused children. These children tend to form insecure attachments with their caregivers, probably in response to the difficulties these parents have in providing a nurturing and sensitive environment for the child. Thus, the child approaches the world with an internal representation of others as hostile and threatening. Physically abused children also tend to be more aggressive toward other children and to perceive hostile intent from other children even in ambiguous situations. Other studies have indicated a lack of social sensitivity in abused children. Abused toddlers, for example, seem to show no sign of concern when witnessing the distress of other toddlers. Instead, abused toddlers tend to respond with fear, physical attack, and anger. This is reminiscent of studies in which abusive parents show stronger physiological reactions and irritability in response to infant crying and suggests that physically abused children in turn may be negative and hostile in reaction to the distress of others.

Long-term Consequences. Adults who have been abused as children are more likely to exhibit both nonfamilial and marital violence than are nonabused adults. This association seems especially strong for males, for those who also witnessed parental conflict and aggression, and for those with a concomitant neuropsychological impairment or psychosis. Furthermore, it is estimated that approximately 30 percent of physically abused and neglected children will grow up to inflict abuse on their own children. Substance abuse, including alcohol and drug use, also may be associated with a history of physical abuse, but studies indicate inconsistent results. Emotional problems in adults abused as children include self-injurious or suicidal behavior, depression, anxiety, somatization (physical complaints that are due to an emotional problem), dissociation, and psychosis. The association between child abuse and such emotional problems seems particularly strong for females. In addition to aggression and violence, interpersonal difficulties among abused adults include feeling shy and self-conscious around others, negative feelings about interpersonal interactions, feeling disliked and misunderstood by others, and overall excessive interpersonal sensitivity.

Future Directions

It is important to note that while the physical abuse of children substantially increases their risk for problems, many abused children are resilient to such adversity and grow up to lead healthy lives. As long as physical abuse continues to be an unfortunate reality in our society, future studies of these resilient children will be fruitful in understanding the factors that can protect children from the negative consequences associated with physical abuse. Moreover, scientific investigations on the causes and consequences of physical child abuse have delineated the influence of multiple biological, psychological, and social dimensions. Programs that address these multiple levels will be most effective in the future prevention and treatment of abuse.

BIBLIOGRAPHY

Barnett, Douglas, Jody T. Manly, and Dante Cicchetti. "Defining Child Maltreatment: The Interface Between Policy and Research." In *Child Abuse, Child Development, and Social Policy,* edited by Dante Cichetti and Sheree L. Toth. Norwood, N.J.: Ablex, 1992.

Belsky, Jay. "Etiology of Child Maltreatment: A Developmental-Ecological Analysis." *Psychological Bulletin* 114 (1993): 413–434.

Finkelhor, David, and Jennifer Dziuba-Leatherman. "Victimization of Children." *American Psychologist* 49 (1994): 173–183.

Kempe, C. Henry, et al. "The Battered Child Syndrome." *Journal of the American Medical Association* 181 (1962): 17–24.

Malinosky-Rummell, Robin, and David J. Hansen. "Long-term Consequences of Childhood Physical Abuse." *Psychological Bulletin* 114 (July 1993): 68–79.

Peterson, Lizette, and Deborah Brown. "Integrating Child Injury and Abuse-Neglect Research: Common Histories, Etiologies, and Solutions." *Psychological Bulletin* 116 (1994): 293–315.

Wekerle, Christine, and David A. Wolfe. "Child Maltreatment." In *Child Psychopathology,* edited by Eric J. Mash and Russel A. Barkley. New York: Guilford, 1996.

ANGELA SCARPA

See also **Corporal Punishment; Developmental Factors; Endocrinology: Hormones in Child Abuse.**

RITUAL

Ritual abuse of children is a brutal, recurrent, and nonaccidental injury (for example, physical or sexual abuse) that involves systematic beliefs or practices in communities within a magical, religious, or supernatural, but not necessarily satanic, context. Sexual abuse is the most prevalent type of ritual abuse. Typically, a trusted person exploits a relationship and persuades a child to engage in sexual activities and remain silent. The media highlight reports of rituals (such as animal sacrifices, drinking blood, and magical surgery), but tend to downplay or ignore less sensational and more common incidents.

In the United States, David Finkelhor estimated that 5.5 children are ritually abused per 10,000 day-care enrollees. He investigated 1,637 "verified" ritual abuse cases in 270 day-care settings with more than six children. These cases were selected because Finkelhor asserted that the thorough investigations by researchers and data collected confirmed (verified) the alleged ritual abuse. Finkelhor's research team retrospectively interviewed 193 original investigators and informants (about six per case). Researchers compared 187 child-care centers with reported child abuse yearly with 61,000 licensed centers without such reports and calculated a rate of 30.7 centers with reported and substantiated sexual abuse per 10,000 centers. In day-care centers, researchers estimated that 5.5

children per 10,000 enrollees are sexually abused. Their comparisons indicated that a child has less risk of ritual abuse in day care than of child abuse at home. One of the most famous cases (and the longest and most expensive) of suspected ritual abuse was the McMartin preschool case in Manhattan Beach, California, where abuse allegedly occurred in 1983 at the day-care school without the parents' knowledge. After allegations of abuse including animal sacrifices, satanic rituals, and nude sexual rituals, Children's Institute International interviewed children who had attended the preschool, and 360 children were determined to be victims of sexual abuse. The media and psychotherapists were fascinated by the children's traumas and eager for more information; they may not have recognized their own influence on the reliability and accuracy of the children's memories. In the spring of 1984, although examinations of 150 children showed no physical evidence of sexual abuse, the physician concluded that 120 of the children were sexually abused. Subsequently, the owner of the preschool, Virginia McMartin; the school administrator, Peggy Buckley (McMartin's daughter); Raymond Buckley (Peggy's son); and four teachers were charged with 208 counts of child abuse. The prosecution's case was weak, and when the first trial began in April 1987, charges had been dropped against McMartin and the four teachers; at the end of the trial two years later, Peggy Buckley was acquitted, and Ray Buckley was cleared of thirty-nine of seventy-five counts of child abuse. At Ray's retrial in 1990 the jury was deadlocked, and the state decided not to pursue the case further.

Ritual abuse also occurs in intrafamilial and extrafamilial settings. Ritual abusers use mind control (for example, brainwashing, humiliation, and starvation) and psychoactive drugs to distort a child's perception of reality, authority, and self and inflict hidden injuries (such as near suffocation and electric shock). Repeated ritual abuse evokes in a child denial, psychic numbing, dissociation, thought suppression, sleep disorders, exaggerated startle response, regression, excessive fears, panic, hypervigilance, and flashbacks. Evaluations of incidents of suspected ritual abuse must reflect how children forget and remember, how children construct their stories and how they are interpreted, and how ritual abuse allegations affect the survivors and perpetrators. Techniques to detect ritual abuse other than children's drawings and the use of anatomically correct dolls are scant. A child's suggestibility and thought processes and false memory syndrome confound a child's ability to report ritual abuse. Coaching and techniques such as cognitive interviewing may increase the child's errors as well as recall.

BIBLIOGRAPHY

Finkelhor, David, Linda M. Williams, and Nanci Burns. *Nursery Crimes: Sexual Abuse in Day Care.* Newbury Park, Calif.: Sage, 1988.

Ney, Tara, ed. *True and False Allegations of Child Sexual Abuse: Assessment and Case Management.* New York: Brunner/Mazel, 1995.

SHARON VALENTE

See also **Children; Cults; Satanism, Modern.**

SEXUAL

Beginning in the 1980s, it became clear that the sexual abuse of children was much more prevalent than previously realized. The Third National Incidence and Prevalence Study, supported by the National Center of Child Abuse and Neglect (NCCAN 1996), documented that each year approximately three hundred thousand children were recognized (by public agencies, such as protective-service and mental-health agencies, and schools) as being sexually abused. This represented an increase in recognized cases of child sexual abuse of more than 100 percent from 1988 (NCCAN 1988) and more than 600 percent from 1980 (Burgdorf 1980; NCCAN 1996). A number of prevalence studies have suggested even higher rates. In separate studies, for example, D. E. H. Russell (1986) and David Finkelhor and his colleagues (1990) reported prevalence rates between 27 percent and 38 percent. Prevalence rates should be expected to be higher than annual incidence rates, since they represent cumulative childhood experiences and because they include more than just those cases recognized by official agencies. Usually, retrospective prevalence studies indicate that in the majority of cases the abuse was never reported to authorities. The conclusion thus is clear: sexual abuse occurs more frequently than previously realized, even though it cannot be stated with certainty how frequently.

These incidence and prevalence studies have also identified other important characteristics of sexual abuse. Almost all reports find that females are the victims more often than males by a ratio of approximately four to one. For female victims as compared with males, the abuser is more likely to be a relative or family friend. Abuse occurs from infancy through adolescence. For females the peak age at onset is between seven and eight years of age, and the mean duration is about two years. For male victims the peak age at onset is also prior to puberty, but the duration of the abuse tends to be less. For both males and females, however, it is important to consider sexual abuse as a repeated trauma rather than a one time event. Poverty is associated with the likelihood of sexual abuse. Little is known about ethnic differences in incidence of sexual abuse, although it is clear that sexual abuse is experienced by children of all ethnic groups.

Federal legislation, specifically the Child Abuse Prevention and Treatment Act (1974), defines sexual abuse as "Employment, use, persuasion, inducement, enticement, or coercion [by a parent or caretaker who is responsible for the child's welfare] of any child [under age 18] to engage in, or assist any other person to engage in, any sexually explicit conduct or any simulation of such conduct for the purpose of and visual depiction of such conduct; or rape . . . , molestation, prostitution, or other form of sexual exploitation of children, or incest with children." Each state is mandated to develop the specifics of the law and of statutes pertaining to the law. More information about federal and state legislation can be obtained from the National Clearinghouse on Child Abuse and Neglect Information (1997).

Research on the effects of sexual abuse proliferated in the late twentieth century. Most of this research consisted of two basic designs, each of which had some inherent limitations. First, short-term or acute impact was assessed using cross-sectional designs in samples of children and adolescents after sexual abuse was officially identified or disclosed. Second, long-term impact was assessed using retrospective designs in samples of adults who reported themselves to have been abused as children. There were very few longitudinal studies. There are particular difficulties with cross-sectional designs in studies of child sexual abuse since aspects of the abuse can easily be confounded with the age or developmental stage of the research subjects.

The most serious problem with retrospective designs concerns the distortions of memory that can occur with the passage of time and with experience. In child-sexual-abuse studies this is particularly problematic for two reasons. First, sexual abuse has been shown to affect memory under cer-

tain circumstances not fully understood. In some cases it has been shown to be associated with amnesias and other types of forgetting. Researchers in the late 1990s were also concerned that "false memories" of sexual abuse experiences could be induced under certain circumstances.

Another problem with the extant research is that the definition and description of the sexual abuse experienced by the research participants has been inconsistent and, in some cases, too sketchy to allow the reader to understand exactly what the child experienced. Finally, it is important to note that most of the research on child sexual abuse, especially research with children, was conducted using all-female samples. More of the adult studies have samples with both males and females in which, usually, sex differences were analyzed.

Other limitations or deficiencies in the research on the impact of child sexual abuse are described in detail in the articles cited in the bibliography at the end of this article.

Effects of Child Sexual Abuse

Physical and Motor Development. Research with samples younger than elementary school age is scant. One study with preschool children found somatic complaints (enuresis, or involuntary urination; stomach aches; headaches) and developmental delays to be common. In adulthood, similar somatic complaints have been found. There is inconsistency in the research with school-age children, although enuresis appears to be common and genital abnormalities (i.e., lasting physical anomalies resulting from injury) have been found. The prevalence of somatic complaints and developmental delays in adolescents who have been abused has apparently not been studied. There is also, in childhood and adolescence, evidence of some psychobiological effects similar to those associated with high levels of stress, for example, disregulated cortisol, elevated catecholamines, and suggestions of immune-system problems. A few late-1990s studies suggested the possibility of hippocampal damage in adults who were abused both physically and sexually as children. Prolonged exposure to elevated levels of cortisol is hypothesized to be at least partly responsible for this damage.

Social and Emotional Development. Internalized problems, generally in the form of depression or anxiety, are found in sexual abuse victims of all ages. Peer relationships are often poor, especially in middle childhood. There also seems to be an enhanced risk of suicide from adolescence onward. Externalized problems such as aggression, conduct problems, and delinquency are found from middle childhood on. Sometimes the form of these problems changes with development (e.g., delinquency emerges in adolescence). There is no evidence of these "acting out" problems in early childhood, but there are few studies. Levels of dissociation, something not examined among younger children, are higher for sexual abuse victims from middle childhood onward. Sexual behavior problems are apparent from early childhood through adolescence. For the younger child this takes the form of sexualized behavior such as excessive masturbation. For the older child and adolescent it takes the form of early onset of sexual activity (i.e., coitus). The adult studies are inconsistent about whether sexual problems persist into adulthood. Of all the problems associated with sexual abuse, the persistence of sexual problems into adulthood seems to be the most exclusively associated with sexual abuse per se, and not with other forms of abuse or violence. The adult studies indicate elevated alcohol or drug abuse and externalizing problems (e.g., diagnoses of antisocial personality) in both men and women. Studies with women show greater revictimization rates (i.e., likelihood of being raped or battered) and problems with child rearing.

Cognitive and Academic Development. Evidence of problems with poor school performance for sexually abused children and adolescents is fairly consistent. Sometimes this poor school performance is not reflected in grades, but rather in teacher ratings and, in some cases, achievement test scores. The nature of these problems is not clear—there has been no research on basic cognitive abilities or memory with this population, although the finding of higher rates of attention deficit hyperactivity disorder and of elevated dissociation suggests there may be attentional problems in these children. With the exception of one study indicating poor short-term memory in adults abused as children, neither cognitive abilities nor educational and occupational attainment in adulthood has been investigated.

Mediators. Most of what is known about possible mediators or moderators of the impact of sexual abuse on development comes from a few adult studies. As noted, most of the research to date is on females—very little is known conclusively about male victims of sexual abuse. These few studies suggest that adult males abused as children are less likely to exhibit depression and anxiety than are previously abused females but are equally or more likely to be diagnosed as having an antisocial personality and to have substance-abuse problems. The studies concerned with marital and sexual relationships tend to be inconsistent for both males and females. No research studies have investigated whether there is a connection between being sexually abused as a child and being a perpetrator of abuse as an adult. Clearly this and other gender-related issues are important areas for further research.

There is also almost no research that focuses on ethnic-group or social-class differences and developmental outcomes. One exception is the research of Gail Wyatt, who studied sexually abused and nonabused African American and white women in terms of their adolescent sexual histories and other aspects of adjustment. For the most part ethnic-group differences were minimal. In the late 1990s there was, however, emerging evidence of ethnic differences in the nature of sexual abuse experiences. For example, in one study, African American females were more likely to be abused at an older age and for a shorter duration than were Caucasian females. To the degree that differences in sexual abuse experiences predict different developmental outcomes (see below), understanding such ethnic differences may be critical. Again this is an area that needs further research.

Some research has been conducted on how different characteristics of abuse—for example, the severity of the abuse (often defined as penetration), the age at which the abuse began, its duration and frequency, the relationship of the victim to the perpetrator, and whether the sexual abuse was accompanied by violence—affect the impact of the abuse on the victim. The findings of these studies are often inconsistent. The variables most consistently associated with a more adverse impact are longer duration of the abuse, force or violence accompanying the abuse, and father or father figure as perpetrator.

Conclusion

The need for further research is clear, and we should be cautious about concluding that we understand the long-term impact of child sexual abuse on development. Several important findings need to be confirmed and expanded. First, the suggestion that there are psychobiological effects of child sexual abuse is extremely important. The few studies in this area implicate cortisol elevation and disregulation. Similar disregulation has been associated with low social competence in preschoolers; with diagnoses of post-traumatic stress disorder and major depression in adults; and, perhaps as a result of associated hippocampal damage, with short-term memory problems and level of dissociation among women. An intriguing and disturbing possibility is that such hormonal disregulation may be related to other findings of long-term impact of sexual abuse on physical health including gynecological problems in women, immune dysfunction, and somatization symptoms.

A second important finding, supported by a number of studies, is the association between sexual abuse and depression, anxiety disorders, and also "acting out" and externalizing problems in females and males, especially in adolescence and adulthood. These problems include delinquency, conduct disorders, antisocial personality, alcohol and substance abuse, and sexual acting out. It now seems clear that maladaptation resulting from sexual abuse takes many more forms, including social deviancies of several types, than was previously thought.

Finally, it is quite important to consider the impact of sexual abuse on educational attainment and occupational attainment and satisfaction. Here, the empirical evidence for abuse during childhood and adolescence is strong: school performance and achievement and certain cognitive abilities are low among sexual abuse victims as compared with nonabused children of comparable socioeconomic standing. This would suggest that a major long-term impact of sexual abuse would be lower educational attainment and, as a result, lower occupational attainment in adulthood, but no studies of adults have examined outcome variables in this domain. The only study related to this subject is one that investigated short-term memory in adults. Since occupational attainment and satisfaction are so central to well-being during adulthood, this area demands more research.

Research has sketched out the impact of sexual abuse on the development of children, adolescents, and adults, but there is much yet to be learned. One especially important emphasis is a developmental framework—how the experience of sexual abuse in childhood interferes with development at the time it is experienced and how it may affect the resolution of later developmental processes or tasks as the individual goes through adolescence and then adulthood. The research needs to include a focus on long-term effects and thus either be lon-

gitudinal and long-term or be a follow-up study of individuals documented to have been sexually abused as children. Finally, a multivariate perspective is required, meaning research needs large sample sizes so that the impact of different forms of abuse—experienced by males as well as females at different ages, and by members of different ethnic groups or social classes—can be teased apart. Only then can the complexities of this phenomena be understood.

BIBLIOGRAPHY

Beitchman, Joseph, et al. "A Review of the Long-term Effects of Child Sexual Abuse." *Child Abuse and Neglect* 16 (1992): 101–118.

———. "A Review of the Short-term Effects of Child Sexual Abuse." *Child Abuse and Neglect* 15 (1991): 537–556.

Burgdorf, K. *Recognition and Reporting of Child Maltreatment: Summary Findings from the National Study of the Incidence and Severity of Child Abuse and Neglect.* Washington, D.C.: National Center for Child Abuse and Neglect, Department of Health and Human Services, 1980.

Finkelhor, David, et al. "Sexual Abuse in a National Survey of Adult Men and Women: Prevalence, Characteristics, and Risk Factors." *Child Abuse and Neglect* 14 (1990): 19–28.

National Clearinghouse of Child Abuse and Neglect. *Child Abuse and Neglect State Statutes Series* 1, no. 1. Washington, D.C.: U.S. Department of Health and Human Services, 1997.

———. *Study of National Incidence and Prevalence of Child Abuse and Neglect.* Washington, D.C.: U.S. Department of Health and Human Services, 1988.

———. *Third Study of National Incidence and Prevalence of Child Abuse and Neglect (Preliminary Findings).* Washington, D.C.: U.S. Department of Health and Human Services, 1996.

Russell, D. E. H. *The Secret Trauma: Incest in the Lives of Girls and Women.* New York: Basic, 1986.

Trickett, Penelope K., and Catherine McBride-Chang. "The Developmental Impact of Different Forms of Child Abuse and Neglect." *Developmental Review* 15 (1995): 311–337.

Trickett, Penelope K., and Frank W. Putnam. "The Developmental Impact of Sexual Abuse." In *Violence Against Children in the Family and the Community,* edited by Penelope K. Trickett and Cynthia Schellenbach. Washington, D.C.: American Psychological Association, 1998.

PENELOPE K. TRICKETT

See also **Developmental Factors; Incest; Sex Offenders.**

CHILD LABOR

It is an old saying that working people built America. What is less well known is that, for most of the nation's history, children labored next to adults on farms, in shops, and in factories. In most cases, these children were working with family members, and their work was a crucial component in the family's survival. At the same time, however, these child workers faced severe dangers to their physical health. Children working without the protection of their families, as indentured servants or slaves, and orphaned children working to support themselves often faced even greater physical, emotional, and psychological danger.

Most children in colonial America worked long hours. Many were apprenticed out to learn a trade, often at seven or eight years of age. Boys might be apprenticed to learn a skilled trade; this could provide them with useful knowledge for the future but could also be demanding, draining work. Girls were apprenticed as domestic servants or to learn sewing or spinning. These girls were highly vulnerable to sexual aggression from the head of the household or from other males in the home or community.

Throughout the nineteenth century and into the twentieth, large numbers of girls were employed as domestic servants, though indenture itself became much less common. In the early nineteenth century girls as young as eight might be working in middle-class homes; these were often the children of Irish immigrant women, who made up two-thirds of the servant workforce. A hundred years later, large numbers of older girls from immigrant families worked as domestic servants in the nation's rapidly growing urban centers.

Another form of child labor was slavery. In the South prior to 1865, slavery was a family affair, with enslaved children working ten, twelve, and even fifteen hours a day alongside their parents and grandparents in plantation fields. Like their elders, children suffered from inadequate food, shelter, and clothing. The threat of violence in the shape of whippings or other punishments was always present; children were emotionally and psychologically damaged by having to watch their parents and other loved ones be punished, and they were sometimes whipped themselves. Perhaps even worse, there was the ever-present danger of families being split apart if an owner chose to sell one or more family members. Slave children regularly suffered what from a modern perspective is considered severe physical abuse and emotional neglect, but at the hands of their owners rather than their parents.

After abolition, most African American families continued to work the land until the middle of the twentieth century. They resisted the developing economic system by withdrawing women and children from farm labor as best they could. In addition, African American parents and communities made extraordinary efforts to give their children some education, and in the early twentieth century they received some aid from white philanthropists. The majority of white working children also worked on their families' farms. In fact, most working children in U.S. history were white children toiling on farms. Both black and white children who were raised on farms continued to work long hours for much of the year to maintain the family's survival.

In the latter third of the nineteenth century, the factory system spread across the nation, and children were drawn into it along with adults. Mechanization led to a number of jobs, such as helping machine operators, that children could manage, and children had the advantage that they could be paid lower wages than adults. The most brutal conditions faced by child workers may have been in southern textile mills, where children from poor white families were indentured at minuscule wages and in dangerous surroundings.

The more intense the discrimination faced by an immigrant group, the more the entire family had to work to survive. Few groups faced higher

A young girl works a spinning machine at a textile mill. Child workers received wages that were far lower than adults'. Photographed by Lewis W. Hine. LIBRARY OF CONGRESS

barriers in the early twentieth century than the Chinese. The 1913 Alien Land Law banned them from purchasing land to farm, and Chinese workers faced severe discrimination in hiring for factory work as well. As a result, many Chinese families opened small businesses, where children worked alongside adults from dawn until late at night.

In the late nineteenth century, some reformers became increasingly aware of child labor as a social problem. Opposition to child labor gained strength with the creation of the National Child Labor Committee in 1904, which in turn helped create the Children's Bureau. Photographs by Lewis Hine in the early 1900s that showed the tragic conditions in which children worked were widely circulated, dramatically increasing public awareness of child labor as a problem needing resolution. In 1916 Congress passed legislation banning certain kinds of child labor used in interstate commerce, but the Supreme Court deemed the law unconstitutional. No congressional child labor legislation survived judicial review until the New Deal of the 1930s, and even then it remained very difficult to enforce.

Child labor in general has become relatively rare in the United States. Yet in the late twentieth century, children in migrant farm labor families, many of which were Mexican or Mexican American, continued to work long hours. Migrant children worked alongside their parents in fields in California, Texas, and elsewhere; the work is seasonal, the pay low, and benefits and social services are virtually nonexistent.

The use of child labor in some of the trading partners of the United States came under scrutiny in the 1990s. Under the North American Free Trade Agreement, nations exploiting child labor can face millions of dollars in fines. President Bill Clinton and the U.S. labor movement pushed for greater awareness and condemnation of international child labor. In practice, however, by 1999 little had been done to persuade businesses in other countries to change their practices.

Compulsory education laws and child labor legislation played a role in the dramatic reduction in child labor during the first half of the twentieth century, as did minimum wage legislation. But other significant factors, including the growing strength of organized labor and the shrinking industrial need for unskilled labor that could be performed by children, finally ended child labor as an important part of working-class life.

BIBLIOGRAPHY

Curtis, Verna Posever. *Photography and Reform: Lewis Hine and the National Child Labor Committee*. Milwaukee, Wisc.: Milwaukee Art Museum, 1984.

Hareven, Tamara K. *Family Time and Industrial Time: The Relationship Between the Family and Work in a New England Industrial Community*. Cambridge, U.K.: Cambridge University Press, 1982.

Trattner, Walter I. *Crusade for the Children: A History of the National Child Labor Committee and Child Labor Reform in America*. Chicago: Quadrangle, 1970.

TIMOTHY A. HACSI

See also **Child Abuse; Children; Sweatshops; Workplace.**

CHILDREN

"Younger and younger children, some of them as young as eight or nine, are becoming involved in crimes of greater and greater violence, even in the most wanton and senseless of murders." This statement is from a 1956 report by Robert Hendrickson, the former chairman of the U.S. Senate Subcommittee on Juvenile Delinquency. Scans of journals and popular media from as far back as the 1920s, 1930s, and 1940s reveal that the fear of unprecedented savagery by children has been a continuing American theme, regardless of the era. In 1996 Jean Hellwege, the senior editor of the journal of the Association of Trial Lawyers of America, used similar words: "Juveniles are committing crimes at younger ages, and the crimes they commit are increasingly more violent."

These declarations usually cite sensational crimes committed by children along with some limited statistics. Shocking incidents in which Chicago elementary schoolchildren dropped a five-year-old to his death from a high building in 1995 and a Richmond, California, six-year-old inflicted a near-fatal beating on an infant the following year received widespread publicity. In 1997 one American child twelve or younger was arrested for a serious violent crime every fifty minutes. Some crime authorities and the news media cite such incidents and statistics as proof that today's children are uniquely violent and, more alarmingly, that they will age into an epidemic of "adolescent super predators" in the near future.

Violence by Children

Is it fair, then, to state that American society at the end of the twentieth century is menaced by ever-younger, murderous bad seeds? In many respects the answer is the other way around: surges in violent acts by adults, especially those of parental age committed around and against children, define America's crisis of violence. U.S. crime statistics show that children (here defined as preteens, ages twelve and younger) were about 25 percent less likely to commit murder in the 1990s than they were in the 1960s and 1970s. However, the rate of children being murdered rose by 80 percent in that period; the fact is the overwhelming majority of child victims were and are slain by adults. Trends in the 1980s and 1990s showed that the worst, most rapidly increasing menace to American children was not their peers but the adults charged with their care.

For all the alarm about "children killing children," little systematic study seems to have been made as to whether grade-schoolers have become more brutal. Federal Bureau of Investigation statistics on crimes committed by children under age thirteen have been available on an annual basis since 1964 (the first year accurate national figures on this age group appeared; 1997 is the most recent yearly statistic available at this writing). Although these crime statistics are suspect because of inconsistent gathering methods and are particularly incomplete for younger age groups prior to 1970, they represent the best measure available.

Homicide, the crime that is both of greatest public concern and the most likely to be accurately tabulated, is rarely committed by children. Annual numbers are small and fluctuate considerably. FBI reports, adjusted to reflect national populations, indicate that an average of sixty-eight children ages twelve and younger were arrested for homicide every year from 1964 through 1974, forty-five per year from 1975 through 1985, and forty-five per year from 1986 through 1997. The total exceeded a hundred only twice, in 1974 and 1995, the latter clearly an anomaly compared with lower totals in surrounding years (see figure 1). Expressed as per capita rates, murder arrests declined from around 3.4 per million children ages eight to twelve in the 1960s and early 1970s to 2.6 in the 1980s and 1990s.

FBI statistics indicate that in a roughly twenty-year period, from the mid-1970s to the mid-1990s, the rate of arrest of children under age thirteen for the other serious violent felonies of rape, robbery, and aggravated assault rose by 45 percent. This compares with rate increases of 65 percent among youths ages thirteen through seventeen, 53 percent

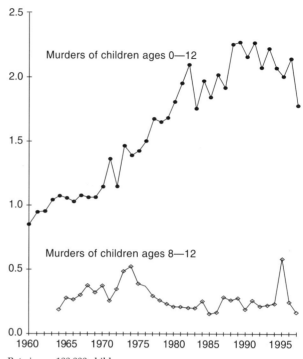

FIGURE 1.   U.S. Child Murders and Murder Arrests of Children, 1964–1997

Murders of children ages 0—12

Murders of children ages 8—12

Rate is per 100,000 children.
SOURCES: U.S. Mortality Detail File (1968–1995) and Vital Statistics of the United States (1965–1967), both from the National Center for

among young adults ages eighteen through twenty-nine (often the parents of younger children), and 78 percent among adults ages thirty through forty-nine (often the parents of older children and teenagers). If measured by arrests tabulated by the FBI, the increase in the incidents of violent crimes among children was accompanied by a similar rise among adults. If measured by estimates from the Bureau of Justice Statistics' National Crime Victimization Survey, the rate of violent crime did not rise appreciably for any group from the 1970s to the 1990s. Whether measured by arrests or by household surveys, children under age thirteen account for less than 2 percent of the nation's violent crime. The rate of children ages eight to twelve arrested for violence remains less than one-tenth that of adults old enough to be their parents.

Violence Against Children

The 1980s and 1990s brought a sharp increase not only in rates of violent crime but also in serious property, drug, and other felony arrests among adults of parental age. The surge in adult crime has created hazardous home and community environments affecting children in profound ways. Much adult violence is directed at children. The rate of murder of children ages twelve and younger nearly doubled from 1970 to 1995 (see figure 1). In 1996 the Department of Justice reported that nine of ten murdered children are killed by adults, not by children or teenage juveniles. Department of Health and Human Services studies (1996) estimate that every year over half a million children and youths are violently victimized and two to three thousand are murdered by their parents or caretakers. (This finding compares with an average of five grade-school and middle-school children murdered at school per year by other children, according to a 1996 Centers for Disease Control and Prevention study.) A 1997 report by the Bureau of Justice Statistics found that violent and sexual assailants of children are substantially older than those who attack adults. The bureau found that the victims of four in ten violent sex offenders were age twelve or younger; of these offenders, one-fourth were over age forty and 90 percent knew their victims.

In addition to criminal acts of child abuse, children often are subjected to other forms of corporal punishment by adults that are not illegal. The 1990 National Longitudinal Study of Youth found that six in ten children ages three to five had been spanked in the week preceding the study, and of these children an average of three spankings per week was recorded. "In view of the widespread acceptance of violent behavior in American culture, it is not surprising that over 90 percent of American parents report using slaps and spankings to discipline their children," Illinois State University psychology professor and child development specialist Laura Berk notes. As with child abuse, studies by Murray Straus (1985) of the Family Research Laboratory at the University of New Hampshire in Durham show that children who receive corporal punishment consistently have been linked to greater levels of violent behavior.

Creating Violent Children

Scholars theorize that violence is transmitted to children through a variety of mechanisms. Being raised in violent families and communities establishes an adult model for violence and may affect children's cognitive development, though not in universal or predictable ways.

Statistical evidence shows that violent behavior among children is a reflection in miniature of the violence witnessed in the adult world around them. Detailed California figures issued by the

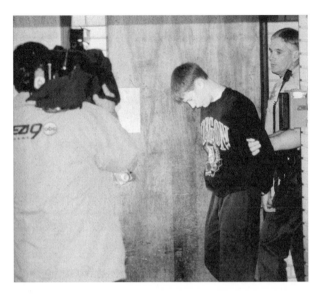

Fifteen-year-old Kipland Kinkel is arrested in May 1998 for first killing his parents and then shooting nine others at his high school in Springfield, Oregon.
CRAIG STRONG/GAMMA/LIAISON AGENCY

California Criminal Justice Statistics Center (1977–1997) showed that children's arrest rates, though much lower, mirror those of adults in the respective categories of racial and ethnic group, gender, locale, and era. African American children, like African American adults, show arrest rates for violent felonies three to five times higher than those of other racial or ethnic groups, and both show cyclical peaks in 1980 and 1990. Males of all races account for 85 percent of teenage and adult arrests and 90 percent of children's arrests for serious violent crimes. Among all racial and ethnic groups, the rate of arrest of children (male and female) for violence in poorer, urban California counties is several times higher than in wealthier urban counties—a pattern also true among adults. This suggests that violence is a learned behavior strongly connected to communities, families, and socioeconomic conditions.

A number of controlled studies have found that the statistical link between child and adult violence is also a personal one. Children who are violently abused are more likely to be arrested for violent offenses than are nonabused children. A 1990 study, by Kenneth Dodge and his colleagues, of three hundred students found that grade-school pupils with recorded histories of abuse were observed to be three times more aggressive—and consistently were rated as more aggressive by teachers and peers—than nonabused pupils even when family income, divorce and single-parent statistics, and family discord were taken into account. A 1996 Child Welfare League of America study of seventy-five thousand Sacramento, California, children ages nine through twelve found that those who had records of abuse and neglect constituted just 1.4 percent of the child population but accounted for half the criminal arrests among children.

In certain children, histories of parental violence, harsh and inconsistent discipline, and family conflict are likely to breed youths who view the world as filled with unpredictable menace. Highly aggressive youths appear particularly likely to misinterpret the innocent behaviors of other people as threatening and to react hostilely. Children raised among violent adults have greater odds of learning aggression from those adults, whom they perceive as role models, and of adopting strategies by which aggression is rewarded immediately rather than controlling behavior for rewards in an uncertain, remote future. There is reason to believe, Straus concludes, that "family training" is the genesis of children's violence.

Yet even so, 1990s children were not as violent as adult trends suggested they should be. The general rule seems to be that children's acts of violence are similar to those of the adults around them, except in cases in which children are less violent than would be expected. Further, it should be noted, most abused children apparently do not become pathologically violent, either in childhood or adulthood. So being a victim of abuse and poor role models, though the most consistent predictors, do not completely explain why certain children express violence whereas others do not.

As for other mechanisms, the American Psychological Association's Commission on Violence and Youth reported in 1993 that "hundreds of studies" have reached the "irrefutable conclusion that viewing [media] violence increases violence," and that prolonged viewing "can lead to emotional desensitization toward violence" (American Psychological Association 1993, p. 33). The effect of violent media on subjects of all ages (not just children) has been reported in four decades of laboratory studies. In particular, aggressive individuals evidently seek out violent media in a reciprocal, mutually reinforcing pattern that appears to stimulate violent expressions and exacerbate other problems linked to violence, such as poor academic achievement. As a rule, however, exposure to violence

through television, movies, music, toys, and video games is a poor predictor of violence in real-life settings. Large-scale studies that attempt to correlate aggression levels among children with their exposure to media violence in fact reveal only weak correlations or none at all; even those finding the largest effects suggest that only a very small fraction of violence in society might be associated with media depictions.

The American Psychological Association study reported that 98 percent of households have a television, and the "level of violence on commercial television has remained constant during nearly two decades." In addition, 60 percent of today's households subscribe to cable channels, where "more graphic violence, sexual content, and mature themes are readily accessible" to children (p. 32). Yet, as noted, homicide arrest rates have declined among children since the 1970s, and other violent crime trends are similar for children and adults. Consumer surveys show that middle- and upper-income families are more likely to subscribe to cable channels with the most violent programming, yet lower-income groups display the highest rates of homicide and violent crime arrest. In short, media violence is an unreliable predictor of violence in society and, if ultimately found to be important, apparently affects children and adults alike.

When Children Are Not Violent

The study of violence in children appears hampered by adherence to incomplete theories that do not account for intriguing anomalies that surfaced in the 1990s. California provides a striking example. California children are exposed to as much or more media violence, violence in the home, and violent crime in the community as children anywhere. Poverty rates have doubled among California's children in the last twenty-five years. By any theory of criminal behavior, the state should be facing an epidemic of homicidal grade-schoolers.

Yet California's consistent and detailed crime and vital statistics reveal a surprising pattern: children's violent crime trends have remained stable even as adult violence has doubled, and children's murder arrest rates of the 1990s were about one-third lower than those of the 1970s. Of the eight thousand Californians arrested for murder from 1995 to 1997, only a dozen were under age thirteen—a child murder arrest rate well below the national average in a state whose teenagers and adults are considerably more murder-prone than the national norm. The state's transition in child and youth population from a more affluent European white majority to a less affluent, African American, Asian, and Hispanic majority has not been accompanied by an increase in children's violence. Why not?

It may be that California's large numbers of families and communities composed of recent Asian and Latin American immigrants are adept at raising and protecting their children and that the resilience of children and youth amid harsher environmental conditions is greater than previously suspected. California's evolution to a nonwhite majority will be repeated in major states across the country in the new millennium, and its surprisingly hopeful trends in behavior among the young demand more objective study. In particular, the "demographic fallacy"—the dubious idea advanced by traditional crime theorists that a large (especially a large minority) child population such as that of the 1990s predicts future hordes of violence-prone teenage and young adult super predators—requires extensive rethinking in light of new evidence. American violent crime trends over the last quarter of the twentieth century have been driven by higher crime rates among aging baby boomers, not by children or adolescents.

In many ways, the United States has framed the question of children's violence backward. It is understandable that brutal attacks, especially homicide, perpetrated by young children should draw public concern and media attention. This focus is not, however, because such incidents signal an ominous trend toward legions of murderous grade-schoolers, but because they remain very rare. Such tragedies indicate an extreme pathology in the individual perpetrators not shared by tens of millions of other children who, however stressed, do not commit such acts. The most crucial research challenge of the new millennium is not why a small number of children (like those of past eras) display extreme savagery, but why so many millions of American children remain reasonably pacific even as stresses such as poverty, family breakup, community disorganization, and adult violence against the young escalate.

BIBLIOGRAPHY

American Psychological Association. *Violence and Youth: Psychology's Response.* Vol. 1. New York: American Psychological Association, 1993.

Bender, David, and Bruno Leone, eds. *Crime.* San Diego, Calif.: Greenhaven, 1998.

Berk, Laura E. *Child Development.* 4th ed. Boston: Allyn and Bacon, 1997.

Dodge, Kenneth A., John E. Bates, and Gregory S. Pettit. "Mechanisms in the Cycle of Violence." *Science* 250 (21 December 1990).

Novaco, Raymond W. "Aggression." In *Encyclopedia of Mental Health.* Vol. 1, edited by Howard S. Friedman. San Diego, Calif.: Academic Press, 1998.

Sedlak, Andrea J., and Diane D. Broadhurst. *Executive Summary of the Third National Incidence Study of Child Abuse and Neglect.* Washington, D.C.: U.S. Department of Health and Human Services, 1996.

Straus, Murray A. "Family Training in Crime and Violence." In *Crime and the Family,* edited by Murray A. Straus and A. J. Lincoln. Springfield, Ill.: Charles C. Thomas, 1985.

U.S. Advisory Board on Child Abuse and Neglect. *A Nation's Shame: Fatal Child Abuse in the United States.* Washington, D.C.: U.S. Department of Health and Human Services, 1995.

U.S. Department of Justice, Bureau of Justice Statistics. *Juvenile Offenders and Victims: A National Report,* and *Juvenile Offenders and Victims: 1996 Update on Violence.* Washington, D.C.: U.S. Department of Justice, 1995, 1996.

MIKE A. MALES

See also **Child Abuse; Developmental Factors; Domestic Violence; Gangs; Teenagers; Television: Children's Television; Toys and Games.**

CHILDREN'S LITERATURE. *See* Literature: Children's and Young Adult Literature.

CHILDREN'S TELEVISION. *See* Television: Children's Television.

CHINESE AMERICANS

The first wave of Chinese immigrants arrived on the West Coast in the late 1840s; they were miners during the gold rush. More arrived in the 1860s to be railroad workers. Their arrival coincided with the great national controversies surrounding the emancipation of slaves, the internment of Native Americans, and the agitation against Spanish Americans. Unlike any of these groups, the Chinese had arrived in this country as "free laborers," the first "colored" immigrants to do so. Because of this—and the willingness of the Chinese to work for low wages—white hostility toward them was intense. They were subjected to unfair taxes and legal persecution. In 1854 the state of California ruled that "Chinese shall not be witnesses in an action . . . wherein a white person is a party." Not surprisingly, they were robbed, assaulted, and murdered regularly by whites who were not held legally accountable.

Attacks against the Chinese escalated during the nationwide campaign for the passage of the Chinese Exclusion Act, which was designed to bar Chinese laborers from legal immigration and to deny those already in the United States the right to naturalization. The grassroots white prejudice was typified by an incident of anti-Chinese rioting and vigilantism in Los Angeles (1871), which led to the loss of eighteen Chinese lives. The main anti-Chinese movement at the time was led by Denis Kearney of San Francisco, and it eventually evolved into the Workingmen's Party of California.

Even after the act's passage in 1882, vigilante attacks persisted, aimed to expel the remaining Chinese from white neighborhoods and workplaces. Murdering of Chinese had become so common that newspapers seldom bothered to report it. Police officials winked at the attacks, and politicians' rhetoric incited even more violence, including riots in a number of cities. In Tacoma (1885) and Seattle (1886), Washington, Chinese were rounded up and ordered to leave. In 1885, fifty-one Chinese were killed in the coal-mining town of Rock Spring, Wyoming, and in 1887 ten Chinese gold miners were murdered at Log Cabin Bar, Oregon, in the course of a brutal robbery attempt. Lawless violence against the Chinese became so serious that President Grover Cleveland in 1885 had to order federal troops on the West Coast to maintain law and order.

Coerced out of towns and small communities, the Chinese began to congregate in major metropolitan centers for self-protection. "Chinatowns" expanded in San Francisco, Los Angeles, and Portland, Oregon, and others emerged in cities like Chicago, New York, and Boston as the Chinese migrated eastward, where the overall Chinese population was small enough to avoid hostile attention. Their convergence into Chinatowns, however, turned the violence against them to their own kind.

Since they were legally barred from citizenship and voting, the Chinese had no political leverage to demand regulatory services from American courts and law-enforcement agencies. Therefore, the Chinese had to establish informal political structures to police themselves. Transplanted from

traditional rural China, these structures were erected around clan, village, surname, district, dialect, fraternal, and trade associations, which functioned as charitable, mutual-aid, credit, and employment agencies. They set rules for financial transactions and arbitrated disputes within the communities. Each association was independent in principle, but to avoid conflicts most Chinatowns established umbrella organizations, such as the Chinese Consolidated Benevolent Association in New York City, as supreme authorities.

Even with the seemingly orderly and hierarchical structures, without American courts and police to impose ultimate sanctions, major quarrels inside Chinatowns generally could not be resolved except by means of physical violence. That being the case, tongs—secret fraternal organizations known for their members' ability in physical combat—became powerful, particularly with regard to critical disputes over territorial and commercial rights inside the communities. To insure self-preservation, almost everyone chose to join a tong. The conduct of community affairs was thus reduced to its lowest common denominator. Periodic "tong wars" erupted, exposing residents to physical harm. At other times, tongs used their monopoly on violence to engage in gambling, drug trafficking, extortion, and prostitution to enrich their members, further degrading the Chinese communities into chaos and humiliation. At the same time, the community members with means (i.e., landlords and owners of shops, stores, and restaurants) used their economic resources to take control of the associations and, in turn, of the whole community. They thus emerged as an "extraterritorial" ruling class within American borders, which law enforcers avoided interfering with under the pretext of keeping out of "internal affairs of the Chinese," while the welfare and safety of Chinese working people were left unprotected.

Although the Chinese Exclusion Act was finally repealed in 1943 during World War II, when China allied with the United States against Japan, official neglect and discrimination against the Chinese in the United States eased only after the Civil Rights movement of the 1960s. Then, with the passage of the liberal, nondiscriminatory 1965 Immigration Act, more Chinese immigrants poured into the country, many of them middle-class professionals. Beginning to penetrate deeper into white American neighborhoods and job sites, they were seen as unwelcome intruders, and instances of anti-Chinese incidents mushroomed. Moreover, Chinese

233

Americans often were blamed for events occurring in Asia. The most appalling case was that of a Chinese American engineer, Vincent Chin, who was murdered in June 1982 by two Detroit autoworkers who believed that Japan was responsible for the domestic unemployment in the auto industry and who had mistaken Chin for Japanese. At the same time, the image of Chinese as hard working and upwardly mobile and worthy of others to model themselves after has provoked resentment and strife from other racial minorities.

Internal oppression within Chinese communities continued in the late twentieth century. Beginning in the 1970s, Chinatowns across the country expanded rapidly as more working-class immigrants arrived, most of them able to take advantage of job opportunities and the congenial ethnic and cultural environment. However, immigrants in many Chinese ethnic enclaves in the late 1990s were working in dead-end service jobs and in declining industrial jobs for Chinese subcontractors who maintained sweatshop conditions by using actual and threatened violence of the old political order. Immigrants in such conditions were trapped: working over sixty-hour weeks alongside other Chinese, they would never learn English and find better jobs in the mainstream American labor market.

Beginning in the mid-1980s, international ethnic Chinese crime syndicates engaged in smuggling heroin and humans moved into Chinatowns in the United States to use them as bases of operations. Human-smuggling networks import yearly thousands of illegal immigrants who have to work for years to pay off huge smuggling debts, which run from $30,000 to $40,000. To avoid being kidnapped and tortured for not paying, these aliens are forced to work under almost subhuman conditions. The local employers are able to take full advantage of these defenseless laborers to depress the wages of all other workers. The labor situation in Chinese communities has deteriorated to such a point that women who cannot pay their debts as seamstresses are forced into prostitution, and men into drug-dealing.

BIBLIOGRAPHY

Chin, Ko-lin. *Chinese Subculture and Criminality: Non-traditional Crime Groups in America.* New York: Greenwood, 1990.

Kaplan, David. *Fires of the Dragon: Politics, Murder, and the Kuomintang.* New York: Atheneum, 1992.

Kwong, Peter. *Forbidden Workers: Chinese Illegal Immigrants and American Labor.* New York: New Press, 1998.

Saxton, Alexander. *The Indispensable Enemy: Labor and the Anti-Chinese Movement in California.* Berkeley: University of California Press, 1971.

Storti, Craig. *Incident at Bitter Creek: The Story of the Rock Springs Chinese Massacre.* Ames: Iowa State University Press, 1991.

Tsai, Shih-shan Henry. *The Chinese Experience in America.* Bloomington: Indiana University Press, 1986.

PETER KWONG

See also **Asians; Immigration; Nativism.**

CHINESE EXCLUSION ACT

The Chinese Exclusion Act of 1882 was both a deliberate discrimination against prospective Chinese immigrants and the hinge on which American immigration policy turned. Prior to the passage of the 1882 act, except for the ineffective Page Act of 1875, which tried to limit the immigration of Chinese women, immigration of free persons to the United States was unrestricted. Once Congress had legislated against Chinese immigrants in 1882, it proceeded to pile restriction upon restriction for the next forty-two years, culminating in the Immigration Act of 1924.

Chinese began immigrating to the West Coast for economic reasons just as the gold rush of 1849 began. The campaign for Chinese exclusion was, in the first instance, a response to racist and economic protest against Chinese stemming from California in particular and the West in general. By the 1870s one can speak of an organized anti-Chinese movement, led eventually by the Irish immigrant Denis Kearney, whose slogan was "The Chinese must GO!" In the 1870s all political parties in California adopted anti-Chinese planks. The only defenders of the Chinese were entrepreneurs, who wanted Chinese labor, and missionaries, who were chiefly concerned with saving their souls. The anti-Chinese movement was accompanied by violence throughout California and the West. The worst episode before 1882 was the Los Angeles riot of 1871, in which at least twenty-one Chinese were shot, hanged, or burned to death by white mobs.

The national political history of Chinese exclusion was complicated by the 1868 Burlingame Treaty between the United States and China, which, in addition to its main provisions giving Americans access to the China market, contained a clause recognizing "the inherent and inalienable

Denis Kearney

Denis Kearney (1847–1907) was born in County Cork, Ireland. Orphaned at an early age, he went to sea at age eleven and rose to be chief mate. He came to San Francisco in 1868, married there, established a hauling business in 1872, and became a citizen in 1876. In 1877 he became the acknowledged leader of the existing anti-Chinese movement and was the key figure in the formation of the Workingmen's Party that year. His violence was largely rhetorical, but his threats "to kill every wretch that opposes it" alarmed both the Chinese and San Francisco's white establishment. The legislature passed a "gag law" making it a felony to encourage riots, and Kearney and his colleagues were repeatedly arrested. The Workingmen's Party, which had a broad anticapitalist agenda, dominated two elections—in 1878 and 1879—and then fell apart. Of all the party's demands, only the anti-Chinese provisions it succeeded in placing in the California Constitution of 1879 took effect. Kearney retired from politics to resurface briefly in 1892 in a vain attempt to start an anti-Japanese movement. He died in Alameda, California.

right of man to change his home and allegiance." When Congress passed a bill in 1879 limiting the number of Chinese who could arrive on one vessel to fifteen, President Rutherford B. Hayes vetoed it on the ground that it conflicted with the treaty and promised to renegotiate the treaty. In the renegotiated treaty, ratified and proclaimed in October 1881, China agreed to give the United States the right to "regulate, limit, or suspend" the immigration of Chinese laborers but gave Chinese coming as "teachers, students, merchants, or from curiosity" and their servants, as well as "Chinese laborers already in the United States," the right "to go and come of their own free will and accord." In 1882 Congress passed a bill suspending the immigration of Chinese laborers for twenty years and allowing in precisely the categories of persons specified in the treaty. President Chester A. Arthur

A cartoon satirizing American anti-Chinese sentiments. The cartoon appeared in 1882, the year the Chinese Exclusion Act was passed. CORBIS/BETTMANN

vetoed the bill on the grounds that twenty years was too long but indicated that he would approve "a shorter experiment." Congress took his suggestion and repassed what became the Chinese Exclusion Act in May 1882 with a ten-year suspension; it was later renewed for another ten years and made permanent in 1904, during Theodore Roosevelt's administration.

The passage of the 1882 act and its sequelae was punctuated by increasing anti-Chinese violence centered in the Rocky Mountain and Pacific Northwest regions. Denver and Rock Springs, Wyoming, were the sites of the worst anti-Chinese violence, but everywhere Chinese went there was violence against them. Attackers were rarely prosecuted; the few who stood trial were almost always exonerated by all-white juries.

In 1943, as a gesture of solidarity with its ally in the war against Japan, Congress repealed the fifteen laws effecting Chinese exclusion, gave Chinese a quota, and allowed Chinese to be naturalized. This, too, was a turning point in immigration policy: over the next twenty-two years all of the overt racial bars to immigration and naturalization were removed.

BIBLIOGRAPHY

McClain, Charles J., Jr. *In Search of Equality: The Chinese Struggle Against Discrimination in Nineteenth-Century America.* Berkeley: University of California Press, 1994.

Miller, Stuart C. *The Unwelcome Immigrant: The American Image of the Chinese, 1785–1882.* Berkeley: University of California Press, 1969.

Opdycke, Sandra. "Denis Kearney." In *American National Biography,* edited by John A. Garraty and Mark C. Carnes. New York: Oxford University Press, 1999. Vol. 12, pp. 421–422.

Peffer, George Anthony. *'If They Don't Bring Their Women Here': The Regulation of Chinese Female Immigration to the U.S., 1852–1882.* Urbana: University of Illinois Press, 1999.

Salyer, Lucy. *Laws Harsh as Tigers: Chinese Immigrants and the Shaping of Modern Immigration Law.* Chapel Hill: University of North Carolina Press, 1995.

Sandmeyer, Elmer C. *The Anti-Chinese Movement in California.* 2d ed. Urbana: University of Illinois Press, 1973.

Saxton, Alexander. *The Indispensable Enemy: Labor and the Anti-Chinese Movement in California.* Berkeley: University of California Press, 1971.

ROGER DANIELS

See also **Asians; Chinese Americans; Government Commissions; Immigration.**

CHURCH BOMBINGS

Although attacks on churches have been a facet of violence in America through much of the country's history, it was not until the Civil Rights movement of the 1950s and 1960s that explosives were used. Attacks on churches and other religious structures date back to the early 1800s, when some Protestants, referred to as Nativists, protested the flow of Irish Catholics into the country. Verbal and printed attacks flared into physical violence. On 11 August 1834, a mob stormed an Ursuline convent in Charlestown, Massachusetts, and set it on fire. Nuns managed to safely evacuate sixty students, many of them Unitarians from wealthy families in nearby Boston.

In May 1844 Irish Catholics and a group of Protestants skirmished in the Philadelphia suburb of Kensington. The confrontation triggered another outburst several days later, when hundreds of Protestants surged through the Irish section of the city. Two churches, St. Michael's and St. Augustine's, were burned by the rioters; more than thirty homes were destroyed; and thousands of Catholics fled the area. In July 1844 another mob encountered state militia troops guarding the Saint Philip de Neri Church in the Philadelphia suburb of Southwark. Gunfire erupted, with both sides employing cannons as well as muskets. When the struggle ended, thirteen were dead and fifty others wounded.

In the latter half of the twentieth century, white terrorists in the South, many of them members of the Ku Klux Klan (KKK), placed bombs at churches that blacks used for rallies and marshaling areas for nonviolent protest marches. Most of the bombing attacks took place in Birmingham, Alabama, which became known as "Bombingham"; church attacks began a few days after a year-long boycott by blacks of city buses in Montgomery, Alabama. The majority of attacks occurred at night when the buildings were empty, but a few occurred when there were services or choir rehearsals in progress. The boycott, which started in December 1955 and was headed by Martin Luther King, Jr., age twenty-seven, led to open seating on buses, but within a few days violence began. Snipers fired at blacks waiting at bus stops, a group of white toughs beat several black passengers, and a campaign of telephone threats was waged. King's Montgomery home was bombed on 30 January 1956; King's wife, Coretta, and daughter, Ylonda, as well as a church member, Mrs. Roscoe Williams, were in the house but were not injured. On 20 December 1956 the U.S. Supreme Court upheld a lower court ruling by federal judges Frank M. Johnson, Jr., and Richard Rives, of Montgomery, which declared segregation on Montgomery city buses to be unconstitutional.

In Birmingham, Fred Shuttlesworth, leader of the Alabama Christian Movement, declared that he and other blacks intended to ride city buses in "an unsegregated fashion." On Christmas Day 1956 Shuttlesworth's church, the Bethel Baptist Church, was bombed, the blast throwing the minister and his wife out of their bed. Then, on 10 January 1957, bombs went off at four churches in Montgomery (Bell Street Baptist Church, Hutchinson Street Baptist Church, First Baptist Church, and Mount Olive Baptist Church) and at the homes of two ministers. There were no injuries. Shuttlesworth said the bombings were an attempt to frighten blacks who sought full civil rights, but that they only made people more determined. White terrorist groups apparently reasoned that if the churches were bombed, blacks would not hold civil rights rallies, and, therefore, the movement for civil and voting rights would cease.

The worst bombing event of the period took place on 15 September 1963, when an explosion at the Sixteenth Street Baptist Church in Birmingham killed four girls and injured about twenty-two other members of the parish. The explosion occurred at approximately 10:22 A.M., in the midst of morning services, instantly killing Cynthia Wesley, Carole Robertson, and Addie Mae Collins, all age fourteen, and Denise McNair, age eleven. The Federal Bureau of Investigation estimated that sixteen to twenty sticks of dynamite were used in the explosive device, which had been placed outside the ground-level window of the women's lounge. Investigators theorized that the bomb had been placed during the night and might have had a timing device that malfunctioned, setting off the bomb later than planned. In 1997 the film director and producer Spike Lee made a documentary about the incident; the film, entitled *Four Little Girls*, was nominated for an Academy Award.

In the early 1970s the attorney general of Alabama, William Baxley, reopened the probe of the church bombings in Alabama, concentrating on the Sixteenth Street Baptist Church case. In 1977 a Ku Klux Klan member, Robert "Dynamite Bob" Chambliss, was convicted in the death of Denise

McNair. He died in prison in 1985. The same investigation later led to the conviction of a Georgia man in the bombing of the Bethel Baptist Church in Birmingham. J. B. Stoner was sentenced to ten years in prison.

In addition to the bombings in Birmingham and Montgomery, a synagogue was bombed in Atlanta in October 1958, and more than forty churches were burned or bombed in Mississippi during the mid-1960s, most of them rural structures. The majority of these arsons occurred in the months after three civil rights workers, James Chaney, Andrew Goodman, and Michael Schwerner, disappeared on 21 June 1964 near Philadelphia, Mississippi. On 4 August their bodies were found buried in an earthen dam. Church fires began to erupt around the state as the FBI pressed its probe of the KKK. Ultimately, more than a dozen KKK members were arrested; a federal court jury convicted seven of them on the charge of conspiring to violate the civil rights of the three workers.

In 1965, when King, Jr., led voting rights marches in Selma, Alabama, the bombing scare in Birmingham flared anew. No bombs exploded, but many were found at different locations, including some churches and a synagogue. All were in green boxes, and no arrests were ever made. For a time there was a lull in attacks on churches, but in 1981 a group of Ku Klux Klansmen and neo-Nazis conspired to bomb a synagogue in Nashville, Tennessee. The plan was thwarted when federal agents of the Bureau of Alcohol, Tobacco, and Firearms were informed. They infiltrated the group, even replacing the dynamite with phony sticks. Several arrests were made and four group members were convicted, receiving sentences of up to fifteen years.

Then, in the mid-1990s, a number of rural black churches were set on fire in Alabama, Tennessee, Mississippi, and South Carolina. In Greene County, Alabama, four churches burned within a few weeks during early 1995. Another burned in Dallas County, Alabama, near Selma. Federal and state law-enforcement officers made a number of arrests of whites but were not able to link the arsons to one organized effort.

Morris Dees of the Southern Poverty Law Center, in Montgomery, Alabama, a nonprofit group that has battled the terrorism of the KKK, neo-Nazi, and so-called biblically inspired groups since the 1970s, said that the 1990s burnings of black churches were not an organized effort by white terrorists. In only two cases were the KKK found responsible; both were in South Carolina. Sometimes the attacks were perpetrated by individuals working independently of any organization but sharing beliefs in common with such organizations. In Alabama, the man arrested for torching the Liberty Baptist Church in Dallas County was a volunteer fireman. "There is a long, sorry history of white vigilante groups burning black churches," Dees said in a January 1999 interview. "Back in the 1920s black churches burned across the South, and again in the 1960s. It's a lot easier to burn a church than to bomb it. The church was the soul of the black community, the only place they could meet. The church was not only the spiritual center, but the social and cultural center."

In the late 1990s the FBI and the state of Alabama again resumed the investigation into the 1963 bombing of the Sixteenth Street Baptist Church, and a federal grand jury convened to question witnesses. The FBI viewed several men as suspects, all cohorts of Robert Chambliss, the Klansman convicted in 1977. As of 1999, no indictments had been returned in the renewed probe.

BIBLIOGRAPHY

Billington, Ray Allen. *The Protestant Crusade.* Gloucester, Mass.: Peter Smith Publishing, 1963.

Manis, Andrew M. *A Fire You Can't Put Out: The Civil Rights Life of Birmingham's Rev. Fred Shuttlesworth.* Tuscaloosa: University of Alabama Press, 1999.

Sikora, Frank. *Until Justice Rolls Down: The Birmingham Church-Bombing Case.* Tuscaloosa: University of Alabama Press, 1991.

FRANK SIKORA

See also **Bombings and Bomb Scares; Catholics; Civil Rights Movements; Ku Klux Klan; South; Vandalism and Violence Against Property.**

CIVIL DISOBEDIENCE

Civil disobedience, most closely associated in the United States with 1960s-era political protest, is the refusal to obey governmental authority or law as a way of agitating against, challenging, changing, or removing that authority or law. *Civil disobedience*—especially in the forms associated with two of its most famous practitioners, Henry David Thoreau and Mohandas K. Gandhi—implies non-violent protest; when it is violent, the violence is extremely low level and virtually never interpersonal. Examples of violent civil disobedience are tree spikes deployed by Greens, trespassing, and window breaking by antiwar demonstrators in the 1960s. Civil disobedience can include just about any protest action short of riot or insurrection, and it always refers to breaking the law.

Civil disobedience can take the form of picketing, sit-ins, unauthorized marches and demonstrations, sit-down strikes, hunger strikes and other forms of public agitation or noncooperation with objectionable rules and regulations, limited property destruction, trespassing, "jail not bail" campaigns (aimed at creating overflowing conditions in the jails so that, for instance, civil rights issues become more visible), obstruction of traffic, disruption of public ceremonies, and some boycotts. It can also include private acts, such as refusing to pay one's taxes in protest of a law or policy or refusing induction into the military.

The Eighteenth and Nineteenth Centuries

The American Revolution. Civil disobedience was first employed in America during the Revolutionary era, as colonists began to resist erratic English policies that resulted, for example, in the hated 1765 Stamp Tax, the first direct tax on American colonists. Perhaps the most famous single act of civil disobedience in American history was the Boston Tea Party of 1773, a protest against a discriminatory tax on tea. Leading up to the outbreak of war, colonists harassed tax collectors, refused to pay their tariffs, and committed other acts designed to impede the implementation of policies felt to be discriminatory and unjust. Such acts of defiance led the British to crack down, sometimes violently, and helped drive the colonies toward open rebellion.

Abolitionism. Careful, well-planned use of civil disobedience did not appear again in the United States until the early 1840s, in the context of abolitionism. In the decades before the Civil War, a network of abolitionist activity that became known as the Underground Railroad helped thousands of fugitive slaves make their way to freedom in contravention of state and federal law. Though not generally thought of as civil disobedience, and clearly more than a single protest action, the aiding of runaway slaves occupied the borderland between civil disobedience and insurrection, as did acts of liberation by slaves themselves who attacked their owners or ran away. Nevertheless, the mostly black "conductors" on the Underground Railroad and the operators of safe houses—both in slave and free states—worked in absolute defiance of the state and federal laws that protected property rights of slave owners.

In the North, activists such as Frederick Douglass used civil disobedience to advance the cause of civil rights for blacks, sometimes blocking streets or boarding white-only carriages to protest segregation in horse-drawn streetcars. Blacks who refused to sit in the black-designated section of Boston's public transportation forced conductors to choose between conceding the issue or (as more often happened) dragging them from their seats or ejecting them from the train altogether. Ultimately the Massachusetts state legislature repealed the state's segregationist transportation laws in 1843.

The Influence of Thoreau. Arguably the most celebrated proponent of civil disobedience in the nineteenth century was the transcendentalist writer and philosopher Henry David Thoreau, who in 1846 refused to pay his poll taxes and briefly went to jail in protest of the Mexican War and against a government "which buys and sells, men, women, and children, like cattle" (1960, p. 118). In his famous essay "On the Duty of Civil Disobedience" (first delivered as a speech, in 1848), Thoreau outlined his position on the moral necessity of resisting laws that are in conflict with individual conscience. "The State never intentionally confronts a man's sense, intellectual or moral, but only his body," he declared. "It is not armed with superior wit or honesty, but with superior physical strength. I was not born to be forced. I will breathe after my own fashion. Let us see who is the strongest" (1960, p. 234).

Thoreau also addressed the reluctance of many citizens to engage in acts of civil disobedience. "When I converse with the freest of my neighbors, I perceive that, whatever they may say about the magnitude and seriousness of the question . . . the long and the short of the matter is . . . they dread the consequences of disobedience to [the existing government] to their property and families" (p. 232). His argument—that a government that forces its citizens to violate their personal morals lacks legitimacy—provided some of the philosophical underpinning for the Indian nationalist movement led by Mohandas K. Gandhi nearly a century later and also served as inspiration for much of the American social and political protest of the 1960s era.

The Twentieth Century: Before Martin Luther King, Jr.

Gandhi. In the early decades of the twentieth century, Mohandas K. Gandhi embraced many of the ideas that the American Thoreau had developed in the name of individualism, and applied them in the cause of Indian nationalism, seeing civil disobedience as a way for Indian people to free themselves from colonial rule without resorting to violence. Gandhi called his form of civil disobedience *satyagraha yoga*, a Sanskrit expression that describes a disciplined combination of *satya*—"truth and love"—with *graha*—"firmness, persistence"—undertaken as a way of creating social change. Gandhi preferred to translate *satyagraha* as "nonviolent direct action" rather than "passive resistance," in order to avoid the connotation of inaction; nonviolent direct action, unlike civil disobedience, need not involve violating the law. Pacifism was also central to Gandhi's vision of overturning anti-Indian laws in South Africa and gaining "home rule" for India itself; a devout Hindu, Gandhi was also heavily influenced by New Testament ideas of loving one's enemy and turning the other cheek. Satyagraha created a form of protest that sought "the vindication of truth not by infliction of suffering on the opponent but on one's self."

Gandhi employed nonviolent resistance in the campaign in South Africa for Indian minority rights. Later, this form of civil disobedience became the prime weapon in the struggle against British colonial rule in India, a struggle that ended with Indian independence in 1947. This anticolonial campaign included a number of spectacular incidents of nonviolent direct action. Most notable was the salt campaign, which lasted a full year. During this time, one hundred thousand Indians went to jail for deliberately violating British salt laws. The British commanded a monopoly on salt production and sale in India. When Gandhi and his followers marched to the sea, he picked up a lump of salt—a symbolic violation of the salt law. It touched off the beginning of civil disobedience in India. Gandhi sought to demonstrate the immorality of British oppression by steadily escalating his pressure tactics while simultaneously offering to negotiate with the colonial government.

When talks failed, Gandhi stepped up his agitation. In winning public support through demonstrations of superior morality and resolve, Gandhi utilized legal protest measures such as mass marches, picketing, strikes, boycotts, and ultimately, as the final stage in the campaign, outright civil disobedience such as the salt law protests.

The Beginning of the U.S. Civil Rights Era. Through the first part of the twentieth century, blacks refrained from most forms of overt protest in the face of racial discrimination, usually limiting their action to boycotts. Many times acts of civil disobedience accompanied boycotts or other legal forms of protest. With the release of the motion picture *Birth of a Nation* (1915), blacks began a picketing campaign that grew into the first mass protest marches in American history (thousands marched in Boston and Philadelphia) and eventually led to the first arrests for nonviolent direct action against racial prejudice. The film depicts black Union army troops as depraved men lusting after white women and presents the Ku Klux Klan as the heroic saviors of the South; such historical inaccuracy deeply offended black leaders and ignored the contributions made by rank-and-file blacks during the Civil War and Reconstruction. When the film was shown, the Boston *Guardian* editor William Monroe Trotter and others staged a form of sit-in when they refused to leave the ticket line and theater lobby, provoking their arrest. Other blacks set off stink bombs in the theaters during the screening of the film. When the newly created Boston board of censors refused to ban the movie, blacks purposefully violated a recently enacted antipicketing ordinance. However, these acts of civil disobedience designed to block the movie failed completely: the antipicketing ordinance made the protests illegal, and the movie continued to play.

As early as 1922, the writer James Weldon Johnson had suggested that blacks pay attention to the nationalist movement unfolding in India. "If noncooperation brings the British to their knees in India," he wrote, "there is no reason why it should not bring the white man to his knees in the South." But the vast majority of black leaders in the years prior to World War II thought that the cause of racial equality would best be served by accommodation. They advised a prudent course of good citizenship and patriotism and frowned upon acts of civil disobedience, which, they feared, not only tainted the cause but had proven potential for backfiring—fomenting repressive legislation and even violence against blacks.

Meanwhile, however, civil disobedience had proved critical to the fight for women's suffrage (granted by constitutional amendment in 1920) and to achieving many of the goals of the labor movement. In the 1930s, radical laborites, especially the Industrial Workers of the World (IWW) and the Communist Party USA, staged actions such as free-speech confrontations against authorities, while the United Auto Workers employed sit-down strikes in auto plants from 1936 to 1937 that ultimately resulted in the recognition of the UAW. Thus in 1941 the activist A. Philip Randolph decided the time had come for blacks to embrace the strategy of direct-action protest, and he called for "an all-out thundering March-On-Washington, ending in monster demonstrations at Lincoln's monument [that] will shake up white America" (Meier and Rudwick 1976, pp. 346, 345). Ten thousand blacks would "wake up and shock official Washington as it has never been shocked before." Although Randolph advocated "broad, organized mass action," he advised against civil disorder and acts of violence.

The proposed March on Washington was called off when the Franklin Delano Roosevelt administration created the Fair Employment Practices Committee (responding to pressure from Randolph's activist organizing) to push for nondiscriminatory hiring in war plants and elsewhere. Despite the cancellation of the march, Randolph remained optimistic about the potential for using Gandhi's tactics of civil disobedience to gain civil rights for blacks. He began cautiously to urge southern blacks to integrate white railway coaches and waiting rooms, labeling such actions "constitutional obedience" and asserted that "a citizen is morally bound to disobey an unjust law." Many black leaders felt that civil disobedience was still far too dangerous—the sociologist E. Franklin Frazier warned in 1923, "I fear we would witness an unprecedented massacre of defenseless black men and women in the name of Law and Order" (Meier and Rudwick 1976, p. 348)—but in Chicago the interracial peace group Fellowship of Reconciliation staged sit-downs against discrimination in the 1940s and then in 1947 sponsored the far more spectacular "Journey of Reconciliation" to contest segregated interstate transportation. Though this forerunner of the Freedom Rides—in which whites and blacks traveled by bus through the South to challenge Jim Crow interstate transportation laws—failed to attract public attention and change laws, it became an important first step in the Civil Rights movement.

The Twentieth Century: After Martin Luther King, Jr.

The Black Civil Rights Movement. The phrase *nonviolent direct action* entered popular usage in the United States in the 1940s during protests against racial discrimination organized by the Congress of Racial Equality (CORE). CORE synthesized Mohandas K. Gandhi's philosophy of nonviolent resistance and tactics of gradual, step-by-step escalation of protest with the methods employed by activists engaged in the sit-down strikes of the 1930s. This marked a major divergence from the past protest tactics of African Americans toward an embrace of Gandhi's philosophy of pacifist confrontation. CORE leader James Farmer explained the adoption by civil rights activists of Gandhi's principle of satyagraha: "We . . . believed that truth alone, the transparent justice of our demands, would convert the segregationists, once they agreed to listen. That was why satyagraha as 'the firmness engendered by love' was so essential to our discipline." Nonetheless, in developing its protest protocols, the Civil Rights movement never wholly relied upon Gandhi-style pacifism. CORE and other civil rights groups introduced a more militant element to the use of civil disobedience.

The sit-in movement that began on 1 February 1960 with the sit-in protests at Woolworth's in Greensboro, North Carolina, initiated the broad wave of civil disobedience that came to characterize the Civil Rights movement. Stirred and made impatient by the success of the Montgomery Bus Boycott from 1955 to 1956, activists in the Student Nonviolent Coordinating Committee (SNCC) began violating southern segregation ordinances in bold and imaginative ways.

Although most of these tactics had been applied on a much smaller scale in the previous century, the Gandhian nonviolent civil disobedience and direct action of the early 1960s were essentially indigenous creations of black America, reinvented by movement activists. Nonviolence and pacifism were not philosophies of life that underpinned the protest protocols of the Civil Rights movement. They were tactics, adopted through necessity. Nevertheless, philosophical nonviolence played a significant role in the direct-action and other civil disobedience campaigns of the era. In a very real way

Gandhi's pathbreaking efforts against British colonial rule in India as articulated by Martin Luther King legitimized the civil rights efforts in the minds of a wary white public. However, even if Thoreau or Gandhi or Randolph (or CORE for that matter) had never existed, the possibility remains that civil disobedience—specifically, breaking a law in order to protest it—would have emerged during the civil rights revolution in America.

Following the firestorm of sit-ins at lunch counters and other facilities, activists staged wade-ins at segregated beaches and pools, kneel-ins at white churches, and sleep-ins at whites-only motels. CORE revivified the dramatic Freedom Rides through the South. SNCC and CORE joined with King's Southern Christian Leadership Conference (SCLC) to wage nonviolent campaigns of civil disobedience against segregation in Birmingham, Alabama, and throughout the South. Attracting 240,000 participants, the 1963 March on Washington for Jobs and Freedom (in part a tribute to the venerable Randolph) also aimed at lobbying for the Civil Rights Act (passed in 1964).

Martin Luther King's abiding belief in agape (Christian brotherly love) and Christian ethics molded and gave the moral high ground to student-led acts of civil disobedience. King provided the wisdom and the rhetoric. Students provided the moral force. After reading Thoreau, King came to believe that "one honest man could set in motion a moral revolution!" He rejected the thinking of Karl Marx because it conflicted with his religious faith. He also could not accept the Marxist notion that the end justifies the means. King also rejected the accommodationism advocated by Booker T. Washington, believing that racial self-help provided at best a partial solution while placing the onus for success on blacks.

It was Gandhi, however, who influenced King most profoundly. From the Indian leader he learned that one could redirect anger into a positive and moral force for change. To both men, nonviolence did not mean weakness. Reacting to violence with charity and "love-force" became a show of superior physical and moral strength. Nonviolent direct action in the face of outright repression was not weakness but noncooperation with evil. Gandhi provided the blueprint for using strikes, protests, and civil disobedience without lapsing into bitterness and hatred for one's oppressor. Ultimately, both men believed, one had to trust that divine justice would reward the expression of moral integrity, and that it would produce the loving and just society for which they struggled.

Other Protest Movements of the 1960s and After. The Civil Rights movement inspired subsequent reform and protest movements to embrace its tactics of nonviolent civil disobedience, although outside of the context of civil rights, the concept was largely divested of its importation of divine justice. Beginning with civil disobedience (sit-ins and trespassing on federal property) at the Pentagon in October 1967, antiwar movement activists staged sit-ins at draft centers, blocked traffic, burned draft cards, destroyed draft files—at least once by pouring blood on them—and staged mass demonstrations that often erupted into violence. Five hundred thousand people turned out for a 1969 march in Washington, D.C., called the New Mobilization to Stop the War, and a year later one million went to the capital city to protest the killing of four students by National Guardsmen during a protest at Kent State. The May Day 1971 protest against the war led to the blocking of traffic in Washington, D.C., in which over ten thousand people were arrested. If one excludes acts of resistance by slaves, civil disobedience was more prevalent during the later decades of the twentieth century than at any other time in American history. The antiwar movement and other protests by New Left radicals actually relied more heavily on civil disobedience

than the Civil Rights movement did. Most of these acts of civil disobedience were nonviolent, but antiwar protests employing civil disobedience with such low-level violence as property destruction, pouring blood on draft files, and smashing windows occasionally developed into insurrectionary riots.

Gandhi had demonstrated that essential to any civil disobedience campaign, especially in the face of unfavorable governmental and popular reaction, is widespread awareness of the selfless acts of submission on the part of protesters to beating, arrest, and occasionally death—most often conveyed through the news media. To be effective, protesters involved in acts of civil disobedience cannot meet violence with violence. Instead, they have to submit to sometimes brutal measures. Accordingly, civil rights and antiwar demonstrators practiced folding into a protective fetal position to guard against injury and to make removal of their limp bodies from a protest site more difficult.

The year 1968 proved critical for nonviolent protest in America. That year two separate incidents demonstrated just how fragile nonviolent civil disobedience was and how disciplined its progenitors had to be in avoiding insurrectionary and criminal violence. At Cornell University in the spring about one hundred militant Black Powerists, carrying shotguns and rifles and wearing ban-

An antiwar protester at the U.S. Capitol. LIBRARY OF CONGRESS

doliers, occupied the student union building on Parents' Day to protest the curriculum, which they claimed was limited in scope to the interests of the white middle class and therefore racist. That same spring black and white students seized several buildings at Columbia University to protest in loco parentis regulations as well as university plans to build a gym on the site of a neighborhood park in the predominantly black Morningside Heights section of New York City.

In that same turbulent year the Mexican American activist Cesar Chavez began a hunger strike to protest discrimination against Hispanics in California and elsewhere, particularly migrant farmworkers. Influenced heavily by Gandhi and King, Chavez had founded La Causa in 1965. Early La Causa protests, such as a national campaign to boycott grapes, resembled early Civil Rights movement actions. Repression of Hispanic activists was strong (members of La Causa had been arrested simply for chanting "Huelga!"—that is, "Strike!"), and La Causa was slow to adopt civil disobedience until Chavez brought national and international attention to the cause of civil rights for Hispanics with his dramatic twenty-five-day hunger strike in 1968.

Fasting as a form of protest is not in itself civil disobedience unless it takes place in a public place, whereupon the protester can be charged with trespassing and possibly other violations. In 1984 Mitch Snyder of the Washington, D.C.–based Community for Creative Nonviolence went on a hunger strike to protest the Reagan administration's refusal to renovate the Federal City Shelter. Earlier that year, it had taken a lengthy occupation of the deserted building in order for activists to gain the right to convert the building into a homeless shelter. Snyder's hunger strike, though not itself an act of civil disobedience, succeeded in galvanizing public opinion and in winning public support for acts of civil disobedience related to the seizure of federal property.

In 1973 three hundred members of the American Indian Movement seized the village at Wounded Knee, South Dakota. They took eleven hostages and set up barricades at this historical site. Unlike their siege of the Bureau of Indian Affairs in Washington, D.C., several months before, they were armed and declared their intention to outlast authorities. After several exchanges of gunfire with U.S. marshals, the activists began to disperse and the protest ended. The action lost credibility with the American public when threats of violence became open acts of violence. Such hostage-taking, itself not a form of civil disobedience, is another example of how civil disobedience (e.g., at the historical site) can become outright insurrectionary or criminal violence.

Since the 1960s era, women's liberation, environmentalist, and antinuclear protestors have staged dozens of actions at nuclear weapons research installations, storage areas, missile silos, test sites, military bases, corporate and government offices, and nuclear power plants from Seabrook, New Hampshire, to the Diablo Canyon reactor in California. Protest against apartheid in South Africa in the 1980s expanded the scope of civil disobedience in the United States. Demonstrations in front of the South African Embassy in 1984 included prominent citizens and members of Congress and resulted in arrests. Activists also sought to block various government policies in Central America, such as support for the Nicaraguan contras during the mid-1980s, through various forms of trespass and unauthorized demonstrations at the White House, the Capitol, Central Intelligence Agency offices, military bases, and congressional and federal offices.

Gay rights activists have employed civil disobedience since the 1969 Stonewall riots in New York City. ACT UP (AIDS Coalition to Unleash Power) has staged hundreds of acts of civil disobedience that have called attention to the AIDS crisis and homophobia. At the same time, antiabortion activists in the pro-life movement adopted civil disobedience tactics such as blocking entrances to abortion clinics and picketing the private homes of physicians who perform abortions.

BIBLIOGRAPHY

Anderson, Terry H. *The Movement and the Sixties: Protest in America from Greensboro to Wounded Knee.* New York: Oxford University Press, 1995.

———. *The Sixties.* New York: Longman, 1999.

Branch, Taylor. *Parting the Waters: America in the King Years, 1954–1963.* New York: Simon and Schuster, 1988.

———. *Pillar of Fire: America in the King Years, 1963–1965.* New York: Simon and Schuster, 1998.

Carson, Clayborne. *In Struggle: SNCC and the Black Awakening of the 1960s.* Cambridge, Mass.: Harvard University Press, 1981.

Garrow, David J. *Bearing the Cross: Martin Luther King, Jr., and the Southern Christian Leadership Conference.* New York: Vintage, 1988.

Meier, August, and Elliott Rudwick. *Along the Color Line: Reflections in the Black Experience.* Urbana: University of Illinois Press, 1976.

———. *CORE: A Study in the Civil Rights Movement, 1942–1968.* New York: Oxford University Press, 1973.

Thoreau, Henry David. *Walden and "Civil Disobedience."* New York: Signet, 1960.

HOWARD SMEAD

See also **Antiwar Protests; Civil Disorder; Civil Rights Movements; Free Speech Movement; King, Martin Luther, Jr.; Nonviolence; Social Control.**

CIVIL DISORDER

Civil disorder, a violent breach of order by the citizenry against one another or against the government, comes in many forms. Although the term *civil disorder* covers war and criminal violence, most often it is used to refer to collective or mob violence such as rioting, lynching, vigilantism, and labor strikes, as well as recreation and entertainment. Taken collectively, these forms of group violence have been at least as commonplace as criminal violence and much more so than war in the history of the United States. Violence in its group form has been, as the historian Michael Wallace puts it, "a basic device used to change or preserve the system," but most often in the United States social violence is initiated with a "conservative bias," to maintain the status quo. Repressive rioting, for example, has generally sought to protect "the American, the Southern, the white Protestant, or simply the established middle-class way of life and morals."

Historically in the United States, such private enforcement of the social order has been so widespread as to be commonplace. And its signature has always been that the end justifies the means: such violence generally carries strong extralegal elements. Participants—regardless of whether they are lynchers, vigilantes, or rioters—knowingly and willfully break the law with the expressed intent to enforce *their* view of the law (or of morality, or social, racial, ethnic, or religious tradition).

One of the paradoxes, therefore, of American civil violence has been the way it has coexisted with institutional stability. Remarkably little social violence has been directed against governmental authority. In this point lies a major distinction between American civil disorder and European mobbing, which has more often been directed against the government. Most social violence in the United States has been decidedly non-insurrectionary. In

Civil Disorder as Recreation

From the colonial period to the early nineteenth century, backcountry violence along the frontier, especially east of the Mississippi and south of the Ohio River, often included a peculiar form of disorder known as rough-and-tumble fighting or eye-gouging matches. These were no-holds-barred battles in which men used any tactic possible to damage their opponents. Men often grew and sharpened their fingernails to use as weapons. They bit and scratched, pulled each others' hair, bit off fingers, ears, and lips, pulled at their opponent's "cods." Most especially, combatants inserted their nails into the eye socket of an opponent and popped out the eye, a technique much bragged about. Travelers were stunned to see one-eyed men, men missing an ear, men with fingers severed at the joint or with their lips bitten off. Occasionally men died.

A typical rough-and-tumble match might attract drinkers and bettors and often spawned additional fights or spread into a general melee. Rough-and-tumble provided entertainment in areas desolate of diversion from the rigors of survival. They also provided a crude social hierarchy and a way to earn honor in areas dominated by wild game, outlaws, and hostile Indians. Champion gougers sat at the top of a barbaric local "society."

fact, throughout the decades many incidents of civil disorder have served governmental policy, and the historical record is replete with incidents of civil disorder in which local authorities sided with or actually participated in the mob action.

With the major exception of the Civil War, the United States remained fairly untroubled by antigovernment violence until the 1960s, when a great deal of the rioting and terrorism was aimed directly at the federal government: rioting, for example, by antiwar demonstrators and extreme terrorism by the Weather Underground. Thirty years later, right-wing militias conducted a great deal of antigovernment posturing but little open violence. Violence associated with militias was almost always the result of an individual militia member resisting arrest for various violations of the law, precipitating a showdown with law-enforcement officials. The most destructive act of antigovernment terrorism ever to occur in the United States, the bombing on 19 April 1995 of the Alfred P. Murrah Federal Building in Oklahoma City, in which 168 people were killed, was executed by two men (Timothy McVeigh and Terry Nichols) who shared the militia ideology but nonetheless were acting on their own, not as members of a group.

Causes of Civil Disorder

The American propensity toward violence is often explained as being the legacy of the nation's violent frontier heritage. The reality, however, is that over the centuries since U.S. independence, race has been the preeminent cause of American civil disorder, and most collective violence in U.S. history has been urban violence, occurring far from the frontier. The harshest collective violence in America has been that erupting from racial and ethnic conflict, with America's cities serving as the centers for a cosmopolitan but volatile mixture of race and ethnicity.

Violence as a means of enforcing white dominance over blacks was not restricted to the cities, neither before nor after slavery. Whenever and wherever the white population felt even vaguely threatened by black revolt or peaceful progress toward equality, whites were likely to resort to violence, whether it was to punish a perceived criminal or to prevent black political participation or economic progress. This formula for using violence to maintain supremacy also applied to post–Civil War nativist reaction to Roman Catholic immigration in the East and to Chinese railroad-construction workers in the West. Ironically Protestants were willing to join forces with Catholics in a form of racial solidarity when they felt economically threatened by the Chinese, as when rampaging white miners massacred twenty-eight Chinese workers in the Rock Springs, Wyoming, riot of 1885, the worst case of anti-Chinese violence on record.

No single factor, however—including race—sufficiently explains the history of civil disorder in the United States. Historically, reaction to change has been the engine of collective violence around the world, and the United States has been no different. During the Gilded Age, America's cities, as indeed the countryside, underwent massive, rapid social transformation; at the same time, the late nineteenth century's disposition toward laissez-faire politics meant local governments were weak and disinclined to act. Many U.S. cities had not even had a police force until the Civil War era, and

nineteenth-century law enforcement in general was notoriously inefficient and corrupt. Minimal urban government combined with maximum laissez-faire meant that as immigrants began to flood into American cities in the 1820s and again after the Civil War the authorities who should have protected them were unwilling and unable to do so. (The pervasiveness of guns among the civilian population after 1820, when arms production became industrialized and firearms widely marketed, only exacerbated the law's inability to thwart rioters, lynch mobs, and vigilantes.) Local lawmen often supported riots—either through nonintervention or active participation—rather than stopping them. Without the high-speed communications and automobiles that in the twentieth century would enable law enforcement to react quickly to civil disorder, state governments in the 1800s, on the rare occasions they disagreed, found it easiest to honor the tradition of localism and avoid interference. After the turn of the century, public outrage at the continued frequency of civil disorder, in combination with an improved ability to respond on the part of law enforcement, led to increased state intervention.

At the federal level, the traditions of localism and laissez-faire politics translated into a prevailing assumption that states should manage their own affairs, and this combined with a general lack of concern for acts of racial and ethnic repression to preclude federal intervention at least through the turn of the century. During the nineteenth century, the federal government stayed out of riot and lynching control (whether in the city or the countryside) altogether, but did respond to labor violence, invariably siding with management against the strikers. Not until the gruesome lynching of Claude Neal in Florida in 1934 did federal authorities even begin to instruct concerned citizens how they might induce their state governments to act against social violence. Moreover, with the sole exception of the prosecution of the Ku Klux Klan in South Carolina during Reconstruction, not until the Claude Screws case in 1943 did the federal government bring charges against citizens for acts of social violence.

Psychology of the Mob

Crowds—random gatherings of people—are not mobs, even when they are demonstrating or protesting. The frequent and large antiwar demonstrations during the Vietnam War were not mobs, though a few occasionally gave birth to tangential rioting; neither are the often boisterous gatherings of abortion opponents at pro-life rallies. A *mob* implies a group or crowd of people that has become highly emotional and exhibits behavior that anyone outside the mob would view as beyond the norm, behavior that is virtually always illegal.

One of the most peculiar aspects of this type of civil disorder is that anyone, given proper circumstances, can become a participant. A group might plan a demonstration in the hope it becomes a riot, but the centripetal forces involved in the transformation of a group or crowd into a mob are entirely unpredictable. The emergence and contagion of civil disorder happens more or less spontaneously, with events fortuitously drawing people into the vortex until the action convulses outward. Even police units can turn into a mob and riot, as the Chicago police did at the Democratic National Convention in 1968.

Factors in Mob Formation. In order for a crowd to become a mob, several factors must occur:

1. *Numbers.* First, there must be a sufficient number of people—by law a bare minimum of three—to enable those present to develop an "impression of universality," that is, a feeling of safety in numbers. Mobs generally grow to multiple dozens and often thousands.

2. *Communication.* Whatever their numbers, the assembling people must have freedom of movement and the ability to communicate with one another. Over a period of time that can last from minutes to half a day, the crowd shares information about whatever event is under way or whatever topic has drawn it together. Information may pass from person to person nearly instantaneously, and galvanize a crowd. In other circumstances, the information sharing happens more slowly: the crowd becomes visibly excited; "milling around" grows in intensity, and as the information circulates it stimulates feelings of mutual assurance, a sense that the mood and the opinions within the crowd are universally shared and morally right. Regardless of the speed at which the information travels, rumor may play an important role. Often by the time the crowd reaches the point of transformation into a mob, the shared and assimilated information has become wildly inaccurate.

3. *Trigger event.* The crowd reaches a critical stage at which point it will either act or dissolve. The gathering has grown to encompass a volatile mass of people inflamed by the information being communicated among themselves, poised for something to happen, and, as social psychologist Roger Brown frames it, "having the physical possibility of acting out the impulse they would not ordinarily act out." Yet even at its most excited a crowd might not become a mob, especially if superior force or outright violence is introduced against it. A trigger is required to ignite the mobbing. The trigger can be a leader who issues a call to act. It could be a drunken individual who shouts an epithet or throws a bottle. It might be a clap of thunder. In the case of the riots in South Central Los Angeles in 1992, the trigger event was the withdrawal of law enforcement from the flash point at the corners of Florence and Normandy Avenues. Liberated from police presence, the angry crowd began attacking passing motorists, and the riot was under way. Victory in a sporting event can be a trigger for celebratory rioting, while in New York City in 1977, an electrical blackout was the trigger event after which thousands of people, emboldened by the darkness and the perceived lack of law enforcement, swept through the city looting, smashing windows, and spreading general havoc.

Mob Behavior. The sociologist Roger Brown argues that "the wildness and folly of the mob are not created de novo in the crowd. The impulses are always there" (1965, p. 734). Mob behavior is more extreme than individual behavior would be, but as members of a developing mob increasingly feel a sense of mental unity, their group-inspired confidence unleashes what Brown calls "pre-existing primitive urges" to abandon civilized standards of behavior. At the same time, "the anonymity that comes with large numbers causes a loss of responsibility"(pp. 734–735). Individual members become homogeneous in their thought and action while they are part of a mob: standard of living, character, and intelligence, as well as family background, race, and ethnicity are all irrelevant to the mob's collective state of mind.

Part of the transformation of a crowd into a mob involves overcoming instincts toward normative behavior, and indeed, from the outside mobs ap-

Police subdue antiwar demonstrators near the Conrad Hilton Hotel on Chicago's Michigan Avenue during the Democratic National Convention, August 1968. CORBIS/ BETTMANN

pear disturbingly emotional and irrational. However, from the perspective of someone inside of a mob, once action begins, that action makes sense and does not seem at all irrational, even when the behavior it produces is bizarre and antisocial to a degree beyond normal comprehension. For instance, in Lowndes County, Alabama, in 1918, a lynch mob randomly killed eleven blacks out of frustration at being unable to track down its intended victim. Among the murdered was a black woman protesting the innocence of her husband; the mob strung the woman up by her heels, then cut out and tore apart her eight-month-old fetus before dousing her with gasoline and setting her afire.

Such emotionality obviously exceeded the individual expression of individual participants, which describes the function of the mob in the first place. Mobs often contain rather commonplace, inoffensive people who psychologically get swept up and transformed by the dynamics of the mob. The temporary union of often disparate individuals creates an entirely new entity, starkly different from any single individual in the mob. The independent energy of the mob does not allow for averaging out of emotions or creating a balance between high intensity and low. The mob is greater than the sum of its parts and more extreme than any individual within it. Once formed, mobs are powerful entities and are not easily contained.

Although a mob manifests singularity of purpose, it is not altogether monolithic. In a lynch mob, for example, a division of labor often occurs. Some members hold the victim, others may build the pyre or light the fire. Still others might shoot the victim. The vast majority simply—and ghoulishly— watch the proceedings.

Riots

By far the most common manifestation of civil disorder is rioting, which can be repressive, insurrectionary, or expressive. Repressive mobs restrict, subjugate, or punish in order to maintain the status quo; insurrectionary mobs are rebellious. Expressive mobs may be celebratory, as in the post–Super Bowl riots; panic-driven; or they may be anxious, as with people who rush a gate as they leave a concert. Repressive mobs have been most common and have generally sought to preserve the racial, ethnic, and religious or moral order.

Throughout its tumultuous history, America has had well over a thousand riots. Although several periods have been marked by intense rioting —for instance, during the Jacksonian era beginning in the 1830s and lasting through the 1860s; again in the 1890s; and then notably in the 1960s —no period has been entirely free of rioting.

The Jacksonian Era. The Jacksonian period saw intense social, cultural, political, and ethnic change, as well as the use of greater democracy and reform movements such as abolitionism. It was a period of social upheaval and violence, both criminal and group. Riots broke out in all quarters over the influx of Roman Catholic Irish and other immigrants, for example. The historian David Grimsted generously describes Jacksonian mobs as "social exclamation points" that were "but a piece of the ongoing process of democratic accommodation, compromise, and uncompromisable tension between groups with different interests" (1998, p. viii). They were also acts of outright repression, usually surrounding slavery and abolitionism. Quite often the rioters were nativist (that is, antagonistic toward immigrants) and anti–Roman Catholic. From 1830 to 1865, 70 percent of America's cities of twenty thousand or more experienced major civil disorder. There were 147 riots in 1835 alone, covering the gamut of mob activity: thirty-five were against abolitionists, eleven were in response to imagined slave insurrections, and fifteen of them were race riots. Of the race riots, eleven were against blacks, three were to help fugitive slaves, and one was by blacks. Hezekiah Niles, a Baltimore newspaper editor writing in 1835, bemoaned "the spreading spirit of riot . . . in every quarter." The reign of "King Mob seemed triumphant," Supreme Court justice Joseph Story quipped upon witnessing the celebratory riots in Washington, D.C., at Andrew Jackson's inauguration in 1829. Thirty-five major riots occurred in Baltimore, Philadelphia, New York, and Boston between 1830 and 1860.

In the antebellum South, rioters faced little challenge from local law enforcement, which expressed scant objection. Southern mobs generally killed, injured, and burned with impunity. In the North the police often sought to impede the progress of a mob's activity, resulting in loss of life among the rioters.

Pre–Civil War social violence was often driven by ethnic, political, or religious frictions, or was related to various social reform movements. After the Civil War, rioting became almost exclusively racial. White mobs in Wilmington, North Carolina, in 1898 successfully drove black elected officials from office and from the city, in a racial coup d'état that effectively ended any black prosperity advanced by Reconstruction.

The Twentieth Century. In the early years of the twentieth century, race riots began to shift in character—repressive rioting by whites gradually gave way to insurrectionary rioting by blacks.

Blacks had long fought back, lending racial riots a communal nature; for instance, in Atlanta, Georgia, in 1906, blacks armed themselves to return fire at bands of whites marauding through their neighborhoods. As early as 1917, when black soldiers in Houston rioted against Jim Crow discrimination, and to a lesser extent again in the so-called Red Summer of 1919, during which twenty-six race riots broke out across the nation between the months of April and October, blacks were rioting in protest against segregation that ensured poor education, inadequate job opportunities, substandard housing, and police brutality.

At the close of World War I, white GIs had returned from Europe to encounter competition for jobs and housing from blacks. The result, in the words of historian Herbert Shapiro, was "a collision between racism and an enhanced black consciousness that rejected deference to white supremacy." White mobs found this challenge unacceptable. Wreaking havoc in industrial cities across the country during the Red Summer of 1919, urban rioters joined their companion rabble, rural lynch mobs, in an unplanned wave of repressive civil disorder. The actions were local, but the ultimate goal of the white violence everywhere it occurred was to prevent change—in other words, to maintain the preexisting racial equilibrium.

Other riots sought to bring change about, or at least to protest the lack of it. Blacks rioted in Harlem in 1943 in response to job discrimination in the defense industry, discrimination that carried par-

---

The Chicago Rioting of 1919

One of the bloodiest episodes of the Red Summer began in Chicago on 27 July 1919, after a black teenager named Eugene Williams joined the throngs swimming in Lake Michigan to escape the ninety-six-degree heat. Offshore, he strayed into the swimming area designated for whites only, was stoned for this breach of racial etiquette, and drowned. His death touched off a flurry of rock throwing between outraged blacks and whites. Police refused to arrest the initial white rock thrower. Indeed, they went after a black man. This episode triggered a seven-day riot in which bands of whites ranged into black neighborhoods burning and pillaging. Twenty-three blacks died. Blacks fought back, killing fifteen whites.

ticular insult while blacks were fighting overseas in the name of freedom and democracy. Such insurrectionary rioting against the inequality of America's social balance continued to be counter-weighted by the rioting of repressive mobs. In June of that same year, over the course of several nights more than a thousand white servicemen attacked black and especially Mexican American youths in the streets, theaters, and shops of Los Angeles, singling out those wearing the zoot-suits that were in fashion among urban Chicanos at the time. The attacks were said to be in retaliation for an assault on white servicemen by Mexicans. For the most part, police allowed the mobs a free hand. The "Zoot-Suit Riot" was yet another example of the determination of white society to use any means necessary to maintain the primacy of their native culture. Commented the Los Angeles district attorney: "Zoot-suits are an open indication of subversive character." The city council followed the riot by making the wearing of such garb a misdemeanor. "All that is needed to end lawlessness is more of the same action as is being exercised by the servicemen," proclaimed the Los Angeles county supervisor.

World War II and the second Red Scare quelled black protest violence. However, the forces of dissatisfaction erupted once again during the insurrectionary "long hot summers" of the mid-1960s. The first riot occurred in Harlem in 1964. The following year a four-day riot in the Watts section of Los Angeles touched off a wave of insurrectionary rioting in black ghettos that did not really end until the spring of 1968, when mobbing at the death of Martin Luther King, Jr., swept the country. All told nearly three hundred riots and disturbances involving half a million blacks broke out during these years, marking it one of the worst periods of peacetime turmoil in history, eclipsing even the lynch-filled 1890s and rivaling Jackson-era rioting.

Labor Strikes

America possesses the most violent labor history of any Western nation. Labor actions in the United States have often developed into riots, if not localized, armed insurrection, and just as frequently spawned officially sanctioned counterviolence. The incidents of disorder resulting from strikes, lockouts, and attempts at union organizing lasted until the New Deal, when the labor movement and unionization at last became an integral part of the U.S. industrial economy. The most violent era, however, came during labor's infancy, from Reconstruction until the 1920s.

Police arrest looters in Harlem, New York City, during riots in 1943. CORBIS/BETTMANN

Strikes or lockouts frequently deteriorated into violence. Often management hired armed thugs to break up strikes or prevent unionization. Workers just as often picked up weapons as part of their protest. During the riotous summer of 1877, state and federal troops violently suppressed a nationwide railroad strike over wage cuts. In cases such as the 1894 strike in the Pullman factory or the 1892 strike by Pennsylvania steel mill workers at Homestead, management attempts to enforce its labor practices led to violent conflagrations with multiple deaths. One of the most telling strikes took place in 1897 at the Lattimer mines in eastern Pennsylvania. Sheriff's deputies, acting as strikebreakers, were infuriated at the sight of foreign-born mine workers carrying the American flag as part of their protest and casually massacred nineteen unarmed Slavic miners. After the bloody shooting, the deputies left the scene laughing and joking about how many "Hunks" they had killed.

Lynching

Even more gruesome than rioting was a distinctly American form of repressive mob action, the lynch mob. Lynching, or lynch law, is said to be named for Colonel Charles Lynch of Virginia, who during the American Revolution formed a vigilante band to arrest and try loyalists and highwaymen. He tried them in his home. If found guilty they received thirty-nine lashes "well laid on." As time passed those tried in "Judge Lynch's Court" were invariably put to death.

According to the 1940 Tuskegee Guidelines for lynching, compiled by documenters of lynchings at the library of Tuskegee University, the following criteria must be met in order to define an event as a lynching.

1. There must be legal evidence that a person was killed.
2. The person must have met death illegally.
3. A group must have participated in the killing.
4. The group must have acted under pretext of service to justice, race, or tradition.

Although lynching is commonly thought to involve death caused by hanging, the specific method used by a mob to kill its victim is not relevant in defining a murder as a lynching: what counts is *why* the victim is murdered. The Wild West "necktie party" that resides in the popular imagination was largely a product of Hollywood movie writing. Of roughly five thousand lynchings that have taken place since 1882, when re-

cords were first kept, nearly four fifths of the victims have been black and 90 percent of the lynchings have taken place in the South. Like riots, lynchings have occurred most often in the hot summer months, with August being the most typical. Unlike rioting, lynchings have been predominantly a rural phenomenon.

The sociologists Stewart Tolnay and E. M. Beck have explained the motivations of southern lynch mobs in a way that can be extrapolated to account for most lynchings in the United States, regardless of geography or of the race or ethnicity of the victim. The white South lynched blacks, they say, "first, to maintain social control over the black population through terrorism; second, to suppress or eliminate black competitors for economic, political, or social rewards; and third, to stabilize the white class structure and preserve the privileged status of the white aristocracy" (1995, pp. 18–19). This final point was often unarticulated by the rioters and may have been largely subliminal. More than anything, however, lynching was a matter of upholding the honor of the lynchers (as expressed in their control of local society) and assuring the continued domination of their race or religion.

The historian W. Fitzhugh Brundage (1993) has identified four types of lynch mobs: mass mobs, posses, private mobs, and terrorist mobs. He places the size of mass mobs as ranging from over fifty into the thousands. By far the most spectacular, lynchings by mass mobs usually involved ritualized death employing torture, dismemberment, and the victim's self-cannibalism. Newspapers and radios spread the word of the impending event, and special trains might be set up to transport people to the lynching. Oftentimes a festive atmosphere prevailed, with participants dressing as though for a picnic, vying for good viewing positions, hoisting their small children onto their shoulders to give them a better view. The mob might sell the victim's body parts for souvenirs.

For example, ten thousand people attended the 1893 lynching in Paris, Texas, of Henry Smith, a black man who was alleged to have raped and killed a three-and-a-half-year-old white child. Captured after an extensive manhunt, Smith was brought back to Paris by train whereupon the mob transported him through the town on a chair atop a cotton wagon. Lynchers built a platform ten feet high and lashed Smith to a pole atop the platform to create a better view for the audience of Smith's demise. Special trains brought in hundreds of onlookers. The murdered girl's father burned the flesh from Smith's feet with a hot iron. His tongue

The Lynching of Claude Neal

Early on 27 October 1934, a white mob lynched a twenty-three-year-old black man named Claude Neal outside Marianna in the Florida Panhandle. Neal had been arrested for the murder of his nineteen-year-old white neighbor, Lola Cannidy, with whom he may have been intimate. His barbaric torture and execution outraged the nation and changed attitudes about lynching.

Fearing for Neal's safety, the sheriff of Jackson County transferred Neal from jail to jail, eventually taking him across the state line into Brewton, Alabama, where he "confessed." Despite the lack of any evidence, rumors spread that Cannidy had been raped. Newspapers and local radio stations touted the impending lynching. Several carloads of lynchers removed Neal from the Brewton jail. They stopped short of the Cannidy home, where a crowd numbering in the thousands was waiting, and executed Neal by means of torture and mutilation. The impatient mob at the Cannidy house meanwhile burned down the Neal family home.

An eyewitness offered this description of the lynching to the National Association for the Advancement of Colored People:

> After taking the nigger to the woods about four miles from Greenwood [in Jackson County], they cut off his penis. He was made to eat it. Then they cut off his testicles and made him eat them and say he like it . . . Then they sliced his sides and stomach with knives and every now and then somebody would cut off a finger or toe. Red-hot irons were used on the nigger to burn him from top to bottom.

The mob dragged Neal's body from the back of a car to the Cannidy house, where family members further mutilated it. Eventually the naked corpse was hanged in the courthouse square.

The governor failed to intervene until heightened emotions, possibly inflamed by depressed economic conditions, led to a riot in Marianna, in which blacks were attacked and white-capped. In this case, lynching was the trigger event that sent whites on a rampage against local blacks to remove them from competition for scarce economic resources and jobs. Local law enforcement remained inactive throughout both events. Neither lynchers nor rioters were punished, but the federal government, reflecting national outrage, began its slow transition toward thwarting lynching and racist violence.

The Department of Justice shifted its policy from noninvolvement in lynchings to advising citizens how they might elicit more action from state authorities. This reflected a general acknowledgment nationwide that no matter what its cause, lynching must end in the United States.

was cut out to silence his wailing and profanity. Eventually Smith was immolated. An eyewitness remarked, "Fathers, men of social and business standing, took their children to teach them how to dispose of Negro criminals. Mothers were there too, even women whose culture entitles them to be among the social and intellectual leaders of the town" (Williamson, 1984, pp. 185–186).

Posses, according to Brundage, often swelled into the hundreds. They frequently crossed the line from the quasi-legal to the extralegal by summarily executing the apprehended suspect. At that point they became a mob and a contributor to the overall pattern of civil disorder.

Private mobs were small and, for whatever reason, tended to try to operate in secret. The lynchers of Mack Charles Parker in Poplarville, Mississippi, broke into the county jail under cover of darkness and, aided by local law enforcement, spirited Parker out of town to his death. Such lynchings

The body of Claude Neal hangs from an oak tree in the courthouse yard in Marianna, Florida, in October 1934. CORBIS/BETTMANN

depended on local support or acquiescence. By 1959, when this occurred, the probability of public, indeed national, identification was high. Prosecution remained rare, however, for any type of lynching, until the 1960s. The two men who lynched fourteen-year-old Emmett Till in 1955 were local heroes until tried. Although acquitted by an all-white jury in less than an hour, they were disgraced more for having been caught than for their misdeeds. In 1912 a private mob actually broke *into* the federal prison at Marietta, Georgia, to kidnap and lynch Leo Frank, a Jewish businessman wrongfully sentenced to life for the murder of an employee in his pencil factory. The mob felt he should have been sentenced to death and proceeded to enforce its own verdict.

The fourth category of lynch mob identified by Brundage is the terrorist mob, such as the Ku Klux Klan or other "white-cappers" (so named for the white hoods they wear to hide their identities) and vigilante organizations. Both terrorist mobs and private mobs take it upon themselves to enforce local social order, but while private mobs act primarily to exact vengeance for some real or imagined crime or offense against the people, terrorist mobs choose their victims less on the personal level, seeking rather to convey a more general message and to foster fear and intimidation. In 1964 during the civil rights project known as Freedom Summer, a terrorist mob made up of local law enforcement and members of the KKK kidnapped and murdered three civil rights workers —James Chaney, Michael Schwerner, and Andrew Goodman—who were in Mississippi as part of a drive to register black voters and help provide other basic services to blacks in the South. The young men were murdered not just in retaliation for their civil rights activism but, more importantly, to discourage other activists from entering that section of rural Mississippi.

All lynch mobs contain conscious elements of terrorism; they have the intent of sending a message, of creating a sense of fear and intimidation directed not just at the victim but at the entire group he or she represents. Lynchings are often accompanied by cries of "that'll teach 'em," "that'll show 'em we mean business," or "that'll keep 'em in their place." In 1991 in Crown Heights, New York, a group of black men lynched a rabbinical student named Yankel Rosenbaum—who simply happened to be in the wrong place at the wrong time—apparently just to "teach Jews a lesson." The black mob that killed Rosenbaum was roaming the neighborhood and expressing its anger with calls to "get a Jew" in retaliation for the death hours earlier of a local black boy, who had been killed by a reckless driver in a religious motorcade of Hasidic Jews. The events were the beginning of anti-Semitic rioting that lasted for the next four nights.

Vigilantism

Localism and the absence of effective government along the eighteenth-century frontier bred a distinct form of American civil disorder known as vigilantism. The historian Richard Maxwell Brown described vigilante groups as an "organized, extralegal movement, the members of which take the law into their own hands." They are distinguishable from lynch mobs in that vigilance committees have an organized structure and are semipermanent, though few last more than a short period of days or weeks. They are also illegal. Regardless of their intended purpose, they have no legal authority to enforce the law, or morals, or tradition.

The first vigilante movement appeared in 1767 along the South Carolina frontier. The Regulators, as they called themselves, formed to carry out Indian removal and to protect against highwaymen when the colonial government refused to do either. They got so out of hand in administering their own interpretation of law and order that a counter-vigilance group developed called the Moderators. From that point forward there have been at least 326 identifiable vigilante movements in the United States. This does not include the dozens of militia movements that formed in the 1990s.

Vigilante movements sprang up all over the frontier and tended to focus on lawbreakers. The San Francisco Vigilance Committees of 1851 and 1856 were urban and focused on political corruption and the unruly ethnic poor. They marked a shift from the old-style, frontier-based, law-and-order vigilantism to "new vigilantism," which sought to maintain community, racial, ethnic, and moral standards whether or not the law was being broken.

Vigilante movements were usually formed and led by members of the local elite, generally businessmen seeking to ensure a hospitable business and commercial environment. Brown argues, somewhat dubiously, in favor of "good" or socially constructive vigilante movements that brought stability to an area and were supported by the populace. On the other hand, he asserts, "bad" vigilante movements became socially destructive and anarchic. They generally operated without community approval and weakened the social order. These movements often sparked counter- or anti-vigilante movements. But regardless of the extent of their local support, and despite their widespread popularity throughout U.S. history, all vigilante movements by definition have been extralegal, making them a form of civil disorder—an important and distinctly American form.

Historical Amnesia

Ironically, while the history of civil disorder is widely documented, until the widespread social disorder of the 1960s it remained absent from historical studies. To this day it remains absent from public awareness. This phenomenon, remarked upon by a select few scholars, is known as "historical amnesia." Or as Richard Hofstadter elaborates, "The United States has a history but not a tradition of domestic violence." What makes American civil disorder so extraordinary comes not so much from its voluminous record, but from the public's remarkable ability to convince itself that it is peace-loving and peaceable. The historical record does not support such a conclusion.

The reasons for this collective memory loss amount to much more than a simple, though understandable, desire to forget unpleasant events. Rather it is because American civil disorder has lacked an ideology. Mob action and vigilantism share no common philosophical or political thread, save that of localism. Although there are pronounced racial and ethnic themes, rioters have come from all shades of the political spectrum and have been black and Latino as well as white. Similarly, social violence has appeared in all parts of the nation. It lacks a geographical locus. Although the South has been the most violent region, owing to its connection to the inherently violent institution of slavery, lynchers, antilabor thugs, duelers, and eye gougers have cropped up in every quadrant of the map.

Thus, social violence has lacked the sort of cohesion that might have caused it to become a sustained phenomenon. While most repressive acts of violence have been perpetrated by whites against blacks, whites have died defending blacks. White mobs frequently lynched and white-capped white abolitionists. The same Protestant mobs that rioted against Irish-Catholic immigrants joined forces with the Irish against Chinese workers.

BIBLIOGRAPHY

Ayers, Edward L. *Vengeance and Justice: Crime and Punishment in the Nineteenth Century South.* New York: Oxford University Press, 1984.

Brown, Richard Maxwell. *Strain of Violence: Historical Studies of American Violence and Vigilantism.* New York: Oxford University Press, 1975.

Brown, Roger. *Social Psychology.* New York: Free Press, 1965.

Brundage, W. Fitzhugh. *Lynching in the New South: Georgia and Virginia, 1880–1930.* Urbana: University of Illinois Press, 1993.

Dinnerstein, Leonard. *The Leo Frank Case.* New York: Columbia University Press, 1968.

Feldberg, Michael. *The Turbulent Era: Riot and Disorder in Jacksonian America.* New York: Oxford University Press, 1980.

Graham, Hugh Davis, and Ted Robert Gurr, eds. *The History of Violence in America: A Report to the National Commission on the Causes and Prevention of Violence.* New York: Bantam, 1969.

Grimsted, David A. *American Mobbing, 1828–1861: Toward Civil War.* New York: Oxford University Press, 1998.

Hofstadter, Richard, and Michael Wallace, eds. *American Violence: A Documentary History.* New York: Knopf, 1970.

Litwack, Leon F. *Trouble in Mind: Black Southerners in the Age of Jim Crow.* New York: Knopf, 1998.

McGovern, James. *Anatomy of a Lynching: The Killing of Claude Neal.* Baton Rouge: Louisiana State University Press, 1985.

Olson, James S. *The Ethnic Dimension in American History.* 2d ed. New York: St. Martin's, 1994.

Report of the National Advisory Commission on Civil Disorders. New York: Bantam, 1968.

Shapiro, Herbert. *White Violence and Black Response: From Reconstruction to Montgomery.* Amherst: University of Massachusetts Press, 1988.

Smead, Howard. *Blood Justice: The Lynching of Mack Charles Parker.* New York: Oxford University Press, 1986.

Tolnay, Stewart E., and E. M. Beck. *Festival of Violence: An Analysis of Southern Lynchings, 1882–1930.* Urbana, Ill.: University of Illinois Press, 1995.

Williamson, Joel. *The Crucible of Race: Black-White Relations in the American South Since Emancipation.* New York: Oxford University Press, 1984.

Wright, George C. *Racial Violence in Kentucky, 1856–1940: Lynchings, Mob Rule, and "Legal Lynchings."* Baton Rouge: Louisiana State University Press, 1990.

Wyatt-Brown, Bertram. *Southern Honor: Ethics and Behavior in the Old South.* New York: Oxford University Press, 1982.

HOWARD SMEAD

See also **Antiwar Protests; Civil Disobedience; Civil Rights Movements; Lynching; Riots; Strikes; Vigilantism; Zoot-Suit Riot.**

CIVIL LIBERTIES

Although Americans place a high priority on reducing violence, none of the various competing concerns of American society is more important or enduring than the protection of civil liberties. The conflict between maintaining order and securing liberty has taken several forms during the course of U.S. history. One perennial controversy concerns whether the First Amendment's "freedom of speech" clause provides warrant for demonstrations, speeches, or materials that contain descriptions of, or are capable of inciting, violence. Another controversy arises from competing interpretations of the Second Amendment "right to bear arms" clause. A final contentious issue, which has surfaced at various times in U.S. history, centers on efforts to restrict civil liberties during wars, rebellions, or other civil disturbances.

The twentieth century has witnessed the development of an increasingly libertarian approach to these controversies. In fact, viewed in a comparative context, the United States has adhered to a more libertarian ethos than has prevailed in practically any other country. The conventional categories of "liberal" and "conservative" do not work well in regard to civil liberties controversies (hate speech and gun-control are good examples of issues that confound the usual categorization of liberals as those against state-imposed restrictions and conservatives as those in favor of state-imposed restrictions). Thus it makes more sense to speak of a libertarian approach (which favors very few governmental restrictions of individual liberties) as distinct from a communitarian approach (which is more willing to tolerate governmental restrictions of individual liberties as is necessary to secure some sort of common good).

Freedom of Speech

The dominant free-speech issue throughout much of U.S. history concerns efforts to restrict subversive speech. Beginning with the passage of the Sedition Act of 1798, and continuing with the enactment of the Espionage Act of 1917 and the Smith Act of 1940, Congress has tried on several occasions to restrict speech that advocates the violent overthrow of the government. In addition, beginning in the early twentieth century, a number of state legislatures enacted their own sedition and criminal-syndicalism acts, and thereby sought to prohibit advocacy of violence for the purpose of achieving political and social reform.

Although a number of convictions were obtained under the federal Sedition Act during the closing years of John Adams's administration, these cases did not give rise to any Supreme Court decisions on the subject, and the law was allowed to expire at the beginning of the Jefferson administration in 1801. The nineteenth century witnessed very few prosecutions for seditious speech. During the course of the twentieth century, however, prosecutions under the Espionage and Smith Acts, as well as the various state sedition and syndicalism laws, produced a fair number of judicial decisions.

As the century progressed, the Court became increasingly hesitant to uphold these prohibitions on subversive speech. In several of the early-twentieth-century cases, such as the 1925 case *Gitlow v. New York* and the 1927 case *Whitney v. California,* the Court relied on a "bad tendency" test, under which speech could be (and usually was) prohibited if it merely evinced a tendency to produce violent action. In another group of cases, the Court relied on a more stringent "clear and present danger" test. Under this approach, which was first articulated by Justice Oliver Wendell Holmes in a 1919 case, *Schenck v. United States,* and then

Antiabortion activists, including the Polish Freedom Fighters, Inc., demonstrate in Washington, D.C., in January 1984. CORBIS/BETTMANN

adopted by the Court in a 1951 case, *Dennis v. United States*, words could be prohibited only when they were "used in such circumstances and are of such a nature as to create a clear and present danger" of violence. Beginning with its decision in the 1969 case *Brandenburg v. Ohio*, the Court has employed an even more exacting standard (which in practice is very difficult to meet), under which speech can be restricted only when it is "directed to inciting or producing imminent lawless action." In the absence of any other significant decisions in this area, the *Brandenburg* ruling remains the controlling precedent.

The late twentieth century saw the emergence of a whole new set of free-speech conflicts. Many legislatures and courts grappled, in one way or another, with the question of whether it is permissible to prohibit the utterance of "fighting words," words that are capable of provoking a violent response from listeners, bystanders, or audiences. Throughout the course of the twentieth century, state legislatures targeted a number of different groups. In the 1920s states enacted laws primarily for the purpose of restricting Ku Klux Klan demonstrations. In the 1930s and 1940s the chief target was Jehovah's Witnesses, whose proselytizing efforts during this period occasionally included vicious condemnations of Catholics and, to a lesser

extent, Jews. In the 1950s and 1960s the principal concern was silencing civil rights activists and antiwar demonstrators. In the 1980s and 1990s antiabortion protestors were also a frequent target.

Once again, the Supreme Court demonstrated an increasing unwillingness to sustain these restrictions on freedom of speech, especially in the period following the 1940s. In the 1942 case *Chaplinsky v. New Hampshire*, the Court held that fighting words were not protected by the First Amendment and could be prohibited, but over the next several decades the Court changed course. In a 1971 case, *Cohen v. California*, the Court determined that fighting words could be punished only if they were "directed to the person of the hearer," and, because this requirement was not satisfied in a case where an individual entered a courthouse wearing a jacket emblazoned with the words "Fuck the Draft," his conviction was overturned. In a 1977 case, *Smith v. Collin*, the conflict between free speech and the prevention of violence arose in perhaps its most dramatic fashion, when neo-Nazi members of the National Socialist Party of America sought to obtain a permit to parade through Skokie, Illinois, which was home to a large Jewish community, including a number of Holocaust survivors. In this case the Seventh Circuit Court of Appeals, and eventually the U.S. Supreme Court, sided with the Nazi marchers, as well as with the American Civil Liberties Union, in concluding that the threat of a violent confrontation was insufficient grounds for banning a demonstration.

State legislatures have been equally active in prohibiting hate crimes, and the Supreme Court has undergone a similar evolution in its approach to these laws. Early in the twentieth century, several states responded to instances of racist and anti-Semitic speech by enacting group-libel laws (which prohibited speech that defamed members of various racial or religious groups); when one of these laws was challenged in the 1952 case *Beauharnais v. Illinois*, the Court deemed it to be fully consistent with the First Amendment. In the late 1980s and early 1990s, however, as a much larger group of states moved to enact hate-crime laws, the courts were less willing to sustain them. To be sure, in the 1993 case *Wisconsin v. Mitchell*, the Supreme Court upheld the use of sentence-enhancement laws (which provide for harsher penalties when crimes are motivated by animus toward a particular racial or religious group). But when judges have considered the validity of hate-speech laws (which prohibit speech that targets racial or religious groups), they have consistently sided with free-speech claimants. In 1989 and 1991 a pair of federal district courts struck down campus speech codes that were enacted by the Universities of Michigan and Wisconsin, respectively. Then, in a 1992 case, *R.A.V. v. City of St. Paul*, the Supreme Court overturned a similarly crafted ordinance under which an individual had been prosecuted for an incident of cross burning.

The dissemination of descriptions of violence—through books, magazines, television programs, or the Internet—has historically elicited much less legal activity. For various reasons, legislatures and courts have been more preoccupied with regulating obscenity and indecency, and, consequently, they have given less attention to regulating violent material. In fact, the lone Supreme Court decision in this area is a 1947 case, *Winters v. New York*, which featured a challenge to a New York law that was enacted in the late nineteenth century in an effort to prohibit books, newspapers, and magazines that contained accounts of "deeds of bloodshed, lust, or crimes." In this instance the Court struck down the law for being excessively vague, and in the aftermath most other states proceeded to eliminate these laws from their statute books.

In the 1980s and 1990s, in response to growing concerns about violence in comic books, in movies, on television, and on the Internet, several states moved to reenact these sorts of laws and to focus on restricting the distribution of violent material to minors. Once again, though, when these laws were challenged in the federal and state courts, as was the case with laws enacted by Missouri and Tennessee, they were struck down as violative of free-speech guarantees.

The Supreme Court's increasingly libertarian approach to free-speech issues has not gone unchallenged. In the 1990s several prominent law professors criticized the Court for granting insufficient weight to the harms that members of minority groups suffer when they are the target of incendiary demonstrations or hate speech. Many of these critics pointed out that a number of other countries, such as Canada, Germany, and Italy, have gone much further than the United States in taking action to reduce these threats. Nevertheless, while a number of state legislatures and public and private universities have experimented with prohibitions on this type of speech, Congress has generally resisted the call to enact such measures, and the Supreme Court has repeatedly overturned most laws that have come in conflict with its staunch libertarian interpretation of the First Amendment's free-speech guarantee.

The Right to Bear Arms

Another enduring conflict revolves around the proper means of interpreting the Second Amendment, which states that "a well regulated Militia, being necessary to the security of a free State, the right of the people to keep and bear Arms, shall not be infringed." Those who favor limitations on firearms call attention to the first clause, with its mention of a "well regulated Militia," and conclude that the amendment poses no obstacle to laws that regulate guns for individual use. Critics of gun regulation emphasize the second clause, with its focus on the "right of the people to keep and bear Arms." In light of the fact that the militia was originally understood, at the time of the ratification of the Bill of Rights, to include all able-bodied citizens, these individuals argue that the amendment stands as a bar to nearly all gun-control measures.

Although one might expect that the Supreme Court would have provided a definitive interpretation of this guarantee, in fact there have been very few Court decisions in this area, and these decisions have dealt only tangentially with the principal issue. In an 1869 case, *Presser v. Illinois*, in a decision that has never been overturned, the Court held that the Second Amendment was not "incorporated" by the "due process" clause of the Fourteenth Amendment and therefore it did not apply to acts of state and local governments. Even in the Court's most direct confrontation with the meaning of the Second Amendment, in the 1939 case *United States v. Miller*, although the justices addressed the merits of the question and appeared to side with those who emphasize the importance of the "well regulated Militia" clause, they eventually resolved the case on the basis of a minor point.

In the absence of a definitive judicial ruling, the battle over the legitimacy of gun-control measures has been fought mainly in the legislative and political arena. Although in the nineteenth century several states required licenses for the carrying of a gun, the first modern gun-control measure is generally considered to be New York's Sullivan Law of 1911, which stipulated that individuals had to obtain a license in order merely to purchase or possess a gun.

Federal gun-control laws have been enacted at various times during the course of the twentieth century, usually in response to specific events or crises. In response to the gang violence that raged during the Prohibition era, Congress enacted the National Firearms Act of 1934 and the Federal Firearms Act of 1938, which restricted the possession of sawed-off shotguns and automatic weapons, and regulated the activities of gun manufacturers and dealers, respectively.

In the 1960s the assassinations of several prominent political figures, including John F. Kennedy, Robert F. Kennedy, and Martin Luther King, Jr., along with widespread rioting and a general increase in violent crime rates led to the passage of the Gun Control Act of 1968. Among the various restrictions included in the law were bans on the ownership of submachine guns, the interstate sale of handguns, or the sale of any firearms to minors or felons.

In the 1980s the failed assassination attempt on President Ronald Reagan, during which White House press secretary James Brady was shot and partially paralyzed, spurred yet another call for the passage of stricter and more effective gun-control measures. Owing in part to the lobbying efforts of Brady, as well as to popular revulsion at a spate of multiple handgun killings in the late 1980s and early 1990s, Congress enacted the Brady Handgun Violence Prevention Act of 1993 (Brady Act), which imposed a five-day waiting period and a criminal background check on all handgun purchases. Then, in 1994, Congress approved a ban on nineteen types of semiautomatic (or assault) weapons. Meanwhile, state legislatures enacted all sorts of gun-control measures, including bans on gun sales to minors and laws limiting individuals to one gun purchase per month.

Even with the passage of these laws, American gun regulations at the close of the twentieth century remained among the least restrictive among Western industrialized nations, on account of the constitutional commitment to a right to bear arms, a long-standing tradition of gun ownership, and intense lobbying efforts on the part of the National Rifle Association.

Civil Liberties in Times of Crisis

Commitments to preserving civil liberties are at no time more strained than during wars, rebellions, or other civil disturbances. In fact, many countries' constitutions allow for this eventuality by stating explicitly that civil liberties may be restricted insofar as is necessary to maintain order. Although the U.S. Constitution makes no such formal provision for relaxing the protection of civil liberties in emergencies, in terms of actual practice, judges, legislators, and executives have all been willing to interpret constitutional guarantees in a more flexible manner during crisis situations.

The prosecution of the Civil War provoked the first widespread instances of wartime deprivations of civil liberties. Especially in the first few months of the conflict, President Abraham Lincoln took a number of steps to maintain order in the mid-Atlantic and border states, including censoring the mail, imposing martial law, and suspending the privilege of the writ of habeas corpus (the procedure by which individuals can request a judicial inquiry into whether they are being detained for legitimate reasons). Defending his suspension of the writ of habeas corpus, which was the most controversial of the measures, Lincoln asked whether it would be better to allow "all the laws, but one, to go unexecuted, and the government itself go to pieces, lest that one be violated." Whereas Congress generally answered this question in the negative, and, accordingly, supported Lincoln's actions, the Supreme Court's reaction was more mixed. Although in an 1861 case, *Ex Parte Merryman*, Chief Justice Roger Taney challenged Lincoln's authority to suspend the writ, this challenge had little practical effect. Then, in an 1866 case, *Ex Parte Milligan*, the Court ruled that martial law could not be imposed in an area of the country that was not in a state of insurrection; but because the decision was not handed down until after the war's end, it was of limited utility.

U.S. entry into World War I and World War II produced similar controversies, including debates over censorship of the mail and the imposition of various other wartime security measures. But the most dramatic incident was the internment of over one hundred thousand Japanese Americans in the aftermath of the Japanese attack on the U.S. Navy base in Hawaii at Pearl Harbor in 1941. This action received the support of all three branches of the federal government. President Franklin Roosevelt issued an executive order authorizing military leaders to undertake this measure. Congress then enacted a statute that embodied its approval of the policy. And when the Supreme Court heard challenges to the imposition of a curfew, in a 1943 case, *Hirabayashi v. United States,* and the forced exclusion policy, in a 1944 case, *Korematsu v. United States,* the justices upheld both actions. As

Chief Justice Harlan Stone explained in his *Hirabayashi* opinion, the war power must be understood to include "the power to wage war successfully."

Although questions surrounding the legitimacy of restrictions on press freedoms surfaced at various times during each of these wars, the Supreme Court did not confront the issue until the Vietnam War. The precipitating event was an effort by the Nixon administration to enjoin the *New York Times* and *Washington Post* from publishing excerpts from the Pentagon Papers (which consisted of a number of purloined volumes of classified material describing the United States' entry into the war). In its 1971 decision in *New York Times Company v. United States,* the Supreme Court refused to grant such an injunction, and publication of the documents continued.

In the 1990s the chief threats of violence were seen as emanating not so much from foreign powers but rather from domestic and international terrorist groups, as was demonstrated by the bombings of the World Trade Center in New York City and the Alfred P. Murrah Federal Building in Oklahoma City in the early 1990s. In the wake of these incidents, Congress began deliberating about how best to prevent future terrorist attacks. Among the various measures introduced at this time were several calls for a reexamination of the Foreign Intelligence Surveillance Act of 1978, which outlines the procedures and criteria by which the Federal Bureau of Investigation can undertake electronic surveillance efforts. A number of members of Congress advocated increasing the FBI's capacity to conduct domestic wiretapping. By contrast, others cautioned against lowering the threshold, on the grounds that this would significantly imperil the civil liberties of unpopular political groups. In the ensuing debate over the Antiterrorism and Effective Death Penalty Act of 1996, the libertarian arguments proved more persuasive, and the more controversial surveillance provisions failed to achieve congressional support.

What stands out from a review of these wartime controversies is the degree to which the United States has maintained a high level of protection for civil liberties, even in the face of strong countervailing pressures. The distinctiveness of the American experience becomes all the more evident when it is contrasted with the record of other countries, many of whose constitutions provide for the explicit relaxation of civil liberties guarantees in crisis situations.

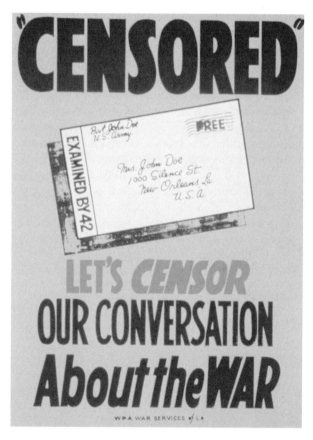

Freedom of speech was suspended during World War II. A 1943 poster. Corbis

In fact, on the whole, Americans have been much less willing than citizens of other countries to tolerate deprivations of liberty for the purpose of maintaining order. Whether one considers restrictions on freedom of expression, on the right to bear arms, or on various guarantees in times of crisis, Congress and the state legislatures have been generally hesitant to pass laws that might have the effect of curtailing civil liberties. Moreover, even when these measures have been enacted, as they have been at various times in U.S. history, the Supreme Court has generally invalidated them, especially in the late twentieth century, on the grounds that they violate constitutional guarantees.

BIBLIOGRAPHY

Cottrol, Robert J., ed. *Gun Control and the Constitution: Sources and Explorations on the Second Amendment.* New York: Garland, 1994.

Delgado, Richard, and Jean Stefancic. *Must We Defend Nazis? Hate Speech, Pornography, and the New First Amendment.* New York: New York University Press, 1997.

Downs, Donald Alexander. *Nazis in Skokie: Freedom, Community, and the First Amendment.* Notre Dame, Ind.: Notre Dame University Press, 1985.

Greenawalt, Kent. *Fighting Words: Individuals, Communities, and Liberties of Speech.* Princeton, N.J.: Princeton University Press, 1995.

Heumann, Milton, and Thomas W. Church, eds. *Hate Speech on Campus: Cases, Case Studies, and Commentary.* Boston: Northeastern University Press, 1997.

Neely, Mark E. *The Fate of Liberty: Abraham Lincoln and Civil Liberties.* New York: Oxford University Press, 1991.

Rehnquist, William H. *All the Laws but One: Civil Liberties in Wartime.* New York: Knopf, 1998.

Saunders, Kevin W. *Violence as Obscenity: Limiting the Media's First Amendment Protection.* Durham, N.C.: Duke University Press, 1996.

Spitzer, Robert J. *The Politics of Gun Control.* Chatham, N.J.: Chatham House, 1995.

Walker, Samuel. *Hate Speech: The History of an American Controversy.* Lincoln: University of Nebraska Press, 1994.

JOHN J. DINAN

See also **Civil Disobedience; Film: Film Violence and Censorship; Pornography; Right to Bear Arms; Television: Censorship.**

CIVIL RIGHTS MOVEMENTS

The history of civil rights movements in the United States has its roots in concepts of freedom that long antedate the American Revolution. Such concepts embody both opposition to the exercise of arbitrary, absolute power and the idea that the people have rights that society's ruling classes and institutions shall not violate. The European struggle against autocracy facilitated the growth of civil rights movements. A historic statement of rights was found in the English Magna Carta of 1215, which included provision for redress of any infringement upon its terms. Although the Great Charter specifically addressed relations between king and barons, in time it came to be seen as a broad-gauged weapon against oppression. A deeply ingrained belief in "the rights of Englishmen" emerged and helped shape movements far beyond England. The right to justice was affirmed and all persons were to be free to come and go except outlaws, prisoners, and enemy aliens.

In subsequent years a variety of protest movements in Europe challenged the rich and powerful in the name of popular rights, and in the mid-seventeenth century English revolutionaries overthrew what they viewed as a tyrannical monarchy. After the Glorious Revolution of 1688 established a constitutional monarchy, the English Declaration of Rights (1689) was enacted to affirm specific privileges guaranteed to the people such as the right to petition, the right of Protestants to bear arms for their own defense, and the right of the members of Parliament to speak freely within the legislature. In his *Two Treatises of Government* (1690), John Locke argued that government is instituted to safeguard the individual's rights to life, liberty, and property. The rights of freedom of thought, speech, and religion, he said, are to be upheld; nevertheless, Locke had no quarrel with slaveholding by colonial planters. He helped draft, and perhaps authored, the Fundamental Constitutions of South Carolina, containing the assurance to whites that "Every Freeman of Carolina, shall have absolute power and authority over Negro Slaves, of whatever opinion or Religion soever."

The Colonial Era

American colonial history is marked by struggles for civil rights. Among early pioneers in that struggle was Roger Williams, founder of Rhode Island. Williams opposed persecution of religious dissenters and urged recognition of the rights of Native Americans to the lands they cultivated. In 1639 émigrés from Massachusetts drafted the Fundamental Orders of Connecticut, embodying Thomas Hooker's declaration that "the foundation of authority is laid . . . in the free consent of the people, to whom belongs the choice of public magistrates, by God's own allowance."

In early American history a wide variety of persons were denied civil rights—slaves, indentured servants, women, prisoners, and apprentices. Voices calling for recognition of the rights of Africans to self-ownership were raised. In 1700 the Massachusetts Puritan Samuel Sewall stated in a pamphlet, *The Selling of Joseph,* his argument against slavery. "All Men," Sewall declared, "as they are the Sons of Adam, are Coheirs; and have equal Right unto Liberty, and all other outward Comforts of Life."

Later in the eighteenth century the Quakers, led by John Woolman and Anthony Benezet, found slaveholding immoral, basing their stand on the idea that the divine spirit speaks through every human being and the right of each person to express that divinity shall not be denied. In his essay "Some Considerations on Keeping of Negroes," Woolman wrote: "That the Liberty of Man was, by the inspired Law-giver, esteemed precious, appears in this; that such who unjustly deprived Men of it, were to be punished in like Manner as if they had murdered them. *He that stealeth a Man, and selleth him; or if he be found in his Hand, shall surely be put to death.* (New Testament, I Tim. i. 10.)" In 1774 the Philadelphia Yearly Meeting stated that slaveholding was a practice "so evidently contrary to our Christian profession, and principles and common rights of mankind." During the colonial era there were also numerous attempts by slaves to gain freedom, efforts that extended to forcible uprisings such as the Stono, South Carolina, revolt of 1739 and the New York conspiracies of 1712 and 1741. Risking their lives and sometimes hanged or burned at the stake for their deeds, slaves asserted their right to individual freedom.

The Age of Democratic Revolution

The American Revolution codified a natural-rights philosophy that would henceforth undergird civil rights movements. In his 1775 essay "African Slavery in America," Thomas Paine observed that a succession of eminent men had proved the holding of slaves "contrary to the light of nature, to every principle of justice and humanity, and even good policy." The slave, Paine wrote, as the proper owner of his freedom, "has a right to reclaim it, however often sold," and he ranked man-stealing as among the most enormous crimes.

The Declaration of Independence is the great foundation stone of American civil rights. That document proclaims "that all Men are created equal, that they are endowed by their Creator with certain unalienable Rights, that among these are Life, Liberty, and the Pursuit of Happiness." When government becomes destructive of securing such ends, "it is the right of the People to alter or abolish it, and to institute new Government, laying its Foundation on such principles, and organizing its Powers in such Form, as to them shall seem most likely to effect their Safety and Happiness." In 1776 the first American society for the abolition of slavery was organized in Pennsylvania. In 1773 a group of Massachusetts slaves petitioned the Massachusetts Assembly for the right to immigrate to Africa. They based their petition on the colonists' struggle against enslavement by the British, proclaiming that "the divine spirit of *freedom,* seems to fire every humane breast on this continent, except such as are bribed to assist in executing the execrable plan." In 1774 blacks in Massachusetts had petitioned the governor and the legislature for the enactment of legislation recognizing the "natural right" to freedom of themselves and their children "without Being depriv'd of them by our fellow men as we are a freeborn Pepel and have never forfeited this Blessing by any compact or agreement whatever."

In Connecticut in 1779 blacks in the towns of Stratford and Fairfield urged the state's general assembly to release them from bondage. They declared they were convinced of their right "(by the Laws of Nature and by the whole Tenor of the Christian Religion, so far as we have been taught) to be free; we have endevored rightly to understand what is our Right, and what is our Duty, and can never be convinced that we were made to be Slaves." In 1783 Chief Justice William Cushing of Massachusetts, in the case of *Commonwealth v. Jennison,* charged the jury that whatever had previously been the views held about slavery, "a different idea has taken place with the people of America, more favorable to the natural rights of mankind, and to that natural, innate desire of Liberty, with which Heaven (without regard to color, complexion, or shape of noses-features) has inspired all the human race."

The U.S. Constitution of 1787 and the subsequently adopted Bill of Rights amendments established a political system incorporating a variety of civil rights, although failing to come to grips with slavery. The Constitution, as originally adopted, conveys the right of electing the House of Representatives to "the People of the several States" (still without defining precisely who are the people) and bars prosecution of members of the House and Senate for any speech in Congress. Under the Constitution the writ of habeas corpus (in which a person alleges that he is being detained illegally and is entitled to a speedy judicial inquiry into the legality of the detention) shall not be suspended except in case of invasion or rebellion, where the protection of public safety may require it. No bill of attainder (in which the rights of a defendant are waived) or ex post facto law may be passed. In these features the Constitution upholds the right of the people to protection from arbitrary governmental actions that had been experienced while the colonists were under British rule. The crime of treason and the requirements for convicting any person of treason are carefully defined. Implicit in the Constitution but fundamental to its meaning is that the people shall have the right to a government that is not absolute in its power.

Responding to demands from several states and from such prominent revolutionary leaders as Thomas Jefferson, the Bill of Rights was framed by Congress and duly ratified by the states. There is, of course, that most precious First Amendment, which enjoins Congress from making any law "respecting an establishment of religion, or prohibiting the free exercise thereof or abridging the freedom of speech, or of the press; or the right of the people peaceably to assemble, and to petition the government for a redress of grievances." Following in sequence are the right of the people to bear arms, premised on the need for a well-regulated militia; protection from the quartering of troops in houses; the right of the people to security from unreasonable searches and seizures; the Fifth Amendment protection against self-incrimination; the right to speedy and public trial with an impartial jury; and the guarantee against cruel and unusual punishments.

The American Revolution formed a part of what the historian R. R. Palmer termed "the age of democratic revolution." A great landmark of that age was the French Revolution, which in August 1789 promulgated the Declaration of the Rights of Man. Such rights included liberty, equality, the right to hold property, and the right to resist oppression. The declaration also set forth that since all persons were equal before the law, all in accord with their abilities were eligible to hold public office. The revolutionary age was also was marked by the Haitian Revolution of the 1790s, characterized by the waging of a successful slave insurrection and the defeat of Napoleon Bonaparte's attempt to reconquer Haiti.

Civil Rights and Slavery

In the period between the Revolution and the Civil War the questions of civil rights and slavery were indissolubly linked. African American slaves were considered as having no claim to rights, and the rights afforded free blacks were severely limited. Furthermore, following the immediate post–Revolutionary War years, during which some abolition societies functioned in the South, especially in Virginia, slaveholders adamantly suppressed criticism of slavery and attempted to destroy the growing abolitionist movement of the North. They would not abide by the 1820 Missouri Compromise limiting the extension of slavery, prevented Congress in the period between 1836 and 1844 from even receiving antislavery petitions, and in 1850 secured passage of the Fugitive Slave Act, which required citizens throughout the nation to assist, when called upon, in the capture of fugitive slaves. In 1857 Chief Justice Roger Taney, himself from a slaveholding family, asserted in the *Dred Scott* case that a Negro "had no rights which the white man was bound to respect."

Ultimately the majority of northerners came to realize that without opposing slaveholder aggression there was no security for the rights of any American. Slavery was a national institution, with the southern planters allied with those northerners who viewed the abolitionists as troublemakers. Among events dramatizing this reality was the November 1837 murder in Alton, Illinois, of the abolitionist newspaper editor Elijah Lovejoy. The murder of Lovejoy, as John Quincy Adams wrote, sent "a shock as of an earthquake throughout this continent." The memorial meetings in the wake of Lovejoy's death produced a new generation of radical abolitionists, among them Wendell Phillips, who eloquently championed the cause of antislavery as an orator and a journalist in the decades before the Civil War, and John Brown, whose militant twenty-year crusade against slavery ended in a failed 1859 raid on the federal arsenal at Harpers Ferry, Virginia.

A feature of the pre–Civil War period was antiabolitionist and antiblack riots by mobs in several northern cities. Mobs in such places as Cincinnati, Ohio; Utica, New York; New York City; and Philadelphia rioted against abolitionists; gentlemen of the propertied classes were prominent among the rioters. Interference with the free movement of

A nineteenth-century painting depicting a meeting of the Anti-Slavery Society in 1840.
CORBIS/BETTMANN

mail was also one of the slaveholders' stratagems. When in 1829 a clothes salesman named David Walker, who was black, attempted to distribute his pamphlet *Walker's Appeal,* which asserted the right of slaves to do what was necessary to obtain their freedom, sacks of mail containing the publication were destroyed in southern post offices.

The struggle between slavery and freedom that exploded in Kansas following passage of the 1854 Kansas-Nebraska Act further dramatized the connection between antislavery and constitutional rights. That struggle was fought out with guns in Kansas, but it also resounded in the United States Senate. In May 1856 Senator Charles Sumner of Massachusetts, in his "Crime Against Kansas" speech, condemned the "swindle" of the Kansas-Nebraska Act, attacked as specious the rationalizations given for that legislation, and noted the "shameful imbecility" produced by slavery. On 22 May 1856 South Carolina Representative Preston S. Brooks put into action his conviction that he could not represent his state "if he permitted such things to be said." Brooks came up to Sumner at his desk in the Senate chamber and struck him repeatedly with his gutta-percha cane. Southerners

were quoted as saying that if Congress dared debate the assault on Sumner, the House would ring with volleys from revolvers. Many in the North were aroused by this event, and in the long run Brooks's violence succeeded in hardening hostility to slavery and its political representatives. Public meetings of indignation were held in both the cities and small towns of the North; a meeting of five thousand at Faneuil Hall in Boston condemned Brooks's assault "as a crime against the right of free speech and the dignity of a free State."

The linkage between constitutional rights and antislavery was also exhibited in the *Amistad* case in which slaves recently transported from Africa had overpowered the officers and crew of a Spanish slave ship, only to be captured by a U.S. Coast Guard ship and charged with murder, mutiny, and piracy. The arrest of the Africans was quickly followed by formation of a defense committee organized by abolitionists. When the case ultimately reached the Supreme Court in 1841, former president John Quincy Adams argued the case for thirty-six of the surviving slaves, insisting that their rights had been trampled upon by the piratical Spanish slavers. Adams also excoriated the federal government's attempt to spirit the slaves out of the country before any appeal could be filed, invoking the linkage between the constitutional rights of black persons and those of every American.

The growing antislavery sentiment led to the enactment of state personal-liberty laws excluding state officials from participating in the return of fugitive slaves. The Supreme Court decision in *Prigg v. Pennsylvania* (1842) encouraged such exclusion in its finding that the federal government could not force state officials to help enforce the 1793 Fugitive Slave Law, which authorized a claimant or his agent to arrest runaway slaves in any state or territory. Following the adoption of the 1850 Fugitive Slave Act, which added U.S. commissioners to the courts to issue warrants for the arrest of fugitives and certificates for their removal from the state, abolitionists like Henry Highland Garnet increasingly asserted the right of self-defense against slave catchers. Frederick Douglass, who previously had supported William Lloyd Garrison's pacifism, took his stand with Garnet. In 1852 Douglass told a Pittsburgh audience: "The only way to make the Fugitive Slave Law a dead letter is to make a half a dozen or more dead kidnappers." The call to a 1853 National Negro Convention listed the violations of black people's rights beginning with the Fugitive Slave Act of 1850, followed by legislation in several states to expel free blacks, the exclusion of blacks from taxpayer-supported public schools, exclusion from serving on juries, barriers against learning trades, and the efforts of the American Colonization Society to deport black people from the United States. Opposition to the right of black children to receive even private education was made manifest in the mob violence that forced the closure of the integrated Connecticut school operated by the Quaker teacher Prudence Crandall.

Civil War and Reconstruction

Following the bloody violence of the Civil War, after Union victory secured the freedom promised to slaves by President Abraham Lincoln's Emancipation Proclamation of 1863, white supremacists perpetrated murderous assaults upon freedmen and white Republicans in a variety of incidents, such as the 1866 racial riots in New Orleans and Memphis. Congress established a Joint Committee on Reconstruction, which heard extensive testimony, much of it presented by blacks, concerning the repeated acts of violence inflicted by white southerners upon blacks.

Seneca Falls Convention

The wave of reform ignited during the Jacksonian era was also expressed in the emergence of a self-defining women's movement for equality. At Seneca Falls, New York, in July 1848 a women's rights convention adopted a trailblazing Declaration of Sentiments. Modeled after the Declaration of Independence, it proclaimed that all men *and* women were created equal, repeated the words concerning life, liberty, and pursuit of happiness, and upheld the right to overthrow such government that "evinces a design to reduce them to absolute despotism." The declaration itemized the "injuries and usurpations" inflicted by men upon women: the denial of the right to vote, the denial of rights "given to the most ignorant and degraded men," the denial of the right to property, including wages, and the denial of the right to enter such professions as theology, medicine, or law. Basing its resolutions on the truth that the equality of rights rests on the equality of the sexes in capabilities and responsibilities, the declaration asserted that all laws enforcing an inferior position upon women had no force or authority. Women, as well as men, were to have the right "to promote every righteous cause by every righteous means." The declaration minced no words in its assertion that women had the duty "to secure to themselves their sacred right to the elective franchise." A number of men attended the convention, but according to Philip S. Foner in his *Frederick Douglass: A Biography* (1964), only Douglass actively took part in the proceedings. Following the convention Douglass wrote in his newspaper, the *North Star*, "that in respect to political rights, we hold women to be justly entitled to all we claim for man. We go farther, and express our conviction that all political rights which it is expedient for man to exercise, it is equally so for women."

In 1866 Congress, overturning a presidential veto, enacted the Civil Rights Act. This act defined all persons born in the United States (except Native Americans) as national citizens and specified rights to be enjoyed regardless of race—the right to make contracts and bring lawsuits, and the protection of all laws for security of person and property. Federal officers were authorized to bring suit

Elizabeth Cady Stanton addresses the first women's rights convention in Seneca Falls, New York, 19 July 1848. CORBIS/BETTMANN

against violations, and such cases were to be heard in federal courts. The Civil Rights Act invalidated numerous discriminatory statutes in both the North and the South. As Eric Foner writes, blacks "quickly employed on their own behalf the Civil Rights Act of 1866. . . . Only in 1867 would blacks enter the 'political nation,' but in organization, leadership, and an ideology that drew upon America's republican heritage to demand an equal place as citizens, the seeds that flowered then were planted in the first years of freedom." This act was a harbinger of the Fourteenth Amendment, adopted in 1868. But even with the setting in place of this measure, racists persisted in their use of intimidation and terror to destroy the democratic reforms of Reconstruction. They created the conspiratorial Ku Klux Klan, which drove the freedmen

from the polls, assassinated Republican officeholders, and burned down schools.

In 1870 and 1871 Congress responded to southern racist violence with a series of Enforcement Acts. Presidentially appointed election supervisors were empowered to bring cases of election fraud and intimidation of voters to federal courts. The Ku Klux Klan Act of 1871 outlawed conspiracies to deprive citizens of their voting rights, with federal district attorneys now empowered to prosecute the conspirators. Provision was also made for military intervention and suspension of the writ of habeas corpus, and in 1871 President Ulysses Grant declared martial law in thirteen upcountry counties of South Carolina where the Klan had been waging a reign of terror. The federal action was at that moment successful in suppressing the Klan, but the North's commitment to federal protection of civil rights gradually dwindled. The 1875 Civil Rights Act was more the marking of a passing era than a sign of reinvigorated commitment to equal rights. A kind of farewell tribute to Charles Sumner, it prohibited discrimination by hotels, theaters, railroads, and other public facilities, but in 1883 the Supreme Court ruled the law unconstitutional. The secret negotiations in 1877 that resolved the disputed presidential election between Rutherford B. Hayes and Samuel J. Tilden centered around agreement that federal troops would be withdrawn from the South, allowing the former slave states to manage their own affairs.

Post-Reconstruction

In the mid-1870s a decades-long era began when no further civil rights legislation emerged from Congress. African American leaders and organizations spoke up repeatedly for the realization of the rights won in the bitter struggles of the Civil War and Reconstruction. The 1879 exodus of southern blacks to Kansas and emigration of hundreds of black people to Africa was an expression of protest at the denial of rights as well as a consciousness of group identity. But although Republicans during election campaigns might wave the "bloody shirt" of antisecessionism, in effect the racial question in the South was placed in the hands of those who had fought to dismember the Union. In 1890 the Republicans in the House of Representatives succeeded in passing a "Force Bill" that would protect black voting rights in the South, but Republicans in the Senate gave way to a southern filibuster in order to secure passage of a tariff bill. The barbarism of lynching, the ritual of sadistic killing of blacks by white mobs, became a regular feature of southern society. White supremacists insisted that sexual assaults by black men upon white women necessitated the resort to lynching, but as the crusading African American journalist Ida. B. Wells reported, in the great majority of lynchings not even the allegation of sexual assault was made. Lynching was a means of racial subjugation, a system of terror. Civil rights were subordinated to mob rule, the system of debt slavery known as peonage, and the cruel, dehumanizing realities of southern prison camps.

Segregation and Disfranchisement

The 1890s fastened upon the South the systems of segregation and disfranchisement. Segregation had previously been a feature of southern society, but it now became a comprehensive system mandated by law, affecting almost every public interaction between whites and blacks. From 1877 to the 1890s, thousands of blacks still voted and numerous blacks were elected to public office, although this was a society already under white domination. The 1890s witnessed a massive assault on the role of African Americans in the southern political process. Grandfather clauses, literacy tests, poll taxes, and resort to naked terror reduced the black voting population in the South almost to the vanishing point. The nation lived a remarkable lie, with whites avoiding the truth by embracing so-called "scientific" notions of racism and paying attention to demagogic politicians who claimed that blacks were allegedly undergoing a process of degeneration that endangered civilization. American law in the 1890s put its seal of approval on segregation with the 1896 Supreme Court *Plessy v. Ferguson* finding. The high court, laying down a precedent that stood until 1954, found that state-mandated segregated facilities did not violate the equal protection clause of the Fourteenth Amendment as long as facilities provided for blacks and whites were approximately equal.

The 1890s triumph of white supremacy climaxed in the Wilmington, North Carolina, massacre of 1898. Following statewide elections in which Democrats defeated a Republican-Populist fusion ticket, Wilmington racists organized a mass assault upon the black community, destroyed the newspaper owned by the black editor Alexander L. Manly, drove hundreds of blacks from the city, and forced Republican officeholders under threat of violence to resign. Scores of blacks were killed. The white-supremacy campaign openly rested on the claim that economic power rather than majority rule was to determine political power. The Republican administration of William McKinley did precisely nothing in response to the Wilmington violence, leaving no doubt that the federal government would not intervene on behalf of civil rights in the South.

Parallel to the victimization of blacks was mounting discriminatory treatment against persons of Asian origin in the West, with restrictions on immigration and naturalization and segregation of schools in San Francisco beginning in 1906. The turn-of-the-century situation regarding civil rights was a counterpart to the American commitment to empire. The denial of constitutional rights and self-determination to the peoples of the newly acquired colonies of Puerto Rico and the Philippines, and the transformation of Cuba into a virtual U.S. protectorate, corresponded to the denial of civil rights at home. Much of the rationale for empire rested upon an assumption of Anglo-Saxon superiority, the denial that other peoples had the capacity for self-government.

Resurgence of Civil Rights

The imposition of segregation and disfranchisement, the unchecked prevalence of lynching, such events as the bloody 1906 assault by whites on the Atlanta black community, and the spread of racial violence to the North spurred a reawakening of civil rights activism. In 1905 the Niagara Movement, led by W. E. B. Du Bois and the Boston editor William Monroe Trotter, held its founding meeting and announced its "protest against the curtailment of our civil rights." The Niagara Movement was a forerunner of the interracial 1909 National Conference on the Condition of the Negro, held in New York City, which in turn led to the formation of the National Association for the Advancement of Colored People. The NAACP formulated a program of demands featuring insistence upon enforcement of the rights guaranteed under the Fourteenth Amendment and also enforcement under the Fifteenth Amendment of "the right of the Negro to the ballot on the same terms as other citizens." The NAACP launched an organized movement that would make civil rights a centerpiece of twentieth-century life in the United States.

The early-twentieth-century Civil Rights movement, linked in ideology and in some cases by family lineage, to pre–Civil War abolitionism, built a national network of local affiliates, mounted a many-sided publicity campaign seeking to arouse public awareness of racist atrocities, and lobbied and marched for enactment of an antilynching law. The magazine of the NAACP, the *Crisis*, edited by Du Bois, achieved a circulation in the tens of thousands, eloquently championing the cause of civil rights and illuminating the international ramifications of the U.S. race question. In 1917 supporters of civil rights succeeded in having the Supreme Court strike down a Louisville, Kentucky, ordinance that mandated segregated residential zones for whites and blacks. In 1925 the NAACP took charge of the legal defense in the case of the Detroit physician Ossian Sweet and members of his family, who were brought to trial for having fired shots into a white mob threatening the home into which the Sweets had moved. One member of the mob had been killed. The defense team was led by the great trial lawyer Clarence Darrow, who vividly portrayed the very real fear of immediate violence instilled by the presence of the mob. The jury found for the defendants, but the NAACP did not succeed in *Corrigan v. Buckley*, the lawsuit against restrictive housing covenants it had taken to the Supreme Court.

World War and Racism

The World War I era and its aftermath were marked by an array of violations of the civil rights of African Americans. There was the vicious East St. Louis racial riot of 1917, and the notorious "Red Summer" of 1919 in which a number of cities exploded in racial violence. Blacks had migrated north in search of better economic conditions and to escape the omnipresent deprivation of civil rights that characterized the South. But at the end of the war, white America made clear to African Americans its determination that existing patterns of racial subordination would not change. This period was marked by the rebirth of the Ku Klux Klan, a resurgence that directly coincided with the impact in 1915 of the D. W. Griffith film *Birth of a Nation*, which presented Radical Reconstruction as an interval of Negro misrule from which the South was rescued by the heroic Ku Klux Klan.

The 1930s and World War II

In the 1930s the political left became substantially involved in defense of civil rights. The stratagem of raising the cry of rape against black men that would lead either to outright lynching or to the "legal" lynching of death sentences was challenged by campaigns of mass agitation combined with competent legal defense. The highlight of this

struggle was the Scottsboro case of 1931, in which Alabama authorities had obtained death sentences against eight out of nine black youths charged with rape. In form and substance the youths had been denied a fair trial, but it took a whirlwind, worldwide defense campaign organized by the communist-led International Legal Defense to stay the hand of the Alabama executioners. In the 1930s labor organizers, in many cases communists or socialists, helped to form such militant organizations as the Sharecroppers Union and the Southern Tenant Farmers Union. Southern landlords and sheriffs considered such activity subversive conspiracy, repeatedly assaulting those involved. These struggles were an early test of labor's right to organize. Such violence played a role in encouraging New Deal congressmen to expose the system of labor espionage and intimidation instituted by much of corporate America.

Despite many New Deal reforms, the federal government failed to confront the issue of civil rights. President Franklin D. Roosevelt refused to push for antilynching legislation. During World War II, the federal government refused to take any action to remedy the conditions of housing discrimination, police brutality, and abuse of black servicemen out of which came the 1943 race riots in Detroit and Harlem. Underscoring the federal government's indifference to civil and human rights was the 1942 decision to relocate all persons of Japanese ancestry residing in the Pacific Coast states in concentration camps.

During the 1930s and World War II, a considerable segment of American opinion became sensitized to issues of civil rights. The anti-Semitism that permeated Nazi Germany was a major factor in creating this consciousness. Reinforcing this mindset was the shift by many historians toward a more positive view of Radical Reconstruction (a view long championed by W. E. B. Du Bois) and the change in anthropology, heralded by the work of Franz Boas, that refuted notions of inherent racial inferiority. Those concerned with civil rights and alarmed by fascism supported President Roosevelt's 1941 establishment of the Fair Employment Practices Committee (FEPC), which oversaw hiring in industries under government contract. The FEPC was a foreshadowing of the extension of civil rights into economic issues. President Roosevelt took this action only under the pressure of a threatened march on Washington organized by the African American activist A. Philip Randolph; but finally he himself saw that the government could no longer continue its stance of indifference toward the pervasive system of segregation and discrimination. In 1942 an interracial group of pacifists formed the Congress for Racial Equality (CORE) with the objective of infusing the civil rights cause with the spirit of nonviolence. Sit-ins were organized in various eating places located in northern cities and the upper South.

Postwar Civil Rights

Despite ongoing incidents of racial violence, the years after World War II brought an increasingly rapid progression toward recognition of civil rights for black Americans. The disfranchisement of blacks in the South still prevailed, and, North and South, blacks were still excluded from many areas of employment. But countervailing pressures were asserting themselves: increased activism by civil rights organizations, global competition ignited by the Cold War that rendered American racism more vulnerable to international pressure, and the emergence of new independent states in Africa. In 1947 a panel appointed by President Harry Truman produced *To Secure These Rights,* a report that itemized the various inequities still imposed upon African Americans and called for such measures as strengthening the civil rights section of the Justice Department's Criminal Division, enactment of an antilynching statute, and an act that would target police brutality. Public interest in civil rights was also intensified by the 1947 Journey of Reconciliation, a nonviolent, anti–Jim Crow project initiated by the religious pacifist Fellowship of Reconciliation.

A landmark success in the civil rights struggle was the Supreme Court's unanimous 1954 decision in the case *Brown v. Board of Education of Topeka, Kansas.* The court found that racial segregation by public institutions—"separate but equal" notwithstanding—violated the clause of the Fourteenth Amendment guaranteeing that the state shall not "deny to any person within its jurisdiction equal protection of the laws." In a decision bringing together cases from several states relating to public education, the justices drew upon an array of social science evidence in support of their conclusion that segregation was inherently a program for enforcement of inequality. In 1955 the Supreme Court rendered its decision as to how *Brown* was to be implemented—based on the concept of "all deliberate speed." The school desegregation rulings were a product of a long legal battle waged by such NAACP attorneys as Charles

Houston, Thurgood Marshall, and Jack Greenberg that chipped away at various facets of segregation in education. It was also framed in an international setting where racial segregation hung like a millstone around the neck of U.S. foreign policy, especially as that policy increasingly applied to relations with people of color. In the final analysis, however, the rulings depended upon the willingness of African American families, at considerable risk to their own safety, to challenge segregation.

The focus of the struggle for civil rights moved from the courtroom into the larger public arena. The Montgomery Bus Boycott of 1955–1956, led by the young minister Martin Luther King, Jr., and embracing his principle of nonviolence, garnered national and international attention. The boycott challenged the segregated seating practices on Montgomery's buses and was ultimately successful despite arrests and bombings. Montgomery's black women played a major role in the mobilization of this movement. They printed the leaflets announcing the boycott, carried on much of the routine organizational work, and formed a large percentage of those boycotting the buses. Drawing upon the heritage of the black church, the American tradition of nonviolence symbolized by such figures as Henry David Thoreau, and the principles of nonviolent resistance to evil championed by Gandhi, mass nonviolent direct action became a central component of the U.S. Civil Rights movement. In 1957 King and his associates took on a larger field of action as they formed the Southern Christian Leadership Conference (SCLC). Stimulated by this resurgent Civil Rights movement, Congress in 1957 enacted a Civil Rights Act, the first such legislation since 1875, establishing the Civil Rights Commission, which was authorized to gather evidence on voting violations.

The 1960s

Along with the SCLC, the NAACP, and CORE, the Student Nonviolent Coordinating Committee (SNCC) and the predominantly white Southern Conference Educational Fund (SCEF) became the leading organizations of the movement. Within the movement there was some argument about strategy and tactics, as differences emerged over a reliance on individual charismatic leadership as against dependence on grassroots organization with an emphasis on participatory democracy. But while no one formula was sufficient, the movement's center of gravity remained the local community organizations and churches. In 1960 lunch-counter sit-ins erupted across the South, and the following year brought the Freedom Rides (by blacks and whites on segregated buses to Alabama and Mississippi), with their numerous instances of violent assault on the riders and the jailing of many of them in Mississippi's medieval prison, the Parchman State Farm.

The wave of activism marking the early 1960s climaxed in the civil rights demonstrations that unfolded in Birmingham, Alabama, in 1963. These protests dramatized for a world audience the contrast between the snarling police dogs and water hoses employed by Birmingham's commissioner of public safety, Eugene "Bull" Connor, and the demeanor of the peaceful demonstrators, many of them children, seeking basic civil rights. The sequel to Birmingham was President John F. Kennedy's commitment to civil rights, followed by the August 1963 March on Washington, which brought tens of thousands to the nation's capital in a massive demonstration for jobs and civil rights. This was the setting for King's historic "I Have a Dream" speech, which placed opposition to discrimination and segregation at the heart of the American democratic tradition.

The enactment of the Civil Rights Act of 1964 brought enlarged protection of voting rights, prohibition of discrimination in public accommodations and public facilities, provisions for accelerating school desegregation, and prohibition of job discrimination on account of race, color, religion, sex, or national origin. The 1964 legislation also established an Equal Employment Opportunity Commission. The Civil Rights Act struck a blow at segregation from which the Jim Crow system could not and would not recover.

During subsequent months two major confrontations carried forward the momentum of the struggle that had culminated in the Civil Rights Act. The first was the Mississippi Freedom Summer Project, initiated by SNCC and supported by much of the civil rights community, both within Mississippi and beyond. Mississippi was the hard core of segregation, disfranchisement, and racial violence in the United States. Hundreds of student volunteers from an assortment of college campuses converged to challenge the system. Tragically, it was only after Klansmen murdered three civil rights volunteers, James Chaney, Andrew Goodman, and Michael Schwerner, in Neshoba County, that the extreme case of Mississippi received national attention.

At the conclusion of the March on Washington, 28 August 1963, more than two hundred thousand people gather around the Lincoln Memorial to hear Martin Luther King, Jr., deliver his "I Have a Dream" speech.
HULTON GETTY/LIAISON AGENCY

The second episode was the 1965 struggle at Selma, Alabama, for voting rights in the southern states that had long practiced racial disfranchisement. The objective was to prod President Lyndon Johnson to champion enactment of a voting rights statute; protesters hoped that by creating a situation of great tension in Selma they would arouse whatever was decent in American public opinion. The events in Selma vividly contrasted peaceful demonstrators with sheriff's deputies and state troopers who eagerly used their clubs and cattle prods against blacks seeking to register and then against marchers attempting to take their grievances to the state capital at Montgomery. At Selma, James Reeb, Jimmie Lee Jackson, Viola Liuzzo, and Jonathan Daniels entered the ranks of the nation's martyrs. Johnson threw his power behind passage of a voting rights law, ending the systematic disfranchisement of hundreds of thousands of African Americans and opening the door for blacks to participate significantly in the process of elections and officeholding.

In the Wake of the 1960s

In subsequent years issues of civil rights remained central in national policymaking. The use of affirmative action guidelines (federally sanctioned practices designed to protect women and minorities from discrimination) in education and the workplace has provoked heated controversy, its supporters arguing that affirmative action is a necessary means of realizing legal guarantees of equality, its detractors that it is a form of reverse discrimination. In 1988 Congress passed the Civil Liberties Act, recognizing the wrong inflicted upon Japanese Americans in the World War II detention program and awarding $20,000 to each survivor of the camps. Laws have been written against sexual harassment as connected to the workplace. Other notable legislation includes the Education for All Handicapped Children Act (1975) and the Americans with Disabilities Act (1990). In *Roe v. Wade* (1973), viewed by many as a civil rights decision, the Supreme Court held that the Constitution protected a woman's right to abortion. Some progress has been made toward extending the protections of constitutional rights to prisoners; as the prison population has grown so has the concern of civil rights organizations.

At the end of the twentieth century, certain civil rights issues had yet to be resolved—indeed, there was continuing debate as to what constitutes civil rights. To what extent are economic rights also civil rights? Is there or should there be a right to gainful employment that provides a decent living standard above the poverty line? The black middle class had grown considerably, but masses of African Americans were still locked in poverty; the widening income gap between whites and African Americans deprived millions of the opportunity to fulfill their potential. The actions of such states as California and Texas in abolishing affirmative action in university admissions threatened to reduce minority presence in certain quarters of higher education. Some argued that it is the human and civil right of every American to have access to competent health care and that it is government's responsibility to implement this right. There was intense debate as to whether or not the death penalty, a penalty disproportionately inflicted upon the poor and people of color, violates the constitutional right to protection from "cruel and unusual punishments." The gun-control debate, heightened by a spate of school shootings in the 1990s, pitted those who assert the constitutional right to bear arms against those who see the security of life as a right. Incidents of police brutality against minority individuals undermined the transformation of formal rights into living reality. In a modern world in which decisions by powerful institutions can generate great social benefit or incalculable destructiveness, does access to information constitute a basic civil right?

Expanding the scope of civil rights may make possible the elimination of conditions that breed violence. In the final analysis, civil rights rests on respect for the dignity and worth of all persons, respect manifested not only in words but, above all, in deeds.

BIBLIOGRAPHY

Aptheker, Herbert. *Abolitionism: A Revolutionary Movement.* Boston: Twayne, 1989.

Blaustein, Albert P., and Robert L. Zangrando. *Civil Rights and the American Negro.* New York: Trident, 1968.

Bell, Derrick. *And We Are Not Saved: The Elusive Quest for Racial Justice.* New York: Basic, 1987.

Blumberg, Rhoda L. *Civil Rights: The 1960s Freedom Struggle.* New York: Twayne, 1984.

Branch, Taylor. *Parting the Waters: America in the King Years, 1954–1963.* New York: Simon and Schuster, 1988.

———. *Pillar of Fire: America in the King Years, 1963–1965.* New York: Simon and Schuster, 1998.

Cagin, Seth, and Philip Dray. *We Are Not Afraid: The Story of Goodman, Schwerner, and Chaney and the Civil Rights Campaign for Mississippi.* New York: Macmillan, 1988.

Carson, Clayborne. *In Struggle: SNCC and the Black Awakening of the 1960s.* Cambridge, Mass.: Harvard University Press, 1981.

Carter, Dan. *Scottsboro: A Tragedy of the American South.* Baton Rouge: Louisiana State University Press, 1979.

Chafe, William H. *Civilities and Civil Rights: Greensboro, North Carolina, and the Black Struggle for Freedom.* New York: Oxford University Press, 1980.

Curry, Constance. *Silver Rights.* Chapel Hill, N.C.: Algonquin, 1995.

Daniels, Roger. *Asian America: Chinese and Japanese in America Since 1950.* Seattle: University of Washington Press, 1989.

Dittmer, John. *Local People: The Struggle for Civil Rights in Mississippi.* Urbana: University of Illinois Press, 1994.

Du Bois, W. E. B. *The Souls of Black Folk.* Millwood, N.Y.: Kraus-Thomson, 1973.

Durr, Virginia. *Outside the Magic Circle.* Tuscaloosa: University of Alabama Press, 1985.

Farmer, James. *Lay Bare the Heart: An Autobiography of the Civil Rights Movement.* New York: Arbor House, 1985.

Filler, Louis. *The Crusade Against Slavery, 1830–1860.* New York: Harper, 1960.

Flexner, Eleanor. *A Century of Struggle: The Women's Rights Movement in the United States.* Cambridge, Mass.: Harvard University Press, 1975.

Formisano, Ronald P. *Boston Against Busing: Race, Class, and Ethnicity in the 1960s and 1970s.* Chapel Hill: University of North Carolina Press, 1991.

Graham, Hugh Davis. *The Civil Rights Era: Origins and Development of National Policy, 1960–1972.* New York: Oxford University Press, 1990.

Hampton, Henry, and Steve Fayer. *Voices of Freedom: An Oral History of the Civil Rights Movement from the 1950s Through the 1980s.* New York: Bantam, 1990.

Harding, Vincent. *Hope and History: Why We Must Share the Story of the Movement.* Maryknoll, N.Y.: Orbis, 1990.

Kluger, Richard. *Simple Justice: The History of Brown v. Board of Education and Black America's Struggle for Equality.* New York: Vintage, 1977.

Konvitz, Milton. *A Century of Civil Rights.* New York: Columbia University Press, 1961.

Mills, Kay. *This Little Light of Mine: The Life of Fannie Lou Hamer.* New York: Dutton, 1993.

Morris, Aldon D. *The Origins of the Civil Rights Movement: Black Communities Organizing for Change.* New York: Free Press, 1984.

Oshinsky, David M. *Worse Than Slavery: Parchman Farm and the Ordeal of Jim Crow Justice.* New York: Free Press, 1996.

Rakove, Jack N. *Declaring Rights: A Brief History with Documents.* Boston: Bedford, 1998.

Robinson, Armstead L., and Patricia Sullivan, eds. *New Directions in Civil Rights Studies.* Charlottesville: University Press of Virginia, 1991.

Shapiro, Herbert. *White Violence and Black Response: From Reconstruction to Montgomery.* Amherst: University of Massachusetts Press, 1988.

Sitkoff, Harvard. *The Struggle for Black Equality, 1954–1980.* New York: Hill and Wang, 1981.

Tsai, Shih-shan Henry. *The Chinese Experience in America.* Bloomington: Indiana University Press, 1986.

Weisbrot, Robert. *Freedom Bound: A History of America's Civil Rights Movement.* New York: Norton, 1990.

HERBERT SHAPIRO

See also **Abortion; African Americans; Black Panthers; Church Bombings; Civil Disobedience; Civil Disorder; Dred Scott Decision; Du Bois, W. E. B.; Freedom Rides; Free Speech Movement; Gay Bashing; King, Martin Luther, Jr.; Malcolm X; Montgomery Bus Boycott; Race and Ethnicity; Reconstruction; Riots; Southern Christian Leadership Conference; Suffrage; Watts Riot.**

CIVIL WAR

During the worst fighting of the bloodiest day of the Civil War, Union soldiers fell at the rate of more than a hundred per minute. By nightfall at the Battle of Antietam (also known as the Battle of Sharpsburg), more than twenty-five thousand men had been killed, wounded, or reported missing. The date 17 September 1862 remains the most violent in U.S. history. "No tongue can tell, no mind can conceive, no pen portray the horrible sights I witnessed this morning," a soldier wrote afterward. One horrified officer reported that his men had been too exhausted to move and simply slept among the corpses.

The images of those fallen soldiers soon became a vivid part of the national memory when photographer Mathew Brady opened an unprecedented exhibition of pictures his assistants had taken of the Antietam dead. It was a pivotal moment in the history of violence in America. "Mr. Brady has done something to bring home to us the terrible reality and earnestness of war," wrote a stunned correspondent for the *New York Times* on 20 October 1862. "If he has not brought bodies and laid them in our door-yards and along streets, he has done something very like it."

There were few American families from the era who escaped the "terrible reality" of this conflict. Approximately half of the adult white men in the North and three-fourths of the adult white men in the South served in the armed forces. Nearly 200,000 African Americans, risking not only death but also a return to enslavement, also fought in uniform. Altogether more than three million soldiers served in the Union and Confederate armies. The best estimates suggest that there were over 620,000 combatant deaths, approximately 360,000 for the Union and 260,000 for the Confederacy. Another 275,000 federal soldiers and about 200,000 rebel soldiers survived their wounds, placing total casualties at well over one million. Historians have speculated that at least 50,000 Southern civilians died from war-related causes. It is nearly impossible to calculate the cost of the physical damage wrought by the conflict, but the national government spent more than $20 billion from 1861 to 1865—more than eleven times all previous federal spending combined.

The Coming of War, 1850–1861

In many ways, the scale of the violence makes a mockery of any attempts to explain why the Civil War happened. Nevertheless, historians have argued over the causes of the Civil War for years, and the topic remains a matter of debate. In 1865 Abraham Lincoln stated in his second inaugural address that slavery "was, somehow, the cause of the war." Few scholars would dispute that conclusion, but many have explored how other factors in the decade before the war, such as political blundering, cultural antipathy, economic regionalism, and partisan realignment, also contributed to the political crisis.

"Unutterable Horrors of War"

Most Southerners blamed their defeat on Northern industrial resources. Nonetheless, it would be unfair to conclude that factories and machines won a war that required such immense human sacrifice. Civil War battlefields were scenes of unfathomable chaos. Most battles took place in at least partially forested areas, and the smoke from the firearms and artillery and the occasional haphazard nature of regimental uniforms contributed to a general melee. Adding to the disorientation of battle were the deafening sounds. "It seemed as if earth and heaven were coming together, such was the roar of cannon," wrote one scared Union soldier. At Spotsylvania (12 May 1864) an oak tree some twenty inches in diameter was reportedly cut down by rifle shots alone.

In many ways the postbattle conditions were even more frightening because of inadequate medical care. One surgeon wrote to his wife, "The unutterable horrors of war most manifest in a hospital, *two weeks* after a battle, is terrible." Another surgeon confessed, "I have amputated limbs until it almost makes my heart ache to see a poor fellow coming in the Ambulance to the Hospital." The sad fact was that a Civil War soldier was two times more likely to die from disease than combat. Yet most Union soldiers endured to earn the most hard-fought victory in American history. The question was at what price did freedom and the preservation of the Union come? "We think no more of going out to fight now," wrote William Wallace of the Third Wisconsin Regiment, "than if we were going down to shoot ducks in the old marsh."

Without doubt, there was a steady and ominous escalation of violence preceding the outbreak of war. Following the Compromise of 1850 (and the strengthening of the Fugitive Slave Act), there were several dramatic shoot-outs between Southern bounty hunters who ventured into the free states and mobs of outraged abolitionists. Disturbances over the extension of slavery into the western territories also led to bloodshed. More than two hundred people died when Free-Soilers and proslavery settlers battled to determine whether the territory of Kansas would enter the Union free or slave. After Senator Charles Sumner of Massachusetts spoke out against this violence in 1856, Representative Preston Brooks of South Carolina assaulted him on the Senate floor and beat him senseless with a cane. While Sumner fell into a coma, a deranged abolitionist named John Brown vowed revenge and formed a plot that ultimately led to his notorious raid on the federal arsenal in Harpers Ferry, Virginia, in 1859.

When Southern states, led by South Carolina, began seceding from the Union following the Republican Party's victory in 1860, there was a grim sense of inevitability to the crisis. "The tug has to come," President-elect Lincoln wrote privately, "and better now than later." Yet for all of the tense anticipation, the nation was sorely unprepared for what was to come. At the outset of the conflict, there were fewer than twenty thousand soldiers in the federal army, mostly stationed west of the Mississippi River and preoccupied with fighting Indians. Union arsenals contained just over a half million small firearms—almost entirely outdated flintlock muskets—out of which nearly one-third immediately fell into Confederate hands following the attack on Fort Sumter in April 1861. Faced with the surreal prospect of invading their own nation, Union military planners reportedly had to purchase current maps of the Southern states from local bookstores.

Mobilizing the Armies, April 1861–February 1862

Mobilization thus proved challenging for both sides, but ultimately the North's greater industrial capacity provided the critical difference, especially in the production of weapons and ammunition. In 1860 there were more than 110,000 factories across the North but only about 18,000 in the South. By the end of the conflict, Northern factories and armories had produced over 2.5 million small firearms, more than ten times the Southern production. The Confederacy was forced to rely mainly upon British imports and captured Union rifles to keep pace in the deadly small-arms race. The South proved more capable at mass-producing heavier artillery. The Tredegar Iron Works in Richmond alone manufactured about a thousand of the Confederates' three thousand cannon. Nevertheless, the Union still held a significant advantage, producing twice as much heavy artillery as the rebels. In addition, federal troops were better clothed and better fed than their Confederate counterparts. By the middle of the war, one Union

Civil War Casualties

	Union	Confederate
Combat deaths	110,070	94,000 (est.)
Killed in action	67,088	N.A.
Mortally wounded	43,012	N.A.
Deaths from disease	249,458	164,000 (est.)
Deaths from dysentery	44,558	N.A.
Deaths from typhus	40,656	N.A.
Deaths from pneumonia	19,971	N.A.
Imprisoned by enemy	194,743	214,865
Died during confinement	30,218	25,976
Desertion	200,000 (est.)	104,000 (est.)
Caught and returned	80,000 (est.)	21,000 (est.)
Executed	147	N.A.
Wounded survivors	275,175	194,026 (est.)
Civilian war-related deaths	N.A.	50,000 (est.)

general reported, "A French army of half the size of ours could be supplied with what we waste."

The Union and Confederate armies were organized in similar but not identical fashion. Each contained three combat branches—artillery, cavalry, and infantry—with the regiment as the fundamental organizational unit. Without question, the infantry was the most important branch of both armies, inflicting (and suffering) 80 to 90 percent of the war's casualties. The infantry soldiers from each side typically carried a single-shot rifled musket. Union troops favored a .58-caliber Springfield rifle produced at the Springfield Armory in Massachusetts. The primary Confederate rifle was the .577-caliber Enfield imported from England. Both weapons were nearly five feet long, weighed about nine pounds, and required a complicated protocol to load and shoot, but experienced soldiers learned to fire two or three rounds per minute at an effective range of a few hundred yards. Late in the war, Union troops, especially in the cavalry, benefited from new breech-loading and repeating rifles, but such modern inventions were slow to gain acceptance and prone to malfunction.

For most of the war's first year, there were only occasional skirmishes as each side tackled logistical and organizational problems. The few battles did little more than demonstrate the woeful inexperience of federal troops and officers. At the first Battle of Bull Run (also known as the Battle of Manassas), on 21 July 1861, members of the press and Washington society watched in horror as the Confederates routed the Union forces and sent them fleeing back to the nation's besieged capital. Following this debacle Lincoln devoted himself prin-

cipally to keeping border states within the Union and effectively ceded control of the army to a thirty-four-year-old general, George McClellan, who prepared to fight a textbook-style campaign against the Confederate armies and delayed major action until the spring of 1862.

Fighting Through Stalemate, March 1862–February 1864

From 1862 to 1864, however, Union troops not only failed to break the Confederate defenses in northern Virginia but also endured several embarrassing defeats and even occasional rebel invasions of northern territory—such as at Antietam in Maryland (1862) and Gettysburg in Pennsylvania (1863). McClellan (who was dismissed shortly after the brutal standoff at Antietam) and his successors seemed baffled by the audacity of the Confederate general Robert E. Lee and by the logistical challenge of subduing 750,000 square miles of rebel territory. Only in the western theater of the war did Union troops seem to earn significant victories on Confederate territory, as General Ulysses S. Grant led a series of hard-fought campaigns along the Mississippi River that effectively split the Confederacy in two by the summer of 1863.

When the Army of the Potomac, under the command of General George Meade, finally won a decisive victory against Lee's Army of Northern Virginia at the Battle of Gettysburg (1–3 July 1863), it marked the costliest human sacrifice in American military history, with combined casualties of nearly fifty thousand men. During this battle at a small Pennsylvania crossroads, Lee lost one-third of his fighting force of seventy-five thousand men.

The continued intensity of the carnage frustrated segments of the Northern home front and led to escalating criticism of the Lincoln administration. In one of the saddest ironies of the war, several Union regiments that helped save the nation in Gettysburg found themselves only days later shooting down antidraft protestors in New York City, causing at least 120 civilian deaths in one of the worst riots in American history. Nor was the South immune to such civil disturbances. Several hundred housewives rioted in Richmond during the spring of 1863 over food shortages.

But if civilians were growing weary of the stalemate, somehow the troops managed to persevere. Only about 8 percent of the Union troops and 20 percent of the Confederates were conscripts or draftees. When three-year enlistments in the Union Army were up in 1864, more than half of those veterans remained to fight. The average Confed-

The Battle of Gettysburg, Pennsylvania, 1–3 July 1863. Lithograph by Currier and Ives. THE GRANGER COLLECTION

erate soldier was disabled at least six times during the course of the conflict by battle wounds or sickness—and yet continued to fight. Who were these brave souls? About half of the Union soldiers were farmers, more than one-third were skilled artisans, and one-tenth were laborers; nearly one-quarter were foreign-born, a figure roughly equivalent to their proportion in the northern population. According to one of the most complete studies, only forty-seven out of every thousand soldiers had any education beyond grammar school—although more than 90 percent were literate. The average age at enlistment in the Union army was just under twenty-six.

Small-unit cohesion, religion, local pride, and other cultural factors provide some explanation for the determination of these soldiers, but arguably the most critical factor as the war dragged on was ideological. From a dispute over the legal rights of states, this conflict had evolved by 1863 into a struggle for freedom. That was why Lincoln's brief memorial at the military cemetery in Gettysburg on 19 November 1863 struck such a resonant chord when he equated Northern war aims with a "new birth of freedom." Since the issuance of the Emancipation Proclamation on 1 January 1863, the war had been about ending the evil of slavery as much as restoring the Union. Not only did the proclamation promise to end slavery in the rebel territories, it also paved the way for nearly two hundred thousand African Americans to serve on the Union side during the critical final months of the war. Higher moral stakes meant even fiercer resis-

tance from the rebels, but the rising body count seemed to demand a nobler purpose both in the field and at home.

Destroying the Confederacy, March 1864–April 1865

On the other hand, the countless battlefield deaths also translated into expressions of revenge and a steady escalation in brutality. Approximately ten thousand Missouri civilians along the Kansas border were banished from their homes in 1863 by Union commanders angered by Confederate guerrilla warfare. It was an ominous precedent. "They cannot be made to love us," wrote the Union general William T. Sherman, "but they can be made to fear us." Recognizing that he needed a general who had demonstrated an ability to inspire fear, Lincoln brought Ulysses Grant to the East and promoted him to general-in-chief in March 1864. Grant devised a plan that sent Sherman and his troops toward Atlanta while he helped direct the Army of the Potomac on yet another campaign toward Richmond. The purpose of these simultaneous assaults, coupled with other raids on rebel strongholds, was to destroy the Confederacy and finally finish the war. The results would anticipate at least some of the awful effects of modern total war.

However brutal, Grant's plan contained elements of strategic genius rooted in his adaptation to the new conditions of mechanized warfare. Grant, a former leather-store clerk from Galena, Illinois, continued the nineteenth-century tradition

A Union artillery battery during the Civil War. THE GRANGER COLLECTION

of maneuvering massed armies in persistent attempts to flank or "turn" the enemy, but he coupled this tactic with a grand strategy of constant pressure and raids designed to break the Confederate war-making capacity. What Grant recognized was that the increased accuracy and greater range of rifled muskets—created by the spiraled groove cut inside the barrel—and the more efficient, elongated bullets called "minie balls" that expanded when fired, allowed relatively few defenders to hold off assaults from forces in much greater numbers. Grant appeared to be the only leading Union general willing to authorize the relentless and wide-ranging campaigning necessary to overcome this defensive stalemate.

However, Grant still faced one even more imposing human obstacle. In addition to his reputation for offensive brilliance, General Robert E. Lee proved equally adept on the defensive as he maneuvered his depleted armies and employed trenches and earthen field fortifications around Richmond. The clashes between Grant and Lee from the spring of 1864 until the war's end in April 1865 were some of the war's most horrific. At Cold Harbor (3 June 1864), Union forces suffered over seven thousand casualties compared to only fifteen hundred for the Confederates. Combat-hardened

veterans pinned their names and addresses to their uniforms before the battle in forlorn recognition of their likely fate. One prescient soldier found dead had carried a diary into combat that read, "June 3. Cold Harbor. I was killed."

Near the end of August 1864, President Lincoln actually began to prepare for the likelihood that his Democratic opponent and former subordinate, George McClellan, would win the election of 1864 and negotiate an end to the war. Many observers questioned Northern resolve, and several Republicans considered the prospect of dumping Lincoln from the ticket. But Sherman's capture of Atlanta in September was arguably the most significant single moment in the war, a military victory that essentially guaranteed Lincoln's political success and the continuation of the Union war effort.

The more traditional reason for Sherman's fame (or infamy) surrounds the reports of atrocities committed by his marauding troops known as "bummers" during the final months of the war. Although the atrocities have been the subject of some controversy, the extent of Sherman's war crimes against civilians has probably been overstated. Maps of the area surrounding the path of Sherman's march from Atlanta to Savannah indicate that very few civilian homes were actually destroyed—one document shows only three buildings burned across a sixty-mile stretch. Sherman himself estimated that the damage done by his bummers was about $100 million, most of which he admitted was probably "simple waste and destruction."

Coming to some judgment about civilian atrocities committed during Sherman's marches in Georgia (and later the Carolinas), and in the "campaign of fire and vandalism" conducted in 1864 by Generals David Hunter and Philip Sheridan in the Shenandoah Valley, remains terribly sensitive. One result, however, is indisputable. The strategy was brutally effective. During the winter of 1864–1865, the Confederate resistance crumbled. By the spring of 1865, Grant finally captured Richmond and cornered Lee and his exhausted Army of Northern Virginia at Appomattox. Although Lee's surrender on 9 April 1865 marked the effective end of the Confederacy, President Jefferson Davis and several armies continued sporadic fighting for another two months.

Facing the Aftermath

Clearly, the Civil War's unprecedented explosion of violence, and the subsequent adjustment to its terrible reality, had a lasting impact on American history. For the next thirty-five years, U.S. politics was bitter, divisive, and violent. Reconstruc-

tion, which lasted in at least some areas of the South until 1877, provoked political crises that rivaled the antebellum period, leading at one point to the first presidential impeachment in American history. More troubling, in the next thirty years, the nation endured the assassination of three presidents—Lincoln in 1865, James Garfield in 1881, and William McKinley in 1901. No president was elected from a former Confederate state until Lyndon Johnson of Texas won the presidency in 1964. Political reconciliation came slowly to a nation still divided.

For the freed slaves, however, reconciliation meant little. African Americans enjoyed a brief period of economic and political independence in the South before an explosion of racial violence and legal segregation denied them the full reality of the freedom Lincoln had once promised. During Reconstruction, Ku Klux Klan violence reached epidemic proportions. More than three hundred African American voters were reportedly murdered by Klansmen during one election campaign in Arkansas in 1868. Over the years the continued lynching of black males ultimately led to a great migration of Southern black families to the North.

Yet the aftermath could have been worse. Only one Confederate, Henry Wirz, the commandant of the notorious Andersonville prison camp, was executed for war crimes. Although disabled veterans

The Union general William T. Sherman and troops march through Georgia to the sea, 1864. THE GRANGER COLLECTION

Two women in mourning move among the ruins in Richmond, Virginia, April 1865.
CORBIS

were common sights in towns across the nation, the public celebration of their sacrifices helped ease their transition back into the peacetime society. Many wrote colorful recollections of their experience. According to the most recent estimates, more than fifty thousand books have been written on the Civil War and the total rises steadily. There are still hundreds of Civil War roundtables and reenactments. Over the years, the realities of the war's violence have given way to an almost romantic sensibility. One veteran, later a famous jurist, described the process of that transformation with typically sardonic flair: "War when you are at it, is horrible and dull," Oliver Wendell Holmes, Jr., concluded. "It is only when time has passed that you see that its message was divine."

BIBLIOGRAPHY

Boritt, Gabor S., ed. *Why the Confederacy Lost*. New York: Oxford University Press, 1992.

Donald, David Herbert. *Lincoln*. New York: Simon and Schuster, 1995.

Foner, Eric. *Reconstruction: America's Unfinished Revolution, 1863–1877*. New York: Harper and Row, 1988.

Fox, William F. *Regimental Losses in the American Civil War, 1861–1865*. Albany, N.Y.: Albany Publishing, 1889.

Grimsley, Mark. *The Hard Hand of War: Union Military Policy Toward Southern Civilians, 1861–1865*. Cambridge, England: Cambridge University Press, 1995.

Hagerman, Edward. *The American Civil War and the Origins of Modern Warfare*. Bloomington: Indiana University Press, 1988.

Hattaway, Herman, and Archer Jones. *How the North Won: A Military History of the Civil War*. Urbana: University of Illinois Press, 1982.

Hess, Earl J. *The Union Soldier in Battle: Enduring the Ordeal of Combat*. Lawrence: University Press of Kansas, 1997.

Livermore, Thomas L. *Numbers and Losses in the Civil War in America: 1861–65*. 1900. Reprint, New York: Kraus Reprint. 1969.

McPherson, James M. *Battle Cry of Freedom: The Civil War Era*. New York: Oxford University Press, 1988.

———. *For Cause and Comrades: Why Men Fought in the Civil War.* New York: Oxford University Press, 1997.

Royster, Charles. *The Destructive War: William Tecumseh Sherman, Stonewall Jackson, and the Americans.* New York: Knopf, 1991.

MATTHEW PINSKER

See also **Dred Scott Decision; Harpers Ferry, Raid on; Lincoln, Abraham; Military Culture; Prisoners of War; Quantrill's Raid; Reconstruction.**

CLANTON GANG
Newman (1816–1881); Phin (1845–1906); Ike (1847–1887); Billy (1862–1881)

The Clanton family is remembered chiefly as the foil of the Earp brothers in the sanguinary affairs of Tombstone, Arizona, between 1880 and 1882. Without the Fremont Street fiasco commonly called the "gunfight at the O. K. Corral," the Clantons might have escaped the light of history altogether. The Clantons were among the early settlers of southeastern Arizona, arriving there first in 1873, when the Apache still reigned in the region. That they were hardy folk there is no doubt, but they were always linked to the violence of the time.

The patriarch of the family, Newman Haynes Clanton, usually called "Old Man" Clanton in the popular literature, was born in Davidson County, Tennessee, in 1816. In 1840 he married Mariah Sexton Kelso in Callaway County, Missouri. She bore five sons and two daughters: John W. (1841–1916), Phineas F. "Phin," Joseph I. "Ike," Mary E. (1852–1916), Esther A. (1854–1919), Peter A. (1859–?), and William H. "Billy." Old Man Clanton left his family in 1849 for the California gold rush. Returning home in 1851, he moved first to Illinois and then to Texas. There in 1861 he and his oldest son, John, enlisted in the Confederate army. John promptly deserted but later received minimal punishment and reenlisted, serving out the rest of the Civil War. After the war Newman moved his family again, this time to southern Arizona and then to California.

Most of the family returned to Arizona in 1873, where Newman established a farming community named Clantonville, which failed by 1877. He next established a cattle ranch south of Charleston, just in time for the silver boom at Tombstone. He turned the ranch over to his boys, Phin and Ike, in 1880. With the increased demand for beef created by military contracts and the demands of the min-ing camps, the Clantons supplemented their herds by stealing Mexican cattle. The so-called Clanton gang was initially little more than a motley crew of drovers, some of them from Texas and New Mexico.

But Tombstone presented a threat as well as an opportunity. The boom brought the cowboys' operations under closer scrutiny. Probably few locals cared about the origin of the beef on their tables, but other activities of the gang, including stage robberies, shootings, and rowdyism, soon brought them into collision with the Tombstone business elite and the Earps. Tensions mounted after a failed stage robbery near Benson resulted in the deaths of the Earps's driver and passenger. Wyatt Earp offered Ike Clanton $6,000 if he would help him bring in the culprits from the Clanton gang. This secret deal precipitated the Earp-Clanton feud.

Before Ike could bring in the culprits, Mexicans killed Old Man Clanton and four others, including the only survivor of the bunch that had tried to rob the stage, at Guadalupe Canyon. On the evening of 25 October 1881, Ike had a confrontation with John Henry "Doc" Holliday, whom he suspected of knowing about his deal with Wyatt. Afterward, he went on a drunken binge that was the direct cause of the O. K. Corral fight on 26 October. He fled the fight while his youngest brother, Billy, and Tom and Frank McLaury died.

Following the street fight, Ike tried to have the Earps convicted of murder. When he failed, he joined others in a vendetta against the Earps that left Virgil Earp with a crippled arm and Morgan Earp dead. Wyatt Earp then sought revenge, killing four cowboys allied with the Clantons before leaving the territory in the spring of 1882. Ike and Phin Clanton soon left Cochise County as well, settling two hundred miles north in Apache County.

Over the next few years both brothers were accused of various shootings, thefts, and other crimes but were never convicted. Then on 1 June 1887 Ike Clanton was killed by Jonas V. Brighton, an agent of a cattlemen's association. Four months later Phin Clanton was sentenced to ten years in prison for grand larceny. He was pardoned five years later, but he was accused of various crimes during the 1890s. He married in 1902 and died in 1906.

The Clanton gang, whose name was a misnomer for the collection of criminals and ne'er-do-wells that caused so much trouble in Tombstone and southern Arizona in the early 1880s, became a staple part of the popular literature of the Earp-Clanton feud, with Old Man Clanton elevated to patriarch of a vast criminal combine and Ike made into the symbol of the crude, violent, and cowardly thugs who faced the Earps in the Tombstone melodrama.

BIBLIOGRAPHY

Tefertiller, Casey. *Wyatt Earp: The Life Behind the Legend.* New York: Wiley, 1997.

Traywick, Ben T. *The Clantons of Tombstone.* Tombstone, Ariz.: Red Marie's Bookstore, 1996.

GARY L. ROBERTS

See also **Earp Brothers; Frontier; Gunfighters and Outlaws, Western; Holliday, John Henry "Doc"; O. K. Corral Gunfight.**

CLASS

Throughout American history, class-based inequalities have thwarted the country's democratic promise of political inclusiveness and upward economic mobility. From the beginning of colonial settlement onward, the expansiveness of the landscape combined with the relatively open and liberal nature of American political and economic institutions have held out the possibility that a wide range of groups would have the opportunity to prosper and participate in self-governance. At the same time, successive class systems have denied to certain groups the means of mobility—access to land, education, artisanal skills, and entrepreneurship—and have sustained exploitative labor relationships between elites and workers. This tension between rhetoric and reality, between the ideal of freedom and the fact of subordination, helps to explain distinctive patterns of violence stemming from class relationships within the British North American colonies and later within the United States.

It is possible to outline four contexts in which class-related violence occurs; yet individual instances of violence often blur these contexts, suggesting that they overlap and reinforce each other. First, in its most dramatic forms, class-related violence derives not only from efforts on the part of the powerful to use force to maintain their political prerogatives and exploit the powerless (and especially their labor) but also from efforts among the powerless to resist such exploitation. Second, when avenues of upward mobility and respectability are blocked to them, certain groups of non-

elites vent their rage not on their oppressors but on persons as vulnerable as, or even more than, themselves, within a specific political economy.

A third context of class-related violence reveals the historic injustices committed against persons of African descent; these injustices possess a class component—that is, in some respects the oppression of black people is a variation on the theme of the oppression of poor people—but at the same time, racial ideologies transcend class relationships and spawn unique forms of violence. Indeed, in certain circumstances blacks constitute a caste —a group of people targeted for discrimination regardless of their socioeconomic status. Thus, lynch mobs in the Jim Crow South murdered relatively well-to-do black shopkeepers as well as sharecroppers accused (falsely) of various crimes.

Finally, at times the state (in the form of individual heads of state and groups as diverse as local law enforcement agents, congressmen, and federal health and safety inspectors) upholds through the force of law and the threat of violence a wide variety of unequal relationships, and at other times intercedes on behalf of people who cannot protect themselves from the depredations of lawless groups and individuals. Violent activities of the state, ranging from the prosecution of wars to the prosecution and punishment of criminals, inevitably reveal a class dimension when they place the weak and the poor at risk and preserve the privileges of the powerful in the process.

Class-related violence, then, can take many forms. The slave driver wielded a whip over workers in the fields, and the late-nineteenth-century industrialist relied on private security guards to intimidate striking workers with pistols and billy clubs. Eighteenth-century backwoods farmers engaged in skirmishes with land speculators and their minions, the land surveyors; and members of Depression-era tenant associations used violence to turn back officials charged with evicting families from their homes. Those particular uses of physical force are straightforward enough. Yet violence can also assume indirect forms, for example, when state governments deinstitutionalize public mental-health programs with the result that impoverished, mentally ill persons are left homeless and vulnerable to attacks by criminals on the street or when federal inspectors turn a blind eye toward dangerous worksites.

Class systems are ultimately fluid relationships, and in order to understand the roots of the violence undergirding them, it is necessary to examine the ways those systems have changed over time. It is possible to outline, at least in broad terms, three successive class systems in American history and explore the sites of conflict characteristic of each system. These class systems were most prominent in the period when most workers were bound laborers of some sort (the early colonial period through the Revolution in the North and the Civil War in the South), the period when heavy manufacturing drove the economy (for a century, beginning in the mid-nineteenth century), and the period characterized by relatively small numbers of highly paid, well-educated "information managers" and large numbers of ill-paid service workers (roughly the latter half of the twentieth century). The transitions between these systems were especially contentious points in American history, as patterns of state authority and labor deployment shifted and aggrieved groups reacted violently.

Violence and the Creation of Social Hierarchies in the Colonial and Early National Periods

During the colonial period in the North, and until 1865 in the South, Anglo elites derived their power from commercial activities and (especially in the South) from the control of large tracts of land and large numbers of bound laborers to work the land. Compared with many European societies, the colonies boasted a large percentage of landed male household heads. Nevertheless, landownership had as its counterpoint the dispossession of hundreds of thousands of Native Americans; the ideal of the yeoman farmer thus came at the expense of the natives who were killed or driven away from their ancestral homelands. The American Revolution furthered this process of conquest, highlighting the conjunction of liberal, republican ideals with unbridled viciousness.

As sites of economic production, the colonial household and later the southern slave plantation were marked by violence between workers and their masters. In the seventeenth-century Chesapeake, tobacco planters desperate to keep ahead of declining prices worked their indentured servants mercilessly, foreshadowing patterns of physical brutality that would become routine on slave plantations. In England the comparable institution of servants-in-husbandry had built-in safeguards against such abuse; servants had the opportunity to contract with a new master at the end of every harvest season. In contrast, colonial servants were bound to work for long periods of time—seven years was the standard, but in fact many were forced to work much longer—in order to repay their transportation costs. Colonial records are replete with accounts of male and female servants who resisted the demands made upon them, either by retaliating violently against their tormentors or by running away.

Bacon's Rebellion reveals overlapping contexts of class-related violence. This uprising, which engulfed the colony of Virginia in 1676, originated in a conflict between backcountry settlers and the Susquehannock Indians. Resentful over the lack of land available to freed servants and angered over the refusal of the colonial elite to commit troops to protect them from the Indians, the settlers, under the leadership of the well-born Nathaniel Bacon, Jr., launched an offensive against the colonial capital, drawing support from poor farmers, servants, craftsmen, and slaves along the way. Eventually, twenty-three of the rebels were executed (Bacon died of disease before he could be apprehended). What began as a battle between colonists and Indians had mushroomed into a challenge to elite authority. Within the coming years, colonial officials would seek to divert the attention of poor farmers from the injustices of colonial rule by bolstering the system of black slavery and awarding all white men regardless of status the right to bear arms and own land.

The hierarchical lines of authority of the southern slave plantation resembled those of a ship, where more often than not the discipline of the crew assumed violent forms. Local governments ceded to individual slave owners total power over their workers. Unlike English servants, American slaves had no rights that the courts or their masters were bound to respect. By the time of the Revolution, slave owners had begun to differentiate Africans and their descendants from the poor in general; the resulting racial ideology, which posited stark differences in the temperament and intelligence of black people compared with white people, provided the philosophical foundation for the unbridled exploitation of slaves. The institutionalized use of violence—whippings, brandings, mutilations, and even public executions—allowed slave owners not only to discipline recalcitrant workers but also to terrorize enslaved workers in general.

The Revolution crystallized a number of class relationships and the political crosscurrents that sustained them. Colonial elites, thwarted in their attempts to achieve Crown-appointed positions of power and influence and deprived of representation in the British Parliament, threw off the yoke of monarchy while simultaneously seeking to maintain their economic and political interests at home. Indeed, the Patriots fought battles on a number of fronts. Within their own households, white men in the South especially sought to solidify the institution of bondage by protecting their holdings in the face of British attack and, later, by securing constitutional authority for slavery. Some slaves joined the British forces to fight against slaveholders and on behalf of their own freedom; others resisted the wartime demands imposed upon them by their Patriot masters by working carelessly or not at all.

Even as enslaved Americans were rendered marginal within the emerging new nation, a variety of groups, including urban artisans, backcountry squatters, and the tenants on huge Hudson Valley estates, launched violent challenges to patterns of class privilege and feudalism. These groups embraced the rhetoric of revolution, with an emphasis on self-determination and equal economic opportunity, and thereby heralded the emergence of a new class system characterized by free, and not bound, white labor. These uprisings met with mixed results. In 1786 a group of armed men in western Massachusetts demanded financial relief from an eastern elite class of merchants and creditors. These followers of the Revolutionary War veteran Daniel Shays sought to close the courts of the new commonwealth and thereby stymie anti-debtor, hard-currency policies. The Massachusetts militia crushed the rebels. And too, between 1790 and 1809, in more than one hundred different incidents, backwoods insurgents in Maine, calling themselves Liberty Men, dressed in Indian clothing and attacked the surveyors and agents hired by landowners; in at least some cases they managed to disrupt the process of rampant land speculation in the backcountry.

From the cauldron of the Revolution flowed distinctive class systems in the North and South. In the South slavery benefited from the protection of the Constitution and from the territorial expansion that followed the defeat of the British, the French, and their Indian allies to the west. In the North during the late eighteenth century, the demise of slavery and indentured servitude testified to the growth of a dynamic economy that relied on flexible labor arrangements, especially wage labor.

It is worth noting at this point that some historians have suggested that the entry of women into the urban paid-labor force as domestics or needleworkers contributed to a form of collective misogyny that manifested itself in the form of male sexual predatory behavior. If we define "classes" as groups with varying degrees of access to power and material resources, then it is possible to argue that, throughout much of American history, females have constituted a separate class from males. In some instances men commit sexual assaults against women who are considered the cause of the struggling (male) breadwinner's humiliating precariousness in the labor market. Certainly the time-honored double standard that accepted forms of male sexual aggression and condemned as immoral the female victims of that aggression represented an enduring form of class-related violence.

Emergent Racial Ideologies and Class Violence

In the North the transition from an agricultural-commercial economy to an industrial economy pitted various groups against each other. Jacksonian rhetoric elevating the "common man" to a position of political-symbolic significance was counterbalanced by dramatic transformations in the economy that threatened to condemn whole groups to poverty. In 1828 striking weavers in New York City protested the low wages paid them by the city's largest textile employer, Alexander Knox, by destroying his home, attacking his son, and dismantling the looms of their nonstriking coworkers.

The routinization of manual labor and the decline in patriarchal relationships (master-servant) meant that more and more workers were toiling under the direction of a boss whose primary consideration was efficient, time-oriented production. At worksites like canals, where workers were ill-paid, housed in tents, and subjected to harsh discipline on the job, fights broke out among men who defined themselves on the basis of "tribalistic" loyalties, arraying whites against blacks, Protestants against Catholics, the native-born against immigrants, and even, for example, Irishmen against each other (based on their county and kin loyalties). In many instances alcohol played a major part in these intraclass skirmishes, which often resulted less from convictions based on principle or politics than from the raw social antagonisms among the powerless themselves.

These conflicts played themselves out on a larger stage throughout the antebellum North, where workers increasingly identified themselves according to their gender, race, ethnicity, religion, and skills (or lack thereof) and scrambled to stay off the bottom rungs of the labor-market ladder. In certain cities workers organized themselves into fire companies during after-work hours, and the pitched battles between members of rival companies amounted to turf wars within the laboring classes. Fearful of their own insecure position within a transformed economy, native-born workers attacked immigrants and their institutions, especially during the 1830s and 1840s. In 1834 native-born Protestants burned an Ursuline convent near Boston, demonstrating their fear of newly arrived Catholic immigrants from Ireland. A year later, Protestants and Catholics fought each other during a major riot in the Five Points slum of New York City.

It was during this period that workers of west European descent, regardless of religion or ethnicity, embraced the notion of "whiteness" to distinguish themselves from slaves and the descendants of slaves. In the North demonstrations of African American political protest (and even cultural celebrations like parades and festivals) served to provoke whites, who feared that large numbers of freed slaves would ultimately migrate out of the South and work as cheap laborers in the North. Angry mobs of whites targeted individual abolitionists and their white supporters as well as ordinary black men and women workers and black communities in general.

Irish immigrants in particular were forced to compete with blacks for jobs at the lowest echelons of the workforce—as teamsters, construction workers, waiters, and other kinds of manual laborers. (Black workers referred to the bricks lobbed at them by their antagonists as Irish confetti.) At least some antiblack violence during this period stemmed from the fact that black workers tended to toil in the out-of-doors, visible to the white laboring classes and therefore presumably more threatening as a public presence. At the same time, white elites, such as merchants and cotton manufacturers, provided tacit support to such violent activity, for they relied on the southern slave system for their profits and feared that abolition would directly harm their economic interests.

On the West Coast white working men, disappointed that gold mines, factories, and fields had not yielded the riches they had hoped for, directed their wrath against Chinese immigrants. Discriminatory tax provisions leveled at Chinese workers in the 1850s escalated into a full-blown nativist movement by the 1870s, as whites persisted in blaming the newcomers for the drop in wages that was in reality precipitated by the completion of the transcontinental railroad and the importation of manufactured goods from the East. Anti-Chinese riots proved destructive in Los Angeles in 1871 and San Francisco in 1877. A wave of terror swept over Chinese communities in towns throughout the West in 1885; that year a mob of white miners destroyed the Chinatown in Rock Springs, Wyoming, and killed twenty-eight Chinese.

The social turmoil characteristic of the antebellum North and Far West illustrated several principles of class relations that would continue to shape American industrial capitalism and spur class-related violence for the next century or so. First, employers would engage in a ceaseless quest to reduce labor costs by seeking out groups who would work for the longest hours at the lowest wages. At times the solution to this problem came in the form of labor-saving machines, which became additional sources of violence (injuries and life-threatening illnesses) affecting workers of all kinds. Employees initiated turnouts and strikes in an effort to wrest concessions from their employers in the areas of wages and working conditions; employees also sought to control by means of force the entry of certain groups—blacks, white women, or strikebreakers, for example—into the labor force. Employers benefited from this type of intra-class warfare, for they relied upon "reserve armies" of laborers, chronically underemployed men and women who stood ready and willing to work for little pay whenever the opportunity presented itself.

Southern planters expressed their contempt for northern "free labor" and its raw racial and ethnic animosities. Yet southern elites also had to contend with violent rebellions; the history of the region was punctuated by slave revolts. An unknown number of slaves and free people of color conspired to liberate themselves from the southern racial caste system. Among the best-known conspiracies and, for southern whites, most frightening were those of Gabriel Prosser, a slave blacksmith (in Richmond, Virginia, in 1800); Denmark Vesey, a black who had purchased his own freedom (in Charleston, South Carolina, in 1822); and Nat Turner, a free black preacher (in Southampton County, Virginia, in 1831). In this 1831 uprising slaves murdered fifty-seven white men, women, and children, and Turner and sixteen of his followers were eventually executed. John Brown's raid on the federal armory in Harpers Ferry, Virginia, in 1859—intended to provoke a general insurrection among slaves—struck terror in the hearts of many white Southerners and gave rise to widespread rumors about other slave uprisings in the making. To protect themselves against a revolution from below, southern planters acted at once defensively and aggressively by seceding from the Union.

The Civil War brought to the fore various class relationships that ultimately turned violent in the course of the conflict. The governments of both the United States and the Confederate States of America relied upon manpower mobilization policies that favored the rich over the poor—by allowing wealthy men to purchase substitutes to serve in their place in the army and by exempting certain favored classes (but not ordinary farmers) from military service altogether. Responding to the Union Conscription Act of 1863, workers in northern cities directed their wrath both toward blacks and toward the rich. In New York City white rioters lynched six blacks, beat many more, and burned the Colored Orphan Asylum; they also vandalized the homes of prominent abolitionists and attacked well-dressed whites on the street.

In the South the ranks of Confederate political leaders and military officers were dominated by large planters who sought to preserve the institution of slavery at all costs. These men approved policies like the "twenty slave law," which permitted each plantation to withhold from military service one white man (a planter, his son, or an overseer) for every twenty slaves on the place. During the course of the war, nonslaveholding farmers and other poor Southerners expressed their resentment toward elites in a variety of ways. Principled Unionists engaged in guerrilla warfare against Confederate troops, especially in the hill country of southern states. Poor women and their children staged bread riots in protest of the high prices for food and the lack of food. As a group, enslaved Americans became freedom fighters and "enemies at home," and they carried out other acts of subversion within the heart of the Confederacy—black men became Union soldiers and men, women, and children abandoned their master's plantation in favor of the uncertainty of life on the road.

The efforts of a new southern elite to assert its authority after the war assumed violent forms. Men of various classes transformed the Democratic Party into a white man's fraternity dedicated to the forceful subordination of all African Americans, both in the cities and the countryside. The Ku Klux Klan and other white supremacist organizations left class divisions among whites intact but preserved the economic and political interests of large landowners and fledgling industrialists in opposition to landless whites. In May 1866 terrorists (including many policemen) attacked blacks in Memphis, Tennessee, leaving forty-five blacks and three whites dead. In New Orleans that same summer, another forty people (most of them black) died at the hands of a white mob. During the period leading up to the election of 1868, white vigilantes killed two hundred black Republicans in St. Landry Parish, Louisiana, thus eliminating the Republican vote in that parish altogether.

Well into the twentieth century, the redeemed South operated on principles of state-sanctioned terror, as lynch mobs hanged, multilated, and burned black people, some of whom had committed the crime of resisting Jim Crow, while others were chosen randomly to better intimidate the whole black population. In parts of the South, a new generation of blacks, born as free men and women, engaged in public demonstrations against Jim Crow streetcars and other forms of racial segregation. In 1906 white rioters in Atlanta killed twenty-five blacks, injured many more, and destroyed black neighborhoods. Between 1900 and 1916, lynch mobs claimed eleven hundred victims, mostly black men and women in the South and Midwest. By refusing to support antilynching legislation until the mid-twentieth century, successive U.S. presidents and congresses implicitly condoned such violence.

Forced labor persisted in the South after emancipation. Most rural southern blacks and an increasing number of rural whites worked as sharecroppers and tenant farmers, many in a state of debt peonage or neoslavery. These families were kept at work on a plantation at the point of a gun or by the threat of incarceration presumably because of their indebtedness to the landowner. In the swamps of Florida, eastern European immigrants who had been lured south with promises of gainful employment found themselves at work on railroad beds and in turpentine camps guarded by armed men and attack dogs. It was also in the South that the convict lease and convict labor systems were used most extensively; these systems funneled poor, mostly black, men out of the towns and rural areas and into public works projects like the construction of roads. The chain-gang prisoner wielding a pickax under a blistering summer sun offered a particularly grim representation of the New South.

Industrial Capitalism and Patterns of Class Violence

The emergence of the United States as a major industrial world power in the late nineteenth century was marked by bloody battles between workers and employers. In contrast to western European countries, where labor parties served as a mediating force between these two groups, the late-nineteenth-century United States offered no legitimate political voice to members of the working classes or their allies. Bosses had virtually unlimited power to impose long hours on workers vulnerable to accidents and other industry-related hazards. The principle of laissez-faire was a decidedly one-sided affair, with the states and the federal government attempting to facilitate the growth of monopoly capital while constraining (at the point of the bayonet) the efforts of workers determined to organize themselves.

Once again, the brutality of the economic system stood in stark contrast to the rhetoric of freedom and opportunity—rhetoric that drew twenty-six million immigrants to American shores between 1880 and 1916. Violent industrial strikes claimed the lives of men and women workers, both black and white, in the North, Midwest, and South. The Great Strike of 1877, a nationwide work stoppage of railroad workers, was marked by pitched battles between workers arrayed on one side, and local police forces, private security agents, state militias, and federal troops on the other. In Pittsburgh state militiamen imported from Philadelphia killed twenty-six people, as strikers looted and burned railroad property. During the depression of the early 1890s, strikes initiated by the Amalgamated Association of Iron, Steel, and Tin Workers at the Homestead steel plant near Pittsburgh and by the American Railway Union in Pullman, Illinois, again pitted U.S. troops and security guards against workers; the first incident resulted in the deaths of sixteen people, the latter twelve.

In New York City in 1911, the Triangle Shirtwaist Factory fire left 147 workers (most of them young women) dead, the victims of employer callousness (fire exits were locked) and state indifference (safety inspectors were never numerous enough to monitor all of the city's worksites). The conflagration followed the Uprising of the Twenty Thousand, a strike of garment workers throughout New York and Philadelphia, in 1909.

World War I heightened class tensions as workers felt squeezed between rising prices and stagnant wages. Phosphate workers in the South and lumber workers in the Northwest were among the groups of workers that sought to take advantage of wartime dislocations and press for concessions from employers. Repression followed swiftly. In 1917 in Bisbee, Arizona, managers of local copper mines rounded up eleven hundred members of the Industrial Workers of the World, a militant industrial union, transported them one hundred miles into the desert, and abandoned them.

During this period, the Great Migration of southern blacks into cities provoked an angry reaction among whites who encountered, or who feared they might in the near future encounter, integrated worksites and neighborhoods for the first time. Riots against blacks claimed at least forty-eight lives in 1917 in East St. Louis and thirty-eight lives in 1919 in Chicago.

Predictably, the crisis of American capitalism known as the Great Depression intensified a variety of class conflicts that resulted in bloodshed. In 1932 the Bonus Army, made up of twenty thousand unemployed veterans of World War I, marched on Washington, D.C., demanding early payment of the bonus promised them for their service. When police tried to evict the marchers, who had erected a tent city in Anacostia Flats, a pitched battle broke out between two thousand of the veterans and eight hundred police, resulting in the deaths of two marchers. The beginnings of the Farmers Holiday movement in the Midwest, organized to protest evictions and declining crop prices, and the Share Croppers Union, an organization of black and white farmers in Alabama, were marked by violence (both in 1932). In 1935 protests by residents of Harlem over high unemployment rates and lack of federal aid turned bloody, claiming the lives of four people.

The founding of the Congress of Industrial Organizations in 1935 proved especially threatening to employers, for the new union sought to organize groups of workers that had traditionally remained alienated from one another, including skilled and unskilled workers, men and women, and blacks and whites. During the sit-down strike of the United Automobile Workers in Flint, Michigan, in 1937, company guards and city police attacked strikers with guns, clubs, and tear gas, killing fourteen and injuring thirty-seven. A year later, a peaceful outing of workers employed at Republic Steel's plant in Chicago was attacked by police; ten died and ninety were wounded. Organizing drives by textile workers throughout the South and by miners in Harlan County, Kentucky, were also marked by bloodshed.

The Violent Destruction of Jim Crow

Ironically, the creation of hundreds of thousands of relatively well-paying defense jobs during World War II heightened tensions among members of the working classes, especially between blacks and whites. Two issues in particular fueled the antagonism of white workers toward blacks. The first centered on the integration of worksites that had historically been reserved for whites only; in the aircraft industry, for example, whites predominated as skilled workers and blacks were excluded from the better jobs until well into the war years. In some instances the introduction of black workers into all-white workplaces provoked hate strikes.

Working-class neighborhoods constituted a second site of violent contention. In cities like Detroit, where thousands of black and white southern migrants were seeking employment, housing shortages exacerbated racial prejudice among whites and led to pogromlike campaigns against the black population. In 1943 a battle between blacks and whites left twenty-five blacks and nine whites dead. That same year more than 240 cases of anti-black violence occurred in forty-seven cities throughout the nation.

Beginning in the 1950s and continuing through the early 1970s, civil rights demonstrations in the South and North elicited violent reactions from whites within a variety of contexts. Police and crowds attacked freedom riders (integrated groups that challenged segregation on interstate buses) and beat hundreds of ordinary black citizens, whites assassinated black leaders like Medgar Evers and killed black children (in 1963 four girls were murdered in a Birmingham church), and organized groups like the White Citizens Council orchestrated campaigns of violent intimidation against the black population. In the North members of suburban "neighborhood improvement associations" firebombed the houses of black people, and white parents forcibly blocked the integration of formerly all-white schools (as in Boston in 1974). The violent resistance of white people to the Civil Rights movement stemmed from a two-pronged impulse—the fear among elites that blacks would no longer serve as a subordinate workforce and the fear among white working classes that black people would be able to compete with them on the open market for jobs and housing.

By the early 1950s technological innovations, combined with the growth in union membership (one-third of the total American labor force), had encouraged employers to streamline their workforces, especially at the lowest levels. This process had devastating consequences for black workers. Moreover, racially discriminatory patterns of residential growth kept large numbers of urban blacks confined to inner cities, excluded from the burgeoning suburbs and new public schools that offered members of the white working classes and their children an entrée into the middle class. These factors helped to account for patterns of intraclass violence within black ghetto communities.

The civil rebellions that rocked major American cities in the 1960s stemmed from several factors: the cumulative impact of long-term structural unemployment among black men, routinized forms of white police brutality directed against blacks, the unfulfilled promise of the Civil Rights movement and of President Lyndon Johnson's "Great Society" social-welfare initiatives, and (in 1968) the assassination of Martin Luther King, Jr. In 1965 the black Watts neighborhood of Los Angeles went up in flames; thirty-four persons died and nine hundred were injured. The following year, seventy-five major riots left 87 people dead, with the bloodiest incidents occurring in Newark, New Jersey, and Detroit.

By the last decade of the twentieth century, the plight of the poorest people trapped in all-black ghettos had not improved substantially, though the ethnic and class dynamics of inner-city economies had changed over the years. In 1992 the acquittal of three white policemen who had beaten, clubbed, and kicked a black motorist, Rodney King, sparked rage among blacks in South Central Los Angeles. Yet the social landscape of that city was considerably more complicated than stark black-white divisions would suggest. An influx of illegal refugees from Mexico and Central America worsened the plight of black job seekers. Beginning in the mid-1970s, Korean immigrants, many of whom came with sufficient capital to start small businesses, became a visible presence in poor black and Hispanic neighborhoods. The 1992 South Central rebellion gave expression to class antagonism among blacks and these various groups of newcomers as well as between the black poor and the Los Angeles city law enforcement establishment.

The Violent Marketplace

In the latter part of the twentieth century, threats to the health and well-being of workers came not from gun-toting security guards but from hazards related to certain jobs that were no less dangerous because they relied on sophisticated forms of technology. Migrant workers suffered from the extensive use of pesticides, textile workers were felled by brown lung, miners remained in danger of losing life and limb as a result of cave-ins and explosions, and industrial workers labored in worksites polluted by asbestos and lead. In 1992 twenty-five black and white workers in Hamlet, North Carolina, were burned alive when a vat of chicken grease caught on fire; the escape doors had been nailed shut.

In the 1970s large numbers of refugees from Southeast Asia, Latin America, and Central America began to take the lowest-paying service and agricultural jobs. Not far from the shadow of glittering skyscrapers, deaf Mexicans, easily exploited and held against their will, peddled trinkets on the sidewalks of New York City. On the West Coast, Thai immigrants and Chinese peasants who were smuggled into the country toiled in garment sweatshops, and Mexican strawberry pickers worked sixteen-hour days for pennies a day.

Once again, the transition to a new economy and a new class system resulted in social upheaval, though patterns of violence were muted compared with earlier years. By this time it was clear that even large strikes overseen by relatively militant union leaders would not be marked by the same kind of violence that had characterized other labor-management conflicts earlier in the century. Large corporations guarded their public images carefully and eschewed the rough tactics that led to the spilling of blood. Nevertheless, the international dimension of American capitalism suggested that even image-conscious companies were willing to engage in brutality toward their workers. The Nike Corporation admitted in the mid-1990s that supervisors at one of its plants in Vietnam had disciplined a group of women employees (who had failed to wear the proper footwear to work) by forcing them to run around the factory in the midday heat, causing several to collapse from exhaustion.

By the late twentieth century, when most Western democracies have accepted responsibility for upholding minimum standards of health and welfare among their citizens, the absence of such standards in the United States—especially in the areas of health, housing, and employment opportunity—constitutes a form of state-sanctioned violence directed at the poor. The institutionalization of poverty will no doubt continue to produce intraclass violence within households (parents against children, husbands against wives) and on the streets (drug dealers against their own neighbors, native-born job seekers against immigrants). Thus, conflicts among the poor themselves have become the hallmark of the American class system, and the normal workings of the marketplace have replaced the overt brutality of former systems as a source of class violence.

BIBLIOGRAPHY

Aptheker, Herbert. *American Negro Slave Revolts.* New York: International Publishers, 1963.

Avrich, Paul. *The Haymarket Tragedy.* Princeton, N.J.: Princeton University Press, 1984.

Bailyn, Bernard. *The Peopling of British North America: An Introduction.* New York: Vintage, 1988.

Bernstein, Iver. *The New York City Draft Riots: Their Significance in American Society and Politics in the Age of the Civil War.* New York: Oxford University Press, 1990.

Branch, Taylor. *Parting the Waters: America in the King Years, 1954–1963.* New York: Simon and Schuster, 1988.

Gilje, Paul. *The Road to Mobocracy: Popular Disorder in New York City, 1763–1834.* Chapel Hill: University of North Carolina Press, 1987.

Jones, Jacqueline. *American Work: Four Centuries of Black and White Labor.* New York: Norton, 1998.

Lichtenstein, Alex. *Twice the Work of Free Labor: The Political Economy of Convict Labor in the New South.* London: Verso, 1996.

Lott, Eric. *Love and Theft: Blackface Minstrelsy and the American Working Class.* New York: Oxford University Press, 1993.

Montgomery, David. "The Shuttle and the Cross: Weavers and Artisans in the Kensington Riots of 1844." *Journal of Social History* 5 (summer 1972).

Morgan, Edmund S. *American Slavery, American Freedom: The Ordeal of Colonial Virginia.* New York: Norton, 1975.

Roediger, David R. *The Wages of Whiteness: Race and the Making of the American Working Class.* London: Verso, 1991.

Stansell, Christine. *City of Women: Sex and Class in New York, 1789–1860.* New York: Knopf, 1986.

Sugrue, Thomas J. *The Origins of the Urban Crisis: Race and Inequality in Postwar Detroit.* Princeton, N.J.: Princeton University Press, 1996.

Way, Peter. *Common Labour: Workers and the Digging of North American Canals, 1780–1860.* Cambridge: Cambridge University Press, 1993.

JACQUELINE JONES

CLEAVER, ELDRIDGE
(1935–1998)

On 6 April 1968, in the aftermath of the assassination of Martin Luther King, Jr., Eldridge Cleaver engaged in a violent confrontation with law-enforcement officials in Oakland, California. Speaking of that day in a 1997 interview with Henry Louis Gates, Jr., Cleaver said, "We were well armed and we had a shoot-out that lasted an hour and a half. I will tell anybody that that was the first experience of freedom that I had." The confrontation became the central experience in Cleaver's life. A decade of incarceration and violence had set the stage for the event, and thirty years of exile and renunciation followed.

Leroy Eldridge Cleaver was born in Wabbaseka, Arkansas, in 1935. From the age of twelve to twenty-one he was in and out of prison. He was incarcerated for possession of marijuana, rape, and assault with intent to murder during these years, and while in prison he became an enthusiastic follower of Malcolm X. "Malcolm X had a special meaning for black convicts," he wrote in *Soul on Ice* (1968), a collection of letters and memoirs written while he was in prison. "A former prisoner himself, he had risen from the lowest depths to great heights. For this reason he was a symbol of hope, a model for thousands of black convicts who found themselves trapped in the vicious PPP cycle: prison-parole-prison" (p. 58). Cleaver was devastated to hear of Malcolm X's murder in 1965.

As a model prisoner and a writer for *Ramparts* magazine, Cleaver earned his parole in 1966. In February 1967 he met Huey Newton and Bobby Seale, who had recently founded the Black Panther Party, and he became the party's minister of information. With the 1968 publication of *Soul on Ice*, Cleaver's stature as a leading black radical grew. Cleaver saw the Black Panthers as a revolutionary group that provided the military "backbone" to the Civil Rights movement. He viewed black convicts as prisoners of war in a socioeconomic struggle between capitalists and the proletariat.

The Oakland shoot-out left Black Panther Bobby Hutton dead and two police officers wounded; Cleaver himself was savagely beaten while in police custody. The shoot-out came about after King's murder on 4 April had incited riots in Oakland. The Panthers knew that the riots would require police reaction; seeking an armed confrontation with police, fourteen Panthers, including Cleaver, went down to the area in Oakland where the rioting was the worst and initiated the shoot-out. Reluctant to return to jail, Cleaver jumped bail and fled the country in November, first to Cuba and then to Algiers. In 1971 he broke with the Black Panthers and in 1975 returned to the United States. He avoided jail time by pleading guilty to the assault charges stemming from the shoot-out in exchange for five years' probation.

Later in life Cleaver renounced his militancy. He criticized Louis Farrakhan and the Nation of Islam as "racist" and for taking black America on a "detour through the swamps of hatred." Before dying of cancer in 1998, Cleaver became a born-again Christian and aligned himself with the Republican Party. Despite the evolution of his views, Cleaver will be remembered for his involvement in the 1968 shoot-out and the rhetoric of alienation and

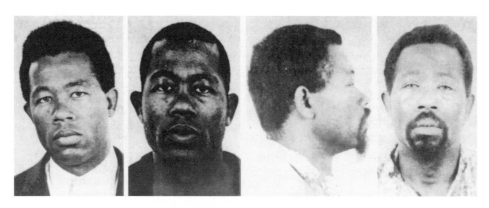

Photos of Eldridge Cleaver in a 1968 FBI poster. LIBRARY OF CONGRESS

militant revolutionary fervor that he espoused in *Soul on Ice.*

BIBLIOGRAPHY

Cleaver, Eldridge. *Soul on Ice.* New York: McGraw-Hill, 1968.

———. Interview by Henry Louis Gates, Jr. "The Two Nations of Black America." *Frontline.* Public Broadcasting System, 1997 (aired 10 February 1998). Available at http://www.pbs.org/wgbh/pages/frontline/shows/race/interviews/ecleaver.html.

Lockwood, Lee. *Conversations with Eldridge Cleaver: Algiers.* New York: McGraw-Hill, 1970.

ADAM MAX COHEN

See also **Black Panthers; Malcolm X; Newton, Huey.**

CODE OF SILENCE *See* Police.

CODY, WILLIAM "BUFFALO BILL"
(1846–1917)

William Frederick "Buffalo Bill" Cody was a plainsman, scout, Indian fighter, and showman whose feats were immortalized in dime novels and whose Wild West Show made him an international celebrity.

He was born 26 February 1846, in LeClaire, Iowa, and settled with his family in 1854 in Salt Creek Valley, Kansas. His father, Isaac Cody, was stabbed during a free-state speech and was hounded by proslavery forces. After his father's death, William Cody, age eleven, went to work for the overland freighters Russell, Majors, and Waddell. On his first trip, twenty miles west of Fort Kearney in Nebraska, the party was attacked by Indians. During the group's escape, Cody fell behind, encountered an Indian, and shot him. This incident led to the newspaper story "The Boy Indian Slayer." At age fourteen Cody joined the Pony Express to deliver mail and news. On one trip he was able to overcome a holdup man who demanded his saddlebags. He tied the man to his own horse and towed him along, apologizing to the Pony Express for being slowed down.

During the Civil War he joined irregular military companies, then enlisted in the Union Army. Early in 1864 he was sent to spy behind Confederate lines, then served as a scout and guide for the Ninth Kansas Regiment and won acclaim for

William Cody, also known as Buffalo Bill, in a January 1892 portrait. HULTON GETTY/LIAISON AGENCY

his courage, especially during the bloody repulse of Confederates at Pilot Knob, Missouri, on 27 September 1864. He was often used as a courier. Several horses were shot out from under him, but he emerged from the war unscathed.

After the war he worked irregularly as a scout and guide. He was dubbed Buffalo Bill when he began supplying buffalo meat to workers on the Kansas Pacific Railroad. He used a .48-caliber breech-loading Springfield rifle to kill more than four thousand buffalo a year. Cody also served as chief of scouts for the Fifth U.S. Cavalry (1868–1872), out of Fort Larned in Kansas. He participated in sixteen Indian fights, including the defeat of Indians on 11 July 1869 at Summit Springs, near present-day Sterling, Colorado, during which Cody purportedly killed the Sioux chief Tall Bull with a single shot through the skull. By 1870 his fame had spread beyond the Great Plains, and he became a hunting guide for notables, including

Grand Duke Alexis of Russia in 1872. E. Z. C. Judson, who wrote dime novels under the name Ned Buntline, met Cody and began writing about his exploits, including *Buffalo Bill's First Trial; or Will Cody, the Pony Express Rider* (1888). Judson also wrote the play *The Scouts of the Plains* (1872), in which Cody played himself on the Chicago stage in 1872–1873.

During the summer of 1876 Cody took part in the Sioux Wars and the battle to avenge the death of George A. Custer. On 17 July he opened the fight on War Bonnet Creek in Nebraska by killing Yellow Hair (Hay-o-wei). He held Yellow Hair's scalp aloft before the charging Fifth Cavalry and cried, "The first scalp for Custer." Although Yellow Hair's father offered Cody four mules for his son's scalp, Cody refused.

In 1883 he organized Buffalo Bill's Wild West Show (the precursor to the rodeo), an extravaganza that combined sharpshooting and riding exhibitions with dramatizations of moments in the West's history, including noisy and dramatic reenactments of Custer's last stand and stagecoach robberies. The show toured in Europe and was an international success. The show's stars included the markswoman Annie Oakley and, for one season (1885), the Sioux chief Sitting Bull. During the last Sioux outbreak, 1890–1891, Cody volunteered his services to Major General Nelson A. Miles. It was thought that Cody, the only white man Sitting Bull ever trusted, could bring in the chief for a conference with Miles (actually an arrest order), but the arrest order was rescinded.

Cody died on 10 January 1917 and was buried on Lookout Mountain in Colorado. His heroics remain a vivid example of violence in the Old West, especially during the Indian wars. Although Cody was awarded the Medal of Honor in 1872 after an Indian fight at the Platte River, the medal was revoked in 1917 because scouts were considered civilians and were therefore ineligible for the Medal of Honor. In 1989, however, sixty-two years after his death, the U.S. Army restored his name to the Medal of Honor list, citing him for "gallantry."

BIBLIOGRAPHY

Blackstone, Sarah J., ed. *The Business of Being Buffalo Bill: Selected Letters of William F. Cody, 1879–1917.* New York: Praeger, 1988.

Russell, Don. *The Lives and Legends of Buffalo Bill.* Norman: University of Oklahoma Press, 1960.

Sorg, Eric V. *Buffalo Bill: Myth and Reality.* Santa Fe, N. Mex.: Ancient City, 1998.

Wetmore, Helen Cody, with a foreword by Zane Grey. *Last of the Great Scouts: The Life Story of Col. William F. Cody, "Buffalo Bill."* New York: Grosset and Dunlap, 1899, 1918.

White, Richard. "Frederick Jackson Turner and Buffalo Bill." In *The Frontier in American Culture,* edited by James R. Grossman. Berkeley: University of California Press, 1994.

LOUISE B. KETZ

See also **Custer, George Armstrong; Sitting Bull; West.**

COLD WAR

The Cold War, generally defined as the protracted rivalry between the United States and the Soviet Union from the late 1940s to the late 1980s, required Americans to confront the possibility of violence on a scale unprecedented in world history. Recurrent crises—over Berlin at various times, over Cuba in 1962, over the Middle East in 1973—raised the specter of nuclear war, with projected American casualties in the scores of millions or more. Although nuclear war was avoided, the threat of such a holocaust strongly influenced American thinking and produced new genres of literature, film, and television movies that often depicted the violent rending, sometimes to the point of extinction, of American society. Jonathan Schell's 1982 book, *The Fate of the Earth,* provided a detailed account of the damage a nuclear bomb would do to Manhattan; the following year, the ABC film *The Day After* graphically depicted Kansas City in the wake of a nuclear attack.

The fear of an impending nuclear war affected American society in other ways as well. In the past, the United States had maintained only a small peacetime army. During the Cold War, when there was the possibility that an enemy might destroy the United States within a matter of hours, Americans endorsed permanent military mobilization. Defense budgets soared far beyond anything conceived of before the Cold War; an entire sector of the economy was devoted to producing weapons. To ward off the large war that all feared, the nation engaged in smaller but still violent wars in Korea and Vietnam, and interventions by American military forces in Latin America and the Middle East. American deaths under arms during the Cold War totaled some ninety thousand.

Domestic dissatisfaction with the Vietnam War contributed to the culture of protest that emerged during the 1960s; some antiwar protestors engaged in violent activities avowedly intended to "bring the war home." Draft boards were bombed, as were Reserve Officers' Training Corps buildings and defense-related laboratories. Actual and anticipated violence caused local and state governments to deploy police and National Guard troops against the protestors. In 1968 antiwar protestors, among others, disrupted the Democratic National Convention in Chicago; police responded with batons and tear gas, injuring hundreds severely enough to require medical attention. In 1970 National Guardsmen fired on antiwar demonstrators at Kent State University in Ohio; four people were killed and nine wounded. Shortly thereafter, lethal violence erupted at an antiwar protest at Mississippi's Jackson State University, where two were killed and nine wounded.

The perceived danger to American society during the Cold War encouraged an acceptance of inroads against civil liberties. During the late 1940s and early 1950s, a second Red Scare developed. Although less broadly violent than the original Red Scare of the post–World War I era, the anti-dissent campaign that became associated with the name of Senator Joseph McCarthy of Wisconsin included loyalty tests and the creation of blacklists. It also produced the only peacetime executions for espionage in American history, those of Julius and Ethel Rosenberg in 1953.

BIBLIOGRAPHY

Brands, H. W. *The Devil We Knew: Americans and the Cold War.* New York: Oxford University Press, 1993.

Englehardt, Tom. *The End of Victory Culture: Cold War America and the Disillusioning of a Generation.* New York: Basic, 1995.

Sherry, Michael S. *In the Shadow of War: The United States Since the 1930s.* New Haven, Conn.: Yale University Press, 1995.

H. W. Brands

See also **Antiwar Protests; Foreign Intervention, Fear of; Literature: Nuclear War Fiction; McCarthy, Joseph R.; Militarism; Red Scare.**

COLT, SAMUEL
(1814–1862)

Without Samuel Colt and his revolving pistol, the history of violence in the United States might well have been different, and the American West's most enduring legend, the gunfighter, would likely not have existed at all. Born 19 July 1814 in Hartford, Connecticut, Samuel Colt was a precocious youngster with a fascination with firearms. At the age of six, he allegedly rebuilt an old horse pistol (a large pistol carried by horsemen). His mother died the next year, and his father placed him in the care of a farmer at Glastonbury. While there, he got into trouble for firing a pistol on the Sabbath. He then went to work in his father's factory. He was preoccupied with the practical application of science and afterward attended Amherst Academy. His stay there was brief; he was expelled for firing a pistol.

At fifteen Colt exploded an underwater device using electric current. Later he went to sea and, while on a voyage, he carved a model for a revolving pistol with six chambers. After he returned home, he had a prototype built, which he paid for with the proceeds of nitrous oxide (laughing gas) demonstrations. His invention was patented in 1835 in England and in 1836 in the United States. He began manufacture at his Paterson, New Jersey, plant in 1836. Colt even wangled a demonstration with President Andrew Jackson, but the economic

Samuel Colt, about 1855. Hulton Getty/Liaison Agency

crisis of 1837 and the weak construction of his first models delayed his success. He closed his plant in 1842.

The American military was slow in adopting his novel idea. His first real break came in Texas when Major John Coffee Hays used Colt's revolvers effectively against the Comanches. Afterward, the Texas Rangers adopted the weapon, and in 1846–1847 Colt worked closely with Samuel Walker in the development of the Walker Colt. Walker persuaded the government to purchase one thousand of the revolvers for use by the U.S. Mounted Rifles during the Mexican War. Not having a factory of his own at the time, Colt had the Walker Colts manufactured at the Whitney Armory in Connecticut. With his profits Colt opened his own firm in Hartford, Connecticut. Later Colt designed the Colt Dragoon for the U.S. Cavalry. In 1851 he introduced the Navy Colt, which proved to be one of his most popular models, and in 1860 he began production of the Model 1860 Army.

The Civil War provided the ultimate proving ground for Colt, and although he died on 10 January 1862, well before the war ended, Colt Firearms dominated pistol production for the rest of the century. The Model 1873 Army, commonly known as the "Peacemaker," fired a metallic cartridge (earlier cartridges were made of paper or linen) and became the standard military firearm during the Indian wars and the weapon of choice of frontier lawmen, outlaws, and gunfighters in the last decades of the nineteenth century. Sam Colt's revolving pistol played a major role in the violence of the last frontier and an even greater role in the myth of the Old West.

BIBLIOGRAPHY

Keating, Bern. *The Flamboyant Mr. Colt and His Deadly Six-Shooter.* Garden City, N.Y.: Doubleday, 1978.
Sutherland, R. G., and R. L. Wilson. *The Book of Colt Firearms.* New York: Random House, 1971.
Wilson, R. L. *Colt: An American Legend.* New York: Abbeville, 1985.

GARY L. ROBERTS

See also **Deringer, Henry; Remington, Eliphalet; Weapons.**

COLUMBINE HIGH SCHOOL SHOOTINGS. *See* Schools.

COMICS

Violence comes in many forms, and in the early days of American comic books, a rich assortment was to be found. Modern format four-color comic books were invented and first flourished in the middle 1930s, offering the slapstick action and roughhouse behavior that was at least as old as newspaper strips such as *The Yellow Kid* (1895) and *The Katzenjammer Kids* (1897), as well as the more realistic, gun-toting violence of new strips like *Dick Tracy* (1931). Initially, comic books specialized in fairly wholesome violence that took place in such Saturday matinee locations as the jungle, the Wild West, the big city, and distant planets.

Superman

In 1938, with the advent of Jerry Siegel and Joe Schuster's Superman in *Action Comics,* a more flamboyant type of violence came to the newsstands. This was still pretty innocent stuff, involving a sort of costume-party approach to fierce action, with a lot of special effects tossed in—explosions, crashes, battles between musclemen and engines of destruction. It was just the thing to appeal to the restless, hyperactive boys who made up the majority of readers of this new medium. After Superman hundreds of other superheroes followed, among them Batman (1939), the Human Torch (1939), the Sub-Mariner (1939), Captain Marvel (1940), and Captain America (1941).

These heroes were not above criticism, and criticism arose. As early as 1940 the *Chicago Daily News* accused funny books of being a "national disgrace" and "pulp-paper nightmares." It was feared that the violence depicted would act as "a violent stimulant" and "their hypodermic injection of sex and murder made the child impatient with better stories." The newspaper warned that "unless we want a coming generation even more ferocious than the present one, we must band together to break the 'comic' book." More critics joined the battle, but comic-book titles and sales continued to multiply.

The United States entered World War II in December 1941, and while attacks on comic books continued, they did not seem especially important in a country that was now engaged in a violent conflict and encouraging ferocity toward its enemies. The makeup of the comic-book audience changed, too. Millions of young men entered military service and comics became best-sellers at camp and base post exchanges. With many more adult readers, content changed. At many publishing houses violence became much more explicit and bloody. Pretty young women, often scantily clad, showed up increasingly in stories and, particularly at houses like Fox and Fiction House, on covers. Then in 1942 appeared the comic book that would become the best-selling title of the decade, whose influence would nearly topple the comics industry a decade or so later.

True Crime

The first regularly issued true-crime comic, *Crime Does Not Pay*, was published by Lev Gleason and Arthur Bernhard and edited by cartoonists Charles Biro and Bob Wood. It appeared in the spring of 1942 and stayed in business until the spring of 1955. Bernhard left fairly soon, and Gleason continued alone as publisher. Major influences on the genesis and evolution of the magazine were hard-boiled periodicals such as *True Detective*, *Master Detective*, and *Official Detective*. Printed on somewhat better paper than the pulp-fiction magazines and illustrated with grainy photos of vicious criminals, blowsy gun molls, and bloody corpses, they offered breathless, nonfiction accounts of daring bank robberies, brutal murders, and assorted crimes of passion. *Crime Does Not Pay* came closer than any comic book had before to emulating this particular blend of grim reality, bullet-riddled action, and titillation.

Gleason contended that the magazine was "dedicated to the eradication of crime," and for a time covers carried the slogan "A force for good in the community!" *Crime Does Not Pay* chronicled crooks of recent vintage, such as Legs Diamond and Lucky Luciano, and older heavies like Billy the Kid. Most of the cases were packed with shooting, violence, and action, but initially little actual bloodshed was depicted. Mild sexual activity was typical, usually provided by the lady friends of the various crooks and killers. Despite the fact that the crooks and gangsters always came to bad ends, for most of the story they were the center of the action and filled the space usually occupied by heroes in other comics.

By 1945 the combined sales of all Gleason titles had climbed to 1.5 million, and by 1947 to over 2 million. Late in 1947 the covers of *Crime Does Not Pay* boasted, "More Than 6,000,000 Readers Monthly!" (Gleason and Biro apparently assumed that each copy sold was passed around among several readers.) Despite the impressive sales, the magazine had the field pretty much to itself for several years. But after the war, because of the uncertain economic conditions and the decline of interest in supermen, other publishers turned to crime. Among the dozens of titles that followed were *Real Clue*, *Headline*, *Law Breakers*, *Crime Can't Win*, *Crimes by Women*, *True Crime*, *Inside Crime*, *Crime and Punishment*, *Penalty*, *War Against Crime*, *Guilty*, and *Crime SuspenStories*.

Many of these new titles went far beyond what Gleason had been doing. The gore content increased and readers were provided full-color depictions of shootings, stranglings, stabbings—with knives, ice picks, meat cleavers—drownings, acid throwings, and electrocutions. Blood flowed from every sort of wound and from the mouths of the corpses that decorated most of the true-crime tales. In addition, the sex content increased, with women being shown not only as the objects of desire but as the victims of beatings, torture, and a wide range of other brutal assaults. A separate comic-book horror genre had grown up parallel with the crime material, and the many titles in this category also provided violence and bloodshed.

Backlash

Criticism of comic books accelerated in the years after World War II. The Cold War era encouraged the hunting of scapegoats of all sorts, and comics—the good, the bad, and the ugly—found themselves blamed for the increase in juvenile delinquency and sundry other crimes and misdemeanors. By the mid-1950s, after attacks from psychiatrists, parents' groups, and investigations by Senate committees, the comic industry was in very sad shape. In fact, it never fully recovered.

The psychiatrist Fredric Wertham made public the conclusions of his two-year study of comic books in 1948. He charged that they undermined morals, glorified violence, and were "sexually aggressive in an abnormal way." The media picked up on Wertham's charges, and national magazines like *Collier's* and the *Saturday Review* ran pieces on the dangers of comic-book violence. The attacks accelerated and many newsdealers refused to distribute comics that parents' groups considered objectionable. Police departments threatened newsstands, and numerous citizens' committees were set up to evaluate comic books.

In 1954 Wertham's book, *The Seduction of the Innocent*, was published, the Senate Subcommittee on the Judiciary held hearings in Manhattan on comic books, and the self-regulatory Comics Code

A Senate Subcommittee on the Judiciary, including Senators Thomas Hennings (left) and Estes Kefauver (center), holds a hearing in 1954 to determine whether comic books are factors in a nationwide increase in juvenile delinquency. CORBIS/BETTMANN-UPI

Authority was established. The Wertham book, expanding on the topic on which he had been writing and lecturing for the previous several years, stated that "the bad effects of comic books exist potentially for all children." The Senate hearings were presided over by Senators Thomas Hennings and Estes Kefauver, and among the witnesses were Wertham and William Gaines, publisher of titles such as *Mad, Tales from the Crypt,* and *Crime SuspenStories.* Gaines might have avoided nationwide notoriety if he had not engaged in a discussion of good and bad taste with Senator Kefauver. Holding up the cover of *Crime SuspensStories #22,* Kefauver stated, "Here is your May issue. This seems to be a man with a bloody ax holding a woman's head up, which has been severed from her body. Do you think that's in good taste?"

Gaines answered, "Yes, sir, I do—for the cover of a horror comic. A cover in bad taste, for example, might be defined as holding the head a little higher so that the blood could be seen dripping from it, and moving the body over a little further

so that the neck of the body could be seen to be bloody."

"You've got blood coming out of her mouth."

"A little," Gaines had to admit.

Subsequently, the comic-book publishers formed the Comics Magazine Association of America and named a respected judge to administer a Comics Code. The code stipulated that "No comics shall explicitly present the unique details and methods of crime. . . . Scenes of excessive violence shall be prohibited. Scenes of brutal torture, excessive and unnecessary gun play, physical agony, gory and gruesome crime shall be eliminated." Additionally, "All scenes of horror, excessive bloodshed, gory or gruesome crimes, depravity, lust, sadism, masochism shall not be permitted." Comic books had come a considerable way since the innocent days when Superman could impress his youthful readers simply by leaping over a tall building in a single bound.

Many publishers, including Gaines, cut back or ended their crime and horror lines. The stipulations of the code made it difficult, if not impossible, for most crime and horror comics to continue, since if the publishers did not abide by the code their comic books would almost certainly not even be distributed.

Superheroes made a comeback in the middle 1950s, when characters such as the Fantastic Four (1961), the Hulk (1962), and Thor (1962) were introduced and new versions of the Flash (1956) and Green Lantern (1959) made successful comebacks. The stories became wordier and more complex, and were continued from issue to issue. The audience for this sort of fare was chiefly among high-school and college-age readers. The violence was of the sort to be found in action films and televised wrestling matches. The Comics Code remained in force for some years and then gradually faded away. By the late twentieth century interest in comic books had waned and sales dropped. Superbeings dominated the remaining titles. Costumed like rock stars and motorcycle hoods, these superbeings practiced violence of a cosmic, grandiose, and essentially unreal sort.

BIBLIOGRAPHY

Goulart, Ron. *Great History of Comic Books.* Chicago: Contemporary Books, 1986.

Harvey, Robert C. *The Art of the Comic Book.* Jackson: University of Mississippi Press, 1996.

Wertham, Fredric. *Seduction of the Innocent.* New York: Rinehart, 1954.

RON GOULART

See also **Film: Animation; Literature: Children's and Young Adult; Popular Culture; Television: Children's Television.**

CONFESSIONS, COERCED

For much of recorded Western history, coerced confessions were routinely used as a means to investigate crime. In Europe, the Inquisition, originating in the decrees of Pope Innocent III at the close of the twelfth century, led to a system of canon law in which sectarian judges would extract confessions from suspected heretics through the use of torture and prolonged imprisonment in dark, damp, and foul-smelling dungeons.

The example set by the Roman Catholic Church gradually spread throughout most of continental Europe. The practice of coercing confessions from those suspected of criminal acts was adopted by the secular courts of northern Italy in the thirteenth century. By the sixteenth century torture was regularly and legally employed to investigate and prosecute crime by all of the great nations of Europe except England. The authorized use of judicial torture was not abolished in continental Europe until the second half of the eighteenth century. Much of the impetus for abolition came from the writings of Voltaire, Cesare Beccaria, and other Enlightenment scholars who pointed to cases in which innocent persons had confessed to and had been executed for crimes later revealed to have been committed by others.

Although torturous punishments for convicted criminals were routinely meted out in medieval England, the use of torture as a means to induce confessions was never officially condoned. The English system of criminal justice rejected the inquisitorial methods of other European governments and instead relied on an accusatorial model in which judges presided over jury trials and had no authority to initiate a prosecution and no duty to collect evidence or secure a defendant's confession. Throughout the Middle Ages there were many cases in which English judges, in defiance of the common law and with the authority of the reigning monarch, permitted the use of the rack, the thumbscrew, and other instruments of torture as a means to obtain evidence and force confessions from suspected criminals. Nevertheless, the belief that the use of torture or any cruelty in forcing confessions was unfair and generally illegal became increasingly accepted both in England and the American colonies by the middle of the seventeenth century.

American Historical Developments

As Leonard Levy stresses in his magisterial *Origins of the Fifth Amendment* (1986), the right to protection against coercive methods of interrogation was not easily or uniformly adopted in America. But as English common law gradually became American law, there was a growing respect for the view that forcing people to incriminate themselves violated fundamental principles of fairness and due process of law. On 15 December 1791 the requisite number of states ratified the Bill of Rights—the first ten amendments to the United States Constitution, including the Fifth Amendment's guarantees of due process of law and protection against self-incrimination.

This historic event, however, did not end coercive methods of interrogating suspected criminals. The Bill of Rights, as the U.S. Supreme Court made clear in *Barron v. Baltimore* (1833), applied only to the federal government and provided no protection against abuses by state or local authorities. Confessions shown to be coerced were generally inadmissible in federal courts, but this was not the case in most state courts until well into the twentieth century.

Three key historical developments led to the contemporary American rule of law that governs coerced confessions in all American courts: Confessions that are proved to have been obtained by the use of physical force, threats of physical violence, or other forms of extreme psychological pressure are involuntary and untrustworthy and cannot be admitted as evidence in a criminal trial. First, in a series of decisions beginning with *Hopt v. People of Territory of Utah* in 1884, the U.S. Supreme Court made it clear that the federal courts would follow the common-law rule prohibiting the use of confessions obtained by physical force or threats of violence. Since *Hopt*, federal courts have barred coerced (and other involuntary) confessions either as a matter of traditional federal evidentiary rules or, depending upon the circumstances of the case, the Sixth Amendment right to counsel, the Fifth Amendment right against self-incrimination, or the Fifth Amendment due process clause (which prohibits violations of due process rights by federal officials).

The second major development that led to present-day rules against the use of coerced confessions was the ratification of the Fourteenth Amendment in 1868. The due process clause of the Fourteenth Amendment commands that "no State shall . . . deprive any person of life, liberty, or property without due process of law." This clause has been interpreted by the Supreme Court to protect individuals from arbitrary, unjustified, and lawless actions by state and local officials. Moreover, in a gradual case-by-case process generally known as the "nationalization of the Bill of Rights," the Supreme Court has made most of the provisions of the Bill of Rights binding upon the states under the theory that the due process clause should be understood to protect certain fundamental rights, including the rights of criminal defendants against misconduct by state or local officials.

The third major event that shaped contemporary coerced-confession jurisprudence was the Supreme Court's landmark decision in *Brown v. Mississippi* (1936). In the *Brown* case, the Supreme Court for the first time reversed a state criminal conviction on the ground that the conviction was based upon a coerced confession. The case grew out of "third-degree" tactics that had long been employed against blacks, poor whites, and other powerless people suspected of crime in the American South. After the murder of a white man in Mississippi and amid reports of a lynch mob gathering at the scene of the crime, police and sheriff's deputies quickly arrested three young black men and charged them with the crime.

One of the suspects, Arthur Ellington, was taken from his home by a deputy sheriff and handed over to the mob that had gathered at the crime scene. With the participation of the deputy, the mob twice hanged Ellington by a rope attached to the limb of a tree. When he began to lose consciousness, they let him down, tied him to the tree, and flogged him unmercifully. When he refused to confess, he was taken home, only to be arrested two days later by the same deputy and another deputy. The deputies took Ellington to jail by a circuitous route that led into Alabama, where they stopped, whipped him, and told him they would continue to whip him until he confessed. At that point, he agreed to sign any statement they gave him and he was taken to jail.

Two other suspects, Ed Brown and Henry Shields, were taken to the same jail, where they were forced to strip and bend over chairs. Police, deputies, and several white male "volunteers" proceeded to whip them with a leather belt containing metal buckles until their backs were bleeding and their skin, as one Mississippi judge later put it, had been "cut to pieces." Told that the whipping would continue until they confessed to the murder, Brown and Shields screamed out their confessions. But the whipping did not end; the police continued it until the suspects confessed to every specific detail demanded by their torturers. All three suspects were then warned that the whipping and strapping would be resumed if they complained of their treatment or if they changed even a single detail of their "confessions."

At the trial, a sheriff's deputy and several others admitted to beating the suspects. But when asked if the whippings were particularly severe, the deputy insisted that the whippings were "not too much for a Negro; not as much as I would have done if it were left to me." Less than one week after the commission of the crime the defendants were convicted and sentenced to death. The Mississippi

Supreme Court twice rejected the defendants' claim that the trial judge had erred in admitting the confessions into evidence. However, with the financial support of the National Association for the Advancement of Colored People and other interest groups, an appeal was taken to, and accepted by, the U.S. Supreme Court.

The convictions were overturned on 17 February 1936, when Chief Justice Charles Evans Hughes, writing for a unanimous Court, declared that the use of coerced confessions to secure criminal convictions violated the due process clause of the Fourteenth Amendment. The due process clause, wrote Hughes, permitted the states broad latitude in regulating criminal trial procedures, but "the rack and torture chamber may not be substituted for the witness stand. . . . It would be difficult to conceive of methods more revolting to the sense of justice than those taken to procure the confessions of these petitioners."

Coerced Confessions After *Brown v. Mississippi*

In the years following *Brown,* the Supreme Court continued to employ the due process clause to reverse convictions based on coerced confessions. In *Chambers v. Florida* (1940), the Court unanimously invalidated confessions made by four black murder suspects who were isolated from friends, family, and counsel; threatened with mob vengeance and police violence; and relentlessly interrogated by relays of officers for six days. Although it was not proven that physical force had been used to obtain the *Chambers* confessions, Justice Hugo Black's opinion for a unanimous Court made it clear that the use of mental torture, especially when accompanied by threats of violence, would sometimes be enough to justify the suppression of a confession.

In 1944, in *Ashcraft v. Tennessee,* the Court held a confession to be involuntary and inadmissible as evidence because the suspect had been interrogated almost continuously for thirty-six hours under the glare of bright lights. A year later, in *Malinski v. New York* (1945), the Court again took the view that intense psychological pressure, even in the absence of physical brutality, could render a confession inadmissible. In *Malinski,* the defendant had been stripped and held incommunicado for ten hours in a hotel room in an effort to "let him think that he is going to get a shellacking."

Between 1945 and 1967 the Supreme Court invalidated numerous state and federal convictions on the ground that guilty verdicts had been obtained by means of physical or psychological coercion. In a separate, though closely related, series of cases, the Court established that even when coercion could not be proved, an involuntary or untrustworthy confession obtained from a suspect who was unlawfully detained or deprived of other fundamental rights could not be used to secure a criminal conviction. Thus in the landmark case of *Miranda v. Arizona* (1966), the Court held that suspects held in police custody, prior to undergoing interrogation, must be informed of their right to counsel, told of their right to remain silent, and warned of the likelihood that their words will be used against them. A confession obtained in violation of *Miranda* is not necessarily a coerced confession, but it nonetheless will generally be inadmissible as evidence in a criminal trial on the ground that the suspect was deprived of his opportunity to exercise his Fifth Amendment privilege against self-incrimination in an intelligent manner.

One year after *Miranda,* the Supreme Court announced a stringent rule against the use of coerced confessions. In *Chapman v. California* (1967), the Court made it clear that coerced confessions were to be governed by the so-called "rule of automatic reversal." Under this rule, the use of a coerced confession in a criminal trial could not be considered a "harmless error." An appellate court was duty bound to overturn a criminal conviction resting in whole or in part on a coerced confession, regardless of how much evidence of guilt existed, apart from the confession, to support the conviction. The *Chapman* Court stressed that coerced confessions were not only untrustworthy but that their use in a criminal trial would offend the principle that the United States' is an accusatorial and not an inquisitorial system of criminal justice.

A 1991 Supreme Court decision regarding coerced confessions, however, arguably represents a step backward toward the days when police were permitted to employ coercive methods to wrest confessions from suspects. In *Arizona v. Fulminante,* a sharply divided Court overruled *Chapman* by ruling that the use of a coerced confession as evidence in a criminal trial was simply one of those inevitable errors that occur in the course of a criminal trial. An appellate court, Chief Justice William Rehnquist explained in his majority opinion, should assess such an error in the context of other evidence presented during the trial in order to determine whether the error may have been "harmless." If it appears that the trial's outcome would have been the same with or without the use of the coerced confession, the guilty verdict will stand.

In a bitter dissenting opinion, Justice Byron White declared that the use of a coerced confession violates a defendant's fundamental constitutional rights and should never be subjected to harmless-error analysis by a reviewing court. White pointed out that the confession of Oreste Fulminante had been obtained by a fellow jail inmate who was working as a paid informant for the FBI and who had told Fulminante that he would not protect him from being attacked by other prisoners as a "child killer" unless he admitted involvement in the murder of his eleven-year-old stepdaughter. According to White, this was a classic example of a coerced confession—one obtained by conveying "a credible threat of physical violence." He chided the majority for its unwillingness to provide suspects with sufficient protection against erroneous convictions based on false confessions and he warned "that in the end life and liberty can be as much endangered from illegal methods used to convict those thought to be criminals as from the actual criminals themselves."

Conclusion

Ideally, this essay would conclude with the assertion that coerced confessions are no longer used in American law enforcement. However, the *Fulminante* decision, by giving appellate courts a tool for affirming otherwise invalid confessions, arguably gives police subtle encouragement to break the rules. It will always be difficult to prove that a confession resulted from physical violence, threats of violence, or undue psychological pressure. Police officers, especially when other evidence is unavailable, will naturally try very hard to persuade suspects to confess, and there will always be a temptation to resort to coercive methods. Juries are unlikely to rule out a confession unless it appears to have been extorted by outright police brutality. In the long run, the remedy lies in better police recruitment and training, improved court procedures, and the development of a national consensus against modern variations of the rack and the thumbscrew.

BIBLIOGRAPHY

Cortner, Richard C. *A "Scottsboro" Case in Mississippi: The Supreme Court and Brown v. Mississippi*. Jackson: University Press of Mississippi, 1986.
Grano, Joseph D. *Confessions, Truth, and the Law*. Ann Arbor: University of Michigan Press, 1993.
Levy, Leonard W. *Origins of the Fifth Amendment: The Right Against Self-Incrimination*. New York: Macmillan, 1986.
Stephens, Otis H., Jr. *The Supreme Court and Confessions of Guilt*. Knoxville: University of Tennessee Press, 1973.

KENNETH C. HAAS

See also **Police: Police Brutality; Torture.**

CONFLICT RESOLUTION

This entry is divided into two parts: **International and Institutional** *and* **Interpersonal.**

INTERNATIONAL AND INSTITUTIONAL

Conflicts have always been part of human social life, and so has their resolution. Large-scale social conflicts have been resolved not only by one side's overwhelming use of violence but also by various combinations of violence, nonviolent coercion, persuasion, and the promise of benefits. In the late twentieth century an array of new methods to resolve conflicts constructively were developed. The first section of this article describes the core ideas of the new approach to conflict resolution (CR). Next, the article examines sources of this new approach, and finally, it notes international and institutional applications of the approach.

Problem-Solving Conflict Resolution

A core idea of the new approach to CR is that conflicts can be redefined as problems that can be solved in ways that satisfy at least some of the concerns of each of the adversaries. Analysts and practitioners disagree, however, whether such win-win or mutually beneficial outcomes are possible always, often, or only occasionally.

A problem-solving CR approach is utilized in a wide variety of conflicts waged between various adversaries, in diverse settings, and about different matters. The adversaries may be national governments in the same global region, ethnic communities within a neighborhood or a country, organizations in a city or a country, or individuals in a family setting. They may be struggling over the allocation of material resources such as land or about differences in ideology or values. Furthermore, these various conflicts may occur together sequentially, with each adversary engaged in many other conflicts concurrently. This very complexity provides opportunities for a specific conflict to become transformed. For example, the reduced salience of a particular conflict, perhaps fostered by an intermediary, can help change a destructive conflict into a constructive one, conducted within agreed-upon rules.

The problem-solving approach may be used in each stage of a conflict, including its emergence, escalation, transformation, settlement, and resolution. Practitioners and analysts of CR give particular attention to negotiations to reach an agreement. They stress the importance of separating the persons involved from the positions espoused, searching for the interests that underlie the stated positions, and constructing many options that may satisfy the interests.

Many advocates of this CR approach emphasize contributions made by mediators. Mediators may facilitate negotiations by providing a safe setting, helping the adversaries to communicate with each other, and assisting them to generate possible solutions to their conflict. Depending upon the disputants' expectations and the mediators' resources, mediators may provide compensation for the risks assumed by the adversaries in making an agreement, increase the pressure to reach an agreement, or help ensure compliance to the settlement reached. The U.S. government made such a contribution in the course of the transformation of the protracted Arab-Israeli conflict beginning in the 1970s.

Since the 1980s, attention has been given to prenegotiation and how intermediaries help bring adversaries to the negotiation table. In the prenegotiation stage, mediators may help adversaries explore each side's readiness for negotiations, help determine which adversaries should try to meet with each other, and help shape an acceptable agenda for negotiations.

In the 1990s the new CR approach increasingly was applied to preventing the destructive escalation of conflicts and to building durable, peaceful relations between former adversaries. Some analysts and practitioners of CR problem solving have drawn attention to nonprovocative methods of defense (such as deploying weapons in defensive positions rather than in a threatening manner), to devising confidence-building measures (such as agreeing on certain procedures in order to avoid any surprises that might appear threatening), and to other ways to avert destructive conflict escalation. Additional methods may even enable adversaries to escalate a struggle constructively, as demonstrated in the 1960s civil rights struggle in the southern United States; such constructive escalation is possible when the adversary is not dehumanized and when an appeal is made to shared values and interests. What seems to be crucial to such efforts is the assurance made to the other side that its continued existence is not threatened.

A variety of methods for building an enduring, peaceful accommodation after a conflict seems to have ended have been discussed and applied. These may pertain to reconciliation, coexistence, superordinate institutional arrangements, and legal systems, and they may include structural arrangements to enhance and ensure equity, such as human rights safeguards and institutions fostering superordinate identities. They also include such experiential methods as interactive workshops, dialogue groups, and truth commissions as well as such interpersonal methods as therapeutic counseling and personal meetings and friendships across antagonistic cleavages. Interethnic and interdenominational workshops and dialogue groups are held in many communities in the United States with the support of government agencies, religious organizations, corporations, and foundations.

The Development of Problem-Solving Conflict Resolution

The new CR approach developed in three periods: (1) 1946–1969, a period of early practices and basic research; (2) 1970–1985, years of crystallization and expansion, during which CR growth was particularly strong in the United States; and (3) since 1986, a time of extension, diffusion, and institutionalization. The emergence of CR, of course, had many antecedents. At the close of the nineteenth century, many thinkers and political leaders believed that spreading economic development, democracy, and trade ties could produce a relatively peaceful world. Efforts to limit or reduce armaments, to assure arbitration of international disputes, and to restructure societies to end war were pursued by peace movement and socialist party activists, such as Bertha von Suttner and Jean Juarès, both active in the late nineteenth century and the early twentieth. The ferocity and devastation of World War I undermined those optimistic beliefs. The Great Depression, the rise of fascism, and the horrors of World War II further undermined faith in progress and the attainment of enduring peace.

Nevertheless, the failures of previous efforts, such as the League of Nations, helped shape the new efforts after World War II, including the treatment of former enemies and the creation of new international governmental and nongovernmental organizations. Furthermore, new ideas about domestic relations with respect to political and industrial democracy emerged. For example, during the economic depression of the 1930s, trade-union activity was aided by new legislation, such as the National Labor Relations Act of 1935, and collective bargaining became institutionalized.

Early Efforts, 1946–1969. Scholarly and practitioner activities that provided the foundations of problem-solving CR grew rapidly immediately after World War II. Some of the work was spurred by the specter of nuclear annihilation that the Cold War evoked, but many other components of the foundations had independent origins. Thus, basic research in sociology, psychology, and other academic disciplines contributed to the development of the new CR approach.

Spurred by concerns about the possible eruption of nuclear as well as nonnuclear wars, an important body of scholarly work contributed to CR using quantitative methods. Researchers, such as J. David Singer, Rudolph J. Rummel, and Edward Azar, among others, began to collect and analyze data on the incidence and correlates of wars and on conflicting and cooperative interactions among the countries of the world, testing CR as well as traditional international-relations ideas.

Another important body of work, produced by Karl Deutsch and others, examined how cooperative activities and institutions provided a basis for increasing integration and bonds, thus lessening the possibility of destructive conflict. Comparative analyses of variations in the integration and co-operation between countries found that highly integrated pairs of countries formed communities and were unlikely to go to war with each other. According to an important strand of thought, functional integration among countries would help create a common interest in peace; this helps explain the process that led from the European Coal and Steel Community established in 1950 to the development of the European Union in the 1980s and 1990s.

Game theory also was influential in the development of CR, helping analysts think about the conflict implications of various payoff matrices and the strategies chosen by interacting players. The prisoner's dilemma (PD) payoff matrix especially was and is the basis of considerable analysis and experimentation. Rather than assuming a zero-sum game (where what one side wins the other loses), the PD payoff assumes a variable-sum game (where both sides may variably win or lose), better reflecting reality.

In the 1950s and 1960s, research was conducted on the relations between contending groups and how overt struggle is prevented, waged constructively, or resolved amicably. For example, much work was done regarding race and ethnic relations by Morton Deutsch, Kenneth B. Clark, Joe Feagin, and Robin M. Williams, Jr. One clear finding was that equal-status interaction between members of different ethnic groups reduces prejudice and antagonistic behavior between them. Another relevant finding was that the creation of superordinate goals—that is, broad, inclusive, or overarching goals—can bring contending groups into cooperative relations.

The practice and the analysis of nonviolent action provided another important element in the development of CR. As articulated by leaders of some nonviolent campaigns, waging a struggle nonviolently recognizes the humanity of the opponent, which limits the conflict's destructive escalation and enhances the likelihood of later attaining an enduring and mutually acceptable outcome. In addition, during the civil rights struggle in the American South, the Community Relations Service of the U.S. Department of Justice mediated many disputes, helping to sustain the constructive character of that struggle. The role of the government in mediating labor-management disputes was evident in the establishment of the Federal Mediation and Conciliation Service in 1947.

Finally, the field of peace studies influenced the development of CR. Workers in peace studies stress the socialization of individuals (by parents, teachers, and peers) to believe that certain ways of waging conflicts are proper and others are not. In addition, research on the military-industrial complex and other interests vested in pursuing conflicts contributed to the demystification of wars and other large-scale conflicts. Understanding how protracted conflicts are de-escalated is particularly germane to CR. For example, the idea behind "graduated reciprocation in tension-reduction" is that de-escalation in tension between long-standing adversaries can occur if one side announces it is undertaking conciliatory actions, invites reciprocation, and persists in conciliatory moves, even when there is no immediate reciprocation. This idea has been influential, and there is evidence that it has been effective under certain conditions when applied in protracted international conflicts, as was the case in the late 1980s with the Soviet leader Mikhail Gorbachev's contribution to ending the Cold War.

Crystallization and Expansion, 1970–1985. In the early 1970s, the practice of problem-solving CR began to flourish. Publications disseminated CR ideas and reports of experience with more and more specialized types of mediation as new fields of CR activity were cultivated and expanded. Training in negotiation and mediation was increasingly provided by academic institutions, such as Harvard University and Syracuse University, and nonacademic institutions, such as Search for Common Ground.

The rapid expansion of CR in the United States was fostered by the convergence of several factors, including the social movements of the 1960s and 1970s as well as the great increase in lawyers, in litigation, and in congested courts. The alternative dispute resolution movement, which sought to provide an alternative to adversarial proceedings and to appealing to the judiciary, seemed attractive to some lawyers and many nonlawyers as a way to reduce the burden on the courts.

Feminist theory and research also contributed to the development of problem-solving CR. Feminism provided a critique of and an alternative to the traditional emphasis on hierarchy and coercive power as the essential forms of decision-making in social life. Feminists stressed the importance of social relationships and the possibility of reaching integrative agreements through consensual decision-making processes.

An extensive body of social-psychological theory and research also contributed greatly to CR, with theories pertaining to cognition, interaction, personality, and many other matters. Some work, by Jeffrey Z. Rubin, for example, focused on how entrapment contributes to escalating conflicts and how that process can be interrupted.

The considerable work done on the emergence, expansion, and effects of various social movements also enriched the CR field significantly. The influential resource-mobilization approach stresses the importance not simply of a sense of grievance but of the belief that grievances can be redressed. The emergence and transformation of large-scale conflicts, therefore, is largely shaped by the apparent strength of the opposition, the capabilities of the social-movement members, and the leaders' formulation of credible goals.

Increasingly during this period, problem-solving interactive workshops were conducted. In this method, a convenor, often academically based, brings together a few members of the opposing sides and guides their discussions about their conflict, fostering mutual understanding and exploration of new options. The participants are often persons with ties to the leadership of their respective parties or those who may become leaders. Many workshops have been held in relationship to protracted communal struggles, such as those in Northern Ireland, Cyprus, and the United States.

Extension, Diffusion, and Institutionalization Since 1986. Problem-solving CR spread into many new settings, with training and practice in mediation increasingly done at all levels of schooling, in private corporations, and in government agencies. CR was also introduced in more regions of the world, for example, in Eastern Europe and the former Soviet Union, Latin America, and southern Africa. Furthermore, CR work increased at each stage of a conflict's course and in the development of structural and normative patterns that reduce the probability of conflicts erupting and becoming destructive. This effort was particularly noteworthy in work settings and in societies with deep ethnic, religious, or other communal cleavages.

CR increasingly became institutionalized, as indicated by several developments. Its practice was officially mandated in certain circumstances, for example, in the development of certain U.S. federal regulations and in child custody cases in some jurisdictions. Institutionalization was also evident in the establishment of many theory-building and research centers, several of them based at universities. In addition, many universities provided graduate training in conflict analysis and resolution, including certificate programs and master's and doctorate programs in CR—for example, the Program on the Analysis and Resolution of Conflict at Syracuse University and the Institute for Conflict Analysis and Resolution at George Mason University. Moreover, many other independent centers were founded to offer training in CR and mediation and also to provide mediating and consulting services.

Finally, workers in the field of CR also gave increasing attention to institutional arrangements for managing recurrent conflicts before they became protracted and destructive. This was especially noteworthy for persons concerned about working together in large, bureaucratic organizations and living together in multiethnic societies.

Applications

Applications of the problem-solving CR approach occur at each major conflict stage, preventing conflict eruption, limiting destructive escalation, transforming seemingly intractable conflicts, negotiating settlements, and sustaining accommodations. Persons engaging in the CR activities noted here may not have identified their work as problem-solving CR, but their actions nevertheless illustrate the approach.

Prevention. Many institutions train people in the use of negotiation and mediation, offering alternatives to violence and other eruptions of destructive conflicts. This process includes training employees about the cultural diversity of the workforce and ways to interact cooperatively with coworkers from different cultural backgrounds. Schools at the primary, secondary, and college levels increasingly are establishing centers and curricula for dispute settlement with peer mediation. In some prisons private groups train inmates in alternatives to violence.

In foreign affairs the U.S. government and citizens have been engaged in preventing eruptions of destructive violence. The breakup of the former Yugoslavia in the early 1990s is an example of a destructive escalation of ethno-nationalist conflicts. Even in this context, however, many potentially destructive conflicts did not erupt. In the former Yugoslav republic of Macedonia, for example, a variety of preventive measures—including the nonprovocative policies of the Macedonian leadership—averted destructive conflict between Serbia and Macedonia and between Albanians and Macedonians inside Macedonia. In addition, international governmental and nongovernmental organizations took appropriate measures, including the deployment of U.S. and other military personnel in peacekeeping missions.

Limiting Destructive Escalation. Obviously, most conflicts do not escalate to immense mutual destruction. Often, careful policies by at least one side limit the destructiveness of a conflict. This was the case in the American civil rights struggle from the mid-1950s into the late 1960s. Those engaged in the struggle to win basic civil rights for African Americans sought alliance with other Americans, appealing to the shared values of most Americans. The reliance on nonviolent action was justified by the premise that even the opponents were human and would recognize the humanity of those seeking their civil rights. In the 1980s emerging environmental conflicts were prevented from becoming destructive by early meetings bringing together the major stakeholding parties. In the 1980s controversy over the uses of the South Platte River in Nebraska and Colorado, the stakeholders included persons who engaged in sport fishing, raising cattle, and farming, as well as residents who wanted fresh water for their households and environmentalists who wanted to preserve a natural habitat for cranes.

Transformation. Although some conflicts seem intractable, eventually even they are transformed and become tractable or even resolved. This was the case in the United States in the transformation of long-standing conflicts involving differences between Protestants and Catholics and between Christians and Jews. By the mid-1950s prejudice and discrimination against Catholics and Jews had greatly decreased in many arenas. Demographic and political shifts, the horrors of the Holocaust, and the growth of inclusive norms of justice strengthened the resistance to ethnic animosity for the most part; at the end of the twentieth century, some organized anti-Semitic groups persisted, but their anti-Jewish attacks were widely condemned. Other conflicts involving ethnic identities also became tractable. In the late 1990s efforts were under way to find common ground between groups holding opposing positions regarding the right to abortion.

Even the seemingly most intractable international conflicts do become transformed, often without one side imposing an outcome upon the other side, and sometimes in a mutually acceptable manner. The immensely destructive threats characterizing the Cold War gradually became moderated by policies of mutual reassurance, as exemplified in the agreements reached during the period of détente in the early 1970s. These official policies were aided and supplemented by a variety of nongovernmental policies and interactions. For example, in 1957, nuclear physicists and others from the United States, Great Britain, and the Soviet Union who had previously worked on the development and possible use of nuclear weapons began meeting to exchange ideas about ways to reduce the chances that nuclear weapons would be used in war. The meetings became the Pugwash Conferences on Science and World Affairs and contributed to the signing of many U.S.-Soviet arms control agreements.

Negotiating Settlements. Increased understanding of problem-solving CR enabled negotiators in disputes about environmental issues, ethnic relations, international conflicts, and many other matters to reach agreements more quickly and with greater equity. Speed is often important to reach a settlement when the opportunity to conclude a settlement is present.

Institutional arrangements in many spheres also increased the availability and legitimacy of mediators. In domestic matters this was evidenced in the increased roles of nongovernmental as well as governmental organizations. In international affairs, the role of the United Nations increased after the Cold War. The United States played and will continue to play major roles in mediating international conflicts, as in Israeli-Arab relations, by helping to initiate negotiations, facilitate the process, and reach an equitable agreement.

Sustaining Agreements. Reaching an agreement does not ensure its implementation and survival. Workers in the field of CR are giving increasing attention to this matter in relation to the transitions from authoritarian rule, from intense ethnic violence, and from other protracted and bitter conflicts. Ways of enhancing the legitimacy and resources needed to sustain an agreement are increasingly sought and found. This approach may include efforts at bringing about reconciliation and a belief that justice is being served.

External support is often important to help implement and maintain an agreement made by long-standing adversaries. Nevertheless, the policies and skills of persons at each social level within each antagonistic party can contribute—or undermine—the durability of any agreement that has been reached. Organizations can be constructed to help develop common identities and vested interests in cooperation.

Conclusion

The expanding use of the problem-solving approach to the management of conflicts increases the repertoire of ways to prevent, limit, and durably conclude destructive conflicts. More and more people are applying a great variety of new methods in various conflicts. Admittedly, such methods are not always well executed or effective in avoiding destructive waging of conflicts and in preventing destructive outcomes. When considering the appropriateness and effectiveness of problem-solving methods, however, we must ask, compared to what? Resorting to brutal violence and other efforts at unilateral imposition of will also often fail; indeed, they are often counterproductive, resulting in widespread destruction.

BIBLIOGRAPHY

Burton, John W. *Conflict: Resolution and Prevention.* New York: St. Martin's, 1990.

Fisher, Ronald. *Interactive Conflict Resolution.* Syracuse, N.Y.: Syracuse University Press, 1997.

Fisher, Roger, and William Ury. *Getting to YES.* Boston: Houghton Mifflin, 1981.

Hampson, Fen Osler. *Nurturing Peace: Why Peace Settlements Succeed or Fail.* Washington, D.C.: United States Institute of Peace, 1996.

Kressel, Kenneth, and Dean G. Pruitt. *Mediation Research.* San Francisco and London: Jossey-Bass, 1989.

Kriesberg, Louis. *Constructive Conflicts: From Escalation to Resolution.* Lanham, Md.: Rowman and Littlefield, 1998.

———. "The Development of the Conflict Resolution Field." In *International Conflict Resolution,* edited by I. William Zartman and Lewis Rasmussen. Washington, D.C.: United States Institute of Peace, 1997.

———. *International Conflict Resolution: The US-USSR and Middle East Cases.* New Haven, Conn.: Yale University Press, 1992.

Lederach, John Paul. *Building Peace: Sustainable Reconciliation in Divided Societies.* Washington, D.C.: United States Institute of Peace, 1997.

Lund, Michael S. *Preventing Violent Conflicts.* Washington, D.C.: United States Institute of Peace, 1996.

Moore, Christopher W. *Dispute Management Systems Design.* Boulder, Colo.: LDR Associates, 1994.

Susskind, Lawrence. *Dealing with an Angry Public: The Mutual Gains Approach to Resolving Disputes.* New York: Free Press, 1996.

Weiner, Eugene, ed. *The Handbook of Interethnic Coexistence.* New York: Continuum, 1998.

LOUIS KRIESBERG

See also **Antiwar Protests; Disarmament and Arms Control; Nonviolence; Peacemaking; Prevention: Violent-Crime Prevention.**

INTERPERSONAL

Interpersonal conflict can be defined broadly as situations in which the needs and desires of two or more people or groups of people appear to be incompatible and in danger of being thwarted. Many theories have been put forward as to what conflict is, how it develops, and how it may be resolved. James Schellenberg (1996), in his effort to categorize conflict theories, discusses four main types or "families" of conflict theories:

1. *Individual characteristics* theories focus attention on individual behavioral factors and

consider their role in creating or maintaining conflict. The underlying idea is that social conflict is a result of aggression by individuals; the key to managing conflict is understanding the aggressive impulse.

2. Proponents of the *social structure* perspective view conflict as a product of the way society is organized. In this view, the major divisions of society (and the inequities between and within such divisions), such as race, ethnicity, class, and gender, are seen as the underlying foundations of conflict.

3. Theories from the *social process perspective* focus on the social interaction between individuals or groups. Although the seeds for a specific dispute may lie in individual or structural characteristics, social conflict is understood to be not strictly the result of such factors but rather of people's perceptions and interactions over time.

4. Theories from the *formal perspective* characterize conflict development and its resolution in logical and mathematical terms. Disputants are viewed as "super-rational," calculating costs and benefits and then choosing the most rewarding options.

Each of these perspectives offers a piece of the conflict puzzle, but none can explain conflict in general. The theories are suggestive of the kinds of questions we may wish to ask when observing conflict. How much of the behavior is due to the character of those involved? How much is a result of social, political, or economic inequities between the groups of whom the disputants are members? How much is a reflection of an escalatory process, for example, us-versus-them thinking? Do these factors come together in some logical, predictable way? Is there an optimal solution? These perspectives also permit us to think more broadly about possible strategies for dealing with various conflicts.

Individual approaches to managing conflicts fall into three general categories (Pruitt and Carnevale 1993): (1) Parties working together to determine what the outcome will be—for example, through negotiation or mediation—are engaged in *joint decision making*. (2) *Third-party decision-making* methods involve a party external to the dispute who determines its outcome—for example, in cases involving adjudication by the legal system, arbitration, or the exercising of legitimate author-

ity, such as by a manager or parent. (3) Parties who make independent decisions are engaged in *separate action*—they may retreat (one yields to the other), struggle (fight against each other), or try tacit coordination (accommodate each other without discussion).

Professionals working in the field of conflict management have tended to emphasize joint-decision-making methods of negotiation and mediation. Such methods are less costly (in terms of money, time, lives), more likely to reflect the parties' own interests, and more likely to honor and support the parties' relationship than the other two types of procedures. However, joint-decision-making procedures are based on voluntary participation, open and direct communication between the parties, trust, shared values, and positive (or at least manageably negative) feelings—factors, needless to say, not inherent in all conflictual situations and relationships.

Joyce L. Hocker and William W. Wilmot (1995) have suggested that people adopt particular preferred styles of responding to conflict. The *collaborator* tries to manage conflict by maintaining interpersonal relationships and ensuring that both parties in the conflict achieve their personal goals; he or she acts not only out of self-interest but on behalf of the opposing parties' interests as well. The *compromiser* assumes that a win-win solution is not possible; the objective is to find some expedient, mutually acceptable solution that partially satisfies the parties involved. The *accommodator* strives to maintain the interpersonal relationship at all costs, with little or no concern for the personal goals of the parties involved. The *controller* takes the necessary steps to ensure that his or her personal goals are met, whatever the cost to the relationship involved. The *avoider* views conflict as something to be shunned at all costs; a central theme of this style is hopelessness, with personal goals remaining unfulfilled and the interpersonal relationship rarely maintained.

Although all the styles have utility in certain situations, flexibility is a key to success in conflict situations. Well-managed conflict can result in better and more appropriate working agreements, heightened appreciation for others' points of view, enhanced relationships, increased self-esteem and confidence, and better health.

BIBLIOGRAPHY

Bolton, Robert. *People Skills: How to Assert Yourself, Listen to Others, and Resolve Conflicts.* Englewood Cliffs, N.J.: Prentice Hall, 1979.

Fisher, Roger, and William L. Ury, with Bruce Patton, ed. *Getting to Yes: Negotiating Agreement Without Giving In.* 2d ed. New York: Penguin, 1991.

Hocker, Joyce L., and William W. Wilmot. *Interpersonal Conflict.* 4th ed. Madison, Wis.: Brown and Benchmark, 1995.

Katz, Neil H., and John W. Lawyer. *Communication and Conflict Resolution Skills.* Dubuque, Iowa: Kendall/Hunt, 1985.

Pruitt, Dean G., and Peter J. Carnevale. *Negotiation in Social Conflict.* Pacific Grove, Calif.: Brooks/Cole, 1993.

Schellenberg, James A. *Conflict Resolution: Theory, Research, and Practice.* Albany: State University of New York Press, 1996.

WILLIAM C. WARTERS

See also **Prevention: Violent-Crime Prevention; Schools: Antiviolence Curricula.**

CONTRAS

The Contras, or *contra-revolucionarios* (counter-revolutionaries), were a U.S.-supported, armed force that was intent on overthrowing the Sandinista government of Nicaragua in the 1980s. The Contra war against Nicaragua cost at least thirty thousand lives, provoked human rights violations, devastated the already weak infrastructure of that Central American nation, and caused the Nicaraguan government to divert scarce resources from social programs to the military and to declare a state of emergency that limited civil liberties. In the intense Cold War and anticommunist atmosphere of the times, the Ronald Reagan administration judged the Sandinistas (Frente Sandinista de Liberación Nacional, or FSLN) as Marxist radicals and communists who had aligned themselves with another U.S. enemy, Fidel Castro's Cuba. U.S. backing of the Contras spurred prolonged debate between the Reagan administration and Congress over the use of foreign aid, covert operations, and low-intensity warfare. U.S. assistance to the Contras also led to the Iran-Contra scandal that exposed abuses of power in the Reagan administration.

The Contras, called freedom fighters under the Reagan doctrine of aiding anticommunists, grew into an armed force of some twenty thousand. Directed, supplied, and funded by the United States, particularly by the Central Intelligence Agency (CIA), the Contras consisted of former followers of the regime of Anastasio Somoza Debayle (which the Sandinistas had ousted in July 1979), including ex-members of Somoza's notorious national guard; Miskito Indians, who had long sought independence from the central Nicaraguan government and who had resisted strong-arm Sandinista efforts to relocate them; peasant farmers who opposed Sandinista programs that disturbed traditional ways or who were coerced into Contra service; soldiers of fortune; disaffected Sandinistas who thought the FSLN was becoming too radical; and businesspeople aggrieved by increased state control of the economy. The Contras operated mostly in northern Nicaragua, using bases in nearby Honduras and Costa Rica as bases of operation to stage hit-and-run attacks.

Origins and Sabotage

In November 1981 President Reagan signed National Security Decision Directive 17. This order provided the CIA with $19 million to create a Contra force. Reagan officials attempted to quiet suspicious members of the U.S. Congress by arguing that the project was intended only to interdict arms shipments from Nicaragua to rebels in El Salvador who were seeking to overthrow the U.S.–backed government there. In reality, the purposes of the directive reached beyond interdiction to the overthrow of the Sandinista government. When Reagan signed his directive, a nucleus Contra force in effect already existed, made up of ex-Nicaraguan national guardsmen trained by the pro-Somoza military government of Argentina, guard leaders who had fled to Miami, and anti-Sandinista Nicaraguan exiles in camps in Honduras. Reagan officials believed that the Contras' sabotage of Nicaraguan facilities, combined with a U.S. trade embargo and the blocking of World Bank loans to Nicaragua, would destabilize the Sandinista government by creating economic havoc, which, in turn, would spawn social and political unrest. The former CIA director Stansfield Turner criticized Contra actions as "terrorism."

The Contras first struck on 14 March 1982, when former national guardsmen trained by CIA agents blew up two bridges in northern Nicaragua. The Contras soon sabotaged crops, warehouses, and other nonmilitary sites. They also assassinated government officials and attacked military patrols. As the war continued through the decade, oil tanks, boats, communications equipment, airports, farm cooperatives, and health clinics became targets. The Contras proved incapable of seizing and holding towns, but they inflicted considerable suffering on the Nicaraguan people. Human rights groups, such as Americas Watch, detailed the kidnapping and torture of civilians. In the mid-1980s, newspaper reporters broke the story that some

Contras were smuggling drugs (especially cocaine) that reached the United States.

Congress and the Iran-Contra Scandal

News about the Contras soon became public in the United States, and many members of Congress questioned the U.S. subversion of another nation's sovereignty, the destruction of life and property, and the emphasis on military rather than diplomatic methods for dealing with the Sandinistas. As a result, the Boland Amendment of December 1982 prohibited the use of U.S. funds for the overthrow of the Nicaraguan government. The Reagan administration winked at this congressional restriction and thwarted the repeated efforts of Latin American leaders to arrange peace negotiations. Instead, the United States continued to enlarge Contra operations in Nicaragua. In late 1983 Congress became more obliging, appropriating $24 million for the Contras. In early 1984 CIA operatives mined Nicaraguan harbors, damaging British and Japanese commercial ships. Nicaragua appealed to the World Court, which, in 1986, declared the United States in breach of international law. In mid-1984 news reports revealed that a CIA manual used in Nicaragua instructed assassins on how to "neutralize" officials, including judges. In response to these CIA activities, Congress passed the second Boland Amendment in October 1984, requiring an end to all military aid to the Contras.

Refusing to be prevented by Congress from overthrowing the Sandinista government, the CIA and National Security Council, under the guidance of Lieutenant Colonel Oliver North, schemed to finance the Contra war. Saudi Arabia, Taiwan, and other countries were asked to give millions of dollars—which they did. Right-wing groups in the United States were also encouraged to make contributions. In addition, the National Security Council diverted funds to the Contras that were derived from the secret sale of arms to revolutionary Iran, a nation that the United States condemned as a haven for terrorists and with which it did not have diplomatic relations. Uninformed about the clandestine arms sale to Iran, Congress approved $27 million in nonmilitary aid for the Contras in June 1985. A year later, Congress voted another $100 million in both military and nonmilitary aid for the Contras. Then, in July 1986, the Iran-Contra connection broke into the news. North and other officials were dismissed or resigned under charges that they had lied to Congress. Several of them were convicted of withholding informa-

tion from Congress, and President George Bush granted presidential pardons to many of them.

The Peace Process and Disbanding of the Contras

As the Contras' military campaign faltered and their U.S. aid dwindled, the peace process accelerated. At a meeting of Central American presidents in January 1988, President Daniel Ortega of Nicaragua agreed to open direct talks with the Contras and to hold national elections. Two months later, the Sandinistas and Contras signed a cease-fire agreement. The Nicaraguan government then granted a general amnesty to all Contras, and Congress voted $49.7 million in humanitarian aid for them. Hurricane Joan ravaged Nicaragua in October; a drought in 1989 seriously reduced agricultural production. When combined with the Contras' destruction of property, these blows staggered Nicaragua's economy and bankrupted the government. In the February 1990 elections a coalition of opposition parties financed by the United States defeated the Sandinistas.

The new Nicaraguan government soon clashed with the Contras. The Central American presidents had devised plans to disarm, dissolve, and resettle the Contra forces. But the Contras protested their exclusion from the new government and initially refused to hand in their arms as required by agreement. Finally, on 10 June 1990, most Contras surrendered their weapons and received U.S.$50 in cash, as well as food, clothing, and farm tools. When the land that the Contras were promised was not available and several of their number were murdered, perhaps by Sandinistas, some Contras rearmed and once again unleashed violence. These "Recontras" disbanded in early 1992 under an agreement that provided them with houses and land.

The Contras ultimately proved ineffective as fighters and politicians. Their reputation was soiled by associations with former Somoza henchmen, corruption, factionalism, and the violence they committed against Nicaraguan villages. The Contras never won popular favor in their homeland, and, met by increasingly successful Sandinista counterattacks, they failed to hold territory. Nevertheless, the devastating economic crisis that their terrorist attacks caused helped to create a popular discontent that led to the electoral defeat of the Sandinistas. The funding of the Contra war cost the United States $300 million in aid, as well as widespread condemnation for the high death toll, the blatant violation of Nicaraguan sovereignty, and the political crisis at home in the Iran-Contra affair.

BIBLIOGRAPHY

Coatsworth, John H. *Central America and the United States: The Clients and the Colossus.* New York: Twayne , 1994.

LaFeber, Walter. *Inevitable Revolutions: The United States in Central America.* 2d ed. New York: Norton, 1993.

LeoGrande, William M. *Our Own Backyard: The United States in Central America, 1977–1992.* Chapel Hill: University of North Carolina Press, 1998.

Pastor, Robert A. *Condemned to Repetition: The United States and Nicaragua.* Princeton, N.J.: Princeton University Press, 1987.

Walker, Thomas W., ed. *Revolution and Counterrevolution in Nicaragua.* Boulder, Colo.: Westview, 1991.

THOMAS G. PATERSON

See also **Central Intelligence Agency; Drug Trade; Military Interventions.**

COPYCAT VIOLENCE

It has become a commonplace of public discourse on crime that depictions of violence in the mass media engender further violence through imitation. The first comprehensive theory of copycat violence extends as far back as the late nineteenth century, when the French criminologist and sociologist Gabriel Tarde, challenging Cesare Lombroso's then-prevalent view of crime as biologically determined, argued for the social determination of crime in his *Penal Philosophy* (1890). Tarde's theory focuses on imitative crimes, which proceed along a well-established route from the nobility to the lower classes "through the spread and attraction of their pleasures, their luxuries, and their vices" (Tarde 1912, p. 341). Tarde posits a simple and direct connection between the initial crime and its imitations: representations of violence arouse a desire to commit violence. He labels such crimes "suggesto-imitative assaults" and cites as the "most striking example" of such assaults the recent murder spree of Jack the Ripper: "Never perhaps has the pernicious influence of *general news* been more apparent. The newspapers were filled with the exploits of Jack the Ripper, and, in less than a year, as many as eight absolutely identical crimes were committed in various crowded streets of the great city. ... There followed a repetition of these same deeds outside of the capital and very soon there was even a spreading of them abroad" (p. 340; emphasis in original). Tarde sums up his theory of copycat crime succinctly: "Infectious epidemics spread with the air or the wind; epidemics of crime follow the line of the telegraph." Though later theorists questioned Tarde's simple notion of causality, the two main elements of his theory—crime as contagion and the role of the media in transmitting the disease—remain at the center of discussions of copycat violence to this day.

According to turn-of-the-twentieth-century criminology, women were more vulnerable to the contagion of violent representations than men and were consequently more likely to commit imitative crimes. The Austrian criminologist Hans Gross (1911) argued that this greater tendency to be influenced by depictions of violence could be traced to a difference in female psychology: "The imaginative power of woman is really more reproductive than productive, and it may be so observed in crimes," he asserts and, indeed, goes so far as to argue that when one is confronted with an imitative crime, "the woman must be fixed upon as the intellectual source of the plan, even though the criminal actually was a man" (pp. 300, 310).

Discussions of copycat violence have typically relied on anecdotal evidence, and the investigations begun at the turn of the century were not really picked up in earnest until the mid-1960s, when researchers began to study imitative violence quantitatively. Leonard Berkowitz and Jacqueline Macaulay studied criminal activity following two widely reported crimes—the assassination of President Kennedy in November 1963 and Richard Speck's multiple murders of nursing students in the summer of 1966—and found "unusual increases in the number of violent crimes," while "non-violent crimes did not appear to be affected" (Berkowitz and Macaulay 1971, p. 238). Though they cautiously assert that "other determinants undoubtedly are more important in the great majority of these incidents," they nevertheless conclude that "contagious influences operate on top of these determinants, and probably in conjunction with a number of them" (p. 260). Reports of sensational crimes, according to their theory, provoke further violence through a two-step process: eliciting aggressive impulses in the spectator and reducing inhibitions to act on these impulses. In place of Tarde's emphasis on desire and Gross's emphasis on an innate lack of immunity, Berkowitz and Macaulay suggest that violent representations lessen restraints on violent actions. Other

305

quantitative studies have similarly argued for the contagious nature of other acts of violence, repeatedly recording, for example, an increase in suicides following both well-publicized suicides and fictional accounts of suicide. David Phillips has argued, for example, that the much-publicized suicide of Marilyn Monroe in 1962 was responsible for well over 300 "excess suicides" in the following two months and that fictional suicides on television soap operas "appear to trigger a rise in U.S. suicides."

Other studies, however, have argued that there is no evidence that representations of violence provoke further violence. Ray Surette (1992) concluded that the media do indeed exert an important influence on violent behavior, but their effect "is more likely qualitative (affecting criminal behavior) than quantitative (affecting the number of criminals)" (p. 131). In other words, media reports of crimes affect how crimes are committed rather than whether they are committed.

Over the years there have been a number of well-publicized accounts by criminals claiming to have been prompted to commit their crimes by representations of violence. These range from Peter Kürten, the "vampire of Düsseldorf," who confessed to thirty-five murders during the 1920s and 1930s and claimed during his trial that "the sensational reports in certain scandal sheets turned me into the man who stands before you today," to John Hinckley, Jr., who claimed that his 1981 attempted assassination of President Reagan was an emulation of the film *Taxi Driver* (1976) and an attempt to impress one of the film's stars. Indeed, simulation and serial killing are, in popular and clinical discourse, always linked. As Mark Seltzer (1998) has argued, "repetitive, compulsive, serial violence" is marked by a "radical entanglement between forms of eroticized violence and mass technologies of registration, identification, and reduplication, forms of Copy-catting and simulation" (p. 3). Copycat violence thus exhibits a crisis of subjectivity in which "the boundaries have come down between inside and outside" (p. 264), between representation and perception, between bodies, images, and machines. However, most criminals who have been interviewed about the copycat nature of their crimes downplay media influence as a source of their criminality.

Attempts to fix legal blame for copycat crimes on those responsible for the fictional representations of violence have repeatedly met with failure. Oliver Stone was sued over the rash of copycat crimes attributed to his gruesomely violent film *Natural Born Killers* (1994). The novelist John Grisham (himself a best-selling author of violent crime stories) provoked a public debate with Stone when he wrote that the director should be held legally responsible under the product-liability law for any violence inspired by his film.

Since the "discovery" of copycat violence as a social problem over a century ago, analysts have pondered solutions to this syndrome. Neither lawsuits nor censorship have been effective. If novelty is the fuel of copycat crimes, then perhaps their essentially repetitive nature, which quickly renders the new old, will prove a built-in self-corrective; in the words of a commentator following a series of copycat product tamperings in 1982, "There seems to be only one way to end the copycat tamperings. I think it will be short lived. . . . Before long copycat tamperings will become so common that they will no longer provide thrill seekers with the excitement they crave" (Surette 1992, p. 139).

BIBLIOGRAPHY

Berkowitz, Leonard, and Jacqueline Macaulay. "The Contagion of Criminal Violence." *Sociometry* 34, no. 2 (1971).

Gross, Hans. *Criminal Psychology: A Manual for Judges, Practitioners, and Students.* Translated by Horace M. Kallen. Boston: Little, Brown, 1911.

Phillips, David. "The Impact of Fictional Television Stories on U.S. Adult Fatalities: New Evidence of the Effect of Mass Media on Violence." *American Journal of Sociology* 87, no. 6 (1982).

———. "The Influence of Suggestion on Suicide: Substantive and Theoretical Implications of the Werther Effect." *American Sociological Review* 39, no. 3 (1974).

Seltzer, Mark. *Serial Killers: Death and Life in America's Wound Culture.* New York: Routledge, 1998.

Shnayerson, Michael. "Natural Born Opponents." *Vanity Fair.* July 1996.

Surette, Ray. *Media, Crime, and Criminal Justice: Images and Realities.* Pacific Grove, Calif.: Brooks/Cole, 1992.

Tarde, Gabriel. *Penal Philosophy.* Translated by Rapelje Howell. Boston: Little, Brown, 1912.

TODD HERZOG

See also **Children and Violence; Film: Film Violence and Censorship; Spectacle, Violence as; Television: Censorship.**

CORONA, JUAN
(1934–)

In early May 1971 migrant workers in the Yuba City, California, area began to disappear. By the end of the month, gravesites of the murdered workers were discovered, and by early June a total of twenty-five bodies had been unearthed. Juan Vallejo Corona's murder spree had lasted only six weeks, yet he had killed at a rate of nearly one person every other day. The victims were all migrant workers, most of them were elderly, and many were alcoholics. They were the perfect victims, easy to pick up and unlikely to be missed. Indeed, the disappearance of some of the men probably would not have been noted if their bodies had remained undiscovered. The bodies were often found with the trousers missing or pulled down, stabbed, and with their heads brutally chopped with a large, sharp instrument, most likely a machete.

Corona was in the ideal situation to have access to his victims. In the 1950s he had come to California as a migrant worker himself and had since built up a labor contract business. Housing migrant workers in a bunkhouse at his home, he would hire out the men to local farmers, earning a commission for each worker. Thus, it was not unusual for him to be seen with one of the many migrant workers that were flocking to California for the summer work.

Corona seemed to be a happily married man with several children. Corona's defense lawyers cited his apparent heterosexuality in claiming that another man had committed the murders, and some still believe that Corona must have had an accomplice. It is possible that Natividad Corona,

Juan Corona's half brother and a convicted sex offender, was the killer. The characteristics of the murders were similar to an attack for which Natividad Corona was convicted, although some argue that Juan Corona was the true perpetrator of that act.

The murders were clearly premeditated, because the graves were sometimes prepared days in advance. Goro Kagehiro, a local farmer, discovered a large, freshly dug hole on his property that had been filled in when he later returned. Upon investigation, it was found to conceal the body of one of the victims. Receipts with the name of Juan Corona were found in the graves of two of the victims, and several witnesses claimed they had last seen the victims alive in Corona's presence. A search of Corona's house yielded bloodstained clothes, a pistol (one of the victims had been shot), as well as a bloodstained knife and a machete. Perhaps the most substantial piece of evidence was a ledger that listed the names of the victims, along with their date of arrival at the bunkhouse and the date they "departed."

In 1973 Corona was sentenced to twenty-five consecutive terms of life imprisonment. He sought an appeal on the grounds that he had not received a proper legal defense and was retried in 1982. Corona was found guilty a second time and was sentenced to twenty-five terms of imprisonment ranging from twenty-five years to life. Natividad Corona died in Mexico in 1973 and was never tried for any of the murders.

BIBLIOGRAPHY

Cray, Ed. *Burden of Proof: The Case of Juan Corona.* New York: Macmillan, 1973.

Kidder, Tracy. *The Road to Yuba City.* Garden City, N.Y.: Doubleday, 1974.

TRACY W. PETERS

See also **Serial Killers.**

Juan Corona leaving the courthouse in Fairfield, California. CORBIS/BETTMANN

CORPORAL PUNISHMENT

From the earliest days of primitive society, corporal punishment—the infliction of physical pain or bodily harm without necessarily causing death—has been used to punish crime and as a disciplinary measure. In the late twentieth century corporal punishment continued to be legally practiced as a means of criminal punishment in some of the nations of Africa, the Middle East, and the

English-speaking Caribbean. Among the nations that employ corporal punishment are Afghanistan, the Bahamas, Bangladesh, Brunei, Iran, Libya, Malaysia, Pakistan, Qatar, Saudi Arabia, Singapore, Sudan, Swaziland, Trinidad and Tobago, United Arab Emirates, Yemen, and Zimbabwe.

Corporal Punishment as a Method of Disciplining Children

In 1994 the case of Michael Fay—an American youth caned by Singapore authorities for the crime of vandalism—became a cause célèbre in the United States. Public opinion polls revealed deep disagreement about Fay's treatment, but they also showed that many Americans were in favor of corporal punishment of the type Fay received. Indeed, in many American families, spanking and other physical punishments are commonly used to punish children. Moreover, in the 1990s twenty-seven states still permitted corporal punishment in schools (although it had been banned in some local school districts in those states). The paddling of recalcitrant schoolchildren by public-school officials was especially prevalent in Arkansas and Texas.

The distinction between the use of corporal punishment to discipline unruly schoolchildren and the use of corporal punishment to punish criminals is historically and legally significant. In *Ingraham v. Wright* (1977), the U.S. Supreme Court held that the administration of corporal punishment in public schools, even when inflicted in a severe and painful manner, is not prohibited by the cruel-and-unusual-punishment clause of the Eighth Amendment. One of the petitioners, a student at Drew Junior High School in Dade County, Florida, suffered a hematoma requiring medical treatment after receiving more than twenty strikes on his buttocks with a flat wooden paddle. Another student in the same school was beaten on his arms as well as his buttocks and lost the full use of his arms for a week. Altogether, sixteen Drew students testified to having received severe paddlings from teachers or the principal.

The Supreme Court acknowledged that the corporal punishment regime at Drew was arguably arbitrary, excessive, and degrading. The Court nevertheless held that the Eighth Amendment protects only those convicted of crimes and was never meant to limit the range of noncriminal punishments that could be imposed on schoolchildren. Writing for the five justices in the majority, Justice Lewis Powell explained that the ban on cruel and unusual punishment clearly was intended to protect convicted criminals from barbaric, torturous, or illegal methods of punishment. The use of corporal punishment as a means of disciplining schoolchildren, on the other hand, was widely practiced in colonial days, and the framers of the Constitution never intended to ban the paddling of schoolchildren.

Powell added that the contemporary Court would not be justified in extending Eighth Amendment protection to paddled schoolchildren because corporal punishment still plays a role in disciplining schoolchildren in the United States and "[this Court] can discern no trend toward its abolition." Justice Powell conceded that critics of the *Ingraham* decision would be quick to point out that it was now clear that schoolchildren could be beaten without constitutional redress, "while hardened criminals suffering the same beatings at the hands of their jailers might have a valid claim under the Eighth Amendment." Justice Powell concluded, however, that this anomaly was no reason to "[wrench] the Eighth Amendment from its historical context and [extend] it to traditional disciplinary practices in the public schools."

Corporal Punishment as a Criminal Sentence

As the *Ingraham* majority pointed out, the use of corporal punishment as a means of punishing convicted criminals was generally considered unconstitutional throughout the United States by the early 1970s. It is noteworthy, however, that the contemporary ban on the sanctioned use of corporal punishment as a means of punishing criminals is a relatively recent development in American criminal jurisprudence. In Anglo-Saxon England, criminals were often killed, mutilated, whipped, or sold into slavery. The Anglo-Saxons whipped offenders with knotted cords, and it was not uncommon for masters and mistresses to whip their erring servants to death. After England's Whipping Act of 1530 authorized the public whipping of vagrants, flogging, branding, burning, placement in the pillory (wooden frames with holes for the head, hands, and sometimes the feet), and other tortures were routinely inflicted on beggars, thieves, prostitutes, and other minor offenders. Indeed, until the pillory was abolished in England in 1837, the spectacle of a man helpless in its grasp, his head protruding through its beams and his hands through two holes, was not uncommon. The more serious misdemeanants were sometimes nailed through their ears to the pillory, branded, and shaved bald.

No doubt many of the miscreants so punished considered themselves to have been blessed by God, for they at least had not fallen victim to the executioner. The Anglo-Saxons relied heavily on capital punishment, imposing death by hanging, by beheading, by drowning, by stoning, by boiling, and by burning, as well as by flogging. Although hanging had become the most common method of inflicting death by the late eighteenth century, burning—a fate generally reserved for heresy, treason, or the murder of a husband by a wife—remained lawful in England until 1790. At that time, these offenses were among more than 240 offenses punishable by death. Others included pickpocketing, adultery, stealing sheep, stealing a handkerchief, and associating with gypsies.

Not surprisingly, the criminal punishments employed in the American colonies were quite similar to those prevailing in England. Over a dozen offenses considered serious, including murder, treason, rape, and robbery, were punishable by death, and corporal punishments were routinely meted out to vagrants, trespassers, blasphemers, adulterers, Sabbath breakers, petty thieves, and others unfortunate enough to have offended colonial moral standards. The early settlers in northern America brought with them a firm belief in the efficacy and morality of flagellation. Consequently, the whipping post and other means of corporal punishment—the stocks and pillory, branding, the brank, and the ducking stool, among others—were among the most popular forms of punishment in seventeenth- and eighteenth-century America.

As in England, such punishments were imposed even for minor offenses, and they were often designed to convey shame and humiliation as well as physical pain and discomfort. Victims of the rod, the cane, the birch, the lash, the strap, and the cat-o'-nine-tails were typically tied to a wooden whipping post or some other immovable structure usually located in or near the town square. Firmly secured to the post or perhaps a cart's tail or even the carriage of a gun, the offender was stripped to the waist and publicly lashed with the requisite number of strokes decreed by colonial authorities. Sometimes salt was thrown upon victims' bleeding backs to increase the pain.

Colonial Delaware was notorious for its use of the whipping post. Whipping posts were erected in all three of Delaware's counties in the late seventeenth century. The Sussex County post was painted red and became known as Red Hannah because whipped slaves would often speak of the pains they suffered when they "hugged Red Hannah." Robert Caldwell's classic study, *Red Hannah* (1947), chronicles the history—and ineffectiveness—of Delaware's use of the whipping post. Typical was the case of Agnieta Hendriks, publicly whipped with twenty-seven lashes on 3 April 1679 for the crime of "giving birth to three bastard children." Unfortunately, in November of 1680, the unrepentant Hendriks was convicted of having still another bastard child. This time the court ordered her to endure thirty-seven lashes and to leave the county for five years.

Caldwell found that over time the opportunity to hug Red Hannah increasingly became reserved for blacks. Gender differences were apparent as well. Delaware abolished the whipping of white women convicted of theft in 1855 but did not ban the whipping of women convicted of other crimes until 1889. Despite a 1963 Delaware Supreme Court decision (*State v. Cannon*) upholding the constitutionality of whipping as a method of punishing criminals, the whipping post gradually fell into disuse in the second half of the twentieth century and was removed from Delaware prisons in the 1970s.

The stocks and pillory were found in the town squares of nearly all early New England communities. The culprit, typically a petty thief, drunkard, adulterer, or vagrant, could expect to be pelted with insults and ridicule as well as with sticks and stones. Some offenders were whipped or branded while secured to the frame and a few experienced the agony of ear nailing and the subsequent removal of one or both ears.

Branding was a common form of punishment in colonial America. The laws of colonial New Jersey, for example, stipulated that for burglary the first offense was to be punished with a *T* (for "thief") burned into a hand and the second offense with an *R* (for "rogue") burned into the forehead. A 1662 Maryland law ordered that a person twice convicted of hog-stealing was to have an *H* burned into his shoulder. This law was widely perceived as being too lenient and was amended four years later to apply to first-offense hog-stealers, who were to receive the brand on their forehead. *The Scarlet Letter*, Nathaniel Hawthorne's 1850 novel of Puritanism and punishment in seventeenth-century Boston, accurately depicted the somewhat kinder and gentler practice of forcing adulterous wives to attach an *A*, cut from scarlet cloth, to their upper garments. Others who offended the strict tenets of Puritan morality were similarly adorned; blasphemers wore a *B*, paupers a *P*, and drunkards a *D*.

The brank was a metal frame placed around the head. Also known as the "dame's bridle" and the "gossip's helm," it contained a spiked plate that entered the mouth over the tongue so as to inflict severe pain if the offender spoke. The brank was generally reserved for gossips, perjurers, and blasphemers, but in colonial New York it could also be used for husband beaters and drunkards. Those found guilty of particularly serious cases of blasphemy often received a worse fate—the piercing of the tongue with a hot iron.

The ducking stool was a well-known device employed as a form of corporal punishment for lesser crimes. The miscreant, typically a village scold or gossip, was strapped to a chair that had been fastened to a long lever and situated at the bank of a river or pond. Once secured to the chair, the victim was repeatedly submerged in the water before a jeering crowd. Colonial law generally required ducking stools to be set up at the body of water closest to the county courthouse.

The Spanish Mantle was another device commonly used to inflict discomfort and humiliation. This was a barrel with a single hole for the head and arms. The malefactor, typically a thief or a blasphemer, was forced to wear the barrel while marching through the street to the jeers of onlookers. Similarly, iron masks and cage-like helmets were often attached to offenders in an effort to produce discomfort and humiliation. Miscreants were frequently confined in *jougs,* iron collars attached to a wall or post. Very often the particular method of punishment indicated to onlookers the particular crime that had been committed. For example, citizens convicted of libel or slander—causing an innocent citizen to be ridiculed—typically were shackled by the feet to a wooden stake, a punishment known as the bilboes, which exposed the convict to jeers, taunts, laughter, whispering, and other ridicule.

Corporal Punishment in Prisons

It was in part in reaction to the cruelty of methods of corporal punishment that an influential group of Philadelphia Quakers in 1790 established the Walnut Street Jail. Generally considered to have been the first true penitentiary in the world for the housing of convicted criminals, the Walnut

Street Jail and the Eastern State Penitentiary, opened in 1829, became the centerpieces of the Pennsylvania penal reform movement. Whippings and beatings were not used in the Pennsylvania system of prison discipline. Each prisoner was isolated in his solitary cell twenty-four hours a day under a rule forbidding inmates to speak. Prisoners who refused to maintain their silence and work at hard labor in their cell were removed to a dark cell with reduction in food. As Gustave de Beaumont and Alexis de Tocqueville explained in their 1833 treatise, *On the Penitentiary System in the United States and Its Applications in France,* "it is rare that more than two days of such discipline are required to curb the most refractory prisoner."

No other state, however, strictly followed the Pennsylvania model. All of the other states that opened new penitentiaries in the first half of the nineteenth century relied heavily on the whip to enforce inmate discipline. New York State, which opened its Auburn State Prison in 1817 and the Sing Sing prison in 1828, locked prisoners in their solitary cells at night but allowed them to work together in common work areas during the day. As in Pennsylvania, the rule of silence was enforced, but the punishment for those who violated this or any rule was a severe whipping.

Connecticut opened its Wethersfield Penitentiary in 1827 and soon established a combination of whipping, solitary confinement, bread-and-water diets, and the use of chains to enforce discipline. By the middle decades of the nineteenth century, all of the state penitentiaries, in their efforts to enforce discipline, increasingly reverted to the very kinds of corporal punishments that were characteristic of medieval England and colonial America. The whip became common in southern prisons as well as in New York, Virginia, and Ohio. Maine began to resort to the ball and chain, and Pennsylvania, still reluctant to employ the whip, turned to the use of the iron gag, because as one Pennsylvania warden explained, inmates were "men of idle habits, vicious propensities, and depraved passions."

Whippings and other corporal punishments were commonly used to enforce prison rules through the early 1900s. In 1927 the North Carolina Supreme Court held that prison officials could continue to whip prisoners so long as state law or administrative regulations specifically authorized the use of corporal punishment. Concerns about corporal punishment and other harsh practices in state prisons and county jails led Congress in 1891 to enact legislation establishing federal prisons. Corporal punishments were rarely applied in the Leavenworth, Atlanta, and McNeil Island Penitentiaries—the first three federal prisons of the early twentieth century. However, in some cases prisoners were put in segregation cells with their wrists handcuffed to the bars at chest height and left there during the working hours of the day. By the early 1930s, the U.S. Bureau of Prisons banned corporal punishment in federal prisons; at that time, all of the top officials in the bureau agreed that it was inhumane, ineffective, and detrimental to the bureau's increasing emphasis on rehabilitation.

Beginning in the 1930s, whippings by state prison officials in northern states began to decline significantly. Whippings and other physical punishments—including the everyday pains inflicted on chain-gang inmates—continued as lawfully imposed punishments in most southern states through the 1950s. Nevertheless, a clear trend toward the abolition of corporal punishment as a method of disciplining prisoners had begun. Virginia, for example, enacted legislation banning the use of corporal punishment in adult prisons in 1946 (although whipping continued in juvenile institutions until 1973). In 1955 North Carolina enacted a statute forbidding the use of corporal punishment on any prisoner.

By 1968 only two states—Arkansas and Mississippi—still permitted official use of corporal punishment for prison disciplinary purposes. In the mid-1960s Arkansas prisoners brought a series of lawsuits challenging the use of the strap, which was a wooden-handled leather belt from three to five feet in length, about four inches wide, and a quarter inch thick. As a routine disciplinary measure, prisoners were forced to lower their trousers, lie facedown on a cot or a table, and receive ten lashes on their buttocks. In *Talley v. Stephens* (1965), a federal trial court had upheld the use of the strap so long as the lashings were limited to ten blows and were administered by "responsible people" in a "dispassionate" manner and with "appropriate safeguards."

Talley, however, was overruled three years later in the landmark case of *Jackson v. Bishop* (1968). Writing for a unanimous panel of the U.S. Court of Appeals for the Eighth Circuit, Judge Harry Blackmun (who would be appointed to the U.S. Supreme Court in 1970) declared that the use of the strap, irrespective of any precautionary measures that may be imposed, violated the cruel-and-unusual-punishment clause of the Eighth Amendment. Blackmun stressed that "corporal punishment is easily subject to abuse in the hands of the sadistic and the unscrupulous . . . and is degrading to the punisher and the punished alike." He concluded that the use of the strap "offends contemporary concepts of decency and human dignity and precepts of civilization which we profess to possess."

Jackson v. Bishop had the practical effect of ending many other methods of corporal discipline that had been used in Arkansas prisons. These included hitting inmates with blackjacks and clubs, inserting needles under fingernails, crushing knuckles or testicles with pliers, and the use of the infamous "Tucker telephone"—an electrical device whose terminals were attached to the genitals and big toe of the inmate. A prison staff member would then turn the crank, sending electrical shocks through the inmate's body until he passed out.

The *Jackson* decision led to the end of the officially sanctioned use of corporal punishment as a method of enforcing prison discipline or punishing criminals. Although the U.S. Supreme Court has never directly ruled on the question of the constitutionality of inflicting corporal punishments on accused or convicted criminals, the Court's opinion in *Ingraham v. Wright* (1977) cited *Jackson* approvingly. Moreover, since 1968 no federal or state court has contradicted the *Jackson* holding.

Conclusion

Corporal punishment persists as a child-rearing practice in many American families. And it remains lawful as a disciplinary measure to be taken against schoolchildren in at least some areas of the majority of American states. However, corporal punishment is no longer officially permitted as a method of punishing criminals or disciplining prisoners. This is not to say, however, that corporal punishment could not reemerge as part of the American criminal justice system. In the book *Just and Painful* (1995), the criminologist Graeme Newman advocates painful but not tissue-damaging electric shocks as a method of punishing certain offenders. Newman argues that a properly administered regimen of electric shocks would be less costly and far less cruel and destructive of prisoners' lives than is the contemporary practice of imprisonment. In Delaware, bills to bring back the whipping post are introduced every several years, and although no such bill has been enacted into law, many citizens strongly support such a measure.

It should also be noted that corporal punishment continues as an unofficial disciplinary method in many American prisons. Prisoners have won numerous lawsuits against prison staff and officials for unauthorized beatings and other forms of brutality. In *Hudson v. McMillian* (1992), the U.S. Supreme Court upheld an award of $800 in damages against two Louisiana prison guards who beat a shackled prisoner after being told by their supervisor, "Don't be having too much fun, boys." After exchanging angry words with Keith Hudson, a black inmate, the two guards placed him in handcuffs, leg irons, and waist chains. They punched and kicked Hudson in the face and stomach, bruising his body, loosening his teeth, cracking his dental plate, and causing a swelling of his face.

Louisiana officials argued that the beating had not violated the Eighth Amendment because it had not inflicted "significant injury." But by a seven-to-two vote, the Court held that an inmate who is the victim of unauthorized, excessive, and unnecessary force by prison staff does not have to prove that he suffered a significant injury in order to assert his right to be free from cruel and unusual punishment. In a concurring opinion, Justice Blackmun argued that to allow the significant-injury standard might permit prison officials to bring back the leather strap and other torturous punishments of the past. The majority opinion seemed to agree: "When prison officials maliciously and sadistically use force to cause harm, contemporary standards of decency are always violated." At the turn of the twenty-first century, *Hudson v. Palmer* and *Jackson v. Bishop* remained the law of the land.

BIBLIOGRAPHY

Adams, Robert. *The Abuses of Punishment.* New York: St. Martin's, 1998.

Barnes, Harry Elmer. *The Story of Punishment: A Record of Man's Inhumanity to Man.* Boston: Stratford, 1930.

Caldwell, Robert. *Red Hannah: Delaware's Whipping Post.* Philadelphia: University of Pennsylvania Press, 1947.

Christianson, Scott. *With Liberty for Some: Five Hundred Years of Imprisonment in America.* Boston: Northeastern University Press, 1998.

Newman, Graeme. *Just and Painful: A Case for the Corporal Punishment of Criminals.* 2d ed. New York: Harrow and Heston, 1995.

KENNETH C. HAAS

See also **Child Abuse: Physical; Cruel and Unusual Punishment; Prisons: Prison Conditions; Schools.**

CORPORATIONS

The corporation developed first in Rome but found greater utility in England during the late seventeenth century, when it was the hub of business activity. However, by the mid-eighteenth century corporations had gone out of favor with the English commonwealth due to the exorbitant speculation that they typically engaged in and that eventually resulted in the failure of the South Sea Company (1765). Indeed, while people were literally starving to death, owners of English corporations restricted the sale of foodstuffs in order to drive up prices, thereby ensuring a hefty profit. In response, the British Empire passed the Bubble Act (1720), which for more than one hundred years restricted the activities of corporations. Unmoved by the English experience, however, the United States saw corporations gaining prominence during the Industrial Revolution. This era in American history was a time of substantial social and political change and, for a brief period, of unrestricted and absolute corporate authority.

Spurred by new and innovative means to produce materials and goods for sale and export, joint-stock ventures proved to be an efficient mechanism to pool the resources of investors. Mid- and late-eighteenth-century English inventions, such as the spinning jenny and the steam engine, set the stage for technological advances in America that led to a greater reliance on machinery for increased processing efficiency.

In the late eighteenth century Eli Whitney contributed to the American Industrial Revolution by inventing the cotton gin and interchangeable parts for weapons. Across nations affected by the boom in industrial production, laws were changed to allow unrestricted growth in corporate business enterprises. Corporations became legally recognized as "juristic persons," or entities accorded legal rights and protections. Missing from this calculus, however, were laws ascribing to this "person" any specific legal obligations. Therefore, measures designed to curb potentially abusive, if not violent, business practices were left unaddressed. The stage for the Industrial Revolution in America (1848–1878) was thus set by innovations in the means to produce materials and by laws that encouraged rapid economic expansion without fear of personal liability. Historians would come to call this era the "years of violence."

The impact of the Industrial Revolution on the American social landscape was phenomenal. What had been an economy based largely on agrarian commodities, in which most citizens lived on farms and produced items for self-sufficiency, turned quickly into an economy based on the mass production of goods for others to consume. This new economy required substantial numbers of unskilled laborers. In rapid succession, factories took the place of farms as sources of income, and tenements and slums became home to hard-pressed workers. It was during this time period that the term *hoodlum* was coined to describe roving youths who banded together in what today are referred to as gangs. While it is true that the growth of the American system of production eventually led to a higher quality of life for most citizens, decades of suffering and violence preceded the realization of widespread social benefits.

The Labor Movement

While legions of laborers poured into the cities to find work, others, far fewer in number, were busy laying the plans for future capital investments. In the mills and foundries of the Northeast and South, laborers faced daunting conditions. In the absence of workplace safety laws, workers often were injured, crippled, and killed by the machines they toiled over. Moreover, it was not unusual for the older buildings that housed production facilities to catch fire. Many workers died because adequate safeguards such as exit doors and fire escapes were not in place. Workweeks were long and difficult, averaging over sixty hours. Aside from being dangerous places, factories were often unsanitary, unhealthy, and demeaning environments. It was not uncommon to find entire families, children included, working on the factory floor. And since young males could be paid less than the prevailing wage, many industries, including coal, silk, glass, and cotton, located in areas where male children were plentiful.

Employers at this time were not required by law to protect workers from foreseeable harm. There were no regulations or laws concerning the treatment of employees, no social safety nets, and no recourse for workers left injured or unemployed. Indeed, the Supreme Court ruled frequently that employers could not be held accountable for workplace mishaps. The risks of working in unsafe and dangerous factories, the Court argued, were incurred solely by the employee.

Against this backdrop of hardship, a relatively small number of individuals were profiting in sums never before achieved. Known as robber bar-

ons, these men were the magnates of industry and finance. Their names have left an indelible mark on American history and social thought. James Fisk, a speculator and financier, who together with the most rapacious of the barons, Jay Gould, looted the coffers of businesses across the States; Cornelius Vanderbilt, a railroad magnate and America's first multimillionaire; and John D. Rockefeller, the founder of Standard Oil, stood out as examples of the promise that capitalism fulfilled.

According to the historian Eric Hobsbawm (1996), there were three characteristics that distinguished American robber barons from prior business leaders. First, the absence of governmental regulation over economic activity made it possible for business owners to employ ruthless and violent means against both laborers and competitors. The long reach of business, moreover, sparked the corruption of politicians and police at the local, state, and national levels. Second, the robber barons were driven by the sole purpose of making as much money as possible in any area ripe for profiteering, not in constructing single business enterprises. Finally, American owners of industry were often "self-made" as opposed to "old money." They were driven opportunists who understood that accumulation was a moral imperative in capitalism. Thus, they employed any and all means to garner wealth, sometimes at the expense of human life.

The Civil War slowed the pace of the Industrial Revolution and, for a short while, provided a distraction from the hardship of labor. After the war, however, two competing images emerged in the American economic landscape that defined and justified the relationship between employees and owners. First, Karl Marx and Friedrich Engels's critique of capitalism, published in the *Communist Manifesto* (1848), resonated with the thoughts and experiences of workers. Capitalism, Marx and Engels argued, degraded humanity and served only a few individuals whose fortunes grew at the expense of the masses. On the other hand, the theories advanced in Charles Darwin's influential *On the Origin of Species* (1859), especially as applied by the English philosopher Herbert Spencer, proffered a view of the evolution of mankind in which the strong climbed quickly the ladder of success while the weak and the meager were left to perish. "Social Darwinism," or more precisely "economic Darwinism," was extended into industrial relationships: business leaders were simply better suited to lead a business, brighter and more aggressive than average laborers, and thus worthy of the fortunes bestowed upon them.

The American labor movement can be viewed through the lens of these competing frameworks and serves as an excellent example of how corporations relied on violence to pursue their interests. Although scattered across the nation, labor unions attracted many workers and thus affected many industries (estimates place the number of craft unions at around thirty in 1870, with collective membership of about three hundred thousand). This changed rapidly with the advent of the railroad and the great economic depression of 1873. Railroads opened markets that before were closed and made possible the movement of materials across great distances. The depression, on the other hand, led to massive economic instability, lower wages, and, for many, unemployment.

Amid these changes, unions became a fractured but potent voice for workers, a voice that was despised by most employers. The strike, the most powerful weapon in a union's arsenal, shook the foundations of the railroad and mining industries, but even against the collective force of workers, the strike paled in comparison with the power mustered by business owners. In Pennsylvania, for example, large corporations, particularly the railroads, were given the authority to hire armed police and to use them as they deemed fit. The armed representatives of business owners were often ruthless in their pursuit to divest unions of their power, employing rifles instead of the law to squelch opposition. With the clear aim of intimidation, and without fear of punishment, the armed police of the railroads and mines often engaged in vigilante action, killing some 530 known individuals from 1850 to 1889. It was during this period that the most despised and brazen group of corporate thugs and spies, known as the Pinkertons, were employed widely across industries.

When the corporation was unable to halt the actions of organized labor unions, the U.S. Army was called in to do the job. Time and again, when up against striking workers, state governors, backed by their close association with business leaders, called in the National Guard to ensure the continued operation of industry. By the mid-1880s more than one thousand union strikes had occurred across the states, from Idaho and Colorado to New York. In their wake were thousands of dead and injured workers, either shot or struck down by the bayonets of American soldiers. Some of the worst incidents occurred in the minefields

of Colorado where, with the assistance of Republican governor James H. Peabody, troops indiscriminately arrested union loyalists and sympathizers and deported anyone who refused to disavow the union. The dispute came to a climax when, after a bomb killed thirteen strikebreakers, the government and mine owners responded by killing or wounding a half-dozen men during an assault on their union headquarters.

Battles raged as well in Michigan, where dozens of miners were killed in clashes with authorities and where in 1913 company loyalists were rumored to have provoked a stampede at a crowded Christmas party for workers following a ten-month strike; sixty-two children were killed. Later, in April 1914, violence was revisited on the mines of Colorado when union laborers battled National Guardsmen. In what came to be known as the Ludlow Massacre, National Guardsmen attacked and burned a camp full of women and children; some thirteen died. In total, at least seventy-four people, on both sides of the conflict, were killed. While employees were able to garner new rights from the company's owners, the Rockefellers, the union all but perished.

Violence Against Citizens and Consumers

The dark side of corporate behavior extends well beyond working conditions and labor disputes. Often, corporate violence is not aimed directly at employees or adversaries, but indiscriminately and indirectly at bystanders and consumers. The New York Central Railroad, known for its dubious stock dealings, operated a freight train that traversed some of the most crowded streets in New York. One particular stretch of track became infamous as "Death Avenue." The people who lived in this area were poor, and their children often played on or alongside the tracks. The trains were not subject to an enforced speed limit and passed unyieldingly through the crowded streets. For more than twenty-five years, residents had tried to enact legislation that would restrict train speeds or require elevation of the tracks. Such legislation always met with resistance from the railroad lobby, which effectively silenced citizen demands for safety. While the battle of finances and political will was being waged in legislative committees, over 325 people lost their lives to trains that passed Death Avenue; almost half of those who died were children. It was not until 1908 and a public protest in which five hundred children and parents lined the streets that the state legislature passed a law to elevate the tracks.

Consumers, too, have often been the unwitting victims of corporate carelessness and disregard. The nation's food supply, for example, has at various times been adulterated with spoiled, toxic materials. Nowhere was this better illustrated than in Upton Sinclair's *The Jungle* (1906). Sinclair exposed the sordid conditions of America's meat-processing and packing plants. Animals that were sick, dying, and even dead as a result of infection were routinely processed to later fill the shelves at stores across the country. Rancid meat, mixed with animal parts and chemically treated to prevent the overt appearance of spoilage, also found its way to the plates of soldiers engaged in the Spanish-American War. Exposés soon followed that chronicled the exploits of chicken-processing plants and dairy distributors. Largely due to the outrage generated by Sinclair's novel, however, the force of public opinion was enough to outweigh the power of the processors, and Congress passed the Pure Food and Drug Act in 1906.

The nation's health was also put at risk by corporations that placed profits above human life. Shipping port operators in the South, for example, routinely concealed the existence of serious communicable diseases that could easily spread across the country. Harbor operators in San Francisco denied knowledge that the plague had entered the harbor, although they had gone to some length to hide its existence. Waste products dumped into the rivers that fed Scranton, Pennsylvania, were attributed to an epidemic of yellow fever, while the sludge from processing plants that contaminated the drinking water of Ithaca, New York, was blamed for a typhoid epidemic. At the time, it was not illegal to dump waste into the waterways and basins that provided a city with its drinking water.

Modern Corporate Violence

The size and operational scope of contemporary corporations means that the harm they are capable of inflicting is substantial and potentially widespread. And given the complexity of the modern corporation, with its layers of bureaucracy and diffuse decision-making processes, it is often difficult to assign responsibility for corporate crime to any one individual or group of executives.

Corporate wrongdoing often damages entire communities. Certain businesses, such as textiles and meat processing, often locate in economically depressed areas of the country where labor is plentiful and cheap and where regulation and oversight is at a minimum. Plants and mills in these areas are typically the largest, or only, employer and they exert tremendous political clout.

In September 1991 a deadly fire erupted at the Imperial Food Products plant in Hamlet, North Carolina. Meat-processing plants dot the southern United States, where they have been able to avoid regulation and inspection. As an industry, meat processing has a history of contaminating waterways and land with the waste byproducts of its operations. The plant in Hamlet, which was the primary employer of the community, caught fire after a hydraulic line burst, spraying the flammable fluid into hot oil. Ninety employees were in the plant at the time of the fire. Twenty-five died and fifty-six were injured. Almost immediately, employees who escaped the fire reported that the exit doors had been locked or blocked, that the plant had no fire sprinkler system, no windows to provide for escape, and too few exit doors. The resulting investigation found that the company's owners had locked the fire doors to prevent employees from stealing chickens and that the building, which was over one hundred years old, had never been inspected in eleven years of plant operations. The community was devastated by the loss of life and the loss of its largest employer.

Communities are also affected by corporate violence when businesses knowingly contaminate drinking water, pollute the air, and illegally dump toxic wastes. In 1988 the Environmental Protection Agency (EPA) estimated that some 88 billion pounds of toxic wastes were produced in the United States. The EPA also estimated that almost 90 percent of this waste was disposed of improperly—that is, in unapproved landfills, in waterways, in ditches, or in containers that eventually decompose and allow the toxic contents to seep into the ground. The Allied Chemical Company, as an example, was convicted for dumping Kepone, a toxic pesticide, in Virginia's James River. As a result, the governor closed almost one hundred miles of the river, which bankrupted the regional fishing industry.

Minority communities appear to be particularly victimized by certain types of corporations. Chemical companies, for example, have historically established their businesses in areas where minorities live. The resulting pollution of the air, land, and water has been termed "environmental discrimination," because minorities are disproportionately affected. Minorities are also more likely

---

Hawk's Nest

No treatment of the history of corporate violence in America would be complete without mention of Hawk's Nest, an incident that eventually claimed the lives of 764 workers. Hawk's Nest is an area on the western side of West Virginia where the New River—the largest river in the state—meets the Gauley River to form a strong rushing current. In 1930, plans were made to channel the strong current into a hydroelectric dam. Engineers, however, would have to direct the strong current down a three-mile-long tunnel that descended 162 feet.

The lowest bidder was granted the contract to build the dam and the tunnel. Rinehart and Dennis Company, under the direction of Union Carbide and Carbon Corporation, assumed responsibility for construction and immediately hired thousands of laborers, mostly black migrants from the South. The migrant workers were used primarily to drill the tunnel, a dangerous job responsible for several deaths caused by accidental explosions and mishaps involving the large drill rigs. But the men had understood the dangers of working with dynamite and machines; what they had not known was that a far greater threat loomed inside the mountain through which they were drilling.

Core samples taken from the tunnels showed that the sediments were 96 percent to 99 percent pure silica, a fine granular substance much like sand. Drilling and blasting sent large amounts of this material airborne, where it was likely to be inhaled by tunnel workers. As a basic precaution, practiced often in other mines, the company could have issued face masks that would have filtered most of the material from workers' lungs, or hosed down with water the inside of the tunnel to dissipate the airborne cloud of sand. It did neither.

Some men became sick immediately and died on site. Accounts from survivors indicate that the dead were buried quickly in makeshift graves to minimize work stoppages and avoid the scrutiny of officials. Indeed, a large grave site containing the remains of almost seventy men was found on property belonging to a Union Carbide employee—the medical examiner who had given the workers a clean bill of health. Other accounts were more graphic and told a story of men exiting the tunnel covered in silica, barely recognizable and barely breathing. Many of these men, the stories went, walked into the woods or into their encampments to die.

The tunnel was completed but the damage done to the men who had constructed it was ongoing. Although it is difficult to calculate, epidemiological estimates indicate that many more men died in the years following the opening of Hawk's Nest than during the time it took to construct it. Acute silicosis, or lung disease caused by the ingestion of silica found in the tunnel, killed or maimed almost eight hundred men. The camps where the men worked, slept, and died were later burned by the company, and Union Carbide and Carbon Corporation ultimately avoided financial and criminal responsibility for damages incurred by the workers at Hawk's Nest.

---

than others to be the direct victims of corporate malice. For example, Film Recovery Systems, Inc. (FRS), was a company that recycled silver from spent photographic plates. This process involves soaking the plates in a mixture of cyanide, a lethal chemical. To "contain costs," however, FRS employed mainly illegal aliens who could not read or speak English. Also to contain costs, FRS refused to supply workers with adequate ventilation or basic protective equipment, such as gloves, boots, and respirators. Moreover, management personnel at the plant approved the removal of the poison symbol (a skull and crossbones) from the containers of cyanide to avoid employees' questions. One person died from cyanide poisoning and at least two-thirds of the employees suffered from symptoms related to cyanide poisoning. In 1985 five executives were initially convicted of manslaughter, but their convictions were overturned on a technicality after years of appeals.

The harm from pollution, unsafe working conditions, and adulterated foods pales in comparison with the harm exacted on communities and individuals by the tobacco industry. Estimates by the Centers for Disease Control and Precention (CDC) show that over four hundred thousand people die each year due to tobacco-related health problems. The cost of all tobacco-related health problems runs to over $50 billion in medical expenses each year. Eighty percent of long-term smokers started smoking prior to the age of eighteen; nearly three thousand youths start smoking each day. The CDC estimates that more than five million children alive today will have their lives ended prematurely by tobacco.

While advocates of tobacco point out that smoking is legal and subject to free choice, critics point to numerous exposés undertaken in the 1990s revealing how tobacco producers covered up scientific data pertaining to the addictiveness of nicotine and the link between tobacco use and cancer. It has been suggested that manufacturers genetically engineered tobacco plants to make them more addictive, thereby ensuring addiction and long-term profit. Moreover, the tobacco industry has long targeted minority communities, women, and young people in marketing campaigns. These groups now make up the majority of new smokers.

Conclusion

For the first half of the twentieth century Americans were exposed to the carnage of unfettered capitalism. Labor disputes were put down with ferocious violence, workers toiled in unsafe and unhealthy factories, children worked from sunup to sundown, while consumers thousands of miles away from corporate boardrooms felt the adverse effects of amoral decisions made in them. For its part, government was a willing agent of unrestricted capitalism, as were the courts.

The social movement against corporate violence has done much to better the lives of ordinary people. The laws that have been passed, such as fair labor laws, workplace safety laws, and environmental laws, now set limits on the behaviors of corporations. Specialized regulatory agencies also interact with businesses large and small to ensure and aid in compliance with the law. Moreover,

criminal law has been used to punish malfeasant corporations and executives. Still, corporations are capable of exacting a devastating toll on communities and individuals alike. The modern global economy will likely bring with it new challenges and new forms of violence caused by corporations that operate across continents, where laws and enforcement powers vary considerably. History stands as a testament to the harm that can be caused by corporations, and reminds us of the price associated with unrestricted capitalism.

BIBLIOGRAPHY

Brady, Kathleen. *Ida Tarbell: Portrait of a Muckraker.* Pittsburgh: University of Pittsburgh Press, 1989.

Bruce, Robert. *1877: Year of Violence.* 1959. Chicago: Ivan R. Dee, 1989.

Cherniack, Martin. *The Hawk's Nest Incident.* Binghamton, N.Y.: Vail-Ballou, 1986.

Darwin, Charles. *On the Origin of Species.* London: J. Murray, 1859.

Geis, Gilbert. "From Deuteronomy to Deniability: A Historical Perlustration on White-Collar Crime." *Justice Quarterly* 5, no. 1 (1988).

Green, Gary S. *Occupational Crime.* New York: Nelson Hall, 1990.

Hills, Stuart L., ed. *Corporate Violence: Injury and Death for Profit.* Totowa, N.J.: Rowman and Littlefield, 1987.

Hobsbawm, Eric. *The Age of Capital: 1848–1875.* New York: Vintage, 1996.

Marx, Karl, and Friedrich Engels. "The Communist Manifesto." In *Marx and Engels: Selected Works.* Vol. 2. Moscow: Foreign Language Publishing House, 1948, 1962.

Nelson, Daniel. *Shifting Fortunes: The Rise and Decline of American Labor, from the 1820s to the Present.* Chicago: Ivan R. Dee, 1997.

Sinclair, Upton. *The Jungle.* 1906. New York: Harper and Brothers, 1951.

Swados, Harvey. *Years of Conscience: The Muckrakers.* Cleveland: World, 1962.

JOHN PAUL WRIGHT

See also **Capitalism; Environment, Violence Against; Private Security: Private Police; Sexual Harassment; Tobacco Industry; Workplace.**

COSA NOSTRA. *See* Mafia; Organized Crime.

COSTELLO, FRANK
(1891–1973)

Frank Costello was born Francesco Castiglia in January 1891 in Calabria, Italy; he migrated to New York in spring 1895. Although most famous as a bootlegger, gambler, and political fixer, he was

Frank Costello. LIBRARY OF CONGRESS

first arrested in April 1908 for assault and robbery and subsequently in March 1915 for carrying a concealed weapon. On this later charge he was sentenced to a year in prison. During the 1920s Costello became a major bootlegger. According to some reports, he worked in partnership with the notorious "Big Bill" Dwyer. In the middle of the decade the two men were charged with rum-running, but although Dwyer was convicted, Costello was not. The federal judge in his case was eventually charged by the House Judiciary Committee with corruption and judicial misconduct and promptly resigned from the bench.

Costello's criminal activities continued to flourish, particularly in gambling. In the late 1920s he joined forces with Philip "Dandy Phil" Kastel, who had once been the manager of a Montreal nightclub but had become known in New York as an extortionist with major interests in slot machines. Together Costello and Kastel cornered a large share of the gambling market, with interests in casinos as well as slots. In the 1930s New York's reform mayor Fiorello La Guardia successfully destroyed their slot machine racket, which was supposedly worth $50 million with yearly profits of around $3 million. Costello and Kastel then moved their operation to New Orleans at the invitation of Huey P. Long, Louisiana's colorfully corrupt senator and presidential hopeful.

Costello and Kastel's original Louisiana company was named Bayou Novelty. Over time it metamorphosed into Pelican Novelty and then Louisiana Mint—for each play of the slot, a package of mints was supposed to be dispensed. The organized-crime boss Meyer Lansky was a partner in Louisiana Mint as well as in Costello's Beverly Country Club, acknowledged by the Internal Revenue Service as "the finest supper club and gambling casino in the south." Joining them in ownership of the Beverly was Carlos Marcello, Louisiana's top mobster.

While operating in Louisiana, Costello remained an exceptionally powerful criminal figure in New York. The Kefauver Committee, the Senate subcommittee that completed a massive, countrywide investigation of organized crime in the early 1950s, stated that by 1942 Costello "unquestionably had complete domination over Tammany Hall," the nickname for the New York County Democratic Party. As far as the committee could tell, Costello was likely the nation's most influential racketeer, and his prime political connection was the corrupt mayor of New York, William O'Dwyer, who succeeded La Guardia in 1946.

The Kefauver Committee cited Costello for contempt when he balked at testifying after several days on the stand, and he was found guilty in 1952. That same year the government attempted to strip him of citizenship, and the following year he was tried for tax evasion. Costello was convicted and sentenced to the federal penitentiary in Milan, Michigan. He was out on bail and back in New York in the spring of 1957 when the hoodlum Vincent "The Chin" Gigante tried to assassinate him, but Gigante's bullet only grazed Costello's skull. Costello was finally released from prison in the summer of 1961, having paid his debt for evading taxes and contempt of Congress.

At the age of seventy-nine Costello supposedly had one last fling as an active crime boss. In 1970 he was called in to manage the affairs of a crime syndicate whose leaders were either in prison or handicapped by illness, but this interlude did not last long. Costello died in 1973 of natural causes.

BIBLIOGRAPHY

Walsh, George. *Public Enemies: The Mayor, the Mob, and the Crime That Was.* New York: Norton, 1980.

Wolf, George. *Frank Costello: Prime Minister of the Underworld.* New York: Morrow, 1974.

ALAN A. BLOCK

See also **Genovese, Vito; Lansky, Meyer; Organized Crime.**

COSTS OF VIOLENT CRIME

The cost of crime in the United States is staggering. Estimates vary, but $450 billion a year is not unrealistic. That estimate includes only the direct costs of the losses Americans incur as well as the costs to the criminal justice system of catching, judging, and punishing the perpetrators. It is estimated that Americans spend an additional $450 billion on security against the involuntary transfer of goods. Violent crime creates 3 percent of U.S. medical expenses and results in wage losses equivalent to 1 percent of all U.S. earnings. Crime also entails social costs, negative consequences that distort the way people live and relate to one another —a climate of fear and distrust of one's neighbors, a sense that one must limit one's activity to avoid danger.

Most scholars distinguish between the direct and indirect costs of crime. The direct cost includes dollars lost because of victimization; injuries suffered as a result of victimization, including pain and suffering; risk avoidance, that is, measures taken to reduce the probability that crime will occur; and, of course, lives taken. Indirect costs of crime include the increased cost of insurance, increased anxiety owing to the fear of crime, and the entire criminal justice system. Most scholars who undertake the problematic task of estimating these costs focus on personal victimizations, excluding white-collar crimes (crimes against businesses or the government) and so-called victimless crimes (drug offenses, gambling, and prostitution). The discussion here follows that lead.

Crime is not something that can be eradicated completely, whether because of human nature or because the logical consequence of making a rule is breaking it. Crime necessarily entails costs—of preventing it, managing it, and recuperating from it. A perennial question for economists and social scientists, as well as the public, concerns determining a reasonable cost of crime for U.S. society, given national values and the ability to control human behavior.

Reduced Crime Rates and Spending

From 1993 to 1998 crime rates in many of the largest U.S. cities declined dramatically. To what extent was this reduction attributable to spending since the late 1970s? The answer to this question has implications for future spending. The reductions were unmistakable and profound. In New York City, for example, in 1993, 600,000 felonies were committed; in 1998 approximately 330,000 were committed. Many other cities experienced similar declines. In 1996 the national crime rate dropped to its lowest level since 1973, when the government began keeping track of victimizations systematically. In 1996 violent crime rates dropped 10 percent, and property crime dropped 8 percent from the previous year. The homicide rate was down significantly across the country (9 percent lower than in 1995) and was the lowest since 1969. The burglary rate was almost half of what it had been in 1980.

It appears that the crime situation in the United States is, if not solved, then at least under control. This trend ought to give most Americans a sense that they are safer than they once were and that the criminal justice system is doing a better job, with the money spent on controlling crime finally paying off. As crime rates were plummeting all over the country, with the greatest drops in violent crimes, incarceration rates were climbing steeply in the 1980s and 1990s, with penalties stiffened for a variety of illegal activities. Victimizations decreased substantially. Although other factors helped account for the decline (not the least of which was a booming economy), changes in policing policies in big cities, tougher sentencing practices, and the concomitant growth of prisons and their populations had an important impact.

The Economic Perspective

The cost of crime should largely be judged by the extent to which the dollars spent reduce the amount of crime Americans experience. Some argue that the crime-rate level reflects not crime's natural state but the amount of money the criminal justice system has chosen to allocate to the goal of reducing crime; a cost approaching zero would be realized only if society were willing to pay infinite sums for protection and control. For the reductions experienced in the 1990s, U.S. society paid a substantial price—in terms of both money and social costs. If the cost-benefit ratio favored an increase in benefits, most would say the money was well spent—if it was certain that the dollars led directly to the reductions.

While crime costs Americans a considerable amount of money, it also creates jobs and wages. For example, the corrections industry has been booming since the early 1980s. By more than tripling the number of persons incarcerated, state governments created high-paying construction jobs and jobs inside prisons once they were built. California, for instance, built more prisons under Governor George Deukmejian in the 1980s than it had in the previous one hundred years. The question of whether imprisonment is a good investment in terms of the cost-benefit ratio has been addressed by many scholars. Anne Morrison Piehl and John DiIulio (1995) have argued that $2.80 is saved for every dollar spent incarcerating the "median offending prisoner." President Bill Clinton's Violent Crime Control and Law Enforcement Act of 1994 funneled millions of dollars to municipalities, allowing police departments to increase their number of officers. Many of these jobs went to people at the lower end of the labor market and replaced jobs lost to manufacturing and other labor-intensive industries that had reduced their manpower needs. The private-security field also created jobs for those with lower education levels. Almost every dollar spent on crime went to employ someone. Of course, if those dollars had not been spent on crime, they might have been available for other purposes; but it is not clear that the alternative spending possibilities would benefit the same segment of the population.

The 20 percent decline in real wages of men aged sixteen to twenty-four since the mid-1970s has led to about a 15 percent rise in the crime rates among that same age-group of males (Grogger 1996). The cost of crime increases as a function of the decline in real wages among potential offenders. It may well be that money has to be transferred either through wages or victimizations and that the choice of transfer policies is made by the society at large through market and command mechanisms. Corporations may try to socialize their labor costs by offering lower wages and absorbing the consequences of that policy through increased corporate and personal taxes. Those taxes are then spent on increased criminal justice organizational costs brought about by increases in victimizations. Given the picture at the end of the 1990s, it is possible that violent and property crime can be reduced not by increasing wages at the lower end of the labor market but by keeping those wages low, while at the same time taxing working Americans at a rate sufficient to generate resources for increasing the penalties for criminal activity. Low wages and more prisons seemed to form a winning strategy at the close of the twentieth century.

The Social-Science Perspective

Another approach to the cost of crime, which can be called the victimization perspective, comes not from economists but from social scientists. This perspective was developed in the early 1980s and begins with a new definition of crime, one that treats crime as an event rather than as a behavior. The work of John Conklin and others (1975) discussed how these events or victimizations affected not just the victim of the crime but also other members of the community whose lives and subsequent behavior were shaped by the event's occurrence. Rather than drawing people together—which is the classic sociological notion of the impact of crime put forth by Émile Durkheim—crime destroyed community by generating fear and distrust. Thus, the cost could be seen in terms of lost community solidarity and cohesiveness, the isolation and fear that followed criminal acts.

Following this line of thinking, scholars theorized that, if communities could nurture collective rather than individual responses to crime, the costs of crime could be reduced as well as the actual amount of crime committed in a given community. A great deal of research and many demonstration projects went into testing these hypotheses in the early 1980s, some of which led to the community policing initiatives that proved so useful in reducing crime in the 1990s in Chicago, New York, and several other cities.

Ironically, though greater police presence can lead to less concern about crime, it can also fuel one's sense of risk. By contrast, collective action not deriving from the criminal justice system can build a community's sense of informal social control and thereby reduce the social and emotional costs of crime. Such collective action can be sponsored and delivered by the state or sponsored by nongovernmental organizations. Low-cost community crime-prevention programs played an important role in reducing violent crime in the 1990s.

"Get Tough" Strategies

Another approach to crime reduction emphasizes making crime so expensive for criminals that they will determine that its costs far outweigh its benefits. The unfortunate consequence of this approach is that it is very expensive for taxpayers. Increasing the costs of crime to the perpetrator requires increasing his or her chances of getting caught, which requires hiring more police officers. The system then requires more district attorneys to press charges, more judges and juries to sentence criminals, and more prisons and prison guards to incarcerate those criminals. The costs of "get tough" strategies are apparently ones that taxpaying citizens are ready to bear. Indeed, the unique mix of these strategies with the less expensive community crime-prevention policies has produced impressive results.

Advanced industrial nations have developed complex systems—whether market or governmental command mechanisms—to manage the delivery of needed services and products. No matter what the system, the nation's citizens pay for the service or product. If the market is used to distribute the product, the consumer, with some important qualifications, chooses how to spend his or her money. But when governmental command mechanisms are used, the choice of service and the price of that service are outside the citizens' control. Although democratic representation is meant to ensure that choice is part of the process, when citizens do not trust their government, those command choices are often questioned, especially when they are expensive and seen as ineffectual. Until the last decades of the twentieth century, expenditures on crime in the United States fell into that category of governmental choices. The broader context of an expanding economy and a shrinking federal deficit, both features of the late 1990s, affects the crime problem in unmeasured but important ways. In a situation in which spending has had good results, the problem for citizens and scholars alike is to determine precisely which expenditures in what combination have produced the desired result.

BIBLIOGRAPHY

Cohen, Mark A. "Pain, Suffering, and Jury Awards: A Study of the Cost of Crime to Victims." *Law and Society Review* 22, no. 3 (1988).

Conklin, John E. *The Impact of Crime*. New York: Macmillan, 1975.

Greer, William W. "What Is the Cost of Rising Crime?" *New York Affairs* 8, no. 39 (1987).

Grogger, Jeffrey. *Employment and Crime*. Sacramento, Calif.: State of California, Department of Justice, Division of Law Enforcement, Criminal Identification and Informa-

tion Branch, Bureau of Criminal Statistics and Special Services, 1996.

Karmen, Andrew. *Crime Victims: An Introduction to Victimology*. 3d ed. Belmont, Calif.: Wadsworth, 1996.

Klaus, Patsy. *The Costs of Crime to Victims*. Washington, D.C.: U.S. Department of Justice, 1994.

Laband, David N., and John P. Sophocleus. "An Estimate of Resource Expenditures on Transfer Activity in the United States." *Quarterly Journal of Economics* 107, no. 3 (August 1992).

Lindgren, Sue A. "The Cost of Justice." In *Report to the Nation on Crime and Justice*. 2d ed. U.S. Department of Justice. Washington, D.C.: Bureau of Justice Statistics, 1988.

Miller, Ted R., Mark A. Cohen, and Shelli B. Rossman. "Victim Cost of Violent Crime and Resulting Injuries." *Health Affairs* 12, no. 4 (1993).

Miller, Ted R., Mark A. Cohen, and Brian Wierseman. "Victim Costs and Consequences: A New Look." *National Institute of Justice: Research Report* (January 1996).

Phillips, Llad, and Harold L. Votey, Jr. *The Economics of Crime Control*. Beverly Hills, Calif.: Sage, 1981.

Piehl, Anne Morrison, and John J. DiIulio, Jr. " 'Does Prison Pay?' Revisited." *Brookings Review* 13, no. 1 (1995).

Reynolds, Morgan O. "The Economics of Criminal Activity." In *The Economics of Crime*, edited by Ralph Andreano and John J. Siegfield. Cambridge, Mass.: Schenkman, 1980.

Rottenberg, Simon. "The Social Cost of Crime and Crime Prevention." In *Crime in Urban Society*, edited by Barbara N. McLennan. New York: Dunellen, 1970.

Spelman, William. *Criminal Incapacitation*. New York: Plenum, 1993.

DAN A. LEWIS

See also **Capitalism; Prisons: Overview; Structural Violence; Victims of Violence.**

CRAZY HORSE
(1841–1877)

Crazy Horse, a major war chief of the Oglala Sioux, is best remembered for the important role he played in the Sioux Indian wars against the United States beginning in the early 1860s and ending with the defeat of Colonel George Armstrong Custer's Seventh Cavalry on 25 June 1876 at the famous Battle of Little Bighorn in Montana (also known as Custer's Last Stand).

Crazy Horse was born in the fall of 1841, the second child and first son of a Brulé Sioux woman, in the region of the Black Hills in South Dakota. His father was an Oglala holy man, also called Crazy Horse. The child was given the name Curly because, unlike most Oglalas, he was fair-skinned and had light, curly hair. He took his father's name shortly before his sixteenth birthday, having demonstrated great bravery and humility in a war party against the Arapaho in which he killed two enemy warriors with his pistol and bow.

Crazy Horse came of age as a young warrior at a critical juncture of American and Native American history: the Oregon Trail, leading American settlers west through the ancestral homelands of the Teton Sioux (a loose confederation of seven tribal groupings that stretched west from Minnesota to Montana), had opened in the early 1840s. By 1849, with the discovery of gold in California, forty-niners were streaming into Sioux territory and trampling the fertile grazing ranges of the Great Plains—those vital grasslands that fed some fifteen million buffalo, which, in turn, were the life source of the diet, economy, and culture of the Plains tribes. The encroaching settlers often strewed garbage, tools and wagon parts, and dead animals in their wake. The foul smell of rotting carcasses and garbage often drove the buffalo away.

Eventually this influx of whites led to violent skirmishes (the Grattan massacre in 1854) and full-blown warfare (the Sand Creek massacre of the Cheyenne in 1864) between the Plains Indians and soldiers sent to protect the American settlers. As a leading Oglala warrior and an *akicita* (a shirt wearer, one who governed the Sioux tribal councils and enforced the laws of the tribe), Crazy Horse soon developed a reputation for military leadership and reckless bravery in battle. A taciturn man who kept to himself, Crazy Horse developed a reputation among the Oglala Sioux for being strange (they called him Tasunke Witko, the "strange one"). He had few close friends with the exception of his brother, Little Hawk, and Hump, a well-known Minneconjou-Oglala warrior. Crazy Horse would ride into battle wearing only a single hawk feather tied to his braided hair. He painted his face with jagged lightning streaks and hailstones, tied two small stones behind his ear, and brushed dirt over himself and his horse because he had been told in an early vision that he could never be killed if he rode into battle in this fashion.

Although Red Cloud received much of the credit for being the Sioux chieftain with whom the U.S. government eventually had to sign a peace treaty, much of Red Cloud's military success against the whites came under the strategic direction of Crazy Horse, his young war leader. Crazy Horse, for example, designed the strategy that led to the Fetterman massacre on 21 December 1868, a major Indian victory, in which the Sioux, led by Crazy Horse, wiped out Captain William J. Fetterman and eighty of his cavalry. (The Sioux called it the Battle of the Hundred Slain.)

Ultimately, Crazy Horse broke with Red Cloud, who in 1868 signed a peace treaty with the United States. When told of Red Cloud's willingness to make a deal with the government to sell off the rights to his people's beloved and sacred Black Hills in 1875, Crazy Horse is reputed to have said, "One does not sell the land the people walk on."

An unfinished model of Crazy Horse, in front of Thunderhead Mountain in the Black Hills of South Dakota. CORBIS/BETTMANN

Crazy Horse played a key strategic role in the Battle of Little Bighorn by cutting off all possibilities for retreat on Calhoun Hill. As a result, George Armstrong Custer and 225 troopers of the elite Seventh Cavalry were wiped out by a combined force of some twenty-five hundred to three thousand Sioux and Cheyenne under the leadership of Sitting Bull, Gall, and Crazy Horse. However, the Sioux failed to capitalize on their great victory and, still divided by old tribal custom, split up and went their separate ways. Sitting Bull fled with his Hunkpapas to Canada, and Crazy Horse and his small band, after continuing their struggle through the difficult winter of 1876–1877, finally surrendered at Fort Robinson, Nebraska, on 6 May 1877.

Crazy Horse had a difficult time adjusting to reservation life. The authorities, as well as some jealous Sioux leaders, feared he would again take the younger men with him and go off to war. In September 1877, betrayed by Red Cloud and his uncle, a Brulé chief called Spotted Tail, the authorities set out to arrest Crazy Horse. At first he fled but was finally convinced that he would be treated fairly if he surrendered. Immediately surrounded by soldiers when he arrived at Fort Robinson, he realized that he had been betrayed and that he would be jailed. As he tried to fight his way free, he was bayoneted twice by a soldier and died a few hours later. His mother and father took his body and placed it at rest somewhere in his precious Black Hills. To this day, no one knows where.

Crazy Horse in Popular Culture

In nineteenth-century dime novels, Western adventures, and even in films through the 1990s, Crazy Horse is generally shown as a stereotyped fanatic savage. From the 1926 silent film *The Flaming Frontier* to Cecil B. DeMille's 1936 Western epic *The Plainsman* and the 1941 Errol Flynn movie saga of George Custer *They Died with Their Boots On* (in which Custer is killed in the last reel by Crazy Horse), there is no resemblance to historical reality.

Little changed in the shoot-'em-up Technicolor extravaganzas of the 1950s. In *Sitting Bull* (1954), the Indian actor Iron Eyes portrays Crazy Horse as a fanatical war chief. In *Chief Crazy Horse* (1955), the man depicted by Victor Mature (a white actor), although a little more sympathetic, bears little resemblance to the real Oglala chief. The 1990s saw a little more accuracy in two television movies depicting the legendary Indian. In *Son of the Morning Star* (1991), Crazy Horse is portrayed with remark-

able accuracy by Rodney A. Grant. *Crazy Horse* (1996), in which an Indian actor, Michael Greyeyes, plays the lead convincingly, has a script that succeeds in presenting a realistic depiction of Crazy Horse's brief life.

BIBLIOGRAPHY

Ambrose, Stephen E. *Crazy Horse and Custer: The Parallel Lives of Two American Warriors.* New York: New American Library, 1975.

Goldman, Martin S. *Crazy Horse: War Chief of the Oglala Sioux.* New York: Franklin Watts, 1996.

Josephy, Alvin M. *The Patriot Chiefs: A Chronicle of American Indian Resistance.* New York: Viking, 1961.

Sandoz, Mari. *Crazy Horse: The Strange Man of the Oglalas.* Lincoln: University of Nebraska Press, 1942.

MARTIN S. GOLDMAN

See also **American Indians: American Indian Wars; Custer, George Armstrong.**

CRIME, LEGAL DEFINITIONS OF

Historical Origins

Legal definitions of violent crimes have changed during the course of American history due to a wide variety of factors, including religious influences, technological advances, divorce rates, the women's movement, urbanization, and evolving moral standards. While definitions of some crimes have remained remarkably unchanged, others have evolved into creatures significantly different from what they originally were. In addition, new crimes have been created that could not have been imagined by early American lawmakers.

The Colonial Period. The examination of legal definitions of violent crime begins, quite naturally, with English law and the law of the early American colonies. The two were not, however, one and the same. For a number of reasons, the American colonists did not engage in a wholesale importation of English law, and it is in the selective adoption and adaptation of this law that the genesis of uniquely American definitions of crime can be found.

Often, early American settlers were religious dissidents seeking freedom from persecution. Their mission in the New World was to build godly societies, or societies governed by the word of God as revealed in the Bible. They relied heavily on Scripture to define what conduct was criminal (against God or sinful), and to determine the precise punishment to be imposed (Friedman 1993). As a result, while the death penalty was heavily used in seventeenth-century England for a wide variety of crimes, it was much less frequently employed in colonial America and in most cases could be imposed only for those crimes for which the Scriptures clearly prescribed death, including murder, treason, arson, and several moral offenses. But while the general practice of most colonies was to limit the use of the death penalty as compared to its liberal application in England, there was great variance among the different colonies.

The harsh and isolated conditions of life on the frontier required strictly defined rules for survival. Unique issues involving native tribes and slavery led to the creation of special courts for slaves and differing punishments depending upon the race of both the perpetrator and the victim. The combination of novel living conditions, the relatively open American social and political structure, and strong religious influences led to the rejection of the complicated English court system, the monarchical system of property rights, and harsh English punishments, which failed, in the colonists' minds, to match the punishment with the crime.

The Eighteenth Century. The definitions of the most prominent violent crimes of murder, rape, assault and battery, and robbery remained largely unchanged from the 1600s to the mid-1700s. Perhaps one of the greatest early departures from English law was the division in the colonies of murder into degrees of seriousness, which was undertaken out of a desire to more closely fit the punishment to the crime. More secularized attitudes, the increasing number of professionally trained lawyers, and greater urbanization and mobility caused American criminal law to become more closely aligned with that of England. As the noted scholar Lawrence Friedman (1985) put it, after independence "the English overlay was obvious, pervasive—but selective" (p. 113).

The Nineteenth Century. The law of England was common law—law created by judges on a case-by-case basis. Americans distrusted the degree of power the common-law system vested in the judiciary and showed an early preference instead for a statutory system, in which crimes are defined by a legislative body. If a statute characterizing a particular action as criminal did not exist, the action was not considered a crime. Common law, however, continued to play an important role, since the enactment of statutory definitions of crime required consensus building and therefore took a great deal of time, and also since the statutory definitions were haphazard, varying from community to community. Therefore, when states were formed, English common law existing at the time the colonies were founded generally applied unless expressly or implicitly repealed by statute. By the 1850s there was a strong move toward enacting comprehensive penal codes to define all crime by statute. Some statutes incorporated common-law definitions of crime, some completely replaced common-law definitions, and others relied on a combination of both.

The Modern Penal Code. The trend toward comprehensive penal codes continued into the 1950s, when the American Law Institute began its work on a Model Penal Code. After more than a decade of work, the first Model Penal Code was published in 1962. Recognizing the appropriateness of local variations in the definitions and application of criminal law, the drafters of the Model Penal Code did not intend that it be adopted intact. A majority of states have used the Model Penal Code as a resource and guide in accomplishing substantial renovations of their penal codes.

Violent Crimes

While many crimes employ what most people would consider violent means, "the crimes that concern Americans the most are those that affect their personal safety—at home, at work or in the street," according to a 1969 report by the President's Commission of Law Enforcement and the Administration of Justice. Homicide, assault and battery, rape, and robbery are almost universally viewed as the most serious violent crimes. These crimes are classified in the only national system of criminal reporting presently available, the Uniform Crime Reports, published annually by the Federal Bureau of Investigation. Suicide (the only one of these crimes not separately classified by the FBI) and kidnapping are also commonly included in discussions regarding violent crime and merit treatment here as well.

Legal Definitions of Selected Violent Crimes

Homicide. The importance placed on human life makes the taking of the life of one human being by another human being the most extensively analyzed of violent crimes. The high value of human life also makes homicide the most widely defined of all crimes, encompassing intentionally caused as well as unintentionally caused deaths. But not all homicides (killings of another human being) are murders (criminal homicides). Rather, when there is a legal excuse (such as an accident devoid of unlawful intent), or justification (such as self-defense), or when the killings are authorized by the state, they are not criminally punishable.

Murder has always been a crime, has always been the most serious form of homicide, and has always been punishable by death. Until the 1550s, there was only one kind of murder: the unlawful killing of another human being with malice aforethought (express or implied). Thus, murder originally required a premeditated intent to kill. The difficulty of proving a literal premeditated intent to kill, along with the recognition that killings which should be severely punished were not receiving appropriate treatment, led to the development in the common law of several new classifications of murder, many of which exist today.

The requirement of premeditation was one of the first to be eliminated in the new legal definitions beginning in the 1600s. Murder committed in the heat of passion, for example, did not require malice aforethought. Eventually, any death caused by an individual evincing an unpremeditated intent to kill (including in the heat of passion) would be subject to the charge of murder (unless legally excused or justified). The felony-murder rule also developed in England and was adopted in varying forms in the United States. This allowed murder charges to be brought even in cases of unintentional killings if committed during the course of a felony. Two additional types of murder also developed: so-called "depraved heart" murder (that which results from extremely negligent conduct, such as throwing a rock onto a busy highway) and intent-to-do-serious-bodily-injury murder (that which results, for example, from choking a person without an intent to kill him or her). None of these types of murder had been addressed in English common law.

Only five states (Iowa, Kansas, Missouri, Pennsylvania, and Virginia) do not statutorily define murder but instead adopt the common law definition. In all U.S. jurisdictions, the crime of murder requires (1) conduct on the part of an individual (either by commission or omission); (2) a malicious state of mind (defined as intent to kill, a depraved heart, or an intent to commit a felony); and (3) the resultant death of a human being within (in many states) a prescribed period of time.

American law departed from that of England in dividing murder into degrees as well as kinds or classes. The degrees reflect differing levels of culpability and allow for a more precise tailoring of the punishment to fit the crime. In 1794 Pennsylvania became the first state to enact murder laws that used degrees to narrow the application of the death penalty. Greater precision and uniformity in sentencing has been the goal of categorizing murder in subsequent decades. Premeditation, while not required for murder, serves as the distinguishing factor in those states that divide murder into first and second degrees.

First-Degree Murder. First-degree murder is the only crime now punishable by death in the United States. First-degree murder encompasses the intentional, premeditated (with malice aforethought), deliberate killing of another human being. Many states also include killings occurring during the commission of a felony in the category of first-degree murder. California's definition of first-degree murder reflects a modern statutory approach to homicide: the "unlawful killing of a human being, or a fetus, with malice aforethought," except where the death of the fetus is the result of an abortion performed with the mother's consent (California Penal Code, section 187).

The law of homicide requires that the victim be a living human being, a frequent issue in deaths involving a fetus. In the United States a fetus must be "born alive," that is, fully brought forth and capable of independent circulation. The application of the "born alive" requirement varies widely from jurisdiction to jurisdiction. While abortion was a common law crime, and many states continued to make it a statutory crime, the United States Supreme Court in the 1973 decision *Roe v. Wade* made abortion a constitutionally protected right under some circumstances.

The typical common law definition of murder also required that the death occur within a year and a day after the fatal injury was inflicted. This rule was necessary in the past because of the difficulty of pinpointing the causal connection between the homicidal act and the ultimate death of the victim. Medical advances in measuring brain activity and its cessation have now made the question of causation relatively clear, thus making the rule obsolete. Several states have abolished the rule altogether, while others, such as California, have extended the time frame to three years and a day.

Due to medical advances, another area of concern involves the termination of life support. The question of criminal liability for ending life support has received cautious treatment by the courts. (See, for example, *Barber v. Superior Court*, 195 California Reporter 484 [California Appellate Reports 1983]). No criminal liability is attached to good-faith discontinuance of life support based on competent medical advice and with the consent of a competent patient and patient's family.

The malicious state of mind required for first-degree murder may include both intent in the form of desiring a particular result, regardless of the likelihood of that result occurring (intentional killings), and knowing that a result is substantially certain to occur (knowing killings). Most states require the former definition of intent, or classify intentional and knowing killings into different degrees of murder.

Felony murder is one of the most controversial yet enduring types of first-degree murder. The basic premise appears to be that a felon is a depraved person in a criminal state of mind. Therefore, the law does not concern itself with the fact that the felon may accomplish a result quite different from the one he or she intended. As originally formulated, the felony-murder rule allowed the defendant to be charged with murder whenever a death occurred in the commission of any felony, including a felony not involving risk to life or bodily injury. The rule applied even when the death was that of a co-felon, when the death was not caused by the felon, and when the death occurred after the felony was completed.

Because of the controversy over imposing the severe penalties attached to first-degree murder on individuals who did not intend, let alone plan, to kill, efforts have been made to limit the application of the felony-murder rule. Approximately nineteen states limit its application to certain defined felonies, typically rape, robbery, kidnapping, arson, and burglary, which are considered to involve the risk of serious bodily injury. At least another nine states allow the charge of first-degree murder to be considered for any felony case in which death results. Felony murder has been abolished in at least five states, and was abolished in England in 1957.

Another restriction on felony murder involves limiting its application to killings caused by the felon rather than by a third party, such as a police officer who accidentally kills a bystander or co-felon. One notable exception is when human beings are used as shields during the commission of a felony. In such cases, the felon may be charged with murder even if he or she did not kill the person used as a shield.

Second-Degree Murder. Second-degree murder is defined in some states as all murder that does not fall under the definition of first-degree murder. Second-degree murder includes intentional, but not premeditated, killings. A person who acts knowing that death is substantially certain to occur is subject to being charged with second-degree murder, which is punishable by imprisonment but not death. A person who kills during the commission of a felony not listed by the relevant jurisdiction as one subject to the charge of first-degree murder might also face charges of second-degree murder.

Manslaughter. Killings committed without malice are considered a form of homicide, but are less severely punished than murder. Some states divide manslaughter into voluntary (or first-degree) and involuntary (or second-degree) forms. The tendency in modern revised penal codes is to restrict the definition of manslaughter to a single degree of severity.

Voluntary manslaughter is often defined as an intentional killing that occurs during the heat of passion as the result of an "adequate provocation." Although the killing is intentional, the fact that it was the result of an adequate provocation (that which would cause a normal person to lose his or her self-control) is considered a mitigating factor.

Involuntary manslaughter is an unintentional killing characterized by gross or wanton negligence. In determining the latter, most states require a high degree of risk of death or serious bodily injury under circumstances in which the potential danger is known to the defendant (i.e., recklessness). The mishandling of firearms resulting in death is a common form of involuntary manslaughter.

A separately defined form of manslaughter developed around the automobile: vehicular manslaughter. This form of manslaughter often involves a reduced degree of negligence, sometimes as little as ordinary negligence (failure to exercise the standard of care that a reasonable person should have exercised under the circumstances), sometimes more, but still less than criminal negligence or recklessness. Florida's statute is typical: "Vehicular homicide is the killing of a human being by the operation of a motor vehicle by another in a reckless manner likely to cause death of, or great bodily harm to, another" (West's Florida Statutes Annotated, section 782.071).

New Defenses to Homicide Charges. In the late twentieth century, a group of so-called abuse excuses gained recognition and acceptance in criminal law. Most prominent of these are the "battered wife syndrome" and "post-traumatic stress disorder." In a number of cases, women who killed their spouses after a long history of spousal abuse have been successful in avoiding criminal liability altogether or have been able to reduce their convictions from murder to voluntary manslaughter. Post-traumatic stress disorder has also gained acceptance as an explanation used to mitigate the severity of the crimes charged or to reduce the penalties imposed.

Assault and Battery. Although technically separate crimes, the terms *assault* and *battery* are often used together to describe a particular form of criminal conduct.

Assault is defined as an attempted battery: an unlawful attempt to do bodily harm to another by using force or violence. Under common law, all assaults and batteries were characterized as misdemeanors. Now, most assaults are misdemeanors, but if committed against public officers, or of an aggravated nature involving the use of deadly weapons or force likely to cause great bodily injury, they are classified as felonies.

Some states require that the perpetrator of the crime have the actual ability to commit a battery. For example, if a person, thinking an unloaded gun is loaded, fires it at another person, there is no actual ability to commit a battery, and thus no assault. However, this act may qualify as an assault in those jurisdictions that extend assault to include the threat of injury to another. Such acts must arouse a reasonable apprehension of bodily harm; threatening looks or words are usually not enough. Performing such acts as throwing a rock at a person, firing a shot in the victim's direction, raising a fist against someone, or otherwise threatening a person with a weapon would all constitute an assault in most states. Depending on the weapon used, close proximity may not be required. A gun fired from a distance, but within the victim's line of vision or comprehension, would suffice.

Battery, on the other hand, requires actual physical contact. It is generally defined as the unlawful application of force or violence upon the person of another. Bodily injury is not necessarily required. Offensive, insulting, provoking, or rude touching, such as spitting at or kissing another, against the victim's will, is sufficient to constitute a battery. Use of force that may otherwise be permissible, such as disciplinary action by teachers or physical restraint by police officers, becomes a battery if excessive. A moderate spanking does not give rise to a battery, but infliction of serious wounds would. A physician can commit a battery by performing a procedure for which he or she has not obtained the patient's consent.

Statutes recognizing the crime of stalking (enacted in a majority of states by 1993) began as a way to protect victims from conduct that did not fit within the traditional definitions of assault and battery. Such statutes usually require a continuous and willful course of conduct, and the making of a credible threat that reasonably causes the target to fear for his or her safety.

Mayhem. The crime of mayhem is rarely defined independently in modern criminal codes. Most often, it is incorporated into the law of assault and battery, and usually falls under aggravated battery. Mayhem started as a crime against the sovereign, because it was defined as the permanent injuring or disabling of a part of another's body, thereby depriving the ruler of the effective military assistance from his or her subjects. In modern law, the focus is on the right to preserve the natural condition and functioning of one's body. For example, throwing acid at a victim's face or body; cutting off a finger, arm, or nose; knocking out a front tooth; or putting out an eye all constitute acts of mayhem.

Rape. Of all the definitions of violent crimes, that of rape has probably changed the most over time, both in terms of the class of potential victims and the manner in which the crime is prosecuted. Rape used to be defined as carnal knowledge of a woman by a man not her husband, by force and against her will. Statutory rape is a separate form of rape applicable to females, and sometimes males, under a particular age, and is premised upon the assumption that a young female cannot legally "consent" to sexual intercourse. The age of consent varies from ten to eighteen years of age in different states. The Model Penal Code recommends ten years as the cutoff age for statutory rape.

Spousal rape is a relatively new form of rape; it was not recognized under the common law. Under common law, a wife was considered the property of her husband; upon marriage, she was deemed to have given her irrevocable consent to sexual intercourse with her husband. Modern thinking has recognized the fallacy of this rule and has acknowledged the criminal nature of spousal rape. The rise in the divorce rate was a factor leading to the extension of the crime of rape to estranged husbands. By 1989 only eight states refused to recognize spousal rape. Some states limit the scope of spousal rape to situations in which the wife has filed for divorce and is living apart from her husband. Lesser penalties for spousal rape are usually applied than for other forms of rape.

Additional significant developments in the law of rape include the elimination of the requirement that the woman "resist to her utmost" and the advent of rape shield laws that prevent the victim's sexual history from being used as evidence in a jury trial. The death penalty for rape was ruled unconstitutional by the United States Supreme Court in *Coker v. Georgia* (1977). Date rape is another late-twentieth-century development in the ongoing reform and refinement of the law of rape. Date rape is defined as forced, unwanted sex with a person the victim knows, and it can occur during a first meeting, on a subsequent date, or even after being engaged to be married.

Arson. Arson is the common-law felony designed to protect the sanctity of a dwelling place. It involves the deliberate burning of another's dwelling without justification or excuse. Modern statutes have extended the definition of arson to include the intentional burning of buildings, structures, and vehicles of all types. While not so in common law, current statutes include the burning of one's own property, and the burning of any property with intent to defraud an insurance company.

Robbery. Robbery has been on the books in a form we recognize since at least the twelfth century, and in different forms even earlier. Under the older English common law, as it is now in a number of states, robbery was defined as "the felonious taking of personal property in the possession of another, from his person or immediate presence, and against his will, accomplished by means of force or fear" (see, e.g., California Penal Code section 211). The common-law definition is the definition generally used by a number of states. The remaining states primarily adopt the definition promulgated by the Model Penal Code. Robbery

was a felony punishable by death in colonial times, and remained so even into the early 1960s.

The use of force or fear is the key feature of robbery that differentiates it from ordinary theft or larceny. Pickpocketing is not considered robbery, because there is no force applied nor fear instilled—the victim is typically unaware of the crime while it is in progress. Many jurisdictions also have some form of aggravated robbery in cases in which especially violent means are used or a particularly vulnerable class of victims such as the elderly are involved.

In the 1990s carjacking became a federal crime punishable by a fine, imprisonment, or both depending on the severity, in terms of injury or death, inflicted during its commission (Anti-Car Theft Act of 1992; 18 United States Code Annotated section 2119).

Suicide. Although suicide was a crime at common law, American jurisdictions have never imposed penalties for a successful suicide. England's Suicide Act of 1961 abolished suicide and attempted suicide as a crime in England. However, in the United States, criminal liability does attach to attempted suicides that result in injury or death to bystanders or rescuers, as well as to those who aid or abet a suicide. Charges of involuntary manslaughter, assault and battery, and an assortment of other criminal charges could be brought against those who endanger the life or safety of others when attempting suicide.

Assisted suicide as a separate crime gained national attention in Michigan due to the activities of the physician Jack Kevorkian in helping persons who wished to commit suicide accomplish their goals. The definition of this crime was in a state of flux in the late 1990s.

Kidnapping. Under common law, the crime of kidnapping required the forcible taking of a person to another country. Eventually, the crime of kidnapping was broadened to include any asportation (carrying away or removing feloniously), regardless of geographical boundaries. Passage of the "Lindbergh Law" in 1932 made it a federal crime to transport a victim across state lines. For a period of time kidnapping was punishable by death, but the death penalty for kidnapping was ruled unconstitutional by the United States Supreme Court in 1968.

Under state law, either the transporting of a victim or confinement in a secret place suffice in most jurisdictions. The Model Penal Code approaches the matter of kidnapping differently, emphasizing the danger or terror to the victim as the essential component of the separate crime of kidnapping.

A relatively recent development in the crime of kidnapping involves parental abductions of children involved in custody disputes. The Parental Kidnapping Prevention Act of 1980 and the Uniform Child Custody Jurisdiction Act are federal laws enacted to address the rising number of abductions by parents in violation of custody orders (see, e.g., 18 United States Code Annotated section 1204; 28 United States Code Annotated section 1738A). Potential penalties include a fine, imprisonment, or both.

Plea Bargaining

The existence of different degrees of seriousness with respect to violent crime gave rise to choice and flexibility on the part of prosecutors in pursuing a negotiated plea of guilty and made such a plea more attractive to the accused.

It is unclear exactly when or how plea bargaining originated. In general, the role of the jury began to decline in the 1800s. Early juries were in many cases called upon to decide not only the facts but the law. By the end of the nineteenth century, the United States Supreme Court started to rein in the power of the jury, which at the same time increased the importance of the prosecutor. The criminal justice system was overwhelmed with cases awaiting trial. There was tremendous need for a quick and definitive way to dispose of criminal charges short of dropping them. During the late nineteenth century, plea bargaining became an important and frequently used method for accomplishing that goal. It is estimated that anywhere from 65 percent to 90 percent of crimes are disposed of by plea bargaining.

Of course, plea bargaining is not without controversy. The negotiated guilty plea has many desirable features such as certainty, speed, and convenience when guilt is obvious. It is sometimes necessary because witnesses become unavailable or unwilling to testify, or victims do not want to prosecute. The ability to tailor the sentence to the particular circumstances is another beneficial aspect of plea bargaining.

On the other hand, critics complain of the potential for abuse in a process that is not subject to public scrutiny. There is concern that plea bargaining reduces or dilutes the severity of criminal penalties out of a desire to dispose of the case without consideration of the true merits. Victims and family members alike feel deprived of their day in court and believe that justice is not done by acceptance of a guilty plea, no matter how uncertain the outcome if submitted to a jury. Sometimes, prosecutors may "overcharge" the crime in order to leave negotiating room for a plea to a lesser offense.

Despite these criticisms, plea bargaining has been called "an essential component of the administration of justice" (*Santobello v. New York*, 1971). The realities of the overburdened American criminal justice system seem to dictate that plea bargaining is here to stay, at least until another and better method for disposing of an ever-increasing caseload is introduced.

Conclusion

The definitions of the primary crimes of interpersonal violence have in many ways remained unchanged over the years. The desire for fair punishment had a significant impact on the differentiation of crimes by degree or level of intent, thus preserving their fundamental definitions. As new technology arises, so do new crimes, such as vehicular manslaughter and euthanasia. As social relationships change, so do the boundaries defining criminal and noncriminal behavior. The ebb and flow of criminal jurisdiction is both necessary and appropriate. As the legal writer Robert Traver has aptly said, "For all its lurchings and shambling imbecilities, the law—and only the law—is what keeps our society from bursting apart at the seams, from becoming a snarling jungle. No other system has yet been found for governing men except violence."

BIBLIOGRAPHY

American Bar Association. "Plea Bargaining: Nemesis or Nirvana." Annual Meeting, American Bar Association, Section of Criminal Justice. Chicago, 9 August 1977.

American Law Institute. *Model Penal Code: Proposed Official Draft.* Philadelphia: ALI, 1962.

Friedman, Lawrence M. *Crime and Punishment in American History.* New York: Basic, 1993.

———. *A History of American Law.* 2d ed. New York: Simon and Schuster, 1985.

Jacobs, James B. "Criminal Law, Criminal Procedure, and Criminal Justice." In *Fundamentals of American Law,* edited by Alan B. Morrison. Oxford, U.K.: Oxford University Press, 1996.

Kadish, Samuel H. *Encyclopedia of Crime and Justice.* New York: Free Press, 1983.

LaFave, Wayne R., et al. *Substantive Criminal Law.* Minneapolis: West, 1986.

Mueller, Gerhard. *Crime, Law, and the Scholars: A History of Scholarship in American Criminal Law.* Seattle: University of Washington Press, 1969.

Mulvihill, Donald J., and Melvin M. Tumin. *Crimes of Violence: A Staff Report Submitted to the National Commission on the Causes and Prevention of Violence.* Vol. 2. Washington, D.C.: U.S. Government Printing Office, 1969.

Reckless, Walter C. *American Criminology: New Directions.* New York: Meredith, 1973.

Scheb, John M., and John M. Scheb II. *Criminal Law and Procedure.* 3d ed. Belmont, Calif.: West/Wadsworth, 1999.

Walker, Samuel. *Popular Justice: A History of American Criminal Justice.* Oxford, U.K.: Oxford University Press, 1980.

Wharton, Francis. *Wharton's Criminal Law.* 15th ed. New York: Clark, Boardman, Callaghan, 1993.

LANN G. MCINTYRE

See also **Arson and Fire; Assault; Crime and Punishment in American History; Criminal Justice System; Deadly Force; Drive-by Shooting; Drunk Driving; Hate Crime; Hijacking; Homicide; Incidence of Violence; Kidnapping; Plea Bargaining; Rape; Robbery; Sentencing; Statistics and Epidemiology; Thrill Crime; Uniform Crime Reports.**

CRIME AND PUNISHMENT IN AMERICAN HISTORY

The history of American criminal justice begins, conventionally, in the seventeenth century, with the arrival of European colonists in what is now the United States. Of course, long before that time the native tribes had their own norms of crime and punishment. Those tribes did not leave behind written records. They had oral traditions, and many of the native peoples that survive today maintain their own legal systems, which preserve at least some of the spirit of their older laws.

The dominant group of settlers came from England, and they brought with them English ways of dealing with crime. It is hard to sum up the colonial period in a single formula—there were at least thirteen separate colonies, and the period covers more than 150 years, from the early seventeenth to the late eighteenth century. In all of the colonies, however, the core of the criminal justice system was derived from the law of the motherland. Terms like *judge, jury, felony,* and *arrest* were common English words, and they were familiar to every colonist too.

Conditions in the colonies, however, were strikingly different from those in England, and the colonial criminal justice system deviated markedly

The whipping-post and pillory at New Castle, Delaware, 1868. Wood engraving in *Harper's Weekly,* 12 December 1868. LIBRARY OF CONGRESS

from the system in the mother country. The court system was much simpler—not surprising in small, tight-knit communities. One innovation was the development of the office of a public prosecutor, called the district attorney or the county attorney, whose job was to prosecute crime on behalf of the community. There was no such position in England. In the colonies punishments were, on the whole, less bloody and severe than in England. Whipping, however, was a standard punishment. There was also much use of shaming punishments—sitting in the stocks, for example. For some crimes the offenders were branded or mutilated (loss of an ear). Religious influence was strong in America, particularly the northern colonies, and what was considered sinful—fornication, for example—was also apt to be punished as a crime.

Punishment in the colonies was always a public affair—if you were whipped for your offenses, you were whipped in public. Hangings were also public. These were great didactic occasions: the condemned man often made a statement in the very shadow of the gallows, confessing his sins and begging the community not to follow in his footsteps. The yoke of punishment was borne most notably by servants and the underclass; and, especially in the South, by the growing numbers of black slaves.

The adoption of the Constitution and the Bill of Rights in the late eighteenth century enshrined as a matter of fundamental law a list of protections for defendants in criminal trials—the right to trial by jury, freedom from unreasonable searches and seizures, and a prohibition of cruel and unusual punishment. In the nineteenth century, the Supreme Court held that the Bill of Rights was binding only on the federal government and not on the states. The states, to be sure, had their own constitutions and their own bills of rights—much influenced by the federal Bill of Rights. But there was no enforceable national standard.

Nonetheless, the nineteenth century was an age of reform in criminal law and criminal procedure. Criminal codes were simplified and rationalized. Many states eliminated "common law crimes" and established the principle that nobody could be punished for any wrongdoing not listed in the penal code. In the North and the Midwest, the list of capital crimes was cut down radically. In Pennsylvania, as early as 1790, the death penalty was abolished for the crimes of robbery, burglary, and sodomy. Essentially, in some states only murder remained punishable by death—and not even all murders. Pennsylvania in 1794 introduced the idea of dividing murder into "degrees"; only first-degree murder ("wilful, deliberate, or premeditated") carried the death penalty. A few states (Michigan in 1846; Wisconsin and Rhode Island a few years later) did away with the death penalty altogether. The South lagged behind on this score. Most of those condemned to death in the South were black, as had been true in the colonial period as well.

In the disorderly cities of the early nineteenth century, public hangings came to be seen as barbaric spectacles—as incitements to violence, rather than as good moral theater. The states (for example, New York in 1835) began to shift their executions from public squares to enclosed yards within the bounds of prisons and jails. Later, in the 1880s, with new technology and the invention of the "electrical chair," executions retreated deep inside the bowels of the prison.

There were two innovations of the utmost significance in nineteenth-century criminal justice. The first was the penitentiary. In the colonial period there had been jails and workhouses, but they were crude affairs architecturally speaking, and

they were most definitely not the dominant mode of punishing criminals. Jails were primarily for debtors and for men and women charged with crime who were waiting for their trials and had not made bail. But in the nineteenth century, the prison became the centerpiece of a new system of corrections. The essence of prison life was discipline and regimentation. The prisoners dressed alike in prison uniforms, ate the same food, marched in lockstep, and performed hard labor. There were no distinctions of class. The early prisons, for example, Cherry Hill in Pennsylvania (1829), were massive stone buildings surrounded by strong, high walls and guarded day and night; individual wings or cell blocks radiated out of a common core. In these prisons absolute silence was the rule.

The prisoner, in other words, was totally stripped of all individuality. This was part of the theory that underlay the penitentiary system. In colonial times, as has been noted, punishment was invariably inflicted in public: shame and stigma were deliberately used, both to warn and deter any members of the community who might be tempted by sin or crime and to teach and reform any straying lambs in the flock. This was a system that perhaps worked well in small, tight, fairly isolated communities, with clear lines of authority and a strong religious superstructure. It worked much less well in the larger, brawling world of nineteenth-century cities. Now respectable people came to believe very firmly that exposure to society was the cause of criminality: bad company and the temptations of vice, especially hard liquor. The penitentiary was run on the model of a stern, disciplined family. The prisoner was removed from the temptations of society and subjected to the kind of iron discipline that presumably builds character.

The other major innovation of the nineteenth century was the development of a police force. A police force, in essence, is a full-time, quasi-military force, on duty night and day, whose job is to keep order on the streets and to find and arrest those who break the law. Before there were police forces, constables acted as a kind of daytime shift in the law-enforcement business; night watchmen made the rounds in cities and towns. This was a loose and fairly amateur system. Cities were growing rapidly in the nineteenth century and becoming more and more unruly, violent, disorderly places. A wave of riots in the 1830s and 1840s, in Philadelphia, Baltimore, New York, Cincinnati, and St. Louis, underscored this point. In 1834 a Boston mob burned down an Ursuline convent.

The London system, the Metropolitan Police, which came into existence in 1829, served as a model for American police forces. New York City and Philadelphia each established a police force in 1845. New Orleans followed in 1852 and Chicago in 1855. The first police typically were in plain clothes, except for their badges; but by 1858, the Boston police were in uniform, and uniforms soon became the norm. This change underscored the fact that the police were a kind of urban army, with its own system of ranks—sergeant, lieutenant, captain, and so on. A uniformed police force is a visible display of law and order. It deters by its very presence. At a date slightly later than the first police force, the first detective squads were organized (New York, for example, in 1857). The uniformed police were overt and obvious. Detectives were covert, sly, and underground. They were supposed to prevent crime and ferret out the slicker, more hidden, more elusive criminal elements in society.

The police did not, of course, end urban turbulence. Perhaps the worst example of violent disturbances in American history was the so-called draft riots of 1863, in New York City. These riots began as a protest against conscription, but turned into a wave of violent riots. Hundreds died, many of them blacks killed by rampaging white laborers. Nineteenth-century police departments were quite commonly tainted with corruption and machine politics. The Lexow Report (1894) declared the New York City police department to be "thoroughly impregnated with . . . political influence" and also venal and ineffective: "houses of ill-repute, gambling houses, policy shops, pool rooms, and unlawful resorts of a similar character were being openly conducted under the eyes of the police." This investigation was only the first of a series in New York and other cities; each one tended to find the same problems and to announce the same short-lived solutions.

In the twentieth century, to be sure, problems of corruption and brutality remained. The police did become more professional—subject to civil service exams, for example, and also to educational requirements. Police work and detective work also became more scientific. Fingerprinting came in about the turn of the century, and forensic science developed rapidly. The first police were all men, of course, but women began to move into this male preserve in the early twentieth century. In 1910, for example, Los Angeles hired its first woman to serve as a regular member of the department. The numbers of women on police forces, however, remained quite small at first, as did those of minorities. Blacks made up 4 percent of the force in Philadelphia in 1930, 1 percent or less in such cities as Cleveland, Detroit, and New York. This situation did not change until the Civil Rights movement in the 1950s and 1960s.

The Criminal Trial

The basic shape of the criminal trial has in some ways maintained itself over the years: crimes were divided into serious crimes (felonies) and less serious ones (misdemeanors), although the exact definition and the dividing line between them tended to differ from state to state. For felonies there was a kind of two-stage process. First came indictment by a grand jury. This was a select body (made up usually of twenty-three members) that sat for a term and reviewed cases on a preliminary basis. If the grand jury concluded there was enough evidence to warrant a trial, then the defendant was delivered over to a trial court. The trial itself was largely an oral contest between opposing lawyers, with each side presenting its case and calling witnesses and with the right of each lawyer to cross-examine the witnesses of the opposing side. The audience for this was a jury of twelve men (women were not eligible until the twentieth century), selected at random. At the close of the trial, the judge instructed the jury, that is, he told them about the legal rules that applied to the case. The jury then retired to a closed room to discuss the case and mull over the evidence. The guilt or innocence of the defendant was entirely in their hands.

This was the system on paper. Over the course of the century the system changed considerably. A few states (California, for example) largely abandoned the grand jury system in the later nineteenth century. They replaced indictment with the information system. This too was a two-stage process, but instead of a grand jury, the preliminary hearing was held before a judge or magistrate; it was this official who decided if there was evidence enough to go to trial.

During the nineteenth century the percentage of cases that went to trial declined dramatically. What replaced trial was the guilty plea. By 1900, in many parts of the country, only a small number of convictions resulted from actual jury trials; the rest were the result of guilty pleas. In New York three

A twelve-person jury depicted in a 1964 drawing by Franklin McMahon.
CORBIS/FRANKLIN MCMAHON

times as many defendants pleaded guilty as went to trial.

Why did so many defendants—and more and more over the years—give up without a fight? Perhaps some were motivated by remorse or hopelessness. Most were not. As time went on, increasingly these pleas resulted no doubt from plea bargaining—a "deal." That is, the defendant would agree to plead guilty in exchange for a promise by the prosecutors to drop some charges or to ask for a lighter sentence. There is unmistakable evidence of plea bargaining from the late nineteenth century on; and there is strong evidence, in Theodore Ferdinand's study of Boston courts, that it existed in some locations in the early part of the nineteenth century as well. Certainly, the percentage of guilty pleas rose dramatically in Boston between 1826 and 1850.

The trend away from trials continued in the twentieth century. By the late twentieth century, in some parts of the country, as many as 90 percent or more of all convictions came after the defendant "copped a plea." Plea bargaining was attacked from all sides, and some places tried to abolish it altogether; but it had a stubborn way of persisting. Whatever its faults, it is an expedient way of handling large numbers of cases; full trial by jury in the modern world is extremely expensive and time consuming. This fact makes the temptation to strike a deal almost overwhelming on both sides.

At the bottom of the pyramid of courts, in the numerous police, municipal, and justice-of-the-peace courts, proceedings were quick and slap-dash, lawyers and juries were uncommon, and justice was rough and ready. Here thousands and thousands of drunks, disturbers of the peace, and vagrants were fined, sent to county jail for short terms, or otherwise disposed of. At the other end of the spectrum—the top of the pyramid—were the great show-trials, cases of great drama and high theater. These were the cases that made headlines, with people fighting for a seat in the courtroom. Perhaps the most famous of all was the 1893 trial of Lizzie Borden in Fall River, Massachusetts. Abby Borden and her husband, Andrew, one of the leading citizens of the town, had been brutally hacked to death with an ax the year before. Andrew's daughter, Lizzie, an unmarried woman in her thirties, was arrested and charged with the murder of her father and stepmother. After a sensational trial, Lizzie Borden was acquitted. What was really on trial was the concept that a woman of her class and background was capable of murder. This trial, and others of its type, performed the same didactic and dramaturgic function that criminal justice as a whole had filled in the colonial period.

This function was, if anything, heightened in the twentieth century. In 1924 Richard Loeb and Nathan Leopold murdered a young boy, Bobby

An inspector studies fingerprints in January 1919.
CORBIS/BETTMANN

Hiss for perjury (1949–1950), Cold War issues were sensationally in the foreground.

The celebrity trial became still more prominent in the age of mass media. In *Sheppard v. Maxwell* (1966), the defendant, a doctor, was accused of murdering his pregnant wife. Sheppard was convicted, but the Supreme Court thought the case such a media circus that it reversed the conviction. (He was later acquitted.) Television dramatically ratcheted upward the entertainment and sensation value of great criminal trials—the unholy climax, perhaps, was the murder trial of O. J. Simpson in the 1990s.

Sentencing and Corrections

In the late nineteenth century, the classic penitentiary system fell into a kind of decay. Crowded conditions probably doomed the silent system, which depended on solitary confinement. States balked at spending the money necessary to keep up these huge establishments. During the last third of the nineteenth century, there was a wave of penal reform. The basic aim of the reforms was to devise some way to classify prisoners—to separate those who might be reformed and returned to society from those who were thought hopelessly corrupt. By 1869, twenty-three states had laws that allowed "time off" for good behavior in prison. By the end of the century more than half the states had some form of parole law, under which prisoners with good records could get conditionally released from prison before their time was up.

Another innovation was the indeterminate sentence. The basic plan was simple: when a person was convicted of a crime, the judge would no longer fix the sentence; rather he would fix a minimum sentence. The criminal would go to prison and after the minimum time was up (often one year), the prison authorities, who had had a chance to observe the prisoner, would fix a sentence, either long or short, depending on their assessment of the case. Good behavior in prison was one factor in this assessment, but not the only one: an Illinois law of 1899 spoke also of "improvement or deterioration of character" and the prisoner's "constitutional and acquired defects and tendencies." Here too the idea was to lock up for a long time those criminals who were not yet "cured" of their criminal tendencies, or who were downright incurable. The indeterminate sentence became mandatory for all first-time offenders in New York in 1901. "Habitual criminal" laws had something of the same philosophy; for example, in Ohio under

Franks, apparently just for the thrill of it. Clarence Darrow, the most sensational lawyer of the day, argued for the defense, and the trial (actually, a penalty hearing, since the defendants had confessed) was a media sensation. So too was the 1935 trial of Bruno Hauptmann, who was accused of kidnapping and killing the infant baby of Charles Lindbergh. Some cases had important political overtones. At key moments in history, by reason of their inherent drama and wide public interest, some trials seemed to sum up an era or project a particular issue onto the larger screen of debate. In the Scopes trial (1925), a teacher was accused of teaching Darwinian theories in school, which was against the law in Tennessee; the trial heightened a national debate over evolution, science, and religion. The Sacco-Vanzetti case in the 1920s pitted liberals against conservatives. In the trials of Alger

a law of 1885, a man or woman convicted of a third felony could be detained in prison for life.

Probation was yet another correctional reform. The idea was to give a convicted criminal another chance; it was a kind of parole system, but it set in before any prison time was served at all. A Boston bootmaker, John Augustus, pioneered a form of the system on his own as early as the 1840s. In 1878 Massachusetts formalized the system and provided for a paid probation officer in the criminal courts. Other states later adopted the system (for example, California in 1903).

Another innovation of the turn of the century was the development of a special system of juvenile justice. In general, in the nineteenth century young offenders could be, and were, tried as adults, although children under fourteen were deemed *prima facie* incapable of possessing a "guilty mind." (Under the age of seven, children could not be tried at all.) In some states there were special homes for destitute and delinquent children—so-called houses of refuge. Massachusetts in 1847 created a State Reform School for boys, and in 1855 a similar reform school for girls. But the trial process for these boys and girls was the same as for adults. A pioneer Illinois law of 1899, which applied at first only to Cook County (Chicago and its suburbs), created a special juvenile court. The terms of the law swept into its net all children in need of institutional handling, whether they had been delinquent or simply abandoned or neglected. In theory, this was not a criminal court at all; the boys and girls sent to detention homes or reform schools were not going to prison but to places where they would be nurtured and trained.

The idea spread rapidly; Colorado passed a juvenile court law in 1903, and other states followed. How the juvenile court actually worked is not easy to tell. It was certainly popular with parents of difficult children; most delinquents were boys, but their delinquencies in the early twentieth century seem mild in comparison with the tougher, more deadly delinquents of the period after the Second World War. Girls were subject to a double standard: they were dragged into court for the same sexual activity that went unpunished among boys.

Juvenile courts were, as noted, not supposed to be criminal courts, and juveniles were not criminals; but a boy or girl sent to a juvenile hall could be forgiven for not seeing the distinction. Eventually the Supreme Court came to agree in the landmark case of *In re Gault* (1967). Young Gerald Gault had been committed to the State Industrial School in Arizona. This was punishment, whatever you called it, said the Supreme Court, and the juvenile court had to recognize the constitutional rights of its young people.

Three boys in the judge's chambers in a Denver juvenile court in the early twentieth century. CORBIS

In the period after the Second World War, young criminals became more violent and dangerous: young killers and rapists increased, creating a public backlash. From the late 1970s on, state after state passed laws allowing juveniles who committed grave crimes to be tried as adults. The slogan was, if they're old enough to do the crime, they're old enough to do the time.

Lawless Law

Any account of the history of criminal justice, and especially any account of violent crime and its punishment, would be seriously lopsided if it did not take into account violence within the legal system or the ways in which the official legal order allowed, encouraged, or ignored violence "outside" the jurisdiction of the law.

Every society defines an area, outside the regular legal system, in which a private citizen may use force. This may be nothing more than spanking a child or "correcting" a servant. The line that separates legitimate force from illegal force changes over time—what was once serious spanking now verges on child abuse, beating one's wife becomes taboo, and so on. Under the regime of slavery, the master had full authority to whip and otherwise punish his slaves. Even masters who killed slaves were rarely prosecuted—and then only for truly egregious cruelty. In effect, slave owners ran their own private legal systems on the plantation; slave owners and overseers were accusers, judge, jury, and punishers rolled into one.

Emancipation did not end violence against former slaves. In the late 1860s the Ku Klux Klan acted to enforce a kind of unwritten code of white supremacy. The Klan murdered a black legislator in Alabama in 1870, for example, for no better reason than that he was successful and influential. Local officials turned a blind eye to the Klan's violence, and federal laws enacted against their activities were ineffectual in the face of the strong support for the Klan's goals among many white Southerners.

The Klan was a kind of organized lynch mob, killing some four hundred blacks between 1868 and 1872. Lynching itself had its "golden age" in the years after 1880. A report issued by the National Association for the Advancement of Colored People (NAACP) in 1919, covering a thirty-year period, recorded more than three thousand lynchings. Almost 90 percent of them took place in the South; and 78 percent of the victims were black. (One famous white victim was Leo Frank, who was also Jewish, accused—almost certainly wrongly—of murdering a thirteen-year-old girl; Frank was lynched by a Georgia mob in 1913.) Lynch mobs were often incredibly brutal. In 1899 a black man, Sam Holt, accused of murdering a white man and raping his wife, was tortured, mutilated, and burned at the stake in Newman, Georgia, as two thousand people watched. Punishment for taking part in a lynch mob was almost unheard of.

Vigilante movements flourished in the West in the period after the Civil War. These were, in Richard Maxwell Brown's formulation, organized, extralegal movements, whose members "take the law into their own hands." Two early and famous examples were the "vigilance committees" of raw, booming San Francisco in the 1850s, led by merchants and other prominent citizens and directed against thieves, criminals, and corrupt politicians. But there were outbursts of vigilantism in all of the western states—Texas, Montana, Alaska, and elsewhere. In Casper, Wyoming, in 1889, Ella Watson ("Cattle Kate") and a henchman were hanged for rustling livestock—a rare example of a woman victim. The vigilantes claimed to be upholding law and order, and they sometimes conducted "trials"; but the outcomes were pretty much foreordained. "Law and order" was the excuse, too, for the widespread use of brutality and the "third degree" among urban police.

Laws Against Vice

In the late nineteenth century, there was a dramatic upsurge of interest in laws against vice and what we would now call victimless crime. There were frequent crackdowns on gambling. Abortion was criminalized; between 1860 and 1880 the majority of the states passed antiabortion laws. Also notable was a heightened interest in laws controlling sexual behavior. The climax, perhaps, was the passage in 1910 of the Mann Act, the famous "White Slave Traffic Act." The Mann Act was the product of a campaign against "white slavers"—men who allegedly seduced or kidnapped innocent young women and forced them into the sex trade as virtual slaves. The Mann Act made it a federal crime to "transport . . . any woman or girl" across state lines "for the purpose of prostitution or debauchery, or for any other immoral purpose."

In the late nineteenth and early twentieth centuries, many states also raised the "age of consent." A male who had sex with a female who was below the age of consent was guilty of rape, no matter how old he was—or how willing a partner the female had been. By 1913, in California the age of consent was eighteen; in Tennessee it was twenty-one. Laws such as these in effect made teenage sex a crime (for the male at least), although they were only fitfully enforced. There were also campaigns in many cities against "red-light districts"—areas of vice that the police ignored (or were bribed to ignore).

By far the most important laws aimed at stamping out vice were those passed against liquor and drugs. There had always been a strong temperance movement in the United States, but it gained renewed vigor in the early twentieth century. The Eighteenth Amendment to the Constitution—forbidding the making, shipping, importing, or selling of liquor—went into effect on 29 January 1920, beginning an era of Prohibition. Congress backed up the amendment with a strong enforcement law, the Volstead Act. Many states also passed their own "little Volsteads."

Prohibition had a short, turbulent life. Many thought that Prohibition was a total failure. This is debatable, but it was certainly a political failure, especially in the cities, where millions of people continued to drink and to get liquor by hook or by crook. But there were continued efforts by "drys" to put more teeth into the law to stamp out the demon rum. Tens of thousands were arrested, fined, and jailed, both by the federal government and by the states, before Prohibition was repealed at the beginning of the 1930s.

Drug laws had a slower start but a longer life. In the nineteenth century there were only scattered laws and ordinances against drug use, mainly against opium dens. A New York law of 1905 declared that cocaine, morphine, and opium were "poisons" and could not be sold without a warning label. A landmark on the road to criminalization of drugs was the Harrison Narcotic Drug Act of 1914. This federal law was in form a tax statute, but it was aimed at ending the drug traffic. The statute applied to heroin, morphine, and "coca leaves" and their derivatives. At first, federal drug laws were not vigorously enforced, but in 1930 Congress established a Federal Bureau of Narcotics, a tireless source of propaganda against drugs and drug use. The Marihuana Tax Act of 1937 added marijuana to the list of the damned substances.

Police destroying barrels of beer during Prohibition. Corbis/Bettmann

Backlash—or the Triumph of Vice?

In retrospect, Prohibition was the high-water mark of the war against vice. With one powerful exception (drugs), the trend since 1930 has run strongly in the direction of removing the "criminal" label from victimless acts. The laws against gambling that existed years ago cease to mean much in the age of Las Vegas, Atlantic City, state lotteries, and Mississippi riverboat casinos. The trend away from criminalization is particularly notable in the case of laws governing sexual behavior. Connecticut repealed its law against fornication in 1967; other states did the same, and many swept away their laws against adultery as well. In 1975, California made a fairly clean sweep of its "victimless" sex laws, so that any sexual act between consenting adults is now legal. The Mann Act was overhauled in 1986. The new version was gender-neutral, and it applied to a more limited range of behaviors. It is now effectively dead.

A trend away from restrictive abortion laws reached its climax in 1973 when the Supreme Court decided *Roe v. Wade*. This decision held that the constitutional right of privacy meant that states could not forbid women to have an abortion, at least in the first and second trimesters of pregnancy. The case rested, in part, on *Griswold v. Connecticut* (1965), which struck down Connecticut's archaic laws against the sale or use of "any drug, medicinal article or instrument for the purpose of preventing conception."

There were, to be sure, pockets of resistance to all of these trends—particularly in the South, where, for example, sodomy laws still remain on the books. In 1986 the Supreme Court, in *Bowers v. Hardwick*, upheld the Georgia sodomy law by the narrowest of margins. Enforcement is mostly half-hearted, but the threat of enforcement is always there. The antiabortion movement continues to be a strong (occasionally violent) political force; the Supreme Court came within a single vote of over-ruling *Roe v. Wade* in 1992. By the late twentieth century people were able to print, buy, sell, or watch pornography on a scale that would have seemed unthinkable in the nineteenth century. Here, too, there have continued to be dissenting voices; pornography on the Internet is an issue newly added to the debate.

Drug laws constitute the single greatest exception to the liberalizing trend. Enforcement has tightened over the years, especially for heroin and cocaine. Since the 1960s successive presidents have waged increasingly stringent crusades against

---

Prisoners of War?

The rate of arrest and imprisonment for drug offenses skyrocketed in the 1980s and 1990s; some of the punishments that are handed out are truly draconian. In 1980 there were more than half a million arrests for drug violations, in 1990 more than a million. By that year, more than half of all federal inmates were in prison because they had violated drug laws. Life imprisonment was possible in some states even for first-time drug offenders whose offenses were deemed serious; thus, the maker or seller of a narcotic drug in an amount of 650 grams or more could be jailed for life. In fact, in 1989 about a thousand defendants did receive life imprisonment for drug violations in state courts. Toughness on drug crimes continues to enjoy a high level of public support; few public officials speak out against tougher drug policies.

---

pushers and users. President George Bush declared "war" on drugs in 1989 and appointed a drug "czar" (head of the National Office of Drug Control Policy) to act as the commander in chief.

Federalizing Crime

One of the most striking features of the history of criminal justice since 1900 is the increased involvement of the federal government. In the nineteenth century, crime was almost entirely a state matter. It was in the states that men and women stood trial for murder, arson, rape, robbery, and all other crimes, including petty offenses. There were a few federal crimes—smuggling, tax evasion, and crimes committed in the armed forces, for example—but they were not of overwhelming importance. Until 1891, when Fort Leavenworth opened in Kansas, the federal government did not have its own prison system (except for the military); it boarded out its prisoners in state and local jails. A second prison opened in Atlanta in 1902.

In the course of the twentieth century, the picture altered considerably. The federal role in the economy increased enormously in the age of radio, movies, and television. It was inevitable, then, that Washington's role in criminal justice would also increase. Prohibition, as noted, had been a federal responsibility (shared, to be sure, with the states).

The Mann Act was federal. The Dyer Act of 1919 (the National Motor Vehicle Theft Act) made it a federal crime to transport a stolen car across state lines. The federal income tax (from 1913), and the dozens of regulatory statutes passed during the New Deal and afterward, created dozens of new federal offenses such as stock fraud, insider trading, and cheating on income tax returns. The number of federal prisoners grew steadily over the years, from about three thousand in 1915 to more than one hundred thousand (over half of whom were drug offenders) in 1998. The Bureau of Prisons controls over ninety institutions in various parts of the country.

Federal law enforcement had also become a significant factor. In 1908 the attorney general, Charles J. Bonaparte, created a Bureau of Investigation inside the Justice Department. Out of this nucleus the Federal Bureau of Investigation (FBI) developed. J. Edgar Hoover became director of the bureau in 1924, and ran it until his death in 1972. He exercised immense power and was a genius at publicity and public relations—his list of the "ten most wanted" criminals was a master stroke. Hoover's work, however, was marred by his right-wing zeal and his paranoia; he became obsessed with ferreting out anarchists, communists, and leftists, and he was not above using wiretaps and other dirty tricks against such civil rights leaders as Martin Luther King, Jr. Nevertheless, under Hoover the FBI came to stand for the latest in forensic science. It was perhaps necessary to have such a national law enforcement body at a time when crime itself took on organized and interstate aspects. The FBI also made an attempt to gather decent crime statistics. The Uniform Crime Reporting program, from about 1930 on, produced the most widely used index of American criminality.

Crime was also federalized in an important way by decisions of the U.S. Supreme Court, which "incorporated" parts of the Bill of Rights into the Fourteenth Amendment and made them enforceable against the states. This meant that the Court could impose a national standard, a standard of criminal justice that applied to all the states. A landmark decision was *Powell v. Alabama* (1932). This case arose out of the notorious Scottsboro case, in which two women (falsely) accused nine poor, young black men of gang rape; the men were convicted after a slapdash trial before an all-white jury. The Supreme Court reversed the convictions, on the grounds that the defendants had not had

competent lawyers. In so doing, the Court "incorporated" the Sixth Amendment (right to counsel) into the Fourteenth Amendment and applied it to the states.

The process accelerated in the 1950s and 1960s, when Earl Warren became chief justice of the United States. In *Gideon v. Wainwright* (1963), a case coming up from Florida, the Supreme Court expanded the right to counsel; according to this decision the state had to provide a lawyer for a defendant accused of a serious crime if he could not afford one. *Miranda v. Arizona* in 1966 ruled that the police had to respect the rights of the men and women they arrested; if the suspects wished, they could remain silent and consult with a lawyer before the police were to question them; and the police had to tell the accused about these rights—they had to give the accused what came to be called the "Miranda warning."

These decisions and others of the Warren Court formed a kind of high-water mark. The Court has become more conservative in the years since Warren retired, and its decisions often reflect the tension, anger, and fear in society over the problem of violent crime. The post-Warren Court has certainly not extended the rights of defendants, and some of the doctrines have been nibbled a bit around the edges. The Court, however, has never repudiated or overruled the key decisions of the Warren Court.

Meanwhile, the national political importance of crime has continued to grow, and this has moved the criminal justice system onto center stage. No nineteenth-century president was expected to talk about crime in his State of the Union Address as was the case in the late twentieth century. President Hoover appointed a crime commission in 1929, but the idea of a national "war on crime" is essentially a product of the years from the 1960s on.

Punishment and Corrections

The early twentieth century continued and expanded the correctional reforms and innovations of the late nineteenth century. For example, by 1925 all but two states had passed parole laws; the two exceptions, Mississippi and Virginia, fell into line by 1942. The reforms, however, ran into serious trouble in the period after the Second World War, when the rate of violent crime skyrocketed, and demands for toughness reverberated throughout the system. In the 1970s many states began to tinker with the indeterminate sentencing system;

some replaced it with a "flat-time" system that was notably tougher than what came before. Parole also came under fire; Illinois, for example, abolished it in 1977.

Conditions inside prisons were often crowded, unsanitary, and inhumane. There were constant investigations and exposés, but they usually came to nothing. The correctional system in the South was particularly brutal—especially the notorious chain gang, in which men were shackled night and day and forced to work killing hours under subhuman conditions. The experience was vividly described in 1932 in Robert E. Burns's *I Am a Fugitive from a Georgia Chain Gang*; the book created a sensation and inspired a popular movie, but Georgia did not abolish the chain gang until the 1940s.

The 1960s, the period of the Civil Rights movement, saw the beginnings of a prisoners' rights movement. In a notable series of court cases, prisoners (and their attorneys) argued that their prison conditions—and in some cases conditions in the whole state system—were so substandard that they amounted to "cruel and unusual punishment." Indeed, in one 1970 case, a federal court declared the whole Arkansas prison system unconstitutional. The court ordered immediate reforms, stating that the situation was "shocking to the conscience of reasonably civilized people." Arkansas was not alone in falling under the lash of the federal courts. Prisons, however, remained plagued with violence and unrest. The 1971 riot in Attica, New York, was one of the worst and the bloodiest. After 1980 the rate of imprisonment rose dramatically in response to the cry for tougher sanctions. States then embarked on an orgy of prison building; the total population of men and women under lock and key passed the one million mark sometime in the early 1990s.

The Death Penalty

There has been opposition to the death penalty in the United States since independence. Capital punishment came under renewed attack in the twentieth century. The NAACP, disturbed by the fact that blacks were put to death out of all proportion to their share of the population, was one of the organizations that campaigned strongly against it. Public opinion began to shift, and the use of the death penalty declined. In 1936, 62 percent of a sample of the population told the Gallup poll they approved in general of capital punishment; by 1966, only 42 percent said so. About two hundred men and women were put to death in

Two death-penalty protesters in Jackson, Georgia, 12 December 1984, on the eve of the electrocution of Alpha Otis Stephens. CORBIS/BETTMANN

1933, eighty-two in 1950, and only two in 1967. Five states (Oregon, Iowa, West Virginia, Alaska, and Hawaii) abolished the death penalty altogether in the twentieth century. In *Furman v. Georgia* (1972), the Supreme Court swept away every existing death penalty statute and emptied every state death row.

Furman was a narrow (5-4) victory, and the majority was itself deeply divided. Two of the justices, Brennan and Marshall, thought the death penalty was inherently unconstitutional, but the other three justices who made up the majority had certain reservations. In their opinion all the existing statutes were defective, because they allowed random, arbitrary imposition of this most drastic form of punishment. After *Furman* many states passed new statutes, trying to come up with laws that would pass constitutional muster. In 1976 in a cluster of cases, the Supreme Court struck down all new statutes that made death mandatory for certain crimes, but approved a Georgia law that took a different, more complex and nuanced tack. Other states followed, modeling their new statutes on those that had won approval in the high court. Today death penalty cases typically have two stages: there is a guilt stage, and then, after conviction, a separate trial, the penalty stage, in which the jury (or, in a few states, the judge) weighs various aggravating and mitigating circumstances to decide on life imprisonment or death.

The tide had turned in the public's opinion. In the 1970s the polls began to show a majority of the population again in favor of capital punishment; by the 1980s the majority was huge. In the 1990s New York and Kansas joined the ranks of states with the death penalty. But neither state, as of 1999, had actually executed anybody. In fact, the vast majority of executions take place in the southern states; Texas is the undisputed leader in legal executions. Everywhere, however, the process has slowed to a crawl. In 1933 Giuseppe Zangara tried to shoot Franklin D. Roosevelt; his bullet hit the mayor of Chicago, Anton Cermak, who died of his injuries. Zangara was indicted, pleaded guilty, and was sentenced to death and executed in the electric chair, all in little more than a month. But in June 1991, when Jerry Joe Bird died in Texas of a lethal injection, he had been on death row for seventeen years—and this is by no means an unusual situation. The Supreme Court—and the legislatures— have indicated their displeasure and impatience, but the long wait to die continues almost unabated.

Gender and Justice

One dramatic change in the twentieth century has been the entry of women into the criminal justice system. Before 1900 there were no women judges or jurors and virtually no women lawyers. Even after women gained the right to vote, there was a certain reluctance to let them into the all-male club of criminal justice. The Louisiana Constitution of 1921 specified that no woman was to serve on a jury unless she wanted to and said so in writing. The U.S. Supreme Court struck down this provision in 1975. Today women are as common as men on juries, and there is a reasonable chance of seeing a woman as lawyer or judge as well.

Crime itself is not an equal opportunity employer. In 1950, 3.5 percent of the adult prisoners in state and federal prisons were women. In 1975 the figure was 3.6 percent; in 1996 the figure was 6.5 percent. In 1905 in New York City, men were arrested at a rate five times that of women. Most of these women were arrested for vagrancy or prostitution. Robbers or burglars are rarely women, and women account for a very small percentage of violent crimes.

Women, unfortunately, do figure prominently as victims in the criminal justice system. This is particularly true in cases of domestic violence and rape. Until fairly recently, the police were loath to intervene in "domestic disturbances." Pressure from the women's movement has brought about significant changes; in the 1970s shelters for battered women began to appear in towns and cities. At the same time, case law for the first time took seriously women's rights to plead self-defense in instances where battered women killed their husbands or lovers.

Rape has always been defined as a serious crime, but in the nineteenth century and well into the twentieth, the prosecution of rape was hardly enforced with vigor. As late as 1969, in New York there were 2,415 complaints, 1,085 arrests, and only 18 convictions for rape. A study of jury behavior published in the 1960s showed that juries tended to acquit the defendant in cases of acquaintance rape—indeed, in most cases where the rapist was not a stranger or had not been extremely violent. In practice, too, only "respectable" white women had any chance of getting justice in a rape case. A husband had absolute immunity from any charge of raping his spouse; this was written into the statutory law. The case law tended to require an act of extreme resistance; if a woman did not fight back, even to the point of risking her own death, she could be considered as legally "consenting." The law allowed the defense to parade the victim's sex life before the jury. This was relevant, because, as Benjamin N. Cardozo put it in a New York case decided in 1918 (*People v. Carey*), a woman's "honor has been lost" once she has "yielded" her chastity, and a woman who had lost her "honor" had also lost the "great motive which inspired resistance even unto death."

This view changed rather dramatically in the 1970s and 1980s, thanks to the women's movement and to changing ideas about chastity, sex, and the role of women in society. "Rape shield" laws made it more difficult for the defendant to bring in the woman's sexual history as evidence; the husband's immunity from charges of spousal rape was eliminated in most states, and the requirement of "utmost resistance" was dropped. The concepts of "date rape" and "acquaintance rape" made a mark, too, on judges and juries.

The Era of Hard Feelings

Throughout American history, people have complained about crime and crime rates. But crime became a truly national issue only after the end of the Second World War. There is no question that the rate of violent crime rose dramatically in this period. The major response, politically, has been to advocate more "toughness." Politicians, federal and state, vied with each other in promising to tighten the screws in the criminal justice system. One result was a dramatic increase in the rate at which men and women were sent to prison. In many states there were attacks on the parole system and the indeterminate sentence, draconian laws against habitual defenders (including "three strikes" laws) were passed in many states, and there was a definite turn of the wheel toward renewed use of the death penalty. Rates of violent crime were dropping in the 1990s, to uncertain effect on public policy.

BIBLIOGRAPHY

Ayers, Edward L. *Vengeance and Justice: Crime and Punishment in the Nineteenth-Century American South*. New York: Oxford University Press, 1984.

Bodenhamer, David J. *Fair Trial: Rights of the Accused in American History*. New York: Oxford University Press, 1992.

Brown, Richard Maxwell. *Strain of Violence: Historical Studies of American Violence and Vigilantism*. New York: Oxford University Press, 1975.

Ferdinand, Theodore. *Boston's Lower Criminal Courts, 1814–1850*. Newark: University of Delaware Press, 1992.

Friedman, Lawrence M., *Crime and Punishment in American History*. New York: Basic Books, 1993.

Friedman, Lawrence M., and Robert V. Percival. *The Roots of Justice: Crime and Punishment in Alameda County, California, 1870–1910*. Chapel Hill: University of North Carolina Press, 1981.

Gordon, Diana R. *The Return of the Dangerous Classes: Drug Prohibition and Policy Politics*. New York: Norton, 1994.

Hindus, Michael S. *Prison and Plantation: Crime, Justice, and Authority in Massachusetts and South Carolina, 1767–1878*. Chapel Hill: University of North Carolina Press, 1988.

Hirsch, Adam J. *The Rise of the Penitentiary: Prisons and Punishment in Early America*. New Haven, Conn.: Yale University Press, 1992.

Jacobs, James B. *Stateville: The Penitentiary in Mass Society*. Chicago: University of Chicago Press, 1977.

Johnson, David R. *American Law Enforcement: A History*. St. Louis: Forum Press, 1981.

Lane, Roger. *Murder in America: A History*. Columbus: Ohio State University Press, 1997.

———. *Roots of Violence in Black Philadelphia, 1860–1900*. Cambridge, Mass.: Harvard University Press, 1986.

———. *Violent Death in the City: Suicide, Accident, and Murder in Nineteenth Century Philadelphia*. Cambridge, Mass.: Harvard University Press, 1979.

Langum, David J. *Crossing over the Line: Legislating Morality and the Mann Act*. Chicago: University of Chicago Press, 1994.

McGrath, Roger D. *Gunfighters, Highwaymen, and Vigilantes: Violence on the Frontier*. Berkeley: University of California Press, 1984.

Schwarz, Philip J. *Twice Condemned: Slaves and the Criminal Laws of Virginia, 1705–1865*. Baton Rouge: Louisiana State University Press, 1988.

Spindel, Donna J. *Crime and Society in North Carolina, 1663–1776*. Baton Rouge: Louisiana State University Press, 1989.

Steinberg, Allen. *The Transformation of Criminal Justice: Philadelphia, 1800–1880*. Chapel Hill: University of North Carolina Press, 1989.

Tonry, Michael. *Malign Neglect: Race, Crime, and Punishment in America*. New York: Oxford University Press, 1995.

Walker, Samuel. *Popular Justice: A History of American Criminal Justice*. 2d ed. New York: Oxford University Press, 1998.

———. *Taming the System: The Control of Discretion in Criminal Justice, 1950–1990*. New York: Oxford University Press, 1993.

LAWRENCE M. FRIEDMAN

See also **Capital Punishment; Crime, Legal Definitions of; Crime and Violence, Popular Misconceptions of; Cruel and Unusual Punishment; Death Row; Drugs and Crime; Execution, Methods of; Hate Crimes; Organized Crime; Police; Prisons: Overview; Theories of Violence; Torture.**

CRIME AND VIOLENCE, POPULAR MISCONCEPTIONS OF

Violent crime in many respects has become a way of life for many Americans. There is little doubt, in any event, that the problem of violence is serious and one that needs to be addressed. On the other hand, it is also true that some popular and political conceptions regarding the nature of violence (including juvenile and adult crime) and solutions for reducing it are often ill conceived and misguided.

Juvenile Violent Crime and Justice

Juvenile arrest rates for the violent index offenses (murder, forcible rape, robbery, and aggravated assault) increased dramatically from 1980 through 1994 (50 percent from 1987 to 1991). Although the rate of juvenile arrests for violent crime began to drop in 1995, it still remains at an extremely high level compared to other violent offenses. Even so, these data do not tell the entire story and may well present a misleading picture of youth crime. For example, the largest proportion of crime committed by juveniles is property, not personal, crime. Of crimes that are classified as violent, the vast majority are simple assaults and relatively minor confrontations. Moreover, the ways in which juvenile crime, both property and violent, is measured may be problematic in themselves and lead to unknown errors. Police statistics, for example, may over- or underestimate youth violence in that most crime committed by young people occurs in groups. Thus, it may be more of a question of who is "unlucky" enough to get caught. For instance, an entire group, including only a few perpetrators, may be apprehended (overestimation), while police may also take in only a few members of a group when all members are perpetrators (underestimation). The reliability of such estimates is therefore variable. The most common juvenile violent offense is non-life-threatening assaults. How these offenses are counted and classified is really a matter of police discretion. Crime definitions are also a problem. Robberies may run the gamut from schoolyard extortion to liquor store holdups and home invasions. Surveys have also been used to measure youth crime, often asking youth to self-report their own criminal activity. These measures often give us a different picture of youth violence, but they also suffer from an array of well-known biases (e.g., errors in recall, honesty in reporting) and therefore are not error free.

A study conducted in 1996, which examined disproportionate minority confinement within five Wisconsin counties (Milwaukee, Waukesha, Rock, Brown, and Fond du Lac), illustrates this point. As part of this effort, juvenile court records were analyzed to determine differences in case processing between minority and majority youth. The analysis also included the offenses for which these youth were arrested and processed over a three-year period from 1991 to 1993. While few differences in processing were attributed to race alone, there were interesting patterns with regard to the distribution of juvenile offenses within these five counties. The analysis of the data revealed that serious violent offenses were not the norm for any of the counties, including the state's most urban area, Milwaukee. Rather, the most common crimes were property offenses such as auto theft and retail theft (shoplifting). Violent encounters were generally of a less serious nature, such as simple battery (i.e.,

without the use of a weapon). An additional level of analysis included the use of focus groups conducted with juvenile justice decision-makers in each of the five counties. The overall consensus was that popular and political images of violent youth crime were a misperception and that the problem of violent youth crime was not as serious as it was often portrayed. Unfortunately, this misperception was not benign and had serious ramifications within the state.

Despite the clear conclusions of the Wisconsin study, the state legislature authorized funding to build two new juvenile confinement facilities designed to hold seriously violent juvenile predators. Later they were changed to house young adult offenders because there were not enough seriously violent offenders to fill them. Obviously, the original decision to build secure confinement facilities for violent youth was misguided and not informed by actual data that were available at the time. Politicians and government officials in other states would do well to learn from the experience in Wisconsin that while violent juvenile crime remains a serious problem, it does not overwhelm the juvenile justice system.

A Note on School Violence. Political and popular conceptions of school violence often revolve around an image of "gun toting" young predators who make schools dangerous places. Media accounts often serve to perpetuate this myth. Incidents in the 1990s involving school shootings served to reinforce this belief, especially with the intense news attention that they received. The reality, however, is that such incidents are few and far between and are certainly not the norm. Most schools are relatively safe and may in some cases be safer than one's home environment, according to homicide data. A substantial number of killings occur in family settings, among relatives and those who know one another. For example, the Centers for Disease Control and Prevention reports that while homicide is the second leading cause of death among youngsters, fewer than 1 percent of child homicides occur in and around schools. Students aged twelve through eighteen are more likely to be the victims of serious violent crime away from schools rather than at schools. Furthermore, a study conducted in the Milwaukee Public Schools suggests that in 1999, for instance, the most common problems in the schools were noncompliant and disruptive behavior. Overall, the nature of crime outside the school is far more serious than in school, and within Milwaukee County and across the country the popular perception of schools as extremely dangerous places is a perception that is not supported by the available data.

Adult Violent Crime and Justice

As with juveniles, the violent offending rate for adults in the United States is extremely high, higher than that for any other industrialized nation. According to data from the World Health Organization, the United States leads all other G7 countries (Canada, France, Germany, Italy, Japan, and the United Kingdom) in homicides. The homicide rate for the United States in 1990 was 9.4 per 100,000 persons, which is over three times higher than that of the next country, Italy, with a rate of 2.6 per 100,000. Moreover, according to figures for 1995 from the Department of Health and Human Services, not only was homicide the tenth leading cause of death in the United States, but among young black males it was the leading cause of death. The rate at which Americans kill one another is truly astounding.

However, it is important to note that violent offenses represent less than ten percent of all crimes. Most violent crimes are not index offenses (murder, robbery, forcible rape, aggravated assault). In both the Federal Bureau of Investigation's Uniform Crime Reports (UCR) and the National Crime Victimization Survey (NCVS), the most common violent crime is simple assault. Moreover, there are problems associated with the collection of both UCR and NCVS data. For example, the UCR is not a complete enumeration of all crimes that occur, nor does it accurately reflect all arrests for property and violent crime. UCR data are dependent upon police-reporting practices that have been found to vary across departments. The NCVS relies on victim recall and honesty, which may introduce unknown distortions. More important, both sets of data are aggregated for the entire country and may not provide an accurate representation of what is occurring on a local level.

While the rate of violent offending, especially black-on-black crime, is still at an unacceptably high level, there have been some positive trends. The rate of violent offending dropped substantially from 1995 to 1999, especially homicide. According to FBI data, the nation's murder rate in 1997 fell to a level last seen more than twenty years before that. Much of the decline in the murder rate was posted in the nation's largest cities. While

some argue that this is merely the calm before the storm, most scholars agree that this is not an aberration but rather is indicative of a real reduction in violence that is likely to continue in the twenty-first century. Numerous reasons have been offered for this downward trend, ranging from the increased effectiveness of law enforcement to changes in the demographic structure of the population. As in most debates, some arguments make more sense than others. One of the more popular policing strategies has been termed "quality of life" enforcement. The rationale behind this approach is that attention to the smaller problems will have an impact on the larger ones, including violent crimes. Consequently, many police departments increasingly target minor offenses such as loitering, vagrancy, jaywalking, drinking in public, and the like, which were previously ignored or given a low priority. Many politicians and police chiefs across the country have argued that this policy has greatly contributed to the national reduction in crimes of violence, claiming that increased police presence has led to the discovery of other, more serious crimes. But such claims have not been substantiated. In some cities, the violent-crime rate has dropped even without "quality of life" enforcement. Furthermore in some instances, such as in New York City, "quality of life" enforcement has resulted in claims of aggressive police practices, including harassment and brutality.

Another argument advanced for the drop in violent crime has been an increase in the severity of sentencing (especially at the federal level), coupled with the rise in the prison population. However, in the past, while the incarceration rate increased, so did the violent-crime rate; it is only since 1996 that this relationship has reversed itself. Moreover, supporters of this strategy have not addressed crimes, violent and otherwise, which occur within prison settings. There is no way of accurately assessing "get tough on crime" approaches other than the fact that they are extremely expensive.

Demographic shifts in the population have long been associated with changes in crime patterns. In the 1960s the dramatic increase in the youthful segment of the population was seen as one factor associated with the rise of crime, both property and violent. So the argument today is that as we moved toward an older and more elderly population, the rate of violent crime has dropped and will continue to do so. Again, while there might be some truth to this argument, it is extremely difficult to assess its overall effect. More viable explanations focus on changes in the economy and the drug market. In the strong economy of the 1990s, higher wages and increased employment opportunities lessened the lure of criminal involvement. The steady increase in violent crime long associated with control of drug markets and the epidemic of crack cocaine came to a halt; nationally, the use of and trafficking in crack cocaine and other drugs decreased dramatically. Drug wars lessened as they increasingly drew police and political attention, which interfered with the dealers' economic transactions. Together, these forces had a major impact on the nature of violent crime.

A Note on "Three Strikes and You're Out." Perhaps the most famous and hotly debated crime-control policy in the 1990s was "three strikes and you're out." Drawing from a baseball analogy, the principle is straightforward: if offenders are convicted of three offenses, they face life imprisonment. While all states have had "habitual" offender statutes focusing on repeat offenders, "three strike" statutes generally impose much longer prison sentences. More than twenty states and the federal system have enacted this policy, which usually focuses on violent felonies. However, it has rarely been used; for example, as of 1999 only five offenders had been sentenced under Wisconsin's 1994 statute.

It is instructive to examine the situation in California, the only state where the statute has been consistently implemented. Over 40,000 offenders have been imprisoned in the state since the statute was enacted in 1994. Of these, over 4,400 were sentenced to twenty-five years to life. The California "three strikes" policy is especially severe; it is not limited to violent offenses but includes conviction for any three crimes, even, in one case, the theft of a slice of pizza. About 85 percent of those convicted under the California statute have been convicted of a nonviolent crime. In the aftermath of this policy, the California correctional population has risen dramatically, leading to increased violence and tension in prisons, because ethnic hatred and racial antagonisms are bottled up at close quarters. Moveover, there seems to be a pattern of racial disparities under this statute; African Americans are sent to prison thirteen times as often as whites. While "three strikes and you're out" is politically popular during a time in which the violent crime rate is dropping, there is no evidence to suggest that it significantly reduces the rate of violent offending. What it does is increase tensions between African Americans and law enforcement

and contribute to the massive growth in the prison population, which has had deleterious effects on the social organization of California's prison system.

Criminal Sentencing. As noted above, criminal sentences are long and getting longer. In fact, American prison sentences are among the longest in the world. Many states (twenty-eight as of the turn of the century) have passed life-without-the-possibility-of-parole statutes as well mandatory sentences for many violent offenses, drug offenses, crimes committed with guns, as well as for habitual offenders. (Mandatory sentences usually require a specific minimum or maximum term, while most statutes give judges more discretion in sentencing.) California has the most inmates in its correctional system—over 160,000 in 1999—followed by Texas with approximately 140,000 inmates. Together, these two states account for about one quarter of the entire population of state prisons. A policy of what the researcher Samuel Walker in *Sense and Nonsense* (1998) calls "gross incapacitation" (locking up a lot of people and sending them to prisons for long terms) served to triple the prison population nationally between 1980 and 1995. According to the Bureau of Justice Administration, the average time served by violent criminals rose to forty-nine months in 1997 from forty-three months in 1993. The proportion of time actually served by inmates increased from 47 percent of the sentence in 1993 to 54 percent in 1997. Overall, the state-prison population has been growing at a rate of 7 percent annually since 1990.

The ultimate question is what effect these policy changes have on recidivism among inmates and the overall crime rate. The answer is simply "not much." There is no clear evidence that increased incarceration is responsible for the significant drop in the rate of violent crime that began in the 1990s. A policy of gross incapacitation predated the drop in the crime rate. In fact, it has been evident for a long time that the incarceration rate has little effect on the crime rate. In 1968 the Model Sentencing Act proposed a sentencing structure in which ordinary terms for offenders, including those committing violent crimes (with the exception of homicide and certain atrocious crimes), would not exceed five years' imprisonment. The rationale behind this proposal (the act did not become law) was the lack of any deterrent effect for sentences exceeding five years. Nevertheless, lawmakers like to be seen as "tough on crime."

There are concrete statistics related to increased incarceration, and they show negative effects. One is the increasing imprisonment rate for minority offenders, especially African Americans. On the average, almost half of the inmates of state prisons are black. If the current incarceration trend continues, there is little doubt that even more African American inmates will populate prisons, and over-representation will occur for other minority groups as well.

Homicide and Parole Risk. Those in prison for homicide convictions have the opportunity to kill again under two circumstances, while still in prison and when back in the community. As noted earlier, most prisons are dangerous places where assaults and other violent crimes, including murder, are not uncommon. However, the public and politicians are most concerned about the potential for homicide and other violent crimes that may occur when convicted murderers are released from prison. The concern has some basis, since most convicted homicide offenders will be released to the community. Although there is the possibility of "life without parole," proportionately few offenders are sentenced under that option. The question, of course, is whether this concern of future crime on the outside is justified. Do homicide offenders make poor parole risks? In order to address this question, one first has to distinguish between types of homicides. Some homicide offenders are imprisoned for acts arising from domestic disputes. These offenders are most often model inmates and do well upon release from prison. After the object of their frustration has been removed, they feel no need to kill again.

The offenders deserving more attention are the predatory criminals, those convicted of homicides during the commission of violent crime such as armed robbery, sexual assault, or premeditated murder. A 1980 national study of parolees who had been convicted of murder showed that, in a three-year follow-up after release, 4.5 percent returned to prison for commission of a new crime and 0.31 percent for the commission of another homicide. The reality is that homicide offenders are less likely to commit murder on parole than persons originally sentenced for armed robbery, forcible rape, or aggravated assault. The truly dangerous, both in and outside of prison, are young, male offenders involved in the distribution of illegal drugs.

Additional evidence can be drawn in the aftermath of *Furman v. Georgia*, a Supreme Court deci-

sion handed down in 1972. The majority of the Court ruled that the administration of capital punishment constituted cruel and unusual punishment, and the decision returned death-row inmates to the general prison population and made them eligible for parole. One decade later, 75 percent of the inmates affected by the *Furman* case and 70 percent of a similarly situated comparison group did not commit a serious violation of institutional rules. With regard to parole behavior of those released into the community, 14 percent of the *Furman* inmates whose death sentences had been commuted committed a new felony upon release. This rate is similar to those non-*Furman* inmates who had been originally sentenced to death and those originally sentenced to life in prison. In a 1987 follow-up study of the *Furman* parolees, 4.5 percent committed another violent crime while on release. The repeat homicide rate for this same group was 1.6 percent. (An increase in the number of parolees between 1972 and 1980 is not reported.) The reality is that few convicted murderers kill again. Common fears that these individuals would be a menace to society if released would seem to be unfounded, since these rates of recidivism are acceptable by most scholarly and political standards. (Notwithstanding *Furman*, the Supreme Court later upheld the constitutionality of capital punishment.)

Sexual Assault. Sexual assault can occur both in prison and in outside society. While females are the most likely victims of this crime, males may also be victimized. There is a widespread misconception that sexual assaults (rapes) are common within prisons. In fact, while forced sexual contact among prisoners does occur, it is not widespread. Most sexual activity that does occur is consensual. There are no national statistics on this topic, and much of what we do know is obtained through surveys and interviews with inmates. While there is obviously room for error in this type of information-gathering, much of the research regarding sex in prison is remarkably consistent.

Sexual relationships in prison are not the same within men's and women's facilities. One reason is that female correctional facilities are very different from men's prisons with regard to social organization. Racial gangs and violence are not common in women's prisons, where integration of racial groups is the norm. Social organization centers on families, pseudo families, friendships, and homosexual liaisons. Pseudo-family relationships, which often involve consensual sex, reinforce the traditional role of the family outside the walls. Allegiances are frequently based upon emotional and personal connections.

Although racial strife and gang violence do not permeate the entire prison structure, they are common occurrences in many men's prisons. Violence is often condoned and approved and is part of the existing subculture. When rapes do occur within men's prisons they are more likely to express a need for power, domination, and control. This is actually similar to what studies of sexual assaults in the outside world conclude. While sex is part of the act, the prevailing need is to control one's victim. However, it bears repeating that nonconsensual sex in prison is still a relatively rare event, even though the "myth of sex in prison" continues in the public's mind. Further, sexually aggressive prisoners are often not successful in their attempts to dominate other inmates.

There is a widespread misconception that women are the only victims of rape outside of prison. However, men can be the victims of rape in the ouside world as well. This can include both homosexual and heterosexual attacks. Again, it is a longstanding myth that rape is a sexually motivated offense. In reality rape serves essentially nonsexual needs. Rape is the sexual expression of aggression. While the victims of serial killers are sexually exploited, for example, the underlying motivations for the attack is again power, domination, and control. Interviews conducted with those convicted of serial murder consistently support this premise. The reality is that victim selection is frequently determined by availability and vulnerability and not primarily by sexual desirability. Anyone can be the victim of a sexual assault. Rape happens not only to young adult women but also to both sexes and all age groups.

Domestic Violence. As with sexual assault, there is also a prevailing misconception that only women are the victims of domestic violence. While available data suggest that females are the most likely victims of abuse, it is also true that males can be the victims of domestic violence both as adults and children. A 1980 National Family Violence Survey showed that 16 percent of the respondents reported some kind of violence between spouses during the year of the survey, while 28 percent reported marital violence at some point in the marriage. During the twelve months prior to the interview, 3.8 percent of the women reported

being the victim of abusive violence. However, a larger number of the wives, 4.6 percent, admitted, or were reported by their husbands to have engaged in, violence of some sort. Another National Family Violence Survey revealed that the overall rate of wife-to-husband violence increased slightly over a ten-year period. These data suggest that women can be as violent, or even more violent, within a family as men. Yet it should also be noted that much of the violence by women against their husbands is in retaliation or for self-defense.

It is interesting to note that one of the major criminal justice policies dealing with domestic violence makes no distinction among perpetrators, men or women. This pro-, or mandatory, arrest policy, which is in effect in most jurisdictions, states that if there is evidence of a misdemeanor assault the police must make an arrest. The main premise is that a "taste of the bars" will deter future assaults. The first implementation of this policy was in the early 1980s in Minneapolis, Minnesota. The research there suggested that a pro-arrest policy was effective in reducing future domestic violence. However, later replications in other cities found that a pro-arrest policy may in fact increase recidivism. In Milwaukee, for example, this policy was found to have no long-term positive effect and, in fact, increased repeat offenses among offenders who were unemployed.

Drugs. When trying to understand the relationship between drugs and violence, there are three factors that need to be identified. The first deals with the pharmacological effects of various types of drugs. Historically, alcohol has been and continues to be the number-one drug of choice in the United States and has often been associated with the commission of violent crime. Alcohol acts first as a stimulant that may reduce inhibitions to the use of violence. A substantial amount of violent crimes, including homicide, robbery, and domestic abuse, are alcohol related. Barbituates, amphetamines, certain hallucinogens, and various stimulants such as PCP and methamphetamine ("crank") have also been linked to violent encounters. On the other hand, reality is much more complicated than the myth of the "drug crazed" criminal who consistently robs and murders while high on drugs. Some drugs may tend to ameliorate violence; examples are tranquilizers, marijuana, and cocaine (although the evidence for cocaine is somewhat mixed). Drug use may also increase the chances of violent victimization. Moreover, it should be noted that not everyone who partakes of such drugs as alcohol or cocaine are addicts in the traditional use of the term. Some drug users can function in society and do not necessarily engage in violence. Recreational drug use is widespread and does not often lead to violence and other destructive behaviors.

The second factor involves what might be termed economically compulsive violence. This is the traditional way in which many citizens and politicians associate drugs with violence. The assumption is that drug addicts commit crimes of violence in order to support their habits. The question is, which comes first: drugs then crime; crime then drugs; or both simultaneously? While the evidence is far from conclusive, it does suggest that most crime committed by most drug users is nonviolent. Few robberies can be directly related to drugs. Even if a perpetrator tests positive for drug use, it does not necessarily mean that drugs caused a violent crime. Moreover, research suggests that heroin users tend to avoid violence if other alternatives are available.

The third and last link of drugs to violence is found in aggressive patterns of drug distribution. These activities frequently involve territorial disputes leading to homicides, drive-by shootings, and robberies. In a larger sense, drug cartels like those in Colombia have contributed much to international violence. Similarly, street wars among gangs involved in the distribution of drugs have certainly contributed to the murder and injury rate in the United States. In this case a popular perception—that the drug trade is violent—is not misguided.

Conclusion

This brief entry has attempted to place a selection of high-profile problems of American violence in context. There is no doubt that violence in the United States has been and remains a very serious problem, more so than in any other industrialized nation. Obviously, this is a cause for concern and a reason for concerted action. On the other hand, it does make sense to try to understand the true nature of the problem before rushing to conclusions and implementing purported solutions. Reality is almost always more complex than myth, and popular perceptions are often only partly true. Solutions to the problem are not easy, but balanced analysis reveals that many policies enacted to combat violence may well do more harm than good. This article has attempted to provide some insight into the violence problem in discussing what we think we know and, perhaps more important, what we do not know.

BIBLIOGRAPHY

Felson, Marcus. *Crime and Everyday Life.* 2d ed. Thousand Oaks, Calif.: Pine Forge, 1998.

Kappeler, Victor E., Mark Blumberg, and Gary W. Potter. *The Mythology of Crime and Criminal Justice.* 2d ed. Prospect Heights, Md.: Waveland, 1995.

Maguire, Kathleen, and Ann L. Pastore, eds. *Sourcebook of Criminal Justice Statistics.* Washington, D.C.: U.S. Department of Justice, Bureau of Justice Statistics, 1998.

Pope, Carl, et al. *Wisconsin's Minority Overrepresentation Study, Final Report.* Wisconsin Office of Justice Assistance and the Governor's Juvenile Justice Commission, 1996.

Snyder, Howard. *Juvenile Arrests 1997.* Washington, D.C.: Office of Juvenile Justice and Delinquency Prevention, 1998.

Tonry, Michael, and Mark H. Moore, eds. *Youth Violence.* Chicago: University of Chicago Press, 1998.

Walker, Samuel. *Sense and Nonsense About Crime and Drugs: A Policy Guide.* 4th ed. Belmont, Calif.: Wadsworth, 1998.

Zimring, Franklin E. *American Youth Violence.* New York: Oxford University Press, 1998.

Zimring, Franklin E., and Gordon Hawkins. *Crime Is Not the Problem: Lethal Violence in America.* New York: Oxford University Press, 1997.

CARL E. POPE

See also **Drugs and Violence; Drug Trade; Prisons: Overview; Rape; Schools.**

CRIMINALISTICS. *See* Forensic Science.

CRIMINAL JUSTICE SYSTEM

Systems of justice across time and around the world are of numerous types. For more than two thousand years trials by ordeal, or perhaps by battle, were the cornerstone of the inquisitorial system of justice. The assumption of guilt was the guiding factor, and the accused was considered guilty until he could prove himself innocent. Inquisitorial justice became manifest when some form of divine intervention spared the accused from pain, suffering, or death or when the accused would readily admit his or her guilt, which was usually elicited through torture or other forms of corporal punishment. This system—which might more properly be called the inquiry system so as to remove the aura of terror associated with the word *inquisition*—still exists in a modified form in most countries of the world that did not evolve from English or American colonial rule. In the modern inquiry court, all persons—judge, prosecutor, defense attorney, defendant, and witnesses—are obliged to cooperate with the court in its inquiry into the crime. Out of this inquiry (an inquisition, in a value-free sense of the term) it is believed that the truth will emerge.

By contrast, the judicial process in the United States reflects the adversary system in which the innocence of the accused is presumed and the burden of proof is placed on the court. In the adversary court, the judge is an impartial arbiter or referee between battling parties—the prosecution and the defense. Within strict rules of procedure, the opposing sides fight to win, and it is believed that the side with truth will be victorious. Adversary proceedings are grounded in the right of the defendant to refrain from self-incrimination (as opposed to the lack of such a right in an inquiry court) and in due process of law, a concept that asserts fundamental principles of justice and implies the administration of laws that do not violate the sacredness of private rights.

The Bill of Rights

During the First Congress in June 1789, James Madison of Virginia proposed a dozen constitutional amendments. Congress approved ten of them in September 1791, and they have become known as the Bill of Rights. The significance of the Bill of Rights is that it restricts the government rather than individuals and private groups. It was added to the Constitution at the insistence of those who feared a strong central government.

Within the Bill of Rights, the First Amendment prohibits laws and practices that have the effect of establishing an official religion, and it protects the freedoms of speech, the press, religion, assembly, and the right to petition the government for redress of grievances; the Second Amendment ensures the right to keep and bear arms as part of a well-regulated militia; the Third Amendment forbids the government to quarter soldiers in people's homes; and the Fourth Amendment protects a person's right to be secure in his or her person, house, papers, and effects against unreasonable searches and seizures. The Fifth Amendment requires indictments for proceedings in serious criminal offenses, and it forbids compelling an individual to incriminate himself or herself or trying a person twice for the same offense (double jeopardy); it also contains the initial constitutional statement on

Albert DeSalvo, also known as the "Boston Strangler," being escorted to the Cambridge, Massachusetts, superior court in 1967. CORBIS/BETTMANN

due process of law. The Sixth Amendment sets out certain requirements for criminal trials, including the defendant's right to counsel, notification of the charges, a speedy and public trial before an impartial jury in the jurisdiction in which the crime was allegedly committed, and the related rights to confront hostile witnesses and to have compulsory processes for obtaining defense witnesses. The Seventh Amendment preserves the right to a jury trial in common-law civil suits involving twenty dollars or more. The Eighth Amendment forbids excessive bail, excessive fines, and cruel and unusual punishments. The Ninth Amendment has never been cited as the sole basis of a U.S. Supreme Court decision, and there has long been a debate over what the founding fathers intended it to mean. On its face, it states that the enumeration of specific rights elsewhere in the Constitution should not be taken to deny or disparage unenumerated rights retained by the people. The Tenth Amendment clearly was designed to protect states' rights and guard against the accumulation of excessive federal power; but it, like all of the amendments, is subject to a variety of interpretations by judges and legal scholars.

Due Process of Law

The concept of due process of law as stated in the Fifth Amendment (and later in the Fourteenth Amendment) is anything but precise. In general, however, due process should be understood as asserting a fundamental principle of justice rather than a specific rule of law. It implies and comprehends the administration of laws that do not violate the very foundations of civil liberties; it requires in each case an evaluation based on a disinterested inquiry, on a balanced order of facts exactly and fairly stated, on the detached consideration of conflicting claims, and on a judgment mindful of reconciling the needs of continuity and change in a complex society. A better understanding might be achieved by considering due process in its two aspects: substantive and procedural.

Substantive due process refers to the content or subject matter of a law. It protects persons against unreasonable, arbitrary, or capricious laws or acts by all branches of government. In the criminal justice process, one illustration of substantive due process is the void-for-vagueness doctrine. Under its precepts, due process requires that a criminal law must not be so vague and uncertain that, in the words of the Supreme Court, "men of common intelligence must necessarily guess at its meaning." The Court has struck down criminal statutes and local ordinances that, for example, made it unlawful to wander the streets late at night "without lawful business," to "treat contemptuously the American flag," and willfully to "obstruct public passages." In all of these cases, the issue of substantive due process and the void-for-vagueness doctrine came into play because the statutes were neither definite nor certain as to the category of persons referred to or the conduct that was forbidden.

Procedural due process is concerned with the notice, hearing, and other procedures that are required before the life, liberty, or property of a person may be taken by the government. In general, procedural due process requires the following: notice of the proceedings; a hearing; an opportunity to present a defense; an impartial tribunal; and an atmosphere of fairness.

The Criminal Justice Process

Criminal justice in the United States exists for the control and prevention of crime, and as a process it involves those agencies and procedures set

The Dallas, Texas, courtroom where Jack Ruby was tried in February 1964 for murdering Lee Harvey Oswald. CORBIS/BETTMANN

up to manage both crime and the persons accused of violating the criminal law. As an organizational complex, criminal justice includes the agencies of law enforcement charged with the prevention of crime and the apprehension of criminal offenders; the court bureaucracies charged with determining the innocence or guilt of accused offenders and with the sentencing of convicted criminals; and the network of corrections institutions charged with the control, custody, supervision, and treatment of those convicted of crime.

There are many steps in the criminal justice process, and although there are some differences from one jurisdiction to the next, the federal system is the general model followed by most state and local courts.

Prearrest Investigation. Although the first phase of the criminal justice process would seem logically to be arrest, this is usually the case only when a crime is directly observed by a police officer. In other situations, the process begins with some level of investigation. Prearrest investigation can be initiated when police receive a complaint from a victim or witness, knowledge from informers, or information through surveillance. Typically, investigative activities include an examination of the scene of the crime, a search for physical evidence, interviews with victims and witnesses, and a quest for the perpetrator. Data from an informer or general surveillance can suggest that some suspicious activity is occurring—perhaps drug sales, prostitution, or systematic theft—at which point an officer's or detective's "go out and look" investigation takes place.

Prearrest investigations can also occur in another manner, sometimes even before a crime has been committed. Law-enforcement agencies at the local, state, and federal levels become involved in long-term investigations when crime is not necessarily known but is strongly suspected or believed to be about to occur. This type of investigation is most typical of federal enforcement agencies, such as the Federal Bureau of Investigation, the Internal Revenue Service, the Customs Service, and the Drug Enforcement Administration. Such investigations, which include the use of informers, undercover agents, surveillance, sting operations, and perhaps wiretapping and other electronic eavesdropping devices, were common in the last decades of the twentieth century in investigations of drug trafficking, international money-laundering operations, and organized crime, to name but a few.

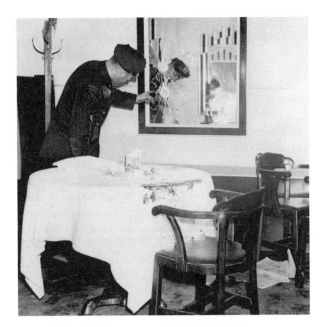

The police investigate the crime scene at the Palace Chop House, Newark, New Jersey, where the gangster Dutch Schultz was gunned down in October 1935. CORBIS/BETTMANN

In all types of prearrest investigation, the investigation activities may continue beyond the point at which the evidence necessary for an arrest has been gathered.

Arrest. When an investigation suggests that a crime has been committed or when a crime has been directly observed by a police officer, an arrest is made. Although the legal definition of *arrest* tends to vary from one jurisdiction to another, it is simply the action of taking a person into custody for the purpose of charging him or her with a crime. In most jurisdictions an arrest warrant is necessary in cases of misdemeanor (a crime less serious than a felony, or grave crime), unless the crime has been observed by a police officer. In some jurisdictions a warrant is also unnecessary for misdemeanor arrests in cases of domestic violence. The warrant is a written order giving authorization to arrest and is issued by a magistrate or someone of equal authority. Felony arrests can be made without a warrant if the officer has reasonable certainty that the person being arrested is the offender. Reasonable certainty (or probable cause) refers to the arresting officer's "rational grounds of suspicion, supported by circumstances sufficiently strong in themselves to warrant a cautious man in believing the accused to be guilty."

Arrests can be made not only by police and other law-enforcement officers but also by private citizens under the following circumstances: (1) a criminal offense is committed or attempted in his or her presence; (2) the person arrested has committed a felony, although not in his or her presence; and (3) a felony has been committed, and he or she has reasonable cause for believing the person arrested to have committed it.

The statutes of most jurisdictions governing arrest are quite specific. Criminal codes designate who can make arrests, the circumstances under which arrests can be made, and the conditions under which an arrest warrant is and is not mandatory. There are exceptions, however, that can place police agencies, private citizens, and other individuals in criminal justice proceedings in a tenuous position with regard to the constitutionality of how they make an arrest.

Booking. For some lesser offenses the police may be permitted to issue a citation, which is an order to appear before a judge at some future date. In all other circumstances, however, a physical arrest occurs when the suspect is present, and the process continues to the booking phase.

Booking refers to the administrative steps and procedures carried out by the police in order to record an arrest properly and officially. At the time of booking, the accused's name and address, the time and place of arrest, and the arrest charge are entered into the police log. Booking can also include fingerprinting and photographing the suspect.

The booking phase is the first point at which the accused can drop out of the criminal justice process with no further criminal proceedings. Charges may be dropped if the suspect has been arrested for a minor misdemeanor or if there was a procedural error by the police, such as a lack of probable cause for arrest or illegal search and seizure. In the case of a procedural error, the decision to drop the charges can be made by an assistant prosecutor or by someone of high rank in the police system. Booking is also the first point at which some defendants can be released on bail.

The word *bail*, taken from the French term *baillier*, meaning "to deliver" or "to give," is the most common form of temporary release. It involves the posting of financial security by the accused (or by someone on his or her behalf), guaranteeing an appearance at trial.

Initial Appearance. Due process requirements mandate that within a reasonable (not extreme or arbitrary) time after arrest the accused must be brought before a magistrate and given formal notice of the charge. Such notice occurs at the initial appearance. At this time, the accused is also notified of his or her legal rights, and bail is determined for those who did not receive such temporary release during the booking phase. Release on recognizance (ROR), a substitute for bail, can also occur, typically at the recommendation of the magistrate when there seems to be no substantial risk that the accused will fail to appear for trial. The accused is released on his or her recognizance, or obligation.

For some kinds of minor offenses, such as being drunk and disorderly or in other cases where a simple citation has been issued, summary trials and sentencing are conducted at this initial appearance, with no further court processing. In other situations, the magistrate presiding at the initial appearance may determine that the evidence available is not sufficient to warrant further criminal processing and consequently may dismiss the case.

Preliminary Hearing. Because of the complexity of criminal processing and the delays generated by overloaded court calendars, in many jurisdictions defendants have the option to bypass the initial appearance and instead proceed directly to the preliminary hearing.

The major purpose of the preliminary hearing is to protect defendants from unwarranted prosecutions. Thus, the presiding magistrate seeks to do the following:

- Determine whether a crime has been committed
- Determine whether the evidence establishes probable cause to believe that the defendant committed it
- Determine the existence of a probable cause for which the warrant was issued for the defendant's arrest
- Inquire into the reasonableness of the arrest and search and the compliance of the executing officer with the requirements of the warrant
- Fix the appropriate bail or temporary release, if this was not already done

Preliminary hearings are rarely held. In some jurisdictions, the defense may waive this hearing in order to keep damaging testimony temporarily out of the official records in the hope that by the time the trial does occur witnesses may have forgotten some things, become confused, or disappeared. However, some defense attorneys insist on this hearing as a tactic for gaining insight into the strengths and weaknesses of the state's case.

Determination of Formal Charges. Whether the initial court processing does or does not include an initial appearance or preliminary hearing, the next step in the criminal justice process is the formalization of charges. One mechanism is indictment by a grand jury. The indictment is a formal charging document based on the grand jury's determination that there is sufficient cause for a trial. The decision must be a majority decision, and when it is reached, a true bill (a bill of indictment endorsed by a grand jury as warranting prosecution of the accused) is signed, containing the following information:

- The type and nature of the offense for which the accused was arrested
- The specific statute alleged to have been violated
- The nature and elements of the actual specific charges brought against the accused
- The time and place of the occurrence of the crime
- The name and address of the accused or, if not known, a description sufficient to identify the accused with reasonable certainty
- The signature of the foreperson of the grand jury to verify that the decision of the grand jury has been returned as a true bill
- The names of all codefendants in the offense charged, as well as the number of criminal charges against them

Because the grand jury does not weigh the evidence presented, its finding is by no means equivalent to a conviction; it simply binds the accused over for trial. If this tribunal returns a no bill—that is, if it fails to achieve the required majority vote and thus refuses the indictment—the charges are dropped and the accused is released.

Grand juries are available in about half of the states and in the federal system, but in only a limited number of jurisdictions are they the exclusive mechanism for sending a defendant to trial. The most common method for bringing formal charges is the information, a charging document drafted by a prosecutor and tested before a magistrate. Typically, this testing occurs at the preliminary hearing. The prosecutor presents some, or all, of the evidence in open court—usually just enough to convince the judge that the defendant should be

bound over for trial. As indicated earlier, however, the preliminary hearing is sometimes waived, and in those circumstances the information document is not tested before a magistrate.

Arraignment. After the formal determination of charges through the indictment or information, the trial process begins. The first phase in this segment of the criminal justice process is the arraignment, at which the accused is taken before a judge, the formal charges are read, and the defendant is asked to enter a plea. There are four primary pleas in most jurisdictions:

1. Not guilty: If the not-guilty plea is entered, the defendant is notified of his or her rights, a determination is made of competence to stand trial, counsel is appointed if indigence is apparent, and in some jurisdictions the defendant can elect to have a trial by judge or a trial by jury.
2. Guilty: If a plea of guilty is entered, the judge must determine if the plea was made voluntarily and if the defendant has an understanding of the full consequences of such a plea. If the judge is satisfied, the defendant is scheduled for sentencing; if not, the judge can refuse the guilty plea and enter "not guilty" into the record.
3. Nolo contendere: This plea, not available in all jurisdictions, means "no contest" or "I will not contest it." It has the same legal effect as the guilty plea but is of different legal significance in that an admission of guilt is not present and cannot be introduced in later trials.
4. Standing mute: Remaining mute results in the entry of a not-guilty plea. Its advantage is that the accused does not waive his or her right to protest any irregularities that may have occurred in earlier phases of the criminal justice proceedings.

The Trial Process. The complete trial process can be long and complex. It may begin with a hearing on pretrial motions entered by the defense to suppress evidence, relocate the place of the trial, discover the nature of the state's evidence, or postpone the trial. After the pretrial motions (if there are any) the jury is selected and the trial proceeds as follows:

1. Opening statements by prosecution: The prosecutor outlines the state's case and how the state will introduce witnesses and

physical evidence to prove the guilt of the accused.

2. Opening statements by the defense: The defense, if it elects to do so, explains how it plans to introduce witnesses and evidence on its own behalf.

3. Presentation of the state's case: The state calls its witnesses to establish the elements of the crime and to introduce physical evidence; the prosecutor accomplishes this through direct examination of the witnesses (after which they are allowed to be cross-examined by the defense).

4. Presentation of the defense's case: The defense may open with a motion for dismissal on the grounds that the state failed to prove the defendant guilty "beyond a reasonable doubt." If the judge concurs, the case is dismissed and the accused is released. If the judge rejects the motion, the defense may still choose to rest without presenting a case on those same grounds; usually, however, the defense's case proceeds in the same manner as the state's presentation.

5. Prosecutor's rebuttal: If the defense presents a case, the prosecutor may elect to present new witnesses and evidence, following the format of the state's original presentation.

6. Defense's surrebuttal: The defense may again make a motion for dismissal; if denied, it too can introduce new evidence and witnesses.

7. Closing statements: The defense attorney and the prosecutor make closing arguments, which sum up their cases and the deductions that can be made from the evidence and testimony.

8. Charging the jury: In jury trials, the judge instructs the jury as to possible verdicts and charges the members to retire to the jury room to consider the facts of the case, to deliberate on the testimony, and to return a just verdict.

9. Return of the verdict: Once the jury members have reached a decision, they return to the courtroom with a verdict, which is read aloud by a member of the court. The jury may be polled, at the request of either the defense or the prosecution; that is, each member is asked individually whether the verdict announced is his or her individual verdict.

In the case of a trial by judge, the steps involving the jury are eliminated and the judge makes the determination of guilty or not guilty. In the majority of jurisdictions, the victim may have a role in the process through active participation.

Posttrial motions can also occur if the defendant is found guilty and the defense is given the opportunity to seek a new trial or have the verdict of the jury set aside (revoked).

Sentencing. Although the jury in many instances is involved in the sentencing procedure, especially in death penalty cases, it is the judge that imposes the penalty. After conviction or the entry of a guilty plea, the defendant is brought before the judge for the imposition of the sentence. The sentencing process may begin with a presentence investigation, which summarizes the offender's family, social, employment, and criminal history and serves as a guide for the presiding judge in determining the type of sentence to impose. Depending on the nature of the offense and the sentencing guidelines established by statute, a simple fine or adjudication to probation in the community might be imposed. Sentences can also include other forms of community-based corrections, imprisonment, or even death.

Appeals and Release. Subsequent to conviction and sentencing, defendants found guilty may appeal their cases to a higher court. Appeals are based on claims that due process was not followed, that new evidence has become available, or that the sentence imposed was "cruel and unusual," in violation of constitutional rights.

Release from imprisonment occurs after the time specified in the sentence has been served or if the offender is released on parole—a conditional release that occurs after only a portion of the sentence has been served. Release from prison, or from any type of sentence, can also occur through pardon—a forgiveness for the crime committed that bars any further criminal justice processing. Other factors that can affect a sentence are a reprieve, which delays the execution of a sentence, and a commutation, which reduces a sentence to a less severe one.

Criminal Justice as a System

The preceding summary of the various stages in the criminal justice process might suggest that the administration of justice is a system—an orderly flow of managerial decision making that begins with the investigation of a criminal offense and ends with a correctional placement. However, the notion of criminal justice operating as an orderly system is problematic. The justice process is composed of a series of bureaucracies (such as police departments; probation, parole, and prison agencies; and legal defense systems) operating along alternative and often conflicting paths; also, one segment of the system often serves as a dumping ground for each of the others.

Questions of definition and interpretation can confound the complexities of criminal procedure even further. Police officers interpret a situation to determine if a law has been violated. Prosecutors and defense attorneys interpret the law of an alleged offense and the social situation of an alleged offender to determine which laws were violated and to assess the culpability of the accused. Juries interpret the information provided by the police and courts to determine the innocence or the extent of guilt of the defendant. Judges interpret the evidence presented and the character of the offender to determine the nature and type of sentence and to ensure that due process has been achieved. And finally, correctional personnel use their knowledge of the law, social science, correctional administration, and human behavior to determine the appropriate custodial, correctional, rehabilitative, and punitive treatment for each convicted criminal.

Not only is there a lack of unity of purpose and organized interrelationships among police, courts, and corrections, but also individual interpretations of crime, law, evidence, and culpability at every phase of the process create further inefficiency. Criminal justice in the United States, therefore, is hardly a system. However, this is to be expected from a process of justice in a democratic society where checks and balances have been built in at every level to ensure that the fairness of due process can be achieved.

BIBLIOGRAPHY

Alderman, Ellen, and Caroline Kennedy. *In Our Defense: The Bill of Rights in Action.* New York: William Morrow, 1991.

Cox, Archibald. *The Court and the Constitution.* Boston: Houghton Mifflin, 1987.

Horwitz, Morton J. *The Transformation of American Law, 1870–1960.* New York: Oxford University Press, 1992.

Inciardi, James A. *Criminal Justice.* 6th ed. Fort Worth, Tex.: Harcourt Brace, 1998.

Rembar, Charles. *The Law of the Land: The Evolution of Our Legal System.* New York: Simon and Schuster, 1980.

JAMES A. INCIARDI

See also **Capital Punishment; Crime and Punishment in American History; Legal Definitions of Crimes; Police; Prisons: Overview; Sentencing.**

CROWN HEIGHTS RIOT

Racial and ethnic tensions erupted in violence in 1991 during a three-day riot in the Crown Heights section of Brooklyn in New York City.

On a Monday evening, 19 August, Grand Rabbi Menachem Schneerson of the Lubavitch Hasidic sect was returning from a visit to the grave sites of his wife and father-in-law in an automobile entourage that included a police escort. The last car in the three-car motorcade proceeded through an intersection, where it collided with another vehicle. The car careered onto the sidewalk and struck Gavin and Angelo Cato, seven-year-old cousins who were playing outside their homes. An angry crowd quickly assembled and assaulted the driver, Yosef Lifsh.

Within minutes an ambulance from the Hasidic-run Hatzolah service and two from New York City Emergency Medical Services (EMS) arrived. The EMS ambulances took both children to the hospital; Gavin Cato had suffered blunt trauma to the head and died immediately. The Hatzolah ambulance was instructed by the police to attend to Lifsh.

A rumor quickly spread that the Hatzolah crew arrived at the accident scene first but refused to treat the children. Adding fuel to the fire was the fact that police did not arrest Lifsh. Within an hour there was a flood of 911 calls reporting altercations between blacks and Hasidim. Later that evening, a large crowd of blacks, mostly young males, broke into smaller groups and rampaged through the neighborhood.

At 11:20 P.M. Yankel Rosenbaum, a twenty-nine-year-old rabbinical student from Australia, was attacked by a mob of a dozen or more black youths shouting "There's the Jew! Let's get the Jew!" He was stabbed four times and taken to Kings County Hospital, where he died a few hours later. Lemrick Nelson, sixteen, was quickly arrested for the stabbing. New York City mayor David N. Dinkins visited Rosenbaum in the hospital and called the attack a "lynching." Some Jewish leaders called it a "pogrom." Dinkins's remark may have been meant to be taken as an acknowledgement of a common experience of persecution shared by

The police guard a Hasidic center in the Crown Heights section of Brooklyn, New York, during a demonstration following racial riots in August 1991. CORBIS/AGENCE FRANCE PRESSE

blacks and Jews. Jewish leaders, however, saw the mayor's rather mild response to the subsequent demonstrations and rioting as biased; he was accused of allowing the rioters to engage in a state-sponsored attack on the Jewish community, thus providing fodder for the political mills.

Violence continued for three more days as police in riot gear followed a policy of restraint while blacks and Hasidim confronted each other across police lines. As blacks marched in protest, some carried anti-Semitic signs and shouted "Death to Jews" and "Kill the Jews." On Thursday of that week, according to a report in the *Daily News*, the command was given to "take back the streets," and order was restored in the ninety-four-square-block area.

Relative to other riots in U.S. history, the Crown Heights disturbance caused minor damages. It was limited to a small area, and only six businesses reported property damage. There was also damage to twenty-seven police cars. During the rioting 263 emergency calls and 129 arrests were made. Claims of disturbance-related injuries were made by 152 police officers and 38 civilians. There was one death—Yankel Rosenbaum's. Gavin Cato, because he was killed before the riot, is generally not included in the toll.

Nevertheless, the impact of Crown Heights was felt nationally. After rapid "white flight" from the district in the late 1960s and early 1970s, the relatively high-crime, low-income area contained about 180,000 black and 30,000 Hasidic Jewish residents. The violence of 1991 reflected the alienation of the neighborhood's African American and Caribbean American residents, who felt that their needs and rights were being subordinated by city officials to those of the Hasidim.

Nelson was tried in state court in 1992 and was found not guilty on three counts of manslaughter. In 1997 he was convicted in federal court for violating Rosenbaum's civil rights and sentenced to nineteen years in prison. Much of the blame for the violence was placed on Dinkins, New York City's first African American mayor. Criticism of how Dinkins had handled the crisis contributed to his loss in the 1993 mayoral race to Rudolph Giuliani. In 1999 Mayor Giuliani publicly apologized for the riots and agreed to pay $1.1 million to settle a federal lawsuit by ninety-two mostly Jewish Crown Heights residents.

BIBLIOGRAPHY

Crown Heights Coalition. *Crown Heights: A Strategy for the Future. A Report of the Crown Heights Coalition Prepared in*

Cooperation with the Office of the Brooklyn Borough President Howard Golden. 1992.

Girgenti, Richard. *Report to the Governor on the Disturbances in Crown Heights.* New York: Rector, 1993.

Krase, Jerome. "The Anatomy of Inter-Ethnic Conflict: Brooklyn's Italians, Jews, and Blacks." In *Origins and Transitions,* edited by Mario A. Toscano. Los Angeles: Ipermedium, 1996.

Krase, Jerome, and Charles LaCerra. *Ethnicity and Machine Politics.* Lanham, Md.: University Press of America, 1992.

Smith, Anna Deavere. *Fires in the Mirror: Crown Heights, Brooklyn, and Other Identities.* New York: Anchor Books, 1993.

JERRY KRASE

See also **Jews; New York; Race and Ethnicity.**

CRUEL AND UNUSUAL PUNISHMENT

The cruel-and-unusual-punishment clause of the Eighth Amendment to the U.S. Constitution has raised difficult moral issues. The ban on cruel and unusual punishment is traceable to early English documents, in which the concept was first used to condemn punishments unauthorized by statute and outside the jurisdiction of the sentencing court as well as to disapprove of excessive or disproportionate punishments. As early as the eleventh century, the laws of Edward the Confessor (1042–1066) declared that "extreme punishment . . . shall be inflicted according to the nature and extent of the offense." The Magna Carta, signed by King John in 1215 under compulsion from barons as a condition for swearing their loyalty to him, contained three provisions condemning disproportionate punishment.

In the sixteenth century this English concept was extended to include torture and other inhumane methods of punishing criminals. For those convicted of a crime, punishment typically consisted of whipping, mutilation, or other tortures that often led to death. In fact, in sixteenth- and seventeenth-century England, over two hundred offenses, including picking pockets, theft of a handkerchief, and associating with gypsies, were commonly punished by death. A concern over brutal and disproportionate punishments led Parliament in 1641 to issue a statute abolishing the Star Chamber, an executive tribunal that had become notorious for ordering brutal punishments.

Public outrage over excessive and barbaric punishments led to the 1689 adoption of the English Bill of Rights, which stated: "Excessive bail ought not to be required, nor excessive fines imposed; nor cruel and unusual punishments inflicted." This bill, however, did not immediately end the use of harsh punishments. Nevertheless, the English retreat from cruel punishments had begun: in 1790 the burning of women was ended, and in 1841 Parliament banned the whipping of women; drawing and quartering was abolished in 1814, gibbeting (hanging in chains) in 1834, pillorying in 1837, and beheading in 1870. Finally, Parliament abolished all methods of extinguishing life in 1965.

In America, Massachusetts passed the first law against cruel and unusual punishment, drafted by Reverend Nathaniel Ward and published in 1641 as Clause 46 of the Body of Liberties: "For bodilie punishments we allow amongst us none that are inhumane, barbarous or cruel." This language suggests that the early colonists were concerned about barbaric punishments, such as burning at the stake, breaking on the wheel, and crucifixion. Nonetheless, no other colonial legislature enacted a similar statute until 1776, when Virginia passed a Declaration of Rights that contained a provision with the identical wording used in the English Bill of Rights. By 1790 eight of the original thirteen states—Virginia, Delaware, Maryland, Massachusetts, North Carolina, New Hampshire, Pennsylvania, and South Carolina—had added a provision against cruel and unusual punishment to their constitutions. Finally, on 15 December 1791, the Eighth Amendment, echoing the English Bill of Rights and the Virginia Declaration of Rights, was ratified: "Excessive bail shall not be required, nor excessive fines imposed, nor cruel and unusual punishments inflicted."

The meaning of this ban was not clear in 1791, and debate among scholars and jurists as to the original meaning of the clause has never ceased. Certainly, the framers of the Constitution did not intend to end capital punishment or all forms of corporal punishment. In 1791 citizens routinely witnessed public executions and whippings. Over a dozen offenses were punishable by hanging, and whipping, branding, and the pillory were widely accepted forms of punishment.

The First U.S. Supreme Court Interpretations

The Supreme Court's first attempt to interpret the meaning of the cruel-and-unusual-punishment clause came in *Wilkerson v. Utah* (1879), in which a condemned man challenged Utah's use of the firing squad as a method of execution. The Court noted that shooting was a common way to execute criminals and thus found execution by firing squad neither cruel nor unusual. The Court, however, commented that a punishment involving torture or some other type of "unnecessary cruelty" might, in some contexts, be defined as violating the Eighth Amendment.

Eleven years later, the Court considered whether or not executions in the newly invented electric chair qualified as cruel and unusual punishment. In *In re Kemmler* (1890) the Court refused to invalidate a death-by-electrocution statute. Instead, the Court commented on the quick and painless nature of death in the electric chair:

> Punishments are cruel when they involve torture or a lingering death; but the punishment of death is not cruel within the meaning of that word as used in the Constitution. It implies there something inhuman and barbarous, something more than the mere extinguishment of life.

In 1910 the Court broadened its previous interpretations of the Eighth Amendment by deciding that a punishment that involved neither torture nor a lingering death offended the proscription against cruel and unusual punishment. In *Weems v. United States* an American employed by the Philippine government had been convicted of falsifying an official document and condemned to twelve to twenty years' imprisonment while chained at ankle and wrist and sentenced to endure a long list of other hardships, including permanent loss of his rights to privacy and to participate in political activities. In finding a punishment cruel and unusual for the first time, the Court declared that future efforts to apply the Eighth Amendment should take into account the nature of the crime, the purpose of the law, and the severity of the penalty imposed.

The constitutionality of the death penalty was challenged—and upheld—in the 1947 case *Louisiana ex rel. Francis v. Resweber*. Willie Francis had been convicted of murder, sentenced to death, and led to the electric chair. However, the usually reliable mechanism failed to supply enough current to kill Francis, and an appeal was sought on Eighth Amendment grounds to prevent a second attempt. By a five-to-four vote, the Court declared that only "an unforeseeable accident prevented the prompt consummation of the sentence," that Francis would not be forced to undergo excessive pain, and that the authorities' intentions in adopting electrocution were humane. The two most significant developments in *Francis* were the majority's view that the legislative purpose of a punishment has a bearing on its validity and the nine justices' agreement that the cruel-and-unusual-punishment clause would prohibit a statute that was fashioned to inflict unnecessary pain.

The Supreme Court invoked the cruel-and-unusual-punishment clause in a way that puzzled many Court watchers in 1958 in *Trop v. Dulles*. The petitioner had been convicted of wartime desertion by a military court in 1944; consequently, his 1952 application for a passport was rejected on the ground that he had lost his U.S. citizenship and become stateless by reason of his wartime conviction. Chief Justice Earl Warren, in his plurality opinion, held that "the Eighth Amendment forbids Congress to punish by taking away citizenship." In so doing, he called attention to what has always been the most vexing problem of adjudicating the cruel-and-unusual-punishment clause—striking a balance between respect for the legislative prerogative to determine punishments and the diligence required by the judiciary's responsibility to preserve the Constitution's guarantees of individual rights against governmental encroachment.

In *Trop*, Warren resolved this problem by stating that the Eighth Amendment would be "little more than good advice" from the founding fathers to future legislators if the mere legislative authorization of a punishment automatically established its constitutional validity. Most important, Warren wrote that "the Amendment must draw its meaning from evolving standards of decency that mark the progress of a maturing society." The *Trop* decision, however, did not open the cruel-and-unusual-punishment clause to the broad application some had hoped for. The plurality opinion expressly pointed out that capital punishment "cannot be said to violate the constitutional concept of cruelty in a day when it is still widely accepted."

Four years later, in *Robinson v. California* (1962), the Court again found a punishment violative of the Eighth Amendment. Walter Lawrence Robinson had been convicted under a California statute that made his narcotic addiction a crime, and he had been sentenced to ninety days in jail. Writing for the majority, Justice Potter Stewart reiterated the theme of the plurality opinion in *Trop*: the Constitution's prohibition of cruel and unusual punishment was not a static concept but one which should be continually reexamined "in the light of contemporary human knowledge."

By punishing an individual who had become addicted to a narcotic, the state, according to the majority, had punished a status rather than an act. Importantly, the state law contained no remedial objectives. Thus, the Court repeated the theme expressed in *Francis* requiring scrutiny of the legislative intentions of a statute. The decision in *Robinson* also made it clear that the Fourteenth Amendment's due-process clause incorporated the cruel-and-unusual-punishment clause, thereby making it applicable to the states as well as to the federal government.

The Modern Era

Capital Punishment. After *Robinson*, most of the Court's Eighth Amendment decisions concerned the constitutional status of capital-punishment and death-penalty laws. In 1972 the Court's *Furman v. Georgia* decision temporarily halted all executions in the United States. But *Furman* did not hold that capital punishment in and of itself violated the Eighth Amendment. The Court held only that all then-existing state and federal death-penalty laws violated the cruel-and-unusual-punishment clause because they did not provide sufficient guidelines for judges and juries and therefore caused death sentences to be meted out in an arbitrary, capricious, and discriminatory manner. Four years later, in *Gregg v. Georgia* (1976), the Court upheld new death-penalty laws that require the jury (and in a few states, the judge) to conduct a separate sentencing hearing after a guilty verdict in order to consider "aggravating" and "mitigating" factors of the defendant's crime and character. Under most of these guided-discretion laws, the sentencing jury or judge is instructed to weigh all of the relevant facts and circumstances and to return a sentence of either death or life imprisonment.

On the same day that *Gregg* was announced, the Court struck down another type of death-penalty law that several states had enacted in the aftermath of *Furman*. In *Woodson v. North Carolina* (1976) a narrow majority declared mandatory death-penalty laws in violation of the Eighth Amendment because they undermined the *Gregg* mandate that capital sentencers consider all relevant information concerning the defendant's crime and character. After *Woodson*, the Court consistently invalidated mandatory death-penalty laws on Eighth Amendment grounds. In *Blystone v. Pennsylvania* (1990), however, the Court upheld a state death-penalty statute that, while not man-

datory, has an element of mandate in it: the statute requires capital juries to impose a death sentence if they find that aggravating circumstances outweigh mitigating circumstances.

For the most part, the contemporary Court has rejected Eighth Amendment challenges to the death penalty. For example, in *Penry v. Lynaugh* (1989) it upheld the death sentence of a man with the mental age of a six-year-old. And although the Court held that the proscription against cruel and unusual punishment bars the execution of fifteen-year-olds who commit crimes (*Thompson v. Oklahoma*, 1988), it refused to extend the same protection to sixteen- and seventeen-year-old offenders (*Stanford v. Kentucky*, 1989). In an important 1987 case, *McCleskey v. Kemp*, the Court held that statistical evidence of racial discrimination in capital sentencing is not, in and of itself, a violation of the Eighth or the Fourteenth Amendment. As of 1999, thirty-eight states and the federal government had capital-punishment laws, more than thirty-five hundred people were on death row, and it was highly unlikely that the Court would declare capital punishment violative of the ban on cruel and unusual punishment in the foreseeable future.

Prison Litigation. The proscription against cruel and unusual punishment played a significant role in prison-reform litigation in the second half of the twentieth century, but, as with capital punishment, a limit seemed to have been reached. Although numerous lower federal courts invoked the cruel-and-unusual-punishment clause to condemn prison conditions in the 1960s and 1970s, the Supreme Court did not find the Eighth Amendment applicable to prison conditions until *Estelle v. Gamble* in 1976. J. W. Gamble, an inmate in Texas, alleged that his Eighth Amendment rights had been violated because he received inadequate treatment for a painful back injury. The Court ruled that, under some circumstances, the failure to provide adequate medical care for prisoners violates the Eighth Amendment. The majority, however, made it clear that mere negligence or medical malpractice was not enough for an Eighth Amendment claim. Stressing that to invoke the Eighth Amendment prisoners must prove "deliberate indifference" on the part of prison officials to serious medical problems, the Court found that Gamble had failed to do so and rejected his claim.

In *Wilson v. Seiter* (1991) the Court held that the *Gamble* standard of deliberate indifference would be applied in all inmate conditions-of-confinement cases, not just medical-care cases. Thus, whether a lawsuit involves allegations of overcrowding, rotten food, poor ventilation, inadequate heating, unsanitary cells, or failure to protect inmates from other inmates, the plaintiff must show both that the alleged condition is present and that prison officials demonstrated deliberate indifference to it. The *Seiter* standard gives prison authorities latitude to cite inadequate funding as a defense, and the vast majority of conditions-of-confinement suits have been decided in favor of prison officials. Nevertheless, as of 30 June 1998, at least thirty-six states were under court order to improve conditions in one or more prisons.

The cruel-and-unusual-punishment clause also has been invoked in cases where prisoners claim to have been victimized by excessive and unnecessary use of force by prison staff. Although the Court has never decided whether the lawfully prescribed use of corporal punishment to discipline prisoners would violate the Eighth Amendment, the U.S. Court of Appeals for the Eighth Circuit held in *Jackson v. Bishop* (1968) that whipping or flogging prisoners was unconstitutional. As of 1999, no state or federal prison had corporal punishment as an official policy, but inmate allegations of improper use of force were common. In *Whitley v. Albers* (1986) the Supreme Court reviewed the case of a guard who in the course of trying to stop an inmate disturbance fired his shotgun and hit the left knee of a prisoner not involved in the disturbance. The guard was found not to have violated the inmate's Eighth Amendment rights because, as the majority explained, he had applied force in "a good faith effort to maintain or restore discipline" and not "maliciously and sadistically for the very purpose of causing harm."

This standard was applied to all inmate use-of-force claims in *Hudson v. McMillian* (1992). Two Louisiana prison guards beat Keith Hudson, a handcuffed and shackled prisoner, after one of them had argued with him. The guards' supervisor approved the beating, merely telling them "not to have too much fun." Hudson suffered minor bruises, facial swelling, loosened teeth, and a cracked dental plate. A federal magistrate found that the guards had violated Hudson's right to be free from cruel and unusual punishment and awarded him damages of $800. A federal appeals court reversed that finding, holding that prisoners who bring claims of excessive force in violation of the Eighth Amendment must prove "significant injury" and that Hudson's injuries were "minor" and

required no hospitalization. By a seven-to-two vote, the Supreme Court rejected the "significant injury" standard and held that even when significant injury is not proven, the malicious, sadistic, and purposeless use of force by prison staff amounts to cruel and unusual punishment. To hold otherwise, wrote Justice Sandra Day O'Connor in her majority opinion, "would permit any physical punishment, no matter how diabolic or inhumane, inflicting less than some arbitrary quantity of injury." She added that "such a result would have been as unacceptable to the drafters of the Eighth Amendment as it is today."

Conclusion

The *Hudson* ruling indicates that the Eighth Amendment provides a reasonable measure of protection to prisoners maliciously victimized by prison officials or staff. However, the Supreme Court has made it difficult for prisoners to challenge the imposition of unusually lengthy prison terms for relatively minor crimes on Eighth Amendment grounds.

For example, in *Harmelin v. Michigan* (1991), the Court rejected an Eighth Amendment claim brought by Ronald Harmelin, a forty-six-year-old air force veteran with no prior criminal record who was caught transporting 672.5 grams of cocaine for a drug dealer. Harmelin was subsequently convicted and sentenced under a Michigan statute that mandated life imprisonment without parole for anyone convicted of possessing 650 or more grams of cocaine.

The five justices of the *Harmelin* majority agreed that Harmelin's sentence could not be considered cruel and unusual, but the majority split in its reasoning. Justices Antonin Scalia and William Rehnquist argued that federal courts should never overturn a lawfully imposed prison sentence on the ground that it is disproportionate to the offense. In all such cases "the length of the sentence actually imposed is *purely* a matter of legislative prerogative."

The remaining members of the majority—Justices Anthony Kennedy, O'Connor, and David Souter—contended that there was a proportionality principle inherent in the Eighth Amendment but only a very narrow one. The ban on cruel and unusual punishment, they stressed, applies only to "exceedingly rare" cases in which prison sentences are grossly disproportionate to the crimes. Harmelin's sentence, they concluded, did not fall into this category, primarily because his crime was "extremely serious" in that the cocaine could have led to other crimes, including drug-related violence.

By the end of the twentieth century, the era of Eighth Amendment activism exemplified by cases such as *Trop v. Dulles* (1958) and *Robinson v. California* (1962) appeared over. Perhaps the most telling evidence was Justice Scalia's plurality opinion in *Stanford v. Kentucky* (1989). In justifying the Court's repudiation of arguments against executing sixteen- and seventeen-year-olds, Scalia pointedly noted in *dicta* (comments not essential to the holding and without the force of law) that the language of the Eighth Amendment "proscribes only those punishments that are both 'cruel and unusual.'" In other words, Scalia left open the possibility that a future Court might uphold the constitutionality of a punishment conceded to be cruel if it is frequently imposed. It is not at all clear that the framers of the Eighth Amendment intended to sanction punishments that were cruel but not unusual, but as of 1999 it appeared that the Court might very well do so in the not-too-distant future.

BIBLIOGRAPHY

Berkson, Larry Charles. *The Concept of Cruel and Unusual Punishment.* Lexington, Mass.: D. C. Heath, 1975.

Branham, Lynn S., and Sheldon Krantz. *The Law of Sentencing, Corrections, and Prisoners' Rights.* 5th ed. St. Paul, Minn.: West Group, 1997.

Coyne, Randall, and Lyn Entzeroth. *Capital Punishment and the Judicial Process.* Durham, N.C.: Carolina Academic Press, 1994.

Granucci, Anthony F. "'Nor Cruel and Unusual Punishments Inflicted': The Original Meaning." *California Law Review* 57 (1969).

Hoffmann, Joseph L. "The 'Cruel and Unusual Punishment' Clause: A Limit on the Power to Punish or Constitutional Rhetoric?" In *The Bill of Rights in Modern America: After Two Hundred Years,* edited by David J. Bodenhamer and James W. Ely, Jr. Bloomington: Indiana University Press, 1993.

KENNETH C. HAAS

See also **Capital Punishment; Corporal Punishment; Death Row; Execution, Methods of; Prisons: Prison Conditions; Sentencing; Tarring and Feathering.**

CUBAN AMERICANS

Cuban immigrants in the United States have been both the victims and the perpetrators of violence directed at advocates of liberal and radical causes. In the late nineteenth and early twentieth centuries, Cuban cigar workers in Florida came under attack for supporting militant trade unionism and radical ideologies. Following the Cuban Revolution of 1959, Cuban exiles in the United States employed violence against individuals, especially fellow Cuban Americans, who support improved relations with Cuba.

Antilabor Violence

Nineteenth-century migrants from Cuba followed the cigar industry to Florida when cigar manufacturers from Havana relocated their factories first to Key West during the 1860s and then to Tampa during the 1880s, searching for unrestricted markets and labor peace. These Cuban cigar makers who produced luxury hand-rolled cigars brought with them a commitment to trade unionism and various radical ideologies, including socialism, that led to confrontations with employers and their allies among local elites. In addition, Cuban workers supported Cuba's independence from Spain, the birthplace of most of the cigar manufacturers who opened factories in Tampa and who hired Spanish-born workers for some of the most coveted positions, such as factory foreman.

Conflicts over issues of class and nationhood erupted in Florida and occasionally led to violence and repression by vigilantes. In 1887 two Cubans were arrested in Tampa for the murder of a fellow cigar worker in a union dispute. When hostility between Cuban and Spanish workers continued to disrupt production in the cigar factories that had recently opened in Tampa, leading businessmen organized a vigilance committee that forced nine Cuban union leaders to leave Tampa. In 1892, following a series of strikes and violent encounters between Cuban and Spanish cigar workers, Tampa businessmen organized another vigilance committee to police the cigar industry. Tampa cigar workers subsequently formed La Resistencia, a radical union that sought "to resist the exploitation of labor by capital," and in 1901 they struck in support of a closed shop to restrict employment to union members. Once again they encountered repression. An armed Citizens' Committee kidnapped fifteen Resistencia leaders, most of them Cubans, and put thirteen of them on a chartered ship that dumped them in Honduras with a warning never to return to Tampa. During subsequent strikes in 1910 and 1921 vigilantes again intimidated striking cigar workers and forced at least one Cuban-born union leader to leave Tampa.

Immigrant cigar workers lost every one of these Tampa strikes, in part because of the intervention of members of the local elite, who organized vigilance committees that used violence and threats of violence to break strikes by the largely Cuban workforce. Although often identified by name in the press, vigilantes escaped prosecution because they were prominent citizens who worked in league with government officials.

Anti-Castro Terrorism

The Cuban Revolution of 1959 produced another exodus of refugees to the United States. Their growing communities in south Florida and New York City's metropolitan area provided strong support for U.S. policies against the government of Fidel Castro, notably the failed invasion at the Bay of Pigs in 1961 and the subsequent embargo on trade. Cuban exiles, including veterans of the Bay of Pigs, also mounted a campaign of terror against Cuban targets in the United States and against anyone who sought dialogue with Cuba. After several isolated incidents in the 1960s, the domestic violence reached its peak in the 1970s when the United States and some Cuban Americans took steps to improve relations with Cuba. Between 1973 and 1976, one hundred bombs exploded in the Miami area, which the Federal Bureau of Investigation called "the terrorist capital of the United States" (García 1996, p. 141). These attacks took the lives of several Cuban Americans and blew off the legs of a Spanish-language radio commentator who spoke out against the terrorism. Following talks in Havana during 1978 between Cuban officials and a delegation of Cubans living in the United States, prominent members of the delegation, known as the Committee of 75, came under attack, and bombs exploded at their homes and businesses in the Miami area.

A similar wave of violence swept through New York City and northern New Jersey, which had the country's largest Cuban community outside south Florida. From 1975 to 1980, some twenty bombs exploded at sites such as the diplomatic missions of Cuba and the Soviet Union, Lincoln Center, where Cuban artists performed, and the offices of New York's most prominent Spanish-language newspaper, which supported travel to Cuba. Responsibility for these acts was claimed by a group of Cuban extremists calling themselves Omega 7, which also killed a member of the Committee of 75 living in New Jersey and a minor Cuban diplomat based in New York. Some fifteen members of Omega 7 were arrested and convicted, including

three Cubans who participated in the 1976 bombing death of Orlando Letelier, a former Chilean diplomat living in Washington, D.C. At the time the FBI called Omega 7 the most dangerous terrorist organization in the country.

During the 1980s, when the Reagan administration proved sympathetic to exile groups demanding a hard line against Cuba, the incidence of violence by anti-Castro Cubans temporarily declined, but it revived in 1988 following renewed calls for dialogue by other Cuban Americans. In Miami bombs exploded at the Cuban Museum of Art and Culture, which displayed works by Cuban artists, at the home of a professor who organized a conference on U.S.–Cuban relations, and at a travel agency offering trips to Cuba. When the *Miami Herald* opposed federal legislation tightening the embargo against Cuba in 1992, the Cuban American National Foundation organized a boycott of the paper, and its vending machines were vandalized. These attacks led Americas Watch, a division of Human Rights Watch, to condemn Miami's "repressive climate for freedom of expression" (*New York Times*, 19 August 1992, p. 18). Given the number of unsolved bombings and the level of intimidation, Americas Watch expressed concern that government authorities had failed to prosecute those responsible.

Since the 1880s official inaction in the face of criminal acts helps explain the prevalence of violence to repress Cubans in the United States who advocated change. The one significant difference is that since 1959 Cubans and Cuban Americans have been not only the victims but also the perpetrators of repressive violence that has gone largely unpunished.

BIBLIOGRAPHY

Bardach, Ann Louise. "Our Man in Miami." *New Republic,* 3 October 1994.

García, María Cristina. *Havana USA: Cuban Exiles and Cuban Americans in South Florida, 1959–1994.* Berkeley: University of California Press, 1996.

Ingalls, Robert P. *Urban Vigilantes in the New South: Tampa, 1882–1936.* Knoxville: University of Tennessee Press, 1988.

ROBERT P. INGALLS

See also **Immigration; Labor and Unions; Miami.**

CUBAN MISSILE CRISIS

The Cuban Missile Crisis occurred in October 1962 when the United States demanded the withdrawal of nuclear-capable missiles that the Soviet Union had placed in Cuba. Fidel Castro's radical Cuban government alarmed U.S. officials because it advocated revolution throughout Latin America and because Castro had built economic and military ties with the Soviet Union, the United States' primary Cold War adversary. Since 1959, when Castro came to power after driving out U.S. ally Fulgencio Batista's regime, the Eisenhower and Kennedy administrations had sought to intimidate, weaken, and overthrow Castro's government using any means: hit-and-run raids carried out by Cuban exiles backed by the Central Intelligence Agency; assassination plots against Castro; economic embargo; the Bay of Pigs invasion; military maneuvers in the Caribbean; contingency plans for a U.S. invasion; the ousting of Cuba from the Organization of American States; and, under Operation Mongoose, the sabotage of Cuban facilities. "If I had been in Moscow and Havana at that time [1962]," Secretary of Defense Robert McNamara later remarked, "I would have believed the Americans were preparing for an invasion."

Soviet Missiles and American Options

In the summer of 1962, Cuba and the Soviet Union, at the height of the U.S. multitrack campaign to unseat Castro, struck an agreement intended to deter invasion: the Soviets would install on the island forty-eight medium-range ballistic missiles (SS-4s with a range of 1,020 miles), thirty-two intermediate-range ballistic missiles (SS-5s with a range of 2,200 miles), numerous surface-to-air missiles (SAMs), and forty-two light IL-28 bombers (with a range of 600 miles). Soviet Premier Nikita Khrushchev sought not only to defend Cuba but also to counter the threat of the U.S. Jupiter missiles deployed in Turkey and targeted against the Soviet Union. Khrushchev also calculated that missiles in Cuba would improve the Soviet ranking in the nuclear arms race.

As Republican Party partisans such as Senator Kenneth Keating of New York criticized President John F. Kennedy for tolerating a Soviet military buildup in Cuba, the CIA monitored the island with U-2 reconnaissance flights. On 14 October 1962 a U-2 spy plane photographed missile sites. Two days later, the president gathered a group of key advisers called the Executive Committee (ExComm) of the National Security Council and told it to find a way to force the missiles out of Cuba. For several days, Kennedy and ExComm debated options while the CIA predicted that the Soviet missiles could shortly become operational and

could reach as far as Dallas, Texas, and Washington, D.C., threatening ninety-five million Americans. Despite the case made by the Joint Chiefs of Staff for an air strike on the missile bases, ExComm advisers rejected this course because of the possibility that some missiles might survive and be fired against the United States. The president readied U.S. forces for an invasion, but he hesitated to exercise that option because of an expected high casualty rate and possible Soviet retaliatory action, perhaps against Berlin. (U.S. leaders did not know then that the Soviets had sent tactical nuclear weapons to Cuba to blunt an invasion or that more than forty thousand Soviet troops, not ten thousand as thought, stood ready on the island.) ExComm also discussed negotiations but shelved that option because U.S. officials refused to talk with Castro, and they feared that Khrushchev would drag them out. In the end, especially following the advice of Secretary of Defense Robert McNamara, Kennedy endorsed a naval blockade or "quarantine" to stop further Soviet military shipments and to force Khrushchev to retreat in the face of superior U.S. power in the region.

Losing Control and Defusing the Crisis

On 22 October 1962, having rejected private negotiations in favor of public confrontation, Kennedy announced the naval blockade on national radio and television. U.S. war vessels patrolled the Caribbean Sea to intercept ships and 140,000 U.S. troops assembled in Florida for a possible invasion of Cuba. Some observers sketched scenarios of a nuclear holocaust. Moscow denounced the blockade as a violation of international law and an intrusion into sovereign Soviet-Cuban affairs. On 26 October 1962, in one of several letters that Khrushchev exchanged with Kennedy during the crisis, the Soviet premier proposed a deal: he would remove the "defensive" Soviet missiles if the United States pledged not to invade Cuba. The next day Khrushchev asked for more: the removal of the U.S. Jupiter missiles from Turkey. Meanwhile, the president's brother Attorney General Robert Kennedy met privately with Soviet Ambassador Anatoly Dobrynin, exploring the missile-swap option. That day, 27 October, the crisis escalated when a Soviet SAM shot down an American U-2 over Cuba and an Alaska-based U.S. spy plane strayed into Soviet territory. The crisis was "so near to spinning out of control," recalled National Security Adviser McGeorge Bundy.

President Kennedy then agreed to the no-invasion pledge in exchange for withdrawal of the

Soviet missiles. As part of the crisis-ending bargain, Robert Kennedy privately assured Dobrynin that the Jupiters in Turkey would be dismantled. On 28 October 1962 Khrushchev accepted these terms. He, too, feared losing control over events and over Castro, who might ignite some incident. The conclusion of the crisis proved messy. Not until mid-November did the Soviets agree to pull out the IL-28 bombers (the SS-5s had never arrived). Khrushchev had not consulted Castro, who resented the settlement and rejected UN on-site inspections that were to confirm missile removal. Although the missiles and bombers departed Cuba, a formal Soviet-American agreement was never signed, and Kennedy's public no-invasion pledge, issued at a press conference on 20 November 1962, included provisos.

Consequences

Taking credit for effective crisis management, Kennedy enhanced his carefully cultivated image as a bold, decisive leader. In retrospect, Kennedy's handling looks less impressive, as McNamara has put it, because of the "misinformation, miscalculation, misjudgment, and human fallibility" that dogged all leaders in the crisis and constantly raised the level of danger.

The outcome of the missile crisis both slowed and accelerated the Cold War. Having found communication difficult during the crisis, the two powers afterward installed a "hot line," or teletype link, between the White House and the Kremlin. After the crisis Kennedy's public comments raised questions as to whether or not he was seeking a thaw in the Cold War. Washington and Moscow did sign a Limited Test Ban Treaty on 5 August 1963. Some analysts have argued that Kennedy's success in driving the missiles from Cuba emboldened him to become more interventionist in Vietnam. U.S. policy toward Cuba became more hardline, with new assassination plots and CIA sabotage activities that aggravated Cuban-American relations for many more years. The Soviets vowed to end their nuclear inferiority by building more weapons, thus escalating the nuclear arms race. Soviet leaders in 1964 deposed Khrushchev, who could not claim a public victory for the secret deal requiring withdrawal of the Jupiters.

BIBLIOGRAPHY

Alison, Graham, and Philip Zelikow. *Essence of Decision: Explaining the Cuban Missile Crisis.* 2d ed. New York: Longman, 1999.

Blight, James G., Bruce J. Allyn, and David A. Welch. *Cuba on the Brink: Castro, the Missile Crisis, and the Soviet Collapse.* New York: Pantheon, 1993.

Blight, James G., and David A. Welch. *On the Brink: Americans and Soviets Reexamine the Cuban Missile Crisis.* New York: Hill and Wang, 1989.

Chang, Laurence, and Peter Kornbluh, eds. *The Cuban Missile Crisis, 1962: A National Security Archive Documents Reader.* New York: New Press, 1992.

Fursenko, Alexandr, and Timothy Naftali. *One Hell of a Gamble: Khrushchev, Castro and Kennedy, 1958–1964.* New York: Norton, 1997.

May, Ernest R., and Philip D. Zelikow, eds. *The Kennedy Tapes: Inside the White House During the Cuban Missile Crisis.* Cambridge, Mass.: Belknap Press of Harvard University Press, 1997.

Nathan, James, ed. *The Cuban Missile Crisis Revisited.* New York: St. Martin's, 1992.

Paterson, Thomas G. *Contesting Castro: The United States and the Triumph of the Cuban Revolution.* New York: Oxford University Press, 1994.

THOMAS G. PATERSON

See also **Central Intelligence Agency; Cold War; Cuban Americans; Foreign Intervention, Fear of; Kennedy, John F.**

CULTS

The November 1978 mass suicide of nearly one thousand members of the People's Temple in Jonestown, Guyana, established an indelible link between cults and violence. That connection was strengthened when seventy-four Branch Davidians perished in flames outside Waco, Texas, in April 1993 and when thirty-nine followers of Marshall Applewhite gave their lives in order to reach the "evolutionary level beyond human" in the Heaven's Gate incident of 1997. Although those three examples suggest that there may be an inherent connection between violence and groups identified as cults, there are actually thousands of new and alternative religious groups in the United States, the overwhelming majority of which conduct themselves peacefully. A fuller account of the nature and activities of cults is needed in order to put any incidents of cult violence into perspective.

Defining Cults

Since the mid-1970s a loose coalition of former members of cults, aggrieved parents of cult members, mental health professionals, law enforcement officials, and others has aggressively attempted to portray many new religious movements as cults.

They argue that cults have proliferated in the late twentieth century and that they constitute urgent social, political, economic, religious, and public health problems. The danger of cults lies in a psychological manipulation that opponents describe as brainwashing, thought reform, or coercive persuasion, which is exercised by leaders who are so powerful as to be literally irresistible. The victims suffer psychological violence and physical deprivation, lose their sense of self, and adopt new, externally imposed identities. They become, in effect, pawns of the unscrupulous cult leader (usually a man), willing to die, or even to kill, for him.

Although the negative view of cults has enjoyed wide currency in the news media and among certain professions (such as law enforcement and among some psychologists), it has been vigorously opposed by new religious groups themselves and by many academics in sociology and religious studies. Those who oppose the prevailing popular understanding have forcefully argued that brainwashing and its associated concepts provide an inadequate descriptive and theoretical account of conversion, that the interaction between leaders and followers cannot accurately be described solely as manipulation, and that participation in a new religious group is most often the result of conscious choice. They prefer terms like "new religious movement," a relatively value-free category. They also promote historical and cross-cultural comparisons, since new religions have been prominent in the last third of the twentieth century in U.S. history. The Church of Jesus Christ of Latter-day Saints, for example, is a vigorous world religion that began in New York State in the mid-nineteenth century. Those who reject the "cult" stereotype also stress the dynamic nature of new religions; imported or homegrown religious movements can lose their novelty and achieve wide acceptance, just as sects can move so far from their parent bodies that they become new religions. The term *cult*, therefore, is highly problematic. There are significant disputes about its precise definition, and it is often used in polemical, rather than descriptive and analytical, contexts. It offers a very unsteady platform from which to assess the connections between certain religious groups and violence.

Throughout history new religious groups have suffered persecution and violence; the murder of the Mormon prophet Joseph Smith is only one example. Also, millenarian groups, like the Jehovah's Witnesses, the Branch Davidians, and the Church

A member of the Children of God, a radical communal sect, holds a vigil in New York City near the United Nations headquarters to warn fellow Americans to leave the country. Members of the sect believed that the comet Kohoutek, which appeared in the skies in January of 1974, was a sign of impending disaster for the United States. CORBIS/BETTMANN

Universal and Triumphant of Elizabeth Claire Prophet, have frequently anticipated the eschatological violence of God's coming judgment. On occasion, groups or individuals have committed violent acts, either against themselves or others, which they perceived as being expressions of their religious convictions. But the widespread academic rejection of the negative stereotype of cults, including their intrinsic link to violence, underscores the need for more nuanced explanations. In order to appreciate the distinctiveness of each group within its appropriate context, it is helpful to distinguish rhetorical, episodic, programmatic, and defensive forms of violence, to identify carefully the perpetrators and victims, and to determine to what extent violent actions are intrinsically related to the beliefs and practices of any group.

Religious groups outside the mainstream often use violent rhetoric. Isolated in a hostile world, members feel duty-bound to express God's judgment on the intellectual poverty, moral laxity, and religious errors of the majority even as they attempt to draw more recruits. Especially those groups that expect the imminent end of the world may depict their mission in military terms to emphasize its urgency. The Branch Davidian leader David Koresh, for example, asserted that "theology really is life and death" and expected the apocalyptic battle of Armageddon to be fought in his lifetime. In contrast, isolated episodes of violence that have no central justification in a group's religious worldview reveal more about individual actors than the group to which they belong. Programmatic violence, however, refers to acts undertaken as the necessary expression of a group's beliefs. For example, several contemporary groups or individuals on the American radical right base their calls for an apocalyptic race war on novel and idiosyncratic understandings of either Christian or Aryan mythology. Finally, defensive violence refers to actions taken by groups in response to imagined, anticipated, or actual attacks by outside forces. Different kinds of violence may well be intertwined, as the following examples illustrate.

Jonestown

For most of its history the People's Temple received public praise, particularly for its advocacy of racial integration. Founded by Jim Jones in 1955, the group moved away from mainstream Christianity as Jones became increasingly worried about nuclear war, enamored of socialism, and convinced of his own messianic mission. In 1977 Jones responded defensively to increasing criticism by moving the entire community from California to an outpost in Guyana (a republic in northeastern South America, between Venezuela and Suriname). But the group remained dogged by accusations from concerned relatives and by government investigations. As external pressures mounted and defections from his inner circle occurred, Jones began to envision a mass suicide as a way of preserving the integrity of his utopian community. During the final "white night" at Jonestown, in Guyana, Jones justified the deadly attack on the U.S. congressman Leo Ryan's entourage as a reaction against the attempt to remove people from the community. (Ryan had gone to Jonestown on a fact-finding mission even though Jonestown had initially refused him permission to visit. Members of his group included concerned relatives hoping to persuade family members to leave with them.) As men, women, and children were dying all around him from having drunk or injected themselves with a soft drink laced with cyanide and tranquilizers, Jones finally exhorted his followers to commit "revolutionary suicide" as a protest against an inhumane world. Although most of the People's Temple's violence was directed inward toward themselves, it was also symbolically intended to strike at external enemies.

Feeling besieged from without and betrayed from within, Jones tried to lead his followers through death to another world. The violent end of the People's Temple was the result of a complex set of specific interlocking factors, including the geographical isolation of the community, Jones's deteriorating physical and mental health, the pressure applied by the concerned relatives and the U.S. government, and the dedication of the People's Temple members to Divine Socialism, an ideology that mixed Jones's interpretative Marxist and socialist doctrine with his ideosyncratic gnostic mythology and his claim to be the messiah.

Waco

The Branch Davidians located themselves within a 150-year-old Adventist tradition that was saturated with biblical apocalyptic rhetoric. Throughout the Bible studies that were David Koresh's characteristic mode of teaching, his conversations with federal agents during the fifty-one-day siege at the Mount Carmel Center, and his partially completed manuscript on the Seven Seals, Koresh consistently reserved for God the execution of the final judgment and repudiated retaliatory violence against his enemies. Koresh's teachings gave little reason to anticipate that either he or the Branch Davidians would lash out violently at anyone. The causes of the violence during the initial raid of the Bureau of Alcohol, Tobacco, and Firearms (BATF) on 28 February 1993 and throughout the fifty-one-day siege of the Mount Carmel Center were not central to Koresh's theology.

How one evaluates the conflicting claims of the Branch Davidians and of the outsiders will determine whether the violence of the raid and siege is considered defensive or programmatic. As at

Jonestown, the violence at Mount Carmel should be understood as the result of factors specific to the group, including the eagerness of the BATF for a televised success, the impenetrability of Davidian doctrine to outsiders, the "gun culture" of rural Texas, the failure of the Federal Bureau of Investigation's behavioral scientists and negotiators to persuade tactical forces to wait, and the climate of fear surrounding cults in the fifteen years since Jonestown.

Heaven's Gate

Like the Branch Davidians, the followers of Marshall "Do" Applewhite and Bonnie Lu "Ti" Nettles believed that this earth was in its final days. Followers of "the Two" saw themselves as a small elite besieged by human and cosmic enemies, all of whom would soon be annihilated. To be saved one would have to become a student of a representative of the Next Level, overcome one's mammalian nature, and train one's soul to become a match for a new, perfect body in the Kingdom.

Like Jim Jones, Applewhite redefined suicide. Because he believed that bodies were only containers for souls, suicide became a desired transformation, a way of realizing one's full potential. The Two and their followers did not see themselves as enacting the violent final judgment on this civilization. In fact, they did not conceive their own actions as violent at all, preferring instead to see them as a "willful exit of the body." In one of their final messages they claimed that "the true meaning of 'suicide' is *to turn against the Next Level when it is being offered*." Although the group expressed some concern about hostile outsiders, it did not experience the same kind of immediate, forceful external pressure that the People's Temple and the Branch Davidians did. Applewhite's followers embraced suicide as a programmatic necessity, a bridge to the Next Level, and a final demonstration of all that they had learned.

Christian Identity and the Radical Right

The Oklahoma City bombing (19 April 1995) and other acts of domestic terrorism have brought to light in the mid-1990s a shadowy world of militias, tax-resisters, self-styled patriots, constitutionalists, and others on the radical right. Religion is often an essential part of their ideologies. Despite their often extreme differences, many independent Christian Identity churches, for example, blend the conviction that Europeans are the descendants of the lost tribes of Israel with virulent racism and anti-Semitism, an abiding hostility to the Zionist Occupation Government (ZOG) of the United States, and an image of a militant, revolutionary Jesus. Alongside Identity churches are individuals and groups who treat the preservation of the white race as a sacred duty and find inspiration for their crusade in Aryan mythology. Violent rhetoric abounds on the radical right, both in the appropriation of biblical, apocalyptic imagery and in the calls for radical action. For example, the hero of *The Turner Diaries,* an influential novel about the Second American Revolution, embraces a bloody struggle to reclaim America for the white race. Similarly, the Identity church group the Covenant, the Sword, and the Arm of the Lord looked forward to an apocalyptic battle between the children of God and the spawn of Satan. Despite the ubiquitous violent rhetoric, however, there have been few instances of sustained programmatic violence on the radical right. One episode that stands out, however, is the crusade of the Bruders Schweigen (Silent Brotherhood), also known as the Order. Founded in 1983 by Robert Jay Mathews, the Order financed its revolutionary campaign against ZOG with several armored-car robberies. As in the previous cases, however, the factors that led the Order from rhetorical to programmatic violence were specific to its leadership, members, and situation.

Conclusion

While violent rhetoric often appears in small religious groups outside the mainstream, actual programmatic violence occurs much less frequently. Even on the radical right, federal initiatives, such as the siege of the Weaver family's cabin in Ruby Ridge, Idaho, in August 1992, suggest that groups may be the victims of officially sanctioned violence, rather than its initiators. At Ruby Ridge, U.S. Marshal William Degan and fourteen-year-old Sammy Weaver died in a gun battle when the marshals attempted to arrest Randy Weaver for failing to appear in court on gun charges. One day later, Weaver's wife, Vicki, was killed by FBI sharpshooter Lon Horiuchi. Defensive violence, especially by groups that already feel themselves to be persecuted minorities, is more widespread. The successful ending of the standoff between federal agents and the Montana Freemen in 1996, however, suggests that government agents may have grown more adept at defusing potentially violent situations by exercising patience, continuing to negotiate, maintaining a loose perimeter, avoiding the escalation of tactical pressure, and refusing to amplify the believers' feelings of persecution.

In addition to the complexity, diversity, and long history of new religious movements in the United States, those who would link cults and violence need to recognize that established religions are no strangers to violence, as events in Ireland, Israel, and India in the twentieth century indicate. While some would want to characterize violence in mainstream religions as a peripheral phenomenon, a sustained consideration of those traditions reveals a more complicated situation. Thus, because of the nature of religion itself, the diversity of new religious movements, and the complicated nature of the situations in which violence does occur, there can be no simple characterization of the links between cults and violence.

BIBLIOGRAPHY

Barkun, Michael. *Religion and the Racist Right: The Origins of the Christian Identity Movement.* Chapel Hill: University of North Carolina Press, 1994.

Chidester, David. *Salvation and Suicide: An Interpretation of Jim Jones, the People's Temple, and Jonestown.* Bloomington: Indiana University Press, 1988.

Gallagher, Eugene V. "God and Country: Revolution as a Religious Imperative on the Radical Right." *Terrorism and Political Violence* 9 (1997): 63–79.

Hall, John R. *Gone from the Promised Land: Jonestown in American Cultural History.* New Brunswick, N.J.: Transaction Books, 1989.

Kaplan, Jeffrey. *Radical Religion in America: Millenarian Movements from the Far Right to the Children of Noah.* Syracuse, N.Y.: Syracuse University Press, 1997.

Singer, Margaret T. *Cults in Our Midst: The Hidden Menace in Our Everyday Lives.* San Francisco: Jossey-Bass, 1995.

Smith, Jonathan Z. "The Devil in Mr. Jones." In *Imagining Religion: From Babylon to Jonestown,* by Jonathan Z. Smith. Chicago: University of Chicago Press, 1982.

Stark, Rodney, and William Sims Bainbridge. *The Future of Religion: Secularization, Revival, and Cult Formation.* Berkeley: University of California Press, 1985.

Tabor, James D., and Eugene V. Gallagher. *Why Waco? Cults and the Battle for Religious Freedom in America.* Berkeley: University of California, 1995.

Wessinger, Catherine. *When the Millennium Comes Violently.* Chappaqua, N.Y.: Seven Bridges, 1999.

———, ed. *Millennialism, Persecution, and Violence.* Syracuse, N.Y.: Syracuse University Press, 1999.

EUGENE V. GALLAGHER

See also **Extremism; Heaven's Gate; Jonestown; Koresh, David; Religion; Ruby Ridge; Waco; Wovoka.**

CUNANAN, ANDREW
(1969–1997)

Andrew Cunanan, the spree killer who gained worldwide notoriety in the summer of 1997 after murdering the fashion designer Gianni Versace, grew up in Rancho Bernardo, California, an upscale suburb of San Diego. He attended an elite preparatory school in La Jolla, California, where he distinguished himself by his flamboyant behavior. In 1988, when Cunanan was a nineteen-year-old freshman at the University of California at San Diego, his father, a stockbroker who had been accused of embezzlement, fled to Manila in the Philippines, plunging the family into hardship. Cunanan dropped out of school to join his father but soon returned to the States.

By the early 1990s Cunanan had become a conspicuous figure on the San Francisco gay scene. Assuming a variety of guises—a Hollywood mogul with a mansion on the Riviera, a naval officer, and a graduate of Choate and Yale University—

A photograph of Andrew Cunanan that appeared on FBI posters in 1997. FBI/GAMMA LIAISON

he dined at the trendiest restaurants, dressed impeccably in blazers and ascots, and drank only the finest champagne. In truth, the unemployed Cunanan was entirely dependent on the largesse of others. Though his mother would later describe him as a "high-class male prostitute," Cunanan was in fact a gay gigolo—the kept companion of a succession of older, wealthy men. By the fall of 1996, however, something caused Cunanan's world to fall apart. Seemingly overnight, he went from a life of comfort and glamour to a sordid, desperate existence.

In mid-April 1997 Cunanan traveled to Minneapolis to visit a former lover, David Madson, an architect. Two nights after his arrival Cunanan invited a twenty-eight-year-old friend named Jeffrey Trail to Madson's apartment. Later that evening, neighbors reportedly heard violent shouting and loud thuds coming from the location. Two days later the police found Trail's body rolled up in a carpet in Madson's apartment. He had been savagely bludgeoned with a hammer. Two days after this discovery Cunanan drove with Madson to a lake about fifty miles north of Minneapolis and—using a handgun that had belonged to Trail—fired several .40-caliber bullets into Madson's head.

By the time a fisherman discovered Madson's corpse, Cunanan had fled in the victim's red Jeep. He next turned up in Chicago, where he gained entrance to the home of a seventy-two-year-old real estate mogul named Lee Miglin. For reasons unknown, he subjected Miglin to a horrific form of torture, wrapping the victim's head in duct tape, then stabbing him with pruning shears before sawing open his throat. Heading east in Miglin's 1994 Lexus, Cunanan next killed a forty-five-year-old cemetery caretaker named William Reese in Pennsville, New Jersey, shooting the victim in the head. He then made off in Reese's red Chevrolet pickup.

With the killing of Reese, Cunanan earned a spot on the Federal Bureau of Investigation's Ten Most Wanted list. Making his way south, he eventually arrived in Miami Beach, Florida, where he checked into a down-at-the-heels hotel on 12 May. In early June he moved his stolen pickup to a South Beach parking garage, two blocks from Gianni Versace's palatial residence, Casa Casuarina. At about 8:30 A.M. on Tuesday, 14 July, Versace—following his morning routine—stepped out to purchase coffee and magazines at a local café. Returning home, Versace was opening the front gates of his estate when Cunanan strode up and shot him twice in

the head with a .40-caliber pistol. Cunanan then fled into a nearby parking garage, where police investigators subsequently found the stolen red pickup. Inside the truck were Cunanan's passport and bloody clothes.

During the manhunt that followed Versace's murder, Cunanan proved maddeningly elusive, spurring a media frenzy. Although the public quickly demonized Cunanan, endowing him with almost supernatural powers of both omnipotence and ubiquity (countless Cunanan sightings poured in from every state to FBI offices and the Miami Police Department), his ability to elude capture had more to do with police blunders and bad luck than with any particular cunning of his own. Indeed, most authorities agreed by then that Cunanan fit the profile of an out-of-control spree killer whose rampage was likely to climax with his death, either by his own hand or in a shoot-out with law enforcement.

That prediction bore out on Wednesday, 25 July, when the caretaker of a houseboat docked in a marina forty blocks from the site of Versace's murder entered the vessel and found evidence of an intruder. As the man left the boat to call the police, he heard a single gunshot. When SWAT team members entered the houseboat several hours later, they found Cunanan sprawled on a bed, dressed only in boxer shorts. He had shot himself in the mouth, foreclosing the possibility that the world would ever learn what had triggered his rampage.

BIBLIOGRAPHY

Chua-Eoan, Howard. "Dead Men Tell No Tales." *Time*, 4 August 1997.
Lacayo, Richard. "Tagged for Murder." *Time*, 28 July 1997.
Lambert, Pam. "Point Blank." *People*, 28 July 1997.
Orth, Maureen. *Vulgar Favors: Andrew Cunanan, Gianni Versace, and the Largest Failed Manhunt in U.S. History.* New York: Delacorte, 1999.
Schechter, Harold, and David Everitt. *The A to Z Encyclopedia of Serial Killers.* New York: Pocket, 1997.
Thomas, Evans. "End of the Road." *Newsweek*, 4 August 1997.

HAROLD SCHECHTER

See also **Serial Killers.**

CURSES, HEXES, AND CHARMS. *See* Folk Culture.

CUSTER, GEORGE ARMSTRONG
(1839–1876)

The most famous and controversial of the army's Indian-fighting officers, George Armstrong Custer has been alternately glorified and vilified for his campaigns against Native Americans. In 1868 he won a major victory against Black Kettle's Southern Cheyenne followers along the banks of the Washita River in Indian Territory. Eight years later, however, his entire command was shattered by Lakota and Northern Cheyenne warriors at the Little Bighorn River in Montana.

Born on 5 December 1839 in New Rumley, Ohio, Custer received an appointment to the U.S. Military Academy in 1857. Habitually in danger of expulsion for his poor conduct, he graduated in 1861, ranked last in his class of thirty-four. Custer served as a staff officer in the Union Army of the Potomac until June 1863, when he was named brigadier general at the tender age of twenty-three. Tenacious, courageous, and audacious during the battles of Gettysburg, Yellow Tavern, and Trevillian Station and throughout the Shenandoah Valley campaigns, he emerged from the Civil War a major general.

For Custer it had been a glorious war, but the next decade proved much more difficult. The much reduced postwar army left him only a lieutenant colonel in the Seventh Cavalry Regiment. Since his colonels (Andrew Jackson Smith was succeeded in 1869 by Samuel Sturgis) were usually absent, Custer was the unit's de facto commanding officer. But overseeing seven hundred troops scattered among several western posts hardly compared to the glories of his Civil War years. He first led troops against Indians in 1867 as part of General Winfield Scott Hancock's campaign into central Kansas. Frustrated by his inability to catch his more mobile enemies, in mid-July Custer left his command in order to dash across Kansas to see his wife. A military court found him guilty of having been absent without leave but handed down a relatively light punishment of one year's suspension from the army.

Despite the court-martial Custer remained a favorite of General Philip Sheridan, under whom he had served during the Civil War. In the fall of 1868, Custer spearheaded Sheridan's winter campaign into Indian Territory. Discovering an Indian village along the Washita River, on 27 November, Custer struck at dawn. Coming from four different directions, the Seventh Cavalry quickly overran resis-

George Armstrong Custer, 1872. LIBRARY OF CONGRESS

tance, with Indian casualties probably numbering over one hundred. Fearing that enemy forces from nearby encampments would make a counterstrike, he ordered the village burned and escaped to safety. His victory was marred, however, by the death of Major Joel Elliott and nineteen troopers, who had been out of contact with Custer as the main column withdrew and were later found to have been killed.

In 1873 Custer participated in the army's Yellowstone Expedition, designed to further the westward expansion of the Northern Pacific Railroad. The following year he commanded an expedition into the Black Hills, during which prospectors accompanying Custer discovered traces of gold. Public pressure to open the region, once reserved for Native Americans, led to open warfare by 1876. Custer nearly missed the campaign because his public denunciations of corruption within the Grant Administration had led the president to remove him from command. He was restored to combat duty only through the personal intercession of General Sheridan and General Alfred Terry, who was to lead one of the army's three columns but had no experience fighting Indians.

The campaign began in earnest in May 1876. Hoping to track down the enemy, Custer, leading 655 men, cut loose from Terry's main column and moved up Rosebud Creek. On the morning of 25 June, scouts discovered signs of an Indian encampment along the Little Bighorn River. Fearing that a delay might allow the enemy to escape, relying on experience suggesting that Indian groups rarely cooperated with one another, and hoping that some spectacular deed might restore his reputation, Custer opted for an immediate attack. He divided his force in hopes of converging upon the surprised Indians from different directions, as he had at the Washita.

But circumstances were different this time. The Lakota and Northern Cheyenne had remained together. With numbers estimated at anywhere from fifteen hundred to seven thousand, the Indians repulsed Major Marcus A. Reno's detachment as it began its attack from the east. Three companies with Captain Frederick W. Benteen managed to reinforce Reno but did nothing to relieve the pressure on Custer, whose two hundred scouts and soldiers were maneuvering north of the Indian encampment. Badly outnumbered and hampered by the broken terrain, Custer's column was wiped out; not a single soldier survived. Custer's body was later found among a circle of troopers who had killed their horses to form a rude breastwork near the crest of the battlefield's highest point, now known as Custer Hill.

Controversy has dogged subsequent portrayals of Custer and his "last stand." Those sympathetic to Custer blame Reno and Benteen for failing to pressure the Indians sufficiently, thus allowing the full weight of the tribes to be concentrated against Custer. Others, however, have asserted that Custer was the victim of his own rash actions. By dividing his command in the face of the enemy and attacking without proper reconnaissance, his critics contend, Custer had violated fundamental rules of warfare. A few even charge that Custer committed suicide.

Reality probably lies somewhere between these extremes. Most serious scholars now believe that Custer fell during the middle of the battle, with many of his command later dying in an unsuccessful breakout attempt through Deep Ravine. Reno and Benteen were encountering enough troubles of their own; had they joined Custer, they might have suffered a similar fate. Rash as it may seem, Custer's decision to attack immediately was based upon his frontier experience, which had taught him the importance of decisive action and the element of surprise. This time, however, the Lakota and Northern Cheyenne had gathered in unusually large numbers and were confident of victory, having recently defeated another army column at the Battle of the Rosebud. And although many in the Seventh Cavalry panicked in the face of the approaching disaster, no credible evidence suggests that Custer died in a manner other than what would be expected from a man who loved warfare and whose career had been built upon violence—fighting to the end.

During his lifetime George Custer was a ceaseless self-promoter, a project that his wife, Libbie, enthusiastically assumed after his death. His raffish appearance—from the black velvet, gold-trimmed coat he wore during the Civil War to the fringed buckskin suit he often donned in the West, crowned by a flowing, reddish-blonde mane—was a calculated attempt to draw attention to himself. As the subject of countless books and movies, Custer has become enshrouded in legend and stereotype. The interest in Custer and his "last stand" says much about America's interest in violence. Perhaps, however, it might be most fruitful to see the Battle of Little Bighorn not through the prism of the defeat of Custer, but as a victory for the Indians.

BIBLIOGRAPHY

Gray, John S. *Custer's Last Campaign: Mitch Boyer and the Little Bighorn Reconstructed.* Lincoln: University of Nebraska Press, 1991.

Leckie, Shirley A. *Elizabeth Bacon Custer and the Making of a Myth.* Norman: University of Oklahoma Press, 1993.

Rankin, Charles E., ed. *Legacy: New Perspectives on the Battle of the Little Bighorn.* Helena: Montana Historical Society, 1996.

Utley, Robert M. *Cavalier in Buckskin: George Armstrong Custer and the Western Military Frontier.* Norman: University of Oklahoma Press, 1988.

ROBERT WOOSTER

See also **American Indian Wars; Crazy Horse.**

D

DAHMER, JEFFREY
(1960–1994)

A ghastly novelty only thirty years earlier, serial killers had become almost commonplace by the 1990s. Indeed, when police discovered that Long Island gardener Joel Rifkin had butchered seventeen prostitutes in the early 1990s, the story was considered fairly prosaic and attracted little attention outside the New York metropolitan area. Confronted as the country had been by so many tales of remorseless multiple murder, only the most shocking case could truly capture people's attention. In such jaded times, it took not only serial homicide but the violation of the most sacrosanct taboos to transform a seeming nonentity like Jeffrey Dahmer into a *People* magazine cover story.

Dahmer grew up in a middle-class family in Milwaukee, Wisconsin. Early on he indulged in sadistic fantasies that he would later inflict, in real life, upon small animals. He was fond of dissecting roadkill and, when tired of that, moved on to trapping live chipmunks and squirrels and slaughtering them. Some of them would end up gutted, skinned, and nailed to trees behind his house.

He applied his gruesome hobbies to human beings for the first time in 1978. Dahmer, eighteen at the time, picked up a young male hitchhiker and brought him back to his house for a sexual encounter. Dahmer crushed the young man's skull with a barbell, strangled him, and dismembered the body.

For the next seven years, Dahmer kept his horrific impulses in check. He enrolled in Ohio State University but dropped out after a few months; he then enlisted in the army but was soon drummed out because of drunkenness. By 1985 he was working a menial job at the Ambrosia Chocolate Factory in Milwaukee. In his spare time, he began murdering young men once again.

Typically Dahmer would find his victims at gay bars. After bringing them back to his apartment, Dahmer would drug them and strangle them. Sometimes he would have sex with the corpses. At other times he would devour parts of their flesh. At his most horrendous, he would perform his version of a lobotomy while his victim was still alive, drilling a hole into the skull and injecting muriatic acid into the brain. He thought that this would turn the victim into a zombie who would obey his every command. In the end, he would inevitably carve up the body with an electric saw and store the parts around his apartment.

Ten of Dahmer's seventeen murder victims were African American. In early 1991, a fourteen-year-old Asian boy escaped from the killer's apartment, naked and bleeding, but was returned by the police, who accepted Dahmer's explanation that he and the boy were just having a lovers' spat.

The police discovered Dahmer's crimes in July 1991, when another intended victim escaped and stopped a patrol car. Inside Dahmer's apartment, the police found decapitated heads in the freezer, skulls in the closet, and various rotting body parts

Jeffrey Dahmer in Milwaukee Circuit Court, July 1991.
REUTERS/CORBIS-BETTMANN

stored in a lobster pot. A series of Polaroid pictures provided a visual record of Dahmer's victims, some of whose remains were corroded by acid.

Dahmer's crimes, incorporating not only dismemberment but also necrophilia and cannibalism, elicited both revulsion and fascination, perhaps more than any other murder case since police uncovered the crimes of Ed Gein over thirty years earlier. Newspapers and magazines clamored for the most grisly updates. Paperbacks chronicled all the gruesome details just months after Dahmer's arrest. The so-called Milwaukee Monster even found his way, in fictionalized form, into more legitimate literature. *Zombie,* a 1995 novel by the acclaimed author Joyce Carol Oates, featured a character named Quentin P——— whose atrocities are clearly modeled after Dahmer's deranged lobotomy experiments.

While the Oates book brought Dahmer lore to the pages of the *New York Times Book Review,* most people probably became familiar with the murderer's pop-culture legacy through the folk-oriented oral tradition. Within days of the first news about the case, a host of Dahmer jokes began to circulate across the country, giving the public a chance to laugh nervously at the mind-boggling horrors that the media were presenting to them. A particularly memorable example: Jeffrey Dahmer's mother goes to his apartment for dinner one night. She says, "You know, Jeffrey, I don't like your friends." Dahmer says, "So try the salad."

Dahmer's confessions led to his conviction and sentencing to fifteen consecutive life terms. He would serve only three years in prison; in 1994 a fellow inmate beat him to death.

BIBLIOGRAPHY

Baumann, Ed. *Step into My Parlor.* Chicago: Bonus, 1991.
Norris, Joel. *Jeffrey Dahmer.* New York: Pinnacle, 1992.
Schwartz, Anne E. *The Man Who Could Not Kill Enough: The Secret Murders of Milwaukee's Jeffrey Dahmer.* Secaucus, N.J.: Carol, 1992.

DAVID EVERITT

See also **Cannibalism; Serial Killers.**

DALLAS

In the 1950s and 1960s, Dallas avoided the ugly racial discord that characterized other southern cities, such as Birmingham, Alabama, and Little Rock, Arkansas. The Dallas journalist Jim Schutze once suggested that although Dallas had more than its share of Ku Klux Klan "sheets and lynching," the city's business-led Dallas Citizens Council, prudently realizing that bloodshed would discourage outside investment, managed to smother racial violence and maintained a de facto "Jim Crow" regime, even after court-ordered desegregation.

In the past the Dallas elites often resorted to brutality to maintain power. This oppression, in turn, inspired resistance by dissenters, from abolitionists and freedmen in the mid-nineteenth century to marginalized African Americans and Latinos in the twentieth century. Despite its straight-arrow, corporate image, Dallas has often conducted its politics on the margins of the law.

Frontier disorder marked the city's early years, with community leaders often resorting to burglary and theft to maintain land claims in Peters Colony, a land grant awarded originally by the Republic of Texas that included modern-day Dallas. Early residents often settled there without company agents present to establish property lines. To settle land disputes, in 1852 the state granted back a million acres of the best land in the colony to owners of the Texas Emigration and Land Company. To prevent a company takeover of disputed land, a committee that included future Dallas mayor Samuel B. Pryor broke into the office of company representative Henry Hedgcoxe and seized maps and land claims. The raiding party celebrated its victory in the "Hedgcoxe War" by burning one company official in effigy and riding another out of town on a rail.

Violence by the elites continued up to the Civil War. Much of downtown Dallas burned on 8 July 1860. The village suffered an estimated $400,000 in damages. Reported fires in nearby Denton and Pilot Point sparked rumors of a slave revolt incited by northern abolitionists. A "committee of vigilance" warned of a slave plot to set fires, seize weapons, and poison whites throughout Texas. The committee interrogated nearly one hundred slaves, whipping them to extract confessions. Three slaves were blamed for the fire and hanged. Authorities also whipped two suspected abolitionists. An ensuing statewide panic resulted in the slayings of an estimated eighty slaves and thirty-seven whites statewide, but many reports of fires proved false.

After the Civil War, Confederate veterans whipped, shot, and harassed freed blacks as well as white Republicans who were thought to support the federal army's occupation of the town. In its spring 1867 session, the Dallas County grand jury failed to indict a single defendant in thirteen murder cases in which the victims were former slaves and Unionists. The first Freedman's Bureau agent, William H. Horton, left town following accusations of corruption; in 1868 an assassin murdered Horton's successor, George Eben, before he even reached town. Such violence restored power to unreconstructed Confederates.

After the Houston and Central Texas Railroad opened a line through Dallas in 1872, the once-quiet village was transformed into a lawless boomtown as an infusion of cash from the cattle and cotton industries attracted lawbreakers. Notorious gunslingers such as Sam Bass, Frank James, and Doc (John Henry) Holliday soon called Dallas home. In the early twentieth century, crime-saturated prostitution "reservations" like the Frogtown neighborhood sprouted on ground that later

proved equally fertile for Depression-era criminals. Clyde Barrow struggled with poverty in West Dallas while his partner in crime, Bonnie Parker, grew up in the hardscrabble Dallas community of Cement City before they launched a robbery career that made them national celebrities in the 1930s. Gangsters such as Benny Binion attracted front-page headlines and assassination attempts in the 1950s. Despite its law-and-order image, by the mid-1970s Dallas often had a higher homicide rate than larger cities like Los Angeles and Chicago in annual surveys of murder rates.

At times criminal violence received official sanction. A revived Ku Klux Klan commandeered the city and county government in the 1920s. The Dallas chapter of the Klan became the largest in the nation. A local dentist, Hiram Wesley Evans, rose to the rank of Imperial Wizard, or national leader. With the police commissioner and the police chief as members, the Klan operated with impunity, beating black men suspected of sexual dalliances with white women and publicly whipping whites charged with gambling and other moral offenses.

During and after World War II, segregated African American neighborhoods became too small to hold the city's black population. In 1940 and 1950, a series of bombings rocked homes sold to blacks in bordering white neighborhoods. A special grand jury uncovered several prominent citizens' involvement in the bombings, although no one was ever convicted.

Despite its brutish past, civic boosters promoted Dallas as a haven for business development and political order. Nevertheless, widely publicized assaults by mobs in Dallas in the early 1960s on vice presidential candidate Lyndon Johnson and United Nations ambassador Adlai Stevenson underscored the city's reputation for political extremism. It was into this politically charged atmosphere that President John F. Kennedy ventured in November 1963 to patch a feud within the Texas Democratic Party. Kennedy was riding in an open limousine through downtown Dallas on his way to a speech at the Dallas Trade Mart when several shots rang out in Dealey Plaza on 22 November 1963. The president suffered severe injuries, including a fatal head wound, and critics called Dallas a "city of hate" and a magnet for right-wing crackpots, and many blamed the extremism for the president's death. Dallas's image suffered further when local nightclub owner Jack Ruby murdered the accused assassin, Lee Harvey Oswald, before national television cameras.

Dallas's image slowly recovered as the city skirted the riots and political convulsions that shook the rest of the nation in the 1960s. Dallas avoided uprisings that seized communities like Detroit and Watts. Tensions did boil over in July 1973 after a police officer fatally shot twelve-year-old Santos Rodriguez as the child sat handcuffed in a squad car. A downtown demonstration led by Mexican American activists turned violent, with protesters fighting police and looting more than forty stores.

Not even this incident dislodged Dallas from its perch of civic pride, at least in the eyes of the American public. A 1983 Gallup survey found that more people associated the city with the Dallas Cowboys football team than with the Kennedy assassination. Almost as many people associated the city with the television drama *Dallas* as with the assassination. Extensively remodeled in rich public relations veneers of sports glamour and wealth, Dallas by the 1990s seemed to have successfully cloaked nearly 150 years of violence.

BIBLIOGRAPHY

Payne, Darwin. *Dallas: An Illustrated History.* Dallas: Windsor, 1982.

Phillips, John Neal. *Running with Bonnie and Clyde: The Ten Fast Years of Ralph Fults.* Norman: University of Oklahoma Press, 1996.

Schutze, Jim. *The Accommodation: The Politics of Race in an American City.* Secaucus, N.J.: Citadel, 1986.

Smith, Thomas H. "Conflict and Corruption: The Dallas Establishment vs. the Freedmen's Bureau Agent." *Legacies* 1, no. 2 (1989).

MICHAEL PHILLIPS

See also **Kennedy, John F.; Oswald, Lee Harvey; Ruby, Jack; Urban Violence.**

DALLAS, CLAUDE

(1950–)

"Mountain Man" Claude Lafayette Dallas, Jr., was convicted of killing two Idaho conservation officers in 1982. Dallas's crime, fifteen-month flight, trial, and subsequent prison break inspired three books, a film, and a song by the country-and-western singer Ian Tyson. Many saw Dallas as an Old West hero who had resisted overbearing government and then lived off the land until betrayed for a bounty.

Dallas was born on 11 March 1950 in Winchester, Virginia. Little is known about his childhood, except that he liked to hunt and to read about the West, and he graduated sixty-fifth out of eighty in his high school class. In 1968 Dallas, an outsider, adopted the life of a ranch hand and trapper in the arid lands of southeastern Oregon, Nevada, and Idaho. Always armed and constantly practicing his draw, he seemed menacing to some but impressed his few friends as an independent cowboy who would neither start nor run from trouble.

By Dallas's own account, on 5 January 1981 wardens William Pogue and Conley Elms caught him in his camp on federal land, in southwest Idaho's Owyhee County, with illegal game and attempted to arrest him. He claimed he argued that the arrest was unreasonable, drew his handgun after Pogue threatened him, won the subsequent shoot-out, and then, using his rifle, shot both men in the head as they lay on the ground. He left Elms's body in the river, hid Pogue's, and escaped into the desert. Dallas's friend Jim Stevens witnessed the killings and helped him remove Pogue's body; but he subsequently notified the authorities. For a $20,000 reward, an informant revealed Dallas's location. Agents of the Federal Bureau of Investigation eventually captured him after a helicopter chase and gunfight, and Dallas was charged with first-degree murder. In his defense, he portrayed himself as an old-time "buckaroo" who ignored unreasonable game laws and had the moral and legal right to stand his ground against an aggressive officer, thus appealing to the concept of "no duty to retreat," which the historian Richard Maxwell Brown sees as a core American value. Although he could have avoided violence by consenting to arrest, the Idaho jury convicted him of voluntary manslaughter, not murder, and would have freed him but for the fact that he had shot both victims in the head. The judge rejected the self-defense argument, however, and sentenced Dallas to thirty years in prison.

On 30 March 1986 Dallas escaped from the Idaho penitentiary and was named to the FBI's Ten Most Wanted list. He eluded capture for almost a year while admirers cheered him on. Claiming that he had been convinced that guards planned to kill him, he won acquittal on prison-escape charges. To ensure his security he was transferred first to Nebraska and then to a Kansas prison.

The prosecuting attorney in the Dallas case believed that Dallas had lied and charmed his way out of a murder charge, but more than Dallas's per-

Claude Dallas is escorted by FBI agents for an arraignment on charges of fleeing from justice, in San Bernadino, California, on 9 March 1987. CORBIS/ BETTMANN-UPI

vatized, Dallas could have been arrested for trespassing. As it was, rival public land users, not bureaucrats, had sent the game wardens to his camp. They were state lawmen, not federal agents, who acted the part of no-nonsense frontier sheriffs while they protected western hunters' game from poachers. Even so, to his many sympathizers, Dallas embodied the frontier virtues of independence and self-reliance. His guns, his lonely lifestyle, his defiance of authority, and his resort to violence reflected widely held ideals of the mythic West.

BIBLIOGRAPHY

Brown, Richard Maxwell. *No Duty to Retreat: Violence and Values in American History and Society.* New York: Oxford University Press, 1991.

Cawley, R. McGreggor. *Federal Land, Western Anger: The Sagebrush Rebellion and Environmental Politics.* Lawrence: University Press of Kansas, 1993.

Long, Jeff. *Outlaw: The True Story of Claude Dallas.* New York: Morrow, 1985.

Olsen, Jack. *Give a Boy a Gun: A True Story of Law and Disorder in the American West.* New York: Delacorte, 1985.

CHARLES COATE

See also **West.**

suasive personality was involved in the jury's decision to find him guilty on a lesser count. At the time the killing of the wardens occurred, many westerners believed that distant bureaucrats and environmentalists were waging "war on the West," and that it was time to fight back to save their way of life. In 1979 Dallas's adopted state of Nevada had demanded state control of federal land and launched the so-called Sagebrush Rebellion. The demand to recover federal land was endorsed by many counties in the West. Dallas's Idaho trial followed that state's 1980 landslide vote for Ronald Reagan, a self-styled Sagebrush rebel. The movement declined when the Reagan administration expressed sympathy and pledged that federal land policy would be more responsive to local interests.

Whether Dallas was justified in his hostility toward the federal government is open to debate. If the federal land where he trapped had been pri-

DALTON GANG
Grattan (1865–1892); William Marion (1866–1893); Robert (1867–1892); Emmett (1871–1937)

The legacy of violence along the Kansas-Missouri border in the nineteenth century was already well established by the time the Dalton brothers were born in Missouri. Their father was a rambler and ne'er-do-well, and their mother was a cousin of the Younger brothers, whose legend was already linked to that of the James brothers. Of Lewis and Adeline Dalton's fifteen children, five would make their way into the history of the violent frontier. Their son Franklin, a deputy U.S. marshal in the Indian Territory, was killed by fugitives in 1887.

After Frank's death, Grattan and Robert Dalton also became deputy marshals, and Emmett rode with them as a member of the posse. Bob eventually became the chief of the Indian police of the Osage nation, but it soon became apparent that their badges were a cover for the Daltons' illicit activities as horse thieves and extortionists and, in Bob's case, as a killer. By 1890, however, they were operating openly as horse thieves in

Oklahoma Territory and Kansas. The federal authorities were soon after them and they fled Kansas, with Bob, Emmett, and other members of the gang taking refuge in New Mexico while Grattan visited brother Bill in California. After robbing a gambling hall in Santa Rosa, New Mexico, the gang split up, and Bob followed Grat to California.

The arrival of his outlaw brothers was hardly good news for Bill Dalton, who had hoped for a career in politics. When a train was robbed shortly after Bob and Grat arrived, the Dalton brothers were blamed, and Grat and Bill were arrested. Grat was convicted but escaped from the Vidalia, California, jail in September 1891 before sentencing. Although Bill was exonerated, his political career in California was finished, and he soon followed his brothers back to Oklahoma. Through the months that followed, Bob, Emmett, and Grat Dalton robbed and killed, staying just ahead of federal and local law officers.

In October 1892 Bob and Grat decided to strike the two banks in Coffeyville, Kansas, where they had lived for a time when they were growing up. Not all the gang members agreed with this decision, but Bob, Grat, and Emmett, backed by Dick Broadwell and Bill Powers, attempted the daring robbery anyway. The Daltons were recognized, and the townspeople took them on in a street fight that left four citizens and all the gang members except Emmett dead. The Coffeyville raid ended the Dalton gang.

Disillusioned and bitter, Bill Dalton joined Bill Doolin's gang for a time before organizing his own gang in 1893. The new Dalton gang was short-lived. The robbery of a bank in May 1894 in Longview, Texas, resulted in the death of one lawman and one of the outlaws. The survivors fled to Oklahoma, where someone in the gang spent the money stolen in the robbery too freely. Bill Dalton was killed on 8 June at his wife's home near Elk, Oklahoma, in a shootout with lawmen. Emmett was sentenced to life in prison for the Coffeyville robberies; he was paroled in 1908 and eventually wrote two books about his life outside the law.

Emmett proved to be charming and persuasive as he romanticized the crimes of his brothers, claiming that many crimes attributed to them were actually committed by others. He effectively used the romantic model of the James gang, portraying the Daltons as good-hearted, brave, generous boys driven to lives of crime. It was a myth that resonated with the attitudes of the late nineteenth and early twentieth century, and the chances are good that the Daltons, steeped in the lore of the Jameses and Youngers before them, actually believed it.

BIBLIOGRAPHY

Samuelson, Nancy B. *The Dalton Gang Story: Lawmen to Outlaws.* Eastford, Conn.: Shooting Star, 1992.
Smith, Robert Barr. *Daltons! The Raid on Coffeyville, Kansas.* Norman: University of Oklahoma Press, 1996.

GARY L. ROBERTS

See also **Gunfighters and Outlaws, Western; James, Jesse.**

DANCE

The dancing body is always a potential site for the enactment of violence. In dance, as in sports, martial arts, and many forms of work, destructive impulses can be discharged, deflected, and often redirected toward healthier goals. Dance performance and dance ritual, in fact, are often created to give participants a chance to confront their own aggression, even to test it. But in the dance an affinity for physical violence is countered by a need to survive. Paradoxically, when violent behavior is structured and rehearsed to produce a performance, the behavior becomes less violent, less harmful. Thus, dance converts destructive energy into socially or aesthetically acceptable action.

Intentional violence has recurred in a wide range of contexts throughout twentieth-century dance and performance art. In formal ballets and modern dance, it is signified through mimetic or metaphoric actions that entertain and sometimes offer the spectator catharsis or a vicarious experience of violence. Experimental work—often combining syncretically with other arts, media, technology, and quasi-religious practices—employs real violence or extreme risk as an instrument for physical or social transformation that can extend to the audience as well as the performers.

Physical Metaphors

Theater history is strewn with mimetic portrayals of violence. When expressionism and the modern dance released the body from the conventions of classical ballet, both the look and the actions of the dancer could stand for tormented emotions. The dancer and choreographer Martha Graham, influenced by the techniques of the Stanislavsky method of training actors, built a vocabulary of dance gesture based on the body's experience of psychological trauma. Graham's "contraction and release" employed a sudden, strong mobilization of the muscles in the center of the body to galvanize a total action: turning, falling, locomotion, or jumping. Initially, dancers would practice these moves as if they had been punched, or would accompany the moves with shouts and screams. The body absorbed an imagined blow or emotional spasm, then projected the impact outward in dance movement. As in Method actor training, an emotional residue embedded itself in the movement as it became codified, so that the trigger of the original impetus (or sense memory) was no longer needed. Graham's mature choreography depicted the epic rage of the Greek myths and the sexual desire of individuals, using a contorted and aestheticized body language of inner torment.

Graham's fellow modern dancers worked out individual movement styles with a similar aim of externalizing the most divisive and dramatic inner states. Modern dance movement enacts emotional qualities, but it usually avoids the literal, pantomimic depiction of everyday action. For instance, in Helen Tamiris's *Negro Spirituals* (1931), the Crucifixus is represented by the solo dancer standing with one shoulder slightly lower than the other. As the words "They pierced him in the side" are sung, the dancer stabs her flattened hands toward her flanks with a harsh, rebounding impulse. The viewer doesn't see a literal piercing but an abstract representation of pain that induces our kinesthetic empathy.

Although the early modern dancers and their styles passed on, the expressive potential of movement became an essential resource for their dance successors. This liberated body expressivity has even penetrated the domain of classical ballet. In the fairy tale classics of the nineteenth century, the audience was persuaded to sublimate and romanticize the dancer in courtly love scenes. But modernists, intrigued with the body as a physical presence on the stage, acknowledged that the couple in a pas de deux has to exert force, control, and sometimes harsh maneuverings to create the illusion of love. Toward the end of the twentieth century, distortion, asymmetry, and extremes of virtuosity came to symbolize a modern sensibility in ballet as its mechanics were exposed and even exaggerated to depict troubled relationships instead of euphemistically idyllic ones. The American choreographer William Forsythe (based since 1984 in Frankfurt, Germany) specializes in antag-

onistic duets where women are literally jerked around by their male partners. Instead of graciously placing the woman in refined positions, the man shoves and yanks her so that her body inverts, angles, over-rotates, or hangs precariously off-balance. The only thing that saves these dances from being abusive is that the woman is a technically equal partner to the man. She can counterbalance his brutal treatment, sustain any contorted position he thrusts her into, and spin as fast as he propels her, while retaining her authority as a ballerina.

Forsythe's beaten-up but tough ballerina is a latter-day relative of the Chosen One in the most famous modern ballet of all, Vaslav Nijinsky and Igor Stravinsky's *Le Sacre du printemps* (1913). A girl is chosen at random to complete the sacrificial spring ritual of the tribe. She must dance herself to death to ensure the bounty of the crops and the harvest and the birth of children, and so preserve the tribe for another year. The choreography of

Lydia Sokolova in *Le Sacre du printemps*. CORBIS/E. O. HOPPÉ

this final solo makes punishing demands on the dancer, and the curtain falls as her inert body is triumphantly lifted by the ancestors.

When the contemporary modern dance choreographer Paul Taylor adapted the theme of *Le Sacre* in 1980, he sidestepped its morbidity by transposing it into the idiom of American popular violence, the comic strip, with flat, jerky movement, a disjointed storyline, and cartoonish characters. Taylor made far more harsh pieces when exploring psychosexually traumatized individuals. In *Last Look* (1985) and other plotless works, the dancers wrench into distorted shapes, torture themselves with frantic energies, and project a foreboding sense of inner torment. With these dark essays Taylor has pushed Martha Graham's movement imagery to its most extreme limits of eroticized violence.

Sexuality Reconfigured

In dance, it is difficult to talk about violence without also talking about sex. While Forsythe and other contemporary choreographers reflect the ambivalence felt in Western culture at large toward the increased independence and sexual autonomy of women, Graham's legacy opened the way for women to perform their suppressed feelings of sexual desire and predation. Some of the most strident assertions of women's power and anger coincided with the performance counterculture of the 1960s. Carolee Schneemann, a visual artist who participated in the early Judson Dance Workshops, staged her feminist identity in visceral performance pieces that celebrated the erotics of the forbidden object. In her most famous work, *Meat Joy* (1964), men and women disrobed each other, dressed each other in newspaper, painted each other's bodies and faces, and orgiastically rolled on top of each other among piles of paper, paint, fish, chickens, and frankfurters. Schneemann evoked the body's primal sensuality, calling *Meat Joy* "flesh jubilation" (Schneemann 1979, p. 62). Although her performance pieces were mostly heterosexual and benign, Schneemann's theater of feminist transgressiveness featured her own body as an art object laden with symbolic messages. In *Interior Scroll* (1975) she painted her naked body, then took a long strip of twisted paper from her vagina and read from feminist texts printed on it.

Body art was developed in the early 1960s when dancers, visual artists, and other performers were redefining theater itself, and the presence of a human body—sometimes not even a moving body

—could constitute a dance. Taking their cue from the futurists and Dadaists of the fin de siècle, American avant-gardists devised elaborate attacks against the social conventions of the late 1950s, and shock became a primary tool for performance artists with a personal or political platform. The French theorist Antonin Artaud had proposed an extremist theater of cruelty, where the human body would be transformed in "the exercise of a dangerous and terrible act." Artaud's fixation on the violent act, linked to psychopathology and to possession states and other religious practices, remained a mostly unconsummated potential for dancers. Although performance art's politically motivated physical distortions were escalating—from face painting and simulated orgies to bondage, self-mutilation, and plastic surgery—transformational body art became less feasible for dancers as they returned to their primary concern with new dance and choreography.

Cruelty and Excess

Since the cultural revolution of the 1960s, theater dance has applied experimental strategies to the finished techniques of formal ballet and modern dance in order to project explosive ideas without altogether relinquishing the virtuosic aspect of dance. Tanztheater, pioneered by the German choreographer Pina Bausch, makes pointedly political statements about sexual manipulation and its relation to a commodity-obsessed culture. Working more from theater-games techniques than from dance composition, Bausch and her many followers in Europe and North America produced spectacles of combat, torture, exploitation, and consumption that some critics have seen as angry or ironic comments on the crimes of Nazi Germany and the bourgeois excesses of postwar society. During the 1980s Tanztheater was especially valued by feminist theorists.

Bausch's works often feature gigantic sets and elaborate costumes. Scenic elements such as water, dried leaves, or dirt claustrophobically enclose the space and cover the floor with impediments to movement. As each piece proceeds, the sets, props, and costumes, along with the performers themselves, become sensual objects to be handled, scuffed, torn, smeared, and soaked in frenzied episodes of sensuality. Couples encounter one another and play power games, almost always involving verbal and physical abuse, with the women as victims. Partners touch each other in ritualistic seductions; caresses turn to squeezing, torturous tickling, licking, slapping, and wrestling until the performers are physically spent and humiliated. Neither partner shows any emotion beyond the physical rage or desire required to do the action. The "game" is repeated over and over with the same depersonalized intensity and the same or different partners.

Tanztheater's dramaturgical framework is that of the music hall revue. Sketches, recitations, and musical numbers invoke a Brechtian alienation with their vernacular style, cabaret dances, and exaggerated intimacy. Given its pervasive theme of sadomasochistic sexual dysfunction and domination, Tanztheater glamorizes violence even as it condemns it. The audience is required to participate in both the performers' semipornographic pleasure and their degrading sense of shame. What began in the 1960s as permissiveness—an opening up of the senses to new creative possibilities—led to these displays of extreme cruelty and voyeurism, sanctioned in the name of political reparations. Tanztheater operates in an ambiguous realm: as metaphor it writes a harsh corrective message by exposing the evils of power, but as real theatrical action, it sensationalizes the same evils.

Outcry from the Margins

In America the counterculture gave access to the anger of marginalized groups, especially women and blacks. The modern dance choreography of Alvin Ailey, Talley Beatty, Eleo Pomare, and Rod Rodgers often focused on oppression, frustration, and the edgy life of the ghetto through graphic theatricalizations and impassioned technique. By the 1990s, minorities had regrouped and the issues had changed. Along with race and ethnicity, gender and AIDS became major themes on the modern dance stage. As a gay, HIV-positive African American, Bill T. Jones made some of the strongest statements in mainstream dance.

Jones and his partner Arnie Zane formed a duo in the countercultural days of the 1970s. Jones created a series of confrontational solo dances that combined eclectic movement with spectacular monologues in which he would alternately confront and beguile the audience, keeping it constantly off-balance as to his intention. Zane was the more structural and objective artist of the two. Neither of them had a conventional dance education, and they both engaged in the experimental studies of the time, including contact improvisation. They went on to make acrobatic duets together, and eventually created a whole repertory

Bill T. Jones performs *Last Night on Earth* in Edinburgh, Scotland, in 1993. Corbis/Robbie Jack

of dances utilizing their contrasting physical and creative types.

After Zane's death in 1988, Jones made deeper and more serious pieces for the Jones/Zane company, partly as a memorial to Zane and perhaps also as a way of expressing fear for his own medical future. *Still/Here* (1994) used many of the countercultural techniques that had become highly evolved and polished in Jones/Zane's hands. Before choreographing the dance, Jones conducted and videotaped a series of quasi-therapeutic workshops with terminally ill people, eliciting their sadness and apprehension and their grim courage. In the staged work, the subjects' movements became part of the choreographic vocabulary of the dancers, and the edited videotapes were played as a scenic montage behind the live performers. Jones's use of actual patients as a subject for the dance was severely criticized, although his intent was to create a work of affirmation in the face of death. Dance critic Arlene Croce's condemnation of the piece as "victim art" ignited a bitter national debate that touched on the subjects of authority, aesthetics, and public funding for controversial artwork.

Remedial Contacts

Contact improvisation, encounter groups, and other antitheatrical processes allowed performers for the first time to explore physical and emotional forces in their lives that would not have been acceptable on the stage. Contact improvisation developed in the aftermath of the counterculture as a means of exploring movement and as a meditative practice similar in effect to Eastern physical disciplines like tai chi and yoga. Contact improvisation activated the dancer's body weight, balance, and flexibility during a continuous interaction with a partner. Acknowledging some of the same hazards of physical and sexual dominance addressed by Tanztheater, contact improvisation from its earliest years presupposed a nongendered body; seduction and other sexual power plays were taboo. Even when the movement became rough or a sexual attraction manifested itself, the rules required a constant adjustment and change, or exchange, of weight, so that destructive or dominating impulses would immediately have to modulate into new actions. As a nonverbal and nontheatrical form, it was relieved of the provocations of everyday life, and participants could enter the studio with a minimum of anxiety or aggression.

In their earliest experiments, around 1972, contact improvisers were absorbed with the liberated physicality of falling, rolling, carrying, and jumping that was afforded by working with a cooperative partner in the absence of strict dance technique. Their intention was to focus on the inner experience of the body and to become sensitized to their own latent physical powers. Contact soon spread to many nondancers interested in body sensitivity, and concurrently became a skilled performance form. As in the case of Jones and Zane, it became a resource for movement and a philosophical underpinning for a choreographic way of life.

An obvious analogue to contact improvisation is the Brazilian form *capoeira*. Like many martial arts practices, *capoeira* developed among colonized peoples as a way of maintaining the skills of combat without provoking official censure. A syncretized practice with influences from the cultures of Africa, native Indians, and Portuguese whites, *capoeira* was a key element in what the scholar Lowell Lewis has called the culture of slavery: "a complex system with the constant threat of violence, but with recourse to that violence only when other channels broke down. It is the value of deception, of apparent accommodation, which . . . is at the heart of the play in capoeira" (Lewis 1992, p. 40). From the plantations, *capoeira* moved to urban centers where it crystallized into a street dance form.

Although *capoeira* has become a showcase for virtuosic dancers, its original function was not theatrical but social. Unlike contact improvisation, it actually precludes body contact, since its main ob-

Capoeira **dancers in Brazil, 1990s.** CORBIS/INGE YSPEERT

jective is to evade and deceive the opposing partner. But it results in a remarkably similar performance, where the body draws on an endless supply of spatial possibilities and a reservoir of quick, smooth flexibility that allows the dancer/player to make instantaneous, full-body changes of direction, level, and shape.

Capoeira is also closely related to the challenge that is at the heart of American tap dance. Challenge, whether underlying the intricate skills of martial arts or the structured explosions of rhythm dance, is a way of asserting power without bringing the full destructiveness of aggression into play. Discharging their energy in the grounded actions of a step dance, the hitting patterns of a stick dance, the slaps and taps of body music, and the clattering of spoons, bones, stones, or drums, people the world over have found a safety valve for their discontents and their tribal animosities in rhythm dance. During the 1990s rhythm dance grew into a multicultural phenomenon, with popular stagings of tap, Irish step dancing, and other traditional forms and invented genres like American hip-hop, the gumboot dances of South Africa, and the urban trash-can sonorities of the show *Stomp*. The audience gains a vicarious relief through these performances of bravado and controlled ferocity, which are often staged with the high-powered sound and light technologies of a rock concert so that the pounding beat assaults the whole theater.

Rituals and Recovery

Along with self-awareness and tolerance for differing styles of behavior, the counterculture opened up the range of acceptable performance material, both on and off the conventional stage. The ubiquitous eye of television meanwhile was looking at accidents, births, deaths, crimes in progress, and drugs changing hands. In 1967 Anna Halprin's *Parades and Changes* offered nudity on the New York dance stage for the first time, and Halprin left town before she could be arrested. By 1998, nudity could no longer shock a dance audience. Choreographers like Jones and Zane had a place in their companies for dancers of a variety of body types. In 1990 Jones moved to the intersection of theater and therapy. In the final act of his full-length piece about slavery and sexuality, *Last Supper at Uncle Tom's Cabin/The Promised Land*, the dancers, with about forty laypersons from whatever community the company visited on tour, took off all their clothes and moved toward the audience in a mass metaphor of vulnerability and communal harmony.

The 1990s saw the development of serious choreography for retired dancers, elderly people, and the disabled. Advances in extending the physical capabilities of severely injured patients through medical rehabilitation programs and sports medicine fostered the development of wheelchair dance. Troupes of paralyzed people and amputees teamed with walking dancers to offer dramatic and often physically demanding performances, in which bodies that are often seen as deformed or disfigured become heroic, poetic—Artaud's theater of cruelty in reverse.

Wheelchair dance epitomizes a resolute, optimistic sensibility in millennial American dance. Only a technologically confident generation could assume that a body can be remade with superhuman capacities. Dancers live close to the culture of physical training and bodybuilding, rehab, marathons, and cosmetic surgery during their daily encounters with injury and the effects of aging. In its dual nature as both a physical and a metaphoric act, dance has adapted readily to the notion of cyborg or manufactured bodies. If dancers can't actually absorb lethal bullets or re-grow severed limbs, they can sculpt and condition their bodies to translate stress into entertainment.

Elizabeth Streb's *Ringside* has perfected the choreographed conquest of specially designed obstructions and risks. In her dance, steel-muscled performers hurl themselves against walls, bounce on and off trampolines in close coordination, rotate high in the air on circular harnesses, and create precisely timed ensemble effects of rolling, falling, diving, sliding, and smacking into one another. Streb thinks of her "pop action" dance as a means of transcending human limits. Hers is a theater where the body surpasses itself by inviting risk and courting danger. But more than a theater, a circus, or a spectacle, *Ringside* is an inexhaustible harangue. At every performance it flings down the gauntlet in the face of death.

BIBLIOGRAPHY

Artaud, Antonin. "Theatre and Science." In *Antonin Artaud Anthology,* edited by Jack Hirschman. San Francisco: City Lights Books, 1965.
Croce, Arlene. "Discussing the Undiscussable." *New Yorker,* 26 December 1994.
Jones, Bill T., with Peggy Gillespie. *Last Night on Earth.* New York: Pantheon, 1995.

Lewis, J. Lowell. *Ring of Liberation: Deceptive Discourse in Brazilian Capoeira*. Chicago: University of Chicago Press, 1992.

Novack, Cynthia J. *Sharing the Dance: Contact Improvisation and American Culture*. Madison: University of Wisconsin Press, 1990.

Schneemann, Carolee. *More Than Meat Joy*. New Paltz, N.Y.: Documentext, 1979.

Servos, Norbert, and Gert Weigelt. *Pina Bausch-Wuppertal Dance Theater or The Art of Training a Goldfish*. Translated by Patricia Stadié. Cologne: Ballett-Bühnen Verlag, 1984.

Siegel, Marcia B. "Carabosse in a Cocktail Dress." *Hudson Review* (spring 1986).

———. "Virtual Criticism and the Dance of Death." In *The Ends of Performance*, edited by Peggy Phelan and Jill Lane. New York: New York University Press, 1998.

Tracy, Robert. *Goddess—Martha Graham's Dancers Remember*. New York: Limelight Editions, 1997.

MARCIA B. SIEGEL

See also **Performance Art.**

DAYS OF RAGE. *See* Weatherman *and* Weather Underground.

D-DAY

On 6 June 1944 Allied forces landed on the German-occupied Normandy coast in the largest amphibious operation of World War II. Officially named Operation Overlord but commonly referred to as D-Day ("D" being the coded designation for the date of an amphibious assault), the attack involved nearly three million U.S., British, Canadian, Free French, and Polish military personnel, supported by eleven thousand aircraft and five thousand ships. Combining air, naval, and ground operations, the invasion gave the Allies a foothold from which they liberated France and the Low Countries and went on to defeat Germany.

Anglo-American planners had long recognized the need to open a second front to help out their eastern ally, the Soviet Union. American strategists favored an early strike against western Europe. Their British counterparts, however, were wary of German military prowess. Stung by a disastrous amphibious raid against Dieppe, France, on 19 August 1942, during which three-quarters of the attackers had been killed, wounded, or taken prisoner, most British strategists preferred operations in the less well-defended Mediterranean. At the Trident Conference in May 1943, President Franklin D. Roosevelt and Prime Minister Winston Churchill finally agreed upon the cross-channel invasion, with a target date of 1 May 1944.

General Dwight D. Eisenhower was named supreme commander, with British Air Chief Marshal Sir Arthur Tedder as deputy chief. Overall command of ground forces went to Field Marshal Bernard Montgomery. Deeming the German defenses in the Pas de Calais region (the shortest channel crossing) too strong, the Allies instead chose Normandy, with its reasonably good beaches and harbor facilities at nearby Caen and Cherbourg. The Allies developed a plethora of special devices, such as pontoon-laden amphibious tanks, chemically treated uniforms, and two huge prefabricated harbors. To encourage enemy suspicions that the assault would come at Pas de Calais, the Allies mounted an elaborate deception campaign (Operation Fortitude), flooding the airwaves with false radio traffic, constructing huge encampments of empty tents, and conducting a massive aerial bombardment of the region.

The German commander in chief in the west was Field Marshal Gerd von Rundstedt, a respected veteran. Field Marshal Erwin Rommel—in principle von Rundstedt's subordinate but retaining direct access to Adolf Hitler—was the "Desert Fox" who had bedeviled British forces in North Africa for nearly two years. Both von Rundstedt and Rommel, who commanded Army Group B, believed the invasion would strike at the Pas de Calais but differed as to the best means of defense. Von Rundstedt thought it impossible to stop the landings themselves, instead hoping to build a reserve force strong enough to launch an overwhelming counterattack once the site of the invasion had been determined. Rommel, however, concluded that the overwhelming Allied air superiority would chew up any counterattack before it began and believed it essential to stop the invasion at the water line. As a result, German defensive preparations were somewhat divided.

Nevertheless, the Allied forces faced a daunting task in launching an amphibious invasion in the face of a determined enemy and overrunning defenses studded with antilanding craft, antitank obstacles, concrete strong points, and machine-gun nests. Original plans had called for a three-division assault, but Eisenhower's insistence on five divisions delayed the operation until 5 June, the next best combination of tide, moon, and light conditions. Poor weather forced another day's postponement, but just after midnight the operation began. To hold strategic inland positions and help

View from the landing barge on the beach at Normandy, D-Day, 6 June 1944. Public Relations Division, U.S. Coast Guard/Library of Congress

fend off any counterattacks, three United States and British airborne divisions landed in the early hours of 6 June. Air and naval forces began pounding the coast shortly thereafter. The first amphibious landing craft were scheduled to hit the beaches—designated from west to east as Utah and Omaha (American), and Gold, Juno, and Sword (British and Canadian)—just after dawn.

As was inevitable in any operation of this size, much went wrong. Instead of being concentrated near their targets, the sixteen thousand American paratroopers were scattered wildly about the French countryside. Poor visibility and inadequate coordination with forward observers reduced the effectiveness of the bombardment. High waves swamped many amphibious vehicles, and lateral currents often pushed those who survived ashore far from their designated areas. The American landing at Omaha, where the bluffs overlooking the beaches were stoutly defended, nearly turned into a disaster. For a time frightened soldiers huddled for cover behind a low seawall under heavy German fire. Eventually, however, simple courage won the day. "Two kinds of people are staying on this beach," proclaimed Colonel George Taylor, "the dead and those who are going to die. So let's get the hell out of here!" Sparked by such inspirational leadership, the Americans resumed the attack and their assaults cleared the enemy from the bluffs.

Elsewhere, the attackers often met less resistance and by the end of the day had moved as far as five miles inland. Allied casualties had totaled about nine thousand, far fewer than planners had feared but still a heavy cost for those among the first assault waves. Many German strategists, including Hitler, still insisted the main invasion would come later, at Pas de Calais, and thus held most of their armor in reserve. The Allied forces quickly checked local counterattacks and secured a foothold, though they did not gain all their immediate objectives.

The successful D-Day landings resulted from battlefield gallantry, careful planning, and the prodigious weight of the Allied war machine. In a tremendous feat of logistics and organization, 175,000 men had landed, either by air or sea. Ironically, the emphasis on the landings themselves had initially left the Allies unprepared to deal with the heavily defended hedgerow country of Normandy. Caen, which the British had hoped to take on D-Day, was not actually occupied until the second week of July. But following six weeks of hard fighting, Allied troops broke out of Normandy and began racing across France. Within a hundred days they had reached the German border, well ahead of what even the most optimistic official estimates had predicted.

The massive D-Day landings have become something of a barometer of how American motion pictures have portrayed wartime violence. In 1962 Twentieth-Century Fox released *The Longest Day*, based upon the popular history of the same name by Cornelius Ryan. A three-hour spectacular boasting some of Hollywood's greatest stars, this black-and-white epic showed much violence but little gore. In 1998 Dreamworks Pictures and Paramount Pictures released *Saving Private Ryan*, directed by Steven Spielberg, which many observers quickly hailed as the most authentic war movie ever made. The first half-hour of *Saving Private Ryan* depicts the assault on Omaha Beach with horrific, exacting fidelity, conveying to millions of viewers the shock, horror, panic, and courage of the D-Day invasion.

BIBLIOGRAPHY

Ambrose, Stephen E. *D-Day, June 6, 1944: The Climactic Battle of World War II*. New York: Simon and Schuster, 1994.

Ellis, John. *Brute Force: Allied Strategy and Tactics in the Second World War*. New York: Viking, 1990.

Keegan, John. *Six Armies in Normandy: From D-Day to the Liberation of Paris*. New York: Penguin, 1982.

Ryan, Cornelius. *The Longest Day: June 6, 1944*. New York: Simon and Schuster, 1959.

ROBERT WOOSTER

See also **World War II.**

DEADLY FORCE

The use of deadly force is perhaps inherent in the concept of a public police force, but its scope can vary. In Anglo-American systems beginning in medieval times and continuing into the late twentieth century, its implementation was governed by the ancient common-law rule that permitted the use of deadly force against a "fleeing felon," whether the fugitive was considered dangerous or not.

Policies concerning the use of deadly force have varied widely. In England very few police officers are authorized to carry guns, and as a consequence few citizens are killed by police; in contrast, in the United States virtually all sworn officers carry guns, and the rate of killings was from five to six times higher. Despite the widespread use of firearms by police in the United States, until the 1970s American police departments had virtually no guidelines or training with respect to when to use them. And even after several years of widespread adoption of guidelines by the late 1970s, studies continued to show that African Americans were

shot and killed at alarmingly higher rates than whites; that such killings, whatever the circumstances, were almost always found by police officials to be "justifiable homicides"; and that in a great many instances the victim was neither armed nor posed a danger to civilians or police.

Two closely related developments that emerged in the 1960s and gained ground in the 1970s and 1980s led to the near universal adoption of formal procedures regarding the use of deadly force. The Civil Rights movement publicized the racist results of the absence of such procedures, and the Supreme Court's "due process revolution" imposed checks on the discretion of all public officials, including the police. Prodded by these pressures, progressive law-enforcement officials promoted policies to govern police use of deadly force. They rejected the "fleeing felon" rule and developed regulations that (a) restricted use of firearms to situations in which they were needed to protect against death or serious injury, (b) required firing warning shots, (c) mandated systematic monitoring of all instances in which firearms were discharged, and (d) provided for sanctions against officers who violated these restrictions. In 1985, in *Tennessee v. Garner*, the Supreme Court formally rejected the use of deadly force against an apparently unarmed, nondangerous fleeing suspect and concluded that police departments had to develop rules narrowly restricting the use of deadly force. By the time the Court acted, almost all large police departments had developed such regulations, spurred on by local court rulings, civil rights activists, and internal departmental review.

These policies had salutary results. From the mid-1970s through the 1980s, the number of police shootings as well as the number of citizens killed by the police decreased by 30 percent or more. The disparity between the number of blacks and whites killed by police officers decreased sharply, and the numbers of police officers killed in the line of duty declined as fewer suspects returned shots. However, the so-called code of silence, the unwritten fraternal rule that keeps police from informing on one another, continues to protect many officers who violate these policies, and the disparity between white and black victims of police violence, though reduced, persists. Still, the revised approach to the use of deadly force can be regarded as one of the most successful police reforms of the twentieth century. It has served as a model for policies governing such actions as the use of choke holds, tear gas, pepper spray, handcuffing, high-speed auto pursuits, and the like.

BIBLIOGRAPHY

Fyfe, James J. "Police Use of Deadly Force: Research and Reform." *Justice Quarterly* 5 (June 1988): 164–205.
Sherman, Lawrence W., and Ellen G. Cohn. *Citizens Killed by Big City Police, 1970–1984.* Washington, D.C.: Crime Control Institute, 1986.
Walker, Samuel. *Taming the System: The Control of Discretion in Criminal Justice, 1950–1990.* New York: Oxford University Press, 1993.

MALCOLM M. FEELEY

See also **Crime, Legal Definitions of.**

DEATH ROW

Death rows have a certain unchanging, even time-less quality. This is the case because all death rows share one preeminent purpose: to warehouse con-demned prisoners—in effect, to store their bodies—until they are put to death. Conditions of con-finement have changed over the centuries, as have methods of execution, but the essential state of life under sentence of death remains unchanged. To suffer fear and degradation, to become more an object and less a person—these have been and re-main the enduring realities of death-row confine-ment.

Before the twentieth century, prisons were dungeons—dark places of close confinement, of-ten built underground. Life there could be un-imaginably grim. Most prisoners were destitute and lived in a state of desperation and hopeless-ness. For the wealthy few, prison life was a differ-ent matter altogether. In the eighteenth century, English prisoners, including those under sentence of death, were allowed to purchase comforts to make their confinement easier. Some had access to the modern equivalent of gyms or health clubs within the prison walls. Others could have meals catered, including last meals, which they were al-lowed to consume in the presence of friends, some-times amid considerable revelry. Renwick Wil-liams, also known as the Monster of London, executed in the late eighteenth century, provides a case in point. Some twenty couples were in atten-dance on the eve of his execution. The festivities included a tea, a dance, and a supper served with a variety of wines.

In the nineteenth century prison conditions be-came more uniform—and more uniformly de-priving—for all offenders, rich and poor. The daily regimen afforded prisoners, and especially con-demned prisoners, was sterile and controlled. Of-ficials regulated every aspect of the lives of their charges. Farewell festivities on death row became a thing of the past.

Yet whether condemned prisoners in earlier times were allowed much or little personal free-dom, and whether they whiled away their last hours drunk or sober, the experience of death row was always shaped by fear. Indeed, condemned prisoners awaited the executioner in nothing less than dread. Some suffered mental breakdowns. A few aged visibly, seemingly growing old over-night. Fear ruled the lives of condemned prisoners because executions were a terrifying spectacle—replete with torture and mutilation and sometimes agonizingly extended deaths, all conducted before crowds often hungry for bloody entertainment.

Most condemned prisoners were defeated psy-chologically and dehumanized; they went to their deaths without resistance. Noted one mid-nine-teenth-century observer, characterizing the typical American prisoner on the threshold of execution, "you behold a man already half dead:—his coun-tenance has fallen, his eyes are fixed, his lips are deadly pale and quivering, while his whole aspect, in anticipation of the reality, gives you the per-sonification of death's counterpart" (Spear 1994, p. 50). Those who attempted suicide on the eve of their executions—the last resort of a not insub-stantial number of prisoners—might be dragged to the gallows with open, bleeding wounds.

Fearful conditions persisted on death rows well into the twentieth century. The death row at the state prison in Ossining, New York, known as Sing Sing, remodeled in 1922 and in operation until the 1960s, was called "the slaughterhouse." Prisoners lived virtually around the clock in solitary cells. Brief periods of recreation offered no relief, for re-lease from the cell brought with it the threat of violence from other desperate men. "In the mood of despair that gripped us all," noted one prisoner, Isidore Zimmerman, "tempers were short, nerves frayed. It was enough to put one prisoner within striking distance of another for murder to be done." Prisoners had no privacy; they were always on dis-play for their keepers, under unremitting surveil-lance. "It was enough to leave a prisoner alone for seconds, if he meant to take his own life" (1964, pp. 119–120). The death chamber was housed on death row, behind a door that was visible to prisoners when they left their cells for recreation. Executions occurred every few weeks; fellow prisoners, former neighbors, would be marched a few feet down the hall and put to death. The sounds of execution—the hum of the electric chair motor, the opening and closing of the doors of the execution chamber—were readily heard on death row. Autopsies of executed prisoners, conducted immediately and featuring drills and saws, unnerved even the strongest prisoners.

By the late twentieth century, prisoners on death row were no longer housed in close proximity to the execution chamber. Nor were death-row regimes as uniform as they had once been. Solitary confinement, the norm on death rows in American prisons until about 1975, has been replaced in some jurisdictions with less oppressive regimes, where prisoners congregate in small groups for recreation and work, sometimes for hours each day. These more relaxed regimes were established in part because the average stay on death row increased—from days in the nineteenth century to weeks and then months over most of the twentieth century to years and even decades as the century came to a close. At the same time, executions became, for a time, quite rare. (A number of Supreme Court holdings in class-action cases emptied death rows in the 1970s.) Legal holdings and consent decrees were fashioned to allow more freedoms to prisoners who, although technically under sentence of death, had a long wait ahead of them and a fairly good likelihood of winning release from death row.

At the end of the twentieth century executions made a resurgence; in any given year fifty or more American prisoners were put to death. Fewer condemned prisoners won release from death row by court action. Perhaps inevitably, conditions of confinement became more restrictive as executions became more common. Oklahoma's death row provides a revealing case study. Known as H Unit, this death row is a kind of futuristic rendering of solitary confinement. A solid concrete structure, built underground, H Unit is a testimonial to the capacity for technology to separate and isolate prisoners and staff. Prisoners are confined for up to twenty-three and even twenty-four hours a day in these subterranean concrete cells, which are bereft of decorations and windows; no natural air circulates, and the only natural light emanates from distant skylights. Heavy surveillance strips inmates of privacy and individuality; there is no work, no

recreation, and no vocational training. Computers, cameras, and intercoms control communication; control is impersonal and near total. Death-row conditions have gone "back to the future," creating what might be termed a modern dungeon—clean but unremittingly barren and utterly cut off from the outside world.

Death rows may differ in the details of their administration, but no death row offers prisoners a way of life that might in any way prepare them for the violent death that they must face. In this basic and profound sense, all death-row prisoners have been and are warehoused for death.

BIBLIOGRAPHY

Gatrell, V. A. C. *The Hanging Tree: Execution and the English People, 1770–1868.* New York: Oxford University Press, 1994.

Jackson, Bruce, and Diane Christian. *Death Row.* Boston: Beacon, 1980.

Johnson, Robert. *Death Work: A Study of the Modern Execution Process.* 2d ed. Belmont, Calif.: West/Wadsworth, 1998.

Lawes, Lewis E. *Life and Death in Sing Sing.* Garden City, N.Y.: Doubleday, 1928.

Spear, Charles. *Essays on the Punishment of Death.* Littleton, Colo.: Fred B. Rothman, 1994. Originally published in 1845.

Zimmerman, Isidore, with Francis Bond. *Punishment Without Crime.* New York: Clarkson N. Potter, 1964.

ROBERT JOHNSON

See also **Capital Punishment; Crime and Punishment in American History; Executions, Methods of; Prisons and Prisoners.**

DENVER

Denver was conceived in violence. Colonel Edwin V. Sumner's troops defeated the Cheyenne in 1857, paving the way for gold seekers to make discoveries at the base of the Rocky Mountains in 1858. When real-estate speculator William Larimer and his party arrived at the confluence of Cherry Creek and the South Platte River in November 1858, they found a potentially valuable tract of land already occupied. Its lone defender, Charles Nichols, was warned that if he did not renounce his claim, "a rope and a noose would be used on him." Nichols submitted, and Larimer founded Denver.

Individual Perpetrators

A rope and a noose were used a few months later on John Stoefel, condemned for committing the town's first murder on 7 April 1859. He started a trend. On 12 June 1860 Marcus Gredler killed Jacob Roeder by cutting off his head with an ax. Gredler was hanged on June 15. A few days later William Hadley used a butcher knife to murder a man named Card. Hadley escaped. In July, Charles Harrison, a gambler, slew a free African American named Stark who had claimed to be equal to a white man. Harrison was not prosecuted. The same month James Gordon murdered John Gantz. Gordon escaped, but thanks to Sheriff William H. Middaugh, who traveled some two thousand miles in the process, Gordon was retaken and hanged.

After the excitement of the gold rush faded, the city calmed down for a time. Between 1861 and 1865 Denverites focused their blood lust on Native Americans more than they did on each other. Shortly after Christmas 1863 a pimp killed a soldier named Bill Duffield. In retaliation, Duffield's friends torched Aunt Betsy's whorehouse, but Colonel John Chivington, the local military commander, prevented his men from doing worse. The next year Chivington led volunteers to Sand Creek in southeastern Colorado, where on 29 November they massacred more than 160 Native Americans, many of them women and children, thereby igniting years of warfare.

The Union Pacific Railroad pushed into southern Wyoming in the late 1860s, bringing into the region a new crop of ruffians. In *Hands Up; or, Twenty Years of Detective Life in the Mountains and On the Plains* (1882), the pioneer detective David J. Cook recalls desperadoes such as Sanford Duggan and L. H. Musgrove, both of whom were lynched in Denver late in 1868. He tells of the Italian murderers who on 15 October 1875 hacked two of their companions to death while another one of them played the harp. And he devotes a chapter to the anti-Chinese riot of 31 October 1880, during which a mob hanged an innocent Chinese man and did more than fifty thousand dollars in damage.

In *Going to Meet a Man* (1990), William King discusses the murder on 19 May 1886 of Joseph Whitnah by Andrew Green, an African American. That led to Green's execution, the city's last legal public hanging, on 27 July 1886, witnessed by some fifteen thousand people in a carnival-like atmosphere. Less attention has been paid to the city's last lynching, on 26 July 1893, of barkeeper Daniel Arata, who killed one of his customers.

In *Denver's Murders* (1946), the editor Lee Casey and others review eight of the city's most famous murders, most between 1901 and 1942. Included is the October 1941 killing of Philip Peters by Theodore Coneys, dubbed the "spider man" because he eluded the police until July 1942 by hiding in the attic of the house where he had committed the crime. Casey does not include, except in passing, the robbery on 18 December 1922 of a Federal Reserve truck as it delivered money to the U.S. Mint. One guard and one gangster died, and the government lost more than $200,000. Nor does Casey treat Prohibition-spawned violence such as the 18 February 1933 killing of Joe Roma, described by the *Denver Post* as "the little half-pint big shot of Denver gangland."

Nearly a decade after *Denver Murders* was published, one man outdid all of Casey's murderers. On 1 November 1955 John Gilbert Graham planted a bomb aboard United Airlines Flight 629 in an attempt to blow up his mother, Daisie, and collect her insurance. Forty-four people died when the plane exploded eleven minutes after taking off. Graham was executed a little more than a year later. Joseph Corbett, Jr., was luckier. Linked to

John Gilbert Graham is led to court in Denver on 9 December 1955. Graham admitted to bombing a United Airlines plane, which resulted in forty-four deaths. CORBIS/BETTMANN

the February 1960 kidnap-murder of the brewer Adolph Coors III, one of the Denver metropolitan area's richest men, Corbett was sentenced to life in prison because the evidence against him was circumstantial.

High-profile crime continued to bedevil the Denver area in the 1980s and 1990s. Stephen Singular in *Talked to Death: The Life and Murder of Alan Berg* (1987) details the background and aftermath of the 18 June 1984 slaying of Berg, an outspoken talk radio host who allegedly was gunned down by white supremacists. The murder of JonBenet Ramsey, a six-year-old beauty queen, in Boulder, northwest of Denver, sometime during the night of 25–26 December 1996 baffled police and sparked a news media feeding frenzy. On 20 April 1999 national attention again focused on Denver when two disgruntled teenagers, Eric Harris and Dylan Klebold, killed themselves, twelve of their fellow classmates, and one teacher during a shooting and bombing rampage at Columbine High School in suburban Jefferson County.

Social Unrest

Like most large cities, Denver has suffered violence engendered by social, economic, religious, and racial rancor. In the 1920s a powerful Ku Klux Klan intimidated many, although no record that it killed anyone has come to light. In mid-August 1932 racial hatred inflamed whites to drive African Americans out of Washington Park, where they had attempted to go swimming. Thirty-six years later African American anger exploded after the assassination of Martin Luther King, Jr. Busing to integrate schools apparently prompted someone to blow up forty-six school vehicles in February 1970. During the same period tensions between mainstream Denverites and Chicanos fostered the St. Patrick's Day blowout in 1973, in which the Chicano activist Luís Martínez was killed, twelve policemen injured, and a building blown up.

Labor-management clashes have similarly disturbed Denver's repose. Alfred Horsley, better known as Harry Orchard, who claimed to be working for the Western Federation of Miners, confessed that in a botched attempt to dynamite a Colorado Supreme Court justice, he accidentally killed Merritt Walley in 1905. During the Tramway strike of early August 1920, the city's deadliest, strikers derailed streetcars, sacked the offices of the *Denver Post*, and beat strikebreakers. The trigger-happy scabs, commanded by "Black Jack" Jerome,

responded by killing seven people, many of them curious bystanders.

Denver's violence has mirrored national patterns. When it was a frontier outpost it temporarily suffered, like many other western towns, from a surfeit of unbridled, well-armed young men. When it became a city it reacted, as many cities did, to social and economic tensions by attacking newcomers such as the Chinese. Like most sizable cities it has witnessed lynchings, bloody labor-management clashes, and race riots. In the late twentieth century, gang violence, drug murders, road rage, and the Columbine High School tragedy have reminded the Mile High City that altitude and relative affluence are not antidotes for the violence that infects American life.

BIBLIOGRAPHY

Barker, Bill, and Jackie Lewin. *Denver! An Insider's Look at the High, Wide, and Handsome City.* New York: Doubleday, 1972.

Leonard, Stephen J. "Bloody August: The Denver Tramway Strike of 1920." *Colorado Heritage* (summer 1995).

Leonard, Stephen J., and Thomas J. Noel. *Denver: Mining Camp to Metropolis.* Niwot: University Press of Colorado, 1990.

Secrest, Clark. *Hell's Belles: Denver's Brides of the Multitudes . . . And a Biography of Sam Howe, Frontier Lawman.* Ann Arbor, Mich.: Braun-Brumfield, 1996.

STEPHEN J. LEONARD

See also **Urban Violence.**

DEPRESSIONS, ECONOMIC

Economic depressions in the United States have spawned several popular protest movements that ended in violence. Depressions also precipitated some of the most violent strikes in American labor history.

Violence and Economic Protest

One of the most significant violent economic protest movements in American history, Shays's Rebellion was also the earliest. In 1786, during the depression that followed the end of the Revolutionary War, farmers in western Massachusetts organized to resist high state taxes and farm foreclosures. From August to December, Shaysites closed county courts at gunpoint to prevent forfeiture of farms in lieu of back taxes, but they were defeated by Continental troops and the Massachusetts militia on 26 December; of some two dozen casualties among the Shaysites, four died. Shays's Rebellion forced Americans to face fundamental questions about the new nation's ability to maintain public order and became an important factor in the calling of the Constitutional Convention in 1787.

Subsequent depression-era protest movements were both less violent and less revolutionary. Two such movements, Coxey's Army of 1894 and the Bonus Army of 1932, were planned as peaceful demonstrations in Washington, D.C. The Ohio businessman Jacob S. Coxey's "army" of unemployed workers marched from Massillon, Ohio, to Washington, D.C., to demand passage of a bill that would have created a massive federal highway project designed to provide jobs for the unemployed. Inspired by Coxey's idea, several "regiments" of unemployed workmen from the West Coast and the mountain states also attempted to join him. The sporadic violence attendant on the movement came largely from the western contingents' penchant for train-stealing and the final dispersal of Coxey's camp by Washington police on 10 August.

The Bonus Army of 1932, formed at the height of the Great Depression (1929–1941), was composed of World War I veterans and their families who made a similar pilgrimage to Washington to demand early payment of a bonus that a 1924 act of Congress promised to deliver in 1945. Some twenty thousand Bonus Army veterans camped out for several weeks in a shantytown at Anacostia Flats. At the end of July, after Congress had refused the army's demands, federal troops under Douglas MacArthur stormed the camp, burning the shantytown and teargassing the veterans and their families.

The Farmers' Holiday Association (FHA) of 1932–1933 was a protest movement of the Great Depression that had more in common with the Shaysites than it did with either Coxey's Army or the Bonus Army. Like Shays and his men, FHA members organized to resist mortgage foreclosures on farms during a period of rock-bottom agricultural prices. Unlike the Shaysites, however, the FHA did not organize military resistance to state authority, but instead foiled mortgage auctions by intimidating bidders, buying up farms for a dollar, and returning them to their original owners. The FHA also organized farm strikes in Iowa and Wisconsin, during which FHA members seized control of rural highways to prevent nonmembers from marketing milk and corn. Martial

law was declared in several Iowa counties in the spring of 1933. FHA activity tapered off after 1933, but sporadic disruptions of farm sales continued as late as 1936.

The Dearborn, Michigan, massacre that ended the Ford Hunger March of 1932 might also be classified as the violent suppression of an economic protest movement. On 7 March some three or four thousand unemployed workers marched to the Ford Rouge plant in Dearborn to demand back pay, shorter work days, the rehiring of laid-off employees, and other concessions. When protesters ignored the orders of the Dearborn police to halt at the city limits and continued on to the Ford plant, the police fired into the crowd, killing four and wounding at least twenty.

Strike Violence

Depressions were periods of severe strike violence in American history, especially in the years since the Civil War. Widespread railroad strikes paralyzed large sections of the nation's rail system in 1877 and 1894 before being crushed by the violent intervention of federal troops. The railroad strike of 1877, perhaps the bloodiest incident in American labor history, began as a response to a 10 percent wage cut announced by the nation's largest railroads in June and July of that year. Baltimore and Ohio Railroad employees in Martinsburg, West Virginia, took control of railroad property in that city on 18 July. During the next ten days, the strike, accompanied by rioting and violent clashes between strikers, militia, and townspeople, spread to Baltimore; Pittsburgh; Buffalo, New York; Chicago; and St. Louis. Nationwide, over a hundred citizens, strikers, and soldiers died in the riots.

The Pullman strike of 1894 also began with demands to restore cut wages. Pullman Palace Sleeping Car Company employees particularly resented high rents in company housing. When Pullman employees struck, members of the newly organized American Railway Union supported the strike by refusing to work on trains that included Pullman cars. Because Pullmans were ubiquitous, the resulting walkout of railroad employees halted rail traffic in and out of Chicago. Declaring that the strike was interfering with the U.S. mail, President Grover Cleveland sent federal troops to protect strikebreakers. As in 1877, bloody riots were the result.

The Great Depression also witnessed several major episodes of strike violence. A general strike in San Francisco and a cotton strike by the United Textile Workers in the South made 1934 one of the most turbulent years in American labor history. The San Francisco general strike capped a two-month longshoremen's walkout that had been marred by rioting and the deaths of two protesters at the hands of police. The cotton workers' strike brought the National Guard into Georgia, North Carolina, and South Carolina.

On 11 January 1937, in one of the most famous labor-capital conflicts of the Depression, supporters of United Auto Workers' sit-down strike at the Chevrolet plant in Flint, Michigan, fought police in the so-called Battle of the Running Bulls. No one was killed and General Motors was ultimately unionized. But the Congress of Industrial Organizations' attempt to organize "Little Steel" the same year was much bloodier. In the Memorial Day massacre of 1937, Chicago police fired into a crowd of two or three thousand strikers marching outside the Republic steel plant, killing ten and injuring fifty-eight.

Historians debate the role of socialists and communists in each of these incidents. Although each organization had some radical members, in most cases the demands of strikers and protesters were limited to wages, prices, or working conditions, and did not extend to social or political revolution.

BIBLIOGRAPHY

Bruce, Robert V. *1877: Year of Violence.* New York: Bobbs-Merrill, 1959.

Hofstadter, Richard, and Michael Wallace, eds. *American Violence: A Documentary History.* New York: Knopf, 1970.

Jeffreys-Jones, Rhodri. *Violence and Reform in American History.* New York: New Viewpoint, 1978.

McElvaine, Robert S. *The Great Depression: America, 1929–1941.* New York: Times Books, 1984.

Selvin, David F. *A Terrible Anger: The 1934 Waterfront and General Strikes in San Francisco.* Detroit: Wayne State University Press, 1996.

R. RUDY HIGGENS-EVENSON

See also **Capitalism; Labor and Unions; Pullman Strike; Riots; Strikes.**

DERINGER, HENRY, JR.
(1786–1868)

Henry Deringer, Jr., is the only American gun maker whose name became synonymous with his product (with the possible exception of Samuel Colt). During the late 1850s and early 1860s, the deringer pistol (commonly misspelled "derringer") achieved national, even international, renown.

The inventor of the "pocket pistol" was born in Easton, Pennsylvania, on 6 October 1786. He was the son of a German couple who had come to America around the time of the Revolutionary War. His father had had at least some experience as a gunsmith, making so-called Kentucky rifles. After serving for one year as an apprentice to a firearms manufacturer in Richmond, Virginia, Henry, Jr., moved in 1806 to Philadelphia, where he established his own arms factory and where he and his wife, Eliza Hillebush Deringer, raised a large family (nine children are mentioned in Deringer's will). By 1845 Deringer was, by all accounts, a wealthy man, having made money not only from the sale of arms but also from real estate holdings and shares in several banks. Having spent more than sixty years of his life in Philadelphia, he died on 26 February 1868 at the age of eighty-one.

Early in his gun business, Deringer supplied the U.S. government with flintlock muskets and rifles. At the same time he manufactured for the civilian market various hunting rifles and dueling pistols. Wilson and Eberhart have estimated that between the end of the War of 1812 and the start of the Mexican War in 1846, Deringer made more than twenty thousand weapons for the U.S. Army and some fifty thousand trade rifles. In 1842 Deringer produced a martial percussion pistol for the U.S. Navy. It may very well have been his success with this "box-lock" firearm (which uses percussion rather than flint ignition) that led Deringer to develop and expand production of the compact, concealable, large-caliber single-shot pistol for which he became famous.

Deringer's handgun was never patented and consequently was widely imitated. Eventually making the transition from the percussion to the cartridge era, the weapon has remained in production. In its heyday, just prior to the Civil War, the deringer was typically sold in pairs. Such pistols were most sought after not by soldiers, pioneers, or homesteaders, but by riverboat gamblers, gold miners, confidence men, dance hall women, newspaper editors, and politicians. They were also prized by ladies and gentlemen and regarded as fashionable. Indeed, they could be purchased in jewelry stores, including Tiffany's in New York, as well as in gun shops. They attained their greatest popularity in the South, in California, and, more specifically, in newly or provisionally settled cities such as New Orleans and San Francisco. The gun attained its greatest notoriety in 1865, when John Wilkes Booth used a deringer in his deadly assault on President Abraham Lincoln.

BIBLIOGRAPHY

Eberhart, L. D., and R. L. Wilson. *The Deringer in America.* Vol. 2, *The Cartridge Period.* Lincoln, R.I.: Andrew Mowbray, 1993.

Parsons, John E. *Henry Deringer's Pocket Pistol.* New York: William Morrow, 1952.

Wilson, R. L., and L. D. Eberhart. *The Deringer in America.* Vol. 1, *The Percussion Period.* Lincoln, R.I.: Andrew Mowbray, 1985.

DONALD D. KUMMINGS

See also **Colt, Samuel; Gatling, Richard Jordan; Remington, Eliphalet; Weapons.**

DESALVO, ALBERT
(1931–1973)

A murderous mind often has its roots in a brutal childhood. Albert DeSalvo (also known as the Boston Strangler) would seem to be a case in point. Born in Chelsea, Massachusetts, in 1931, DeSalvo witnessed family violence as a fact of life. Frank

Albert DeSalvo, the "Boston Strangler," on 25 February 1967, after his escape from Bridgewater State Hospital and subsequent capture in a West Lynn, Massachusetts, uniform store. CORBIS/BETTMANN

DeSalvo, Albert's father, would explode at the slightest provocation. Once, he beat one of his sons with a rubber hose until the boy was a mass of visible bruises. The boy had been guilty of toppling a box of fruit. Violence was also Frank's way of expressing his dissatisfaction with his wife. On one occasion he methodically broke every one of her fingers. In all, six children grew up in the DeSalvo household, experiencing and witnessing these savage acts. Only Albert, though, would become a murderer—clearly this sort of upbringing is only a partial explanation for homicidal impulses. He may have harbored some brutal predisposition of his own, perhaps even inherited from his father. Whatever the reason, by the age of thirty-one he would become known as the Boston Strangler, the killer of thirteen women in an eighteen-month period.

As is common among many serial killers, Albert DeSalvo first dabbled in violence as a child by torturing small animals. Years later, his sadism took a less overt form. Passing himself off as a representative of a modeling agency, DeSalvo would persuade women to allow him to take their measurements. At the age of thirty, in 1961, he was convicted of lewd and lascivious behavior; the police called him the Measuring Man. After his release from prison a year later, his crimes turned violent. As the serial rapist who wore green pants when he talked his way into the homes of his victims, DeSalvo was dubbed the Green Man by the police. His sexual perversions probably had been cultivated during his childhood. As a boy, DeSalvo and his siblings had witnessed their brutish father having sex with prostitutes. As an adult, Albert went beyond his father's cruel excesses. Sex and violence now forged into one desire in Albert DeSalvo's increasingly deranged mind.

At the same time that he was finagling his way into women's homes for the purpose of rape, DeSalvo was also using his glib tongue to enter apartments for even deadlier reasons. In the summer of 1962, he began raping and strangling elderly women. Typically, he would leave a nylon stocking knotted into a bow around his victim's neck. Within months he moved on to younger victims. His methods also became more ferocious. He would bite his victims and, in some cases, would force a broomstick into the vagina.

Hunted now as the Boston Strangler, DeSalvo terrorized his native city for a year and a half. Ultimately, the police arrested him without even realizing they had captured Boston's most infamous serial murderer. He was jailed instead for one of his nonlethal Green Man rapes, and the truth came out only when DeSalvo began boasting of his more serious crimes to a fellow inmate. Even then, the courts never brought the Boston Strangler to trial. DeSalvo's lawyer, the famed F. Lee Bailey, arranged an unusual sentencing deal: DeSalvo avoided receiving the death penalty for his thirteen killings by accepting a life sentence for the Green Man attacks. The life sentence did not last very long. In 1973, nine years after his final arrest, DeSalvo was stabbed to death by a fellow prisoner.

BIBLIOGRAPHY

Frank, Gerold. *The Boston Strangler.* New York: New American Library, 1966.

Newton, Michael. *Hunting Humans.* Port Townsend, Wash.: Loompanics Unlimited, 1990.

Wilson, Colin, and Donald Seaman. *The Serial Killers.* New York: Carol, 1991.

DAVID EVERITT

See also **Serial Killers.**

DETERRENCE. *See* Cold War; Disarmament and Arms Control.

DETROIT

Founded in 1701 by Antoine Laumet de la Mothe Cadillac as a French garrison, Fort Pontchartrain du Détroit evolved from trading post to garrison town to commercial center before becoming, between 1920 and 1940, the leading producer of automobiles and fourth-largest city in the United States. Since then its industrial growth, population size, and ethnic composition have fluctuated, with a thread of socioethnic tensions and violence running throughout its history.

The Nineteenth Century

From its mixture of French (1701), English (1760), and American (1796) heritages, Detroit bore ethnic and cultural conflicts that characterized later periods of city strife. The first intergroup frictions occurred in the 1830s between French Catholics and Protestant New Englanders who resented the lingering French feudalistic social order and land tenure. But it was the city's black population preventing the return of fugitive slaves to Kentucky in 1833 that sparked the first major social explosion, in a riot against white authorities; though it did not involve street fighting among city residents, the clash served to highlight free black resistance and intensify local white fear.

Conflicts during Detroit's commercial-industrial stage, from the mid-nineteenth century to 1900, turned on issues of race, crime, and labor, in part indicating demographic and geographic influences. The influx of Irish and German immigrants in the late 1840s ignited disorders from 1855 to 1859, largely involving the assault by working-class Germans on black bordellos threatening their eastside neighborhood. Criminal activities, including gambling and theft, provided economic mobility to segments of black society, and other ethnic groups would follow suit. Since many of these activities, carried on by blacks and others, occurred close to downtown, business elites sought to establish spatial and social control and, by the early 1860s, were considering the creation of a municipal police force.

Detroit's second major social upheaval occurred on 6 March 1863, during the Civil War. The city had recently received a draft call when two nine-year-old girls, one black and one white, claimed that they had been raped by publican William Faulkner, a mulatto. (This accusation was later proved to be false.) Faulkner's conviction drew a life sentence, angering whites who wanted Faulkner to hang. Failing in their attempt to lynch him, they turned on the black community, killing two people, injuring scores, and burning thirty homes. The rioting was dominated by Irish immigrants— mostly lower-class transients, resentful of federal conscription and fearful of job competition (though blacks made up only 3.1 percent of the population of 45,619). They destroyed much of black Detroit in the Midwest's only major riot of the Civil War.

Public concern about disorder and crime, especially in the well-to-do residential and business districts, led to the creation by the state in 1864 of the Metropolitan Police Force of the City of Detroit. In the 1870s it served reputable citizens by concentrating on unlawful activities by lower-class Irish and African Americans in the downtown area. Ironically, Irish males were overrepresented in both the ranks of prisoners and policemen, whereas the first black patrolman was not hired until 1893. During the last three decades of the nineteenth century, the city was subject to several strikes, but these resulted in little bloodshed. In the economic crisis of 1893, however, the police were called in to quell bloody work stoppages by unemployed foreign-born residents— notably recently arrived Poles—against American-born workers, who soon moved to disfranchise aliens.

The Early Twentieth Century

Between 1900 and 1945 Detroit's transformation into a center of modern industrialization was marked by violence. Both Henry Ford's five-dollar-a-day wage and World War I labor demands brought thousands of newcomers into the city during the Great Migration (1916–1920). The influx of racial and ethnic groups continued through World War II, expanding the municipal population from 465,766 in 1910 to 1,849,568 in 1950 and raising the city's rank from ninth- to fourth-largest as early as 1920. By that year the number of black residents had increased to 40,838, or 4.1 percent of the total, sparking interethnic competition over jobs and housing.

Although Detroit avoided upheaval during the Red Summer of 1919, when whites threatened by postwar changes attacked blacks in twenty-five riots across the nation, it encountered ethnoreligious tension and racial bloodshed throughout the next decade. Ku Klux Klan members supported a mayoral candidate and promoted antiblack, anti-Catholic, and anti-Jewish propaganda, complete with cross burnings and campaign violence, in 1924 and 1925. They were repulsed at the polls by blacks, Catholics, and European immigrants. Klan beliefs nonetheless resonated with many whites who felt threatened as the number of black residents nearly doubled by the mid-1920s and members of the black middle class entered all-white neighborhoods. In the most publicized incident, a mob, including many foreign-born Catholics, attacked the home of Dr. Ossian Sweet and drew gunfire that killed one demonstrator. Jurors acquitted Sweet and his brother Henry, both benefiting from the skill of defense attorney Clarence Darrow and support by the National Association for the Advancement of Colored People. Nonetheless, the Klan's legacy, if not its citywide membership of thirty-five thousand, carried into the decade of the Great Depression. Meanwhile, smaller in number, yet more violent and involving some Detroit area policemen, a Klan splinter group calling itself the Black Legion targeted blacks, Catholics, Jews, communists, and unionists, until several Legionnaires were convicted of murdering a federal employee in

1936. Organized crime also shook Detroit in the 1920s and 1930s, the result of its location and ethnic population combined with illegal opportunities that arose in the wake of the national Prohibition. The Jewish Purple Gang and the Italian Pascuzzi Combine competed for the Canadian liquor trade that supplied most midwestern cities, including Al Capone's Chicago. Their activities, ranging from bootlegging to murder, drew citizens, policemen, officials, and residents of nearby Ecorse, Hamtramck, and Wyandotte into bloodshed and corruption. From the aftermath of "Bloody July" in 1930—when gang fratricide occurred daily—until repeal of Prohibition three years later, Italian mobsters emerged to dominate syndicated crime in the city.

Meanwhile, efforts to organize industrial workers made little headway until the Great Depression. Strikers had clashed with police in pre- and postwar Detroit, for example, Industrial Workers of the World in 1913 and Carriage, Wagon, and Automobile Workers in 1919. Conflict intensified in the 1930s, when factory speed-ups, economic crisis, and government recognition ushered in unionization and collective bargaining, especially in the auto industries for which Detroit had become known worldwide. Labor competition, in which the United Automobile Workers (UAW), the American Federation of Labor, and the Communist Party challenged management, produced bloodshed. From the Detroit Unemployed Council's Hunger March to the Ford River Rouge plant in Dearborn on 7 March 1932 to the UAW's drive at Ford Motor Company, accentuated by the "Battle of the Overpass" on 26 May 1937, violence erupted intermittently between unionists, police, company thugs, and strikebreakers, until the UAW won the National Labor Relations Board election four years later.

On the eve of the United States' entry into World War II, the UAW had established union consciousness but not complete solidarity. As Detroit became the "arsenal of democracy," racial conflict intensified over jobs and especially living space in the face of in-migration, inadequate housing, and wartime sacrifices. Blacks had entered the union in an uneasy alliance with white workers, only to experience discrimination over upgrading and the hiring of black women. Thus, throughout the war both races engaged in "wildcat strikes," Klan influence emerged in some locals, and the potential for violence loomed large. It erupted most notably at the federally built Sojourner Truth Homes in

The aftermath of the July 1967 race riot in Detroit. Forty-three people were killed and at least six hundred injured. UPI/CORBIS-BETTMANN

1942 and in side-by-side communal and commodity riots along the city's major thoroughfare on 20–22 June 1943. White rioters—younger, unattached, and employed—traveled great distances to protest the changing racial order by attacking blacks on Woodward Avenue, while black rioters—older, married, and employed—remained in the eastside to protest their blocked opportunities by looting and destroying white-owned property. Neither southerners nor riffraff were responsible for the twenty-five black and nine white deaths; injuries to more than 675 persons requiring hospital care; $2 million in property damage; or one million hours of lost defense work. Just as police officers —98.5 percent white—had assisted management in the labor wars, they aligned with white rioters in the worst urban upheaval to that time in U.S. history.

The Post–World War II Decades

Postwar Detroit entered its most acclaimed and most difficult era, reaching its largest population shortly before undergoing industrial automation, job losses, plant relocations, and sociopolitical tensions. During the Cold War, the UAW purged its ranks of leftists and strengthened itself in a series of protracted, largely peaceful strikes. Wildcat stoppages protesting black upgrading also marked the late 1940s, yet black hiring—for the least desirable jobs—continued into the 1960s. Some mob violence against supposed radicals occurred in the period of the Korean War and Senator Joseph McCarthy's campaign against American communists.

By 1960 Detroit experienced full-blown deindustrialization, economic recessions, black influx and white exodus, as well as continued violence over contested neighborhoods and job discrimination against poorer blacks. Liberal efforts by Mayor Jerome P. Cavanagh from 1961 to 1969 failed to resolve the ethnic, racial, and increasing class conflicts, which burst forth in the city's worst riot on 23 July 1967. The riot lasted four days, claimed forty-three lives, injured over six hundred people, and damaged between $150 and 200 million in property. The mostly black participants struck at white-owned property and police as symbols of authority, protesting their condition relative to whites and completing the historical transition from communal to commodity disorders—that is, from interracial combat initiated by whites to assaults on businesses and looting incited by blacks. Greater percentages of black women joined black males, who, compared with their counterparts in 1943, appeared to be somewhat younger, and with fewer married and employed. Black rioters were joined by a contingent of whites, who made up 12 percent of those arrested. All the rioters, in general, were longtime city residents, motivated by the Civil Rights movement and by the violent atmosphere of both urban life and the Vietnam War.

The riot resulted in efforts to improve race relations in Detroit, as well as further economic decentralization; yet it also accelerated white flight and strain in the police community, which led to the transition of municipal political power from white to black society. In 1973 Coleman Young began twenty years of unbroken mayoral rule over what would become the nation's first predominantly African American metropolis. Significantly, he challenged the Detroit Police Department, whose overwhelmingly white composition, role in the riots, and reputation for brutality infuriated black residents. He succeeded in making the force an integrated unit that better represented the city's demography; in 1976 William Hart became the first black to serve as chief of police. Young empowered black Detroiters and, doubtless, reduced the chance of race riots as the city's African American population increased from 44.5 to 60.7 percent from 1970 to 1990.

Amid economic woes, population loss, shrinking tax base, and reduced federal assistance, however, Young found other forms of bloodshed intractable. Italian mobs carried gambling, racketeering, and violence from wartime contacts with Henry Ford to postwar control of the Teamsters Union, allying with Chaldean drug dealers and bookmakers. Much as Prohibition in the 1920s led to increased crime, in the 1980s and 1990s the illegality of drugs spawned crime by black and Hispanic gangs. Less centralized, younger, and more nihilistic than their predecessors, they killed competitors and (mostly black) bystanders in turf wars that fostered the city's reputation as the nation's murder capital. Police corruption exacerbated violence, as Chief Hart and other officials were involved in drug-related scandals. So did the city's postindustrial socioeconomic plight, which continued with the new mayor, Dennis W. Hatcher, who began his term in 1993.

Detroit's Violent Celebrations

Postindustrial Detroit has been the location of several revelous riots—celebrations that have gotten out of hand—most notably over sporting events and over the city's unique way of celebrating Halloween. Following victories by the Detroit Tigers in the 1968 and 1984 World Series and by the Detroit Pistons in the 1990 National Basketball Association championship, ecstatic fans became destructive crowds: looting stores, setting fires, hurling objects, and engaging in assaults (including rape and murder). The riots escalated over time—in 1990 they claimed seven dead, several hundred injured, and 140 arrested —and spread to other major cities with sports franchises. More notorious has been the carnival-like observance of setting buildings afire as prelude to Halloween, a tradition that began in 1986 and became routinized as Devil's Night. While both forms of outbursts share characteristics of emotion, contagious nature, and release from everyday pressures, Devil's Night momentarily turned socioeconomic patterns of behavior askew: mostly lower-class individuals targeted and ignited hundreds of structures, but spectators from all classes gathered to watch the infernos.

BIBLIOGRAPHY

Capeci, Dominic J., Jr., and Martha Wilkerson. *Layered Violence: The Detroit Rioters of 1943.* Jackson: University Press of Mississippi, 1991.

Conot, Robert. *American Odyssey.* New York: Morrow, 1974.

Fine, Sidney. *Violence in the Model City: The Cavanaugh Administration, Race Relations, and the Detroit Riot of 1967.* Ann Arbor: University of Michigan Press, 1989.

Holli, Melvin G., ed. *Detroit.* New York: New Viewpoints, 1976.

Oestreicher, Richard Jules. *Solidarity and Fragmentation: Working People and Class Consciousness in Detroit, 1875–1900.* Urbana: University of Illinois Press, 1989.

Peterson, Joyce Shaw. *American Automobile Workers, 1900–1933.* Albany: State University of New York Press, 1987.

Schneider, John C. *Detroit and the Problem of Order, 1830–1888: A Geography of Crime, Riot, and Policing.* Lincoln: University of Nebraska Press, 1980.

Sugrue, Thomas J. *The Origins of the Urban Crisis: Race and Inequality in Postwar Detroit.* Princeton, N.J.: Princeton University Press, 1996.

Widick, B. J. *Detroit: City of Race and Class Violence*. Chicago: Quadrangle, 1972.

DOMINIC J. CAPECI, JR.

See also **Urban Violence.**

DEVELOPMENTAL FACTORS

*From the moment of conception, the first years of a person's life play an important role in behavioral patterns in adult years. The following four entries present developmental factors in chronological order: **Prenatal, Perinatal, Childhood,** and **Puberty and Adolescence.** See also "Age and the Life Cycle" for a study of violence throughout life. "Endrocrinology," "Genetics," and "Health and Medical Factors" examine closely related factors contributing to violent behavior.*

PRENATAL

Prenatal disturbances have a variety of negative effects on fetuses. One potential outcome of these negative effects is antisocial behavior, in particular criminal violence, in childhood and adulthood. Among the prenatal risk factors that predict antisocial behavior are poor nutrition and physical injury to a developing fetus. The introduction of a teratogen, an agent that causes developmental malformations, during fetal development can also have negative effects; drugs and alcohol are examples of teratogens that, if abused by the mother during her pregnancy, can adversely affect the formation of the fetus. A virus may also work as a teratogen, and influenza in particular has been the subject of large epidemiological studies.

The timing of exposure to an agent may be a critical factor in determining whether or not it will pose a risk to the fetus. Studies indicate that exposure to certain viruses, such as influenza, during critical periods of development may increase the risk for certain mental and behavioral disorders. For example, if a mother has influenza during the second trimester of her pregnancy, there may be an increased risk that her child will develop schizophrenia during adulthood and major affective disorders, which are characterized by a disturbance in mood, such as depression. Exposure to influenza during the first and third trimesters of fetal development, however, has not been associated with an increased risk of mental disorder. This finding has been replicated in independent studies completed in a number of international settings.

Helsinki Influenza Project

Data from the Helsinki Influenza Project that was conducted from 1985 to 1987 suggest a potential link between exposure to influenza during specific periods of fetal brain development and criminal violence. Within the context of the project, Jasmine Tehrani and colleagues examined whether a fetus's exposure to maternal influenza during the second trimester was associated with an increased rate of violent offending during childhood and adulthood.

The researchers searched the Finnish Police Register for all Helsinki residents born in the nine months after the 1957 influenza epidemic and who therefore had been exposed to the virus in utero. The register includes information only on violent and major property offenses. The research uncovered no relationship between property offenses and exposure to the epidemic. However, a significant association was observed between convictions for violent crimes and exposure to the virus during the second trimester of gestation, as indicated in figure 1. Most of the violent offenders had been exposed to influenza at the cusp of the sixth and seventh months of gestation.

Because the data regarding the influenza exposure and criminal convictions were recorded as they occurred, this study does not rely on recall and is therefore, to date, the only nonretrospective study to examine the association between the timing of influenza exposure and criminal violence. Other data support the contention that violent behavior may be related to exposure to influenza during the second trimester of gestation. Peter Venables found that a significant proportion of violent young Mauritius children were also exposed to influenza during this trimester.

Timing of Teratogens and Neural Development

The brain develops sequentially. If a region of the brain does not develop during its assigned period, the area will be left with a deficit, because the brain does not return to correct undeveloped areas. The maternal influenza infection may be a teratogenic disturbance that disrupts the development of the fetal brain. Sarnoff Mednick and colleagues (1988) have proposed a working model that may help structure the interpretation of the Helsinki results. To increase the risk for criminal violence, this neural disruption must satisfy two conditions: first, it must occur during a period (or periods) of rapid development of specific brain regions; and

FIGURE 1. Violence in Helsinki Cohort Born After the 1957 Influenza Epidemic

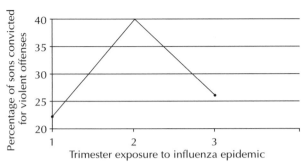

second, a deficit in these specific brain regions must play a significant role in increasing the risk for criminal violence.

Regions of the brain are especially vulnerable during periods of rapid development, and a teratogen will have exaggerated effects on the region undergoing rapid growth. This period of vulnerability must span some days in the second trimester of gestation. For example, if a failure of development of a subarea of the prefrontal cortex or thalamus is a risk factor for criminal violence, then one period of vulnerability might comprise those days of gestation during which the prefrontal cortex or thalamus is most rapidly developing. If the teratogen is introduced during a gestational period different from the one identified as critical, the risk for criminal violence will not increase. It is possible that a teratogen introduced during a different gestational period may increase risk for other behavioral disorders.

It is further hypothesized that normal mental functioning depends on the brain's developing during gestation without serious disturbance. Each brain area, system, and circuit has its appointed time during gestation to flourish. If this assigned developmental period is disturbed (by genetic or teratogenic influence), that area, system, or circuit will suffer a developmental deficit; such a deficit may be associated with specific mental, behavioral, and cognitive disorders.

The Drosophila as Model

The development of the drosophila (a small two-winged fly used in genetic research) provides an instructive model of this hypothesis. The effect of teratogens on drosophila development has been the subject of intense study since research was conducted by H. Gloor in 1947. The most commonly studied teratogen has been heat shock, a term that can refer to exposure to chemicals, stress, or extreme temperatures (for example, exposure to a temperature of 40.8 degrees Celsius for thirty-five minutes), which stops the synthesis of RNA (ribonucleic acid) and protein. This teratogen has been introduced at different stages of the drosophila's development, and systemic structural abnormalities have been observed. These abnormalities resemble mutant-gene defects and are termed *phenocopies*. Phenocopies result from interruptions of gene expression at critical developmental periods, that is, when rapid changes are occurring.

After the heat-shock teratogen is introduced, cell activity is dominated by heat-shock proteins, and normal gene expression is put on hold. When the danger is past, the genes begin to express normally again. There is, however, an internal timing process that informs the cell which part of the drosophila is scheduled for rapid development. Thirty-seven hours into pupal development, the wings are scheduled to develop rapidly. This wing development must be completed in the next four hours because at forty-one hours the head will begin rapid development, and that of the wings will cease or be severely reduced. The genes will express on schedule and will not return to an organ to repair errors. If the heat-shock teratogen is presented between thirty-seven and forty-one hours, the development of the wings will be disturbed, and wings will develop abnormally or not at all. That is, whichever part of the drosophila should have developed during the teratogen-inspired interruption will be incomplete or abnormal.

Other teratogens have been tested on the drosophila. For example, in Gloor's 1947 study (published in German in the *Revue Suisse Zoologique*), ether was also an effective teratogen. Many other chemical teratogens have been tested and found to yield equivalent effects. The term *heat-shock proteins* is also used for teratogens other than heat.

The relevance of this model for the effects of teratogens on human-brain development is clear. In response to a teratogen (such as maternal influenza, severe stress, or maternal alcohol consumption or tobacco use), the cells assume a defensive stance. Heat-shock proteins will dominate cell behavior; normal gene expression will be put on hold. If a list of human-brain areas is substituted for the different parts of the drosophila and the time scale is changed, it is clear that when the influence of the teratogen dissipates, gene expression will skip a brain area and move on to the next one scheduled for rapid development.

Implications for Human Fetal Development

The timing of a teratogen is crucial in determining its effect on the specific sequence of fetal organ development. For example, thalidomide, a sedative and hypnotic drug, only has teratogenic effects during one week in the first trimester. Taken by the mother in another period, it has no known negative effect. It is likely that the same principle applies to brain development in the latter part of gestation. The timing of a teratogen may help determine the nature of a major mental or behavioral disorder. It is possible that the great diversity of behaviors seen in violent individuals is related to the consequences of teratogens encountered at certain times during gestation. The type and timing of the teratogen may also influence a person's cognitive ability, personality, or temperament.

BIBLIOGRAPHY

Machon, Ricardo A., and Sarnoff A. Mednick. "Adult Schizophrenia and Early Neurodevelopmental Disturbances." *Confrontations Psychiatriques: Epidemiologie et Psychiatrie* 35. Specia Rhône-Poulenc Rorer (1994).

Mednick, Sarnoff A., et al. "Adult Schizophrenia Following Prenatal Exposure to an Influenza Epidemic." *Archives of General Psychiatry* 45 (1988).

Mednick, Sarnoff A., et al. "Influenza and Schizophrenia: Helsinki vs. Edinburgh." *Archives of General Psychiatry* 47 (1990).

O'Callaghan, Eaubhard, et al. "Schizophrenia After Prenatal Exposure to 1957 A2 Influenza Epidemic." *Lancet* 337 (1991).

Tehrani, Jasmine A., et al. "Mental Illness and Criminal Violence." *Social Psychiatry and Psychiatric Epidemiology* 33 (1998).

Venables, Peter H. "Maternal Exposure to Influenza and Cold in Pregnancy and Electrodermal Activity in Offspring: The Mauritius Study." *Psychophysiology* 34 (1997).

Waddington, John L. "Schizophrenia After the 1957 Influenza Epidemic in Ireland." Paper presented at the meeting of the Royal Society of Psychiatry, 24–27 July 1992, Dublin, Ireland.

SARNOFF A. MEDNICK
JASMINE A. TEHRANI

See also **Alcohol and Alcoholism; Drugs and Violence; Maternal Prenatal Violence.**

PERINATAL

In 1861 William John Little, a pioneer London orthopedic surgeon, observed that "the act of birth does occasionally imprint upon the nervous and muscular systems of the nascent infantile organism very serious and peculiar evils." Prior to major advances in medical care in the twentieth century, most infants suffering from perinatal complications died in infancy or very early childhood. However, improvements in health care and an increased focus on pediatrics resulted in a significantly lower mortality rate for children who had suffered early developmental insults. By the 1950s these children were the focus of widespread concern. Public-health physicians began to suggest that prevention programs focus on children along the entire "continuum of reproductive casualty," ranging from studies of cerebral palsy and epilepsy to learning disabilities and behavior disturbances (Pasamanick and Knobloch 1960). Subsequent studies focused on potential negative long-term outcomes among children who had suffered from perinatal difficulties. One such long-term focus is the exhibition of violent behavior. Research evidence suggests that infants who suffer from perinatal difficulties and who are exposed to further environmental risks in childhood are more likely to exhibit violent behavior as they grow older.

Perinatal factors may be related specifically to violence, rather than to nonviolent delinquency or property crimes, such as thievery. Most of the studies that have found no relationship between perinatal factors and criminal outcomes have failed to examine a connection with violent offenses in particular. Investigators who have separated offenders as to their propensity for violence have noted that the more violent offenders have histories of perinatal difficulties.

Perinatal factors can be separated into two primary types: pregnancy complications (including those that result in minor physical anomalies) and birth complications.

Pregnancy Complications

Complications during pregnancy may arise from certain high-risk illnesses of the mother (for example, influenza or hypertension), from eclampsia (an attack of convulsions during pregnancy or parturition), from maternal exposure to stress or to teratogens (for example, radiation, nicotine, and alcohol), and from maternal bleeding during pregnancy. These complications have been associated with behavior problems such as impulsivity and aggression in children, but they have rarely been examined in relation to violence.

One study, by Elizabeth Kandel and Sarnoff A. Mednick, that explicitly examined the relationship between subjects whose mothers had experienced pregnancy complications and their history of arrests for violence found nonsignificant results. A methodological weakness may explain the study's failure to find a significant relationship. Measures of pregnancy complications are subjective and often retrospective. Therefore, prenatal complication measures may not be reliable or valid. There is one prenatal complication measure, however, that can be reliably and objectively measured years after birth—minor physical anomalies. Minor physical anomalies are small aberrations in external physical characteristics that are believed to reflect genetic defects or disruptions of pregnancy. These anomalies, which can be caused by teratogens or stress during pregnancy, are not noticeable to the untrained observer and are largely unrelated to overall physical attractiveness. Some of the most commonly measured minor physical anomalies include extra hair whorls, small head circumference, low-set ears, asymmetrical ears, curved fingers, a single transverse crease on the palm of the hand, and abnormal toe lengths. For example, as the ears develop during gestation, they drift upward to their normal position on the side of the head. If there is some disruption in fetal growth, the ears' drift upward may be slowed or stopped, resulting in low-set ears.

Because minor physical anomalies reflect general disruptions in fetal growth, they can serve as an observable index of central nervous system deficits resulting from less than optimal gestation. These deficits in the development of the brain of the fetus might in turn increase the propensity for behavior problems, including aggression and violence, later in life. Minor physical anomalies have been found to be related to aggression, attentional problems, and hyperactive behavior in children. A study by Elizabeth Kandel, Patricia A. Brennan, Sarnoff A. Mednick, and Niels M. Michelsen noted a significant relationship between minor physical anomalies and arrests for violent behavior. In this study of 129 males, minor physical anomalies measured at ages eleven to thirteen were related to arrests for violence through age twenty-two, providing preliminary evidence for a relationship between minor physical anomalies and violence. But this sample consisted largely of males whose parents had been hospitalized for a psychiatric illness. These males therefore would have been exposed to multiple social risk factors during development, including stressful life events, family conflicts, and socioeconomic adversity. It is likely that the combination of minor physical anomalies and the ad-

ditional social risks produced the increased rates of violent behavior in these males.

Birth Complications

Birth or delivery complications include forceps extraction, breech delivery (where the hind end of the body emerges first), umbilical cord prolapse (where the umbilical cord slips from its usual position), and preeclampsia (a toxic condition that can develop in late pregnancy and that is characterized by a sudden rise in blood pressure, excessive weight gain, edema, the presence of albumin in the urine, severe headaches, and visual disturbances). Birth complications have been found to predict arrests for violent crimes when they occur in combination with other potential risk factors. For example, birth complications and early institutionalization of the child were found to predict arrests for violent crimes in a study of 4,269 Danish males conducted by Patricia A. Brennan, Sarnoff A. Mednick, and Adrian Raine. These risk factors did not predict arrests for property offenses such as thievery. Similar increases in violent criminal behavior were found in a study of males who had a history of birth complications and early maternal rejection (Raine, Brennan, and Mednick 1994). In this study, males who had a history that included both delivery complications and early maternal rejection were three times as likely as other males in the sample to have a record of criminal violence. In addition, these males at risk constituted a relatively large percentage of the arrests for violence in the cohort (a group of individuals having a statistical factor in common in a demographic study). Although they made up only 4.5 percent of the overall sample, they committed 18 percent of the total number of violent crimes.

Most of the research on perinatal factors and violence has been focused on males and on official criminal outcomes, such as arrests. Generalization to females and self-reported violence or aggression is not yet possible. Preliminary research evidence, however, suggests that there may be a relationship between birth complications and criminal violence, particularly for males who are exposed to other risk factors as well. These findings suggest that violence-prevention strategies might begin very early in life with improved perinatal care.

BIBLIOGRAPHY

Brennan, Patricia A., Sarnoff A. Mednick, and Adrian Raine. "Perinatal and Social Risk Factors for Violence." In

Biosocial Bases of Violence, edited by Adrian Raine, Patricia Brennan, David Farrington, and Sarnoff Mednick. New York: Plenum, 1997.

Kandel, Elizabeth, Patricia A. Brennan, Sarnoff A. Mednick, and Niels M. Michelsen. "Minor Physical Anomalies and Recidivistic Adult Violent Criminal Behavior." *Acta Psychiatrica Scandinavica* 79, no. 1 (1989).

Kandel, Elizabeth, and Sarnoff A. Mednick. "Perinatal Complications Predict Violent Offending." *Criminology* 29, no. 3 (1991).

Lewis, Dorothy O., Shelley S. Shanok, and David A. Balla. "Perinatal Difficulties, Head and Face Trauma, and Child Abuse in the Medical Histories of Seriously Delinquent Children." *American Journal of Psychiatry* 136, no. 4 (1979).

Little, William J. "On the Influence of Abnormal Parturition, Difficult Labours, Premature Birth, and Asphyxia Neonatorum on the Mental and Physical Condition of the Child, Especially in Relation to Deformities." *Transactions of the Obstetrical Society of London* 3 (1861).

Pasamanick, Benjamin, and Hilda Knobloch. "Brain and Behavior: Session II. Symposium 1959. 2. Brain Damage and Reproductive Casualty." *American Journal of Orthopsychiatry* 30, no. 2 (1960).

Raine, Adrian, Patricia A. Brennan, and Sarnoff A. Mednick. "Birth Complications Combined with Early Maternal Rejection at Age One Year Predispose to Violent Crime at Age Eighteen Years." *Archives of General Psychiatry* 51, no. 12 (1994).

PATRICIA A. BRENNAN

See also **Children; Nature vs. Nurture; Teenagers.**

CHILDHOOD

Biological, psychological, and social factors converge in childhood to shape developmental trajectories of violent behavior. Although there are many competing theories regarding what causes individuals to become violent, nearly all of them reference the importance of childhood influences on later violent behavior. Where these theories diverge is in their explanation of the precise mechanisms through which childhood factors affect violent outcomes. Theoretical explanations of the relationship between childhood influences and violent outcomes all wrestle with the same empirical fact: nearly all violent adults were aggressive children, but most aggressive children do not become violent adults. Explorations of the relationship between childhood development and violence, then, must be able to account for both stability and change in violent behavior over time. Recognizing the interplay between fairly stable individual characteristics and dynamic sociocultural influences that shape behavioral outcomes affords the best starting point for those explorations.

Biological Influences

There is growing evidence that violent behavior is influenced by certain genetic and biological factors. High levels of testosterone, for example, appear to increase an individual's baseline tendency to engage in violence. Further, tendencies toward violence emerge in infancy, with some babies displaying notably more aggressive behaviors (such as kicking, biting, and hitting) than others. Such infants are more likely to become aggressive children who bully, threaten, punch, or even use weapons on other children. Whereas behavioral expressions of genetic and biological tendencies toward aggression change over time in ways that may suggest an increase or decrease in such behavior, an individual's relative rank (the degree of aggressiveness an individual exhibits relative to others) does appear to remain relatively stable. This stability in rank is partly rooted in biology, affected by such things as neurotransmitters and hormones (e.g., serotonin and testosterone), early exposure to environmental toxins (e.g., lead), and early physical trauma (e.g., severe head injury). However, as individuals progress through childhood, these biological factors, which manifest as an aggressive temperament, interact with various psychological and social mechanisms to shape the developmental course of aggression and violent behavior.

Psychological and Sociological Influences

Despite the relative stability of aggressive behavior over time, most aggressive children do not, in fact, grow up to be violent adults. This suggests that, despite biological antecedents that shape aggressive temperaments, various psychological and sociological mechanisms determine the degree to which this temperament is manifest in actual aggressive behavior. Theoretical frameworks in both psychology and sociology stress the importance of early family experiences in shaping the course of violence. From the perspective of both these disciplines, childhood socialization is a crucial determinant of the degree to which an aggressive temperament will manifest as violent behavior. Under ideal socialization conditions—proper monitoring and a consistent system of punishment and rewards in the context of a warm and nurturing environment—even a child with a highly aggressive temperament may not become violent. Conversely, under less than ideal conditions—poor supervision, erratic punishment, and a cold emotional climate—a child with a low predisposition to aggression might exhibit aggressive behaviors. In most cases, however, the interaction between temperament and socialization is such that children with an aggressive temperament are likely to have the most adverse socialization experiences.

Both control and learning theories offer useful perspectives. From the perspective of control theories, children with aggressive temperaments have difficulty developing internal controls and do not respond well to external controls. As such, they are unable to cultivate the psychological mechanisms and social bonds that inhibit violent behavior. In response, parents and other agents of socialization respond to these children by either ignoring them or imposing harsh discipline in an effort to squelch their violent behavior. These children are also likely to be rejected by their peers and to perform poorly in school. This further restricts the development of social bonds and reduces the likelihood that these children will be motivated to inhibit their aggressive tendencies.

Learning theories recognize that, in addition to the cultivation of strong social bonds, the learning and modeling of prosocial behavior is an important aspect of development that works to inhibit aggressive behavior. Unfortunately, many children with aggressive temperaments who have difficulty developing social bonds also develop within environments that present them with numerous opportunities to learn and model aggressive responses. The erratic and often harsh discipline they may receive from parents or other caretakers in response to early expressions of their aggressive tendencies ironically serves to enhance the likelihood that their aggressive behavior will continue via mechanisms of social learning and modeling. Further, since such children have difficulty cultivating friendships with their nonaggressive peers, they tend to seek out and model the behavior of similarly aggressive peers. The likelihood of continued violence is even stronger for those children who grow up in poor, disorganized neighborhoods where violent peer influences are more numerous and where they are more likely to hear of, witness, or even be directly involved in violent crime. In this context, recurring media images of violence may be especially harmful. Although numerous prosocial messages accompany these antisocial messages, children with aggressive temperaments and weak social bonds may have more difficulty identifying and modeling these prosocial messages.

Violent behavior is firmly rooted in early life experiences. However, such experiences (even those that can be linked to biological development) are not deterministic. As children develop, early biological, psychological, and social experiences are processed through current experiences, which have the potential to shape the trajectory of future behavior. As such, it is nearly impossible to predict who will become violent. We can, however, identify those mechanisms that serve to enhance or reduce the likelihood of later violence. Early aggressiveness in the context of weak social bonds, poor social control, and models for violent behavior characterize a childhood ripe for the development of violent behavior.

BIBLIOGRAPHY

Cairns, Robert, and Beverly Cairns. *Lifelines and Risks: Pathways of Youth in Our Time.* Cambridge, U.K.: Cambridge University Press, 1994.

Gottfredson, Michael, and Travis Hirschi. *A General Theory of Crime.* Stanford, Calif.: Stanford University Press, 1990.

Loeber, Rolf, and Magda Stouthamer-Loeber. "Development of Juvenile Aggression and Violence: Some Common Misconceptions and Controversies." *American Psychologist* 53 (February 1998).

Olweus, Dan. "Stability of Aggressive Reaction Patterns in Males: A Review." *Psychological Bulletin* 86, no. 4 (July 1979).

Rutter, Michael, Henri Giller, and Ann Hagell. *Antisocial Behavior by Young People.* Cambridge, U.K.: Cambridge University Press, 1998.

LISA MARIE BROIDY

See also **Children; Endocrinology; Genetics; Health and Medical Factors: Lead; Neurotransmitters.**

PUBERTY AND ADOLESCENCE

There is a robust relation between age and crime. A person is more likely to be arrested in the second decade of life than in any other time period. In 1996 individuals between the ages of ten and nineteen accounted for 45.3 percent of all arrests for property crimes and 28 percent of all arrests for violent crimes (Maguire and Pastore 1998). When rates of crime are plotted against age, the rates are highest during mid- to late adolescence; in fact, for all types of crime, there is a dramatic increase in the number of offenders from early to mid-adolescence (ages thirteen to fifteen) that peaks in mid- to late adolescence (ages sixteen to eighteen) and declines thereafter, decreasing more slowly than it increased. For example, in 1996 the violent-crime rate increased from a low of 0.22 per 1,000 among those under twelve years of age to 9.96 among sixteen- to eighteen-year-olds and dropped to 8.78 among nineteen- to twenty-one-year-olds with a steady decline thereafter. Important to note is the fact that this increase during adolescence reflects an increase in prevalence rather than incidence, meaning that more individuals are joining the ranks of offenders rather than the same set of offenders committing more crimes. The basic form of this age-crime relation appears to be stable across crime type, although violent crimes tend to peak somewhat later. Additionally, the relation between age and crime is maintained across gender. Finally, the age-crime curve is identifiable across data sources, countries, and historical periods. The robustness of this relation has led some to assert that the relation between age and crime is one of the "brute facts" of criminology.

Many researchers have attempted to explain this remarkable upsurge by relating it to individual or environmental factors that change during this same time period of a person's life. Given the myriad biological, psychological, and social changes that occur during adolescence, there is no shortage of such age-related factors. The following sections review the major changes of adolescence that are relevant to understanding violent crime and examine a particularly influential theory that draws distinctions between types of offenders.

Biological and Physical Changes

During adolescence, hormonal shifts lead to a sequence of visible, physical developments that include changes in body size and type and the appearance of secondary sex characteristics. Any of these changes are capable of contributing to the increases in crime and violence observed during adolescence.

Testosterone. During puberty, males and females experience dramatic changes in their levels of so-called sex hormones. Although testosterone is considered the male hormone and estrogen the female hormone, both sexes experience a rise in both hormones at puberty. The rate of increase, however, is dramatically sex-specific: testosterone levels rise up to eighteen times over the level in childhood for males, and estrogen levels rise up to eight times in females. The increase in testosterone is especially important because testosterone has been linked strongly to aggression. Experimental

animal research suggests that testosterone plays an important role in the genesis and maintenance of some forms of aggression in rodents, and early exposure to testosterone has been found to increase aggression in a wide range of animal species. Other studies have found a positive correlation between testosterone levels and human aggression and violence; this correlation is particularly strong when violence is measured using behavioral indices (e.g., history of violent crimes) rather than personality inventories. Further, the few quasi-experimental studies (e.g., castration of sex offenders, and administration of antiandrogens) that have been conducted found results consistent with a causal relation between testosterone and violence.

Several cautions, however, are in order. Although it appears that testosterone is related to violence, no research has examined the relations between testosterone levels and violence during adolescence. Thus, it cannot be said with certainty that changes in testosterone are responsible for changes in violence. In fact, although testosterone increases in adolescence and declines during adulthood, it does not peak in the teenage years in the same way that crime does. Further, because few studies have included females, it is not known whether the smaller testosterone-level increases experienced by female adolescents are responsible for increases in their crime rate.

Changes in Physical Size. In response to hormonal changes, an individual's size changes drastically during puberty. These changes may be more significant for male than for female violence. Overall, the typical girl gains about thirty-eight pounds and 9.5 inches during puberty, while the typical boy gains about forty-two pounds and 10 inches. Although their weight gains are similar, boys and girls differ in how that weight is distributed. Boys finish adolescence with a muscle-to-fat ratio of about 3:1, whereas the ratio for girls is about 5:4. The muscle increase is particularly notable in boys' upper bodies; between ages thirteen and eighteen, male arm strength more than doubles. To the extent that physical size and ability plays a role in crime and violence (e.g., physical intimidation requires a certain body size and purse snatching requires speed), these increases in size and strength may contribute to the increases in crime. However, it should be noted that apart from some research on body type and crime, this possibility has not been investigated directly.

Changes in Secondary Sex Characteristics. In addition to increases in body size, adolescents experience changes in their secondary sex characteristics—changes in the genitals and breasts; the growth of pubic, facial, and other body hair; and the further development of the sex organs. This sexual maturation may have implications for crime, particularly for early maturing females. Several studies have found that sexually mature girls, especially those maturing early, are at risk for adolescent crime when they are exposed to adolescent males. For example, some research has found that sexually mature girls in mixed-sex contexts (such as schools or peer groups) have higher rates of offending than females in same-sex contexts and sexually immature girls in mixed-sex or same-sex environments. Furthermore, increases in the rates of offending in these contexts parallel physical maturation. At age thirteen the early maturing girls in the mixed-sex school were the worst offenders, but at age fifteen these girls were joined in their offending by girls attending mixed-sex schools who had experienced puberty in the intervening years. The likely reason behind this increase in offending is the recruitment of the sexually mature girls by older boys who are already engaged in crime.

Cognitive Changes

During adolescence an individual's ability to think and reason changes dramatically. Whether these changes are described using the language of the psychologist Jean Piaget (e.g., attaining "formal operations") or information-processing models (e.g., gains in "underlying capacity" and "effective representations"), experts agree that adolescents become more capable of thinking abstractly and in terms of possibility rather than only in terms of reality. This capacity for abstract thinking brings with it other changes that may influence crime and violence, namely increases in argumentativeness and self-importance. The ability to reason more effectively, for example, is frequently used by adolescents in disagreements with parents and peers and in challenging societal rules. More important, adolescents also experience an egocentrism in which they regard themselves as much more central and significant than they actually are. One outgrowth of this egocentrism has been called the invincibility fable, meaning some adolescents feel that they have the unique ability to escape the consequences of dangerous or illegal behavior. Both the questioning of authority and the feeling of invincibility may contribute to the rise in crime and violence during adolescence.

Social Changes

Adolescents generally spend less time with parents, more time with peers, and more time in unstructured activities than they did when they were younger. These changes have important implications for adolescent crime.

Parents. Relations between children and their parents change during adolescence. The frequency of interaction between adolescents and their parents is lower in adolescence than in earlier life periods, and there is a relatively steady decline in the amount of time they spend together as adolescence progresses; this reaches its nadir around the height of pubertal change. Finally, although feelings between parents and children remain generally positive in adolescence, the incidence of contentious exchanges between parents and children increases during this period. These changes heighten conflict in the family and reduce the parents' ability to effectively monitor, supervise, and discipline their children. All of these factors are strongly related to delinquency.

Peers. As the adolescent spends less time with parents, he or she spends more time with peers. In fact, adolescents experience friends as the most satisfying of all companions, and teenagers in the United States spend more time talking to their friends each day than doing anything else. Familiarity and time spent with deviant peers (such as peers who engage in delinquency or illegal substance use) increase dramatically during adolescence, an important development given that the delinquency of an individual's peers is one of the strongest predictors of the individual's own delinquency. In fact, the relations between age and the number of delinquent friends and between age and time spent with peers look remarkably like the age-crime curve itself. Several studies have found that the age-crime relation is markedly reduced when one takes into account time spent with peers.

Activities. As time spent with peers increases, the nature of social activities changes as well; in turn, these activities have repercussions for crime. The most important of these changes is the increase in unstructured socializing with peers in the absence of responsible authority figures. During adolescence, individuals spend more and more time in activities that carry no agenda for how time

405

is to be spent and that have no adult supervision (i.e., riding around in a car for fun, getting together with friends informally, and going to parties). According to a "routine activities" perspective on crime, such activities are conducive to crime because the absence of structure leaves no one in charge and creates more time and therefore opportunity for deviance.

Subtypes of Offenders

Terrie E. Moffitt has argued that the upsurge in adolescent crime and violence conceals two subtypes of offenders. Specifically, she distinguishes between life-course persistent (LCP) offenders, whose antisocial tendencies become apparent early in childhood, who account for a disproportionately large percentage of all criminal activity, and who are likely to continue offending throughout adulthood, and adolescent-limited (AL) offenders, whose antisocial behavior begins relatively late and who are likely to desist offending upon entering adulthood. The key difference between these two groups is thought to lie in the distinct developmental trajectories leading to each type of antisocial outcome. LCP offenders are thought to be characterized by early emerging neuropsychological deficits (such as deficits in verbal or executive functions) that set in motion a series of social and academic failures, which cumulate in a pattern of undercontrolled, explosive behavior that persists across the life course. On the other hand, AL offenders are thought to offend because of a felt maturity gap between their biological and social status. Biologically mature but socially still children, these adolescents offend as a means of gaining access to those things that are denied them (such as status, money, relationships, and power). Once these coveted adult assets become available through more legitimate means, the AL offenders cease their offending. Although LCP and AL offenders commit roughly equivalent levels of nonviolent offenses, the LCP offenders have been found to be somewhat more violent than their AL counterparts.

BIBLIOGRAPHY

Archer, John. "Testosterone and Aggression." *Journal of Offender Rehabilitation* 21, nos. 3–4 (1994): 3–39.

Berger, Kathleen S., and Ross A. Thompson. *The Developing Person Through the Life Span*. 4th ed. New York: Worth, 1998.

Caspi, Avshalom, et al. "Unraveling Girls' Delinquency: Biological, Dispositional, and Contextual Contributions to Adolescent Misbehavior." *Developmental Psychology* 29, no. 8 (1993): 19–30.

Hirschi, Travis, and Michael Gottfredson. "Age and the Explanation of Crime." *American Journal of Sociology* 89, no. 3 (1993): 552–584.

Maguire, Kathleen, and Anne L. Pastore. *Sourcebook of Criminal Justice Statistics 1997*. Washington, D.C.: U.S. Government Printing Office, 1998.

Moffitt, Terrie E. "Adolescence-Limited and Life-Course Persistent Antisocial Behavior: A Developmental Taxonomy." *Psychological Review* 100, no. 4 (1993): 674–701.

Osgood, D. Wayne, et al. "Routine Activities and Individual Deviant Behavior." *American Sociological Review* 61 (August 1996): 635–655.

Warr, Mark. "Age, Peers, and Delinquency." *Criminology* 31, no. 1 (1993): 17–40.

DONALD LYNAM

See also **Children; Endocrinology: Testosterone; Teenagers.**

DEVIL WORSHIP. *See* Satanism.

DIAMOND, JACK "LEGS" (1896–1931)

Jack "Legs" Diamond, a fast-running thief, gunman, murderer, bootlegger, and likely narcotics dealer, was born John Nolan in Philadelphia in 1896. His father was a minor Democratic ward politician. As youngsters, Jack and his brother, Eddie, joined a local street gang of little consequence in the northeastern section of Philadelphia. In 1913 Jack moved to New York City and there teamed up with a gang of package thieves (also called "truck bouncers") active on Manhattan's Lower West Side. One year later he was arrested in Brooklyn for burglary and sentenced to a short term in the New York Reformatory. Over the course of the next seventeen years, he was arrested twenty-four more times on charges ranging from assault and robbery to grand larceny, burglary, and homicide.

In his early New York years Diamond came to the notice of such infamous organized-crime racketeers as Owney Madden and "Monk" Eastman. In time, Diamond's propensity for violence propelled him into the role of bodyguard for Jacob "Little Augie" Orgen, a labor racketeer whose mob began its criminal activities as strikebreakers. Ultimately, Diamond's protection was of little value, because, despite his presence, an emerging criminal duo—Louis "Lepke" Buchalter and Jacob "Gurrah" Shapiro—murdered Orgen in a drive-by

Philadelphia police's photo of Jack "Legs" Diamond, in September 1930. CORBIS/BETTMANN

shooting on 15 October 1927. Next, Diamond joined with the legendary organized-crime figure Arnold Rothstein, a gambler and political fixer as well as a suspected underworld financier of narcotics and assorted rackets. Rothstein allegedly paid Diamond a thousand dollars a week both to protect him and to make sure gambling debtors paid off.

According to the celebrated *New York Times* reporter Meyer Berger, Rothstein and Diamond had a falling out in the autumn of 1928. In a pique Rothstein sent a crew to murder Eddie Diamond, who was in a tuberculosis sanatorium in Denver. They failed, and soon enough, six of them were murdered. Two days before the 1928 elections, Rothstein was shot in the groin by a disgruntled gambler. He died on election day, 6 November 1928. The murder of Rothstein was pivotal in New York City politics for a decade after Fiorello La Guardia made fighting organized crime his major campaign issue in his failed bid for New York City's mayoralty in 1929.

Diamond's most important criminal activity was bootlegging. Indeed, the criminologist and historian Mark Haller holds that Diamond was one of the New York area's top bootleggers, although

he probably made his major mark in rural Greene Country, New York. Through violence and intimidation, Diamond tried to corner the local "applejack" market and to force saloon owners to buy his beer. Not only was this a war of small proportions, but by instigating it, Diamond alienated much of the local community and Governor Franklin D. Roosevelt, who ordered his attorney general to investigate and prosecute Diamond. Diamond had already estranged a score of New York City gangsters and been shot numerous times in the past. In December 1931 he was murdered in Albany, New York, to no one's surprise.

BIBLIOGRAPHY

Curzon, Sam. *Legs Diamond*. New York: Monarch, 1962.
Haller, Mark H. "Bootleggers and American Gambling, 1920–1950." Staff and Consultant Papers. Washington, D.C.: Commission on the Review of the National Policy Toward Gambling, October 1976.

ALAN A. BLOCK

See also **Organized Crime.**

DIET. *See* Anorexia and Bulimia; Health and Medical Factors.

DILLINGER, JOHN
(c. 1903–1934)

John Dillinger was the most notorious bandit–bank robber of the 1932–1936 period, when a rash of automobile bandit crimes occurred throughout the Midwest and Southwest. Between 1933 and 1934 he and his gang had ten murders, twelve bank robberies, and three police-arsenal robberies attributed to them. Dillinger's crime spree captured the imagination of the U.S. public, and, even more than sixty years after his death, he was the subject of countless legends and conspiracy theories.

Although he perpetuated most of his crimes in rural areas alone or as part of a small gang, he had contacts with more prominent organized-crime figures of the St. Paul, Minnesota, and Chicago areas. For the most part, he led his own small gang in a series of exploits that drew even more attention than the crimes of contemporaries such as Bonnie Parker and Clyde Barrow, Ma "Arizona Kate" Barker and her sons, Alvin Karpis, and "Pretty Boy" Floyd.

John Dillinger. LIBRARY OF CONGRESS

Born in Indianapolis probably on 22 June 1903, Dillinger demonstrated an early penchant for violence and crime. After his mother's death in 1906, his father had difficulty controlling him and eventually moved to rural Mooresville, Indiana, in 1920, where Dillinger spent his late adolescence. While there, Dillinger resisted going to school and embarked on a career of crime, committing progressively more serious crimes. He joined the navy in 1923 but soon deserted. In 1924 he was sentenced to ten to twenty years in the Pendleton Reformatory after he robbed and beat a local store owner.

Dillinger first achieved notoriety on 17 July 1933, when he and Homer Van Meter, both recently paroled from prison, robbed a bank in Daleville, Indiana. The two were apparently funding an escape attempt for their friends John Hamilton, Harry Pierpont, Charles Makley, and Russell Clark, each of whom would become part of the Dillinger gang. During the robbery, witnesses remarked on Dillinger's confidence, good looks, and fashionable clothes. He appeared to enjoy the thrill of robbing banks, and he became well known for

the athleticism he displayed in leaping over a teller's gate.

Arrested soon after the robbery of the bank in Daleville, Dillinger managed his first escape from jail with the help of the gang members whose escape he had made possible through money he had had smuggled to them. Fully assembled, the gang robbed a police arsenal and one bank of $75,000 and then sought shelter in Chicago, where, apparently, they were able to purchase safe haven through underworld connections. While there, Dillinger met Evelyn "Billie" Frichette, who would later become his best-known gun moll when the gang fled farther west to Arizona and after Dillinger escaped again from jail. On 25 January 1934, the gang was finally captured, and Dillinger was extradited to Indiana.

With Dillinger already a national figure, government officials in Crown Point, Indiana, made much of their captive; several officials even posed for pictures with Dillinger. They were soon humiliated, however, when he accomplished his most notorious escape. On 3 March, brandishing what appeared to be a pistol yet never firing a shot, Dillinger made his way out of his cell and stole the sheriff's car. (Later reports held that he had carved the pistol out of wood.)

Reuniting with Frichette and the gang and fleeing to the St. Paul area, Dillinger found himself relentlessly pursued. He narrowly escaped law-enforcement officials several times and enhanced his reputation as someone cool under fire and clever enough to outsmart the government. Among the new members of his gang was Lester Gillis, also known as "Baby Face" Nelson and a notorious bandit in his own right. On 22 June 1934, J. Edgar Hoover, director of the federal Division of Investigation (the predecessor to the Federal Bureau of Investigation), declared Dillinger "Public Enemy Number One," the first time the term had been used in a national context, and announced a reward, for his capture or killing, of $10,000. Dillinger and his gang began to splinter under the pressure; Frichette was arrested when she returned with Dillinger to Chicago, and Hamilton, Van Meter, and Gillis would all be killed in separate shoot-outs.

Dillinger was finally killed by federal agents under the direction of Melvin Purvis, the special agent in charge, on 22 July in front of the Biograph Theater in Chicago. Exiting the gangster movie *Manhattan Melodrama* accompanied by the moll Polly Hamilton and Anna Sage, a brothel madam,

Dillinger was shot by sharpshooters positioned on top of neighboring buildings. Sage, who had tipped off the authorities as to Dillinger's whereabouts, gained fame as "the lady in red" for wearing a bright red dress as a signal that the man with her was Dillinger, who often traveled in disguise and who reportedly had had plastic surgery to alter his appearance.

Even in death, Dillinger remained controversial. A famous photograph of his body from the morgue showed a prominent bulge under the sheet covering it. Although caused by the position of his hands and the onset of rigor mortis, the bulge, alongside the many stories of Dillinger's sexual prowess, gave birth to the legend that he had an enormous penis. Subsequent legendary stories that the Smithsonian Institution kept his penis in its collection were utter fabrications. In addition, legends continued to circulate even in the 1990s that someone other than Dillinger was shot in front of the Biograph Theater. Supporters of that claim, stated most completely by Jay Robert Nash and Ron Offen in their 1970 book, *John Dillinger: Dead or Alive*, held that Dillinger lured someone else into a trap in order to cover up his own escape.

As the object of one of the most publicized manhunts in U.S. history, Dillinger became a figure alternately condemned and celebrated. Law-enforcement officials, most notably Hoover, cast him as a ruthless outlaw and an enemy of the state. The unprecedented scope of federal involvement in the search for Dillinger—involvement made possible because authorities succeeded in depicting him as a national threat—helped lay the groundwork for the influence the Federal Bureau of Investigation would have in U.S. affairs from the mid-1930s until the early 1970s. Throughout Hoover's career as director of the FBI, he kept a plaster death mask of Dillinger in a display case just outside his office door.

At the same time, much of the U.S. public saw Dillinger as a symbol of the individual resisting the power of the state. Dillinger, whose family experienced many of the economic hardships common to rural areas caught between a long-term declining farm economy and a national economy ravaged by the Great Depression, proved effective as such a symbol. Many found him sympathetic through his association with small towns—his family moved to Mooresville, Indiana, from Indianapolis when he was a teenager—and through his attacks on banks, which were seen as culprits in farm foreclosures of the period. His general cha-

risma and demonstrated ability to outwit government officials led many to attempt to see him in person, to write letters in support of his exploits, and to cheer when he appeared on-screen in newsreel reports. As the subject of three movies, two titled *Dillinger* (1945 and 1973) and *The Lady in Red* (1979), and countless newspaper articles, Internet sites, and books, he was a representative of the dramatic but doomed bandit figure overwhelmed by the forces of modern America.

BIBLIOGRAPHY

Gentry, Curt. *J. Edgar Hoover: The Man and the Secrets*. New York: Norton, 1991.
Girardin, G. Russell, with William J. Helmer. *Dillinger: The Untold Story*. Bloomington: Indiana University Press, 1994.
Potter, Claire Bond. *War on Crime: Bandits, G-Men, and the Politics of Mass Culture*. New Brunswick, N.J.: Rutgers University Press, 1998.
Toland, John. *Dillinger Days*. New York: Random House, 1963.

JOE KRAUS

See also **Hoover, J. Edgar; Robbery.**

DISARMAMENT AND ARMS CONTROL

At least two traditional themes have formed the basis of official and nongovernmental attitudes toward disarmament and arms control in the United States—one is based on national self-interest and the other on humanitarian reform. If these two have occasionally worked in tandem, they have been more frequently at cross-purposes. The self-interest theme has been the more dominant, especially in the post–World War II decades, and was grounded on a conservative, even Hobbesian, view of the world that endorsed arms control measures as a means of enhancing national security and reducing military expenditures. Adherents of the reformist theme, generally advocates of antiwar, pacifist, and utilitarian ideals, have sought more universal and humanitarian objectives aimed at ending martial violence, but have met with only limited success. Nevertheless, grassroots advocates of restrictions or limitation of armaments and their use have had, at times, an impact on national policies.

Defining Terms

The terms *arms control* and *disarmament* have been and are used as umbrella terms to encompass specific techniques to limit and regulate armaments and to reduce martial violence should war occur. But the terms are also used independently to suggest two separate approaches; indeed, some people have emphasized the distinctions between them in tones bordering on theological cant.

Actually, the term *disarmament* is the older and more widely used of the two. During the nineteenth century it became fashionable, particularly after the Hague conference of 1899, to use "disarmament" to describe all international efforts to limit, reduce, or control the implements of war. The former director of the UN Disarmament Affairs Division William Epstein wrote in *Disarmament: Twenty-five Years of Effort* (1971) that in the United Nations and its subsidiary agencies "the term 'disarmament' has in practice been used not as meaning total disarmament but as a generic term covering all measures relating to the field—from small steps to reduce tensions or build confidence, through regulation of armaments or arms control, up to general and complete disarmament" (pp. 3–4).

It was U.S. academic specialists—those linking the technology of nuclear weaponry to the politics of the Cold War—who in the early 1950s began insisting upon the use of "arms control" in place of "disarmament." To these experts, the term *disarmament* lacked semantic precision; moreover, it carried a tone of utopianism that these self-styled realists felt inappropriate for the new, emerging military-technological-diplomatic relationship. "Arms control to be meaningful must be devised in relation to the technological factors which produced the need for it," Henry A. Kissinger wrote in *Necessity of Choice* in 1960. "It cannot be conceived in a fit of moral indignation. Effective schemes require careful, detailed dispassionate studies and the willingness to engage in patient, highly technical negotiations. Otherwise arms control may increase rather than diminish insecurity" (p. 213). Only later did Kissinger discover the significance of the political dimension of arms control.

Aside from the semantic differences between the two terms, there often exists a difference of emphasis in priorities. Those post-1945 reformers who explicitly advocated disarmament objected to national policies heavily dependent upon military force; they especially rejected total reliance upon a nuclear deterrence system. They were impatient with limited partial measures because these provided, at best, only short-term, piecemeal benefits while ignoring the unprecedented peril posed by the still vast arsenals of strategic weapons and delivery systems capable of destroying Western civilization. During the Cold War, the disarmers argued that the limited arms control measures were essentially cosmetic and concealed the lack of progress in general reduction of tactical and strategic nuclear weapons systems.

For their part, "arms controllers" dismissed the disarmers as "utopian dreamers" and argued that the way to achieve a peaceful world in the Cold War era was by linking limited, step-by-step measures to the nuclear deterrence system and ensuring the strategic military balance. They sought international stability; consequently, they gave little thought to the prospect of a warless world. Indeed, they were exceedingly cautious about significant arms reductions because this might disrupt the strategic balance.

Historical Developments

The tendency of American presidents, policy makers, and ordinary citizens to characterize the United States as a uniquely peace-loving nation is based more on myth than reality. The twentieth-century version of this self-image developed, in large measure, because of the emphasis on the distinctions between democracies and totalitarian states. Large democracies have not militarily threatened other large democratic states—in contrast to the actions of totalitarian nations. While there is a measure of validity in this distinction, it does not mean that democracies are by definition peace-loving societies. The considerable number of military campaigns that the United States has engaged in—both prior to 1945 and since—belie this comfortable self-perception. Similarly, Americans have often condemned arms buildup by foreign nations as stimulating world tensions and increasing the likelihood of war, while at the same time arguing that the stockpiling of U.S. armaments is to "protect the peace."

America's antipathy to militarism and military institutions can be traced back to George Washington's 1796 farewell address, in which he warned that "overgrown military establishments are, under any form of government, inauspicious to liberty, and are to be regarded as particularly hostile to republican liberty." During the Cold War anti-

410

militarists warned against the influence upon policies of the growing U.S. "military-industrial complex." Ironically, it was a former general, President Dwight D. Eisenhower, who coined the phrase in his 1961 farewell address when he pointed to individuals, groups, and institutions in government, science, industry, and the military who had vested interests in high levels of armament expenditures. Antimilitarists and others have stressed the fact that the military-industrial complex usually stood in opposition to disarmament policies.

National self-interest has been the guiding principle of the United States in its past dealings with arms control and disarmament issues. This can be seen in the historical examples that follow.

From Colonial Days Until World War I

In the period before World War I the United States pursued four arms control undertakings: (1) regulating arms sales to Native Americans; (2) demilitarizing the Great Lakes; (3) formulating "rules of war" to govern the actions of its armed forces; and (4) participating in the two international peace conferences at The Hague.

Shortly after the War of 1812—the last of the Napoleonic Wars—a small number of Americans along the Atlantic seaboard formed one of the earliest secular peace movements, which sought means other than war to resolve international disputes. Such efforts, however, did not begin to influence U.S. foreign policy until it combined with internationalism at the end of the century with the same lack of success.

From early in the seventeenth century, British authorities—usually unsuccessfully—sought to prohibit frontier traders from dealing arms to Native Americans. After the Revolution, the United States tried to continue the practice of prohibiting arms sales to the Indians. New treaties made with, or forced upon, Native Americans frequently included provisions calling for relocation and disarmament.

The Rush-Bagot agreement of 29 April 1817 resulted in what was perhaps the most successful U.S. arms control undertaking—the demilitarization of the Great Lakes. The agreement between the United States and Great Britain saved each nation considerable cost as it introduced both quantitative and qualitative arms restrictions. It limited the naval forces of each party "on Lake Ontario, to one vessel, not exceeding one hundred tons burden, and armed with one eighteen-pound cannon. On the upper lakes, to two vessels, not exceeding

like burden each, and armed with like force," and "on the waters of Lake Champlain, to one vessel not exceeding like burden, and armed with like force." Land fortifications were left intact, however, after the Treaty of Washington (1871), in which both parties agreed to submit all outstanding disputes to joint commissions and third-party arbitrators, and demilitarization gradually expanded to create the "unguarded frontier" between Canada and the United States.

During the Civil War, the Columbia College professor Francis Lieber submitted to the War Department his *Instructions for the Government of Armies of the United States in the Field*, which sought to make war more civilized. The so-called Lieber Code, drawn from the writings of medieval jurists, was incorporated into the Union Army's General Orders No. 100 (1863). Among other things, the code recognized the status of noncombatants, regulated treatment of prisoners of war, prohibited the use of poison and the seizure of private property without compensation, and insisted that cultural treasures not be willfully destroyed. Lieber's contribution later influenced the Declaration of Brussels (1874) on the rules and customs of war.

The first Hague conference (1899) was called by Russian czar Nicholas II to deal with the mounting international arms race. American peace activists and internationalists optimistically viewed the Hague process as the best hope for peace even though the U.S. government had just concluded a war with Spain and was preparing for a brutal struggle in the Philippines. Washington officials were committed to building up the navy and modernizing the army, and consequently had little interest in arms limitations or controls on new military technology. Captain Alfred T. Mahan, a senior U.S. delegate, joined with his British counterpart to prevent the conference from limiting naval forces; however, despite U.S. opposition, declarations prohibiting the use of asphyxiating gas and expanding (dumdum) bullets, as well as the dropping of projectiles from balloons, were approved. The rules of war were agreed upon, granting additional protections to noncombatants and prisoners of war, and the International Court of Justice was created.

The second Hague conference took place in 1907 amid growing international rivalries. Earlier, President Theodore Roosevelt had indicated that the United States might now be willing to support arms limitations; however, none of the major European powers was willing to reduce or limit its military forces and the conference failed to lessen tensions. Later, in June 1910, both houses of the U.S. Congress officially endorsed naval limitations without a dissenting vote. This decision was prompted by a new class of battleship, the dreadnoughts, which had started another round of expensive ship construction. The proposal failed to gain support abroad, but pointed to new proposals a decade in the future.

The Interwar Years, 1919–1939

U.S. interest in disarmament undertakings, sparked by President Woodrow Wilson's endorsement as stated in point four of his famous Fourteen Points and Article Eight of the League of Nations Covenant, grew unevenly during the first fifteen years of this period. These undertakings, frequently hindered by the United States' insistence upon avoiding "entangling alliances," included (1) sponsorship of the Washington Naval System, 1922–1939; (2) initiation of the Kellogg-Briand Pact, which sought to outlaw war; and (3) ambivalent, belated support of the League's disarmament efforts.

Motivated largely by a desire to reduce expenditures, the Harding administration promoted the limitation of naval forces at the Washington Conference, in 1921–1922. The proposal by Secretary of State Charles Evans Hughes to reduce the number of existing capitals ships (battleships and cruisers) and limit future construction, which was tied to national security issues, was quickly endorsed by public opinion worldwide. The ensuing treaty placed limits on the battleships and aircraft carriers of the major naval powers—the United States, Great Britain, and Japan—as well as France and Italy. It slowed an impending naval-building race, provided the basis for extending limitations to other classes of warships, and eventually established the most complete system of arms control yet achieved.

The Geneva conference of 1927 failed to extend the limits to include cruisers, destroyers, and submarines because the naval delegates—criticized for viewing the world through a porthole—adopted a purely technical approach to determining parity. This approach, which concentrated on technical rather than broad political issues, would also plague American arms control efforts throughout the Cold War era. A subsequent attempt in 1930 in London, where political leaders agreed to share the risks involved, saw the limits extended to other classes of warships of the three major navies. President Hoover claimed that the

United States had saved $1 billion ($100 billion in late-twentieth-century currency), but naval professionals in the United States, Great Britain, and Japan were outraged, attesting to the fact that no power had achieved an advantage in the agreements.

The Washington treaty system was the most extensive arms control undertaking up to that time, a forerunner of nuclear-age strategic arms limitations efforts. It was successful until Japanese militarists terminated the limitations because they were no longer satisfied with the political arrangements and were willing to employ military force to incorporate China and Southeast Asia into their sphere of interest.

Salmon O. Levinson, a successful Chicago lawyer, is credited with founding the grassroots movement to "outlaw war." Before any world body could maintain peace, he argued, international law must declare war an illegal and criminal act. Secretary of State Frank B. Kellogg used this basic idea in negotiating a pact with France; subsequently, all other nations were invited to join. Since the United States was not a member of the League of Nations, Kellogg did not attempt to link the pact to an international tribunal that might enforce it, a failure that prompted harsh criticism.

The United States, insisting on retaining its "freedom of action," had rejected membership in the League because of its emphasis on "collective security." The U.S. rejection of political-military commitments that might require it to contribute troops, France's insistence on a security guarantee, and Germany's aggressiveness doomed the League's attempt to develop a world disarmament system between 1932 and 1935.

American peace advocates, especially the Women's International League for Peace and Freedom, chaired by Jane Addams, the War Resisters' International, and the National Council for the Prevention of War, were quite active in promoting disarmament during the interwar years. They rallied public support for the Washington Naval Treaty, the Kellogg-Briand Pact, and the unfulfilled efforts of the League of Nations. Their activities were frequently fragmented and not particularly effective in influencing policy; however, they did succeed in initiating some arms control ideas and mobilizing public support.

The Cold War Years and After

The Cold War years brought radical changes in military technology, but the driving forces behind American arms control policies had not changed.

The fourteenth annual assembly of the League of Nations in Geneva, Switzerland, October 1933. Members are discussing the problem of disarmament. CORBIS/BETTMANN

U.S. policy makers developed plans that invariably corresponded to traditional goals: to enhance the security of the nation and its allies, to lower military expenditures, and to achieve partisan domestic political advantage. The latter was increasingly significant as arms control issues, such as the test ban and the nuclear freeze, became a factor in election campaigns.

The Truman administration put forth the Baruch Plan in 1946 as a bid to control nuclear weapons. This detailed, technically oriented scheme, designed to continue the atomic monopoly of the United States, was unacceptable to the Soviet Union, which, in turn, suggested an uncomplicated accord prohibiting the manufacture and ownership of nuclear weaponry. "The American government," Freeman Dyson wrote in the 1984 book *Weapons and Hope*, "having made heroic efforts to achieve an internal consensus for the negotiation, was in no mood to examine carefully the merits of the Soviet proposal. So far as American public opinion was concerned, there were only two alternatives: either total international control of nuclear energy through the Baruch Plan, or none at all" (p. 171).

Dyson's observations point to two major factors that largely governed arms control and disarmament policies during the Cold War: the intense intragovernmental negotiations required to construct a proposal and the increasingly ideological

nature of the American public. Astute observers understood that negotiations between competing government bureaucracies, such as the State and Defense Departments, were more fiercely waged than those between U.S. and Soviet diplomats. As the decades passed, politicians, "defense" and "patriotic" interest groups, and media pundits appear to have become increasingly anti-Soviet and anticommunist; indeed, these themes created an American ideology and a political arena in which candidates competed to be the staunchest Cold War warrior. Driven by this ideology, analysts often gave policy makers and the public exaggerated assessments of the USSR's capabilities and the vulnerability of the United States. Any U.S.-Soviet arms control agreement grounded on "mutual national interests" faced severe challenges. Cold War arms control negotiations became deadlocked most frequently over the issues of verification and compliance. For most of these years, the United States insisted on on-site inspection and other "intrusive" verification systems to prevent the possibility that "cheating" might provide its adversaries with a significant military advantage. However, as noted by analysts Albert Carnesale and Richard N. Haass (1987), "The entire verification and compliance problem [became] difficult for another reason as well: the [domestic] political requirements for verification and compliance [were] increasingly more demanding than . . . the security

413

Disarmament Treaties

Limiting or Reducing Weapons

Intermediate/Strategic Nuclear Weapons

- *SALT I Interim Agreement (U.S.-USSR), 1972.* Froze the number of intercontinental ballistic missiles (ICBMs) and regulated the number of submarine-launched ballistic missiles (SLBMs) in relation to ICBMs.
- *ABM Treaty (part of SALT I) and ABM Protocol (U.S.-USSR), 1972, 1974.* Limited anti–ballistic missile (ABM) systems to one base site for each country and prohibited nationwide systems and the development, testing, and deployment of sea-based, air-based, and space-based ABMs.
- *SALT II Treaty (U.S.-USSR), 1979.* Limited the total number of strategic nuclear delivery vehicles, the launchers for multiple independently targetable reentry vehicles (MIRVs), bombers with cruise missiles, warheads on ICBMs, and other weapons, and prohibited the testing and deployment of new ICBMs. Not ratified by the United States.
- *INF Treaty (U.S.-USSR), 1987.* Eliminated ground-launched intermediate-range nuclear forces (INF) and included comprehensive verification procedures.
- *START Treaty (U.S.-USSR), 1991.* Furthered the limitation of strategic nuclear delivery vehicles, etc., begun in SALT I and II.

Conventional Forces

- *CFE Treaty, 1990.* Limited and reduced conventional (nonnuclear) forces in Europe.

Demilitarization or Denuclearization

- *Antarctic Treaty, 1959.* Prohibited the military use of Antarctica.
- *Outer Space Treaty, 1967.* Prohibited nuclear weapons in earth orbit and outer space.
- *Treaty of Tlatelolco, 1967.* Established nuclear-free zones prohibiting the possession, deployment, and testing of nuclear weapons in Latin America.
- *Seabed Treaty, 1971.* Prohibited placing nuclear weapons on the seabed.

Outlawing of Weapons

- *Biological Weapons Convention, 1972.* Prohibited the development, production, and stockpiling of biological weapons and required the destruction of existing stockpiles.
- *Chemical Weapons Convention, 1993.* Prohibited the development, production, and stockpiling of chemical weapons and required the destruction of existing stockpiles. Not ratified by the United States.

(continued)

requirements" (p. 348). Despite critics' fears, arms control efforts did not weaken the United States' strategic position, nor did they particularly enhance that of the Soviet Union.

Nongovernment organizations attempted, with varying success, to influence government policy during the Cold War. Scientists involved in the Manhattan Project founded the Federation of

---

Disarmament Treaties (*continued*)

Regulating Arms Trade and Traffic

- *1950 Tripartite Declaration (U.S.-G.B.-France), 1950–1955.* Building upon the UN Middle East arms embargo, 1948–1949, these nations agreed to limit the trade or granting of arms to Israel and its enemies. The arrangement ended when the USSR signed an arms deal with Egypt in 1955.
- *Non-Proliferation Treaty, 1968.* Prohibited nuclear weapons or technology transfers to *nonnuclear* nations.

Stabilizing the Military and Political Environment

- *Environmental Modification Convention, 1977.* Prohibited attempts to alter the weather and environment for military purposes.

Nuclear Testing

- *Limited Test Ban Treaty, 1963.* Prohibited nuclear-weapon tests in the atmosphere, in outer space, and under water.
- *Threshold Test Ban Treaty (U.S.-USSR), 1974.* Prohibited underground nuclear tests above an explosive yield of 150 kilotons.
- *Peaceful Nuclear Explosions Treaty (U.S.-USSR), 1976.* Prohibited "group explosions" with a yield of over 150 kilotons when using nuclear devices in place of conventional explosives for "digging" canals, tunnels, etc.

Reducing the Risk of Nuclear War

- *Hot Line Agreements, 1963, 1971; Accidents Measures Agreement, 1971; Prevention of Nuclear War Agreement, 1973;* and *Nuclear Risk Reduction Centers Agreement, 1987.* All were aimed at improving communications, consultations, and safeguards between the United States and Soviet Union to prevent the accidental or unauthorized use of nuclear weapons, especially during political crises.

Atomic Scientists (now the Federation of American Scientists), stating that "the value of science to civilization has never been more clear, nor have the dangers of its misuse been greater." Its magazine, the *Bulletin of Atomic Scientists*, remains the principal vehicle for the nongovernment arms control community. In 1955 Albert Einstein and Bertrand Russell warned scientists that the escalating arms race depended on the contributions of science. They urged scientists to examine the ethical implications of their professional activities and to recognize the danger of nuclear war. In response, a small group of scientists met two years later at Pugwash, Nova Scotia. Subsequent Pugwash conferences have provided scientists with a forum for pointing out the advantages of arms control.

Two examples of peace activism and popular support for arms control are the Test Ban Treaty and the nuclear freeze movement. In the mid-1950s the American public became concerned that above-ground nuclear testing was introducing an unacceptable amount of radiation into the atmosphere. Physicians for Social Responsibility collected and publicized data showing that Strontium 90 was entering the food chain, and the Council for a Livable World worked for a treaty barring nuclear tests. Peace advocates are credited with providing the added support necessary to gain the U.S. Senate's ratification of the Limited Test Ban Treaty (1963).

The National Freeze Campaign, initiated by Randall Forsberg in 1980, demanded a bilateral freeze on further nuclear weapons development, testing, production, and deployment until a definitive agreement could be worked out by the two superpowers. In 1982 nearly six hundred thousand people gathered in New York City to demonstrate for the freeze. So responsive was the public that congressional candidates were forced to take a stand on the issues and the House of Representatives narrowly passed a resolution calling upon the president to negotiate a bilateral freeze with the Soviet Union. This did not happen, but President Reagan did introduce the Strategic Defense Initiative and renew efforts for nuclear weapons limitations.

During the Cold War years, several series of arms control negotiations were under way, often at the same time, seeking to limit and reduce strategic nuclear weapons systems, outlaw chemical and biological weapons, halt the testing of nuclear devices, limit and reduce conventional weapons in Europe, and establish means of preventing accidental nuclear war. These undertakings frequently resulted in interim agreements, bilateral accords, or multilateral treaties. Below is a list of some the arms control agreements that the United States signed, sometimes with substantial reservations, in the years since 1945.

It is most difficult to briefly summarize the Cold War arms control experience, but a few basic considerations warrant mentioning. First, U.S. public opinion was ambiguous regarding arms control and disarmament activities, particularly those involving the Soviet Union. The majority of Americans, according to various opinion polls, favored bilateral agreements with the Soviets; at the same time, a majority expected the Communists to "cheat" if given an opportunity. Second, it is evident that nuclear deterrence held a far, far higher priority than arms reductions among policy makers. After 1946 the United States never seriously considered a program that would lead to general and complete disarmament and, despite the strategic arms agreements, the numbers and destructiveness of nuclear weapons systems continued to grow during the Cold War years as arms control measures tended to focus on enhancing the deterrence system rather than reducing the nuclear stockpile.

Conclusion

U.S. statesmen have frequently put forward proposals involving the employment of various arms control and disarmament mechanisms. Several officials have suggested that progress in the development of international arms control agreements is due largely to U.S. leadership. Yet while American diplomats played a significant role in arms control negotiations, especially during the twentieth century, the United States failed to endorse a number of major arms control and disarmament activities. In the 1920s, for example, the United States refused until 1975 to ratify the Geneva Protocol outlawing the use of chemical weapons. During the Cold War era, the United States often rejected proposals for nuclear-weapons-free zones, showed little enthusiasm for negotiating any treaty predicated on "complete and total disarmament," resisted a total test ban agreement, and—along with the Soviet Union—urged other nations to forgo nuclear weapons while constantly expanding its own arsenal. In 1997 President Bill Clinton, after initially supporting a treaty to outlaw the use of land mines, refused to sign it, at the Pentagon's urging. Additionally, the Clinton administration was not able to secure ratification of the chemical weapons convention, nor satisfactorily carry out the intent of the strategic arms limitation agreements.

On the positive side, U.S. leadership has utilized various disarmament and arms control techniques to enhance its national security, reduce or contain its military expenditures, and stimulate worldwide efforts to find alternatives to war and lessen the severity of military violence.

BIBLIOGRAPHY

Burns, Richard Dean, ed. *Encyclopedia of Arms Control and Disarmament*. 3 vols. New York: Scribner, 1993.

Burrows, William, and Robert Windrem. *Critical Mass*. New York: Simon and Schuster, 1994.

Caldwell, Dan. *The Dynamics of Domestic Politics and Arms Control: The SALT II Ratification Debate*. Charlestown: University of South Carolina Press, 1991.

Carnesale, Albert, and Richard N. Haass, eds. *Superpower Arms Control: Setting the Record Straight*. Cambridge, Mass.: Ballinger, 1987.

Dando, Malcomb. *Biological Warfare in the Twenty-first Century*. London: Brasseys, 1994.

Krepon, Michael, and Dan Caldwell, eds. *The Politics of Arms Control Treaty Ratification*. New York: St. Martin's, 1991.

Lalsen, Jeffrey A., and Gregory J. Rattray, eds. *Arms Control: Toward the Twenty-first Century*. Boulder, Colo.: Lynne Rienner, 1996.

Pierre, Andrew J., ed. *Cascade of Arms: Managing Conventional Weapons Proliferation*. Washington, D.C.: Brookings Institution, 1997.

Price, Richard M. *The Chemical Weapons Taboo*. Ithaca, N.Y.: Cornell University Press, 1997.

Spector, Leonard S., Mark G. McDonough, and Evan S. Medeiros. *Tracking Nuclear Proliferation: A Guide in Maps and Charts*. Washington, D.C.: Carnegie Endowment, 1995.

RICHARD DEAN BURNS

See also **Antiwar Protests; Conflict Resolution, International and Institutional; Militarism; Nonviolence in the United States; Peacemaking; Weapons.**

DODGE CITY

There are two Dodge Cities, the historical and the metaphorical. Frontier businessmen founded the real Dodge City in 1872 astride the path of the Santa Fe Railroad in southwest Kansas. During its first three years it served as the busy center of the buffalo-hide trade of the southern plains. After the rapid extermination of the buffalo, Dodge in 1876 became one of the West's principal cattle towns, a sale and shipping point for Texas livestock driven north on the Western Trail.

A three-year drought beginning in 1878 temporarily frustrated agricultural settlement of the area, unexpectedly prolonging the town's career as a cattle-trading center for several years. But in 1885 farmers overran its surrounding ranges, legislators closed Kansas to direct importations of Texas cattle, and Texas ranchers fenced off the trail. Dodge subsided into its permanent role as a typical county seat.

The second Dodge City belongs to the imagination. It thrives as a cultural icon, the archetypical rendezvous of cowboy-hatted characters with itchy trigger-fingers. As such, it is a widely employed metaphor for violence, crime, and civil anarchy.

Dodge City as Metaphor

As late as the 1920s, inhabitants of the real Dodge resisted this image. But publication of Stuart Lake's best-selling *Wyatt Earp: Frontier Marshal* (1931), a fictionalized biography of Dodge's assistant marshal of the late 1870s, brought tourists and dollars. Since then townspeople have collaborated in reifying the mythical Dodge and elevating Earp and another local lawman, W. B. ("Bat") Masterson, into historical celebrities.

Hollywood followed suit. Such films as *Dodge City* (1939), *Masterson of Kansas* (1954), and *The Gunfight at Dodge City* (1959) lent realism to a genre already devoted to astronomical levels of violent death. Even more influential in the late 1950s through the early 1970s were three popular television serials set in Dodge: *The Life and Legend of Wyatt Earp, Bat Masterson,* and especially the long-running *Gunsmoke,* whose two-decade television tenure exceeded the real town's "wild and woolly" era by six years.

The metaphorical Dodge City came into its own during the Vietnam War, when American service personnel used it to designate any fearsomely defended venue, whether hostile or friendly (for example, Hanoi). To "get out of Dodge" meant to speedily vacate a dangerous area.

Some usages from the 1990s suggest the metaphor's versatility. A rash of killings in New York City in 1990 put Mayor David N. Dinkins on the defensive. "Things are not out of control," he insisted, "and this is not Dodge City." In 1992 Jack Kemp, former secretary of Housing and Urban Development, asserted that one crime-plagued Washington, D.C., neighborhood "was so bad it was called Dodge City." In 1994 Baruch Goldstein, an Israeli militant, emptied his weapon into a crowd of Muslims; a report was headlined "Hebron: Dodge City on the West Bank." The latest crime fad, said *Newsweek* that same year, was sticking up tollway booths; toll collectors were arming, and officials worried about "turning the nation's highways into something out of Dodge City." In 1995 a congressman described ruinous competition among fertility clinics: "It's kind of like Dodge City before the marshals show up." In 1997 the columnist George Will praised an active Republican organization whose fax machine, he exulted, "is the quickest gun to clear its holster since Dodge City simmered down." In early 1998 New York was bedeviled by jaywalkers, pitting pedestrians against cars. The *New York Times* headline read: "Dodge City, in More Ways Than One." And by this date the metaphor had been internationalized. A 1997 dispatch from Serbia reported that the most flourishing business in one war-ravaged town was prostitution. "Dodge City," grumbled a citizen.

Body Counts Versus Homicide Rates

By the 1950s the theatrical image of Dodge had been incorporated into serious historical literature as fact. But in 1968 Robert R. Dykstra's *The Cattle Towns* revealed the unglamorous truth: deadly violence at Dodge was rare rather than commonplace. Although no systematic data exist for the pre-1876 town, local newspapers documented the

Front Street, Dodge City, Kansas, in the 1880s. THE KANSAS STATE HISTORICAL SOCIETY, TOPEKA, KANSAS

homicides of its cowboy years. They disclose that adult deaths from violence (murder, justifiable or excusable homicide, and manslaughter) numbered only fifteen—an average of one and a half per cattle season.

All victims were killed with firearms, including a local tailor clubbed with a rifle. Six were cowboys or ranchers. Three were lawmen, one of whom died in a private quarrel stemming from a business rivalry. One was a woman, inadvertently shot in an attempted assassination of the mayor. The others were a freighter, a railroader, a dance hall proprietor, a farmer. None died in a Hollywood-style street fight. Six were not even armed.

Dodge's body count was modest principally because the arrival of the cattle trade had prompted its businessmen to organize a town government, hire multiple peace officers, and institute gun control. Lawmen thereafter felt obliged to kill just four men—one by mistake and two, in separate incidents, being cowboys firing their pistols while galloping from town. Assistant Marshal Wyatt Earp helped kill one of these equestrians; on another occasion Sheriff Bat Masterson also killed one violator.

This revisionist view prevailed among historians, if not the public, until the 1980s, when scholars appropriated the Federal Bureau of Investiga-

tion's Uniform Crime Reporting Program method for calculating homicide rates "per 100,000 inhabitants." Since then, a few statistically naive re-revisionists have asserted that the myth is essentially correct, in that frontier Dodge was a much more dangerous place than America's most violent modern metropolis. They relish such comparisons as Dodge City's 78.4 homicide rate in 1880, as against that for greater Miami of 32.7 in 1980. But the underlying *body counts* are these: Dodge, 1; Miami, 515. Clearly, the reason Dodge's 1880 rate was more than twice that of Miami's a century later is simply that its population was tiny (1,275, as against Miami's million-plus). Only if Dodge had possessed at least five thousand residents would its rate have been smaller than Miami's. The scholarly debate continues.

Meanwhile, the public's take on Dodge City seems unchanged. The movie *Wyatt Earp* (1994) at least depicted Earp attempting to maintain gun control. But a popular 1992 nonfiction television series, *The Real West*, offered a segment titled "Bloody Dodge City," its producers having refused to allow reference to the low body count. In that series and in various reformatted versions, "Bloody Dodge City" became a History Channel staple in the late 1990s. The cattle town of the imagination seems here to stay.

Law and Order at Dodge City

Dodge City never depended on a lone lawman to keep order. In the fiscal year 1884–1885, peace officers' salaries totaled 42 percent of the town budget. Taxes supported a city marshal, an assistant marshal, and as many policemen as needed, all closely supervised and (not always successfully) regimented. Police regulations imposed in 1882 included the following:

1. Each and every member of the Police force shall devote his whole time and attention to the business of the department, and is hereby prohibited from following any other calling. . . .

3. Each and every member must be civil, quiet, and orderly; he must maintain decorum, command of temper, and discretion. . . .

5. All officers on duty must wear the star or shield on the outside garment on the left breast.

6. No member of the police force while on duty shall drink any intoxicating liquor. . . .

9. Every member will be furnished with a copy of these regulations and is expected to familiarize himself with the same and also with the ordinances.

10. The members of the police force will as soon as practicable after making an arrest report the same to the City Attorney and execute, under his directions, the proper papers. . . .

11. Every officer will be held responsible for the proper discharge of his duties; following the advice of others will be no excuse, unless he be a superior officer.

12. The City Attorney will furnish information on legal matters on any officer's request. . . .

13. The presence of any infectious disease must be promptly reported to the Mayor.

BIBLIOGRAPHY

Courtwright, David T. *Violent Land: Single Men and Social Disorder from the Frontier to the Inner City.* Cambridge, Mass.: Harvard University Press, 1996.

Dykstra, Robert R. *The Cattle Towns.* New York: Knopf, 1968; Bison, 1983.

———. "Overdosing on Dodge City." *Western Historical Quarterly* 27 (winter 1996).

———. "To Live and Die in Dodge City: Body Counts, Law and Order, and the Case of *Kansas* v. *Gill.*" In *Lethal Imag-ination: Violence and Brutality in American History,* edited by Michael A. Bellesiles. New York: New York University Press, 1999.

———. "Violence, Gender, and Methodology in the 'New' Western History." *Reviews in American History* 27 (March 1999).

ROBERT R. DYKSTRA

See also **Earp Brothers; Frontier; Masterson, William "Bat."**

DOMESTIC VIOLENCE

The following definitional overview will guide the reader to the extensive coverage of domestic violence elsewhere in this *Encyclopedia.* The reader should consult the index for further references.

Domestic violence is a pattern of assaultive and coercive behaviors—physical, social, psychological, and economic—at home. The abuser creates fear and intimidation through physical means, pressured or forced sex, threats of violence, humiliation, and other forms of emotional abuse. Studies show that violence during childhood continues throughout life; abusive behavior is learned through past observations of family and peers. Men who have experienced violence tend to bring this violence into relationships with women.

Domestic violence crosses all socioeconomic and ethnic boundaries. According to the Department of Justice, 21 percent of crime in California is related to domestic violence. In the United States, a woman is physically abused by her husband every nine seconds. It is estimated that twelve million women will be abused by a current or former partner at some point in their lives.

Until the 1970s, domestic violence was largely considered a private family matter by law enforcement and the courts. Thanks to greater awareness and efforts of grassroots organizations and the women's movement, domestic violence is now recognized as a serious problem that requires coordinated prevention and intervention efforts by law-enforcement and government agencies, the legal and medical professions, and social workers.

Police are usually called upon to curb and control domestic violence, but imprisonment and the use of restraining orders are not necessarily effective. Medical professionals often have to choose between respecting a patient's confidentiality and reporting an incident to the police. When confronted by police and doctors, many victims deny that a problem exists, usually because they fear retaliation by the abuser. Even if the victims acknowledge the problem, fear, intimidation, and physical harm force many of them to stay in the abusive situation. Effective prevention and intervention measures include validating and acknowledging the injustices and experiences of each victim, respecting the victims' needs and gaining their trust, and helping them realize that they are not alone and that there are resources available to them.

In this *Encyclopedia* the following entries are especially relevant: **Age and the Life Cycle; Child Abuse; Conflict Resolution: Interpersonal; Elder Abuse; Incest; Maternal Prenatal Violence; Parricide; Psychological Violence; Rape; Sibling Abuse; Spousal and Partner Abuse; Women.**

FORREST HONG

DRAFT RIOTS

During the week of 13 July 1863, working-class rioters protesting their conscription to fight in the Civil War swept through New York City. Looting, arson, and mayhem resulted in widespread destruction of public and private property. Upwards of one hundred rioters, police, militia, local elites, merchants, and innocent bystanders were killed or murdered, including many African Americans who were lynched by crowds of mostly, but not exclusively, Irish Americans. Union Army regiments, having just fought Confederate troops at Gettysburg earlier in the month, were called to the city and on 16 and 17 July quelled the riots.

Under the auspices of the March 1863 Conscription and Enrollment Acts, initiated by President Abraham Lincoln's Republican Party, the first national conscription mandated the enlistment of white males between twenty and forty-five years of age, excepting married men between thirty-five and forty-five. Draftees providing a substitute conscript or three hundred dollars were exempt from military service. Conscription was thus biased against poor and working-class whites, whose racial antipathies and resentment of local elites were exacerbated by the perceived injustice of the law. State Democratic Party leaders saw the draft as an attempt on the part of the federal and state Republicans (merchants and industrialists—the native born) to undermine their authority by setting New York State draft quotas disproportionately high

with the result that New York City had to yield up an unfair share of its young men (who were likely to be working-class or poor or immigrants as well as Democratic Party members). State courts had been expected to declare conscription unconstitutional. Short of this, New York Democratic Party officials, particularly Horatio Seymour, the Democratic governor of New York, had been expected to protect the male populace from the draft by ordering city officials not to enforce the lottery system. Democratic Party leaders, however, were unable to prevent federal marshals from proceeding house to house, beginning March 1863, to register all eligible New Yorkers.

While the legitimacy of Lincoln's Republican Party was at stake in the controversy surrounding the draft, the New York City draft riots did not indicate pro-Confederate sympathies per se. The main issue was the expansion and centralization of federal authority and the social and political order of a heavily Democratic New York City. New York City did, however, have long-standing ties to southern slavery, and it was the capital of both the antiabolitionist and the abolitionist press.

The first protests against the draft took place on Monday morning, 13 July, the day of the lottery. Crowds gathered, speeches were made, factories were shut down, and their workers joined the mob in the streets. Resistance on the part of merchants, landlords, factory owners, and their sympathizers was met with violence. In short order, buildings, factories, shops, and homes were looted and set on fire, their occupants killed or injured. Republican sympathizers, elites, blacks, German and Jewish store owners, Chinese peddlers, and bystanders of higher social status than the protesters were attacked indiscriminately. African Americans were especially in danger—earlier in the year African Americans had been used to break a longshoremen's strike on the docks and working-class racial antagonism, always prevalent, was at an extreme. On the first day of rioting, a crowd razed the Colored Orphan Asylum and later lynched a black man whose body they set on fire. Throughout the insurrection, hangings of African Americans were accompanied by mutilations and other acts of brutality and defilement.

Union victory and freedom for black slaves would, in the minds of many, lead to displacement of white workers by low-wage blacks. Fear of racial amalgamation ran high, especially among oppressed groups like Irish-Catholics, who competed with the blacks in the trades. The draft riots be-

Antidraft rioters in July 1863. Wood engraving from *Frank Leslie's Illustrated Newspaper,* **25 July 1863.** LIBRARY OF CONGRESS

came another opportunity for all white workingmen, but especially Irish longshoremen, street pavers, cartmen, hack drivers, and dock laborers, to institute the "white only" rule for their trades.

By week's end, military regiments had restored order and steps were taken to reinstitute conscription. The effects of the riots were widespread. William Tweed's Tammany Hall political machine solidified its hold on party politics for a decade to come; Tweed and his machine were able to use the political chaos of the riots to harness working-class sympathy—especially among the Irish—while preserving civil peace at the same time. The legitimacy of the national Republican Party was bolstered. By not declaring martial law in New York City the Republicans forestalled further violence (the draft resumed without incident in August 1863). (On the other hand, Lincoln undermined the potential political ascendancy of radical Republicans in New York City, who would have used martial law to reconstruct the city in their political favor.) Not least, enough Union troops were raised to defeat the Confederacy. The working class frustrated Republican rule in New York City and effectively brought about its own political inclusion. The unfortunate situation of African Americans,

however, remained little changed in the aftermath of the riots.

BIBLIOGRAPHY

Bernstein, Iver. *The New York City Draft Riots: Their Significance for American Society and Politics in the Age of the Civil War.* New York: Oxford University Press, 1990.

Burrows, Edwin G., and Mike Wallace. *Gotham: A History of New York City to 1898.* New York: Oxford University Press, 1999.

Cook, Adrian. *The Armies of the Streets: The New York City Draft Riots of 1863.* Lexington: University Press of Kentucky, 1974.

Jacobson, Matthew Frye. *Whiteness of a Different Color: European Immigrants and the Alchemy of Race.* Cambridge, Mass.: Harvard University Press, 1998.

MATTHEW E. ARCHIBALD

See also **Civil War; Labor and Unions; New York; Race and Ethnicity; Riots.**

DRED SCOTT DECISION

Few decisions issued by the U.S. Supreme Court have achieved as notorious a place in history as that reached in the 1857 case of *Dred Scott v. John*

F. A. Sandford. The Dred Scott decision, having since become a symbol of racism in the pre–Civil War United States, remains closely identified with the unfolding crisis immediately preceding the outbreak of that war. Although it was decided four years before the shelling of Fort Sumter, South Carolina, which began the Civil War, the position taken by the Supreme Court respecting the limits of congressional power seriously exacerbated tensions between North and South and further weakened a political process struggling to contain sectional conflict and to preserve national unity.

No one could have foretold in 1846, when Dred Scott's lawsuit was first heard in the state courts of Missouri, that the efforts of a slave to secure his and his family's freedom would have had such a profound impact. Born in Virginia around 1800, Scott had been purchased in 1833 by John Emerson, an army surgeon then stationed in St. Louis, Missouri, where slavery was legal. In 1842, after postings to Illinois as well as Minnesota, then a part of the Wisconsin Territory, Emerson, newly discharged and now married to Eliza Irene Sanford, returned to St. Louis. He died the next year, and his estate, which included Scott and Scott's

Dred Scott. CORBIS/BETTMANN

family, was inherited by Emerson's wife. In 1846 Scott filed suit against Eliza Emerson, claiming that he had become a free man during the years he had resided with John Emerson in Illinois, a state that did not recognize slavery, and in the Wisconsin Territory, which, by the terms of the act providing for its territorial status, forbade slavery within its boundaries. Scott lost his first bid for freedom because of a failure of the evidence to prove some of the basic and necessary elements of the charges leveled against Emerson, but Scott obtained an order for another trial. This new trial, in 1850, resulted in a decision in Scott's favor, the jury having satisfied itself that he had indeed once resided in free territory and thus, according to the judge's instruction, could no longer be considered a slave.

Eliza Emerson appealed, and the matter was brought eventually to the Missouri Supreme Court. Much, however, had changed since the lawsuit had originally been filed. The Compromise of 1850, through which Congress had attempted to address the status of slavery in newly acquired territories from Mexico, had failed to resolve the bitter feelings and suspicions that had arisen prior to its enactment. To appease the southern states, the compromise also included a more stringent fugitive slave law that required the authorities of the different states to cooperate fully with federal officials in the apprehension and return of runaway slaves. Enforcement of the law, sometimes carried out in disregard of the affected states' legal procedures and the rights guaranteed under their separate constitutions, produced mixed and, from the southern point of view, entirely unsatisfactory results. The reluctance of many courts in the northern states to recognize the force or legitimacy of southern state laws and decisions respecting the status of slaves, specifically those in transit to and from the South, proved particularly irksome and unsettling. This practice of ignoring southern legal precedent and law, undoubtedly, was what the Missouri Supreme Court had in mind when, on 22 March 1852, it overturned the judgment rendered in Scott's favor. In view of these new developments, the Missouri Supreme Court was reluctant to give either Illinois or territorial law "full faith and credit" as specified under the U.S. Constitution. Instead, and despite the weight of established legal precedent in Missouri recognizing the application of another state's laws in circumstances similar to those in Scott's case, the Missouri court elected to apply the state law in determining Scott's status.

In 1854 a new lawsuit was filed on Scott's behalf. Emerson had since moved to Massachusetts, remarried, and turned over matters concerning her former husband's estate to her brother, John F. A. Sanford, a resident of New York with strong business ties to St. Louis. Sanford, whose name was subsequently misspelled in the court's records, was made the defendant in a new attempt to obtain Scott's freedom through legal action in the federal courts. Sanford immediately objected to the federal court even hearing the matter. Scott, Sanford argued, was a slave and, under the laws of Missouri, could not be considered a citizen of that state. For that reason, the suit did not involve citizens of different states and therefore did not fall within federal court jurisdiction. This "plea in abatement," as it was then called, was rejected by the federal judge hearing the matter, Robert W. Wells, the same judge who would later instruct the jury to use Missouri law to determine Scott's status. Since the Missouri Supreme Court had already decided that issue, the jury did not delay in reaching a similar conclusion. Not content, however, to let the matter rest there, Scott's lawyers, in 1854, appealed the decision to the U.S. Supreme Court.

In 1854 the Kansas-Nebraska Act did away with the traditional boundary between free and slave territory in what had been the Louisiana Purchase and gave the occupants of those territories the right to determine whether to be admitted to the Union as free or slave states. This act was soon followed by the appearance of the Republican Party and its "free soil" message to which many in the North proved receptive. Moreover, incidences of violence in Kansas, including the destruction of Lawrence, a center of free-state sentiment in the state, by a proslavery raiding force and John Brown's retaliatory executions of proslavery men at Pottawatomie Creek, underscored Congress's inability or unwillingness to effect a true and lasting basis for sectional harmony. In 1856, however, when the Dred Scott case finally came before the Supreme Court, the issue it posed was relatively limited: Had the lower federal court acted correctly in accepting the case for adjudication, and since neither side had appealed the decision made in connection with the plea in abatement, could the Supreme Court consider this issue at all? Not quite a year later, perhaps frustrated by Congress's continuing reluctance to assume responsibility for de-

ciding who should regulate slavery in the territories, the majority of the justices of the Supreme Court, unmindful of the fundamentally political nature of the issue, crafted their own solution.

The decision they reached, by a seven-to-two vote, that Congress could not exclude slavery from the territories, seemed to fly in the face of the moral standards of some and clearly lacked a historical or well-reasoned basis upon which to persuade a majority of the American people of its wisdom and finality. The decision reinforced, on the one hand, northern suspicions regarding a southern slave conspiracy and, on the other, the intransigence of southerners' demands respecting the unimpaired exercise of their property or slaveholding rights throughout the nation. The Supreme Court's ruling made it virtually impossible for Congress to find a middle position respecting slavery and the territories and shook the confidence of many Americans in the inviolability of the national values incorporated in the Constitution. Two very different and contentious worlds were emerging from one, and the possibility of armed conflict was becoming increasingly real.

BIBLIOGRAPHY

Ehrlich, Walter. *They Have No Rights: Dred Scott's Struggle for Freedom.* Westport, Conn.: Greenwood, 1979.

Fehrenbacher, Don E. *The Dred Scott Case: Its Significance In American Law and Politics.* New York: Oxford University Press, 1978.

Finkelman, Paul. *Dred Scott v. Sandford: A Brief History with Documents.* Boston: Bedford, 1997.

Hopkins, Vincent C. *Dred Scott's Case.* New York: Fordham University Press, 1951.

Potter, David M. *The Impending Crisis, 1848–1861.* New York: Harper and Row, 1976.

G. JACK BENGE, JR.

See also **Civil War; Slavery.**

DRIVE-BY SHOOTING

A drive-by shooting is a gang-related or gang-motivated incident in which the perpetrator discharges a firearm from a vehicle: for purposes of definition, it does not matter whether injury or homicide results. Drive-by shootings are a powerful element of urban street-gang violence in the United States. As a terror tactic, a drive-by shooting can be easily camouflaged within the normal activity of driving a car. Not until the last second, when escape for the intended target is almost impossible, is a drive-by shooting revealed for the deadly hit-and-run maneuver that it is.

History

The phenomenon has two possible sources. The first is the gangster violence of the Prohibition era (1919–1933), when a hit-and-run maneuver known as "drive-by murder" was rumored to be a daily and normal occurrence surrounding the business of bootlegging. The tactic, said to have been originated by Al Capone, was used to help establish and maintain gangsters' rule and influence throughout business and politics.

The second antecedent is a World War II military strategy used by Japanese soldiers, who created an unconventional form of "mobile warfare" that allowed them to shoot at the enemy from hidden positions behind Allied lines. After the war, these mobile tactics were adopted and modified by American gangs; the drive-by became an alternative to the rumble or gangbang, which involves gang members meeting to fight at a specific place and time.

Gang activity increased in the 1950s, but the limited availability of guns kept drive-by shootings rare. It was not until the 1970s, when high unemployment rates contributed to a surge of gang membership and a surplus of firearms came into the hands of gangs, that drive-by shootings began to develop into a large-scale problem. The rate of drive-by shootings continued to rise throughout the 1980s as gangs began to engage in turf wars over drug distribution, in particular that of crack cocaine. In the San Diego, California, area, the number of drive-by shootings almost doubled between 1981 and 1988, increasing from 23.7 percent to 40.8 percent of all shootings. From 1989 through 1993, one-third of all Los Angeles gang-related homicides were the result of drive-by shootings.

Characteristics and Trends

Although drive-by shootings cause thousands of injuries and deaths each year (the precise number is unavailable because local law enforcement does not necessarily categorize a drive-by as such but often as an assault or a homicide), the primary objective of this type of assault is not murder but rather the creation of fear. The intent of drive-by shootings carried out by gangs at the end of the twentieth century was much the same as the purpose of Prohibition-era drive-by murders: to promote one's own gang by intimidating rival gangs.

Unlike the drive-by shootings of the 1920s, however, which involved planning and were directed toward a specific target, the post-1970 drive-by shootings are impulsive acts of violence—targets were usually unspecified, and often innocent bystanders were caught in the crossfire.

Participation in a drive-by shooting is encouraged and expected of gang members—such involvement brings respect from others within the gang and is also a means to improve one's status within the gang's hierarchy. The riskier the situation, the more bizarre and violent the act toward the perceived enemy, the more the perpetrator is esteemed and honored within the gang. This enhancement of reputation and the ego gratification it represents are not necessarily related to whether or not someone has been killed. By contrast, gang members who will not participate in a drive-by shooting are considered to lack "heart" or true dedication, and although they are allowed to continue as members of the gang, they are not given any high ranking or meaningful status.

Drive-by shootings most commonly occur in conjunction with one or more of the following situations: as part of an initiation ritual, as a proactive or reactive measure connected to gang reputation or to other gangs' violent activity, as an element of business competition between gangs, and simply as a search for excitement.

For example, as part of an initiation ritual a car filled with gang members may go out in the evening and drive purposely without putting the headlights on; when an oncoming car flashes its headlights out of courtesy, the individual who wants to become a gang member shoots at the oncoming car. A drive-by shooting as a proactive measure may involve gang members driving into the neighborhood of rivals and shooting to display power, to pose a challenge, to offset any potential act of violence from the rival gang, or some combination of these motives.

Equally numerous are the reasons for shootings that are carried out reactively, often in retaliation: they may be for an incursion by rival gang members into the neighborhood, for a physical or verbal attack on a fellow gang member by a rival, or for a verbal attack by rivals on a gang as a whole. A drive-by shooting may be used for the purpose of attempting to expand a drug distribution area or to protect territory already held. Sometimes gang members go riding in a car just for fun, and engage in a drive-by shooting because it is something to do and the opportunity arises.

Drive-by shootings have few commonalities. They usually occur in the evening or at night, when it is difficult to identify license plates, perpetrators, and vehicles. The most common weapon used is the handgun; victims are more likely to be injured than killed in a drive-by shooting; and the arms and legs are the most commonly injured areas of the body. The majority of drive-by shootings also involve drugs, alcohol, or both.

Gang violence is characteristically sporadic. As a result, it is difficult to associate drive-by shootings with any particular location. Areas with many violent gangs, areas with lengthy or year-round fair-weather conditions, low-density neighborhoods, and automobile-dependent areas are particularly prone to these shootings. The West Coast, particularly southern California, best fits the aforementioned list and fosters a large percentage of recorded drive-by shooting incidents in the United States.

Prevention

The Federal Bureau of Investigation launched the National Gang Strategy in 1993, implemented by so-called Safe Streets task forces. The 1994 omnibus federal crime bill increased penalties for drive-by shootings. In 1995 the U.S. Department of Justice's Office of Juvenile Justice and Delinquency Prevention established the National Youth Gang Center, which serves as a resource for comprehensive, accurate, consistent, and timely national information on youth gangs and gang-related crimes. Federal, state, and local authorities have used such information to develop policies and programs aimed at reducing gang violence, including drive-by shootings. In Los Angeles, for example, the police department's Operation Cul de Sac, applying information acquired from the center, uses traffic barriers to block vehicle access to streets in neighborhoods where gang violence, specifically drive-by shootings, has spun out of control. A 1998 study of this program by the National Institute of Justice concluded that homicides and aggravated assaults fell and were not displaced to other neighborhoods. Because drive-by shootings are such a powerful and deadly tactic for gangs, they are unlikely to cease.

BIBLIOGRAPHY

Covey, Herbert C., Scott Menard, and Robert J. Franzese. *Juvenile Gangs.* 2d ed. Springfield, Ill.: Charles C. Thomas, 1997.

Davis, R. H. "Cruising for Trouble: Gang-Related Drive-by Shootings." *FBI Law Enforcement Bulletin* 64 (January 1995).

Diver-Stamnes, Ann C. "Gangs." In *Lives in the Balance: Youth, Poverty, and Education in Watts.* Albany: State University of New York Press, 1995.

Fagan, J. "Gangs, Drugs, and Neighborhood Change." In *Gangs in America.* 2d ed., edited by C. Ronald Huff. Thousand Oaks, Calif.: Sage, 1996.

Hutson, H. Range, Deirdre Anglin, and M. J. Pratts. "Adolescents and Children Injured or Killed in Drive-by Shootings in Los Angeles." *New England Journal of Medicine* 330, no. 5 (1994).

Hutson, H. Range, et al. "The Epidemic of Gang-Related Homicides in Los Angeles County from 1979 Through 1994." *Journal of the American Medical Association* 274, no. 13 (1995).

Sanders, William B. "Drive-bys." In his *Gangbangs and Drive-bys: Grounded Culture and Juvenile Violence.* New York: Aldine de Gruyter, 1994.

Yablonsky, Lewis. *Gangsters: Fifty Years of Madness, Drugs, and Death on the Streets of America.* New York: New York University Press, 1997.

ADRIANA N. TORRES

See also **Carjacking; Crime, Legal Definitions of; Los Angeles; Road Rage; Urban Violence.**

DRUGS

The first two entries below discuss the relationship between **Drugs and Crime** *and between* **Drugs and Violence.** *The third entry examines types of* **Drug Prevention and Treatment** *programs. The final entry chronicles violence in the* **Drug Trade.**

DRUGS AND CRIME

During the early years of the twentieth century, two competing models of the drug "problem" emerged that served to shape the nature and direction of federal policy formation. On the one hand, there was the criminal model of addiction. This posture, actively pursued by the police establishment, held that "addicts" ought to be the objects of vigorous enforcement activity because the great majority of them were members of criminal subcultures, gangs, and organizations. To support this view, law-enforcement groups pointed to the experiences of their officers and agents and to several studies that demonstrated that most addicts were already criminals before they began using drugs.

The counterpoint to the criminal model was the medical model of addiction, a notion fostered by the medical community as early as the late nineteenth century. Although physicians had been

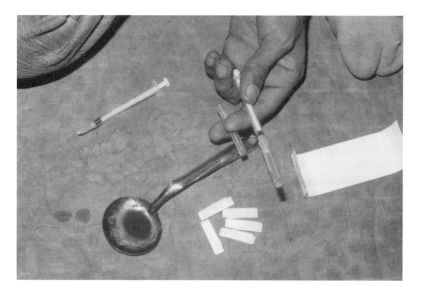

Drug paraphernalia for mixing heroin. CORBIS/JEFFREY L. ROTMAN

among the first to contend that "morphinism" and "cocainism" were the result of a moral weakness, they also emphasized that addiction itself was a chronic and relapsing disease. As such, the medical model argued that the addict should be treated in the same manner as any patient suffering from some physiological or medical disorder.

Influenced more by the criminal than the medical model, state and federal approaches to drug abuse control evolved a variety of avenues for reducing the supply of and the demand for illicit drugs. Supply-and-demand reduction strategies were initially grounded in the classic deterrence model: through legislation and criminal penalties, individuals could be discouraged from using drugs; by making an example of traffickers, the government could force potential dealers to seek out other economic pursuits.

The Harrison Act of 1914

The ultimate triumph of the criminal model of addiction was the Harrison Act of 1914, a piece of federal legislation that required all people who imported, manufactured, produced, compounded, sold, dispensed, or otherwise distributed cocaine and opiate drugs to register with the Treasury Department, pay special taxes, and keep records of all transactions. As such, it was a revenue code designed to exercise some measure of public control over narcotics and other drugs. Certain provisions of the Harrison Act permitted physicians to prescribe, dispense, or administer narcotics to

their patients for "legitimate medical purposes" and "in the course of professional practice." But how these two phrases were to be interpreted was another matter entirely.

On the one hand, the medical establishment held that addiction was a disease and that addicts were patients to whom drugs could be prescribed to alleviate the distress of withdrawal. On the other hand, the Treasury Department interpreted the Harrison Act to mean that a doctor's prescription for an addict was unlawful. The U.S. Supreme Court quickly laid the controversy to rest. In *Webb v. United States* (249 U.S. 96 [1919]), the Court held that it was not legal for a physician to prescribe narcotic drugs to an addict-patient for the purpose of maintaining his or her use and comfort. Two years later, in *Whipple v. Martinson* (256 U.S. 41 [1921]), it was held that within the framework of governmental responsibility for the public health and welfare, the state had a legitimate interest in regulating the use of "dangerous habit-forming drugs." The following year, the decision in *United States v. Behrman* (258 U.S. 280 [1922]) not only reaffirmed this position but went one step further. The *Behrman* decision declared that a narcotic prescription for an addict was unlawful, even if the drugs were prescribed as part of a "cure program." The impact of these decisions combined to make it almost impossible for addicts to obtain drugs legally. In 1925 the Supreme Court emphatically reversed itself in *Linder v. United States* (268 U.S. 5), disavowing the *Behrman* opinion and holding that addicts were entitled to medical care like other patients, but the ruling had almost no effect. By that time, physicians were unwilling to treat addicts under any circumstances, and well-developed illegal drug markets were catering to the needs of the addict population, which was estimated to be as high as three million although the data collection methods used were not very precise.

In retrospect, numerous commentators on the history of drug use in the United States have argued that the Harrison Act snatched addicts from legitimate society and forced them into the underworld. This, however, is a considerable overstatement, because subcultures of criminal addicts existed long before the passage of the Harrison Act. However, the Harrison Act further contributed to the criminalization and marginalization of narcotics addicts and other users of illegal drugs.

Drugs-Crime Studies

The relationship between drug use and street crime has been discussed and examined for decades, with the range of questions addressing issues of sequence, causality, and the nature and frequency of criminal acts. Is criminal behavior, for example, antecedent to addiction; or does criminality emerge subsequent to chronic drug dependence? Stated differently, is crime the result of, or a response to, circumstances associated with addiction to illegal drugs, or is addiction per se but one more aspect of an established criminal lifestyle? If criminality is indeed a preaddiction phenomenon, does the onset of continuous illegal drug use bring about a change in the nature, intensity, and frequency of criminal behavior? Does criminal involvement tend to increase or decrease subsequent to addiction? And what kinds of criminal offenses do street-drug users typically commit—violent predatory crimes, or profit-oriented economic crimes, or both?

Attempts to answer these questions empirically began in the 1920s, and through the close of the 1960s many dozens of studies targeting the relationship between crime and addiction were carried out. In the mid-1970s, both the National Institute on Drug Abuse and the National Institute of Justice began funding studies in many parts of the United States for the purposes of developing a useful database on the drugs-crime connection and addressing many of the unanswered questions.

In extensive follow-up studies of addicts' careers in Baltimore in the early 1980s, for example, John C. Ball and David N. Nurco found that there were high rates of criminality among heroin users during those periods in which they were addicted and markedly lower rates during times of nonaddiction. This finding was based on the concept of the "crime-days per year at risk." The "crime-day" was defined as a twenty-four-hour period during which an individual committed one or more crimes. Thus, "crime-days per year at risk" is a rate of crime commission that can vary anywhere from 0 to 365. Over the addiction careers of the Baltimore addicts studied, the average crime-days per year at risk was 230, suggesting that their criminal involvement was persistent not only on a day-to-day basis, but also over an extended number of years and periods of addiction.

Another major series of studies was done in the early 1980s by investigators in New York who operated from a storefront, conducting interviews with hundreds of criminally active drug users recruited from the streets of East and Central Harlem. The findings about the economics of the drugs-crime relationship documented the wide range of heroin usage rates among addicts and the clear correlation between amount of heroin needed and amount of crime committed, in spite of the many legal and illegal ways in which heroin users obtained the necessities of life—from heroin to bed and board—without money.

Still other studies conducted in Miami demonstrated that the amount of crime committed by drug users was far greater than anyone had previously imagined, that drug-related crime could at times be exceedingly violent, and that the criminality of street-drug users was far beyond the control of law enforcement. Research conducted elsewhere arrived at similar conclusions.

Altogether, these varied research findings imply that while the use of heroin and other drugs does not necessarily initiate criminal careers, it tends to intensify and perpetuate them. That is, street drugs were freezing users into patterns of criminality that are more acute, dynamic, unremitting, and enduring than those of other offenders.

Crack Cocaine and Street Crime

Crack is a variety of cocaine base, produced by "cooking" cocaine hydrochloride in boiling water and baking soda. It has been called the "fast-food" variety of cocaine, popular because it is cheap, is easy to conceal, and vaporizes with practically no odor. The gratification is swift: a short-lived (up to five minutes) but nevertheless intense, almost sexual, euphoria. Smoking cocaine as opposed to

427

snorting it results in more immediate and direct absorption of the drug, producing a quicker and more compelling "high," greatly increasing the dependence potential. Moreover, there is increased risk of acute toxic reactions, including brain seizure, cardiac irregularities, respiratory paralysis, paranoid psychosis, and pulmonary dysfunction.

Users typically smoke for as long as they have crack or the means to purchase it—money, personal belongings, sexual services, stolen goods, or other drugs. It is rare that smokers have but a single "hit" of crack. More likely they spend $50 to $500 during what they call a "mission"—a three- or four-day binge, smoking almost constantly, three to fifty crack "rocks" per day. During these cycles, crack users rarely eat or sleep. And once crack is tried, for many users it is not long before it becomes a daily habit. The tendency to "binge" on crack for days at a time, neglecting food, sleep, and basic hygiene, severely compromises physical health. Consequently, crack users appear emaciated most of the time. They lose interest in their physical appearance. Many have scabs on their faces, arms, and legs—the results of burns and picking at the skin (to remove bugs and other insects imagined to be crawling under the skin). Crack users tend to have burned facial hair from carelessly lighting their smoking paraphernalia; they have burned lips and tongues from the hot stems of their pipes; and many cough constantly.

The use of crack first became popular in many inner-city communities in the United States during the mid-1980s, and shortly after the drug was noticed by the media, press and television reports began describing crack use as an "epidemic" and "plague" that was devastating entire communities. Considerable focus was placed on how the high addiction liability of the drug instigated users to commit crimes to support their habits, how youths were drawn into the crack-selling business, how the violence associated with attempts to control crack distribution networks turned some communities into urban "dead zones" where crime was totally out of control, how crack engendered a "hypersexuality" among users, and how the drug was contributing to the further spread of HIV and AIDS.

In terms of crime, however, much of the drugs-crime research had been conducted, or at least initiated, before the arrival of crack cocaine in America's inner cities. Therefore, research on the drugs-crime connection related primarily to narcotics users, not crack users. By the late 1980s, empirical studies of the criminality of crack users began examining rates of crack-related violence in several urban areas, crime associated with crack distribution, and prostitution linked to the bartering of sex for crack or sex for money to purchase crack.

On the whole, research demonstrated that crack users were committing crimes with considerable frequency. Furthermore, the greater the involvement in the manufacturing, sale, and distribution of crack, the greater the criminal involvement. This criminogenic effect of the crack trade is the result of the interactive pattern typical of crime-drug relationships for addictive, expensive drugs: crime finances use, use encourages more use, more use encourages more crime. More specifically, crack dealing finances crack use, crack use encourages more crack use, and more crack use requires more profit-making crimes to support an ever-growing addictive use pattern.

Sex-for-crack exchanges in crack houses have been associated with this pattern. Although prostitution has always been to some degree a drug-related crime, the nature of crack addiction seems to have intensified this connection. Because crack makes its users ecstatic, yet is so short-acting, it has extremely high addiction potential. Use rapidly becomes compulsive use. Crack acquisition thus becomes enormously more important than family, work, social responsibility, health, values, modesty, morality, or self-respect. This makes sex-for-crack exchanges psychologically tolerable as an economic necessity. Further, the disinhibiting effects of crack enable users to engage in sexual acts they might not otherwise consider.

BIBLIOGRAPHY

Ball, John C., John W. Shaffer, and David N. Nurco. "The Day-to-Day Criminality of Heroin Addicts in Baltimore: A Study in the Continuity of Offense Rates." *Drug and Alcohol Dependence* 12 (1983): 119–142.

Inciardi, James A. *The War on Drugs II: The Continuing Epic of Heroin, Cocaine, Crack, Crime, AIDS, and Public Policy.* Mountain View, Calif.: Mayfield, 1992.

Johnson, Bruce D., Paul J. Goldstein, Edward Preble, James Schmeidler, Douglas S. Lipton, Barry Spunt, and Thomas Miller. *Taking Care of Business: The Economics of Crime by Heroin Abusers.* Lexington, Mass.: Lexington Books, 1985.

Tonry, Michael, and James Q. Wilson, eds. *Drugs and Crime.* Chicago: University of Chicago Press, 1990.

JAMES A. INCIARDI

See also **Alcohol and Alcoholism.**

DRUGS AND VIOLENCE

History and Scope of the Problem

The relationship between drug use and violence concerned society for most of the twentieth century. Drugs are defined as any substance that alters mood and has psychoactive effects. Drugs may be legal or illegal and can be used for a wide variety of purposes. Violence is defined as any physically threatening or injurious confrontation. Drug policy in the United States is based on the presumed relationship between drug use and violence. Many of the original arguments to regulate or criminalize alcohol and drug use made in the early part of the twentieth century were based on the presumed causal relationship between substance use and violence. During this era, a wide variety of materials produced by the federal government and the media portrayed drug users as brutal, routinely engaging in murderous and sexually crazed violent behavior. These assumptions about the drugs-violence relationship were widely accepted and continually portrayed until the 1960s.

The 1960s brought a rapid increase in the use of a wide variety of substances. Conventional cultural wisdom about the effects of drugs, including violence, came under increased scrutiny. The federal government and independent scholars closely examined data on the drugs-violence relationship. Government commissions, as well as most research reports, generally concluded that individuals abusing illegal drugs were actually less likely to engage in violent behavior than non-drug-using criminals. It was thought that users focused instead on nonviolent property crimes, such as burglary and larceny, and on prostitution to obtain money for relatively expensive drugs. In addition, it was concluded that there were no psychopharmacological effects that increase aggressive violent behavior in many commonly used illegal drugs, such as marijuana and heroin. These drugs were viewed as more likely to calm a user than to cause violence. Such views led to widespread consensus that marijuana and narcotics users were very unlikely to engage in violent crime (McBride and McCoy 1993).

The accepted absence of a relationship between drug use and violence began to be challenged with the rediscovery of crack cocaine in the 1980s. A wide variety of clinical observations and research reports began to note increasing rates of violence among drug users, especially pointing out the extent of cocaine use among violent criminals. Reports from the Drug Use Forecasting Program showed a high rate of drug use (mostly cocaine use, likely in the form of crack) among felony arrestees in the United States. In many cities the majority of those arrested for robbery had cocaine metabolites in their bodies at the time of arrest. Further, these same data also showed that violent juvenile offenders are more likely to have cocaine in their bodies than juveniles arrested for crimes against property (National Institute of Justice 1996).

Additional data showed a high rate of violent behavior among nonincarcerated drug users. In a population of street cocaine users, Inciardi and Pottieger found that as crack use increases, users engage in an increased number of robberies. The U.S. Department of Justice has found a consistent correlation between cocaine use and homicide. As cocaine use rises (as measured by the analysis of urine from felony arrestees), homicide rates increase and vice versa (National Criminal Justice Reference Service 1997). Broader population studies also show a strong correlation between the use of illegal drugs and violence. An important study in the *Journal of the American Medical Association* reported that violent death was eleven times higher in homes where illegal drugs were used (Rivara et al. 1997). This information has made researchers rethink the effect of drugs on violent behavior and has caused a reevaluation of existing national drug policies and enforcement practices that might sustain or even increase the drugs-violence relationship.

Theoretical Framework

In a classic 1985 article, Paul Goldstein suggested that the drugs-violence relationship be interpreted within a framework involving the following three types of factors: (1) psychopharmacological—considering the actual biological effects of specific drugs on violence; (2) economic—observing how drug cost and market competition affect violent behavior, and (3) systemic—examining the ways the values and behaviors of drug-using subcultures affect violent behavior.

Within this framework, clinicians and researchers began to focus on the specific psychopharmacological effects of various drugs that might relate to violence. Particularly, stimulants such as cocaine were examined for their effects on aggressive behavior as well as their effects on an individual's ability to assess accurately the risk of violence in given situations. Economic analysis focused on the expense of drugs and the large amounts of cash to be made from street-level drug distribution (particularly cocaine). In many communities, the most lucrative economic opportunities involve drug sales. Research on drug-using subcultures often noted that acting tough and aggressive, or giving the appearance of someone who easily could become extremely violent, was a crucial part of self-presentation on the street. Such a presentation was seen as essential for success and safety.

In addition to Goldstein's tripartite scheme, researchers have noted also that the relationship between drug use and violence is strongly affected by macrolevel social changes in American and world culture. In the United States, the wide distribution and availability of very powerful lethal weapons probably has played a significant role in increasing the violence level of aggressive behavior within drug-using subcultures. Fists, knives, and small-caliber handguns have given way to powerful automatic pistols and heavy weapons. Further, the billion-dollar international drug trade has certainly supported the use of violence to protect drug distribution. Finally, the role and growth of juvenile gangs in street and school violence may involve conflicts over drug distribution.

While data revealed that violent crime had declined slightly in the United States in the 1990s, the data still indicated that drug use—particularly cocaine use—virtually saturated the criminal justice system. Cocaine and other illegal drug use remained very common among violent offenders. The psychopharmacology, cost and profit of drugs, and subcultural values among drug users amid the availability of lethal weapons continued to result in a strong empirical relationship between drug use and violence. While these empirical facts were widely accepted, there was disagreement about possible solutions to the problem.

Strategies for Reduction

Many scholars, politicians, and other observers have argued that much of the drugs-violence connection is a result of current drug policy. They argue that many—if not all—drugs should be legalized. Supporters of the legalization movement do not claim that their proposed policy action would provide a panacea to such issues as widespread societal violence and drug abuse. Rather, they state that without legalization, violence will continue to rise unchecked (Trebach and Inciardi 1993). Legalization advocates argue that (1) economically driven violence would be reduced if

drugs were readily available and cheap, and (2) systemic violence associated with the values of drug-using subcultures would be reduced. That is, since drugs would be both readily available and cheap, there would be no need to engage in crime to obtain large amounts of money for drugs; there would be no violent conflict over drug distribution; and there would be no need to be violent (or to seem violent) in order to distribute or use drugs.

Opponents of legalization have argued that connections between violence and drug use existed well before free-market drug distribution was prohibited by the Harrison Act in 1914 (Trebach and Inciardi 1993). In addition, any decrease in economically driven violence resulting from drug legalization would likely be erased by a corresponding increase in psychopharmacologically driven violence because of increased drug use in a nonprohibitionist environment. At the end of the twentieth century, the political climate and accepted scientific research indicated that widespread drug legalization was not likely to occur. It therefore became important to focus on other strategies that could be employed to reduce the relationship between drug use and violence given the existing policy environment.

Research focusing on drug use and violence has been based on criminal justice settings. While crime includes both violent and nonviolent acts, studies of drug use onset and first crime committed show that, on average, age at first crime committed precedes age at first use of all drugs except alcohol. For both crime and drug use, age of onset is below sixteen (Trebach and Inciardi 1993). Intervention and prevention of further violence and drug use is therefore critical among the juvenile population. Reviews of intervention programs within juvenile justice settings indicate that collaborative approaches—involving social service agencies, juvenile justice systems, families, schools, and communities—have the best chance of preventing further drug use and violent activity (McBride et al. 1997).

Unfortunately, collaboration among local agencies alone is not enough to curb the increasing violence associated with drug use. The cultural and structural issues that drive drug use and violence involve all three levels of society: micro (familial and individual interactions between directly connected persons), meso (local agency and other activity based on formal or informal community structure and policy), and macro (national-level policies, economics, and cultural influences). Macrolevel policy decisions must be made that create and enhance sustainable and viable education, employment, and resource opportunities for individuals and organizations in local communities. Educational opportunities must provide accessibility to quality education that will give individuals the skills needed to become and to stay competitive in the job market. Employment opportunities should include enough income and security to make it possible for individuals to succeed economically without turning to involvement in the drug market. Resource opportunities need to involve funding and support for local communities to establish needed employment and educational opportunities, as well as to continue and to expand social service agencies. These opportunities must be lobbied for and made available at the macro level if individuals and local collaboratives are to have a chance—that is, the chance for individuals at the micro level to choose positive alternatives to drug use and violence, and the chance for mesolevel collaborative agencies to be able to provide resources for juveniles currently needing help.

BIBLIOGRAPHY

Goldstein, Paul J. "The Drugs/Violence Nexus: A Tripartite Conceptual Framework." *Journal of Drug Issues* 15 (fall 1985).

Inciardi, James A., and Anne E. Pottieger. "Kids, Crack, and Crime." *Journal of Drug Issues* 21 (spring 1991).

McBride, Duane C., and Clyde B. McCoy. "The Drugs-Crime Relationship: An Analytical Framework." *Prison Journal* 73 (September–December 1993).

McBride, Duane, Curt VanderWaal, Holly VanBuren, and Yvonne Terry. *Breaking the Cycle of Drug Use Among Juvenile Offenders.* Paper presented to the National Institute of Justice, Washington, D.C., December 1997.

National Criminal Justice Reference Service. *Homicide in Eight U.S. Cities: Trends, Context, and Policy Implications.* Washington, D.C.: U.S. Department of Justice, December 1997.

National Institute of Justice. *1995 Drug Use Forecasting: Annual Report on Adult and Juvenile Arrestees.* Washington, D.C.: NIJ, June 1996.

Rivara, Frederick P., Beth A. Mueller, Grant Somes, Carmen T. Mendoza, Corman B. Rushforth, and Arthur L. Kellerman. "Alcohol and Illicit Drug Abuse and the Risk of Violent Death in the Home." *Journal of the American Medical Association* 278 (August 1997).

Trebach, Arnold S., and James A. Inciardi. *Legalize It? Debating American Drug Policy.* Washington, D.C.: American University Press, 1993.

DUANE C. McBRIDE
YVONNE M. TERRY

See also **Alcohol and Alcoholism; Developmental Factors: Prenatal Factors; Maternal Prenatal Violence; Self-Destructiveness.**

DRUG PREVENTION AND TREATMENT

Much of the violence in the United States arises from substance abuse and illicit drug trafficking. Despite the urgency of the problem, rigorous research on drug-related violence is relatively recent. Throughout most of the twentieth century, whenever the use of an illicit drug became prominent, the drug was often viewed by the media, law enforcement, treatment and prevention agencies, and some researchers as a cause of violent crime. Heroin occasioned such responses in the 1920s and 1950s, marijuana in the 1930s, PCP in the 1970s, and cocaine and crack in the 1980s.

Examining the extent to which drug prevention and treatment programs can reduce drug-related violence is justified because of the many adverse consequences of such violence, which include death, serious injury, medical costs and lost earnings, and immeasurable instances of pain, suffering, and reduced quality of life.

Drug-Related Violence

In 1985 Paul J. Goldstein, a leading researcher in drug-related violence, emphasized that improved methods of assessing drug-related violence were crucial for developing effective interventions. He noted that official statistics obtained in the criminal justice and health-care systems could not link acts of criminal violence (and resultant death or injury) to drug use or trafficking by victims and perpetrators. Goldstein and his colleagues therefore undertook research in New York State and City, using innovative data collection procedures to determine more precisely the nature and extent of the connection between drugs and violence. In examining homicides, the researchers and detectives obtained information on the relationships and drug involvement of victims and perpetrators, the possible role of drugs in the events, and characteristics of crime scenes (e.g., drug market, "shooting gallery"). In associated ethnographic studies, the investigators conducted weekly interviews with heroin and cocaine addicts and dealers under conditions of strict confidentiality and immunity from prosecution. In these interviews, subjects provided detailed data on their drug use, drug dealing, and associated violent activities.

The research of Goldstein and coworkers found that drugs and violence could be related in three different ways: (1) psychopharmacologically—through the short- or long-term ingestion of a drug; (2) economic-compulsively—needing money to finance addiction; and (3) systemically—resulting from disputes between participants in the drug distribution system (e.g., territorial disputes between dealers, eliminating informers, retribution for selling adulterated drugs, punishment for not paying one's debts). This schema determined that 40 percent to 53 percent of violent events were drug related. Systemic factors predominated in two studies of homicide, whereas systemic and psychopharmacological aspects were equally prominent in two "street" studies of addicts. Most systemic and economic-compulsive events involved heroin in the early 1980s and cocaine, particularly crack, during the late 1980s and early 1990s. Most psychopharmacological violence involved the use of alcohol. Finally, the probability of both violent perpetration and victimization were greater for subjects involved in drug distribution than for those who were only users.

Drug-Related Violence Among Drug Treatment Clients

Remarkably little research has targeted the nature and extent of drug-related violence among drug treatment clients. In one such study conducted in New York City, Barry Spunt and his colleagues (1990) interviewed forty-six male methadone clients and seventy-two male heroin addicts not in treatment about their involvement in violence over the preceding eight-week period. No significant group differences were found in violent crime rates, proportion of violent events that were drug-related (49 percent for methadone clients versus 42 percent for the comparison group), or factors (psychopharmacological, economic-compulsive, systemic) associated with violence. In both groups most psychopharmacological violence was alcohol-related and most economic-compulsive violence was cocaine-related. A major group difference, however, was that violence in treatment clients was less likely to involve heroin. For those not in treatment, heroin was the drug most frequently related to systemic violence and second most frequently associated with both psychopharmacological and economic-compulsive violence. In contrast, treatment clients evidenced no systemic or psychopharmacological events related to heroin. The researchers concluded that because much of the treatment group continued to abuse nonnarcotic drugs (mainly cocaine and alcohol)

and commit violence, treatment programs should focus on reducing these violent behaviors as well as heroin use. They also emphasized the need for research on the effect of methadone treatment on drug-related violence.

Drug Treatment and Crime Reduction

The extent to which drug abuse treatment reduces drug-related violence needs to be rigorously examined. Evaluations of treatment effectiveness typically do not use measures of drug-related violence that might clarify circumstances under which violent behavior occurs. However, considerable research evidence indicates that for most individuals, involvement in certain kinds of treatment (methadone maintenance, therapeutic community, and drug-free approaches, or any of these combined with criminal justice supervision) significantly reduces drug use (measured by both self-report and urinalysis), assault, robbery, theft, drug dealing, and arrest. Although studies have found that relapse to drug use and crime frequently occurs within three months after treatment, twelve-month post-treatment rates of drug use and crime are generally lower than twelve-month pretreatment rates. While most of these studies have involved heroin addicts, a nationwide study of ten thousand drug abuse clients, conducted from 1991 to 1993, found reductions in drug use and crime up to twenty-four months after treatment. The primary drug of abuse for most of these clients was cocaine.

The effects of drug treatment tend to vary among individuals. There is evidence that the more criminally active and violent drug abusers (especially those using heroin or cocaine or both) will have poorer treatment outcomes. Unlike most other heavy users of heroin or cocaine or both, these individuals tend to commit disproportionately high rates of several different types of crime, including violent crimes, regardless of addiction status. Individuals with favorable treatment outcomes are generally older, employed, less predisposed to violence, and more stable psychologically; they become involved in crime later in life.

The impact of drug treatment also varies with the types of offenses committed. Among heroin addicts, property crime and, ironically, violent crime (assault and robbery) tend to decline over time at greater rates than drug distribution and other organized crimes. One of the most comprehensive evaluations of the effects of treatment on the types of offense committed was conducted by John C. Ball and Alan Ross (1991), who analyzed the reduction in fifteen types of criminal activity among 491 male heroin addicts who had been in methadone maintenance treatment for six months or more. There was an overall reduction in the annual crime-days rate from 244 during the addiction period before treatment to 91 during treatment. Although there was a marked decline for all offenses, the reduction was greater for theft (auto theft, 89 percent; shoplifting, 90 percent; burglary, 87 percent; other theft, 93 percent) and violence (assault, 91 percent; robbery, 89 percent) than for organized crimes (drug business, 81 percent; pimping, 76 percent; loan-sharking, 73 percent; confidence games, 79 percent; illegal gambling, 47 percent).

Preventing Drug Abuse

There has also been a paucity of formal studies of the impact of drug prevention programs on violence. Evaluations of prevention programs have not made extensive use of measurements expressly designed to gauge drug-related violence. Also, most evaluations have not followed youths into later adolescence and adulthood.

Comprehensive literature reviews by James Howell (1995), David Hawkins (1995), and their colleagues provide evidence that prevention programs that focus on reducing risk factors and enhancing protection factors can be effective in reducing drug use, violence, and other deviant behavior in children and adolescents. Such programs recognize that the more risk factors one is exposed to in early childhood (e.g., poor parental or family functioning, deviant peers, poor neighborhood, school failure), the greater the probability of early deviance. While most youths who experiment with alcohol, tobacco, or marijuana do not subsequently abuse heroin or cocaine (the only drugs that are likely to cause increased crime with increased use), the earliest users are far more likely to do so. Similarly, while most youths involved in minor delinquency do not become serious criminals, those with early involvement are disproportionately likely to become chronic violent offenders. One of the most consistent findings in the social scientific literature is the earlier the onset of youthful deviance, the greater the severity, variety, frequency, and persistence of deviance, such as violent crime, drug dealing, and heroin and cocaine addiction, throughout adolescence and adulthood.

There is, therefore, a growing consensus among social scientists that prevention programs need to start as early as possible in an individual's life in order to identify risk and protection factors. Early childhood programs designed to reduce multiple risk factors and enhance protection factors are most likely to prevent or at least delay the onset of drug use. Promoting certain factors such as social skills, close relationships with supportive, conventional family members and peers, and school achievement are particularly important because they can, in many instances, counteract negative influences.

Future Directions

Drug treatment and prevention programs appear to be promising approaches for reducing drug-related violence. Methadone maintenance, drug-free outpatient programs, and therapeutic communities all help to reduce predatory crime and drug use, especially for individuals remaining in treatment for at least six months. Criminal justice supervision can be effective in assuring that clients stay in treatment. However, individuals with the highest rates of pretreatment violence generally have poor outcomes. Criminologists emphasize that conventional drug abuse treatment is not likely to be effective with chronic violent offenders because their deviant behavior patterns typically begin early in life, encompass a wide variety of serious offenses, and persist despite changes in addiction status.

Drug abuse treatment programs would probably be more effective in curbing drug-related violence if, in addition to addiction, they focused on reducing predatory crime, drug dealing, and other deviant behaviors. Of the types of drug-related violence identified by Goldstein and colleagues, economic-compulsive violence is apparently most likely to be reduced by treatment. The primary goal of treatment is to eliminate drug dependence, and economic-compulsive violence most directly reflects dependence on expensive drugs (e.g., heroin, cocaine). Psychopharmacological violence is more closely associated with abuse of alcohol than the use of illicit drugs. Systemic violence mainly concerns illicit drug distribution, and drug business crimes seem less likely to be reduced by treatment than other offenses.

Treatment programs have an especially challenging task in intervening with individuals entrenched in addiction and criminal careers. Given the strong link between early problem behavior and the variety, frequency, severity, and persistence of subsequent deviance, prevention would apparently be more effective than treatment in reducing drug-related violence. Since conditions facilitating severe, long-standing deviance occur very early in life, comprehensive interventions beginning in early childhood that address multiple deficits (e.g., school, family, peers, neighborhood) and are enhanced by protection factors would probably be the most effective prevention approaches. School screening programs could help in detecting early risk factors, including child abuse or neglect, neurological impairments, parental substance abuse, and learning disabilities, all of which increase the likelihood of drug abuse and violence.

An increased understanding of how at-risk young people avoid serious drug and crime involvement is crucial to guiding prevention and early intervention efforts. A focus of research initiatives in the 1990s by both the National Institute on Drug Abuse and the National Institute of Justice is to follow at-risk youths into adulthood to learn more about how protection factors work in real-life situations and under different circumstances. Such information is also particularly valuable for addressing how drugs and violence are intertwined in the development of criminal careers. Further, drug prevention programs need to focus not only on the dangers of drug use but also on illicit drug distribution. Violence tends to be more closely related to drug dealing than to drug use, and many successful dealers are not addicts.

Finally, techniques for measuring drug-related violence, similar to those developed by Paul Goldstein and his colleagues, need to be incorporated into evaluations of the effectiveness of drug treatment and prevention programs. Such data are likely to be helpful in understanding what types of interventions are effective in reducing drug-related violence, both generally and for specific types of individuals.

BIBLIOGRAPHY

Ball, John C., and Alan Ross. *The Effectiveness of Methadone Maintenance Treatment*. New York: Springer-Verlag, 1991.

Goldstein, Paul J. "The Drugs-Violence Nexus: A Tripartite Conceptual Framework." *Journal of Drug Issues* 15, no. 4 (1985).

———. "Questions and Answers in Lethal and Non-Lethal Violence." In *Proceedings of the First Annual Workshop of the Homicide Research Working Group, Ann Arbor, Michigan, June 14–16, 1992*, edited by Carolyn Rebecca Block and Richard L. Block. Washington, D.C.: National Institute of Justice, 1992.

Hawkins, J. David, Michael W. Arthur, and Richard F. Catalano. "Preventing Substance Abuse." In *Building a Safer Society: Strategic Approaches to Crime Prevention*. Volume 19 of *Crime and Justice: A Review of Research*, edited by Michael Tonry and David Farrington. Chicago: University of Chicago Press, 1995.

Howell, James C., Barry Krisberg, J. David Hawkins, and John J. Wilson, eds. *Sourcebook on Serious, Violent, and Chronic Juvenile Offenders*. Thousand Oaks, Calif.: Sage, 1995.

Leshner, Alan I. "NIDA Seeks New Keys to Preventing Drug Abuse Among Adolescents." *NIDA Notes*, May/June 1996.

Spunt, Barry J., Paul J. Goldstein, Patricia A. Bellucci, and Thomas Miller. "Drug Relationships in Violence Among Methadone Maintenance Treatment Clients." *Advances in Alcohol and Substance Abuse* 9, no. 3 (1990).

This article is dedicated to the memory of Dr. David Nurco, a prominent investigator in the field of drug abuse and an exceptional mentor.

TIMOTHY KINLOCK

See also **Alcohol and Alcoholism; Prevention: Violent-Crime Prevention.**

DRUG TRADE

As argued by the White House's Office of National Drug Control Policy, illegal drugs lead to levels of violence that challenge the very security of American citizens. The office's 1999 *National Drug Control Strategy Report* (*NDCSR*) posits further that drugs and crime are linked in "an undeniable nexus" where "drug trafficking and violence go hand in hand." By the late 1990s, according to the *NDCSR*, the numbers of drug-related arrests were over 1.5 million and rising. Arrestees testing positive for drugs had fallen from the high levels of the 1980s but still comprised over 60 percent of total arrests in major cities. Drug-related murders still took place but continued their decline from the high levels of the late 1980s.

Arguments linking drugs and violence are not new to the United States. Government officials have made similar claims beginning in the nineteenth century, during California's antiopium campaigns, and continuing during subsequent national campaigns against drugs. However, these arguments often reflected political opportunism more than actual concerns with violence. The Reagan administration's campaign against drugs, especially against crack cocaine in the mid-1980s, led to a backlash among scholars, with many calling for greater conceptual clarity and research on the relationship between drugs and violence.

The efforts of Paul J. Goldstein to disaggregate the drug-violence nexus (1985) significantly influenced scholarship on the nature and sources of drug-related violence. Goldstein called for greater clarity in the concepts of drugs and violent crime, arguing for the need to study both concepts by type of drug (such as heroin, crack, and cocaine) as well as type of violence (such as homicide and assault). Goldstein's threefold typology of drug-related violence posits a first type of violence linked to the effects of drug usage; a second stemming from the addict's need to commit crimes to finance a drug habit; and a third linked to the dynamics of the drug trade as an illicit market.

Though all three dimensions often are conflated in the *NDCSR* and media reports, the work of Goldstein and others suggests that the primary sources of drug-related violence lie in the broader systemic dynamics of the drug trade. These dynamics include territorial disputes between trafficking organizations, robberies and retaliation by rival organizations, punishment of informers, disputes between dealers and consumers over drug quality or debt payments, and enforcement of "normative codes" within trafficking organizations. It is important to stress, however, that the drug trade is not always distinguished by violence. Instead, violence appears to play two primary functions. First, violence serves as a selective tool of market regulation in the broader illicit economy, more commonly invoked by individuals or groups seeking to consolidate their market share. Second, violence serves as a tool of political challenge and control used by drug traffickers and governments alike.

Violence and Illicit Drug Markets

By designating the drug trade as illegal, governments in the United States and abroad have helped to create one of the most dynamic sectors in the illicit economy. In general, illicit markets emerge when high levels of demand exist for prohibited activities and where governments lack the capacity or political will to engage in total enforcement. Prohibition increases the profitability of illegal activities and the incentives for new competitors to enter the market. These participants in the illicit economy lack many of the tools found in licit markets for settling disputes and enforcing discipline within their own organizations. Simply put, criminals do not have recourse to legal contracts, nor can they appeal to the enforcement apparatus of the government, except in cases of official corruption.

Because of this lack of legal recourse, threats and use of physical force play important roles in the regulation of illicit activities. But the actual use of violence varies. Economists studying the dynamics of crime, for example, have observed that violence is usually bad for business. Violence incurs costs, including the risk of retaliation against business activities by competitors. More important, violence tends to attract greater levels of interference from government authorities, which increases the risks of arrest and loss of assets. As a result, criminals often seek less disruptive solutions to resolving disputes in the illicit economy. These solutions include turning to financial accommodation, temporary alliances of convenience, and more extensive organizational frameworks.

The drug trade illustrates these dynamics of an illicit market. Despite a long history of government control efforts, people continue to demand illegal drugs. The presence of a mass market for illegal

Houston police officer Roland Johnson gathers loose marijuana after local police make a landmark drug bust on 8 January 1985. More than five thousand pounds of high-grade marijuana, worth over $2.5 million on the street, were seized in a warehouse on the southeast side of the city. Photographed by Ira Strickstein. UPI/CORBIS-BETTMANN

drugs in the United States since the 1960s, for example, facilitated the expansion of trade in cannabis, heroin, cocaine, and an array of synthetic products (e.g., LSD, ecstasy, and methamphetamine). Prohibition is the official U.S. policy, but in practice, for an array of reasons too extensive to explore here, the federal government has lacked the capacity and the will to engage in total enforcement. The result is a lucrative illicit market in the United States. Though facts and figures in the illicit economy must be taken with caution, estimates of the revenues generated by the drug trade in the United States alone place annual sales at more than $50 billion.

Despite such stakes, the incidence of violence linked to the drug trade varies. Anecdotal evidence, for example, suggests that disputes over drugs between users, between users and dealers, or between dealers and their street-level retailers (dealers sometimes but not always use representatives to sell the drugs on the street for them) often lead to violence. Larger-scale incidents of violence, however, tend to reflect the extent to which distribution networks are at issue. The more extensive the disputes over distribution networks, the more likely the incidence of large-scale violence. This variation can be illustrated by brief examples drawn from the marijuana, cocaine, and crack trades in the United States.

Violence and the Marijuana Trade. During the 1960s, Mexico was the primary source for marijuana consumed in the U.S. market. Mexican trafficking organizations emerged as the primary suppliers for this demand, relying on extensive distribution networks in the central and western portions of the United States. During the 1970s, Colombian traffickers began to seek inroads into the U.S. market but avoided a direct confrontation by exploiting the weaker Mexican presence in the eastern part of the United States and by introducing a higher-quality product into these new networks. Ironically, the U.S. campaign against the Mexican cannabis trade during the 1970s further helped to facilitate a relatively nonviolent transition in market control. Under pressure from the United States, the Mexican government began spraying marijuana fields with herbicides. Afraid of the potential health risks of Mexican drugs laced with herbicides, U.S. consumers shifted their strong domestic demand to Colombian cannabis. By the late 1970s, Colombian trafficking networks dominated the U.S. market.

Cocaine Trafficking. During the late 1970s, Colombian traffickers also began to expand their distribution networks to meet the growing U.S. demand for cocaine. Earlier in the decade, Colombian cocaine producers had shipped limited amounts of the drug into the United States through Cuban networks active in southern Florida. By the early 1980s, however, conditions began to change. Turf battles between rival Colombian and Cuban cocaine-trafficking organizations took place in southern Florida, leading to levels of violence not seen since the days of alcohol prohibition. Drug-related murders numbered in the hundreds, and street battles between rival gangs with automatic weapons dominated the headlines in Dade County, Florida.

The Colombians consolidated their areas of control over cocaine distribution networks by the middle of the 1980s, with representatives of two Colombian organizations dividing the U.S. market. The Medellín cartel was firmly in place in southern Florida, and the Cali organization and its Dominican subcontractors were entrenched in New York. As this market consolidation took place, the levels of violence linked to cocaine began to fall. By the late 1980s, however, the U.S. cocaine wars resurfaced. Incidents of violence, including drug-related murders, increased as the Medellín cartel began to challenge Cali's control of the New York City distribution networks. The growing saturation of the U.S. market for cocaine had forced a new wave of violent competition over market share.

By the early 1990s, levels of violence linked to the cocaine trade once again began to fall. Efforts by the Colombian and U.S. governments against the Medellín cartel had been successful; the cartel's top leaders were either dead or in prison. Rather than halting the cocaine trade, however, the crackdown against Medellín had shifted control to the Cali organization and indirectly resolved the violent disputes over U.S. distribution networks. As government officials from both countries shifted their focus to the Cali organization in the mid-1990s, the cocaine trade once again survived. With the top Cali leadership in prison, Colombian traffickers opted for a lower profile and turned to Mexican crime groups to facilitate the transshipment of cocaine into the United States. By the late 1990s, Mexican trafficking organizations had gained from this relationship such that they began to emerge as a dominant force in the U.S. cocaine trade. Through the late 1990s, the disarray in the

Colombian soldiers patrol a town in the southern Caquetá province in July 1999, after an intense rebel attack by the Revolutionary Armed Forces of Colombia a few days before. Photographed by Carlos Linares.
CORBIS/REUTERS NEWMEDIA INC.

Colombian cocaine industry and the diversification of a growing number of Colombian traffickers into the higher-end heroin trade made this transition relatively nonviolent in the United States.

Violence and Crack. In contrast to marijuana and cocaine, the introduction of crack cocaine into the United States during the mid-1980s revealed a different pattern of violence. Crack cocaine created new market dynamics as well as disputes over the nature of distribution. Rather than challenging the Colombian distribution networks, crack producers in the United States offered a new outlet for foreign cocaine exporters. Domestic producers utilized Colombian cocaine hydrochloride as a raw material for crack cocaine: an addictive, low-cost, and high-profit product targeted at poorer consumers in the inner cities.

The lucrative nature of the crack trade and the initial absence of established organizations and distribution networks contributed to a wave of inner-city violence in the United States. Studies of conditions in New York City during the late 1980s, for example, revealed that over 52 percent of homicides were drug related, with over 75 percent of these linked to the crack trade. But by the late 1990s, these levels of violence had begun to recede. The sources of this change remain an issue of de-

bate among scholars and government officials but appear to reflect a combination of market consolidation, new enforcement efforts targeted at major U.S. cities, severe and extensive incarceration of those arrested for crack offenses, and a gradual decline in the popularity of the drug.

Violence and Politics

Many arguments linking violence and the drug trade point to the challenge that drug traffickers pose to governments. At a narrow level, this challenge has consisted of attacks against those enforcement officials seeking to curtail the trade. At a broader level, this challenge has entailed more politically motivated attacks against the integrity of the state.

Violence Against Enforcement Officials. Violent attacks against enforcement officials can occur at all stages of the drug trade and focus on all levels of the criminal justice system. In the United States, undercover police officers have been the primary victims of violence. Buy-and-bust operations and surveillance activities put police officers at risk. Officers in undercover drug operations, especially those that place them in direct contact with drug dealers, tend not to use bullet-proof vests because at close range the vest looks rather suspicious and might blow the officer's cover. Often this reluctance leads to tragic results. In 1998 alone, drug traffickers were blamed for the deaths of officers in Chicago, Cleveland, Detroit, Kansas City (Missouri), New York City, and Tampa. Street-level retailers are not the only participants in the drug trade that engage in violence. Eradication campaigns against growers and producers and larger-scale interdiction efforts against traffickers also place U.S. enforcement officials at risk. Between 1973 and 1995, for example, forty-two employees of the U.S. Drug Enforcement Agency (DEA) were killed in the line of duty. Perhaps the most well-known of these incidents took place in 1985 with the kidnapping and murder in Mexico of the DEA agent Enrique (Kiki) Camarena.

Violence against enforcement officials has been more extensive in Colombia than in the United States. During the 1980s, government control efforts against the cocaine trade sparked a backlash of retaliation against the agents of the criminal justice system. The Medellín cartel stood at the forefront of the violence. The cartel's strength stemmed from an organizational structure that placed extensive resources in the hands of its leader, Pablo Escobar. His willingness to resort to violence to maintain discipline within the organization also characterized the cartel's response to the government's efforts at drug control. In contrast, the loosely organized Cali cartel sought a lower profile. It tended to avoid direct confrontation and the use of violence against enforcement officials; Cali traffickers instead relied more on tools of corruption to facilitate the cocaine trade. The government's focus on the more visible activities of members of the Medellín cartel enhanced the Cali cartel's efforts and suggested to those dealing with the latter group that accommodation was more preferable than becoming the target of Medellín-style violence.

The Colombian government's efforts to control the cocaine trade during the 1980s and 1990s were uneven at best. Colombian leaders sought to balance the demands of U.S. pressure for action against the cocaine cartels with the need to devote resources against what they saw as the more urgent challenge posed by political insurgent groups. In this context, the Medellín cartel expanded its trafficking operations by offering enforcement officials the simple choice of "lead or silver." Rather than risking death, many officials accepted bribes from the Medellín cartel to look the other way or more actively advance the cartel's interests.

When Colombian officials turned to enforcement efforts against the Medellín cartel during the mid-1980s, the cartel responded with violence. Attacks took place targeting a wide array of officials including the police, judges, government ministers, and political candidates. These levels of violence escalated during the late 1980s. Fearing prosecution and imprisonment in the United States, cartel members sought to dissuade Colombian officials from entering into extradition treaties. The cartel's tactics soon shifted from attacks on individual enforcement officials to larger-scale incidents of violence against enforcement officials and civilians, including the use of car bombs. By the early 1990s, the Medellín cartel was responsible for the deaths of nearly five hundred police officers, forty judges, and an untold number of civilians. The more notable victims of the cartel included a minister of justice, an attorney general, and a number of political candidates and officials.

Narco-Terrorism. The Medellín cartel's attacks against civilians were intended to increase the stakes of the Colombian government's control efforts and destabilize the government. As such the attacks appeared to illustrate a broader pattern of politically motivated violence linked to the drug trade, or "narco-terrorism." Though the term was commonly used during the wars on drugs waged by the adminstration of U.S. President Ronald Reagan during the 1980s, the extent of narco-terrorism remains difficult to determine. This problem is in large part due to the ill-defined and contested nature of the concept itself.

The most common definitions of narco-terrorism refer to the involvement of terrorist activities with the narcotics trade. However, even the U.S. Department of State acknowledges that terrorism lacks a single, accepted definition. Similarly, government officials have defined the narcotics trade with little consistency, at times including everything from marijuana and cocaine to opium and heroin. Even the nature of involvement by terrorists in the narcotics trade is problematic. Terrorists can produce drugs and precursor chemicals, engage in trafficking and retail distribution, launder drug proceeds, or provide protection and logistical support for others directly engaged in the trade. Terrorists can participate in the drug trade simply to raise funds for purchasing weapons or to further alliances of convenience with traffickers in the face of government crackdowns. Finally, terrorists can use the drug trade as a tool of violence against civilians by spreading addiction and, in turn, challenging the credibility of government institutions.

Officials in the Reagan administration used references to the threat of narco-terrorism to generate congressional support for steps against leftist insurgency movements and Latin American drug traffickers. The drug-trade activities engaged in by U.S.-backed freedom fighters, such as by the mujahideen in Afghanistan and the contras in Nicaragua, were categorically denied by the administration. This selective emphasis on narco-terrorism by the Reagan administration facilitated similar arguments by South American governments seeking to obtain U.S. financial support. Leaders in Peru and, to a lesser extent, Colombia also used references to the threat of narco-terrorism in domestic political debates both to undermine challenges from the left and the drug cartels and to divert attention from military involvement in the drug trade.

In retrospect, however, the actual ties between leftist movements and narcotics traffickers in South America during the 1980s appear limited at best. In Colombia, leftist movements and the Medellín cartel were more adversaries than allies during the early 1980s. The newfound wealth of the Medellín traffickers, their conservative leanings, and their tendency to purchase large-scale landholdings in rural areas ran contrary to the aims of groups such as the Revolutionary Armed Forces of Colombia (Fuerzas Armadas Revolucionarias de Colombia, or FARC) and the Revolutionary Movement of April 19 (Movimiento 19 de Abril, or M-19). As a result, these insurgency movements initially targeted drug traffickers as just another portion of wealthy Colombian society whose families could be kidnapped for ransom. The violent response of the drug traffickers soon dissuaded further attacks. For example, traffickers quickly banded together under the auspices of a new organization, Death to Kidnappers (Muerte a Secuestradores). The message was not lost on the insurgency movements.

By the mid-1980s, relations between insurgency movements and drug traffickers in Colombia appeared to have changed. The 1984 government raid on the cocaine laboratory at Tranquiladora revealed evidence of a possible linkage between FARC and the Medellín cartel, with FARC providing protection services for the remote location. Colombian and U.S. officials also attributed the 1985 attack by M-19 against the Colombian Palace of Justice to the influence of the Medellín cartel. Having failed to stop extradition agreements through threats and limited violence, the cartel had purportedly contracted M-19 to engage in larger-scale violence against the Colombian government.

However, the extent of the actual linkage between drug traffickers and leftist insurgents remained unclear. Evidence from the Palace of Justice attack, for example, was initially incomplete. Subsequent investigations of the connection between the Medellín cartel and M-19 were inconsistent and contested. A greater problem for narco-terrorist arguments during the 1980s, however, was that Medellín cartel members continued to provide financial support to right-wing paramilitary groups that were seeking to eradicate groups such as FARC and M-19.

Where cooperation between traffickers and leftists did take place in Colombia, it appeared to be more a temporary marriage of convenience based on economic and security considerations. For example, as the Colombian government's campaign against the drug cartels intensified, FARC expanded its protection services to local growers and helped drug-trafficking organizations retain access to clandestine airfields. Similarly, in Peru increased activity by the government against traffickers and leftist groups had the unintended effect of increasing ties between drug traffickers and insurgency movements such as Shining Path (Sendero Luminoso).

By the late 1980s and early 1990s, these dynamics began to change. Seeking to generate greater revenue, FARC and Shining Path began to bypass the trafficking organizations and directly enter the drug trade. FARC, for example, expanded its financial operations into growing, refining, and trafficking drugs. This pattern of terrorist organizations moving beyond protection rackets for growers and traffickers to more extensive participation in the drug trade clearly was not limited to FARC and the Shining Path. By the late 1990s, the U.S. Department of State was reporting that major terrorist organizations such as the Liberation Tigers of Tamil Eelam and the Kurdistan Workers' Party also were active in the drug trade. However, FARC and Shining Path remained the organizations most commonly identified by U.S. officials as being engaged in narco-terrorism.

BIBLIOGRAPHY

Brownstein, Henry H. "The Drugs-Violence Connection: Constructing Policy from Research Findings." In *The New War on Drugs: Symbolic Politics and Criminal Justice Policy,* edited by Eric L. Jensen and Jurg Gerber. Cincinnati: Anderson, 1998.

Clawson, Patrick L., and Rensselaer W. Lee III. *The Andean Cocaine Industry.* New York: St. Martin's, 1996.

De la Rosa, Mario, Elizabeth Y. Lambert, and Bernard Gropper, eds. *Drugs and Violence: Causes, Correlates, and Consequences.* Washington, D.C.: U.S. Government Printing Office, 1990.

Friman, H. Richard, and Peter Andreas, eds. *The Illicit Global Economy and State Power.* Boulder, Colo.: Rowman and Littlefield, 1999.

Goldstein, Paul J. "The Drugs/Violence Nexus: A Tripartite Conceptual Framework." *Journal of Drug Issues* 15 (1985).

Goldstein, Paul J., et al. "Crack and Homicide in New York City: A Case Study in the Epidemiology of Violence." In *Crack in America: Demon Drugs and Social Justice,* edited by Craig Reinarman and Harry G. Levine. Berkeley: University of California Press, 1997.

Gordon, Diana R. *The Return of the Dangerous Classes: Drug Prohibition and Policy Politics.* New York: Norton, 1994.

Inciardi, James A. *The War on Drugs II: The Continuing Epic of Heroin, Cocaine, Crack, Crime, AIDS, and Public Policy.* Mountain View, Calif.: Mayfield, 1992.

Lee, Rensselaer W., III. *The White Labyrinth: Cocaine and Political Power.* New Brunswick, N.J.: Transaction, 1989.

MacDonald, Scott B. *Mountain High, White Avalanche: Cocaine and Power in the Andean States and Panama.* New York: Praeger, 1989.

Shannon, Elaine. *Desperados: Latin Drug Lords, U.S. Lawmen, and the War America Can't Win.* New York: Signet, 1989.

Stares, Paul B. *Global Habit: The Drug Problem in a Borderless World.* Washington, D.C.: Brookings Institution, 1996.

U.S. Department of State. Bureau for International Narcotics and Law Enforcement Affairs. *International Narcotics Control Strategy Report.* Washington, D.C.: U.S. Government Printing Office, 1998, 1999 (available at www.state.gov).

U.S. Department of State. Office of the Coordinator for Counterterrorism. *Patterns of Global Terrorism Annual Reports.* Washington D.C.: U.S. Government Printing Office, 1996, 1997, 1998, 1999 (available at www.state.gov).

U.S. Office of National Drug Control Policy. *National Drug Policy Control Strategy Report.* Washington, D.C.: U.S. Government Printing Office, 1999 (available at www.whitehousedrugpolicy.gov).

H. RICHARD FRIMAN

See also **Contras; Crime and Violence, Popular Misconceptions of.**

DRUNK DRIVING

Contemporary public perception of the drunk driver, shaped by anti–drunk driving activist groups and proponents, is that of the killer drunk or sociopath with a long criminal record and an impaired moral sense. Accordingly, traffic accidents resulting in fatalities, in which the driver at fault is determined to have a blood-alcohol concentration (BAC) above the legal limit, are seen as criminal acts. The drunk driver is subject to criminal sanction consistent with that applied to perpetrators of other violent crimes resulting in death. For anti–drunk driving advocates, culpability is measured by the level of harm the impaired driver inflicts and his or her recklessness in inflicting it. Drunk driving involves a degree of risk-taking that displays a wanton disregard for human life. The assumption of unnecessary risk-taking, and the damage and suffering sustained by the innocent victim and his or her loved ones, underlies anti–drunk driving advocates' claim that drunk driving is a violent crime.

According to the National Highway Traffic Safety Administration (NHTSA), in 1997, 39 percent of the 41,967 traffic fatalities in the United States were alcohol-related. For Americans between the ages of five and twenty-five, motor vehicle fatalities are the leading cause of death.

In the early days of the automobile, field sobriety tests were used to assess levels of impairment and convictions were infrequent. After World War II, so-called per se laws based on Scandinavian drunk driving legislation were established in industrialized countries. Per se laws, commonly referred to as DWI (driving while intoxicated), DUI (driving under the influence), or DUIL (driving under the influence of liquor) laws, specify that a certain blood-alcohol concentration entails standard penalties such as license revocation, jail time for recidivists, drinking-driving education, and so on. Each year there are approximately 1 million to 1.5 million arrests for driving under the influence of alcohol. Over time, public campaigns have advocated harsher penalties and lower BAC standards.

In the mid-1960s the NHTSA established traffic safety as a federal concern. In 1975 the U.S. Department of Transportation and the NHTSA set up the Fatal Accident Reporting Service (FARS), which provides systematic reports of vehicular fatalities for drivers and pedestrians. The mission of FARS is to improve traffic safety through dissemination of fatality information (which includes data on blood-alcohol levels in alcohol-related crashes). Lobbying efforts of groups such as Mothers Against Drunk Driving (MADD, 1980), Students Against Destructive Driving (SADD, 1981), and Remove Intoxicated Drivers (RID, 1978) were successful in obtaining major changes in state laws affecting stricter enforcement, lower BACs, and harsher sanctions. Significantly, these groups have been able to define drunk driving in the mind of the public as a criminal act. Poster and media campaigns depicting the traumatic, violent, and often gruesome consequences of drunk driving have been undertaken for the purposes of general deterrence.

The fact that most traffic fatalities are not related to alcohol consumption suggests that the emphasis on alcohol impairment is a moral, as well as a utilitarian, consideration for anti–drunk driving proponents. In any case, most official agencies and bureaucracies are strongly supportive of deterrence-based anti–drunk driving policies. Yet, H. Laurence Ross (1992), Joseph R. Gusfield (1996), and others argue that the long-term general deterrent effects of legal sanctions remain unclear. Ross's seminal study of the British Road Safety Act (1967) showed that the deterrent effect dissipated in two years. In a similar study conducted in France in 1981, Ross again came to the same conclusion. Studies in New Zealand and Australia supported this claim. Nonetheless, while such studies have shown that the general deterrent effects of public anti–drunk driving campaigns are short-lived, national trends indicate a marked decline in the number of traffic fatalities and drunk driving crashes over the long run. The number of alcohol-related traffic fatalities in 1997, for example, represents a reduction of about a third from a decade earlier.

Despite controversy surrounding methodology and interpretation of outcomes, some suggest that the adoption of well-publicized anti–drunk driving sanctions in which punishment appears to be certain and swift, if not severe (questions abound on this point), heightens perceptions of punishment, which affects drinking norms and may thus act as a deterrent. Although the causal connection between sanctions and drinking and driving for the public at large cannot be unambiguously established (a requirement for causality in the sciences), it is argued that citizen campaigns and legal threats provide people with reference points for redefining their behavior, which over the long run result in changes in norms and patterns of behavior. Thus, it is not so much the legal sanctions themselves but the redefinition of drunk driving as a public health issue that alters social institu-

tions (such as advertising and public drinking), which in turn affects drinking and driving.

Drunk Driving as a Violent Offense

It is argued that the drunk driver whose actions result in injury or fatality to another is not simply in violation of traffic laws but has acted in a grossly negligent fashion that increases culpability. It is this high degree of culpability that warrants the charge of homicide by criminal negligence, vehicular manslaughter, and other special homicide statutes, according to movement activists and federal and state officials. The crash is portrayed as both criminal and violent, one in which the drunk driver willfully acts in a dangerous manner by drinking, then climbing behind the wheel of an automobile, thereby causing the dismemberment or killing of the innocent bystander. If the underlying responsibility of a driver is to operate the motor vehicle in a careful, safe, and considerate way, then the incapacitated driver violates these precepts in the extreme. Moreover, when fatality results, the driver, whose incapacity is self-inflicted, is regarded by anti-DUI advocates as a murderer.

General Causes

Drunk driving is a result of complex social forces. Like other social problems, the origins of drunk driving have social antecedents. Two primary institutions to which one might look to understand the phenomenon are transportation and recreation. On the one hand, modern industrial societies at the end of the twentieth century created a social and cultural context, and a physical environment, in which private automobile use is necessary, if not compulsory, for most activities. Consequently, automobile injuries and fatalities reflect the amount of automobile use, regardless of exacerbating factors.

On the other hand, alcohol consumption has been and continues to be viewed as a central facilitator of social interaction. Conformity to the norms of alcohol consumption, then, implies that people will drink to varying degrees on social occasions. Given Western societies' dependence on the automobile, conformity to both sets of norms will result in people driving after they have been drinking. In addition, since some Western subcultures (e.g., youth) have higher rates of alcohol consumption than others, to the degree that both activities flourish, drunk driving will take place within the subculture, perhaps even defiantly so. Drunk driving will therefore persist to the degree that social institutions remain unchanging. As indicated above, social mores regarding drinking and driving are the forces most likely to alter behavior. Citizen movements, public health agencies, educational institutions, the advertising industry, and the criminal justice system are all instrumental in addressing the problem of drunk driving and reducing driving fatalities.

BIBLIOGRAPHY

Ross, H. Laurence. *Confronting Drunk Driving: Social Policy for Saving Lives.* New Haven, Conn.: Yale University Press, 1992.

Gusfield, Joseph R. *Contested Meanings: The Construction of Alcohol Problems.* Madison: University of Wisconsin Press, 1996.

National Highway Traffic Safety Administration. *Traffic Facts 1997: Alcohol.* Washington, D.C.: NHTSA, 1998.

MATTHEW E. ARCHIBALD

See also **Alcohol and Alcoholism.**

DU BOIS, W. E. B.
(1868–1963)

W. E. B. Du Bois, one of the most influential Americans of the twentieth century, had an unparalleled impact as race leader, educational and inspirational force, writer, theorist, and activist. He wrestled with some of the most complex social and political issues of his time and sought to uplift his people and all the dispossessed, the alienated, and the marginalized. Devoted as he was to the black struggle for civil rights, his writings inevitably touch on the subject of violence.

Life

The early life of William Edward Burghardt Du Bois, born on 23 February 1868, was inauspicious. Of French Huguenot and African descent, he grew up in Great Barrington, Massachusetts, where his mother worked as a domestic, and was kindly treated by townspeople after a stroke limited her physical abilities. His father disappeared from Great Barrington by the time his son was two. Willie, as Du Bois was known, was recognized for his intelligence in the town's integrated school system. At the urging of the high school principal, local churches and townspeople contributed money to send Du Bois to Fisk, a black college in Nashville, Tennessee, where he received a bachelor of arts degree in 1888. He then went to Harvard, where he received another B.A. and an M.A. and Ph.D. in

history. At various times he taught at Wilberforce and Atlanta Universities, but was never asked to teach at a predominantly white school.

Among Du Bois's groundbreaking academic works are *Suppression of the African Slave-Trade* (1896), *The Philadelphia Negro* (1899), and *Black Reconstruction in America* (1935). *The Souls of Black Folk* (1903) is a brief, intense volume of compelling prose that is considered one of the most important works on race ever published. *Darkwater* (1920), *Dusk of Dawn* (1940), and the posthumously edited *Autobiography of W. E. B. Du Bois* (1968) intertwine memoir and social commentary. In 1905 Du Bois founded the Niagara Movement—a precursor to the National Association for the Advancement of Colored People (NAACP), of which he was also a founding member, in 1909. He became director of publications and research for the NAACP in 1910, editing the organization's official publication, *The Crisis*, and the *Brownies' Book* for children. Du Bois participated extensively in the Harlem Renaissance, a time of great black cultural achievement from roughly 1918 to the early years of the Great Depression. Most notably he celebrated black writers in *The Crisis* and instituted prizes for them; he also founded the Krigwa Players, a distinguished theatrical group based in Harlem that specialized in plays dealing with black life. Additionally he wrote for popular audiences a number of novels such as *The Quest of the Silver Fleece* (1911) and essays on aspects of black life such as *The Negro* (1915), *The Gift of Black Folk* (1924), and *Black Folk, Then and Now* (1939).

The Souls of Black Folk

It is impossible to overstate the significance of *The Souls of Black Folk* as an elucidation of the African American experience and of the sociopolitical importance of race. In the early years of the century, figures as disparate as the African American writer and activist James Weldon Johnson and the German sociologist Max Weber testified to its power and insights. Every serious discussion of race in America must acknowledge its primacy. Part polemic, part prophecy, part sociopolitical analysis, part cultural criticism, part history, part autobiography, the work contains passages of lyric beauty as well as bitter, if sometimes ironically veiled, indictment. Its purpose is always clear: to set forth black life in America; to reveal the achievements and oppression of the community; and to expose the unfairness with which it has been treated.

Two of the century's oft-repeated pronouncements on race involve quotations from *The Souls of Black Folk*: "the problem of the Twentieth Century is the problem of the color line"; and the idea that African Americans must look at themselves "through the eyes of others" in a "world that looks on in contempt and pity," creating in black Americans a feeling of "twoness,—an American, a Negro; two souls, two thoughts, two unreconciled strivings ... in one dark body, whose dogged strength alone keeps it from being torn asunder." The latter remark demonstrates Du Bois's rhetorical skill, employing the imagery of violence in a fashion entirely appropriate to the African American experience.

Reworked from Du Bois's earlier writings, the book, like the author's own life, is both varied and unified. He tells of his New England childhood, of the spirituals black Americans created to help them deal with the evils of slavery, of slavery and Reconstruction with their legacy of prejudice and discrimination, of poor black children in an impoverished South, of race leaders such as Frederick Douglass and Alexander Crummel, whom he praises and offers as models of how to deal with race prejudice. In a famous chapter on Booker T. Washington, he criticizes the most influential black of the day for focusing his racial improvement strategies too greatly upon "industrial education" and for seeming to exchange black political power, civil rights, and the "higher [i.e., professional] education of Negro Youth" for a temporary and uncertain financial gain.

The Souls of Black Folk cannot avoid reporting and discussing violence. Sometimes this violence is psychological, a result of the slaver's attitude that "classed the black man and the ox together." At least as often, it was physical, caused by "the hell of war" and war's aftermath, when "the former slaves were intimidated, beaten, raped and butchered by revengeful men," a time when "lynching" emerged as a form of "lawless" southern justice. Violence is in the air of the "black belt" of Tennessee that Du Bois recalls from his years of teaching among the black mountain folk. He tells of meeting a justifiably sullen sharecropper who had labored forty-five years at the same farm, "beginning with nothing, and still having nothing." Bitter and "hopelessly in debt," the man recalls a black boy killed by police "for loud talking on the sidewalk": "Let a white man touch me, and he dies. ... I mean it. I've seen them whip my father

W. E. B. Du Bois, around 1918. Library of Congress

and my old mother in them cotton-rows till the blood ran."

A man of strong, vocal opinions, Du Bois was a highly controversial civil rights theorist and activist, attacked by those who feared his demands for absolute equality. He quarreled with other black leaders, most famously with Booker T. Washington (over the latter's tight control over the black press and what Du Bois considered Washington's too passive and nonconfrontational accomodationism) and also with Marcus Garvey, and sporadically with fellow NAACP board members, with whom he broke in 1934 and again in 1948, because he was more radical than the board. Always outspoken, even into his nineties, against the United States' treatment of its black and other marginalized citizens, he ran for the Senate on the American Labor Party ticket in 1950. He was indicted in 1951 by a federal grand jury for failing to register as an agent of a foreign principal, but the Cold War charge was ultimately thrown out of court. The State Department twice refused him permission to leave the United States, but in 1958, with his passport reinstated, he left to become a citizen of Ghana, where he joined the Communist Party. He died in Ghana on 27 August 1963.

Responses to Violence

Du Bois's firsthand introduction to the intense and systematic violence of racial oppression came during his years at Fisk and the "black belt" surrounding Nashville, an experience he describes in the memoir *Dusk of Dawn*. As a student in Tennessee, he encountered a range of violence from potential to actual that he "had never realized in New England." Fisk students carried guns. Lynching was on the rise in the late-Reconstruction South; Du Bois wrote that each of these violent deaths left "a scar upon my soul." In one incident he was shocked to see a door pitted with buckshot when an offending white newspaperman was publicly gunned down. Once, when the young Du Bois lifted his hat to apologize to an older white woman for bumping into her, she venomously cursed him. Even his first sexual experience was a kind of attack, by the lonely mother of one of the black students he taught outside the city.

As a professor at Atlanta University (1897–1910, 1934–1944), Du Bois several times experienced the racial violence whose political, social, and economic origins (and consequences) he tried to analyze and understand. But it was difficult for him in 1899 to be reasonable about the lynching and dismembering of Sam Hose, a black farmer whose knuckles were hung like smoked meat in an Atlanta grocery store. After the Atlanta race riot of 1906, which resulted in the deaths of as many as two dozen blacks and about six whites, he bought a shotgun to protect his wife and child—and wrote the impassioned and accusatory elegiac poem "A Litany at Atlanta."

Although he notes in his *Autobiography* that "he could not be a calm, cool, and detached [social] scientist while Negroes were being lynched, murdered, and starved," he consistently abjured retaliatory violence except as a last defense against violent aggression. "The Challenge of Detroit," in the November 1925 *Crisis,* answered the question "Must black folk shoot and shoot to kill in order to maintain their rights?" with an implied "Yes." "Social Planning for the Negro, Past and Present," a 1936 *Journal of Negro Education* article, reaffirmed that "we black men say ... we do not believe in violence, and we will fight only when there is no other way." John, the fictional hero in "Of the Coming of John" in *The Souls of Black Folk*, kills a white man he catches trying to rape his sister. As for himself, Du Bois asserted in his *Autobiography*, "I revered life. I have never killed a bird nor shot a rabbit." The shotgun he bought after the Atlanta riots of 1906 "was fired but once and then by error into a row of *Congressional Records*, which lined the lower shelf of my library." The two civil rights organizations he helped found, though aggressive, were nonviolent.

Du Bois's examinations of the history of black people in the United States began with investigations of the slave trade, with its horrific punishments and the slaves' violent insurrections. He found this history to be filled, he declared in his essay "The Souls of White Folk" (in *Darkwater*) with narratives "of orgy, cruelty, barbarism, and murder done to men and women of Negro descent," a flood "of hatred, in wilder, fiercer violence."

Du Bois always recognized that African Americans were not alone in being brutally oppressed. "Condemn lynching men," he wrote in the essay "[Frederick] Douglass as a Statesman," "and not merely lynching Negroes." In *Dusk of Dawn* he wrote that the "community that mobbed" William Lloyd Garrison, the crusading abolitionist, in 1835 also "easily hanged" the poor, immigrant anarchists Nicola Sacco and Bartolomeo Vanzetti in 1927. He frequently commented on violence against women and workers and on violence inspired by ethnicity, declaring himself strongly against the "horror of World War—of ultimate agitation, propaganda, and murder." Yet in his *Autobiography* he justified state violence in the name of communism, welcoming the Soviet Union's ruthless suppression of the rebellion in Hungary in 1956, suppression he viewed as necessary to counter the influence of "pushing businessmen" and "reactionaries."

Most typical of Du Bois was the continuing struggle he carried on throughout his life against violence by powerful oppressors against peoples they considered inferior and less entitled to full participation in determining their rights. Lynching was in the United States the clearest and most cruel manifestation of this violence. In *Dusk of Dawn* he calls lynching a "horror" responsible for seventeen hundred Negro deaths "from 1885 through 1894." Each of these deaths scarred his soul, he wrote, but also made him ponder "the plight of other minority groups" in America, such as Italians, Chinese, and Jews. Thus his sympathies along with his activism spread. On 28 July 1917 Du Bois led a march of some ten thousand African Americans in New

York City to protest a recent deadly race riot in East St. Louis and to express outrage against lynching (then still not a federal crime) generally. This dramatic achievement—the ability to rally the oppressed against injustice—can perhaps be seen as the defining symbol of Du Bois's adherence to the principle of equality.

BIBLIOGRAPHY

Lewis, David Levering. *W. E. B. Du Bois: Biography of a Race, 1868–1919.* New York: Holt, 1993.

Moore, Jack B. *W. E. B. Du Bois.* Boston: Twayne, 1981.

Rampersad, Arnold. *The Art and Imagination of W. E. B. Du Bois.* Cambridge, Mass.: Harvard University Press, 1976.

JACK B. MOORE

See also **African Americans; Civil Disorder; Civil Rights Movements; Lynching; National Association for the Advancement of Colored People.**

DUELING

A custom of limited duration in the United States, dueling was a means for members of a local elite to vindicate their reputation as gentlemen of valor according to the rules of the ancient code of honor. European dueling, based on military and aristocratic foundations, had roots stretching back to the early medieval period. But in colonial America, which was steeped in provincial manners, duels were a rarity. Dueling was not widely accepted until the American Revolution, when officers in the Continental armies imitated the dueling practices of their French counterparts. After the Treaty of Paris in 1783, the convention spread to the ranks of lawyers, editors, politicians, and others whose status as gentlemen might be questioned in the fluidity of American society.

Dueling in the United States

In the absence of instruction in French swordplay, duelists in the United States relied on pistols, fashioned especially for the purpose in England and Philadelphia. Americans followed European manuals in issuing, or posting, challenges by public proclamation on courthouse doors, in newspaper columns, or in circulated letters. According to the imported code, seconds, or the assistants of duelists, were obliged to exhaust possibilities of peaceable outcomes. If a duel materialized, the principals, or antagonists, were allegedly acting not in fury. Rather, they were to display a cool regard for defending untarnished reputations—not only their own and that of their lineage but also that of groups and communities to which they belonged. By mutual agreement, principals and seconds established the meticulous rules of engagement. A physician and a handful of witnesses were supposed to assure fairness and supervise all regulations punctiliously.

Despite the apparent social utility of dueling, slave states set such penalties as abrogating the duelist's right to hold public office. Politicians largely determined their self-esteem in contests before the voters. Sometimes to avoid such a stigma as well as charges of murder or maiming, duelists conducted their business across the nearest state line. Extradition of participants was rare. Even when a fatality occurred on home ground, the subsequent trial usually acquitted the victor; he presumably had acted in self-defense. Moreover, if powerful enough, the dueling politician could often induce his legislative friends to free him from the penalty against office holding by special resolution.

Justifications for Dueling

Confident of public acquiescence, advocates of dueling defied the strictures of church and state. Justifying a 7 January 1845 duel (a fortuitously bloodless one) with Thomas L. Clingman, his political opponent, William L. Yancey of Alabama proclaimed that the "laws of God, the laws of [his] own state," and "solemn obligations" to his wife and children "yielded, as they have ever done from the earliest times to the present, to those laws" of society "which no one, however exalted his station, violates with impunity" (quoted in Brown 1968, p. 120). In 1838 the former governor of South Carolina John Lyde Wilson argued in a dueling manual he wrote that the causes of wars among nations, dread of shame and defense of honor, ought to apply "with equal force to individuals." Wilson had little faith that "our eloquent clergy" or judges could "suppress" so utilitarian a device for policing moral boundaries. George Tucker, a Virginia essayist, raised the familiar argument that the threat of a challenge compelled all and sundry to cultivate gracious manners or risk misunderstanding. Thus the violence of the duel served, its proponents thought, as a social balance wheel.

Duels were less fatal than one might expect. In Irish duels of the late eighteenth century 30 percent died on the spot or were mortally wounded. English duels were less frequent with a casualty rate of 12 percent. American duels may have come close to the English pattern. The purpose of the duel was to demonstrate a willingness to risk life, as if such a demonstration was a gift to family, friends, and honor itself. Shooting to kill was sometimes half consciously rejected. On 8 April 1826, for instance, furious over a purported insult on the Senate floor, Henry Clay, the secretary of state, challenged the truculent John Randolph, Virginia's senior senator. They both fired twice but were immensely relieved that neither struck the other. Colonel Alexander K. McClung of Mississippi, a notoriously busy duelist, on the other hand, usually killed his adversaries. Likewise, in 1806, General Andrew Jackson, the only duelist to reach the presidency, determined in cold fury to kill Charles Dickinson, his rival in Nashville, Tennessee, politics. He did so with such hard-heartedness that his political popularity was temporarily fractured.

By fighting duels, politicians like Jackson demonstrated loyalty to their clients and peers, the young men and colleagues on whom they depended for gaining or retaining public office. Representing the Federalist clique, in 1804 the former secretary of the treasury Alexander Hamilton and Vice President Aaron Burr, bitter rivals in New York politics, fought the most significant duel of the era. Without an exchange of fire, the followers of both men would have registered contempt of their leaders' cowardice. Hamilton, however, was a devout Episcopalian and feared divine punishment for murder. In addition, mourning the recent death of a son in a duel, he plunged into suicidal despair. Beforehand, Hamilton determined to miss. Burr was less conflicted and killed his opponent. Northerners elevated Hamilton's spirit to Christian martyrdom. Thereafter, as politics became more complex, loyalty to party replaced allegiance to a leader, a change that undermined the need for self-sacrificing fealty. No longer need a patron prove his willingness to "lay down his life for his friends."

Decline of the Duel

At the end of the eighteenth century in the North, evangelical revivalism, a spirit of democratic reform, and the consequent withdrawal of a politically active upper class eroded the foundations of the duels. Many of them had been based on political rivalries. Also, men of business began to require written contracts instead of the less reliable "word of a gentleman," which, upon challenge, often prompted conflict. These factors only gradually challenged dueling in slave states. There kinship, neighborliness, and planter wealth, rather than the more impersonal institution of a political party, still determined leadership and sometimes required a display of valor on the field of honor. Even college students engaged in duels over trivial

The 1804 duel between Alexander Hamilton and Aaron Burr. CORBIS/BETTMANN

matters, perhaps as preparation for future careers as gentlemen of discrimination.

The duel—formal and exclusive—contrasted with the "ungrammatical" violence of the lower classes in the South and West. The famous gunslingers at the O. K. Corral and elsewhere required no seconds to regulate a cooling-off period, no ritual encounter at dawn. Back stabbing and ambushes could be executed without regard to gentlemanly rules of combat. But the duel could not survive the process of democratization and fervent religious revival that swept the South in the aftermath of Confederate and planter-class defeat. To a degree, common principles of political discourse reappeared with the postwar reunion of the sections. Thenceforward the duel became merely a subject of literary romance and no longer the functional though savage custom it once had been.

BIBLIOGRAPHY

Brown, William Garrott. *The Lower South in American History.* 1902. Reprint, New York: Haskell House, 1968.

Eaton, Clement. *The Freedom-of-Thought Struggle in the Old South.* New York: Harper and Row, 1964.

Greenberg, Kenneth S. *Honor and Slavery.* Princeton, N.J.: Princeton University Press, 1996.

Stowe, Steven M. *Intimacy and Power in the Old South: Ritual in the Lives of the Planters.* Baltimore: Johns Hopkins University Press, 1987.

Williams, Jack K. *Dueling in the Old South: Vignettes of Social History.* College Station: Texas A & M University Press, 1980. Reprints John Lyde Wilson, *The Code of Honor; or, Rules for the Government of Principals and Seconds in Dueling.* Charleston, S.C.: n.p., 1838.

Wyatt-Brown, Bertram. *Southern Honor: Ethics and Behavior in the Old South.* New York: Oxford University Press, 1982.

BERTRAM WYATT-BROWN

See also **Honor; South.**

E

EARP BROTHERS

**Newton Jasper (1837–1928); James C.
(1841–1926); Virgil W. (1843–1906);
Wyatt B. S. (1848–1929); Morgan S.
(1851–1882); Baxter Warren (1855–1900)**

The "fighting Earps" of Tombstone, Arizona, fame were born in the Midwest. The patriarch of the clan was Nicholas Porter Earp, a tough, sometimes profane wanderer who found it difficult to settle down. His eldest son, Newton Jasper Earp, was born in Kentucky. After Newton's mother died, Nicholas remarried, and his new wife, Virginia Cooksey Earp, bore six children, James C., Virgil W., Martha E. (1845–1856), Wyatt B. S., Morgan S., Baxter Warren, and Adelia D. (1861–1941).

The Earps spent most of their early lives in Illinois and Iowa. During the Civil War, Newton, James, and Virgil served in the Union army, and in 1864 Nicholas moved the rest of the family to San Bernardino, California. In 1868 Wyatt and Virgil went to work for the Union Pacific Railroad, and Nicholas and the rest of the family returned east, eventually settling down in Lamar, Missouri. On 17 November 1869 Wyatt, who had rejoined his family, replaced his father as constable of Lamar Township and was later appointed the first town constable of Lamar when it was incorporated in February 1870. His brother Newton challenged him for the office, but Wyatt beat him in the election. Wyatt also married Urilla Sutherland in Lamar in January 1870, but she died less than a year later. To make matters worse, he was accused of misappropriating funds while he was constable.

Wyatt left Lamar in the winter of 1870–1871, just ahead of allegations that he mishandled funds, and in March 1871 he was arrested in Indian Territory for stealing horses. Before he could be brought to trial, he escaped from the Van Buren, Arkansas, jail and fled into Kansas. His wandering father soon left Missouri as well, settling for a time in Peace, Kansas. Virgil was driving stages in Nebraska when he met his lifelong companion, Alvira "Allie" Sullivan. Wyatt witnessed the murder of Chauncey B. Whitney by a Texan, Billy Thompson, in Ellsworth, Kansas, in 1873. The next year Wyatt went to Wichita, Kansas, where his brother James was tending bar. Wyatt served as a Wichita policeman from 1875 to 1876, winning a reputation as a game fighter and a good officer. His career in Wichita ended abruptly when he became embroiled in a fistfight with William Smith, a candidate for town marshal.

Wyatt moved on to Dodge City, Kansas, where he was hired as a policeman. Morgan became a Forel County deputy sheriff. Other members of the Earp family moved through Dodge that summer. Virgil and even Nicholas served briefly as peace officers, before they and other members of the family moved west. Again Wyatt proved to be an effective officer. In 1877 he and Morgan went north to Deadwood. Wyatt did not stay long; Morgan moved on to Montana where he eventually became an officer in Butte and met his wife, Lou. Wyatt returned to Dodge, then struck the gambler's circuit in Texas, working for a time in a Fort Worth saloon where his brother James tended bar.

Wyatt rejoined the force in Dodge City in 1878 and served until September 1879. He was consid-

Wyatt Earp, in an 1886 photograph. CORBIS/BETTMANN

ered a tough and fair officer and may have killed his first man, a young cowboy named George Hoy, who was shooting up the town. Early in September 1879 Wyatt left Dodge with his brother James and headed west. Wyatt was accompanied by his second wife, Celia Ann "Mattie" Blaylock. They paused briefly in Las Vegas, New Mexico, before moving on to Prescott, Arizona, where Virgil was living. Virgil had served as a peace officer in Prescott and seemed well established there, but he packed his belongings and moved with his brothers to Tombstone, which was founded after silver was discovered in the area. On 1 December 1879 Virgil was appointed deputy U.S. marshal.

The Earp brothers expected to take advantage of the silver mining boom. They dabbled in mining claims and gambled, but within a short time they were once again earning their living with their guns. Wyatt briefly worked as a guard for Wells Fargo before being appointed deputy sheriff of Pima County. Morgan then replaced Wyatt. Upon the death of the town marshal, Fred White, in 1880 Virgil took over that post temporarily. At the next election he was defeated by Ben Sippy but suc-

ceeded him after Sippy skipped town under questionable circumstances. Wyatt hoped to be appointed sheriff of the newly formed Cochise County, but the job went to John H. Behan, a man with more political experience and connections in Arizona.

The Earps aligned themselves with the Republican power structure in Tombstone and hoped to establish themselves as respectable businessmen and citizens. Unfortunately they soon collided with a loosely connected crowd of cowboys, cattle thieves, and stage robbers with ties to the Democratic machine in Cochise County. This rivalry created problems both for the Earps and for the Republicans in general that eventually led to the street fight erroneously called the "gunfight at the O. K. Corral" on 26 October 1881. This fight of the Earps against the Clantons and McLaurys upset the Earps' plans in Tombstone. Although they were exonerated at a preliminary hearing on the gunfight, Virgil lost his job as town marshal, and public sentiment became more divided over their role in the town.

The cowboys planned revenge, and on the night of 28 December 1881, Virgil was shot in an ambush by friends of the Clantons and never regained full use of one arm. Wyatt, who was appointed deputy U.S. marshal in Virgil's place, appealed to Ike Clanton and tried to end the feud, but on 18 March 1882 Morgan was murdered as he played pool at Hatch's Billiard Parlor in Tombstone. Wyatt sent James and the wounded Virgil to California with their families, and at the head of a posse that included his youngest brother, Warren, he went after the cowboys. Frank Stilwell, "Indian Charley" Cruz, Curly Bill Brocious, and Johnny Barnes died before the Earp party left Arizona, with warrants for the Earp brothers' arrest outstanding in both Cochise and Pima Counties.

For the next few years, most of the Earp brothers drifted. Wyatt gambled, working as an agent for various businesses, including the Southern Pacific Railroad, Wells Fargo, and the Santa Fe Railroad. Virgil also worked for the Southern Pacific as an officer before being elected town marshal of Colton, California, in 1887. James pursued his career as a saloonkeeper, and he and Wyatt were together in Eagle City, Idaho, when Wyatt served briefly as deputy sheriff of Kootenai County and acted as peacemaker in a land dispute that had turned violent. In the early 1890s Wyatt operated gambling halls and dabbled in horse racing. In 1896, at Mechanics Pavillion in San Francisco, he acted as referee in the controversial Tom Sharkey–

Bob Fitzsimmons boxing match, which he gave to Sharkey on a foul.

Wyatt departed for Alaska the next year with his third wife; he operated a saloon in Nome. While he was there, his brother Warren was killed in a saloon fight in Willcox, Arizona. Virgil was again living in the Prescott area. In 1905 Virgil moved to Goldfield, Nevada, where he and Wyatt were reunited briefly before Virgil died of pneumonia in 1906. Newton Earp, who had avoided the Tombstone troubles, served as a peace officer in Garden City, Kansas, and eventually moved to California, where he died in 1928.

For most of the rest of his life, Wyatt divided his time between Los Angeles, California, and Parker, Arizona. Although he pursued a variety of mining enterprises, he was never successful. He was well known, however, and associated with a number of prominent people who respected him. He died on 13 January 1929. At the time of his death, Wyatt Earp was working with a young journalist named Stuart N. Lake on a biography. *Wyatt Earp: Frontier Marshal*, which was published in 1931, ensured that Wyatt Earp and his brothers would become a permanent part of the legend of the West.

BIBLIOGRAPHY

Chaput, Donald. *Virgil Earp: Western Peace Officer.* Norman: University of Oklahoma Press, 1994.
Terfertiller, Casey. *Wyatt Earp: The Life Behind the Legend.* New York: Wiley, 1997.

GARY L. ROBERTS

See also **Clanton Gang; Dodge City; Frontier; Gunfighters and Outlaws, Western; Holliday, John Henry "Doc"; Masterson, William "Bat"; O. K. Corral Gunfight.**

EATING DISORDERS. *See* Anorexia and Bulimia.

ELDER ABUSE

America is an aging society. Indeed, one of the most impressive achievements of the twentieth century was the increase in life expectancy from about fifty years of age in 1900 to more than seventy-five years in 1995. This increase in life expectancy combined with a lower birthrate has resulted in a gradual aging of the population, the "graying of America." In 1999, the sixty-five-and-over group was the fastest-growing segment of the population, growing at more than twice the rate of the rest of the population. Within this senior group, the oldest members, eighty-five and older, were experiencing the most dramatic growth. Increases in the senior population will accelerate even more dramatically starting in 2011, when members of the largest generation in the history of the country, the baby boomers, begin to turn sixty-five.

As population aging transforms U.S. society, affecting areas as diverse as family relationships, work and retirement, and the organization and delivery of health care and social services, how will society respond? And how will it address one of its major challenges—the burgeoning problem of elder abuse?

Contrary to stereotypes, the vast majority of older people are healthy, with less than 5 percent living in institutional settings such as nursing homes. Nevertheless, older adults are more likely than younger persons to suffer from chronic health conditions. When conditions such as arthritis, disability from stroke, and emphysema impair functioning, older people may need to turn to others to help them manage their day-to-day activities. Unfortunately, relying on others makes older adults more vulnerable to abusive situations such as domestic violence, neglect, and financial exploitation. At the same time, fear of losing their independence may discourage older individuals from seeking the help they need to protect themselves from abuse. Failure to recognize the problem of elder abuse and to identify and reach out to its victims compounds their isolation and empowers perpetrators of violence, exploitation, and neglect.

The case study in the sidebar illustates many of the issues inherent in situations of elder abuse and the tragic consequences that can ensue when such abuse is not recognized.

What Is Elder Abuse?

Elder abuse encompasses an array of abusive situations, including battery and domestic violence and other physical abuse as well as neglect, psychological abuse, and financial abuse. In most states, an older adult is defined as an individual sixty-five years of age or older, although some states use sixty as the age for eligibility. Because it focuses on a variety of abuses perpetrated on victims who have attained a defined age, elder abuse is distinct from domestic violence. Whereas responses to domestic violence were initially

Case Study of Elder Abuse

Mrs. D., a sixty-five-year-old widow, lived alone in a quiet residential neighborhood of single-family homes. Like many older adults, she had lived in her home for most of her adult life and owned it free and clear. Over the years, many of her friends in the neighborhood had moved away and, although she was well liked and knew most of her current neighbors by sight, she seldom socialized with them. Most were busy with young children and full-time jobs and generally kept to themselves.

Over time, several of the neighbors became aware that a middle-aged man, Mr. H., was paying frequent visits to Mrs. D. Ultimately Mr. H. moved into Mrs. D's home, bringing with him a parade of visitors. These "guests" arrived at all hours of the day and night; many drove expensive cars, and few stayed long. Neighbors saw less and less of Mrs. D., and when they caught a glimpse of her coming or going, she ignored them. They reported that she seemed disengaged and harried. At one point she accused the family living next door of stealing expensive jewelry that had disappeared from her home. They sometimes heard yelling coming from the home, yet were reluctant to interfere in what they believed was none of their business.

One day, Mrs. D.'s next-door neighbor answered the door to find a social worker from the local senior center. A friend had called the center, concerned about Mrs. D.'s increased isolation. The worker wondered if the neighbor knew where Mrs. D. was since there was a for-sale sign on the home and no one appeared to be living there. Upon reflection, the neighbor seemed to recall that she had last seen Mrs. D. driving her car out of the driveway about three weeks earlier. After subsequent efforts failed to locate Mrs. D., the social worker filed a missing-persons report. When the police investigator located Mr. H. through a realtor, Mr. H. told the investigator that Mrs. D. was traveling, that he had recently seen her off on a flight to a distant city.

Two months later Mrs. D. was picked up by the police in Brooklyn, New York. She was confused, dirty, and combative. They assumed that she was homeless. She gave them her name but could provide little else in the way of information. She was hostile, aggressive, and physically threatened the officers, whereupon they put her in the back of the patrol car and took her to the hospital.

After forty-eight hours in a hospital emergency room, Mrs. D. was placed in a locked psychiatric facility. To control her violent and disruptive behavior, she was sedated with high doses of psychotropic drugs and kept tied to either her bed or a chair.

Over time, she lost the ability to walk and her speech became increasingly incoherent. Three months after she was found, a persistent social worker at the psychiatric hospital, attempting to find Mrs. D.'s relatives, came across the missing-persons report and contacted the police in Mrs. D.'s hometown. They in turn notified the social worker who had filed the original report.

Meanwhile, Mr. H., who had obtained legal control over all of Mrs. D.'s property before her departure, sold her home, absconding with the proceeds and all of her remaining assets. Mrs. D., who had enjoyed a comfortable pension and income from several investments, was now penniless, homeless, and in legal limbo as she could not be discharged from the hospital and moved to her home state unless authorized to do so by a person with legal authority to sign her out. Such authority could be granted only by petitioning the court for legal guardianship in New York. Yet guardianship, a state-based policy, is difficult to arrange between parties from different states. The two social workers, one in New York and one in Mrs. D.'s home city, persisted. More than six months after she had been located, guardianship was granted to the social worker who had filed the original report, and Mrs. D. was returned to her home city.

As a result of the high dose of drugs administered in the psychiatric facility, Mrs. D. had developed tardive akasthesia, a neurological disorder characterized by agitation, inability to sit still, involuntary arm movements, and constant humming. Unable to walk or to communicate her needs and suffering from debilitating physical and psychiatric problems, Mrs. D. required twenty-four-hour care in a skilled nursing facility. This care was paid for by Medicaid, the combined state and federal program that serves low-income people. Neurological tests indicated that Mrs. D. had "probable Alzheimer's dementia." After several months of treatment, she gradually regained the ability to walk, but her cognitive functioning (her memory and reasoning ability) showed little improvement. Once she was ambulatory, she wandered around the facility taking things and at times threatening other residents. Eventually, she was moved to a more restrictive psychiatric facility, where she died three years later. Although information about Mr. H. was provided to law enforcement, little effort was made to locate him. In all likelihood, he continues to victimize older persons.

developed for battered women, most efforts to address elder abuse have not focused on abuse by spouses or partners. Thus, older victims of domestic violence may not receive the attention they need from either service system. Common types of elder abuse are defined as follows:

Physical Abuse. Physical abuse is hitting, kicking, pushing, slapping, sexually abusing, or otherwise assaulting an older person, resulting in physical trauma. It also can include unreasonable use of physical restraints or otherwise restricting an older person's freedom of movement as well as excessive or inappropriate medication. Indicators of physical abuse include injuries such as bruises, burns, lacerations, fractures, or sprains; signs of physical confinement; and evidence of previously untreated injuries that are incompatible with explanations of how the injuries were received. Conflicting accounts or questionable explanations are also red flags. Elders who have been abused may appear depressed, indifferent, anxious, or fearful. Partners or caregivers who do not give the older victim the opportunity to speak for him- or herself also suggest the possibility of abuse. Unfortunately, professionals may contribute to the problem by ignoring the older person if the caregiver is present or by discounting the explanation of the older person if he or she appears to be impaired.

Neglect. Neglect is indicated by the failure of a caregiver adequately to meet the basic needs of a dependent older person: to provide food, shelter, and clothing, as well as failure to assist with activities of daily living, to provide medical care, and to protect a dependent person from safety hazards. Neglect also can include abandonment or social isolation. Indicators of neglect include poor hygiene, poor nutritional status, untreated injuries, and lack of necessary help with self-care.

Psychological Abuse. This form of abuse includes intimidation, threats, belittling, and insults resulting in emotional trauma. It can also include intentionally confusing or manipulating an older person or withholding support and affection to create an environment of fear and insecurity.

Financial Abuse. Also referred to as financial exploitation, exploitation of resources, material exploitation, material abuse, fiduciary abuse, financial mistreatment, financial or economic victimization, extortion, theft, and fraud, financial abuse is the theft or misappropriation of an older person's money or other financial resources. It includes persuading, tricking, or coercing an older person to take out a loan, make a will, deed property, turn over money or other assets, and other ruses that result in using assets in ways other than what the older adult intended. Although older adults are often victims of dishonest contractors, mail-order scams, questionable loan arrangements, and telemarketing fraud, it is those closest to the victims—their family members and friends—who are most likely to commit financial abuse.

As Mrs. D.'s case illustrates, financial abuse may go hand in hand with other forms of mistreatment. Studies show that physical and psychological abuse are more likely to occur when the perpetrator is financially dependent on the victim. Problems such as substance abuse and mental disorders that create financial dependency may also inhibit the perpetrator's ability to control aggression. In Mrs. D.'s case her home provided a front for Mr. H.'s drug dealing while her property and assets offered an additional source of income to support his drug habit. Social workers and adult protective service workers report that drug dealers are increasingly using older adults as unwitting pawns in their business deals. In one scenario, the dealer takes the older adult for "a walk." Prior to the outing, drugs are stashed in the older person's purse or pockets. The drugs are then retrieved as sales are transacted, permitting a quick getaway and leaving the older person literally holding the bag if the police show up. Such a ploy also puts the older adult at risk of attack or reprisal if conflict arises between those purchasing and those selling drugs.

Self-neglect. In addition to abuse inflicted by others, elders may be victims of self-neglect, which is defined as the individual's failure to provide his or her own basic necessities (food, shelter, and self-care). Self-neglect is one of the most common forms of abuse and one of the most challenging to address. As Mrs. D.'s case illustrates, self-neglect may result when the elder has been abandoned by a significant other. Typically this occurs when the perpetrator has depleted or gained control of the elder's resources. Self-neglect also can occur when an older person, challenged by health problems, functional difficulties, or cognitive impairment, struggles to maintain his or her independence.

How Often Does Elder Abuse Occur?

A recent study by the National Center on Elder Abuse estimates that the incidence or number of new cases of elder abuse occurring outside institutions such as nursing homes was about a half million during 1996. The study points out that this number is more than four times higher than the number of cases reported to adult protective services. Moreover, there is evidence that elder abuse is on the rise, with many states seeing increases in the number of cases reported to protective service agencies.

As Mrs. D.'s case illustrates, abuse can occur both in the elder's own home and in institutional settings. Scandals in nursing homes reported in the popular press in the 1980s and 1990s reveal a litany of abuses, including sexual abuse, battery, and neglect. Nursing-home reform legislation, supported by advocates and leaders in the nursing home industry, was enacted by Congress in 1987, resulting in improved oversight and regulations. This legislation also tightened restrictions against using physical and chemical restraints (e.g., drugs) to control behavior. Nevertheless, because of their high level of dependency, persons in long-term care settings are extremely vulnerable to the behavior and whims of their caregivers. Direct-care providers in nursing homes typically have high turnover rates, receive low pay, bring few skills to the workplace, and receive minimal training. Although some reforms appear to be meeting with success, there is still room for improvement. As Mrs. D.'s case shows, the common practice of restraining institutionalized persons can be highly detrimental to the health, well-being, and quality of life of the nursing home or psychiatric facility resident.

Elder abuse in nursing homes has been well documented and appeared to be declining somewhat by the late twentieth century. Sadly, as has been mentioned, most elder abuse is committed by those closest to the older persons: their family members, typically spouses and adult children.

Corrective Measures

As a result of the increasing recognition of the problem of mistreatment of older persons, elder-abuse statutes have been enacted in all fifty states and the District of Columbia. Many elder-abuse laws are patterned after child-abuse laws, suggesting that older persons are childlike and dependent. In general, these laws are based on the premise that older persons require protection because of the association of age with physical and cognitive impairments that increase vulnerability to abuse. Forty-three states have provisions for man-

datory reporting by professionals who suspect that an older person or dependent adult is a victim of abuse. The agency Adult Protective Services (APS) receives reports of abuse for persons who live in the community. For persons in institutions, the nursing-home ombudsman program handles reports. Of course, reports can also be made directly to law enforcement.

Unresolved Problems

Specific instances of elder abuse may be difficult to identify because definitions of what is and is not abuse are sometimes unclear. Elder abuse may occur as a result of patterns of spousal battery that continue into old age or it may begin in later life as a result of dementia, a caregiver's poor coping ability, substance abuse, or a new relationship.

The paradigm for elder abuse, modeled after child abuse, focuses on dependency and caregiving problems rather than physical violence perpetrated by domestic partners. Unfortunately, services designed for victims of domestic violence may fail to address the needs of older adults. Similarly, financial exploitation, which is seldom a factor in child-abuse situations, is too often unaddressed in responses to elder abuse.

Although professionals may be mandated to report instances of abuse, the older person may refuse help, resulting in a conflict between what the professional views as the elder's best interest and what the elder chooses to do. And as with other public policies designed to "protect" vulnerable persons, the state's efforts to promote safety may interfere with an individual's freedom, autonomy, and self-determination. When freedom and safety are in conflict, the current wisdom is that freedom, which is founded upon civil liberties inherent in our society, should prevail. Some argue, however, that elder abuse is a crime against humanity that should be pursued regardless of what the victim wants. Pursuing it as a crime, it is also argued, can prevent the elder's being forced to fall back on public benefits and can stop the perpetrator from victimizing others.

The obligation of service providers to help also may conflict with autonomy in situations of self-neglect, making it difficult to determine what is the most ethical and appropriate way to offer support and assistance. If it is determined that an elderly person lacks the cognitive ability to make an informed choice, then his or her desire to remain in dangerous or neglectful situations may be overridden. For example, if Mrs. D. had demonstrated the ability to understand her circumstances, it is unlikely that she would have been admitted to a facility in New York.

Financial abuse represents a particularly problematical area because its detection and investigation may interfere with the legally guaranteed rights and responsibilities of adults to enter into contracts, buy and sell property, and give major assets as gifts to other persons. In such instances, a critical issue for those involved is to determine whether the situation is an abusive one that requires intervention or if it is a legitimate private transaction.

Another issue that complicates the field of elder abuse is that diverse cultures have conflicting ideas about what constitutes abuse. For example, in some cultures money and property are viewed as belonging to the family rather than to individuals within the family. Yet such sharing, particularly when it involves public benefits such as Social Security or supplemental security income payments, may constitute financial abuse in the eyes of public officials.

Potential Remedies

Since elder abuse was first recognized as a significant problem in the 1970s, a number of responses have been developed. Although reporting of abuse, discussed above, has been mandated by law, once a crime has been reported there is often little available in the way of prevention or treatment. Adult Protective Service agencies, burdened with high caseloads and inadequate funding, concentrate their efforts on crisis intervention rather than preventing abuse or providing ongoing treatment to victims. Agencies need to be better informed as to prevention, just as families and caregivers must be better educated about caring for dependent older persons. Education is especially important for families where norms of behavior permit physical violence as a means to address problems.

Those most likely to encounter elder abuse, including gerontologists, health-care workers, and law enforcement personnel, need training in how to identify and address abuse. Police officers and health-care workers, who are often most likely to encounter evidence of abuse, typically have little training or knowledge concerning how to work with elder-abuse cases. In fact, there is evidence that professionals often fail to identify elder-abuse situations in the first place, accepting such explanations for physical injury as accidental falls. A

lack of intervention studies makes it hard to know which approaches offer effective treatments. Intervention with the perpetrators themselves, through education, self-help, support groups, and substance-abuse programs, is extremely rare. Where punishment and not treatment is the likely outcome, older victims may be unwilling to turn in or to testify against their abusers, who are likely to be close family members. And without the help and support of the older victim, intervention may not be possible.

Although more and better efforts to prosecute perpetrators also are needed, a number of problems confront those who try to prosecute elder-abuse cases. Because Mrs. D. lacked close family members or friends, by the time anyone had become aware of the crime, the perpetrator had vanished. Even if the police had been able to locate Mr. H., there were no credible witnesses available to testify about what had happened. Unfortunately, given its comparatively low risk, financial abuse is becoming the crime of choice for con artists, who are rarely held to account for victimizing an older person.

Studies are needed to determine how many people are victimized, by whom, in what way, and with what results. The wide dissemination of information about elder abuse obtained through research and reporting could aid providers, family, neighbors, and friends. Those who prey on older people are less likely to strike when they know that someone is paying attention. The graying of America makes it incumbent on all citizens to ensure that those who are blessed with long life are not robbed of the dignity, material necessities, and physical well-being needed to enjoy it.

BIBLIOGRAPHY

Abused Elders or Older Battered Women. Report on the AARP Forum. Washington, D.C.: American Association of Retired Persons, 1993.

Dejowski, Edward D., ed. *Protecting Judgment-Impaired Adults: Issues, Interventions and Policies*. Binghamton, N.Y.: Haworth, 1990.

Johnson, Tonya Fusco, ed. *Elder Mistreatment: Ethical Issues, Dilemmas, and Decisions*. Binghamton, N.Y.: Haworth, 1995.

Kosberg, Jordan K., and Juanita L. Garcia. *Elder Abuse: International and Cross-Cultural Perspectives*. Binghamton, N.Y.: Haworth, 1995.

Pillemer, Karl A., and David Finkelhor. "The Prevalence of Elder Abuse: A Random Sample Survey." *The Gerontologist* 28 (1988).

Quinn, Mary J., and Susan K. Tomita. *Elder Abuse and Neglect: Causes, Diagnosis and Intervention Strategies.* 2d ed. New York: Springer, 1997.

U.S. Department of Health and Human Services. Administration on Aging and Administration for Children and Families. *The National Elder Abuse Incidence Study.* Washington, D.C., 1998. Also at http://www.aoa.gov/abuse/report/default.htm.

U.S. House of Representatives. *Elder Abuse: A Decade of Shame and Inaction.* Select Committee on Aging, Subcommittee on Health and Long-Term Care, 101st–102d Cong., Hearing 1 May 1990. Washington, D.C.: U.S. Government Printing Office, 1990.

Wolf, Rosalie S., and Karl A. Pillemer. *Helping Elderly Victims: The Reality of Elder Abuse.* New York: Columbia University Press, 1989.

KATHLEEN H. WILBER

See also **Age and the Life Cycle; Domestic Violence; Medicine and Violence: Emergency Medicine; Psychological Violence.**

EMERGENCY MEDICINE. *See* Medicine and Violence: Emergency Medicine.

EMOTION

So often is violence accompanied by rage that it is common to think of violent action against people or property as an inevitable part of anger that has somehow gone out of control. A 1984 movie dramatized the difference between emotion and action. In *The Terminator* an emotionless android is sent back from the future to the late twentieth century. This humanoid machine had been programmed to destroy anything or anyone in the path of its mission to kill the young woman who would some day bear the child destined to oppose the merciless culture of war machines represented by that android. Audiences watched spellbound as the Terminator killed without anger, guilt, shame, remorse, fear, distress, excitement, or joy. Deadly action was executed with swift efficiency by a character incapable of emotion; many film critics described the scenes of carnage as more like ballet than anything they might have associated with murder or war.

In this sense, violence (like ballet) may be understood as a set of skills, the end result of learned and perhaps practiced sequences of actions culminating in effects such as damage, destruction, or death. A child who has been frightened or humiliated by older or bigger kids often wishes for enough skill at some martial art to defend himself or herself. In the mythic frontier West, a gun was called an "equalizer," a device that gave a little guy with no physical prowess the ability to match the capacity for violence of more powerful opponents. To the victim of violence, it may make little or no difference whether an attack was launched during a moment of rage or as a dispassionate decision. Yet essential to an appreciation of violence is a good grasp of the nature of human emotion and the forces that can motivate any individual to accept the idea that violent action is acceptable or even necessary.

The Affect System

The study of emotion is something like the subject of color in paintings. From the pigments for a few primary colors, the skilled artist can mix the most delicate shade or variation of any hue seen in nature, as well as many never seen before. From the hundreds of labels that have been given the wide range of human emotional experience, a few may be selected to represent the equivalent of primary colors—basic elements from which all the others can be derived. The first scientist to make such a list was Charles Darwin, who in 1872 pointed out that it was possible to group all of the known emotions into a limited set of families of emotion, each of which was characterized by a highly specific facial expression. The American psychologist and philosopher Silvan S. Tomkins (1911–1991) kept that part of Darwin's contribution, but in the four-volume *Affect Imagery Consciousness*, published between 1962 and 1992, Tomkins introduced what is now known as "affect theory" and "script theory." With minor variation (Ekman 1972; Izard 1971, 1977; Nathanson 1992), Tomkins's system has provided the dominant language in contemporary psychology, and the one most useful for our purpose here.

The language of computers affords a good analogy for human emotion. All machinery that whirs, buzzes, and makes noise is known as hardware. The basic programs that tell the hardware how to be a computer, like the operating system or the BIOS, are stored on chips as immutable instructions called firmware. It is through software that we introduce the sets of variable and easily altered instructions that make a computer function as a word processor or game or other tool of our era. In the human being, the structures, circuits, and other chemical and physical components of our bodies may be thought of as hardware, whereas the way we grow up in a family, a neighborhood, or an era provides the software for emotion. The firmware for emotion is encrypted in the brain as the affect system described by Tomkins, a discrete set of nine innate mechanisms that when modified by the software of life become the infinitely variable language of adult emotion. In this entry the term *affect* is used to describe any of this group of physiological events, *feeling* represents our awareness that an affect has been triggered, and *emotion* designates the combination of an affect with our memory of previous experiences of an affect. Affect is biology, while emotion is biography.

Each innate affect starts out as the equivalent of a computer program, a sequence of purely biological actions set in motion when the button for it is pushed; affect is the bridge between biology and psychology. For example, any time the central nervous system processes a message that begins suddenly, lasts very briefly, and ends quickly (like a thunderclap or a pistol shot), an affect is triggered that both resembles the form or contour of its stimulus and makes that stimulus more important and urgent for the organism. In the case of the sudden, brief stimulus just described, the affect triggered is named for the range between surprise and startle, and is known formally as *surprise-startle*. You experience it as the reaction in which you are motivated to drop your attention to whatever else might have been going on at the moment and to focus on that noise, flash of light, suddenly occurring idea (like the "Eureka!" of Archimedes), or any other sudden, brief stimulus. If you watch people who have been startled, you may notice that they blink, curl their bodies forward, and make a sharp intake of breath sometimes associated with the sound "Oh!" That is the firmware for surprise-startle. If through most of your life startling events have become associated with pleasant revelations, then your general attitude toward the affect is positive; to the extent that what follows the awareness brought by the affect proves unpleasant, your association to the affect will be negative. The physiological affect program itself is in no way altered by the actual nature of the stimulus that turned it on; affect is only a response to the speed or rhythm at which information enters the central nervous system. It is the software of life that makes each individual's experience of an affect so personal.

Actually, surprise-startle is the only one of the nine innate affects that has no intrinsically pleasant or unpleasant flavor, which conforms to its evo-

TABLE 1. The Innate Affects

Positive Affects	Neutral Affect	Negative Affects
interest-excitement enjoyment-joy	surprise-startle	fear-terror distress-anguish anger-rage dissmell disgust shame-humiliation

lution as an amplifier of an event that may last only a few hundredths of a second. For stimuli that drone on and on as steady-state events, like feeling cold, the relentless hum of overwork, or the unyielding noise of a jackhammer in the street, an unpleasant or *negative affect* is triggered that represents the range from mild distress to awful anguish. *Distress-anguish* is characterized in the infant by sobbing, which is also a steady-state event, and distinctive alteration of the muscles of the face in which the corners of the lips turn down and the eyebrows form a straight line.

A steady-state stimulus of even greater unpleasant intensity triggers another negative affect in which nearly all the muscles of the body are tensed and the face of the infant becomes hot and red as a cry of rage is emitted. As an innate affect program, *anger-rage* is the physiological reaction to high-density overmuch. Only the affect anger-rage is intrinsically associated with violent action, as is obvious to anyone who has ever watched a screaming, crying, raging infant flail its arms and legs wildly in tune with the physiological affect program. Sometimes you will see a toddler become angry when unable to move something in its way, then (assisted by the muscularity innately associated with the affect anger-rage) kick or punch the offending object and burst into laughter as it yields to this sudden powerful action. Football coaches often push players to get angry at their opponents in order to guarantee what they hope will be focused and effective violent action. Paradoxically, martial arts instructors teach calm and disciplined action, knowing that power is most useful when managed with skill.

Tomkins showed that although each of the innate affect protocols makes things happen all over the body, it is the facial display that provides the most information both to the growing infant and the observing other. We adults tend to smile when we see babies or children react with the full, innate expression of an affect, for when we can see so easily what another person is feeling it is almost as if we are reading that person's mind. Part of emotional maturity is the learned ability to mute or regulate the degree to which we allow the visible or audible expression of any affect.

If surprise-startle is our prewired, innate reaction to a stimulus that begins and ends suddenly, what happens when a stimulus rises in intensity less rapidly? It seems that there is an optimal range of stimulus increase to which the organism responds with the *positive affect* we call *interest-excitement*. No matter how old we may be, whether newborn babies or senior citizens, we will respond to such an optimal gradient of stimulus acquisition with the kind of facial expression described as "track, look, listen," while our heartbeat and rate of breathing increase to a pleasant degree. This evolved response to novelty is the affect that powers the kind of attention we give the study of books, classes, road maps, and anything else that we find "interesting." Since all of the innate affects act to amplify any stimulus so that it becomes more noticeable, we may say that the affect system brings things into consciousness. No stimulus may become the subject of our attention unless it has first triggered an affect, and nothing may enter the special channel of neocortical function we call consciousness until the door to awareness has been opened by an affect. Interest-excitement provides the range of attention from the attitude that makes us search for the source of a barely audible sound when we are walking in the woods, or makes us wildly excited by the action of a fast-moving basketball game. As for all the affects, what triggers the emotional aspect of our involvement is not the exact information generated at the moment, but the way that information is being received by the affect system.

Yet there are many situations in which the gradient at which information enters the system is greater than that which may be accepted as a trigger for interest-excitement but not so sharp as that which triggers surprise-startle. Stimuli that occur at an unpleasantly rapid gradient activate an innate mechanism that makes the heart pound uncomfortably fast and breathing increase to an unpleasant degree, while remapping the face with cold cheeks and a frozen stare. The range of affect from mild fear (anxiety) through sheer terror is handled by the innate affect Tomkins called *fear-terror*, and it is a prominent member of the cast of negative affects. The ways we learn to behave when we are frightened, the actual source of whatever has triggered this negative affect, the thoughts we experience when scared—all of this important data is quite different from the innate mechanism that has called us to anxious attention. Many people have a tendency to lump all unpleasant feeling under the label "anxiety," but the more you know about the affect system, the more it becomes important to distinguish among the negative affects on the basis of the trigger required by each.

There is, of course, an affective reaction to stimulus decrease, and intuitively you might have guessed that it would be pleasant. The range of affect between mild contentment and absolute joy was named *enjoyment-joy* by Tomkins, and it is the mechanism through which we are motivated to pay attention to anything associated with the action of reduced activity. The affect protocol sculpts the face to a smile when the gradient of stimulus reduction is gradual and makes us laugh when it is sudden. Throughout life we can observe the muscles of the face relax, the corners of the mouth widen, and the eyes shine brightly as we are suffused with pleasant thoughts brought into consciousness not by the actual nature of the stimulus that has been reduced but by the sheer fact that it has been reduced. What we adults think of as having a good time or enjoying ourselves may be understood as a series of events during which we experience sequences of both interest-excitement and enjoyment-joy. Fun, like most common words for emotional experience, is more complex than one might think! It is the kind of combination of mental functions that is best understood as an ideoaffective complex—somewhat different each time we use the word, and certainly different for each of us on the basis of our personal histories.

Of the three remaining negative affects, two have evolved from our programmed reaction to possibly dangerous food. The mechanism for which Tomkins coined the term *dissmell* (the innate reaction to a foul odor) wrinkles the nose and upper lip while drawing the head back from the offending substance and often forcing a noise like "eeoo!" Although in the infant this is purely a response to odor, in the adult (as an ideoaffective complex) this becomes the cornerstone of prejudice, the way we reject what or who we have neither examined nor sampled. *Disgust*, initially a response to bad-tasting food, makes the infant thrust tongue, lower lip, and head forward with a characteristic sound of "yucch." In the adult, this mechanism lends its peculiar flavor to our feelings about anyone we had once loved and now find noxious.

One affect remains, the mechanism responsible for the shame family of emotions. The affect mechanism is triggered not by anything particularly social or related to higher brain function, but when something interferes with the expression of either of the two positive affects (interest-excitement or enjoyment-joy). The physiological mechanism for shame affect produces the blush, averts our gaze, and by interfering with the positive affect responsible for attention and consciousness at that moment causes a cognitive shock. (No one can think clearly in the moment of shame.) The affect *shame-humiliation* sets in motion a pattern of responses called the compass of shame that may include *withdrawal* from the suddenly shaming situation, the *attack self* form of defensively deferential behavior, narcissistic *avoidance* of any unpleasant information about the self, or a form of attack on the self-esteem of another person called *attack other* behavior. The *attack other* library of learned behavior scripts most of the spontaneous displays of anger and associated violence in our society, for in response to what they experience as an insult or a blow to their self-esteem, many people will fly into rage that may be truly dangerous to others. Nathanson (1992) has estimated that perhaps 90 percent of the public hostility and assault we see in contemporary society is mobilized as such a response to shame. Shame-humiliation may start out as a relatively simple amplification of an impediment to either of the positive affects, but it results in highly complex alterations of our view of ourselves and our associations with others.

We Have Evolved with a Blueprint for Emotional Life

We have, then, nine mechanisms that have evolved to register and bring into consciousness a wide range of physiological conditions representing all possible ways information can enter the central nervous system. Two of them, interest-excitement and enjoyment-joy, feel wonderful; because surprise-startle brings into consciousness events that are so brief, it may be considered neutral. The negative affects (fear-terror, distress-anguish, anger-rage, dissmell, disgust, and shame-humiliation) provide six different ways of feeling awful for six very different reasons.

Tomkins points out that we have therefore evolved to be "wired" or programmed with four rules for psychological functioning. First, because

positive affect feels so good, we are motivated to maintain and to maximize it. Second, because negative affect feels so bad, we are motivated to minimize it. Third, the system works best when we express whatever affect has been triggered so we can obey the first two rules. Fourth, anything that fosters the working of these three rules is good for mental health, while anything that interferes with them is bad for our emotional health.

The several hundred labels with which we adults describe our emotional experience are all made up of these nine components, just as in chemistry the atoms of several elements may be joined to make complex molecules. For example, contempt may be understood as the fusion of dissmell (because I find you noxious, stay distant from me) with anger (or I will hurt you); guilt as the fusion of shame (of discovery) with fear (of punishment); humiliation as the experience of shame after exposure by someone who wanted to hurt you; grief and sadness as distress-anguish triggered by loss, stress, and tension, the same affect triggered when we feel unable to do anything about the cause of the steady-state stimulus. Even though there are many neurochemical circuits that can go wrong to produce the cluster of illnesses known as "depression," each form of depression is characterized by the unyielding presence of one or more of the negative affects, for any unpleasant emotional experience must involve a negative affect. Suicide is only superficially "violence against the self," for at a much deeper level it represents the individual's decision that the only way to get relief from mental pain associated with an unremitting, intense negative affect is to end the self that suffers.

Just as the physician may use medication to normalize the dysfunctional neurochemistry associated with the biological depressions, an individual may use "street drugs" for their effects on the affect system. In modest doses, alcohol reduces shame and therefore allows us a momentary increase in self-confidence; it is called a "disinhibiting" drug because it counters the inhibiting effects of shame on certain kinds of public action. If an individual is angry and contemplating violent action in order to express that anger, and if the anger is being held in check by the idea that it would be embarrassing to be seen as angry, then alcohol can disinhibit and thus facilitate violent action. Similarly, cocaine and the amphetamines can increase anyone's level of excitement to the degree that no action can be restrained by shame in the normal social system. Heroin is involved with a complex sequence of affects that are responsible for much violence in society: at its best, those who use this drug say that it offers a level of enjoyment-joy far in excess of anything that can be achieved normally. So intense and horrific are the periods of negative affect that ensue as these effects wear off that drug users will engage in whatever kind of action seems required to fund their addiction, notwithstanding the danger to others associated with these actions.

Implications for Society

This separation between the evolved system for the expression of innate affect and the behavior with which it may become associated offers much hope for a society troubled by violence. The human cannot learn to live without negative affect—distress, anger, shame, fear, dissmell, and disgust have remained with us through evolution because they offer considerable advantages in dealing with our experienced world. Yet any and all affective expression may be modulated through training. Children of our era are free to study violent behavior by watching over and over on videotape the actions of their heroes and antiheroes on a video screen; they often pick up and practice maneuvers with guns and knives left in their milieu; they may learn any of the martial arts; and they may even choose to emulate the most dangerously competent of their elders. Needed is a system of education that incorporates the idea of affect modulation into entertainments, education, and training—material produced and provided at a level of sophistication through which children now learn the techniques of violent action. It is incumbent on those who understand the firmware for emotion and its link to the software of daily life that we educate ourselves and our children toward a new emotionality that fosters the survival of our society.

BIBLIOGRAPHY

Darwin, Charles. *The Expression of the Emotions in Man and Animal.* 1872. Reprint, New York: St. Martin's, 1979.

Ekman, Paul. "Universals and Cultural Differences in Facial Expressions of Emotion." In *Nebraska Symposium on Motivation 1971,* edited by J. Cole. Lincoln: University of Nebraska Press, 1972.

Izard, Carroll E. *The Face of Emotion.* New York: Appleton-Century-Crofts, 1971.

———. *Human Emotions.* New York: Plenum, 1977.

Nathanson, Donald L. *Shame and Pride: Affect, Sex, and the Birth of the Self.* New York: Norton, 1992.

Tomkins, Silvan S. *Affect Imagery Consciousness.* Vol. 1, *The Positive Affects,* 1962. Vol. 2, *The Negative Affects,* 1963. Vol. 3, *The Negative Affects: Anger and Fear,* 1991. Vol. 4, *Cognition,* 1992. New York: Springer.

DONALD L. NATHANSON

See also **Neuropsychology; Psychological Violence; Shame; Temperament; Victims of Violence: Social Suffering.**

ENDOCRINOLOGY

Following the **Overview***, three subentries examine the role of hormones and the endocrine system on violence and aggression:* **Hormones in Child Abuse, PMS and Female Violence,** *and* **Testosterone.**

OVERVIEW

Efforts to stem the worldwide tide of violence will be successful only if they are based on a comprehensive understanding of the causes and consequences of violent behavior. Violent behavior is the product of multiple, interacting influences that converge in unique ways to prompt individuals to participate in violent activities. These influences include biological, experiential, situational, and social processes. In the field of nonhuman biology, the endocrine aspects of aggressive behavior are the subject of much research.

Definitions of violence, aggression, and dominance and of acting out and oppositional or disruptive behaviors are evasive, as the boundaries between the categories are not clearly designated. "Violence" implies physical force with the intent of injury; it is a violation of criminal laws. "Aggression" carries many definitions but is generally considered to describe behavior aimed at harming or injuring another; it may or may not involve breaking a criminal law. "Dominance" may or may not involve injury but its apparent intent is to achieve or maintain high status. "Acting out" and "oppositional" and "disruptive" behaviors refer to defiance, disobedience, and lack of respect for adults but may include aggressive acts as well. Endocrine aspects of the entire spectrum of these behaviors have been considered in past research.

Endocrinology is the study of the biochemical integrative mechanisms that regulate both the physiological functioning of bodily systems (e.g., reproduction, metabolic and homeostatic processes, growth and development, adaptive responses to stress) and behavior. The field of endocrinology is extremely diverse and includes not only the traditional study of hormones (e.g., their synthesis, transport, site of action, and mode of action) but also the study of the interdependent functions of the closely linked nervous and endocrine coordinating systems, that is, the neuroendocrine system. Hormones elicit a wide variety of biological responses and can be categorized according to their biochemical structures into three major subclasses: (1) the amino acid derivatives, which include several of the major neurotransmitters, (2) the peptides and polypeptides, the largest and most diverse group of hormones, and (3) the lipophilic steroids, the group of hormones that are often the focus of hormone and behavior research.

The lipophilic steroidal hormones are all cholesterol derivatives and share very similar biochemical structures. Steroidal hormones include the commonly termed sex or gonadal steroids (testosterone and other androgens, estrogens, and progestins), corticosteroids and adrenal androgens originating from the adrenal cortex, and neurosteroids that appear to be synthesized directly from cholesterol in several locations throughout the nervous system. Historically, it has been repeatedly demonstrated that steroidal hormones from the hypothalamic-pituitary-gonadal (HPG) and hypothalamic-pituitary-adrenal (HPA) axes have important roles in the development of the central nervous system and behavioral expression in many species of animals. However, the roles steroidal hormones play in human behaviors, and particularly violent behaviors, have been difficult to ascertain accurately. Few studies directly examine hormones and the behavior of violent individuals, but much of what is known about hormones and aggressive behavior provides a basis for understanding hormones and violence.

Hormones and Aggressive and Violent Behavior

Steroids may influence violent behavior by contributing to the shaping and reshaping of brain structure and functioning. It is theorized that during brief, sensitive periods in prenatal and early postnatal life gonadal steroids influence the structural and functional potential of the highly plastic developing nervous system. These structural and functional hormone-mediated changes are referred to as organizational effects. Beginning at puberty and continuing into adulthood, gonadal steroids bring to expression the patterns of behavior that

were previously organized in early development and are referred to as activational effects. Commonly observed human sexual differences in brain structure, function, and behavioral expression are believed to originate from the differential organizational and activational effects of gonadal hormones in males and females. For instance, since males are exposed to higher concentrations of androgens than females during prenatal development and males are more aggressive than females, androgens are implicated in the observed sexual dimorphisms in aggression and dominance. Although prenatal hormonal influences may be important, evidence also indicates that the nervous system can be characterized by its structural and functional plasticity not only in early development but throughout the life span. Steroidal hormones collectively modulate brain biochemistry and influence neuronal functioning in multiple ways, thereby potentially contributing to and responding to human behavioral expression continuously throughout life. In short, hormones and behavior are reciprocally interactive throughout the life span.

The role of steroids in violent and aggressive behavior is derived primarily from correlational studies of males in adolescence and adulthood. Adolescence is the developmental period when hormones are expected to be related to behavior because of the activational influences of rising hormones at puberty, the period of reproductive maturation. Testosterone, estrogen, and adrenal androgens (dehydroepiandrosterone, dehydroepiandrosterone sulphate, and androstenedione) increase rapidly during puberty. Adolescence is also the time when antisocial behavior and delinquency increase. In older adolescents, testosterone concentrations have been linked to self-reports of physical and verbal aggression resulting from provocation and have been causally related to provoked and unprovoked aggression. In younger adolescents, the relationship between testosterone and aggression is less consistently demonstrated. Lower concentrations of testosterone have been linked to delinquent behavior problems in adolescent boys, and dominance has been linked primarily to estrogen and the adrenal androgens in adolescent girls. In adult males, high concentrations of endogenous (internally produced) testosterone seem to foster dominance behavior, which sometimes is aggressive.

These studies are correlational in nature, thereby ruling out simple cause-and-effect relationships between hormones and aggressive behavior. The most convincing evidence for the effects of sex steroids on aggressive behavior during adolescence is derived from endocrine experiments of removal and replacement of a hormone. A randomized, double-blinded, placebo-controlled clinical trial with delayed-puberty adolescents showed that estrogen administered to girls and testosterone to boys increased aggressive behavior (Finkelstein et al. 1977). Girls given a low dose of estrogen (early puberty) showed an increase in aggressive impulses and physical aggression against peers. Boys showed no treatment effects of testosterone at the low dose. At the mid-dose of estrogen (midpuberty), girls showed an increase in aggressive impulses and physical aggression against peers and adults. At mid-dose of testosterone, boys showed an increase in aggressive impulses and physical aggression against peers and adults. At the high dose there were no significant increases in aggressive behaviors for either boys or girls. (The reasons for this seeming anomaly are uncertain.) This experimental study showed for the first time the direct effects of sex steroids on aggressive behavior in adolescents.

The role of endogenous hormones on aggression and violence is much more complicated. The notion that steroidal hormones, and the androgens in particular, are simple yet major causal factors in violence is no longer appropriate. The endocrine-violence link appears to be much more complex and subtle than supposed by the pioneers in human behavioral endocrinological research. Previous thinking held that the effect of hormones on behavior was unidirectional; this notion has been replaced by theories and findings of a reciprocal relationship: that is, that behavioral expression (e.g., competition, aggression, and dominance) has consequences on hormone concentrations and on subsequent biochemical interactions within the nervous system.

In an important development, it has been demonstrated by Allan Mazur and Alan Booth that behavioral expression influences the concentrations of steroidal hormones and thus that reciprocal relationships exist between hormones and behavior. Testosterone, for instance, not only influences dominance; dominance also influences testosterone concentrations. Evidence for the effect of dominance on testosterone is derived from studies of the effects of competitive challenges on steroid concentrations. Testosterone rises when a person faces a competitive challenge, as if to prepare that person for confrontation. After the competition,

testosterone rises in winners and declines in losers, supporting a reciprocal cause-and-effect relationship between testosterone and dominance.

Longer-term effects of behavior on hormone concentrations are evident in a longitudinal study of boys. Aggressive and disruptive behavior predicted lower concentrations of testosterone at puberty in anxious boys, suggesting that aggressive behavior affects the development of the endocrine system. Hormones secreted under stressful circumstances, like cortisol, may suppress testosterone. The emphasis on testosterone and aggression in males has resulted in an incomplete assessment of the complex interactions among sex steroids, adrenal androgens, and cortisol in aggression.

Controversy exists as to whether aggression is a concomitant of under- or overarousal (activation) of the endocrine system. It should be noted that different hormones may be related to violence in different ways. Although overarousal of the endocrine system, reflected in higher concentrations of testosterone, is usually considered a correlate of aggression, both under- and overarousal of the endocrine system reflected in cortisol concentrations are correlates of aggressive behavior. The relationship between cortisol and aggression appears to vary across the life span. In children, higher concentrations of saliva cortisol were associated with greater conduct disorder symptoms (acting-out behavior). In adolescence, low cortisol concentrations when a person was confronted with a challenging situation predicted acting-out behavior later in development. Cortisol concentrations also were lower in sons whose fathers had conduct disorder as children. Similarly, in habitually violent adult criminals and in males with a violent history of abusing others, cortisol concentrations were low. Underarousal may allow a person to engage in aggressive behavior or commit violence without accompanying guilt and anxiety.

Much more is to be learned regarding the relationship between hormones and the expression of violent behavior. Nonetheless, certain demonstrated facets of the testosterone and aggression link merit particular attention. Despite the popular portrayal in the media and literature of steroidal hormones as causes of violent behavior in humans, the accumulated research findings suggest multiple possible interactive roles for hormones and behavior. Hormones may appropriately be viewed as risk factors and potential mediators or moderators of the link between temperament and personality on the one hand and aggressive behavior on the other. Further, we must remember that behavior can actually influence hormone changes. Hormones seem to be more appropriately viewed as risk factors in the development of behavioral capacities than as strict causes of violent behavior. The differences that exist in hormone-behavior relationships across individuals indicate that, at the individual level, the biological and behavioral relationship to steroidal hormones is most often determined by a number of coacting influences, including biochemical profile, the environment, and the individual's life experiences.

Administering hormones to treat or control violent behavior cannot be justified at this time. To understand further the role of endocrine factors in violence, three directions are worthy of pursuit. First, research may examine hormones in combination with psychological and contextual factors. This multivariate approach is needed in a case-by-case as well as in a large epidemiological approach to assessing the contribution of hormones to violence. The context in which hormones and violence are examined is especially important. Some contexts, such as with peers where dominance issues are often salient, are likely either to increase or decrease the probability of identifying hormone-behavior relationships. Second, increasingly sophisticated, sensitive, and accurate endocrine measurements, in combination with new brain imaging techniques, have the potential to reveal the developmental connections between hormones and brain functioning. Third, the inclusion of females in future studies will contribute to a more comprehensive view of the endocrinology of violence. Aggression and dominance take different forms universally in females and males, and a different configuration of hormonal profiles may be involved.

BIBLIOGRAPHY

American Psychological Association. *Reducing Violence: A Research Agenda. A Human Capital Initiative Report.* Washington, D.C.: APA, 1996.

Brain, Paul, and Elizabeth J. Susman. "Hormonal Aspects of Antisocial Behavior and Violence." In *Handbook of Antisocial Behavior,* edited by David M. Stoff et al. New York: Wiley, 1997.

Coie, John D., and Kenneth A. Dodge, "Aggression and Antisocial Behavior." In *Handbook of Child Psychology.* Vol. 3, *Social, Emotional, and Personality Development,* edited by Nancy Eisenberg. New York: Wiley, 1998.

Finkelstein, Jordan W., et al. "Estrogen or Testosterone Increases Self-Reported Aggressive Behaviors in Hypogonadal Adolescents." *Journal of Clinical Endocrinology and Metabolism* 82, no. 8 (1997).

McEwen, Bruce S. "Steroid Hormone Actions on the Brain: When Is the Genome Involved?" *Hormones and Behavior* 28, no. 4 (1994).

Mazur, Allan, and Alan Booth. "Testosterone and Dominance in Men." *Behavioral and Brain Sciences* 21, no. 3 (1998).

Rubinow, David R., and Peter J. Schmidt. "Androgens, Brain, and Behavior." *American Journal of Psychiatry* 153, no. 8 (1996).

ELIZABETH J. SUSMAN
JEFFREY T. QUIRK

See also **Developmental Factors; Health and Medical Factors.**

HORMONES IN CHILD ABUSE

The relationship between a developing child and his or her environment or experience involves a dynamic interchange of influences. In other words, the environment and the child are continually acting upon and changing one another. Thus, the experience of the child can have effects on the child's social, psychological, and biological development.

Scientists have investigated hormonal changes in maltreated children. The primary hormones studied reflect functioning of the sympathetic nervous system and of the hypothalamic-pituitary-adrenal (HPA) axis. The hormones released through sympathetic activation include epinephrine (adrenaline) and norepinephrine (noradrenaline). The hormones involved in the HPA axis include corticotropic releasing hormone (CRH), which stimulates the release of adrenocorticotropic hormone (ACTH), which in turn stimulates the release of cortisol. Furthermore, the HPA system has a circadian rhythm, with increased morning levels that continually decrease into the afternoon and evening. Both systems are activated as part of human physiological responses to stress, which suggests that they may be particularly vulnerable to change in reaction to the chronic stress of maltreatment.

Overall, the results vary widely from study to study. Of two studies noting ACTH changes in response to CRH in maltreated children, one found attenuated ACTH responses, while the other found increased ACTH responses. Several studies have investigated changes in cortisol secretion. In one study maltreated children exhibited a restricted range of morning cortisol secretion over thirty-one days, suggesting dampened tonic HPA activity. Another study indicated heightened afternoon cortisol levels in maltreated children. Two studies of depressed maltreated children have consistently found suppressed midmorning levels and either a rise or smaller decrease in afternoon levels. These studies indicate a flattened circadian rhythm of cortisol in maltreated children that is different from the usual diurnal decrease of cortisol noted in the general population. In a sample of sexually abused girls, however, morning cortisol levels were higher and afternoon levels lower than controls, suggesting a more marked diurnal decrease than is typical. Increased daily output of cortisol, norepinephrine, and epinephrine (averaged over twenty-four hours) has also been found in adult women with post-traumatic stress disorder (PTSD) secondary to childhood sexual abuse. These findings suggest that the development of PTSD in sexually abused girls may be related to increased HPA and sympathetic activation. Finally, in a study of children attending a clinic for severe disruptive behaviors, physically abused children did not differ overall from nonabused clinic controls in morning cortisol levels either before or after a stressful laboratory task. Patterns of individual differences were noted, however. Abused children with low basal cortisol levels and heightened reactivity to the laboratory stressor exhibited the highest rates of aggression in the clinic.

Although these studies do not indicate a clear pattern of hormonal changes in all maltreated children, one implication is clear: the hormones involved in HPA and sympathetic activation are different in maltreated children and nonmaltreated children. These studies suggest dysregulation of the HPA axis and physiological responsivity to stress in abused children. Such dysregulation may underlie vulnerability to behavioral and emotional problems as a consequence of the adversity of maltreatment.

BIBLIOGRAPHY

Hart, Jordan, et al. "Salivary Cortisol in Maltreated Children: Evidence of Relations Between Neuroendocrine Activity and Social Competence." *Development and Psychopathology* 7, no. 1 (Winter 1995).
———. "Altered Neuroendocrine Activity in Maltreated Children Related to Symptoms of Depression." *Development and Psychopathology* 8, no. 1 (winter 1995).
Lemieux, Andrine M., and Christopher L. Coe. "Abuse-Related Posttraumatic Stress Disorder: Evidence for Chronic Neuroendocrine Activation in Women." *Psychosomatic Medicine* 57 (1995).
Scarpa, Angela, and David J. Kolko. "Aggression in Physically Abused Children: The Role of Distress Proneness." *Annals of the New York Academy of Sciences* 794 (1996).

ANGELA SCARPA

See also **Child Abuse.**

PMS AND FEMALE VIOLENCE

Changes in the menstrual cycle, with particular focus on the premenstrual syndrome, have been explored as a biological factor associated with female violence. First coined by Katherina Dalton in 1953, the term *premenstrual syndrome* (PMS) refers to the cyclic recurrence of a cluster of behavioral and physical symptoms in the luteal phase—the phase between ovulation and the onset of menses (the menstrual flow). The symptoms typically begin to remit (or abate) within a few days of the onset of menses (the follicular phase) and are absent in the week following it. The more than one hundred symptoms that have been reported in association with PMS fall into five basic categories: (1) depression, including crying, confusion, social withdrawal, and insomnia; (2) anxiety, including impatience, irritability, mood swings, and nervousness; (3) pain, including backaches, breast tenderness, cramps, and joint and muscle pain; (4) water retention, including abdominal bloating, weight gain, and swelling; and (5) hypoglycemia, including craving sweets, increased appetite, fatigue, and headaches.

Although the types of symptoms and the degree of their severity vary from individual to individual, they occur during a specific and relatively constant period of the menstrual cycle and have a definite beginning and ending. A high proportion of women of reproductive age experience premenstrual emotional and physical changes. Estimates of the incidence of PMS range from 20 to 90 percent, depending on factors such as the definition of symptoms, sampling procedures, and research methodology. Efforts to define the diagnostic criteria of PMS more rigorously have resulted in suggestions for prospective documentation (that is, documentation kept on a daily basis rather than composed retrospectively from memory) and quantification of the level of symptom change for at least two consecutive months.

According to the *Diagnostic and Statistical Manual of Mental Disorders-IV* (American Psychiatric Association, 1994), when the behavioral and physical symptoms associated with PMS are of a level of severity that interferes with social or occupational functioning, they are classified as premenstrual dysphoric disorder (PMDD). An estimated 5 percent of reproductive-age women meet PMDD criteria. Typically, PMDD symptoms are of comparable severity (but not duration) to those of a major depressive episode. Depressed feelings and marked impairment in social or occupational functioning during the luteal phase are in great contrast to the mood and capabilities displayed during the rest of the month. A diagnosis of PMDD requires the presence of an affective symptom among other behavioral and physical symptoms and prospective daily self-ratings during at least two connective symptomatic cycles; symptoms must be present during the last week of the luteal phase and remit within a few days of the onset of the follicular phase. PMDD differs from PMS in its characteristic pattern of symptoms, their severity, and the resulting impairment.

Although the etiology of PMS and PMDD is unknown, the most widely accepted theories focus on hormonal changes, nutritional deficiencies, and stress. The primary method of treatment for most cases of PMS involves a combination of regular exercise, nutritional therapy, and avoidance of stress. More severe cases require drug therapy, including hormone treatments, antidepressants, sedatives, analgesics, and diuretics.

Diagnosing PMS and PMDD as clinical conditions has been controversial. Arguments both for and against doing so have been presented by feminists. On the one hand, acknowledging PMS and PMDD as clinical disorders would allow affected women to be treated; on the other hand, such acknowledgment may undermine efforts toward equal opportunities for women. Feminist scholars who question the validity and legitimacy of PMS as a true medical entity view it as socially constructed and specific to western culture. Some argue that the term *syndrome* connotes an abnormal condition and that, because PMS is so prevalent, it is the women who do not have PMS who are statistically abnormal.

An association between PMS and criminal behavior is supported by a number of investigations. Studies have shown that female criminal deviant behavior occurs most often within the eight-day paramenstruum phase—the four premenstrual days and the first four days of menstruation. Often cited as evidence of a connection between PMS and crime, Katherina Dalton's influential studies in the 1960s found that 49 percent of the crimes committed by a sample of female prison inmates took place within the paramenstruum phase and 63 percent during the premenstrual phase. Another study indicated that of the inmates who had been reported for behavioral problems within the prison, 54 percent displayed these problems during the paramenstruum phase. An association between PMS and the infliction of physical and verbal abuse on others was also found among prison inmates. Other studies reported that women make more suicide attempts and are more likely to succeed in committing suicide during the premenstrual phase. So convincing was Dalton's research that several legal cases were won on the basis of PMS as the causal factor in violent crimes.

The use of menstrual-cycle changes as a legal defense dates back to 1833, when it was used in the defense of a woman accused of pyromania. Several legal cases in England during the late 1970s and the 1980s were won on the basis of PMS as an extenuating factor in violent crimes. In each case, the PMS defense was accepted in mitigation of punishment. A PMS defense has been used successfully in some state civil cases in the United States; however, it has not been tested in a criminal case.

Much of the research that linked PMS to female crime was based on self-reported data collected retrospectively with highly variable definitions of the syndrome. Some of the research focused on special populations, including prisoners and patients in mental institutions, so the extent to which such findings can be generalized to the average, cycling female is questionable. The most widely recognized symptomatology of PMS and PMDD does not include violent or aggressive acts, and even among those with severe symptoms, the number involved with violent crimes is small. Despite its reported association with female violence, few experts consider PMS an important factor in female violence and point instead to individual, social, and economic factors as more significant.

BIBLIOGRAPHY

Birnbaum, Carol, and Lee Cohen. "The Psychiatric Evaluation and Treatment of Premenstrual Dysphoric Disorder." In *Challenges in Clinical Practice: Pharmacologic and Psychosocial Strategies*, edited by Mark H. Pollack, Michael W. Otto, and Jerrold F. Rosenbaum. New York: Guilford Press, 1996.

Cowen, Barbara. "Women and Crime." In *Violence and the Prevention of Violence*, edited by Leonore Loeb Adler and Florence L. Denmark. Westport, Conn.: Praeger, 1995.

Dalton, Katherina. *The Premenstrual Syndrome*. Springfield, Ill.: Charles C. Thomas, 1964.

Lewis, James W. "Premenstrual Syndrome as a Criminal Defense." *Archives of Sexual Behavior* 19, no. 5 (1990).

Rittenhouse, C. Amanda. "The Emergence of Premenstrual Syndrome as a Social Problem." *Social Problems* 38, no. 3 (1991).

HSIU-ZU HO

See also **Sex Differences; Women.**

TESTOSTERONE

The belief that the testes promote virile behavior largely predates the 1889 report by the seventy-two-year-old physiologist Charles-Édouard Brown-Séquard about his rejuvenation following self-injections of extracts of dog or guinea pig testicles. Later evidence for the effect of testosterone on physical aggression stems from rodent studies: the depletion of testosterone by castration and its replacement by injection in male neonates significantly affect aggression in adulthood. Similar studies with nonhuman primates and humans were not as conclusive. Although some influence of testosterone on human physical aggression has been suggested, it is difficult to disentangle it from other influences, such as social dominance and sexual behavior.

Testosterone in Human Development

Testosterone is mainly produced by the testes and regulated by the hypothalamic-pituitary-gonadal axis. By ten to twelve weeks of gestation, males have higher levels of testosterone than females. Fetal testosterone secretion influences the development of male secondary sexual characteristics and has long-term effects on behavior. Human female fetuses exposed to high levels of androgens (because of adrenocortical dysfunction or maternal drug treatment) can later evince masculinized genitals and display male-oriented social or play activities and cognitive abilities.

The postnatal course of testosterone is different for females and males. At birth, females have plasma testosterone levels similar to adult females, but these levels decrease rapidly and reappear only at puberty. Relative to females, males have higher birth levels of plasma testosterone, which decrease rapidly one week after birth and increase again from the second week. By the second month, they reach mid-adolescence levels (i.e., half the adult levels). Male testosterone levels then decrease until the seventh month, when no sex differences can be noted. These differences reappear only at puberty. It has been suggested that sex differences in testosterone during postnatal months influence further sexual differentiation of the hypothalamus and account for behavioral sexualization. Between the ages of seven and ten to twelve, testosterone is mainly produced by the adrenal glands and rises slightly in both males and females. Male levels of plasma testosterone (in nanomols per liter) rise sharply with puberty from a mean of 0.28 at eight years to 4 around thirteen years, 15 by sixteen years, and 20 at the end of adolescence. The rise of female testosterone during puberty is much less spectacular. At eight years, both sexes evince similar levels; by the end of adolescence, female levels fluctuate according to the menstrual cycle between 0.75 and 1.28. At the end of a pregnancy, a woman's average testosterone levels reach 2.35. The pubertal rise of testosterone is highly correlated with the growth of genital organs, the differentiation of secondary sexual characteristics, and somatic growth. Sexual motivation and behavior also parallel the increase in testosterone, but no clear causal link between testosterone increase and development of sexual motivation and behavior has been shown. However, synthetic testosterone is used to treat certain conditions in males (e.g., delayed puberty, hypogonadism, impotence, lack of libido, aging) and females (e.g., breast tumors, lack of libido, aging). It has also been extensively used in both sexes for its anabolyzing properties in the building up of, for example, muscle tissue.

Testosterone and Aggression During Adulthood

A low, but significant, association between testosterone levels and measures of aggressiveness has been noticed in adults (in comparative studies of samples selected for high or low aggressiveness, as well as in correlational studies in nonselected samples). Experiments probing for variations in violent behavior following manipulation of testosterone levels are difficult to conduct in humans. It has been easier to demonstrate that controlled life experiences can modulate an individual's level of testosterone. For example, winning a competition (e.g., a tennis or a chess match) increases testosterone levels. Studies on nonhuman primates and adult humans indicate that the impact of stress on the hypothalamic-pituitary-gonadal axis may mediate competition-related testosterone fluctuations. Thus, the testosterone-aggressiveness relation evidenced in comparative and correlational studies may result from the complex interplay of hypothalamic-pituitary-gonadal physiology, dominance behavior, stress, and physical aggression.

The Need to Define Aggression

A major problem in clarifying the aggression-testosterone link has been the definition of *aggression* used. Boxers or tennis and chess players can all be ranked on an aggressivity continuum. In this context, the term *aggressive* usually means assertive, energetic, and vigorous, a behavioral style characterized by attacking the opponent rather than taking a defensive position. This aggressivity concept may also be applied to the style of a politician during an election campaign, a board chairman, a court lawyer, a scientist, or a car salesman. This assertive style is often considered a key to success; that is, it leads to social dominance. The link between testosterone and aggressive behavior must be differentiated from the link between testosterone and physically violent behavior. Unfortunately, most studies of human aggression, including those focused on the link between aggression and testosterone, have not clearly differentiated aggressive individuals who prefer physical aggression as a means of solving problems from aggressive individuals who use other means of achieving their goals. An aggressive-assertive behavioral style is generally considered an asset in modern societies, whereas physical aggression is generally condemned.

Testosterone and Aggression During Childhood and Adolescence

That adolescence is the best time to study the influence of testosterone changes on aggressive behavior is a recurrent suggestion. Over the pubertal years, male testosterone levels are multiplied by a factor of 20. If increased testosterone levels lead to more frequent physical aggression, a substantial increase of physical aggression should be observed during adolescence. Official criminal statistics indicate that prosecution for violent crimes increases from early to late adolescence. However, this phenomenon could be attributed to a number of factors other than increased testosterone levels. For example, courts may selectively prosecute older adolescents. As they grow older, adolescents also have more opportunities for socially unacceptable behavior because of weaker parental supervision, increased involvement in deviant groups and access to weapons, and stronger competition for mates. To a certain extent, all these changes are related to pubertal maturation, which is strongly associated with increased levels of testosterone. However, none of the few longitudinal studies (that is, those involving repeated observation or examination of a set of subjects) of adolescents shows clear evidence that the increase in testosterone, rather than the increase in height, physical

strength, cognitive abilities, or liberty to roam, leads to the increase in prosecutions for violent offenses.

There is in fact good evidence that the frequency of physical aggression decreases rather than increases during adolescence. Longitudinal studies from early childhood through adolescence show a steady decline in the frequency of physical aggression. The highest frequency of physical aggression for both males and females is observed around age twenty-four months. As they become socialized, most children learn to use means other than physical aggression to dominate, that is, to gain access to what they want or to retaliate. There is a small proportion of children who apparently do not learn to inhibit physically aggressive responses. Longitudinal studies reveal that chronic physically aggressive adolescents and adults were generally those who had not learned to inhibit physically aggressive behavior during childhood.

Developmental studies of physical aggression from early childhood to adulthood challenge the simple idea that increased levels of testosterone lead to increased levels of physical aggression. Testosterone levels are at their lowest at two years and at their highest at eighteen years. Studies of aggression in two-year-olds count the frequency of physically aggressive acts within periods of fifteen minutes, while similar studies in adolescents count them over periods of twelve months. If the pubertal testosterone increase explains adolescent and adult physical aggression, it becomes difficult to explain why physically aggressive adolescents and adults were already showing chronic patterns of physical aggression during childhood.

The Need for Further Research

There is no clear evidence that an increase in testosterone level directly leads to an increase in physical aggression. However, adolescent and adult studies suggest that individuals with a history of physically violent behavior tend to have higher levels of testosterone than individuals without such a trajectory. The origin of this association is multifactorial. Testosterone levels result from multiple, interactive determinants, including genetic factors, perinatal factors, age, daily and seasonal rhythms, food, physical activity, substance use, sexual behavior, stress, and social dominance status. Physical aggression among humans is most frequent in early childhood, when testosterone levels are at their lowest. During the preschool years most children learn to control their physical aggression. Those who do not are at high risk of becoming chronically violent adolescents and adults. It may be more difficult for males with high perinatal levels of testosterone to learn to control physical aggression in early childhood. The more a child has a neuroendocrine system that favors assertive and vigorous behavior, the more the environment must be supportive of his or her achieving control over physically aggressive actions or reactions during the first three or four years after birth, when this control is generally learned. This developmental process may explain why physically aggressive preschoolers who become physically aggressive adolescents and adults have higher levels of testosterone. One would also expect higher levels of adolescent and adult testosterone in physically aggressive preschoolers who learned alternatives to physical aggression. Unfortunately, there have been very few studies of testosterone levels during the perinatal period, when testosterone has a strong organizational impact on the nervous system, and no longitudinal studies on the links among perinatal testosterone levels, early childhood physical aggression, and later chronic physical aggression. These studies will be necessary to elucidate the role testosterone plays in the development of physically violent behavior.

BIBLIOGRAPHY

Archer, John. "Testosterone and Aggression." *Journal of Offender Rehabilitation* 21, no. 3–4 (1994).

Farrington, David P. "Childhood, Adolescent, and Adult Features of Violent Males." In *Aggressive Behavior: Current Perspectives,* edited by L. Rowell Huesmann. New York: Plenum, 1994.

Forest, Maguelone G. "Physiological Changes in Circulating Androgens." In *Androgens in Childhood: Biological, Physiological, Clinical, and Therapeutic Aspects.* Vol. 19, edited by Maguelone G. Forest. Basel, Switzerland: Karger, 1989.

Hoberman, John M., and Charles E. Yesali. "The History of Synthetic Testosterone." *Scientific American* 272 (1995).

Mazur, Allan, and Alan Booth. "Testosterone and Dominance in Men." *Behavioral and Brain Sciences* 21, no. 3 (1998).

Tremblay, Richard Ernest, et al. "Male Physical Aggression, Social Dominance, and Testosterone Levels at Puberty: A Developmental Perspective." In *Biosocial Bases of Violence,* edited by Adrian Raine et al. New York: Plenum, 1997.

Tremblay, Richard Ernest, et al. "Do Children in Canada Become More Aggressive as They Approach Adolescence?" In *Growing Up in Canada: National Longitudinal Survey of Children and Youth/Grandir au Canada: Enquête longitudinale nationale sur les enfants et les jeunes.* Vol. 1, edited by Human Resources Development Canada and Statistics Canada. Ottawa: Statistics Canada, 1996.

RICHARD E. TREMBLAY
BENOIST SCHAAL

See also **Developmental Factors: Puberty and Adolescence; Gender; Masculinity; Sex Differences.**

ENFORCEMENT ACTS

During the approximately twelve years of Reconstruction (1865–1877), as the United States adjusted to the end of slavery, three constitutional amendments sought to establish the rights of national citizens, white and black, and to make those national rights enforceable upon and within the states. In the Thirteenth Amendment of 1865, the Fourteenth Amendment of 1868, and the Fifteenth Amendment of 1870, Congress included an enforcement clause giving itself the "power to enforce, by appropriate legislation" the new constitutional laws. But white southerners resisted these attempts to establish black rights. White southerners hoped to preserve their social traditions; they hoped to redeem their state governments from northerners, Republicans, and blacks and reestablish law and order—that is, white law and black order.

Extralegal groups that began as harmless fraternal organizations of Confederate Army veterans soon became political actors in this redemption effort. In effect, the night-riding Ku Klux Klan and Knights of the White Camelia and other such groups (riders on horseback disguised in hoods or masks) became, in the words of the historian James M. McPherson, "armed auxiliaries of the Democratic party." Because voting rights implied equality with whites, the Klan intimidated blacks to prevent them from exercising suffrage. Blacks, as well as white Republicans, were threatened, physically assaulted, and sometimes even murdered. Terrorist tactics proved so successful in the 1868 elections that the Klan managed to limit Republican turnout at the polls in Louisiana, Georgia, Arkansas, and Tennessee. In Opelousas, Louisiana, in St. Landry Parish, a race riot killed more than two hundred blacks, and in the following November elections not a single Republican vote was cast in the parish.

How to control the Klan and protect white and black Republicans posed a dilemma for state officials, especially since in many states, members of the Klan were also members of the state militia. Often the state militias opposed the Republican-controlled state governments and worked to undermine those governments. In some states with Reconstruction Republican governments, such as South Carolina, governors established black state militias to keep order. Yet Reconstruction governors were reluctant to deploy black militias for fear of sparking worse outbreaks of violence. Further, most state militias were infantrymen who simply could not catch the mounted Klan members. Effective state action against the Klan occurred in only a few states with white militias. In Arkansas, Governor Powell Clayton declared martial law, relied on loyal militia companies, and tried Klansmen in military courts (to avoid sympathetic juries); the state executed several convicted Klan members. North Carolina's Governor William W. Holden was not as successful. Democrats impeached and removed him from office for declaring martial law and prosecuting Klansmen.

First Enforcement Act

Failure at the state level to control the widespread unpunished violence led to pressure for federal action. Congress responded by passing civil rights acts known as the Force or Enforcement Acts. On 31 May 1870, Congress passed the first Enforcement Act (*U.S. Statutes at Large* 16, 140) pursuant to the enforcement clauses of the Fourteenth and Fifteenth Amendments. This act made it a federal offense for state election officials to discriminate against voters on the basis of color. Bribery and intimidation of voters by private persons became a federal offense, which was a new development in American federalism. Aimed at the Klan, section 6 of this act made it a felony to conspire or ride the public highways to deprive any citizen of "any right or privilege granted or secured to him by the Constitution or laws of the United States." In its most controversial provision, section 7 extended federal power over actions and crimes which previously had been solely the concern of the states by making it a federal felony to deprive another person of civil or political rights. For example, if a Klansman committed a murder, he would be charged in federal court with violating the deceased person's civil rights, not with homicide, which was a traditionally state-defined crime. Also under section 7, the state-defined penalty for the crime determined the punishment for a civil rights violation; in other words, federal courts could prescribe the death penalty, the state punishment for murder, for a violation of a person's civil rights.

Second Enforcement Act

Although this law was strong on paper, President Ulysses S. Grant and Attorney General E. Rockwood Hoar initiated few prosecutions under it. When unpunished assaults continued—and grew especially fierce in North and South Carolina—the Grant administration asked Congress for further legislation. On 28 February 1871, Congress passed and Grant signed the Second Enforcement Act (*U.S. Statutes at Large* 16, 433), which placed under direct federal supervision congressional elections in cities of more than twenty thousand persons. Normally, states control congressional elections, but under this legislation Congress assumed direct control over its elections within states.

Third Enforcement Act

Grant's administration requested further power to deal with lawlessness in the Carolinas, and Congress responded on 20 April 1871 by passing the Third Enforcement Act, popularly known as the Ku Klux Klan Act (*U.S. Statutes at Large* 17, 13). This act has been described as "the most far-reaching assertion of federal legislative power to enforce civil rights in the Reconstruction Era." It provided a civil, federal remedy to individuals deprived of their constitutional rights by private persons. Further, the Third Enforcement Act authorized the president to use federal and state military forces to suppress domestic insurrections when states were unable or unwilling to do so. Furthering this iron-fist approach, the act empowered the president to determine when a rebellion was in existence and allowed him to suspend the writ of habeas corpus (which provides the right to a hearing before a judge to inquire into the legality of one's imprisonment or arrest) in such areas. In order to purge juries of Klansmen, the Third Enforcement Act required that every federal juror take an oath that he had not voluntarily or involuntarily taken part in Klan activities. In practice, this oath excluded almost all southern white Democrats from federal jury service and filled juries with southern white Republicans and blacks. This act dramatically expanded federal authority to act directly on individuals within states, which further altered traditional boundaries of American federalism.

On 12 October 1871, armed with this new statute, Grant and his new attorney general, Amos T. Ackerman, issued a proclamation disbanding all illegal conspiracies and urging persons to turn in their weapons to federal authorities. Grant followed this proclamation with a second one on 17 November in which he declared nine counties in the upcountry of South Carolina in rebellion and suspended habeas corpus in those counties. Assisted by the Seventh Cavalry, federal marshals arrested large numbers of suspected Klansmen. Hundreds fled the region or disappeared into the mountains to avoid the anti-Klan sweep. More than three thousand people were indicted by the federal grand jury; of these, several hundred pleaded guilty and received suspended sentences. In time, the federal government dropped charges against approximately two thousand of those indicted, in large part to clear the clogged federal court dockets. Of the 600 major offenders tried, juries acquitted about 250. Most of the persons who were found guilty received short jail sentences, but sixty-five of them served up to five years in the federal prison in Albany, New York, for violating civil rights.

Grant's actions and this far-reaching statute achieved their goals: the Klan collapsed and relative domestic peace returned as night-riding dramatically decreased throughout the South. Resistance to black rights and voting did not cease, but unpunished violence against black voters and their white supporters slowed, at least for some time.

Three persons convicted under the Enforcement Acts appealed their convictions to the U.S. Supreme Court. In *United States v. Hiram Reese*, 92 U.S. 214 (1876), the Court held that the Enforcement Act of 1870 unconstitutionally placed elections under federal oversight because the Fifteenth Amendment did not grant the right to vote to anyone; control of suffrage stayed with the states. That same year, the Supreme Court in *United States v. Cruikshank*, 92 U.S. 542 (1876) announced its state-action doctrine: the Fourteenth Amendment authorized federal intervention only in cases where direct state action denied rights. Ordinary private criminal actions, without a showing of racial bias, could not be reached through the Fourteenth Amendment or the Enforcement Acts. Lastly, the Court decided in *United States v. R. G. Harris*, 106 U.S. 629 (1883), that indictments brought under the Ku Klux Klan Act were invalid because those indictments affected private persons, not actions by the state or its officers. Plaintiffs had to demonstrate that the state, acting through its officers, had denied citizens their federal rights, and punishment of routine assaults between private persons was left to the states.

After Reconstruction

Democratic Congresses repealed much of the Enforcement Acts in 1894 and 1909, but the prohibitions against night-riding and conspiracies to deprive citizens of rights survived. Civil lawsuits contending the denial of citizens' federal rights at the state level were brought under the vestige of the Enforcement Acts in the key statute of *U.S. Code*, vol. 28, sec. 1983.

BIBLIOGRAPHY

Hyman, Harold M., and William M. Wiecek. *Equal Justice Under Law: Constitutional Development, 1835–1875.* New York: Harper and Row, 1982.

Kaczorowski, Robert J. *The Politics of Judicial Interpretation: The Federal Courts, Department of Justice, and Civil Rights, 1866–1876.* New York: Oceana, 1985.

Williams, Lou Falkner. *The Great South Carolina Ku Klux Klan Trials, 1871–1872.* Athens: University of Georgia Press, 1996.

THOMAS C. MACKEY

See also **Civil Liberties; Government Commissions; Ku Klux Klan.**

ENVIRONMENT, VIOLENCE AGAINST

What exactly constitutes "violence against the environment"? The term *the environment* was broadly circulated in the 1960s in response to a series of crises in the supply of natural resources; that decade also saw the consequent rise of the environmental movement. The environment today is of course a buzzword, conjuring images ranging from beached whales to Sierra Club lobbyists to edenic images of the rain forest. Generally, the environment refers to the spheres inhabited by human beings, wildlife, and vegetation, but also to the earth's protective atmospheric layer and to other "natural," that is, nonhuman, entities such as rocks and soil. In the more technical sense the environment refers to the totality of physiochemical and social phenomena that surround a given organism and that affect as well as are affected by it. The size of a given environment cannot be delineated with any exact precision because organisms are generally on the move and different environments are constantly overlapping. Sometimes the terms *habitat* and *ecosystem* are seen as synonymous with environment; but they connote smaller, more specific areas. Every species transforms its environment through subsistence. In this respect no species has had a greater impact on the environment than humans.

Violence that results from "natural" (i.e., non-human) force, such as a hurricane, does not pertain to this discussion. It is violence in the sense of "abusive or unjust exercise of power" (as defined in the *American Heritage Dictionary*) that most closely applies to environmental issues. Sometimes what appears to be violence against the environment is actually a good and necessary thing, as when the U.S. Forest Service practices controlled burning in the national forests in order to create the ash that replenishes the soil and prepares the ground for future growth. Normally humans do not willingly or consciously damage or destroy the nonhuman world; they extract its natural resources in order to survive. But when the carrying capacity of an environment is exceeded—when an organism consumes too much of its environment's resources so that it cannot survive in its habitat over the long run—then an "abusive or unjust exercise of power" results and violence against the environment is committed.

The developed nations of the world are gluttonous consumers of fossil fuels, foods, and water; it has been documented that the average American today consumes eighty times more energy resources per year than the average resident of the sub-Sahara. During the Industrial Revolution the consumption of the earth's resources grew exponentially. In the modern era the environmental movement arose in response to the fear of depletion of the earth's resources. It is environmentalism—defined here as an ethical, political, and social movement that argues on behalf of the health, harmony, and integrity of the natural environment—that has led to the recognition of the problem of violence against the environment. Environmental philosophy, an outgrowth of environmentalism, has led the way in arguing for the existence of ethical values inherent in the nonhuman world. To speak of violence against something is to presume that it has been wronged, that is, that it has certain rights of existence. Laws like the Endangered Species Act recognize that species other than humans have the right to exist. "To love what *was* is a new thing under the sun," wrote Aldo Leopold in 1949 (p. 112), in telling of the extinction of the passenger pigeon, a species that once numbered, it is estimated, three to five billion.

Reasons for Environmental Degradation

Degradation of the environment is not a modern phenomenon. Evidence suggests that tribes

---

Mass Extinction

Since the birth of the Earth some five billion years ago paleoecologists have been able to document five separate waves of mass extinction, each occurring about every fifty million years. The most famous is the extinction of dinosaurs, theorized to have been caused by the collision of a meteor with Earth approximately sixty-five million years ago during the Cretaceous period. The resulting dust cloud blocked the rays of the sun and cooled the planet's temperature by several degrees, wiping out virtually all of the giant reptiles who could not adapt quickly enough to changing global temperatures.

An even greater mass extinction took place some 250 million years ago, at the end of the Permian period, when 96 percent of all species disappeared. One estimate has it that of the billion species that once inhabited the earth, 99.9 percent of them are now extinct as a result of nonhuman causes. Clearly, however, the latest wave of mass extinction, or biodepletion, is occurring at a much faster rate than during any previous period—perhaps as much as one hundred to one thousand times the previous natural levels.

---

that inhabited what is now North America ten to twenty thousand years ago at times overexploited their own environments. Extinction of certain megafauna through overhunting occurred during the Ice Age. Prior to contact with Euroamericans, certain Native cultures on the Great Plains wasted enormous numbers of bison at kill sites.

In 1967, in a controversial article that has sparked debate ever since, the historian Lynn White, Jr., argued that Christianity is the primary cause of environmental degradation. As White put it, Christianity, because of the language in Genesis granting humans the power to have "dominion" over the earth and its resources, is "the most anthropocentric religion the world has seen." Christian conquest of the Western Hemisphere made it possible "to exploit nature in a mood of indifference to the feeling of natural objects" (p. 32). White's interpretation remains compelling. It can be argued that this particular religious worldview, together with improved technology resulting from the scientific and industrial revolutions and the effective separation of humans from nature, gave us the incentive to increase our exploitation and consumption of natural resources at an exorbitant rate.

The birth of Manifest Destiny—authorizing Americans to proceed westward across the continent as part of their divine mission as a country—is a cultural explanation of why the United States in particular has enacted such violence against the environment. Yet the United States has not been the sole country to commit "sins" against the environment through expansion of its national boundaries; colonialism, defined as the takeover of other cultures' land, people, and resources, is as old as humankind. Furthermore, no single economic system—capitalism, socialism, and so on—has exerted a monopoly on environmental degradation.

A more basic, behavioral, explanation for environmental degradation has been offered by Garret Hardin in a famous essay entitled "The Tragedy of the Commons." Hardin argued that human individuals seek short-term private benefit, even when it is disadvantageous to the community at large. Thus (as the situation existed in ancient Britain), sheepherders who might have refrained from grazing their flock on publicly owned land—"the commons"—because of the prospect of overgrazing would nevertheless do so to prevent others from taking advantage of their own altruism. The result is that the commons suffers degradation through everyone's greed until it no longer can sustain a population. In the larger application of the commons metaphor, then, the earth itself becomes the commons or shared resource, with all the world's population, nations, and cultures competing for its resources. As the world's population grows, the size of the commons remains the same or even shrinks because of overuse and nonsustainable practices; thus the environment suffers increased degradation.

Practices that have resulted in violence against the environment include agriculture, the building of dams, and mining; these, along with the related problems of water and air pollution and the handling of hazardous wastes, are discussed here in turn. Before discussing the future of environmental problems, tactics, and attitudes, the subject of the endangerment and extinction of species is treated as an especially significant outcome of violence against the environment.

Agriculture

Agriculture, which dates back to the Neolithic revolution ten thousand years ago, has done more to alter the earth's environment than any other form of human activity. Today agricultural land occupies 37 percent of the world's total land mass. Over the years it has deleteriously affected the environment in a number of ways. Wildlife habitat has been eliminated, contributing to the decline of some species (e.g., the American bison) and the extinction of others (e.g., the passenger pigeon). Farming also contributes to soil degradation in the forms of nutrient exhaustion, erosion, and salinization. Agricultural pollution occurs with the production of animal wastes and, in the modern era, chemical fertilizers, pesticides, and herbicides. Finally, agriculture was the pivotal factor in bringing about the most profound human impact of all on the environment: significant population increases. While the population of hunter-gatherer societies is generally limited by the food supply to about one person per square mile, farming in the twentieth century has allowed the human population to grow to more than two hundred times as dense.

The Colonial Period. The gradual replacement of Eastern Woodlands tribes of Native Americans by English settlers in the seventeenth and eighteenth centuries transformed the New England landscape from one of forests and meadows to one of fields and fences. The change in land-use practices from hunting and gathering to farming led to the eventual dispossession and decline of the region's indigenous peoples and the wreaking of ecological havoc. True, native cultures had certainly manipulated their environment prior to the arrival of Europeans in various ways, such as through the hunting and trapping of fur-bearing mammals and the deliberate use of fire to create clearings in the forest for hunting and horticultural purposes. But their impacts on the New England ecology were minimal compared to the effects of Old World practices applied to the New World landscape. Unlike in England, where land was scarce and labor plentiful, New England colonists encountered an abundance of "free" land and sparse populations. Farmers thus resorted to the easiest, and most wasteful, techniques to clear the forests for crops: girdling the trees or burning them outright.

By the 1850s as much as three-fourths of southern New England had been deforested. Deforestation eventually led to a warmer climate (because of the elimination of the temperature-moderating effects of the tree canopy), increased erosion and sedimentation, and the reduction of wildlife. The introduction of grazing animals such as cattle and hogs led to further impacts on the forest, since grazing required fenced pasture lands and wood provided the cheapest material for fencing. Corn, the most important crop Indians taught the English how to plant, increasingly became the dominant staple in the colonies' growing participation in an international market economy; the resulting practice of monoculture caused soil exhaustion (no other grain puts such nutrient demands on the soil). All in all, "ecological abundance and economic prodigality went hand in hand: the people of plenty were a people of waste" (Cronon 1983, p. 170).

Following independence from Britain and expansion westward, the pattern of ecological abundance and economic prodigality was repeated endlessly. The Land Ordnance of 1785 stipulated that land be surveyed and sold in mile-square sections, eventually leading to a pattern of squares and rectangles imposed on much of the American landscape, as a cross-continental flight today reveals. Over the next hundred years, a series of inventions resulted in massive transformation of the Great Plains from prairie to farmland: Cyrus McCormick's reaper and the steel plow in the 1830s; the gasoline tractor by the turn of the century; and dry farming techniques permitting the planting of wheat and other crops on land where less than the required twenty inches of annual rainfall occurred. The Homestead Act of 1862, allowing settlers to own 160 acres of land if they farmed it for five years, further encouraged westward expansion and agriculture.

The 1930s. Overfarming along with a period of severe drought led to what has become known as the "Dirty Thirties," "the most severe environmental catastrophe in the entire history of the white man on this continent" (Worster 1979, p. 24). As the native prairie grasses that held the land together were broken and replaced by farmland, desertification resulted when rain failed to fall and wind blew away the topsoil. About one-third of the Great Plains, totaling nearly a hundred million acres, was affected, and in 1938, the worst year of wind erosion, more than four hundred tons of dirt blew away from the average acre of cultivated land. In May 1934 the dust blew with such intensity and volume that Washington, D.C., was engulfed by black clouds—even as President Franklin D. Roosevelt was convening his cabinet to address the issue. The administration responded with an infusion of New Deal dollars for soil conservation; the Plains residents' response was often emigration further westward, with a mass exodus of over a million to California (as portrayed in John Steinbeck's *The Grapes of Wrath*). Donald Worster argues that the chief cause of the Dust Bowl was not drought but capitalism, the same economic mindset that had led to the Depression: "a capitalist-based society has a greater resource hunger than others, greater eagerness to take risks, and less capacity for restraint" (1979, p. 7).

Post–World War II. Following World War II, further technological advances were made that once again revolutionized farming practices and worsened environmental degradation. Pesticides, herbicides, and cheap fertilizers became widely available, resulting in broadcast applications of each; since 1945 the use of synthetic pesticides, for example, has risen thirty-three fold. The benefits of these chemicals has been substantial: DDT helped to eliminate mosquito transmission of malaria by 1953; yields for key crops such as corn, wheat, and cotton more than doubled between 1945 and 1965; and food prices in the United States have dropped to the lowest percentage of family expenditures of any country in the world. Yet there have been concomitant harms. Pesticide use in the United States has resulted in approximately sixty-seven thousand poisonings and six to ten thousand cancer cases, with as many as twenty-seven accidental deaths, every year. Domestic animals are also poisoned, along with wildlife (e.g., wild bees, fish, and birds). A common form of contamination occurs through seepage into groundwater supplies. And while pesticides have undoubtedly reduced crop losses in specific cases, the share of crop yields lost to insects overall almost doubled from 1940 to 1990—despite more than a tenfold increase in both the amount and toxicity of synthetic insecticides applied. Overall, the known costs of environmental harms resulting from pesticides amounts to $8 billion each year. Rachel Carson's *Silent Spring* (1962), an exposé of the harms of indiscriminate use of pesticides, is generally regarded as signaling the birth of the modern environmental movement; and although the book did eventually result in the ban of DDT in the United States in 1972, violence against the environment in the form of pesticides remains a major problem. Worldwide, the development and application of pesticides continues to grow, especially in developing countries.

The herbicide Agent Orange (a combination of 2,4-D and 2,4-T) illustrates the problems resulting from indiscriminate use. Originally developed in 1945 to kill broadleaf plants but not grass and related grain crops, it was recognized as a potentially important weed killer and used as such on thousands of farms in this country. In the 1960s, during the escalation of the Vietnam War, the U.S. military decided to employ it to defoliate vast areas of South Vietnam in order to expose the activities of communist guerrilla forces and destroy their agricultural fields. Agent Orange was eventually sprayed over nearly 9 percent of the total surface area of South Vietnam. However, the strategy failed miserably in two ways: not only were the communist forces unfazed by the broadcast application, it also resulted in the contamination of many U.S. soldiers.

Another way modern agriculture contributes to environmental degradation is through fertilizers and animal waste. Farms are a major source of "nonpoint" pollution in that the way they contaminate the earth, water, and air is diffuse and scattered. And because of its episodic, unpredictable discharges, farm pollution is a difficult form of contamination to control. The exponential growth in application of fertilizers containing nitrogen and phosphorus since World War II has led to their leaching out into streams and rivers and to the consequent eutrophication (oxygen-deprivation) of waterways. Feedlots are another source of pollution. Where domestic animals such as cattle, pigs, and turkeys are raised and fattened in enclosed spaces for eventual slaughter, the concentration and runoff of animal waste is enormous. This form of nonpoint pollution also contributes to eutrophication of rivers and contamination of groundwater supplies.

There are those who argue that the growth of U.S. agribusiness has been the root cause of environmental harms caused by agriculture. Wendell Berry, a leading critic of modern agribusiness, argues that the bigger-is-better mentality of government, science, and the farming industry has led to a shocking degree of agricultural violence against the environment. Even as farm output doubled since the 1950s, the number of farms has fallen from 5.6 to 2.4 million, and the farming population has shrunk from 23 to 6 million (from 15 percent to 2.7 percent of the population). Worse, the top 15 percent of the farms in terms of size produced almost 80 percent of total farm income by the mid-1990s. Critics such as Berry maintain that the ecological and social costs are inextricably connected: "a generalization of the relationship between peo-

ple and the land" (p. 33) has led to a lack of concern for humans and the consequences of farmer's actions against the environment.

Remedial actions have been taken. For example, scientific research has been conducted to employ safer applications of pesticides along with more natural means of controlling pests. More farmers practice no-till farming as a means of reducing sedimentation of streams and erosion. An organic farm movement, originating in the 1970s, has spread among a minority of farmers to practice and preach a more environmentally friendly means of agriculture. Farmers have been encouraged to take environmentally valuable lands (such as wetlands) out of production. Awareness of the environmental problems caused by agriculture is slowly mounting, so that today a movement known as sustainable agriculture is clearly evident—though it remains a minority force within international agribusiness as a whole.

Dams

Over millennia and around the world, dams have been built by various cultures to irrigate crops and provide drinking water, to generate hydroelectric power, to foster navigation, and to control flooding. Dams on the whole produce less environmental damage than nuclear power or coal-fired generators as a source of electricity, but they have not been without environmental and social consequences. Dams result in the decline of riverine habitat and biodiversity, as well as invasion of exotic species; increased sedimentation and eutrophication; displacement of human settlements; and aesthetic loss as wild rivers are replaced by stagnant reservoirs.

In 1902, when the U.S. government passed the Reclamation Act, dam construction—especially in the American West—began to accelerate, causing a myriad of environmental problems and a growing controversy over the advantages and disadvantages of dams. It was out of conflict over the building of a dam in Yosemite National Park that the modern conservation movement emerged in the early twentieth century as a major U.S. social and political movement. The 1902 Reclamation Act, which federalized state water-reclamation projects, allowing dam-building to proceed on a massive scale, was passed in response to a series of severe droughts in the late nineteenth century that afflicted farmers and ranchers in the arid West. Congressmen representing western states feared that further settlement could not occur until an adequate and dependable water supply was in place. At this time Progressives, who believed that the government's duty was to make the most efficient use of our natural resources for the greatest number of its citizens, influenced policy. Thus the federal government essentially established a system of socialized state irrigation to help farmers and ranchers succeed in the West; the great dam construction projects were further stimulated by the advent of the Depression thirty years later and the New Deal response to unemployment. Theodore Roosevelt Dam on the Salt River in Arizona; Hoover Dam on the Colorado River in Nevada; Grand Coulee Dam on the Columbia River in Washington; Glen Canyon Dam on the Colorado River in Arizona: these are the greatest monuments to a sixty-year era of epic construction.

By 1978 the Census of Agriculture reported that there were over forty-five million acres of irrigated land in the western United States, amounting to one-tenth of the world's total. But even before this time, environmentalists had begun to raise the question, what destruction had progress wrought? At various times and locations, dams have been to blame for massive flooding, entailing death of humans and animals and destruction of property; poisoning of humans and animals by pesticides applied to irrigated farmlands surrounding dams; and higher levels of salinization—the increased concentration of salt in the soil that occurs when groundwater evaporates—rendering water undrinkable and unsuitable for agricultural purposes. Dams have galvanized the environmental movement in at least two important ways. Proposed dam projects within national parks caused environmentalists to band together to lobby Congress to vote down dam projects. In the 1950s in Colorado the Bureau of Reclamation proposed a dam in Echo Park within Dinosaur National Monument for hydroelectric purposes. Environmentalists protested that a spectacular series of canyons would be destroyed. Conservationists won the battle in an effort that served as a crucible for the emerging post–World War II environmental movement in the United States. Wilderness recreation and aesthetics took precedence over utility.

The celebrated case of the snail darter in Tennessee in the 1970s expanded the argument against dams to include not only aesthetic and recreational losses but biological losses as well. The identification of a tiny fish found in no other waters but the Little Tennessee River (as it was believed at the time) led to the temporary halting by the Supreme

The Hoover Dam, on the Colorado River in Nevada.
CORBIS/ROBERT HOLMES

Court of the Tellico Dam in Tennessee, despite the fact that the all-powerful TVA (Tennessee Valley Authority) backed the project. Though the dam was ultimately completed, it was through the debate surrounding it that environmentalists realized they could protect rivers and their biotic inhabitants from dam-building through various legal protections of endangered species.

Mining

Like dam-building, mining has been integral to human activity and the growth of civilizations around the globe. The various forms of mining—underground, surface, placer, and hydraulic—produce severe environmental impacts, including topsoil loss, erosion, and sedimentation; the disruption of native ecosystems; and the leaching of hazardous substances.

Surface mining represents the most blatant form of violence against the environment and now accounts for over 60 percent of the world's total mineral production. It is employed when a vein of valuable minerals (such as coal) lies close enough to the surface to be more easily extracted with power shovels than by means of excavating deep tunnels. As the surface materials, known as the overburden, are removed in order to access the valuable materials below, the resulting piles are set aside and create spoil banks. Surface mining was used in the nineteenth century but became much more widespread with the advent of large-scale, commercial mechanized mining following World War II. The several types of surface mining—area, contour, open-pit—occur throughout the United States. The world's biggest open-pit mine is located near Bingham, Utah, and operated by Kennecot Copper Corporation. A seemingly endless series of terraces that have been dug out over a period of seventy years at the base of picturesque, snow-capped mountain ranges, the pit is now so deep that the world's tallest buildings could easily fit within. The harms to the environment from such a mine are obvious: the destruction of vegetation and wildlife habitat, the decline in air quality through increase in dust, and the loss of aesthetic beauty.

More insidious is the contamination of groundwater supplies. Surface mining for coal (which accounts for 41 percent of the land disturbed by this activity) has led to acid mine drainage, which occurs when pyrite-bearing rocks, exposed to the air by strip mining, come into contact with water through rainfall or groundwater. The result is highly acidic water, bright orange to rusty red in color. In Appalachia nearly seventy-five hundred miles of streams and rivers and thirty thousand acres of land have been seriously affected by the discharge of uncontrolled acid mine drainage, killing fish and other forms of wildlife and contaminating drinking water supplies.

The reasons for uncontrolled acid mine drainage have been the historic "rape and run" mentality of coal-mining companies and the laissez-faire environmental policies of the state and federal governments. This culture of neglect began to come to an end with the publication in 1963 of Harry Caudill's exposé, *Night Comes to the Cumberlands.* Caudill laid bare the horrific environmental and human costs of unregulated strip mining in Appalachia: widespread deforestation, the pollution of rivers and creeks, the boom-and-bust economic cycles endemic to the mining industry. Not until 1977, however, was adequate federal legislation passed in the form of the Surface Mining Control and Reclamation Act.

Air Pollution

Pollution is a naturally occurring phenomenon: for example, smoke produced by volcanic eruptions and forest fires ignited by lightning strikes has long been a feature of earth history. Yet there is no question that air and water pollution intensified with the development of agriculture and the concentration of populations in towns and cities.

Cities in the United States such as Cincinnati and Chicago passed laws in the 1880s to try to regulate air pollution. But it was not until the post–World War II era that serious national regulations were passed, mainly as a result of numerous deaths resulting from air pollution. Air pollution, perhaps more than any other form of violence against the environment, demonstrates the global nature of the problem; it is a harm that recognizes no arbitrary political boundaries.

Air pollution introduces many harmful elements into the atmosphere. The burning of fossil fuels produces sulfur dioxide and nitrogen oxide. Vehicles using hydrocarbon fuels produce carbon monoxide. These primary pollutants then set off photochemical reactions resulting in secondary pollutants such as smog. Although automobiles are now the key source of air pollution in urban areas, industrial burning of fuels releases fly ash and introduces dioxin, chlorine, and PCBs (polychlorinated biphenyl) into the atmosphere as well. These pollutants have had a number of deleterious effects on humans—respiratory diseases such as black lung disease and asthma, eye irritation, and brain damage caused by lead poisoning—and on the environment—principally, devegetation and habitat loss.

The four main kinds of harm done to the atmosphere are smog, acid rain, ozone depletion, and the greenhouse effect. The term *smog* was coined around the turn of the twentieth century to describe the lethal combination of smoke and fog characteristic of the air in London during the winter. Los Angeles has gained notoriety as the smoggiest U.S. city. A number of factors make it so: long summer days, sea winds that push pollution against the mountains that surround the city, frequent air inversions that prevent pollutants from dispersing vertically, and more cars per capita than any other major metropolitan area. Acid rain is a by-product of smog and other forms of air pollution. It occurs when sulfur dioxide and nitrogen oxides are formed during the combustion of fossil fuels, which are then transported and deposited on land and water through rain or cloud droplets or in dry form. Although some acid rain naturally occurs through volcanic activity and forest fires, emissions from electric utilities and motor vehicles are the greatest contributors to this phenomenon. The eastward drift of pollutants emanating from the tall smokestacks of factories and utilities in the Midwest has created serious acid rain effects in the northeastern United States. Alpine lakes in

Smokestacks in Pittsburgh in the 1890s. CORBIS-
BETTMANN

the Adirondack Mountains of upstate New York
have suffered from increased acidity, with an estimated 24 percent of the lakes in the region now
devoid of fish as a result. Along with ozone pollution, acid rain has also led to significant diebacks
of conifers at higher elevations in the Adirondacks
and Great Smoky Mountains in North Carolina.

Ozone pollution, or more accurately ozone-
layer depletion, demonstrates perhaps better than
any other form of pollution the global nature of
the source and effects of environmental problems.
In 1974 several chemists discovered that chlorine
from chlorofluorocarbon (CFC) molecules had the
potential to break down ozone in the stratosphere,
where it exists as a nine- to thirty-mile layer shield-
ing life on Earth from the sun's radiation. The chief
sources of CFCs are propellants in aerosol spray
cans, thermal insulation, cleaning solvents, cooling
agents in refrigerators and air conditioners, and
foaming agents in plastics. NASA satellites in the
mid-1980s then discovered dramatically lower
ozone levels over Antarctica—some as low as 45
percent below normal. By 1992 the "hole" in the
ozone layer over the South Pole had grown to a

size three times bigger than the United States, and
ozone depletion over highly populated areas of
North America, Europe, South America, Australia,
and New Zealand had increased by 3 percent.

The resultant real and potential harms of increased ultraviolet radiation are many: depletion
of phytoplankton in the oceans, the foundation of
the marine food chain (or web); increased carbon
dioxide and greenhouse warming through the decrease of phytoplankton, which absorbs great
amounts of carbon dioxide; the destruction of
crops; and a dramatic rise in malignant melanoma,
or skin cancer, which is now the fastest-increasing
form of cancer in the world. On this last point, scientists were particularly alarmed by evidence indicating that in the United States the area of greatest thinning of the ozone layer ran in a line roughly
from Philadelphia to Reno, with the depletion lasting into late spring, when more people were likely
to be spending time outdoors. In response to this
new environmental threat, the United States
banned CFC aerosols in 1978, and in 1987, along
with twenty-two other nations, signed the Montreal Protocol, which required that signatory countries agree to cut CFC production in half by the
year 2000 and to phase out two particularly harmful ozone-destroying gases.

The Greenhouse Effect. Even more daunting an
atmospheric problem is the greenhouse effect, or
global warming. As with many other forms of pollution, to a certain degree greenhouse warming is
a natural phenomenon, a process that traps radiation within the earth's atmosphere through the
accumulation of water vapor, carbon dioxide, nitrous oxide, methane, and ozone, all of which effectively and essentially retain heat from the sun.
Accounting for half of all greenhouse gases is carbon dioxide, the chief sources being the burning of
fossil fuels and the destruction of the rain forests
across the world; since 1765 its presence in the atmosphere has increased 27 percent. The predicted
consequences of global warming are dire: drought;
increased sea levels due to the warming of the po-
lar icecaps, which in turn would result in the in-
undation of coastal settlements around the world;
more intense hurricanes and tornadoes; and a general shifting of biogeographic zones north in the
Northern Hemisphere and south in the Southern
Hemisphere.

Greenhouse effects will remain for many years
the most significant, invisible, and insidious form
of violence against the environment—even as we

477

Global Warming

Global temperatures recorded since consistent scientific records were first kept in the nineteenth century indicate that by the year 2100 it may be two to three degrees centigrade warmer on average on Earth than before 1800. To put this rise in perspective, it took a three- to four-degree-centigrade increase for the planet to emerge out of the last ice age twelve thousand years ago. It is noteworthy that, as of the 1990s, the six warmest years on record—1995, 1990, 1991, 1994, 1988, and 1983—were in the last quarter of the twentieth century.

The issue of global warming caused by greenhouse gases may be the very issue necessary to bring about worldwide cooperation in solving our environmental crisis. Or it may be the very issue that dooms us. Developing countries rightfully point to the hypocrisy of developed nations like the United States, which balk at signing treaties calling for reductions in emissions because they would inhibit economic development, while at the same time urging developing countries to sign such agreements. Why should residents of India, Brazil, and Nigeria not enjoy the same degree of affluence and profligate overconsumption of resources that citizens of the United States have for so long enjoyed?

improve air quality itself through such landmark laws as the Clean Air Act (1963, 1970, 1990). This legislation established three major provisions: (1) the federal government, not the individual states, would be the major determinant of air pollution policy, with the Environmental Protection Agency the key regulatory body; (2) national ambient air-quality standards were created for six major pollutants (carbon monoxide, lead, nitrogen dioxide, ozone, particulates, and sulfur dioxide); and (3) each state was then required to devise its own implementation plan in order to meet the federal standards. Since the 1970s progress has been made in reducing air pollution by requiring industries to install scrubbers on smokestacks and car manufacturers to install catalytic converters in automobile exhaust systems. Mainly as a result of the Clean Air Act, lead has been reduced by 96 percent, and particulates by over 60 percent. Yet many states and cities remain noncompliant.

Water Pollution

The struggle to control water pollution in the United States has on the whole been more successful than efforts to stem air pollution. A series of environmental disasters involving various forms of water pollution in the 1960s and 1970s called attention to the befouling of our waters and galvanized the environmental movement into forcing the federal government to better regulate how we interact with oceans, rivers, and lakes. The cleanup of Boston Harbor has been one of the more notable success stories of modern environmentalism. Through the 1970s and 1980s Boston built $3.4 billion worth of sewage treatment facilities—amounting to one of the world's largest public works projects—and 80 percent of the cleanup has been completed. The harbor now supports thriving lobster and fishing industries.

The Cuyahoga River, a tributary of Lake Erie that flows through Cleveland, Ohio, gained notoriety in 1969 for catching on fire, an event that provided the final impetus for the passage of the Clean Water Act. Long a sink for the industries that line its banks, the river had become virtually devoid of life because of its deadly mix of cyanide, phosphates, and raw or inadequately treated sewage. Ten years later chemical pollution of the river had been decreased by 20–40 percent, and local residents witnessed ducks on the water for the first time in memory.

The grounding of the supertanker the *Exxon Valdez* in southern Alaska in 1989, resulting in the spewing of over ten million gallons of crude oil into the waters of Prince William Sound, led to the passage of the Oil Pollution Act in 1990 and the regulation of oil tankers. The *Valdez* spill also contributed to the defeat of efforts to open up the Arctic National Wildlife Refuge on Alaska's north coast to oil drilling, mainly because of the threat posed to the rich resident megafauna (principally caribou).

Point sources of water pollution involve a specific source of discharge. Nonpoint sources of pollution are scattered and diffuse and thus much harder to regulate and control. Nonpoint sources include runoff from farms, golf courses, lawns, construction sites, roads, and parking lots. A possible example of nonpoint-source water pollution is the occurrence of deformed frogs in southern Minnesota. In 1994 students on a field trip discovered a number of frogs with deformed limbs in a pond near Henderson. Frogs are considered an "indicator species," that is, one that serves as a gauge of the health of a given ecosystem. To date the cause of the abnormalities has not been iden-

Rescue workers hold a cormorant soaked in oil, a victim of the *Exxon Valdez* spill that contaminated a wildlife refuge in Prince William Sound, Alaska. CORBIS/GARY BRAASCH

tified. Thirty other states besides Minnesota have now also reported the existence of deformed frogs.

The Clean Water Act (1972, 1977, 1987), like the Clean Air Act, was passed in acknowledgment of the fact that the federal government could best regulate and prevent pollution of our nation's water and air. Its provisions included the establishment of water quality levels protecting fish, shellfish, and wildlife; the prohibiting of the discharge of toxic pollutants from point sources; the allocation of federal financial assistance to states to construct publicly owned waste treatment works; and the control of nonpoint-source pollution. As with the Clean Air Act, the EPA was designated the chief federal regulatory agency involved in overseeing enforcement of these and other provisions. Water pollution, in contrast with the doomsday global threats posed by global warming and ozone-layer depletion, represents less of a problem in the United States. Remarkable comebacks in terms of river and lake cleanups have been made since the 1960s. Drinking water is generally safer than it was thirty years ago. Yet over seven hundred contaminants have been identified in drinking water supplies across the country. Contamination of drinking water supplies in Pennsylvania and Wisconsin affected thousands of people in the 1990s and attested to the need for continued vigilance.

Hazardous Waste

Some hazardous material, such as radon, the decay product of radium, is naturally occurring.

But the well-publicized incidents involving hazardous waste and the environmental laws passed since the 1960s apply mainly to human-made waste. Hazardous waste is that which contributes to or causes human death or illness or, in its storage, handling, transportation, or disposal, poses a threat to the environment. The four main kinds of hazardous wastes are pesticides (such as DDT, discussed above under agriculture), petrochemicals (e.g., plastics), organic chemicals (e.g., PCBs), and heavy metals (e.g., lead); nuclear waste is of course another form. The chief sources of hazardous wastes are industry (including the nuclear industry), landfills, and illegal dumping, both in point form (specific, such as an industry pouring arsenic into a river from a drainpipe) as well as nonpoint form (nonspecific, such as toxic substances in a landfill leaching into groundwater supplies).

Several notorious examples of human exposure to hazardous wastes illustrate the dire threats posed by improper use, storage, and disposal of these materials. In 1971 in Times Beach, Missouri, located thirty miles southwest of St. Louis, chemical wastes (gathered from service stations and industrial plants) were mixed with oil and sprayed on roads as a dust suppressant. Over the next two years sixty-two breeding horses died on nearby farms. When soil samples were taken it was discovered that dangerous levels of dioxin were present. Dioxin is a chemical by-product of manufacturing processes and is considered toxic to humans at one part per billion (ppb) in soil levels; a decade

479

later, when Times Beach experienced the worst floods in town history, the dioxin levels were measured at 100 to 300 ppb. Virtually every resident of the community of two thousand experienced some kind of health disorder ranging from nosebleeds to skin disorders to cancer and heart disease. Most of the families were relocated and Times Beach became a modern industrial ghost town.

Love Canal, New York, is unquestionably the most infamous nonnuclear hazardous waste site. Between 1942 and 1953 an estimated 21,800 tons of chemical wastes were buried by Hooker Chemical Company in a human-made canal in a neighborhood of Niagara Falls. In 1953 the land was sold to a local board of education, and a school was built in 1954—in spite of the fact that in the deed of sale it was specified that chemicals were buried under the property. Homes were also built in the area. By 1976 it became obvious that a serious problem existed when flooding raised water levels and houses began to reek of chemicals. When birth defects started to occur (in 1979 only two pregnant women out of nineteen gave birth to children without defects), residents formed a homeowners' association and demanded that the government relocate affected families. In 1980 President Jimmy Carter declared a federal emergency for Love Canal—the first-ever anthropogenic federal envi-

ronmental disaster. The costs of cleanup amounted to $250 million. Eventually 459 out of 564 single-family homes were purchased from residents, and Love Canal was sealed by a concrete cap with assurances by government officials that the danger from hazardous waste would be prevented. Yet, in a mind-boggling case of short-term historical memory, by 1988 families and businesses were once again relocating to the Love Canal neighborhood.

Nuclear Waste. The accident at the Three Mile Island nuclear reactor near Harrisburg, Pennsylvania, in 1979 involved the direct production of power for residents and businesses and is the most infamous example in the United States of the potential dangers of the nuclear age. In the 1970s, following the Arab oil embargo and growing concerns over declining supplies of fossil fuels, great optimism was expressed about the potential of nuclear power to solve our energy needs. Proponents of the nuclear industry predicted that five hundred power reactors would be built by the year 2000. But a series of events at Three Mile Island significantly changed the outlook for nuclear power. During routine maintenance at the plant a human mistake in replacing a water purifier occurred and several safety devices subsequently failed to perform, resulting in radioactive steam escaping into

Three Mile Island, Harrisburg, Pennsylvania, 1979, after an accident leaked radioactive steam into the atmosphere. Franken; Owen/Corbis

the atmosphere and radioactive water introduced into the Susquehanna River. Worse, the possibility arose that the reactor's core might experience a meltdown, threatening millions of people living in the New York–Philadelphia–Washington corridor. No one was killed by the accident, though subsequent studies have revealed that for residents downwind from the reactor cancer incidence has been higher than normal. The greatest effect of the accident was to thwart the construction of future nuclear power plants; since 1979 not one new plant has been built; however, 109 plants remain in operation in the United States, not to mention more than 400 others around the world. The threat of another nuclear accident remains real.

An even greater threat than nuclear accident is the problem of disposing of nuclear waste. The waste generated from nuclear reactors, as well as from the military production of nuclear weapons, produces spent fuel that contains high concentrations of radioactive elements. These elements have very long half-lives and require storage up to ten thousand years before their radioactivity is reduced to harmless levels by natural decaying processes. A number of temporary storage sites for nuclear waste, civilian and military, exist across the country. The ideal storage site must be stable, dry, isolated, and subterranean. Not surprisingly, the decision to locate a single, permanent storage site has been a difficult one, leading to a classic example of the NIMBY phenomenon: not in my back yard. Eventually the U.S. government chose Yucca Mountain, about a hundred miles southeast of Las Vegas, Nevada, as the sole site for a high-level nuclear waste storage facility. Into this barren desert ridge of Yucca Mountain over a hundred miles of tunnels have been drilled more than a thousand feet beneath the surface, despite geologists' doubts as to the stability of the terrain. The earliest date at which nuclear waste can be stored there is now projected to be 2010. Meanwhile over thirty thousand tons of spent fuel are sitting at more than one hundred sites in thirty-four states, a nuclear time-bomb awaiting detonation. Of the many federal laws passed to regulate hazardous waste, the most well-known is the Comprehensive Environmental Response, Compensation, and Liability Act, better known as Superfund. Passed in 1980 in response to the Love Canal disaster, the law authorizes the EPA to clean up hazardous waste sites and is funded by a tax on pollution producers. The EPA was also charged with prioritizing the list of hazardous sites. As of 1990 some thirty-three thousand sites were identified as potentially hazardous, and the estimated cleanup bill amounts to more than $500 billion. The threats posed by hazardous wastes to the human and nonhuman environment remain real and deadly, defying easy, immediate solutions.

Species Endangerment and Extinction

Extinction is both a natural and anthropogenic phenomenon. In 1988 the scientist E. O. Wilson estimated the current rate of extinction at up to 17,500 species each year, with much of it coming in the world's greatest source of biodiversity, tropical rain forests. Many of these species are unknown to us, have never even been seen by humans. Some 50–150 species of plants and animals may be disappearing each day, and in the next twenty-five years this could mean the disappearance of 5–10 percent of the world's species. At least one out of every eight known plant species is now threatened with extinction or nearly extinct. According to some conservation biologists, we are on the verge of a biotic holocaust.

There have been various causes of this dramatic and recent acceleration in species extinction, and they fall into two general categories: unintentional and deliberate. The primary cause is habitat loss as resource extraction and ever-expanding human populations eliminate and encroach on territory occupied by other species. People unknowingly or uncaringly eliminate the homes of animals as they provide for their own subsistence. But we have also deliberately sought to control or eliminate certain animals and plants, sometimes in the name of predator control. Moreover, people have caused animal populations to plummet as a result of hunting and fishing, and because of the value of a particular animal's fur or other bodily parts.

Prior to the arrival of Europeans in the fifteenth century, the American bison ranged from the Appalachian Mountains in the East to the Rocky Mountains in the West to Florida in the South. The entire bison population is estimated to have been over sixty million at its peak. But the herds east of the Mississippi were eliminated by the mid-nineteenth century. In the West the railroad, territorial expansion of Euroamerican settlers, and a campaign to eliminate Native American tribes or drive them onto reservations largely contributed to the bison's decline. Millions of buffalo were shot for their hides, for their tongues (the meat was considered a delicacy in eastern restaurants), for sport, and to reduce the independence of Plains Indians, who depended heavily upon the animal for subsistence. The population was ultimately reduced to some five hundred, mostly in captivity. A campaign to save the bison came just in time, and in the 1990s the largest herd (of about five thousand animals) roamed within the borders of Yellowstone National Park.

One of the chief predators of the bison in the West was the wolf. In the late nineteenth century and well into the twentieth, the U.S. government, together with farmers and ranchers who feared wolves would attack and kill their livestock, conducted a campaign to eradicate the wolf. The desire to kill the "big bad wolf" is rooted in longstanding, atavistic prejudices against the animal, reflected in numerous stories in Western culture. By the twentieth century most wolves had been eliminated from the lower forty-eight states. With wolves eradicated there were fewer checks on the deer population, and the results were too many deer, devegetated mountainsides, and horrific starve-offs. In 1999, only in Minnesota did a significant wolf population still exist (around two thousand members of the gray wolf subspecies). Attempts were being made to restore wolf populations in Yellowstone National Park and in Arizona, as well as in the South. Alaska retains a significant population, but its state government conducts periodic campaigns to control wolf numbers through aerial hunting in order to protect moose and caribou populations. And the Department of Agriculture's Bureau of Animal Damage Control (ADC) continues to kill animals considered by farmers and ranchers to be threats to their crops and livestock, among them thousands each of coyotes, beavers, skunks, and raccoons, as well as numerous snapping turtles, musk turtles, wild turkeys, mountain lions, gray wolves, and black bears.

No one intended to eliminate the U.S. national emblem, the bald eagle, but this was exactly the effect of pesticide campaigns carried out beginning in the 1950s. DDT and related pesticides had the deleterious effect of causing reproductive problems in eagles and other raptors. By 1982 the estimated eagle population in the lower forty-eight states had fallen to fifteen hundred pairs. But with the banning of DDT in 1972 and the inclusion of the bald eagle on the endangered species list, its numbers have slowly recovered. By 1999 it was estimated that about twenty-four hundred pairs were thriving (some thirty thousand eagles live in Alaska). The recovery of the bald eagle has been one of the great success stories of modern-day conservation, and the bird has actually been removed from the list of endangered species.

Three main groups have argued on behalf of species protection: the government, private conservation organizations, and scientists. The Endangered Species Act has been the key to preservation of critically threatened species. Passed in 1973, this law has been the bane of promoters of industrial and commercial development. Conversely, it was a landmark in the history of the animal rights movement. The law creates two categories: endangered and threatened. The former is defined as a species "in danger of extinction throughout all or a significant portion of its range," whereas the latter is one likely to become endangered. In 1990, 596 species were listed as threatened or endangered in the United States. The most controversial aspect of the act required that no action by a federal agency would be allowed that could result in threatening the population or habitat of an endangered species. Long before the Endangered Species Act was passed, however, the federal government established national wildlife refuges to preserve the habitat of threatened species. In 1999 there were over five hundred separate national wildlife refuges on a hundred million acres. Scientists have formed the new subfields of conservation biology and restoration ecology in response to the widespread endangerment and extinction of many species and habitats, arguing for the scientific and economic as well as intrinsic value of all things natural.

A Vision of the Future

Over the course of the twentieth century, the United States was transformed from a rural into an urban nation. A certain attitude toward nature went along with this change: nature was a place to escape to rather than an integral part of everyday life. Thus, throughout the year, at home and at work, we might tolerate or even contribute to violence against the environment and then declare ourselves in harmony with nature during two weeks of vacation at a cabin in the woods. The environment must be redefined not only as the place where we play but where we work and live.

It is also time to recognize that certain parts of the population are suffering the effects of violence against the environment more than others. The term *environmental racism* was coined in 1987 in a study documenting the correlation between the siting of hazardous waste sites and the location of low-income, minority communities. Subsequent reports have confirmed that exposure to environmental risks is significantly greater for racial and ethnic minorities than for nonminority populations. The NIMBY stance of white middle- and upper-class families in response to the possible location of hazardous wastes has led to increased risks for the economically—and thus politically—disadvantaged. The problems of environmental quality and poverty are inextricably related.

Environmentalists now recognize the critical importance of teaching humans how to live sustainably with their environments. The Sierra Club, the National Audubon Society, the Wilderness Society, and the National Wildlife Federation have used the power of their memberships to lobby Congress and presidents to pass environmental laws for over a century; without their influence, it is doubtful that such landmark legislation and agencies such as the Wilderness Act of 1964, the Clean Air and Water Acts, the U.S. Park Service, and the Environmental Protection Agency would have been created. However, as environmental organizations grew in membership and influence through the 1970s and 1980s a perception developed among some environmentalists that these groups had become, through institutionalization, a part of the very system they were attacking and trying to change. Thus emerged radical environmentalism and groups like Greenpeace and Earth First!, which advocate and carry out direct, and sometimes illegal, action against government and industry.

Radical environmentalism has succeeded in calling attention to certain environmental causes and in shifting the goals of environmentalism from anthropocentric toward biocentric strategies. Anthropocentrism essentially holds a human-centered view of the universe and argues for actions on the basis of whether and to what extent they will benefit humans. Biocentrism, in contrast, extends the recognition of rights to nonhuman and even nonliving natural objects in attempting to place all things on the same level of equality, while recognizing that every species must live off other entities if it is to continue to exist. Biocentrism has been linked to the philosophy of deep ecology espoused by the Norwegian philosopher Arne Naess. Deep ecology—as opposed to the "shallow" ecology of traditional environmentalism—maintains that every thing has an intrinsic value and should be recognized as such. The rain forest then should be preserved not only because of the potential cures for cancer that may exist in its plants and animals but for its own biodiversity. Environmental historians now identify in the latest phase of environmentalism a distinct move from conservationism and environmentalism to ecologism: a recognition on the part of environmentalists of the importance of maintaining the ecological web that binds all living and nonliving things on Earth.

BIBLIOGRAPHY

Berry, Wendell. *The Unsettling of America: Culture and Agriculture.* San Francisco: Sierra Club, 1977.

Brown, Lester R., et al. *State of the World 1998: A Worldwatch Institute Report on Progress Toward a Sustainable Society.* New York: Norton, 1998.

Carson, Rachel. *Silent Spring.* Boston: Houghton Mifflin, 1962.

Caudill, Harry. *Night Comes to the Cumberlands.* Boston: Little, Brown, 1963.

Cronon, William. *Changes in the Land: Indians, Colonists, and the Ecology of New England.* New York: Hill and Wang, 1983.

———, ed. *Uncommon Ground: Toward Reinventing Nature.* New York: Norton, 1995.

Devall, Bill, and George Sessions. *Deep Ecology: Living as if Nature Mattered.* Salt Lake City, Utah: Gibbs Smith, 1985.

Easterbrook, Gregg. *A Moment on the Earth: The Coming Age of Environmental Optimism.* New York: Viking, 1995.

Hardin, Garret. "The Tragedy of the Commons." *Science* 162 (1961): 1243–1248.

Jackson, Wes, et al. *Meeting the Expectations of the Land: Essays in Sustainable Agriculture and Stewardship.* San Francisco: North Point, 1984.

Leopold, Aldo. *A Sand County Almanac and Sketches Here and There.* New York: Oxford University Press, 1949.

Limerick, Patricia. *The Legacy of Conquest: The Unbroken Past of the American West.* New York: Norton, 1987.

Lopez, Barry. *Crossing Open Ground.* New York: Scribners, 1988.

———. *Of Wolves and Men.* New York: Scribners, 1978.

Marsh, George Perkins. *Man and Nature; or, Physical Geography as Modified by Human Action.* 1864. Cambridge, Mass.: Harvard University Press, 1965.

Matthiessen, Peter. *Wildlife in America.* Rev. ed. New York: Viking, 1987.

McGurty, Eileen Maura. "From NIMBY to Civil Rights: The Origins of the Environmental Justice Movement." *Environmental History* 2, no. 3 (July 1997): 301–323.

McKibben, Bill. *The End of Nature.* New York: Random House, 1989.

Nash, Roderick. *Wilderness and the American Mind.* 3d ed. New Haven, Conn.: Yale University Press, 1982.

Palmer, Tim. *Endangered Rivers and the Conservation Movement.* Berkeley: University of California Press, 1986.

Ponting, Clive. *A Green History of the World: The Environment and the Collapse of Great Civilizations.* New York: Penguin, 1991.

Pyne, Stephen. *Fire in America: A Cultural History of Wildland and Rural Fire.* Princeton, N.J.: Princeton University Press, 1982.

Reisner, Marc. *Cadillac Desert: The American West and Its Disappearing Water.* New York: Viking, 1986.

Robbins, Jim. *Last Refuge: The Environmental Showdown in Yellowstone and the American West.* New York: Morrow, 1993.

Sullivan, Walter. *Landprints: On the Magnificent American Landscape.* New York: Times Books, 1984.

U.S. Department of the Interior. "Impact of Surface Mining on Environment." In *Man's Impact on Environment,* edited by Thomas R. Detwyler. New York: McGraw Hill, 1971. Pp. 348–369.

White, Lynn, Jr. "The Historical Roots of Our Ecological Crisis." *Science* 155 (1967): 1203–1207.

Worster, Donald. *Dust Bowl: The Southern Plains in the 1930s.* New York: Oxford University Press, 1979.

———. *Rivers of Empire: Water, Aridity, and the Growth of the American West.* New York: Pantheon, 1985.

DON SCHEESE

See also **Animals, Violence Against; Corporations.**

EPIDEMIOLOGY. *See* Gun Violence: Epidemiology of Injuries; Statistics and Epidemiology.

ETHNICITY. *See* Race and Ethnicity.

EUGENICS

Darwin's great discovery was that the mechanism of evolutionary progress is the process of natural selection, which results in the survival of the fittest. It was Darwin's cousin, Francis Galton, who recognized in 1865 that "one of the effects of civilization is to diminish the rigour of the application of the law of natural selection. It preserves weak lives that would have perished in barbarous lands" (p. 325). Darwin agreed: "We civilized men do our utmost to check the process of elimination; we build asylums for the imbecile, the maimed, and the sick; we institute poor laws; and our medical men exert their utmost skills to save the life of everyone to the last moment. Thus the weak members of civilized societies propagate their kind. No-one . . . will doubt that this must be highly injurious to the race of men" (Darwin 1871, p. 501).

By the second half of the nineteenth century, lower-class parents in Europe and America were having larger families than were parents from the managerial and professional classes. Better sewage disposal, cleaner drinking water, improved control of infectious diseases, all reduced infant mortality and especially so for the poor. Middle- and upper-class persons were marrying later and beginning to employ birth control to limit family size. To the extent that there was social mobility, so that stronger, more talented individuals could rise in status while the sickly or less gifted settled downward, this greater fecundity of the lower classes meant that a larger proportion of each new generation was derived from the genetically less fit of the parental stock, a phenomonen described by the term *dysgenics.*

One possible counter to these dysgenic tendencies would be to institute in human society some form of selective breeding similar to that which had proven so successful in animal husbandry. Galton coined the name *eugenics* for such endeavors, and many biological and social scientists during the first two-thrids of the twentieth century endorsed the need for eugenic measures. They included such eminent figures as Karl Pearson and Sir Ronald Fisher, two of the founders of modern statistical theory; Sir Julian Huxley, evolutionary biologist and grandson of T. H. Huxley, Darwin's feisty protagonist; the psychologists Sir Cyril Burt, Sir Godfrey Thomson, and Raymond Cattell; and Nobel Laureates Hermann Muller, Joshau Lederberg, and Francis Crick.

The most prominent supporter of eugenics by far, however, was Adolf Hitler, whose slaughter of millions of Jews, gypsies, and other "inferiors" was alleged to be in the interest of eugenics or "racial purification." So horrific was the Nazi Holocaust that *eugenics* became a term of opprobrium and many educated people, including many scientists, became suspicious of any human genetical research concerning psychological traits. Following World War II, the study of psychological differences between people went through a period of radical environmentalism. Psychodynamic theorits, on the one hand, and learning theorists, on the other, proffered competing explanations for behavioral diversity based on differences in experience from infancy onward. Invoking genetic differences to explain behavioral variation was considered to be not only scientifically misguided but also probably fascistic.

Twin Studies

During the same postwar period, however, a relatively small group of behavior geneticists persisted in studying twins as well as the psycholog-

484

ical similarities between adopted children on the one hand, and their adoptive versus their biological parents on the other. By the last decade of the twentieth century, two surprising facts had become firmly established by these efforts. First, nearly every psychological trait that can be reliably measured owes from 20 to 80 percent of its variation in the population to genetic differences between people. Second, being reared together in the same home does not make children more alike psychologically by the time they reach adulthood. (One important exception to the principle that parents are largely interchangeable is that parents who fail to socialize one child—because the parents are themselves abusive, incompetent, or unsocialized—are likely to fail in a similar way with any other children in their houlsehold.) Identical (or monozygotic) twins are remarkably similar psychologically and, as adults, they are just as similar even if they were separated in infancy and reared apart as single children in separate adoptive homes (Bouchard et al., 1990).

It has been established through both twin and family studies that the general factor of intelligence that is measured by the IQ (intelligence quotient) test owes about 75 percent of its variation in the population to genetic differences between people. That is, the broad-sense heritability of IQ is therefore about 75 percent. We also know that traits like aggression, self-control, responsibility, conscientiousness, constraint, empathy, altruism, callousness, and antisocial behavior, which together constitute the supertrait of socialization, all owe from 40 to 60 percent of their variation in the population to genetic factors (Lykken, 1995; Lynn, 1996). Proponents of genetics assert that if it can be shown that there is a negative correlation between intelligence or socialization, on the one hand, and fertility, on the other, then the dysgenic problem posed originally by Galton must once again be faced: should a civilized society preserve "weak lives" when doing so appears to interfere with natural selection by condoning the conception of children who will be genetically ill equipped to become self-sustaining, law-abiding citizens?

Dysgenic Trends

Richard Lynn (1996) explored the correlations between high fertility and both intelligence and socialization and found that in the developed countries, both IQ and family size are inversely related to social class. That is, being from a lower social class is statistically associated with having a lower IQ and a larger family size. This would suggest that the average IQ should have been slowly but steadily decreasing throughout the twentieth century. The problem, as Lynn acknowledges, is that there was instead a substantial secular *increase* in measured IQ over this period, in Britain and in European countries, in Japan, and in the United States, a trend most persuasively documented by James Flynn (Flynn, 1984). Flynn himself concluded that these massive gains could not be genuine improvements in intelligence, partly on the grounds that such substantial increases in the brilliance of college students and in the number of geniuses amongst us would have been noticed and commented upon.

The gains, however, seem to have been largely at the lower end of the bell curve of IQ, and Lynn concludes that they are genuine, reflecting improvements over this period in the standards of living and especially in prenatal fetal nutrition. From these observations, Lynn argues that there have indeed been real gains in *phenotypic* (realized, or functioning) IQ, especially at the lower end of the distribution, but that these gains have hidden a simultaneous decrease in *genotypic* (inherited, or potential) IQ due to the dysgenic effects of higher fertility on the part of less-intelligent parents. At least for a time, therefore, the mean IQ may not decrease because of continuing improvements in environmental support for the less privileged. Lynn predicts that once nutritional and other environmental improvements stabilize, a decreasing trend in phenotypic, as well as in genotypic, IQ will begin to be observed that is due to the dysgenic fertility differential between the social classes.

The dysgenic trends for traits of socialization are rather easier to demonstrate. The prevalence of conduct disorder in children and of antisocial personality in adults has been increasing alarmingly in recent decades. In the United States, for example, the rate of violent crime increased nearly 400 percent from 1960 to 1991 (Federal Bureau of Investigation 1996). Both sociopaths (unsocialized primarily because of incompetent parenting) and psychopaths (whose temperaments make them difficult to socialize) tend to breed carelessly and to be dreadful parents. Lynn reviews numerous studies showing that criminals and delinquent adolescents are likely to have more siblings than do law abiders. In the United States, more than 50 percent of incarcerated delinquents have a member of their immediate family who has also been incarcerated (U.S. Department of Justice 1988). Lynn himself examined the relative fertility of criminal versus noncriminal parents of the working-class boys in London sampled and followed in the famous Cambridge study (Farrington and West 1990; Lynn 1995). Parents who had been convicted of an indictable offense had produced, on average, 3.91 children, significantly more than the working-class parents who had no criminal convictions and some 77 percent more than for the British population as a whole.

If less-intelligent parents are producing relatively more offspring than are parents with higher IQs and if criminals and other less socialized parents are producing relatively more offspring than are the law-abiding, socialized majority (and if these numerous offspring tend to be doubly disadvantaged, by having inherited difficult-to-socialize temperaments and by receiving poor or negligible parental guidance), what, if anything, can be done about this problem? Mass sterilization of persons classified as "genetically unfit" is not an option. Galton's own hope to redress the balance by inducing intelligent persons of good character to increase their family sizes also holds little promise.

At least in respect to criminal violence, something already seems to be working. After peaking in 1991–1992, the U.S. violent crime rate decreased regularly each year through 1997 (although it was then still more than three times the 1960 level). The most obvious explanation for this trend is the fact that the number of inmates of U.S. prisons increased from about 200,000 in 1975 to more than 1.3 million in 1998. Donohue and Levitt (1999) provide evidence that nearly half of the post-1992 reduction in the American crime rate can be attributed to the eugenic effect of the legalization of abortion in 1973. The number of documented abortions in the United States rose from 750,000 in 1973 (when live births totaled 3.1 million) to over 1.6 million in 1980 (when live births totaled 3.6 million; statistics distinguishing abortion rates for male versus female fetuses are not available). Donohue and Levitt cite estimates that, compared to mothers who gave birth during this period, those who received abortions were 70 percent more likely to be teenage or single women. This means that the cohort of young men who reached the high-crime ages of 15 to 25 after 1990 was relatively depleted of young men reared without fathers. It can be shown for both whites and African Americans that boys reared without fathers are some seven times more likely to become engaged in crime and violence (Lykken 1997). Thus it appears that crime and violence can be reduced by aborting the fetuses of women at high risk of producing violent or criminal offspring and by segregating those youngsters who break the law through the imposition of long prison terms. Massive imprisonment seems cruel, however, and it is certainly expensive, while abortion is widely opposed and in fact has been sharply curtailed in the United States since 1980 by statutes prohibiting the use of tax monies for this purpose.

Eumemic Solutions

The term *eumemics*, coined by the anthropologist Vincent Sarich, is based on another new word, *meme*, coined by the British evolutionary biologist, Richard Dawkins (Sarich 1993; Dawkins 1976). Just as the gene is the unit of genetic influence upon the development of the individual, so the meme is the unit of experience or environmental influence. Thus *eumemics* is a program for maximizing the good memes and minimizing the bad ones in the developmental experiences of children.

In addition to his eugenic proposals, Galton had a eumemic suggestion, parental licensure, which seems to hold more promise. The criteria for licensure in the twenty-first century might be kept simple: any mature, self-supporting, married couple who had completed a three-month college-level practicum in parenting would be eligible, providing that neither member had been convicted of a violent crime nor abondoned a prior family containing prepubertal children. Persons not meeting these basic requirements (e.g., homosexual couples) could appeal to family court for an exception. A child born to an unlicensable mother would be removed from her custody at birth and placed for permanent adoption. The objective of such a program would be to reduce the number of children being reared by abusive, immature, unsocialized, or otherwise incompetent parents.

Advocates of parental licensure (e.g., Lykken 1997, in press; Westman 1994) argue that the objective is not just for the welfare of the self-sufficient, socialized majority who have to support the less competent and to tolerate the misbehavior of the unsocialized. Advocates contend that the primary concern is for the innocent children of incompetent parents, who might else be deprived of their birthrights of life, liberty, and the pursuit of happiness. Opponents of parental licensure advocate instead improved policing (Sampson, in press), waiting for the social pendulum to swing the other way (Harris, in press), or adding a harmless contraceptive to the water supply, while providing antidotes ad libitum to those requesting them (Scarr, in press).

Parental licensure, while intended as a eumemic program, would also have an indirect eugenic effect. The question that remains for society to address is whether, for the sake of the children, persons who cannot control or support themselves, and who would not be permitted to adopt someone else's child, must be permitted to continue producing children biologically.

BIBLIOGRAPHY

Bouchard, Thomas J., Jr., et al. "Sources of Human Psychological Differences: The Minnesota Study of Twins Reared Apart." *Science* 237 (October 1990).

Darwin, Charles. *The Descent of Man and Selection in Relation to Sex.* London: Murray, 1871.

Dawkins, Richard. *The Selfish Gene.* Oxford, U.K.: Oxford University Press, 1976.

Donohue, John J., and Steven D. Levitt, "Legalized Abortion and Crime." *Stanford Law School Working Paper,* 1999.

Farrington, David P., and Donald J. West. "The Cambridge Study in Delinquent Development: A Long-Term Follow-up of 411 London Males." In *Criminality: Personality, Behavior, and Life History,* edited by Henry J. Kerner and George Kaiser. Berlin: Springer Verlag, 1990.

Federal Bureau of Investigation. Uniform Crime Reports for the United States, 1993. Washington, D.C.: U.S. Department of Justice, 1996.

Flynn, James R. "Massive IQ Gains in Fourteen Nations: What IQ Tests Really Measure." *Psychological Bulletin* 98, no. 2 (1987).

———. "The Mean IQ of Americans: Massive Gains, 1932 to 1978." *Psychological Bulletin* 95, no. 1 (1984).

Galton, Francis. "Hereditary Talent and Character." *Macmillan's Magazine* 12 (June 1865).

Harris, Judith R. "The Outcome of Parenting: What Do We Really Know?" *Journal of Personality.* In press.

Lykken, David T. *The Antisocial Personalities.* Mahwah, N.J.: Lawrence Erlbaum, 1995.

———. "The Case for Parental Licensure." In *Psychopathy: Antisocial, Criminal, and Violent Behaviors,* edited by Theodore Millon, E. Simonsen, and M. Birket-Smith, New York: Guilford, 1997.

———. "The Causes and Costs of Crime and a Controversial Cure." *Journal of Personality.* Forthcoming.

Lynn, Richard. "Dysgenic Fertility for Crime." *Journal of Biosocial Science* 27, no. 3 (1995).

———. *Dysgenics: Genetic Deterioration in Modern Populations.* Westport, Conn.: Praeger, 1996.

Maguire, Kathleen, and Ann L. Pastore, eds. *Sourcebook of Criminal Justice Statistics.* Washington, D.C.: U.S. Department of Justice, Bureau of Justice Statistics, 1999.

Sampson, Robert J. "Crime, Criminals, and Cures: Medical Model Revisted." *Journal of Personality.* Forthcoming.

Sarich, Vincent. Letter to *Scientific American,* June 1993.

Scarr, Sandra. "Toward Voluntary Parenthood." *The Journal of Personality.* Forthcoming.

U.S. Department of Justice. *Survey of Youth in Custody, 1987.* Washington, D.C.: U.S. Department of Justice, Bureau of Justice Statistics, 1988.

Westman, Jack. *Licensing Parents: Can We Prevent Parental Abuse and Neglect?* New York: Plenum, 1994.

DAVID T. LYKKEN

See also **Euthanasia; Genetics; Holocaust; Medicine and Violence; Sterilization, Involuntary.**

EUTHANASIA

The standard definition of *euthanasia*—literally, a "good death" (from the Greek)—is the deliberate ending of a person's life in order to prevent further suffering. The word is sometimes used interchangeably with the term *mercy killing* and in the 1990s gained both famous and infamous association with its most visible advocate and practitioner, the Michigan doctor Jack Kevorkian. But there are actually several different types of euthanasia; without additional descriptive qualifiers, the term is vague to the point of being meaningless.

Active euthanasia is when someone, usually a physician, puts the death-causing agent into a suffering person's body with the intent of ending that person's life. The agent could be administered through a variety of means (e.g., injection into a vein or infusion into a person's intravenous tube).

Passive euthanasia occurs when life-sustaining treatment is withheld or withdrawn, allowing the person to die.

Voluntary euthanasia takes place when a person makes an explicit, informed request for someone else to administer a death-causing agent.

Involuntary euthanasia occurs when a death-causing agent is administered to a person who has not requested or has refused such an action.

Nonvoluntary euthanasia occurs when a person who is incompetent or incapable of giving informed consent has a death-causing agent administered to him or her, presumably because the decision maker believes that such an action is in the best interests of that person as a result of advance directives completed by him or her.

These terms can be combined, so that a death can be described as the result of *active voluntary*

Jack Kevorkian

Jack Kevorkian's rise to fame began in 1990 when he assisted a woman in the early stages of Alzheimer's disease to die. Since then he admitted to being involved in over 120 deaths, most of those occurring between 1994 and the end of 1998. Although the medical examiner in Michigan declared all these deaths to be homicides, Kevorkian described the deaths as if they were assisted suicides. He was brought to trial four times for the deaths of six of these people but was found not guilty in three cases, and the fourth was declared a mistrial.

In November 1998, Kevorkian presented a videotape to the television news program *60 Minutes* showing him injecting a man who had amyotrophic lateral sclerosis (ALS, or Lou Gehrig's disease) with medication that first made the man unconscious and then stopped his heart. The videotape showed that Kevorkian directly caused the man's death. After a quick trial he was found guilty of second-degree murder and delivery of a controlled substance (the charge of assisting a suicide was dropped).

For the first time, Kevorkian himself described his action as voluntary active euthanasia. Some critics charged that it was actually involuntary active euthanasia because they believed the man did not really want to die. Kevorkian was convicted primarily because consent is not a defense to actively causing the death of another person; the man's apparent request that Kevorkian take this action was legally irrelevant. In addition, the judge had ruled that Kevorkian could not use the man's suffering as evidence nor could the man's family testify in Kevorkian's behalf.

euthanasia (e.g., a lethal injection at the request of the person); *passive voluntary euthanasia* (e.g., an individual requests that artificial nutrition and hydration be discontinued); *active involuntary euthanasia* (e.g., a physician decides that a person would be better off dead and injects a death-causing agent into her intravenous tube, even though the patient has explicitly said that she wants to continue receiving treatment).

Euthanasia in its many forms must be differentiated from *rational suicide* and *assisted suicide*. (Some feel that because the word *suicide* is associated with irrationality, it should not be used in this context; nevertheless, "suicide" is ubiquitous in the discussion surrounding personal decisions about death and so is used here.) In *rational suicide* the person makes a well-reasoned decision that death is her or his best option and takes the action necessary to die without requesting help from, or otherwise involving, other people. *Assisted suicide* is a form of rational suicide where a person obtains information and perhaps the means of death from another person but self-administers the death-causing agent.

History

The practice of euthanasia was recorded by the ancient Greeks and Romans but likely goes back much earlier in the history of humankind. In the United States, the public debate over euthanasia dates back to at least 1906, when the first bill to legalize the practice was introduced in the Ohio legislature. Prior to this time there had been only isolated discussions in the medical community focusing on the role of physicians in helping patients to die peacefully so as to relieve suffering. There is no documentation of how often the different forms of euthanasia occurred.

In 1937 the state of Nebraska voted on legislation proposed by advocates of euthanasia; that attempt to legalize euthanasia failed, but in the following year the Euthanasia Society of America was formed, and shortly thereafter what appears to be the first article in a medical journal advocating the legalization of euthanasia in the United States was published. However, whatever support existed for any form of euthanasia soon declined after the concept became associated with the program of eugenics practiced by the Nazi regime in the years before and during World War II.

Although advocates for voluntary active euthanasia point out that what the Nazis perpetrated was clearly murder, the Nazis themselves characterized the extermination of selected groups of people in the name of racial hygiene as "euthanasia." Moreover, the killing of vulnerable individuals by Nazi physicians began as a program in which hospitals routinely euthanized mental patients, old people who were incurably ill, and babies born with birth defects, and it ultimately expanded to include wholesale executions of millions of Jews and other citizens deemed "defective" or "biologically inferior" by the German state. Following World War II, as the world came to learn more about the extent of the genocide in central Europe and how this so-called euthanasia had been largely overseen by the German scientific and medical communities, advocates of euthanasia in the United States had slim hope of persuading the public to give American physicians the power to kill, even at the apparent request of a suffering and dying person. Opponents of euthanasia pointed to Nazi Germany as demonstrating the dangers of the "slippery slope," arguing that once a certain line is crossed—that is, that physicians should never intentionally help a person to die—it is impossible to prevent the narrow definition of individuals considered "eligible" for such an action (for example, mentally competent individuals who have less than six months to live) from expanding to include ever-larger numbers of people.

In the second half of the twentieth century, improvements in medical technology enhanced physicians' ability to treat and prevent illnesses and other conditions and generally to keep people alive longer. Along with these changes came a growing belief that in some circumstances it was inhumane for physicians to do everything in their power, and at any cost, to prolong life. As a result, withholding and withdrawal of treatment emerged as ethical issues, although they were distinct from directly ending a person's life.

Two court cases are credited with moving the public debate around different forms of euthanasia forward. The first concerned twenty-one-year-old Karen Ann Quinlan, who was in a persistent vegetative state and required a respirator for life support after she fell into a coma while partying with friends. Quinlan's parents asked her physicians to disconnect her from the respirator; they refused, saying that disconnecting her would be the same as killing her. Joseph Quinlan sought court permission to have the machine turned off, and in 1976, following a nearly year-long court battle, the New Jersey Supreme Court ruled in his favor. As a result of this decision, legislation was introduced in a majority of states allowing for the withholding or withdrawal of life-sustaining treatment in some circumstances (in other words permitting passive euthanasia), and many states legalized the use of living wills (documents in which a person can state what kinds of treatments she or he does or does not want done in certain circumstances) and durable powers of attorney for health care (documents in which a person gives the power to make health-care decisions to another individual in the event that she or he cannot make such decisions for herself or himself).

The second decision to have a great impact on the euthanasia debate came in 1990, when the U.S. Supreme Court ruled on its first "right to die" case (what is defined here as nonvoluntary passive euthanasia). Nancy Cruzan had been in a persistent vegetative state for over seven years following an automobile accident. When Cruzan's parents sought to discontinue her artificial nutrition and hydration, the Missouri Supreme Court ruled that there was not enough proof to demonstrate what the patient's wishes would have been regarding her treatment, and that in the absence of such proof the state was compelled to preserve her life. The U.S. Supreme Court affirmed the Missouri ruling, holding that it was acceptable for Missouri to require a high level of proof in order to make life-and-death decisions based on what a patient, now incompetent, "would have wanted," but within the same decision the Court implicitly declared that *competent* people do have a constitutional right *not* to receive medical treatment against their will, even if stopping or not starting such treatment might result in death. After the Supreme Court decision, the case went back to a lower court, where several of Nancy's friends testified that she had expressed her wishes not to live in a state like the one she was in, so her physician dropped his opposition to her parent's action to remove Nancy's feeding tube. She died less than two weeks later.

Following the Cruzan decision, Washington State in 1991 and California in 1992 introduced ballot initiatives that would have allowed a physician to participate in voluntary active euthanasia (in which the physician administers the death-causing agent at the explicit request of the patient) or physician-assisted suicide (in which the physician advises the patient and provides the medication, but the patient self-administers the death-causing agent). Both measures were defeated. Since then almost every ballot initiative and proposed legislative bill has focused solely on physician-assisted suicide (for instance, the Oregon Death with Dignity Act), although bills introduced in Nebraska have continued to allow voluntary active euthanasia in addition to assisted suicide. (The 1997 Supreme Court cases *Washington v. Glucksberg* and *Vacco v. Quill* dealt only with physician-assisted suicide.)

Voluntary Active Euthanasia and Physician-Assisted Suicide

Involuntary euthanasia (either active or passive) has no serious advocates, and voluntary and nonvoluntary passive euthanasia have become accepted medical practice. Thus, it is voluntary active euthanasia (VAE) and physician-assisted suicide (PAS) that remain complex and provocative issues.

Many more organizations and individuals support PAS than VAE; but most opponents of VAE are also against the legalization of PAS. The leading organization in the United States advocating for VAE is the Euthanasia Research and Guidance Organization (ERGO!); two of the major opponents of PAS and VAE are the American Medical Association and the National Hospice Organization. Although both ERGO! and its opponents contend that legalizing PAS is a step toward allowing VAE, most proponents of PAS oppose legalizing VAE because PAS keeps control over the timing of the death in the hands of the patient whereas in VAE the physician has control.

Arguments for VAE. One of the primary arguments for allowing physicians to help a suffering person to die is the belief in personal autonomy— that is, individuals should be allowed to determine for themselves how and when they will die. The belief is that people can make well-reasoned decisions about what is their best option, given their own personality and their unique circumstances. Further, it is asserted that the personal or religious beliefs of someone else should not be forced upon an individual who believes that death is better than life.

Another argument centers on mercy: from this perspective, it is wrong to force people to continue to suffer against their will, especially when something can be done to alleviate that suffering. Not all pain can be managed, and some pain can be controlled only by making the person unconscious and therefore unable to enjoy his or her remaining days. Also, not all suffering is related to physical pain but may also derive from other physical problems such as nausea, itching, and diarrhea. For some people, treatment of symptoms is less than adequate, and the side effects of drugs may be worse than the condition being treated.

Proponents of VAE also argue that safeguards can be put in place to ensure that no one is forced to die. In order to protect vulnerable populations and avoid the slippery slope of ever-broader eligibility for euthanasia, most proposals have stated that, among other things, only terminally ill individuals who are mentally competent and who have been given six months or less to live by two or more physicians would be eligible.

Arguments Against VAE. Those who argue against VAE declare that a slide down the slippery slope is inevitable, even if safeguards are present. At first, they say, voluntary euthanasia may be limited to people who are terminally ill with six months to live, but once society is comfortable with allowing physicians to euthanize one group of people, it opens up the possibility of eventually extending eligibility to more people—for example, to everyone who has a terminal illness, and perhaps next to people with chronic illnesses, and so on. Might the criteria of "competence" eventually be extended to people who had *once* been competent but are no longer (such as people who develop Alzheimer's disease)? Ultimately, might the requirement of competence be abandoned altogether, so that people who have never been competent (such as individuals with severe mental retardation) would also be considered eligible for "voluntary" active euthanasia?

Opponents also say that pain and suffering can be managed and controlled for everyone who is willing to experiment with alternatives. In the most extreme cases the person can be made unconscious, so that the pain and suffering are no longer experienced, until he or she dies. Further, some state, in keeping with the Hippocratic oath, that a physician's duty is to heal or at least do no harm. In addition, it has been argued that suffering can be enriching and should not be eliminated. Related to this last point is the religious perspective that the Sixth Commandment, which prohibits killing, encompasses euthanasia.

Those opposed to euthanasia also contend that most people who think they want to die are experiencing a clinical depression; treatment of this mental illness can eliminate the desire for death. Societal and familial pressure is also of concern: people may be coerced to "choose" death by health-care institutions and providers or by greedy or overwhelmed family members (all of whom may be concerned about the costs of keeping a dying person alive indefinitely).

Conclusion

Voluntary active euthanasia is an extremely controversial issue in the United States and in many other countries. It is inevitably a part of any debate about options at the end of life. The fact that well-informed, compassionate people are on both sides of what has been called the "death with dignity" debate only ensures that it will continue.

BIBLIOGRAPHY

Horan, Dennis J., and David Mall, eds. *Death, Dying, and Euthanasia*. Frederick, Md.: University Publications of America, 1980.

Humphry, Derek, and Ann Wickett. *The Right to Die: Understanding Euthanasia*. Eugene, Oreg.: National Hemlock Society, 1990.

Johnson, Gretchen L. *Voluntary Euthanasia: A Comprehensive Bibliography*. Los Angeles: National Hemlock Society, 1987.

Meisel, Alan. *The Right to Die*. 2d ed. New York: Aspen Law and Business, 1995. Annual supplements.

Miller, Ronald Baker. "Assisted Suicide and Euthanasia: Arguments for and Against Practice, Legalization, and Participation." In *Drug Use in Assisted Suicide and Euthanasia*, edited by Margaret P. Battin and Arthur G. Lipman. Binghamton, N.Y.: Pharmaceuticals Products, 1996.

Moreno, Jonathan D., ed. *Arguing Euthanasia: The Controversy over Mercy Killing, Assisted Suicide, and the "Right to Die."* New York: Simon and Schuster, 1995.

Roberts, Carolyn S., and Martha Gorman. *Euthanasia*. Santa Barbara, Calif.: ABC-CLIO, 1996.

Steinbrook, Bonnie, and Alastair Norcross, eds. *Killing and Letting Die*. 2d ed. New York: Fordham University Press, 1994.

JAMES L. WERTH, JR.

See also **Assisted Suicide and Euthanasia; Eugenics.**

EXECUTION, METHODS OF

Most early forms of execution induced terrible pain and a slow, excruciating death. The goal was often to maximize suffering. In contrast, modern American techniques attempt to minimize the suffering. Although even modern executions are sometimes botched, they are quicker, cleaner, and more regulated than those of the past. Since the late nineteenth century, the advent of each new execution technique (electrocution, then lethal gas, then lethal injection) has been accompanied by the claim that the new technique is less painful and more "humane."

Early Forms of Execution

A mere listing of the myriad methods of execution could fill several pages. Early forms made use of readily available materials or features of the natural environment. Drowning, burying alive, and throwing off a cliff required little preparation or equipment. Stoning was widely used in the Middle East during ancient times and is still occasionally used in some parts of the world. In biblical times the condemned person was often stripped naked and pushed off a tall rock or cliff before the assembled crowd began throwing the rocks that would reduce the victim's body to a broken, bloody heap. Sometimes the condemned were bound to a stake or buried in the ground up to the waist before the first stone was cast.

Sticks, clubs, iron bars, whips, and other tools have also been widely used to beat prisoners to death. At times the goal was to kill, but death might also be the unintended result of an overzealous beating. The severe floggings given to slaves and prisoners of war as punishment often ended in death. In China, Persia, and Turkey, long pieces of wood or bamboo were used as whips to tear away thin strips of flesh from the body. This slow form of killing could take hours and hundreds of strokes. "Breaking at the wheel" was first used by the Romans around 190 A.D. to execute slaves and Christians. In its earliest form, the victim was tied face up to a large bench or table and a spoked wheel was laid on top of him. The wheel was repeatedly hit with a club or hammer so that the rim, hub, and spokes of the wheel shattered the bones of the victim. A later variation of this technique was used in Belgium, Denmark, France, Holland, Germany, and Russia during the sixteenth, seventeenth, and eighteenth centuries. The technique involved binding the criminal faceup to a large wagon wheel. An executioner used an iron bar to methodically smash the legs and arms before bringing death by a final blow to the throat or heart.

Local beasts of burden were also enlisted in the service of the executioner. In India during the rule of the Rajahs, lawbreakers were sometimes tied to the leg of an elephant using a short rope. Then, the elephant was forced into a run so that the victim was violently jerked along the ground. Finally, the criminal's head was crushed under the elephant's foot. Many people have heard of Christian martyrs being thrown to hungry lions in the Roman amphitheaters, but leopards, hyenas, crocodiles, and wild boars have also been used as animal executioners. In seventeenth- and eighteenth-century Europe and in the American West, horses were occasionally used to make executions especially excruciating. Each arm and leg of the person was tied to a strong horse; the horses were then whipped so that they galloped in four different directions. If this was not sufficient to rip arms and legs from the body, deep cuts could be made at the hips and shoulders to help the process along.

Cutting, stabbing, and decapitating have long been popular forms of execution. One of the ear-

---

The First Electric Chair

By the end of the nineteenth century, public officials had begun the search for more modern, civilized methods of execution. Hangings were often botched and were strongly associated with lynchings and vigilante justice. The European alternative to hanging—the guillotine—was more efficient and certain but left behind a bleeding, decapitated corpse. A cleaner method was needed. In 1886, the governor of New York, David B. Hill, established a commission to find a "humane" alternative to hanging. One member of the commission, a dentist named Alfred Southwick, advocated the newly harnessed power of electricity (Thomas Edison had invented the electric light bulb only a few years earlier, in 1879). Southwick was convinced by his investigation of the accidental death of a drunken man by electrocution that electricity could provide a quick, clean method of killing. A wooden chair was rigged up with wires and electrodes, and a cat, a dog, and a monkey were executed to demonstrate the effectiveness of the new technique.

The animal executions went well, and on 6 August 1890 William Kemmler, who had murdered his lover with an ax, became the first man to die in the electric chair. Kemmler wore a business suit to his execution at Auburn Prison, in Auburn, New York. Unfortunately, his execution did not go smoothly. Kemmler strained against his straps, bloody foam dripped from his mouth, his face turned purple, and smoke rose from the scorched skin under the electrodes. When the first jolt of electricity failed to kill, a second jolt was applied. Witnesses became sick. The unpleasant spectacle led one physician in attendance to comment, "The electrical system of execution can in no way be regarded as a step in civilization. The guillotine is better than the gallows, the gallows is better than electrical execution." Despite the complications, Southwick declared that Kemmler's execution was the "grandest success of the age." Public officials were impressed with the new technology and by 1906 one hundred condemned prisoners had been killed in electric chairs across the United States.

---

liest and most hideous versions of death by the blade was used by the Assyrians against prisoners of war. The technique involved slicing and peeling away the flesh while the victim was still alive. Chinese variations on cutting away the flesh are sometimes known as "death by a thousand cuts." Here a skilled executioner wielding a razor-sharp knife systematically severed appendages from the body or cut away parts of the victim's flesh in a predetermined sequence (e.g., calves, thighs, biceps, fingers, toes, nose, and ears). Death might come to the prisoner early or late in the gruesome process.

Beheading has been accomplished in a variety of ways. When the executioner used an ax, the victim's neck rested on a wooden block. To be decapitated with a sword, the victim sat or knelt or stood—no block was used because too often the end of the sword hit the block first before the rest of the blade sliced through the neck. The guillotine, first used in 1792, was the most successful early execution machine. Compared with a stroke from the blade of a human executioner, the guillotine produced a swifter, more humane beheading. Because of dull blades, clumsy executioners, and terrified or unconscious victims, beheadings conducted by humans often required hacking off the head using several blows of an ax or sword.

Burning at the stake was generally reserved for women. Though burning is surely a horrible way to die, it was considered far less excruciating than the disemboweling and quartering that men faced for similar crimes. In England, from the thirteenth through the eighteenth century, men convicted of capital crimes could be hanged, drawn, and quartered. First, the prisoner was nearly strangled to death by hanging. Then, the executioner cut down the prisoner, disemboweled him, threw the entrails into a nearby fire, cut the head off, and cut the body into quarters. The five parts of the corpse were often displayed at conspicuous sites as visible

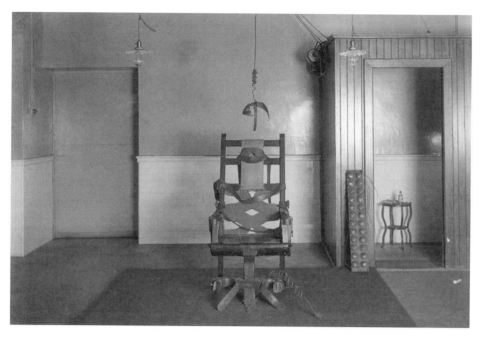

The first electric chair, seen here in Auburn Prison, New York, around 1908. COURTESY OF THE CAYUGA MUSEUM

warnings to potential wrongdoers. During the sixteenth and seventeenth centuries many major crossroads in London were decorated with decaying corpses hanging from trees or stuck on poles. London Bridge was festooned with the heads of the recently executed.

The major justification for these sadistic practices was deterrence. It was supposed that the threat of execution would cause others to refrain from illegal activities. Torturing a criminal before execution and mutilating the corpse after execution was thought to boost deterrent power. Indeed, for most of human history, rulers and local governments encouraged the masses to watch the execution ceremony—in the belief that viewing these hideous spectacles would instill fear in the heart of anyone who might be tempted to commit a crime. In Europe and some American colonies, hangings, often several in a day, were festive public spectacles witnessed by hundreds or thousands of rowdy spectators.

Worldwide, hanging and shooting are still the most popular forms of execution. Early forms of hanging involved slow strangulation as the person dangled from the end of a rope. In modern hangings, the goal is to snap the prisoner's spine. A noose is tightened around the neck and a trapdoor beneath the prisoner's feet swings open. If all goes well, the cervical vertebrae are dislocated and death comes quickly. Execution by shooting brings

death by massive damage to internal organs, or damage to the central nervous system, or hemorrhage. In many parts of the world, prisoners are shot in the head at close range. In the United States, the condemned prisoner is strapped into a wooden armchair and a hood is placed over the head. A stethoscope is used to locate the heart and a red cloth target is pinned to the site. A large pan sits under the chair to collect draining blood. Five anonymous sharpshooters fire on command.

Modern Forms of Execution

During the nineteenth century bloody, sadistic execution rituals became repugnant to a large segment of citizens, religious authorities, and public officials. Executions became less public, less cruel, more precise, and more mechanized. In the United States (the only Western democracy that still permits capital punishment), executions are generally conducted late at night, using well-defined and specialized procedures, and witnessed by only a handful of observers. The three methods of execution most familiar to Americans—electrocution, poisonous gas, and lethal injection—are used only in the United States.

In 1889 the electric chair began to replace the noose because killing by electrocution was thought to be more humane, modern, and scientific. In theory, a mysterious, invisible force would pass through the prisoner's body and death would

493

occur almost instantly. To prepare for electrocution, part of a prisoner's leg and head are shaved to afford good contact with electrodes. The prisoner is strapped to the chair and a powerful surge of electricity (about 1,900 volts) is passed through the body. The official goal is paralysis of the heart and respiratory system through the burning of internal organs. In the case of lethal gas, the prisoner is strapped to a steel chair in an airtight chamber. A stethoscope is taped to the chest to monitor heartbeat and fix the time of death. The executioner pulls a lever to drop capsules of sodium cyanide into a vat of sulfuric acid. Cyanide gas fills the chamber and death is caused by asphyxiation.

Lethal injection, first used in 1977, was the last innovation in the twentieth century in the technology of execution. The prisoner is strapped to a gurney on his back, and needles that deliver the poison are inserted in both arms, usually just opposite the elbow. Three substances are injected: the first is a fast-acting anaesthetic, the second is a drug that paralyzes the diaphragm and respiratory muscles, and the third drug stops the heart. At the end of the twentieth century, more than three-quarters of the states that authorized capital punishment used lethal injection. If this trend continues, lethal injection will become the only method of execution in the United States.

The execution procedure has also become more impersonal, bureaucratic, precise, and sanitized. Every step in the process is spelled out in meticulous detail: After the death warrant is issued, the prisoner is moved to a special cell next to the death chamber. Guards are posted outside the cell to prevent the prisoner from committing suicide. The prisoner receives a final visit with loved ones as well as a visit by a "spiritual advisor." Personal possessions are boxed for distribution to relatives after the execution. The execution machinery is tested. After a final meal and a final shower, the prisoner is dressed in a clean execution uniform and is photographed. The death warrant is read aloud. After the execution, the corpse is removed from the chamber. Each prison official who participates in the process has a specific and limited duty (e.g., to watch the prisoner for a six-hour shift to prevent suicide, to escort the prisoner to the chamber, to tighten one or more of the leather straps that hold the prisoner to the chair or gurney).

Of course, even modern American techniques do not work perfectly on every occasion. Botched executions can be the result of mistakes by the executioners, errors in combining or delivering drugs, equipment problems, or struggling by the condemned prisoner. Such problems prolong the process of killing and cause unpleasant spectacles of suffering. Politically, it is important that executions *appear* clean and humane. Though most politicians and much of the public still favor the death penalty in the abstract, we are far more ambivalent about the act of killing condemned prisoners.

BIBLIOGRAPHY

Abbott, Geoffrey. *The Book of Execution.* London: Headline, 1994.
Costanzo, Mark. *Just Revenge: Costs and Consequences of the Death Penalty.* New York: St. Martin's, 1997.
Johnson, Robert. *Death Work: A Study of the Modern Execution Process.* Pacific Grove, Calif.: Brooks-Cole, 1990.
Trombley, Stephen. *The Execution Protocol: Inside America's Capital Punishment Industry.* New York: Crown, 1992.

MARK COSTANZO

See also **Capital Punishment; Crime and Punishment in American History; Cruel and Unusual Punishment; Death Row.**

EXPERIMENTATION. *See* Animals, Violence Against; Medicine and Violence; Medical Experimentation on the Mentally Ill; Methodologies of Violence Research.

EXTORTION. *See* Crime, Legal Definitions of; Organized Crime.

EXTREME FIGHTING. *See* Ultimate Fighting.

EXTREMISM

To understand the role of extremism and extremist groups in American life, it is best to distinguish between extremist thought and extremist style. In a general sense, extreme beliefs are those furthest removed from what most people appear to believe. What constitutes extreme belief changes over time. For instance, those who advocated the abolition of slavery before the Civil War in the United States were considered extremists. In the late twentieth century defenders of slavery or any other form of racial oppression were regarded as extremists. Given the shifting nature of extreme belief, it is probably best to begin with an analysis of the extremist style.

Extremist Style

Many twentieth-century observers (historians and political scientists) have noted distinctive characteristics of the extremist style. While there is no consensus on what constitutes extremism, some common attributes are often linked to such an outlook. Extremists are intolerant of ambiguity; they see the world in stark black-and-white terms. Concomitantly, they are highly moralistic and judgmental, in that they interpret events and people as strictly good or evil. If there is only one right answer to a problem or only one virtuous path to follow and everything else is error and villainy, there is no reason to permit public discussion of what is manifestly false. As a consequence, extremists wish to shut down the marketplace of ideas, which is central to a pluralistic democratic society. Adversaries or opponents, those in error, are defined as enemies who possess no redeeming qualities, so one need not abide by rules of fair play in confronting these evildoers.

Then there is what the historian Richard Hofstadter referred to as the "paranoid style" in U.S. politics. Not only are extremists highly suspicious, but they also believe the world is in the grip of a comprehensive conspiracy. They claim that a small group of powerful individuals (e.g., insiders, financiers, monopoly capitalists, Jews) have devised and are implementing a comprehensive plan (e.g., the new world order) to control and dominate all aspects of American life. Extremists view seemingly random events or minor political setbacks as manifestations of the conspiracy. Rarely if ever do events occur by accident or as the result of normal human shortcomings. For extremists these events are explained in terms of the unfolding conspiracy.

Many extremists have an apocalyptic view of the world. Whether derived from the book of Revelation, the writings of Karl Marx, or science-fiction films and literature, this view leads many extremists to believe that some type of catastrophic event is imminent, one that will dramatically change the nature of American life. Some of those who have this apocalyptic vision attempt to force the end by carrying out acts of violence intended to ignite the fire. Before the Civil War, the abolitionist John Brown sought to do this. In the last decades of the twentieth century, Charles Manson and a long list of other extremists hoped to spark a racial holy war by perpetrating highly publicized attacks on celebrities and randomly selected members of the African American community. By murdering prominent members of minority communities, the hope was to polarize the races and create a spiral of violence, with spokespeople for the different groups blaming the other race for a mounting wave of reciprocal killings.

If the characteristics listed above represent key elements of the extremist style, it should not be difficult to imagine a link between this approach to the world and violence. Over the course of U.S. history, extremist groups have engaged in violent campaigns to halt the conspiracy, defeat the enemy, and bring on the apocalypse, or they have retreated from the world into sacred or secular compounds or encampments (e.g., Justus Township in Montana, the Branch Davidians in Waco, Texas, MOVE in Philadelphia, Elohim City in Arkansas, Charles Manson's Family in the Mojave Desert, California). Sometimes these groups have oscillated between these two ways of coping with the menacing world in which they live.

Extremist Thought

Bearing in mind that beliefs once considered extreme may come to be regarded as mainstream or vice versa, some general statements may be made about extremism in the United States by examining the central issues around which it formed. When discussing U.S. extremism, it is useful to keep in mind that the history of the United States differs from that of Europe and consequently the causes for extremism have differed.

U.S. history is exceptional when viewed against the European experience. Struggles against absolute monarchies, an established church, and a system of inherited class privilege were at the core of European political history during the eighteenth and nineteenth centuries. Close to the core if not always part of it were conflicts over the economic and political status of the urban working class and rural peasantry. These conflicts shaped the politics of extremism in Europe.

The United States was different: it had no monarchy, no established church, no inherited aristocracy, and no traditional peasantry. Some policies that in Europe seemed extreme, for example, near-universal access to state-supported primary and secondary education, were quickly adopted and became conventional in the United States. On the other hand, American society had other problems that provided the bases for extremism and political violence. These problems involved questions of national identity, race and the legacy of slavery, and the role of the federal government in American life.

First, who is and who is not American has been a matter of widespread concern from the earliest days of the Republic. Much more than in Europe, nationality in the United States, a country of immigrants, has been a question of belief and conduct rather than birth. As a consequence, nativist social and political movements have arisen from time to time that have sought to deny the status of being an American to members of newer immigrant groups. Spokespeople for nativist movements, such as the nineteenth-century American and Know-Nothing Parties and the American Protective Association, often have asserted not only that the ways of the immigrant group are incompatible with authentically American ones but also that members of the group owe their allegiance to some foreign power. During the nineteenth century Roman Catholics from Germany and Ireland, and later southern and eastern Europe, were the principal targets of these accusations. Their loyalty, so the allegation went, was to the Vatican and the pope, not the U.S. Constitution. During the early decades of the twentieth century, particularly in the period between the Russian Revolution and the outbreak of World War II, Jewish immigrants aroused similar fears. Depression-era demagogues such as William Dudley Pelley and Gerald Winrod claimed that communism was part of a Jewish plot to take over the United States.

Some scholars have maintained that extreme nativist sentiment waned after World War II. The dominant fears became communism and the threat posed by the Soviet Union and its allies. The important right-wing groups of the 1950s and 1960s such as the John Birch Society and the Christian Anti-Communist Crusade stressed the dangers of domestic communist conspirators but did not identify them with any particular immigrant group. While it may be true that extreme nativism waned after the war, nativism and nativist movements enjoyed something of a revival in the 1970s, 1980s, and 1990s. The White Aryan Resistance in southern California and various Christian Identity churches throughout the West consistently expressed fears that the land assigned by God to white Aryan yeomen was being overrun by "dusky hordes" of Asian and Hispanic immigrants under the control of a powerful Jewish world conspiracy.

The second major source of extremism in American life involved race and the legacy of slavery. From the Civil War forward the maintenance of white racial supremacy has stimulated the formation of numerous groups committed to the exclusion of African Americans from previously all-white institutions and places of residence. Not uncommonly, groups such as the Ku Klux Klan have been willing to use violence in order to maintain white racial dominance. The period between the Supreme Court's 1954 *Brown v. Board of Education* ruling concerning school desegregation and the passage of the 1964 Civil Rights Act was especially brutal. In that era the Civil Rights movement's commitment to the use of nonviolent techniques to promote the integration of public facilities and the voting rights of African Americans was met by largely self-defeating violence from White Citizens Councils and Klan groups throughout the South. In the context of this struggle the American Nazi Party of George Lincoln Rockwell and its successor, the National White People's Party, were formed.

There is another side to the coin. From time to time elements within the African American community have supported the idea of black nationalism, the idea that blacks should withdraw from other U.S. citizens. During the 1920s this sentiment took the form of Marcus Garvey's Back to Africa movement. Throughout the second half of the twentieth century the Nation of Islam, or Black Muslims, advocated African American social and economic separatism, sometimes including the establishment of an independent black republic to be carved out of the current United States. The Black Panther Party, which was active during the 1960s and underwent something of a revival in the 1990s, was another group committed to African American social and economic autonomy within the United States and willing to use violence on occasion to further this objective.

A third source of extreme belief and action in U.S. life involved the role of the federal government. Almost from its inception the government's right to rule has been challenged by what the historian Catherine Stock has identified as "rural radicalism." In the early years of the Republic this took the form of Shays's Rebellion and the Whiskey Rebellion, challenges to the government's ability to tax and regulate. In frontier times the belief developed that when the government seemed unresponsive or unwilling to enforce the law, as defined by the frontiersmen, the latter acquired the right to enforce the law themselves, to apply vigilante justice. Local citizens, for example, carried out attacks on Native Americans, Mormons, Chinese immigrants, and others in the nineteenth century when they perceived that the federal government was unable or unwilling to act against them. Vigilante justice and defiance of the federal government did not disappear in the twentieth century and came to be linked to the idea that Washington had fallen under the control of alien elements. From the Minutemen organizations of the 1960s, paramilitary units prepared to defend their localities against communist attack, through the Posse Comitatus of the 1980s, to the Michigan and Montana militia associations of the 1990s, there continued to be thousands of Americans who believed the federal government posed a mortal danger to their fundamental rights and who were willing to take up arms against its representatives. The bombing of the Alfred P. Murrah Federal Building in Oklahoma City in 1995 was a dramatic expression of this sentiment.

During the 1990s vigilante justice also manifested itself in a series of abortion clinic bombings and in the murder of a number of publicly identified physicians who performed abortions. Frustrated by the refusal of the federal courts to outlaw abortion, individuals inspired by Identity theology, Reconstructionism (a splinter of mainstream Presbyterianism), and an apocalyptic strain of Catholicism waged a campaign of religiously inspired violence against those they saw as violating God's law by killing the unborn. Those involved in antiabortion (one might add antihomosexual) violence not uncommonly were drawn to and supported by the militia and "patriot" movements.

Finally, opposition to the country's capitalist form of economic development and organization stimulated a certain amount of extremist reaction.

In the late nineteenth and the early decades of the twentieth century, anarchists, including members of the Industrial Workers of the World, or Wobblies, carried out violent attacks on prominent political figures as well as on a number of captains of industry, often individuals linked to the repression of strikers. But despite the widespread fear sometimes bordering on hysteria it stimulated, the Communist Party (organized in 1920) never amounted to much. During the Depression era of the 1930s, the party made some headway within the trade unions here and there, and later some individuals linked to the party carried out espionage on behalf of the Soviet Union. Compared with its counterparts in France, Italy, Finland, and a few other European countries, however, communism in the United States never posed a serious challenge to the existing order. Nor, for that matter, did such minuscule but violent groups as the Symbionese Liberation Army and the Weather Underground of the post-Vietnam era.

BIBLIOGRAPHY

Bennett, David. *The Party of Fear: From Nativist Movements to the New Right in American History.* New York: Vintage, 1995.

George, John, and Laird Wilcox. *American Extremists: Militias, Supremacists, Klansmen, Communists, and Others.* Amherst, N.Y.: Prometheus, 1996.

Sargent, Lyman Tower, ed. *Extremism in America.* New York: New York University Press, 1995.

Stock, Catherine McNicol. *Rural Radicals: Righteous Rage in the American Grain.* Ithaca, N.Y.: Cornell University Press, 1996.

LEONARD WEINBERG

See also **Abortion; Cults; Heaven's Gate; Immigration; Jonestown; Ku Klux Klan; Militias, Unauthorized; Neo-Nazis; Oklahoma City Bombing; Religion; Skinheads; Terrorism; Vigilantism; Waco; Weatherman and Weather Underground.**

F

FAMILY. *See* Domestic Violence.

FASHION

What people wear is one of the most essential marks of identification: clothing can convey its wearer's gender, sexual orientation, class, race, or regional origin; it can indicate ethnic, cultural, or religious identity. Clothing thus often separates insiders from outsiders, distinguishing family, friends, and allies from foreigners, outlaws, and enemies. At the same time, fashion has been the field on which many kinds of violence have played out, in practice as well as symbolically.

Although there are undoubtedly many ways to consider the topic of fashion within the context of violence, it can be loosely grouped in two categories: fashions that in some way represent or connote violence, and fashions that are themselves violent. However, the broader context is the same: fashion, like other aspects of art and culture, reflects the concerns and anxieties common to American culture in general and American ambivalence toward violence in particular. A deep fascination with representations of violence coexists with anxiety and concern over widespread social problems such as riots, homicide, rape, police brutality, and handgun sales, among other issues.

Interest in the themes and images of violence within fashion varies with the times—violence within fashion generally is the result of other cultural or social forces and trends. For instance, images within fashion magazines often borrow from street styles and from what is known as subculture styles—the styles of groups who coalesce around a particular social or cultural movement, public figure, music, or other especially powerful public presence. In the pages of the fashion magazine *Vogue* in 1994, the critic Luc Sante discussed the way violence was glamorized in the images of 1990s fashion photography in a way that directly reflected the culture of the moment, as exemplified by movies like *Reservoir Dogs* and *Natural Born Killers* and the musical performances of "industrial rock" groups such as Nine Inch Nails, as well as in the music and personas of heavy metal and rap artists.

Background

Although fashion is often associated with the expression of identity, historically it has also been used as a way to exert control. For example, slaves in the United States were governed by strict rules about their clothing, and limitations on slaves' time for personal grooming and adornment was one way for slaveholders to control the sense of individual and group identity gained through style. Descriptions in ads for runaway slaves included clothing and, especially in the eighteenth century, hair, in addition to name, age, and color.

American history is rife with clothing styles that originated in some sort of violent practice but later became common idioms of fashion. Indeed, the founding myths of American history appear regularly in fashion trends, far removed from their original contexts. In general, these fashions tend to be reminders of fashion as a form of control.

Native Americans. Colonizing Europeans who encountered Native Americans here were determined to bring them not just Christianity but also standards of dress more suitable to their new religion. Hundreds of years later, though, Native American style made a comeback, when the partly shaved head called a Mohawk—by some accounts, a style used as a way to identify the enemy—reappeared as a punk hairstyle. In the twentieth century, other Native American styles, such as ornamental beads, fringe, and turquoise and silver jewelry, made their way into the mainstream. Meanwhile, the war bonnet, which is based on the traditional headgear of the Sioux, ultimately became a universalized symbol of the American Indian.

Military Garb. Perhaps the example par excellence of fashion as way of both identifying others and exerting control is military clothing, in styles too numerous to describe in detail. Military clothes first became a part of everyday clothing after the Mexican War, when U.S. Army surplus was sold at auction and given to slaves to wear. At the end of World War II, the development of leisure activity coincided with the appeal of American military leaders' uniforms to provide the basis for the emerging fashion known as sportswear. Many people found the clothes of wartime, like khakis, both comfortable and attractive.

Western Wear. Yet another important way in which violence appears as fashion is in the American fascination with outlaws. The myth of the cowboy battling savages and conquering the wilderness, for instance, infuses American fashion as it does other aspects of American culture. Western style, especially during the 1930s and 1940s, became popular as a projection of the wearer's self-image (which had more to do with the myth of the cowboy's rugged individualism than with the actual history of the cowboy experience).

Despite fluctuating interest in explicitly Western fashion idioms, the myth of the West—with all its real and implied violence—endures at least symbolically in the longstanding appeal of denim, which was considered revolutionary when it was introduced. According to Lee Hall, a historian of American fashion, Levi's-brand denim pants and the Stetson hat—work clothing for conquering the West—are "two of the most identifiable products contributing to the development of American sportswear" (1992, p. 93). The introduction of denim was especially important, according to Ted Polhemus, because jeans "mark a critical juncture in the seemingly unstoppable shift from formal to casual, [since] they also constitute the first important example of Dressing Down, in which middle-class people adopt working-class style" (1994, p. 24).

Outlaws and Outsiders. Whereas the cowboy as outsider is perceived as the embodiment of American culture, the gang member is considered a threat to that culture. Thus some schools prohibited the color combinations, oversize jeans and T-shirts, and other styles associated with gangs in the late twentieth century.

Clothing prohibitions have been enacted before, notably in the period that culminated in the Zoot-Suit Riot of 1943. Worn by Mexican American and black men, zoot-suits were characterized by their luxurious cut and fabric—typically, a knee-length draped jacket with wide shoulder pads worn with a showy tie and long key chain, and high-waisted, deeply pleated, full trousers pegged at the ankle. Zoot-suits seemed to flaunt wartime fabric rationing, and an effort was made to imprison those who wore them. The controversy over the suits erupted into violence in Los Angeles in June 1943 and then across the country, culminating in the Detroit race riots just three weeks later. These riots were about more than fabric or pants cut. Zoots were thought to be affiliated with gangs, and they incited widespread anger about crime, violence, and lack of patriotism. In the face of such antagonism, a zoot-suit was a mark of identity and communal allegiance. The furor over the zoot-suits radicalized both César Chavez and Malcolm X and sowed in others the seeds of identity politics that would blossom in the 1960s.

Images of Violence

Perhaps the most influential style associated with violence is punk, which though usually considered English in origin can just as easily be traced to American musicians like Richard Hell and Patti Smith and, before them, to Lou Reed and Iggy Pop. The black leather, metal studs, and dyed Mohawks characteristic of punk borrowed from the iconography of fetishism popular in the 1960s (seen, for instance, in the cat suits worn in the television show *The Avengers*). In its eventual incorporation into the mainstream, punk was enormously influential not only stylistically but also socially; it refined the premises of the 1960s sexual revolution to contend with issues of gender and power through its appropriation of sadomasochistic notions of dominance and submission.

Punk's revolutionary eclecticism influenced all subsequent fashion. High fashion incorporated the explicit sexual images of violence and murder first associated with punk and other subcultures. Numerous fashion photographers have since drawn on the conventions of pornography—particularly hard-core porn—including Madonna videographer Jean-Baptiste Mondino and the photographers Helmut Newton, Chris von Wangenheim, Guy Bourdin, and Ellen Von Unwerth. The enormously influential German-born photographer Helmut Newton, whose magazine work first drew attention in the 1960s, appears to have bypassed punk in drawing directly from sadomasochistic and fetishist stylistic idioms. Fetishistic and sadomasochistic images on MTV and in magazines, fairly common in the 1970s and later, can be traced at least in part to Newton's recurring interest in sexually charged themes and to the tension and aggression more generally characteristic of his work.

Body Art

Many forms of fashion bring to mind acts of violence done to the body. These trends evoke outsider or outlaw sensibilities and draw on a variety of violent images. The shaved heads of some gay and post-punk subcultures, for instance, can be seen as alluding to the penitentiary, military, or concentration camp. Similarly, piercing and tattooing make reference to gangs and slavery. The association of piercing with slavery, which appears in the images of hard-core pornography, reaches back to the Bible. Tattoos, which were once associated with working-class masculinity, began to enjoy wider popularity in the 1960s, and by the 1990s they were as likely to be seen on college students and supermodels as on brawny workingmen.

The late-twentieth-century interest in body art, or "body modification," appeared within the context of the nostalgia and celebration of tribalism that accompanied the close of the millennium. One critic, writing about heroin and needles, sees body modification—which includes scarification and branding in addition to piercing and tattooing—as an act of defiance against the cultural conventions that demand a clean body in working order prepared to labor in a consumer economy. At the

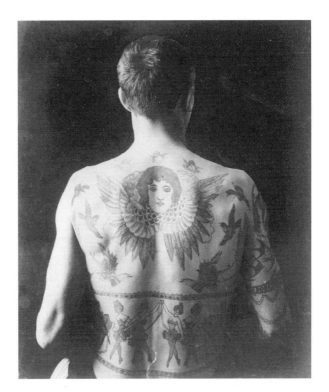

In this photograph from the 1930s, a man's back is covered with tattoos of angels and dancing women. HULTON GETTY/LIAISON AGENCY

very least, if American fashion is fundamentally about change and obsolescence, the relative permanence of piercing and tattoos represents a resistance to fashion—although the widespread popularity of such body art in the 1980s and 1990s (and even the subsequent trend toward the surgical removal of tattoos) seems to suggest a paradox within this expression of cultural rebellion.

In the face of fairly broad acceptance of tattoos and piercing, the needle itself continues to be stigmatized. This helps explain the outrage against a 1990s trend in fashion photography called "heroin chic"—couture-clad models portrayed with the dissipated, worn-out "druggy" look—associated with the work of the photographer Nan Goldin. Because of such images, the fashion industry was criticized for what was seen as an aestheticization of drugs, especially heroin. That this controversy coincides with the continued presence of AIDS—often spread through the use of contaminated needles—should come as no surprise.

Violence in Pursuit of Beauty

Any account of fashion must also consider beauty conventions and practices, for they are

501

inextricably linked. Feminists have long criticized American standards of female beauty, which at one time required women to fasten their bodies into corsets and which continue to promote wearing high heels, waxing and plucking body hair, augmenting breast size, removing fat through liposuction, and staying thin (an obsession that can lead to extreme eating behaviors including anorexia and bulimia), among other procedures and practices. In addition to the pain and cost of these beauty regimens, they perpetuate a gender inequality that can be connected, directly or indirectly, to the harassment, abuse, and rape of women.

Similarly, the pressure to conform to white standards is at least in part responsible for the many products embraced by African Americans to straighten or relax their hair, including the painful hair-straightening formula made with lye, potatoes, and eggs that was ancestor to the "conk" of the 1930s and 1940s. At the same time, such practices—like the rituals and pain involved with body modification—can also be seen as promoting group identity and personal self-expression.

BILBIOGRAPHY

Hall, Lee. *Common Threads: A Parade of American Clothing.* Boston: Little, Brown, 1992.

Hebdige, Dick. *Subculture: The Meaning of Style.* New York: Routledge, 1988.

Hollander, Anne. *Seeing Through Clothes.* New York: Avon, 1980.

Lurie, Alison. *The Language of Clothes.* New York: Random House, 1981.

Mazón, Mauricio. *The Zoot-Suit Riots: The Psychology of Symbolic Annihilation.* Austin: University of Texas Press, 1984.

McRobbie, Angela. *Zoot Suits and Second-Hand Dresses: An Anthology of Fashion and Music.* Boston: Unwin Hyman, 1988.

Nickerson, Camilla, and Neville Wakefield, eds. *Fashion: Photography of the Nineties.* New York: Scalo, 1996.

Polhemus, Ted. *Streetstyle: From Sidewalk to Catwalk.* London: Thames and Hudson, 1994.

Santé, Luc. "The Glamorization of Violence." *Vogue,* September 1994.

Wilson, Elizabeth. *Adorned in Dreams: Fashion and Modernity.* Los Angeles: University of California Press, 1985.

Wolf, Naomi. *The Beauty Myth: How Images of Beauty Are Used Against Women.* New York: William Morrow, 1991.

KETURA PERSELLIN

See also **Dance; Gangs; Mutilation of the Body; Popular Culture; Sadism and Masochism; Zoot-Suit Riot.**

FEDERAL BUREAU OF INVESTIGATION

Created in 1908 as the investigative division of the Department of Justice, the Bureau of Investigation, which was formally renamed the Federal Bureau of Investigation in 1935, had a limited mission: to investigate suspected violators of federal antitrust and interstate-commerce laws. The bureau had no policing role; local and state police forces retained exclusive responsibility for investigating and apprehending violent criminals. The bureau's mission, however, changed during the 1930s.

The lawlessness engendered by Prohibition and the increased ability to cross state lines that the automobile provided to gangsters confirmed that local and state police could not contain a perceived crime wave. The exploits of John Dillinger—when orchestrating a string of bank robberies throughout the Midwest from 1933 to 1934 and when escaping from a local jail after being apprehended—the 1932 kidnapping and murder of the infant son of the aviator Charles Lindbergh, and the 1933 gun battle in the Kansas City, Missouri, railroad station that resulted in the deaths of bureau agents and police officers who were escorting the convicted gangster Frank Nash to the Leavenworth, Kansas, penitentiary caused many to reassess the principles of states' rights. Exploiting this emotionally charged setting, Attorney General Homer Cummings succeeded by 1934 in obtaining congressional approval for much of his Twelve Point Crime Program. Congress enacted legislation that extended federal jurisdiction to bank robbery, kidnapping, and extortion and authorized FBI agents to carry firearms. Then a number of highly publicized raids that led to either the violent death or the capture of notorious gangsters, including Dillinger, George "Machine Gun" Kelly, "Pretty Boy" Floyd, and "Baby Face" Nelson, captured the public's imagination. G-men, or special agents of the FBI—highly trained professionals who "always got their man"—came to be synonymous with crime control and represented the nation's frontline defense against violent criminals.

While the war against gangsters catapulted the FBI to national prominence and undercut libertarian and states' rights concerns about the threat posed by a secretive federal bureaucracy, crime fighting became a lesser FBI priority. The succeeding international crises of World War II and the Cold War led to a new mission: to monitor suspected spies and to identify their ideological supporters in order to protect the national security first from Nazi Germany and then from the Soviet Union. FBI efforts, however, were not confined to counterintelligence and criminal prosecution under the espionage law but extended to containing suspected communist influence, whether in Hollywood, labor unions, or the Civil Rights movement. Toward this end the FBI orchestrated leaks to favored reporters and members of Congress to discredit individuals and organizations who might promote radical change or influence public opinion. As a by-product of this shift in focus, investigations of increasingly more powerful organized-crime families became secondary.

FBI priorities changed dramatically after 1957, when a New York state police officer discovered that prominent crime leaders from around the country had convened a meeting in Apalachin, New York. Because the FBI director, J. Edgar Hoover, had publicly denied the existence of a nationwide crime conspiracy, or mafia, the FBI had a potential public-relations fiasco on its hands. In response, FBI officials launched a code-named Top Hoodlum Program to identify the nation's more influential crime bosses. This war against organized crime was abetted by the passage of two

Director J. Edgar Hoover outside the FBI building in Washington, D.C., in 1950. UPI/Corbis-Bettmann

laws: the Omnibus Crime Control and Safe Streets Act in 1968, which legalized the use of wiretaps and bugs, or concealed listening devices, during criminal investigations; and the Racketeer Influenced and Corrupt Organizations (RICO) Act in 1970, which relaxed the standards of proof to promote prosecution of criminal conspiracies. A perceived law-and-order crisis—evidenced by the sharp increase in urban crime and by the climate of lawlessness that gave rise to urban race riots and violent anti–Vietnam War demonstrations during the 1960s—triggered the enactment of these two laws to expand federal law-enforcement authority, thereby negating Congress's earlier concerns about Big Brother, which had led it to ban wiretapping in 1934 and to stymie the efforts of Presidents Franklin D. Roosevelt and Harry S. Truman to expand federal regulatory power after 1937.

The upsurge of domestic and international terrorism in the 1970s, including publicized incidents of hostage taking and airplane hijacking, raised new questions over the need to expand FBI authority and over whether or not FBI methods included excessive use of force. To meet these new threats, FBI officials created a specially trained Hostage Rescue Team. Both before and after the collapse of the Soviet Union and of communist governments in Eastern Europe during 1989–1991, increased resources were devoted to monitoring and apprehending individuals engaged in domestic terrorism. The result was a complicated and contradictory legacy.

On the one hand, the actions of the FBI's Hostage Rescue Team in violent confrontations—for instance, when attempting to apprehend Randall Weaver at Ruby Ridge, Idaho, in 1992, which led to the deaths of Weaver's son and wife, and when forcing the surrender of David Koresh and his Branch Davidian adherents at Waco, Texas, in 1993, which led to the deaths of women and children inside his compound—raised questions about the militarization of federal law enforcement and the FBI's use of excessive force. On the other hand, the bombing of the World Trade Center in New York City in February 1993 and of the Alfred P. Murrah Federal Building in Oklahoma City in April 1995 suggested that insufficient resources were being devoted to containing a potentially serious terrorist threat of diverse origins. Whereas foreign-born Islamic fundamentalists were responsible for the World Trade Center bombing, U.S. citizens identified with conservative anti–gun control and antigovernment militia movements were responsible for the Murrah Building bombing. Other domestic bombing incidents occurred at the 1996 Olympics in Atlanta and at abortion clinics, notably in Birmingham, Alabama, in 1998. The bombing attacks on the U.S. air base Khobar Towers in Saudi Arabia in 1996 and on U.S. embassies in Kenya and Tanzania in 1998 and the confirmed links between U.S. and overseas organized-crime gangs (notably, in Italy and Russia) led FBI officials to effect better coordination with foreign police agencies. By the 1990s the FBI no longer focused on uncovering evidence to convict those accused of violating federal statutes; the FBI's mission and methods also included acquiring advance intelligence essential to anticipating and averting the commission of violent crime.

BIBLIOGRAPHY

Burnham, David. "The FBI." *Nation,* 11–18 August 1997.

Gentry, Curt. *J. Edgar Hoover: The Man and the Secrets.* New York: Norton, 1991.

Kelly, John, and Phillip Wearne. *Tainting Evidence: Inside the Scandals of the FBI Crime Lab.* New York: Free Press, 1998.

Kessler, Ronald. *The FBI: Inside the World's Most Powerful Law Enforcement Agency.* New York: Pocket, 1993.

McGee, Jim. "The Rise of the FBI." *Washington Post Magazine,* 20 July 1997.

Powers, Richard Gid. *Secrecy and Power: The Life of J. Edgar Hoover.* New York: Free Press, 1987.

Theoharis, Athan, and John Stuart Cox. *The Boss: J. Edgar Hoover and the Great American Inquisition.* Philadelphia: Temple University Press, 1988.

Theoharis, Athan, with Tony Poveda, Susan Rosenfeld, and Richard Gid Powers, eds. *The FBI: A Comprehensive Reference Guide.* Phoenix, Ariz.: Oryx, 1998.

ATHAN G. THEOHARIS

See also **Central Intelligence Agency; G-Men; Government Violence Against Citizens; Hoover, J. Edgar; Organized Crime; Police Violence.**

FEMINISM. *See* Theories of Violence: Feminism; Women.

FEUDS

Historically, feuds in the United States have been associated with the dozen or so conflicts that occurred in southern Appalachia (especially eastern Kentucky) between 1880 and 1900 and with a series of cattle wars and outlaw gangs in Texas, Montana, and Wyoming at about the same time. However, the term *feud* is problematic when used to describe conflicts in the United States. In other cultures, such as premodern Europe and the tribal societies of Africa and Latin America, feuds, or vendettas, were based on rigid rules of behavior for each party and, however violent, functioned to preserve order within or between communities. That these conflicts were governed by regulations and were associated with order differs greatly from the American concept of feuds. In the United States feuding was seen as deriving from a lack of education and as a primitive and chaotic response to a lack of central state authority (as in the mountains of Appalachia or the frontier West). Analogies with foreign cultures, however, suggest that the participants in feuds were aware that they were engaged in a private war, or even system of revenge, and had clear expectations of how it would proceed.

History of the Term *Feud*

In the United States the term was not generally invoked until the late nineteenth century, and when, on rare occasions, it was used in the press, it usually referred to a private conflict between gentlemen over questions of honor. Frequently these private vendettas resulted in a duel, which resolved the issue; rarely did the conflict carry over from the two individuals into an ongoing family conflict. Although there was a rigid set of expectations associated with duels, they were only incidentally related to feuds or vendettas.

In the antebellum United States the public became more aware of what the term meant because of the proliferation of newspapers and popular literature. In Kentucky in the 1850s, the Hill-Evans conflict over the ownership of some slaves turned violent and resulted in widespread newspaper coverage and the publication of a popular pamphlet. Mark Twain popularized feuds with his story of the Grangerford-Shepherdson feud, which he later incorporated into *The Adventures of Huckleberry Finn* (1884) and *Life on the Mississippi* (1883). Twain's feud was based on incidents he had witnessed while working as a pilot on a riverboat on the Mississippi from 1857 to 1861—the Darnell-Watson feud. These early accounts of feuding, both real and fictional, are significant because they apply the term *feuding* to a set of family conflicts in which the participants themselves did not use the term and in which there was no lack of a local justice system (which in both cases intervened to end the violence).

Only in the late nineteenth century, particularly the 1880s and 1890s, did feuding come to have a more specific meaning to most Americans—a meaning very much symbolized by the widely publicized story of the Hatfield-McCoy feud of southern West Virginia and northeastern Kentucky. Sensationalistic journalism of the era constructed an image of feudists as impoverished, ignorant mountain dwellers routinely engaged in family-clan violence. To explain this behavior journalists pointed to the feudists' isolation from centers of civilization, the weakness of governmental and legal systems in these areas, and a culture inherited from the feuding clans of Scotland. Furthermore, the southern mountains came to be seen as the most violent place in America, with the possible exception of the lawless western frontier. The cure was said to be civilization—that is, education, government, religion, and economic development, always symbolized in this era by the railroad.

Causes of Feuds

An examination of the context and course of events in the approximately dozen social conflicts that provided the raw material for this enduring image of poor mountain dwellers as inherently feudists reveals other causes for the conflicts. The post–Civil War South—both the mountainous and the nonmountainous regions—was a violent place. Two processes escalated the violence that had been an intrinsic part of antebellum plantation society. First, as whites resisted African American participation in politics, they turned increasingly to violence and terror, especially lynching. Thus, racial violence became more embedded in southern culture than ever before. Second, some white southerners as well as northerners saw an opportunity for economic development, which in the cotton South meant manufacturing and in the mountain South required building railroads and digging coal mines. Both of the latter enterprises required capital investment beyond that available at the local level and an accompanying increase in state as well as federal authority. In many parts of the South, poorer farmers, such as those who populated Appalachia, resented the intrusion of outside capitalists and state officials, while others saw a chance to make fortunes by allying themselves with these forces. These differing perceptions often resulted in violent confrontations—shootings, stabbings, ambushes—that were frequently fought out in elections and battles for physical possession of the local courthouse. These

racial and economic conflicts often overlapped and were related. The story of Appalachian feuds reflects the evolution of such conflicts.

The Appalachian Feuds

The earliest feuds to become famous through their coverage in the *New York Times* occurred in the mid-1870s in the eastern Kentucky mountains. In Breathitt County the Strong-Little feud and in Carter County the Underwood-Holbrook war were clearly related to the Civil War and its racial politics. In both cases, one side had been organized as Union guerrillas during the war and afterward supported the right to vote for the few black men who lived in those counties. Although engaged in violence, all participants were determined to assume the high ground by assembling votes and taking control of local government. In Breathitt County this resulted in the fatal shooting of the local magistrate and a battle at the courthouse door. The governor sent in troops to see that court was held in a peaceful manner but did nothing to prevent the lynching of one of the black participants (blacks actually rarely participated in such feuds). The press responded to this political and racial violence by calling it deplorable but typical of Kentucky and the South. The term *feud* was used (by the press, not the participants) to describe the conflict, but it was also applied to political and racial violence in other parts of the South and often used interchangeably with terms such as *vigilantism, lynching, war,* and *riots.*

In the mid-1880s came a series of mountain conflicts that led to the almost exclusive identification of the term *feud* with the southern Appalachians. The most famous feuds took place in Kentucky: Martin-Tolliver in Rowan County, French-Eversole in Perry County, Turner-Howard in Harlan County, Hatfield-McCoy in Pike County (as well as in Logan County, West Virginia), Baker-Howard in Clay County, and Hargis-Cockrell-Marcum-Callahan in Breathitt County. By the time most of these feuds had emerged in 1884, the Democrats had regained power at the national level with the election of Grover Cleveland as president; thus, local Democrats had reason to hope they could regain some political control from Republicans, and Election Day contests took on increased importance. Race was still an issue, but the most important factor was the heightened interest in the eastern Kentucky mountains as a source of economic recovery for the South. The economic depression of the 1870s had been severe for the whole

Some members of the Hatfield clan, in 1899. THE GRANGER COLLECTION

country but worse for the South, which was already in serious economic decline after the Civil War. The rich coalfields of Kentucky and West Virginia were proving very attractive to New York capitalists and state leaders of Kentucky and West Virginia, and it was in this context that local politics became important far beyond the local community. Issues such as local taxation, local financial support of railroad building, and the buying of mineral rights by outside speculators became crucial to the future of these mountain communities, and feuds reflected these battles over the developing political economy.

The Martin-Tolliver war of Rowan County, the first portrayed by the press as irrational family animosity, began as a gun battle on Election Day in August 1884 between partisans of candidates for a local office. There was already a railroad and considerable industry in Rowan County, but the political contest would determine who might reap the economic rewards of continued development. Although the Martin-Tolliver feud generated the most national newspaper coverage of all the feuds, it never gained the folkloric reputation of the

Hatfield-McCoy feud, which began with a dispute over some land that had gone in a period of five years from being virtually worthless (too steep for farming) to extremely valuable because of the coal that had been discovered there. This land dispute revived the political conflict of the Civil War, when some McCoys had sympathized with the Union and the Hatfields had fought for the Confederacy. Economic position, however, was much more important than family loyalties, since there were Hatfields on the McCoy side and McCoys on the Hatfield side. The McCoys were poorer than the Hatfields, who were moderately well-to-do if not wealthy. This economic conflict led to a series of confrontations involving accusations of pig stealing, fatal Election Day stabbings, and a Romeo and Juliet romance between a son of the leading Hatfield and the daughter of a McCoy. These more colorful events obscured the economic undercurrent in which the poorer McCoys joined with wealthy outside developers and state officials to arrest and try the Hatfields for murder. Although the leader of the Hatfields, "Devil Anse," escaped arrest and trial, he lost the economic contest and was forced to sell his land for much less than it was worth.

This pattern was repeated in other feuds. In the French-Eversole conflict, for example, Benjamin French was rapidly buying up mineral and timber rights to land in Perry County and was opposed by Joseph Eversole, a local lawyer and merchant. Eversole was killed, and a series of gun battles in mountain hollows followed. In the press both sides, seen as representative of the entire population of the mountains, were described as "desperadoes" or "bandits." In such descriptions distinctions were lost between those who sought to keep economic development within some kind of local control and outsiders who saw local people, even educated, middle-class people, as obstacles to their economic plans. In the pattern that emerged, the wealthiest side in these feuds (usually Republicans and relative newcomers to the region) hired the poorest young men in these mountain communities to conduct their violent warfare in the streets, courthouses, and hollows while the localists (usually Democrats of middling economic standing) fought back with violence in kind. The object, however, was rarely personal revenge but rather control of the political system and economic resources. Rarely did the men involved in these violent conflicts perceive of themselves as "feudists," and they resented being portrayed that way by the press. But the image has persisted despite the fact that the worst violence in the southern Appalachians actually took place after "civilization"—in the form of railroads and coal mining—had come to dominate the region. The labor conflicts between coal miners and management that took place in the first third of the twentieth century were far more bloody and encompassing than the earlier feuds (in the Hatfield-McCoy feud, only twelve were killed over a period of twelve years). Yet, public memory in the United States today characterizes southern Appalachians as unusually violent because of this supposed tradition of feuding when, in reality, it was the industrialization of the mountain region that produced the most virulent violence.

Labeling these conflicts as feuds between ignorant mountaineers obscured the economic contest over development, which one historian, Alan Trachtenberg, has termed the "incorporation" of America. As this process accelerated in the post–Civil War era, it inspired violence in a variety of places from the Appalachian south to the frontier West. Historians at the end of the twentieth century began to realize that many cultural myths that feature feuds, cattle wars, gunfights, and outlaw gangs are not aberrant, bizarre stories of a peculiarly lawless frontier but part of a pattern of economic development that escalated the very violence it claimed to pacify.

BIBLIOGRAPHY

Brown, Richard Maxwell. *No Duty to Retreat: Violence and Values in American History and Society.* New York: Oxford, 1991.

Otterbein, Keith F. *Feuding and Warfare: Selected Works of Keith F. Otterbein.* Langhorne, Pa.: Gordon and Breach, 1994.

Pearce, John Ed. *Days of Darkness: The Feuds of Eastern Kentucky.* Lexington: University of Kentucky Press, 1994.

Trachtenberg, Alan. *The Incorporation of America: Culture and Society in the Gilded Age.* New York: Hill and Wang, 1982.

Waller, Altina L. *Feud: Hatfields, McCoys, and Social Change in Appalachia, 1860–1900.* Chapel Hill: University of North Carolina Press, 1988.

———. "Feuding in Appalachia: Evolution of a Cultural Stereotype." In *Appalachia in the Making: The Mountain South in the Nineteenth Century,* edited by Mary Beth Pudup, Dwight B. Billings, and Altina L. Waller. Chapel Hill: University of North Carolina Press, 1995.

ALTINA L. WALLER

See also **Dueling; Honor; South; West.**

FICTION. *See* Literature: Fiction.

"FIFTY-FOUR FORTY OR FIGHT"

According to the historian Edwin A. Miles, leading American textbooks of the 1940s and 1950s in mentioning the 1840s dispute between the United States and Britain over the boundary of the Oregon territory proclaimed "fifty-four forty or fight" as the campaign slogan that "virtually won the presidential election of 1844 for James K. Polk and the Democratic Party." With help from the scholar Hans Sperber, in 1957 Miles demolished this wisdom, reducing it to a myth that decades later was still believed by some. Polk had been on record in favor of the "reoccupation" of Oregon (a euphemism for endorsement of the "fifty-four forty" boundary claim), but in the 1844 campaign he did not emphasize it, and he never used the slogan attributed to him. Oregon was not a factor in the election, and the phrase "fifty-four forty or fight" did not become current until spring 1846.

The Oregon matter hinged on the negotiation of a boundary line to divide the vast "Oregon country" that since 1818 had been jointly occupied by Britain and the United States. The northern extent of this domain was the latitude fifty-four degrees and forty minutes forming the lower boundary of the Russian colony of Alaska. Several times since 1818, British-American negotiations aimed at dividing Oregon had become deadlocked over the traditional U.S. position in favor of the forty-ninth parallel (the present mainland boundary between British Columbia and the state of Washington) versus British insistence on a border to follow the Columbia River from the forty-ninth parallel south and then westward to the Pacific Ocean. The crux of this long-running but unheated diplomatic disagreement was a geographic triangle formed by the Columbia on the east and south, Puget Sound and the Pacific on the west, and the forty-ninth parallel on the north—an area composing two-thirds of the present state of Washington. Both Britain and America wanted that triangle.

The "great migration" of midwestern immigrants to Oregon began in the early 1840s. When midwestern ruralists got wind of Secretary of State Daniel Webster's 1843 proposal to abandon the traditional American position and yield to the British the disputed triangle save for a narrow enclave along Puget Sound, they angrily reacted with public meetings supporting an extravagant "all-Oregon" claim of fifty-four forty. Webster's plan went nowhere, but the rural agitation against it led to the 1844 Democratic Party platform plank calling for the "reoccupation" of Oregon. Although Polk adhered to the 1844 plank in his inaugural address of 1845, later that year he retreated in diplomacy to the customary U.S. offer of the forty-ninth parallel. When that offer was almost insultingly rejected by the British minister even as an overture for renewed negotiations, an outraged Polk reverted to the all-Oregon position (although he never used the words "fifty-four forty or fight").

Polk declared that should "any European interference on the North American continent" be attempted, the United States would "be ready to resist it at any and all hazards." This was a veiled but clearly understood reference to Britain's Oregon claim, and "at any and all hazards" meant military action by the United States. Through diplomatic channels the British replied that it would not yield to "Yankee braggadocio" and, if necessary, would undertake military preparations. In fact, neither Polk nor the British wanted war, but

Polk's official language was so blunt that U.S. commercial and financial interests took alarm.

The crisis over Oregon came in the early months of 1846, during which the boundary dispute was the subject of impassioned oratory in the U.S. Senate. However, when the British at last offered to compromise on the forty-ninth parallel (with a detour south around Vancouver Island), Polk immediately accepted, and the Senate overwhelmingly ratified the agreement by a vote of forty-one to fourteen on 18 June 1846. The nation readily accepted this settlement; the American settlers in Oregon even held a celebration.

As Donald A. Rakestraw concluded in 1995, it turned out to be a case of "fifty-four forty or fold," and fold the United States did with its forty-ninth parallel compromise. The kernel of truth behind the myth of "fifty-four forty or fight" is that the bellicose motto accurately caught the mood of eagle-screaming nationalism often marking political oratory and popular feeling in the expansionist 1840s—the decade of Manifest Destiny. Such radical rhetoric was, however, more significantly expressed by the annexation of Texas (1845), the war with Mexico (1846–1848), and the acquisition of California and the Southwest (1848).

BIBLIOGRAPHY

Hietala, Thomas R. *Manifest Destiny: Anxious Aggrandizement in Late Jacksonian America.* Ithaca, N.Y.: Cornell University Press, 1985.

Merk, Frederick. *The Oregon Question: Essays in Anglo-American Diplomacy and Politics.* Cambridge, Mass.: Harvard University Press, 1967.

Miles, Edwin A. " 'Fifty-four Forty or Fight'—An American Political Legend." *Mississippi Valley Historical Review* 44 (September 1957).

Paterson, Thomas G., J. Garry Clifford, and Kenneth J. Hagan. *American Foreign Relations: A History to 1920.* 4th ed. Lexington, Mass.: D.C. Heath, 1995.

Rakestraw, Donald A. *For Honor or Destiny: The Anglo-American Crisis over the Oregon Territory.* New York: Peter Lang, 1995.

Sellers, Charles. *James K. Polk, Continentalist, 1843–1846.* Princeton, N.J.: Princeton University Press, 1966.

Sperber, Hans. " 'Fifty-four Forty or Fight': Facts and Fictions." *American Speech* 31 (February 1957).

RICHARD MAXWELL BROWN

See also **West.**

FIGHT-OR-FLIGHT SYNDROME

The term *fight-or-flight* refers to the body's physiological reaction to perceived threat. A perceived threat elicits hormonal changes that in turn create an internal condition of disequilibrium, which results in such symptoms as elevated heart rate, rapid breathing, perspiration, and trembling limbs. From a biological perspective, the fight-or-flight response stimulates the defense area of the hypothalamus. This stimulation "results in widespread cardiovascular adjustments, including increases in muscle blood flow and constriction of the cutaneous vasculature" (Eves and Gruzelier 1984, p. 342).

Walter Cannon, a young physiologist, first examined this "stand-and-fight" or "turn-and-run-away" response to stress in 1942. In 1975, Hans Selye made stress and its effects his lifetime study. Selye measured changes in the body's physiology under stress and postulated that the body always reacts to stress in the same way, irrespective of the source of the stress. Carl R. Stephens (1987) identified two problematic assumptions in Selye's findings: (1) that arousal is primarily mediated through the sympathetic division of the autonomic nervous system (ANS), and (2) that the ANS is autonomous and does not respond to conscious controls. This implies that will and awareness do not impact one's response to stress and that treatment for stress should rely on physiological interventions only.

Precipitators of the Fight-or-Flight Response

The fight-or-flight response comes about as a result of events that threaten one's safety or events that are psychologically threatening. Psychological stress results from a cognitive appraisal of threat or the anticipation of impending harm. Anticipated harm that seems ambiguous or unpredictable contributes in yet a greater way to the stress reaction. Perceived control, on the other hand, reduces emotional arousal, even if the perception is illusory. The same is true for voluntary loss of control (such as willingly sacrificing control for the greater good or goal). An example of this is when a soldier runs into battle, drawing fire upon himself in order to preserve the integrity of the troops left behind.

Evolutionary psychology proposes that while the fight-or-flight response seems to have existed always, the stimuli, or the events that elicit the response, have changed over time. Evolutionary psychologists account for this change by postulating that humans' brains did not develop at a pace needed to keep up with the demands of twentieth-century stressors. Jobs in the twentieth century, for example, often demand that people be aware of social norms and attain social approval in order to be promoted. The fight-or-flight response, then, is called into play for "incidental" events such as inappropriate statements or actions. These events are embarrassing and are perceived as a threat to a person's self-esteem or how a person defines him- or herself in relation to the world.

Cathartic Theory: Responses to Extreme Threat

For extreme threats (traumatic events), the mind and body's responses include both the fight-or-flight response and other, more severe, after-the-fact responses such as numbing of emotion, hyperarousal, and intrusive thoughts. These symptoms constitute post-traumatic stress disorder. Cognitive theory postulates that a traumatic event crushes one's deeply held values regarding safety and fairness and rearranges one's cognitive schema. Rebuilding the shattered cognitive schema requires intervention of a type specified by cathartic theory, which addresses the mind and body's response to traumatic events. The Pavlovian model of cathartic theory, used by William Sargant (1957; see Straton 1990), shows how dogs who were trapped in cages during a flood forgot conditioned reflexes that had been recently implanted. This suggests that under severe mental distress, disturbances in the brain tend to discard old patterns of thought as new beliefs are instilled. Treatments derived from cathartic therapies arouse emotions in order to allow a person to embrace a new belief.

Three functions of the brain are involved in a traumatic experience: memories, emotions, and decisions. Cathartic theory suggests that these functions might be "frequency-specific" to the state the brain was in when the traumatic incident occurred. Efforts to change a life decision will be maximized if the brain is "tuned into" the same "frequency" as when the decision was made or "recorded" (Straton 1990). This points to the importance of replicating the physiological state one experienced during the event in order to examine old ways and make a new belief.

Other Responses for Managing Stress

The opossum response—wherein the threatened individual rolls over and plays dead—is yet another response to threat. Theorists have suggested three explanations for the opossum response: (1) a failure in the autonomic arousal system to control for threats; (2) a learned response, much like submission in the face of overwhelming odds; and (3) parasympathetic dominance, dominance by that part of the autonomic nervous system that functions in opposition to the sympathetic system, serving to inhibit heartbeat or to contract the pupils of the eyes (Stephens 1987). One manifestation of parasympathetic dominance is depression, the body's attempt to control hyperarousal and subdue rage and anxiety.

Another response to threat is self-awareness and self-regulation. Stephens (1987) suggests that emotions are the result of seeking to obtain and keep one's objects of desire. A threat, then, is the perceived *in*ability to gain or keep the objects of one's desire. Self-awareness of emotions needs to be coupled with self-regulation to avoid self-indulgence; self-regulation needs to be coupled with self-awareness to avoid rigid fanaticism, suppression, and destructive emotional outbursts.

Barbara Winstead (1984) recorded her observations of the stress responses of many Polish people who were engaged in the Solidarity movement. She created two broad classifications for people's responses to stress: direct action and palliative responses. Direct action consists of the fight-or-flight response. Direct actors believe that stress is best mediated by affecting their environment. In the case of the unrest in Poland, direct actors decided to try to affect their environments by either fighting the Polish government or by leaving Poland.

Palliative responders, on the other hand, do not alter the environment, but alter the emotional impact of the situation by redirecting attention, mentally reframing the situation, or taking such somatic interventions as tranquilizers. Within the palliative response category are two subcategories: sensitizers and avoiders (Lazarus 1975). Sensitizers are vigilant types, seeking out information and thinking and talking often about the situation. Avoiders minimize the situation and ask others not to speak of it as a means of controlling their own intake of information. Winstead noted that the direct actors in the Polish crisis had a strong sense of self-efficacy, or belief that they could perform a desired task. Direct actors experienced less anxiety than did sensitizers and avoiders.

The benefits of conflict-engaging (with the possibility of finding a mutually acceptable solution) hold true for spouses' and children's communication patterns. Social deficits (the lack of compromising skills) often account for maladaptive approaches to settling disputes.

In summary, the fight-or-flight response is an automatic response, and it exists to counter perceived threats, both psychological or physiological. Human responses to mediate the effects of stress differ, but recognition of the source of stress, preparation to face the threat, and action to change one's environment seem to be the prescriptions for managing stress after the initial, involuntary fight-or-flight response passes.

BIBLIOGRAPHY

Eves, Frank, and John Gruzelier. "Individual Differences in Cardiac Response to High Intensity Auditory Stimulation." *Psychophysiology* 21, no. 3 (1984): 342–352.

Geer, James H., Gerald H. Davison, and Robert I. Gatchel. "Reductions of Stress in Humans Through Nonveridical Perceived Control of Aversive Stimulation." *Journal of Personality and Social Psychology* 16, no. 4 (1970): 731–738.

Janoff-Bulman, Ronnie. *Shattered Assumptions: Towards a New Psychology of Trauma.* New York: Free Press, 1992.

Lazarus, Richard S. "A Cognitively Oriented Psychologist Looks at Biofeedback." *American Psychologist* 30, no. 5 (1975): 553–561.

Peterson, Candida C., and James L. Peterson. "Fight or Flight: Factors Influencing Children's and Adults' Decisions to Avoid or Confront Conflict." *Journal of Genetic Psychology* 151, no. 4 (1990): 461–471.

Stephens, Carl R. "Stress: An Unnecessary Fact of Life." *Military Medicine* 152, no. 1 (1987): 19–23.

Straton, David. "Catharsis Reconsidered." *Australian and New Zealand Journal of Psychiatry* 24, no. 4 (1990): 543–551.

Valentine, Pamela V. "Traumatic Incident Reduction: Treatment of Trauma-Related Symptoms in Incarcerated Females." *Proceedings of the Tenth National Symposium on Doctoral Research in Social Work.* Columbus: Ohio State University College of Social Work, 1999.

Winstead, Barbara. "Coping with Stress: Naturalistic Observations of the Polish Crisis." *Journal of Clinical Psychology* 40, no. 6 (1999): 1516–1524.

PAMELA VEST VALENTINE

See also **Aggression; Sociobiology; Theories of Violence: Psychology.**

FILIBUSTERING EXPEDITIONS

In the historiography of early and mid-nineteenth-century America, the term *filibusters* refers to irregular armies of U.S. adventurers and the individuals who joined such armies. Mixing political and economic motives, filibusters sought territorial conquests and material gain through involvement in foreign conflicts in which the United States was a neutral party. Although some filibusters targeted Canada, most sailed and marched toward Latin America.

The word descends from the Dutch *Vrijbuiter*, which means "freebooter." During the seventeenth and eighteenth centuries, the term referred to English buccaneers, maritime pirates who roamed the Caribbean in search of Spanish quarry. Although the term was not applied to private clandestine armies until the 1850s, it has been retroactively applied by historians to earlier figures in U.S. history such as Aaron Burr and James Wilkinson. Although those and other filibusters were independent of—and even conspired to wrest territory from—the federal government, still other early filibusters acted with the tacit approval of, and, in some cases, with quiet support from, Washington. The administrations of Thomas Jefferson, James Madison, and James Monroe—viewing some filibusters as advancing U.S. diplomatic interests—occasionally gave unofficial support to clandestine armies, many of them Texas- and Florida-bound.

The phenomenon's liveliest run, however, came during the 1840s and 1850s, when colorful filibusters such as Narciso López, William Walker, Henry A. Crabb, and Joseph Morehead—independent of the federal government and often at odds with it—became fixtures of the nation's new penny press and the popular imagination. In its efforts to defeat filibuster armies, the federal government employed, at various times, presidential proclamations, spies, indictments, and the U.S. Navy.

Narciso López

Narciso López, the son of a prosperous plantation owner, was born in Venezuela in 1797. After fighting in his native country alongside the Spanish army in its unsuccessful war against the rebel José Martí, he fled to Cuba. During the 1830s he rose to high rank in civil and political offices in both Spain and Cuba. During the late 1840s, embittered by personal, political, and business reversals, López began conspiring to overthrow Cuba's colonial government.

When that uprising failed, López, in July 1848, fled to the United States and began plotting to invade Cuba; his motive—perhaps to create an independent republic, perhaps to establish U.S. dominion over the island—remains a subject of debate. Between 1848 and 1851, first in New York and Washington and then in New Orleans, López

organized four successive expeditionary armies. The federal government thwarted two before they could sail. Two others reached Cuba and engaged the Spanish garrison. López's final landing in Cuba, with roughly four hundred filibusters, occurred on 12 August 1851. Over the coming weeks all of the filibusters were either killed in battle, executed, or captured and sent to prison. López himself was executed—by garrote—on 1 September in Havana.

William Walker

William Walker—the "grey-eyed man of destiny" to his admirers—was born in Nashville, Tennessee, in 1824. He graduated from the University of Nashville in 1838 and in 1843 earned an M.D. from the University of Pennsylvania. After further medical studies in Paris and a year of European travel, he returned to the United States disillusioned with medical practice. He studied and briefly practiced law in New Orleans and then moved on to journalism. Between 1848 and 1850 he was an owner and editor of the New Orleans *Daily Crescent.*

After moving to California, Walker resumed his legal practice, participated in Democratic Party politics, and fought several duels. In 1853, after Mexican authorities rebuffed his plans for an American colony in that country, he organized an armed expedition of forty-five filibusters. Sailing from San Francisco, they seized the coastal town of La Paz on 3 November. Walker declared Lower California an independent republic with himself as president.

On 18 January 1854 Walker declared the annexation of the neighboring state of Sonora, unmolested until then. His empire, however, proved short-lived. Federal officials in San Francisco blocked the shipment of supplies to the filibusters, and they soon faced starvation. As Mexican resistance hardened, the invaders retreated northward and surrendered to federal authorities at the U.S. border. A jury in San Francisco acquitted Walker on charges of federal Neutrality Act violations.

Undaunted—and lured by promises of land and money—in 1855 Walker accepted a commission from a faction in a civil war then rending Nicaragua. Sailing from San Francisco, Walker and fifty-seven filibusters landed on Nicaragua's northern coast that May and joined the fighting. Cornelius Vanderbilt's Accessory Transit Company, which operated a rail line across the country, assisted Walker's faction by transporting American reinforcements, free of charge, to the battle theater. When his band won, Walker became commander in chief of the army. In May 1856 the new government won diplomatic recognition from the United States. Walker was inaugurated as president, and—with plans to introduce slavery to the country—began devising an ambitious program of internal improvements, including the building of a transoceanic canal.

Walker tactically erred, however, by taking sides in a power struggle between rival capitalists seeking to control the Accessory Transit Company. When Cornelius Vanderbilt, whom Walker had opposed, won the struggle, the industrialist began intriguing against Walker's government. Vanderbilt's steamship operations cut off reinforcements from the United States, and his agents assisted anti-Walker forces in Central America. The U.S. government broke off relations and joined the opposition, and in May 1857 Walker surrendered to the American navy.

Six months later, having eluded federal authorities, Walker undertook another expedition—this time from Mobile, Alabama—and landed near Greytown (today's San Juan del Norte, Nicaragua). The filibusters were quickly arrested by U.S. Navy forces and returned to the United States.

In August 1860 Walker returned to Central America. Dodging U.S. and British Navy ships waiting off Nicaragua's coast, the filibusters landed in Honduras with plans to march overland to Nicaragua. On 3 September, however, British naval forces captured the Americans and turned them over to Honduran authorities. Nine days later Walker fell before a Honduran firing squad.

Young, single, white men, both Americans and immigrants, dominated most filibuster armies. Their motives ranged from genuine idealism to a quest for booty and martial adventure. Although earlier historians identified filibustering—especially the mid-nineteenth-century raids on Latin America—with the planter interests of the southern Democratic Party, recent scholarship suggests a broader national base that defies classification by region, party, or economic interest. The practice had disappeared by 1861, and by the late nineteenth century the term *filibuster*—with its connotation of lawless enterprise—had evolved into a pejorative term for protracted parliamentary debate designed to obstruct the passage of legislation.

BIBLIOGRAPHY

Brown, Charles H. *Agents of Manifest Destiny: The Lives and Times of the Filibusters.* Chapel Hill: University of North Carolina Press, 1980.

Carr, Albert Z. *The World and William Walker.* New York: Harper and Row, 1963.

Chaffin, Tom. *Fatal Glory: Narciso López and the First Clandestine War Against Cuba.* Charlottesville: University Press of Virginia, 1995.

May, Robert E. *The Southern Dream of a Caribbean Empire, 1854–1861.* Baton Rouge: Louisiana State University Press, 1973.

TOM CHAFFIN

See also **Privateers.**

FILM

*The first three subentries introduce violence in film: **Overview**, **Landmark Films**, and **Directors**. They are followed by three subentries that examine **Violent Genres**, **Animation**, and **Documentary Film**. The concluding three entries focus on specific issues in film violence: **Censorship; Aesthetics of Violence;** and **Representing Gender, Race, and Ethnicity.***

OVERVIEW

Violent action has been a conspicuous feature of American cinema from its earliest years, evident in films produced both within and without the commercial motion picture industry. The pervasiveness and durability of screen violence may stem in part from the graphic power and plasticity of motion pictures, their ability to register the visceral impact of aggressive movement, composed within and across a series of edited shots. The appeal of violence in films, hence, can be viewed as a logical extension of the attraction of movie audiences to kinetic spectacle, to physical acts that arrest attention or carry an emotional charge.

It would be a mistake, however, to treat violence in motion pictures as a single phenomenon. What general account would adequately explain the function of violence in Hollywood genres as diverse as crime films, horror films, disaster films, action-adventure films, sports films, social-problem films, war films, Westerns, science fiction, costume epics, domestic melodramas, slapstick comedies, screwball comedies, and animated cartoons, not to mention avant-garde films or documentaries produced independently of the entertainment industry? Screen violence may be construed as fictional or nonfictional, emancipating or oppressive, legal or criminal, purposeful or anarchic, tragic or comic. It may be tightly inter-woven with the narrative trajectory of characters, carefully choreographed in largely abstract, formal patterns, or consigned to isolated or intermittent effects. The significance of film violence hinges on the viewers' understanding of its motivation and consequences, their familiarity with genre conventions, their topical or historical knowledge, and the social conversations, both immediate and long-term, through which screen events accrue, and lose, meaning over time.

Surviving films and printed commentary suggest that the peak years of screen violence—calculated quantitatively, as a percentage of total screen time—may well have occurred in the fifteen years after the introduction of Thomas Edison's Kinetoscope in 1893. Emerging out of the nineteenth-century tradition of popular public amusements, early motion pictures thrived on sensational material. The early Edison catalog included films of wrestling matches, animal fights, and staged locomotive collisions. In the wake of Edison's success with films of the Mike Leonard–Jack Cushing and Jim Corbett–Peter Courtney prizefights in 1894, rival production companies vied for the right to present or restage boxing bouts featuring Bob Fitzsimmons and Corbett (1897), Tom Sharkey and Charles McCoy (1899),

Fitzsimmons and Jim Jeffries (1899), and Jeffries and Sharkey (1899). Violent public rituals were reenacted in Edison's *The Execution of Mary, Queen of Scots* (1895) and *Execution of Czolgosz with Panorama of Auburn Prison* (1901). In 1898 a film version of *The Passion Play of Oberammergau*, climaxing in a reenactment of Christ's crucifixion, gained cultural capital for the Eden Musee in New York; this photographed drama was then distributed widely to major cities and, finally, to churches and other religious groups after its commercial run.

War films, often containing faked combat scenes, exploited news reports during the Spanish-American War (1898), the Boxer Rebellion in China (1900), the U.S. occupation of the Philippines (1904), and the Russo-Japanese War (1904–1905). Trick films depicted a dreamlike world of frenetic, aggressive transformations, with bodies and objects appearing, disappearing, and mutating in fantastic ways. Young mischief makers performed slapstick pranks and suffered slapstick punishments in short comic vignettes. Influenced by the popular success of Biograph's *The Escaped Lunatic* and Edison's *The Great Train Robbery* (both 1903), chase and rescue scenarios—motivated by burglaries, kidnappings, prison escapes and the like—became staples of nickelodeon programs, providing filmmakers with a simple narrative premise

A scene from *Execution of Czolgosz with Panorama of Auburn Prison* (1901). COURTESY OF CHARLES MUSSER

A scene from Thomas Edison's *The Great Train Robbery* (1903). PHOTOFEST

around which to developed sustained sequences of physical action, with moving locomotives and automobiles often quickening the pace and adding a sense of modern danger to the mix.

Depictions of violence in early films also helped spawn the first wave of organized protest against the movies. For many Progressive Era critics, storefront nickelodeons were yet another symptom of a general cultural disorder that modern urban life had wrought. Crime films were denounced for making vice appear attractive to impressionable children and working-class immigrants. Seeking to elevate the reputation of their product, filmmakers in turn increasingly drew upon literary or historical source material, cast distinguished theatrical actors in their films, and extended the length of feature productions to match that of dramatic works on the legitimate stage. These changes occasioned the promulgation of new standards for depicting violent physical action on the screen. Movie violence was deemed defensible as long as it was not "gratuitous" or "excessive," if it was placed in service of well-told stories and bore proper moral weight. Fistfights, gunfights, swordplay, car chases, collisions, and explosions were incorporated into Westerns, Civil War films, costume epics, detective films, and urban and rural comedies—all emergent genres in the 1910s, with roots in nineteenth-century American literature

and drama. The careers of D. W. Griffith, Thomas Ince, and Cecil B. DeMille, legendary directors of the silent era, advanced through their mastery of filming stories of this kind and on their ability to provide legitimizing narrative contexts for the screen violence that remains in evidence in genre fiction today.

From this social angle, the history of violence in commercial movies is the story of its regulation, first through recurring narrative conventions. A central trope of popular American cinema, Linda Williams has convincingly argued, is the revelation of moral virtue through victimization, figured climactically in either paroxysms of pathos (in women's film and related family melodramas) or virile acts of combat and rescue (in various action genres). Revenge plots—a narrative tit for tat, built around acts of retaliation—are common to slapstick comedies, Westerns, and regional feud films. Physical encounters with demonized aliens or savages recur in horror films, science fiction, Westerns, historical epics, jungle travelogues, and other action-adventure films. Physical violence as a displaced form of sexual attraction can be found in screwball comedies, horror films, and many varieties of crime films, prototypically film noir. In the social-problem film, moreover, a host of disorders or afflictions—alcoholism, racism, juvenile delinquency, prostitution, labor exploitation, and so on—are given visible expression. In these narrative contexts, violence has the power to make manifest, complicate, or resolve social or psychological conflicts. As an instrument of conventional genre fiction, then, violence appears structural rather than aberrant, articulating a relationship between criminal and sanctioned forms of aggression, defining social boundaries, and setting the terms for the renewal of social order.

Film producers also have worked in concert to regulate violent material in an overtly public manner through the adoption of formal guidelines and the establishment of official reviewing agencies. Self-regulatory efforts of this kind, dating from the Motion Picture Patents Trust's sponsorship of the National Board of Censorship in 1909, have been designed to bring movie censorship under industry control, free of government constraints on trade practices. Toward this end, aesthetic and moral principles concerning the treatment of screen violence often have been codified. Included in the "Thirteen Point" guideline drawn up in 1921 by the short-lived National Association of the Motion Picture Industry, for example, was an explicit prohibition against "stories or scenes which unduly emphasize bloodshed and violence without justification in the structure of the story." Following his appointment in 1922 as head of the newly formed Motion Picture Producers and Distributors Association, Will H. Hays led an even more high-profile campaign to deflect the complaints of social watchdog groups and government officials through initiatives of this kind, culminating in the introduction of a full-scale Production Code in 1930. The code proscribed, among other items, the sympathetic or explicit depiction of criminal behavior or methods, and prescribed caution in the representation of "repellent subjects" such as executions, "third degree" interrogations, brutality, gruesomeness, brandings, and surgical operations. Variously interpreted and applied over the years, the Production Code nevertheless survived as an official industry document until 1966, replaced two years later by a voluntary, age-based ratings system. In slightly modified form this system remains in effect today.

Filmmakers, however, also have pressed hard against these regulatory restrictions, modifying screen conventions for representing violence in the process. Their willingness to challenge such restriction follows in part from the normal and routine effort of directors, cinematographers, editors, and sound designers to manipulate formal conventions, finding creative ways to extend, elaborate, or intensify the experience of a violent event on screen without necessarily altering the underlying logic of its function in a narrative. Over time technological innovations have made available new stylistic options. Thus we can trace a path from the stop-action trick shot employed by the cinematographer William Hesse for Edison's *The Execution of Mary, Queen of Scots* to the fragmentation and morphing of bodies through computer-video technologies in a futuristic action film such as James Cameron's *Terminator 2* (1991), or we can chart a line of development from the rapidly edited Civil War battle scenes of Griffith's 1915 epic *The Birth of a Nation* to the subjective camera work and surround-sound effects of the D-Day invasion that open Steven Spielberg's 1998 war drama, *Saving Private Ryan*. Stylistic treatments of violence also have been strongly shaped by foreign film aesthetics: scenes of foreboding or terror in horror films and film noir by German Expressionist and French Impressionist cinematography of the 1920s, love-on-the-run crime narratives by elliptically edited French New Wave films of the 1960s, and the percussive rhythms and sound effects of fight sequences by Hong Kong action films of the 1970s and 1980s. Hollywood filmmakers have continually reworked and revitalized stylistic conventions to arrest the attention of successive generations of audiences inured to older techniques.

To the extent that the surprise or shock of violence has been central to its aesthetic function in motion pictures, moreover, filmmakers have felt compelled not simply to enhance or refine stylistic techniques but to toy with the narrative implications of violent acts and test the limits of prevailing taboos. Throughout the heyday of the studio era, film comedians and cartoon animators retained a license to violate standards of narrative plausibility and good taste in their depiction of aggressive acts, often in parody of more sober film genres. A cycle of popular gangster films in the early 1930s featured gun battles of unprecedented harshness and duration, embedded in plots that focused on the lives of ambitious and willfully violent Prohibition-era mobsters, played with considerable magnetism by emerging male stars such as Edward G. Robinson, James Cagney, and Paul Muni. Skirting code prohibitions on sadistic and sexualized violence, film noir crime melodramas in the 1940s and 1950s presented intricately narrated and visually stylish stories of betrayal and corruption,

The D-Day invasion, as depicted in Steven Spielberg's *Saving Private Ryan* (1998). PHOTOFEST

darkly counterpointing the optimism of much official wartime and postwar culture.

By the mid-1960s, various factors favored a broad-based assault on the industry's self-regulatory constraints. The divorce of theater chains from major producers and distributors, mandated by a Supreme Court ruling in 1948, weakened the hold of Hollywood studios on exhibition programs. Yet another Supreme Court ruling in 1952 granted all film distributors First and Fourteenth Amendment protection against state and federal censorship. In the 1950s television-viewing habits skewed motion picture demographics toward youths in their teens and early twenties, viewers most likely to seek entertainment outside the home, an audience producers believed demanded a higher quotient of sensation and thrills on the screen. Thus, by the time that media images of assassinations, civil rights protests, urban riots, and the war in Vietnam heightened attention to public acts of violence in the 1960s, institutional constraints on Hollywood filmmakers had loosened. In the wake of the dismantling of the Production Code Administration in 1966, critically acclaimed if controversial films by a new generation of directors—*Bonnie and Clyde* (Arthur Penn, 1967), *The Wild Bunch* (Sam Peckinpah, 1969), *The Godfather* (Francis Ford Coppola, 1972), *The Exorcist* (William Friedkin, 1973), and *Taxi Driver* (Martin Scorsese, 1976)—orchestrated scenes of operatically explicit carnage that would have been unthinkable even a decade earlier.

Since the introduction of the ratings system in 1968, institutional pressures on commercial filmmaking have taken more intricate and subtle forms. An economic incentive remains for producers to avoid a more restrictive rating (currently R or NC-17), which limits the potential size of a film's audience. Yet according to industry wisdom, the coveted viewers in their teens or twenties tend to shun films with a general audience (G) rating, which signals the absence of violence, sex, or coarse language. Furthermore, the growing dependency of Hollywood on a global market has favored the production of high-impact action blockbusters that are less dependent on carefully wrought dialogue or other forms of culturally specific knowledge. In this economic environment new cycles of violent films have flourished, many of which rework older genre themes. Vengeful Western heroes have been recast as errant cops, rape victims, and futuristic knights or cyborgs; gothic monsters return as neighborhood miscreants, including affectless psychokillers, who stalk, slash, and slay; and immigrant gangsters have been relocated to the suburbs or Florida, while black gangsters—a staple of "race films" for African American audiences in the 1930s and 1940s—have resurfaced in crossover independent films and more mainstream Hollywood fare. Even cinematic critiques of violence in critically acclaimed films such as *Glory* (Edward Zwick, 1989), *Unforgiven* (Clint Eastwood, 1992), and *Schindler's List* (Spielberg, 1993) employ a familiar rhetoric of consecrated valor or victimization to make their point. "B" serials have been upgraded into big-budget action films in the Indiana Jones, Superman, and Batman series, and pulp fiction has been given an art-cinema sheen in the films of Quentin Tarantino and David Lynch. Cool, high-tech thrillers—the durable James Bond series, *Speed* (Jan De Bont, 1984)—subordinate plot line to a principle of pure spectacle and movement, embracing the fundamental logic of the chase and rescue film of nearly a century ago.

Still other models for the use of violence can be found in the films produced outside the motion picture industry. Dating from the amateur cinema of the 1920s, American avant-garde or experimental filmmakers have employed violent imagery in ways that escape convenient genre categorization, exploring the power of the medium to disturb or subvert both social and aesthetic norms. Influenced by modernist literature and art, 1940s psychodramas such as *Meshes in the Afternoon* (Maya Deren, 1943) and *Fireworks* (Kenneth Anger, 1947) depict suicidal or sadomasochistic fantasies through densely figurative imagery and startling transpositions of bodies and settings. From found footage the collage artist Bruce Conner conjures a comic and horrifying vision of death-defying stunts and apocalyptic disasters in *A Movie* (1958),

orchestrates images of cheesecake nudes, naval weaponry, and Mickey Mouse to a mock-orgasmic climax in *Cosmic Ray* (1961), and interweaves fragmentary images and sounds to decompose the numbing media coverage of the assassination of John F. Kennedy in *Report* (1963–1967). Confidence in the inviolability of the human body comes under direct assault in Stan Brakhage's *The Act of Seeing with One's Own Eyes* (1971), a sensuous document of hospital autopsies, a routine medical practice that polite society keeps comfortably out of sight. Violent film images in these instances give haunting expression to personal and public traumas and the stark physicality yet social invisibility of permeable bodily forms.

Violence also has played a critical role in the history of newsreel and documentary filmmaking, raising a host of issues that are unique to these genres. In the years prior to television journalism, commercial newsreels carried on the tradition of early nonfictional spectacle, offering passing views of accidents, disasters, and military maneuvers in packaged short subjects. But social documentary filmmaking also has long circulated outside commercial channels, drawing on a tradition of socially engaged literature, painting, and photography in which violent images are employed for polemical political ends. The Workers Film and

Clint Eastwood in *Unforgiven* (1992). PHOTOFEST

Photo League and its left-labor offshoots in the 1930s took as their principal subject public acts of economic exploitation and oppression; handheld camerawork and abrupt, discontinuous cutting often provided a visceral sense of charged protest and conflict. (This endeavor was briefly reprised by Newsreel filmmaking collectives in New York and San Francisco in the late 1960s and early 1970s.) Social-documentary filmmaking under New Deal and liberal corporate sponsorship in the 1930s and 1940s relied on powerful imagery of rural and urban disasters to advance an argument for new social programs and policies. Wartime documentaries used graphic depictions of global militarism and fierce combat on behalf of somber arguments for the legitimacy of the Allied cause. Direct Cinema documentaries by the Drew Associates in the early 1960s exploited the inherent drama of potentially violent events, including capital punishment and school desegregation in the South.

Structural violence in American institutions has been a recurring theme of the extensive documentary corpus of Frederick Wiseman, and brutal murder mysteries provide the narrative core of several powerful contemporary documentaries, including *The Thin Blue Line* (Errol Morris, 1988), *Who Killed Vincent Chin?* (Christine Choy and Renee Tajima, 1989), and *Brother's Keeper* (Joe Berlinger and Bruce Sinofsky, 1992). Meanwhile, documentary images that have left the deepest impression on collective media memory—the liberation of Nazi concentration camps, an atomic cloud mushrooming from the New Mexico desert, Kennedy's assassination in Dallas—endlessly recirculate. At once mesmerizing and politically controversial, these images possess a cultural power beyond the boundaries of any particular film in which they appear.

Contemporary critics of motion pictures often treat the escalating intensity or explicitness of movie violence as either a sign or cause—sometimes both sign and cause—of social breakdown or moral decay. But crisis-oriented analysts would be wise to review the history of such critiques, most especially the recurring positing of an earlier state of innocence from which the "new" violence of any given era presumably departs. Without question, styles of representing screen violence have changed greatly over the decades, and depictions of violent acts once deemed taboo have become commonplace in movies. But contemporary portrayals of violence are not necessarily more exciting or disturbing than audiences once found, say, the last-minute rescue scene in a Griffith melodrama, the gunning down of a 1930s gangster, or the sudden attack of an outsized, genetically altered insect in a 1950s science fiction film, however tame or quaint these scenes may appear today. A crisis model, after all, does not much help explain the deep—and decidedly precinematic—roots of motion picture violence in comic and tragic tales of greed, aggression, revenge, and deliverance in American culture; nor does that model account for the coexistence of violent and more peaceable film imagery and plotting, across many different genres, in every period of U.S. motion picture history since the late nineteenth century. The challenge is to assess the sources, functions, and range of effects of different varieties of film violence in specific aesthetic and social contexts, a task that requires careful distinctions and multiple angles of approach.

BIBLIOGRAPHY

Browne, Nick, ed. *Refiguring American Film Genres: Theory and History.* Berkeley: University of California Press, 1998.

Brownlow, Kevin. *Behind the Mask of Innocence.* New York: Knopf, 1990.

Couvares, Francis G. *Movie Censorship and American Culture.* Washington, D.C.: Smithsonian Institution Press, 1996.

French, Karl, ed. *Screen Violence.* London: Bloomsbury, 1996.

Goldstein, Jeffrey H., ed. *Why We Watch: The Attractions of Violent Entertainment.* New York: Oxford University Press, 1998.

Hill, Annette. *Shocking Entertainment: Viewer Response to Violent Movies.* Luton, U.K.: University of Luton Press, 1997.

Keough, Peter. *Flesh and Blood: The National Society of Film Critics on Sex, Violence, and Censorship.* San Francisco: Mercury House, 1995.

Mast, Gerald, ed. *The Movies in Our Midst: Documents in the Cultural History of Film in America.* Chicago: University of Chicago Press, 1982.

Musser, Charles. *The Emergence of Cinema: The American Screen to 1907.* New York: Scribners, 1990.

CHARLES WOLFE

See also **Popular Culture; Representation of Violence; Television.**

LANDMARK FILMS

From the disreputable depths of drive-in fare to mainstream Hollywood cinema, a surprising number of American movies have featured moments of particularly intense graphic violence. Celebrated examples from recognized classics include James Cagney smashing a grapefruit into girlfriend Mae

Clarke's face in *The Public Enemy* (1931); crazed gangster Richard Widmark pushing an elderly woman in a wheelchair down a flight of steps while cackling gleefully in *Kiss of Death* (1947); the bizarre opening fight between a bald prostitute and her trick in *The Naked Kiss* (1964); and the alien bursting forth from John Hurt's chest in *Alien* (1979). Indeed, violent action is a defining feature of Hollywood cinema, foundational to the pleasures of many genres. But while American film is saturated with violence, the true landmark movies regarding violence are those that have pioneered new strategies for representing something that is so frequently shown, and to which viewers have become somewhat inured, in such a way as to make us rethink our response to it. It might be said that in so doing such films make violence their theme as well as their subject.

Violence was an essential element of American film from the beginning of the century. Edwin S. Porter's *Great Train Robbery* (1903), the one-reeler often said to have initiated the development of classic Hollywood cinema, contains a great deal of violence given its rather short length and seen in the context of its time. An early example of the Western, the very first shot in the narrative features two black-clad villains who break through a door at a railroad station, brandish pistols, and beat and bind the stationmaster. Just two shots later the robbers force their way into the car car-rying the money, kill the guard in the ensuing shootout, and dynamite the strongbox. Subsequently, one of the engineers is bludgeoned unconscious and a rather obvious dummy is thrown from the moving train, a fleeing passenger is shot in the back, and all the bandits are killed by a posse in the final showdown.

The Great Train Robbery, moreover, used the technical resources available at the time to enhance the depiction of these violent actions. The gunfire and explosion, for example, were tinted yellow to add to their visual impact. The film also ended with a close-up, which has no relation to the story, of a cowboy pointing and firing his pistol directly at the camera—that is, at the viewer. This final shot encapsulates the film's violent appeal and so was sometimes shown at the beginning rather than at the end of the film, thus engaging the spectator's desire for violent action at the outset.

The Sounds of Violence

Howard Hawks's *Scarface* (made in 1930 but not released until 1932), one of the most famous gangster films of the early sound era, similarly exploited the new technology of synchronized sound to enhance the affective impact of violence. The film was part of a wave of gangster films that appeared in the early 1930s; but Hawks's film, while ultimately celebrating the charisma and energy of its violent protagonist, as does *Little Caesar* (1930)

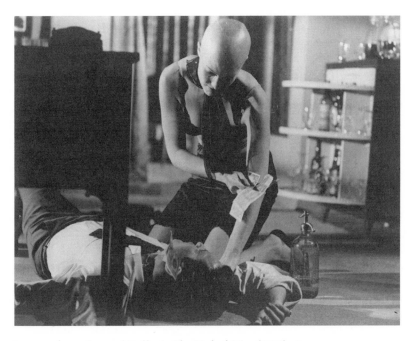

A scene from Samuel Fuller's *The Naked Kiss* (1964). Photofest

and *The Public Enemy* (1931), in fact featured considerably more violence than the other films in the cycle.

Scarface's conventional rise-and-fall narrative unfolds rapidly, like the machine gun that gangster Tony Camonte (Paul Muni) so lovingly fetishizes. The film features almost two dozen deaths, counting innocent bystanders and undeveloped characters, an impressive body count even by today's standards. The film's breakneck pace is abetted by an exciting soundtrack that adds a new dimension to the depiction of violence in film: the screeching of tires as cars careen around corners in exciting chases, rapid-fire dialogue, and, above all, the rat-a-tat fire of machine guns. One transitional montage features a shot of pages flying off a calendar, already a cliché image of time passing, but superimposed with a close-up of a blasting machine gun—a concise image that bespeaks the violent nature of the film as a whole.

Despite a pious entreaty tacked on before the opening credits, "This is an indictment against gang rule in America and the careless indifference of the government. . . . What are you going to do about it?," *Scarface* in fact revels in rather than reviles the violence it so often shows. The film happily draws attention to its violent moments by working an *X* into the mise-en-scène of every killing. After the victims of the St. Valentine's Massacre are gunned down, for example, the camera moves up to show seven cross braces of a steel support beam. The consequences of violent death are thus minimized as the viewer is invited to play with the text, waiting for the next violent scene with aesthetic anticipation.

Domestic Violence

Alfred Hitchcock's *Psycho* (1960), adapted from Robert Bloch's novel, which in turn was based in part on the real-life exploits of multiple murderer Ed Gein, has proved to be perhaps the most influential horror film ever made. Set in contemporary hotel and motel rooms, offices, hardware stores, and used-car lots, *Psycho* forever relocated the site of horror from the Gothic trappings of Universal Studio's 1930s cycle of films and the exotic locales of Val Lewton's films of the 1940s to the more mundane, quotidian world of the viewer. *Psycho* showed that horrifying violent acts were not necessarily committed only by gangsters like Tony Camonte and that violence was present in middle-class America, repressed beneath its seemingly placid exterior.

The scenes of violence in the film are actually few, and they are in fact more suggestive than graphic. The murder of the detective Arbogast happens out of frame as the image fades. And the film's most famous violent scene, the murder of Marion Crane (Janet Leigh) in the shower by the mysterious Mrs. Bates, is rendered entirely through the kinetic violence of montage. The rapid rhythm of the editing during the shower sequence simultaneously repositions and disorients the viewer, and aside from one quick shot in which the point of the knife seems to be pressing against Marion's abdomen, it is never shown actually piercing her flesh. Hitchcock's bravura editing, along with the piercing strings of Bernard Herrmann's music, mirrors the frenzy of the knife we imagine slashing Marion's naked flesh.

The sequence's powerful effect is achieved also through the charged images of its aftermath: the dead eye staring from the face lying on the tile floor, the folded newspaper with the forty-thousand dollars hidden inside it, and, above all, the close-up of the white porcelain bathtub spattered with the dark droplets of Marion's blood.

The physical location of the murder in a shower initially suggests Marion's moral cleansing, making viewers feel more at ease with a character with whom they had been encouraged to identify but whose actions had been ethically questionable. In other words, viewers are momentarily made more comfortable only to feel more violated subsequently. The sequence's powerful effect is thus in part achieved as a result of the violent thwarting of viewer expectation, as the star is killed off when the film is only half over and spectators are jerked out of their identification with the apparent protagonist. In this scene, then, the violence reaches out from the screen to the audience.

Ultraviolence

A number of historical factors in the 1960s converged to push American films toward more graphic representations of violence. Audiences had grown more accustomed to the visual representation of violence as a result of daily television coverage of the war in Vietnam; the classical studio system, along with the Production Code (since 1930, Hollywood's self-imposed means of eliminating or diluting any politically or morally contentious issues and images from its films), was crumbling; and the rift in American society regarding American intervention in Southeast Asia was growing. Given these developments it is not

The shower scene in Alfred Hitchcock's *Psycho* (1960). PHOTOFEST

surprising that the period witnessed a number of significant violent films.

Arthur Penn's *Bonnie and Clyde* (1967), a much romanticized treatment of the life of two real but rather minor criminals of the 1930s, had the most immediate cultural impact; its influence extended beyond the screen to inspire a retro fashion fad and several pop songs. With the two attractive actors Warren Beatty and Faye Dunaway in the title roles, the film's vision of romantic rebels versus stern, retributive lawmen captured the cultural zeitgeist. The film's graphic violence reflects the depth of existing social tensions, and it even positions viewers on the side of the rebels.

Bonnie and Clyde generated considerable controversy upon its release. Its uneasy mixture of tones suggested to some a casual, even amoral attitude toward violence. In several sequences the Barrow gang is shown escaping from pursuing police cars accompanied on the soundtrack by jaunty banjo music. This combination of sound and image has the effect of making the action seem somewhat humorous, like Mack Sennett's Keystone Kops comedies in the silent era.

The film's violence, however, was clearly no laughing matter. *Bonnie and Clyde* brought a new visceral quality to the depiction of gunshot wounds and their impact on the body. When, for example, Clyde attempts to drive the gang away from an ambush, we see him take a bullet in his left arm; the impact is clearly discernible and is followed by an explosion of red blood gushing over the white sleeve of his shirt. Clyde's brother Buck (Gene Hackman) is shot in the head, and we watch as he lies on the ground deliriously regressing into childhood while his wife Blanche (Estelle Parsons), herself injured in the face, screeches hysterically. Even when the impact of a bullet is not shown, as when Clyde shoots a pursuing banker in the face as he clings to the running board of the getaway car, Penn immediately inserts a close-up of the man's wounded face to emphasize the consequences of violence.

The most famous instance of graphic violence in *Bonnie and Clyde* is the concluding scene, in which the couple, betrayed by the father of a fellow gang member, C. W. (Michael Pollard), are ambushed on a country road. As their bodies are being riddled in slow motion with machine-gun fire from several directions, we see them jerking crazily as their bloody wounds multiply. This graphic "dance of death" influenced the depiction of violence in many subsequent films, as in the killing of the impulsive Sonny (James Caan) in a hail of bullets at a tollbooth in *The Godfather* (1972). In *Bonnie and Clyde*'s last shot, the camera tracks behind the bullet-riddled car as the lawmen gather by the two bodies, showing us the Texas Ranger and his men through its cracked glass window. Violence has irredeemably shattered the social order.

Sam Peckinpah's *The Wild Bunch* (1969) continued in the graphic manner of *Bonnie and Clyde*, but added the use of exploding "squibs" to show blood spurting and spraying upon the bullet's entry into the body. The machine gun is introduced into this Western to add to the graphic potential of the violence, as in *Scarface* and *Bonnie and Clyde*. But Peckinpah expands the violence in the large-scale massacres that frame *The Wild Bunch*, and the dance of death becomes cinematically constructed choreography.

In the opening and closing sequences editing fractures time and space in a manner as violent as the action depicted. In both cases the film cuts rapidly from one part of the massacre to another, as wounded bodies seem to fly in all directions. Peckinpah also employs slow motion to give the violence, paradoxically, a balletic grace. Montage is used to isolate and elongate violent motion, similar to Leni Riefenstahl's pioneering treatment of the divers in *Olympia* (1938). Often the violent action is intercut and matched with other actions occurring simultaneously, as when the film cuts back and forth three times between a horse and rider crashing through a shop window and another rider tumbling to the ground in the street.

Peckinpah thus aestheticizes violence in the film, an approach he would experiment with further in *The Getaway* (1972) and *Straw Dogs* (1971) in an attempt to demonstrate cinematically the allure of violence. The two massacres in *The Wild Bunch* become orgies of bloodlust in which spectators are often more enthralled than appalled, conveying our collective attraction to violence in spite of any intellectual objections on our part. Before and at the end of the opening bloodbath on Main Street, Peckinpah inserts several close-ups of children enjoying the spectacle of a few scorpions bravely but futilely trying to fight off an army of swarming ants. These images suggest both that brutal violence is inherent in the natural world (also the theme of *Straw Dogs*)

and that people are socialized by the violence to which they are witness.

George A. Romero's *Night of the Living Dead* (1968) pushed the horror genre beyond *Psycho* by similarly locating the monstrous in the quotidian world and by violently subverting viewer expectations, but also adding an emphasis on graphically portrayed violence absent from Hitchcock's film. The farmhouse where a small band of people fight to survive through a long night under siege by a horde of zombies is thoroughly commonplace, but the violence is extraordinary. Romero's cannibalistic zombies look like stiff-legged plain folks, but they are shown ghoulishly chewing arms, legs, and steaming entrails. Among the living within the farmhouse, discord results in horrible, even taboo-breaking violence: two are burned by an exploding gas tank, one is shot in the stomach and another in the head, and a father shoots his daughter, who then returns as a zombie to kill her mother by stabbing her with a garden trowel and then eating her.

Night of the Living Dead outflanks the viewer by combining such horrifying graphic imagery with a consistent violation of generic conventions. For example, the military, usually a symbol of civilized order in horror films, is depicted as disorganized, incompetent, and dishonest; the romantically involved teenage couple is summarily torched; and Ben (Duane Jones), the apparent hero, is black. As well, the violence begins within minutes of the beginning of the film and continues well into the film before any exposition is provided, and the explanation for the sudden widespread plague of zombification, when finally given, is equivocal. The film also consistently eliminates the horror narrative's conventional means of dealing with monsters, as both religion and reason ultimately prove ineffective in halting the threat of the living dead. Finally, all the protagonists die, including Ben, our figure of identification, and the collapse of civilization seems uncomfortably imminent.

Made independently in Pittsburgh on a paltry budget of $114,000, *Night of the Living Dead* was an astounding commercial success, grossing over $30 million worldwide. The film became the first cult and midnight movie, and it inaugurated a cycle of similar zombie movies that established the mythology of the living dead as securely as that of vampires and werewolves. Even more significantly, *Night* shifted the horror genre's emphasis from mere suggestion to graphic violence, particularly as it relates to the human body. The first "meat movie" or "splatter film," *Night of the Living Dead* set the stage for the often sadistic and misogynist slasher and stalker movies to follow.

Ten years later Romero's sequel *Dawn of the Dead* (1978) took splatter to a new dimension through advances in prosthetic gore effects and heavy excess. In this film Romero ingenuously used his obviously larger budget, bright color cinematography, and more sophisticated violent effects. The film's brutal opening sequence exceeds even that of the opening massacre in *The Wild Bunch*. Here, again without the comfort of exposition, we see a confusing scene of chaotic violence: ethnic minorities are slaughtered by special SWAT teams, zombies bite chunks of flesh out of their spouses, the living and dead are indiscriminately shot, and a pit full of zombies and body parts writhes and twitches in blood. The violence is so pervasive that we are not quite sure how to react. When an apparently naive soldier is suddenly shot between the eyes, we are at first horrified but then relieved when we realize that he is now able to rest in peace, unable to reanimate as a zombie.

But the film is so full of people and zombies being dismembered, shot, and killed—the shot of the top of a zombie's head sheared away by rotating helicopter blades showing blood spurting out the top as it continues to lurch mechanically toward its victim is a particularly vivid one—that after a while the violence comes to seem more like a decorative texture than meaningful acts with painful consequences. Romero's point in *Dawn of the Dead* is that when we forget the true impact of representations of violence, which its proliferation in the media encourages, we come to feel detached from its gruesome reality, as unemotional as the zombies for whom the living are merely food.

Political Violence

Spike Lee's *Do the Right Thing* (1989) is a film about the racial tensions that explode into mob violence on a hot summer's day. The psychological and physical violence in the inner city world it depicts seem to spill over into the film's angry, confrontational style. The film itself is violently aggressive, like the graffiti it features throughout—a minority voice demanding to be heard. Recalling Sergei Eisenstein's notion of the "kino-fist," *Do the Right Thing*'s belligerent tone is established immediately from the opening credits, behind which Rosie Perez, dressed as a boxer, dances to Public Enemy's ominous rap song "Fight the Power" while throwing punches at the camera. The frequent use of vibrant colors, oblique angles, and distorting lenses demands our attention and prevents us from maintaining the conventional position of uninvolved voyeur. The busy soundtrack frequently blares rap music—the very auditory invasiveness that precipitates the climactic riot when Sal (Danny Aiello), the owner of the pizza shop, smashes Radio Raheem's ghetto blaster. In one scene violent racial epithets are hurled directly at the camera by a series of ethnic characters, an explicit encapsulation of the aesthetic strategy of the film as a whole.

Do the Right Thing features many elements of traditional narratives, including the classical dramatic unities of time, place, and action. There is even the equivalent of a Greek chorus in the form of three black men who sit in the street and offer periodic comments. But there is no major character, no traditional hero, with whom viewers may comfortably identify, and the film's lack of closure—none of the dramatic conflicts presented in the film are resolved—fails to generate a satisfying sense of catharsis. The film even offers two seemingly contradictory epigraphs, one from Martin Luther King, Jr., espousing nonviolent civil disobedience, the other from Malcolm X, defending violent resistance. We are emotionally trapped by *Do the Right Thing*, caught within the tangled web of racism, just as the characters are trapped in their ghetto world.

Lee's black take on mainstream movie style was highly influential, initiating a cycle of "hood" films, such as *Boyz N the Hood* (1991), *Juice* (1992), and *Menace II Society* (1993), that aimed to present a more authentic view of the inner-city black experience, including the omnipresent threat of violence, both by having more radically charged content and by "fighting the power" of mainstream cinema's more conventional style.

Postmodern Violence

Henry: Portrait of a Serial Killer (1990), based partly on the life of Henry Lee Lucas, achieves its powerful effect, paradoxically, through a flat, minimalist style. The film is as bland as the drab, blue-collar world in which Henry (Michael Rooker) lives with his friend and accomplice, Otis (Tom Towles). The film treats its gruesome violence with a kitchen-sink neutrality that captures the matter-of-fact manner in which Henry does everything, from buying a pack a cigarettes to brutally murdering another victim. *Henry*'s style seems to embody the "waning of affect" often said to characterize the postmodern era. Even when Henry is shown hacking Otis's dead body into smaller pieces in order to pack it in a suitcase—the head is removed with a sickening slurping noise—director John McNaughton eschews any overt visual embellishment.

Some of the violence in *Henry* is in fact not shown, only its aftermath. The nude, mutilated bodies of Henry's female victims—one with a pop bottle wedged into her face—are shown in elegantly composed tableaux while we hear the sounds of the struggles that had transpired earlier. Thus McNaughton is able to focus on the horrible results of Henry's murderous impulses without having to show a violent spectacle. The film's very first shot is a close-up of a woman's face in peaceful, almost erotic repose. As the camera zooms back, we are shocked to realize that this is the face of a dead, violated woman. But it is too late: we have been seduced by murder, not unlike Henry.

In the film's most disturbing sequence, Henry and Otis force their way into a suburban home and kill the family living there while videotaping their horrible deed, which they choreograph for the camera. The man is tortured and stabbed, the woman strangled and violated, and the teenage son wrestled to the ground where his neck is audibly snapped. We see this sickening event unfold on television, as the two killers watch their home video. For them, this is merely good video, nothing more consequential.

This postmodern connection between the pervasive sensationalism of violence in the media and our concomitant desensitization regarding violence is also the theme of Oliver Stone's *Natural Born Killers* (1994), a fictional story about a pair of outlaw serial killers, Mickey and Mallory Knox (Woody Harrelson and Juliette Lewis). Stone takes the opposite approach from McNaughton, packing his movie with wild visual hyperbole. The film's mise-en-scène is filled with other media images and compositions that refer to them, and Stone's camera shoots from strange angles, tilts and wobbles oddly, and moves strangely. In the opening slaughter at the roadside cafe, for example, the camera flies through the air behind one of Mickey's bullets, pauses before a frightened waitress, and then enters her head, blood splattering the wall.

Highly stylized, *Natural Born Killers* constantly shifts between film and video imagery. Television figures prominently in the plot as well, and in the climax a video camera replaces a person as sole witness to the pair's deeds. The "I Love Mallory" sequence shows the domestic violence and abuse in Mallory's family from her point of view as a sitcom complete with canned laughter at all the wrong moments, emphasizing the extent to which our very consciousness and memory are shaped by television. The sensationalist style of *Natural Born Killers*, thick with blood and bodies, is insistently contextualized in the film as a reflection of the manner in which the news media treat the subjects of mass murder and multiple murder in American culture.

Conclusion

American cinema has arrived at the postmodern point where it is at once fully aware of its history regarding such contentious issues as representations of violence and at the same time able to mock the treatment of violence in these films, and other media, while employing their very same techniques. This aesthetic contradiction informs Quentin Tarantino's influential *Pulp Fiction* (1994), the primary influence on a subsequent wave of seriocomic crime films.

A pastiche of many other movies, *Pulp Fiction* combines the matter-of-factness of *Henry* with a stylistic bravado almost equal to *Natural Born Killers*, providing an uneasy mix of tones that goes far beyond that of *Bonnie and Clyde*. Professional killers mumble small talk about foot massages and fast-food hamburgers while driving to work just like the rest of us—the only difference is that their job today just happens to be to intimidate and kill four young men who have welshed on a drug deal. The film's moments of violence, which are startlingly visceral, manage to be at once humorous and horrible. For example, when one of the two hit men (John Travolta) accidentally shoots a hostage in the face at point-blank range, the pair become hapless comic figures who, ignominiously bespattered with blood and brains, must figure a way out of the mess they have gotten themselves into.

When the gun goes off it is pointed directly at the camera, and the screen momentarily turns red. The shot recalls the famous final shot of *The Great Train Robbery*, both in camera placement and in the use of color to heighten the image's affective impact, seeming to bring us full circle in the treatment of violence on the screen. However, whereas Porter's film sought to create a unified viewing subject, the ideal of classic narrative cinema, Tarantino's pulls the viewer in different directions. The blown-apart head comes to represent the frac-

John Travolta and Samuel L. Jackson in Quentin Tarrantino's *Pulp Fiction* (1994). PHOTOFEST

tured subjectivity of the viewer, who shrinks in horror from the situation even while laughing at it.

By contrast, Steven Spielberg's *Saving Private Ryan* (1998) seeks to restore the full affective power to the cinematic representation of violence. In its powerful opening, a depiction of the carnage involved in the D-Day landing at Normandy, the film attempts to present the horrible reality of combat, stripped of the patina of glory that characterizes battles in the conventional war film genre. Soldiers vomit in anticipation, and scores of men are peremptorily massacred. The blood runs so thick it tints the ocean water. One soldier, in obvious shock, clutches his severed arm in bewilderment. The hand-held camera lends a documentary immediacy to the chaos of the battle. In the hand-to-hand combat in the climax of the film, physicality is again emphasized as heroic soldiers die in pools of their own blood while cowards freeze, unable to act. But although *Saving Private Ryan* succeeds in subverting the war film as powerfully as Godard's *Les Carabiniers* (1963) and Stanley Kubrick's *Full Metal Jacket* (1987), it succumbs to ideological convention.

While *Saving Private Ryan* appears to subvert the myth of patriotic glory that informs the genre of the war film as successfully as (but differently than) Godard's *Les Carabiniers* or Kubrick's *Paths of Glory* (1957) and *Full Metal Jacket*, it ultimately endorses it. In the classic war film, individualism must always be sacrificed for the collective welfare of the fighting team. Traditional war film heroes come to understand this lesson, and if they die in battle, it is usually as noble. In the climactic battle scene of *Saving Private Ryan*, Captain Miller (Tom Hanks) becomes a typical war film character who selflessly fights to the death in a glorious last stand that recalls the mythic tradition of Davy Crockett and the Alamo popularized by Walt Disney.

BIBLIOGRAPHY

Cawelti, John G., ed. *Bonnie and Clyde.* Englewood Cliffs, N.J.: Prentice-Hall, 1973.

Clarens, Carlos. *Crime Movies: An Illustrated History.* New York: Norton, 1979.

Gagne, Paul R. *The Zombies That Ate Pittsburgh: The Films of George A. Romero.* New York: Dodd, Mead, 1987.

Naremore, James. *Filmguide to "Psycho."* Bloomington: Indiana University Press, 1973.

Prince, Stephen, ed. *Sam Peckinpah's "The Wild Bunch."* New York: Cambridge University Press, 1998.

Reid, Mark A. *Spike Lee's "Do the Right Thing."* New York: Cambridge University Press, 1997.

Rothman, William. *Hitchcock—The Murderous Gaze.* Cambridge, Mass.: Harvard University Press, 1982.

Russo, John. *The Complete "Night of the Living Dead" Filmbook.* New York: Harmony Books, 1985.

Seydor, Paul. *Peckinpah: The Western Films.* Urbana: University of Illinois Press, 1980.

Sharrett, Christopher, ed. *Mythologies of Violence in Postmodern Media.* Detroit: Wayne State University Press, 1999.

Wood, Robin. *Arthur Penn.* New York: Praeger, 1969.

———. *Hitchcock's Films Revisited.* New York: Columbia University Press, 1989.

BARRY KEITH GRANT

DIRECTORS

The important American directors of Hollywood narrative cinema are a diverse group, but it would be hard to find even a handful whose work does not deal in violence of some kind. Violence, after all, is a manifestation of the conflict that is so crucial to story, and it takes multiple forms on celluloid as in life. Looks, language, and the weather can be violent to powerful effect—as in Spike Lee's examination of racial conflict in *Do the Right Thing* (1989)—and there is gut-wrenching emotional violence in the melodramas of Douglas Sirk, such as *Written on the Wind* (1957). Cinematic violence, however, primarily brings to mind shootouts, dismemberment, and death. The body in pain or under threat is a common concern for many of the American cinema's major directors. Sam Peckinpah, Stanley Kubrick, Arthur Penn, Martin Scorsese, and Brian De Palma have all made important individual films about violence and have developed consistently violent oeuvres. Younger directors such as David Cronenberg, David Lynch, Ridley Scott, David Fincher, Oliver Stone, and Quentin Tarantino also address the violent culture and subcultures in which Americans live.

Violence is not a recent phenomenon in the American cinema. Corpses are thrown violently from the train in Edwin S. Porter's *The Great Train Robbery* (1903), and in the same film an outlaw shoots right into the eye of the camera (and hence directly at the audience). Certain genres, such as the Western, are inherently violent. The famously explicit violence of Sam Peckinpah's *The Wild Bunch* (1969) was preceded by and may have depended on the barely controlled violence and vicious obsession with revenge that mark both John Ford's *The Searchers* (1956) and Anthony Mann's Westerns such as *Winchester '73* (1950) and *The Naked Spur* (1952). Still, technological advances have allowed directors to make the violence that they show more visceral. We can tell that those are dummies being thrown off the train in Porter's film, and though we see the dead and dying in Ford and Mann, we do not see the squirting blood or oozing organs that corn-syrup-filled squibs and prosthetic limbs now provide. When we find ourselves once again looking down the barrel of the gun at the end of both Peckinpah's *Bring Me the Head of Alfredo Garcia* (1974) and Scorsese's *GoodFellas* (1990), we know, much more vividly than in 1903, the violent consequences of its threat.

Sam Peckinpah

Of the major American directors, Sam Peckinpah probably remains the one whose name is most intimately linked with violence. In his films an individual must be violent in order to retain his self-respect and integrity in the face of the encroachment of the unprincipled, impersonal, and mechanized violence of big business or a faraway authority. Peckinpah's heroes are usually twentieth-century westerners who have lived and must die by a violent, often outdated, personal code tied to their frontier mentality. This is a masculine world in which revenge is a common motive and women are usually encumbrances, as in *Major Dundee* (1965).

Although Peckinpah's cinema is consistently concerned with violence, *The Wild Bunch* is especially noteworthy. The demise of the Production Code in the 1960s and the graphic violence of Penn's *Bonnie and Clyde* (1967), which ends with the director's attempt to capture both the convulsing body at the moment of death and its weight after death, preceded Peckinpah's violent Western. *The Wild Bunch* begins and ends with violent gun battles, characterized by woundings, deaths, and the explosion of blood and flesh from pierced bodies. (Little pieces of raw meat were attached to the actors in addition to squibs of red goo.) These scenes of violent death are choreographed and given still greater impact by Peckinpah's use of slow motion and rapid cutting, two techniques that have found many imitators. Here and elsewhere in Peckinpah's work, these techniques instill a balletic grace and searing beauty into his nostalgic expressions of the Western mythology.

Stanley Kubrick

Although Stanley Kubrick's films are not generally as bloodily violent as those of Peckinpah or Scorsese, his cinema commonly explores the paradox that violence is both integral to human existence and a uniquely powerful dehumanizing force. Its threat is succinctly visualized during the opening sequence of *Full Metal Jacket* (1987), as we see the head of each new recruit being shaved before he is trained as a military killer. Later, the drill sergeant's brutalization of Private Pyle finally prompts Pyle to kill the sergeant and then turn his rifle on himself. The recruit's brains spatter on the scrubbed walls of the latrine, symbolizing a killer created and destroyed by violence.

Kubrick first depicted the horrors of death and war in his World War I drama *Paths of Glory* (1957).

The film's focus is on the violence of the power structure: soldiers debate the best and worst ways to die in battle, but, accused of cowardice during a futile attempt to capture an enemy position, they instead suffer a public, ceremonial death before a firing squad. The early sequence of the attempted advance anticipates the opening sequences of Steven Spielberg's *Saving Private Ryan* (1998): in both cases we see soldiers falling to all sides of—and on top of—their comrades, though there is much greater focus on their pain in the later film.

In *A Clockwork Orange* (1971), Kubrick investigates a society imperiled by both lawless individualism and authoritarian control. We witness a gang of youths commit a series of vicious acts, culminating in the beating of a husband and the rape of his wife by their leader as he dances around, trolling "Singin' in the Rain." The counterpoint of the ruthless violence with the perpetrator's elation

Stanley Kubrick directs a machine-gun point-of-view shot during the filming of *Dr. Strangelove* (1964).
CORBIS/BETTMANN

and the joyous music effectively emphasizes the savagery—and is itself an act of aesthetic violence against one of the American cinema's most beloved sequences from one of its most beloved films. Ironic use of music is characteristic of Kubrick's vision of a violent world. In *Dr. Strangelove: or, How I Learned to Stop Worrying and Love the Bomb* (1964), for example, where bureaucratic intransigence and individual megalomania lead to the supreme act of modern violence, the dropping of a nuclear bomb is accompanied by Vera Lynn's "We'll Meet Again."

David Cronenberg

While Kubrick's films from *Lolita* (1962) on were made in Britain, David Cronenberg, a Canadian, has retained his base in Toronto. By distancing themselves from Hollywood, both men were able to retain an unusual amount of control over their films, while observing and recording aspects of the American milieu. (Alfred Hitchcock, whose menacing thrillers usually depict violence obliquely but very powerfully—as in *Psycho*'s [1960] fast-cut murder sequence, where we only think we see blade pierce flesh—offers an alternative model, leaving a successful career in Britain to flourish as a commentator on American life within Hollywood's studio system.)

Most of Cronenberg's work is characterized by the observation of human bodies and minds taken over by other organisms or powers. Violence in his cinema is often connected to sex and biologically altered bodies (*Shivers* [1975], *Rabid* [1977], *Videodrome* [1983], *The Fly* [1986], *eXistenZ* [1999]). Several of Cronenberg's films suggest that some people and places are especially marked to be violent. (The same is true of Kubrick's *The Shining* [1980].) Although a "mad scientist" is usually the progenitor of the "sickness" (*Shivers*, *The Brood* [1979], *Scanners* [1980]), and sometimes also the film's protagonist (*The Fly*, *Dead Ringers* [1988]), in Cronenberg's cinema there is also frequently a corporate-sponsored violence. In *Scanners*, for example, rival companies vying for control of the mental power of scanners have respectable fronts as international security firms purveying weaponry and private armies.

The themes of pleasure drawn from watching violence and the reconstituting of the human body recur in *Crash* (1996). Cronenberg had used car crashes in several earlier films, but here they take center stage. (One of the most commonly encountered instances of violence in our lives, automobile accidents are also common in the Hollywood cinema. For example, they provide a key structuring principle in David Lynch's *Wild at Heart* [1990].) Peckinpah once remarked that he was afraid of a stupid, purposeless death such as in an automobile accident. In *Crash*, however, the violence of twisted metal impinging on the human body causes sexual excitement. The film's car crashes are purposeful here: they are planned, used, and eroticized.

In *Shivers* one character tells another that "dying is an erotic act," and Cronenberg's films consistently examine the relationship between violence and sexuality. This relationship is perhaps most clearly stated in *Crash*, where views of flesh, metal, and their conjoining are juxtaposed with equal pleasure. Cronenberg's cinema, indeed, rarely presents violence through rapid editing, preferring such strategies as the deliberative combination of dissolves, pans, and, at the end of *Dead Ringers*, a survey of a pietà-like arrangement of bodies in a murder-suicide. In this his work is very different from the much more spectacular presentation of violence we see in Brian De Palma, another director whose suspense films have consistently delved into the relationship between sexuality and death (*Carrie* [1976], *Dressed to Kill* [1980], *Casualties of War* [1989]).

Martin Scorsese

Violence is central to much of Martin Scorsese's work, including the group of films that focus on Italian American Mafia relationships. *Mean Streets* (1973), *GoodFellas* (1990), and *Casino* (1995) all display their own rigorous codes of loyalty and violence. (One might compare here Francis Ford Coppola's *Godfather* trilogy [1972, 1974, 1990], Sergio Leone's *Once Upon a Time in America* [1984], and Abel Ferrara's *The Funeral* [1996].) These films typically feature Joe Pesci and Robert De Niro playing characters who go beyond the bounds, employing violence unwarranted even within the violent community to which they belong. For them violence is a part of life, as quotidian as jokes and dinners; eventually, however, these disturbed, psychotic loose cannons meet gruesome ends themselves.

In *Taxi Driver* (1976) it is Travis Bickle (De Niro), social misfit and Vietnam veteran turned cabdriver, who crosses the line, exploding into violence in an apparent attempt to cleanse the corrupt city that he sees everywhere around him. By the end of his rampage, unable to kill himself with his emptied weapons, Travis turns a bloody finger to his head in mock-suicide. The scene, which has

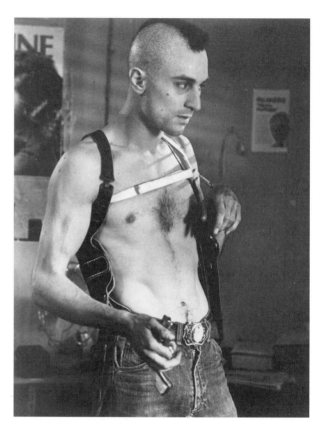

Robert De Niro in Martin Scorsese's *Taxi Driver* (1976).
PHOTOFEST

had no music to this point, is now frozen in a striking and lushly scored tableau of violent bloody death (comparable to those in David Lynch's *Blue Velvet* [1986] and Cronenberg's *Dead Ringers*).

Surprisingly, Travis is publicly feted for his deed at the end of *Taxi Driver*. Scorsese's *Raging Bull* (1980), on the other hand, interrogates a different kind of celebrated violence through a study of the life of boxer Jake La Motta. Shooting in black and white, Scorsese uses slow-motion (sweat or blood spraying from the pummeled face, water poured over the body), close-ups, and a variety of camera angles and movements to capture the violence of the fight scenes. A smoky background envelops the spectators in a dreamlike aesthetic, while on the soundtrack their cries mingle in a distorted melange with the dull, whirring roar of punches. By contrast, the domestic violence that runs like a thread through the film, punctuating it as reliably as the fights, is shot straight, without the stylized camera work.

Quentin Tarantino

Quentin Tarantino's films have all been set in the world of gangsters, where violent responses to events come easily to the characters. His films typically combine the gruesome with the comic. Thus, in *Pulp Fiction* (1994) a hit man who accidentally blows off his backseat passenger's head—when the car in which they are riding hits a pothole—bickers with his colleague about the best way to clean up the mess. Tarantino combines a barrage of violent, "bad" language—loaded with references to film and popular culture—with a visual flair to create a violence that is stylized and distanced through our knowledge of the comic excesses of its perpetrators.

Nevertheless, this violence may still be harrowing. For many moviegoers, the torture sequence from *Reservoir Dogs* (1992), in which a bank robber severs an ear from his hostage policeman, is a defining moment of violence in late-twentieth-century cinema. Although an edit saves us from seeing the actual cutting, the pleasure that the torturer takes in his task, as he dances cheerfully to the tune of "Stuck in the Middle with You," is reminiscent, in its brutality layered with familiar, light-hearted music, of Kubrick's "Singin' in the Rain" sequence.

Oliver Stone

Oliver Stone has made several films that dissect violence, including *Salvador* (1986), *Platoon* (1986), and *Born on the Fourth of July* (1989), as well as *JFK* (1991), which analyzes perhaps the most infamous act of American violence, the assassination of President Kennedy. However, his bloody tale of the media-saturated and celebrated *Natural Born Killers* (1994) is probably his most sustained, and certainly his most controversial, violent film. This is partly because its focus is evidently on the perpetration of violence rather than the suffering that it entails, as in *Born on the Fourth of July*.

The portrayal of violence in *Natural Born Killers* relies heavily on editing—approximately three thousand cuts—and Stone also incorporates several experimental techniques, including cartoons and the back-projection of sequences from famously violent movies onto a wall behind his actors. We may notice, for example, the concluding massacre from *The Wild Bunch* and the chainsaw scene from De Palma's *Scarface*, (1983), where the gangster is spattered with blood from the corpse of his colleague, which is being carved up next to him.

Stone's point, in part, is that we live in a violence-saturated society. Indeed, for many directors, violence is a part of the human condition. "Birth is violent, kids are cruel," Stone has noted.

"We have a natural-born fascination with death because we all know we are going to die" (Bouzereau 1996, p. 68). And we all inhabit bodies that can and do suffer the consequences of violence. Its representation in film has multiple purposes; in the hands of many significant directors, one of the most prominent of these is to further understand our own condition.

BIBLIOGRAPHY

Alloway, Lawrence. *Violent America: The Movies, 1946–1964.* New York: Museum of Modern Art, 1971.

Bouzereau, Laurent. *Ultra-Violent Movies: From Sam Peckinpah to Quentin Tarantino.* Secaucus, N.J.: Citadel, 1996.

Falsetto, Mario, ed. *Perspectives on Stanley Kubrick.* New York: G. K. Hall, 1996.

Fine, Marshall. *Bloody Sam: The Life and Films of Sam Peckinpah.* New York: Donald I. Fine, 1991.

Friedman, Lawrence. *The Cinema of Martin Scorsese.* New York: Continuum, 1997.

Mackey-Kallis, Susan. *Oliver Stone's America: Dreaming the Myth Outward.* Boulder, Colo.: Westview, 1996.

Rodley, Chris, ed. *Cronenberg on Cronenberg.* London: Faber and Faber, 1997.

Seydor, Paul. *Peckinpah: The Western Films, A Reconsideration.* Urbana: University of Illinois Press, 1997.

Sharrett, Christopher, ed. *Crisis Cinema: The Apocalyptic Idea in Postmodern Narrative Film.* Washington, D.C.: Maisonneuve, 1993.

Thompson, David, and Ian Christie, eds. *Scorsese on Scorsese.* London: Faber and Faber, 1989.

CHRIS LIPPARD

VIOLENT GENRES

I'm different from other people—pain *hurts* me!
—*Daffy Duck*

Murder and bloody death are everywhere. In the Hollywood movie as surely as on network television, hardly a crime is worth solving that does not involve a murder. Without the killings of an ape, an astronaut, and a computer, *2001: A Space Odyssey* would have no plot. By the end of *Oklahoma!*, poor Jud *is* dead. (A filmography appears at the end of the essay.)

Since the 1960s, a decade that began with *Psycho*, American filmgoers' tolerance for on-screen violence has steadily increased. The camera looks at awful things instead of looking away, the sounds are sharper and louder, and the makeup, explosions, and optical effects are ever more convincing. Even considering two box-office successes in the same subgenre (killer lovers on the run), both of which were perceived as shocking and irreverent when released, *Natural Born Killers* is far more violent than *Bonnie and Clyde*.

The body count in *Halloween*—the number of people killed or corpses shown on-screen—is four; in *Halloween II*, eleven; in *Henry: Portrait of a Serial Killer*, sixteen; and in *Lethal Weapon*, which is not a horror film but a cops-and-robbers action buddy picture with an upbeat ending, twenty-six. In *The Steel Helmet*, an outright war movie, the number is forty. An earlier mystery, *Vertigo*—as citywise as *Lethal Weapon* but far more obsessive and charged end to end with death—made do with three dead bodies, and each of them, from the policeman to Madeleine to Judy, mattered. If *Halloween* feels more violent and disturbing than *Lethal Weapon*, that is not because it shows more violence. If *Lethal Weapon* is more frightening as an event in American culture than *Halloween* that is because it shows such indifference to death and suffering—unless it wants us to care, in the case of certain favored characters whose pain matters—and because everybody knows that in a movie like this, the "action" isn't real and nobody takes it seriously, so lighten up.

Throughout the 1960s and 1970s the representation of violence had its breakthrough films, and in many of them the action was certainly not meant to be taken lightly. Like *Bonnie and Clyde* and *The Wild Bunch*, Francis Ford Coppola's *The Godfather* and *The Godfather Part II* managed the trick of being bloody and profound, packing the world with violence and confronting it with tragic, romantic

guts. If these films raised the ante of onscreen violence, making it more vivid and direct, they presented violence in the fullness of its pain, its long-term implications, and—in unflinching spectacle—its beauty. In contrast, the James Bond pictures, with their soft-core sex and hard-core effects, led the way for the next generation of action film: the spectacle of deaths whose pain is not explored, of victims who are blown out of their shoes or through plate-glass windows but mainly out of the way, cipher obstacles nobody cares about after they are gone and whose passing is a source of amusement. In the post-*Psycho* horror film, *Night of the Living Dead* and *The Texas Chain Saw Massacre* broke all boundaries of taste in an assault on the gut that evolved (notably in George Romero's *Dead* sequels and in the films of David Cronenberg) into an assault on mindless society as well as on the mind's conventional understanding of limits—not just the limits of behavior, but the limits of what can be shown or categorized or understood, the limits of experience, of identity, of being. These limits were likewise stretched in the family melodrama and the romantic comedy, primarily by director David Lynch (*Blue Velvet*). Physical comedy has always been violent, but the traps set for the villains in *Home Alone* go beyond any banana peel. All these films set new standards, broken by others, as the American cinema became ever more graphically violent, carnal, and foul-mouthed and as its occasionally deep look into the darkness got it somewhere, to a new and terrible vision whose

A scene from John Carpenter's *Halloween* (1978). PHOTOFEST

A scene of mayhem in Oliver Stone's *Natural Born Killers* (1994). PHOTOFEST

politics is *Alien*, whose rite of passage is *Apocalypse Now*, and whose revelation is *Seven*.

The amount of violence in film and its presentation on-screen vary with the times, as Production Codes and ratings systems come and go, and as public acceptance of violence as a part of life rises and falls. Reading genre-analogous films across the decades uncovers not only the development of commercial and artistic strategies but also the symptoms of social change (*Lost Highway* has its roots and double in *The Lady Eve*). If *Natural Born Killers* includes more murders and is more casual about them than *Bonnie and Clyde*, the significant difference is not in the violence but in the attitudes toward it and in fact toward anything: the difference between a world in which everything matters and a world of surfaces whose truth of the day is the image of the day. After Mickey and Mallory have killed her parents (a grotesque sequence in *Natural Born Killers* that demands comparison with the realistic murder of the heroine's father in *Badlands*), Mallory tells her brother that he's free. No matter how difficult it might be for him to go on with his life after this, how hard any real person in his situation would have to work to deal with the murder of his parents, *Natural Born Killers* never again shows the brother or says anything about him. Even a scene of his following Mallory's exploits in the tabloids would have helped. Clyde

(in *Bonnie and Clyde*) at least visits his mother. There is continuity in this earlier world, and with it a sense of consequences and relations, of the human mess and glory that continue to unfold.

The Uses of Violence

To choose violent means of dealing with another person is to put one's project or desire or life above the other's suffering or death. It is also to put everything in physical terms, which are convenient to the motion picture. You can see it, and it moves. By far the easiest way to dramatize conflict for the movies—to make it visual—is to show people hitting each other. And to allow the viewers to enjoy the violence, all the film has to do is allow them to ignore or deny the full reality of the other; that makes slapstick comedy possible, but it also can provide an excuse to dodge the work of creating characters. There are countless cases where the use of violence indicates a failure of dramatic invention, where nothing more interesting or revealing could be imagined, no scene that would allow a character to grow or fester or do anything more than kill or die. In the deeper films, the Michael Corleones survive all the way to the silent scream (*The Godfather Part III*), the abyss of self-knowledge. Much the same thing happens—this going to the bitter end, eyes open—in the extremely violent Western *Heaven's Gate*, the gory mystery

531

Seven, and the thriller *Blow Out,* whose reflexive ending fuses tragic awareness with the absolute horror of violence.

There are, of course, equally serious films that take violence to its logical conclusion and celebrate it, from the Western *The Wild Bunch* and the coming-of-age melodrama *Tol'able David* to the horror movie *The Hills Have Eyes.* And for every one of these pictures, there can be found in the same genre or subgenre a picture that takes violence for granted, as a simple and irrefutable motivator and as a spectacle demanded by the genre as inexorably (and, in the largest sense, neutrally) as a Western demands a gunfight: the horror film has its *Friday the 13th,* the action film its *True Lies.*

If any film can adopt any attitude toward violence, from acceptance to abhorrence, it would obscure matters to say that in an action film the violence isn't "serious," but in a war film it is. This is a question not of genres but of films within genres. Any violent-genre film achieves its vision of violence in its own terms, which it works out in relation to and engagement with the terms of the genre. The genre provides a framework and a set of expectations, not a mandatory formula and attitude. Within any genre, one film may be more violent than another, may use violence for more spectacular or more conceptual ends, and may work with or against audience expectations of violence.

It may be useful, then, to introduce a distinction that applies across genres: between films that make the audience *feel* the violence, much as they might if confronted with the same event in real life (*Henry: Portrait of a Serial Killer, The Last House on the Left,* and the TV movie *The Burning Bed*), and films that urge the audience not to feel or respond to the violence as they would in real life (*Home Alone, Die Hard 3,* and the Road Runner cartoons). In the first group, violence hurts; in the second it is fun, a spectacle not meant to be taken seriously. Either extreme, or any position between them, may occur in any "violent genre." It is not that the action picture presents violence as a fast-paced, enjoyable ride—that the genre has perfected painless death and ought to notify the medical community—but that *True Lies* does this while *Deliverance* does not.

A related distinction worth introducing is between films, in any genre and in the terms of that genre, that *teach* violence, presenting it as the only solution to the character's or culture's problems as defined by the film (*High Noon, Straw Dogs*), and

films that offer other, more creative solutions (*The Boy With Green Hair, The Shawshank Redemption*).

Some genres and subgenres do include violence more readily than others, or are known for it: action, adventure, atrocity, boxing, cops-and-robbers, disaster, gangster, horror, prison, road, science fiction, war, Western, mystery, and thriller. An adventure or science-fiction serial without fistfights and certain-death cliffhangers would be rejected because it failed to deliver not just as a genre piece but as a ritual. Yet many genres usually considered peaceable are rife with violence, decorated and motivated and crammed with it, from the family melodrama (*The Color Purple, Affliction*) and the musical (*West Side Story, Zoot Suit*) to the animated fairy tale (*Snow White and the Seven Dwarfs*) and cartoon comedy (*Duck Amuck*). D. W. Griffith set an enduring pattern for the family melodrama in 1919 with *Broken Blossoms,* in which a drunken boxer beats his daughter to death, and the genre has continued to bring its threat of violence within the family to the many genres it has intersected (as *Psycho* is a horror film as well as a gothic family melodrama, and *Mildred Pierce* is a family melodrama plotted as a murder mystery), but there has never been any expectation or requirement that it be violent. There can easily be a romantic comedy in which no one is murdered, and even a romantic tragedy (marrying the wrong person is bad enough), but it is almost impossible, if not perverse, to make a boxing picture without fights or a gangster picture without guns. The difference appears to be that violence is considered a familiar or essential element of certain genres, but one among many optional elements in others. There is no room here to detail all of the terms of any genre as complex as the gangster film, let alone of all violent genres, even when the discussion is confined, as it is here, to films made in the United States.

The Genres

But it may be possible to indicate some of the characteristic ways violence is dealt with, and what might be called the generic expectations of it, in some of the most routinely violent genres.

The Western demands a showdown. It is the scene in which the values for which the major antagonists stand are tested, and its roots are medieval, in the trial by combat to the death, and let God be the judge. As in many other genres and indeed other narrative arts, it is simple to attach to the good guys the values an artist endorses, and to turn the audience against the bad guys—and the values they are made to represent—by having a bad guy do violence against a good guy or an unfairly easy target (*Shane*). This familiar manipulation works in films that argue for violence (*The Birth of a Nation*) and that argue against it (*Broken Blossoms*).

Genres that pit criminals against each other and against the forces of society—from the cops-and-robbers pictures to the gangster and caper films—are, like the Western, arenas in which personal qualities and social values, united in codes of conduct and degrees of skill, are tested. These standards apply with equal rigor in the original *Scarface* and in *The Godfather Part II*—and in numerous films that cross genres, such as *Mad Max 2* (released in the U.S. as *The Road Warrior*, an Australian road-movie/Western that is also a foundation epic, like a prequel to the *Aeneid*, set in the future) or the horror/adventure/social-criticism/cop-Western *Jaws*.

If these trial-by-combat genres of outlaws, settlers, and wanderers, of enforcers and rebels, carry expectations, codified if not born in literature hundreds of years ago, that God will be on the side of right (as in *Ivanhoe*), to play on and even frustrate those expectations is part of the art of working in a genre and a vital way to express the moods of the artist or reflect those of the culture, where the right may not turn out to be blessed (*Prince of the City*). These codes of honor and visions of the way the world works, or ought to work, are tested from their dark sides in the darker genres, which include not only horror (*Cat People*) and take-no-prisoners satire (*Natural Born Killers*), but also dystopic science fiction (*A Clockwork Orange, Brazil*), radical docudrama (*Salt of the Earth*), atrocity documentary (*Night and Fog, 4 Little Girls*), and, at the heart of darkest Hollywood, film noir (*Out of the Past, Gun Crazy*), whose characters kill to express their love and power and values, to insist that and why they exist, even if all concerned know that they are, as novelist Jim Thompson put it, already dead.

The gunfighters of the West, like the gangsters, police, soldiers, outlaws, and knights—as folklore, pop history, and the genres have chosen to remember them—carried weapons (or were supposed to—*The Man Who Shot Liberty Valance*) and used them. To the extent that the genres are built around these figures, as the war film might be said to fit itself to the soldier and the mystery to the detective, they take on the figure's weapons and his or

her reasons for using them. Thus, the war film and the soldier use violence to survive, to win, and to defend a position (*The Bridges at Toko-Ri, The Steel Helmet*). Malicious, personal violence against fellow soldiers may intrude in the war film (*Platoon*) but belongs properly to those genres, led by the mystery, in which the people who kill each other know each other.

Most mysteries revolve around at least one murder, and someone always turns out to have a compelling reason to commit it. The murder climaxes an earlier, unshown story while starting another, motivating the tale of detection. The decision to murder is followed or uncovered rather than questioned; the genre demands blood. The mystery deploys violent events not only to keep the plot moving, but also to uncover the secrets of the heart and mind and will whose violent expression created the story's world along with its terms and logic, like an evil foundation tale that remains to be translated, a masked and twisted *fiat ego* (let there be me) that in the case of a movie is a literal *fiat lux* (let there be light). The key murder, finally unraveled and revealed, is frequently presented as the climax to the present story. Thus, the world returns to its point of origin—as it usually does in horror when the threat has been annihilated—and the social and personal fractures brought about by the crime are overcome. Unless it is an exposé film (often a real-world mystery solved partly by journalists, as in *All the President's Men* or *Z*), a mystery never solves anything but a mystery; in this respect it is a pure art but rarely a vehicle of political or social change. The courtroom drama, however, often sets out to tell the viewer how to think about an issue; if it gets moving with a crime, it climaxes with a debate (Fritz Lang's German-made *M* and his American film *Fury*). Violence in the courtroom drama may focus on an issue (*To Kill a Mockingbird*); in the murder mystery it may heighten a conflict while reducing it to brutal essentials (*Frenzy*); and in a thriller it is the preferred language of danger and romance (*Niagara*).

The prison picture, a claustrophobic morality play, pits good against evil under pressure, with anger and violence constantly erupting and being suppressed. Evil may take the form of a corrupt penal system (*I Am A Fugitive From A Chain Gang*), a sadistic official (*The Hill*), a brutal roommate or gang of inmates (*American Me*), or a dishonorable rat (*The Criminal Code*). Some prison pictures, like *The Hill*, sincerely denounce violence and present viable alternatives, but the violence happens anyway; it is the genre's almost invariable means of dealing with evil.

The adventure film challenges its heroes to survive violence and unknown danger (*King Solomon's Mines*, *The Most Dangerous Game*, *The Man Who Would Be King*) as they explore the farthest reaches of the world and the limits of their own resources. The spy film proper, from the fact-based *The House on 92nd Street* to the fictional *The Spy Who Came in from the Cold*, is a genre more serious in tone, at least in its treatment of military and ethical issues, than the spy adventure (*North by Northwest*, *Dr. No*). Kin to the spy adventure are the fantasy adventure (*The Wizard of Oz*) and the road movie (*Easy Rider*), so bloodily combined in *Wild At Heart*. And the fantasy adventure, the thrilling visit to the world of impossible realities, of dreams and nightmares, is, like the romance and the thriller, deep kin to the horror film (*A Nightmare on Elm Street*).

Categories of understanding are always shifting in the horror film; things one thought were one way turn out to be another, to answer to another paradigm. What would be a peaceful event in real life or in some other genre may well turn deadly in a horror film (visiting a parent's grave in *Night of the Living Dead*, leaving the bedroom to get a beer in *Halloween*) or put the soul in danger (renting a terrific apartment in *Rosemary's Baby*). In horror movies, violence is the most common way for the monster or the "threat" to express itself, and the violence is usually repeated (Dracula kills in his own way, over and over; so does Norman Bates) until the evil is expelled or destroyed—after which the culture licks its wounds and attempts to return to stability, which formulaically includes romance and reproduction; hence the heterosexual couple that so often survives. Violence—attacking it with *something*, whatever works (shoot them in the *head!*)—is the almost mandatory but not exclusive means of vanquishing the horror: ritual, including prayer and magic, is as effective in this genre as it is in the biblical spectacle, and the best way to get rid of a ghost may be to stop being afraid of it (*The Uninvited*).

While the literature of science fiction is often free of violence, as reconceived for the movies science-fiction almost always demands death—at the hands of a bug-eyed monster (*This Island Earth*), an intriguing technology (*The Fly*, *Forbidden Planet*), things from outer space (*Invasion of the Body Snatchers*), and even close-minded humans (*The Day the Earth Stood Still*). Linked decisively to the genres of romance and adventure as well as to both fantasy and science (unlike fantasy and horror, it must make a scientifically credible case for what it imagines), science fiction is concerned with much more than angry bacteria and mad scientists. But as practiced in Hollywood, the science-fiction film may be difficult to distinguish from the horror film (*Tarantula*). Even pictures that belong squarely within the genre, like *Gog* or *Star Trek II: The Wrath of Khan*, are full of violence, enhanced—appropriately, since it is a genre in which technology counts—by sophisticated, vivid effects.

Realistic violent effects are rampant in the action film (*First Blood*), and, even in the subgenre of the disaster movie (*Earthquake*), such effects are meant to be enjoyed. As in the thriller, sex and violence advance together, reinforcing each other in converging, adrenaline-fueled drives to climax (*Speed*). The action film depends on athletic and mechanical spectacle. Sex, in that context, also becomes spectacle, as it does in other genres. The viewer's reaction to the sex as well as to the violence becomes a blend of distanced voyeurism and engaged identification: an explosion is enjoyed from a safe distance, as an embrace is imagined up close. Good-looking actors, embodying characters who desire each other and act on their impulses, authorize the desires of the viewer who has lusted after them, wanted to be like them, and identified with them. The same is true of violent impulses, authorized by characters who use violence effectively, attractively, and for such compelling reasons as survival and revenge. If this complex of voyeurism, identification, and authorization applies, with modifications, to most sex-and-violence pictures and finally to most bourgeois narrative films, it may be most clearly at work in the action picture, where the enjoyment of violence as thrilling spectacle—like the enjoyment of sex in pornography—is not just authorized, but essential.

The Viewer

The desire to enjoy the spectacle of violence, brought to the theater by the genre fan who expects that desire to be reinforced and satisfied, may be traced to the pleasures of adrenaline. Or the action and disaster pictures may let a caged audience blow off revolutionary and criminal steam in a dream of destruction, where banks are bombed, officials are idiots, smashing somebody in the face solves a problem and really feels good, and right prevails—while outside the theater, of course, nothing changes. In "The Work of Art in the Age of Mechanical Reproduction," Walter Benjamin wrote that mankind's "self-alienation has reached such a degree that it can experience its own destruction as an aesthetic pleasure of the first order."

That may be one more reason it is fun to watch our world blow up. Violence not only keeps viewers entrenched in the ideology, entertaining them with fantasies of blasting away every enemy from the bad guy to the system—so that they will go out into the real world in a post-climactic calm, an energized sense of release and well-being—but also entertains those whose sole rebellious impulse is to watch the house burn down around them, identifying only with the carnage.

Some viewers have deadened themselves to all this violence as a condition of going to the movies; others enjoy it in the first place and, as genre enthusiasts, seek it out. Many have just learned to take it—taking the punches thrown by *Raging Bull* in order to make it through a great film and in the process growing calluses, so that watching the later *GoodFellas* is easy.

It is not that people used to care and no longer do. They can still get upset when the good die young (*Titanic*) or when the painful consequences of violence are left on-screen for a long time (*Unforgiven*). They care when they are given performances and images that reveal what they share with the victim—mortal being, the potential to be in an equally perilous situation, and in some contexts gender and class—and what they recoil from sharing (that wound, that behavior) or see clearly in its otherness (the monster, from Godzilla to the State). They care when they hate the villain. They care when they feel that the victim hurts and matters.

This caring is not necessarily a matter of getting to know a character, for one can recognize the humanity in a group and empathize with the suffering of many to whom one has not been formally introduced (the slaves who are chained and drowned in *Amistad*). Nor is it a matter of the camera's distance from the violence or the amount of time devoted to the event; in *Open City*, the sudden death in long shot of the woman gunned down in the street is at least as affecting as any of the killings shown at length in that film close up. It is a matter of what is considered and presented at all. A bloody murder can be a second of action—bang, they got me, clunk. Or it can hurt, and take a long time, and be a humiliating mess and a shock, and leave people behind, things undone—everything undone—with pieces to be put back together that can never again be put together right.

Filmography

All films are made in the United States unless indicated otherwise.

Affliction (1998, Paul Schrader)
Alien (1979, Ridley Scott)
All the President's Men (1976, Alan J. Pakula)
American Me (1992, Edward James Olmos)
Amistad (1997, Steven Spielberg)
Apocalypse Now (1979, Francis Ford Coppola)
Badlands (1973, Terrence Malick)
The Birth of a Nation (1915, D. W. Griffith)
Blow Out (1981, Brian De Palma)
Blue Velvet (1986, David Lynch)
Bonnie and Clyde (1967, Arthur Penn)
The Boy With Green Hair (1948, Joseph Losey)
Brazil (1985, Terry Gilliam)
The Bridges at Toko-Ri (1954, Mark Robson)
Broken Blossoms (1919, D. W. Griffith)
The Burning Bed (1984, Robert Greenwald)
Cat People (1942, Jacques Tourneur)
A Clockwork Orange (1971, U.K.; Stanley Kubrick)
The Color Purple (1985, Steven Spielberg)
The Criminal Code (1931, Howard Hawks)
Dawn of the Dead (1979, George Romero)
Day of the Dead (1985, George Romero)
The Day the Earth Stood Still (1951, Robert Wise)
Deliverance (1972, John Boorman)
Die Hard 3/ Die Hard With a Vengeance (1995, John McTiernan)
Dr. No (1962, U.K.; Terence Young)
Dracula (1931, Tod Browning)
Duck Amuck (1953, Chuck Jones)
Earthquake (1974, Mark Robson)
Easy Rider (1969, Dennis Hopper)
First Blood (1982, Ted Kotcheff)
The Fly (1958, Kurt Neumann)
Forbidden Planet (1956, Fred M. Wilcox)
4 Little Girls (1997, Spike Lee)
Frenzy (1972, Alfred Hitchcock)
Friday the 13th (1980, Sean S. Cunningham)
Fury (1936, Fritz Lang)
The Godfather (1972, Francis Ford Coppola)
The Godfather Part II (1974, Francis Ford Coppola)
The Godfather Part III (1990, Francis Ford Coppola)
Gog (1954, Herbert L. Strock)
GoodFellas (1990, Martin Scorsese)
Gun Crazy (1950, Joseph H. Lewis)
Halloween (1978, John Carpenter)

Halloween II (1981, Rick Rosenthal)
Heaven's Gate (1980, Michael Cimino)
Henry: Portrait of a Serial Killer (1986, John McNaughton)
High Noon (1952, Fred Zinnemann)
The Hill (1965, Sidney Lumet)
The Hills Have Eyes (1977, Wes Craven)
Home Alone (1990, Chris Columbus)
The House on 92nd Street (1945, Henry Hathaway)
I Am A Fugitive From A Chain Gang (1932, Mervyn LeRoy)
Invasion of the Body Snatchers (1956, Don Siegel)
Ivanhoe (1952, Richard Thorpe)
Jaws (1975, Steven Spielberg)
King Solomon's Mines (1950, Compton Bennett and Andrew Marton)
The Lady Eve (1941, Preston Sturges)
The Last House on the Left (1972, Wes Craven)
Lethal Weapon (1987, Richard Donner)
Lost Highway (1997, David Lynch)
M (1931, Germany; Fritz Lang)
Mad Max 2: The Road Warrior (1981, Australia; George Miller)
The Man Who Shot Liberty Valance (1962, John Ford)
The Man Who Would Be King (1975, John Huston)
Mildred Pierce (1945, Michael Curtiz)
The Most Dangerous Game (1932, Ernest B. Schoedsack and Irving Pichel)
Natural Born Killers (1994, Oliver Stone)
Niagara (1953, Henry Hathaway)
Night and Fog (1955, France, Alain Resnais)
Night of the Living Dead (1968, George Romero)
A Nightmare on Elm Street (1984, Wes Craven)
North by Northwest (1959, Alfred Hitchcock)
Oklahoma! (1955, Fred Zinnemann)
Open City (1945, Italy, Roberto Rossellini)
Out of the Past (1947, Jacques Tourneur)
Platoon (1986, Oliver Stone)
Prince of the City (1981, Sidney Lumet)
Psycho (1960, Alfred Hitchcock)
Raging Bull (1980, Martin Scorsese)
The Road Warrior (see *Mad Max 2*)
Rocketship X-M (1950, Kurt Neumann)
Rosemary's Baby (1968, Roman Polanski)
Salt of the Earth (1953, Herbert Biberman)
Scarface (1930, released 1932, Howard Hawks)
Seven (1995, David Fincher)
Shane (1953, George Stevens)
The Shawshank Redemption (1994, Frank Darabont)

Short Eyes (1977, Robert M. Young)
Snow White and the Seven Dwarfs (1937, prod. Walt Disney)
Speed (1994, Jan De Bont)
The Spy Who Came In from the Cold (1965, Martin Ritt)
Star Trek II: The Wrath of Khan (1982, Nicholas Meyer)
The Steel Helmet (1951, Samuel Fuller)
Straw Dogs (1971, Sam Peckinpah)
Tarantula (1955, Jack Arnold)
The Texas Chain Saw Massacre (1974, Tobe Hooper)
This Island Earth (1955, Joseph Newman)
Titanic (1997, James Cameron)
To Kill a Mockingbird (1962, Robert Mulligan)
Tol'able David (1921, Henry King)
True Lies (1994, James Cameron)
2001: A Space Odyssey (1968, U.K.; Stanley Kubrick)
Unforgiven (1992, Clint Eastwood)
The Uninvited (1944, Lewis Allen)
Vertigo (1958, Alfred Hitchcock)
West Side Story (1961, Robert Wise and Jerome Robbins)
Wild At Heart (1990, David Lynch)
The Wild Bunch (1969, Sam Peckinpah)
The Wizard of Oz (1939, Victor Fleming)
Z (1969, France; Constantin Costa-Gavras)
Zoot Suit (1981, Luis Valdez)

BIBLIOGRAPHY

Benjamin, Walter. "The Work of Art in the Age of Mechanical Reproduction." In *Illuminations*, edited by Hannah Arendt. Translated by Harry Zohn. New York: Schocken, 1968.
Briggs, Joe Bob. *Joe Bob Goes to the Drive-In*. New York: Delacorte, 1987.
Everitt, David, and Harold Schechter. *The Manly Movie Guide*. New York: Boulevard, 1997.
Grant, Barry Keith, ed. *Film Genre Reader II*. Austin: University of Texas Press, 1995.
Haskell, Molly. *From Reverence to Rape: The Treatment of Women in the Movies*. Chicago: University of Chicago Press, 1987.
Kawin, Bruce F. "Me Tarzan, You Junk: Violence and Moral Education in the Paranoia Film." *Take One* 6, no. 4 (March 1978): 29–33.
Keough, Peter, ed. *Flesh and Blood: The National Society of Film Critics on Sex, Violence, and Censorship*. San Francisco: Mercury House, 1995.
Mast, Gerald, ed. *The Movie in Our Midst: Documents in the Cultural History of Film in America*. Chicago: University of Chicago Press, 1982.

Mast, Gerald, and Bruce F. Kawin. *A Short History of the Movies*. 7th ed. Needham Heights, Mass.: Allyn and Bacon, 2000.

McConnell, Frank. *Storytelling and Mythmaking: Images from Film and Literature*. New York: Oxford University Press, 1979.

Warshow, Robert. "The Westerner." In *Film: An Anthology*, edited by Daniel Talbot. Berkeley and Los Angeles: University of California Press, 1967.

Williams, Linda. *Hard Core: Power, Pleasure, and the "Frenzy of the Visible."* Berkeley and Los Angeles: University of California Press, 1989.

Wood, Robin. *Hollywood from Vietnam to Reagan*. New York: Columbia University Press, 1986.

BRUCE F. KAWIN

See also **Television: Violent Genres.**

ANIMATION

Throughout the history of motion picture film, from the late 1800s on, the level of violence depicted on screen has been affected by changing aesthetic standards and varying amounts of censorship. In many ways the rise and fall of violent content in animated films parallels that of live-action cinema; however, it sometimes seems animation has had more freedom of expression than live-action works, since some people find it easy to dismiss animation as "just a cartoon," having little relationship to reality.

Early Animation

Perhaps the first animated film dates from 1899, when Arthur Melbourne Cooper made *Matches: An Appeal*, a British film that depicts animated matchsticks in a war-related message. From that point, animation developed in various directions. Internationally, a number of fine artists experimented with animated images, such as Arnaldo Ginna in *Vita futurista* (*Futuristic Life*, 1916) and Fernand Léger in *Ballet mécanique* (*Mechanical Ballet*, 1924). But better known are the commercial productions that filled theaters and entertained a wide range of moviegoers.

From the very beginning, commercial animation has incorporated violence into its aesthetics, often to add an element of humor. A good example occurs in a popular film directed by Georges Méliès, *Voyage dans la lune* (*Trip to the Moon*, 1902), which employs object animation. Attacking moon creatures disappear in a puff of smoke after they are hit on the head by travelers from Earth.

One of the mainstays of early "silent" cinema in the United States was slapstick humor—physical comedy that relies on visual gags. Early slapstick routines and the people who performed them in films generally developed on the live stage, in vaudeville or variety shows, where the rough and tumble antics of physical comedy were common. Prominent in early American slapstick comedy films were the Keystone Kops of the Mack Sennett Studio and the comedians Charlie Chaplin and Buster Keaton, among others.

Early animated films also drew upon the traditions of physical comedy. One of the most popular animated characters worldwide during the 1920s was Felix the Cat, whose behaviors were strongly influenced by Charlie Chaplin's films. The Felix the Cat series employs a form of "gag" narrative, which became conventional in American animated short films by the early 1920s. Like slapstick comedy, gag animation is based on a model of physical humor, in which pratfalls and "hurt" gags (humor involving potentially painful actions) often occur in rapid succession. A preference for gag formulas in American animation can be seen in the letters of Margaret J. Winkler, the most successful distributor of animated shorts at the time, written to Walt Disney, who was only beginning to establish his reputation in the mid-1920s. Winkler distributed Disney's series of Alice Comedies, which set a live girl in an animated environment, as well as the Fleischer Studios' popular Out of the Inkwell series. In a letter regarding *Alice's Day at Sea* (1924), Winkler underscored her preference for physical comedy when she instructed Disney to "inject as much humor as you can. Humor is the first requisite of short subjects such as Felix, Out of the Inkwell, and Alice" (Merritt and Kaufman 1993, p. 15). The gag formula has continued to dominate American animated shorts to this day; it can be seen in work created throughout the years at the Warner Bros., Disney, and other studios.

Gag narratives have been complemented by another long-standing convention of American animation, the "squash and stretch" technique. Characters are made to metamorphose into relatively short (squashed) and long (stretched) versions of themselves in an effort to caricature movement, creating a form of visual humor. Although squash and stretch animation can be employed to inject personality into regular locomotion, such as walking or running, the technique also is used to create physical humor in exaggerated actions of other types, including hurt gags. An example can be seen in *Clock Cleaners* (1937), the Disney Mickey Mouse classic directed by Ben Sharpsteen, in which Mickey Mouse, Donald Duck, and Goofy clean the inside of a large clock. Mickey's body squashes and stretches as he tries to oust a bird who has settled into the clock. When Donald engages in battle with a renegade clock coil, his body is squeezed and elongated by the feisty object. After a bell that Goofy is cleaning gets struck, causing him to shake violently, his legs stretch into wavy, spaghetti-like strands.

Other examples of hurt gags can be seen in the Wile E. Coyote series made at Warner Bros. and DePatie-Freleng Enterprises between 1949 and 1966. This series centers on variations of one basic scenario: a self-assured, highly creative coyote attempts to trap (in order to eat) a savvy roadrunner who manages to elude all his schemes, with the result that the coyote himself falls victim to his own destructive devices. In every episode, the unfortunate coyote is flattened, burned, or otherwise disfigured several times in the process of hunting his prey. Much of the enjoyment of this series comes with the viewer's anticipation of this unlucky outcome and the knowledge that the persistent hunter will try and try again, despite certain doom.

Other series also use a chase or hunting scenario as a basic premise. For example, the rooster star of the Foghorn Leghorn series (1946–1952), produced by Warner Bros., plays opposite a chicken hawk out to catch himself some chickens. Hunting also occurs as a basic premise in a number of Tex Avery shorts made at Metro-Goldwyn-Mayer, including

King Size Canary (1947) and *Out Foxed* (1949). A different sort of hunt occurs when Bluto chases after the prized Olive Oyl in Popeye the Sailor shorts (1933–1957, released by the Fleischer Studios and the Famous Studios through Paramount Pictures). Popeye always can be counted on to deal the enemy some powerful blows once he has fortified himself with a can of spinach.

During World War II, squash and stretch animation and physical humor were particularly well suited to the animation studios' efforts to create patriotic statements. These sometimes showed the enemy literally being beaten; for example, in the Warner Bros. short directed by Friz Freleng, *Daffy the Commando* (1943), a German military flunky— predictably named Schultz—grows shorter and shorter as his helmet is continually pounded down. At the end of the film, it is Hitler himself who gets a beating on the head, this time by Daffy, who flies to the scene after being ejected from a cannon.

Violence for Humorous Effect

At first, one might think of violence and humor as being opposite poles. But there seems to be something funny about the violence that occurs to the body of a character during physical comedy, whether it appears on stage, in a live-action film, or in an animated production. Whether one likes to admit it or not, humans often derive pleasure from seeing a character being humiliated. Trans-

What's for dinner? A Warner Bros. cartoon featuring Road Runner and Wile E. Coyote. PHOTOFEST

gressions of the social order, including basic codes of civility, lie at the heart of a great deal of film comedy, a point that has been elaborated by Henry Jenkins, Donald Crafton, and others.

Even when physical comedy is potentially painful, the resilience of the performer reassures the viewer that he or she is not really maimed or even bruised. Viewers can laugh at such things partly because they understand that the performance is a fictional event, removed from reality. In variety acts the presence of the stage, which separates the performer from the audience, makes clear that the performances are fictional. The performer in a live-action film is removed from his or her audience in both space and time. However, in both instances viewers realize that the performer, whether on stage or screen, is made of flesh and blood. While it may be funny to watch a live character get thumped on the head, the appearance of blood or the crushing of real body parts would abruptly end the humor. We react to animated characters very differently. When we watch Wile E. Coyote get burned to bits, reduced to a patch of scorched fur on the road, we can laugh because we recognize that there is no real coyote taking part in the act.

There are people who would argue that some viewers—in particular, young children—do not really understand the difference between animation, or film in general, and real life. Throughout the years, in fact, some people have contended that motion pictures of all kinds affect the actions and thought processes of their viewers, especially youngsters. One influential book, Marie Winn's *The Plug-in Drug: Television, Children, and the Family* (1977), fueled peoples' fears about the potential harm of media images upon youth.

Scholars have studied the impact of motion pictures on children from a number of angles. The 1995 anthology *In Front of the Children: Screen Entertainment and Young Audiences*, edited by Cary Bazalgette and David Buckingham, addresses the effects of both film and television. This book attempts to study the production, circulation, and reception of "children's culture" in a relatively objective manner.

Monitoring Content

The golden era of American animation, generally considered to be the 1930s and 1940s, encompassed the period when the Production Code Administration (PCA) was charged with censoring the content of theatrical films and other forms of media. The PCA monitored commercial productions, looking for violence, sexual content, and other material that was considered inappropriate for the screen. Short and feature-length productions created by American animation studios were subject to approval by the PCA, but it appears the PCA was more lenient with animated works than with their live-action counterparts.

An example can been seen in the PCA file for Disney's *Snow White* (1937). PCA reviewers were asked to watch for and note the occurrence of a number of items on a checklist, including depictions of violence and criminal acts. The reviewer of *Snow White* checked neither of these two categories, despite the presence of a number of relevant actions: the attempted murder of Snow White, the terrifying ordeal in the forest (even if it is imagined by Snow White and is largely psychological in nature), the onset of the "sleeping death" of Snow White, and the presumed actual death of Snow White's stepmother, the evil queen. The following remarks were written by the reviewer: "feature length cartoon," "fairy story," "first feature length cartoon in Technicolor. Done superbly." These comments, like the occasional remarks in PCA files on other feature-length animated films, suggest that the production's status as animation may have affected its review—that the evaluators might have found the violent content innocuous because the images are drawn and not live-action. Karl Cohen contends that most animation studios complied with the basic guidelines of the Production Code; thus, the organization felt justified in focusing most of its attention on live-action films, which it seems were constantly challenging the rules.

By the early 1930s Walt Disney was concerned with the wholesomeness of his productions and their appeal to a wide market. In *Snow White* moderation seems to have been used in the interest of young viewers. For example, when Snow White falls into her sleeping death and when the queen plunges to her death, the action occurs offscreen. Because the violence is merely suggested but not actually shown, it probably has less emotional impact on the viewer. In an analysis of the film's adaptation, Jack Zipes has indicated that certain gory elements from the original fairy tale were left out of the Disney film, including the death of Snow White's mother in childbirth and the death of the evil queen by dancing on hot coals. However, some censoring organizations in other countries still found Disney's film too scary for young viewers. In both England and Australia, frames involving the witch interacting with skeletons in the dungeon were removed from the film by censors.

The Production Code was changed to a rating system in 1968, opening the doors for increasingly violent content in motion pictures. Within a few years violence in animation actually found its own showcase: the traveling Sick and Twisted® Festival of Animation programmed by Mellow Manor Productions, which was established in 1977 by Craig "Spike" Decker and Mike Gribble (popularly known as Spike and Mike). The producers of the festival sometimes provide artists with funding to create adult-oriented animation, which may include violence as well as sexual themes.

Among the films showcased at this festival was Mike Judge's *Frog Baseball* (1992), in which two adolescents use frogs for batting practice (the short was later developed into Judge's MTV series *Beavis and Butt-Head*). Another good example of an animation short that uses violence to get laughs is *Lupo the Butcher* (1986), directed by Danny Antonucci, which depicts a man hacking off body parts as he speaks. The film was produced by Marv Newland, who first gained attention for his student film *Bambi Meets Godzilla* (1969), now a cult favorite. The film shows America's favorite animated deer grazing peacefully in a serene forest until the foot of Japan's favorite monster enters the screen directly above, with an unfortunate result.

Bill Plympton is another popular animator who is infamous for his creative use of violence as well as sexual content. His reputation was firmly established with such films as *One of Those Days* (1988), which poses the question, "What would it be like to live the most violent and action-filled day imaginable?", and *Twenty-five Ways to Quit Smoking* (1989), which includes such "cures" as wearing a heat-seeking missile and using a flamethrower as a lighter. A 1997 short, *Sex and Violence,* and its sequel, *More Sex and Violence* (1998), which contained animated versions of print-cartoon ideas considered too extreme for publication, reveal that Plympton continued to build his career by pushing the boundaries of good taste.

Various special-interest groups continue to rally for nonviolent productions for children. A good example can be found in the "UNICEF Amalfi Guidelines," which were generated at the First Conference on the Production of Non-Violent Cartoons, held in Italy at the Cartoons on the Bay festival in 1996. The guidelines discuss the need to monitor the quantitative and qualitative portrayals of violence in many forms: physical and psychological, explicit and implicit. They stress that intelligence, dialogue, and social skills (rather than violence) should be used as a means to solve problems. The guidelines suggest that violent images and expressions be justified by the plot and, whenever possible, be deemphasized. They also say that the message "violence doesn't pay" should be clearly delivered, along with a sense of the consequences of violent action. The "UNICEF Amalfi Guidelines" are largely concerned with the depiction of violence on television, a medium that has received much more scrutiny than film in terms of audience research and the effects of violence on behavior.

BIBLIOGRAPHY

Bendazzi, Giannalberto. *Cartoons: One Hundred Years of Cinema Animation.* London: John Libbey, 1994.

Canemaker, John. *Felix: The Twisted Tale of the World's Most Famous Cat.* New York: Da Capo, 1991.

Cohen, Karl F. *Forbidden Animation: Censored Cartoons and Blacklisted Animators in America.* Jefferson, N.C.: McFarland, 1997.

Crafton, Donald. *Before Mickey: The Animated Cartoon 1898–1928.* Cambridge, Mass.: MIT Press, 1982.

———. "Pie and Chase: Gag, Spectacle, and Narrative in Slapstick Comedy." In *Classical Hollywood Comedy,* edited by Kristine Brunovska Karnick and Henry Jenkins. New York: Routledge, 1995.

Floquet, Pierre. "Tex Avery's Comic Language: A Transgressive Interpretation of Hunting." *Animation Journal* 6, no. 1 (fall 1997).

Furniss, Maureen R. *Art in Motion: Animation Aesthetics.* London: John Libbey, 1998.

Jenkins, Henry. *What Made Pistachio Nuts? Early Sound Comedy and the Vaudeville Aesthetic.* New York: Columbia University Press, 1992.

Maltin, Leonard. *Of Mice and Magic: A History of American Animated Cartoons.* New York: New American Library, 1980.

Merritt, Russell, and J. B. Kaufman. *Walt in Wonderland: The Silent Films of Walt Disney.* Baltimore: Johns Hopkins University Press, 1993.

"The UNICEF Amalfi Guidelines." First Conference on the Production of Non-Violent Cartoons. Cartoons on the Bay (April 1996). URL: http://www.awn.com/cartoonsbay/first/unicef.html.

Zipes, Jack. "Breaking the Disney Spell." In *From Mouse to Mermaid: The Politics of Film, Gender, and Culture,* edited by Elizabeth Bell, Lynda Hass, and Laura Sells. Bloomington: University of Indiana Press, 1995.

MAUREEN RUTH FURNISS

See also **Television: Children's Television.**

DOCUMENTARY FILM

In 1898, barely two years after the public unveiling of cinema, Boleslaw Matuszewski, an obscure

Polish entrepreneur, declared that film would eventually become a source for generating historical evidence. The medium's chief virtue, he wrote, was its "indiscretion," its ability to spontaneously record events lacking a clear focus or coherent structure, scenes not only unposed for the camera but imbued with rapid, chaotic movement. For Matuszewski, examples of what film could uniquely capture included street riots and battlefield combat. There was, however, an obvious problem: "A historical event does not always happen where there is someone waiting for it." The attempt to film occurrences for which there is no prearranged trajectory, the condition of most events deemed "violent," would inevitably result in a partial depiction, a fragmentary mode of documentation that elides beginnings and transitional stages while highlighting peripheral actions and aftermaths.

Despite the fact that in early cinema boundaries between documentary and fictional scenes were often blurred by practices of reenactment, Matuszewski's comments appear remarkably prescient. The issue of violence in documentaries is keyed by constant and irreducible markers of insufficiency, by the absence of footage for crucial intervals of a violent episode, or by existing footage whose meaning or status as evidence is decidedly ambiguous. Perhaps the most famous documentary sequence ever shot is the twenty-six seconds of the assassination of President John F. Kennedy recorded by amateur cameraman Abraham Zapruder. Ever since it was taken in 1963, this footage has been at the center of a seemingly endless controversy fueled not only by conflicting interpretations of information contained in separate frames but by what is missing, what remains unseen, from the event as filmed. Especially since its initial television airing in 1975, the Zapruder material has served as a powerful locus for the American cultural imagination, a dark cipher for what many have claimed as a turning point in the conceptualization of postwar society; in addition, however, it is a cinematic emblem of the visual possibilities and epistemological dilemmas intrinsic to the representation of actual violence.

The various technical reanimations—including magnification of details, looping, freeze-framing, and slow-motion pulsing of frames—performed on the Zapruder footage by official and independent investigators alike have entered our common vocabulary of filmic mayhem through their absorption into a broad range of fictional as well as documentary idioms. Beyond the handful of films that refer or allude to the assassination footage, such as Arthur Penn's *Bonnie and Clyde* (1967) and Oliver Stone's *JFK* (1991), the deployment of visual tropes loosely associated with documentary film's "look" or optical perspective—for example, unsteady handheld movement—has become an omnipresent signifier of heightened realism in the expression of violent action. For documentary features, which do not have the luxury of staging events directly for the camera and thus usually treat violent subject matter in fragmentary fashion or after the fact, the burden of representation shifts from protocols of demonstration to questions of explication: that is, whereas Hollywood genre productions are concerned with how best to show the complex causal mechanics of violent events, American documentaries tend to focus on residual effects, on the social or psychic or philosophical ramifications of a particular act. Thus the status of violence in documentary cinema has little to do with notions of spectacle (the sole exception being a disreputable class of so-called "mondo videos," home-market cult products that string together horrifying newsreel images of crime scenes, riots, and natural catastrophes).

The extent to which organizing a full-length documentary around violence is dependent on—hindered, liberated, or problematized by—the absence of images that could ensure epistemological clarity and completeness in represented violence is amply demonstrated by Errol Morris's *The Thin Blue Line* (1988), in which extensive and contradictory verbal descriptions of a police officer's murder are augmented by reenacted "fictional" scenes shot, edited, and slowed down in order to construct a coherent, convincing narrative explanation for the event. A similar acknowledgment is evident in television shows such as *America's Most Wanted* and *Rescue 911*, nonfictional hybrids that freely intersperse documentary interviews and location footage with staged, often subjectively visualized scenes. Appositely, the series *Cops*, along with a flood of tabloid "specials" focusing on car crashes and other forms of public mayhem, wind up enhancing a viewer's impression of visual inadequacy through the forced repetition of privileged moments caught "on camera."

For the most part, contemporary debates about violence in the media and its relation to criminal behavior bypass the tiny domain of nonfiction theatrical releases, yet the terms in which the debate has been played out are instructive. Disney executive Michael Eisner's response to charges that Hollywood exploits and contributes to violent social impulses is typical: "I don't think anybody thinks that movies like *The Terminator* [1984] are real." Represented violence is claimed to be innocuous in its impact on viewers to the extent that it is seen as "unreal," yet Hollywood studios spend millions of dollars attempting to mimic convincingly authentic, documentarylike styles of graphic depiction. Implicitly, documentaries themselves are exempt from social culpability because the actions they show are "too real," lacking the seductive glamour or ethico-aesthetic capacity to inspire imitative behavior.

Although there is some understandable confusion about the connection among television news programming, feature-length documentaries, and entertainment products, the reason nonfiction cinema has avoided the taint of exploitative violence has less to do with aesthetics or morality than economics. Virtually dormant in the 1970s and 1980s, the market for theatrical documentaries was revived in the 1990s due in part to the rising popularity of television newsmagazine shows, talk radio, and nonfiction publishing. This market, however, remains at the periphery of mass cultural consumption. Less than a dozen features per year are released into specialty theaters located in a handful of urban centers. Even commercially successful nonfiction films such as *Hoop Dreams* (1994) reach but a fraction of the audience attending a Hollywood flop. If $8 million in box-office receipts spells financial disaster for a genre movie, that figure is almost unattainable by a documentary release. Put simply, documentaries lack the cultural clout to be included in the public or, for that matter, academic discourse on media violence. Moreover, of the approximately seventy features released in the United States in the 1990s, fewer than fifteen are thematically grounded in violent events. The vast majority of the films released commercially fit into traditional subgenres such as celebrity portrait (for example, *Truth or Dare*, 1991) or political chronicle (*A Perfect Candidate*, 1996). In summary, of the eight thousand murders and more than one hundred thousand acts of violence witnessed by the average seventh grader in feature films and television shows, according to a 1991 American Psychological Association survey, presumably few if any have seeped from the ranks of documentary cinema.

Violence and Reflexivity

Of course, the rather anodyne prospectus rendered here does not mean that the representation

of violence plays no role in documentary production. In cases where it does function as an integral theme, violence is often presented in distinct and illuminating ways. For example, *Gimme Shelter* (1970), Albert Maysles, David Maysles, and Charlotte Zwerin's chronicle of a free Rolling Stones concert near San Francisco, California, constructs a cogent parallel between the aggressively macho lyrics in songs performed by the group and the escalating crowd violence initiated by a "security" contingent of Hell's Angels. In the film's climactic moments, with Mick Jagger interrupting a rendition of "Under My Thumb" to plead for calm, a black spectator is knifed to death not far from the stage by a member of the motorcycle gang. Jagger's poignant inability to stem the chaotic tide of beatings is positioned as ironic counterpoint to the hostile energies unleashed by rock lyrics, his self-induced aura as a "street fighting man" unmasked by a social code of gang violence beyond his control. In subsequent scenes, the filmmakers examine murky bits of footage of the crime on an editing table, freezing the image flow and magnifying details in the manner of the Zapruder analyses, in order to clarify what actually happened. Realizing that the inadvertent coverage of the murder—the camera was drawn by outbreaks of fighting but had no clear view of the incident in question—will become admissible evidence in the upcoming trial, the film hints at its own culpability as a secondary provocation, and de facto performance, in an obdurate cycle of spectatorship and violence.

The conclusion of William Gazecki's *Waco: The Rules of Engagement* (1997) also hinges on an intricate analysis of movie footage—in this case helicopter surveillance film of the 1993 attack by the Federal Bureau of Investigation on the rear of the Texas religious compound—in arguing that government agents initiated, and possibly planned in advance, the final conflagration that killed seventy-six people. *Waco* consists of a compilation of television news footage, congressional testimony, and interviews with lawyers, mediators, surviving cult members, and other interested parties. The visual and verbal evidence it assembles frequently contradicts government statements and dominant news reporting. Although the inferences drawn by the film are sometimes sketchy, and the witnesses not always credible, *Waco* is an example of post-Zapruder documentary in which the agonized process of interpreting filmic artifacts displaces as it amplifies the historical drama of immediate events. The type of critique rendered here, of government bureaucracy and its manipulation of public information, readdresses the issue of responsibility for violent confrontations from a framework of seemingly intractable institutional assumptions made about the nature of cult groups, the necessity of armed intervention, and the desired "image" of law-enforcement agencies.

In several other documentaries centered on violent events in the 1990s, the consideration of individual motives and responsibility is extended to encompass larger social forces, including the reciprocity between criminal prosecution and media exploitation. Joe Berlinger and Bruce Sinofsky's *Brother's Keeper* (1992) and *Paradise Lost: The Child Murder at Robin Hood Hills* (1996) both concern murder cases in which the accused appear to be convenient prey for a local legal apparatus more interested in disposing of "deviant" outsiders than in conducting a thorough investigation. The films are anchored by courtroom testimony containing vivid descriptions of the alleged crimes, yet the realities of violent death are muffled by a fabric of sympathetic interviews with the defendants and by disparaging accounts of the legal process.

Far more radical in its treatment of celebrity murder is Nick Broomfield's *Aileen Wuornos: The Selling of a Serial Killer* (1992). Rather than adopting a viewpoint that validates documentary film discourse as humanistic and truth-seeking, in contrast to the venal and manipulative reporting of dominant media, Broomfield subverts documentary's claims to a higher moral ground by immersing his portrait of "America's first female serial killer" in a mock-tabloid quest for lurid intimacy. Concern for the victims, or indeed interest in the crimes themselves, is almost entirely vitiated by the ancillary financial wrangling and proprietary competition taking place among Wuornos's closest advisors and between her representatives and the filmmaker—who frequently appears on screen and is constantly heard in offscreen dialogues. When the anticipated interview with the convicted killer finally occurs, the topic of discussion is not remorse or vindication but cash payments. At the core of the film is a tacit admission that since documentary can rarely mediate violent events in a direct manner, the difference between detached, ostensibly objective analysis and blatant self-interest has less to do with empirical research than with ideological posturing. Broomfield suggests that the independent documentarist's investment in sensationalized violence plays on the same fears and voyeuristic urges as other more obviously ex-

ploitative venues. Whether or not one agrees with this argument, it establishes a bracing alternative to conventional methods of framing the issue of violence in cinema.

BIBLIOGRAPHY

Arthur, Paul. "Media Spectacle and the Tabloid Documentary." *Film Comment* 34, no. 1 (January–February 1998).

Barker, Martin. "Violence." *Sight and Sound* 5, no. 6 (June 1995).

Leyda, Jay. *Films Beget Films.* New York: Hill and Wang, 1964.

Simon, Art. *Dangerous Knowledge: The JFK Assassination in Art and Film.* Philadelphia: Temple University Press, 1996.

Wasson, Haidee. "Assassinating an Image: The Strange Life of Kennedy's Death." *CineAction* 38 (September 1995).

PAUL ARTHUR

See also **Kennedy, John F.; Music: Popular; Television; Waco; Wuornos, Aileen.**

CENSORSHIP

Feature films have depicted violence (overt physical action that causes or threatens pain) since the beginning of motion picture production in the United States in the late nineteenth century. From the Payne Fund studies of the early 1930s to the University of California at Santa Barbara media violence studies of the 1990s, social scientists have sought to determine the effects of film violence on viewers. These efforts notwithstanding, the only certain effects of film violence have been controversy and efforts to control film content through censorship.

In *The New Censors: Movies and the Culture Wars* (1997), Charles Lyons defined "film censorship": "In the context of film production, distribution, and exhibition, censorship refers to a set of practices by institutions or groups, either prior to or following a film's release, that result in the removal of a word, scene or entire film from the market place" (p. 6). The institutions engaging in the removal of words, scenes, or entire films that depict violence fall into three categories: government, special interest groups, and the film industry itself. Government censorship has taken place primarily on the state and local levels, where boards review and censor films. Although the federal government has not regulated film content, several decisions by the Supreme Court have had profound effects on the censorship of film violence.

Supreme Court Cases

One of the first significant federal government actions to have broad effects on the censorship of film violence was the Supreme Court's 1915 decision in *Mutual Film Corporation v. Industrial Commission of Ohio,* in which the Court found that motion pictures were a business pure and simple and, as such, did not enjoy First Amendment freedom of speech protections. Motion pictures could be censored and controlled by all levels of government. The years known as the Mutual Film period (1915–1952) were marked by the most extensive censorship of film in American history. By 1952 eight states had created censorship boards to judge the acceptability of film content: New York, Pennsylvania, Maryland, Ohio, Massachusetts, Virginia, Louisiana, and Kansas. Depictions of violence were subjected to close scrutiny, and films were often cut drastically by censorship boards before approval for commercial release was granted.

Prodded by Protestant and Catholic critics of the new medium, as many as ninety cities and towns engaged in the censorship of film during this period. Chicago passed the first movie censorship ordinance in the country in 1907, and its censorship board was one of the most active until the 1960s. An October 1925 issue of *Education Screen* provided an account of local censorship of film violence: "In 1924 our Chicago Board of Censors deleted 1811 scenes of assault with guns with attempt to kill; 757 scenes of attacks on women or attempted rape; 173 scenes of horror as poking out eyes, cutting off ears, etc.; 34 train hold-ups; 37 scenes of dynamiting safes and bridges; 31 scenes of jail breaking . . . these deletions were from 788 pictures only" (p. 475). The sheer number of violent acts deleted by the Chicago censors attests to Philip French's argument that the quantity of film violence has remained largely unchanged throughout film history.

In 1952 the Supreme Court reversed its *Mutual* decision in *Burstyn, Inc. v. Wilson,* overturning a lower court decision that had allowed the New York Board of Censors to restrict the exhibition of Roberto Rossellini's *The Miracle* (1948). The Court concluded that motion pictures were a significant medium for the communication of ideas, designed to inform as well as entertain. The Court extended to film the same First Amendment speech protections enjoyed by newspapers and magazines. This decision placed state and local censorship boards under rigorous procedural requirements, and it helped inaugurate an era of cinematic freedom in

which film violence would be depicted with more graphic intensity than ever before.

Two other Supreme Court decisions influenced the censorship of film violence. Decided on the same day, 22 April 1968, *Ginsberg v. New York* and *Interstate Circuit v. Dallas* both combined to force the film industry to alter its self-regulation. *Ginsberg v. New York* established a legal distinction between the rights of adults and those of children, stating that constitutionally protected material for adults could still be considered obscene for minors, thus providing the foundation for regulations based on age for film and other media. *Interstate Circuit v. Dallas* invalidated a Dallas film classification ordinance because of the vagueness of its standards; however, the Court left open the possibility of upholding more carefully drawn attempts at local classification. The effect of these two cases was to pressure the film industry to introduce a rigorous classification system, a rating system that would replace the thirty-eight-year-old production code.

Film Industry Self-Regulation

Prior to the drafting of the production code in 1930, the film industry made two attempts at self-regulation. In 1921 the industry's first trade association, the National Association of the Motion Picture Industry (NAMPI), suggested Thirteen Points, three of which related to film violence: two prohibited emphasis on "the underworld, vice, or crime," and a third condemned the production and exhibition "of stories or scenes which unduly emphasize bloodshed and violence without justification in the structure of the story" (Inglis 1947, p. 83). Though the list of points was intended to stem the rising demand for censorship, the NAMPI was unable to establish a machinery for enforcing its prohibitions.

In 1922 the NAMPI was replaced by the Motion Picture Producers and Distributors of America (MPPDA). Will Hays, the postmaster general, left Warren Harding's administration to become its president. In 1927 the MPPDA issued the Don'ts and Be Carefuls list of eleven things to be avoided in motion pictures and twenty-six subjects to be treated with special care. None of the eleven don'ts related to film violence. Of the twenty-six carefuls, nine cautioned against violent representation— from the use of firearms to the depiction of cruelty, brutality, rape, execution, and murder. Like the Thirteen Points, the MPPDA's list was not meaningfully enforced. Producers continued to make violent films such as Archie Mayo's *Doorway to Hell* (1930) despite the MPPDA's suggestions.

It was in response to continued criticism by special interest groups that the MPPDA adopted the Motion Picture Production Code in 1930. Authored by a Jesuit priest, Father Daniel Lord, and the Catholic publisher of the *Motion Picture Daily*, Martin Quigley, the production code reflected the growing influence of the Roman Catholic Church on film censorship. Employing evaluative terms such as "sin," "evil," "right," and "good," the code was intended as a standard for moral values in a mass medium.

The production code was more thorough and specific regarding film violence than previous industry self-regulation had been. The code's first section, Crimes Against the Law, prohibited the detailed or graphic representation of crime and violence. In the twelfth section, four of seven Repellent Subjects related to the representation of violence: "actual hangings," "brutality and possible gruesomeness," "branding of people or animals," and "apparent cruelty to children or animals" (Inglis, p. 209). Like the 1927 list of cautions, the code dissuaded but did not prohibit these "repellent subjects"; violence could be depicted under the code "within the careful limits of good taste" (Inglis, p. 209).

Despite government and industry concern, film violence was frequently depicted in the three years following the official adoption of the code. Because of the novelty of sound pictures and the economic effects of the Great Depression, the early 1930s was a period of experimentation by the industry. As box office receipts declined, producers became desperate. In apparent violation of the code, they turned increasingly to graphic violence and sex to attract audiences.

In the case of *Scarface* (1932), producer Howard Hughes made a realistic, exciting, and violent gangster film over the expressed objections of the MPPDA, which had demanded that Hughes reduce the amount of violence indicated in the script. According to Edward de Grazia and Roger Newman (1982), the MPPDA threatened Hughes: "If you should be foolhardy enough to make *Scarface*, this office will make certain it is never released" (p. 36). As a result Hughes compromised with the MPPDA, cutting some of the violence but keeping the ending intact. Such negotiation between industry censors and film producers has been characteristic of industry self-regulation in all of its forms since 1930. In this instance, Hughes had pro-

duced the most violent gangster film of the early 1930s, and the MPPDA was able to claim that it had prevented even greater violence from reaching the screen.

Scarface took advantage of a unique aspect of the production code. Though it reflected certain Catholic values, the code was designed with the understanding that some violence and sex in film was essential to industry economics. Instead of abolishing all representation of violence, for example, Martin Quigley and Father Lord developed the formula of "compensating moral values" to keep violence in films within moral bounds. In the case of *Scarface*, the code allowed the depiction of violence during the gangster's rise, as long as his crimes were punished by the end of the film. Thus violence could be represented and repudiated at the same time.

In 1934 American bishops formed the Legion of Decency to coordinate the boycott of films the church deemed indecent. By distributing pledge forms throughout Catholic dioceses, the legion was able to get millions of commitments to honor any boycott called for by the Catholic Church. The film industry was forced to recognize the economic power behind the church's demands, and it sought to appease Catholics by establishing the Production Code Administration (PCA) in 1934. Headed by a Catholic, Joseph Breen, the PCA's job was to enforce the prohibitions of the production code of 1930. For the first time, the film industry granted a self-regulatory agency enforcement powers: a $25,000 fine would be levied against any MPPDA member company that released a film without a PCA seal, and no theater circuit controlled by an MPPDA member could show a picture without a seal.

For the next twenty years, employing a combination of threat and negotiation, the PCA censored all films released by major American studios. In 1953, a year after the *Miracle* decision granted freedom-of-speech protection to the film industry, United Artists defied the PCA's refusal to approve Otto Preminger's *The Moon Is Blue* and released it without a seal. UA's defiance marked the beginning of the end of the PCA's control over film censorship. In 1966 the PCA created a final, streamlined version of the code that allowed for the approval of certain films with a Suggested for Mature Audiences (SMA) label.

The SMA label reflected the movie industry's recognition of the need to differentiate its product from television. Since the early 1950s television

What Everyone Should Know About The Movie Rating System.

GENERAL AUDIENCES
G

Nothing that would offend parents for viewing by children.

PARENTAL GUIDANCE SUGGESTED
PG

Parents urged to give "parental guidance." May contain some material parents might not like for their young children.

PARENTS STRONGLY CAUTIONED
PG-13
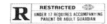

Parents are urged to be cautious. Some material may be inappropriate for pre-teenagers.

RESTRICTED
R

Contains some adult material. Parents are urged to learn more about the film before taking their young children with them.

NO ONE 17 AND UNDER ADMITTED
NC-17

Patently adult. Children are not admitted.

A poster explaining the ratings system. COURTESY OF THE MOTION PICTURE ASSOCIATION OF AMERICA, INC.

had also assumed a role as a provider of mass entertainment. Desperate to recapture audiences lost to television, producers turned to more explicit representations of violence and sex, and the weakened code and the accommodationist post-Breen PCA allowed them to do so. In 1967 *Bonnie and Clyde,* a film that revolutionized the representation and interpretation of violence in film, was released with an SMA label.

In 1968, in the aftermath of the Court's *Ginsberg* and *Interstate Circuit* decisions, Jack Valenti, the new head of the Motion Picture Association of America (MPAA, the renamed MPPDA), replaced the last vestiges of the production code with a new classification system based on letter ratings. (That ratings system still survives.) Under Valenti's plan, all films produced and distributed by MPAA members must be submitted to the Classification and Rating Administration (CARA), which provides "probable" rating decisions to producers and suggestions for gaining a less restrictive rating. In 1968 CARA members were largely holdovers from the PCA staff; in 1997 the board was composed of "average parents" with no ties to the film industry and whose identities were not revealed by the MPAA.

According to the MPAA, the letter ratings are intended to help parents choose suitable films for their children rather than to be evaluative. In 1968 the categories were "G" (for general audiences); "M" (for mature audiences); "R" (restricted, meaning persons under seventeen years are not admitted unless accompanied by a parent or adult guardian); and "X" (persons under seventeen not admitted). In 1970 M changed to "GP" (general audiences, parental guidance suggested); in 1972, GP became "PG" (parental guidance suggested). In 1984, in response to controversy over the graphic violence in the PG-rated *Indiana Jones and the Temple of Doom,* the MPAA added "PG-13" (children under thirteen not admitted unless accompanied by a parent or guardian) between PG and R. Critics have argued that this decision has allowed even more violence to be available to children, because films that might have been rated R for violence are now rated PG-13.

In 1990 the MPAA replaced the X rating with "NC-17" (no children under seventeen admitted, later changed to no one seventeen and under admitted). Though the intention was to allow for quality adult films to be produced without the pejorative X rating, the economic disincentives that discouraged X films—many theaters would not book the films, and many newspapers would not accept their advertising—have continued with films rated NC-17. Many producers have been forced to negotiate with CARA over cuts in order to get the economically favorable R rating, which allows for wide distribution and exhibition.

As with the PCA, CARA has been more restrictive of sex than violence in American film; however, in certain instances, the ratings board has forced cuts or alterations in film violence. In 1976 CARA refused to give Martin Scorsese's *Taxi Driver* a favorable R rating for its violent content unless he altered the color saturation of the film stock in the film's final violent scene to make the violence appear less graphic. After Scorsese experimented with the color in sixty-five edits, CARA gave the film an R. In 1994 Oliver Stone struggled with CARA over the rating of *Natural Born Killers,* which, after some cuts, received an R "for extreme violence and graphic carnage, for shocking images, and for strong language and sexuality" (CARA bulletin no. 1320). Stone had employed a strategy used by other filmmakers to avoid CARA's censorship: he included so much violence in the film that the negotiated cuts did not diminish the film's overall representation of violence.

At the end of the twentieth century, despite occasional calls by politicians for government action, the film industry's ratings system and box-office economics exerted the only censorship of violence in American film. With technological and economic innovations such as the digital delivery of film to the home via fiber-optic cables, changes in distribution will lead to shifts in the regulation of film violence. If film joins television and the Internet in the home, then parents will have to assume the enforcement role for the ratings system, a role traditionally carried out by theater chains. Increasingly, as is the case with the Internet, control over access to violent-film content will become the responsibility of the individual viewer.

BIBLIOGRAPHY

Black, Gregory D. *Hollywood Censored: Morality Codes, Catholics, and the Movies.* Cambridge: Cambridge University Press, 1994.

Couvares, Francis G., ed. *Movie Censorship and American Culture.* Washington D.C.: Smithsonian Institution Press, 1996.

De Grazia, Edward, and Roger K. Newman. *Banned Films: Movies, Censors, and the First Amendment.* New York: Bowker, 1982.

Farber, Stephen. *The Movie Rating Game.* Washington, D.C.: Public Affairs Press, 1972.

French, Philip. "Violence in the Cinema." In *Violence and the Mass Media*, edited by Otto Larsen. New York: Harper and Row, 1968.

Inglis, Ruth A. *Freedom of the Movies*. Chicago: University of Chicago Press, 1947.

Lyons, Charles. *The New Censors: Movies and the Culture Wars*. Philadelphia: Temple University Press, 1997.

BERNIE COOK

See also **Television: Censorship.**

AESTHETICS OF VIOLENCE

Film violence in the cultural scene of late-twentieth-century America had two principal meanings. In its first sense, it was a straightforward term designating the violent action that occurs in particular films. In its second sense, it was a battle cry, designating the site of a political struggle among various social institutions over the power (and corresponding assignment of responsibility) of certain segments of popular culture (including film) to determine behavior and attitudes of the impressionable and the young.

The first meaning refers to forms of representation, in particular the "excessive" and the "graphic," and the second, the manner of response, in particular "imitation" and "acting out." In its first sense, *film violence* belongs to the fictional order of the film image, the conventions that regulate the claims to plausibility and believability of cinematic representation. In its second sense, *film violence* appears, initially, as a medical concern with the harmful personal and social effects of watching violence in an imaginary medium like film. However, since the late 1980s the medical and the political have become condensed. In the political domain, the debate over film violence in the United States Congress in the late 1990s, for example, could be viewed as a strategic simplification and displacement of the many complex social and economic causes of the change of values associated with twentieth-century American culture. Arguably, the debate over movie violence covers and disguises the intimate, ongoing real-world link between the widespread availability of guns and the spread of violent crime.

The Classical Code of Hollywood

The topic of film violence was addressed by Hollywood's self-regulatory Hays Production Code (also known as the Motion Picture Production Code) as early as 1930, but the late-twentieth-century concern with film violence—the "new violence"—is embedded in a cultural era identified with the 1960s. In the classical era of American film, up to the early 1960s, the prohibition against representation of excessive violence and the necessity of a corresponding moral sanction was part of the industry process of self-censorship institutionalized in the Production Code Administration. Representation of violent events—fistfights, shootings, knifings, beatings, and the like—conformed to certain dramaturgical conventions for such action, functioning most notably by suggestion (narrative indirection or simple symbolism), diminishment, or usually the elimination of the details of the actual wounding.

Within classical conventions, for example, a man who had been shot might simply keel over and collapse in the dust. If he was a featured player, he might stagger about in convulsions amounting to a dance of death that prolonged and underlined the seeping away of his stubborn hold on life. In either case, the classical Hollywood film never realistically portrayed wounding or dying, but rather employed a code that signified the loss of life. The actor performed his character's dying, but no blood, cries, or viscera resulting from the wounding itself would be made evident. The wounding—that is to say, the physical intrusion of a weapon into the body and the body's response—could be signified by performance, metaphor, or causal and physiological ellipsis, but not shown in literal detail. Editing of representations deemed unacceptable or excessive—representations that transgressed the classical code—was regularly required before a seal of approval from the Production Code Administration would be issued.

Post-1950s Transformation

In the 1950s the structure of the film industry was transformed by the Supreme Court–ordered "Paramount decrees" that separated the production arm of the industry from exhibition. This change was accompanied by the progressive loss of the traditional film audience to television and the emergence of independent productions that willfully circumvented the Production Code. It also overlapped a series of notable cultural and political events that are usually designated "the sixties." Abraham Zapruder's graphic 8-mm home movie memorialized the image of President Kennedy's head being blown apart in Dallas, Texas, in 1963. Televised pictures of graphic details of American military campaigns in Vietnam, the self-immolation of Vietnamese monks, and the summary execution of a suspected Vietcong guerrilla in the streets of Saigon by a revolver shot to the head led the nightly news. The war in Vietnam dominated the era. With extensive coverage of civil rights struggles, political assassinations, political conventions, and the like, the "in your face" approach to television news altered the content and also the form of the kinds of events that traditionally defined debate within the public sphere. Violent occurrences took on new meaning through the status that television conferred on them as political and narrative events in the life of the nation.

The explicitness, force, and significance of these visual documents of actuality provide the underlying reference for the expansion and exploration of violence that appeared in fictional filmmaking of the era. Three major types of changes—that is, changes in the domains of action, sex, and speech—constituted a fundamental alteration of the conventional narrative decorum that had regulated cinematic representation up to that time: (1) graphic visual documentation of the results of military and political violence (blood spurting, flesh exploding, cries of the wounded); (2) the emergence of unprecedented sexual explicitness, including copulation and particularly ejaculation, as encoded in the early 1970s explosion of pornography as a commercial genre (discoveries and representations wholly repressed in the portrayal of bodies in mainstream cinema); and (3) the nearly wholesale replacement, in certain "with it" dramas, of classical screen dialog with contemporary street vernacular, most evidently in the infinite repetition of the word *fucking* and its proliferating extensions.

In the postclassical era of Hollywood filmmaking the body was present in the fictional scene in a new way—not simply as a medium for the performance or expression of spirit but in its physiological actuality. Picturing violence raised new, fundamental issues. Hence (in a situation in which explicitness in sexual matters was effectively prohibited), explicitness in representation of violence and transgressions of propriety in talk were registers of meaning appropriated by the few directors who saw their potential significance to carry the weight of relevance, seriousness, and authenticity demanded by the cultural subtext. It was through this new paradigm of movie realism that Hollywood sought to renew its failing contact with its emerging audience.

The Violent Sublime

The new language of film violence as established by such defining works as *Easy Rider* (1969), *Bonnie and Clyde* (1967), *The Wild Bunch* (1969),

and—in a different way—*The Godfather* (1972) was a countercultural language of political opposition both to old Hollywood ways and to the reigning values of the culture at large. What Arthur Penn's (*Bonnie and Clyde*) and Sam Peckinpah's (*The Wild Bunch*) films had in common in their key, concluding scenes was an unmatched representational explicitness of agonized wounding of the protagonists' bodies—pierced by torrents of metal from machine guns, rendered in slow-motion cinematography—that opened for examination the duration of death as bodies slowly fell to the ground.

The camera showed how bullets attacked the body and the force of their penetration, spinning it around in an uncontrolled, endless, spasmodic ballet that defined "overkill" for the movies. The emotional force conveyed by the disfiguring destruction of the glamorous bodies of the young stars of *Bonnie and Clyde* (*The Wild Bunch* showed that male beauty personified by William Holden might age but did not disappear) underwrote their status as victims of a massed, illegitimate force and provided proof of the extra-ordinary status of the countercultural, antiestablishment hero, the bank robber. The force of the assault, the force necessary to kill these figures, testified paradoxically to the legendary status of the lives it ended. Indeed the violence of the killing transforms the event and creates the legend. The slow-motion cinematography took the event beyond the temporality of the everyday and aestheticized the outlaw deaths, making them at the same time strange and awesomely beautiful.

Both *Easy Rider* and *Taxi Driver* (1976) created similar aesthetic and mythologizing effects but by use of an elevated, moving camera. The final shot of *Easy Rider* lifts the viewer up, skyward, and away from the scene of the death of Captain America to locate it as being of the land and beside the river. The cinematographic rendering of the concluding mayhem of *Taxi Driver*, the slow-motion movements of the elevated camera peering downward surveying the itinerary of the protagonist's violent ascent, this time in reverse, and marking the results of the awesome path of the alienated protagonist's murderous rampage in the course of his attempt at rescue, lifts the action out of time and makes the stairs a place of heroic transfiguration.

The violence in these particular films is "serious": that is, the films value the lives of the characters and artfully dramatize issues of significance that culminate in violence. The moral assessment per se of the violence is subordinated of course to the design of the work. That is, the work's ideological alignment gives the events their specific meanings—and in these cases, the ideology is a countercultural one. In its "liberal" use, violent assault on the characters by the "establishment" (or by power, however it was personified), was intended to reinforce the myth of the outsider as hero. The constellation of cinematic devices used in the rendering of the action in these films propelled it in the direction of the mythological and even the transcendental; it produced in these specific instances an aesthetic effect that might well be called the "violent sublime." *The Godfather*, by contrast, reversed the strategy and the results but not the fundamental ideological polarities of the late 1960s filmmaking. By employing the protagonist, Michael Corleone, as an initiator of violence at the conclusion of the film (in defense, moreover, of the family), and by intercutting the executions of several mobsters with the religious imagery of the Catholic Church and its language ("Do you, Michael, renounce Satan?"), as Corleone participates in his godson's baptism, Coppola lays bare his protagonist's deceit. The violence diminishes, even profanes, the movie's hero. In *The Godfather* editing, boldly juxtaposing and alternating the setting and ritual of the church with the executions, creates this critical, deconstructive result. Violence

in other words, within the narratives of serious filmmaking of the 1970s, was inflected by the "language" of film either to elevate or condemn. Its value is artistic, not absolute. The meaningful link, however, between the new movie violence and the social subtext was only a temporary conjunction.

Postmodern Modes of Movie Violence

There were several significant, and some novel, features of depicted violence in Hollywood filmmaking at the twentieth century's end. Violent action migrated among genres. The black film and the black man enjoyed a resurgence as an essential component of the action genre. Violent cyborgs and violent women became staples of violent films, and, though hardly new, "gratuitous" violence (and films dedicated to the pleasure of maiming and killing) became the most discussed facet of Hollywood film.

American filmmaking—especially in its signature genres of the Western, the gangster movie, and the horror movie—has always been violent. In the classical era, however, violence was usually confined by stable generic perimeters and its moral import was clearly legible and predictable. However, action elements migrated to other genres. In the 1980s and 1990s most notable was the postmodern mixing of violent genres or situations with

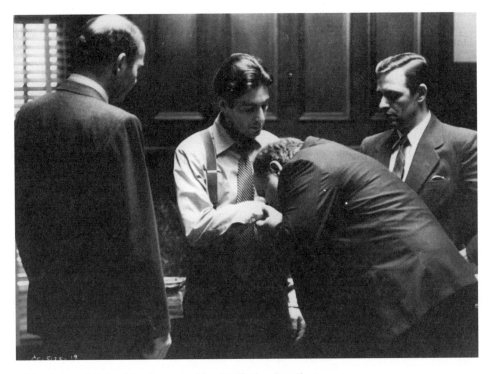

Al Pacino as Michael Corleone in *The Godfather* (1972). PHOTOFEST

comedy, producing an unstable mixture of hilarity and horror and rendering secure responses and moral judgments more difficult. Similarly, audience identification with human types has become less certain.

Movie violence has traditionally been a male prerogative. Competence in beating others and endurance in being beaten are icons of a particular style of American movie masculinity. Beginning in the 1980s, this competence was increasingly vested in some new action figures—the black man, the violent woman, and the cybernetic, robotlike character. These changes all complicate the meanings and responses that had been held in place by dichotomous traditional generic definitions such as man/woman, black/white, human/nonhuman. The powerful or aggressive black man, like the murdering female, is a dangerous challenge to the maintenance of (white, patriarchal) order, and evidently a thrill as well. Yet each new agent of violence is accorded a place in the mainstream cinema and shows a variety of valences; for example, Wesley Snipes (*New Jack City*, 1991), Danny Glover (*Lethal Weapon*, 1987), Sharon Stone (*Basic Instinct*, 1992), and Gina Gershon (*Bound*, 1996).

James Cameron's *Terminator II* (1991) presents a new figuration of the indestructible white male body. An advanced programmed computer machine with a human face and figure, the Terminator is an effective problem solver virtually exempt from the destructive effects of traditional assault —it cannot be stopped or killed by another. The mission of the Terminator is to protect the boy who will lead the forces of humanity in the future war against the machines. His antagonist is a self-healing shape-shifter, a human-like weapon, made of new metal (and produced in the film with the latest digital technology) that reverts to the chosen form regardless of the scale of the damage that is inflicted. The film stages the battle between the countercultural rebel (the Terminator, complete with Harley-Davidson motorcycle and black jacket) and the cyborg policeman. Paradoxically for these high-tech indestructible warriors, the dramatic conflicts of the film are figured through startling anachronism as a series of fights and shootouts.

These figures define a limit point in the evolution of representation of male violence in American movies: indestructible human-like bodies capable of giving and receiving superhuman levels of violence without sustaining fatal injury, making it possible to repeatedly stage fresh episodes of bloodless and painless conflict with powerful but traditional weapons (usually military-type guns).

Of course traditional types and styles persist in some genres, but an increasing number of moviemakers have found it necessary to transcend human vulnerability to invent new figures adequate to the commercial demand for dramatically plausible escalation of violent assault.

"Film violence" and its corresponding modes of filmic representation are cultural constructions that encode historically changing versions of metaphors of the human body. The body of the hero has passed through the stage of the organic (first the idealized body of the classical cinema, then to the vulnerable, wounded body of Vietnam-era dramaturgy) and has emerged as the mechanico-cybernetic postmodern body. The *idea* of the (male, movie) body as an expressive medium has been replaced in some genres by the metaphor of the body as a machine or a force that operates on the laws of physics. The historical appearance of the militarized cyborg in the movies acknowledges, it would seem, both the demands put on the ordinary human body by modern warfare, in particular by the machine gun, and the increasingly warlike character of civil life. The rhythmic body of the contemporary street guerrilla in films that adopt the music-video format seeks to inhabit and re-territorialize this contested arena by integrating military weapons with a hip-hop culture.

Gratuitous violence (sometimes conflated with *graphic violence*) designates violence for its own sake, violence for which there is no narrative justification. Though in practice such indictments often lack an objective basis, there are films whose narrative consists principally of staged combat in a game-like format, the aim of which is the elimination (killing is obligatory for the game to end) of the opponent. In the case, for example, of *Mortal Kombat* (1997), the end of the "game" is accompanied with the outpouring of blood and viscera. The film justifies violence as necessary to save the future of humankind. The Motion Picture Association of America Ratings Board, which gave the film a PG-13 rating, disregarded the resulting gruesome deaths, choosing instead to treat martial arts combat (as opposed to combat with weapons) as an art, and as such not excessively violent. In the end, when push comes to shove, without an agreed set of systematic criteria, "film violence" is what institutions with power say it is.

BIBLIOGRAPHY

Alloway, Lawrence. *Violent America: The Movies, 1946–1964.* New York: Museum of Modern Art, 1971.

Prince, Stephen. *Savage Cinema: Sam Peckinpah and the Rise of Ultraviolent Movies.* Austin: University of Texas Press, 1998.

Shadoian, Jack. *Dreams and Dead Ends: The American Gangster/Crime Film.* Cambridge, Mass.: MIT Press, 1977.

Slotkin, Richard. *Gunfighter Nation: The Myth of the Frontier in Twentieth-Century America.* New York: Atheneum, 1992

NICK BROWNE

See also **Representation of Violence.**

REPRESENTING RACE, GENDER, AND ETHNICITY

This essay explores the intersection of race, gender, and violence in the Western films of two influential American directors, D. W. Griffith and John Ford. It examines the narrative convention that demanded that white women be killed rather than surrendered to Indian attack and the ways in which this recurring motif contributed to an ideology of American empire during the first half of the twentieth century.

The Battle at Elderbush Gulch

D. W. Griffith's three-reel *The Battle at Elderbush Gulch*, released by the Biograph Company in 1913, tells the story of an Indian attack on a white frontier settlement. The climactic attack, precipitated by the settlers' fatal shooting of a chieftain's son (whose trespassing onto the settlement is apparently the product of the native craving for dog meat), unfolds in a fashion that became increasingly familiar to generations of American filmgoers. A small group of white settlers, barricaded inside their cabin and armed with rifles and six-shooters, holds off a multitude of marauding Indians. Alongside the men are a small number of women, including one young mother (Lillian Gish) whose infant child remains lost somewhere in the skirmish outside the cabin.

The settlers, awaiting the arrival of the cavalry, battle bravely until they begin running low on ammunition (a development communicated in the film by one of the protagonists turning his rifle around in anticipation of using it as a club). It is at this moment of maximum dramatic tension that Griffith cuts to a shot of the Gish character, cradled by another woman, cowering and praying at the foot of the stairs. The barrel of a six-gun descends from the top of the frame and comes to a stop inches from her head. The gun is cocked, and the shooter's purpose is clear: he will use his last bullet to spare the young mother from defilement at the hands of savages. This implication is confirmed by

the succeeding shots of the cavalry arriving upon the scene and the would-be angel of mercy withdrawing his weapon in response.

The Battle at Elderbush Gulch, with a running time of approximately thirty minutes, is an early example of Griffith's ability to sustain narrative suspense through an assortment of cinematic conventions that later became staples of the classic Hollywood style. The film, however, is more than merely a technical triumph or a representative of a significant stage in the development of full-length features. Through the use of techniques such as crosscut editing (in which two or more lines of action are shown to occur simultaneously through alternating shots), Griffith succeeds in joining technical innovation to a fantasy of white empire and nationhood. The young white mother who is spared both rape by an inferior racial other and a bullet in her brain is the most overt symbol of the inevitable triumph of white civilization. She represents both the domestication and the population of the frontier. The violence enacted upon her body, whether the imagined rape by the savage Indian or the salvation offered by the bullet from a white man's gun, became one of the recurring symbolic acts through which the West—and the nation itself—was won or lost in our popular culture. Griffith recycled the trope of violence against white womanhood two years later for *The Birth of a Nation* (1915), a Civil War and Reconstruction epic that was the most influential film of the first half of the twentieth century and is an almost perfect articulation of white American empire. (The film recasts the threat of rape in the figure of another culturally defined "savage," the African American male, and features the Ku Klux Klan in the role normally reserved for the cavalry.)

Stagecoach

John Ford's 1939 landmark Western, *Stagecoach*, elevated the genre from perennial B-movie status; made a star out of John Wayne, who had toiled for most of the decade in low-budget Westerns churned out by small studios like Monogram and Republic; and marked the beginning of a thirty-year cycle during which the Western reigned as one of Hollywood's most resilient and profitable products. The film also reinvigorated the trope of the mercy killing pioneered in films such as *The Battle at Elderbush Gulch*. The iconography of the film's climactic scene is almost a direct transcription of the Lillian Gish scene in *Elderbush Gulch*. The cabin is replaced by the stagecoach of the film's title, a frontier settlement on wheels popu-

The Monument Valley desert chase scene in *Stagecoach* **(1939).** PHOTOFEST

lated by an eclectic assortment of characters: the stage driver, a lawman, an alcoholic doctor, a drummer, a banker, a gentleman gambler, the town prostitute, a young army wife who gives birth during the journey, and an outlaw named the Ringo Kid (Wayne).

The stagecoach is overrun by Apaches while attempting to navigate the Monument Valley desert, a locale that became a Ford signature. In one of the Western genre's most memorable chase scenes, the stagecoach attempts to outrun a band of Apaches (who, in this film, possess both horses and rifles) while its male passengers empty their guns in frantic—or, in the case of the Ringo Kid, cool—self-defense. As in *The Battle at Elderbush Gulch*, ammunition is in short supply, and hard decisions must be made. The act of chivalry logically falls to the gentleman gambler, who, discovering that he is down to his last bullet, puts his gun to the head of the young army wife and mother. As with the Gish character, her thoughts are far away and she prays. The gentleman cocks the gun at precisely the moment that the cavalry charge is heard; a gunshot sounds, and the gun falls from his hand. She has been spared, the viewer discovers, by the sound of the bugle and a fortuitous Apache bullet.

The scene's formal choices are significant. The gentleman, Hatfield, reserves his bullet for the Madonna-like character of the army wife (the absence of the husband from the film does much to suggest an almost virginal purity) and not the

prostitute who, in his eyes, has already been defiled. The scene thus acknowledges the distinction between "good" and "bad" women generally advocated by the classic Hollywood production code (a system of industry censorship that prevailed from the 1930s through the 1950s). It also does much to collapse this distinction. Hatfield's attempted execution of the young wife, within the conventions of the genre, is to be understood as necessary and compassionate, but it is also punitive. The "mercy killing" punishes her for an imagined transgression, her imagined participation in the rape fantasy that threatens the establishment of a white civilization on the western plains.

The violence threatened against the body of the white woman—and the violence of the aborted mercy killing, while unfulfilled, is no less stunning—is thus made central to the ideology of American empire propagated by the Western film genre. The fantasy of the rape—the rape that is prevented by the timely arrival of the cavalry but that is nevertheless evoked by the image of the gun to the heroine's head—obscures the actual rape that made possible the expansion of the nation: the rape of the land and the conquest of its native inhabitants by white settlers.

The Searchers

The colossal act of cultural erasure and displacement that underlies the narrative of *Stagecoach* achieved its most complex expression in another

553

Ethan Edwards (John Wayne), left, and Martin Pawley (Jeffrey Hunter) threaten a Comanche woman in *The Searchers* (1956). PHOTOFEST

Ford Western, *The Searchers* (1956), a film built entirely around the generic moment where the male Western protagonist raises his gun to the head of the heroine—or, more accurately, around the conspicuous omission of that moment. In the film, a Civil War veteran, Ethan Edwards (John Wayne), returns home after an unexplained two-year absence following the end of the war. Not long after his arrival, he joins a posse tracking cattle rustlers in the area. The men discover, too late, that the cattle have been taken and slaughtered by Comanches solely for the purpose of luring the posse away from the settlement. They race back to find the remnants of a Comanche raid: the remains of the burning home and the bodies of Ethan's brother, sister-in-law, and nephew. Missing from the scene entirely are Ethan's nieces, Lucy and Debbie (Natalie Wood). They have been taken captive by the Comanches. What follows is a tale of psychological and cultural obsession as Ethan, aided by Martin Pauley (a one-eighth Cherokee who had been adopted by the Edwards family when his parents were killed in an Indian raid), embarks on a five-year odyssey to find Debbie. (He

discovers Lucy dead not long after the Comanche raid).

Ethan and Martin learn that Debbie, now a young woman, is very much alive and married to Scar, the Comanche chief. They press on with their mission, but, apparently, at cross-purposes. Martin is still trying to "fetch Debbie home," whereas Ethan's motivation is less clear. The viewer begins to suspect that his goal is not to bring Debbie home but to set right the genre conventions upset by his absence from the Edwards homestead on the night of the raid. This suspicion is overtly acknowledged when Ethan and Martin temporarily return home for the wedding of Laurie, Martin's sweetheart, to another man: a wedding Martin succeeds in disrupting. Laurie, in an attempt to keep Martin from going on the final raid on the Comanche settlement, tells him that "it's too late . . . [Debbie is] a woman grown. Do you know what Ethan will do if he has a chance? He'll put a bullet in her brain! I tell you Martha [Debbie's deceased mother] would want him to." Laurie, however, is not simply attempting to keep Martin at home; she is voicing the dominant sentiment of the community. The fact that the credo comes from the young woman, and not from Ethan—whose motivation remains unspoken—serves simultaneously to endorse and obscure the misogynist and racist order upon which the convention is based.

In the film's climactic scene, Ethan and Martin participate in the raid on the Comanche settlement. Martin kills Scar, and Debbie, who appears happy to be rescued but fearful of Ethan, is cornered by her uncle in a canyon. She recoils at his feet, expecting the bullet that will cleanse her, only to be swept up in his arms. "Let's go home Debbie," he tells her.

Ethan returns Debbie to the settlement, where she is warmly received by Laurie's family, the Jorgensens. While *The Searchers* appears to overturn the narrative convention of the mercy killing, to extend the promise of redemption (Debbie's and Ethan's) and even unity between the races (in the character of Martin Pauley), the film's resolution does as much to validate the tradition previously established by Griffith and by Ford himself. The viewer is left with the distinct impression that there is really no future for Debbie in the white settlement. The Jorgensens may be kind people, but they will hardly be able to protect Debbie from the prejudices of the larger community. Debbie herself appears to sense that she no longer belongs in this setting. Her entry into the house is hesitant, staggered, and ominous. Nor is Ethan completely redeemed. In the film's final shot, Ethan, framed by the doorway of the house, walks back toward the uncivilized frontier he has been forced to wander for so long. He is the Indian killer of popular mythology, rendered part savage by his deeds, unable and unwilling to completely integrate himself into the incipient white civilization he has helped bring forth.

Conclusion

At the dark heart of each of these films is an act—unrealized but nevertheless imagined—of violence perpetrated against white womanhood, a distinctly white male fantasy of rape and redemption intended both to obscure and justify the very real extermination of a continent of native peoples. The trope achieves its most dramatic and distilled form in the Western, but the logic at its core informs our cinematic culture as a whole. Images of retribution against female "transgression," acts of violence designed to contain ideologically the threat posed by female sexuality, are recurring: from Walter Neff's point-blank execution of femme

fatale Phyllis Dietrichson in Billy Wilder's classic film noir *Double Indemnity* (1944) to Norman Bates's brutal stabbing murder of Marion Crane in Alfred Hitchcock's 1960 masterpiece thriller *Psycho* (a film remade in 1998 by director Gus Van Sant). In each instance, the woman is guilty of both a sexual and a legal transgression—adulteress Phyllis Dietrichson murders her husband for the insurance money, Marion Crane embezzles a large sum of money from her longtime employer and plans to run away with her lover (it is her flight with the money that brings her to the Bates Motel)—and in each instance (as in the Westerns) her punishment is linked to the reassertion of order in the (white, male-centered) world of the film. (In *Psycho*, Marion's murder brings the initial plotline to a close even as it delivers the narrative promised by the film's title.)

These conventions, informing a wide array of American films but finding their most powerful articulation in the Western trope of the mercy killing, would ultimately appear to be telling us as much about our collective selves as about the films we watch.

BIBLIOGRAPHY

Darby, William. *John Ford's Westerns: A Thematic Analysis, with a Filmography.* Jefferson, N.C.: McFarland, 1996.
Gunning, Tom. *D. W. Griffith and the Origins of American Narrative Film: The Early Years at Biograph.* Urbana: University of Illinois Press, 1991.
Simmon, Scott. *The Films of D. W. Griffith.* Cambridge, U.K.: Cambridge University Press, 1993.
Slotkin, Richard. *Gunfighter Nation: The Myth of the Frontier in Twentieth-Century America.* New York: Atheneum, 1992.

GASPAR GONZÁLEZ

See also **Gender; Race and Ethnicity.**

FINE ARTS

The significance of representations of violence in the fine arts has varied over time, as attitudes toward violence have changed and new media have emerged for the creation and contemplation of art. The role of beauty and aesthetics in the fine arts has also changed. Whereas disturbingly violent images seem almost commonplace today, earlier representations of violence tended to be aesthetically pleasing. The classically draped severed heads and limbs of the French artist Théodore

Rape of Europa by Titian (1559–1562). Corbis/Burstein Collection

Géricault (1791–1824), for example, were praised for their naturalism and peaceful beauty. Such aesthetic renderings of the grotesque were rarely considered alarming before the twentieth century, for such artwork usually expressed a clear moral, religious, or educational purpose. Depictions of violence in modernist and contemporary art, on the other hand, are often gruesomely explicit without expressing the beauty, nobility, and grandeur that traditionally made violent subject matter more palatable.

Opinions vary on the purposes and effects of violent images in the fine arts. Some have argued that extremely violent art has no purpose other than to shock. Others claim that shock, fear, and disgust serve the valid purpose of subverting our ability to distance ourselves from violence and horror. Violent art brings the modern viewer, who has been separated from routine encounters with death and disease, closer to a sense of the self as a vulnerable, fleshly being. An opposing view holds that all works of art aestheticize their subject matter; thus, the act of presenting violent images as "art" encourages the viewer to cultivate an attitude of detachment. These issues have become especially pertinent in the ongoing debates about violent images in film, television, and popular music.

Classical Foundations: The European Tradition (800 B.C.E.–1900 C.E.)

Violent art in the United States is part of a Western tradition with origins in ancient Mediterranean culture. Myths, biblical writings, and early Greek and Roman literature, filled with scenes of warfare, brutality, and torture, have served as the primary sources for most of the violent fine art produced in Europe from antiquity until the mid-nineteenth century. Notable examples include Titian's *Flaying of Marsyas* (c. 1570) and *Rape of Europa* (1559–1562); Rubens's *Rape of the Daughters of Leucippus* (c. 1617–1618); Gentileschi's *Judith Slaying Holofernes* (c. 1620); and Rembrandt's *The Blinding of Samson* (1636).

The life and death of Jesus and the persecution of other martyrs have been some of the most popular subjects for violent art. The Last Judgment has provided the basis for numerous depictions of demons and the tortures of the damned, particularly in Gothic cathedrals of the twelfth through fifteenth centuries. Other important examples include illustrations in martyrologies, books on "primitive" rites, and pamphlets describing the torture of criminals, heretics, and witches.

American Art (1700s–1900)

American artists were preoccupied throughout the eighteenth and nineteenth centuries with the search for a distinctive American style. While most of the artistic representations of violence in Europe were to be found in history paintings—the art of the Grand Manner, which depicts dramatic events from history and literature—American artists focused instead on portraits, still lifes, and landscapes, which seldom contained scenes of violence. This turn away from history painting was part of a widespread rejection of European decadence in favor of wholesome American virtues. The lack of established institutions of patronage also contributed to the scarcity of important history paintings in the United States.

The Revolutionary War provided a number of subjects for violent art. John Trumbull's series depicting events of the war, including *Death of General Montgomery in the Attack on Quebec* (1788), is one of the principal examples of violent subject matter in early American painting. An incident in which two Mohawk Indians murdered the young Jane McCrea became a popular subject in paintings such as John Vanderlyn's *The Death of Jane McCrea* (1804). A similar theme was depicted in several paintings and illustrations of James Fenimore Cooper's book *The Last of the Mohicans* (1826), one of the most notable of which is Thomas Cole's *Cora Kneeling at the Feet of Tamenund* (1827). The sculpture and painting of William Rimmer often exhibited themes of death and violence in the European tradition, as in the dramatic *Falling Gladiator* (1861) and *Lion in the Arena* (1873–1876). One of the most famous nineteenth-century paintings of gory subject matter is Thomas Eakins's *The Gross Clinic* (1875), which shows a bloody-handed Dr. Samuel David Gross supervising an operation in his teaching clinic. The picture, denied space in the art gallery at the Philadelphia Centennial of 1876, was displayed in the U.S. Army Post Hospital exhibit.

The American West provided a major source for violent subject matter, exemplified by the works of

Cora Kneeling at the Feet of Tamenund, **an 1827 oil painting by Thomas Cole illustrating a scene of James Fenimore Cooper's book** *The Last of the Mohicans.*
CORBIS/BURSTEIN COLLECTION

557

George Catlin—such as *Buffalo Hunt,* an illustration from Catlin's *North American Indian Portfolio* (1844)—and Frederic Remington (especially *The Last Stand,* 1890; *The Intruders,* 1900; and *Rounded-Up,* 1901). Remington was also noted for his depictions of the Spanish-American War, as in *The Charge of the Rough Riders at San Juan Hill* (1898). Remington is one of the few American artists who is remembered for his journalistic illustrations as well as his sculpture and paintings; consequently, his work straddles a line between fine art and popular media that had begun to blur with the emergence of photography in the mid-nineteenth century.

Photography gave rise to new possibilities for the representation of violence, especially for journalistic purposes. The works of Mathew B. Brady (*On the Antietam Battlefield,* 1862), Timothy O'Sullivan (*A Harvest of Death, Battlefield of Gettysburg, Pennsylvania,* July 1863), and Alexander Gardner (*Gardner's Photographic Sketch-Book of the War,* 1865–1866) documented the brutal aftermath of Civil War battlefields. Jacob Riis, a police reporter for the *New York Tribune,* documented the bleak conditions in the underbelly of the city in *How the Other Half Lives* (1892).

The Twentieth Century

Photography influenced the move toward realism at the turn of the century, exemplified by the literary works of Theodore Dreiser, Upton Sinclair, and Stephen Crane and the art of the Ashcan School, which depicted the everyday life of the streets. Yet, however grim the subject matter, such paintings were almost never overtly violent. At most, the works threaten violence or depict vigorous action, as in George Bellows' boxing paintings *Stag at Sharkey's* (1909) and *Both Members of this Club* (1909). While war-torn Europe produced many graphically violent works, the already scanty tradition of violent art in the United States seemed almost to disappear from view as artists experimented with abstraction. Violence was expressed, instead, in the dynamic, jagged brushstrokes of Franz Kline (*Untitled,* 1948; *Mahoning,* 1956) and the radical fragmentation of the human body in the works of Willem de Kooning (*Excavation,* 1950; *Woman I,* 1950–1952).

That photography, mass media, and current events had become particularly influential on fine art was apparent with the rise of Andy Warhol and pop art. Warhol's obsession with superstar icons and media spectacle influenced his works on

Electric Chair **by Andy Warhol, 1964.** Corbis/Burstein Collection

Marilyn Monroe, begun after her suicide in 1962. Taking his cue from Weegee (Usher H. Fellig), the photographer known for his newspaper shots of homicides and car wrecks in the 1940s and 1950s, Warhol in 1963 created a series of "Disaster" paintings, which featured huge silk-screened photographs of the atomic bomb, car wrecks (*Saturday Disaster,* 1964; *Disaster 22,* 1964), and the electric chair (*Electric Chair,* 1964). Roy Lichtenstein imitated the commercial printing techniques of advertising to create deadpan comic-book-inspired works such as *Blam* (1962), which shows a fighter jet being shot down. "One of the things a cartoon does," Lichtenstein said in a November 1963 interview with Gene Swenson of *Artnews,* "is to express violent emotion and passion in a completely mechanical and removed style." The tensions of the Cold War and Vietnam are also apparent in James Rosenquist's *F-111* (1965), an eighty-six-foot-long mural depicting an F-111 superimposed with images such as a Firestone tire, a cake, a mushroom cloud, a mass of intestinal orange spaghetti, and a little girl under a hair dryer that looks like a missile's nose cone. Another, more extreme anti-Vietnam image is Peter Saul's Day-Glo *Typical Saigon* (1968), which shows surreally grotesque U.S. soldiers assaulting equally misshapen Vietnamese women.

In the radical political atmosphere of the 1960s and early 1970s, many young artists felt that traditional modes of artistic production and display resulted only in objects that too easily became commodities. Performance works by artists such as Chris Burden, who has been shot in the arm with a .22-caliber rifle and nailed to the roof of a Volkswagen; HIV-positive artist Ron Athey, who cuts and bleeds himself; and Orlan, who broadcasts her numerous plastic surgeries via satellite, dissolve the boundaries between art, politics, and everyday life.

In the 1980s and 1990s, sexually provocative and often violent performance art prompted outrage from conservative members of Congress and resulted in funding cuts to the National Endowment for the Arts. Fine-art photographers Richard Misrach, Andres Serrano, and Joel-Peter Witkin became noted for their use of animal and human carcasses. In the popular media, comic book artists, "zine" (as in "magazine") publishers, filmmakers, and television producers continued to explore the boundaries of violent art.

BIBLIOGRAPHY

Fineberg, Jonathan. *Art Since 1940: Strategies of Being.* Englewood Cliffs, N.J.: Prentice Hall, 1995.

Loeffler, Carl E., and Darlene Tong, eds. *Performance Anthology: Source Book of California Performance Art.* San Francisco: Last Gasp and Contemporary Arts Press, 1989.

Puppi, Lionello. *Torment in Art: Pain, Violence, and Martyrdom.* New York: Rizzoli, 1991.

PATRICIA SCHEIERN LEWIS

See also **Dance; Music; Painting; Photography; Sculpture.**

FIRE. *See* Arson and Fire.

FIREARMS. *See* Gun Control; Gun Violence; Right to Bear Arms; Weapons: Handguns.

FISH, ALBERT
(1870–1936)

The great majority of serial killers are psychopaths—or sociopaths, as they are more often called. Considered legally sane, they are in tune with everyday reality, and they understand the distinction between right and wrong, but they believe that rules, including rules prohibiting murder, do not necessarily apply to them. Very rarely does a serial killer qualify as a psychotic, a person who lives mentally apart in his own delusional world. Albert Fish, however, is one example, and perhaps the most horrifying. His appallingly violent crimes did not arise from a conscious indulgence in acts that he knew to be wrong. Instead, they sprang from a deranged religious fervor. He truly believed that he was serving God by killing and cannibalizing his helpless victims.

For Fish, religion and brutality began to merge in a sadomasochistic muddle during the 1870s when, as a small child, he was committed to an orphanage run by a church in Washington, D.C. Discipline could be severe at this institution, much to young Fish's liking. When beaten for a sacrilegious infraction, he became sexually excited.

As an adult, he punished himself. At his most grotesque, he would insert sewing needles into his groin, viewing this practice as an act of contrition. As cruel as he could be to himself, however, his self-inflicted injuries paled in comparison with his assaults on children.

One of Fish's hallucinatory visions instructed him at one point to become a modern-day biblical Abraham. Just as Abraham was willing to kill his own son to prove his devotion to God, so too Fish "sacrificed" children. He found his victims while traveling cross-country as an itinerant handyman. Sometimes he would molest them; other times he would obey his perceived commandments through mutilation and murder.

Fish's murder victims numbered anywhere between five and fifteen. No definitive account of his crimes was ever made. His final homicide, though, was documented in detail. In 1928, when he was fifty-eight, Fish abducted a twelve-year-old girl named Grace Budd, under the pretense of escorting her to a birthday party. At a cottage in Westchester, New York, he strangled the girl and carved up her body. The girl's flesh ended up in a stew that Fish ate over the next few days.

After a six-year manhunt, Fish was finally arrested in New York City in 1934. While in custody,

Albert Fish, in 1935. CORBIS/BETTMANN

he was examined by a psychiatrist, Fredric Wertham, who pronounced the child killer to be the most depraved person he had ever encountered. Lending credence to this assessment was some chilling physical evidence: an X ray of Fish's pelvic region revealed that twenty-seven sewing needles were lodged inside his groin, all of them inserted by Fish himself.

Although there was never any doubt that Fish was insane, the jury at his trial recommended the electric chair, a sentence applicable to a legally sane defendant. The jurors were able to disregard Fish's mental state in the face of Grace Budd's grotesque murder, a crime that, they agreed, demanded his death. Fish, the religiously inspired masochist, probably could appreciate this Old Testament reasoning, "an eye for an eye."

BIBLIOGRAPHY

Heimer, Mel. *The Cannibal: The Case of Albert Fish.* New York: Lyle Stuart, 1971.
Newton, Michael. *Hunting Humans.* Port Townsend, Wash.: Loompanics, 1990.

Schechter, Harold. *Deranged.* New York: Pocket, 1990.

DAVID EVERITT

See also **Serial Killers.**

FLOYD, CHARLES ARTHUR "PRETTY BOY"
(1901–1934)

Charles Arthur Floyd was a strong and hardworking man, but in Oklahoma in the 1920s there simply was not enough opportunity to work. Wind and erosion were already beginning to take their toll on an area which would later become known as the Dust Bowl. More and more frequently the banks were foreclosing on farms in the region. In 1921 Floyd married sixteen-year-old Wilma Hargrove, and after tiring of spending nights in the hobo camps of the area, he soon turned to illicit methods of obtaining income to support his family.

After committing his first series of robberies, in St. Louis, Floyd was sent to the Missouri State Penitentiary in 1925. While he was in prison, his wife gave birth to a child, Jackie. The couple divorced, but Floyd visited his son often throughout the years. Floyd was paroled in 1929 shortly after his father was murdered as a result of a long-standing feud. Floyd was incensed when the murderer, a man named Jim Mills, was acquitted, and is rumored to have murdered Mills and hid the body. If true, this was the first of at least five homicides committed by Floyd.

Floyd continued with his career in crime, including a very successful robbery of the Sylvania bank in Ohio in 1930. He and his accomplices were arrested for this crime, and Floyd narrowly escaped a return to prison by leaping from the window of a moving train. During his bank robberies, Floyd was known for ripping up first mortgages, saving struggling farmers from ruin. The farmers would not forget him for this, and in later years were instrumental in helping Floyd evade capture. He became known throughout the area as "Pretty Boy" Floyd. Some claim that Floyd earned his nickname "Pretty Boy" by the care he took with his hair, while others asserted that it was bestowed on him by a brothel madam. Regardless of how it was attained, Floyd despised the nickname to his dying day.

Yet Floyd, who achieved folk hero status in his lifetime, was by no means merely a misunderstood Robin Hood. His partner, Bill "the Killer" Miller,

"Pretty Boy" Floyd, in a 1931 photograph with his son, Jackie, and former wife, Ruby, at Fort Smith, Arkansas.
CORBIS/BETTMANN

and he gained thousands of dollars as a result of bank robberies, some of which had violent outcomes.

Floyd's girlfriend, Juanita Beulah Baird, accompanied him in his escapades until his death. Baird and her sister had been married to the brothers William and Wallace Ash when they met Floyd and Miller. The brothers, furious that their women had been stolen from them, informed the police of Floyd and Miller's whereabouts. Floyd and Miller retaliated by killing the two men. A short time later, after robbing a bank, Floyd and Miller were stopped by two police officers. Floyd succeeded in shooting one officer dead and managed to escape. Miller was killed in the shoot-out, and Floyd's girlfriend severely wounded.

Floyd continued to run from the law. In 1931 his hideout was discovered, and in his fight to escape he killed Curtis Burks, a federal Prohibition agent. Returning to the area where he had been raised in Oklahoma, Floyd carried on in his career as a bank robber. He once even succeeded in robbing two banks in a single day.

There is considerable debate as to whether Floyd was a participant in the event for which he was finally apprehended. The Kansas City Massacre of 17 June 1933 was a sensational episode in the violent gangland history of the 1930s. The "massacre" occurred when an attempt to free Frank "Jelly" Nash, a bank robber and murderer, resulted instead in the deaths of Nash and four lawmen, including an agent of the Federal Bureau of Investigation, Raymond Caffrey. Two other FBI agents were badly wounded in the shooting, which took place in the parking plaza of Union Station, the most prominent location in Kansas City. After the event, the FBI designated Floyd, who had been identified by several witnesses to the massacre, as "public enemy no. 1." Floyd wrote letters to authorities and the media denying any involvement in the incident.

The one-and-a-half-year manhunt that followed the Kansas City Massacre was one of the emblematic events of the 1930s conflict between public enemies and the FBI. When Floyd was finally shot down near East Liverpool, Ohio, on 22 October 1934 by a party headed by the acclaimed FBI G-man Melvin Purvis, Floyd claimed with his dying breath that he had not been present at the massacre.

BIBLIOGRAPHY

Bruns, Roger A. *The Bandit Kings.* New York: Crown, 1995.
King, Jeffery S. *The Life and Death of Pretty Boy Floyd.* Kent, Ohio: Kent Library State University Press, 1998.

TRACY W. PETERS

See also **Kansas City.**

FOLK CULTURE

Violence as a motif, trait, or theme is as prevalent in oral tradition as it is in many aspects of American life, since folklore often mirrors the larger culture. This widespread theme of crime and violence in folkloric expression usually involves a folk hero who violates the laws of the nation or his or her own folk community or who is a victim of a violent act. Violence in folklore can also be characterized by the harm one does to another, whether by trickery or by supernaturalism.

Folklore consists of forms of cultural expression whose hallmark traits are that they

1. are transmitted orally;
2. are traditional in their form and content; and
3. exist in different variations because they depend on oral circulation.

Violence was not always dealt with thematically in folklore research; instead folklorists studied the transmission of folklore within folk groups or societies in which members shared similar characteristics. Folklorists also looked for cultural characteristics or traits rather than themes and, throughout the twentieth century, focused on such stylized genres as the ballad, the folk song, or the folktale, rather than on a theme that crossed generic boundaries.

Though folklore is often a form of entertainment, it also imparts community standards and teaches the consequences of violating them. Folklore often evolves as a reaction to violence and provides a way to understand and evaluate a criminal or violent event. When a violent act seems incomprehensible or controversial, the folk reaction often is to circulate a joke about it. This happened in 1984 after Bernhard Goetz shot four black teenagers on a subway train in New York City. And in Boston in 1989, when Charles Stuart shot his pregnant wife in the head after they had attended a hospital's birthing class together (and then blamed another man who was nearby at the time of the crime), a joke circulated widely throughout metropolitan Boston: Mrs. Stuart, in response to her husband asking her about wanting a baby, replied, "I need this baby like I need a hole in the head!" This joke, a folk expression, reminds the listener of how Mrs. Stuart died and distills the major elements of the crime.

Though violence appears in many forms of folklore, it is ubiquitous primarily in the Anglo-American folk song and ballad tradition, folktales, urban legends, and personal-experience narratives about urban life (such as crime-victim stories). Violence in folk-expressive forms often appears in folk speech, a jargon that may be shared, for example, by members of street gangs or by confidence men, police officers, or prison inmates, and in forms of urban ethnography, such as detailed descriptions of a criminal's lifestyle. Less apparent is the theme of violence in less-studied genres,

such as folk speech in the forms of curses, hexes, and insults. These forms of folk speech are often included as a component of a group's folk belief system, such as in the Mexican American practice of *curanderismo* (folk healing) or among African American root doctors, folk curers, or people playing "the dozens," a game where African American children hurl insults about their mothers in a verbal duel. With the exception of folk songs, ballads, and local legends, folklorists neglected the study of this urban, "modern" theme until the 1980s.

Places, too, can be identified with acts of violence and made the subject of folklore, such as Fall River, Massachusetts, where in 1892 Lizzie Borden was accused of murdering her parents with an ax. Still, folklore about crime and violence is usually associated with a particular individual as exemplified in the ballad about "Pretty Boy" Floyd, the Oklahoma train robber, or in the "Ballad of Charles Guiteau," about the assassination of President James Garfield. Folklore can also immortalize a particular event, such as the execution of Nicola Sacco and Bartolomeo Vanzetti for the robbery of a shoe factory in Braintree, Massachusetts, in 1927 (in "The Ballad of Sacco and Vanzetti") or the lynching of Leo Frank in 1915 for the alleged murder of Mary Phagan (in "Mary Phagan"). Most often, historical legends and personal-experience narratives related to violent events become localized within a community, such as those told about the infamous Bonnie and Clyde in Lincoln Parish, Louisiana, or New York City crime-victim stories. Sometimes stories related to major events, such as personal-experience stories—where an individual was when President John F. Kennedy was shot in 1963, for example—take on their own nationalistic twist.

Violence in Ballads and Folk Songs

In the Anglo-American ballad tradition, ballads (dramatic, single-episodic narratives sung in stanzas to a repeating tune) are narrated by the individuals who committed the violent act. For example, male suitors who murdered their sweethearts ("The Jealous Lover," "Pearl Bryant," "Naomi Wise," "Tom Dooley") often explain in dramatic detail how, where, and when they committed the murder. Ballads also deal with parents who committed infanticide ("The Murder of Sarah Vail") and those who were attacked and killed ("The Murder of Laura Foster" and "Stella Kenney"). In the type of ballad about a criminal's good night, the criminal imparts a moral lesson, filled with remorse. He often repents close to the hour of his execution and warns listeners not to follow his path, as in the ballad "The Wexford Girl":

Come all ye royal true lovers
A warning take by me
And never treat your own true love to any
For if you do you'll rue like me
Until the day you die
You'll hang like me, a murderer
All on the gallows high.

In the Anglo-American ballad and broadside traditions, ballads about notorious criminals and outlaws and sensational murders are also popular. The ballad scholar G. Malcom Laws, Jr. (1964), classified them as a distinct category of ballad. For example, there are many Robin Hood ballads found in the Francis James Child canon brought from England to America. Robin Hood, like the American outlaw "Pretty Boy" Floyd, was known as a "gentleman killer" who robbed from the rich and gave to the poor, often acting unlawfully to avenge a wrong committed by those in authority. As the historian Lawrence Levine (1977) noted, "Robbing

Robin Hood, as depicted in a late-nineteenth-century lithograph. CORBIS/BETTMANN

from the rich and giving to the poor, they become consciously or inadvertently, public benefactors. . . . They kill primarily in self-defense and almost never harass the unarmed or weak."

The Anglo-American folk song tradition also favors outlaws of the Wild West, as has been documented by both Laws and MacEdward Leach. Most notorious of all the outlaws that Laws and Leach wrote about was Jesse James, murdered by Robert Ford, who shot him in the back for a $10,000 bounty. The following verse describes the essential action:

It was on a Friday night, the moon was shinin' bright
An Jesse was standin' 'fore his glass,
Robert Ford's pistol ball brought him temblin' from the wall,
An' they laid poor Jesse in his grave.

(Leach 1955, p. 754)

Ballads from the broadside tradition often describe murders and local events using the "leaping and lingering" technique, in which the narrative drives into the essential plot of the story. For example, the story of Naomi (Oma) Wise shows how the ballad form centers on a single dramatic incident, that of the girl's tragic end by her suitor's violent act:

O Oma, Oma, let me tell you my mind
My mind is to drown you and leave you behind.
O Lewis, O Lewis, pray spare me my life
And I will deny you and not be your wife.
He kicked her and he stamped her, he threw her in the deep
He mounted his pony and rose in full speed.
The screams of poor Oma followed after him so nigh.
Saying, "I am a poor rebel not fitting to die."

In the Mexican American tradition, the *corrido* (border ballad) was documented. One famous *corrido* narrates the story of a local folk hero, Gregorio Cortéz, whose chase, capture, and imprisonment highlighted problems of unequal justice for Texans and Mexican Americans.

In the African American tradition, the prototype for the badman is encapsulated in the ballad about Stagolee (also known as Staggerlee, or Stacker Lee), which was widely disseminated throughout the South and collected by early ballad hunters. Stagolee also appears as a central character in the "toast," a rhymed, chanted narrative poem that is recited with bravado and well-known in the African American oral tradition. The swaggering braggart—the badman-hero character of the toast—appears in the following verse: "Stagolee, he went a-walking with his .40 gun in his hand / He said, 'I feel mistreated this morning. I could kill any man.'" The ballad goes on to relay the gunfight between Stagolee and Billy Lyons, after the former lost his magical Stetson hat in a gambling match. When Lyons pleads for his life, Stagolee remarks, "What do I care fo' yo' children, what do I care fo' yo' wife / You taken my new Stetson hat, an' I'm goin' to take you' life" (Levine 1977, pp. 414–415).

Violence and Folktales

The Brothers Grimm's *Household Tales* forms the basis of the Indo-European-American folktale tradition. Originally meant for an adult audience because of their violent content, many of the tales, such as that of Hansel and Gretel, were sanitized by Walt Disney and in other makeovers. However, in many communities throughout Europe and America at the end of the twentieth century, these tales were still circulating in variant form and could be collected from tradition bearers. One particularly well-known folktale is "My Mother Slew Me and My Father Ate Me," also known as "The Juniper Tree," in which the stepmother beheads her stepchildren and serves them for dinner to their father. Other examples of tales with violent themes appear in many folktale collections and have not been bowdlerized.

Throughout the Native North American oral tradition, the trickster is a central character. How the trickster is characterized differs from group to group, but he often uses cleverness and transformation to satisfy his consuming need for self-gratification. While he is more a wily character than a violent one, the theme of brutality runs throughout the tales. For example, he slashes a baby's head and props it up for later inspection.

Violence and Folk Belief

In the Southwest tradition of *curanderismo*, the *curandero* (folk healer) uses a complex belief system to enact cures. This system of folk medicine used by thousands of West Texans is a tradition passed down from the time of the Aztecs and was still practiced even after the Anglo infiltration into Texas. While some cures were enacted by a *curandero* to cure physical ills, several dealt with the spiritual realm, such as *mal de ojo* (the evil eye) or *mal puesto*, "imposed upon a person by someone having a willful intent to harm—that is, deliberate

hexing by a brujo or bruja (male or female witch). Remedies for *mal puesto* often involve calling in a *curandero* to remove the spell."

Violence and Urban Folklore

In the 1990s folklorists increasingly turned to urban centers to study violence in the folk tradition. Stories told by prison inmates about their lives of crime were documented by Bruce Jackson, who spent months of fieldwork listening to prisoners brag about their criminal exploits. Others wrote ethnographies of urban street criminals, often gritty accounts of life on the street filled with violence and danger (for example, Mark S. Fleisher, *Beggars and Thieves: Lives of Urban Street Criminals*, 1995).

More popular and more accessible are stories that crime victims tell of encounters with muggers, burglars, and rapists. Often attributing their misfortune to being in the wrong place at the wrong time, victims try to make sense of these incidents of violence in their lives and often see the telling of their story as a badge of survival. Some crime-victim stories continue to circulate because they have a didactic quality, imparting urban survival skills against danger.

BIBLIOGRAPHY

Abrahams, Roger, D. *Deep Down in the Jungle: Negro Narrative Folklore from the Streets of Philadelphia*. Chicago: Aldine, 1964. First revised ed., 1970.

Bottigheimer, Ruth B., ed. *Fairy Tales and Society: Illusion, Allusion, and Paradigm*. Philadelphia: University of Pennsylvania Press, 1987.

Jackson, Bruce. *In the Life: Versions of the Criminal Experience*. New York: Holt, Rinehart and Winston, 1972.

Laws, G. Malcolm, Jr. *Native American Balladry: A Descriptive Guide and Bibliographic Syllabus*. Rev. ed. Philadelphia: American Folklore Society, 1964.

Leach, MacEdward. *The Ballad Book*. New York: Harper, 1955.

Levine, Lawrence. *Black Culture and Black Consciousness: Afro-American Folk Thought from Slavery to Freedom*. New York: Oxford University Press, 1977.

Lindahl, Carl, Maida Owens, C. Renee Harvison, eds. *Swapping Stories: Folktales from Louisiana*. Jackson: University Press of Mississippi in association with the Louisiana Division of the Arts, Baton Rouge, 1997.

Parades, Américo. *"With His Pistol in His Hand": A Border Ballad and Its Hero*. Austin: University of Texas Press, 1978.

Radin, Paul. *The Trickster*. New York: Schocken, 1956.

Thompson, Stith. *The Folktale*. New York: Holt, Rinehart and Winston, 1946.

Trotter, Robert T., and Juan Antonio Chavira. *Curanderismo: Mexican American Folk Healing*. Athens: University of Georgia Press, 1981.

Wachs, Eleanor. *Crime-Victim Stories: New York City's Urban Folklore*. Bloomington: Indiana University Press, 1988.

ELEANOR WACHS

See also **Language and Verbal Violence; Literature.**

FOLK NARRATIVES

*Following the **Overview,** a subentry examines one type of folk narrative: **New York City Crime-Victim Stories.***

OVERVIEW

A mirror of people's innermost feelings as they react to events and changing conditions that affect their lives, folk narratives express in their symbolic language what otherwise could not be expressed. Folk narratives—fictional folktales and realistic legends of many kinds—have been disseminated through time and across boundaries by travelers and migrants—pirates, missionaries, traders, bounty hunters, beggars, and soldiers—who carried their store of knowledge in their cultural baggage. As the means of human communication multiplied beyond the oral, and the audience expanded beyond the village gathering around the fire—particularly from the time printing was invented—the meanings of folk narrative evolved to embrace the global consumer.

Since the end of World War II, with the explosion of the mass media, interpretations of violence have taken center stage in folklore, reflecting certain anxieties that were earlier more constrained. The folklore—including both narrative and customs—of modern Western civilization is intimately connected to the multimedia dissemination of increasingly violent messages in the United States, the country that pioneered in media technology. These messages emerge from narratives about violent acts by violent people; they cluster into episodes, form cycles, and spread copycat-style beyond national boundaries. Folklorization is a process of ongoing transformation.

Narrative Genres

Narrative genres have two things in common: all are autobiographical, individualistic elaborations of personal experience as it relates to socially constructed reality; and all draw on a stock of narrative motifs based on a communal belief system and worldview. Yet folk narratives exhibit a variety of contrasting dimensions of human life. Tales are magical or romantic, comical or anecdotal—

these are considered fiction, products of imagination, told for entertainment. Other narratives tell of encounters by ordinary people on their own premises with the supernatural world of evil spirits and with the horrors of victimization by lunatics and criminals—these are termed legends and are taken as nonfiction, as didactic warnings. Whereas tales represent objective poetry—they take place in another world and happen to other people, not us—legends are highly subjective; they can happen to anyone, here and now. In the modern world, tales have lost much of their relevance, often relegated to the nursery. By contrast, legends such as horror stories, ghost stories, and anecdotes of real-life experiences proliferate and dominate people's concerns; legends are situated in the real world, and play into our current fascination with terror. In part, the purpose of telling legends is to contemplate their feasibility. The media may also play a role in the generating of legends; as headlines announce new threats of violence, seeds for new legend clusters are planted.

Every American parent reading to a child has come across versions of the Grimms' fairy tales that have been sanitized of their violence, the gruesome details edited out, ostensibly to protect children from disturbing images. Yet within the tradition of these folk narratives, the brutal fates of the tales' protagonists are necessary to their rebirth in stronger, smarter, healthier, and more beautiful form. At the same time, in an irony of modern life, many parents and educators take it for granted that vampires, werewolves, skeletons, and broom-riding witches are acceptable, even desirable, images; such images not only populate stories but also decorate lawns at Halloween (amid mock graveyards) and inhabit the shapes of toys. As far as folktales go, today only a few basic plots, episodes, and motifs appear as integral parts of American literature and mass culture, most notably adapted and shaped into normalized formulas by the Hollywood movie industry, in particular the Disney empire.

Attraction to Violence

In the second half of the twentieth century, horror and terror attracted the fascination of American children and young people with growing intensity through the conduit of mass media. Mass media such as comic books, movies, and television often recycle and adapt folk narratives to their particular formats; they blend into, cross over, and interact with each other. Perhaps especially in popular works aimed at an audience of children, violence has become ubiquitous. The psychiatrist Frederic Wertham argued that comic books give children elementary instruction in violent acts by their graphic representation of torture, slashing, rape, murder, and dismemberment. "Comic-books," says the folklorist Gershon Legman, "have succeeded in giving every American child a complex course in paranoid megalomania." Responsible adults do not seem to mind the miring of children in the culture of media violence "because they are themselves addicted to precisely the same violence in reality, from the daily accident or atrocity smeared over the front page of their breakfast newspaper to the nightly prize-fight or murder play in movies, radio, and television coast-to-coast." But news, to be newsworthy, has always been bad news. The folk's attraction to violence, and their simultaneous fear of violence, is the platform of the folkloristic elaboration of horrifying themes filtered through the mass media.

Homo ludens (like the term *Homo sapiens,* which characterizes human beings by their ability to think or reason, *homo ludens* characterizes human beings by their ability to play) partakes in many symbolic and serious games that involve verbal or physical aggression and abuse—some folkloric, others not. But for the *homo narrans* (human beings characterized by their ability to narrate), violence means destruction of the life of innocent people who accidentally encounter their nemesis or enter, in search of knowledge, the forbidden realms of evil. Violation of taboos end tragically, but the hero of the tale always rebounds: the more bloodshed and dismemberment, the better chances of rebirth, happy marriage, and glorious empowerment. For the protagonist of legend the experience is crippling or fatal, yet humans are ready to risk and undertake the adventure to learn what fear is. The prototypical American folk legend—distant kin of the Grimms' "A Tale of a Boy Who Set Out to Learn Fear"—tells of a gruesome visit to a haunted house as a test of courage. A youngster undertakes a hazardous, life-threatening adventure to achieve maturity by learning the taste of fear.

The trip to the designated ghost house, bridge, cemetery, chapel, tunnel, or other hidden and forbidden place that serves as entry to the realm of the dead and monstrous is grafted onto the map of the vast American landscape following the mental map's guidelines. The trip symbolizes a traumatic phase of human life, separation from home and family, entering a strange and hostile world of trials and tribulations without the friendly helpers who direct the folktale hero to fairyland.

A millennial year such as the year 2000 gives rise to widespread belief in the advent of the biblical Apocalypse, with its promise of making contact with the dead. As in so many legends, fear of death is transformed into hope of immortality. If the dead can return, we also will have life after death.

Americans are in fact enamored of the dead. Famous and infamous historic "haunted" houses are listed on a national register for tourists, who may also choose from the many guidebooks and best-selling regional and national ghost-story collections to rationalize irrational belief in the supernatural. Since 1971 a Halloween guided bus tour has ferried screaming seekers on a five-hour, one-hundred-mile ride around Chicago; passengers hear the story of victims and perpetrators whose phantom presence is suggested by the wind and fog.

Yet another American folk tradition is the quest, the legend-trip, in which a person decides to visit a haunted site by car and invites others to join him or her. Examples of such quests or legend-trips are excursions taken by tourists, religious pilgrimages, visits to healers or healing sites or other sites equated with magic or invested with supernatural significance such as Salem, Massachusetts, the site of alleged seventeenth-century witches, or Elvis Presley's mansion, Graceland. Such trips are often taken by high school students or adults; during the trip these traveling companions sometimes condition themselves to a horrific experience by exchanging horror stories. When they reach the site, the group performs a ritual that stimulates the replay of a tragic loss of life—they honk the horn, shine a light, call the victim by name. They might stamp on a grave or climb into a structure, writing their initials to mark their presence. The participants may fear the victim's turning into a vengeful monster intent on punishing intruders by causing their car to crash. American folk narratives tend to express the sense that humans are unsafe and surrounded by uncontrollable hostile forces as soon as they leave their protective nuclear cell. The plea of innocent victims in ghost stories represents the fragility of life in a world of murderers, the enemy present within the familiar world. Common representations of danger are hatchet-wielding killers who lurk in dormitories or in the backseats of cars; escapees from lunatic asylums who attack couples parked in lovers' lanes; predators who pounce when an innocent runs out of gas in a remote and lovely natural setting, decapitating the hapless driver; murderers who prey on children in the care of helpless babysitters; or the evil babysitter herself, who broils the children instead of the turkey intended for dinner; and so on.

Other tales center on the enemy from without: aliens in their powerful flying machines land on our premises, burn circles in the wheat field, kidnap people for medical testing, mingle with humans, even impregnate women. And there is the unseen, unidentifiable enemy, as expressed in recurrent rumors of the poisoning of soft drinks, prescription drugs, and food. Legends portray danger as lurking everywhere.

The context and paraphernalia of the climate of violence are displayed vividly at Halloween, All Saints' Eve, the traditional calendar feast day of the dead. According to the legend, the dead rise from their graves on the night of 31 October and visit the living from door to door. Irish and Scottish immigrants to America imported the ritual of welcoming visitors dressed in spooky costumes (witches, vampires, ghosts, goblins, ghouls) and rewarding them with treats. This pleasant masquerading transformed into the American tradition of trick or treat, a symbolic threat (give me a treat or I'll play a dirty trick on you) and a youthful attack on authority. It is common on Halloween that, while young children extort treats, teenagers vandalize homes and make mischief in neighborhoods. These developments gave rise to a new recurring legend, that of the adult who pays back the mild forms of vandalism by inserting razor blades in apples and poisoning candy. The legend was at times reality, with cases of actual poisoning. Local communities responded by setting up alternatives for the door-to-door ritual. Schools and charitable organizations began to set up haunted houses containing a taste of everything terrifying, monstrous, and disgusting to the happily shuddering visitors: ghosts, skulls and bones, mutilated corpses in pools of blood, vampires, mental patients, execution, autopsy (with children encouraged to touch the exposed "organs").

Folk stories exist only if they are repeated and varied over time. Amid the rapid-fire profusion of media stories about anything and everything, the single but multiplying thread of the folk narrative continues to unwind from our innermost responses and urges.

BIBLIOGRAPHY

Dégh, Linda, with Andrew Vázsonyi. "Does the Word 'Dog' Bite? Ostensive Action: A Means of Legend Telling." In *Narratives in Society: A Performer-Centered Study of Narration.* Helsinki: Academia Scientiarum Fennica, 1995.

Ellis, Bill. " 'Safe' Spooks: New Halloween Traditions in Response to Sadism Legends." In *Halloween and Other Festivals of Death and Life,* edited by Jack Santino. Knoxville: University of Tennessee Press, 1994.

Feshbach, Seymour, and Robert D. Singer. *Television and Aggression.* San Francisco: Jossey-Bass, 1971.

Legman, Gershon. *Love and Death: A Study in Censorship.* New York: Hacker Art Books, 1963.

Schorr, Daniel. "Go Get Some Milk and Cookies and Watch the Murders on Television." In *Impact of Mass Media: Current Issues,* edited by Ray Eldon Hiebert and Carol Reuss. New York: Longman, 1985.

Wertham, Frederic. *Seduction of the Innocent.* New York: Rinehart, 1954.

LINDA DÉGH

See also **Folk Culture; Language and Verbal Violence; Literature.**

NEW YORK CITY CRIME-VICTIM STORIES

Crime-victim stories, a type of modern storytelling, are structured prose narratives that have an identifiable style, form, and function, and most often are related as first-person accounts of crime-centered events. While this type of modern story can be told anywhere, it is a common theme of the folklore of New York City. These crime-based personal-experience narratives describe a confrontation between an alleged criminal offender—for example, a mugger—and his or her victim. Like other types of stories about daily life, crime-victim stories describe in detail the sequential events, usually of a violent and unpredictable encounter of a type perceived to be commonly experienced by urbanites, particularly New Yorkers.

Crime-victim stories that New Yorkers relate have narrative themes, including those of fated victimization and bystander apathy. Some New Yorkers believe that they were just in the wrong place at the wrong time. Others enforce the theme that good Samaritans are few and that most people do not want to be involved when they see crimes taking place. These stories about crime are easy to collect; they are often shared among strangers and casual acquaintances because of the belief among tellers and listeners that the crimes they describe are commonplace happenings. This perception is constantly reinforced by the mass media in and out of New York City. New Yorkers may use these stories as conversational icebreakers, a means to entertain, or a way to embed crime-prevention techniques and urban skills. A key reason that New Yorkers and other urbanites tell these stories is to assert their survival: they have endured an urban ritual. Reiterating the story is a way to work through the emotional impact of a harrowing experience, such as a brush with death.

Stories that at first may seem to be rambling tales about city life often, upon closer inspection, can be found to have a consistent format and a common structure. Tellers often announce that they will impart a story, citing the time and location of the incident to ground it. Next, the confrontation or demand of the offender is announced: "Give me your money and keep walking!" for example. Usually there is some sort of dialogue between the offender and his or her victim. Then, the speaker tells of a resolution. Finally, the speaker will provide a coda to the story evaluating life in New York City or urban life in general: something to the effect, "That's New York! What are ya gonna do?" Oftentimes in a storytelling session, tellers will try to compete with one another for the most harrowing experience that may have happened to them or friends or acquaintances. Many stories are told as secondhand accounts; however, they function the same as firsthand accounts.

These stories, falling under the rubric of the larger narrative framework of the personal-experience narrative, are not traditional in content, but there are times when a crime story is merely a popularly circulated "urban legend," a story told as true and related by a friend of a friend. One example is a story about a runner in Central Park who accuses another runner of stealing his wallet, gets a wallet from the accused, and then is shocked when he finds his own wallet at home. This popular story has been collected by the urban-legend scholar Jan Harold Brunvand and has been attributed to other American locales as well. The same story can be traced back to "The Five Pound Note," in a 1912 British collection, and it was also used by Neil Simon in his 1971 play *The Prisoner of Second Avenue*.

Some purposes of telling stories about crime and violence are to impart skills on how not to be a crime victim and to increase awareness of the dangers of city life, a theme constantly reiterated in the broadcast and print media. It is common to hear people tell each other that they would not walk in a certain area of the city or remind each other to sit in the subway car with the conductor, for example. In this way, crime stories serve a didactic function: know the city well, the tellers admonish; be sure to avoid such dangerous areas or enclosures as elevators and parking lots, and believe in your intuition if you sense danger.

Not all crime-victim stories are told to frighten or to be didactic. Some circulate because they have a humorous or unforgettable twist and are told for entertainment. Oftentimes, these involve a trickster or simpleton, a character well-known in American folklore. For example, crime stories have been collected about burglars who leave their wallets—with identification—in burgled apartments and are subsequently picked up by the police. In another story, a victim has her camera stolen. When it is later found and then reclaimed at the police station, the developed roll of film contains pictures of a burglar known to the police. Another account tells of the rapist who gives his name to the victim, so she can write him a check. As the story goes, the teller's female friend was single, living on the East Side, when two guys broke into her apartment and proceeded to completely loot the apartment and then rape the woman. They also asked her for cash, but she had none. When they threatened her with dire consequences for not producing cash, she offered to write a check made out to cash. One of the assailants declined, saying that he would have trouble cashing it at a bank, and specified that she make it out to him—and he gives her his name. As soon as the rapists left, check in hand, she called the police and gave them the name. Sure enough, they picked him up in a couple of days.

New Yorkers and other urbanites hear about and talk about violence in their daily life. The telling of these crime-victim stories is one way in which they tell their own cautionary tales, a way to spread folk wisdom in a busy metropolis.

BIBLIOGRAPHY

Brunvand, Jan Harold. *The Vanishing Hitchhiker: American Urban Legends and Their Meanings.* New York: Norton, 1986.

Stahl, Sandra K. D. *Literary Folkloristics and the Personal Narrative.* Bloomington: Indiana University Press, 1989.

Wachs, Eleanor, *Crime-Victim Stories: New York City's Urban Folklore.* Bloomington: Indiana University Press, 1988.

ELEANOR WACHS

See also **New York; Victims of Violence.**

FOREIGN INTERVENTION, FEAR OF

Era of Reasonable Fears: 1783–1865

From the end of the American Revolution to the end of the Civil War, there existed a realistic military threat to the fledgling United States. Surrounded by hostile foreign powers (Great Britain in Canada, France in the Louisiana Territory, and Spain in Florida and Cuba), the militarily weak United States responded by attempting to build up its forces and defenses against attack. On numerous occasions during this era, the United States was threatened: by Britain during the War of 1812, by Spain during numerous border clashes over Florida from 1800 to 1809, and by France during the Quasi-War (1798–1800). Continued westward expansion led to conflict between encroaching settlers and Native American tribes, which consumed additional military resources. Consequently, fewer troops were available to defend the strategic but vulnerable coastal cities. In response a massive construction program began along the Great Lakes and in major seaports after the War of 1812, establishing a chain of permanent stone masonry fortifications from Maine to Louisiana. Ironically, these forts were never attacked by European powers, but several became the focal point in some of the most famous battles of the American Civil War, such as Fort Sumter in Charleston Harbor, Forts St. Philip and Jackson guarding the approaches to New Orleans, and Forts Morgan and Gaines guarding Mobile Bay.

In response to fears of foreign invasion, and the fear of economic competition, numerous anti-immigrant organizations arose during this period. The Nativist movement began in the late 1830s as a reaction to an influx of European immigration. Strongly isolationist, anti-Catholic, and anti-Irish, the Nativists became a political force in American politics. Organizations such as the Know-Nothing Party and its later descendant, the Native American Party, pushed for changes in immigration and citizenship laws in the vain hope of keeping new immigrants out of the United States and reducing the rights of those immigrants already in the United States. Reaching its peak in the 1856 election, the Native American Party managed to elect seventy-five congressmen and one governor to office, thus reflecting the existent anti-immigration feeling in America and also contributing to the continuance of bigotry and intolerance throughout the era. Anti-Chinese and anti-Japanese groups

that developed in the American West during the latter half of the nineteenth century, along with present-day racist hate groups, can easily trace their beginnings to the Nativists of the mid-1800s.

The Gilded Age: 1865–1900

Following the Civil War, political instability in Europe prompted the immigration to the United States of persons with radical political views. Called "anarchists," most of these radicals believed in the concept of popular democracy, having been victims of monarchist repression in Europe. Some, however, were enthralled by the new theories of Karl Marx (Marxism) and his emphasis on labor. Consequently, when many of these immigrants went to work in the factories, mines, forests, and mills of the United States, they attempted to organize labor unions, bringing them into direct confrontation with the wealthy industrialists, or "robber barons," of the Gilded Age.

The most famous of these incidents was the 1886 Haymarket Square Riot, when seven police were killed and seventy protesters wounded during a union-organized strike in Chicago. Although Haymarket thwarted the radical labor movement envisioned by Marxists, it aided the growth of moderate labor movements in the early part of the twentieth century, such as the American Federation of Labor (AFL) and the Congress of Industrial Organizations (CIO), which were seen by industrialists and political leaders as less threatening alternatives. At the center of the labor agitation, as many antilabor pundits of the time noted, were "foreign anarchists," without whose influence, it was implied, native-born Americans would not have organized into unions. The attempt by antilabor groups to use the deeply rooted anti-immigrant fears of many Americans of the era to hinder the growth of radical labor unions succeeded. Even the political reform movements of the later Gilded Age, such as the Grangers and the Populists, possessed anti-immigrant planks in their platforms.

America as a World Power: 1898–1945

As the twentieth century began, the United States again faced the possibility of military invasion. Gains from the Spanish-American War of 1898 pushed the nation deeper into international politics and greatly increased the possibility of military conflict. The geostrategic importance of the Panama Canal, completed in 1914, added to the growing fears of international conflict. Military leaders of the time, inspired by the writings of naval theorist Alfred Thayer Mahan, such as *The Influence of Sea Power upon History, 1660–1783* (1890) and *The Influence of Sea Power upon the French Revolution and Empire, 1793–1812* (1892), pressed for additional defenses for American possessions in the Caribbean and Pacific in order to expand the hemispheric influence of the United States. For war planners, the nation's principal enemies were Japan and Great Britain in the Pacific, and Britain, Germany, and France in the Atlantic—either singly or in combination. Color-coded war plans were developed for each contingency (red for Britain, black for Germany, orange for Japan, etc.) and were maintained until the 1930s.

World War I forced a change from the traditional American isolationist, defensive foreign policy to an interventionist and internationalist role. Despite the torpedoing of American merchant vessels, as a result of which American citizens were killed, and the growing economic ties between the Allied Powers and the United States, President Woodrow Wilson resisted U.S. military involvement in the war. This changed in the spring of 1917, mostly because of a perceived threat of a German/Mexican invasion of the United States. The so-called Zimmerman telegram, a diplomatic note passed from the German foreign minister to his ambassador in Mexico, outlined a Mexican-German alliance should war with the United States break out. Intercepted by Britain and passed to the United States, the communiqué infuriated Wilson and the Congress, who authorized the arming of U.S. merchant ships against German attack. Within two months, the United States and Germany were at war.

The end of the Great War and the resurfacing of American isolationism were accompanied by a new surge of antiforeign agitation. Russia's dominance by the Bolsheviks in 1917, communist riots in Austria, Germany, and Italy, and the rise of radicalism in America led to a wave of anti-Marxist sentiment, commonly called the Red Scare. Anti-Red groups, from the American Legion to the Ku Klux Klan to the Department of Justice under Attorney General A. Mitchell Palmer, launched a campaign to stamp out the perceived menace from Moscow. Mass arrests and deportations followed in 1919–1920, with the largest occurring on 2 January 1920, when over twenty-seven hundred persons were arrested. By the mid-1920s, organized communist or Marxist organizations had ceased to exist, ending the first of such periods of anticommunist hysteria in the twentieth century.

American entry into World War II was marked by antiforeign activities by both individuals and the government as a whole. German agents were active in America during the war; in 1942, a group of eight Nazi saboteurs was captured and six were executed after a secret military trial. However, the most famous of the antiforeign actions taken in World War II was the 1942 detainment of Japanese Americans, who were forced from their homes in Hawaii and the West Coast and placed in internment camps in the southern and western United States. After the Japanese attack on Pearl Harbor on 7 December 1941, rumors of a domestic pro-Japanese element that had aided in the assault were rife. As a result, persons of Japanese lineage were banned from U.S. military installations following the attack, while individual Japanese Americans became targets of mob violence. Ostensibly to protect both the military from spies and Japanese Americans from violence, President Franklin D. Roosevelt authorized their internment on 19 February 1942. Approximately 110,000 men, women, and children were moved to "restricted military areas," away from their homes and businesses. The program was ended on 2 January 1945. It was not until 1988, however, that the survivors were recompensed—and then only partially—for the damages they had incurred because of their forced dislocation.

McCarthyism and the Red Scare: 1945–1962

Following World War II and the beginning of the Cold War between the United States and the Soviet Union, a second wave of anticommunist hysteria began that continued well into the 1950s. Leading this crusade was the Wisconsin senator Joseph R. McCarthy, who was able to parlay Midwestern isolationist fears of foreigners and communists into a high-visibility political career. As a member of the House Un-American Activities Committee (formed during World War II as a House investigative committee on foreign espionage and influence in America), McCarthy accused the State Department, the liberal political establishment, the press, and the entertainment community of being under the control or influence of communists. Americans, smarting after the 1949 communist victory in China, the Korean War, and Soviet testing of the atomic bomb, responded by allowing McCarthy's "witch hunt" to continue relatively unhindered. Until 1954, McCarthy succeeded in effectively terrorizing accused communists and their allied "fellow travelers," and encouraging the growth of ultraconservative and reactionary organizations such as the John Birch Society and a rebirth of the Ku Klux Klan. However, it was his attack on the U.S. Army that led to his political downfall. After accusing the army of communist infiltration, McCarthy was publicly humiliated during televised hearings by army counsel Joseph N. Welch, who asked him, "Have you left no sense of decency?"

The end of McCarthyism did not eradicate the fear of foreign intervention in America. The antiwar movement, aimed at American involvement in Vietnam, and the Civil Rights movement were both infiltrated by Federal Bureau of Investigation and military intelligence operatives searching for communist influence, while the domino theory (which held that America must fight communism overseas to prevent it from spreading) had at its heart a basic fear of invasion of the United States by the Soviets or China. The incident most illustrative of post-McCarthy invasion scares was the 1962 Cuban Missile Crisis, when Americans dug fallout shelters and prepared for either a U.S. invasion of Cuba or a Soviet nuclear attack on the United States.

Fear of Invasion: 1962–1999

While the fear of a nuclear Armageddon was dominant in the 1960s and continued through the late 1980s, little concern about physical invasion by a conventional army existed in the United States during that time. With the end of the Cold War, this concern was reduced even further. For the first time in American history, in fact, the United States had no clear reason to fear foreign invasion. And with friendly nations to the north and south, a position as the dominant military power in the Western Hemisphere, and a relatively stable international situation, conditions worked against antiforeign agitation at home. However, the rise of international terrorist organizations with an anti-American agenda did present a danger to the United States at the turn of the twenty-first century. How Americans react to this threat, with forbearance and justice or with the kind of irrationality that produced witch hunts and Red Scares, will have much to do with how the United States defines itself in the twenty-first century.

BIBLIOGRAPHY

Avrich, Paul. *The Haymarket Tragedy*. Princeton, N.J.: Princeton University Press, 1984.

Buhle, Paul, and Dan Georgakas, eds. *The Immigrant Left in the United States*. Albany: State University of New York Press, 1996.

Daniels, Roger. *Prisoners Without Trial: Japanese-Americans in World War II*. New York: Hill and Wang, 1993.

Higham, John. *Strangers in the Land: Patterns of American Nativism, 1860–1925*. New Brunswick, N.J.: Rutgers University Press, 1988.

Kennedy, Paul M., ed. *War Plans of the Great Powers, 1880–1914*. Boston: Allen and Unwin, 1979.

Moore, Leonard J. *Citizen Klansman: The Ku Klux Klan in Indiana, 1921–1928*. Chapel Hill: University of North Carolina Press, 1991.

Skaggs, David C., and Robert S. Browning III, eds. *In Defense of the Republic: Readings in American Military History*. Belmont, Calif.: Wadsworth, 1991.

Tuchman, Barbara. *The Zimmerman Telegram*. New York: Macmillan, 1966.

ROBERT R. MACKEY

See also **Alien and Sedition Acts; Anarchism; Japanese Americans; Military Interventions; Nativism; Red Scare.**

FOREIGN PERSPECTIVES. *See* American Violence in Comparative Perspective.

FOREIGN POLICE, U.S. TRAINING OF

In 1990, sixteen years after Congress abolished most U.S. programs to assist foreign police, the United States had 125 police programs abroad, a 225 percent increase in the number of countries given police assistance under pre-1974 programs and an almost 400 percent increase over that of 1968, the peak year for countries receiving such aid. The many agencies and secret funds historically involved in police training suggest that the 1990 foreign-police assistance authorization of $117 million is an underestimation of the actual funds so allocated. In any case, despite the long and unenviable record of this training and the violence and authoritarianism associated with it, the United States continues in its efforts to influence and train foreign police.

Seldom an explicit component of foreign-policy analysis, foreign-police assistance has been important to U.S. foreign policy. Seemingly a relatively benign, low-key, nonmilitary intervention, foreign-police assistance has been used to bolster the U.S. image abroad and at home with the claim that it makes recipient police more democratic and responsive and less corrupt and violent. However, direct military incursions can be difficult to sell to Congress and the American public, as well as abroad. In fact, police programs are often perceived as attempts by the United States to penetrate foreign states by turning their police into instruments of U.S. foreign policy. Indeed, instead of fostering and protecting human rights, U.S. police programs abroad have been linked to a range of human rights abuses. Moreover, the United States has found that foreign police who have received American training do not demonstrate consistent loyalty to U.S. programs and policies, calling into question even the covert value of Washington's assistance to foreign police.

A Questionable History

In 1898 U.S. occupation forces began establishing police constabularies in the Philippines and Cuba, launching a long period of uncoordinated ad hoc police training in the Caribbean and Central America, and later in postwar Germany and Japan, Greece, and Turkey. In 1957 the United States started a more systematic foreign-police training program under the Overseas Internal Security Program (OISP), a top-secret National Security Council initiative to counter communist subversion before it became a military problem. OISP operated through many agencies and institutions—the International Cooperation Administration (predecessor to the U.S. Agency for International Development, or USAID), the International Association of Chiefs of Police, U.S. universities (Michigan State, Northwestern, University of Southern California), private-police-training organizations—all conduits for intelligence gathering and training on the part of the Central Intelligence Agency and the U.S. military (Huggins 1998). U.S. police did some training, including that by Daniel Mitrione, a one-time staffer at the Office of Public Safety (OPS) of USAID; in 1970 Mitrione was murdered in Uruguay by Tupamaro guerrillas for his assumed involvement with the CIA.

President John F. Kennedy had established OPS in 1962, to consolidate foreign-police-training agencies. Through OPS, the CIA continued its clandestine collaboration in foreign-police training. Except for South Vietnam, Latin America received the most OPS aid, and of the Latin Ameri-

can countries, Brazil got the largest share of the funds. In Brazil, U.S. advisers worked with police known to be linked to death squads and to employ torture, and helped internal security officials write and promote wholly undemocratic national security laws. In the 1990s Brazil's police were among the most violent in South America. In Guatemala, where the United States has had police-training programs since the mid-1950s, the police have participated with the army in torturing, killing, or "disappearing" at least 130,000 civilians, according to the human rights organization Americas Watch. In 1999 President Bill Clinton made a public apology for U.S. involvement in these offenses.

In 1974, in the wake of congressional investigations of widespread human rights abuses by U.S.-trained police and a firestorm of criticism over atrocities committed by such police, Congress banned most U.S. assistance to foreign police. Past police assistance was shown to have fostered violence while fortifying authoritarian governments. Congress exempted from the ban police assistance for narcotics control.

Late-Twentieth-Century Expansion

At the close of the twentieth century, police assistance operated under twelve presidential exceptions to the 1974 Foreign Assistance Act section 660 prohibition against such aid, with training provided by an array of U.S. government agencies and civilian police specialists. The Federal Bureau of Investigation's "rule of law" program trains police throughout the world, focusing especially on Eastern Europe, Russia, and Asia. The Department of Defense Program to Assist National Police Forces is reorganizing police in Latin America, including Bolivia, Peru, Ecuador, Colombia, Panama, and Mexico. In the late 1990s the State Department's Anti-Terrorism Assistance Program sponsored police training in sixty-five countries with a 1997 budget of over $1.6 billion—a twenty-three-fold increase over its initial (1986) budget of $5 million. The Drug Enforcement Administration is involved in police training for drug interdiction, with a 1996 budget for "international narcotics and law enforcement affairs" of just over $153 million. The U.S. Justice Department's International Criminal Investigative Training Assistance Program, with a 1997 budget of just over $23 million, had seen an almost 1,500 percent increase over its 1986 budget of $1.5 million.

The vast expansion of foreign-police training after the funding of such activity was brought to a halt by Congress demonstrates political bad faith and violates the spirit of the 1974 congressional legislation. In addition, almost a century of U.S. involvement with foreign police has not significantly reduced police violence in recipient countries as such programs promised. The United States has trained Salvadoran police since the 1940s, yet the *United Nations Truth Commission Report on El Salvador* (1993) confirmed widespread and murderous brutality by U.S.-trained Salvadoran police throughout the 1980s—even as the United States was assisting these police. In Honduras between 1988 and 1989, following almost thirty years of almost continuous U.S. police assistance, the torture and beatings of civilians by Honduran security forces tripled. In Colombia, where the United States has trained police since the early 1920s, the police are among the most militarized in the hemisphere, engage in systematic violence against citizens, and have been implicated in narco-corruption (Huggins 1998). The United States has been working with Mexican justice and drug officials since the 1980s, yet in 1998 it was disclosed that military, police, justice officials, and elite drug units—all trained by the United States—were tied to drug traffickers.

Institutionalized Violence

The United States has supported foreign police organizations—in Brazil, El Salvador, Guatemala—that make systematic use of torture. Congressional testimony by the CIA shows that its operatives and their superiors have known that the police they assisted engaged in systematic human rights abuses. In the late 1980s and early 1990s CIA torture manuals were discovered. U.S. congressional reports from the 1960s through the 1980s argued that the training of foreign police soiled the U.S. image abroad, refuting the claim that training foreign police makes them more neutrally "professional," less deadly and corrupt, and more humanitarian and democratically responsive to civilian control. In fact, much research suggests that the opposite can be expected, since the underlying goal of U.S. police training seems to have been to centralize internal security, regardless of the consequences for human rights and democratic control.

U.S. assistance to foreign police has directly and indirectly promoted institutionalized violence in recipient countries. By emphasizing a war model of policing, U.S. assistance has encouraged recipient police to see ever larger numbers of citizens as "deviant others"—criminals, communists, terrorists, narco-traffickers—to be eliminated. It has provided the technology and know-how for waging internal war—machine guns, help organizing militarized SWAT teams and improved surveillance systems, and refined interrogation techniques such as the use of sodium pentothal, psychological terror, and "restrained" physical force. Many analysts believe that the United States has indirectly fostered police violence by giving moral and political support to countries whose police are known to engage in human rights abuses (Huggins 1998; Langguth 1978; Weschler 1987).

Rather than eliminating crime, insurgency, terrorism, and drug production and supply, U.S. assistance to foreign police has apparently decreased the quality of democracy and increased human rights abuses in recipient countries. "Rule of law" has been overshadowed by police brutality, torture, murder, and death squads. From a social planning standpoint, either there is a disconnect between the lofty goals of U.S. foreign-police assistance and the actual means for achieving these, or the means are in fact the real goals of U.S. foreign-police assistance: to fortify internal control and increase U.S. power over recipient states without regard for democracy and human rights.

BIBLIOGRAPHY

Americas Watch. "Closing the Space: Human Rights in Guatemala." *Americas Watch Report.* New York: Americas Watch Committee, 1988.

Call, Charles T. "Police Aid and the New World Disorder: Institutional Learning Within the U.S. International Criminal Investigative Training Assistance Program (ICITAP)." In *Policing the New World Disorder: Peace Operations and the Public Security,* edited by Robert Oakley and Michael Dziedzic. Washington, D.C.: National Defense University, 1997.

Government Accounting Office. *Foreign Aid: Police Training and Assistance Report to Congressional Requestors.* Washington, D.C.: U.S. Government Printing Office, 1992.

Huggins, Martha K. *Political Policing: The United States and Latin America.* Durham, N.C.: Duke University Press, 1998.

Klare, Michael, and Cynthia Arnson. *Supplying Repression: U.S. Support for Authoritarian Regimes Abroad.* Washington, D.C.: Institute for Policy Studies, 1981.

Langguth, A. J. *Hidden Terrors.* New York: Pantheon, 1978.

National Security Archive, George Washington University, SEAS.gwu.edu/NSArchive.

United Nations. *United Nations Truth Commission Report on El Salvador.* Report prepared for the Committee on Foreign Affairs, U.S. House of Representatives,

Congressional Research Service. Washington D.C.: U.S. Government Printing Office, 1993.

Weschler, Lawrence. *A Miracle, a Universe: Settling Accounts with Torturers.* 2d ed. Chicago: University of Chicago Press, 1998.

MARTHA K. HUGGINS

See also **Government Violence Against Citizens; Mass Murder: Collective Murder; Military Interventions; Torture.**

FORENSIC PSYCHIATRY

The role of forensic psychiatrists and psychologists in the criminal court is to provide scientific expertise that aids in the decision-making process of the judge or jury. Typically, however, the legal need for clear-cut answers conflicts with the medical view of disease and pathology as a continuum. In fact, the relationship between attorneys and mental-health clinicians in the courtroom has never been comfortable. The general public also has questioned psychiatry's role in court: during the late 1970s and early 1980s a public impression was formed that psychiatric and psychological defenses (resulting in verdicts of not guilty by reason of insanity) were being abused in criminal trials. Nevertheless, the legal profession and psychiatry maintain their difficult relationship because it is in the best interest of society as a whole that they do so.

In the common-law system of jurisprudence, followed in most English-speaking countries, judicial decisions are based solely on evidence presented in court. Ordinarily, witnesses are constrained to testify about things of which they have personal knowledge. One notable exception to this rule is the expert witness, whose opinions—conclusions, assessments, or inferences based on his or her area of expertise, not necessarily personal knowledge—may be admitted as evidence. Expert witnesses, by virtue of their specialized knowledge, education, or experience, can contribute information that is beyond the ability of ordinary witnesses. Expert opinions are thought to assist in the decision-making process on matters outside the ordinary knowledge and experience of judicial fact finders such as judges and juries.

Incompetency

Questions of competency arise in several areas of criminal-court proceedings, and forensic psychiatrists and psychologists are often called on to help determine such cases. Before a trial even begins, at the moment a person is arrested, competency is an issue in terms of his or her ability to understand certain legal protections provided by the Bill of Rights: those against unlawful police searches and seizures and those against self-incrimination, which often involves the nature of confessions. These rights are protected because their violation could lead to information that would help to establish an individual's guilt. As a consequence of the Supreme Court's decision in *Miranda v. Arizona* (1966), police or prosecuting agencies must explain the right not to give statements (which could later be interpreted as self-incrimination) to everyone they arrest and solicit his or her cooperation. However, a person may choose to forgo these rights and permit a search or give a statement. In criminal litigation a question often arises as to whether the defendant's permission was freely given.

A separate but related protection for criminal defendants relates to the prosecution's responsibility to show that any statement by the defendant was given by choice and not coerced, whether or not he or she waived the constitutional right against self-incrimination. That is, a self-incriminating statement may not be used if it was obtained through threats, unlawful promises, or undue pressure. Such an involuntary statement is considered inherently unreliable and therefore inadmissible at a trial or hearing. Whether assessing the capacity of the defendant to consent or determining the voluntariness of his or her statement, the forensic psychiatrist must be alert to such matters as brain damage or organic disorders, functional disorders, medication, intoxicants, vulnerability to inducement, and lack of sophistication (for example, because of age, educational deficits, or cultural differences).

Competency is also an issue in another pretrial procedure: the selection of witnesses. In most jurisdictions witnesses are presumed capable of observing and recalling the matter about which they are testifying, of communicating what they know, of recognizing the difference between truth and falsehood, and of understanding the obligation to tell the truth in accordance with the oath they take, that is, they are presumed to be competent to testify. This presumption posits a low, and therefore rebuttable, threshold. On occasion forensic psychiatrists assess the competency of witnesses as measured by their ability to comply with the above-noted tests. These assessments may relate to the testimony of children or to that of individuals with mental disabilities.

The common-law system presupposes the criminal defendant's active participation in the court process on the belief that this participation contributes to the efficacy of the proceedings and assures the appropriate impact of the process on the defendant. It also addresses the injustice inherent in trials in absentia. When individuals with disabilities such as mental illness or mental retardation become defendants in criminal prosecutions, qualitative issues arise with respect to their potential inability to participate. In the lexicon of the criminal law, the defendant may be incompetent or unfit to stand trial.

In most jurisdictions within the United States, issues of competency are addressed by a special ancillary court process that attempts to determine the defendant's current mental capacity either (1) to participate meaningfully in the criminal proceedings or (2) to cooperate with his or her attorney in the preparation or presentation of a defense. If the defendant fails either of these tests, he or she is considered incompetent or unfit for trial, and the prosecution must cease until he or she regains mental competency or fitness. In the interim the

defendant usually is judicially committed, often to a secure mental-health institution, for involuntary mental-health care by clinicians with forensic expertise. In incompetence proceedings the forensic psychiatrist evaluates the defendant with respect to these tests and renders an opinion on the issues of mental incompetence or fitness for trial. Often a written report is submitted to the trial court. On occasion it is necessary for the forensic psychiatrist or psychologist to testify about the issues in contested court proceedings, which resemble truncated trials.

The difficulty of fitting clinical expertise to legal need was well illustrated by the 1998 federal-court prosecution of Theodore Kaczynski, the Unabomber. Kaczynski demanded that his attorneys present a defense that had no legal basis, and he refused to permit them to present a defense based on his mental condition. Thus the attorneys assessed Kaczynski as incapable of meaningfully cooperating with them in the only defense they deemed possible. At the ensuing incompetence proceeding, a forensic psychiatrist diagnosed Kaczynski with the illness of schizophrenia, paranoid type. Although he was clearly severely mentally ill, his judgment significantly impaired with respect to the conduct of his own defense, Kaczynski's superior intelligence and understanding of the court process led the examiner to conclude that he was competent to stand trial. Ultimately, Kaczynski pleaded guilty in exchange for a sentence of life imprisonment without the possibility of parole in lieu of the death penalty.

Intent and Diminished Capacity

To establish culpability, the prosecution must show not only that the defendant committed a prohibited act but also that the crime was committed with criminal intent, or mens rea. Absent this intent, the defendant is less culpable or not culpable at all, and there can be no conviction without both the act and the intent. For most crimes a general intent to behave in a fashion that results in a prohibited harm is sufficient. For some crimes culpability requires that the defendant behave in a purposeful way; this is called specific intent. For example, murder requires a specific intent called malice. Hence, the mental state of the defendant at the time of the crime is a frequently litigated issue in criminal cases in which the defendant is mentally ill. Forensic psychiatrists are called on to provide the testimonial expertise required for the judge or jury to determine this issue.

The Dan White Case

In 1978 Dan White, a former San Francisco county supervisor, was charged with the murders of San Francisco mayor George Moscone and a member of the county's Board of Supervisors, Harvey Milk. Psychiatrists testifying for the defense asserted that White was depressed, a symptom of which was compulsive eating of junk food. This argument became known in the media as the "Twinkie" defense. White was found guilty of the less serious homicide offense of manslaughter. The jury's opting for the lesser verdict is consistent with a finding that White did not have the malice intent required for a conviction of murder but did have a lesser intent merely to kill. This was an example of diminished capacity. In the 1980s the Dan White case and others with less notoriety led to restrictions by courts and legislatures in many jurisdictions on the types of forensic testimony that could be presented with respect to criminal intent and to the abolition of diminished capacity defense in some.

No area of forensic psychiatry or psychology is more controversial than the dual issue of diminished capacity and failure to form intent, which in some cases has led to reduced convictions. Perceived abuses of these arguments in the 1980s led to restrictions on the types of forensic testimony that could be presented with respect to criminal intent in many jurisdictions and to the abolition of diminished capacity in some. Notwithstanding the restrictions on diminished capacity and failure to form intent, mental defenses based on negated intent continue to be asserted in new forms. Most notably during the 1990s, post-traumatic stress disorder was claimed to negate or diminish criminal intent in cases involving spousal and child abuse or war-related trauma; the implication was that the disorder rendered a person incapable of knowing that what he or she was doing was wrong. Characterized by some as legal recognition of reality and by others as the abuse excuse, these new applications of old intent defenses demonstrate that the concept of mens rea is still vital in criminal law and that forensic experts are still required to resolve issues of criminal culpability.

In addition to assessments of competency, which address the defendant's current mental functioning, the forensic psychiatrist provides expertise concerning the defendant's mental state at the time of the crime. That both the defense and the prosecution may use forensic psychiatrists to support their theories of the case related to intent sometimes results in dueling doctors giving divergent opinions.

Insanity

The original common-law defense regarding the mental element of crimes was insanity. From the fourteenth century the English judicial system considered "madness" as negating criminal intent. But not until 1843, when the English House of Lords, acting somewhat like a modern appellate court, clearly defined *insanity* in the case of Daniel M'Naghten, did the insanity defense, in which the defendant may use his or her mental state at the time of the crime to avoid punishment, come into being.

Over the years the insanity defense has been controversial; there have been many changes in its application and effect. Almost all jurisdictions apply some version of the defense, but it is difficult to generalize across them. In most jurisdictions in the United States, insanity is an affirmative defense that must be proved by the defendant. In addition, most jurisdictions require that the defendant prove some variant of the original M'Naghten rule. This requires that the defendant, at the time of the crime, be "labouring under such a defect of reason, from disease of the mind, as not to know the nature and quality of the act he was doing, or if he did know it, that he did not know he was doing what was wrong." This essentially cognitive test, based on nineteenth-century medical and legal notions, has been extremely difficult to reconcile with modern medical knowledge about mental illness. Consequently, alternate tests have been posited. Notable examples are the Durham, or product, rule (established in 1954), which requires only that the defendant establish that his or her conduct was the product of a mental disease or defect, and the irresistible-impulse test, in which the defendant's responsibility is to establish that he or she lost the power to choose between right and wrong to avoid doing the criminal act.

A rule proposed in 1962 by the American Law Institute (ALI) has drawn a great deal of attention: it excuses criminal responsibility if the defendant, as the result of a mental disease or defect, lacked substantial capacity either to appreciate the criminality or wrongfulness of his or her act or to conform his or her conduct to the requirements of law. This hybrid cognitive-volitional approach has been widely praised by both legal and medical commentators as an improvement over the M'Naghten and cognitive tests (although thoroughly embraced by almost no one) and has been adopted by some courts and legislatures. However, because all of the attempts to reform the M'Naghten rule introduce some liberalization in the application of the insanity defense, this movement has been slow, and in some instances reversed. In 1982 the California electorate amended the state constitution in order to revert from the ALI test established by the California Supreme Court in 1978 to a preexisting and more restrictive M'Naghten variant.

In insanity cases forensic psychiatrists and psychologists evaluate the defendant's mental condition at the time of the crime. Validity is difficult to determine and is complicated by potential manipulation and malingering by the defendant. However, legal findings of insanity are rare, even when mental illness is unmistakable. By the end of the twentieth century insanity had become a peculiarly legal concept relating to culpability and punishment. (The word *insanity* was long ago discarded by the medical profession.) Consequently, even when the testimony of experts supports the existence of mental illness, the goal of that testimony is not necessarily a verdict of not guilty by reason of insanity.

A common misconception is that individuals found not guilty by reason of insanity are released without further consequence. This misperception was fueled by the outcome of the trial of John Hinckley, Jr., who attempted to assassinate President Ronald Reagan on 30 March 1981. Hinckley, who was found not guilty by reason of insanity of the shootings of Reagan and his press secretary, James Brady, was subsequently committed to St. Elizabeth's Hospital in Washington, D.C. At the time, federal court practice did not mandate commitment to a mental institution for those found not guilty by reason of insanity. That practice later changed, with all states and the federal courts being able to use some form of judicial commitment subsequent to a finding of not guilty by reason of insanity. Some states commit an individual found not guilty by reason of insanity to a hospital for involuntary treatment by virtue of that finding alone. A few states use an approach dubbed "guilty, but mentally ill," in which the defendant is committed to a mental hospital until he or she no longer requires treatment and then spends the remainder of a sentence in prison.

Post-Conviction Proceedings

In many jurisdictions forensic psychiatrists and psychologists have a significant role in determining the disposition of the criminal case. In cases of not guilty by reason of insanity, for example, these experts assess treatment needs and violence potential for the purpose of determining the place of treatment. It is also common for psychiatric and psychological evaluations to be used by judges in support of sentencing decisions. For example, if the forensic evaluation suggests that a defendant's judgment was impaired by a mental disability or that his criminal conduct was encouraged by susceptibility to duress or domination by a crime partner, a judge could decide to mitigate the sentence or to recommend a rehabilitative disposition such as probation. Conversely, if the forensic evaluation suggests that the defendant's mental condition increases the likelihood of a repeated offense, the sentence imposed could be more severe.

A controversial area for forensic psychiatrists is their participation in capital trials (those cases in which guilt could be punishable by death). Many psychiatrists and psychologists believe that the ethics of their profession are inconsistent with the life-or-death impact their participation might generate. Nevertheless, they regularly testify on behalf of the prosecution and defense in capital trials. Those called to testify by the defense ordinarily are asked to provide clinical assessments of mental illness and its mitigating effects. Those called by the prosecution ordinarily are asked to negate the assessment of mental illness and its mitigating effects or to assess the potential for violence and harm to others if the defendant lives.

Perhaps the most controversial area of forensic psychiatry and psychology is the assessment of violence potential, colloquially called the prediction of dangerousness. Although substantial progress has been made in assessing the pathology and behavioral aspects of violence potential, legal controversy has arisen over the use of such assessments for civil commitments based on public safety. Forensic psychiatrists have been called on to assess violence potential in special court proceedings such as those leading to the commitment of mentally disordered offenders and sexually violent predators.

In 1997 the U.S. Supreme Court validated the Kansas Sexually Violent Predator (SVP) Act in *Kansas v. Hendricks,* a case that clearly illustrates the controversial nature of these laws; similar laws have been enacted in many states. By his own admission, Leroy Hendricks had what the Supreme Court described as a "chilling history of repeated child sexual molestation and abuse." When Hendricks's sentence to prison for a 1984 conviction was about to expire in 1994, the state of Kansas sought to commit him involuntarily under its newly enacted SVP law. Nominally a civil-commitment statute, the SVP law was directed at released prisoners whose risk to the public could not be adequately addressed under traditional civil-commitment laws, according to the Kansas legislature. Under the act, commitment proceedings could be undertaken for "any person previously convicted or charged with a sexually violent offense and who suffers from a mental abnormality or personality disorder which makes the person likely to engage in predatory acts of sexual violence." The statute defined *mental abnormality* as a "congenital or acquired condition affecting the emotional or volitional capacity which predisposes the person to commit sexually violent offenses in a degree constituting such person a menace to the health and safety of others." Hendricks successfully convinced the Kansas State Supreme Court that the SVP law's definition of *mental abnormality* did not satisfy the Constitution's guarantee of due process of law; previous U.S. Supreme Court decisions had required that a mental illness underlie civil commitments for involuntary treatment.

Hendricks repeated this argument to the U.S. Supreme Court, supported by a brief from the American Psychiatric Association, among others. However, the Supreme Court sharply rejected the argument, holding that the term *mental illness* is "devoid of any talismanic significance" and that the Court had "traditionally left to legislators the task of defining terms of a medical nature that have legal significance." Hence, the Court sustained the Kansas SVP statute and paved a broad path for enactment of new public-safety-driven civil commitments based on legislative specification of mental conditions and forensic predictions of dangerousness.

Although the debate rages in both the legal and psychiatric communities about the role of mental-health professionals in criminal law, it is plain that forensic psychiatry and psychology will continue to grow. Finally, although the insanity defense and related issues have generated publicity and controversy, it is, and always has been, extremely rare that psychiatric defenses result in the releasing of criminals from culpability.

BIBLIOGRAPHY

Appelbaum, Paul S., and Thomas G. Gutheil. *Clinical Handbook of Psychiatry and the Law*. 2d ed. Baltimore: Williams and Wilkins, 1991.

Melton, Gary, et al. *Psychological Evaluations for the Court: A Handbook for Mental Health Professionals and Lawyers*. 2d ed. New York: Guilford, 1997.

Moriarty, Jane C. *Psychological and Scientific Evidence in Criminal Trials*. New York: Clark Boardman Callaghan, 1997.

Rosner, Richard, ed. *Principles and Practice of Forensic Psychiatry*. New York: Chapman and Hall, 1994.

Shuman, Daniel W. *Psychiatric and Psychological Evidence*. 2d ed. St. Paul, Minn.: West Group, 1997.

Stone, Alan. *Law, Psychiatry, and Morality*. Washington, D.C.: American Psychiatric Press, 1984.

Ziskin, Jay. *Coping with Psychiatric and Psychological Testimony*. 5th ed. Los Angeles: Law and Psychiatry Press, 1995.

BRUCE H. GROSS
DAVID MEYER

See also **Psychopathy, Biology of.**

FORENSIC SCIENCE

Forensic science is the application of scientific principles and methods to legal problems. The modern guiding principle in forensic science is the concept that when two objects come into contact, there is a transfer of trace evidence. This transfer may lead to the identification of the people and objects involved in a crime as well as a description of what occurred during its commission. Forensic science has, to a degree, involved almost every known scientific discipline and art.

Expert knowledge and opinion is often required to assist the court in understanding physical evidence. In modern times, the court is either a judge or a jury, but historically it was any tribunal whose task it was to determine the truth in a contested matter. Practitioners of forensic science are often scientific detectives who investigate and analyze evidence so as to present it in a format that can aid the court in determining a verdict.

Historical Development

As society evolved laws and enforcement tribunals, it developed a need for experts to render opinions regarding evidence. Legal procedures and substantive law developed to guide the use of expert testimony and findings in the judicial system. To appreciate the present state of forensics one must understand its historical development.

Pre-twentieth-century forensics was primitive compared with today's scientific standards. Many legal issues were products of rigid social paradigms and superstition. For example, in seventeenth-century America the Salem witch trials employed nonscientific forensic techniques for the identification of witches. One technique involved pricking the skin to find spots that produced no pain. If the suspected witch was lucky, she (or he) only had to endure the physical discomfort of this test. Another witch-detecting technique was to see if a person floated or sank when forced under water in a pond, with the former seen as evidence of guilt. If victims did not float or even drowned, they were viewed as innocent.

Forensic science in the United States evolved in accordance with existing scientific knowledge, which meant that it was not until the mid to late twentieth century that modern forensic methods began to appear. Even in the twentieth century there are examples of questionable science and superstition applied in a legal context. The United States Supreme Court case of *People v. Buck* (1927) sanctioned the forcible sterilization of an individual based on the prevailing acceptance of eugenics, which held that the human race could be "improved" through the control of reproduction. It was reported that thousands of mentally disabled or otherwise "undesirable" people were sterilized before this pseudoscience was discredited and eugenics rejected. In the famous trial of *Tennessee v. John Scopes* (1925), a high school teacher was charged with illegally teaching the theory of evolution. The *Scopes* trial demonstrated the conflict between scientific thinking and popular opinion based on religious and social beliefs.

In the early 1950s the American Academy of Forensic Sciences (AAFS) was created to establish a forum in which forensic practitioners from diverse disciplines could set up professional societies. Although some disciplines progressed faster than others, the AAFS provided forensic practitioners the opportunity to develop as a professional community as well as a platform to question the reliability of new forensic practices and techniques.

As science advanced in the twentieth century, professional growth in forensic science increased. Many forensic practitioners, including those specializing in arson, ballistics and firearms, fingerprints, and questioned documents, gained their skills not through scientific training but through traditional police work. Scientifically trained forensic disciplines were limited until the later twentieth century, and some of them inherited certain limitations. For example, forensic pathology is a branch of medicine that manages problems in the legal determination of the cause and manner of death and collects evidence from the body to assist the overall legal investigation. Pathology is the branch of medicine that generally deals with causes of death not related to criminal or legal circumstances. Most medical pathology programs provide little training in forensic pathology. Although the latter became a medical subspecialty in 1959, many forensic determinations continue to be made by general pathologists.

Presently there are two general types of medicolegal investigative systems in the United States: (1) coroner systems, which may involve nonexperts providing forensic opinions, and (2) medical examiner systems. Even in the latter there is a shortage of forensic pathologists, and general doctors are used to provide forensic opinion. Certain public forensic medical investigations have demonstrated the diversity of opinion offered in forensic pathology.

In the 1980s a phenomenal growth in knowledge in molecular biology enabled the forensic human-identification community to be educated and trained by the established scientific communities in genetics, population genetics, computer science, and molecular biology. The forensic community adapted its traditional forensic experience in applying these new technologies to the solving of crimes.

Most forensic science disciplines are internally regulated, unlike medicine, pharmacy, and hospital-related services. The only external check on the forensic profession independent of the forensic community is the degree and skill of lawyers who cross-examine forensic opinion.

Broad categories of development in traditional forensic science include the identification of individuals and the analysis of anatomical injuries, weapons and tools, poisons and chemicals, and trace evidence. All of these subjects are common issues in crimes.

Human Identification

Initially, the identification of suspects was accomplished by matching personal objects found at crime scenes to their owners. Later, forensic science developed techniques for identifying suspects based on minute physical evidence. It was discovered centuries ago that human fingers leave identifiable impressions, called ridge endings, which are now commonly known as fingerprints. The first use of fingerprints may have been to establish ownership and identity, as evidenced by fingerprints found on clay tablets recording business transactions in ancient Babylon and prints found on ancient Chinese seals. Fingerprint impressions have also been found on official government papers from fourteenth-century Persia.

By the late nineteenth century Sir Edward Henry developed general class characteristics of human fingerprints that became the basis in most English-speaking countries of fingerprint classification systems for the storage and retrieval of fingerprint files. Because fingerprint impressions are not controlled genetically but are a result of embryonic development, no two individuals have identical prints, not even identical twins. Today, fingerprints are classified according to three patterns—loops, whorls, and arches. Approximately 60 percent of fingerprints feature loops, 35 percent whorls, and the remaining 5 percent arches. Fingernail types are then further broken down into subcategories based on patterns of lines called ridges. The specific ridge characteristics are the basis for comparison and identification. By 1902 some New York government agencies were using fingerprints in an organized manner for testing, and by 1903 the identification of criminals in New York City was being done through the use of fingerprints.

Today, police departments have on record millions of fingerprints that can be retrieved and identified by computer technology. Government agencies employ automated fingerprint identification systems (AFIS) to process and identify fingerprints. AFIS technology converts images of fingerprints into digital information that can be analyzed and compared by ridge characteristics. The final identification of a fingerprint is accomplished by a fingerprint examiner using modern tools. Technology has improved the methods for detecting and recovering latent prints. Fingerprint analysts today routinely employ fingerprint powders, iodine fuming, ninhydrin, silver nitrate, Super Glue fuming, and laser and UV light fluorescence.

The Development of Blood Evidence

Crime scenes frequently yield biological evidence including blood, semen, tissue, hair, and saliva. In the late nineteenth century scientific development allowed for chemical presumptive tests for blood. During the early twentieth century tests were developed to distinguish between human and nonhuman blood.

In the early twentieth century Karl Landsteiner won the Nobel Prize for his discovery that human blood was of different types. From this finding, Landsteiner developed the A-B-O system of classification, making it possible for blood evidence to be identified as A, B, O, or AB. If a forensic bloodstain was type A, then the victim or suspect could be placed in a class of donors who shared this type, excluding the rest of the population. However, blood typing was limited forensically, since large percentages of the general population have the same blood type. By utilizing advanced techniques such as electrophoresis, research conducted through the 1960s and 1970s uncovered other genetically controlled "biological markers" in blood, such as polymorphic enzymes. These techniques allowed the forensic scientist to further limit the class of donors who could have donated a blood sample or other biological evidence.

In the 1980s, with the development of DNA technology, genes could be directly identified from biological samples. Rather than identifying genetic expressions of genes in the form of general blood types and enzymes, DNA technology allowed the recognition of the genes themselves. The advantage of DNA forensic typing was that the rarity of donor class established was usually one in a mil-

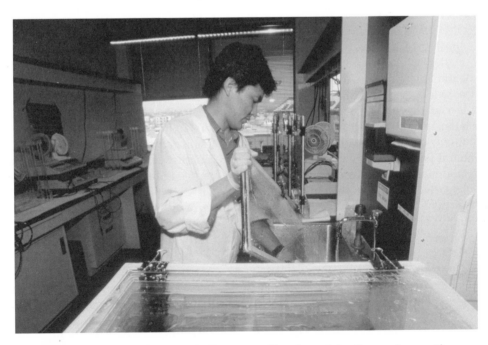

A scientist at Whitehead Institute in Boston readies glass plates for use in genetics experiments in a DNA lab. The plates hold genes and gels that can be read with lasers.
CORBIS/ROGER RESSMEYER

lion, billion, or even trillion. The result was a much more effective matching of biological evidence to individuals.

Forensic DNA Testing

Forensic DNA testing is a process of isolating polymorphic genes, determining the frequency of occurrence of those genes in a given population, establishing whether there is a match of evidence to known samples, and finally assigning the match a statistical frequency of occurrence.

The first widely used forensic DNA test employed restriction fragment length polymorphism (RFLP) genes. RFLP genes are identified based on genetically determined length measured in nucleotide base pairs. Forensic scientists devised matching and statistical strategies to declare a potential correspondence between forensic biological evidence and a suspect or victim. These methods were extremely sensitive to environmental degradation of the DNA, and frequently evidence was not suitable for RFLP DNA testing.

In 1993 Kary B. Mullis won the Nobel Prize for his discovery of the polymerase chain reaction (PCR). The PCR process revolutionized a number of scientific disciplines, including forensic serology. The PCR process is a method by which small quantities of DNA can be replicated from an original sample. Thus PCR technology allowed for very small biological samples from a crime scene to be multiplied and then analyzed and compared with biological samples from suspects. The advantage of using PCR-based DNA testing over RFLP testing was that extremely small quantities of biological material could be tested despite the process of biological degradation that occurs in the crime-scene environment. The forensic serologist could now identify the owner of a discarded cigarette butt, or match a few hairs, as well as trace blood and semen evidence, to an individual.

Forensic serologists select gene systems that are highly polymorphic, or in other words highly variable among individuals for a given population. For example, several loci used in RFLP DNA testing may have hundreds of alleles, or alternative forms of genes, in the human gene pool. Any one individual can have a maximum of only two of these alleles in a specific gene pool. The higher the diversity of a gene pool at a particular locus, the less the probability that two people in a given population will have the same two alleles. Thus gene systems that are highly polymorphic provide higher discrimination among individuals. The loci selected for PCR testing have smaller gene pools than in the RFLP method, but PCR allows for multiple loci testing in the same forensic specimen, thus improving the chance of successful DNA typing. Moreover, the PCR method requires only a few human cells. With PCR testing, by analyzing a small number of cells it is now possible to identify a blood sample as likely having originated from a single individual.

The forensic community displays DNA typing results as genotypes. A genotype is the genetic constitution of an organism, as distinguished from its physical appearance, or phenotype. An example of a genotype is (bl, br), which identifies an individual who received a blue eye gene (bl) from one parent and a brown eye gene (br) from the other. His phenotype would be brown eyes, since the brown gene is dominant. A typical forensic DNA typing report, in this case describing the victim of a sexual assault, the perpetrator (as identified in the sexual assault kit sample), and two suspects, appears in the accompanying table.

Here suspect 1 has the same genetic profile as the individual whose semen was found in the sexual assault kit recovered from the victim. Suspect 2 can be eliminated as a suspect, since his genetic profile is different from the semen recovered in the

TABLE 1. DNA Loci Tested by PCR Methods (Reported as Genotypes)

Source	DQ-alpha	LDLR	GYPA	HBGG	D7S8	GC	D1S80	CSF1PO	TPOX	THO1	Frequency
Victim	1.1,3	BB	BB	AB	AB	Ab	17,21	10,10	8,9	7,9	
Suspect 1	1.1,4	BB	BB	AC	AA	BB	24,17	10,10	7,8	8,8	1 in 36 million*
Suspect 2	1.2,3	BB	BB	BB	AA	BB	20,17	10,10	7,9		
Sexual Assault Kit Sample	1.1,4	BB	BB	AC	AA	BB	24,17	10,10	7,8	8,8	

*Number is fictional but typical of a number generated from a genetic population database for Caucasians.

sexual assault kit. The legal significance of this match is that only one individual randomly selected from 36 million people would be expected to have the same genetic profile as suspect 1. It is not unusual for DNA testing to produce random match probabilities in billions or even trillions. In this case, the court would probably be convinced, based on this DNA typing report, that the semen came from suspect 1. The significance of this type of evidence is expressed statistically by use of a mathematical equation called the product rule. The product rule is the method of calculation based on population genetics that allows individual gene (allele) frequencies to be multiplied together to generate the rarity of a genetic profile. The plausibility of a biological match based on the statistical expression generated by the product rule was the subject of the greatest legal-forensic debate in history.

Legal Challenges to DNA Evidence

When novel scientific evidence is first introduced into a courtroom, its admissibility may be challenged. Rules of evidence vary by jurisdiction. Since 1923, the federal rules have been governed by *Frye v. United States,* in which it was decided that a proponent of courtroom evidence had to demonstrate that there was a general consensus within the appropriate scientific community that a technique was accepted as reliable. This rule was modified in *Daubert v. Merrell Dow Pharmaceuticals, Inc.* (1993) Each state also has their own rules of admissibility with respect to novel scientific techniques. The law provides guidance to the judge in deciding whether proffered scientific evidence is reliable. Initially, issues of DNA admissibility were so complex that widespread litigation occurred before final judicial decisions were made at the highest court levels.

The first use of forensic DNA evidence in American jurisprudence occurred in the case of *State of Florida v. Andrews* in October 1988. Florida and other states rapidly followed with a series of prosecutions based on RFLP DNA testing. In 1989 the first significant legal challenge to RFLP testing was mounted in the case of *State of New York v. Castro.* The evidence in the Castro case was so technically flawed that it instigated a scientific debate regarding the reliability of RFLP evidence. In 1989 the case of *United States v. Yee* (Ohio) was the setting for a clash between world-class scientists, who challenged each other over the reliability of RFLP evidence. Both sides knew that DNA evidence had

great potential but the opponents argued that more scientific work was necessary before it could be acceptable in the courtroom. The debate intensified to a degree that the National Research Council (NRC) initiated a study in January 1990. The NRC is the operational branch of the National Academy of Sciences; one of its functions is to assist government in understanding complex scientific problems. The first NRC report, released in April 1992, was controversial and the debate continued until the NRC issued its second and final report in December 1996. The Federal Bureau of Investigation, the National Institutes of Health Human Genome Center, the National Institute of Justice, the National Science Foundation, and two nonfederal sources, the Sloan Foundation and the State Justice Institute, financially supported the NRC DNA investigation. The second NRC report validated forensic DNA testing despite objections from small minorities of the legal and scientific communities.

Future of DNA Testing

It is anticipated that the newer PCR DNA tests, including Short Tandem Repeat (STR) testing, will replace RFLP DNA testing for use in legal proceedings. (STR genes are smaller than RFLP genes and therefore less susceptible to environmental degradation.) Even in 1990, law-enforcement organizations realized that forensic DNA testing data could be organized in a fashion similar to fingerprint databases. The FBI began to create computerized genetic databases that stored the genetic profiles of criminals as well as ordinary citizens. It became important to standardize the process of DNA testing among law-enforcement agencies so that their forensic DNA testing was compatible with the national genetic databases. Now if a criminal left his blood or other biological sample including hair, semen, saliva, or tissue at a crime scene, he could be identified through his genetic records. Legislation was implemented throughout the United States to help implement the National Genetic Database. Genetic research is expected to produce other genetic databases relating to susceptibility to disease and potential behavioral characteristics. Such databases are controversial, since they provoke constitutional issues concerning the right to privacy.

Analysis of Weapons and Tools

The discharge of firearms leaves microscopic clues that can link a bullet to a particular weapon.

Microscopic marks left on the surfaces of interacting objects allow for object identification. The processes of everyday use and manufacturing impart unique, minute features to the surface of these objects that leave a signature impression on other objects they encounter. Modern firearms employ firing pins, ejector mechanisms, barrels, and standardized cartridges. When a weapon is discharged, the bullet is marked by the lands and groove of the barrel, imparting on it a unique signature that allows the bullet to be identified as having traveled through a specific gun barrel. Likewise, other moving parts of a gun also impart specific signatures on the cartridge of the bullet. A forensic firearm examiner will compare a recovered bullet to the suspect firearm. Tools like pry bars and screwdrivers are capable of leaving telltale signatures on the crime-scene environment. The accuracy of the comparison is highly dependent on the skills of the examiner and the forensic training received. The skill level of the forensic examination varies widely and is a cause of concern in some jurisdictions.

Drug and Chemical Identification

Typical forensic investigations involve the identification of drugs and chemicals. These problems involve the science of toxicology, chemistry, and pharmacology. This area of forensics deals with analyzing blood and urine for the presence of drugs and alcohol and relating the findings to use and behavior. Modern drug analysis involves sophisticated instruments such as mass spectrometers, radio-immuno assay, infrared spectrometers, and other sophisticated instruments that can be supported by computer library systems that can detect and identify nanogram amounts of drugs, explosives, arson-related compounds, and any other chemical compound.

Criminalistics

Forensic science developed as a class of scientific investigators called criminalists cultivated specialties in analyzing trace evidence found at crime scenes. The area of forensics known as criminalistics describes a broad area of forensics whose practitioners evaluate and compare physical evidence found at crime scenes. Such evidence can include arson and explosive residues, blood spatter patterns, broken items, botanical items, gunshot residues, fiber, hair, inks, paint, paper, shoe prints, soil, and wood comparisons. Specialized analysis of trace evidence has dramatically

improved over the last decade. As the pool of scientific knowledge deepens, so does the scope of inquiry and debate. In the late twentieth century substantial technological advances made possible the development of sophisticated tools and techniques, including the personal computer, the scanning electron microscope, x-ray diffraction, mass spectrometry, and even carbon dating, which have joined the forensic arsenal.

Crime-Scene Investigation

Modern forensic analysis requires careful crime-scene investigation and collection of evidence. Police departments instruct their initial on-scene personnel to preserve the crime scene for professional evidence gatherers. Evidence is carefully photographed and cataloged, and its precise location recorded. At the onset of a police investigation critical evidence may not be readily apparent. Therefore specialty teams are employed to decide what evidence should be collected. Even environmental conditions such as lighting and temperature can be critical in determining what happened at the scene of a crime.

Modern forensics involves a wide field of scientific disciplines and frequently employs scientists who are not specialists in forensics. Today there are a wide number of scientific disciplines, from anthropology to nuclear physics, that partake in forensic investigations. As is the case with science in general, forensics faces obstacles when new evidence collides with preconceived notions. The complexity of human interaction at a crime scene can produce so much conflicting evidence that a clear solution is impossible. Specialists from many scientific pursuits are now recruited to solve crimes. The future of forensics is likely to be involved in helping to determine the underlying reasons for crime. Society will be forced to reexamine cultural paradigms in hopes of preventing crimes. And modern technology, as it is used to profile and catalog individuals right down to their genetic makeup, will continue to present challenges to revered constitutional rights.

BIBLIOGRAPHY

FORENSICS

Cowgers, James F. *Friction Ridge Skin: Comparison and Identification of Fingerprints.* Boca Raton, Fla.: CRC Press, 1993.

Di Maio, Vincent J. M. *Gunshot Wounds: Practical Aspects of Firearms, Ballistics, and Forensic Techniques.* 2d ed. Boca Raton, Fla.: CRC Press, 1999.

Houts, Marshall, Randall C. Baselt, and Robert H. Cravey. *Courtroom Toxicology*. 6 vols. New York: Matthew Bender, 1981.

Kirk, Paul Leland, and John D. DeHaan, *Kirk's Fire Investigation*. 4th ed. Englewood Cliffs, N.J.: Prentice Hall, 1997.

Lee, Henry, C., and R. E. Gaensslen. *Advances in Fingerprint Technology*. New York: Elsevier, 1991.

Saferstein, Richard, ed. *Forensic Science Handbook*. 3 vols. Englewood Cliffs, N.J.: Prentice-Hall, 1982.

Sensabaugh, G. F., and E. T. Blake. "DNA Analysis in Biological Evidence: Application of the Polymerase Chain Reaction." In *Forensic Science Handbook*, edited by Richard Saferstein. Vol. 3. Englewood Cliffs, N.J.: Prentice-Hall, 1993.

Spitz, Werner U., ed. *Spitz and Fisher's Medicolegal Investigation of Death: Guidelines for the Application of Pathology to Crime Investigation*. 3d ed. Springfield, Ill.: Thomas, 1993.

Whitehead, P. H. "A Historical Review of the Characterization of Blood and Secretion Stains in the Forensic Laboratory.—Part One: Bloodstains." *Forensic Science Review* 5 (1993).

DNA EVIDENCE

Blake, Edward, Jennifer Mihalovich, Russell Higuchi, P. S. Walsh, and Henry Erlich. "Polymerase Chain Reaction (PCR) Amplification and Human Leukocyte Antigen (HLA)-DQalpha Oligonucleotide Typing on Biological Evidence Samples: Casework Experience." *Journal of Forensic Science* 37, no. 3 (1992): 700–726.

Congress of the United States. Office of Technology Assessment. *Genetic Witness: Forensic Uses of DNA Tests*. Washington, D.C: U.S. Government Printing Office, 1990.

Inman, Keith, and Norah Rudin. *An Introduction to Forensic DNA Analysis*. Boca Raton, Fla.: CRC Press, 1997.

Jeffrey, Alex, A. J. Wilson, and V. Thein. "Individual-Specific 'Fingerprints' of Human DNA." *Nature* 316 (4–10 July 1985): 76–79.

National Research Council. Committee on DNA Forensic Science. *The Evaluation of Forensic DNA Evidence*. Washington, D.C.: National Academy Press, 1996.

National Research Council. Committee on DNA Technology in Forensic Science. *DNA Technology in Forensic Science*. Washington, D.C.: National Academy Press, 1992.

Lander, Eric S. "DNA Fingerprinting on Trial." *Nature* 339 (15 June 1989): 501–505.

———. "Invited Editorial: Research on DNA Typing Catching Up with Courtroom Application." *American Journal of Human Genetics* 48, no. 5 (May 1991): 819–823.

Lewontin, R. C. *Biology as Ideology: The Doctrine of DNA*. New York: HarperPerennial, 1992.

———. "Which Population?" *American Journal of Human Genetics* 52, no. 1 (1993): 205–206.

Lewontin, Richard C., and Daniel L. Hartl. "Population Genetics in Forensic DNA Typing." *Science* 254, no. 5039 (20 Dec. 1991): 1745–1750.

Saferstein, Richard. *Criminalistics: An Introduction to Forensic Science*. 6th ed. Upper Saddle River, N.J.: Prentice-Hall, 1998.

Sensabaugh, George, and Cecilia Von Beroldingen. "The Polymerase Chain Reaction: Application to the Analysis of Biological Evidence." In *Forensic DNA Technology*, edited by Mark A. Farley and James J. Harrington. Chelsea, Mich.: Lewis, 1991.

Weir, "Population Genetics in the Forensic DNA Debate." *Proceedings of the National Academy of Sciences*, 89, no. 24 (15 Dec. 1992): 11,654–11,659.

Witkowski, Jan. "Milestones in the Development of DNA Technology." In *Forensic DNA Technology*, edited by Mark A. Farley and James J. Harrington. Chelsea, Mich.: Lewis, 1991.

WALTER F. KRSTULJA

See also **Genetics; Police.**

FRANK, LEO
(1884–1915)

Born to a Jewish family in Paris, Texas, on 17 April 1884, Leo Frank was raised in the North, educated at Cornell University, and brought to Atlanta in 1908 to help run his uncle's pencil factory. In 1910 he married a native Atlantan, Lucille Selig. But in 1913 Frank's favored life abruptly turned nightmarish. Accused—unjustly, according to many observers and historians—of the brutal murder of his thirteen-year-old employee Mary Phagan, Frank was buffeted by diverse forces: southern resentment over industrialization, an aggressive prosecutor, an incompetent defense team, and a city's vengeful rage.

The last person to see the victim alive, nervous when first interviewed by the police, and not where he claimed to be at about the time the child was killed, Frank quickly became the leading suspect. The case dominated the news in Atlanta from 27 April 1913 (the day after Mary's death) through the end of August, when Frank's trial concluded and Judge Leonard Roan sentenced him to hang.

Circumstantial evidence, however, pointed to the state's main witness against him, Jim Conley, a sweeper whom Frank supervised in the pencil factory, where Mary also worked and met her doom. Conley, an early suspect who had changed his testimony several times after he had been apprehended by the police for having washed blood from a shirt in the factory basement, remained in custody and seclusion for six weeks before the trial. Although he offered interrogators four different versions of how the murder occurred, he consistently claimed that he had helped Frank to dispose of the body. On the witness stand Conley

Leo Frank. LIBRARY OF CONGRESS

gave a brilliant performance for fifteen hours, explaining how he had "watched out" in the past while Frank allegedly entertained young women in his office. Racist observers believed that Conley, an African American, was not intelligent enough to concoct so convincing a story, especially since Frank's lawyers, reputedly two of the best in the South, could not shake his testimony in protracted cross-examination.

Outside the first-floor courtroom mobs of people gathered each day, cheering the prosecutor as he entered and left the building and shouting threats to the jury through the open windows: "Hang the Jew or we'll hang you." Before the trial ended, the judge conferred with attorneys for both sides about how to protect Frank after the jury delivered its verdict. Fearing that Frank might be lynched, Roan suggested that the defendant absent himself when the jurors returned. Thus Frank was safely in jail when the citizens of Atlanta learned that he had been found guilty.

Frank's attorneys launched three appeals to the Georgia Supreme Court and two to the U.S. Supreme Court, but all failed because of legal tech-

nicalities. The case then came to Governor John M. Slaton of Georgia, whose carefully deliberated decision to change Frank's death sentence to life imprisonment sparked riots in Atlanta; menacing hordes converged on the governor's mansion. The National Guard protected Slaton until his term of office ended four days later, when they escorted him out of the state.

In prison only one month, Frank again felt victimized as a fellow prisoner slashed his throat with a knife. A doctor mended the wound, but about a month later, on 15 August 1915, a band of "the best citizens" of Marietta, Georgia, Mary Phagan's hometown, stormed the prison farm at Milledgeville, kidnapped Frank, and then drove him back to Marietta, where they lynched him the next morning.

The Frank case traumatized the Jews of Atlanta, who thereafter shrank from any controversial behavior that might arouse Georgians. Many Jews think Frank was tried, convicted, and lynched because he was Jewish; but in Georgia, Frank—to many southerners at the time a symbol of the depredations of an alien industrialism—was "guilty as sin" and had his sentence commuted because of the influence of rich out-of-state Jews. In one sense they were correct: although no corruption was evident in the posttrial maneuvers, a poor man would not likely have had friends who could finance successive judicial appeals and promote the national outcry that forced Governor Slaton to spend ten days reviewing the case.

The Frank case has remained a horrible memory in the annals of American Jewish history and attracted authors and playwrights over the next several decades. In 1937 MGM produced a movie, *They Won't Forget*, depicting what happened in Georgia in 1913–1915. Books on the subject were written in the 1950s (*Night Fell on Georgia*, by Charles and Louise Samuels), the 1960s (*A Little Girl Is Dead*, by Harry Golden, and *The Leo Frank Case*, by Leonard Dinnerstein), as well as in the 1970s and 1980s.

In 1982 the Nashville *Tennessean* published a special section on the case because it found an eighty-two-year-old man, Alonzo Mann, who had seen Jim Conley carrying Mary Phagan's body on the day of the murder. If Mann, who had remained silent at the time of the murder, had informed police within the next day or two what he saw, it is unlikely that Frank would have been arrested, tried, or convicted. And he certainly would not have been lynched.

In the 1990s the case continued to fascinate. Steve Oney, a journalist, was preparing a book on the case. And Alfred Uhry, a playwright who grew up among the German Jewish elite of Atlanta, wrote the book for a musical, *Parade*, based on the Frank case; it opened at Lincoln Center in New York City in December 1998.

BIBLIOGRAPHY

Dinnerstein, Leonard. *The Leo Frank Case.* New York: Columbia University Press, 1968.

MacLean, Nancy. "The Leo Frank Case Reconsidered: Gender and Sexual Politics in the Making of Reactionary Populism." *Journal of American History* 78 (December 1991): 917–948.

LEONARD DINNERSTEIN

See also **Atlanta; Jews; Ku Klux Klan; Lynching.**

FREEDOM RIDES

Working under the auspices of the Congress of Racial Equality (CORE) in 1961, civil rights activists who became known as freedom riders provoked segregationist violence in the South to pressure President John F. Kennedy into enforcing two Supreme Court decisions banning segregation in interstate travel.

On 4 May 1961 thirteen activists (seven blacks and six whites), who were pledged to nonviolence, set out in two buses from Washington, D.C., heading to New Orleans through the segregated Deep South—Virginia, North and South Carolina, Georgia, Alabama, Mississippi, and Louisiana. Blacks sat in the front of the bus and whites sat in the back to protest the racist seating arrangements of Jim Crowism. They "desegregated" every station along the way by having the black riders use the "white" waiting rooms while the white riders used the "colored" facilities. They encountered little resistance until they reached Alabama.

When the lead bus neared Anniston, Alabama, a mob firebombed it and blocked the exits in an attempt to suffocate the passengers. Twelve riders were hospitalized. Meanwhile, the second bus was met in Birmingham by a mob of Ku Klux Klan members. There, several riders were savagely beaten. After these attacks no Greyhound bus driver would agree to transport the freedom riders, so they reluctantly abandoned their effort and boarded a plane to New Orleans.

Student civil rights activists from Nashville Colleges saw the impasse as a critical moment in the Civil Rights movement. They believed that abandoning the rides because of the threat of violence would encourage other segregationists to use violence to halt integration. When the students arrived in Birmingham to continue the rides, Attorney General Robert F. Kennedy became directly involved. He secured a driver to transport the students after receiving a guarantee from Alabama's staunchly segregationist governor, John Patterson, that the riders would be protected.

At the Birmingham station, state troopers surrounded the bus and a plane circled overhead, but when the bus pulled out of town the state troopers and the plane did not accompany it. In Montgomery a racist mob attacked the bus, shouting "Nigger!" and "Kill the Niggers!" Jim Zwerg, a white freedom rider from Madison, Wisconsin, left the bus first and was immediately pummeled with lead pipes, bricks, and bats. Many other riders were savagely beaten as the police did nothing to intervene. Outraged, Robert Kennedy immediately dispatched six hundred U.S. Marshals to ensure the riders' safety. As Martin Luther King, Jr., gathered with supporters at the First Baptist Church in Montgomery, an angry white mob gathered outside. At around 2:00 A.M., when it seemed as if federal marshals would be unable to keep the mob from burning the church, the governor sent in state troops to restore order.

On 24 May, Alabama troopers led the freedom riders to the state line, and from there they went to Jackson, Mississippi. In Jackson the riders desegregated the waiting rooms and were promptly thrown into a maximum security penitentiary. That summer, over three hundred more freedom riders followed their example, and by September it was estimated that more than seventy thousand students had participated in the movement, with approximately thirty-six hundred arrested. In the fall Robert Kennedy finally convinced the Interstate Commerce Commission to enforce the Supreme Court rulings banning segregation in interstate travel.

The freedom rides were significant in two ways. First, they put the Kennedy administration on notice that campaign rhetoric without action would not be tolerated by civil rights activists. Many activists, according to CORE founder James Farmer, were outraged that President Kennedy had promised a swift end to discrimination in public housing during his 1960 presidential campaign but had

Police officers prepare to arrest Freedom Riders on board the Trailways bus as they arrive in Jackson, Mississippi, on 24 May 1961. Corbis/Bettmann

failed to uphold that promise during his first six months in office. Second, the freedom rides sent a clear message to segregationist white Americans: ugly mob violence could not derail nonviolent efforts to integrate the South. Indeed, the freedom riders had shown that mob violence was actually its own worst enemy, because it turned national opinion against segregation and catalyzed the implementation of integrationist programs on the national level.

BIBLIOGRAPHY

Eyes on the Prize: America's Civil Rights Years, 1954–1965. Public Broadcasting System, 1992. Laser disc and videocassette.

Nash, Diane. "Inside the Sit-ins and the Freedom Rides: Testimony from a Southern Student." In *We Shall Overcome: The Civil Rights Movement in the United States in the 1950s and 1960s.* Vol 3., edited by David J. Garrow. New York: Carlson, 1989.

Riches, William T. Martin. *The Civil Rights Movement: Struggle and Resistance.* New York: St. Martin's, 1997.

ADAM MAX COHEN

See also **Civil Rights Movements; Kennedy, Robert F.**

FREE SPEECH MOVEMENT

In the fall of 1964 student activists at the University of California, Berkeley (UCB), organized the Free Speech Movement (FSM) for the right to conduct political activity on campus. The FSM was both the first major student rebellion of the 1960s and the only one to win total victory. Its triumph inspired activists, both at Berkeley and on other campuses, to stage further protests throughout the decade. Heavily influenced by the Civil Rights movement of the 1960s, the FSM practiced both civil disobedience and nonviolence. The lack of violence (with few exceptions) contrasted greatly with later riotous student demonstrations that erupted out of tensions over race or the Vietnam War.

For years, Berkeley students had routinely set up card tables for political purposes at the edge of campus—the corner of Bancroft and Telegraph. Activists had picked this site because every day a large portion of UCB's twenty-five thousand students passed by and because the university had prohibited on-campus political activity since the 1930s. Conservatives, liberals, and radicals alike distributed literature, gathered supporters' names, and collected funds. Civil rights advocates used the tables to organize local demonstrations. In

Police drag a student demonstrator to jail during the December 1964 sit-in at the University of California, Berkeley, administration building. CORBIS/BETTMANN

September 1964 UCB officials suddenly declared the sidewalk to be school property and banned the tables. Angry, defiant students responded by setting up tables every day in front of the administration building in Sproul Plaza. After lowly bureaucrats cited the protesters for violating university rules, the students invaded Sproul Hall. In a rare violent incident, Mario Savio—a civil rights activist who had just returned from a harrowing summer in Mississippi, where he had been stalked, chased, and beaten repeatedly by angry whites—bit a policeman's leg. He was not charged.

On 1 October 1964 university police visited the tables and arrested Jack Weinberg, a former student and well-known local civil rights leader, and placed him in a police car. Spontaneously, hundreds of students engaged in civil disobedience by sitting down around the vehicle to block its movement. Authorities had never encountered such defiance and did not know what to do; neither side wanted violence. Weinberg remained inside the car for thirty-two hours. During that time, dozens

of students—including Savio, who was a brilliant orator—carefully removed their shoes and climbed atop the car to speak to a crowd of nearly five thousand people. The debate included not only the issues of free speech and political tables on campus, but also the nature and meaning of a college education as well as critiques about society.

Many onlookers later declared the event an epiphany because it had revealed shared hopes and stimulated fresh thinking. The protesters, influenced by Martin Luther King, Jr., and the idea of nonviolence, sang civil rights songs. In the middle of the night, opponents (often from nearby fraternities) harassed the demonstrators by throwing garbage and lighted cigarettes into the crowd, but there were no fights. UCB officials, alarmed by the bad publicity that mass arrests in such a location would bring, ended the demonstration by agreeing to set up an administration-faculty-student committee to change campus rules regarding political speech.

To gain strength during the negotiations, student activists organized the Free Speech Movement. They held a series of rallies at noon in Sproul Plaza and raised money by producing and selling records. Bargaining between activists and administrators over a proposed settlement, however, was stalled. Civil rights supporters insisted that the university could not restrict speech beyond the limits of the U.S. Constitution as interpreted by the federal courts. The administrators, in turn, demanded that students be barred from using the Berkeley campus to plan off-campus demonstrations. Faculty seemed divided and confused; so were students. About one-third favored both FSM goals and nonviolent protests, another third wanted free speech but opposed unlawful demonstrations, and the remaining third backed the administration.

FSM leaders shrewdly concluded that they needed faculty support to overcome the administration's resistance. To gain the professors' backing, the FSM turned to civil disobedience: they organized a massive, nonviolent sit-in in the administration building on 2 December 1964. At a rally beforehand, Savio said, "There is a time when the operation of the machine becomes so odious . . . that . . . you've got to make it stop" (Heirich, pp. 271–272). A large number of students then filed into Sproul Hall. While many FSM leaders came from radical political backgrounds, followers came from diverse political backgrounds. The students who did sit in mirrored fellow students who did not sit in, except that the protesting students had higher grades, an indication that their intentions were serious and not a college prank. As expected, university officials called the police. Borrowing a tactic from the Civil Rights movement, students passively resisted arrest by going limp in order to slow down their removal and thereby maximize the impact of the dramatic arrests on thousands of passersby. Police barred the press from the area and hurled nonviolent demonstrators down terrazzo stairs. They made 773 arrests, which took thirteen hours. Later, enraged faculty organized caravans and bail to retrieve the students from jail.

On 7 December 1964 the administration tried to regain control with a convocation in the outdoor Greek Theatre. The mostly student audience of sixteen thousand or more showed divided opinions. As the meeting ended Savio went onto the stage to announce a student rally. Before he could reach the microphone, however, campus police tackled him and dragged him backstage. The symbolism of a student being physically prevented from speaking in a controversy over free speech was grotesque. The next day the faculty senate voted, 824 to 115, to accept the FSM position demanding no regulation of speech beyond that provided by the U.S. Constitution. University regents overruled the administration and accepted the joint student-faculty position concerning speech on campus. The FSM had won.

Special conditions had produced victory. In part, the FSM won because free speech was embedded both in the Constitution and in popular culture. The FSM, unlike later student groups that focused on narrower issues, rallied supporters from diverse political backgrounds. In addition, university officials were inept compared with protest leaders such as Weinberg and Savio; Weinberg proved to be an experienced civil rights organizer and brilliant strategist, and Savio established himself as a gifted speaker. FSM leaders favored civil disobedience, a tactic that proved effective although controversial among middle-class followers. Both leaders and followers opposed violence, and the police, compared to those involved in later protests at UCB or elsewhere, generally showed restraint.

BIBLIOGRAPHY

Goines, David Lance. *The Free Speech Movement: Coming of Age in the 1960s.* Berkeley, Calif.: Ten Speed Press, 1993.
Heirich, Max A. *The Spiral of Conflict: Berkeley 1964.* New York: Columbia University Press, 1971.
Rorabaugh, W. J. *Berkeley at War: The 1960s.* New York: Oxford University Press, 1989.

W. J. RORABAUGH

See also **Campus; Civil Disobedience; Civil Rights Movements; Nonviolence.**

FRÉMONT, JOHN CHARLES
(1813–1890)

John Charles Frémont, an explorer who became nationally known as "the Pathfinder," probably never killed anyone, but he repeatedly presided

John Charles Frémont. LIBRARY OF CONGRESS

over acts of violence. During his five expeditions to the American West, he gained a reputation for showing defiance toward anyone who blocked his path, and he either countenanced or was responsible for episodes involving charges of cannibalism, the butchery of Indians, and a derring-do defiance toward whoever blocked his path. In that sense, Frémont repeatedly presided over acts of violence, sometimes even against a foreign sovereignty, as during the Mexican War in California.

In 1843, while leading a government surveying expedition, he rashly decided to take his party into the Mexican province of California over the rugged Sierra crest in the dead of winter. During this unauthorized foray, his party was blinded by snow and lashed by cold winds and only narrowly escaped tragedy. Because several of his men had mysteriously disappeared during this adventure, the surviving members of the expedition were later charged with cannibalism.

During 1845, on another western expedition, young Lieutenant Frémont became one of the chief actors in California's conquest by U. S. forces. Outside Monterey, California's provincial capital, while ostensibly heading a scientific expedition, he defied Mexican officials, who had warned him to quit the area, by building a menacing log fort atop Gavilan Mountain; he then withdrew, taking his party northward toward what would later become the California-Oregon border.

While camping in the area inhabited by the Klamath Indians, Frémont failed to post a night guard. During a subsequent raid, several of his men, including two valuable Delaware Indian guides, had their heads split open by enemy tomahawks. Following this outrage, Frémont's guide Kit Carson grabbed the ax of a dead raider and smashed his head with it. A few days later, the explorer gave orders to burn the lodge to "punish these people well for their treachery."

Near Sonoma, Frémont met a band of disgruntled American frontiersmen, most of whom were from Missouri and other midwestern states. On 10 June 1845 these unruly settlers, who would come to be known as Bear Flaggers because their crude banner bore a grizzly bear facing a lone red star, captured a band of Mexican horses and took them to Frémont's campsite. The Bears also imprisoned Mariano Guadalupe Vallejo, the Mexican commandante of northern Calfornia. Frémont indirectly sanctioned the creation of the illegal Bear Flag Republic (June–July 1846)—well before war with Mexico broke out.

In another Indian ambush Kit Carson was almost killed by a poisoned arrow. Frémont saved his life by jumping his horse's hoofs directly upon the Klamath archer. In retaliation, the Klamath was clubbed to death and duly scalped.

Frémont next authorized the violent murder of several Californios (the mostly Mexican and Hispanic settlers) as punishment for their killing of two Americans, Thomas Cowie and George Fowler, at San Rafael. The Californios had tied them to a tree, then shot and hacked the two men to pieces, dumping their bodies into a muddy ditch.

In 1848 Frémont led another western expedition, recklessly plunging into New Mexico's Sangre de Cristo mountains in midwinter. Whipped by chilling winds and deep snowdrifts, he lost a third of his men. Once again, upon his return charges of cannibalism surfaced.

During July 1858 Frémont, carrying only a pistol, defied an armed group of claim jumpers on his Las Mariposas gold-mining property before obtaining legislation that drove them off his land.

Frémont's career was filled with vainglorious escapades that coincided with America's frontier violence. Frémont repeatedly challenged superiors, including military officers and politicians, even President Abraham Lincoln. He died in 1890 at New York City of a burst appendix.

BIBLIOGRAPHY

Harlow, Neal. *California Conquered: War and Peace on the Pacific.* Berkeley: University of California Press, 1982.

Hawgood, John A. "John C. Frémont and the Bear Flag Revolution." *Southern California Quarterly* 4 (June 1962): 67–96.

Marti, Werner M. *Messenger of Destiny.* San Francisco: J. Howell, 1960.

Nevins, Allan. *Frémont: Pathmaker of the West.* New York: D. Appleton-Century, 1939.

Rolle, Andrew. *John Charles Frémont: Character as Destiny.* Norman: University of Oklahoma Press, 1991.

ANDREW ROLLE

See also **Frontier; West.**

FRENCH AND INDIAN WAR

The last and most destructive of the four Anglo-French colonial wars, the French and Indian War (1754–1763) reduced France's New World empire to a few islands, quadrupled the land area of the

British empire, and—together with its European counterpart, the Seven Years' War (1756–1763)—brought the belligerents to the brink of bankruptcy. These dramatic outcomes contributed to the breakdown of Britain's control over its North American colonies and to the American Revolutionary War, which began just twelve years after the return of peace. That the victor so soon fell victim in the aftermath of victory was not the war's only irony. The conflict's decisive outcome resulted from the efforts of European military commanders to limit its violence and bring colonial American patterns of war making into line with the "civilized" practices of European armies.

Contexts and Causes

The first three Anglo-French colonial wars originated in Europe and spread to the New World: King William's War (War of the League of Augsburg), 1689–1697; Queen Anne's War (War of the Spanish Succession), 1702–1713; and King George's War (War of the Austrian Succession), 1744–1748. In this fourth war, hostilities began in North America in 1754 and commenced in Europe two years later. The fighting arose from the confrontation of English and French military forces over control of the Ohio Valley, a circumstance unthinkable before about 1750. This interior region, remote from the core settlements of both empires, had been controlled since the mid-seventeenth century by the Iroquois Confederacy, which claimed ownership on the basis of conquest. Control of the Ohio country, in turn, became a pillar of the confederacy's policy of neutrality in the conflicts between France and Britain.

From the beginning of Iroquois neutrality in 1701, the confederacy's chiefs had allowed European traders to enter the valley and the French to pass through on their way from Canada to France's settlements in the mid-Mississippi Valley (the *pays des Illinois*), but they had forbidden any European settlement. So long as the upper Ohio remained essentially unpopulated, this was an easy policy to maintain, for the French, always more interested in trade than settlement, had benefited from the exclusion of the demographically vigorous British colonists from the interior. The demands of Anglo-American settlers for lands east of the Appalachians, however, led the Iroquois to sell territories of the dependent (previously conquered) tribes that lived under confederacy protection in the valleys of eastern and central Pennsylvania. In the 1730s and 1740s, growing numbers of these peoples—principally Delawares and Shawnees—relocated in the upper Ohio Valley.

Once settled in the region, the Delawares and Shawnees remained in principle subject to Iroquois authority, but in practice they were far enough from the center of Iroquois power to begin acting independently. This so weakened the confederacy's ability to enforce its neutrality policy that, during King George's War, aggressive Pennsylvanian traders set up outposts in the valley and on the south shore of Lake Erie. With the return of peace in 1748, France moved to assert direct control over the region in order to secure communication between its Canadian and its Mississippi Valley settlements. Meanwhile, a syndicate of Virginia land speculators, the Ohio Company, had obtained concessions from the Iroquois that, as they believed, authorized them to found a settlement at the Forks of the Ohio (the site of modern Pittsburgh). The simultaneous efforts of the French and the Virginians to occupy the Forks led to fighting in 1754.

Course of the War

The collision of European powers in the Ohio Valley ended a half-century during which the Iroquois had preserved a three-way balance of power in eastern North America by playing France off against Britain. The war began with the French and their Indian allies (the majority of peoples in the Northeast and upper Midwest) attacking British frontier settlements. The backwoodsmen, incapable of fighting on French and Indian terms, fled; governments built chains of forts along exposed frontiers in a more or less futile effort to protect them; and the New England colonists, always the more aggressive, began planning expeditions against Canada. These patterns, well known from the three previous wars, soon altered as Britain and France sent troops and commanders to direct the war effort. Far more than in any previous conflict, European intervention would shape the French and Indian War.

The war's two phases in America—from 1754 to 1758 and from 1758 through 1760—corresponded precisely to European influences. Virtually uninterrupted French successes characterized the first phase because the French adhered to their proven strategic formula from previous conflicts—guerrilla war. Relying on Indian allies acting in cooperation with Canadian militiamen and the Troupes de la Marine (colonial regulars), the French raided English frontier settlements, killing and capturing many hundreds of civilians and causing tens of thousands more to panic, and attacked fortified outposts whenever the opportunity appeared. This was above all warfare conducted on Indian terms, and it allowed France's Indian allies to act independently in choosing targets and tactics.

Guerrilla tactics violated the norms of war making that eighteenth-century European officers strove to observe. *La petite guerre*, as the French called it, made few distinctions between combatants and noncombatants and gave great scope to Indian cultural practices, which included taking women and children captives, killing wounded prisoners, scalping, and ritual torture. The first commander in chief France sent to take charge of the war in America, the baron de Dieskau, showed so little inclination to meddle with these practices that he even integrated into guerrilla operations the European-trained regiments (Troupes de Terre) that France dispatched to reinforce Canada's defenses.

But Dieskau was wounded and captured at the Battle of Lake George on 8 September 1755, and his successor, the marquis de Montcalm, proved more committed to "civilized" modes of warfare. Montcalm's first campaign, the 1756 offensive against Fort Oswego, a remote Anglo-American post on Lake Ontario, ended with the French-allied Indians killing prisoners, taking captives, and collecting scalps. Montcalm hastily ransomed the hostages with gifts and brandy—and thus succeeded in unintentionally attracting for the coming campaign nearly two thousand warriors from thirty-three nations, the largest Indian contingent ever assembled in North America.

The French offensive of 1757 aimed at destroying another British outpost, Fort William Henry, at the south end of Lake George, New York. Again the French siege succeeded, but this time Montcalm, who was determined that his allies would not behave like savages, strictly forbade killing the wounded, scalping, and seizing captives. When the garrison surrendered on 9 August after a six-day defense, Montcalm granted the British the conventional honors of war: the privilege of retaining their arms and personal property and returning to New York "on parole"—that is, as noncombatants pledged to refrain from campaigning for a year and a half. Montcalm's Indian allies regarded this as a betrayal of trust, since by granting these terms, Montcalm had deprived them of the captives and booty they believed they had earned.

They responded by killing between 69 and 185 Anglo-American soldiers and camp followers and carrying off as many as 500 more into captivity.

This episode, which the Anglo-Americans called "the massacre of Fort William Henry," occurred as a direct result of Montcalm's powerful commitment to the values of European professional military culture. His efforts to contain violence against prisoners and noncombatants drove away the Indian allies on whom New France had always relied for defense. In 1758 virtually the only Indians who offered aid were converts from the St. Lawrence Valley missions; no other warriors cared to submit to the command of a general who clearly despised their values. Thus, ironically, Montcalm's determination to distinguish between combatants and noncombatants—his commitment to "civilized" war making—destroyed the keystone of Canada's security and paved the way to unlimited victory for the British army and its Anglo-American auxiliaries.

While the French were highly successful until 1757, when they began to adopt Europeanized tactics, the commanders whom Britain had sent to direct the Anglo-American war effort had pursued Europeanization from the start with disastrous results. The first British commander in chief, General Edward Braddock, had rejected the use of Indian scouts and mounted a campaign against the French post at the Forks of the Ohio, Fort Duquesne, using European tactics. Having advanced within ten miles of Fort Duquesne, Braddock (accompanied by a young Virginian aide-de-camp, George Washington) suffered a tremendous defeat at the hands of a much smaller contingent of Indians and Canadian militiamen in the Battle of the Monongahela on 9 July 1755. Fully 60 percent of Braddock's force was killed or wounded.

The commander in chief dispatched to replace Braddock, the earl of Loudoun, shared both his predecessor's professionalism and his lack of success. Despite having under his command thousands of regulars—troops trained and disciplined according to European standards—Loudoun won not a single battle in 1756 and 1757. He did, however, alienate the governments of most of the colonies by refusing to consult with them on strategy while demanding that they pay for the war effort. The colonists' reluctance to be subjected to Loudoun's dictates grew by 1757 into virtual refusal to cooperate.

A change of policy in England redressed the balance, however, at almost exactly the same time that

At the Battle of Monongahela outside Fort Duquesne, Ohio, on 9 July 1755, General Edward Braddock is killed and his troops are defeated on 9 July 1755. From Augustus L. Mason's *The Romance and Tragedy of Pioneer Life*, 1883. LIBRARY OF CONGRESS

Montcalm drove away his Indian allies. William Pitt, the erratic, brilliant politician who directed the war effort as secretary of state for the South from late 1757 through 1761, promised to reimburse the colonies in proportion to their participation, restored colonial autonomy by deemphasizing the power of the commander in chief, and recalled Lord Loudoun. Pitt's measures rapidly restored colonial morale and revived England's flagging fortunes. A new offensive in 1758 placed redcoat and colonial forces numbering over thirty thousand in the field against less than half as many French and Canadian defenders. Meanwhile, an Anglo-American diplomatic initiative succeeded in breaking the alliance between the Ohio Valley Indians and the French in 1758.

Two Anglo-American triumphs in that year—the seizure of the Forks of the Ohio and the capture

of Louisbourg, the Cape Breton Island fortress that controlled access to the St. Lawrence River—heralded a decisive change. The war now became a contest on almost purely European terms, a contest that the largest, best-supplied army could scarcely fail to win. Montcalm, forced back to Quebec by British invaders under the command of General James Wolfe in 1759, chose to give battle before the walls of the city on 13 September. In this, the only European-style, open-field engagement of the war, Montcalm preserved his honor and demonstrated his professionalism but lost the city. In the following year, Anglo-American armies would invade once more and annihilate the remaining French resistance.

The conquest of Canada in 1760 has led some historians to assume, erroneously, that the Battle of Quebec was the war's decisive event. Instead, two nearly simultaneous, reinforcing developments determined the outcome: the Battle of Quiberon Bay on the Atlantic coast of France (20 November 1759) and the Iroquois decision to join the Anglo-Americans in the campaign of 1760. The Battle of Quiberon Bay incapacitated the French Atlantic fleet, denying Canada's remaining defenders the reinforcements and supplies they needed to recapture Quebec and resist the invading Anglo-American armies. Although Montcalm's successor, the chevalier de Lévis, lacked Montcalm's aversion to guerrilla tactics, the absence of trade goods and weapons from France prevented him from rebuilding Indian alliances. Thus, when the Iroquois joined forces with the Anglo-Americans, the strategic balance tipped irrevocably against the French.

The Significance of Pontiac's War

The Anglo-American victory in the French and Indian War occurred solely because both sides relied on European methods of warfare, which inevitably gave the advantage to the largest and best-supplied army. The fact that the Anglo-Americans were in no sense fated to triumph can clearly be read in the history of Pontiac's War, which immediately followed the formal conclusion of war and the signing of the Treaty of Paris in 1763. This "rebellion" of Indians formerly allied with the French originated in British efforts to economize and reform long-standing practices in trade and diplomacy. Beginning with the attack of Pontiac, an Ottawa chief, on Detroit, the conflict grew into a pan-Indian war that cost the redcoats at least four hundred lives and the

Anglo-Americans more than two thousand, reduced Britain's presence in the newly conquered West to three isolated posts, and again emptied the frontiers of settlers. In the end, the Indians ceased fighting because they lacked replacement arms and ammunition and because the British restored previous commercial and diplomatic arrangements. Viewed from the Indian perspective, the treaties that ended Pontiac's War in 1766 defined an Indian, not a British, victory.

The Indians who rebelled against British control after the Seven Years' War were trying to maintain local autonomy and customary rights against an imperial authority that was heedless of local conditions. In that sense the breakdown of Anglo-Indian relations was an eerily accurate predictor of the future. Like the failure of Montcalm to transform the Indians into reliable subordinates and the failure of Lord Loudoun to compel the colonists to participate in the war on his terms rather than their own, Pontiac's War demonstrated the futility of coercion as a basis for imperial control. As the events of the next decade would demonstrate, however, this was not a lesson that Britain was prepared to learn.

BIBLIOGRAPHY

Anderson, Fred. *A People's Army: Massachusetts Soldiers and Society in the Seven Years' War.* Chapel Hill: University of North Carolina Press for the Institute of Early American History and Culture, 1984.

Dowd, Gregory Evans. *A Spirited Resistance: The North American Indian Struggle for Unity, 1745–1815.* Baltimore: The Johns Hopkins University Press, 1992.

Hinderaker, Eric. *Elusive Empires: Constructing Colonialism in the Ohio Valley, 1673–1800.* New York: Cambridge University Press, 1997.

Jennings, Francis. *Empire of Fortune: Crowns, Colonies, and Tribes in the Seven Years' War in America.* New York: Norton, 1988.

Selesky, Harold. *War and Society in Colonial Connecticut.* New Haven, Conn.: Yale University Press, 1990.

Steele, Ian K. *Betrayals: Fort William Henry and the "Massacre."* New York: Oxford University Press, 1990.

Titus, James. *The Old Dominion at War: Society, Politics, and Warfare in Late Colonial Virginia.* Columbia: University of South Carolina Press, 1991.

White, Richard. *The Middle Ground: Indians, Empires, and Republics in the Great Lakes Region, 1650–1815.* New York: Cambridge University Press, 1991.

FRED ANDERSON

See also **American Indian Wars; War.**

FRONTIER

In the last decades of the twentieth century the concept of the frontier had become for many U.S. historians the equivalent of an insult in a crowded saloon: an invitation to fight. Many a blow had been leveled at Frederick Jackson Turner's famous account of European-descended whites "advancing" into "free lands" along an "empty" frontier, a notion of national progress that was condemned as oblivious to the existence of the native peoples. Some indignant historians refrained from using the word *frontier* altogether, an extreme reaction that jettisoned a useful analytical concept. Properly understood in a neutral, ecological sense as a shifting, generally westward-moving zone of interaction between indigenous and nonindigenous populations, the idea of the frontier is useful in making sense of the historical pattern of violence in the United States. In fact, it is indispensable.

Peaceful and Not-So-Peaceful Frontiers

The frontier violence of fact and legend was mostly a product of developing regions with an excess of young single males. The historian Walter Nugent calls these type II frontiers and contrasts

The Two Types of Frontiers

Type I	Type II
farming, farm building	mining, ranching, other extraction
families, usually nuclear	individuals
balanced gender distribution	80 to 90 percent (or more) male
a few over forty-five years old	almost none over forty-five years old
many children	few children
high birthrate	low birthrate
women less highly valued	women more highly valued
relatively permanent	transient
limited vice	widespread commercialized vice
peaceful	violent
colonizing	imperialist, exploitative

Source: An elaboration of Walter Nugent, "Frontiers and Empires in the Late Nineteenth Century." *Western Historical Quarterly* 20 (1989): 401.

them with type I farming frontiers, which were generally peaceful, not to say dull. The people of the farming frontiers were the "colorless many, . . . too busy trying to raise families and eke out a living to become legendary." The denizens of the cattle towns and mining camps were the "colorful few," whose lives were more often cut short by accidents, drunken violence, or hygienic neglect.

Type II frontiers were most common in ranching country and in the mining and lumbering regions of the cordillera, the vast elevated region from the eastern Rocky Mountains to the western foothills of the Sierra Nevada and Cascade ranges. With the exception of Mormon-settled Utah, type I frontiers were found in rainier areas with good soil and readier access to the East. In their very earliest stages, they were pioneered by men who came ahead of their families to scout the land, build primitive shelters, and pave the way for agriculture. As soon as they judged conditions to be satisfactory, these men brought their fiancées or wives and children to join them. Though raids by Native Americans or outlaws might bring moments of terror (and retreat to safer lands), populations consisting mostly of young farming families enjoyed relatively stable social lives.

Type II frontiers were far more volatile. In any society young men in their late teens and twenties are responsible for a disproportionate amount of violence and disorder. Statistically, populations that consist mostly of young men have shown a tendency toward violent crime. This is not only because the young men are so numerous or brimful of testosterone, but also because so many of them are unattached. In type II frontiers there simply were not enough eligible women.

In normal circumstances, marriage acts as a brake on rambunctious male behavior: the boys get hitched and settle down. The cliché is grounded in both sociology and evolutionary psychology. When men acquire wives and families, they have more to lose and so behave more cautiously. Other things being equal, a married frontiersman thought twice before wading into the thick of a barroom fray. A married frontiersman was less likely to be in a barroom in the first place.

Vice, another prominent characteristic of type II frontier towns, was linked to violence in several ways. Unattached laborers—cowboys, miners, lumberjacks, fur trappers, navvies, teamsters—were the natural prey of gamblers, pimps, prostitutes, and whiskey peddlers, all of whom followed the frontier. Many vice figures were armed and hardened criminals who used violence or its threat to settle disputes over poker stakes and dance-hall girls. Vice institutions were flash points for trouble.

Nowhere was this clearer than in the Chinatowns of western cities and towns. Chinatowns were, among other things, recreational vice districts for the overwhelmingly male Cantonese laborers who poured into California and other western states and territories after the discovery of gold. They featured gambling parlors, brothels, and opium dens that were controlled by organized gangs called tongs. Tong enforcers (called highbinders or hatchet men) used muscle to collect gambling debts and prevent indentured prostitutes ("slave girls") from running away with customers. They waged pitched battles with other tongs to maintain control of the vice operations, much as rival gangs of bootleggers would later do during Prohibition. The homicide arrest rate for the Chinese in Portland, Oregon, in the 1870s was roughly four times that of the general population, a reflection of the abnormally high ratio of Chinese men to women and the consequent flourishing of vice and organized crime. The Chinese were also preyed upon by white robbers, extortionists, and bullies who found them easy and politically popular targets. The *English-Chinese Phrase Book* (1875, revised 1877) distributed by Wells, Fargo and Company included grimly useful sentences such as "He came to his death by homicide," "He was choked to death with a lasso, by a robber," "He was killed by an assassin," and "He was smothered in his room."

Outside Chinatown the saloon was the central establishment of vice. Spree drinking was common, particularly among workers who had just been paid. When they drank too much, they became careless and clumsy, likelier to give or take offense in dangerous circumstances. Clare McKanna, who studied nearly one thousand homicide cases in three western counties from 1880 to 1920, found that seven in ten of the perpetrators had been drinking, as had about six in ten of the victims. More than one-third of the male victims died in saloons or in the streets in front of them. Thirty-two of them had been shot by bartenders (mostly with pistols, not, according to legend, with a shotgun from behind the counter), while sixteen of the dead were themselves bartenders. Most of the killings took place in the evening or on the weekend, that is, the times when tipsy men were apt to be congregating in saloons and other places of bibulous recreation.

Drunken brawls were not necessarily homicidal. What made them so lethal was the frontier habit of carrying knives or especially guns. Handguns were responsible for 63 percent of the homicides in McKanna's sample; handguns, rifles, and shotguns were responsible for 75 percent. Ready

---

A Stabbing in Idaho

Don Maguire was a Rocky Mountain trader who made his money selling guns, knives, dice, cards, and various other items at a 1,000 percent profit. He kept a journal, which has been edited by the historian Gary Topping. This entry, composed in a hurried, stream-of-consciousness style, was written in the course of an 1877 trip to the mining town of Atlanta, Idaho:

> The two noted characters of the town Coyote Smith and Poker Smith. My attention was first drawn to Coyote Smith. While he was engaged in a quarrel with two carpenters who were working lumber in front of a saloon, he being drunk made much disturbance and at the same time vowing to whip the two carpenters whereupon one of them gave him a kick in the hip. This set him wild. He snarled for a revolver swearing to kill the two. A revolver he could not procure. Midway up the street entered into a second altercation with Poker Smith and seizing a carving knife from the counter of a restaurant he made a stroke [passage obliterated] to sever the jugular vein for Poker Smith but missing his aim the knife struck the collar bone broke and his hand running down the blade he received a horrible wound cutting his hand from the hollow between the thumb and forefinger nearly to the wrist blood flowed freely from both parties but neither was fatally injured. There were no arrests made.

"No arrests made" was the outcome of many a similar confrontation. This sort of affray kept the local surgeon busy, not necessarily the sheriff or vigilance committee. One of the busiest surgeons was George Kenny of Salmon City, Idaho. Before he was through, he managed to fill half a coffee mug with bullets dug from miners.

Source: "A Trader in the Rocky Mountains: Don Maguire's 1877 Diary." *Idaho Yesterdays* 27 (summer 1983): 2–4, 7 (quotation). Where indicated by Maguire's capitalization, periods have been inserted; the spelling of one word, "seizing" for "siezing," has been corrected.

---

access to deadly (and often concealed) weapons greatly increased the odds that a simple assault would escalate to homicide. Most frontier killings and maimings were sordid, unpremeditated affairs that arose from jostling or insults among touchy men who had had too much to drink.

Gun toting also carried the risk of accidental death. The *Caldwell Post*, a cattle-town newspaper, estimated that five cowboys were killed by accidental gun discharges for every one who was shot intentionally. An unjacketed .44- or .45-caliber bullet did tremendous damage. Many of those who survived gun mishaps had to live with terrible injuries: blasted groins, shot-away knees, missing faces, and the like.

Measuring the Violence

The most frequently studied measure of frontier violence is the homicide rate. Killings usually made it into newspapers and official documents and thus into the historical record, while lesser crimes such as assaults were often unremarked or unprosecuted. As Robert Dykstra has argued, even in legendary places like Dodge City the number of murders was actually small, owing to the smallness of their populations. Men did not duel in the streets every noon, nor was killing, criminal or otherwise, a common event.

In proportional terms, however, frontier killings were much more frequent than in the East. When homicide is expressed as a ratio (conventionally the number of cases per 100,000 people per year), type II frontier communities had rates that were at least an order of magnitude greater than those prevailing in eastern cities or midwestern agricultural regions. The homicide rate of Fort Griffin, a central Texas frontier town frequented by cowboys, buffalo hunters, and soldiers, was 229 per 100,000 in the 1870s. That of Boston, a long-settled eastern city whose population included proportionately more women, children, and old people, was only about 6.

Some of the most clear-cut evidence comes from California. Roger McGrath has calculated that the homicide rate for the mining town of Bodie (90 percent male) was 116 per 100,000 from 1878 to 1882, years when eastern homicide rates rarely exceeded single digits. (By contrast, the robbery rates in Bodie and nearby Aurora, Nevada, were comparable to, and burglary rates lower than, those of eastern cities—a reflection, perhaps, of the fear of armed retaliation by potential victims.) Kevin Mullen has estimated that the San Francisco homicide rate ranged from 28 to 80 per 100,000, with an average of about 49, during the city's tumultuous early years (1849–1856). The rate thereafter subsided to a range of 4 to 13 per 100,000 during the 1860s. The main reason for the shift was that the disproportionately youthful and male population characteristic of the early gold rush gradually gave way to a more balanced population that included more women, children, and old people.

This was in fact a universal pattern. Type II settlements did not retain their unbalanced populations forever. Within a decade or two the surplus men moved on to new frontiers, died prematurely, or married and settled down. Women, who were initially scarce, married and began bearing children at an early age, often in their teens. These children were roughly divided between boys and girls. Eventually the children married and further normalized the population. With the increasing numbers of women and children came institutions—schools, churches, and the Woman's Christian Temperance Union—that militated against vice and violence and improved the moral climate of the once-raucous frontier towns.

Frontier violence is thus best understood as a passing migratory anomaly. The nature of the labor demand drew youthful male workers to ranching, mining, and other type II frontier regions. These young men found themselves thrown together in competitive masculine company, isolated from familial influences, tempted by predaceous vice and payday sprees, and at least temporarily unable to find women to marry. When these circumstances changed—when the type II frontiers came to resemble more nearly the type I frontiers—the propensity toward public violence abated or at least stabilized at a lower level.

Cultural Influences

There is more to the story of frontier violence than population structure. Cultural factors also help to explain why men were so quick to fight other men and why there was so much conflict with Native Americans.

Men who come from cultures that stress personal honor are more likely to become involved in fights than those who do not. Such cultures emphasize the importance of responding to any perceived insult or slight, however trivial, lest a man lose face in the eyes of others who determine his social worth. The approved response is to display physical courage, to fight the offender, or, in certain upper-class contexts, to challenge him to a

duel. The addition of deadly weapons to the honor imperative, epitomized by a Colorado grave marker, "He called Bill Smith a liar," explains why hotheaded killings were common on the frontier.

Those portions of the frontier settled or traversed by southerners were especially prone to hotheaded killings. The religiously motivated European immigrants who first journeyed to New England and the littoral regions of the middle colonies—Puritans, Quakers, German Pietists, and the like—were not particularly concerned about honor. However, the Cavaliers who settled in the Chesapeake colonies were. (Maryland's homicide rate from 1657 to 1680 was more than twice that of Massachusetts, though this probably reflects excess males as well as cultural differences.) The Scots, Scots-Irish, border English, and Finns who settled along the backwoods frontier were also highly honor-conscious. They were accustomed to weapons and warfare, because they or their ancestors had come from remote and often violent rural areas on the hardscrabble periphery of northern and western Europe.

As the frontier moved westward, most new settlers situated themselves in places climatically similar to those whence they came. New Englanders moved to Ohio, southerners to the Gulf Plain, and so on. Until the twentieth century, migration tended to follow lines of latitude, as did cultural attitudes toward honor. Frontier regions settled by northerners were less violent than those settled by migrants from the South or Midlands. "All old-timers who know the West will tell you that they did not have so many killings and shooting scrapes after they got up North as they did in Texas," recalled E. C. "Teddy Blue" Abbott in his cowboy memoir, *We Pointed Them North: Recollections of a Cowpuncher* (1939; p. 231). The figures back him up. The statewide homicide rate in Texas was 32 per 100,000 in 1878, far higher than in northern climes.

Conflict with Native Americans

Many frontiersmen, northern as well as southern, had definite ideas about Anglo-Saxon racial superiority and the self-evident correctness of manifest destiny. At best, Native Americans were objects of suspicion; at worst, they were savages, disgusting, incorrigible, and even diabolical obstacles to the advance of civilization. Such extreme ethnocentrism naturally made it easier to justify killing them and appropriating their lands. The classic case was California, where miners enslaved,

Colonel House Nearly Gets Himself Killed

Edward Mandell House (1858–1938) is best known as Woodrow Wilson's adviser and confidant, a man so close to the president that Wilson once called him "my second personality . . . my independent self." But House, who came of age in Texas's most violent era and who counted it nothing to carry a gun, almost did not make it to Washington. In 1879 he was visiting a mining camp near Como, Colorado:

> It was like all other camps of that sort—rough men and rougher women, gambling, drinking, and killing. I was in a saloon, talking to a man whom I had known in Texas, when . . . a big, brawny individual came into the room and began to abuse me in violent terms. I had never seen the man before and could not imagine why he was doing this. I retreated, and he followed. I had my overcoat on at the time and had my hand on my six-shooter in my pocket and cocked it. The owner of the saloon jumped over the bar between us. In five seconds more, I would have killed him. An explanation followed which cleared up the mystery. He had taken me for some one else against whom he had a grudge, and whom he had seen but once. I learned later that he was a popular ex-sheriff of Summit county and that if I had killed him I should have been lynched within the hour.
>
> It always amuses me when I see the bad men in plays depicted as big, rough fellows with their trousers in their boots and six-shooters buckled around their waists. As a matter of fact, the bad men I have been used to in southern Texas were as unlike this as daylight from dark. They were usually gentle, mild-mannered, mild-spoken, and often delicate-looking men. They were invariably polite, and one not knowing the species would be apt to misjudge them to such an extent that a rough word or an insult would sometimes be offered. This mistake of judgment was one that could never be remedied, for a second opportunity was never given.

Source: Charles Seymour, ed., *The Intimate Papers of Colonel House.* New York: Houghton Mifflin, 1926, pp. 24–25.

---

soldiers—together accounted for more than forty-five hundred killings of Native Americans in California between 1848 and 1880.

Of course, the Native Americans in California and elsewhere fought back, often matching and surpassing whites in the ferocity of their attacks. Apaches were known to kindle slow fires under the heads of suspended captives. Tales of such atrocities confirmed the whites' conviction that the elimination of hostile Native Americans was in principle no different from hunting predatory animals. Even when Native Americans were accorded the formalities of a trial, bias against them practically guaranteed convictions. For example, every Apache accused of killing a white in Gila County, Arizona, in the late 1880s was convicted. The only Apaches who were acquitted or had their cases dismissed were those accused of killing other Apaches. For those found guilty, a long sentence was often tantamount to the death penalty. Well over one-third of all Native Americans sent off to prison in Arizona and California were dead within five years.

Native Americans were at a marked demographic disadvantage in their conflict with whites. Their numbers progressively dwindled because of their vulnerability to imported Old World diseases such as smallpox. Too many women and dependents were another military handicap. Braves were in short supply, a legacy of intertribal warfare and, more speculatively, of the greater susceptibility of males to infectious disease. Native American women and dependents were less mobile than the braves and therefore easier to attack. The tactic of destroying villages rather than going after elusive bands of warriors, which emerged in Massachusetts and Virginia as early as the 1620s and 1630s, was used repeatedly in the eighteenth and nineteenth centuries and led to such notorious and lopsided Native American defeats as Sand Creek (1864), Washita (1868), and Wounded Knee (1890).

Ecological violence by Europeans brought further hardship to Native Americans. Hunting was a popular pastime among frontiersmen, particularly during the nineteenth century. Competitive in masculine company and keen on proving their prowess, Europeans often killed more than was necessary to feed their families or sell to others. The rotting carcasses of thousands of Plains buffalo were a stark reminder of the excess slaughter and a signal source of Native American distress. Give the hunters bronze medals with a dead buffalo on one side and a discouraged Native American on

---

raped, or simply shot down Native Americans for no better reason, wrote one French missionary, than "to try their pistols." Miners, ranchers, and militiamen—the latter much more lethal to Native Americans than the better-disciplined regular

the other, General Philip Sheridan admonished the Texas legislature. "Let them kill, skin, and sell until the buffalo are exterminated," he declared. "Then your prairies can be covered with speckled cattle, and the festive cowboy, who follows the hunter as a second forerunner of an advanced civilization."

Native Americans themselves were drawn into overhunting so they could barter meat and skins for European trade goods, thus heightening conflict with other tribes. One of those trade goods, alcohol, had horrific consequences. European memoirs are full of accounts of drunken Native Americans selling their squaws into prostitution, going on wild binges, stumbling into fires, cutting one another to pieces. One theory to account for this extreme behavior is that Native Americans had no knowledge of distilled alcohol before contact with Europeans and thus no store of social knowledge about drinking. Native Americans learned to drink hard liquor from the worst possible tutors: fur trappers, traders, mule skinners, and other denizens of the type II frontier. When they saw white men swill whiskey and become dangerously, obstreperously drunk, they did likewise and suffered the same consequences.

Government's Failure to Control Frontier Violence

Selling liquor to Native Americans was illegal in most places from colonial times on. Neither the British nor the American government was able to suppress the trade, however. The U.S. government, nominally responsible for policing the western territories, was seldom able adequately to enforce any policy to protect Native Americans. The frontier was vast, the settlers numerous and greedy, and the resources of the federal government limited. The army was spread too thin to control the movements of frontiersmen or to prevent them from trespassing on treaty lands. Local courts and juries were invariably sympathetic toward white defendants and hostile toward Native Americans.

In the early stages of frontier expansion, legal institutions were either lacking or inadequate. One response to this situation, patterned after the Regulator movement in South Carolina in 1767–1769 (in which backcountry settlers organized to restore law and order and establish institutions of local government), was vigilantism, or organized extralegal movements against robbers, rustlers, counterfeiters, and other outlaws. The historian Richard Maxwell Brown counted 326 such movements in the country between 1767 and 1904, the majority of which were in southern and southwestern territories and states, the single most important of which was Texas.

When vigilante actions were limited in scope and controlled by local elites, they often served socially constructive purposes. Selected malefactors were whipped, branded, banished, or sometimes hanged in public dramas that affirmed the values of property and order. But vigilantism could also miscarry. In California, racial minorities, particularly Hispanics, made up a disproportionate percentage of those subjected to lynch courts, which were especially swift and merciless if the victims were white. Vigilantism also ran the risk of triggering private warfare, when friends and relatives of the lynch victims sought revenge against the vigilante faction, or of miscarriages of justice, when personal enemies were killed under the guise of the popular will. Vigilantism, in short, was a poor substitute for professional police and regular courts and had been widely superseded by the close of the nineteenth century.

Frontier Violence After 1900

Frontier violence is not entirely a thing of the past. The night, for example, is a present-day frontier where colonization has been made possible by cars and electric lights. Charles Lindbergh wrote in his autobiography that the most spectacular change he had seen in the earth's surface in all his decades of flying was the sprinkling of myriad lights across the United States on a clear night. These lights were signs of "conquest," of human movement into the frontier of darkness. But that movement is highly selective. Midnight finds mostly young men on the streets—and higher rates of drunkenness, accidents, assault, rape, and murder than in the daylight hours. Nighttime, in brief, resembles a type II frontier.

In some respects, inner cities also resemble a type II frontier. Urban women are hardly outnumbered by men, as they were on the nineteenth-century frontier. Nevertheless, many young inner-city males, for economic, subcultural, and demographic reasons, delay marriage or avoid the institution altogether. An increasing number of them have grown up in single-parent households and so have experienced little parental guidance and supervision. Those who have joined gangs, acquired weapons, and become involved with drug traffic and other forms of organized vice are statistically among the most violence-prone members of society, just like their type II frontier counterparts.

The frontier may have passed, but frontier attitudes did not. Wallace-Burke Gun Club, Coeur d'Alene, Idaho, 1894. PHOTOGRAPH BY THOMAS NATHAN BARNARD, #8-X1018A, BARNARD-STOCKBRIDGE COLLECTION, UNIVERSITY OF IDAHO LIBRARY, MOSCOW, IDAHO. USED WITH PERMISSION.

Indeed, urban ghettos can be thought of as artificial and unusually violent frontier societies: vice-ridden combat zones in which groups of armed, unsupervised touchy bachelors, high on alcohol and other drugs, menace one another and the local citizenry.

Some historians have also seen analogies between twentieth-century U.S. involvement in Pacific wars—particularly against Filipino rebels, Japanese soldiers, and Vietnamese communists—and the earlier frontier campaigns against Native Americans. In all these cases, young American men, remote from what they called civilization, were pitted against enemies they deemed treacherous and racially inferior. The conflicts quickly assumed a ferocious quality reminiscent of the worst episodes of the wars against Native Americans. Indeed, the parallel was made explicit in the language of the Vietnam War, when young GIs spoke of forays into "Indian country" and code-named their operations Texas Star and Cochise Green (a reference to the chief of the Chiricahua Apache who waged relentless war against the U.S. Army).

These GIs had grown up in the golden age of the Western, a hugely successful genre in the publishing, film, radio, and television industries (also advertising: a square-jawed cowboy beat out a crusty taxi driver as the emblem of Philip Morris's legendary Marlboro cigarette campaign). That whole generation had been saturated with images of stylized violence and morally simplistic frontier stories of cowboys, Indians, desperadoes, and six-shooters. Did the public's fascination with these stories of frontier violence contribute to the high rates of violence in the United States relative to other industrial democracies? Did it matter that America's mythic hero was a man with a gun, an attitude, and a Stetson hat?

The answer is a qualified yes. We become who we are by emulating other figures in our environment, including the electronic environment with its celebrities and "action figures." Communications researchers have discovered that, for many people, these figures become role models: people act like them, dress like them, talk like them, even talk *to* them. Insofar as larger-than-life frontier figures, played by the likes of John Wayne and James Arness, entered and shaped mass consciousness, they reinforced the belief that gun violence was an appropriate means for resolving conflicts. It is doubtful, however, that their influence was greater than more fundamental social and economic factors—racism, ghetto isolation, subcultures of poverty, deindustrialization, secularization, family decline, homicidal sensitivity about honor, lax gun control laws, drug abuse, and drug trafficking—that have contributed to the ongoing reputation of the United States as a violent land.

BIBLIOGRAPHY

Bartlett, Richard A. *The New Country: A Social History of the American Frontier.* New York: Oxford University Press, 1974.

Brown, Richard Maxwell. "The American Vigilante Tradition." In *The History of Violence in America,* edited by Hugh Davis Graham and Ted Robert Gurr. New York: Bantam, 1969.

Courtwright, David T. *Violent Land: Single Men and Social Disorder from the Frontier to the Inner City.* Cambridge, Mass.: Harvard University Press, 1996.

Dary, David. *Cowboy Culture: A Saga of Five Centuries.* Lawrence: University Press of Kansas, 1989.

Dykstra, Robert R. "Overdosing on Dodge City." *Western Historical Quarterly* 27 (winter 1996).

Fischer, David Hackett. *Albion's Seed: Four British Folkways in America.* New York: Oxford University Press, 1989.

Friedman, Lawrence M., and Robert V. Percival. *The Roots of Justice: Crime and Punishment in Alameda County, California, 1870–1910.* Chapel Hill: University of North Carolina Press, 1981.

Gurr, Ted Robert, ed. *Violence in America.* Vol. 1, *The History of Crime.* Newbury Park, Calif.: Sage, 1989.

Hollon, W. Eugene. *Frontier Violence: Another Look.* New York: Oxford University Press, 1974.

Johnson, David A. "Vigilance and the Law: The Moral Authority of Popular Justice in the Far West." *American Quarterly* 33 (1981).

Jordan, Terry G., and Matti Kaups. *The American Backwoods Frontier: An Ethnic and Ecological Interpretation.* Baltimore: Johns Hopkins University Press, 1989.

Mancall, Peter C. *Deadly Medicine: Indians and Alcohol in Early America.* Ithaca, N.Y.: Cornell University Press, 1995.

McGrath, Roger D. *Gunfighters, Highwaymen, and Vigilantes: Violence on the Frontier.* Berkeley: University of California Press, 1984.

McKanna, Clare V., Jr. *Homicide, Race, and Justice in the American West, 1880–1920.* Tucson: University of Arizona Press, 1997.

Mullen, Kevin J. *Let Justice Be Done: Crime and Politics in Early San Francisco.* Reno: University of Nevada Press, 1989.

Nisbett, Richard E. "Violence and U.S. Regional Culture." *American Psychologist* 48 (April 1993).

Paul, Rodman. *The Far West and the Great Plains in Transition, 1859–1900.* New York: Harper and Row, 1988.

West, Elliott. *The Saloon on the Rocky Mountain Mining Frontier.* Lincoln: University of Nebraska Press, 1979.

White, Richard. *The Middle Ground: Indians, Empires, and Republics in the Great Lakes Region, 1650–1815.* New York: Cambridge University Press, 1991.

DAVID T. COURTWRIGHT

See also **American Indians; Vigilantism; West; Wounded Knee, 1890.**

FUGITIVE SLAVE ACTS

Slavery in early America, because of its inherent unjustness, prompted many bondmen to defy their oppressors through covert or overt resistance or by running away. Among the earliest slave catchers were Native Americans (themselves sometimes taken into slavery) such as the Catawba, who signed treaties with the South Carolina colonial government to guarantee the return of fugitive slaves. During the colonial period most of the legislatures enacted laws prohibiting slaves from running away and specifying punishments for captured fugitives. Until the eighteenth century, however, there were no organized means for actually retrieving runaways; colonial assemblies relied upon Indians, rewards, and individual initiative among the few active slave catchers (such as some Dutchmen living in Virginia) to recapture fleeing slaves.

By the mid–eighteenth century, the legislatures of Virginia, Georgia, and the Carolinas had created slave patrols, composed of white men, who were obligated to catch runaways, but the patrollers' range of activity was limited to the region in which they lived. By the time of the Constitutional Convention in Philadelphia in 1787, slave owners pressed for a more effective means of stopping fugitives from reaching Canada or Spanish Florida, where they might be welcomed as freedmen. The means by which white Americans responded to this growing problem of slave rebelliousness involved nothing less than the authority of the U.S. government and rested upon the cooperation of all the states in the newly formed union.

Southern delegates to the Constitutional Convention proposed a requirement that all states return fugitive slaves to their owners. Passed by a vote of 11–0, with no discussion, this proposal eventually became part of Article IV, Section 2, of the Constitution; it was written without any direct mention of the word *slavery*, perhaps to ease passage of the Constitution among the northern

An 1851 cartoon by Edward Williams Clay on the Fugitive Slave Act of 1850. LIBRARY OF
CONGRESS

states, where opposition to slavery was on the rise.
The clause reads, "No person held to Service or
Labour in one State, under the Laws thereof, escaping into another, shall, in Consequence of any
Law or Regulation therein, be discharged from
such Service or Labour, but shall be delivered up
on Claim of the Party to whom such Service or
Labour may be due." The Constitution, like the
earliest colonial fugitive slave laws, created no
means of enforcement; each slave owner in pursuit
of a slave was responsible for enlisting the cooperation of state or local authorities. The lawmakers
apparently assumed that the states, out of a desire
for law and order, would lend all aid in their
power to slave owners chasing their fleeing
property.

Partially to remedy this defect in the original
drafting of the fugitive slave clause, Congress
passed a law in 1793 that gave judicial authorities
special powers over African Americans claimed as
fugitive slaves. After a master reclaimed an alleged
slave, he would go before a federal court or local
magistrate and give proof (oral or written) that the
individual was indeed an escaped slave. If sufficient proof was given, the judge would provide a
"certificate of removal" allowing the master to return home with his bondman. The hearings were

to be short, and the law did not require the judge
to hear other witnesses or listen to the slave. The
1793 Fugitive Slave Act also provided for a $500
penalty for anyone who concealed a runaway or
obstructed the slave owner in the recovery. Some
northern states like New Jersey created rewards to
supplement the federal law as an incentive for the
capture of runaways.

During the early nineteenth century, as many
northern states began emancipating the slaves
within their borders and manumission or abolition
societies grew more numerous and outspoken in
the region, opposition to the federal fugitive slave
law became more pronounced. In the 1820s several
northern states, including New York, Massachusetts, and Pennsylvania, passed laws that required
full hearings with juries before an alleged fugitive
slave could be taken out of the state by his master.
These "personal liberty laws" were originally designed to prevent free blacks from being kidnapped and taken into slavery under cover of the
federal fugitive slave law. The personal liberty
laws outraged southerners, who claimed that
northern legislatures were violating the sacred
bonds of the Constitution by imposing added requirements upon slave owners who merely sought
to reclaim their property. In *Prigg v. Pennsylvania*

(1842), the U.S. Supreme Court ruled that personal liberty laws were in violation of the Constitution's fugitive slave clause as well as the 1793 law. Northern states then passed new laws that barred the use of jails for holding fugitive slaves (making it more difficult for a master to retain a captured slave) and that banned state or local officials from rendering any assistance to a slave owner hunting a runaway. Southerners claimed that northern states had made it all but impossible for masters to capture runaways.

As part of the Compromise of 1850, southerners demanded and won a tougher fugitive slave law, which required the appointment of federal officials for every county in the nation. These commissioners, not local judges, would determine whether an accused African American was a fugitive slave. The law forbade any testimony by the alleged runaway and provided a financial incentive to the commissioner ($10 for issuing an arrest warrant) to find in favor of the master's claims. The Fugitive Slave Act of 1850 also allowed the army and federal marshals to intervene as security forces to protect masters and commissioners from violence at the hands of slave rescuers, such as those who helped the slaves Shadrach (Boston, 1851) and Jerry (Syracuse, New York, 1851) once again escape from their masters.

Opposition to the new law took many forms. Abolitionists and free blacks criticized the law and attacked courthouses and jails where fugitives were brought for trial by southern whites. The law sparked a series of riots and celebrated rescues in northern states, the most celebrated of which was the case of Anthony Burns in 1854, in which Boston abolitionists killed a U.S. marshal in a failed attempt to free Burns, a Virginia slave being held in the courthouse. By this time, Massachusetts public opinion had swung sharply against the fugitive slave law, and nothing seemed effective except direct action. Following the Burns case, the federal government deployed soldiers and cannons to stave off angry mobs that gathered near the courthouses.

The fugitive slave laws heightened the tensions between North and South and certainly contributed to the onset of the Civil War in 1861. Prior to the Civil War, the violence of slavery was an abstract concept for many northerners, until they witnessed firsthand southern masters who presumed to use northern courts to return slaves to bondage. After the Supreme Court revoked the personal liberty laws in 1842, northerners were prompted to take violent action against southern slave owners, even if that meant attacking a federal courthouse to gain the freedom of a single slave.

BIBLIOGRAPHY

Campbell, Stanley. *The Slave Catchers: Enforcement of the Fugitive Slave Law, 1850–1860.* Chapel Hill: University of North Carolina Press, 1968.

Finkelman, Paul, ed. *Fugitive Slaves and American Courts.* 4 vols. New York: Garland, 1988.

Morris, Thomas D. *Free Men All: The Personal Liberty Laws of the North, 1780–1861.* Baltimore: Johns Hopkins University Press, 1974.

Stevens, Charles. *Anthony Burns, a Narrative.* Boston: J. P. Jewett, 1856.

SALLY E. HADDEN

See also **Dred Scott Decision; Slavery.**